Educational Psychology

First Canadian Edition

John W. Santrock
University of Texas at Dallas

Vera E. Woloshyn
Brock University

Tiffany L. Gallagher
Brock University

Tony Di Petta
Brock University

Zopito A. Marini
Brock University

 **McGraw-Hill Ryerson**

Toronto   Montreal   Burr Ridge, IL   Dubuque, IA   Madison, WI   New York
San Francisco   St. Louis   Bangkok   Bogotá   Caracas   Kuala Lumpur
Lisbon   London   Madrid   Mexico City   Milan   New Delhi
Santiago   Seoul   Singapore   Sydney   Taipei

The McGraw-Hill Companies

McGraw-Hill Ryerson

Educational Psychology
First Canadian Edition

ISBN: 0-07-090969-5

1 2 3 4 5 6 7 8 9 10   TCP   0 9 8 7 6 5 4

Printed and bound in Canada

Statistics Canada information is used with the permission of the Minister of Industry, as
Minister responsible for Statistics Canada. Information on the availability of the wide range
of data from Statistics Canada can be obtained from Statistics Canada's Regional Offices, its
World Wide Web site at **http://www.statcan.ca**, and its toll-free access number 1-800-263-1136.

Care has been taken to trace ownership of copyright material contained in this text; however,
the publisher will welcome any information that enables them to rectify any reference or credit
for subsequent editions.

VICE PRESIDENT, EDITORIAL AND MEDIA TECHNOLOGY: Patrick Ferrier
SPONSORING EDITOR: James Buchanan
SENIOR DEVELOPMENTAL EDITOR: Jennifer DiDomenico
COPY EDITOR: Kelli Howey
SENIOR PRODUCTION COORDINATOR: Jennifer Wilkie
PAGE LAYOUT: ArtPlus Design & Communications
MARKETING MANAGER: Sharon Loeb
SUPERVISING EDITOR: Jaime Duffy
PERMISSIONS AND PHOTO RESEARCH: Alison Derry/Permissions Plus
COVER DESIGN: Dianna Little
COVER IMAGE CREDIT: John Wilkes/Taxi (door) and Photodisc (montage)
PRINTER: Transcontinental Printing Group

National Library of Canada Cataloguing in Publication

Educational psychology / John W. Santrock .... [et al.]. — 1st Canadian ed.
Includes bibliographical references and index.

ISBN 0-07-090969-5

1. Educational psychology.   2. Learning, Psychology of.   3. Motivation in education.
I. Santrock, John W.

LB1051.E386 2003   370.15   C2003-904478-5

Dedications

*To Alan Venable: For caring so much about this book
and improving children's education.*

JOHN W. SANTROCK

*To my husband, Bob, my children, Raymond and Rebecca, and my
parents, Helen and Nykola. Thank you for always listening and sharing
your ideas, but most of all, thank you for your love, patience, and
support—this book would not have been possible without you.*

VERA E. WOLOSHYN

*To the memory of my father, Joseph R. Levay, whose love
inspired me to pursue my dreams.*

TIFFANY L. GALLAGHER

*To my sister Teresa, my brother-in-law Bruce, and my aunt and uncle
Elvira and Domenic Berlingeri, without whose support and Sunday
suppers I would never have attempted this. Thank you one and all.*

TONY DI PETTA

*To the memory of Robbie Case, mentor, friend, and a
modern-day educational Ulysses.*

ZOPITO A. MARINI

About the Authors

John Santrock received his Ph.D. from the College of Education and Human Development at the University of Minnesota. He taught at the University of Charleston and the University of Georgia before joining the faculty at the University of Texas at Dallas. He has worked as a school psychologist and currently teaches educational psychology at both the undergraduate and graduate levels. John's grandmother taught all grades in a one-room school for many years and his father was superintendent of a large school district. John's research has included publications in the *Journal of Educational Psychology* that focus on the contextual aspects of affectively toned cognition and children's self-regulatory behaviour as well as teachers' perceptions of children from divorced families. He has been a member of the editorial boards of *Child Development* and *Developmental Psychology*. His publications include these leading McGraw-Hill texts: *Child Development* (9th ed.), *Adolescence* (9th ed.), *Life-Span Development* (9th ed.), and *Psychology* (7th ed.).

Vera E. Woloshyn, a cognitive-developmental educational psychologist and certified elementary-school teacher, is currently an associate professor in the Faculty of Education at Brock University. Dr. Woloshyn teaches courses in educational psychology, memory development, cognition, literacy, and research methodology at both the pre-service and graduate levels. Her primary research interests include the development and implementation of effective learning and teaching strategies for children and adults. Dr. Woloshyn has been the recipient of several national grants and has written and edited several books and peer-reviewed articles addressing effective literacy instruction and teaching methods. She is a board member for the Learning Disabilities Association of Ontario and has been an active member of her local chapter for more than ten years. Dr. Woloshyn is especially appreciative of the many opportunities she has to work collaboratively with practising teachers and, as the mother of two school-aged children, is especially versed in school life.

Tiffany L. Gallagher, M.Ed., is a lecturer in the pre-service department of the Faculty of Education at Brock University. She is currently a doctoral candidate who is completing her graduate studies on the effects of tutoring students with learning difficulties and the associated experiences of their literacy tutors. Professionally, Tiffany has been an administrator in supplemental education for more than a decade. Tiffany's current research interests include literacy assessment, reading and writing strategy instruction, and the role of the in-school resource teacher.

Tony Di Petta is a career educator with more than 20 years of experience in secondary schools and community colleges and as a training consultant for industry and the military. He has worked as coordinator of training for the Education Network of Ontario, and as an online moderator for the NODE network for distance education. Currently, he is a member of the Faculty of Education at Brock University, where he teaches courses in educational psychology, computers in the classroom, and enterprise education. His research interests include online teaching and learning, creating humanistic virtual environments for professional development, and the impact of technology on society and culture. He can be reached through e-mail at **tdipetta@ed.brocku.ca**.

Zopito A. Marini, Ph.D., a developmental and educational psychologist, is currently a full professor in the Department of Child and Youth Studies at Brock University. Dr. Marini did his graduate work at the University of Toronto (OISE/UT) with Robbie Case, and has been at Brock since 1985, where he was the founding chair of the department. He does research, writes, and lectures on issues related to the prevention and management of family and school conflicts and on the social and emotional impact of technology. At present, Dr. Marini is conducting studies in the areas of victimization by peers (i.e., bullying) and by technology (i.e., computer anxiety).

Brief Contents

Contents

CHAPTER

12   Managing the Classroom   382

CHAPTER

13   Standardized Tests and
Teaching   416

Preface

INTRODUCTION TO THE FIRST CANADIAN EDITION

Welcome to the First Canadian Edition of *Educational Psychology*. We are four Canadian teacher–educators who had used a variety of educational psychology books in our education classes before McGraw-Hill Ryerson invited us to co-author this text. Over the years, we had independently arrived at the conclusion that we needed a textbook with a specific focus on Canadian issues and concerns. We wanted a text that presented and discussed current educational psychology theory and research from a Canadian perspective. We wanted to focus on important academic topics such as the use of the integrated curriculum and information and communication technology, as well as on pressing social issues including multiculturalism, diversity, gender equity, and violence in our schools. And we wanted a mechanism by which to give voice to the lived experiences of Canadian teachers, students, parents, and other educational experts. McGraw-Hill Ryerson provided us with such an opportunity with the development of the First Canadian Edition of John W. Santrock's *Educational Psychology*.

We began the process of writing this text by immersing ourselves in the education literature—first at the general level and then with a specific focus on Canadian contributions to the field. We comprehensively explored and charted the dynamic and changing landscape relating educational psychology to today's schools. We were amazed by the wealth of contributions being brought to bear on education by our fellow Canadians and took great pleasure in highlighting these accomplishments throughout the text; more than 600 references have been added in the First Canadian Edition, over 200 of which were published in 2000–2003. Please see the section "Current, Comprehensive, and Canadian Content" on page xv for a chapter by chapter list of major updates and changes in the First Canadian Edition.

We believe we have created a fresh and innovative approach to exploring and understanding educational psychology. The First Canadian Edition presents a constructivist point of reference that is both informative and engaging to read. We emphasize the most up-to-date research and educational programs from across Canada and combine them with interactive pedagogical exercises and tools such as concept maps, self-assessments, summary tables, and professional development activities. We believe that all readers, especially those who are beginning or continuing their journey as classroom teachers, will be engaged by the pedagogical tools provided in this text along with the explicit focus on Canadian classrooms and teaching practices.

The Themes of Successful Teaching and Learning

Below are some of the key themes about teaching and learning that are emphasized throughout the text, followed by a presentation of the text's pedagogical features.

- Learning is supported when students actively construct meaning on the basis of their personal experiences and background knowledge. Students' learning is enhanced when they assume responsibility for their own learning. Students' minds are not empty vessels into which teachers can pour critical knowledge, nor are they clean slates upon which teachers can record vital skills. Learning works best when it is active, not passive.

- Students learn best when they can develop and effectively use a variety of thinking and reasoning strategies. Learning outcomes improve when teachers guide students in developing and applying these strategies.

- Student learning improves when students develop self-regulatory skills, adapt relevant strategies to the learning context, set appropriate goals, strategically plan how to reach the goals, and monitor their progress toward their goals. Teachers can play a critical role in assisting students in establishing meaningful short-term and long-term goals, developing strategies for reaching these goals, and monitoring goal-directed progress.

- Motivation is a critical aspect of learning. Students benefit enormously when they come to school wanting to learn rather than feeling that they are being made to learn. Teachers can nurture students' motivation and love for learning by providing them with the strategies and skills essential for effective learning, with learning tasks that are relevant to their lives, and with environments that stimulate their curiosity.

- Context, the setting in which learning takes place, plays an important part in both teaching and learning. Learning does not occur in a vacuum. The diverse contexts in which Canadian schools and students are placed are important factors to consider when developing an understanding about how students learn. Teachers need to be especially sensitive to such contextual issues as culture, ethnic background, poverty, and historical changes such as the technology revolution.

- Technology—more specifically, information and communication technology (ICT)—is an important aspect of constructivist approaches to teaching and learning. Teachers and students alike should learn to use and prudently critique ICT, which is increasingly a core feature of the education landscape. Information and communication technology has been shown to enhance student learning and motivation for learning when skilled and creative educators use it in a planned pedagogical approach that focuses on teaching *with* technology rather than *about* technology.

Pedagogical Features: Tools to Help Your Students Succeed

The pedagogical features in the First Canadian Edition have been developed to extend the text's themes to the learning experiences of educational psychology students. Each chapter contains a variety of learning tools that encourage students to forge connections between theory and practice by reflecting on lived experience, applying a variety of strategies, setting goals, providing relevant learning tasks, incorporating technology, and considering different educational contexts. The pedagogical features reinforce the text's commitment to "practising what it preaches," and will help your students succeed in the educational psychology course and in their teaching careers.

The Real Worlds of Canadian Teachers and Students We asked a large panel of expert classroom teachers from across Canada, encompassing a wide range of regions, grade levels, and subject areas, to provide observations, comments, and stories about teaching. Many of these contributors are award-winning teachers, and all have greatly enriched the book with their expertise. Their voices are presented in the following features:

- *Teaching Stories* These are high-interest chapter-opening vignettes about effective teaching as it relates to the chapter's content.

- *Through the Eyes of Teachers* These boxes appear several times in each chapter and profile teachers' observations on relevant topics. In addition, several boxes highlight the voices of other school professionals.

• *Through the Eyes of Students*   In each chapter, these boxes provide insights into students' worlds and how they view themselves, their teachers, and the educational process. Several boxes incorporate parents' viewpoints as partners in education.

Cognitive Maps   Each chapter begins with a chapter outline in cognitive map form that provides information about the chapter's main topics and themes. Three to six times in each chapter, main sections of the text are introduced with mini cognitive maps, which visually present the organization of forthcoming material. The outline cognitive maps reappear at the end of each chapter to aid in student review.

Summary Tables   These tables, organized in a question and answer format, appear at the end of each major subject heading in the text, allowing for periodic review and self-assessment. To ensure continuity, the headings in the summary tables match the headings in the corresponding mini cognitive map. A list of summary tables with page references is found at the end of each chapter.

Teaching Strategies   A critical aspect of an educational psychology text is the extent to which it provides effective and practical strategies that students can apply to the craft of teaching. Empirically validated teaching strategies are highlighted several times throughout each chapter.

Diversity and Education   Diversity is an important theme throughout Canadian classrooms and throughout this text. Each chapter contains a Diversity and Education box that elaborates on relevant concepts or themes presented throughout the chapter. All Diversity and Education boxes are completely new to the First Canadian Edition, and feature subjects such as Canadians in the early history of educational psychology (Chapter 1), Aboriginal role models, mentors, and programs in children's education (Chapter 7), and the Internet and cultural diversity in the classroom (Chapter 10).

Self-Assessment   Reflection is a critical skill in the process of becoming a life-long learner and reflective practitioner. The Self-Assessment feature found in each chapter encourages readers to examine their beliefs and behaviours with respect to chapter content.

Technology and Education   Technology is a principal theme throughout the text. Each chapter features a Technology and Education box that emphasizes technology that is directly relevant to the chapter at hand. More than 95 percent of the Technology and Education boxes are new to the First Canadian Edition, and feature Canadian programs such as Writers in Electronic Residence (Chapter 9) and Frontier College (Chapter 2). Furthermore, in Chapter 10 we provide an in-depth exploration of the role of technology in teaching and learning.

Case Studies   A case study feature entitled Crack the Case is presented at the end of each chapter. These mini cases are closely tied to the content in the chapter and are accompanied by a series of thought-provoking questions and activities.

Professional Development/Portfolio Activities   A number of professional development and portfolio activities related to the chapter content are presented at the end of each chapter. These activities encourage teacher-candidates to reflect on their learning and document their growth in the context of a teaching portfolio.

Internet Activities   Consistent with the increased use of technology in many Canadian classrooms and the overall importance of technology in Canadian society, each chapter contains two end-of-chapter Internet activities that enable readers to gain first-hand experience using educationally relevant information and communication technologies. The Internet activities and links to related Websites are also available on the text's Online Learning Centre, at **www.mcgrawhill.ca/college/santrock**.

Current, Comprehensive, and Canadian Content

Throughout this text, we include contemporary Canadian research, address Canadian educational issues, and provide examples of Canadian projects and programs. Selected major content changes and updates made for the First Canadian Edition are highlighted below.

Chapter 1—Educational Psychology: A Tool for Effective Teaching
- Features two Canadian women pioneers in psychology, Mary Salter Ainsworth and Katharine M. Banham, in the Diversity and Education box
- Profiles exemplary Canadian educators reflecting on their past influential teachers
- Highlights effective use of technology in Alberta schools
- Celebrates the fact that SchoolNet brought all of Canada's schools online in May 2000
- Differentiates between qualitative and quantitative research methods
- Defines "program-evaluation research," "action research," and "ethnic gloss"

Chapter 2—Physical and Cognitive Development
- Features the Heart Healthy Kids™ program
- Provides teaching strategies for primary-grade, intermediate-grade, and secondary-school students at each of Piaget's cognitive stages
- Explains Case's neo-Piagetian theory
- Evaluates and compares cognitive and social constructivist theories
- Discusses Canadian research on how language develops
- Features Frontier College as promoting life-long learning for all Canadians in the Technology and Education box
- Material on reading, writing, and literacy is now covered in greater depth in Chapter 9

Chapter 3—Social Contexts and Socioemotional Development
- Presents Canadian statistics on divorce and single-parent families
- Features Canadian characteristics of low-income families and socioeconomic differences
- Describes research by the Youth Lifestyle Choices Community University Research Alliance on elementary students' leisure time
- Profiles Mary Ann Shadd as an educational pioneer in the Diversity and Education box
- Introduces the multidimensional bullying identification model
- Outlines Ontario's Early Years program
- Features British Columbia's document *Transitions: From Childhood to Youth and Adulthood*
- Presents evolutionary theory to examine moral behaviour
- Cites Lions-Quest Canada as an example of a program promoting service learning
- Discusses extreme forms of peer harassment and school violence
- Covers adolescent pregnancy and STDs in Canada
- Includes recent information on adolescent truancy and school dropout in Canada

Chapter 4—Individual Variations
- Adds Gardner's ninth intelligence, existential intelligence
- Features Project Spectrum, which has an instructional approach consistent with multiple intelligences theory
- Describes the "Flynn effect," which states that IQ test scores are rising
- Presents the issue of cultural bias in IQ testing
- Discusses issues regarding tracking students
- Defines self-fulfilling prophecies, also called the "Pygmalion effect"
- Illustrates creative experiences with computer software, such as Kid-Pix
- Presents contemporary definitions of creativity
- Features the Personal Empowerment through Type (P.E.T.) Inventory

Chapter 5—Sociocultural Diversity
- Presents Canada as one of the most culturally and ethnically diverse countries
- Provides a contemporary definition of poverty and profiles of individuals living in poverty

- Discusses the consequences of poverty on children and their educational experience
- Profiles community and school projects, such as Applecheck
- Features the "Profiles of Canada" project, which shares information about multicultural communities, in the Diversity and Education box
- Summarizes studies on Canadian students' diverse ethnic backgrounds
- Explains prejudice, discrimination, and bias as attitudes that have a negative effect on students' learning
- Presents the distinction between bilingual education, immersion programs, and heritage language programs
- Summarizes Canada's Multiculturalism Act of 1985, which espouses multicultural education
- Highlights programs that connect students from diverse cultures, such as "Teletrip" and "I Have a Dream"
- Explains the concept of multiple masculinities
- Describes how gender stereotyping influences participation rates in school activities
- Discusses gender differences in academic achievement
- Presents statistics on sexual harassment
- Defines sexual orientation

Chapter 6—Learners Who Are Exceptional
- Adds Canadian content to the definition of children with exceptionalities
- Includes a graph of the reasons why children receive special education
- Includes the Learning Disabilities Association's current definition of a learning disability and the characteristics of students with learning disabilities
- Presents current research on identification and intervention strategies for students with learning disabilities
- Presents the Learning Disabilities Association of Ontario's Web-based teaching tool to help promote the early identification of students with possible learning disabilities (Figure 6.2)
- Describes characteristics of students with attention deficit hyperactivity disorder (ADHD) and outlines teaching strategies for working with children with ADHD
- Presents the controversy around medication and ADHD
- Presents Canadian statistics on the number of students with emotional or behavioural disorders
- Draws a distinction between autism and Asperger syndrome
- Provides an updated definition of language disorders and the association with learning difficulties
- Defines and classifies developmental disabilities/intellectual disabilities (mild or severe)
- Provides current statistics on students with visual or hearing impairments and instructional modifications
- Explores the concept of giftedness with contemporary theorists such as Gardner and Gagné
- Describes programs for students who are gifted (e.g., the Shad Valley program)
- Provides historical background for understanding services and individualized education plans for students with exceptionalities

Chapter 7—Behavioural Approaches, Social Cognitive Approaches, and Teaching
- Defines punishment
- Exemplifies time-out as a reactive behavioural strategy
- Highlights Bandura's contributions to educational psychology
- Evaluates the link between media violence and aggression
- Profiles Aboriginal role models, mentors, and programs such as Saskatchewan's Aboriginal Elder/Outreach Program and NWT's Dene Kede Curriculum Program
- Discusses educational lessons in episodes of "Franklin the Turtle" in a new Technology and Education box
- Presents cognitive behaviour modification as a self-instructional method
- Presents Butler's strategic-content learning model as a model of self-regulated learning

Chapter 8—The Cognitive Information-Processing Approach and Teaching

- Presents Canadian research on elaboration
- Updates Baddeley's view of working memory and its components
- Defines mental set
- Defines problem-based learning and provides the example of Marsville
- Highlights the HISTOR!CA organization for supporting the provision of Canadian history education to all students
- Exemplifies scientific problem-solving on the Web and television with *Sci Squad*
- Presents the PASS Reading Enhancement Program as an example of transfer training
- Explains the value of strategy instruction and training teachers to teach strategically

Chapter 9—Social Constructivist Approaches, Domain-Specific Approaches, and Teaching

- Updates definitions of constructivism and social constructivist approaches
- Explains that parental engagement in cognitive apprenticeships is correlated with education and income
- Describes tutoring programs, including volunteer and peer tutoring and Reading Recovery
- Presents the components of cooperative learning and explains how to prepare students
- Describes cooperative learning approaches such as student-teams-achievement divisions (STAD) and the jigsaw classroom
- Provides enhanced coverage of cognitive constructivist approaches to reading
- Explains the balanced-instruction approach to reading supported by the Canadian Psychological Association
- Presents the transactional strategy instruction approach (TSI) as a method for reading instruction
- Illustrates how children's literacy development is enhanced by programs such as the Family Learning Program
- Provides enhanced coverage of cognitive approaches to writing
- Describes programs designed to enhance students' writing, such as WIER
- Presents two approaches to teaching mathematics: the constructivist approach and the practice approach
- Presents innovative Canadian math projects for each of the grade divisions
- Summarizes "Logical Reasoning in Science and Technology," a curriculum that connects science to real-world issues
- Features the Kids as Global Scientists project, Let's Talk Science, and the Ontario Science Centre as examples of programs designed to enhance students' scientific literacy

Chapter 10—Planning, Instruction, and Technology

- Reinforces the importance of instructional planning
- Defines teacher-centred lesson planning as including analyzing behavioural objectives, task analysis, and instructional taxonomies (cognitive, affective, and psycho-motor domains)
- Presents WebQuests as project-based activities for exploring cultural interests
- Explains how advance organizers introduce new material by connecting it to what students know
- Presents the skills of questioning and discussing as key to the teaching and learning process
- Describes the concept of mastery learning, which involves learning a concept to an exemplary degree
- Explores the efficacy of seatwork and homework
- Illustrates learner-centred approaches as moving the focus of planning and delivery toward the student
- Depicts problem-based and project-based learning as engaging students in authentic reality-based tasks
- Explains the concept of discovery learning, which offers students the opportunity to build an understanding based on their experiences
- Offers ideas for integrating the curriculum through multidisciplinary and interdisciplinary approaches

- Presents technological advances such as computer-assisted instruction, word processing, programming, simulations, microworlds, CD-ROMs, videodiscs, hypertext, and hypermedia
- Offers a new Self-Assessment scale for inviting technology in schools

Chapter 11—Motivating Students to Learn

- Updates Maslow's hierarchy to a seven-step model
- Defines the cognitive perspective, which holds that both cognitive and motivational variables account for learning
- Explains the value of promoting students' self-determination and choice in the classroom
- Defines flow as a sense of meaning and happiness when engaged in activities
- Debates the effect of rewards
- Describes the developmental change in adolescence in which intrinsic motivation decreases
- Defines three types of achievement orientation: mastery-oriented, helpless, and performance
- Describes self-efficacy and schools that promote it
- Defines three types of goals: ego-involved, task-involved, and work-avoidant
- Presents planning, time management, and self-monitoring as valuable skills for students
- Provides current research on anxiety management
- Contrasts negative and positive peer-modelling among adolescents
- Describes programs such as Women in Engineering and Science designed to inspire and motivate students
- Profiles Dr. Marie Battiste as an individual who supports achievement motivation
- Presents multimedia animation as a motivating technological tool
- Profiles "Connections," an intervention program to help alienated secondary-school students

Chapter 12—Managing the Classroom

- Contrasts class size with pupil–teacher ratio and investigates the effects of class size on learning outcomes
- Explains the importance of beginning-of-the-year activities
- Describes how instructional interruptions may consume a major portion of the school day
- Defines "ethic of care" as the teacher's development of rapport and trust with the students
- Lists principles for establishing classroom rules and routines
- Provides guidelines for encouraging students to share and assume responsibility
- Offers suggestions to hone the speaking process and discusses the barriers to effective communication
- Provides active listening strategies
- Describes considerations for arranging a classroom
- Includes auditorium, face-to-face, small group, open-concept, and multilevel classroom-arrangement styles
- Provides a new Technology and Education feature on the use of interactive whiteboards
- Presents prevention strategies to counteract problem behaviours
- Describes interventions to address serious behavioural problems
- Explains how parents, peer mediators, and community mentors are a resource to draw upon for support
- Describes how student aggression is demonstrated
- Describes current bullying-prevention programs at the primary, secondary, and tertiary levels

Chapter 13—Standardized Tests and Teaching

- Provides examples of provinces and territories with minimum competency tests
- Illustrates Canadian achievement tests
- Defines and outlines psychoeducational assessment
- Summarizes mandatory provincial and territorial tests individually

- Explains why the Canadian Psychological Association and the Canadian Association of School Psychologists express concern about the public comparison of test results
- Describes the School Achievement Indicators Program (SAIP)
- Describes the Programme for International Student Assessment (PISA) and graphs the results of the most recent test (2000) by country
- Describes basic test-taking skills
- Provides recommendations for calculator use
- Makes a clear distinction between percentile ranks and percentages
- Describes the *Principles for Fair Student Assessment Practices for Education in Canada* as it was developed to ensure equitable assessment of students
- Explains how the Canadian Teachers' Federation adopts a critical position on the use of standardized tests

Chapter 14—Assessing Students' Learning

- Provides a clear distinction between the terms evaluation and assessment
- Describes the classroom teacher's responsibility to assess and evaluate student achievement as stated by the Canadian Teachers' Federation
- Describes the *Principles for Fair Student Assessment Practices for Education in Canada*, which also provides guidelines to ensure that assessment is accurate and fair
- Explains how the "Cross-Cultural Science and Technology Units" (CCSTU) project ensures that instructional units include culturally sensitive strategies for assessing students in science
- Expands coverage of strategies for writing questions for true/false, multiple-choice, and essay tests
- Explains and illustrates performance-based assessment
- Defines portfolio assessment and features the UNITE project as requiring students to complete cross-curricular portfolios
- Provides suggestions for how teachers' comments on report cards could be more specific to improve students' performance
- Illustrates e-portfolios, electronic portfolios that include samples of students' work
- Describes electronic grade books as innovative programs for managing student data and reporting achievement

ACKNOWLEDGMENTS

We are indebted to many individuals who have been instrumental in the creation of the First Canadian Edition of this text. We especially appreciate the support provided by all of the following individuals at McGraw-Hill Ryerson: James Buchanan, Jennifer DiDomenico, Jaime Duffy, Kelli Howey, and Alison Derry. As well, we are grateful for the sincere comments and suggestions that have been offered by our colleagues at Brock University in both the Faculty of Education and the Department of Child and Youth Studies. In particular, Kelly Powick, Anne Elliott, and Susan Drake have offered invaluable assistance and support. Thank you, everyone!

Reviewers of the First Canadian Edition

An extensive number of educational psychology instructors gave us very detailed, helpful information about what they wanted in an ideal textbook for their course. Their ideas significantly influenced the content, organization, and pedagogy of the First Canadian Edition text, and we would like to extend our thanks for their insights and suggestions.

Dr. Anne Archer, Trent University
Professor Paula Barber, Nipissing University
Dr. Katherine Covell, University College of Cape Breton
Dr. Maureen Drysdale, St. Jerome's, University of Waterloo

Dr. Sonja Grover, Lakehead University
Dr. Gary Jeffery, Memorial University of Newfoundland
Dr. Colin Laine, University of Western Ontario
Dr. Anne Marshall, University of Victoria
Dr. Dona Matthews, OISE, University of Toronto
Dr. John J. Mitchell, Okanagan University College
Dr. Warnie J. Richardson, Nipissing University
Dr. Heather Ryan, University of Regina
Dr. Barry H. Schneider, University of Ottawa
Dr. Sonya Symons, Acadia University
Dr. Patrick Walton, The University College of the Cariboo
Dr. Raymond B. Williams, St. Thomas University
Dr. Margarete Wolfram, York University

Panel of Canadian Teachers and Other Professionals Profiled in the First Canadian Edition

A large panel of individuals who teach and work with children at the primary-, intermediate-, and secondary-school levels provided us with material for the Teaching Stories and Through the Eyes of Teachers features. We owe these teachers and other professionals a great deal of thanks for sharing the real world of their experience.

David Adams, Retired Junior High-School Teacher and Guidance Counsellor, Newfoundland
Paul H. Allen, Associate Professor, Faculty of Education, University of New Brunswick
Larry Ash, Head of Mathematics, Science, and Canadian and World Studies, Ontario
Jennifer Auld-Cameron, Instructor, Nova Scotia Community College
Debra Bankay, Teacher, Sacred Heart of Jesus, Halton Catholic District School Board
Arlene Bartolacci, Elementary-School Teacher, Basinview Drive Community School
Erica Bawn, Middle-School Principal, Nova Scotia
Christine Bernardo-Kusyj, Elementary-School Teacher, Nelles School, District School Board of Niagara
Ralph Byng, Elementary-School Teacher, Ontario
Christina Clancy, Secondary-School Science Teacher, Loyola Catholic Secondary School
Juliana Crysler, Elementary Teacher, District School Board of Niagara
Susan Drake, Professor, Brock University
Hillary Elliott, Language Arts Junior High-School Teacher
Lynn Facey, Elementary-School Teacher, Alexander Gibson Memorial, School District 18, Fredericton, New Brunswick
Dan Forbes, Teacher, Arthur Day Middle School; President, Science Teachers' Association of Manitoba, 2002–2003
Karen E. Forgrave, Elementary-School Teacher, Peel District School Board
Barb Gallant, Kindergarten Teacher, Fredericton Christian Kindergarten and Preschool
Anita Ghazariansteja, Secondary-School Science/Chemistry Teacher, Toronto District School Board
John J. Guiney, Elementary-School Teacher, Ontario
Reg Hawes, University of Toronto Schools and the Ontario Institute for Studies in Education
Peter Henderson, School Counsellor, Burnaby Mountain Secondary School, School District 41, British Columbia
David Kanatawakhon-Maracle, Instructor, Brock University and University of Western Ontario
Janice King, Elementary-School Teacher, Newfoundland
Catherine Kitchura, Teacher Candidate (at press)
Dr. Lee Kubica, Director of Programs and Services, Government of Yukon, Department of Education
Alice Kong, Secondary-School Mathematics Teacher, Brampton, Ontario

Catherine Little, Instructional Leader, Science and Technology, Toronto District
    School Board
Kimberly Maich, Special Education Teacher, St. Anthony Elementary, Newfoundland
Liz McAnanama, Elementary-School Teacher, New Brunswick
Carol McCullough, Literacy Coordinator, Bow Valley College, Calgary, Alberta
David Tallach Miller, Secondary-School Teacher, Westlane Secondary School, District
    School Board of Niagara
Tess Miller, Teacher's Assistant/Research Assistant, Queen's University
Jill M. Pickett, Ph.D., C. Psych, Clinical Psychologist, Artemis Centre, Mississauga, Ontario
Michael Riordon, Principal, Niagara Catholic District School Board
Randolph Rodgers, Elementary-School Teacher, Newfoundland
Richard Siler, Science Education Consultant, Retired Teacher, Ministry of Education-
    Sultanate of Oman
Sharon Sulley-Kean, Itinerant Teacher for Speech Programming, Northern Peninsula/
    Labrador South District 2
Karel Sury, Counsellor and Instructor, Brock University
Dr. Vianne Timmons, Vice President Academic Development, University of Prince
    Edward Island
Greg Voigt, Teacher, High-School Sciences, Archbishop O'Leary Catholic High School,
    Edmonton Catholic School Board
Kirk D. White, Instrumental Music Teacher, Montague Intermediate School, Prince
    Edward Island
Alan Wasserman, Guidance Counsellor and Career Education Teacher, Thornhill Secondary
    School, York Region District School Board
Jane Witte, Educational Consultant, Faculty of Education, University of Western Ontario
Anita Wong, Kindergarten Teacher, Huntington Ridge Public School, Peel District
    School Board

Individuals Profiled in Through the Eyes of Students Features in the First Canadian Edition

We wish to convey our heartfelt thanks to the students and parents from across the country who contributed their stories for inclusion in the Through the Eyes of Students features in each chapter. These individuals offered invaluable insights into the pursuit of education through expressing their attitudes and feelings.

Expert Consultants for the U.S. Edition

Finally, we also are indebted to the panel of expert consultants for the First U.S. Edition of the text, who did an outstanding job in helping to create the foundation for the First Canadian Edition.

Dr. Frank Adams, Wayne State College
Dr. James Applefield, University of North Carolina at Wilmington
Dr. Elizabeth C. Arch, Pacific University, Forest Grove, Oregon
Dr. Robert R. Ayres, Western Oregon University
Professor Robert Briscoe, Indiana University of Pennsylvania
Professor Kay Bull, Oklahoma State University
Dr. Mary D. Burbank, University of Utah
Dr. Sheryl Needle Cohn, University of Central Florida
Dr. Rayne Sperling Dennison, Penn State
Dr. Carlos F. Diaz, Florida Atlantic University
Professor Ronna Dillon, Southern Illinois University
Dr. Peter Doolittle, Virginia Polytechnic Institute and State University in
    Blacksburg, Virginia
Dr. David Dungan, Emporia State University

Dr. William L. Franzen, University of Missouri-St. Louis
Dr. Susan Goldman, Vanderbilt University
Dr. Algea Harrison, Oakland Univeristy, Rochester, Michigan
Dr. Jan Hayes, Middle Tennessee University, Murfreesboro, Tennessee
Dr. Alice S. Honig, Professor Emerita, Syracuse University
Dr. Kathryn W. Linden, Professor Emerita, Purdue University
Dr. Richard E. Mayer, University of California, Santa Barbara
Dr. James H. McMillan, Virginia Commonwealth University
Professor Sharon McNeely, Northeastern Illinois University
Dr. Karen Menke Paciorek, Eastern Michigan University
Dr. Peggy Perkins, University of Nevada, Las Vegas
Dr. Nan Bernstein Ratner, University of Maryland, College Park
Dr. Gilbert Sax, University of Washington
Dr. Dale Schunk, Purdue University
Dr. O. Suthern Sims, Jr., Mercer University
Dr. David Wendler, Martin Luther College
Dr. Allan Wigfield, University of Maryland, College Park
Professor Ann K. Wilson, Buena Vista University
Dr. Tony L. Williams, Marshall University, Huntington, West Virginia
Dr. Peter Young, Southern Oregon University
Dr. Steven Yussen, University of Minnesota

INSTRUCTOR RESOURCES

i-Learning Sales Specialist

Your *Integrated Learning Sales Specialist* is a McGraw-Hill Ryerson representative who has the experience, product knowledge, training, and support to help you assess and integrate any of the below-noted products, technology, and services into your course for optimum teaching and learning performance. Whether it's about how to use our test bank software, helping your students improve their grades, or how to put your entire course online, your *i*-Learning Sales Specialist is there to help. Contact your local *i*-Learning Sales Specialist today to learn how to maximize all McGraw-Hill Ryerson resources!

i-Learning Services Program

McGraw-Hill Ryerson offers a unique *i*-Services package designed for Canadian faculty. Our mission is to equip providers of higher education with superior tools and resources required for excellence in teaching. For additional information, visit **www.mcgrawhill.ca/highereducation/eservices/**.

Instructor's Manual

Fully adapted for Canada, this flexible planner includes key terms, discussion/reflection topics, classroom-based activities, video-segment activities, and further readings for each chapter. The complete Instructor's Manual is available for download in the passcode-protected Instructor's Centre on the Online Learning Centre (**www.mcgrawhill.ca/college/santrock**).

Test Bank

This test bank includes approximately 1,000 questions relating to the First Canadian Edition of *Educational Psychology*. The test bank provides multiple-choice questions, short-answer questions, critical-thinking questions, essay questions, and applied assessments for each chapter.

Computerized Test Bank

The questions in the Test Bank are also available on Brownstone, a powerful, accessible test-generating program on a hybrid CD-ROM. With Brownstone, instructors can easily select questions and print tests and answer keys. Instructors can also customize questions, headings, and instructions; add or import their own questions; and print tests in a choice of printer-supported fonts.

Online Leaning Centre

The Online Learning Centre (**www.mcgrawhill.ca/college/santrock**) features a variety of instructor resources, including additional case studies, downloadable supplements, and Weblinks, in a passcode-protected environment.

PageOut™

Build your own course Website in less than an hour. You don't have to be a computer whiz to create a Website, especially with an exclusive McGraw-Hill product called Page-Out. It requires no prior knowledge of HTML, no long hours of coding, and no design skills on your part. With PageOut, even the most inexperienced computer user can quickly and easily create a professional-looking course Website. Simply fill in templates with your information and with content provided by McGraw-Hill, choose a design, and you've got a Website specifically designed for your course. Visit us at **www.pageout.net** to find out more.

Teaching Stories: A Video Collection for Educational Psychology

This brand-new two-video set includes 16 segments and video case studies developed for the Santrock *Educational Psychology* text.

FolioLive

FolioLive makes it easy for students to build Web-based portfolios, and for instructors to review and evaluate them. Visit **www.foliolive.com** to learn more about this unique resource.

STUDENT RESOURCES

Online Learning Centre

The Online Learning Centre (**www.mcgrawhill.ca/college/santrock**) features a variety of resources to help students succeed in the Educational Psychology course. Interactive versions of various text features, Weblinks, self-grading quizzes, videos, and Internet activities are keyed to each chapter of the First Canadian Edition of *Educational Psychology*.

PowerWeb

This unique online tool provides students with premium content such as current articles, curriculum-based materials, weekly updates with assessment, informative and timely world news, Weblinks, research tools, study tools, and interactive exercises.

FolioLive

FolioLive makes it easy for students to build Web-based portfolios. Visit **www.foliolive.com** to learn more about this unique resource.

To the Student

This visual student preface provides you with an overview of the features that will help you to learn the material in each chapter.

BEGINNING OF CHAPTER

Preview

A brief look at what the chapter is about, including a series of questions that will be explored.

Teaching Stories

Each chapter opens with a real-life Teaching Story featuring an outstanding Canadian teacher's commentary on teacher–student interaction, classrooms, and educational issues related to the chapter content.

Chapter Outline

A cognitive map of the chapter shows the organization of topics by heading levels.

Mini Cognitive Map

These mini-maps appear three to five times per chapter and provide a more detailed look at the organization of the chapter.

---

6 Learners Who Are Exceptional

Only the educated are free.
Epicurus
Greek Philosopher, 4th Century B.C.

Preview

For many years, public schools did little to educate students with exceptionalities. However, in the last several decades, legislation has mandated that students with exceptionalities receive a free, appropriate education. And increasingly, students with exceptionalities are being educated in the regular classroom. These are some of the questions we will explore in this chapter:

- What are the challenges of educating students with various exceptionalities and the best strategies for teaching them?
- Should students who are gifted be provided with special educational opportunities?
- What are the legal aspects of working with students who have exceptionalities?
- Should students with exceptionalities be taught mainly in the regular classroom or in a specialized setting?
- What challenges are involved in educating students with exceptionalities in the regular classroom?
- What technologies are available for educating students with exceptionalities?

LEARNERS WHO ARE EXCEPTIONAL

Learners Who Are Exceptional and Strategies for Teaching Them
- Who Are Students with Exceptionalities?
- Learning Disabilities
- Attention Deficit Hyperactivity Disorder
- Emotional and Behavioural Disorders
- Speech and Language Disorders
- Developmental Disabilities/Intellectual Disabilities
- Sensory Impairments and Physical Exceptionalities
- Students Who Are Gifted

Educational Issues Involving Students with Exceptionalities
- Historical Background
- Placements and Services
- Parents as Educational Partners
- Technology

Teaching Stories: Kimberly Maich

Kimberly Maich is a special-education teacher in Newfoundland. Over the years, she has assumed many additional roles beyond special educator including language arts teacher, computer teacher, and vice principal. Here she describes her work with Samuel, a student she met while co-teaching Grade 3.

"Samuel looked like every other boy in the class. In reality, he was profoundly deaf in one ear (unilateral hearing impairment). While a teacher for the hearing impaired monitored his academic progress, Samuel was fully integrated into the classroom setting. We structured his academic program around the accommodations and modifications outlined in his Individual Support Service Plan (ISSP), which for the most part were relatively straightforward and easy to implement. For instance, we ensured that he was seated against the wall with his 'good ear' toward the class, we touched his shoulder when we wanted his attention, and we double-checked that he understood verbal directions. Samuel also wore an FM system, or what is commonly referred to as a phonic ear. The system requires the speaker to wear a small clip microphone that feeds into a receiver headset. The system helped ensure that Samuel was not distracted by other sounds when we were speaking. Samuel removed his headset during whole-class discussions.

"Using the system also provided a unique opportunity to include other students in Samuel's ISSP. The Walkman-like device quickly became a prized possession. When students made presentations (e.g., sharing narratives, performing a play) we allowed them to pass around the microphone so that Samuel would not miss the presentation. His peers enjoyed trying the microphone and were quite amazed that they could hear each other from afar without any wires or buttons to push. Everyone giggled at my jokes about needing to shut the microphone off when entering the bathroom or staff room. Allowing them to wear the microphone demystified the equipment and helped them gain an understanding of how Samuel 'heard' the world around him—it helped them accept Samuel as a valued member of the class."

WITHIN CHAPTER

68 Chapter 3 Social Contexts and Socioemotional Development

Contemporary Theories

- Bronfenbrenner's Ecological Theory
- Erikson's Life-Span Development Theory

CONTEMPORARY THEORIES

A number of theories address children's socioemotional development. In this chapter we will focus on two main theories: Bronfenbrenner's ecological theory and Erikson's life-span development theory. These two theories were chosen because they are the most comprehensive theories to address the social contexts in which children develop (Bronfenbrenner) and major changes in children's socioemotional development (Erikson).

Bronfenbrenner's Ecological Theory

The ecological theory developed by Urie Bronfenbrenner (1917–   ) primarily focuses on the social contexts in which children live and the people who influence their development.

Five Environmental Systems Bronfenbrenner's **ecological theory** consists of five environmental systems: the microsystem, mesosystem, exosystem, macrosystem, and chronosystem (see Figure 3.1) (Bronfenbrenner, 1986, 1997; Bronfenbrenner & Morris, 1998). A **microsystem** setting includes the student's family, peers, school, and neighbourhood. Within these microsystems, the individual has direct interactions with others. For Bronfenbrenner, the student is not a passive recipient of experiences in these settings, but someone who reciprocally interacts with others and helps to construct the settings. The **mesosystem** links microsystems. Experience in one microsystem can affect experience in another microsystem. For example, children whose parents have rejected them might have difficulty developing positive relationships with teachers or with peers. The **exosystem** involves experiences in another setting (in which students do not have active roles) that influence what students and teachers experience. For example, school and park supervisory boards have strong roles in determining the quality of schools, parks, and recreation facilities. Their decisions can help or hinder students' development.

The **macrosystem** involves the broader culture in which students and teachers live, including the society's values and customs. For example, Canada has ratified the UN Convention on the Rights of the Child, which officially recognizes the importance of respecting children's rights. This focus has implications for child development, teaching, and allocation of resources for children. Culture includes the roles of ethnicity and socioeconomic factors in children's development.

The **chronosystem** refers to sociohistorical conditions of students' development. For example, students today are the first daycare generation, the first wired generation, and the first post–sexual-revolution generation.

Evaluating Bronfenbrenner's Theory Bronfenbrenner's theory bridges the gap between behavioural theories that focus on small settings and anthropological theories that analyze larger settings. His theory calls attention to the importance of looking at students' lives in more than one setting—not just what goes on in the classroom, but also what happens in students' families, neighbourhoods, and peer groups.

Critics of Bronfenbrenner's theory say that it gives too little attention to biological and cognitive factors in children's development and does not address the step-by-step developmental changes that are the focus of theories like Piaget's and Erikson's.

Erikson's Life-Span Development Theory

Complementing Bronfenbrenner's analysis of the social contexts in which children develop and the people who are important in their lives, the theory of Erik Erikson (1902–1994) presents a developmental unfolding of people's lives in stages. Let's take Erikson's journey through the human life span.

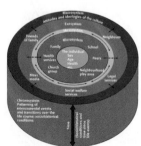

Urie Bronfenbrenner developed ecological theory, a perspective that is receiving increased attention. His theory emphasizes the importance of both micro and macro dimensions of the environment in which the child lives.

FIGURE 3.1   Bronfenbrenner's Ecological Theory of Development Bronfenbrenner's ecological theory consists of five environmental systems: microsystem, mesosystem, exosystem, macrosystem, and chronosystem.

Contemporary Theories **69**

Teaching Strategies
Based on Bronfenbrenner's Theory

✔ Recognize the influences of all environmental systems
- recognize the roles of schools and teachers, parents and siblings, communities and neighbourhoods, peers and friends, media, religion, and culture
✔ Recognize the connection between schools and families
- recognize the role of family and school with respect to students' achievement and attitudes toward school
- recognize that students who are provided with opportunities to communicate and make decisions (at home and school) generally demonstrate greater initiative and achievement than their peers
- encourage and foster meaningful relations between students' families, peers, schools, and parents
- help students establish positive moral goals (e.g., being a role model making a difference in the community)
✔ Recognize the importance of community, socioeconomic status, and culture
- acknowledge that risk factors such as poverty, parenting style, parental substance use, and unemployment can impair students' ability to learn
- recognize that some students demonstrate resiliency in the presence of risk factors
- acknowledge the role of schools and teachers as "buffers" for students who are at-risk

Teaching Strategies

This feature provides clear, practical, and specific strategies for applying theories and principles in the classroom.

www.mcgrawhill.ca/college/santrock

WITHIN CHAPTER

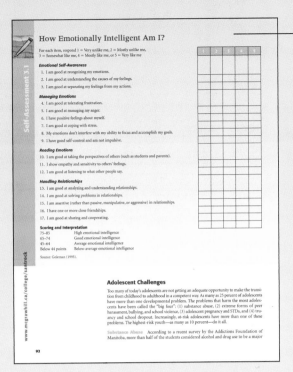

Self-Assessment

This box appears one or more times in each chapter and is closely related to the chapter content. It is a powerful tool that helps you to evaluate and understand yourself in your effort to become an outstanding teacher.

Diversity and Education

In each chapter, these boxes focus on important cultural, ethnic, class, and gender issues related to education.

Summary Tables

To help you to review as you read, each major section of the text concludes with a summary table that recaps the section's main points in a question and answer format.

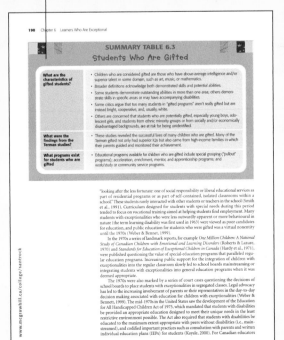

WITHIN CHAPTER

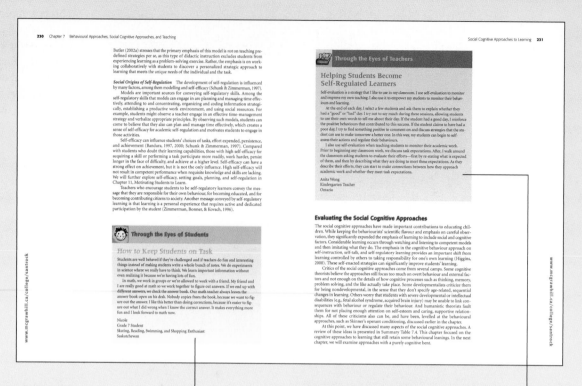

Through the Eyes of Students

This feature provides thought-provoking comments from Canadian students about their attitudes and feelings related to each chapter's content.

Through the Eyes of Teachers

These boxes, appearing several times in each chapter, present motivating and revealing comments on relevant topics from Canadian classroom teachers.

Technology and Education

This box occurs once in each chapter and highlights important issues involving how technology can be used to improve education.

www.mcgrawhill.ca/college/santrock

END OF CHAPTER

Crack the Case

Crack the Case is a case study that gives you a chance to take what you have learned in the chapter and apply it to a real-world teaching issue or classroom problem. Each Crack the Case concludes with a series of questions to help you to think critically about the case.

Chapter Review

The chapter review presents the chapter outline concept map, as well as a list of the summary tables that appear in the chapter, with page references.

Key Terms

Each of the chapter's key terms is listed in the order in which it appears, along with the page number. The key terms also are listed alphabetically, defined, and page-referenced in a Glossary at the end of the book.

Professional Development/Portfolio Activities

This set of activities encourages you to reflect on the material you just learned and to consider how you may apply this knowledge in your teaching career. Depending on your instructor's requirements, your responses could become part of a teaching portfolio.

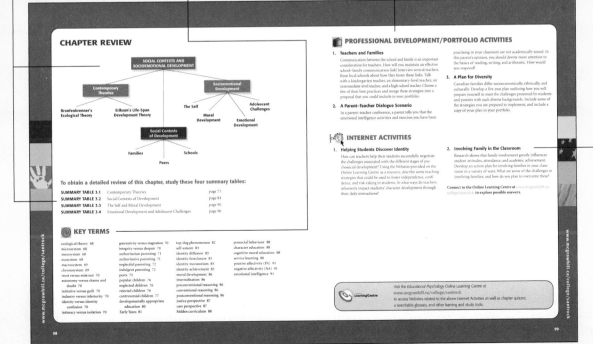

Internet Activities

Visit the *Educational Psychology* Online Learning Centre (**www.mcgrawhill.ca/college/santrock**) for links to Websites that will help you to explore possible answers to the Internet Activities that appear at the end of each chapter.

Online
LearningCentre

www.mcgrawhill.ca/college/santrock

FOR THE STUDENT

- Want to get higher grades?

- Want instant feedback on your comprehension *and* retention of the course material?

- Want to know how ready you *really* are to take your next exam?

- Want the extra help at *your* convenience?

Of course you do!

Then check out your
Online Learning Centre!

- Online Quizzes
- Interactive Exercises
- Additional Case Studies
- Video Observation Activities

FOR THE INSTRUCTOR

- Want an easy way to test your students prior to an exam that *doesn't* create more work for you?

- Want to access your supplements *without* having to bring them all to class?

- Want to integrate current happenings into your lectures *without* all the searching and extra work?

- Want an *easy* way to get your course on-line?

- Want to *free up more time* in your day to get more done?

Of course you do!

Then check out your
Online Learning Centre!

- Downloadable Supplements
- PageOut
- Online Resources

Mc Graw Hill **McGraw-Hill Ryerson**

Higher Learning. Forward Thinking.™

1 Educational Psychology: A Tool for Effective Teaching

Preview

In the quotation on page three, Canadian astronaut Julie Payette comments that education opens the door to the future. As a teacher you will open this door for your students, and you will help shape that future by helping the youth of today become the leaders of tomorrow. In this chapter we will examine what the field of educational psychology is about. These are some of the questions we will explore:

• What are the major challenges of teaching?

• Is teaching more of an art than a science?

• When you imagine yourself as a teacher, what is your image of yourself? What kind of teacher do you want to be?

• What can the science of educational psychology offer to teachers in the classroom?

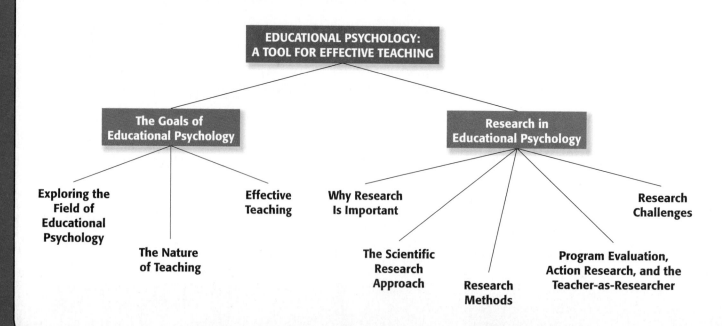

EDUCATIONAL PSYCHOLOGY:
A TOOL FOR EFFECTIVE TEACHING

The Goals of Educational Psychology

Research in Educational Psychology

Exploring the Field of Educational Psychology

Effective Teaching

Why Research Is Important

Research Challenges

The Nature of Teaching

The Scientific Research Approach

Research Methods

Program Evaluation, Action Research, and the Teacher-as-Researcher

Teaching Stories

When preparing for the writing of this text, we asked teachers from around the country to reflect on the craft of teaching. Almost everyone we surveyed included some comments or words of advice for those who were beginning their teaching careers. Below, four award-winning educators from across Canada offer suggestions about how to make teaching a positive experience for yourself and your students.

"I've learned that a teacher's job is never truly finished, so it's important to find a healthy balance between your extended professional life and your personal life. For example, while participating in school co-curricular activities can provide teachers with valuable insights about students' personalities and interests—information that can be used when planning lessons and for classroom management—assuming too many of these responsibilities is problematic for some teachers. Select one or two co-curricular activities that you enjoy but that still leave time for yourself and your family and friends."[1]

"Teachers need to teach students how to learn, but teachers also need to continue in their own professional development and learning. I recommend that teachers attend national or international conferences in their specific subject or interest area. These large conventions can help teachers develop a sense of career direction and focus. They also provide a host of valuable teaching materials and instructional ideas for classroom use."[2]

"Beginning teachers should strive to be flexible and open to new ideas. Teaching the same concept from a variety of perspectives makes your lessons engaging and addresses the learning styles of the students in your classroom. Being flexible also means being sensitive to the perspectives of students and parents. Parents are depending on you to create the best learning environment possible for their children. Put yourself in their shoes and plan accordingly."[3]

"One of the best pieces of advice I'd offer a beginning teacher is to remember to celebrate your students' successes. Acknowledge your students' efforts and accomplishments. If you believe in them and show them that their efforts are valued and recognized, they will respond accordingly. After all, helping students learn to succeed is what teaching is all about."[4]

---

1 Dan Forbes: 18 Years Elementary/Middle Years Teacher, Manitoba; TOBA Award for Physical Education Program, 2001; Roy C. Hill Award for Important Educational Innovation, 1999; Prime Minister's Certificate of Achievement for Teaching Excellence, 1997
2 Anita Ghazariansteja: Secondary-School Science/Chemistry Teacher; Recipient of the 2002 Ontario Secondary School Teachers' Federation Status of Women Award for Outstanding Female Educator
3 David Tallach Miller: Secondary-School Science, Mathematics, & Computer Science Teacher; Recipient of the Teacher of the Year Award
4 Jane Witte: Family Studies Teacher; Independent Educational Consultant; Part-Time Instructor, Faculty of Education, University of Western Ontario; Recipient of the Phyllis Meiklejohn Leadership Award

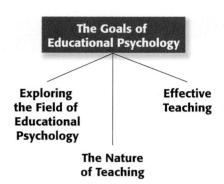

The Goals of Educational Psychology

Exploring the Field of Educational Psychology

The Nature of Teaching

Effective Teaching

THE GOALS OF EDUCATIONAL PSYCHOLOGY

Educational psychology is a vast landscape that will take us an entire book to describe. In this introduction we will explore what the field of educational psychology is about, examine the nature of teaching, and consider what is involved in being an effective teacher.

Exploring the Field of Educational Psychology

Historical Background   The field of educational psychology was founded by several pioneers in psychology just before the start of the twentieth century. One of those pioneers was William James (1842–1910). Soon after launching the first psychology textbook, *Principles of Psychology* (1890), he gave a series of lectures called *Talks to Teachers* (James, 1899/1993) in which he discussed the applications of psychology to educating children. James argued that laboratory psychology experiments often can't tell us how to effectively teach children. He argued for the importance of observing teaching and learning in classrooms for improving education. One of his recommendations was to start lessons at a point just beyond the child's level of knowledge and understanding, in order to stretch the child's mind.

A second major figure in shaping the field of educational psychology was John Dewey (1859–1952), who became a driving force in the practical application of psychology. Dewey established the first major educational psychology laboratory in the United States, at the University of Chicago in 1894.

We owe many important ideas to John Dewey. First, we owe to him the view of the child as an active learner. Before Dewey it was believed that children should sit quietly in their seats and passively learn in a rote manner. In contrast, Dewey believed that children learn best by doing. Second, we owe to Dewey the idea that education should focus on the whole child and emphasize the child's adaptation to the environment. Dewey believed that children should not be narrowly educated in academic topics but should learn how to think and adapt to a world outside school. He especially thought that children should learn how to be reflective problem solvers. Third, we owe to Dewey the belief that all children deserve to have a competent education. This democratic ideal was not in place at the beginning of Dewey's career in the latter part of the nineteenth century, when education was reserved for a small portion of children, many of whom were boys from wealthy families. Dewey was one of the influential psychologist–educators who pushed for a competent education for all children—girls and boys, as well as children from different socioeconomic and ethnic groups.

Another pioneer was E. L. Thorndike (1874–1949), who initiated an emphasis on assessment and measurement and promoted the scientific underpinnings of learning. Thorndike argued that one of schooling's most important tasks is to hone children's reasoning skills, and he excelled at doing exacting scientific studies of teaching and learning (Beatty, 1998).

Educational Psychology: Art or Science?
Educational psychology *is the branch of psychology that specializes in understanding teaching and learning in educational settings.* Both science and practice play important roles in educational psychology (Calfee, 1999; Shuell, 1996). The field draws its knowledge from theory and research in psychology, from theory and research more directly created and con-

William James

John Dewey

James and Dewey created and shaped the field of educational psychology. Many of their ideas are still embodied in current views of how children should be educated.

Diversity and Education
Canadians in the Early History of Educational Psychology

The formal study of educational psychology in Canada dates back to the turn of the twentieth century. The most prominent figures in the early history of educational psychology were individuals like William James, John Dewey, and E. L. Thorndike in the United States; and James Baldwin and Samuel Ralph Laycock in Canada. After the Second World War, more women began to fill academic and research positions in Canadian institutions. Two Canadian women pioneers in psychology were Mary Salter Ainsworth and Katharine M. Banham.

Mary Salter Ainsworth was born in Ohio in 1913 but spent most of her youth in Toronto. She attended the University of Toronto, where she earned her Ph.D. in developmental psychology in 1939. Mary Ainsworth taught at the University of Toronto, where she conducted research into patterns of early emotional attachment in infants. She pursued her interest in attachment in London and Uganda. While in Africa she conducted a longitudinal study of the development of mother–infant attachment, which she wrote about in *Infancy in Uganda: Infant Care and the Growth of Love*.

Mary Salter Ainsworth

Katharine M. Banham, born in 1897, was the first woman to earn a Ph.D. at the University of Montreal. Her research interests included mental development in infancy and early childhood, with particular emphasis on social and emotional development and the rehabilitation of children with cerebral palsy. She was the author of *The Social and Emotional Development of the Child* (1931) and numerous articles, as well as a number of rating scales and psychological test instruments that are still in use today. She was a lecturer in psychology at the University of Toronto from 1921 to 1924, practised as a psychologist for the Canadian National Committee for Mental Health, became a clinical psychologist for the Montreal Mental Hygiene Institute, and held several positions at McGill University. Dr. Banham was the first woman on the psychology faculty at Duke University and a major force in North American psychological research until her death in 1995.

Katharine M. Banham

ducted by educational psychologists, and from the practical experiences of teachers. For example, the theories of Jean Piaget and Lev Vygotsky were not created in an effort to inform teachers about ways to educate children. Yet in Chapter 2, Physical and Cognitive Development, you will see that both of these theories have many applications that can guide your teaching. Other theorists and researchers in educational psychology have tied their activities more directly to learning and teaching in schools. For example, after carrying out a two-year study of 12 secondary schools in British Columbia, Alberta, and Quebec, Henchey and his colleagues (Henchey et al., 2001) offer insights about school and teacher practices that promote high achievement for low-income students. Their findings underscore the importance of holding positive attitudes and high expectations for students, a focus on academic achievement and good teaching, structured classroom instruction, "traditional" standards of behaviour, and a sense of engagement and belonging among teachers and students. Educational psychologists also recognize that teaching sometimes must depart from scientific recipes, requiring improvisation and spontaneity (Gage, 1978).

There is spirited debate about how much teaching can be based on science versus how much of it is art. As a science, educational psychology's aim is to provide you with research knowledge that you can effectively apply to teaching situations. But scientific knowledge alone cannot inform you about all of the teaching situations that you will encounter, and this is where educational psychology is an art. You will need to make some

I have been a student and I have been a teacher. I have seen the pain that comes from not doing nearly well enough. And I have seen the pleasure that can come from the absolute joy of good learning.

Kim Campbell
Former Canadian Prime Minister, Contemporary

www.mcgrawhill.ca/college/santrock

© Banwell & DiPetta, 1998

important judgments in the classroom based on your personal skills and experiences as well as the accumulated wisdom of other teachers. As we see next, those judgments often take place in a classroom that is complex and fast-paced.

The Nature of Teaching

Teaching Is Multidimensional   One reality of teaching is that many events occur simultaneously and in rapid-fire succession (McMillan, 1997; Sumara, 2002). Events happen quickly in the classroom. Researchers have found that a teacher can be involved in as many as 1,000 to 1,500 interactions with students each day (Billips & Rauth, 1987; Jackson, 1968). Amid these interactions, teachers must make immediate decisions to manage the flow of events and keep the time productive (Doyle, 1986).

Teaching also is multidimensional in that it involves many different domains. We often think of teaching in terms of academic or cognitive domains (emphasizing thinking and learning in subject areas such as English, math, and science). However, teaching also involves social, affective, moral, and health domains, as well as many other aspects of students' lives. In school, students gain understanding and skills in academic subject areas. Also, in school they are socialized by and socialize others, learn or do not learn how to control their emotions, gain or do not gain a positive sense of moral values, and do or do not develop good health knowledge and skills. Thus, a teacher's agenda might consist of not only teaching academic subjects but also promoting socialization and personal development. Teaching involves helping students learn how to be self-reliant and monitor their own work, as well as to work cooperatively and productively with others.

Overlapping events and agendas mean that teachers constantly face dilemmas, not all of which can be resolved. And sometimes a decision that resolves one problem fails to address or even intensifies another problem. For example, teachers often must balance what is good for the individual against what is good for the group. A common challenge in the elementary grades is the need to help one student develop better self-control while at the same time maintaining order and activity in the class as a whole.

Teaching Involves Uncertainty   In the hectic world of the classroom it is difficult to predict what effect a given action by the teacher will have on any particular student. Often teachers must make quick decisions that have uncertain outcomes and hope that they have made the best move for that moment. In this book we will extensively examine the best general principles you can use to instruct and motivate students, assess their learning, and manage the classroom. Although these principles will help you make classroom decisions, every situation you encounter will in some way be new. Even the students in the same class change from day to day as the result of additional experiences together and intervening events.

Uncertainty and unpredictability also include the need to teach students in ways that teachers might not have been taught themselves. Current educational reform emphasizes the social contexts of learning, the use of portfolios, and conducting long-term projects (Arends, Winitzky, & Tannenbaum, 1998). Increasingly, the teacher's role is seen as being more like that of a guide who helps students construct their knowledge and understanding than that of a

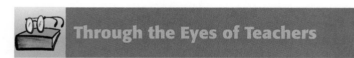

Through the Eyes of Teachers

To Teach Is to Learn Twice

As a first-year teacher, I quickly learned that my pre-service training had not prepared, and could not prepare me for all the situations that I would encounter in the classroom. Teacher education programs stress the importance of initiative, intuition, and life-long learning as skills that teachers need to develop. However, pre-service programs cannot teach those skills—just as they cannot instill in teachers the desire to make a difference in their students' lives.

When teaching, I remind myself that I was once where my students are now—struggling with theories and concepts and relying on teachers as learning guides. Now, however, it is my responsibility to ensure that students understand the very concepts that I once struggled to learn. I realize that what I had learned as a student, I had to learn again as a teacher. I had to revisit this content with the intent of finding ways to make it meaningful to students. I began to see concepts in new ways and I realized that I was learning along with my students. This realization secured my commitment to the processes of life-long learning and professional development that my pre-service instructors had talked about so long ago.

Paul Allen
Associate Professor, Faculty of Education,
University of New Brunswick
Former Secondary-School Teacher

director who pours knowledge into students' minds and controls their behaviour (Brown, 1997; Brown & Campione, 1996; Hogan & Pressley, 1997). In these respects many prospective teachers are being asked to teach in ways that are unfamiliar to them.

Teaching Involves Social and Ethical Matters   Schools are settings in which considerable socialization takes place. The social and ethical dimensions of teaching include the question of educational equity. When teachers make decisions about routine matters such as which students to call on, how to call on them, what kinds of assignments to make, or how to group students for instruction, they can create advantages for some students and disadvantages for others. In some cases, they might unintentionally and unconsciously perpetuate injustices toward students from particular backgrounds. For example, research suggests that teachers generally give boys more instructional time, more time to answer questions, more hints, and more second attempts than they give girls (AAUW Report, 1998; Cole & Willmingham, 1997; Crawford & Unger, 2000).

Teaching Involves a Diverse Mosaic of Students   Your classroom will be filled with students who differ in many ways. They will have different levels of intellectual ability, different personality profiles, different interests, varying motivations to learn, and different family, economic, religious, and cultural backgrounds. How can you effectively teach this incredible mosaic of students?

You will want to reach all of your students and teach them in individualized ways that effectively meet their learning needs. Students' vast individual variations and diversity increase the classroom's complexity and contribute to the challenge of teaching. This diversity is especially apparent in the increasing number of students whose racial, ethnic, linguistic, and cultural backgrounds are quite different from students of Western European heritage, to whom most North American educational systems originally were addressed (Banks & Banks, 1997; Marshall, 1996; Morrison, 2000).

Effective Teaching

Because of the complexity of teaching and the individual variation among students, effective teaching is not like the "one-size-fits-all" sock (Diaz, 1997). Teachers must master a variety of perspectives and strategies, and be flexible in their application. This requires three key ingredients: (1) professional knowledge and skills, (2) commitment, and (3) professional growth. We will evaluate these three needs shortly, but to begin thinking about effective teaching, let's explore students' images of effective and ineffective teachers.

The eye sees only what the mind is prepared to comprehend.

Robertson Davies
Canadian Novelist, 20th Century

Images of Effective and Ineffective Teachers   You have had many teachers in your life, and soon you will be a teacher yourself. Spend a few moments thinking about the teachers you have had and your image of the teacher you want to be. Some of your teachers likely were outstanding and left you with a very positive image. Others probably were not so great.

In a survey of almost 1,000 students ages 13 to 17, having a good sense of humour, making the class interesting, and having in-depth knowledge of the subject matter were the three characteristics listed as being the most important for teachers to have (NASSP, 1997). These results clearly support the belief that a sense of humour is critical for teaching. Consider this humorous incident: A kindergarten teacher was struggling mightily to get a pair of rubber boots onto a student's feet so that he could go out for recess. It was a difficult task that had taken up much more time than the teacher would have liked, but she had finally gotten the boots onto the little boy's feet when he said, "These aren't my boots, you know." The teacher sighed and started taking the boots off. This process proved to be as difficult as putting the boots on, and she had only one of the boots off when the boy continued: "They're my brother's, but my Mom let me wear them today!"

Our childhood images of teachers continue to influence us as adults. Anne Elliot, a professor of education at Brock University, has this image of Mr. McMurtry, her high-school history teacher:

Teaching Strategies
For the Complex, Fast-Paced Classroom

✔ Ground your expectations as a beginning teacher
- expect to be challenged to think
- adapt, and come up with effective solutions to problems not anticipated

✔ Take a long-term view to planning and problem solving
- develop systemic strategies to solve classroom problems
- keep in mind that strategies take time and consistent effort

✔ Focus on all dimensions of teaching: social, ethical, and academic
- children are complex and teachers interact with them in multidimensional ways
- get to know your students as individuals
- recognize that you are a model for their behaviour

The art of teaching is the art of awakening the natural curiosity of young minds.

Anatole France
French Novelist and Poet, 19th Century

He was a quiet, average-looking man, but when he started talking about history it was as if he grew taller and stronger with the stories he told. He was so passionate and knowledgeable about history and he made it come alive for all of us. I still recall listening so intently to his stories that I didn't hear the bell ending the class. He instilled in us the need to always search for the stories behind the story in history. Because of him I studied history in university, and to this day whenever I read a history book I search for the people and the stories that Mr. McMurtry would have brought out in his classes.

Professional Knowledge and Skills Effective teachers have a good command of their subject matter and a solid core of teaching skills. They have excellent instructional strategies supported by methods of goal setting, instructional planning, and classroom management. They know how to motivate, communicate, and work effectively with students from culturally diverse backgrounds. They also understand how to use appropriate levels of technology in the classroom (see Figure 1.1).

Through the Eyes of Students

A Good Teacher Is Someone Who...

A good teacher is someone who gives students a second chance to do their work correctly. She is fair with her students. If she says she is going to do something, she does it. She gives children fun challenges and rewards good work. She helps you learn by spending extra time with you and taking up homework with the class. A good teacher will let you take home the class pet and do chores around the classroom. Most importantly, a really good teacher cares about her students and never yells or gets angry with them.

Jonathon and Raymond
Grade 4 Students, Ontario
Reading, Movie, Video Game, and Sport Enthusiasts

Subject-Matter Competence In the last decade, in their wish lists of teacher characteristics, secondary-school students have increasingly mentioned "teacher knowledge of their subjects" (NASSP, 1997). Having a thoughtful, flexible, conceptual

Used by permission of the estate of Glen Dines

understanding of subject matter is indispensable for being an effective teacher (Borko & Putnam, 1996). Of course, knowledge of subject matter includes a lot more than just facts, terms, and general concepts. It also includes knowledge about organizing ideas, connections among ideas, ways of thinking and arguing, and patterns of change within a discipline; beliefs about a discipline; and the ability to carry ideas from one discipline to another.

Instructional Strategies The principle of constructivism was at the centre of William James' and John Dewey's philosophies of education. **Constructivism** *emphasizes that individuals actively construct knowledge and understanding. In the constructivist view, information is not directly poured into children's minds. Rather, children are encouraged to explore their world, discover knowledge, reflect, and think critically.* Today, constructivism includes an emphasis on collaboration—students working with each other in their efforts to know and understand (Oldfather et al., 1999). Thus, a teacher with a constructivist instructional philosophy would not have students memorize information rotely but would give them opportunities to meaningfully construct the knowledge and understanding themselves (Gibson & MacKay, 2001; Kahn, 1999).

Increasingly, the trend in educational reform is to teach from a constructivist perspective (Bransford, Brown, & Cocking, 1999; Kuhn, 1999; Perkins, 1999). The constructivist belief is that for too long in North American education children have been required to sit still, be passive learners, and rotely memorize irrelevant as well as relevant information. However, not everyone embraces the constructivist view. Some traditional educators believe that the teacher should direct and control students' learning more than the constructivist view implies. They also believe that constructivists often don't focus enough on basic academic tasks or have sufficiently high expectations for children's achievement. Some experts in educational psychology believe that you can be an effective teacher whether you follow the current trend in educational reform and teach more from a constructivist perspective or you adopt a more traditional direct-instruction approach. As you will see in the rest of our journey through evaluating what makes a teacher effective, many other domains and issues are involved.

CHARACTERISTICS OF EFFECTIVE TEACHERS

Characteristics

1. Have a sense of humour
2. Make the class interesting
3. Have knowledge of their subjects
4. Explain things clearly
5. Spend time to help students
6. Are fair to their students
7. Treat students like adults
8. Relate well to students
9. Are considerate of students' feelings
10. Don't show favouritism toward students

CHARACTERISTICS OF INEFFECTIVE TEACHERS

Characteristics

1. Are dull/have a boring class
2. Don't explain things clearly
3. Show favouritism toward students
4. Have a poor attitude
5. Expect too much from students
6. Don't relate to students
7. Give too much homework
8. Are too strict
9. Don't give help/individual attention
10. Lack control

FIGURE 1.1 **Students' Images of Effective and Ineffective Teachers**

Goal-Setting and Instructional Planning Skills Whether constructivist or more traditional, effective teachers don't just go in the classroom and "wing it." They set high goals for their teaching and develop organized plans for reaching those goals. They also develop specific criteria for success. They spend considerable time in instructional planning, organizing their lessons to maximize students' learning. As they plan, effective teachers reflect and think about how they can make learning both challenging and interesting.

Classroom-Management Skills An important aspect of being an effective teacher is being able to keep the class as a whole working together and oriented toward classroom tasks (Borko & Putnam, 1996). Effective teachers establish and maintain an environment in which learning can occur. To create this optimal learning environment, teachers need a repertoire of strategies for establishing rules and procedures, organizing groups, monitoring and pacing classroom activities, and handling misbehaviour (Evertson, Emmer, & Worsham, 2000; Freiberg, 1999; Weinstein, 1997).

Motivational Skills Effective teachers have good strategies for helping students become self-motivated to learn (Boekaerts, Pintrich, & Zeidner, 2000). Educational psychologists increasingly believe that this is best accomplished by providing real-world learning opportunities that are of optimal difficulty and novelty for each student (Brophy, 1998). Effective teachers know that students are motivated when they can make choices that are in line with their personal interests. Such teachers give them the opportunity to think creatively and deeply about projects (Runco, 1999).

Communication Skills   Also indispensable to teaching are skills in speaking, listening, overcoming barriers to verbal communication, tuning in to students' nonverbal communication, and constructively resolving conflicts. Communication skills are critical not only in teaching students, but also in interacting effectively with parents. Effective teachers use good communication skills when they talk "with" rather than "to" students, parents, administrators, and others; keep criticism at a minimum; and have an assertive rather than aggressive, manipulative, or passive communication style (Alberti & Emmons, 1995; Evertson et al., 2000). And effective teachers work to improve students' communication skills as well. This is especially important because communication skills have been rated as the skills most sought by today's employers (Collins, 1996).

Working Effectively with Students from Culturally Diverse Backgrounds   In today's world of increasing intercultural contact, effective teachers are knowledgeable about people from different cultural backgrounds and are sensitive to their needs (Sadker & Sadker, 2000; Spring, 2000; Wilson, 1999). Effective teachers encourage students to have positive personal contact with others and think of ways to create such settings. They guide students in thinking critically about culture and ethnicity issues, and they forestall or reduce bias, cultivate acceptance, and serve as cultural mediators (Banks & Banks, 1997).

Technological Skills   Technology itself does not necessarily improve students' ability to learn. Technology, however, does alter the environment within which learning takes place. Marshall McLuhan (1964) explained that "It is the framework itself that changes with technology, and not just the picture within the frame." A combination of five conditions is necessary to create learning environments that adequately support students' learning with technology. The first condition is vision and support from educational

It is more important to be ingenious than to be a genius.

Pierre Elliott Trudeau
Former Canadian Prime Minister, 20th Century

As you know more you understand less.

Lao Tzu
Chinese Philosopher, 6th Century B.C.

www.mcgrawhill.ca/college/santrock

What are some important aspects of professional knowledge and skills that make up effective teaching?

leaders. The second condition includes clear educational goals, content standards, and curriculum resources. Access to technology is the third condition. The fourth condition includes time, support, and ongoing assessment of the effectiveness of the technology for teaching and learning. This latter condition is based on the 1999 report *Preparing to Implement Learner Outcomes in Technology: Best Practices for Alberta School Jurisdictions.* Finally, the fifth condition is a constructivist focus (Couture, 1997). Each of these conditions is necessary but insufficient in and of itself for increasing teacher and student use of new technologies. The glue that binds these conditions together and makes the parts work as a whole is teachers—teachers who are skilled in the use of technology for teaching and learning, and who integrate information and communication technology appropriately into classroom practice.

Effective teachers know how to use and teach students to use computers for discovery and writing, can evaluate the effectiveness of instructional games and computer simulations, know how to use and teach students to use computer-mediated communication resources such as the Internet, and are knowledgeable about various assistive devices to support the learning of students with exceptionalities.

In the United States, the International Society for Technology in Education (ISTE) established the National Educational Technology Standards (NETS) in 1999. In Canada, a national protocol to enhance the sharing and use of online educational material, called the Canadian Core Learning Resource Metadata Protocol (CanCore), was started in 2001 to provide a standard for describing all multimedia educational objectives. A national education technology consortium of university, government, and industry developed the protocol (see **www.cancore.ca**).

The ISTE and CanCore standards provide a framework for defining:

- what students should know about and be able to do with technology at various stages throughout their academic lives
- what educators need to know about how to use technology effectively and appropriately throughout the curriculum
- what systems, access, staff development, and support services are needed to work with technology in education
- what assessment and evaluation strategies are best suited to monitoring student progress and technological effectiveness in teaching and learning.

Commitment   Being an effective teacher also requires commitment. This includes being motivated, having a good attitude, and caring about students.

Beginning teachers often report that the investment of time and effort needed to be an effective teacher is huge. Some teachers, even experienced ones, report that they have "no life" from September to June. Even putting in hours on evenings and weekends, in addition to all of the hours spent in the classroom, might still not be enough to get everything done.

In the face of these demands, it is easy to become frustrated. Commitment and motivation help get effective teachers through the tough and frustrating moments of teaching. Effective teachers also have confidence in their own self-efficacy and don't let negative emotions diminish their motivation.

In any job it is easy to get into a rut and develop a negative attitude. Initial enthusiasm can turn into boredom. Each day, effective teachers bring a positive attitude and enthusiasm to the classroom. These qualities are contagious and help make the classroom a place where students want to be.

Effective teachers also have a caring concern for their students, often referring to them as "my students." They really want to be with the students and are dedicated to helping them learn. Effective teachers do what they have to do to meaningfully engage students in learning, even if it means spending extra time or resources. Although effective teachers are caring, they keep their role as a teacher distinct from student roles. Finally, besides having a caring concern for their students, effective teachers look for ways to help their students consider each other's feelings and care about each other.

Technology and Education

Schools and Communities

Information and communication technology is helping children learn more effectively in school and it is also helping open schools up to communities. In most parts of Canada, students and parents can communicate with teachers and administrators through e-mail. Teachers can post students' homework assignments and inform parents of upcoming school events on Web pages. Some schools even provide students with take-home laptop or personal hand-held computers.

SchoolNet, a federal government initiative in partnership with the provincial and territorial governments, the educational community, and the private sector, helped connect Canadian libraries and schools to the Internet. By 1999, Canada was the first country in the world to have all of its public libraries and schools, including First Nations schools, on the Net; as of May 2000, there were a half-million networked computers in Canadian classrooms. SchoolNet's current focus is on creating more and better e-learning content for teachers and students. One such project, the Grass-Roots Program, is designed to promote and facilitate the effective integration and use of information and communications technologies (ICT) in the classroom, as well as building unique and relevant Canadian content on the Internet. The Profiling Canada Project, co-sponsored with Statistics Canada, invites schools to develop an electronic portrait of Canada and Canadians based on data available through Statistics Canada. Students use text and images to emphasize relationships or patterns in data that depict the development of their regions and local communities (see **www.statcan.ca/english/kits/grassroots/grass1.htm**).

Professional Growth   Effective teachers develop a positive identity, seek advice from experienced teachers, maintain their own learning, and build up good resources and supports.

Developing a Positive Identity   Your identity is the whole of you, a composite of many pieces. One of life's most important tasks is to integrate the pieces into a meaningful and positive self-portrait (Deaux, 1999; Novak & Purkey, 2001). Fortunately, teaching as a career is gaining more respect. The Ontario Institute for Studies in Education's 2001 public opinion survey of public attitudes and opinions related to educational policy and preferences reported that, while general satisfaction with schools is now at a low point, there is more satisfaction with teachers' performances. The report suggests that support for increased funding of public education is now higher than ever before. Today most teachers see a positive identity in their profession, but there is also an increasing sense of anxiety and stress associated with increased public demands on, and expectations of, teachers (Schaefer, 2001).

Your identity includes more than your role as a teacher. It also includes your personal life, lifestyle, relationships, physical health, mental health, and personal interests. Seek to integrate these various pieces of your life into a positive, meaningful identity of who you are. Also keep in mind that although your identity will stay with you for the rest of your life, it won't be cast in stone. Through the rest of your career as an educator, you will change and grow as the world around you changes, especially if you invite yourself personally and professionally to explore new opportunities and challenges (Novak & Purkey, 2001).

Seek Advice from Competent Experienced Teachers   Competent experienced teachers can be an especially valuable resource for beginning teachers—and for other experienced teachers as well. Increasingly, teachers engage in collaborative consultation in which people with diverse areas of expertise interact to promote competent instruction and provide effective services for students (Hewitt & Whittier, 1997).

www.mcgrawhill.ca/college/santrock

A number of research studies have compared beginning teachers and experienced teachers (Berliner, 1988; Borko & Putnam, 1996; Calderhead, 1996; Webb et al., 1997; Leinhardt & Greeno, 1986; Scott, 1999). In general, experienced teachers are more likely than beginning teachers to:

- Have confidence in their decision-making and problem-solving strategies
- Have expertise in managing their classrooms
- Orchestrate smoothly running classrooms
- Engage in well-practised, virtually automatic routines
- Have extensive knowledge of instructional strategies
- Make deep interpretations of events.

However, researchers have found that too often both experienced and beginning teachers lack the rich and flexible understanding of subject matter that is required to teach in ways that are responsive to students' learning needs (Borko & Putnam, 1996). Indeed, it is important to recognize that not every experienced teacher is a good teacher. Some experienced teachers will say, "Forget everything you learned in school and watch what I do instead." This might or might not be a good idea for you. Many new strategies of teaching have been developed in recent years, especially from a constructivist perspective, so it is important to keep an open mind about whether an experienced teacher is giving you the best advice.

Never Stop Learning   At the start of this chapter we quoted Canadian astronaut Julie Payette's statement that education opens the door to the future. Payette also reminds us that

> The biggest hurdle to progress is the illusion of knowledge. One of the worst mistakes we can make as a people is to think that we know it all. To forget that there is always something more to learn, something new to discover. However far we think we have been, there is much further to go. And we owe it to ourselves and to our children to keep on exploring. For if one day we stop looking, asking, and learning, that day we will start regressing.

Your learning won't stop when you get your degree—learning is ongoing and lifelong. Currently, there is much educational reform taking place, and reform is likely to continue into the foreseeable future. It is an exciting time to become a teacher because of the many new developments. Make a commitment to keep up to date about research and knowledge on effective teaching. This will include taking advantage of workshops, taking courses beyond your initial degree, reading educational journals and books, and seeking information from experts in various educational domains.

Teaching Strategies
For Effective Teaching

✔ Plan on wearing many different hats
- have a sound knowledge of your subject matter
- develop people, collaboration, and organization skills

✔ Put yourself in your students' shoes
- think about how your students perceive you
- model what you want your students to do

✔ Prepare for the future
- reflect on your teaching practice
- look for opportunities to grow personally and professionally
- think about your students' futures

You rarely achieve more than you expect.

Carol Grosse
American Educator, 20th Century

Build Up Good Resources and Supports Don't think that you have to educate your students by yourself. It is especially important to develop good relationships with your students' parents or guardians and encourage them to be partners with you in educating their children. Throughout this book, we will highlight effective ways for you to do this. Developing good working relationships with your administrator and other teachers also can benefit your teaching. Consulting with experienced teachers can be especially effective. One good strategy is to ask a competent experienced teacher to serve as your mentor, someone you can go to for advice and guidance to help you become a more effective teacher.

Also examine other resources of the school system or community you might call on in teaching your students. A school system might have funds available for a teacher's aide or technology equipment. Get to know people in your community who might be willing to come to your class to share their expertise or to serve as mentors for students. Some businesses have mentoring programs for students. For example, Pratt & Whitney Canada, of Longueuil, Quebec, provides a variety of mentoring programs. One of these programs, called Jeunes Entrepreneurs, involves youth in schools across Canada who may be interested in careers in technology. The program has one mentor working with a team of three to four students. Hewlett-Packard is another example of a business that mentors students; HP hosts an online math and science mentoring program for students in Grades 5 to 12.

We have discussed many different characteristics of effective teaching, and we have explored some of the goals of educational psychology. A review of these ideas is presented in Summary Table 1.1.

Research in Educational Psychology

Why Research Is Important

Research Challenges

The Scientific Research Approach

Program Evaluation, Action Research, and the Teacher-as-Researcher

Research Methods

RESEARCH IN EDUCATIONAL PSYCHOLOGY

Research can be a valuable source of information about teaching. We will explore why research is important and how it is done, including how you can be a teacher-researcher.

Why Research Is Important

It sometimes is said that experience is the most important teacher. Your own experiences and those experiences that other teachers, administrators, and experts share with you will make you a better teacher. Research can also make you a better teacher (Charles, 1997; Fraenkel & Wallen, 2000).

We all get a great deal of knowledge from personal experience. We generalize from what we observe and frequently turn memorable encounters into lifetime "truths." But how valid are these conclusions? Sometimes we err in making these personal observations or misinterpret what we see and hear. Chances are, you can think of many situations in which you thought other people read you the wrong way, just as they might have felt that you misread them. And when we base information on personal experiences only, we aren't always totally objective because we sometimes make judgments that protect our ego and self-esteem (McMillan, 2000).

We get information not only from personal experiences, but also from authorities or experts. In your teaching career, you will hear many authorities and experts spell out a "best way" to educate students. But the authorities and experts don't always agree, do they? You might hear one expert one week tell you about a reading method that is absolutely the best, yet the next week hear another expert tout a different method. One experienced teacher might tell you to do one thing with your students, another experienced teacher might tell you to do the opposite. How can you tell which advice to believe? One way to clarify the situation is to look at research that has been conducted on the topic.

Through the Eyes of Teachers

Never Stop Learning

I have always believed that if you are not a good learner, you won't be a good teacher. We grow and develop as persons through learning. Throughout my teaching career, I have attended conferences and workshops in an effort to keep my teaching current, interesting, and relevant for my students and for myself. I believe that I am a model for my students. If I stop learning—so will they. That is one example that I don't want to set.

Christine Bernardo-Kusyj
Elementary-School Teacher
Ontario

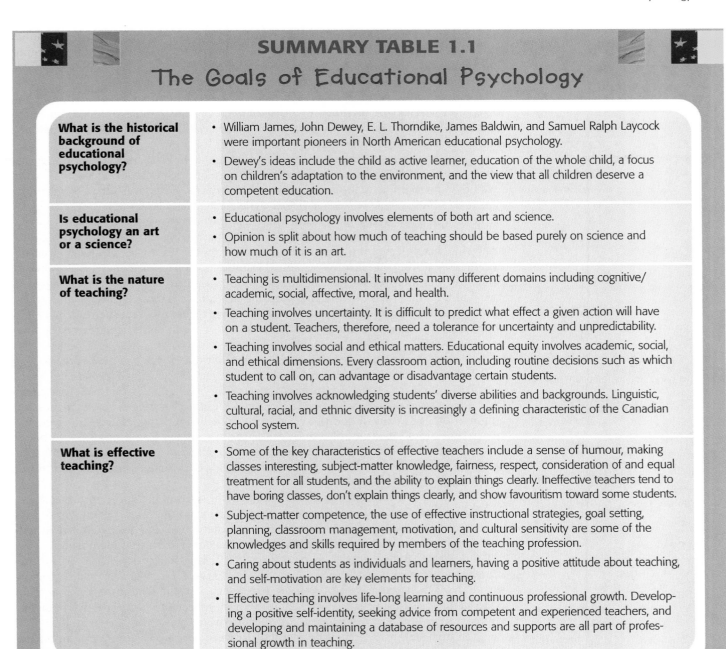

SUMMARY TABLE 1.1

The Goals of Educational Psychology

What is the historical background of educational psychology?	• William James, John Dewey, E. L. Thorndike, James Baldwin, and Samuel Ralph Laycock were important pioneers in North American educational psychology. • Dewey's ideas include the child as active learner, education of the whole child, a focus on children's adaptation to the environment, and the view that all children deserve a competent education.
Is educational psychology an art or a science?	• Educational psychology involves elements of both art and science. • Opinion is split about how much of teaching should be based purely on science and how much of it is an art.
What is the nature of teaching?	• Teaching is multidimensional. It involves many different domains including cognitive/academic, social, affective, moral, and health. • Teaching involves uncertainty. It is difficult to predict what effect a given action will have on a student. Teachers, therefore, need a tolerance for uncertainty and unpredictability. • Teaching involves social and ethical matters. Educational equity involves academic, social, and ethical dimensions. Every classroom action, including routine decisions such as which student to call on, can advantage or disadvantage certain students. • Teaching involves acknowledging students' diverse abilities and backgrounds. Linguistic, cultural, racial, and ethnic diversity is increasingly a defining characteristic of the Canadian school system.
What is effective teaching?	• Some of the key characteristics of effective teachers include a sense of humour, making classes interesting, subject-matter knowledge, fairness, respect, consideration of and equal treatment for all students, and the ability to explain things clearly. Ineffective teachers tend to have boring classes, don't explain things clearly, and show favouritism toward some students. • Subject-matter competence, the use of effective instructional strategies, goal setting, planning, classroom management, motivation, and cultural sensitivity are some of the knowledges and skills required by members of the teaching profession. • Caring about students as individuals and learners, having a positive attitude about teaching, and self-motivation are key elements for teaching. • Effective teaching involves life-long learning and continuous professional growth. Developing a positive self-identity, seeking advice from competent and experienced teachers, and developing and maintaining a database of resources and supports are all part of professional growth in teaching.

The Scientific Research Approach

Some people have difficulty thinking of educational psychology as being a science in the same way that physics or biology is a science. Can a discipline that studies the best ways to help children learn, or the ways poverty affects their behaviour in the classroom, be equated with disciplines that examine how gravity works or how blood flows through the body?

Science is defined not by *what* it investigates but by *how* it investigates. Whether you investigate photosynthesis, butterflies, Saturn's moons, or why some students think creatively and others don't, it is the way you investigate that makes the approach scientific or not.

Educational psychologists take a skeptical, scientific attitude toward knowledge. When they hear a claim that a particular method is effective in helping students learn,

In a world as empirical as ours, a youngster who does not know what he is good at will not be sure what he is good for.

Edgar Z. Friedenberg
U.S. Educator and Sociologist,
Contemporary

they want to know if the claim is based on good research. The science part of educational psychology seeks to sort fact from fancy by using particular strategies for obtaining information (Johnson & Christensen, 2000; Kennedy, 1999).

Scientific research *is objective, systematic, and testable. It reduces the likelihood that information will be based on personal beliefs, opinions, and feelings.* Scientific research is based on the **scientific method**, *an approach that can be used to discover accurate information. It includes these steps: conceptualize the problem, collect data, draw conclusions, and revise research conclusions and theory.*

Conceptualizing a problem involves identifying the problem, theorizing, and developing one or more hypotheses. For example, a team of researchers decides that it wants to study ways to improve the achievement of students from impoverished backgrounds. The researchers have *identified a problem*, which at a general level might not seem like a difficult task. However, as part of the first step, they also must go beyond the general description of the problem by isolating, analyzing, narrowing, and focusing more specifically on what aspect of it they hope to study. Perhaps the researchers decide to discover whether mentoring that involves sustained support, guidance, and concrete assistance to students from impoverished backgrounds can improve their academic performance. At this point, even more narrowing and focusing needs to take place. What specific strategies do they want the mentors to use? How often will the mentors see the students? How long will the mentoring program last? What aspects of the students' achievement do they want to assess?

As researchers formulate a problem to study, they often *draw on theories* and *develop hypotheses*. A **theory** *is an interrelated, coherent set of ideas that helps to explain and make predictions*. A theory contains **hypotheses**, *which are specific assumptions and predictions that can be tested to determine their accuracy*. For example, a theory about mentoring might attempt to explain and predict why sustained support, guidance, and concrete experience should make a difference in the lives of students from impoverished backgrounds. The theory might focus on students' opportunities to model the behaviour and strategies of mentors, or it might focus on the effects of nurturing, which might be missing in the students' lives.

The next step is to *collect information (data)*. In the study of mentoring, the researchers might decide to conduct the mentoring program for six months. Their data might consist of classroom observations, teachers' ratings, and achievement tests given to the mentored students before the mentoring began and at the end of six months of mentoring.

Once data have been collected, educational psychologists *use statistical procedures* to understand the meaning of their quantitative data. Then they try to *draw conclusions*. In the study of mentoring, statistics would help the researchers determine whether their observations are due to chance. After data have been collected, educational psychologists compare their findings with what others have discovered about the same issue.

The final step in the scientific method is *revising research conclusions and theory*. Educational psychologists have generated a number of theories about the best ways for students to learn. Over time, some theories have been discarded and others have been revised. This text presents a number of theories related to educational psychology, along with their support and implications. Figure 1.2 illustrates the steps in the scientific method applied to our study of mentoring.

Quantitative and Qualitative Methods in Research The two philosophies that dominate scientific educational research are the *quantitative* and *qualitative* approaches. Educational research tends to be a blend of both quantitative and qualitative research methodologies. While **quantitative research methods** *are primarily experimental in nature and concerned with the causal relationships between dependent and independent variables,* **qualitative research methods** *are primarily non-experimental and concerned with identifying and describing themes underlying human experience or the experience of a particular phenomenon.*

Quantitative researchers tend to argue that both the natural and social sciences should focus on testable and confirmable theories that explain phenomena by showing

---

Science refines everyday thinking.

Albert Einstein
*American Physicist,
20th Century*

Truth is arrived at by the pains—
taking elimination of the untrue.

Sir Arthur Conan Doyle
*English Physician and Novelist
20th Century*

FIGURE 1.2   **The Scientific Method Applied to a Study of Mentoring**

Step 1
Conceptualize the Problem

A researcher identifies this problem: Many students from impoverished backgrounds have lower achievement than students from higher socioeconomic backgrounds. The researcher develops the hypothesis that mentoring will improve the achievement of students from impoverished backgrounds.

Step 2
Collect Information (Data)

The researcher conducts the mentoring program for six months and collects data before the program begins and after its conclusion, using classroom observations, teachers' ratings of students' achievement, and achievement test scores.

Step 3
Draw Conclusions

The researcher statistically analyzes the data and finds that, for the students being mentored, achievement improved over the six months of the study. The researcher concludes that mentoring is likely an important reason for the increase in the students' achievement.

Step 4
Revise Research Conclusions and Theory

This research on mentoring, along with other research that obtains similar results, increases the likelihood that mentoring will be considered as an important component of theorizing about how to improve the achievement of students from low-income backgrounds.

how they are derived from theoretical assumptions. Quantitative research methods, therefore, view social reality in similar terms to physical reality and attempt to tightly control the variable being studied to see how other variables are influenced. Qualitative researchers, on the other hand, tend to dislike the idea that social sciences (such as education) can be studied with the same methods as the natural or physical sciences and believe that human behaviour is always tied to the context in which it occurs. Thus behaviour should be studied in context rather than being manipulated.

In educational psychology, qualitative methods generally refer to non-experimental approaches that are used to describe or predict behaviour but do not always help identify the causes or underlying reasons for a particular behaviour. Qualitative methods can be used when an experiment isn't practical (i.e., for cost or time considerations), or justified—for example, when a predictor variable such as gender or age cannot be manipulated, or when it is ethically inappropriate to conduct an experiment. Qualitative methods are also approaches to research that most people are familiar with in daily living (e.g., making observations and asking questions).

Quantitative and qualitative research methods are not exclusionary, and often borrow elements or techniques from each other. For example, program-evaluation research, action research, and teacher-as-researcher methods are forms of mixed educational research design that use elements of both quantitative and qualitative methodologies. In the following section we will look at some of the experimental and non-experimental methods that are currently used in educational research.

Research Methods

When educational psychology researchers want to find out, for example, whether watching a lot of TV detracts from student learning, eating a nutritious breakfast improves alertness in class, or getting more recess time decreases absenteeism, they can choose from many methods. We will discuss these methods separately, but recognize that in many instances more than one is used in a single study.

Observation Sherlock Holmes chided his assistant, Watson, "You see but you do not observe." We look at things all the time. However, casually watching two students interacting is not the same as the type of observation used in scientific studies. Scientific observation is highly systematic. It requires knowing what you are looking for, conducting observations in an unbiased manner, accurately recording and categorizing what you see, and effectively communicating your observations (Cone, 1999).

A common way to record observations is to write them down, often using shorthand or symbols. In addition, tape recorders, video cameras, special coding sheets, one-way mirrors, and computers increasingly are being used to make observations more efficient.

Observations can be made in laboratories or in naturalistic settings. A **laboratory** *is a controlled setting from which many of the complex factors of the real world have been removed.* Some educational psychologists conduct research in laboratories at the universities where they work and teach. Although laboratories often help researchers gain more control in their studies, they have been criticized as being artificial. In **naturalistic observation**, *behaviour is observed out in the real world.* Educational psychologists conduct naturalistic observations of children in classrooms, at museums, on playgrounds, in homes, in neighbourhoods, and in other settings.

Interviews and Questionnaires Sometimes the quickest and best way to get information about students and teachers is to ask them for it. Educational psychologists use interviews and questionnaires (surveys) to find out about students' and teachers' experiences, beliefs, and feelings. Most interviews take place face-to-face, although they can be done in other ways, such as over the phone or the Internet. Questionnaires are usually given to individuals in printed form. They can be filled out in many ways, such as in person, by mail, or via the Internet.

Good interviews and surveys involve concrete, specific, and unambiguous questions and some means of checking the authenticity of the respondents' replies. However, interviews and surveys are not without problems. One crucial limitation is that many individuals give socially desirable answers, responding in a way they think is most socially acceptable and desirable rather than how they truly think or feel. For example, some teachers, when interviewed or asked to fill out a questionnaire about their teaching practices, hesitate to admit honestly how frequently they chide or criticize their students. Skilled interviewing techniques and questions that increase forthright responses are crucial to obtaining accurate information. Another problem with interviews and surveys is that the respondents sometimes simply lie.

Standardized Tests **Standardized tests** *are commercially prepared tests that assess students' performance in different domains.* Many standardized tests allow a student's performance to be compared with the performance of other students at the same age or grade level, in many cases on a national basis (Aiken, 2000). Students might take a number of standardized tests, including tests that assess their intelligence, achievement, personality, career interests, and other skills. These tests could be for a variety of purposes, including providing outcome measures for research studies, information that helps psychologists and educators make decisions about an individual student, and comparisons of students' performance across schools, provinces, and countries. Chapter 13 discusses standardized testing in detail.

Case Studies   A **case study** *is an in-depth look at an individual.* Case studies often are used when unique circumstances in a person's life cannot be duplicated, for either practical or ethical reasons. For example, consider the case study of Brandi Binder (Nash, 1997). She developed such severe epilepsy that surgeons had to remove the right side of her brain's cerebral cortex when she was six years old. Brandi lost virtually all control over muscles on the left side of her body, the side controlled by the right side of her brain. Yet at age 17, after years of therapy ranging from leg lifts to mathematics and music training, Brandi is an A student. She loves music and art, which usually are associated with the right side of the brain. Her recuperation is not 100 percent—for example, she has not regained the use of her left arm—but her case study shows that if there is a way to compensate, the human brain will find it. Brandi's remarkable recovery also provides evidence against the stereotype that the left side (hemisphere) of the brain is solely the source of logical thinking and the right hemisphere exclusively the source of creativity. Brains are not that neatly split in terms of most functioning, as Brandi's case illustrates.

Brandi Binder is evidence of the brain's hemispheric flexibility and resilience. Despite having had the right side of her cortex removed because of a severe case of epilepsy, Brandi engages in many activities often portrayed as only "right-brain" activities. She loves music and art, and is shown here working on one of her paintings.

Although case studies provide dramatic, in-depth portrayals of people's lives, we need to exercise caution when interpreting them. The subject of a case study is unique, with a genetic makeup and set of experiences that no one else shares. For these reasons, the findings might not generalize to other people.

Correlational Research   In **correlational research**, *the goal is to describe the strength of the relation between two or more events or characteristics.* Correlational research is useful because the more strongly two events are correlated (related or associated), the more effectively we can predict one from the other. For example, if researchers find that low-involved, permissive teaching is correlated with a student's lack of self-control, it suggests that low-involved, permissive teaching might be one source of the lack of self-control.

However, a caution is in order. *Correlation by itself does not equal causation.* The correlational finding just mentioned does not mean that permissive teaching necessarily causes low student self-control. It could mean that, but it also could mean that the students' lack of self-control caused the teachers to throw up their arms in despair and give up trying to control the out-of-control class. It also could be that other factors, such as heredity, poverty, or inadequate parenting, caused the correlation between permissive teaching and low student self-control. Figure 1.3 illustrates these possible interpretations of correlational data.

Experimental Research   **Experimental research** *allows educational psychologists to determine the causes of behaviour.* Educational psychologists accomplish this task by performing an **experiment**, *a carefully regulated procedure in which one or more of the factors believed to influence the behaviour being studied is manipulated and all other factors are held constant.* If the behaviour under study changes when a factor is manipulated, we say that the manipulated factor causes the behaviour to change. *Cause* is the event being

FIGURE 1.3 Possible Explanations of Correlational Data
An observed correlation between two events does not justify the conclusion that the first event caused the second event. Other possibilities are that the second event caused the first event or that a third, undetermined event causes the correlation between the first two events.

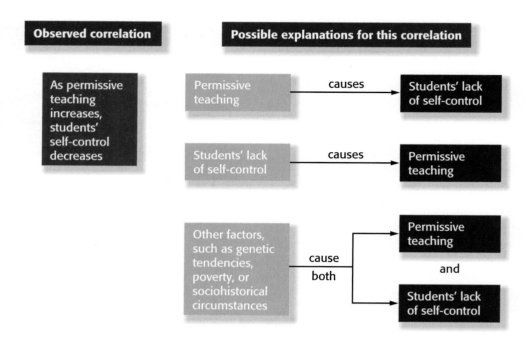

manipulated. *Effect* is the behaviour that changes because of the manipulation. Experimental research is the only truly reliable method of establishing cause and effect. Because correlational research does not involve manipulation of factors, it is not a dependable way to isolate cause.

Experiments involve at least one independent variable and one dependent variable. The **independent variable** *is the manipulated, influential, experimental factor.* The label *independent* indicates that this variable can be changed independently of any other factors. For example, suppose we want to design an experiment to study the effects of peer tutoring on student achievement. In this example, the amount and type of peer tutoring could be an independent variable. The **dependent variable** *is the factor that is measured in an experiment.* It can change as the independent variable is manipulated. The label dependent is used because the values of this variable depend on what happens to the participants in the experiment as the independent variable is manipulated. In the peer-tutoring study, achievement is the dependent variable. This might be assessed in a number of ways. Let's say in this study it is measured by scores on a nationally standardized achievement test.

In experiments, the independent variable consists of differing experiences that are given to one or more experimental groups and one or more control groups. An **experimental group** *is a group whose experience is manipulated.* A **control group** *is a comparison group that is treated in every way like the experimental group except for the manipulated factor.* The control group serves as the baseline against which the effects of the manipulated condition can be compared. In the peer tutoring study, we need to have one group of students who get peer tutoring (experimental group) and one group of students who don't (control group).

Another important principle of experimental research is **random assignment**: *researchers assign participants to experimental and control groups by chance.* This practice reduces the likelihood that the experiment's results will be due to any pre-existing differences between the groups. In our study of peer tutoring, random assignment greatly reduces the probability that the two groups will differ on such factors as age, family status, initial achievement, intelligence, personality, health, alertness, and so on.

To summarize the experimental study of peer tutoring and student achievement, each student is randomly assigned to one of two groups: one group (the experimental group) is given peer tutoring; the other (the control group) is not. The independent variable consists of the differing experiences that the experimental and control groups

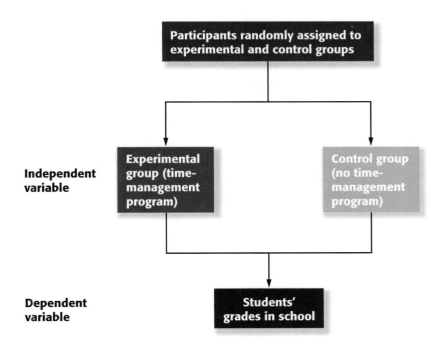

FIGURE 1.4   **The Experimental Strategy Applied to a Study of the Effects of Time Management on Students' Grades**

receive. After the peer tutoring is completed, the students are given a nationally standardized achievement test (dependent variable). For an illustration of the experimental research method applied to a different problem—whether a time-management program can improve students' grades—see Figure 1.4.

Time Span of Research   Another research decision involves the time span of the research. We have several options—we can study groups of individuals all at one time or study the same individuals over time.

Cross-sectional research *involves studying groups of people all at one time.* For example, a researcher might be interested in studying the self-esteem of students in Grades 4, 6, and 8. In a cross-sectional study, the students' self-esteem would be assessed at one time, using groups of children in Grades 4, 6, and 8. The cross-sectional study's main advantage is that the researcher does not have to wait for the students to grow older. However, this approach provides no information about the stability of individual students' self-esteem, or how it might change over time.

Longitudinal research *involves studying the same individuals over a period of time, usually several years or more.* In a longitudinal research study of self-esteem, the researcher might examine the self-esteem of a group of Grade 4 students, then assess the same students' self-esteem again in Grade 6, and then again in Grade 8. One of the great values of longitudinal research is that we can evaluate how individual children change as they get older. However, because longitudinal research is time-consuming and costly, most research is cross-sectional.

At this point we have discussed a number of ideas about why research is important, the scientific research approach, and research methods. A review of these ideas is presented in Summary Table 1.2.

Program Evaluation, Action Research, and the Teacher-as-Researcher

In discussing research methods so far, we have referred mainly to methods that are used to improve our knowledge and understanding of general educational practices. The same methods also can be applied to research whose aim is more specific, such as determining how well a particular educational strategy or program is working (Graziano & Raulin, 2000). This more narrowly targeted work often includes program-evaluation research, action research, and the teacher-as-researcher.

The real voyage of discovery consists not in seeking new landscapes, but in having new eyes.

Marcel Proust
French Author, 20th Century

SUMMARY TABLE 1.2
Why Research Is Important, the Scientific Research Approach, and Research Methods

Why is research important for teachers?	• Teachers can improve their practice by reflecting on personal experiences and listening to advice from experts. • Research determines what strategies to keep and what to avoid. • Research avoids errors in judgment based on personal experience.
What is the scientific research approach?	• Scientific research is objective, systematic, and testable and reduces the probability that information will be based on feelings, opinions, or personal beliefs. • The scientific method involves conceptualizing the problem, collecting data, drawing conclusions, and revising research conclusions and theory. • Theories are coherent sets of ideas and hypotheses that help to explain events and to make predictions.
What are some research methods used by teachers?	• Quantitative methods are primarily experimental and focus on causation. • Qualitative methods are non-experimental (i.e., observation, case study, action research); they are concerned with describing underlying themes or experiences of particular phenomena, but do not always help identify causes. • Observation involves systematic study of behaviours or events in either a lab or a natural setting. • Interviews are a data-gathering method; they are usually conducted face-to-face but can also be done by phone or by video conference. • Case studies provide an in-depth look at an individual or event in a natural setting. Generalizing from case studies can be problematic. • Correlational research describes the strength of the relationship between two or more events or characteristics. • Experiments involve examining the influence of at least one independent variable (the manipulated, influential, or experimental factor) on one or more dependent variables (the measured factor). Experiments also involve random assignment of participants to experimental groups (the ones receiving the manipulation) and control groups (comparison groups treated identically except for the manipulated factor). • The time span of research is either cross-sectional, which studies various groups all at one time, or longitudinal, which studies the same group over time.

Program-Evaluation Research The primary purpose of **program-evaluation research** in education is to examine a particular program or programs to establish effectiveness in meeting stated educational goals or objectives (Lam, 1995). The information or feedback gathered in program-evaluation research can be used to help improve an educational program, as well as adding to the general knowledge base about such programs or research methods. Program-evaluation research often focuses on a specific location or type of program. Because it often is directed at answering a question about a specific school or school system, the results of program-evaluation research are not intended to be generalized to other settings (Charles, 1997). A program-evaluation researcher might ask questions like these:

- Has a gifted program that was instituted two years ago had positive effects on students' creative thinking and academic achievement?
- Has a technology program that has been in place for one year improved students' attitudes toward school?
- Which of two reading programs being used in this school system has improved students' reading skills the most?

Action Research   **Action research** *is used to solve a specific classroom or school problem, improve teaching and other educational strategies, or make a decision at a specific location* (McMillan, 2000; Newman, 2000). The goal of action research is to improve educational practices immediately in one or two classrooms, at one school, or at several schools. Action research is carried out by teachers and administrators rather than educational-psychology researchers. However, the practitioners might follow many of the guidelines of scientific research that we described earlier, such as trying to make the research and observations as systematic as possible to avoid bias and misinterpretation (Mills, 2000). Action research can be carried out by individual teachers in their classrooms, in collaborative action groups involving volunteers, and school-wide through coordinated administration and teacher efforts (Calhoun, E.F., 1993; Calhoun, E.M., 1994). Action research serves to improve the conditions of a school; it also helps teachers in the early detection of problems, teaching problem-solving skills, and gauging the effectiveness of their teaching methods.

Teacher-as-Researcher   The concept of **teacher-as-researcher**, *or what is increasingly referred to as "teacher-researcher," suggests that teachers can conduct their own systematic studies to improve their teaching practice.* This is an important outgrowth of action research. Some educational experts believe that the most effective teachers routinely ask questions and monitor problems to be solved, collect data, interpret it, and share their conclusions with other teachers (Lytle & Cochran-Smith, 1990; Flake et al., 1995; Russell, 2000; Squire, 1998).

What methods can a teacher-as-researcher use to obtain information about students?

www.mcgrawhill.ca/college/santrock

Through the Eyes of Teachers

Using Action Research to Change Classroom Practice

The best action-research project that I ever did involved asking my Grade 7 class to describe their ideal teacher. There was a general consensus that "good" teachers genuinely care about their students and display an interest in their well-being. They said that they learned best when their teachers expressed interest in them as individuals. The project made me curious about my students' perceptions of me as their teacher. I believed that I was a caring teacher, but was curious about whether I demonstrated this care in the classroom. I started an action-research project by asking my class, "How do you know when a teacher cares about you?" Students' responses included, "When the teacher smiles at you and calls you by name," "When the teacher bugs you about getting your homework done," and "When the teacher understands that you have a family or personal problem."

The next step was to try to determine how my students interpreted my behaviours as their teacher. With some fear and trepidation, I videotaped myself teaching. The experience was an enlightening one. I saw that I was very strict and formal, seldom smiling or showing my students that I cared about them. I scared myself to the point where I realized that I had to "lighten up" in class. I now monitor my classroom behaviours by remembering what I saw on that videotape. I smile more, my students smile more, and my classroom is the caring and happy place that I want it to be. My little action-research project helped me create balance between having control and expressing care—it helped me become a better teacher.

Susan Drake
Professor of Education
Former Intermediate-Grade Teacher
Ontario

To obtain information, the teacher-researcher uses methods such as systematic observation, interviews, and case studies. One widely used technique is the *clinical interview*, in which the teacher makes the student feel comfortable, shares beliefs and expectations, and asks questions in a nonthreatening manner. Before conducting a clinical interview with a student, the teacher usually will put together a targeted set of questions to ask. Clinical interviews not only can help you obtain information about a particular issue or problem, but also can provide you with a sense of how children think and feel.

Another popular teacher-as-researcher method is **participant observation**, *in which the observer-researcher is actively involved as a participant in the activity or setting* (McMillan, 2000). The participant-observer often will observe for a while and then take notes on what he or she has seen. The observer usually makes these observations and writes down notes over a period of days, weeks, or months and looks for patterns in the observations. For example, to study a student who is doing poorly in the class without apparent reason, the teacher might develop a plan to observe the student from time to time and record observations of the student's behaviour and what is going on in the classroom at the time.

In addition to participant observation, the teacher might conduct several clinical interviews with the student, discuss the child's situation with the child's parents, and consult with a school psychologist about the child's behaviour. Based on this work as teacher-researcher, the teacher will be able to create an intervention strategy that considerably improves the student's behaviour.

Thus, learning about educational research methods not only can help you understand the research that educational psychologists conduct, but also has another practical benefit. The more knowledge you have about research in educational psychology, the more effective you will be in the increasingly popular teacher-researcher role (Gay & Airasian, 2000).

Research Challenges

Research in educational psychology poses a number of challenges. Some of the challenges involve the pursuit of knowledge itself. Others involve the effects of research on participants. Still others relate to better understanding of the information derived from research studies.

Ethics   Educational psychologists must exercise considerable caution to ensure the well-being of children participating in a research study. Most universities and school systems have review boards that evaluate whether the research is ethical. Before research is conducted in a school system, an administrator or administrative committee evaluates the research plan and decides whether the research can potentially benefit the system.

The code of ethics adopted by the Canadian Psychological Association (CPA) instructs researchers to protect participants from mental and physical harm. The Medical Research Council of Canada, the Natural Science and Engineering Research Council of Canada, and the Social Sciences and Humanities Research Council of Canada prepared a joint report establishing the policy standard for research on human participants (Tri-Council Policy Statement, 1998). Essentially, the policy states that the best interests of the participants must always be foremost in researchers' minds. All participants who are old enough to do so must give their informed consent to participate. If they are not old enough, parental or guardian consent must be obtained. When children and adolescents are studied, parental or guardian consent is almost always obtained. Informed consent means that the participants (and/or their parents or legal guardians) have been told what their participation will entail and any risks that might be involved. For example, if researchers want to study the effects of conflict in divorced families on learning and achievement, the participants should be informed that in some instances discussion of a family's experiences might improve family relationships, but in other cases might raise unwanted family stress. After informed consent is given, participants retain the right to withdraw at any time (Bersoff, 1999).

Because students are vulnerable and usually lack power and control when facing adults, educators always should strive to make their research encounters positive and supportive experiences for each student. Even if the family gives permission for a student to participate in a research study, if the student doesn't want to participate that desire should be respected.

Gender   Traditionally, science has been presented as nonbiased and value-free. However, many experts on gender believe that much educational and other research has been gender-biased (Anselmi, 1998; Chalmers, 1995; Doyle & Paludi, 1998). Educational researchers argue that for too long the female experience was subsumed under the male experience (Tetreault, 1997). For example, conclusions about females have been routinely drawn based on research done only with males. Similarly, with regard to socioeconomic bias, conclusions have been drawn about all males and all females from studies that do not include participants from all income backgrounds.

Ethnicity and Culture   We need to include more students from ethnic minority backgrounds in our research on educational psychology (Graham, 1992; Lee, 1992). Historically, ethnic minority children essentially have been ignored in research or simply viewed as variations from the norm or average. Their developmental and educational problems have been viewed as "confounds" or "noise" in data, and researchers have deliberately excluded these students from the samples they have selected to study (Ryan-Finn, Cauce, & Grove, 1995). Because ethnic-minority students have been excluded from research for so long, there likely is more variation in their lives than research studies have indicated in the past (Stevenson, 1995).

One research challenge involves ensuring that educational research does not involve gender bias. What are some of the questions scholars have raised about gender bias in educational research?

Another research challenge focuses on children from ethnic minority backgrounds. What are some of the ways research has been characterized by ethnic bias? How can this bias be reduced or eliminated?

Researchers also have tended to practise "ethnic gloss" when they select and describe ethnic minority groups (Trimble, 2000; Trimble, 1989). **Ethnic gloss** *means using an ethnic label (e.g., Asian, Italo-Canadian, Latino, or Native Canadian) in a superficial way that makes an ethnic group seem more homogeneous than it really is.* For example, a researcher might describe a sample simply as, "20 Asians, 20 Italo-Canadians, and 20 Native Canadians," when a more precise description of the groups would need to specify that "of the 20 Asian participants, 5 were Canadian-born Koreans from low-income families living in Vancouver; 10 were from homes where Korean is the dominant language spoken; and 10 were from homes where English is now the main spoken language. Five described themselves as Korean, 5 as Korean-Canadian, and 10 as Canadian." Ethnic gloss can cause researchers to obtain samples of ethnic groups that either are not representative or that conceal the group's diversity, which can lead to overgeneralization and stereotyping.

Also, historically, when researchers have studied individuals from ethnic minority groups, they have focused on their problems. It is important to study the problems such as poverty that ethnic minority groups may face, but it also is important to examine their strengths, such as their pride, self-esteem, problem-solving skills, and extended-family support systems.

Being a Wise Consumer of Information about Educational Psychology We live in a society that generates a vast amount of information about education in various media, ranging from research journals to newspapers and television. The information varies greatly in quality. How can you evaluate the credibility of this information?

Be Cautious of What Is Reported in the Popular Media Education is increasingly talked about in the news. Television, radio, newspapers, and magazines all frequently report on educational research. Many professional educators and researchers regularly supply the media with information. In some cases, this research has been published in professional journals or presented at national meetings and then picked up by the popular media. Most universities have a media relations department that contacts the press about current faculty research.

However, not all information about education that appears in the media comes from professionals with excellent credentials and reputations. Most journalists, television reporters, and other media personnel are not scientifically trained and do not have the skills to sort through the avalanche of material they receive in order to make sound decisions about which information to report.

Unfortunately, the media focus on sensational, dramatic findings. They want you to stay tuned or buy their publication. When the information they gather from educational journals is not sensational, they might embellish it and sensationalize it, going beyond what the researcher intended.

Another problem with media reports about research is that the media often do not have the luxury of time and space to go into important details about a study. They often get only a few lines or a few minutes to summarize as best they can what can be very complex findings. Too often this means that what is reported is overgeneralized and stereotyped.

Avoid Drawing Conclusions about Individual Needs Based on Group Research **Nomothetic research** *is research conducted at the level of the group.* Most educational psychology research is nomothetic. Individual variations in how students respond is not a common focus. For example, if researchers are interested in the effects of divorce on children's school achievement, they might conduct a study with 50 children from divorced families and 50 children from intact, never-divorced families. They might find that the children from divorced families, as a group, had lower achievement in school than did the children from intact families. That is a nomothetic finding that applies to children of divorce as a group. And that is what is commonly reported in the media and in research journals as well. In this particular study, it likely was the case that some of the children from divorced families had higher school achievement than children from intact families—not as many, but some. Indeed, it is entirely possible that, of the 100 children in the study, the two or three children who had the highest school achievement were from divorced families—and that this fact was never reported in the popular media.

Nomothetic research can give teachers good information about the characteristics of a group of children, revealing strengths and weaknesses of the group. However, in many instances teachers, as well as the child's parents, want to know about how to help one particular child cope and learn more effectively. **Idiographic needs** *are the needs of the individual, not the group.* Unfortunately, although nomothetic research can point to problems for certain groups of children, it does not always hold for an individual child.

Recognize How Easy It Is to Overgeneralize about a Small or Clinical Sample There often isn't space or time in media presentations to go into detail about the nature of the sample of children on which the study is based. In many cases, samples are too small to let us generalize readily to a larger population. For example, if a study of children from divorced families is based on only 10 to 20 children, what is found in the study cannot be generalized to all children from divorced families. Perhaps the sample was drawn from families that have substantial economic resources, are of Western European heritage, live in a small town, and are undergoing therapy. From this study, we clearly would be making unwarranted generalizations if we thought the findings also characterize children who are from low- to moderate-income families, are from other ethnic backgrounds, live in a different geographical location, and are not undergoing therapy.

Be Aware That a Single Study Usually Is Not the Defining Word The media might identify an interesting research study and claim that it is something phenomenal with far-reaching implications. As a competent consumer of information, be aware that it is extremely rare for a single study to have earth-shattering, conclusive answers that apply to all students and teachers. In fact, where there are large numbers of studies that focus on a particular issue, it is not unusual to find conflicting results from one study to the next. Reliable answers about teaching and learning usually emerge only after many researchers have conducted similar studies and drawn similar conclusions. In our example of divorce, if one study reports that a school counselling program for students from divorced families improved their school achievement, we cannot conclude that the counselling will work as effectively with all students from divorced families until many more studies are conducted.

Always Consider the Source of the Information and Evaluate Its Credibility *Caveat emptor* is a Latin phrase that means "Let the buyer beware"; it should be the motto for the wise consumer of educational psychology. Studies are not automatically accepted by the research community. Researchers usually must submit their findings to a research journal, where they are reviewed by the researcher's colleagues, who make a decision about whether or not to publish the paper. Although the quality of research in journals is far from uniform, in most cases the research has undergone far more scrutiny and careful consideration of the work's quality than is the case for research or any other information that has not gone through the journal process.

At this point we have studied many ideas about program evaluation, action research, teacher-as-researcher, and research challenges. A review of these ideas is presented in Summary Table 1.3. In the next chapter, we will explore the physical and cognitive aspects of children's development.

Both skepticism and wonder are skills that need honing and practice. Their harmonious marriage within the mind of every schoolchild ought to be a principal goal of public education.

Carl Sagan
U.S. Astronomer and Author, 20th Century

www.mcgrawhill.ca/college/santrock

SUMMARY TABLE 1.3

Program Evaluation, Action Research, the Teacher–as–Researcher, and Research Challenges

What are program evaluation, action research, and the teacher-as-researcher?	• Program evaluation is research designed to make decisions about the effectiveness of a particular program or programs. • Action research is used to solve specific classroom or social problems, improve teaching practice, or make decisions about specific locations. • Teachers-as-researchers conduct classroom studies to improve their practice using such techniques as clinical interviews and participant observation.
What challenges are associated with the study of education?	• It is critical to keep the participants' interests in mind. • Every effort should be made to make research equitable for both males and females since research has for too long been biased against females. • More children from minority backgrounds and cultures need to be included in educational psychology research. • Avoid drawing conclusions about individual needs based on group research, don't over-generalize from one sample or study. • Remember that correlational studies are not causal studies. • Always consider the source of information in evaluating its credibility. *Caveat emptor* (or, "Let the buyer beware") is the motto of the wise educational psychology consumer.

Mrs. Vandelaar, an elementary-school principal, felt frustrated when her teachers tried to teach their students about being good citizens. The school and school board lacked appropriate curriculum and materials to assist them with this task. She was aware that there were many programs available that addressed these issues, and she hoped to be able to purchase one for implementation at her school. She worried, however, that the school board might not see the value of such a citizenship program and would refuse to support its purchase or implementation. Mrs. Vandelaar believed that she and her teachers would be called upon to demonstrate the need for such a program, as well as the benefits associated with implementing it.

Some teachers didn't agree with Mrs. Vandelaar's perspective. One believed that it was futile to attempt to change student behaviour because they couldn't change parent behaviour: "After all, the apple doesn't fall far from the tree." Another teacher wanted a "ready-to-use" program that could be applied to all students across Grades 1 to 8. He had read an article in a popular magazine endorsing this program. Yet another teacher wanted to purchase a new version of an old program that she had used when she was a student. Mrs. Vandelaar knew that she had one school year to review existing programs and make a convincing case to the school board for funding.

- How would you carry out the background research necessary to make a sound decision about program selection?
- What issues would need to be considered? Why?
- What type(s) of research would be appropriate? Why?
- What design would you use? Why? Could you use an experimental design? Why or why not?

CHAPTER REVIEW

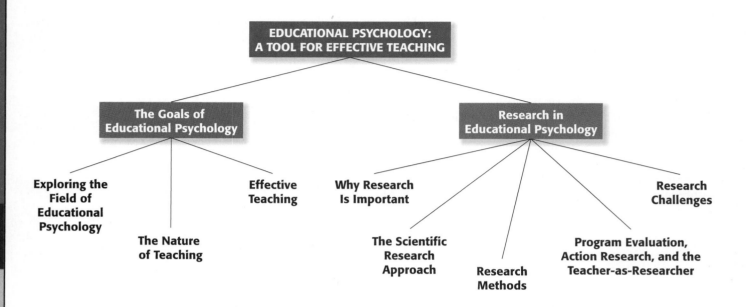

EDUCATIONAL PSYCHOLOGY:
A TOOL FOR EFFECTIVE TEACHING

- The Goals of Educational Psychology
  - Exploring the Field of Educational Psychology
  - The Nature of Teaching
  - Effective Teaching
- Research in Educational Psychology
  - Why Research Is Important
  - The Scientific Research Approach
  - Research Methods
  - Program Evaluation, Action Research, and the Teacher-as-Researcher
  - Research Challenges

To obtain a detailed review of this chapter, study these three summary tables:

KEY TERMS

educational psychology 4
constructivism 9
scientific research 16
scientific method 16
theory 16
hypotheses 16
quantitative research
   methods 16

qualitative research
   methods 16
laboratory 18
naturalistic observation 18
standardized tests 18
case study 19
correlational research 19
experimental research 19

experiment 19
independent variable 20
dependent variable 20
experimental group 20
control group 20
random assignment 20
cross-sectional research 21
longitudinal research 21

program-evaluation
   research 22
action research 23
teacher-as-researcher 23
participant observation 24
ethnic gloss 26
nomothetic research 26
idiographic needs 27

PROFESSIONAL DEVELOPMENT/PORTFOLIO ACTIVITIES

1. What Kind of Teacher Do You Want to Be?

As a teacher candidate, you may be imagining what kind of teacher you aspire to become. As well, you may be setting learning objectives as the means to achieve your goal. These learning objectives often become evident during your teacher training. Write a letter to a friend describing your expectations with respect to your teacher training and the kind of teacher that you want to become. What strengths do you want to develop? What do you believe will be your most significant challenges? Place your letter in an envelope and put it away until the end of the first term. After a few months, read it again; consider what you have learned, and redefine and confirm your goals.

2. Planning for Problems

Teaching environments are fast-paced and complex. Anticipating what might happen and planning ahead will help you to prepare for potential challenges. Try this activity. Make two columns on a piece of notepaper. Consider the grade level and the students that you want to teach. On one side of the paper, brainstorm and list some of the challenges that might happen in the classroom. On the other side, write a strategy for how you might cope with these challenges.

3. Your Teaching Philosophy

Understanding why you are teaching a subject is as important as understanding how you teach that subject. Imagine that you are about to begin your first teaching position in a few weeks. Prepare a letter of introduction for parents that outlines your plans for the class. In this letter, describe your philosophy or approach to teaching. As you explain your philosophy, consider the following questions: Is your focus on the development of basic skills? Will you encourage your students to be "higher-order" thinkers? Will you stress personal growth as a goal for your students? What will you do in your classes to help your students reach the learning objectives? Place this letter in your portfolio.

 ## INTERNET ACTIVITIES

1. Building a Web-Resource Database

The Internet and World Wide Web are powerful resources for teachers, but it takes time and patience to sift through the volume of material available online. Start building a resource database with your colleagues. You could develop a set of criteria for evaluating the educational potential of online resources or Websites. Consider what makes a good educational Website. How can you verify the validity or accuracy of the information you find? Explore three educational Websites or Internet resources; critique them using the criteria that you have developed, and prepare a synopsis. By keeping a log of these Websites and critiques, you are developing a database of online resources for use in your own classroom.

2. Educational Psychology in Different Media

Information about educational psychology appears in journals, magazines, newspapers, and on the Internet or World Wide Web. How do these different media sources compare with respect to how they present information? Find an interesting article in a research journal such as *Educational Psychology Review* or *Phi Delta Kappan*. Search for the same topic on the Internet and compare the content of the information from the two sources. What similarities and differences do you see? What did you learn from this comparison?

Connect to the Online Learning Centre at www.mcgrawhill.ca/college/santrock **to explore possible answers.**

Visit the *Educational Psychology* Online Learning Centre at
www.mcgrawhill.ca/college/santrock
to access Websites related to the above Internet Activities as well as chapter quizzes,
a searchable glossary, and other learning and study tools.

2 Physical and Cognitive Development

Preview

Examining the shape of children's development allows us to understand it better. Every childhood is distinct, and is the first chapter in a new biography. This chapter is about children's physical and cognitive development. These are some of the questions we will explore:

- Do children develop in distinct stages, or is their development smoother and more continuous?

- How do children develop physically, and how does this affect their behaviour and learning?

- What is the best way to characterize students' cognitive development? How might knowledge of students' cognitive development influence the way you teach?

- How does language develop? What is the best way to teach students to communicate verbally?

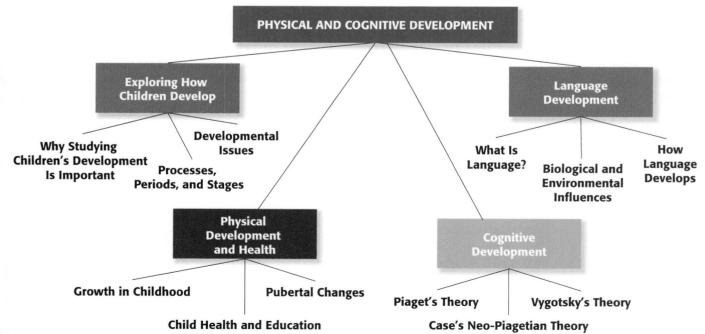

PHYSICAL AND COGNITIVE DEVELOPMENT

Exploring How Children Develop
- Why Studying Children's Development Is Important
- Processes, Periods, and Stages
- Developmental Issues

Physical Development and Health
- Growth in Childhood
- Pubertal Changes
- Child Health and Education

Cognitive Development
- Piaget's Theory
- Case's Neo-Piagetian Theory
- Vygotsky's Theory

Language Development
- What Is Language?
- Biological and Environmental Influences
- How Language Develops

No bubble is so iridescent or floats longer than that blown by the successful teacher.

Sir William Osler
Canadian Physician, 20th Century

Teaching Stories: Debra Bankay

Debra Bankay is an elementary-school teacher who, prior to her certification in Ontario, taught at a private school based in the Froebel philosophy. Friedrich Froebel, best known as the founder of kindergarten, believed that play is critical for healthy child development. Below, Debra explains how she incorporates the Froebel methodology into her classroom instruction.

"I was fortunate to have received training in the Froebel approach prior to teaching in the public system. I try to incorporate the elements of this very child-centred approach in my classes. The Froebelian approach encourages teachers to consider students' emotional, spiritual, mental, physical, and social experiences when planning lessons or assessing student learning.

"Based on my experiences, I believe that play is an important tool for encouraging students' language skills and cognitive development. However, I have also come to realize that as students progress through the elementary grades the nature and design of this play needs to be modified in order to be developmentally appropriate. For instance, while teaching a Grade 7–8 unit on Canadian history, I wanted students to use their research skills to learn about the Fathers of Confederation. I also wanted to incorporate play-based activities that would help them develop a deeper understanding of these early Canadians.

"As part of the unit, students were required to use their research findings to create a detailed character sketch of one of the "Fathers." Specifically, they needed to know how their characters lived and behaved. Toward the end of the unit, students re-enacted the Day of Confederation. They came dressed in costume, made oral presentations, and participated in debates using language that was consistent with the 1800s. They also created activities and games that were representative of the era. The next day, the class discussed the meaning and impact of Confederation on modern-day Canada. The students loved the project and I was able to integrate many elements of the curriculum into the unit. By providing students with opportunities to express their learning across a number of authentic, playful activities, I was able to tailor instruction to meet their diverse developmental levels and learning styles."

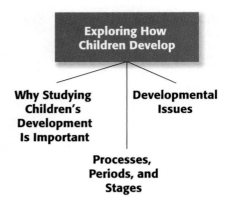

Why Studying Children's Development Is Important

Processes, Periods, and Stages

Developmental Issues

www.mcgrawhill.ca/college/santrock

EXPLORING HOW CHILDREN DEVELOP

Twentieth-century philosopher George Santayana once reflected, "Children are on a different plane. They belong to a generation and way of feeling properly their own." Let's explore what that plane is like.

Why Studying Children's Development Is Important

Why study children's development? As a teacher, you will be responsible for a new wave of children each year in your classroom. The more you learn about children's development, the more you can understand at what level it is appropriate to teach them.

Childhood has become such a distinct phase of the human life span that it is hard to imagine that it was not always thought of in that way. However, in medieval times, laws generally did not distinguish between child and adult offences and children were often treated like miniature adults.

Today we view children quite differently than was the case in medieval times. We conceive of childhood as a highly eventful and unique time of life that lays an important foundation for the adult years and is highly differentiated from them. We identify distinct periods within childhood in which children master special skills and confront new life tasks. We value childhood as a special time of growth and change, and we invest great resources in caring for and educating our children. We protect them from the excesses of adult work through tough child labour laws, treat their crimes against society under a special system of juvenile justice, and have government provisions for helping children when ordinary family support systems fail or when a family seriously threatens a child's well-being.

Each child develops partly like all other children, partly like some other children, and partly like no other children. We often direct our attention to a child's uniqueness. But psychologists who study development often are drawn to children's shared characteristics—as are teachers who must manage and educate groups of same- or similar-age children. As humans, every person travels some common paths—Leonardo da Vinci, Margaret Atwood, Wayne Gretzky, Mother Teresa, and most likely you yourself all walked at about one year, engaged in fantasy play as a child, developed an expanded vocabulary in the elementary-school years, and became more independent as a youth.

Just what do psychologists mean when they speak of a person's "development"? **Development** *is the pattern of biological, cognitive, and socioemotional changes that begins at conception and continues through the life span.* Most development involves growth, although it also eventually involves decay (dying).

An important concept in education related to development is that education should be age-appropriate. That is, teaching should take place at a level that is neither too difficult and stressful nor too easy and boring. As we discuss development in this chapter and the next, keep in mind how the developmental changes we describe can help you understand the optimal level for teaching and learning. For example, it is not a good strategy to try to push children to read before they are developmentally ready; but when they are ready, reading materials should be presented at the appropriate level.

Processes, Periods, and Stages

The pattern of development is complex because it is the product of several processes: biological, cognitive, and socioemotional. Development also can be described in terms of periods and stages.

Biological, Cognitive, and Socioemotional Processes   **Biological processes** *involve changes in the child's body. Genetic inheritance plays a large part.* Biological processes underlie the development of the brain, height and weight gains, changes in motor skills, and puberty's hormonal changes.

Cognitive processes *involve changes in the child's thinking, intelligence, and language.* Cognitive developmental processes enable a growing child to memorize a poem, imagine how to solve a math problem, come up with a creative strategy, or string together meaningfully connected sentences.

Socioemotional processes *involve changes in the child's relationships with other people, changes in emotion, and changes in personality.* Parents' nurturance toward their child, a girl's aggressive attack on a peer, a boy's empathetic feelings for a sick or hurt classmate, and an adolescent's feelings of joy after getting good grades all reflect socioemotional processes in development.

In this chapter, we will focus on physical (biological) and cognitive processes. In the next chapter, we will explore socioemotional processes. Remember as you read about biological, cognitive, and socioemotional processes that they are interwoven. Socioemotional processes can shape cognitive processes, cognitive processes can promote or restrict socioemotional processes, biological processes can influence cognitive processes, and so on.

Periods of Development   For the purposes of organization and understanding, we commonly describe development in terms of periods. In the most widely used system of classification, the developmental periods are infancy, early childhood, middle and late childhood, adolescence, early adulthood, middle adulthood, and late adulthood.

Infancy *extends from birth to 18–24 months.* It is a time of extreme dependence on adults. Many activities, such as language development, symbolic thought, sensorimotor coordination, and social learning, are just beginning.

Early childhood (*sometimes called the "preschool years"*) *extends from the end of infancy to about 5 or 6 years.* During this period, children become more self-sufficient, develop school-readiness skills (such as learning to follow instructions and identify letters), and spend many hours with peers. Grade 1 typically marks the end of early childhood.

Middle and late childhood (*sometimes called the "elementary-school years"*) *extends from about 6 to 11 years of age.* Children master the fundamental skills of reading, writing, and math at this time. Achievement becomes a more central theme of children's lives and they increase their self-control. In this period, they interact more with the wider social world beyond their family.

Adolescence *involves the transition from childhood to adulthood.* It begins around ages 10 to 12 and ends around 18 to 22. Adolescence starts with rapid physical changes, including gains in height and weight and the development of sexual functions. In adolescence, individuals more intensely pursue independence and seek their own identity. Their thought becomes more abstract, logical, and idealistic.

Early adulthood *begins in the late teens or early twenties and stretches into the thirties.* It is a time when work and love become main themes in life. Individuals make important career decisions and usually seek to have an intimate relationship through marriage or a relationship with a significant other. Other developmental periods have been described for older adults, but we will confine our discussion to the periods most relevant for children's education.

Developmental Issues

Three broad theoretical questions repeatedly come up when we study children's development:

- Is a child's development due more to maturation (nature, heredity) or more to experience (nurture, environment)?
- Is a child's development more continuous and smooth or more discontinuous and stagelike?
- Is a child's development due more to early experiences or more to later experiences?

Maturation and Experience (Nature and Nurture)   We can think of development as produced not only by the interplay of biological, cognitive, and socioemotional processes, but also by the interaction of maturation and experience. **Maturation** *is the orderly sequence* *of changes dictated by the child's genetic blueprint.* Just as a sunflower grows in an orderly way (unless defeated by an unfriendly environment), so does a child grow in an orderly way, according to the maturational view. We walk before we talk, speak one word before two words, grow rapidly in infancy and less so in childhood, and experience a rush of sexual hormones in puberty after a lull in childhood. The maturationists acknowledge that extreme environments (those that are physically or psychologically barren and hostile) can harm development. However, they believe that basic growth tendencies are genetically wired into the child's makeup.

In contrast, other psychologists emphasize the importance of experiences in children's development. Experiences run the gamut of inputs from the biological environment (nutrition, medical care, drugs, physical accidents) to the social environment (family, peers, schools, communities, media, culture).

The debate about whether development is influenced primarily by maturation or by experience, which is often called the **nature–nurture controversy**, has been a part of psychology since its beginning. Nature refers to the child's biological inheritance, nurture to environmental experiences. The "nature" proponents claim that biological inheritance is what mainly determines development. The "nurture" proponents argue that environmental experiences are more important.

Continuity and Discontinuity Think about your development for a moment. Did you gradually grow to become the person you are, in the slow cumulative way a seedling grows into a giant oak? Or did you experience sudden, distinct changes as you grew, like the change of a caterpillar into a butterfly? (See Figure 2.1.)

Continuity in development *refers to gradual, cumulative change.* For example, consider the continuity in development when students gradually become better at math or come to understand the importance of treating others fairly. For the most part, psychologists who emphasize experience describe development as gradual and continuous. **Discontinuity in development** *refers to more distinctive, stagelike change.* In this view, each of us passes through a sequence of stages in which change is qualitative rather than quantitative. That is, development does not just produce more of something, it produces something different (Marini & Case, 1994). As a caterpillar changes into a butterfly, it becomes a different kind of organism. Its development is discontinuous. Similarly, at some point in development a student becomes capable of writing a meaningful sentence, which the student could not have done before. This is qualitative, discontinuous change.

Early and Later Experience The **early–later experience issue** *focuses on the degree to which early experiences (especially in infancy and/or early childhood)* or later experiences are the key determinants of development. For example, if infants and young children experience highly stressful circumstances, can those experiences be overcome by later, more positive experiences?

FIGURE 2.1 Continuity and Discontinuity in Development
Is human development like a seedling gradually growing into a giant oak? Or is it more like a caterpillar suddenly becoming a butterfly?

The early–later experience issue has a long history and continues to be hotly debated. Some developmentalists believe that unless infants experience warm, nurturant caregiving in the first year or so of life, their development will never be optimal (Bowlby, 1989). Plato was sure that infants who are rocked become better athletes. Nineteenth-century New England ministers told parents in Sunday sermons that the way they handled their infants determined their children's future character. The emphasis on early experience rests on the belief that each life is an unbroken trail on which a psychological quality can be traced back to a specific origin early in development (Kagan, 1992; 1998).

In contrast, proponents of the influence of later experience argue that development ebbs and flows like an ocean. They say that children are capable of change and that later competent caregiving is just as important as, or more important than, early competent caregiving.

People in Western cultures tend to support the early-experience side of this issue. Many of them have been influenced by the views of famous psychoanalytic theorist Sigmund Freud, who believed that virtually all of a person's important life experiences occur in the first five years of life, especially in relationships with parents. Many people in Eastern cultures, on the other hand, believe that experiences in the elementary-school years are more important than earlier experiences. This stance stems from their view that the key changes in children's cognitive skills, especially their ability to reason, occur after the infant and early-childhood years.

Evaluating the Developmental Issues   Most developmentalists believe it is unwise to take an extreme position on these three developmental questions. Development is not all nature, not all nurture (Plomin, 2000; Wahlsteni, 2000). It is not all continuous, not all discontinuous (Case, 1998). And it is not all early experience or all later experience. Yet how you lean regarding these questions has a bearing on issues that will affect your teaching. For example, are girls less likely than boys to do well in math and science? And if they are, is this because of their "feminine" nature, or because of society's masculine bias? Depending on how you answer this question, you will find different ways to resolve the teaching problem it implies. For children who grew up with poverty, parental neglect, and poor schooling, can enriched experiences in adolescence remove the "deficits"? Your stance on such issues as nature versus nurture also will influence your answer to that question.

PHYSICAL DEVELOPMENT AND HEALTH

As twentieth-century Welsh poet Dylan Thomas artfully observed, children "run all the sun long." And as their physical development advances, their small worlds widen. In this section, we will focus mainly on the normal aspects of physical development.

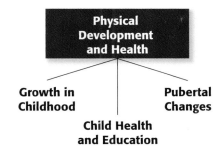

Growth in Childhood

The infant's growth is extremely rapid. The young child's growth is slower. This slower rate continues through middle and late childhood. Otherwise, we would be giants.

An important aspect of physical growth is the development of the brain and nervous system. The number and size of the brain's nerve endings continue to grow at least until adolescence. Some of the brain's increase in size also is due to **myelination**, *a process in which many cells of the brain and nervous system are covered with an insulating layer of fat cells. This increases the speed at which information travels through the nervous system.* Myelination in the areas of the brain related to hand–eye coordination is not complete until about four years of age. Myelination in brain areas that are important in focusing attention is not complete until the end of the elementary-school years (Case, 1992a, 1999; Tanner, 1978). The implications for teaching are that students will have more difficulty focusing their attention and maintaining it for very long in early childhood, but their attention will improve as they move through the elementary-school years. Even in elementary school and later, many educators believe occasional short breaks sustain students' energy and motivation to learn.

Gross motor and fine motor skills develop extensively during childhood. **Gross motor skills** *involve large-muscle activities, such as running and playing basketball.* **Fine motor skills** *involve finely tuned movements, such as the finger dexterity required for writing and drawing.* Children become increasingly venturesome as their gross motor skills improve.

Preschool and kindergarten teachers should implement developmentally appropriate activities for the exercise of gross motor skills. In early childhood, these include exercises that involve fundamental movement, daily fitness, and perceptual–motor activities (Poest et al., 1990). Walking on a beam is one example of an exercise that promotes fundamental movement skills. Daily fitness activities can include a run accompanied by music. Combining fitness with creative movement, music, and children's imagination is a good strategy. Children enjoy moving like snakes, cats, kangaroos, and airplanes.

Avoid recordings and activities that "program" children or involve group calisthenics that are not appropriate for young children. To develop young children's gross motor skills, also include perceptual–motor activities. Teachers can ask students to copy their movements, tap and march to the tune of nursery rhymes, and complete safe obstacle courses.

The development of young children's fine motor skills allows them to draw with more control and skill. Art provides considerable insight into children's perceptual worlds. These insights include what children are attending to, how they view space and distance, and how they experience patterns and forms. Teachers can give students a positive context for artistic expression by providing them a work space where they don't have to be worried about being messy or damaging things.

During the elementary-school years, children's motor development becomes much smoother and more coordinated. Children gain greater control over their bodies and can sit and attend for longer periods of time. However, classes should still be active and activity-oriented. Throughout childhood, boys tend to be better at gross motor skills, while girls tend to be better at fine motor skills.

> Reading is to the mind what exercise is to the body.
>
> *Joseph Addison*
> English Poet, 17th Century

Child Health and Education

Although we have become a health-conscious country, many children as well as adults do not practise good health habits. All too many children eat too much junk food and spend too much time being couch potatoes.

Physical Education Classes   For too long, exercise was relegated to a back seat in children's education. Even today, too little attention is given to the quality of physical education classes, whether children are getting adequate exercise, and whether they eat properly. Recall our earlier discussion of how physical, cognitive, and socioemotional development are interrelated. Children who come to school hungry and who do not exercise regularly (physical development) often do not attend as efficiently in school and are less motivated to study (cognitive development) than their healthier counterparts.

Even when students take a physical education class, they do not always actively participate. Observations of physical education classes at four elementary schools found that students moved through space only 50 percent of the time they were in class, and moved continuously only an average of 2.2 minutes (Parcel et al., 1987).

Does it make a difference if students are encouraged to exercise vigorously in elementary school? One study says yes (Tuckman & Hinkle, 1988). Students were randomly assigned either to three 30-minute running programs per week or to regular attendance in physical education classes. In cardiovascular fitness and creative thinking, the students in the running program were superior to the students who regularly attended traditional physical education classes.

Are Television, Video Games, and the Internet the Culprits?   Some experts argue that television, computer games, and the Internet might be partly to blame for the poor physical fitness of our country's children. Gingras (2001) argues that such claims may be simplistic. She maintains that obesity is a complex problem that is partly genetic and partly environmental. She suggests that it is not uncommon, and certainly is an environmental

As children move through the elementary-school years, they gain greater control over their bodies. Physical action is essential for them to refine their developing skills.

factor of concern, for children to spend three to four hours daily watching television or engaged in computer entertainment. Thus, reducing time spent viewing television, playing video games, or surfing the Net is a wise strategy, not only for improved physical fitness but also for increasing time spent on homework and school-related activities. The amount of time a child spends on these activities may be a topic you will want to explore with parents of students who are having difficulty in school.

A Model School-Health Program: A research report in the *Canadian Medical Association Journal* (Tremblay & Willms, 2000) highlighted an alarming rise in the incidence of child and youth obesity. For example, from 1981 to 1996 the prevalence of overweight children increased from 15 percent to 35.4 percent for boys, and from 15 percent to 29.2 percent for girls. During the same interval the prevalence of obesity in children tripled, from 5 percent to 16.6 percent for boys and from 5 percent to 14.6 percent for girls.

A major concern regarding childhood obesity is that obese children tend to become obese adults, facing an increased risk of diabetes, heart disease, orthopaedic problems, and many other chronic diseases. Increasingly, pediatricians are seeing a rise in the incidences of childhood hyperlipidemia, hypertension, and diabetes.

Efforts are being made to combat the problem. One model school-health program is the Heart Healthy Kids™ physical activity program. Heart Healthy Kids introduces and combines a wide range of movements and skills that could form the basis of daily physical activity in the classroom. Locomotion and travelling skills for each grade level are combined in a variety of sequences to increase cardiovascular fitness, flexibility, and balance. Stability skills are sequenced into easy-to-follow routines. The program also provides students with accurate and detailed information about the heart and how to maintain it. For instance, the program promotes the development of proper eating habits, exercise, and healthy lifestyle choices by including life experiences to which students can readily make personal connections. Heart Healthy Kids supports the healthy living and active participation strands in health and physical education programs at all grade levels.

Am I Physically and Mentally Healthy?

For each item, respond 1 = Never, 2 = Sometimes, or 3 = Always.

Exercise/Fitness

1. I maintain a desired weight and avoid being overweight or underweight.

2. I do vigorous exercises (such as running, swimming, walking briskly) for 15 to 30 minutes at least 3 times a week.

3. I do exercises that improve my muscle tone (such as yoga, calisthenics, and lifting weights) for 15 to 30 minutes at least 3 times a week.

4. I use part of my leisure time to participate in individual, family, or team activities that increase my fitness level (such as gardening, bowling, golf, and baseball).

Eating Habits

5. I eat a variety of foods each day, such as fruits and vegetables, whole-grain breads and cereals, lean meats, dairy products, dry peas and beans, and nuts and seeds.

6. I limit the amount of fat, saturated fat, and cholesterol I eat.

7. I limit the amount of salt I eat.

8. I avoid eating too much sugar (especially frequent candy snacks or soft drinks).

Alcohol/Drugs, Smoking

9. I avoid drinking alcoholic beverages or I drink no more than one or two drinks a day.

10. I avoid using alcohol or other drugs as a way of handling stressful situations or problems in my life.

11. I avoid smoking cigarettes or using other nicotine substances.

Stress Control

12. I have a job or do other work that I enjoy.

13. I find it easy to relax and I express my feelings freely.

14. I have good resources, such as close friends or relatives, whom I can call on in times of stress.

15. I participate in group activities (such as community organizations) or hobbies that I enjoy.

Scoring and Interpretation

40–45	Excellent role model	Excellent physical and mental health
35–39	Good role model	Good physical and mental health
30–34	Potential to be an effective role model	Physical and mental health need some work
15–29	Poor role model	Poor physical and mental health

Pubertal Changes

Puberty *is a phase of maturation that occurs mainly in early adolescence. The changes involve a height and weight spurt and sexual maturation.* The changes start on the average at about $10\frac{1}{2}$ years in females and $12\frac{1}{2}$ years in males (see Figure 2.2). One of the most remarkable

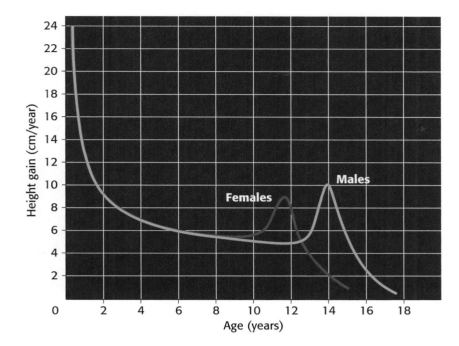

FIGURE 2.2 **Pubertal Growth Spurt**
On the average, the growth spurt that characterizes pubertal change occurs 2 years earlier for girls ($10\frac{1}{2}$) than for boys ($12\frac{1}{2}$).

Youth is the only season for enjoyment, and the first twenty-five years of one's life are worth all of the rest of the longest life of man, even though those five-and-twenty be spent in penury and contempt, and the rest in the possession of wealth, honours, respectability.

George Borrow
English Writer and Traveller, 19th Century

normal variations is that, of two boys (or two girls) of the same chronological age, one might complete the pubertal sequence before the other has begun it. For example, the onset of puberty can occur as early as 8 years of age in girls and $9\frac{1}{2}$ years in boys, or as late as 13 in girls and $13\frac{1}{2}$ in boys, and still be considered within the normal range.

Puberty is coming earlier and has been doing so since the beginning of the twentieth century as a result of improved health and nutrition, although the changes in pubertal timing have begun to taper off. Menstruation is a very late pubertal event, with the height/weight spurt usually appearing about two years earlier. In 1900, a girl's first menstruation (called menarche) occurred at an average of 14 years of age, whereas today it occurs at about 12 years of age.

Because puberty is coming so much earlier, elementary-school teachers are seeing far more students in the late elementary-school grades who have entered puberty, especially girls. Today, an increasing number of nine-year-old girls are entering puberty. The increasingly early appearance of puberty calls attention to the importance of including competent instruction in health and sex education in the elementary-school years.

Think back to when you were in Grade 6 or 7. Some of your classmates had not yet entered puberty, others were just starting, and yet others were far along the pubertal path. Boys and girls who enter puberty earlier or later than their peers might perceive themselves differently. Today, there is a special concern about early maturation in girls. A host of studies in the last decade have documented that early-maturing girls are vulnerable to developing a number of problems (Brooks-Gunn, 1996; Brooks-Gunn & Paikoff, 1997; Petersen, 2000). Early-maturing girls are more likely to smoke, drink, be depressed, have an eating disorder, request earlier independence from their parents, have older friends, and date earlier. Apparently as a result of their

Through the Eyes of Teachers

Growing Up Is Hard Work

Adolescence is a time of difficult decision-making. Adolescents are called upon to overcome many challenges as they face an increased emphasis on body image; drug, alcohol, and sexual experimentation; and school competition. Many of the decisions that these students make will affect them long after they leave high school. As educators, we need to help students understand the implications of their decisions without telling them what to do. We need to help them acquire the skills and perspectives to make decisions that are right for them. For instance, many counsellors use a "decisional balance grid" when educating students about drugs and alcohol. By considering all factors, many students begin to realize that alcohol and drug use is not in their best interests. When students begin to make better decisions for themselves, they can become positive role models for others.

Peter Henderson
School Counsellor
British Columbia

socioemotional and cognitive immaturity, combined with their early physical development, early-maturing girls are easily lured into problem behaviours.

At this point we have discussed a number of ideas about exploring how children develop and children's physical development and health. A review of these ideas is presented in Summary Table 2.1.

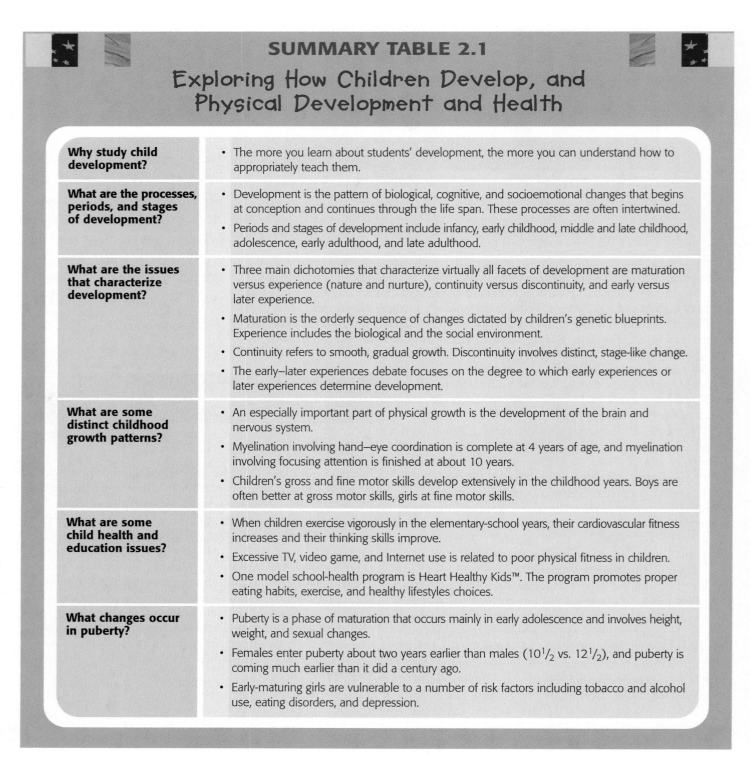

SUMMARY TABLE 2.1
Exploring How Children Develop, and Physical Development and Health

Why study child development?	• The more you learn about students' development, the more you can understand how to appropriately teach them.
What are the processes, periods, and stages of development?	• Development is the pattern of biological, cognitive, and socioemotional changes that begins at conception and continues through the life span. These processes are often intertwined. • Periods and stages of development include infancy, early childhood, middle and late childhood, adolescence, early adulthood, and late adulthood.
What are the issues that characterize development?	• Three main dichotomies that characterize virtually all facets of development are maturation versus experience (nature and nurture), continuity versus discontinuity, and early versus later experience. • Maturation is the orderly sequence of changes dictated by children's genetic blueprints. Experience includes the biological and the social environment. • Continuity refers to smooth, gradual growth. Discontinuity involves distinct, stage-like change. • The early–later experiences debate focuses on the degree to which early experiences or later experiences determine development.
What are some distinct childhood growth patterns?	• An especially important part of physical growth is the development of the brain and nervous system. • Myelination involving hand–eye coordination is complete at 4 years of age, and myelination involving focusing attention is finished at about 10 years. • Children's gross and fine motor skills develop extensively in the childhood years. Boys are often better at gross motor skills, girls at fine motor skills.
What are some child health and education issues?	• When children exercise vigorously in the elementary-school years, their cardiovascular fitness increases and their thinking skills improve. • Excessive TV, video game, and Internet use is related to poor physical fitness in children. • One model school-health program is Heart Healthy Kids™. The program promotes proper eating habits, exercise, and healthy lifestyles choices.
What changes occur in puberty?	• Puberty is a phase of maturation that occurs mainly in early adolescence and involves height, weight, and sexual changes. • Females enter puberty about two years earlier than males ($10^1/_2$ vs. $12^1/_2$), and puberty is coming much earlier than it did a century ago. • Early-maturing girls are vulnerable to a number of risk factors including tobacco and alcohol use, eating disorders, and depression.

From Penguin Dreams and Stranger Things by Berke D. Breathed. Copyright © 1985 by The Washington Post Company. By permission of Little, Brown, and Company.

COGNITIVE DEVELOPMENT

How the mind develops has intrigued many psychologists. We explore three main approaches to how children's thoughts develop: Piaget's theory, Case's neo-Piagetian theory, and Vygotsky's theory. All three theorists are constructivists: they believe that children actively construct knowledge and understanding.

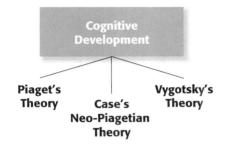

Piaget's Theory

Cognitive Processes   In actively constructing their world, children use schemas. A **schema** *is a concept or framework that exists in an individual's mind to organize and interpret information.* Piaget's interest in schemas focused on how children organize and make sense out of their current experiences.

Piaget (1952) said that two processes are responsible for how children use and adapt their schemas: assimilation and accommodation. **Assimilation** *occurs when a child incorporates new knowledge into existing knowledge*; that is, when children add information about the environment into a schema. **Accommodation** *occurs when a child adjusts to new information*; that is, when children adjust their schemas to the environment.

Consider an eight-year-old girl who is given a hammer and nail to hang a picture on the wall. She has never used a hammer, but from observing others do this she realizes that a hammer is an object to be held, that it is swung by the handle to hit the nail, and that it usually is swung a number of times. Recognizing each of these things, she fits her behaviour into this schema she already has (assimilation). But the hammer is heavy, so she holds it near the top. She swings too hard and the nail bends, so she adjusts the pressure of her strikes. These adjustments reflect her ability to alter her conception of the world (accommodation). Both assimilation and accommodation are required in this example, as they are in many thinking challenges.

Piagetian Stages   Piaget also believed that cognitive development unfolds in a sequence of four stages. Each of the stages is age-related and consists of distinctive ways of thinking. It is the different way of thinking that makes one stage discontinuous from and more advanced than another. Knowing more information does not make the child's thinking more advanced, according to Piaget. The advance is qualitatively different. Piaget's stages are called sensorimotor, preoperational, concrete operational, and formal operational (see Figure 2.3).

Piaget is shown here with his family. Piaget's careful observations of his three children—Lucienne, Laurent, and Jacqueline—contributed to the development of his cognitive theory.

www.mcgrawhill.ca/college/santrock

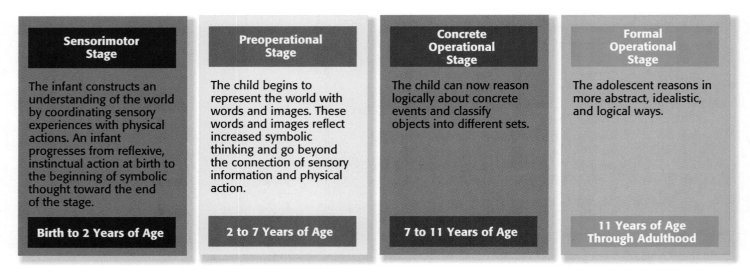

FIGURE 2.3 **Piaget's Four Stages of Cognitive Development**

The Sensorimotor Stage The **sensorimotor stage** *lasts from birth to about two years of age. In this stage, infants construct an understanding of the world by coordinating sensory experiences (such as seeing and hearing) with motor actions (reaching, touching).* At the beginning of this stage, infants show little more than reflexive patterns to adapt to the world. By the end of the stage, they display far more complex sensorimotor patterns.

Piaget believed that *an especially important cognitive accomplishment in infancy is* **object permanence**. *This involves understanding that objects and events continue to exist even when they cannot be seen, heard, or touched.* A second accomplishment is the gradual realization that there is a difference or boundary between oneself and the surrounding environment.

The Preoperational Stage The **preoperational stage** *lasts from approximately two to seven years of age; it is more symbolic than sensorimotor thought. It is egocentric, and intuitive rather than logical.*

Preoperational thought can be subdivided into two substages: symbolic function and intuitive thought. The **symbolic function substage** *occurs roughly between two and four years of age. In this substage, the young child gains the ability to represent mentally an object that is not present.* Expanded use of language and the emergence of pretend play are other examples of an increase in symbolic thought during this substage. Young children begin to use scribbled designs to represent people, houses, cars, clouds, and many other aspects of the world. Their drawings are fanciful and inventive. Suns are blue, skies are green, and cars float on clouds in their imaginative world. The symbolism is simple but strong, not unlike abstractions found in some modern art. As the famous twentieth-century Spanish artist Pablo Picasso once remarked, "I used to draw like Raphael but it has taken me a lifetime to draw like young children." In the elementary-school years, children's drawings become more realistic, neat, and precise (see Figure 2.4a, 2.4b).

Even though young children make distinctive progress in this substage, their preoperational thought still has two important limitations: egocentrism and animism. **Egocentrism** *is the inability to distinguish between one's own perspective and someone else's perspective.*

Piaget and Barbel Inhelder (1969) initially studied young children's egocentrism by devising the three-mountains task (see Figure 2.5). The child walks around the model of the mountains and becomes familiar with what the mountains look like from different perspectives. The child also can see that there are different objects on the mountains. The child then is seated on one side of the table on which the mountains are placed. The experimenter moves a doll to different locations around the table. At each location the child is asked to select from a series of photos the one that most accurately reflects the view the doll is seeing. Children in the preoperational stage often pick the view that reflects where they are sitting rather than the doll's view.

Animism *also characterizes preoperational thought. It is the belief that inanimate objects have "lifelike" qualities and are capable of action.* A young child might show animism by saying, "That tree pushed the leaf off and it fell down" or "The sidewalk made me mad. It made me fall down."

The **intuitive thought substage** *is the second substage of preoperational thought, starting at about four years of age and lasting until about seven years of age.* At this substage, children begin to use primitive reasoning and want to know the answers to all sorts of questions. Piaget called this substage "intuitive" because the children seem so sure about their knowledge and understanding, yet are unaware of how they know what they know. That is, they say they know something but know it without the use of rational thinking.

An important characteristic of preoperational thought is called **centration**. *It involves focusing (or centring) attention on one characteristic to the exclusion of all others.* Centration is most clearly present in young children's lack of **conservation**, *the idea that some characteristic of an object stays the same even though the object might change in appearance.* For example, to adults it is obvious that a certain amount of liquid stays the same regardless of a container's shape. But this is not obvious at all to young children. Rather, they are struck by the height of the liquid in the container. In this type of conservation task (Piaget's most famous), a child is presented with two identical beakers, each filled to the same level with liquid. The child is asked if the beakers have the same amount of liquid. The child usually says yes. Then the liquid from one beaker is poured into a third beaker, which is taller and thinner. The child now is asked if the amount of liquid in the tall, thin beaker is equal to the liquid that remains in the second original beaker. Children younger than seven or eight usually say no. They justify their answer by referring to the differing height or width of the beakers. Older children usually answer yes. They justify their answers appropriately: If you poured the liquid back, the amount would still be the same.

In Piaget's view, failing the conservation-of-liquid task indicates that the child is at the preoperational stage of thinking. Passing the test suggests the child is at the concrete operational stage of thinking.

In our definition of the preoperational stage we indicated that preschool children cannot perform operations. In Piaget's theory, **operations** *are mental representations that are reversible.* As in the beaker task, preschool children have difficulty understanding that reversing an action brings about the original conditions from which the action began. A young student might know that 4 + 2 = 6 but not understand

FIGURE 2.4   **Developmental Changes in Children's Drawings**

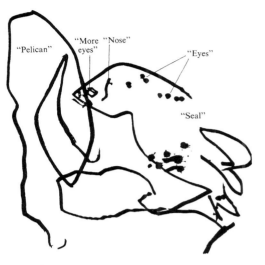

(a) A 3½-year-old's symbolic drawing. Halfway into this drawing, the 3½-year-old said it was "a pelican kissing a seal."

(b) This 11-year-old's drawing is neater and more realistic but also less inventive.

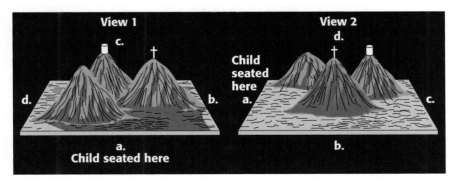

FIGURE 2.5   **The Three-Mountains Task**
View 1 shows the child's perspective from where he or she is sitting. View 2 is an example of the photograph the child would be shown, mixed in with others from different perspectives. To correctly identify this view, the child has to take the perspective of a person sitting at spot *b*. Invariably, a preschool child who thinks in a preoperational way cannot perform this task. When asked what a view of the mountains looks like from position *b*, the child selects a photograph taken from location *a*, the child's view at the time.

"I still don't have all the answers, but I'm beginning to ask the right questions."
Drawing by Lorenz; © 1989 The New Yorker Magazine, Inc.

that the reverse, $6 - 2 = 4$, is also true. Or let's say a preschooler walks to his friend's house each day but always gets a ride home. If asked to walk home from his friend's house, he probably would reply that he didn't know the way because he never had walked home before.

Yet another characteristic of preoperational children is that they ask a lot of questions. The barrage begins around age three. By about five, they have just about exhausted the adults around them with "Why?" "Why" questions signal the emergence of the child's interest in figuring out why things are the way they are.

The Concrete Operational Stage   The **concrete operational stage** *lasts from about 7 to about 11 years of age. Concrete operational thought involves using operations. Logical reasoning replaces intuitive reasoning, but only in concrete situations. Classification skills are present, but abstract problems are difficult.*

Many of the concrete operations identified by Piaget focus on the way children reason about the properties of objects. At the concrete operational level, children can do mentally what they previously could do only physically, and they can reverse concrete operations. For example, to test conservation of matter, the child is presented with two identical balls of clay. The experimenter rolls one ball into a long, thin shape. The child is asked if there is more clay in the ball or in the long, thin piece of clay. By the time children are seven or eight years old, most answer that the amount of clay is the same. To answer this problem correctly, children have to imagine that the clay ball can be rolled out into a long, thin strip and then returned to its original round shape. This type of imagination involves a reversible mental action.

Concrete operations allow the child to coordinate several characteristics rather than focus on a single property of an object. In the clay example, the preoperational child focuses on height or width. The concrete operational child coordinates information about both dimensions.

An important concrete operation is **classifying**, *or dividing things into different sets or subsets and considering their interrelationships.* Reasoning about a family tree of four generations reveals a child's concrete operational skills (Furth & Wachs, 1975). Concrete operational thinkers understand that a person can at the same time be father, brother, and grandson. A preoperational thinker cannot.

Some Piagetian tasks require children to reason about relations between classes. One such task is **seriation**, *the concrete operation that involves ordering stimuli along some quantitative dimension (such as length).* To see if students can serialize, a teacher might place eight sticks of different lengths in a haphazard way on a table. The teacher then asks the student to order the sticks by length. Many young children end up with two or three small groups of "big" sticks or "little" sticks rather than a correct ordering of all eight sticks. Another strategy they use is to evenly line up the tops of the sticks but ignore the bottoms. The concrete operational thinker simultaneously understands that each stick must be longer than the one that precedes it and shorter than the one that follows it.

Another aspect of reasoning about the relations between classes is **transitivity**. *This involves the ability to logically combine relations to understand certain conclusions.* In this case, consider three sticks (A, B, and C) of differing lengths. A is the longest, B is intermediate in length, and C is the shortest. Does the child understand that if $A > B$, and $B > C$, then $A > C$? In Piaget's theory, concrete operational thinkers do, preoperational thinkers do not.

The Formal Operational Stage   The **formal operational stage**, *which emerges at about 11 to 15 years of age, is Piaget's fourth and final cognitive stage. At this stage, individuals move beyond reasoning about only concrete experiences and think in more abstract, idealistic, and logical ways.*

Teaching Strategies
For Primary–, Intermediate–, and Secondary–School Students

Primary Grades: Preoperational Thinkers	Intermediate Grades: Concrete Operational Thinkers	Secondary School: Formal Operational Thinkers
Have students manipulate objects	Encourage students to discover concepts and principles	Recognize the wide range of individual variability across students
Involve students in social interactions	Involve students in operational tasks using concrete materials	Present students with real-world problems and invite them to propose multiple solutions
Ask students to make comparisons	Have students practise the concepts of ascending and descending classification hierarchies	Guide students' efforts when generating potential solutions
Have students draw scenes from different perspectives	Include activities that require conservation of area, weight, and displaced volume	Have students evaluate the effectiveness of potential solutions and select the best one
Ask students to justify their answers when they draw conclusions	Create activities in which students order and reverse order	Ask students to reflect on their cognitive processes when problem-solving
	Ask students to justify their answers when solving problems	Encourage students to create hierarchical outlines for writing and other tasks
	Encourage students to work in groups and exchange thoughts	
	Provide students with materials that stimulate questions	
	Create props and visual aids for complex concepts	
	Actively engage students in the learning process	
Source: Sund (1976)	Source: Labinowicz (1980) and Sund (1976)	Source: Santrock (1998)

The abstract quality of formal operational thinking is evident in verbal problem solving. The concrete operational thinker needs to see the concrete elements A, B, and C to make the logical inference that if A = B and B = C, then A = C. In contrast, the formal operational thinker can solve this problem when it is verbally presented.

Accompanying the abstract nature of formal operational thought are the abilities to idealize and imagine possibilities. At this stage, adolescents engage in extended speculation about the ideal qualities they desire in themselves and others.

At the same time as adolescents are thinking more abstractly and idealistically, they also are beginning to think more logically. As formal operational thinkers, they think more like scientists. They devise plans to solve problems and systematically test solutions. Piaget's term **hypothetical-deductive reasoning** *embodies the concept that adolescents can develop hypotheses (best hunches) about ways to solve problems and systematically reach a conclusion.*

One example of hypothetical-deductive reasoning involves a modification of the familiar game "Twenty Questions." Individuals are shown a set of 42 colour pictures displayed in a rectangular array (six rows of seven pictures each) and asked to determine which picture the experimenter has in mind (that is, which is "correct"). The subjects are allowed to ask only questions to which the experimenter can answer yes or no. The object of the game is to select the correct picture by asking as few questions as possible.

Adolescents who are deductive hypothesis testers formulate a plan and test a series of hypotheses, which considerably narrows the field of choices. The most effective plan is a "halving" strategy (*Q:* Is the picture in the right half of the array? *A:* No. *Q:* Okay. Is it in the top half? And so on). A correct halving strategy guarantees the answer in seven questions or less. In contrast, the concrete operational thinker might persist with questions that continue to test some of the same possibilities that previous questions could have eliminated. For example, they might ask whether the correct picture is in row 1 and are told that it is not. Later, they ask whether the picture is *X*, which is in row 1.

A form of egocentrism also emerges in adolescence (Elkind, 1978). **Adolescent egocentrism** *is the heightened self-consciousness that is reflected in adolescents' beliefs that others are as interested in them as they themselves are. Adolescent egocentrism also includes a sense of personal uniqueness.* It involves the desire to be noticed, visible, and "on stage." Consider 12-year-old Tracy, who states, "Everyone in here is looking at me. This one hair won't stay in place," as she rushes to the restroom to plaster it with hair spray. Perceived uniqueness also is evident in 16-year-old Margaret's feelings after her boyfriend has broken up with her. She tells her mother, "You have no idea how I feel. You have never experienced this kind of pain."

Egocentrism is a normal adolescent occurrence, more common in the intermediate grades than in the high-school years. However, for some individuals, adolescent egocentrism can contribute to reckless behaviour, including suicidal thoughts, drug use, and failure to use contraceptives during sexual intercourse. Egocentricity leads some adolescents to think that they are invulnerable.

Evaluating Piaget's Theory   Piaget's theory has not gone unchallenged. Questions have been raised about these areas: estimates of children's competence at different developmental levels; stages; training children to reason at higher levels; and culture and education.

- *Estimates of children's competence.* Some cognitive abilities emerge earlier than Piaget thought. For example, conservation of number has been demonstrated as early as age three, although Piaget did not think it emerged until seven.
  Other cognitive abilities can emerge later than Piaget thought. Many adolescents and adults still think in concrete operational ways or are just beginning to master formal operations. In sum, recent theoretical revisions highlight more cognitive competencies of infants and young children and more cognitive shortcomings of adolescents and adults (Flavell, Miller, & Miller, 1993; Wertsch, 2000).
- *Stages.* Piaget conceived of stages as unitary structures of thought. Thus, his theory assumes developmental synchrony. That is, various aspects of a stage should emerge at the same time. However, some concrete operational concepts do not appear in synchrony. For example, children do not learn to conserve at the same time as they learn to cross-classify. Thus, most contemporary developmentalists agree that children's cognitive development is not as stagelike as Piaget thought (Bjorklund, 2000; Case, 1998, 1999, 2000).

From you have I been absent in the spring,
When proud-pied April, dress'd in all his trim,
Hath put a spirit of youth in everything.

William Shakespeare, Sonnet 98
English Poet and Dramatist, 17th Century

www.mcgrawhill.ca/college/santrock

- *Training children to reason at a higher level.* Some children who are at one cognitive stage (preoperational) can be trained to reason at a higher cognitive stage (concrete operational).
- *Culture and education.* Culture and education exert stronger influences on children's development than Piaget believed (Gelman & Brenneman, 1994; Greenfield, 2000). The age at which children acquire conservation skills is related to the extent to which their culture provides relevant practice (Cole, 1999).

Still, some developmental psychologists believe we should not throw out Piaget altogether. These **neo-Piagetians** *argue that Piaget got some things right, but that his theory needs considerable revision. In their revision of Piaget, more emphasis is given to how students process information through attention, memory, and using strategies* (Case, 1987, 1997, 1998).

Case's Neo-Piagetian Theory

Growing criticism of Piagetian theory in the late 1960s and the rise of cognitive science in the early 1970s marked the beginning of a new movement in cognitive development dominated by a group of researchers known as the neo-Piagetians (Case, 1985; Pascual-Leone, 1970; Pascual-Leone & Smith, 1969). The neo-Piagetian group built on the important work done by Piaget by taking some of his most classical theoretical components and combining them with more current concepts that provided greater explanatory power (Case, 1998; Pascual-Leone, 1990). One well-known member of this group is Canada's Robbie Case.

Case played a major role in the development of the neo-Piagetian movement. His contributions to educational psychology extend well beyond the confines of cognitive development (Case & McKeough, 1990; Marini, 2000). Case had a genuine interest in both developmental and educational psychology; his theory of cognition allows predictions about development from birth to adulthood and provides new insights about learning and instruction across different content areas (e.g., mathematics, language arts).

Like Piaget, Case characterizes development as a progression though four major stages:

- Sensorimotor stage ($0-1\frac{1}{2}$ years)
- Interrelational stage ($1\frac{1}{2}-5$ years)
- Dimensional stage (5–11 years)
- Vectorial stage (11–19 years)

At the sensorimotor stage ($0-1\frac{1}{2}$ years), children attempt to understand the world by using a range of sensory experiences, particularly touch. At this stage children are particularly interested in cause and effect, such as the dropping of a spoon and the resulting noise (Case, 1992a).

At the interrelational stage ($1\frac{1}{2}-5$ years), children's mental representation consists of objects, people, and actions. Children's thinking is still dominated by relationships between cause and effect, such as the pushing of a button to make a bell ring or the comforting behaviour that produces a smile (Marini & Case, 1989).

Children in the dimensional stage (5–11 years) can focus on multiple dimensions simultaneously, and they begin to make finer discriminations between these operations. Their mental representations involve categories of relationals and dimensions such as *height and weight* and *happy and sad.* For example, children at this stage can consider information related to the discrepancy between what people expect and what they receive when assessing the degree of happiness or disappointment they feel (Marini, 1992).

At the vectorial stage (11–19 years), individuals can operate on mental elements that are second-order categories. These elements tend to be abstract concepts and have properties similar to vectors. An example would be solving two ratios to predict which side of a balance beam would fall. Similarly, in the social domain students at this stage can assess an individual's personality from information provided and then use that information to make predictions about future behaviour (Marini & Case, 1994).

Case believed that children's developmental progression across the stages is a function of more efficient use of working memory, which provides them with a greater ability to process more complex information. An analogy can be drawn between a blackboard and children's working-memory storage capacity (described in greater detail in Chapter 8). A blackboard has a fixed amount of space that can be used to record/store information. The amount of space on the blackboard cannot be changed. However, the working capacity of the blackboard can change depending on how effectively the available space is used. If one writes in very large scribbles and in a messy and unorganized fashion, then the amount of information stored is limited. Similarly, the ability to remember what was written and where it was recorded is also compromised.

If, on the other hand, one writes neatly with small print and presents information in a systematic and organized manner, then much more information can be placed on the blackboard. In this instance, it appears that more space is available even though the surface area (or storage capacity) of the blackboard has not changed. In addition, by presenting the information in an organized manner, the ability to retrieve it is greatly improved.

According to Case, four factors contribute to maturational gains in the capacity of working memory: 1) myelination, 2) automatization through practice, 3) social experience and cultural variation, and 4) the development of central conceptual structures.

1) *Myelination.* Case asserts that synaptic growth and pruning and the increased development of myelin sheaths (which act as a neural insulator and improve neural transmission) increases the efficiency of mental operations and facilitates children's progression from one stage to the next (Case, 1985; 1992b).
2) *Automatization through practice.* Case maintains that by practising certain operations repeatedly, children achieve automaticity in those processes. Automatization frees up attention resources that in turn can be used for other activities, including the execution of more complex operations. An example of this process occurs when people learn to drive. At the beginning, all of the driver's attentional capacity is allocated to keeping the car on the road. However, as operations such as checking the rearview mirror become automatic, other operations such as reading street signs or adjusting the radio can be performed more readily.
3) *Social experiences and cultural variation.* Case argued that social experience and cultural variation plays a major role in children's development. He was quite sensitive to the importance of family and school experiences as well as cultural variation in shaping children's problem-solving abilities. Culture can be interpreted as referring to immediate environments such as school as well as more general contexts such as the larger dominant culture with its scientific paradigms, artistic traditions, and social customs (Case et al., 1996).
4) *The development of central conceptual structures.* As a result of automatization children acquire *central conceptual structures*, networks of concepts that permit them to think about a range of situations in a more complex and advanced manner. Central conceptual structures are best thought of as cognitive structures that are not as broad and universal as Piaget's notion of stages and not as narrow as those of domain-specific proponents. These cognitive structures allow children to understand events that spring from similar concepts and themes such as the behaviours, norms, and expectations surrounding social events (Case, 1997). These structures have large implications for educational and curriculum issues (Griffin & Case, 1997; Kalchman & Case, 1998; Case, Griffin, & Kelly, 1999).

Vygotsky's Theory

Like Piaget, Lev Vygotsky (1896–1934) also believed that children actively construct their knowledge. Vygotsky was born in Russia in the same year as Piaget was born, but died much younger than Piaget did, at the age of 37. Both Piaget's and Vygotsky's ideas remained virtually unknown to North American scholars for many years, not being introduced to North American audiences through English translations until the 1960s. In the last several decades, psychologists and educators have shown increased interest in Vygotsky's (1962) views.

Vygotsky's Assumptions   Three claims capture the heart of Vygotsky's views (Tappan, 1998): (1) The child's cognitive skills can be understood only when they are developmentally analyzed and interpreted; (2) cognitive skills are mediated by words, language, and forms of discourse, which serve as psychological tools for facilitating and transforming mental activity; and (3) cognitive skills have their origins in social relations and are embedded in a sociocultural backdrop.

For Vygotsky, taking a developmental approach means that in order to understand any aspect of the child's cognitive functioning, one must examine its origins and transformations from earlier to later forms. Thus, a particular mental act such as using inner speech (see below) cannot be viewed accurately in isolation but should be evaluated as a step in a gradual developmental process.

Vygotsky's second claim, that to understand cognitive functioning it is necessary to examine the tools that mediate and shape it, led him to believe that language is the most important of these tools. Vygotsky argued that in early childhood language begins to be used as a tool that helps the child plan activities and solve problems.

Vygotsky's third claim was that cognitive skills originate in social relations and culture. Vygotsky portrayed the child's development as inseparable from social and cultural activities. He believed that the development of memory, attention, and reasoning involves learning to use the inventions of society, such as language, mathematical systems, and memory strategies. In one culture this could consist of learning to count with the help of a computer; in another it could consist of counting on one's fingers or using beads.

Vygotsky's theory has stimulated considerable interest in the view that knowledge is *situated* and *collaborative* (Greeno, Collins, & Resnick, 1996; Rogoff, 1998). That is, knowledge is distributed among people and environments, which include objects, artifacts, tools, books, and the communities in which people live. This suggests that knowing can best be advanced through interaction with others in cooperative activities.

Within these basic claims, Vygotsky articulated unique and influential ideas about the relation between learning and development. These ideas especially reflect his view that cognitive functioning has social origins. One of Vygotsky's unique ideas was his concept of the zone of proximal development.

The Zone of Proximal Development   **Zone of proximal development (ZPD)** *is Vygotsky's term for the range of tasks that are too difficult for children to master alone but that can be learned with guidance and assistance from adults or more-skilled children.* Thus, the lower limit of the ZPD is the level of problem solving reached by the child working independently. The upper limit is the level of additional responsibility the child can accept with the assistance of an able instructor (see Figure 2.6). Vygotsky's emphasis on the ZPD underscores his belief in the importance of social influences, especially instruction, on children's cognitive development.

Vygotsky (1987) gave this example of how to assess a child's ZPD: Suppose that, by an intelligence test, the mental age of two children is determined to be eight years. With Vygotsky in mind, we can't stop there. To go on, we seek to determine how each of these children will attempt to solve problems meant for older children. We assist each child by demonstrating, asking leading questions, and introducing the initial elements of the solution. With this help or collaboration with the adult, one of these children solves problems at the level of a 12-year-old child and the other solves problems at the level of a 9-year-old child. This difference between the children's mental ages and the level of performance they achieve in collaboration with an adult defines the zone of proximal development. Thus, the ZPD involves the child's cognitive skills that are in the process of maturing, and their performance level, with the assistance of a more-skilled person (Panofsky, 1999). Vygotsky (1978) called these the "buds" or "flowers" of development, to distinguish them from the "fruits" of development, which the child already can accomplish independently. An application of Vygotsky's concept of the zone of proximal development is the one-on-one instruction provided by many Canadian teachers using the Australian-based Reading Recovery program (Clay & Cazden, 1990). Over time, students participating in these sessions can attain average or close to average grade-cohort reading levels (see Begoray, 2001 for an example of a Canadian-based Reading Recovery program).

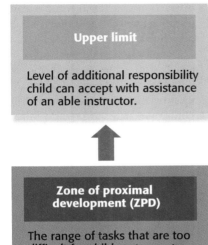

Upper limit

Level of additional responsibility child can accept with assistance of an able instructor.

Zone of proximal development (ZPD)

The range of tasks that are too difficult for children to master alone but that can be learned with guidance and assistance from adults or skilled peers.

Lower limit

Level of problem solving reached on these tasks by child working alone.

FIGURE 2.6   Vygotsky's Zone of Proximal Development

Vygotsky's zone of proximal development has a lower limit and an upper limit. Tasks in the ZPD are too difficult for the child to perform alone. They require assistance from an adult or a more-skilled child. As children experience the verbal instruction or demonstration, they organize the information in their existing mental structures, so they can eventually perform the skill or task alone.

www.mcgrawhill.ca/college/santrock

Through the Eyes of Teachers

The Importance of Scaffolding Instruction

While home schooling my son, I quickly came to understand the importance of scaffolding, or "talking through tasks," in order to help him understand new content and maintain his interest in learning. Over time, my son knew to "talk it out" whenever he ran into a problem. My job was to listen to his thoughts and provide instructional hints and encouragement. By gently guiding his learning, I was able to improve his skills and confidence to learn new things.

For example, while reading *The Underground Railroad* we spent a lot of time exploring the themes of democracy, freedom, slavery, human rights, and political dissent. My son became so involved with the novel that he researched and wrote his own book about the secret symbols and language used by members of the underground railroad. Watching him "talk" his way through the writing of this book convinced me that every skill you teach a child is a springboard for another one. Teaching children means helping them learn to talk their way through activities so that they will gain the confidence to explore new concepts and skills.

Barb Gallant
Home Schooled Three Sons over Four Years
Elementary Teacher
New Brunswick

Scaffolding Closely linked to the idea of the zone of proximal development is the concept of **scaffolding**. *Scaffolding is a technique of changing the level of support. Over the course of a teaching session, a more-skilled person (a teacher or a more-advanced peer of the child) adjusts the amount of guidance to fit the student's current performance level.* When the task the student is learning is new, the more-skilled person might use direct instruction. As the student's competence increases, less guidance is given.

Dialogue is an important tool of scaffolding in the zone of proximal development (John-Steiner & Mahn, 1996; Tappan, 1998). Vygotsky viewed children as having rich but unsystematic, disorganized, and spontaneous concepts. These meet with the skilled helper's more systematic, logical, and rational concepts. As a result of the meeting and dialogue between the child and the skilled helper, the child's concepts become more systematic, logical, and rational. We will have much more to say about scaffolding and other social interactive aspects of learning in Chapter 9, Social Constructivist Approaches, Domain-Specific Approaches, and Teaching.

Language and Thought Vygotsky (1962) believed that young children use language not only for social communication but also to plan, guide, and monitor their behaviour in a self-regulatory fashion. The use of language for self-regulation is called *inner speech* or *private speech*. For Piaget, private speech was egocentric and immature, but for Vygotsky it was an important tool of thought during the early childhood years.

Vygotsky believed that language and thought initially develop independently of each other and then merge. He said that all mental functions have external or social origins. Children must use language to communicate with others before they can focus inward on their own thoughts. Children also must communicate externally and use language for a long period of time before the transition from external to internal speech takes place. This transition period occurs between the ages of three and seven and involves talking to oneself. After a while, the self-talk becomes second nature to children and they can act without verbalizing. When this occurs, children have internalized their egocentric speech in the form of inner speech, which becomes their thoughts. Vygotsky believed that children who use a lot of private speech are more socially competent than those who don't. He argued that private speech represents an early transition in becoming more socially communicative.

Vygotsky's view challenged Piaget's ideas on language and thought. Vygotsky said that language, even in its earliest forms, is socially based, whereas Piaget emphasized young children's egocentric and nonsocial speech. For Vygotsky, when young children talk to themselves they are using language to govern their behaviour and guide themselves, whereas Piaget believed that such self-talk reflects immaturity. Researchers have found support for Vygotsky's view of the positive role of private speech in children's development (Winsler, Diaz, & Montero, 1997).

Evaluating and Comparing Cognitive and Social Constructivist Theories Constructivist theories emphasize that children actively construct knowledge and understanding rather than being passive receptacles of learning. However, the various theories differ in focus and approach to how such learning takes place. Vygotsky's theory is a social constructivist approach that focuses on the social contexts of learning. Piaget's theory does not have such a strong social emphasis, focusing instead on cognitive development and its impact on learning (Hogan & Tudge, 1999). Case's theory combines elements of

Vygotsky's social constructivism and Piaget's cognitive development theories, proposing that students' capabilities for constructing knowledge is facilitated by a skilfully directed social process (McKeough, 2000; Morra, 2002).

All three constructivist theories presented here have been embraced by teachers and applied to education (Doolittle, 1997; McKeough, 2000; Morra, 2001). For example, Vygotsky's view of the importance of sociocultural influences on children's development is consistent with contemporary societal beliefs about the importance of context and culture on learning. Moving from Piaget to Vygotsky to Case, the conceptual shift is from the individual to collaboration, social interaction, and sociocultural activity (Rogoff, 1998). In Piaget's model, students construct knowledge by transforming, organizing, and reorganizing previous knowledge. For Vygotsky, students construct knowledge through social interaction with others (Kozulin, 2000). Case's model argues that, while children construct knowledge by organizing information into more meaningful cognitive structures, this process is facilitated by social interaction and instructional design that is sensitive to their individual memory capabilities.

Teaching Strategies
For Applying Constructivist Theories in the Classroom

✔ Actively engage students in the learning process
  • acknowledge students' prior knowledge and experiences and begin instruction at that level
  • do not push students to achieve too much too early—emphasis on speed of learning and intellectual development encourages passive learning
  • provide maximum amount of instruction, practice, and support
  • encourage students to ask questions, make discoveries, and reflect on them
  • gradually reduce number of explanations, hints, and demonstrations as students begin to master skills

✔ Use scaffolding
  • observe students carefully to discover how they think versus what they think and the product of their thinking
  • provide support for students' self-initiated learning attempts
  • provide instructional assistance and direction only when needed
  • ask questions that stimulate students' thinking
  • ask students to explain their answers
  • provide encouragement and encourage practice

✔ Use skilled peers
  • encourage students to serve as tutors
  • provide structure for small-group work
  • encourage cooperative learning

✔ Monitor and encourage students' use of private speech
  • acknowledge developmental changes from external talk (preschool years) to internal talk (elementary-school years) during problem solving
  • encourage students to internalize and self-regulate their talk
  • balance instructional memory capabilities with task requirements

✔ Use ongoing assessment
  • use tasks of varying difficulty to determine where to begin instruction
  • acknowledge the limitations of standardized tests
  • use authentic assessment measures that reflect students' ongoing efforts, as well as their final products (e.g., portfolios, student–teacher conferences, written and verbal reasoning)

All three theories have implications for classroom teachers. Piaget's theory stresses the need to have students explore the world around them and discover knowledge. Vygotsky's theory suggests that discovery and learning are facilitated by skilful teachers and students' interactions with more-skilled peers. Case's theory calls attention to the need for teachers to plan learning activities that balance learners' individual memory capabilities with the complexity of task requirements and a supportive social environment. In each of these theories, teachers function as facilitators rather than directors of student learning. Figure 2.7 compares the three theories based on their major ideas and their implications for teaching and learning.

At this point we have studied a number of ideas about children's cognitive development. A review of these ideas is presented in Summary Table 2.2. Next, we will explore another key aspect of children's development—language.

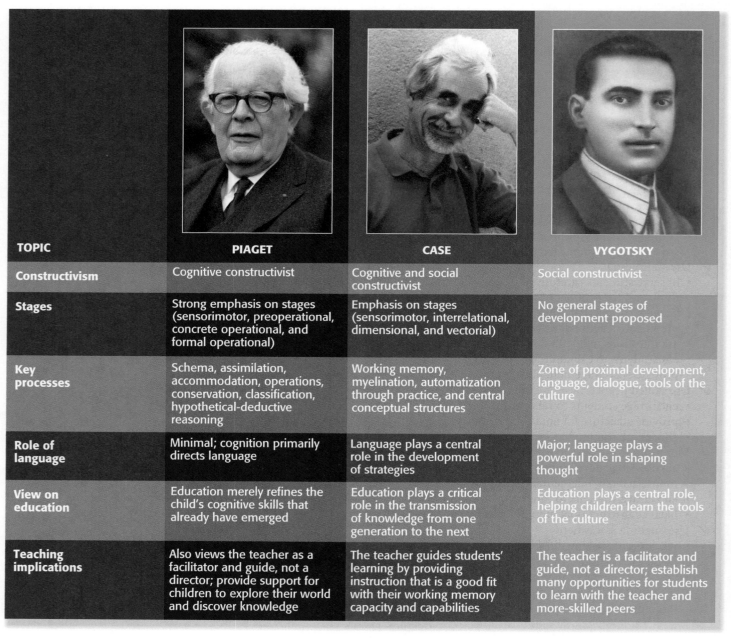

TOPIC	PIAGET	CASE	VYGOTSKY
Constructivism	Cognitive constructivist	Cognitive and social constructivist	Social constructivist
Stages	Strong emphasis on stages (sensorimotor, preoperational, concrete operational, and formal operational)	Emphasis on stages (sensorimotor, interrelational, dimensional, and vectorial)	No general stages of development proposed
Key processes	Schema, assimilation, accommodation, operations, conservation, classification, hypothetical-deductive reasoning	Working memory, myelination, automatization through practice, and central conceptual structures	Zone of proximal development, language, dialogue, tools of the culture
Role of language	Minimal; cognition primarily directs language	Language plays a central role in the development of strategies	Major; language plays a powerful role in shaping thought
View on education	Education merely refines the child's cognitive skills that already have emerged	Education plays a critical role in the transmission of knowledge from one generation to the next	Education plays a central role, helping children learn the tools of the culture
Teaching implications	Also views the teacher as a facilitator and guide, not a director; provide support for children to explore their world and discover knowledge	The teacher guides students' learning by providing instruction that is a good fit with their working memory capacity and capabilities	The teacher is a facilitator and guide, not a director; establish many opportunities for students to learn with the teacher and more-skilled peers

FIGURE 2.7 **Comparing Constructivists' Theories**

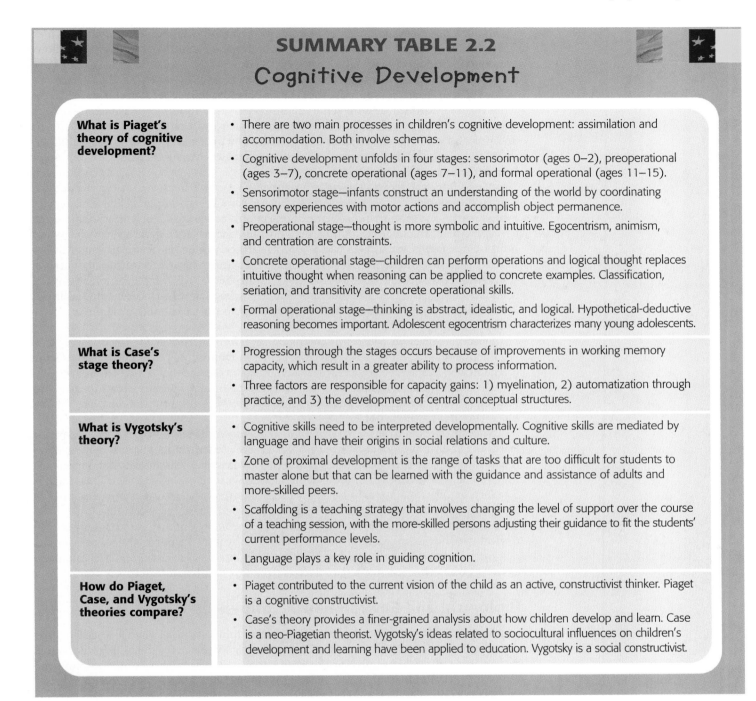

SUMMARY TABLE 2.2

Cognitive Development

What is Piaget's theory of cognitive development?	• There are two main processes in children's cognitive development: assimilation and accommodation. Both involve schemas. • Cognitive development unfolds in four stages: sensorimotor (ages 0–2), preoperational (ages 3–7), concrete operational (ages 7–11), and formal operational (ages 11–15). • Sensorimotor stage—infants construct an understanding of the world by coordinating sensory experiences with motor actions and accomplish object permanence. • Preoperational stage—thought is more symbolic and intuitive. Egocentrism, animism, and centration are constraints. • Concrete operational stage—children can perform operations and logical thought replaces intuitive thought when reasoning can be applied to concrete examples. Classification, seriation, and transitivity are concrete operational skills. • Formal operational stage—thinking is abstract, idealistic, and logical. Hypothetical-deductive reasoning becomes important. Adolescent egocentrism characterizes many young adolescents.
What is Case's stage theory?	• Progression through the stages occurs because of improvements in working memory capacity, which result in a greater ability to process information. • Three factors are responsible for capacity gains: 1) myelination, 2) automatization through practice, and 3) the development of central conceptual structures.
What is Vygotsky's theory?	• Cognitive skills need to be interpreted developmentally. Cognitive skills are mediated by language and have their origins in social relations and culture. • Zone of proximal development is the range of tasks that are too difficult for students to master alone but that can be learned with the guidance and assistance of adults and more-skilled peers. • Scaffolding is a teaching strategy that involves changing the level of support over the course of a teaching session, with the more-skilled persons adjusting their guidance to fit the students' current performance levels. • Language plays a key role in guiding cognition.
How do Piaget, Case, and Vygotsky's theories compare?	• Piaget contributed to the current vision of the child as an active, constructivist thinker. Piaget is a cognitive constructivist. • Case's theory provides a finer-grained analysis about how children develop and learn. Case is a neo-Piagetian theorist. Vygotsky's ideas related to sociocultural influences on children's development and learning have been applied to education. Vygotsky is a social constructivist.

LANGUAGE DEVELOPMENT

Think about how important language is in teachers' and students' lives. They need language to speak to others, listen to others, read, and write. They need language to describe past events in detail and to plan for the future.

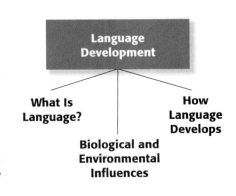

What Is Language?

Language *is a form of communication, whether spoken, written, or signed, that is based on a system of symbols.* All human languages are generative. **Infinite generativity** *is the ability* *to produce an endless number of meaningful sentences using a finite set of words and rules.* This quality makes language a highly creative enterprise. All human language also follows the organizational rules of phonology, morphology, syntax, semantics, and pragmatics.

Spoken language is made up of basic sounds, or phonemes. An example of a phoneme in the English language is /k/, the sound represented by the letter *k* in the word *ski*, the letter *c* in the word *cat*, and the letters *ch* in *Christmas*. **Phonology** *is a language's sound system.* Phonological rules allow some sound sequences to occur (such as *sp*, *ba*, or *ar*) and prohibit others (such as *zx* or *qp*). To learn the phonology of a language, children must learn its sound inventory and permissible sequences of sounds, which are important later for reading (Oller, 2000).

Morphology *refers to the rules for combining morphemes, which are meaningful strings of sounds that contain no smaller meaningful parts.* Every word in the English language is made up of one or more morphemes. Some words consist of a single morpheme (such as *help*). Others are made up of more than one morpheme (such as *helper*, which has two morphemes, *help* + *er*; though not a word itself, the morpheme *-er* means "one who"—in this case, "one who helps"). Just as the rules that govern phonemes ensure that certain sound sequences occur, the rules that govern morphemes ensure that certain strings of sounds occur in particular sequences and conform with other rules (Vander Lely & Ullman, 2001). For example, we cannot reorder *helper* to *erhelp* and we cannot talk about an *undog* or about *desking*.

Syntax *involves the way words are combined to form acceptable phrases and sentences.* If someone says to you "Chelsea gave the pencil to Dominique," you know who was the giver and who was the receiver because you understand the sentence structure. This concept of "who does what to whom" is an important type of syntactic information. You also understand that the sentence *You didn't stay, did you?* is a grammatical sentence but *You didn't stay, didn't you?* is not.

Semantics *refers to the meaning of words and sentences.* Every word has a set of semantic features. For example, *girl* and *woman* share the same semantic denotations of *female* and *human* but differ in their meanings regarding age. Words have semantic restrictions on how they can be used with each other in sentences (Townsend & Bever, 2001). The sentence *The bicycle talked the boy into buying it candy* is syntactically correct but semantically incorrect. The sentence violates our semantic knowledge that bicycles do not talk!

Pragmatics *involves the use of appropriate conversation.* This involves knowledge about context in which to say what to whom and how to say it (Nakamura, 2001). For example, pragmatics is involved when children learn the difference between polite and rude language, as well as when they learn to tell a joke in such a way that it comes across as funny.

Biological and Environmental Influences

Famous linguist Noam Chomsky (1957) argued that humans are prewired to learn language at a certain time and in a certain way. The strongest evidence for the biological basis of language is that children all over the world acquire language milestones at about the same time developmentally and in about the same order, despite vast variations in the language input they receive. For example, in some cultures adults never talk to their infants under one year of age, yet these infants still acquire language.

Children vary in their acquisition of language in ways that cannot be explained by environmental input alone (Hoff, 2001). For example, pioneering language researcher Roger Brown (1973) searched for evidence that parents reinforce their children for speaking grammatically. He found that they sometimes smiled and praised their children for sentences they liked, but they also reinforced sentences that were ungrammatical. From these observations, Brown concluded that processes operating within the child were overriding the environmental input of reinforcement.

However, children do not learn language in a social vacuum (Snow & Beals, 2001). Enough variation occurs in language development when children's caregivers differ substantially in input styles to know that the environment plays a significant role in language development, especially in the acquisition of vocabulary (Tamis-LeMonda, Bornstein, & Baumwell, 2001). Even before they go to school, most children have already been steeped in language. In or out of school, encouragement of language development, not drill and practice, is the key (de Villiers, 1996; de Villiers & de Villiers, 1999). Language development is not simply a matter of being rewarded for saying things correctly and imitating a speaker. Children benefit when their parents and teachers actively engage them in conversation, ask them questions, and emphasize interactive rather than directive language. In one recent study, Farkas (2001) observed that three-year-olds living in poverty showed vocabulary deficits compared to their counterparts in middle-income families, and that these deficits remained when they entered school at six years of age.

Verbal behaviour and its effect on language has been studied by University of Guelph researcher Mary Ann Evans (1996). She found that more than two-thirds of kindergarten students who were nonverbal in the fall term remained nonverbal in the spring term. Evans tracked these students into Grade 1 and noted that the nonverbal kindergarten students obtained lower scores than their verbally active peers on a variety of language tests. The study implies that language and communication skills are a substantial component of verbal participation in the primary classroom.

In sum, children are neither exclusively biological linguists nor exclusively social architects of language (Berko-Gleason, 2000; Gleason & Ratner, 1998). No matter how long you converse with a dog it won't learn to talk, because it doesn't have the human child's biological capacity for language; unfortunately, some children fail to develop good language skills even in the presence of very good role models and interaction. An interactionist view emphasizes the contributions of both biology and experience in language development. That is, children are biologically prepared to learn language as they and their teachers interact. To read about how Frontier College promotes life-long language learning for all Canadians, see the Diversity and Education box on page 58.

"No, Timmy, not 'I sawed the chair'; it's I saw the chair' or 'I have seen the chair.'"
© *Glenn Bernhardt*

How Language Develops

Language acquisition advances through a number of milestones (Bloom, 1998). Babbling begins at about 3 to 6 months. Infants usually utter their first word at about 10 to 13 months. By 18 to 24 months, infants usually have begun to string two words together. In this two-word stage, they quickly grasp the importance of language in communication, creating phrases such as "Book there," "My candy," "Mama walk," and "Give Papa."

As they move beyond two-word utterances, children clearly show that they know some morphological rules (the rules of language that tell how sounds must be combined). Children begin using the plural and possessive forms of nouns (*dogs* and *dog's*); put appropriate endings on verbs (*-s* when the subject is third-person singular, *-ed* for the past tense); use prepositions (*in* and *on*), articles (*a* and *the*), and various forms of the verb *to be* ("I *was going* to the store"). They also tend to overgeneralize these rules. Have you ever heard a preschool child say "foots" instead of "feet," or "goed" instead of "went"? Ask parents who have young children or talk to a young child; you will likely hear some interesting morphological errors.

Some of the best evidence that children develop morphological rules rather than memorize individual words was demonstrated in a classic experiment by Jean Berko-

Through the Eyes of Teachers

Talking to Gain Perspective

Role-playing can be a very effective tool for developing students' understanding and sensitivity to others. When students reach Grades 5 and 6, they can really begin to understand that there are two sides to a conversation. Providing them with a role is one way to let them consider another person's point of view. I also encourage students to develop their problem-solving and negotiating skills as part of their role-play. For example, I have students practise saying no when confronted with unwanted peer pressure (e.g., smoking cigarettes, breaking curfew). By enacting and analyzing the role-plays together in class, students learn to consider a variety of perspectives and to use these perspectives as discussion points. They start to talk *with* each other rather than *at* each other—they begin to engage in meaningful and respectful dialogue.

Ralph Byng
29-Year Elementary-School Teacher
Ontario

Diversity and Education
Frontier College Promotes Life-Long Learning for All Canadians

Frontier College is an institution with a reputation for unlocking opportunity for learners who face closed doors. Alfred Fitzpatrick, the founder of Frontier College, devoutly believed that education should be the right of all people, not just the wealthy. Frontier College is a Canada-wide, volunteer-based literacy organization. The organization focuses on developing an individual's communication and literacy skills by fostering an environment favourable to life-long learning (Fernandez & Thompson, 2000).

At the turn of the twentieth century, Frontier College instructors began to educate labourers at their work sites. In tents and boxcars, some of these men began by learning to write their names. Decades later, in the mid-1960s, Frontier College embarked on the Elliot Lake Project. Due to the decline in the uranium market, laid-off workers in this Northern Ontario town found themselves unemployable due to their lack of literacy skills. Over the course of two years, Frontier College teachers immersed themselves in this community and taught basic reading and writing to hundreds of men. Throughout the 1980s, the College's Beat the Street programs provided peer tutoring in Winnipeg, Regina, and Toronto.

The modern focus for Frontier College is to provide support for students who are disadvantaged by poverty, geographic isolation, or social oppression. It is their belief that life-long learning contributes to individuals' abilities to be self-sufficient and accomplish their goals. Currently, Frontier College runs evening tutorials in inner-city Toronto schools for immigrant children. English instruction is delivered by students from the neighbouring University of Toronto. In fact, Canada-wide there are more than 2,000 university students and community volunteers acting as literacy tutors. Work has begun in isolated locales such as Labrador, the Northwest Territories, and Nunavut to provide distance learning in areas such as literacy and health education. More than 100 years after it was founded, Frontier College is keeping the doors of opportunity open for all Canadians to be life-long learners.

Gleason (1958). Preschool and Grade 1 children were presented with cards like the one shown in Figure 2.8. The children were asked to look at the card while the experimenter read the words on it aloud. Then the children were asked to supply the missing word. Berko was interested in their ability to recall the right word and their ability to say it "correctly." The children showed they knew the morphological rules involved by generating the plural forms of the fictional words (i.e., "wugs").

Although the children's answers were not perfect, they were much better than chance. Moreover, the children demonstrated their knowledge of morphological rules, not only with plural forms of nouns ("There are two wugs") but also with possessive forms of nouns and the third-person-singular and past-tense forms of verbs. What makes Berko's study impressive is that most of the words were nonsensical or made up. Thus, the children could not base their responses on remembering past instances of hearing the words. Instead, they were forced to rely on *rules*.

Young children also learn to manipulate syntax. They can generate questions, passive constructions, clauses, and all the major syntactical structure of their language. Similar evidence that children learn and actively apply rules occurs at the level of syntax. After advancing beyond two-word utterances, children speak word sequences that reflect a growing mastery of complex rules for how words should be ordered. Consider *wh*-questions, such as "Where is Daddy going?" Children typically learn by age three where to put the *wh*- word but might continue for another year learning to put the question as "Where Daddy is going?"

As children move into the elementary-school years, they become skilled at using syntactical rules (the rules about how to combine words to form acceptable phrases and sentences) to construct lengthy and complex sentences (Goldin-Meadow, 2000). They might say something like, "After the man cut the grass, he left and went home." By the end of elementary school, most children can apply appropriate rules of grammar.

Regarding semantics (the rules about the meaning of words and sentences), as children move beyond the two-word stage their knowledge of meanings also rapidly advances (Sanford, 2000). The speaking vocabulary of a six-year-old child ranges from 8,000 to 14,000 words. Assuming that word learning began when the child was 12 months old, this translates into a rate of five to eight new word meanings a day between the ages of one and six. After five years of learning words, the six-year-old child does not slow down. Some children are moving along at the awe-inspiring rate of learning more than 22 words a day. By the time children reach the end of elementary school, many have added another 5,000 to 7,000 words to their vocabulary.

Children who begin elementary school with a small vocabulary may be at risk when it comes to learning to read (Berko-Gleason, 2002). In a two-year longitudinal study of students in Grades 4, 5, and 6, it was found that exposure to print can support vocabulary development and cognitive growth in the verbal domain (Echols, West, Stanovich, & Zehr, 1996). Print exposure is critical for the development of reading and verbal skills (e.g., receptive vocabulary, spelling, reading vocabulary, and reading comprehension).

Changes in pragmatics (the rules about appropriate conversation) also characterize children's language development. A six-year-old is a much better conversationalist than a three-year-old. At about three years of age, children improve in their ability to talk about things that are not physically present. That is, they improve their command of the characteristic of language known as "displacement." Children become increasingly removed from the here and now and are able to talk about things that are not physically present, as well as things that happened in the past, or that may happen in the future. Preschoolers can tell you what they want for lunch tomorrow, something that would not have been possible at the two-word stage in infancy. Preschool children also become increasingly able to talk in different ways to different people. Elementary-school children are more sensitive to the needs of others in conversation than preschool children are. They aren't perfect conversationalists (and neither are most adults), but they are better at talking *with* rather than just *to* someone.

The advances in language that take place in early childhood lay the foundation for later development in the elementary-school years. Children gain new skills as they enter school that make it possible to learn to read and write. Such skills include using language in a displaced way, learning what constitutes a word, and learning how to recognize and talk about sounds (Berko-Gleason, 2002). They have to learn that the alphabet letters represent sounds of the language (alphabet principle). As children develop during middle and late childhood, changes in their vocabulary and grammar also take place.

During middle and late childhood, a change occurs in the way children think about words. They become less tied to the actions and perceptual dimensions associated with words, and they become more analytical in their approach to words.

When asked to say the first word that comes to mind after hearing a prompt, young children typically provide a word that often follows in a sentence. For example, when asked to respond to "dog" the young child may say "barks," or say "lunch" at the prompt "eat." At about seven years of age, children begin to respond with a word that represents the same part of speech as the prompt. For example, a child may now respond to the prompt "dog" with "cat" or "horse." To the prompt "eat," they now might say "drink." This is evidence that children have begun to categorize their vocabulary by parts of speech (Berko-Gleason, 2002).

This is a wug.

Now there is another one. There are two of them. There are two _____.

FIGURE 2.8 Stimuli in Berko-Gleason's Study of Young Children's Understanding of Morphological Rules In Jean Berko-Gleason's (1958) study, young children were presented cards such as this one with a "wug" on it. Then the children were asked to supply the missing word and say it correctly. "Wugs" is the correct response here.

Through the Eyes of Students

Learning the Meaning of New Words

It is important to know what words mean so that you can understand what people are telling you. A good place to learn new words is at school. You can also learn new words at home. I learned the new word "concentrate" at school when my desk partner kept talking to me. I told the teacher and she told my desk partner to let me "concentrate." He did not know what that word meant, so the teacher explained that he was to let me do my work without any interruptions. That is how I learned about the word "concentrate."

Beckie
Grade 2 Student
Likes to Play with Friends; Jujitsu, Soccer, and Bowling Enthusiast
Ontario

Children make similar advances in grammar. The elementary-school student's improvement in logical reasoning and analytical skills helps in the understanding of such constructions as the appropriate use of comparatives (shorter, deeper) and subjectives ("If you were prime minister…").

In adolescence, vocabulary increases with the addition of more abstract words. More complex grammar forms are better understood, as is the function a word plays in a sentence. Adolescents also show an increased understanding of metaphor and satire. In late adolescence, individuals can better appreciate adult literary works. Figure 2.9 summarizes some of the main milestones in language.

Children pick up words as pigeons pick up peas.

John Ray
English Author, 17th Century

FIGURE 2.9 **Language Milestones**

AGE PERIOD	CHILD'S DEVELOPMENT/BEHAVIOUR
0–6 Months	Cooing Discrimination of vowels Babbling present by end of period
6–12 Months	Babbling expands to include sounds of spoken language Gestures used to communicate about objects
12–18 Months	First words spoken Understand vocabulary 50+ words on the average
18–24 Months	Vocabulary increases to an average of 200 words Two-word combinations
2 Years	Vocabulary rapidly increases Correct use of plurals Use of past tense Use of some prepositions
3–4 Years	Mean length of utterances increases to 3–4 morphemes a sentence Use of "yes" "no" questions, *wh-* questions Use of negatives and imperatives Increased awareness of pragmatics
5–6 Years	Vocabulary reaches an average of about 10,000 words Coordination of simple sentences
6–8 Years	Vocabulary continues to increase rapidly More skilled use of syntactical rules Conversational skills improve
9–11 Years	Word definitions include synonyms Conversational strategies continue to improve
11–14 Years	Vocabulary increases with addition of more abstract words Understanding of complex grammar forms Increased understanding of function a word plays in a sentence Understanding of metaphor and satire
15–20 Years	Can understand adult literary works

Note:
1. This is not an exhaustive list.
2. There is a great deal of variation in the ages at which children can reach these milestones and still be considered within the normal range of language development.

Technology and Verbal Language Development

A growing body of research suggests that technology can be used to enhance the social, language, and cognitive skills of students by providing them with appealing and motivating opportunities for language use and social interaction (Senge, 2000). Children acquire spoken language skills in part by participating in dialogue with other people. Computers, games, and technologies equipped with voice-synthesis and text-reader software can help children develop an understanding of sound patterns and language communication patterns. These technologies can also provide students with opportunities for meaningful play and social interactions, from which language skills can further develop.

Tape recorders, talking books, and computer programs can be useful in integrating the many aspects of literacy including speaking, listening, reading, and writing (Novick, 1998). Tape recorders allow students to record stories, songs, or poems and to hear themselves speak aloud. Talking books and computer programs combine audio and visual information in storybook or game formats that enable children to control the pace at which information is presented. Talking books allow learners to see and hear what they are reading as they view accompanying illustrations. Hearing a word or phrase paired with a picture helps young students draw associations between the pictures and verbal language. Talking books encourage vocalizations and word approximations from children, allowing them to control the action and providing them with consistent auditory feedback.

Computer programs such as Symbol Writer (Don Johnston), Muppets on Stage (Sunburst), and Word Heads (Theatrix Interactive) combine graphics, animation, music, and speech-synthesis technologies. For example, Word Heads is a CD-ROM designed for 10- to 14-year-olds that focuses on improving students' vocabulary skills. Students design personalized characters by scanning their own faces from photographs, or drawing custom heads, or importing pictures to use while playing various game shows. Students create narratives by inserting nouns, adjectives, verbs, and idioms into story templates. When the narratives are played back, students learn more about the importance of context for verbal communication.

While games and talking books are useful tools in teaching verbal language, having a teacher or adult participate or supervise is a vital part of providing the scaffolding and guidance needed to make the most of this technology. The critical role of the teacher or parent is in being a receptive and supportive human communication partner.

At this point we have discussed a number of ideas about the nature of language, biological and environmental influences, and language development. A review of these ideas is presented in Summary Table 2.3.

SUMMARY TABLE 2.3
What Language Is, Biological and Environmental Influences, and How Language Develops

What is language?	• Language is a form of communication, whether spoken, written, or signed, that is based on a system of symbols. • Human languages are generative and have organizational rules. • Phonology is a language's sound system. • Morphology is the rules for combining morphemes (the meaningful strings of sounds that contain no smaller meaningful parts). • Syntax is the rules for combining words to form acceptable phrases and sentences. • Semantics is the meanings of words and sentences. • Pragmatics is the use of appropriate conversation.
What are the biological and environmental influences on language?	• Children all over the world reach language milestones at about the same age despite vast differences in their environmental experiences. • Biology and experience interact to produce language development. • Children do not learn language in a social vacuum. • Children benefit when parents and teachers actively engage them in conversation, ask them questions, and talk with, not just to, them. • Language and communication skills are a substantial component of verbal participation in the primary classroom.
How does language develop?	• Language acquistion advances through stages. • Babbling occurs at about 3 to 6 months, the first word at 10 to 13 months, and two-word utterances at 18 to 24 months. • As children move beyond two-word utterances, they acquire some morphological rules. • Children also advance in their understanding of syntax, semantics, and pragmatics and begin to categorize their vocabulary by parts of speech. • By the end of elementary school, most students can apply appropriate rules of grammar. • In adolescence, vocabulary increases with the addition of more abstract words.

Every year, Ms. Nohara required her secondary-school senior history class to read two books about "government or political systems" and to write a brief report about each text.

One student in her class, Liam, selected *1984* and *Animal Farm* by George Orwell. In *1984*, the world turns into a terrible place in which "Big Brother" monitors everyone's actions via two-way television-like screens. Infractions of minor rules are punished severely. *Animal Farm* is a short novel about political systems in which the characters are portrayed as farm animals such as pigs and dogs. Liam enjoyed both books and finished them both before mid-term. His reports were insightful, reflecting on the symbolism contained in the novels and the implications for present-day government.

Liam's friend, Pita, had put off reading her first book until a few days before the reports were due. She knew Liam enjoyed reading about government and had finished his reports. Pita asked Liam if he knew of any "skinny" books that she could read. Liam gladly shared his copy of *Animal Farm* with her. Pita accepted the book, very pleased that it was so short. However, as she began reading the book, she wondered why Liam had given it to her. It didn't seem to fit the requirements of the assignment at all.

The day before the reports were due, Ms. Nohara overheard the students talking. Pita complained to Liam, "I don't get it. It's a story about pigs and dogs." Liam responded, "They aren't really supposed to be farm animals. It's a story about the promises of communism and what happened in the Soviet Union once the communists took over. It's a great story! Don't you see? The pigs represent the communist regime that overthrew the czars during the Russian Revolution. They made all kinds of promises about equality. The people supported them because they were tired of the rich and powerful running everything while they starved. Once the czars were expelled, the communists set up a new government. But they didn't keep any of their promises. Instead, they controlled everything and began acting just like the czars. They even began a secret police force—like the dogs in the story. Remember how they bullied the other animals? That was just like the secret police in the Soviet Union."

"I still don't get it. How can a pig or a dog be a communist or a police officer? They're just animals."

Liam looked at his friend, dumbfounded. How could she *not* understand this book? It was so obvious.

- Using Piaget's theory, explain why Liam understood the book and Pita didn't.
- What could Ms. Nohara do to help Pita better understand the novel?
- How could Ms. Nohara have structured this assignment so that Pita would not need to rush through the texts to complete the assignment?

CHAPTER REVIEW

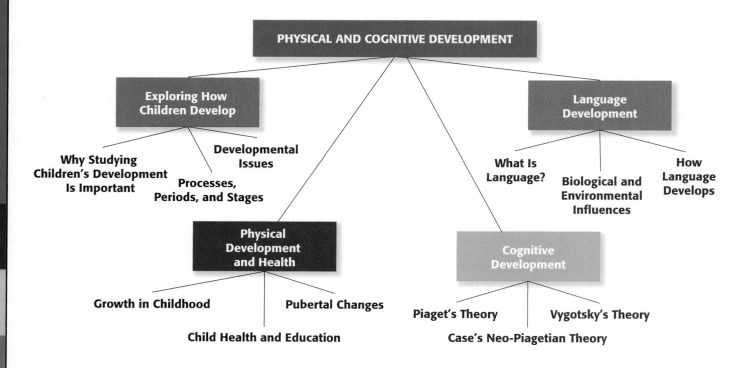

PHYSICAL AND COGNITIVE DEVELOPMENT

- Exploring How Children Develop
  - Why Studying Children's Development Is Important
  - Processes, Periods, and Stages
  - Developmental Issues
- Physical Development and Health
  - Growth in Childhood
  - Child Health and Education
  - Pubertal Changes
- Cognitive Development
  - Piaget's Theory
  - Case's Neo-Piagetian Theory
  - Vygotsky's Theory
- Language Development
  - What Is Language?
  - Biological and Environmental Influences
  - How Language Develops

To obtain a detailed review of this chapter, study these three summary tables:

 KEY TERMS

development 34
biological processes 34
cognitive processes 35
socioemotional processes 35
infancy 35
early childhood 35
middle and late childhood 35
adolescence 35
early adulthood 35
maturation 35
nature–nurture controversy 36
continuity in development 36
discontinuity in development 36

early–later experience issue 36
myelination 37
gross motor skills 38
fine motor skills 38
puberty 40
schema 43
assimilation 43
accommodation 43
sensorimotor stage 44
object permanence 44
preoperational stage 44
symbolic function substage 44
egocentrism 44

animism 45
intuitive thought substage 45
centration 45
conservation 45
operations 45
concrete operational stage 46
classifying 46
seriation 46
transitivity 46
formal operational stage 46
hypothetical-deductive reasoning 48
adolescent egocentrism 48

neo-Piagetians 49
zone of proximal development (ZPD) 51
scaffolding 52
language 55
infinite generativity 55
phonology 56
morphology 56
syntax 56
semantics 56
pragmatics 56

PROFESSIONAL DEVELOPMENT/PORTFOLIO ACTIVITIES

1. Kids Will Be Kids

Do children of the same age all think and behave in the same manner? Consider the students whom you hope to teach. Based on your observations of children and the information presented in this chapter, develop a list of characteristics. How do children think? How do they behave? Then make a second list of the ways in which you, as an adult, think and act. Compare the lists and note the differences between how the children and adults cognate. How will you ensure that you are teaching these students in a manner that is appropriate for their cognitive development level?

2. Thinking about Thinking

Understanding how children think is a step toward helping them learn. Make two lists: one of the characteristics of students who are thinking in formal operational ways, and the other of students who are thinking in concrete operational ways. Below the lists of characteristics, note how you might help these students develop better study skills. Use your ideas to write lesson activity plans that aim to help each of these groups develop study skills. Place the lesson activities in your portfolio as examples of your planning for instruction.

3. Developing Language Skills

Language development is complex, but it generally follows a natural progression in child development. Recall the sections related to language development in this chapter. What information and ideas did you find that were insightful? How will you use these ideas in your own teaching practice? Create some activities based on these ideas for use with Grade 1, Grade 3, and Grade 5 students. What do the activities have in common and how do they differ?

4. Thinking about Learning

Piaget, Case, and Vygotsky are developmental theorists who presented different perspectives on how children learn. Piaget believed in the personal discovery of ideas. Vygotsky believed in the social discovery of ideas. Case presented elements of both views, in combination with aspects of information-processing theory. Based on your experiences, readings, and reflections, how do you view learning? Is learning an individualized discovery of ideas, is it socially constructed, or is it a combination of both? Write a 500-word essay outlining your views and include it in your portfolio.

INTERNET ACTIVITIES

1. Reading, Writing, and E-mail

Giving students frequent opportunities for reading, writing, oral presentations, or collaborative group work can reinforce language skills. The Internet provides some interesting ways for students to practise their reading and writing skills. Access the Flat Stanley Website (http://flatstanley.enoreo.on.ca) and explore how the site uses e-mail and a clever story to promote language and literacy skills. What are the potential problems that you might need to address when using e-mail as a vehicle for teaching writing?

2. Physical Development and Learning

Healthy physical development is an important factor in students' academic achievement. Working with a partner, develop a list of the health risk factors that might inhibit students' success. Discuss and note local programs or resources that are accessible to address these risk factors. What Internet resources are available to help teachers working with these students? Retain this information for future reference.

Connect to the Online Learning Centre at www.mcgrawhill.ca/college/santrock **to explore possible answers.**

Visit the *Educational Psychology* Online Learning Centre at
www.mcgrawhill.ca/college/santrock
to access Websites related to the above Internet Activities as well as chapter quizzes,
a searchable glossary, and other learning and study tools.

3 Social Contexts and Socioemotional Development

Preview

Parents cradle children's lives, but children's development is also shaped by successive choirs of peers, friends, and teachers. Children's small worlds widen as they become students and develop relationships with many new people. In this chapter, we will explore these social worlds and examine students' socioemotional development. These are some of the questions we will address:

- What are some good and bad parenting strategies? How can teachers foster partnerships between school and family?
- How can teachers improve students' social skills?
- What is the best way to provide a developmentally appropriate education for students?
- What does it take for teachers and students to be emotionally intelligent?
- What are the best strategies for helping adolescents who have problems?

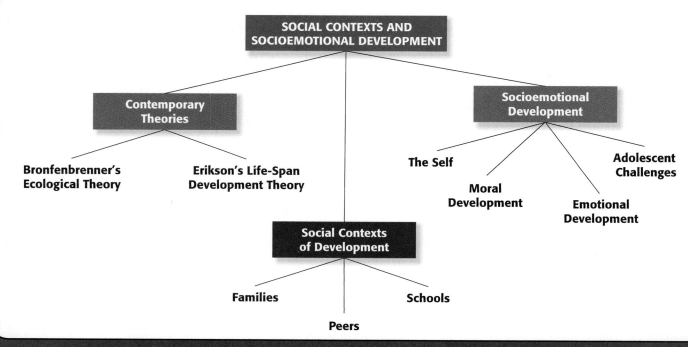

SOCIAL CONTEXTS AND SOCIOEMOTIONAL DEVELOPMENT

Contemporary Theories
- Bronfenbrenner's Ecological Theory
- Erikson's Life-Span Development Theory

Social Contexts of Development
- Families
- Peers
- Schools

Socioemotional Development
- The Self
- Moral Development
- Emotional Development
- Adolescent Challenges

> *In the end the power behind development is life.*
>
> Erik Erikson
> *European-Born American Psychologist, 20th Century*

Teaching Stories: Dan Forbes

Dan Forbes has taught in urban and rural elementary schools across Manitoba for more than 18 years and has been the recipient of many awards including the Prime Minister's Award for Teaching Excellence (1997), the Roy C. Hill Award for Educational Innovation (1999), and the TOBA Award for Physical Education Programming (2001). Below, he recalls one of the many times that a student's socioemotional circumstances have factored into his classroom instruction.

"One of my brightest students came into class very sad and reluctant to talk about what was bothering her. During language arts, I provided the students with a topic for their journals. The students knew that I would read each of their responses. Rather than writing about the assigned topic, Susan used the journalling session to describe what was making her so unhappy.

"Susan lived with her grandmother and mother and it was Susan's responsibility to wake up her grandmother. On the weekend, she become so engrossed with the morning cartoons that she forgot to wake her grandmother at the usual time. When she remembered to go upstairs, she found that her grandmother had passed away.

"After talking with Susan, I realized that she blamed herself for her grandmother's death. I decided to share this information with Susan's mother, whose initial reaction was disbelief. We realized that Susan was trying to be 'strong' for her mother. We decided to stay in touch and to work together to help Susan deal with this traumatic event.

"During the days before the funeral, I arranged to have Susan put together a booklet about her grandmother and to share stories of her life with the class. A few months later, a student in a lower grade lost a grandparent. When Susan learned about this, she volunteered to speak with the student about how to cope with the loss.

"Susan's experience taught me about how important it is to provide our students with a variety of ways to communicate with us. It reminded me about the importance of listening, watching, and reassuring students that they can turn to us for support. Throughout my teaching career, I have seen many tragedies including the explosion of Challenger, September 11th, and the death of a student. I have learned that it is important to make time to address students' feelings and fears. When we work through events together as a class, we all feel better and a special bond is created."

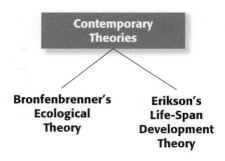

Contemporary Theories

Bronfenbrenner's Ecological Theory

Erikson's Life-Span Development Theory

CONTEMPORARY THEORIES

A number of theories address children's socioemotional development. In this chapter we will focus on two main theories: Bronfenbrenner's ecological theory and Erikson's life-span development theory. These two theories were chosen because they are the most comprehensive theories to address the social contexts in which children develop (Bronfenbrenner) and major changes in children's socioemotional development (Erikson).

Bronfenbrenner's Ecological Theory

The ecological theory developed by Urie Bronfenbrenner (1917–   ) primarily focuses on the social contexts in which children live and the people who influence their development.

Five Environmental Systems   Bronfenbrenner's **ecological theory** *consists of five environmental systems: the microsystem, mesosystem, exosystem, macrosystem, and chronosystem* (see Figure 3.1) (Bronfenbrenner, 1986, 1997; Bronfenbrenner & Morris, 1998).

A **microsystem** *setting includes the student's family, peers, school, and neighbourhood.* Within these microsystems, the individual has direct interactions with others. For Bronfenbrenner, the student is not a passive recipient of experiences in these settings, but someone who reciprocally interacts with others and helps to construct the settings.

The **mesosystem** *links microsystems.* Experience in one microsystem can affect experience in another microsystem. For example, children whose parents have rejected them might have difficulty developing positive relationships with teachers or with peers.

The **exosystem** *involves experiences in another setting (in which students do not have active roles) that influence what students and teachers experience.* For example, school and park supervisory boards have strong roles in determining the quality of schools, parks, and recreation facilities. Their decisions can help or hinder students' development.

Urie Bronfenbrenner developed ecological theory, a perspective that is receiving increased attention. His theory emphasizes the importance of both micro and macro dimensions of the environment in which the child lives.

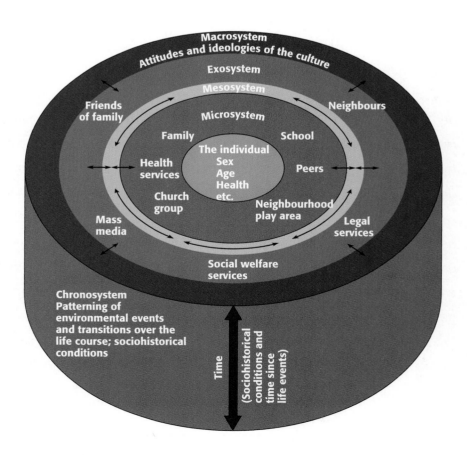

FIGURE 3.1   Bronfenbrenner's Ecological Theory of Development
Bronfenbrenner's ecological theory consists of five environmental systems: microsystem, mesosystem, exosystem, macrosystem, and chronosystem.

The **macrosystem** *involves the broader culture in which students and teachers live, including the society's values and customs.* For example, Canada has ratified the UN Convention on the Rights of the Child, which officially recognizes the importance of respecting children's rights. This focus has implications for child development, teaching, and allocation of resources for children. Culture includes the roles of ethnicity and socioeconomic factors in children's development.

The **chronosystem** *refers to sociohistorical conditions of students' development.* For example, students today are the first daycare generation, the first wired generation, and the first post–sexual-revolution generation.

Evaluating Bronfenbrenner's Theory   Bronfenbrenner's theory bridges the gap between behavioural theories that focus on small settings and anthropological theories that analyze larger settings. His theory calls attention to the importance of looking at students' lives in more than one setting—not just what goes on in the classroom, but also what happens in students' families, neighbourhoods, and peer groups.

Critics of Bronfenbrenner's theory say that it gives too little attention to biological and cognitive factors in children's development and does not address the step-by-step developmental changes that are the focus of theories like Piaget's and Erikson's.

Erikson's Life-Span Development Theory

Complementing Bronfenbrenner's analysis of the social contexts in which children develop and the people who are important in their lives, the theory of Erik Erikson (1902–1994) presents a developmental unfolding of people's lives in stages. Let's take Erikson's journey through the human life span.

Teaching Strategies
Based on Bronfenbrenner's Theory

✔ Recognize the influences of all environmental systems
 • recognize the roles of schools and teachers, parents and siblings, communities and neighbourhoods, peers and friends, media, religion, and culture

✔ Recognize the connection between schools and families
 • recognize the role of family and school with respect to students' achievement and attitudes toward school
 • recognize that students who are provided with opportunities to communicate and make decisions (at home and school) generally demonstrate greater initiative and achievement than their peers.
 • encourage and foster meaningful relations between students' families, peers, schools, and parents
 • help students establish positive moral goals (e.g., being a role model making a difference in the community)

✔ Recognize the importance of community, socioeconomic status, and culture
 • acknowledge that risk factors such as poverty, parenting style, parental substance use, and unemployment can impair students' ability to learn
 • recognize that some students demonstrate resiliency in the presence of risk factors
 • acknowledge the role of schools and teachers as "buffers" for students who are at-risk

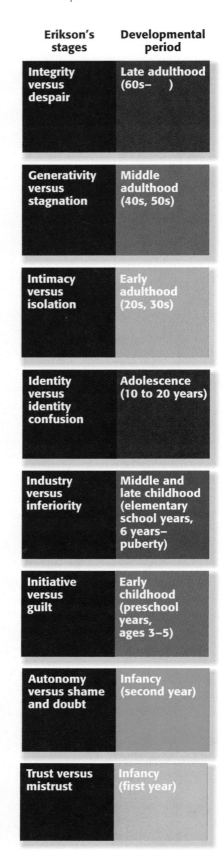

Erikson's stages	Developmental period
Integrity versus despair	Late adulthood (60s–)
Generativity versus stagnation	Middle adulthood (40s, 50s)
Intimacy versus isolation	Early adulthood (20s, 30s)
Identity versus identity confusion	Adolescence (10 to 20 years)
Industry versus inferiority	Middle and late childhood (elementary school years, 6 years– puberty)
Initiative versus guilt	Early childhood (preschool years, ages 3–5)
Autonomy versus shame and doubt	Infancy (second year)
Trust versus mistrust	Infancy (first year)

FIGURE 3.2 **Erikson's Eight Life-Span Stages**

Eight Stages of Human Development In Erikson's (1968) theory, eight stages of development unfold as people go through the human life span (see Figure 3.2). Each stage consists of a developmental task that confronts individuals with a crisis. For Erikson, each crisis is not catastrophic, but a turning point of increased vulnerability and enhanced potential. The more successfully an individual resolves each crisis, the more psychologically healthy the individual will be. Each stage has both positive and negative sides.

Trust versus mistrust (preschool years) *is Erikson's first psychosocial stage.* It occurs in the first year of life. The development of trust requires warm, nurturing caregiving. The positive outcome is a feeling of comfort and minimal fear. Mistrust develops when infants are treated too negatively or are ignored.

Autonomy versus shame and doubt (preschool years) *is Erikson's second psychosocial stage.* It occurs in late infancy and the toddler years. After gaining trust in their caregivers, infants begin to discover that their behaviour is their own. They assert their independence and realize their will. If infants are restrained too much or punished too harshly, they develop a sense of shame and doubt.

Initiative versus guilt (preschool years) *is Erikson's third psychosocial stage.* It corresponds to early childhood, about three to five years of age. As young children experience a widening social world, they are challenged more than they were as infants. To cope with these challenges, they need to engage in active, purposeful behaviour. In this stage, adults expect children to become more responsible and require them to assume some responsibilities for taking care of their bodies and belongings. Developing a sense of responsibility increases initiative. Children develop uncomfortable guilt feelings if they are irresponsible or are made to feel too anxious.

Industry versus inferiority (elementary-school years) *is Erikson's fourth psychosocial stage.* It corresponds approximately with the elementary-school years, from six years of age until puberty or early adolescence. Children's initiative brings them into contact with a wealth of new experiences. As they move into the elementary-school years, they direct their energy toward mastering knowledge and intellectual skills. At no time are children more enthusiastic about learning than at the end of early childhood, when their imagination is expansive. The danger in the elementary-school years is developing a sense of inferiority, unproductiveness, and incompetence.

Identity versus identity confusion (intermediate and high school) *is Erikson's fifth psychosocial stage.* It corresponds to the adolescent years. Adolescents try to find out who they are, what they are all about, and where they are going in life. They are confronted with many new roles and adult statuses (such as vocational and romantic). Adolescents need to be allowed to explore different paths to attain a healthy identity. If adolescents do not adequately explore different roles and don't carve out a positive future path, they can remain confused about their identity.

Intimacy versus isolation (early adulthood) *is Erikson's sixth psychosocial stage.* It corresponds to the early adult years, the twenties and thirties. The developmental task is to form positive close relationships with others. Erikson describes intimacy as finding oneself but losing oneself in another person. The hazard of this stage is that one will fail to form an intimate relationship with a romantic partner or friend and become socially isolated. For such individuals, loneliness can become a dark cloud over their lives.

Generativity versus stagnation (middle adulthood) *is Erikson's seventh psychosocial stage.* It corresponds to the middle adulthood years, the forties and fifties. Generativity means transmitting something positive to the next generation. This can involve such roles as parenting and teaching, through which adults assist the next generation in developing useful lives. Erikson described stagnation as the feeling of having done nothing to help the next generation.

Integrity versus despair (late adulthood) *is Erikson's eighth and final psychosocial stage.* It corresponds to the late adulthood years, the sixties until death. Older adults review their lives, reflecting on what they have done. If the retrospective evaluations are positive, they develop a sense of integrity. That is, they view their life as positively integrated and worth living. In contrast, older adults become despairing if their backward glances are mainly negative.

Evaluating Erikson's Theory   Erikson's theory captures some of life's key socioemotional tasks and places them in a developmental framework. His concept of identity is especially helpful in understanding older adolescents and post-secondary students. His overall theory was a critical force in forging our current view of human development as lifelong rather than being restricted only to childhood (Kroger, 2000).

Erikson's theory is not without criticism. Some experts believe that his stages are too rigid. Bernice Neugarten (1988) says that identity, intimacy, independence, and many other aspects of socioemotional development are not like beads on a string that appear in neatly packaged age intervals. Rather, they are important issues throughout most of our lives. Although much research has been done on some of Erikson's stages (such as identity), the overall scope of his theory (such as whether the eight stages always occur in the order he proposed) has not been scientifically documented. For example, for some individuals (especially females), intimacy concerns precede identity or develop simultaneously.

At this point we have discussed a number of ideas about Bronfenbrenner's and Erikson's theories. A review of these ideas is presented in Summary Table 3.1.

SOCIAL CONTEXTS OF DEVELOPMENT

In Bronfenbrenner's theory, the social contexts in which students live are important influences on their development. Let's explore three of the contexts in which students spend much of their time: families, peers, and schools.

Families

Children grow up in diverse families. Some parents nurture and support their children. Others treat them harshly or ignore them. Some children experience their parents' divorce. Others live their entire childhood in a never-divorced family. Others live in a stepfamily. Some children's mothers work full-time and place them in after-school programs. Other children's mothers are present when they come home from school. Some children grow up in an ethnically uniform neighbourhood, others in a neighbourhood that is more mixed. Some children's families live in poverty, others are economically advantaged. Some children have siblings, others don't. All of these varying circumstances affect children's development and influence students in and beyond the classroom.

Parenting Styles   There can be times when you as a teacher will be asked to give parents advice. There also might be times when it is helpful for you to understand how parents are rearing their children and the effects this has on the children.

Is there a best way to parent? Diana Baumrind (1971; 1996), a leading authority on parenting, thinks so. She believes that parents should be neither punitive nor aloof. Rather, they should develop rules for children while at the same time being supportive and nurturant. Hundreds of research studies, including her own, support her view (Bornstein, 1995; Grotevant, 1998). Baumrind says that parenting styles come in four main forms:

• **Authoritarian parenting** *is restrictive and punitive.* Authoritarian parents exhort children to follow their directions and respect them. They place firm limits and controls on their children and allow little verbal exchange. For example, an authoritarian parent might say, "Do it my way or else. There will be no discussion!" Children of authoritarian parents often behave in socially incompetent ways. They tend to be anxious about social comparison, fail to initiate activity, and have poor communication skills.
• **Authoritative parenting** *encourages children to be independent but still places limits and controls on their actions. Extensive verbal give-and-take is allowed and parents are nurturant and supportive.* An authoritative parent might put his arm on the child's shoulder in a comforting way and say, "You know you should not have done that. Let's talk about how you can handle the situation differently the next time."

Erik Erikson with his wife, Joan, an artist. Erikson generated one of the most important developmental theories of the twentieth century.

Parenting is a very important profession, but no test of its fitness is ever imposed in the interest of children.

George Bernard Shaw
Irish Playwright, 20th Century

Teaching Strategies
Based on Erikson's Theory

✔ Encourage initiative in young children
  • allow preschool and early-primary-grade students the freedom to explore
  • provide preschool and early-primary-grade students with choices and honour their requests for activities whenever possible
  • encourage social and fantasy play
  • provide children with responsibilities (e.g., putting away toys, taking care of a classroom pet or plant)
  • provide developmentally appropriate tasks and structure tasks for success
  • avoid being critical
✔ Promote industry in elementary-school children
  • provide a classroom environment that promotes a love for learning
  • encourage children to discover that they can accomplish tasks
  • nourish students' motivation for mastery and curiosity
  • challenge students but do not overwhelm them
  • require students to be productive
  • be tolerant of mistakes and avoid being critical
  • structure tasks for success
✔ Promote identity exploration in adolescents
  • recognize that students' identities are multidimensional (e.g., vocational goals, intellectual achievement, interest in sports, hobbies)
  • encourage students to reflect on their identity and future goals (e.g., reflective writing, career counselling, community presentations)
  • encourage students to examine different perspectives (e.g., debate religious, political, and ideological issues)
  • encourage students to think independently and express their views
✔ Model positive characteristics associated with Erikson's stages
  • demonstrate trust and initiative
  • be industrious and model a sense of mastery
  • develop positive relationships with others
  • be motivated to contribute to the next generation in a meaningful manner

If I had my child to raise all over again,

I'd finger paint more, and point the finger less.

I'd do less correcting, and more connecting.

I'd take my eyes off my watch, and watch with my eyes.

I would care to know less, and know to care more.

I'd take more hikes and fly more kites.

I'd stop playing serious, and seriously play.

I would run through more fields, and gaze at more stars.

I'd do more hugging, and less tugging.

I would be firm less often, and affirm much more.

I'd build self-esteem first, and the house later.

I'd teach less about the love of power, and more about the power of love.

Diane Loomans
American Poet, Contemporary

Children whose parents are authoritative often behave in socially competent ways. They tend to be self-reliant, delay gratification, get along with their peers, and show high self-esteem. Because of these positive outcomes, Baumrind strongly endorses authoritative parenting.

• **Neglectful parenting** *is a permissive form of parenting in which parents are uninvolved in their children's lives.* When their offspring are adolescents or perhaps even young children, these parents cannot answer the question "It is 10 P.M. Do you know where your child is?" Children of neglectful parents develop the sense that other aspects of their parents' lives are more important than they are. Children of neglectful parents often behave in socially incompetent ways. They tend to have poor self-control, don't handle independence well, and aren't achievement motivated.

• **Indulgent parenting** *is a parenting style in which parents are highly involved with their children but place few limits or restrictions on their behaviours.* These parents often let their children do what they want and get their way because they believe the combination of nurturant support and lack of restraints will produce a creative, confident child. The result is that these children usually don't learn to control their own behaviour. These parents do not take into account the development of the whole child.

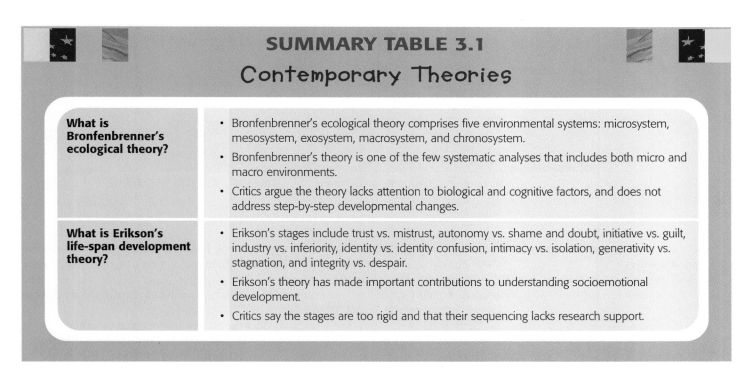

SUMMARY TABLE 3.1

Contemporary Theories

What is Bronfenbrenner's ecological theory?	• Bronfenbrenner's ecological theory comprises five environmental systems: microsystem, mesosystem, exosystem, macrosystem, and chronosystem. • Bronfenbrenner's theory is one of the few systematic analyses that includes both micro and macro environments. • Critics argue the theory lacks attention to biological and cognitive factors, and does not address step-by-step developmental changes.
What is Erikson's life-span development theory?	• Erikson's stages include trust vs. mistrust, autonomy vs. shame and doubt, initiative vs. guilt, industry vs. inferiority, identity vs. identity confusion, intimacy vs. isolation, generativity vs. stagnation, and integrity vs. despair. • Erikson's theory has made important contributions to understanding socioemotional development. • Critics say the stages are too rigid and that their sequencing lacks research support.

Interestingly, a parallel can be made between parenting styles and teaching styles. In Chapter 12, teachers are described as being authoritarian, authoritative, or permissive; these labels describe the style in which a teacher manages the classroom. In general, the authoritative strategy of classroom management is the most effective for encouraging students to become active, self-regulated learners.

The Changing Family in a Changing Society   Increasing numbers of children are being raised in divorced families, stepparent families, and families in which the mother works outside the home. Canada has one of the highest percentages of single-parent families (see Figure 3.3). Although there is considerable disagreement about the reasons why different family structures produce different educational outcomes, students from single-parent-status and low-income families are potentially at risk for social and educational difficulties in childhood (Lipman, Offord, & Dooley, 1996). Ross, Scott, and Kelly (1996b) note that students in low-income families tend to live in risky environments (such as homes that are in poor repair) and tend to engage in risky behaviours (such as smoking, alcohol, drug use, and unsafe sexual practices). These students tend to have lower levels of educational attainment, poorer health, and greater opportunity to be the victims of violence and aggression than their more-affluent peers. Twice as many of these teens tend to drop out of high school than their more-affluent peers, and pregnancy rates for these youth are almost five times higher than those for teens in Canada's highest-income neighbourhoods (Health Canada, 1999).

Children of Divorce   Canada has one of the highest divorce rates among Western industrialized countries. As divorce rates increase, so do the number of children growing up in single-parent families. For example, in 1996 there were about 1.8 million children (almost one in five) living in a single-parent family, usually headed by the mother (Government of Canada, 1996). Considerable research has established that children growing up in single-parent families can be disadvantaged compared to children from two-parent families (Frederick & Boyd, 1998). For instance, children from single-parent families are more likely to drop out of school. However, the effects of divorce on children are complex, depending on such factors as the age of the child, strengths and weaknesses of the child at the time of the divorce, the type of custody involved, socioeconomic status, and

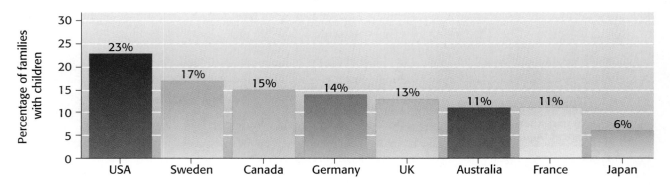

Note: Children are under 18 years of age.

FIGURE 3.3 **Single-Parent Families in Various Countries**

postdivorce family functioning (Hetherington, 1999; Hetherington, Bridges, & Isabella, 1998). The use of support systems (relatives, friends, housekeepers), an ongoing positive relationship between the custodial parent and the ex-spouse, being able to meet financial needs, and quality schooling help students adjust to the stressful circumstances of divorce (Emery, 1999; Parke & Buriel, 1998).

Hetherington's (1995, 1999) research documents the importance of schools when students grow up in a divorced family. Throughout elementary school, students in divorced families had the highest achievement and fewest problems when both the parenting environment and the school environment were authoritative (according to Baumrind's categorization). In the divorced families, when only one parent was authoritative, an authoritative school improved the child's adjustment. The most negative parenting environment occurred when neither parent was authoritative. The most negative school environment was chaotic and neglecting.

Ethnic and Socioeconomic Variations in Families In Canada, families from diverse ethnic groups differ in their size, structure, and composition, reliance on kinship networks, and level of income and education (Jayachandran, 2000). In most Western cultures, child-rearing practices have been found to differ among socioeconomic and cultural groups. In North America, a growing trend is single-parent families. Students from single-parent and low-income families have a greater probability of poor academic attainment than students from two-parent family structures.

Low-income parents often place a high value on external characteristics, such as obedience and neatness. In contrast, middle-class families frequently place a high value on internal characteristics, such as self-control and delay of gratification. Middle-class parents are more likely to explain, praise, accompany their discipline with reasoning, and ask their children questions. Research suggests that low-income parents are more likely to use physical punishment and criticize their children (Hoff-Ginsberg & Tardiff, 1995). As you consider these findings and their implications for your classroom, we believe that a word of caution is warranted. That is, it is especially important for teachers not to over-generalize these findings across all families. That is, these data do not warrant or justify biased expectations about students or parents based on their family composition, ethnicity, or family income.

There are also socioeconomic differences in the way that parents think about education (Mata, 1997). Middle-class parents are more likely to believe that education is something that should be mutually encouraged by parents and teachers. Low-income parents are more likely to view education as the sole responsibility of the schools and teachers. Appropriate linkages between schools and families are therefore of primary importance in helping to establish positive attitudes about education.

School–Family Linkages In Bronfenbrenner's theory, linkages between the family and the school are an important mesosystem. And in Hetherington's study that we just discussed, an authoritative school environment benefited children from divorced families.

www.mcgrawhill.ca/college/santrock

Calvin and Hobbes   by Bill Watterson

Today's teachers think it is extremely important to get parents involved in children's education. In one survey, teachers listed parental involvement as the number-one priority in improving education (Chira, 1993).

What stands in the way of parental involvement? For one thing, education expert Joyce Epstein (1997) says, most parents know so little about their children's education that they can't even ask questions about it. That is why so many conversations begin with a parent asking, "How was school today?" and end with the child responding, "Fine." This low level of parental involvement concerns educators because it is linked with students' low achievement (Eccles & Harold, 1996). For example, in a recent study of more than 16,000 students, the students were more likely to get A's and less likely to repeat a grade or be expelled if both parents were highly involved in their schooling (National Center for Education Statistics, 1997). In this study, high involvement was defined as the parent participating in three or four of the following: school meetings, a teacher conference, a class meeting, or volunteering.

One problem that can interfere with building partnerships between school and family is negative perceptions of families (Workman & Gage, 1997). Some children come to school poorly clothed, on drugs, with knives or guns, and without their homework. They might not be motivated to learn and might show little respect for the teacher. In such circumstances, it can be hard to get past blaming parents for the problems you have inherited as a teacher. However, to get parents more positively involved in their children's education, you have to get past the blaming. Think of parents as having potential strengths that, if adequately tapped, can help you educate the child more effectively.

Peers

In addition to families and teachers, peers also play powerful roles in children's development. Just what are peers?

Exploring Peer Relations   In the context of child development, **peers** *are children of about the same age or maturity level.* Same-age peer interaction plays a unique role. Age grading would occur even if schools were not age graded and students were left alone to determine the composition of their own societies. One of the most important functions of the peer group is to provide a source of information and comparison about the world outside of the family.

Good peer relations might be necessary for normal development (Howes & Tonyan, 2000; Ryan & Patrick, 1996; Rubin, 2000). Social isolation, or the inability to "plug in" to a social network, is linked with many problems and disorders, ranging from delinquency and problem drinking to depression (Kupersmidt & Coie, 1990). Poor peer relations in childhood has been associated with dropping out of school and delinquent behaviour in adolescence (Vitaro, Lorocque, Janosz & Tremblay, 2001). In another study, harmonious peer relations in adolescence was related to positive mental health at midlife (Hightower, 1990).

What Are Elementary-School Students Doing in Their Free Time?

What are elementary-school students doing in their free time? In 2001, the Youth Lifestyle Choices Community University Research Alliance (YLC-CURA), located in Niagara, Ontario, disseminated a survey to more than 7,500 students across Grades 5 to 12/OAC. Students were asked about their after-school leisure activities. The most popular leisure activity reported by elementary-level students (94.4 percent) was watching television. Moreover, 40 percent of the responding students lived in homes with four or more televisions. About 52 percent of the elementary-grade students reported that they watched television after school.

Leisure time is also spent playing video games and on the computer. Approximately 40 percent of elementary-grade students played video games for more than one hour per day. This statistic became inflated on the weekends, with 47.8 percent of these students reporting that they played video games. More than half of the males surveyed (58.4 percent) reported that they most often used the computer to play games. Females, in contrast, used the computer most often to e-mail each other. This survey highlights the fact that elementary-grade students are choosing to spend much of their free time engaged in technological-based media: television, video games, and computers.

Source: Adapted from Report on Youth Lifestyle Choices in the Niagara Region: Findings from the Youth Resilience Questionnaire. Retrieved from www.ylc-cura.ca/publications.html, June 2002.

Peer Status Developmentalists have pinpointed four types of peer status: popular children, neglected children, rejected children, and controversial children (Rubin, Bukowski, & Parker, 1998; Wentzal & Asher, 1995).

Many children worry about whether they are popular or not. **Popular children** *are frequently nominated as a best friend and are rarely disliked by their peers.* Popular children give out reinforcements, listen carefully, maintain open lines of communication with peers, are happy, act like themselves, show enthusiasm and concern for others, and are self-confident without being conceited (Hartup, 1983).

Neglected children *are infrequently nominated as a best friend but are not disliked by their peers.* **Rejected children** *are infrequently nominated as someone's best friend and are*

Children spend considerable time with peers and friends. What peer statuses can children have? How do peer relations change developmentally?

Teaching Strategies
For Forging School–Family Linkages

✔ Provide families with pertinent information
  • provide parents with information about effective child-rearing skills, the importance of family support, child and adolescent development, and home-based strategies for improving student learning
  • invite parents to meet you before or shortly after the school year begins
  • provide parents with positive comments about their children, encourage parents to raise questions and make suggestions, try to obtain information about family structure, rules, roles, and learning style
  • send home students' work each week with a note or letter explaining the nature of the work and how parents can help their children complete it
  • provide interactive homework activities that encourage students to go to their parents for assistance (include information about the objective of the assignment, directions, and tutoring strategies)
  • correspond in the parents' first language whenever possible
  • use computerized telephone systems to record information about study units and homework
✔ Encourage families to attend school meetings and functions
  • encourage school-to-home and home-to-school communications
  • encourage parents to attend parent–teacher conferences and other functions
  • structure meetings to be convenient for families (e.g., lunch and after-work hours, provide child care)
  • monitor the number of families that attend meetings and functions
  • encourage parents to discuss concerns and questions
  • encourage parents to get to know the principal, other parents, and teachers (e.g., create a parent room/centre, organize luncheons with principal)
✔ Include parents in school decisions
  • invite parents to join parent advisory groups, committees, and councils
  • provide parents with information about school structures, initiatives, and programs
  • encourage parents to share recommendations and suggestions with school staff
✔ Encourage volunteerism and collaboration in the classroom
  • match parents' skills with classroom needs
  • provide parents with opportunities to assist outside of school hours (e.g., create materials, clean manipulatives)
  • use the resources of community businesses, agencies, post-secondary institutes, and other groups to strengthen school programs, family practices, and student learning

Source: National Council of Teachers of English (1997)

often actively disliked by their peers. **Controversial children** *are frequently nominated both as someone's best friend and as being disliked.*

Rejected children often have more serious adjustment problems than do neglected children (Dishion & Spracklen, 1996; Rubin et al., 2000). In one study, more than 100 Grade 5 boys were evaluated over a period of seven years until the end of high school (Kupersmidt & Coie, 1990). The most important factor in predicting whether rejected children would engage in delinquent behaviour or drop out of secondary school was aggression toward peers

Diversity and Education
Making a Difference in Canada: Mary Ann Shadd

Mary Ann Shadd was a U.S.–born abolitionist, suffragist, and educator who, along with other members of the Underground Railroad, found Canada to be a more hospitable land than the United States in the 1800s. Born in 1823, Shadd settled in Windsor, Ontario in 1851 and worked tirelessly to help blacks achieve social and educational equality. Her family home was a way station on the Underground Railroad, and her commitment to equality led her to become a teacher and a strong advocate for abolition. Among her many accomplishments were her positions as the first female newspaper editor in Canada and the first black female lawyer in North America. Her enduring legacy also includes the foundation of the first fully integrated non-denominational school in Canada, which was dedicated to the belief that all children, regardless of colour or creed, are entitled to public education. All Canadians owe much to this champion of equality and education.

Mary Ann Shadd was a Canadian hero who made a powerful difference not only in the lives of many blacks in early Upper Canada but also in the present-day lives of all Canadians.

Source: Adapted from McClelland & Stewart (1998); Bearden, Jim, and Linda Jean Butler. 1977. Shadd: The Life and Times of Mary Shadd Cary. Toronto: NC Press Ltd., p. 233.

in elementary school. Aggression, impulsiveness, and disruptiveness characterize the majority of rejected children, although 10 to 20 percent of rejected children are actually shy.

Bullying Bullying is a particular type of peer aggression that can be defined as "the abuse of physical and psychological power for the purpose of intentionally and repeatedly creating a negative atmosphere of severe anxiety, intimidation, and chronic fear in victims" (Marini, Spear, & Bombay, 1999, p. 33). Bullying is a type of abuse perpetrated by peers. The behaviours involved can be severe, pervasive, and have long-lasting consequences (Olweus, 2001; Pepler & Craig, 1995; Smith, Shu, & Madsen, 2001).

The Multidimensional Bullying Identification Model The multidimensional bullying identification model was developed to assist with issues of detection and identification of bullying (Marini, Fairbairn, & Zuber, 2001). The model consists of three distinct components and includes information about a) the five defining characteristics of bullying, b) the four distinct types of bullying, and c) the three major groups of participants.

The first component highlights five distinguishing characteristics of bullying, including a power differential between the victim and the perpetrator; a repeated pattern of aggression; the intent to hurt; an atmosphere of anxiety, intimidation, and fear; and the secretive nature of the bullying behaviour.

The second component describes the direct-to-indirect continuum. Direct bullying is usually characterized by open and overt attacks on the victims, while indirect bullying involves secretive and covert forms of attack (Smith & Sharp, 1994; Rigby, 1996). The second continuum describes different types of aggression from physical to psychological. The combination of the two continua outlines a variety of bullying, including physical, cognitive, social, and emotional (see Figure 3.4).

The third component of the model takes into consideration the complex social dynamics of the three major participants: bullies, victims, and bystanders. It is imperative that educators understand the dynamic and complex sets of relationships at play among all three types of participants so that prevention and management programs can be developed. A more extensive discussion of bullying and its prevention is presented in Chapter 12.

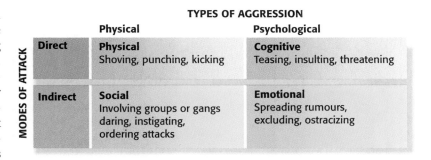

FIGURE 3.4   **The Multidimensional Bullying Identification Model**

Source: Adapted from Marini, Fairbairn, and Zuber (2001)

Friendship   Friendships contribute to peer status and provide other benefits:

- *Companionship.* Friendship gives children a familiar partner, someone who is willing to spend time with them and join in collaborative activities.
- *Physical support.* Friendship provides resources and assistance in times of need.
- *Ego support.* Friendship helps children feel they are competent, worthy individuals. Especially important in this regard is social approval from friends (Berndt & Keefe, 1996).
- *Intimacy/affection.* Friendship provides children with a warm, trusting, close relationship with others. In this relationship, children often feel comfortable about disclosing private, personal information.

Having friends can be a developmental advantage, but friendships are not all alike (Hartup, 2000; Hartup & Stevens, 1997). There are developmental advantages for students in having friends who are socially skilled and supportive. However, it is not developmentally advantageous to have coercive and conflict-ridden friendships. And it sometimes is disadvantageous for students to be friends with someone who is several years older. Some students with older friends engage in more deviant behaviours than their counterparts who have same-age friends (Berndt, 1996). Early-maturing adolescents are especially vulnerable in this regard (Magnusson, 1988).

Developmental Changes in Peer Relations   During the elementary-school years, children's peer groups increasingly consist of same-sex peers (Maccoby, 1995). After extensive observations of elementary-school playgrounds, two researchers characterized the settings as "gender school" (Luria & Herzog, 1985). They said that boys teach one another the required masculine behaviour and strictly reinforce it, and that girls often pass on the female culture and mainly congregate with each other.

In early adolescence, participation in coed groups increases (Dunphy, 1963). Also in adolescence, many students become members of cliques, and allegiance to the clique can exert a powerful influence over their lives. Group identity with the clique can override the adolescent's personal identity. In any secondary school there will be three to six well-formed cliques. Some typical cliques are "jocks," "brains," and "druggies." Although many adolescents want to be in a clique, some are fiercely independent and have no desire to be in one.

Friendship likely plays a more important developmental role in secondary school than in elementary school (Sullivan, 1953). Adolescents disclose more personal information to their friends than younger students do (Buhrmester & Furman, 1987). And adolescents say that they depend more on their friends than on their parents to satisfy their needs for companionship, reassurance of worth, and intimacy (Furman & Buhrmester, 1992).

Schools

In school, children spend many years as members of a small society that exerts a tremendous influence on their socioemotional development.

Schools' Changing Social Developmental Contexts   Social contexts vary through the early childhood, elementary-school, and adolescent years (Minuchin & Shapiro, 1983).

I didn't belong as a kid, and that always bothered me. If only I'd known that one day my differences would have been an asset, then my early years would have been a lot better.

Bette Midler
American Actress and Singer, Contemporary

www.mcgrawhill.ca/college/santrock

Through the Eyes of Students

Good Friends

Good friends are kind and understanding. They always listen to you and are always there to help you out. They are loyal, caring, and forgiving. They are always there to lean on and talk to. You can talk to them about anything—they always try to cheer you up. They never talk about you behind your back or gossip about you. They never push others around or get mad at you when they don't get their way. They forgive you when you mess up. They are sad when you are sad and scared when you are scared. They are happy with your successes. They listen to your problems. Good friends stand up for what they believe in.

When choosing friends, I think about the person within and not the clothes that they wear. Having brand names does not make people good friends. I get to know people well before making any decisions about friendship. I select friends who are caring and not self-centred—those who won't dump you when you don't fit their standards.

Jillian
Grade 9 Student
Skiing, Singing, and Drama Enthusiast
Saskatchewan

The early-childhood setting is a protected environment whose boundary is the classroom. In this limited social setting, young children interact with one or two teachers, usually female, who are powerful figures in their lives. Young children also interact with peers in dyads or small groups.

The classroom still is the main context in elementary school, although it is more likely to be experienced as a social unit than is the early-childhood classroom. The teacher symbolizes authority, which establishes the climate of the classroom, the conditions of social interaction, and the nature of group functioning. Peer groups are more important now, and students have an increased interest in friendship.

As children move into intermediate and high school, the school environment increases in scope and complexity. The social field is now the whole school rather than the classroom. Adolescents interact with teachers and peers from a broader range of cultural backgrounds on a broader range of interests. Many teachers are male. Adolescents' social behaviour becomes weighted more strongly toward peers, extracurricular activities, clubs, and the community. Secondary-school students are more aware of the school as a social system and might be motivated to conform to it or to challenge it.

Developmentally Appropriate Education It is time for a numbers game in an early-childhood class at the Greenbrook School. With little prodding from the teacher, 23 five- and six-year-olds fetch geometric puzzles, playing cards, and counting equipment from the shelves that line the room. At one round table, some young children fit together brightly coloured shapes. One girl forms a hexagon out of triangles. Other children gather around her to count how many parts are needed to make the whole. After about 30 minutes, the children prepare for storytime. They put away the counting equipment and sit in a circle around one young girl. She holds up a giant book about a character named Mrs. Wishywashy, who insists on giving the farm animals a bath. The children recite the whimsical lines, clearly enjoying one of their favourite stories. The hallway outside the kindergarten is lined with drawings that depict the children's own interpretations of the book. After the first reading, volunteers act out various parts of the book. There is not one bored face in the room.

This is not reading, writing, and arithmetic the way most adults remember it. A growing number of educators believe that young children learn best through active, hands-on teaching methods that involve such activities as games and dramatic play. They know that children develop at varying rates and that schools need to allow for these individual differences. They also believe that schools should focus on improving children's socioemotional development as well as their cognitive development. **Developmentally appropriate education** *is based on knowledge of the typical development of children within an age span (age appropriateness) as well as the uniqueness of the child (individual appropriateness).* Developmentally appropriate education contrasts with developmentally inappropriate practice, which ignores concrete, hands-on teaching methods. Direct teaching largely through abstract, paper-and-pencil activities presented to large groups of young children is believed to be developmentally inappropriate. Although we are discussing developmentally appropriate education in this chapter on socioemotional development, the concept applies to children's physical and cognitive development as well.

Developmentally Appropriate Education for Early Childhood and Primary School The U.S.–based National Association for the Education of Young Children (NAEYC) has been instrumental in increasing the number of schools that adopt devel-

Teaching Strategies
For Improving Students' Social Skills

✔ Begin formal or informal intervention as soon as possible
  • recognize that improving students' social skills is easiest when children are ten years of age or younger
  • recognize that in adolescence, peer reputation is more fixed and peer groups have greater importance
✔ Help rejected students communicate with peers in an effective fashion
  • provide students with empathy and active-listening training
  • coach students to refrain from dominating peer relations
✔ Help neglected children attract and sustain positive attention from peers
  • provide training with respect to question asking, listening in a warm and friendly manner, and relating to peers' interests
  • facilitate entry into peer groups (e.g., teacher-assigned groups, randomly determined groups, recess buddies)
✔ Provide formal social-skills training
  • help students develop skills for initiating positive interactions with peers (e.g., asking about favourite activities, inviting others to participate)
  • emphasize the importance of being nice, kind, complimentary, and considerate
  • help students demonstrate caring behaviours
✔ Read and discuss literature about positive peer relations
  • develop thematic units about friendship and positive relationships
  • have relevant literature available in the classroom
  • create or develop supportive games and activities

opmentally appropriate practices (Bredekamp & Copple, 1997; NAEYC, 1996), and has prepared a series of principles for developmentally appropriate education for early childhood and primary school (see Figure 3.5).

Early Childhood Education for Disadvantaged Children   In response to the McCain–Mustard Report (1999) commissioned by the provincial government, Early Years Centres have been established across Ontario. The report highlighted evidence from brain research suggesting that much of the "wiring" in the human brain takes place in the early years. Hence, children's earliest experiences, especially during the first six years of life, are far more important for positive brain development than previously realized. The study suggested that some outcomes for children can now be linked to early brain development. The study emphasized that quality nurturing and learning experiences in early childhood correlate with later academic and social success (McCain & Mustard, 1999).

The **Early Years** *program represents a partnership among government, communities, and parents to positively affect young children's lives and prepare them for school.* Young children and their families are provided access to "early child development and parenting centres" in their neighbourhoods or communities; the program links the services provided by the formal education system (e.g., kindergarten) to other existing infrastructures at the community level (e.g., child care, family resource centres, libraries, and community recreation).

Developmentally Appropriate Education in Elementary School   As children enter elementary school, they interact with and develop relationships with new and significant others. School provides students with a rich source of ideas about how to shape their sense of self. Consider the following two elementary-school classrooms and what

www.mcgrawhill.ca/college/santrock

Goals	Guidelines
Curriculum	• Expect individual differences • Plan experiences for all developmental areas including physical, cognitive, social, and emotional
Teaching strategies	• Provide opportunities for active exploration and interaction with adults, peers, and materials • Provide a range of choices and activities • Expect children to be physically and mentally active
Socioemotional development	• Plan and provide opportunities that promote self-esteem and positive feelings toward learning
Language, literacy, and cognitive development	• Provide opportunities for students to see the value of reading and writing before they begin learning word and sound recognition • Actively involve students in telling stories, listen to stories, participating in dramatic play • Integrate reading and writing across all subject areas in meaningful ways
Physical development	• Provide daily activities for large-muscle use (e.g., sports, games) and fine-muscle use (e.g., puzzles, cutting shapes)
Aesthetic and motivational development	• Provide daily opportunities to interact with and appreciate music, art, drama, and dance

FIGURE 3.5 **Developmentally Appropriate Education for Early Childhood and Primary School**

Source: Adapted from NAEYC, 1996

effect they might have on children's learning and self-esteem (Katz & Chard, 1989). In one, students spend the entire morning making identical pictures of traffic lights as they sit glued to their chairs. The teacher seems uninterested in their work, except when she occasionally comes around and informs them of their mistakes. The teacher makes no attempt to get the students to relate the pictures to anything else the class is doing.

In the other class, students are investigating a school bus. They write to the principal and ask if they can have a bus parked at their school for a few days. They study the bus, discover how it functions, and discuss traffic rules. Then, in the classroom, they build their own bus out of cardboard. The students are having fun, but they also are practising writing, reading, and even some arithmetic. When the class has parents' night, the teacher is ready to report on how each child is doing. But the main thing the parents want to do is to see the bus, because their children have been coming home and talking about the bus for weeks. Which class would you say reflects developmentally appropriate education?

Developmentally Appropriate Education in Intermediate and Secondary School

This transition can be stressful because it coincides with many other developmental changes (Eccles, 2000; Seidman, 2000). Students are beginning puberty and have increased concerns about their body image. The hormonal changes of puberty stimulate increased interest in sexual matters. Students are becoming more independent from their parents and want to spend more time with peers. They are changing from learning in a small, more personalized classroom to learning in a larger, more impersonal school. Achievement becomes serious business and getting good grades becomes more competitive.

As students move from elementary to intermediate or secondary school, they experience the **top-dog phenomenon**. *This refers to moving from the top position (in elementary school,* *where they are the oldest, biggest, and most powerful students in the school) to the lowest position (in intermediate or secondary school, where they are the youngest, smallest, and least powerful students in the school).* One recent study found that when parents were attuned to their young adolescents' developmental needs and supported their autonomy in decision making, the students were better adjusted during the school transition (Eccles, Lord, & Buchanan, 1996).

Schools also play an important role here. In 1999, the British Columbia Child and Youth Advocacy Coalition published *Transitions: From Childhood to Youth and Adulthood*. According to the document, the transition from intermediate to secondary school can have a marked effect on the grades, attendance, and peer relations of Grade 9 students. To facilitate a successful transition and integration into secondary school, school staff should be available, accessible, and sensitive to the needs of these students. Student guidance should be proactive and focus on career goals. In addition, students should be encouraged to participate in peer and social activities.

Three main themes characterize truly outstanding schools:

1. They are willing and able to adapt virtually all school practices to the individual variations in their students' physical, cognitive, and socioemotional development. One effective intermediate school developed an advisory scheme so that each student had daily contact with an adult who was willing to listen, explain, comfort, and prod the student.
2. They take seriously what is known about the development of young adolescents. Too many intermediate schools are simply downward extensions of high schools. But younger and older adolescents differ in many ways. For example, the intense changes of puberty that envelop young adolescents are largely completed by the time high school is reached. One effective intermediate school fought to keep its schedule of minicourses on Friday so that every student could be with friends and pursue personal interests. Two other effective intermediate schools made sure that small groups of students worked with small groups of teachers who could vary the tone and pace of the school day, depending on the students' needs.
3. They give as much emphasis to students' socioemotional development as to their cognitive development. Young adolescents are often emotionally fragile as they widen their social worlds and have more responsibility on their shoulders. In our achievement-oriented society, it is easy to lose sight of just how important students' socioemotional needs are. These effective intermediate schools did not (Lipsitz, 1984).

At this point we have studied many ideas about the roles of social contexts (families, peers, and schools) in children's development. A review of these ideas is presented in Summary Table 3.2.

SOCIOEMOTIONAL DEVELOPMENT

So far we have discussed some of the most important *social contexts* that influence students' socioemotional development: families, peers, and schools. In this section, we will focus more on the *individual students* themselves, as we explore their selves, moral development, emotional development, and adolescent challenges.

The Self

According to twentieth-century Italian playwright Ugo Betti, when children say "I," they mean something unique, not to be confused with any other. Psychologists often refer to that "I" as the "self." Two important aspects of the self are self-esteem and identity.

Self-Esteem   **Self-esteem** *is the global evaluative dimension of the self. Self-esteem also is referred to as self-worth or self-image and reflects an individual's overall confidence and satisfaction with themselves.* For example, a child might perceive that she is not just a person but a *good* person.

www.mcgrawhill.ca/college/santrock

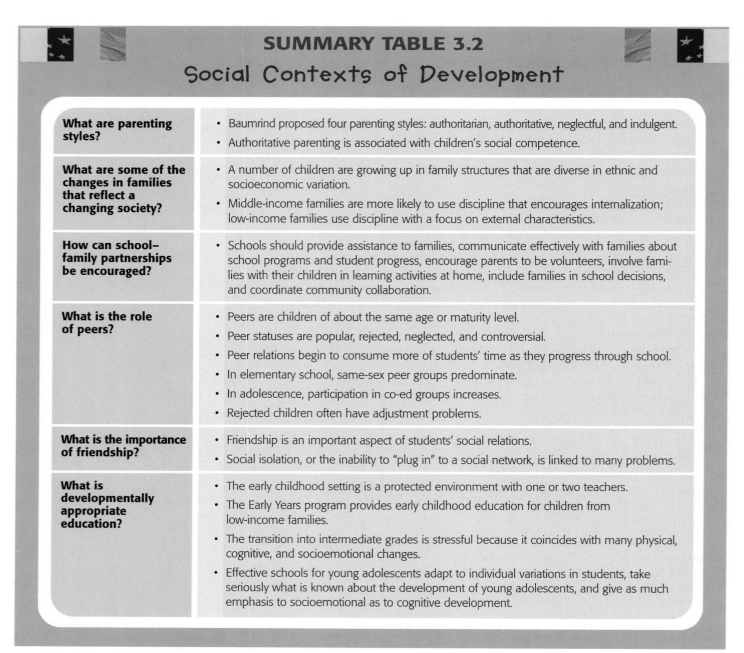

SUMMARY TABLE 3.2
Social Contexts of Development

What are parenting styles?	• Baumrind proposed four parenting styles: authoritarian, authoritative, neglectful, and indulgent. • Authoritative parenting is associated with children's social competence.
What are some of the changes in families that reflect a changing society?	• A number of children are growing up in family structures that are diverse in ethnic and socioeconomic variation. • Middle-income families are more likely to use discipline that encourages internalization; low-income families use discipline with a focus on external characteristics.
How can school–family partnerships be encouraged?	• Schools should provide assistance to families, communicate effectively with families about school programs and student progress, encourage parents to be volunteers, involve families with their children in learning activities at home, include families in school decisions, and coordinate community collaboration.
What is the role of peers?	• Peers are children of about the same age or maturity level. • Peer statuses are popular, rejected, neglected, and controversial. • Peer relations begin to consume more of students' time as they progress through school. • In elementary school, same-sex peer groups predominate. • In adolescence, participation in co-ed groups increases. • Rejected children often have adjustment problems.
What is the importance of friendship?	• Friendship is an important aspect of students' social relations. • Social isolation, or the inability to "plug in" to a social network, is linked to many problems.
What is developmentally appropriate education?	• The early childhood setting is a protected environment with one or two teachers. • The Early Years program provides early childhood education for children from low-income families. • The transition into intermediate grades is stressful because it coincides with many physical, cognitive, and socioemotional changes. • Effective schools for young adolescents adapt to individual variations in students, take seriously what is known about the development of young adolescents, and give as much emphasis to socioemotional as to cognitive development.

"Who are you?" said the caterpillar. "I—I hardly know, Sir, just at present—at least I know who I was when I got up this morning, but I think I've changed several times since then."

Lewis Carroll
English Writer, 19th Century

For many students, low self-esteem is temporary. But in some students, low self-esteem can translate into other, more serious problems. Persistent low self-esteem is linked with low achievement, depression, eating disorders, and delinquency (Harter & Marold, 1992). The seriousness of the problem depends not only on the nature of the student's low self-esteem but also on other conditions. When low self-esteem is compounded by difficult school transitions (such as the transition to intermediate school) or family problems (such as divorce), the student's problems can intensify.

Identity Development   Another important aspect of the self is identity. Earlier in the chapter we indicated that Erik Erikson (1968) believed that the most important issue in adolescence involves identity development—searching for answers to questions like these: Who am I? What am I all about? What am I going to do with my life? How can I make it my own? Not usually considered during childhood, these questions surface as common, virtually universal, concerns during the high-school and post-secondary years.

Teaching Strategies
For Students Who Have Low Self-Esteem

✔ Attempt to determine the causes of low self-esteem
- attempt to determine factors that contribute to low self-esteem (e.g., school performance, family conflict, poor social skills)
- attempt to determine areas of competency that students value (e.g., social approval, academic achievement, physical appearance)

✔ Provide social support and emotional approval
- avoid providing negative feedback and commentary (e.g., "You don't do that right," "How could you not know?" "You should have done better.")
- use community resources that can provide children with additional emotional support and social approval (e.g., Big Brothers, Big Sisters)
- use strategies associated with improving students' social skills

✔ Help students achieve
- provide students with direct instruction in academic skills
- establish individualized goals for students
- help students develop and carry out individualized action plans to achieve these goals

✔ Develop students' coping skills
- help students confront problems directly rather than avoiding them
- help students analyze problems realistically, honestly, and nondefensively

Canadian researcher James Marcia (1980, 1998) analyzed Erikson's concept of identity and concluded that it contains four statuses of identity: identity diffusion, identity foreclosure, identity moratorium, and identity achievement. The extent of an adolescent's exploration and commitment determines the adolescent's identity status. *Exploration* involves examining meaningful alternative identities. *Commitment* means showing a personal investment in an identity and staying with whatever that identity implies.

In **identity diffusion**, *adolescents have not yet explored meaningful alternatives or made commitments.* Not only are they undecided about occupational and ideological paths, they also don't show much interest in such matters. Many young adolescents are identity diffused. In **identity foreclosure**, *adolescents have made a commitment but have not adequately explored alternative avenues.* This most often occurs when parents hand down commitments in an authoritarian manner. In **identity moratorium**, *adolescents are in the midst of exploring alternative courses of action but their commitments either are absent or only vaguely defined.* In **identity achievement**, *adolescents have adequately explored alternative paths and made a commitment.* Marcia's four statuses of identity are shown in Figure 3.6.

Identity status				
Position on occupation and ideology	**Identity moratorium**	**Identity foreclosure**	**Identity diffusion**	**Identity achievement**
Crisis	Present	Absent	Absent	Present
Commitment	Absent	Present	Absent	Present

FIGURE 3.6 **Marcia's Four Statuses of Identity**

www.mcgrawhill.ca/college/santrock

Through the Eyes of Teachers

Learning About One Another

I try to establish a positive tone in my classroom even before the school year starts by creating an "All About Me" bulletin board. During the first day of class, students spend time reviewing the information on the bulletin board and learning about me as their teacher. I fill the board with photos and examples of activities that I have taken part in that reflect the excitement and joy that I receive from teaching.

I keep my bulletin board up for the first week of school. After that, students take turns using the bulletin board to create personal displays about themselves. Students have one week to use the board and are encouraged to post information about their preferences, favourite activities (e.g., books, colours, music, sports, hobbies), and families. At the end of the week, students make a presentation about themselves based on information on the board, with the remaining students being able to ask questions and offer positive comments.

After the presentation students write a story about what they learned about the presenter, including why that person is special. I collect the stories, read them aloud, and place them into a binder titled "All About Us." When the binder is finished, students take turns bringing it home and reviewing it with their families. These activities are wonderful tools for helping students learn about each other and for helping me learn about them.

Karen Forgrave
Elementary-School Teacher
Ontario

"While we're at supper, Billy, you'd make Daddy and Mommy very happy if you'd remove your hat, your sunglasses, and your earring."

Drawing by Ziegler: © 1985 The New Yorker Magazine, Inc.

www.mcgrawhill.ca/college/santrock

Many high-school students will be exploring different areas of their identity, although some will be identity diffused and others will be foreclosed because of the authoritarian ways of their parents. Adolescents can be exploring alternative identities in numerous areas, such as vocational, religious, intellectual, political, sexual, gender, ethnic, and interests (such as sports, art, music, reading, and so on). An adolescent can be farther along the path to identity in some of these areas than in others.

Moral Development

Student's moral development is a consideration for both parents and teachers. **Moral development** *concerns rules and conventions about just interactions between people.* These rules can be studied in three domains: cognitive, behavioural, and emotional.

In the cognitive domain, the key issue is how students reason or think about rules for ethical conduct. In the behavioural domain, the focus is on how students actually behave rather than on the morality of their thinking. And in the emotional domain, the emphasis is on how students morally feel. For instance, do they associate strong enough guilt feelings with an immoral action to resist performing that action? Do they show empathy toward others? (Damon, 2000).

Kohlberg's Theory Lawrence Kohlberg (1976, 1986) stressed that moral development primarily involves moral reasoning and unfolds in stages. Kohlberg arrived at his theory after interviewing children, adolescents, and adults (primarily males) about their views on a series of moral dilemmas, such as whether stealing is ever justified.

Students read stories outlining a dilemma (or, in the case of young children, had the story read to them), then answered a series of questions, such as: Was it right to steal? Is it a person's duty to steal if his family is in need? Would a good person steal? Do pharmacies have the right to charge as much as they want for drugs? Why or why not?

Kohlberg's Levels and Stages of Moral Development Based on the reasons individuals gave in response to the above dilemma and ten others like it, Kohlberg constructed a theory of moral development that has three main levels, with two stages at each of the levels. A key concept in Kohlberg's theory is **internalization**. *This refers to the developmental change from behaviour that is externally controlled to behaviour that is internally controlled.*

Preconventional reasoning *is the lowest level of moral development in Kohlberg's theory, with no internalization of moral values. Moral reasoning is controlled by external rewards and punishment.* **Conventional reasoning** *is the second level in Kohlberg's theory. At this level, internalization is intermediate, but essentially the standards are imposed by other people, such as parents, or by society.* **Postconventional reasoning** *is the highest level in Kohlberg's theory. At this level, morality is completely internalized and not based on external standards.*

The student recognizes alternative moral courses, explores options, and then decides on the moral code that is best.

In studies of Kohlberg's theory, longitudinal data show a relation of the stages to age, although the two highest stages, especially stage 6, rarely appear (Colby et al., 1983). Before age nine, most children reason about moral dilemmas at a preconventional level. By early adolescence, they are more likely to reason at the conventional level.

Kohlberg believed that underlying changes in cognitive development promote more advanced moral thinking. He also said that children construct their moral thoughts as they pass through the stages—that they do not just passively accept a cultural norm for morality. Kohlberg argued that a child's moral thinking can be advanced through discussions with others who reason at the next higher stage.

Lawrence Kohlberg, the architect of a provocative cognitive developmental theory of moral development.

Kohlberg's Critics   Kohlberg's provocative theory has not gone unchallenged (Turiel, 1997). One powerful criticism is that Kohlberg's theory places too much emphasis on moral thinking and not enough on moral behaviour. Moral reasons sometimes can be a shelter for immoral behaviour. Bank embezzlers and prime ministers alike may endorse the loftiest of moral virtues, but their own behaviour can prove to be immoral. No one wants a nation of stage-6 Kohlberg thinkers who know what is right yet do what is wrong.

Another criticism is that Kohlberg's theory is too individualistic. Carol Gilligan (1982, 1998) distinguishes between the justice perspective and the care perspective. Kohlberg's is a **justice perspective** *that focuses on the rights of the individual, who stands alone and makes moral decisions.* The **care perspective** *views people in terms of their connectedness. Emphasis is placed on relationships and concern for others.* According to Gilligan, Kohlberg greatly underplayed the care perspective.

In extensive interviews with girls from 6 to 18 years of age, Gilligan found that they consistently interpreted moral dilemmas in terms of human relationships, not in terms of individual rights. Gilligan (1990, 1996) has argued that girls reach a critical juncture in their development in early adolescence. At about 11 or 12 years of age, they become aware of how much they prize relationships, yet they also come to realize that this interest is not shared by society. The solution, says Gilligan, is to give relationships and concern for others a higher priority in our society. Gilligan does not recommend totally throwing out Kohlberg's theory. She believes the highest level of moral development occurs when individuals combine the care and justice perspectives in positive ways.

Evolutionary Theory   Dennis Krebs and his colleagues have proposed a novel way of examining moral behaviour that is grounded in evolutionary theory (Crawford & Krebs, 1998). Evolutionary theory is a way of thinking about the relationships between human beings and their environments that is based on Darwin's ideas. There are three main models of morality in psychology: psychoanalytic, social learning, and cognitive–developmental. Krebs argues that each of these models neglects important aspects of morality while emphasizing others. His evolutionary-theory approach attempts to integrate psychological approaches to morality and refocus the study of morality to include application in the classroom. He presents questions such as *How does respect for teacher authority develop and how is it maintained?* According to evolutionary theory, respect for authority develops from a series of social commitments and contracts that are fulfilled. Therefore, teachers who do not follow through on their promises are undermining their authority because students are learning that they are not to be trusted.

Moral Education   Moral education is hotly debated in educational circles. We will study one of the earliest analyses of moral education, then turn to some contemporary views.

Through the Eyes of Teachers

Tell Students They Can

Always try to find something in a student's behaviour or response that is correct. Many times students believe that everything they do is wrong! It's easy to say something like "that's almost right" and then ask leading questions to help them arrive at the correct response. It is essential to students' self-esteem that they believe they can make good choices. Students do their best when they are allowed to try without undue criticism or condemnation. I never had a student who did not want to be successful.

Richard Siler
Science Education Consultant, Retired Teacher
Ministry of Education, Sultanate of Oman
Alberta

Carol Gilligan believes that girls experience life differently than boys do; in Gilligan's words, girls have a "different voice." She believes that relationships are central to every aspect of a female's life.

The Hidden Curriculum More than 60 years ago, educator John Dewey (1933) recognized that even when schools do not have specific programs in moral education, they provide moral education through a "hidden curriculum." The **hidden curriculum** *is conveyed by the moral atmosphere that is a part of every school.* The moral atmosphere is created by school and classroom rules, the moral orientation of teachers and school administrators, and text materials. Teachers serve as models of ethical or unethical behaviour. Classroom rules and peer relations at school transmit attitudes about cheating, lying, stealing, and consideration for others. And through its rules and regulations, the school administration infuses the school with a value system (Novak, 2002).

Values and Prosocial Education **Prosocial behaviour** *focuses on the positive side of moral development (in contrast to antisocial behaviour, for example cheating, lying, and stealing). Prosocial behaviour includes being altruistic, fair, sharing, and generally empathetic* (Eisenberg & Fabes, 1998). **Character education** *is a direct approach to moral education that involves teaching students basic moral literacy to prevent them from engaging in immoral behaviour and doing harm to themselves or others.* The argument is that behaviours such as lying, stealing, and cheating are wrong and that students should be taught this throughout their education. Every school should have an explicit moral code that is clearly communicated to students. Any violations of the code should be met with sanctions (Bennett, 1993). Instruction in moral concepts with respect to specific behaviours, like cheating, can take the form of example and definition, class discussions and role-playing, or rewarding students for proper behaviour.

Cognitive Moral Education **Cognitive moral education** *is an approach based on the belief that students should learn to value things like democracy and justice as their moral reasoning develops. Kohlberg's theory has been the basis for a number of cognitive moral education programs.* Teachers act as facilitators rather than as directors. The hope is that students will develop more advanced notions of such concepts as cooperation, trust, responsibility, and community. Toward the end of his career, Kohlberg (1986) recognized that the moral atmosphere of the school is more important than he initially envisioned. For example, in one study a semester-long moral education class based on Kohlberg's theory was successful in advancing moral thinking in three democratic schools but not in three authoritarian schools (Higgins, Power, & Kohlberg, 1983).

Service Learning **Service learning** *is a form of education that promotes social responsibility and service to the community.* In service learning, students might engage in tutoring, help the elderly, work in a hospital, assist at a daycare centre, or clean up a vacant lot to make a play area. An important goal of service learning is for students to become less self-centred and more motivated to help others (Waterman, 1997). In Ontario, one example of service learning is the requirement for secondary-school students to complete 40 hours of community service before graduation.

Tutoring is one example of how adolescents can participate in service learning.

Teaching Strategies
For Improving Students' Prosocial Behaviour

✔ Value and emphasize the importance of being considerate to others
  - model prosocial behaviours
  - encourage students to engage in helping behaviours
  - encourage students to consider the perspectives and feelings of others
  - encourage students to demonstrate empathy and concern for others
  - have students participate in class and school projects that foster altruism (e.g., cleaning up schoolyard, collecting food, visiting older adults in nursing homes)

✔ Label and identify prosocial behaviours
  - explicitly identify prosocial behaviours (e.g., "You are being helpful. You gave him a pencil. That was helpful because he had forgotten his pencil case at home.")
  - avoid making ambiguous statements (e.g., "That was nice," "That's good.")
  - present students with literature and media demonstrating children behaving in prosocial manners
  - explicitly deconstruct antisocial behaviours (e.g., "That's not being nice. How would you feel if he scribbled on your papers like that?")

✔ Attribute positive behaviours to each student
  - attribute positive intentions to positive behaviours (e.g., "You shared because you like to help others")
  - avoid or minimize the use of external rewards when reinforcing prosocial behaviours
  - invite individuals who have contributed altruistically to their communities to the classroom

✔ Use positive discipline strategies
  - adopt proactive strategies for classroom management
  - avoid using punishment
  - discuss the consequences of negative, harmful behaviours, especially for victims

Service learning takes education out into the community (Levesque & Prosser, 1996). One Grade 11 student worked as a reading tutor for students from low-income homes with reading skills well below their grade levels. She commented that until she did the tutoring she didn't realize how many students had not experienced the same opportunities that she had when she was growing up. An especially rewarding moment was when one young girl told her, "I want to learn to read like you do so I can go to college when I grow up." Thus, service learning can benefit not only students but also the recipients of their help.

Researchers have found that service learning benefits students in a number of ways:

- Their grades improve, they become more motivated, and they set more goals (Johnson et al., 1998; Serow, Ciechalski, & Daye, 1990).
- Their self-esteem improves (Hamburg, 1997).
- They become less alienated (Calabrese & Schumer, 1986).
- They increasingly reflect on society's political organization and moral order (Yates, 1995).

Lions-Quest Canada has developed a comprehensive Service Learning Program aimed at linking the home, the school, and the community. Depending on grade level, the program focuses on a variety of life skills such as self-discipline, self-responsibility, and the ability to cooperate and resolve conflicts peacefully. The program provides many opportunities for students to practise good citizenship through cooperative learning, service to

The real test of character is in surprise. It is unforeseen crisis, the sudden calamity, the unexpected shock, when the man is off guard, which shows truly what he is.

Archibald MacMechan
Canadian Author, 20th Century

others, and a healthy, drug-free approach to life. Community-service projects offer students the opportunity to develop personal and social responsibilities by looking beyond themselves and reaching out to others.

At this point, we have discussed a number of ideas about the self and moral development. A review of these ideas is presented in Summary Table 3.3. Next, we will explore the nature of students' emotional development and adolescent problems.

Emotional Development

Students experience emotions—the joy of accomplishing something for the first time, sadness upon learning about a friend's illness, anger during an argument with a peer. Students like or dislike teachers, feel happy when they have been accepted by their classmates, and feel guilty when they don't study hard enough (Graham, 1996).

SUMMARY TABLE 3.3
The Self and Moral Development

What is self-esteem?	• Self-esteem is the global, evaluative dimension of the self. Other terms for self-esteem are self-worth and self-image. • To increase students' self-esteem, identify the causes of low self-esteem and the domains of competence important to the student, provide emotional support and social approval, help students achieve, and develop students' coping skills.
What are the four identity statuses?	• Adolescents have one of four identity statuses: identity diffused, identity foreclosed, identity moratorium, and identity achieved.
What are the domains of moral development?	• Moral development concerns rules and conventions about just interactions between people. • These rules fall into three domains: cognitive, behavioural, and emotional.
What is Kohlberg's theory of moral development?	• Kohlberg identified three levels of moral development: preconventional, conventional, and postconventional. • As the stages unfold, moral thinking becomes more internalized. • Moral development is advanced by cognitive changes, role-taking opportunities, and discussions with others who are at a higher stage of reasoning.
What are the criticisms of Kohlberg's theory?	• Kohlberg did not give enough attention to moral behaviour. • Kohlberg's theory emphasizes the individual and not relationships with others. Gilligan notes that this is a male-oriented-justice perspective.
What is included in values education?	• Each school has a moral atmosphere. • Values and prosocial education is a direct-education approach that advocates teaching students basic moral literacy. • Values clarification emphasizes helping students clarify what their lives are for and what is worth working for. • Cognitive moral education encourages students to develop such values as democracy and justice as their moral reasoning develops. • Service learning involves educational experiences that promote social responsibility and service to the community.

Exploring Emotion   Emotions (also called *feelings* or *affect*) can be classified as either positive or negative. **Positive affectivity (PA)** *refers to the range of positive emotions, whether high energy (enthusiasm and excitement) or low energy (calm and peacefulness). Joy and happiness are examples of positive affectivity.* **Negative affectivity (NA)** *refers to negative emotions such as anxiety, anger, guilt, and sadness.* It is possible to be high on both PA and NA dimensions at the same time. For example, a student might be in a high-energy state and enthusiastic yet also be angry.

Emotional Intelligence   In his book *Emotional Intelligence*, Daniel Goleman (1995) argues that when it comes to predicting a student's competence, IQ as measured by standardized intelligence tests can matter less than emotional intelligence. What is emotional intelligence? **Emotional intelligence** *consists of emotional self-awareness* (such as separating feelings from actions), *managing emotions* (such as controlling anger), *reading emotions* (such as taking the perspective of others), and *handling relationships* (such as solving relationship problems). Goleman believes that self-awareness is especially important in emotional intelligence because it enables students to exercise some self-control. The idea is to encourage students not to repress their feelings but instead to become aware of them so they can cope more effectively.

Childhood innocence

Working with students to help them use anxiety wisely is another aspect of improving their emotional intelligence. Anxiety can serve a useful function as long as it does not spin out of control. Worrying is a rehearsal for danger and can motivate students to search for a solution to a problem. For example, although it is usually a good idea for students to think positively when a test looms on the horizon, if they have not yet adequately prepared for the test a little dose of worry can energize them to do so. Anxiety becomes a problem when worrying becomes an end in itself and blocks thinking.

Perhaps the most visible aspects of emotional intelligence are the "people skills" of empathy, graciousness, and being able to read a social situation. These skills help students get along with others and improve their social interactions.

It is important for teachers to evaluate both the student's emotional and intellectual skills when considering the student's competence. By responding to the items in Self-Assessment 3.1, you can get a sense of how emotionally intelligent you are.

Teachers can help promote emotional intelligence by focusing on feelings, both the student's own and those involved in relationships. Teachers can speak to emotional issues such as hurt feelings over being left out, envy, and disagreements that could erupt into a physical conflict. Some topics for discussion with students include:

- Building self-awareness. Teachers can help students recognize feelings and build a vocabulary for them, and help students see links among thoughts, feelings, and reactions.
- Detecting whether thoughts or feelings are ruling a decision.
- Seeing the consequences of alternative choices.
- Applying insights about feelings to decisions about drinking, smoking, and sex.
- Recognizing strengths and weaknesses: seeing oneself in a positive but realistic light.
- Managing emotions. Teachers help students recognize what is behind a feeling, such as the hurt that triggers anger or depression. Students also learn how to cope with anxiety and sadness.
- Taking responsibility for decisions and actions, as well as following through on commitments.
- Understanding that empathy, understanding others' feelings, and respecting differences in how people feel about things are key dimensions of getting along in the social world.
- Recognizing the importance of relationships and learning how to be a good listener and asker of questions; being assertive rather than passive or aggressive; and learning how to cooperate, resolve conflicts, and negotiate.

The aim of these discussions is to improve students' emotional competence as part of regular education. This contrasts with teaching emotional skills only in remedial classes for students who are faltering or who have been identified as "troubled."

How Emotionally Intelligent Am I?

For each item, respond 1 = Very unlike me, 2 = Mostly unlike me, 3 = Somewhat like me, 4 = Mostly like me, or 5 = Very like me

	1	2	3	4	5

Emotional Self-Awareness

1. I am good at recognizing my emotions.

2. I am good at understanding the causes of my feelings.

3. I am good at separating my feelings from my actions.

Managing Emotions

4. I am good at tolerating frustration.

5. I am good at managing my anger.

6. I have positive feelings about myself.

7. I am good at coping with stress.

8. My emotions don't interfere with my ability to focus and accomplish my goals.

9. I have good self-control and am not impulsive.

Reading Emotions

10. I am good at taking the perspectives of others (such as students and parents).

11. I show empathy and sensitivity to others' feelings.

12. I am good at listening to what other people say.

Handling Relationships

13. I am good at analyzing and understanding relationships.

14. I am good at solving problems in relationships.

15. I am assertive (rather than passive, manipulative, or aggressive) in relationships.

16. I have one or more close friendships.

17. I am good at sharing and cooperating.

Scoring and Interpretation

75–85	High emotional intelligence
65–74	Good emotional intelligence
45–64	Average emotional intelligence
Below 44 points	Below-average emotional intelligence

Source: Goleman (1995).

Adolescent Challenges

Too many of today's adolescents are not getting an adequate opportunity to make the transition from childhood to adulthood in a competent way. As many as 25 percent of adolescents have more than one developmental problem. The problems that harm the most adolescents have been called the "big four": (1) substance abuse, (2) extreme forms of peer harassment, bullying, and school violence, (3) adolescent pregnancy and STDs, and (4) truancy and school dropout. Increasingly, at-risk adolescents have more than one of these problems. The highest-risk youth—as many as 10 percent—do it all.

Substance Abuse According to a recent survey by the Addictions Foundation of Manitoba, more than half of the students considered alcohol and drug use to be a major problem at their school. Eighty-one percent of students reported drinking alcohol in the past year; about 6 percent reported having moderate or serious problems with the use of alcohol. Similarly, 6 percent reported having moderate or serious problems with the use of other drugs. These statistics are quite similar to those from other surveys conducted by the Centre for Addiction and Mental Health in Ontario (1999) and by the Youth Lifestyle Choices–Community University Research Alliance (YLC–CURA, 2001). What roles can schools and teachers play in preventing and intervening in drug abuse? They can do the following:

- Take a K–12 approach, with age-appropriate components.
- Include teacher training in their drug-abuse curriculum. Even the best-designed drug-abuse curriculum is ineffective in the hands of an inadequately prepared teacher.
- Include social skills training that focuses on helping children to develop coping skills and resist peer pressure.
- Use peer-led programs, which often are more effective than teacher-led or counsellor-led programs, especially when senior secondary students are the leaders for intermediate students.
- Make the school-based program part of community-wide prevention that involves parents, peers, role models, media, police, businesses, and youth agencies.

Through the Eyes of Teachers

Helping Students Develop Positive Relationships

Students from 12 to 18 years of age face a variety of social, emotional, and self-esteem issues that are affected by their relationships with others, including their families and peers. Teenagers who have strong, positive relationships with family and friends are, for the most part, better prepared to address these challenges than those who have not developed positive relationships. The lack of positive relationships is linked to feelings of sadness, helplessness, and poor self-esteem.

As teachers and counsellors, we need to help students create positive relationships. School staff can help by creating environments where all students feel safe, valued, and included. Teachers are role models for youth. In many ways, how we relate to students and to each other is more important than what we teach. We need to listen to our students and understand their perspectives. By truly listening to students, we can teach and counsel them in meaningful ways.

Peter Henderson
School Counsellor
British Columbia

Extreme Forms of Peer Harassment, Bullying, and School Violence   On April 28, 1999, one week after two students went on a rampage at the Columbine high school in Colorado, a similar attack occurred in Taber, Alberta. A 14-year-old boy opened fire inside a high school, killing one student and wounding another. Over the last decade we have been seeing an increase in the number of incidents involving students participating in these extreme forms of violent behaviour.

A number of other cases have captured people's attention, including the tragic death of Reena Virk, a Victoria, B.C. teenager, at the hands of a gang made up predominantly of girls. Two other cases have also generated media attention because of the tragic loss of life caused by peer taunting and exclusion. One involved Hasam Hacmed, an adolescent who took his own life because of homophobic taunts, and the other involved a 14-year-old girl who committed suicide because of malicious rumours and exclusion by her peers.

The frequency and severity of these cases makes it clear that schools and communities need to address the underlying causes of adolescent violence in a comprehensive manner. Policies of detention or expulsion, the use of security guards, and corporal punishment have not been effective in reducing antisocial behaviour (Dryfoos, 1998). Yet schools can play an important role in preventing and intervening in antisocial behaviour (Farrington, 2000). Schools with strong governance, fair discipline, student participation in decision making, and high investment in school outcomes by both students and staff have a better chance of curbing antisocial behaviour and violence.

Especially important is upgrading the education of youth from impoverished backgrounds. It is virtually impossible to prevent antisocial behaviour without also considering the quality of education available for youth at risk. Administrators need to implement more systematic and comprehensive programs. One prevention model that has been found useful involves the conception of school violence and bullying as a public health issue (Marini et al., 2000).

Is there any way that psychologists can predict whether a youth will turn violent? It's a complex task, but some clues have been pieced together (Cowley, 1998). Violent youth

Teaching Strategies
For Helping Students Cope Effectively

✔ Address students' stress
  • recognize that students' stress can provide excellent learning opportunities
  • help students identify stress as a challenge rather than a threat
  • attempt to alleviate minor sources of stress so that students can better cope with more relevant issues (e.g., providing a buddy for a child who is having difficulties concentrating due to family turmoil)
✔ Help students discard ineffective coping strategies and adopt effective ones
  • monitor and assess students' strategies for coping while under stress
  • help students acquire effective coping strategies (e.g., develop an optimistic outlook, challenge self-defeating thoughts)
✔ Work cooperatively with others
  • help others (e.g., parents, other teachers) recognize student stress
  • cooperatively attempt to determine causes of stress
  • cooperatively develop a plan to address and alleviate student stress
  • work with parents and extended family members who might help students cope with stress
  • use available in-school resources (e.g., guidance teacher, youth counsellor or social worker), community resources and organizations

Students from Columbine High School in Littleton, Colorado, leave the school after two classmates went on a shooting rampage in April 1999.

One week after the Columbine tragedy, a shooting occurred at W.R. Myers High School in Taber, Alberta. One student was killed and another severely injured in what has been described as a "copycat" shooting. What roles do the media play in these tragedies, and what can teachers do to help prevent further incidents like this from happening?

are overwhelmingly male, and many are driven by feelings of powerlessness and anger. Violence seems to infuse these youth with a sense of power. Youth violence is greatest in the poorest areas associated with large urban centres; urban poverty fosters powerlessness, rage, and frustration, and many inner-city neighbourhoods provide almost daily opportunities to observe violence. Many of the children who live in poverty also lack adequate parent involvement and supervision.

Cornell (1998) and Garbarino (1999, 2000) note that many youth give clear indications of their future violence but are not taken seriously or are largely ignored. Parents, teachers, and administrators often are unable or unwilling to acknowledge what might be a very upsetting reality. Some of the warning signs of potential violent behaviour (Garbarino, 1999; 2000) include:

• frequent loss of temper or threatening others
• frequent physical fighting
• significant vandalism or property damage
• heavy drug or alcohol use
• increased risk-taking behaviours
• detailed plans to commit acts of violence
• strong desire to be in a gang
• trouble controlling emotions like anger
• withdrawal from friends and usual activities and a sense of being rejected and alone
• having been a victim of bullying
• poor school performance
• history of discipline problems or frequent run-ins with authorities
• cruelty toward animals
• feeling constantly disrespected
• failing to acknowledge the feelings or rights of others
• access to or fascination with weapons

Adolescent Pregnancy and STDs   A substantial proportion of Canadian adolescents are sexually active (Health Canada, 1999). Godin and Michaud (1998) estimated that between 47 and 69 percent of students in late high school have had at least one sexual experience. The majority of these youth did not use contraceptives consistently or reliably (Health Canada, 1998a). Among sexually active 15- to 19-year-olds, 51 percent of females and 29 percent of males reported having sexual intercourse without a condom in the past year (Galambos & Tilton-Weaver, 1998). While slightly more than half of the women reported using oral contraceptives (Health Canada, 1998a), fewer than one in five reported using the pill and condoms in combination (Insight Canada Research, 1992).

Participating in high-risk sexual activity may result in a number of negative physical and socioemotional outcomes, including unwanted pregnancy and sexually transmitted disease. Up until the mid-1990s there was a steady rise in the number of pregnancies among young women 15 to 19 years of age (Wadhera & Miller, 1997). There was also a similar increase in the number of abortions (Wadhera & Miller, 1997). Young women who elect to keep their children often do so without the support of a partner. Negative consequences associated with adolescent motherhood can include dropping out of school, failing to gain meaningful employment, and depending on welfare. As a result, the children of adolescent mothers are more likely to grow up in homes with below-average family income.

Adolescents who do not adopt safer-sex practices also risk contracting STDs. While the instances of some STDs are falling, rates for chlamydia and gonorrhea among adolescent women remain high (Health Canada, 1998b). The median age for people with AIDS has decreased from 32 years (1984) to 23 years (1985–1990), indicating that many people become infected during adolescence (Health Canada, 1995). Woloshyn and Rye (1995) indicate that many adolescents possess misconceptions about STDs, sexuality, and safer-sex practices. To promote healthy sexuality, students should be given practical strategies through participation in well-developed sexuality-education programs.

The following are general strategies for reducing unwanted pregnancies and STDs among adolescents:

- *Encourage abstinence in adolescents.* Adolescents are not ready to cope with sexuality's intense, varied feelings or to understand sexuality's complex meanings.
- *Improve and expand sexuality education.* The majority of parents today want sexuality education in the classroom. In fact, 83 percent of Canadian adults favour sexuality education programs (Woloshyn & Rye, 1995). In Sweden, beginning at age seven each child experiences a thorough grounding in reproductive biology. By ages 10 to 12, the Swedish child has learned about different forms of contraception. Swedish teachers are expected to discuss sex-related questions with students regardless of the subject they are teaching.
- *Provide adolescents with the knowledge that they desire.* It is natural for adolescents to have a desire to learn about human sexuality. King, Coles, and King (1991; as cited in Woloshyn & Rye, 1995) found that 39 percent of Grade 11 students were concerned about STDs, and 64 percent of the females were concerned about pregnancy.

Truancy and School Dropout   The fourth main area that keeps adolescents from successfully negotiating the path from childhood to adulthood involves school-related problems. Low school achievement and low grades can lead to dropping out of high school. Students who drop out are more likely than high-school graduates to have fewer job prospects and lower salaries; be unemployed; be on welfare; experience more problem behaviours, such as drug abuse, delinquency, and early sexual intercourse; and become divorced and have unstable marriages.

More positively, in the latter part of the twentieth century the high-school dropout rate declined dramatically in Canada. For example, in 1981 the dropout rate was 23 percent for 16- and 17-year-olds living in poverty, and 14 percent for those not living in poverty. By 1993, the rates had dropped to 8 percent and 5 percent, respectively (Ross, Scott, & Kelly, 1996).

Common Components of Successful Programs   Dryfoos (1998) analyzed the programs that have been successful in preventing or reducing adolescent challenges. The two most important components were (1) intensive individualized attention, and (2) community-wide multiagency collaboration.

Many students develop problems because they have not had someone to care for them, someone who is there when they need help and support (Price, 2000). For instance, in a successful substance-abuse program, a student-assistance counsellor might be available for individual counselling and referral for treatment. In a delinquency program, a family worker might provide support and guidance to a young offender and ask the family to make changes to help prevent delinquent acts.

The basic philosophy of community-wide programs is that a number of different agencies and services need to be in place (Perry, 1999; Dryfoos, 1998). One successful substance-abuse program implemented a community-wide health-promotion campaign that used local media and community education in concert with a substance-abuse curriculum in the schools. In another successful program, local residents belong to a neighbourhood council and work with schools, police, courts, gang leaders, and the media to reduce delinquency.

At this point we have discussed many ideas about children's emotional development and adolescent challenges. A review of these ideas is presented in Summary Table 3.4. In the last two chapters we have examined how students develop, focusing mainly on the general pattern. In the next chapter, we give more attention to individual variations in students.

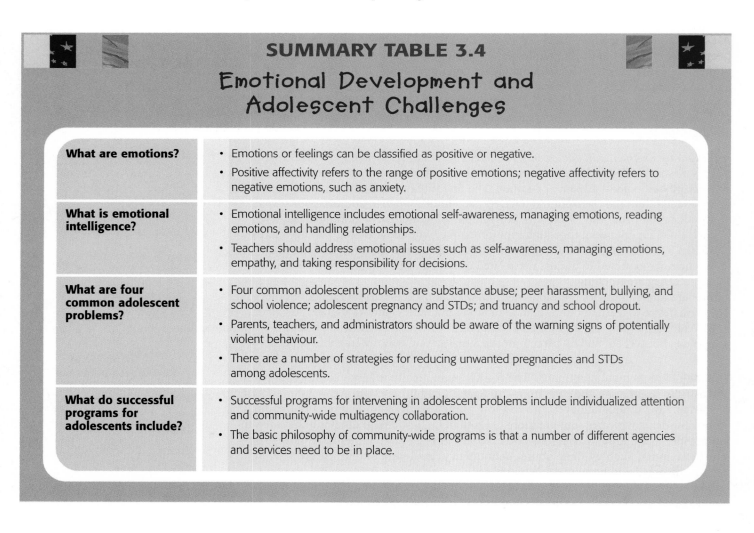

SUMMARY TABLE 3.4
Emotional Development and Adolescent Challenges

What are emotions?	• Emotions or feelings can be classified as positive or negative. • Positive affectivity refers to the range of positive emotions; negative affectivity refers to negative emotions, such as anxiety.
What is emotional intelligence?	• Emotional intelligence includes emotional self-awareness, managing emotions, reading emotions, and handling relationships. • Teachers should address emotional issues such as self-awareness, managing emotions, empathy, and taking responsibility for decisions.
What are four common adolescent problems?	• Four common adolescent problems are substance abuse; peer harassment, bullying, and school violence; adolescent pregnancy and STDs; and truancy and school dropout. • Parents, teachers, and administrators should be aware of the warning signs of potentially violent behaviour. • There are a number of strategies for reducing unwanted pregnancies and STDs among adolescents.
What do successful programs for adolescents include?	• Successful programs for intervening in adolescent problems include individualized attention and community-wide multiagency collaboration. • The basic philosophy of community-wide programs is that a number of different agencies and services need to be in place.

Many schools, including the one in which Miss Mahoney teaches, provide character education in an attempt to reduce problem behaviours. The hope is that by promoting empathy, and by disallowing behaviours such as teasing, name-calling, and threats, the number of violent incidences will decrease. Miss Mahoney has included character education as part of her Grade 5 program. Unfortunately, many of her students, particularly the boys, continue to exhibit the very behaviours she is trying to eliminate.

Ivan and Jacques are on the same soccer team and often get into verbal conflicts with each other, although they appreciate each other's talents on the field. Tuesday night at practice, in violation of the team's rules, Jacques told Ivan that he "sucked." Ivan let the comments pass. He did not want Jacques to suffer a one-game suspension, as they were facing a tough opponent that weekend.

Thursday in class, Jacques accused Ivan of stealing his playing cards. Ivan became angry and denied stealing them. He then found them on the floor and handed them to Jacques. "Here's your dumb cards, Jacques," he said. "See, I didn't steal them."

In anger, Jacques responded, "Fine. Then how come they're all crinkled? You know, I could beat you up—and maybe I just will."

"Yeah, right. You and who else?" asked Ivan with a sneer.

Two other boys working nearby overheard the altercation and began to egg the boys on:

"Yeah, Jacques, Ivan could kick your butt," said Grant.

"I think Jacques would win," said Peter.

"Meet me at the park tomorrow after school and let's just see!" demanded Jacques.

"No problem," retorted Ivan.

Thursday evening they were both at soccer practice. Nothing was said about the fight that was to take place the next day after school.

Friday morning, Jacques's mother called Miss Mahoney to tell her that Jacques was afraid to go to school because Ivan had threatened to "beat him up." Jacques's mother also informed the principal about the situation. However, she didn't know why the threat had been issued and expressed little interest in learning the reason. She wanted her son protected and the other boy punished. That morning Ivan's mother was in the school for another purpose. The principal stopped her to talk about the situation, telling her that Jacques had told his mother he was afraid to come to school because Ivan was going to harm him. Ivan's mother asked for more information and asked that Miss Mahoney and the principal talk to both of the boys and any other children involved.

The story that emerged is the one that you just read. Miss Mahoney and the principal decided that Ivan should serve an in-school suspension the following day and miss recess for the remainder of the week. Jacques received no punishment and walked away from the meeting grinning.

- What are the issues in this case and how might they affect each boy's attitude toward school?
- At what stage of moral development would you expect these boys to be functioning? What predictions can you make regarding each boy's sense of self and emotional development?
- Were Grant and Peter merely bystanders or did they contribute to the situation? What could they have done to help resolve the situation?
- What do you think about the punishment that Ivan received? How would you have handled this situation?

www.mcgrawhill.ca/college/santrock

CHAPTER REVIEW

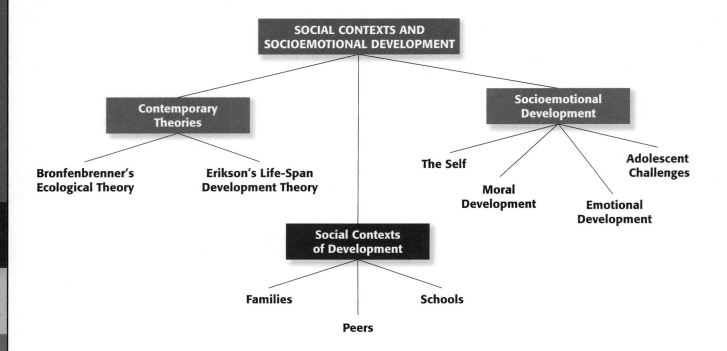

SOCIAL CONTEXTS AND SOCIOEMOTIONAL DEVELOPMENT

Contemporary Theories
- Bronfenbrenner's Ecological Theory
- Erikson's Life-Span Development Theory

Social Contexts of Development
- Families
- Peers
- Schools

Socioemotional Development
- The Self
- Moral Development
- Emotional Development
- Adolescent Challenges

To obtain a detailed review of this chapter, study these four summary tables:

KEY TERMS

ecological theory 68
microsystem 68
mesosystem 68
exosystem 68
macrosystem 69
chronosystem 69
trust versus mistrust 70
autonomy versus shame and
　doubt 70
initiative versus guilt 70
industry versus inferiority 70
identity versus identity
　confusion 70
intimacy versus isolation 70

generativity versus stagnation 70
integrity versus despair 70
authoritarian parenting 71
authoritative parenting 71
neglectful parenting 72
indulgent parenting 72
peers 75
popular children 76
neglected children 76
rejected children 76
controversial children 77
developmentally appropriate
　education 80
Early Years 81

top-dog phenomenon 82
self-esteem 83
identity diffusion 85
identity foreclosure 85
identity moratorium 85
identity achievement 85
moral development 86
internalization 86
preconventional reasoning 86
conventional reasoning 86
postconventional reasoning 86
justice perspective 87
care perspective 87
hidden curriculum 88

prosocial behaviour 88
character education 88
cognitive moral education 88
service learning 88
positive affectivity (PA) 91
negative affectivity (NA) 91
emotional intelligence 91

PROFESSIONAL DEVELOPMENT/PORTFOLIO ACTIVITIES

1. **Teachers and Families**

Communication between the school and family is an important consideration for teachers. How will you maintain an effective school–family communication link? Interview several teachers from local schools about how they foster these links. Talk with a kindergarten teacher, an elementary-level teacher, an intermediate-level teacher, and a high-school teacher. Choose a few of their best practices and merge these strategies into a proposal that you could include in your portfolio.

2. **A Parent–Teacher Dialogue Scenario**

In a parent–teacher conference, a parent tells you that the emotional intelligence activities and exercises you have been practising in your classroom are not academically sound. In this parent's opinion, you should devote more attention to the basics of reading, writing, and arithmetic. How would you respond?

3. **A Plan for Diversity**

Canadian families differ socioeconomically, ethnically, and culturally. Develop a five-year plan outlining how you will prepare yourself to meet the challenges presented by students and parents with such diverse backgrounds. Include some of the strategies you are prepared to implement, and include a copy of your plan in your portfolio.

 INTERNET ACTIVITIES

1. **Helping Students Discover Identity**

How can teachers help their students successfully negotiate the challenges associated with the different stages of psychosocial development? Using the Websites provided on the Online Learning Centre as a resource, describe some teaching strategies that could be used to foster independence, confidence, and risk-taking in students. In what ways do teachers inherently impact students' character development through their daily interactions?

2. **Involving Family in the Classroom**

Research shows that family involvement greatly influences student attitudes, attendance, and academic achievement. Develop an action plan for involving families in your classroom in a variety of ways. What are some of the challenges in involving families, and how do you plan to overcome these?

Connect to the Online Learning Centre at www.mcgrawhill.ca/college/santrock **to explore possible answers.**

Visit the *Educational Psychology* Online Learning Centre at
www.mcgrawhill.ca/college/santrock
to access Websites related to the above Internet Activities as well as chapter quizzes,
a searchable glossary, and other learning and study tools.

Preview

No two students are exactly alike. An important educational task is to provide an education that allows students to competently play out their lives in individual ways. This chapter focuses on students' individual variations. These are some of the questions we will explore:

- What does it mean to be intelligent? Is it more than "book smarts"? Can you teach students to be intelligent?

- What are the best strategies for helping your students become more creative?

- What kind of learning styles are your students likely to have? What kind of learning style do you have? Are some learning styles better than others?

- What kind of temperament and personality traits are you likely to encounter in your students? How might these affect their behaviour in the classroom?

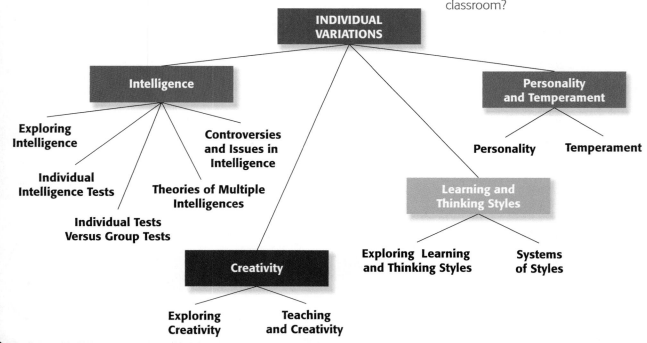

INDIVIDUAL VARIATIONS

Intelligence

- **Exploring Intelligence**
- **Individual Intelligence Tests**
- **Individual Tests Versus Group Tests**
- **Theories of Multiple Intelligences**
- **Controversies and Issues in Intelligence**

Creativity

- **Exploring Creativity**
- **Teaching and Creativity**

Learning and Thinking Styles

- **Exploring Learning and Thinking Styles**
- **Systems of Styles**

Personality and Temperament

- **Personality**
- **Temperament**

Teaching Stories: David Kanatawakhon Maracle

Over the past 12 years, David Kanatawakhon Maracle has worked as an instructor in the aboriginal studies programs at Brock University and the University of Western Ontario. Prior to this, David worked as an elementary-school teacher for the Mohawk of the Bay of Quinte Territory. Below, he reflects on the nature of instruction and assessment in his classroom.

"I've always believed that assessment is as much a reflection of me as it is my students. Culturally, we have been socialized to be independent and pragmatic. It is much more relevant for me to assess students individually while they are working on a project or hands-on activity than it is to assess them as part of a group or on the basis of some abstract, theoretical assignment. Learning needs to apply to students' daily lives and interests or they will not value the process. Accordingly, if the learning process is experiential and pragmatic then the assessment process should also follow the same format. In my experience, parents and teachers listen to children and engage them to discuss *alternative approaches or describe how someone else completed a similar task or project. This approach is more acceptable culturally than telling students 'what to do' or that they are 'doing something wrong.' Comments offered in this manner are not seen as corrective or judgmental but rather as the sharing of experiences.*

"I once had Grade 7 students cut and sew moccasins from moose hide. As they worked with the leather we talked about where the hide came from, how our families created tools and developed processes for tanning and working with such hides, and how these processes are done today. Through observation and dialogue, I was able to assess the students' problem-solving skills, as well as their general learning of history, biology, and the general sciences. In my classes, assessment was a process that allowed me to offer suggestions and gain insights about how students were thinking rather than making formal judgments about their ability."

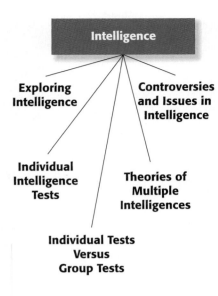

Intelligence

Exploring Intelligence

Controversies and Issues in Intelligence

Individual Intelligence Tests

Theories of Multiple Intelligences

Individual Tests Versus Group Tests

As many people, as many minds; everyone his own way.

Terence
Roman Playwright, 2nd Century B.C.

INTELLIGENCE

The concept of intelligence generates controversy and heated debate, often in reaction to the idea that each person has a general mental capacity that can be measured and quantified in a number. Educational panels and school boards debate whether intelligence tests are useful and fair. They also argue about whether such tests should be used to place students in special classes, streams, or tracks. Educational psychologists debate whether we have a general mental capacity or a number of specific mental capacities. And if we have various mental capacities, what are they? How many do we have?

Exploring Intelligence

Twentieth-century English novelist Aldous Huxley said that children are remarkable for their curiosity and intelligence. What did Huxley mean when he used the word intelligence? Intelligence is one of our most prized possessions, yet even the most intelligent people have not been able to agree on what intelligence is. Unlike height, weight, and age, intelligence cannot be directly measured. You can't peer into a student's head and observe the intelligence going on inside. We can evaluate a student's intelligence only *indirectly,* by studying the student's intelligent acts. For the most part, we have relied on written intelligence tests to provide an estimate of a student's intelligence (Kail & Pelligrino, 1985).

Some experts describe intelligence as including verbal ability and problem-solving skills. Others describe it as the ability to adapt to and learn from life's everyday experiences. Combining these ideas, we can arrive at a fairly traditional definition of **intelligence:** *verbal ability, problem-solving skills, and the ability to adapt to and learn from life's everyday experiences.* But even this broad definition doesn't satisfy everyone. Some theorists propose that musical skills should be considered part of intelligence. And a definition of intelligence based on a theory like Vygotsky's would have to include the ability to use the tools of the culture with help from more-skilled individuals. Because intelligence is such an abstract, broad concept, it is not surprising that there are so many different possible definitions of it.

Interest in intelligence has often focused on individual differences and assessment (Ackerman, Kyllonen, & Roberts, 1999; Lubinski, 2000). **Individual differences** *are the stable, consistent ways in which people are different from one another.* We can talk about individual differences in personality and other domains, but it is intelligence that has been given the most attention and about which the most conclusions have been drawn about the different abilities of students.

Individual Intelligence Tests

The Binet Tests   In 1904 the French Ministry of Education asked psychologist Alfred Binet to devise a method of identifying children who were unable to learn in school. School officials wanted to reduce crowding by placing students who did not benefit from regular classroom teaching in special schools. Binet and his student Theophile Simon developed an intelligence test to meet this request. The test is called the 1905 Scale. It consisted of 30 questions, ranging from the ability to touch one's ear to the abilities to draw designs from memory and define abstract concepts.

Binet developed the concept of **mental age (MA),** *an individual's level of mental development relative to others.* Not much later, in 1912, William Stern created the concept of **intelligence quotient (IQ),** *which refers to a person's mental age divided by chronological age (CA), multiplied by 100.* That is, IQ = MA/CA × 100.

If mental age is the same as chronological age, then the person's IQ is 100. If mental age is above chronological age, then IQ is more than 100. For example, a six-year-old with a mental age of eight would have an IQ of 133. If mental age is below chronological age, then IQ is less than 100. For example, a six-year-old with a mental age of five would have an IQ of 83.

The Binet test has been revised many times to incorporate advances in the understanding of intelligence and intelligence testing. These revisions are called the Stanford-Binet tests (because the revisions were made at Stanford University). By administering the test to large numbers of people of different ages from different backgrounds, researchers have found that scores on a Stanford-Binet test approximate a normal distribution (see Figure 4.1). A **normal distribution** *is symmetrical, with a majority of the scores falling in the middle of the possible range of scores and few scores appearing toward the extremes of the range.*

The current Stanford-Binet is administered individually to people aged two through adult. It includes a variety of items, some of which require verbal responses, others which require nonverbal responses. For example, items that reflect a typical six-year-old's level of performance include the verbal ability to define at least six words (e.g., *orange, envelope*), as well as the nonverbal ability to trace a path through a maze. Items that reflect an average adult's level of performance include defining such words as *disproportionate* and *regard*, explaining a proverb, and comparing idleness and laziness.

The fourth edition of the Stanford-Binet was published in 1985. One important addition to this version was the analysis of the individual's responses in terms of four functions: verbal reasoning, quantitative reasoning, abstract visual reasoning, and short-term memory. A general composite score is still obtained to reflect overall intelligence. The Stanford-Binet continues to be one of the most widely used tests to assess students' intelligence (Aiken, 2000).

The Wechsler Scales   Another set of tests widely used to assess students' intelligence is called the Wechsler scales, developed by David Wechsler. They include the Wechsler Preschool and Primary Scale of Intelligence–Revised (WPPSI-R) to test children 4 to 6½ years of age; the Wechsler Intelligence Scale for Children–Revised (WISC-R) for children and adolescents 6 to 16 years of age; and the Wechsler Adult Intelligence Scale–Revised (WAIS-R).

In addition to an overall IQ, the Wechsler scales also yield verbal and performance IQs. Verbal IQ is based on six verbal subscales, performance IQ on five performance subscales. This allows the examiner to quickly see patterns of strengths and weaknesses in different areas of the student's intelligence. Examples of Wechsler subscales are shown in Figure 4.2.

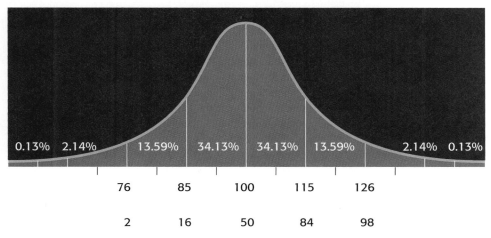

0.13%	2.14%	13.59%	34.13%	34.13%	13.59%	2.14%	0.13%	Percentage of cases under portions

76	85	100	115	126	Approximate IQ score

2	16	50	84	98	Approximate cumulative percentage

FIGURE 4.1   The Normal Curve and the Stanford-Binet IQ Scores
The distribution of IQ scores approximates a normal curve. Most of the population falls in the middle range of scores. Extremely high and extremely low scores are very rare. Slightly more than two-thirds of the scores fall between 85 and 115. Only about 1 in 50 individuals has an IQ of more than 132 and only about 1 in 50 individuals has an IQ of less than 68.

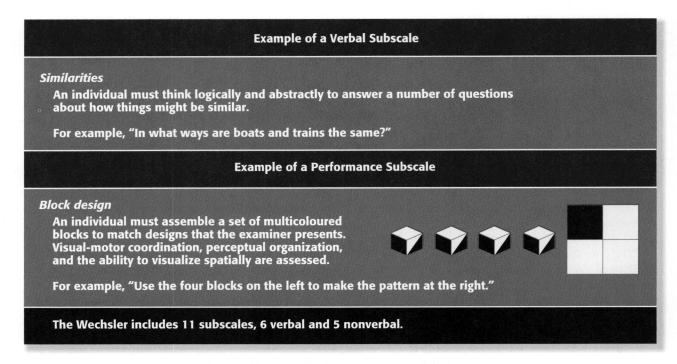

FIGURE 4.2 **Sample Subscales of the Wechsler Intelligence Scale for Children–Revised**

Individual Tests Versus Group Tests

Intelligence tests like the Stanford-Binet and Wechsler are given on an individual basis. A psychologist approaches an individual assessment of intelligence as a structured interaction between the examiner and the student. This provides the psychologist with an opportunity to sample the student's behaviour. During the testing, the examiner observes the ease with which rapport is established, the student's enthusiasm and interest, whether anxiety interferes with the student's performance, and the student's degree of tolerance for frustration.

Students are also given intelligence tests in group settings (Drummond, 2000). Group intelligence tests include the Canadian Cognitive Abilities Test (CCAT), Differential Aptitude Tests (DAT), and the Otis-Lennon School Mental Abilities Tests (French adaptation available 2003; The Psychological Corporation, 2002). Group intelligence tests are more convenient and economical than individual tests, but they do have their drawbacks. When a test is given to a large group, the examiner cannot establish rapport, determine the student's level of anxiety, and so on. In a large-group testing situation, students might not understand the instructions or might be distracted by other students.

Because of such limitations, when important decisions are made about students a group intelligence test should always be supplemented with other information about the student's abilities. For that matter, the same strategy holds for an individual intelligence test. In such instances, an extensive amount of relevant information about the student's abilities outside the testing situation should be obtained (Domino, 2000).

Theories of Multiple Intelligences

Is it more appropriate to think of a student's intelligence as a general ability, or as a number of specific abilities?

Early Views   Binet and Stern both focused on a concept of general intelligence, which Stern called IQ. Wechsler believed it is possible and important to describe both a person's general intelligence and more specific verbal and performance intelligences. He was building on the ideas of Charles Spearman (1927), who said that people have both a general intelligence, which he called *g*, and specific types of intelligence, which he called *s*. As early as the 1930s, L. L. Thurstone (1938) said people have seven specific abilities, which he called primary abilities: verbal comprehension, number ability, word fluency, spatial visualization, associative memory, reasoning, and perceptual speed. More recently, the search for specific types of intelligence has resurfaced as an important issue (Gregory, 2000; Torff, 2000).

Sternberg's Triarchic Theory   According to Robert J. Sternberg's (1986) **triarchic theory of intelligence,** *intelligence comes in three forms: analytical, creative, and practical.*

Analytical intelligence involves the ability to analyze, judge, evaluate, compare, and contrast. Creative intelligence consists of the ability to create, design, invent, originate, and imagine. Practical intelligence focuses on the ability to use, apply, implement, and put into practice. Consider these three students:

- Simone scores high on traditional intelligence tests, such as the Stanford-Binet, and is an excellent analytical thinker.
- Todd does not have the best test scores but has an insightful and creative mind.
- Travis is street-smart and has learned to deal in practical ways with his world, although his scores on traditional intelligence tests are low.

Some students are equally high in all three areas; others do well in one or two.

Robert J. Sternberg, who developed the triarchic theory of intelligence.

Sternberg (1997a, 1999, 2000; Sternberg, Torff, & Grigorenko, 1998) argues that students with different triarchic patterns "look different" in school. Students with high analytic ability tend to be favoured in conventional schooling. They often do well in direct-instruction classes in which the teacher lectures and students are given objective tests. They often are considered to be "smart" students who get good grades, show up in high-level streams, do well on standardized tests, and later get admitted to competitive post-secondary institutions.

Students who are high in creative intelligence often are not on the top rung of their class. Sternberg says that creatively intelligent students might not conform to teachers' expectations about how assignments should be done. Instead of giving conformist answers, they give unique answers, for which they sometimes are reprimanded or marked down. No good teacher wants to discourage creativity, but Sternberg believes that too often a teacher's desire to improve students' knowledge depresses creative thinking.

Like students high in creative intelligence, students with high practical intelligence often do not relate well to the demands of school. However, these students often do well outside the classroom. They might have excellent social skills and good common sense. As adults, they sometimes become successful managers, entrepreneurs, or politicians, despite undistinguished school records.

Sternberg believes that few tasks are purely analytical, creative, or practical. Most require some combination of these skills. For example, when students write a book report, they might (1) analyze the book's main themes, (2) generate new ideas about how the book might have been written better, and (3) think about how the book's themes can be applied to people's lives.

Sternberg believes that it is important to balance instruction related to the three types of intelligence. That is, students should be given opportunities to learn through analytical, creative, and practical thinking, in addition to conventional strategies that focus on "learning" and remembering a body of information. To date, there is no standardized test of Sternberg's triarchic intelligence.

Gardner's Eight Frames of Mind   Educational researchers like Howard Gardner question whether intelligence is a single entity, whether it results from a single factor, and whether it can be measured accurately by IQ tests. Instead, Gardner (1983, 1993) believes there are at least eight types of intelligence. They are described here, along with

"You're wise, but you lack tree smarts."

Howard Gardner, here working with a young child, developed the view that intelligence comes in the forms of at least eight kinds of skills: verbal, mathematical, spatial, bodily–kinesthetic, musical, interpersonal, intrapersonal, and naturalist.

examples of the occupations in which they are reflected as strengths (Campbell, Campbell, & Dickinson, 1999):

- *Verbal skills:* the ability to think in words and to use language to express meaning (authors, journalists, speakers)
- *Mathematical skills:* the ability to carry out mathematical operations (scientists, engineers, accountants)
- *Spatial skills:* the ability to think three-dimensionally (architects, artists, sailors)
- *Bodily–kinesthetic skills:* the ability to manipulate objects and be physically adept (surgeons, craftspeople, dancers, athletes)
- *Musical skills:* a sensitivity to pitch, melody, rhythm, and tone (composers, musicians)
- *Interpersonal skills:* the ability to understand and effectively interact with others (successful teachers, mental health professionals)
- *Intrapersonal skills:* the ability to understand oneself and effectively direct one's life (theologians, psychologists)
- *Naturalist skills:* the ability to observe patterns in nature and understand natural and human-made systems (farmers, botanists, ecologists, landscapers)

Recently, Gardner has postulated the existence of a ninth intelligence, existential intelligence (Gardner, 1999).

- *Existential skills:* the ability to contemplate global questions about life.

Gardner states that the different forms of intelligence can be destroyed by brain damage, that each involves unique cognitive skills, and that each shows up in unique ways in both the gifted and idiot savants (individuals who have developmental disabilities but have an exceptional talent in a particular domain, such as drawing, music, or numerical computation). Presumably, the different forms of intelligence can be enhanced through training. Self-Assessment 4.1 gives you an opportunity to evaluate your strengths and weaknesses in Gardner's eight areas.

Using Multiple Intelligences Theory in the Elementary Grades Project Spectrum is an innovative attempt by Gardner (1993; Gardner, Feldman, & Krechevsky, 1998) to examine the proposed eight intelligences in young children. Project Spectrum begins with the basic idea that every student has the potential to develop strengths in one or more areas. It provides a context in which to more clearly see the strengths and weaknesses of individual children.

What is a Spectrum classroom like? The classroom has rich and engaging materials that can stimulate the range of intelligences. Teachers do not try to evoke an intelligence directly by using materials that are labelled "spatial," "verbal," and so on; rather, they use materials that relate to a combination of intelligence domains. For example, a naturalist corner houses biological specimens that students can explore and compare. This area elicits students' sensory capacities and logical analytic skills. In a story-telling area, students create imaginative tales with stimulating props and design their own storyboards. This area encourages students to use their linguistic, dramatic, and imaginative skills. In a building corner, students can construct a model of their classroom and arrange small-scale photographs of the students and teachers in their class. This area stimulates the use of spatial and personal skills.

Using Multiple Intelligences Theory in Intermediate Grades and Secondary School While Project Spectrum is largely associated with preschool and primary-grade instruction, intermediate-grade and secondary-school teachers can also

Through the Eyes of Teachers

Appealing to Students' Strengths and Interests

Students are motivated by activities that are personally relevant, emotionally involving, and intellectually stimulating. When teaching, I draw on students' strengths and interests to increase their motivation. I always attempt to appeal to their learning styles and multiple intelligences. Students can choose from a variety of assessment options. For instance, if students are musically inclined they can write songs or evaluate music pieces. My classroom is student-centred. I use cooperative learning. I spend most of my time facilitating communications, providing feedback, and encouraging students.

Alan Wasserman
Guidance Counsellor and Career Education Teacher
Ontario

Evaluating Myself on Gardner's Eight Types of Intelligence

For each item, respond, 1 = Not like me at all, 2 = Somewhat like me,
3 = Somewhat unlike me, 4 = A lot like me.

	1	2	3	4

Verbal Thinking

1. I do well on verbal tests, such as the verbal part of the SAT.

2. I am a skilled reader and read prolifically.

3. I love the challenge of solving verbal problems.

Logical/Mathematical Thinking

4. I am a very logical thinker.

5. I like to think like a scientist.

6. Math is one of my favourite subjects.

Spatial Skills

7. I am good visualizing objects and layouts from different angles.

8. I have the ability to create maps of spaces and locations in my mind.

9. If I had wanted to be, I think I could have been an architect.

Bodily–Kinesthetic Skills

10. I have great hand–eye coordination.

11. I excel at sports.

12. I am good at using my body to carry out an expression, as in dance.

Musical Skills

13. I play one or more musical instruments well.

14. I have a good "ear" for music.

15. I am good at making up songs.

Insightful Skills for Self-Understanding

16. I know myself well and have a positive view of myself.

17. I am in tune with my thoughts and feelings.

18. I have good coping skills.

Insightful Skills for Analyzing Others

19. I am very good at "reading" people.

20. I am good at collaborating with other people.

21. I am a good listener.

Naturalist Skills

22. I am good at observing patterns in nature.

23. I excel at identifying and classifying objects in the natural environment.

24. I understand natural and human-made systems.

Scoring and Interpretation

Total your scores for each of the eight types of intelligence. In which areas of intelligence are
your strengths? In which are you the least proficient? It is highly unlikely that you will be strong
in all eight areas or weak in all eight areas. By being aware of your strengths and weaknesses
in different areas of intelligence, you can get a sense of which areas of teaching will be the
easiest and most difficult for you. If you have to teach students in areas in which you are not
proficient, you will need to develop some compensatory teaching approaches and strategies.

Today's classrooms are a diverse mix of learning styles, interests, and ethnic and cultural backgrounds. What are some of the implications for teachers and teaching of the increased cultural and gender diversity in traditionally male-dominated classrooms, such as the transportation class pictured above?

modify their curricula and instructional approaches to be consistent with multiple intelligences theory (Emig, 1997; Guild, 1998; National Council of Teachers of Mathematics, 1998). Karen Goodnough, a researcher at the University of New Brunswick, documented the experiences of one high-school science teacher as he used multiple intelligences theory in his classroom (Goodnough, 2001).

Prior to the project, the teacher described himself as a traditional instructor who relied on didactic instructional approaches and pen-and-paper assessment tools. Concerned that his students, especially those for whom English was a second language, were not demonstrating maximum levels of learning, he joined an action research project and revised a six-week unit on space and astronomy. The revised unit provided students with opportunities to acquire and demonstrate their learning across multiple intelligences. For instance, students worked in groups to produce and perform a rap song containing scientific terms. Assessment included evaluating the accuracy of the scientific information, the quality of the musical components (including beat and rhythm), the creativity of the costumes, and the overall quality of the presentation. In total, students completed 13 different activities as part of the unit, with each activity corresponding to several intelligences. Throughout the unit, students were encouraged to reflect on the intelligences that they were using and whether they enjoyed using them (Goodnough, 2001).

Evaluating the Multiple-Intelligences Approaches   Many educators believe that Sternberg's and Gardner's approaches have much to offer. These approaches have stimulated teachers to think more broadly about what makes up a student's competencies,

---

Teaching Strategies
Related to Gardner's Eight Frames of Mind

✔ Verbal skills
  • read to students and let them read to you
  • discuss book authors with students
  • visit libraries with students
  • have students keep journals of significant events
  • have students summarize and retell a story they have read
✔ Mathematical skills
  • play games of logic with students
  • be on the lookout for situations that can inspire students to think about and construct an understanding of numbers
  • take students on field trips to computer labs, science museums, and electronics exhibits
  • visit virtual science museums and electronic exhibits
  • do math activities with students, such as counting objects and experimenting with numbers
✔ Spatial skills
  • offer a variety of creative materials for students to use
  • have students navigate mazes and create charts
  • invite artists into your classroom to discuss the use of space
  • go on walks with students and later ask them to visualize where they have been and then draw a map of their experiences
✔ Bodily–kinesthetic skills
  • provide students with opportunities for physical activity and encourage them to participate
  • provide areas where students can play indoors and outdoors; if possible, take them to a park
  • have students view and discuss sporting events, dance, and other physical activities
  • encourage students to participate in dance activities

✔ Musical skills
  • provide students with a tape recorder they can use
  • give students an opportunity to play musical instruments
  • create opportunities for students to make music and rhythms together using voices and simple instruments
  • take students to concerts
  • encourage students to make up their own songs
  • integrate music throughout the school day
✔ Insightful skills for self-understanding
  • encourage students to have hobbies and interests
  • listen to students' feelings and give them sensitive feedback
  • encourage students to use their imagination
  • have students keep a journal or scrapbook of their ideas and experiences
  • provide students with relevant literature for discussion
✔ Insightful skills for understanding others
  • encourage students to work in groups
  • help students develop communication and social skills
  • provide group games for students to play
  • encourage students to join clubs
  • have students participate in role-plays with follow-up discussions
  • provide students with relevant literature for discussion
✔ Naturalist skills
  • have students participate in environmentally friendly activities (e.g., recycling)
  • create a naturalist learning centre in the classroom
  • engage students in outdoor naturalist activities, such as taking a nature walk or adopting a tree
  • have students make collections of flora or fauna and classify them
✔ Existential skills
  • ask students to research, discuss, and write about "worldly" issues (i.e., Can animals understand each other? What might life be like on another planet?)
  • encourage students to read about and explore different philosophies and world views
  • invite guest speakers into your classroom to discuss their life experiences
  • have students reflect on and present their own world views

Source: Based on the work of Berger and Pollman (1996); Campbell, Campbell, and Dickinson (1999).

and they have motivated educators to develop programs that instruct students in multiple domains. They also have contributed to the interest in assessing intelligence and classroom learning in innovative ways that go beyond conventional standardized paper-and-pencil memory tasks.

Some critics say that classifying musical skills as a main type of intelligence is off base, because it seems to imply that many other skill domains also should be classified that way. For example, there are outstanding chess players, prizefighters, writers, politicians, physicians, lawyers, ministers, and poets—yet we do not refer to chess intelligence, prizefighter intelligence, and so on. Other critics say that research has not yet been done to support Sternberg's three intelligences or Gardner's multiple intelligences. Notwithstanding these concerns, it may very well be that the ultimate educational value of these theories is that they remind educators to use varied, multi-modality instructional and assessment tools in their classrooms.

Controversies and Issues in Intelligence

As we have mentioned, the topic of intelligence is surrounded by controversy. Controversies include whether nature or nurture is more important in determining intelligence, how much intelligence tests are culturally biased, and whether IQ tests should be used to place students in particular ability groups or streams.

Nature and Nurture   Some scientists proclaim that intelligence is primarily inherited (nature) and that environmental experiences (nurture) play only a minimal role in its manifestation (Herrnstein & Murray, 1994; Jensen, 1969). Heredity is an important part of the intelligence equation (Scarr, 1996). However, the emerging view of the nature–nurture issue is that many complicated qualities, such as intelligence, probably have some genetic predisposition for a particular developmental trajectory (e.g., below-average, average, or above-average intelligence). However, the actual development of intelligence requires more than just heredity.

Most experts today agree that the environment also plays an important role (Ceci et al., 1997). This means that improving children's environments can raise their intelligence. It also means that enriching children's environments can improve their school achievement and the acquisition of skills needed for employment. Craig Ramey and his associates (1988) found that high-quality early educational day care (through five years of age) significantly raised the tested intelligence of young children from impoverished backgrounds. Positive effects of this early intervention were still evident in the intelligence and achievement of these students when they were in intermediate grades (Campbell & Ramey, 1994), and were further maintained in early adulthood (Campbell et al., 2001).

Another argument for the importance of environment in intelligence involves the increasing scores on IQ tests around the world. Scores on these tests have been increasing so fast that a high percentage of people regarded as having average intelligence at the turn of the century would be considered below average in intelligence today (Hall, 1998). In the 1980s James Flynn, a political scientist from New Zealand, observed that IQ test scores have risen about three points every decade (relative to a mean IQ of 100 as measured by Stanford-Binet or Wechsler scales). The "Flynn effect" has been confirmed by numerous studies using various types of intelligence tests with many groups of people in more than 20 countries, including Canada, the United States, and countries in Europe.

Flynn (1984) suggested that people today are better at abstract problem solving than they were generations ago. Better nutrition, universal schooling, improved child-rearing practices, and the increasing relevance of technology are also suggested as factors contributing to the Flynn effect (Neissor, 1997) (see Figure 4.3). If a representative sample of today's children took the Stanford-Binet test used in 1932, about one-fourth would be defined as very superior, a label usually accorded to fewer than 3 percent of the population. Because the increase has taken place in a relatively short period of time, it can't be due to heredity but rather might be due to such environmental factors as the explosion in information people are exposed to and the much higher percentage of the population receiving education.

The interaction of heredity and environment are so complex and dynamic that psychologist William Greenough (1997, 2000) says that to ask what's more important, nature or nurture, is like asking what's more important to a rectangle, its length or its width. Regardless of one's genetic background, growing up "with all the advantages" does not guarantee high intelligence or success, especially if those advantages are taken for granted. Nor does the absence of such advantages guarantee low intelligence or failure, especially if the family and child can make the most of whatever opportunities are accessible to them.

Ethnicity and Culture   Are there ethnic differences in intelligence? Are conventional tests of intelligence biased, and if so, can we develop culture-fair tests?

Ethnic Comparisons   Canadian Native students tend to score below norms for white students on standardized intelligence tests (e.g., Darou, 1992; McShane & Plas, 1984). Specifically, Native students' verbal performance scores are about 20 percent lower.

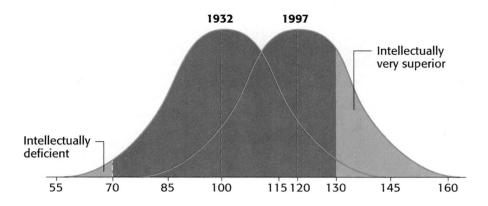

FIGURE 4.3 **Increasing IQ Scores from 1932 to 1997**

Withholding judgment about the appropriateness of using such assessment tools with individuals from diverse cultural backgrounds (see Cultural Bias and Culture-Fair Tests below, and the Diversity and Education box on p. 112), it is important to remember that these scores reflect average differences. That is, there is a great amount of variability within these performance patterns.

Cultural Bias and Culture-Fair Tests Many of the early tests of intelligence were culturally biased, favouring urban children over rural children, children from middle-class families over children from low-income families, and white children over minority children (Miller-Jones, 1989). The standards for the early tests were almost exclusively based on white, middle-socioeconomic-status children. And some of the items were obviously culturally biased. For example, one item on an early test asked what you should do if you find a three-year-old in the street. The "correct" answer was "Call the police." However, children from impoverished inner-city families might not choose this answer if they had had bad experiences with the police, and children living in rural areas might not have had police nearby. The contemporary versions of intelligence tests attempt to reduce such cultural bias.

Another problem is that even if the content of test items is appropriate, the language in which they appear might not be (Serpell, 2000). Some children from minority ethnic groups will have trouble understanding the written language of the test. The language of tests may be especially problematic for learners whose first language is not English and for learners who are less familiar with Western schooling practices, in which students frequently participate in verbal and written question-answering.

There is a growing recognition that in order for a test to be appropriately used across cultures, there must be shared values, shared knowledge, and shared communication (e.g., Greenfield, 1997). Not only must the same items hold the same meanings across cultures, but there must also be an agreement about the value or merit of this knowledge. Furthermore, the value of questioning and communicating with strangers in an impersonal setting about something that is irrelevant to the immediate situation must be an accepted practice. To read further about possible IQ test bias, see the Diversity and Education box.

Culture-fair tests *are tests of intelligence that are intended to be free of cultural bias.* Two types of culture-fair tests have been devised. The first includes items that are believed to be familiar to children from all socioeconomic and ethnic backgrounds, or items that at least are familiar to the children taking the test. For example, a child might be asked how a bird and a dog are different, on the assumption that all children have been exposed to birds and dogs. The second type of culture-fair test has all of the verbal items removed. Figure 4.4 shows a sample from the Raven Progressive Matrices Test, which exemplifies this approach. Even though such tests are

"YOU CAN'T BUILD A HUT, YOU DON'T KNOW HOW TO FIND EDIBLE ROOTS AND YOU KNOW NOTHING ABOUT PREDICTING THE WEATHER. IN OTHER WORDS, YOU DO TERRIBLY ON OUR I.Q. TEST."

© 1991 by Sydney Harris—"You Want Proof?..." W.H. Freeman and Company.

www.mcgrawhill.ca/college/santrock

Diversity and Education
Cultural Bias in IQ Testing

For almost as long as there have been IQ tests, there have been those who believe it is possible to create a culture-free test (e.g., Jensen, 1980). These individuals believe that with an accurate linguistic translation, administration by an "aboriginal" tester, and provision of familiar content, intelligence tests can be transported from one culture to another. However, others caution that it is essentially impossible to create such an instrument (e.g., Cole, 2001; Suzuki & Valencia, 1997). These researchers argue that such attempts basically equate to situations in which a "tester from a dominant culture tests individuals from a minority or less powerful group about information originating from the dominant culture" (Greenfield, 1997).

In an attempt to illustrate the inappropriateness of using the results from "culture-free" tests when making education decisions, Cole (2001) encourages readers to consider the implications of intelligence testing if Binet, the originator of IQ testing in Western society, had been born in Africa. What would be the educational implications if Binet had created his intelligence test based on the knowledge and skills essential to the K'pelle people, a tribal group inhabiting the interior of Liberia? The K'pelle people primarily make their living by growing rice; they supplement their harvest with meat and fish whenever possible. The K'pelle use relatively simple tools like machetes and slingshots to assist their efforts. The roles and responsibilities of men and women are clearly distinguished within the tribe, and there are a few adults who assume specialists' roles (e.g., blacksmiths, bonesetters, weavers). Children attend school in the bush, where they learn to farm, construct houses, track animals, and shoot birds. They are also taught critical lore through ceremonies, stories, myths, and riddles.

What type of intelligence test would Binet develop based on the K'pelle society? Ideally, he would want to identify children who required extra instruction in order to function successfully as adults. With this in mind, he might have created a test where students were required to recall the names of leaves required for making medicine. He could also have tested how many riddles the children knew and their ability to interpret them. Or, more consistent with the K'pelle culture, he could have assessed their ability to use riddles to persuade and influence the behaviours of others.

Cole then encourages the reader to imagine that North American students were required to take the K'pelle-based intelligence test. Leaf-naming items deemed too easy for the K'pelle children would be extremely difficult for our students. Furthermore, because riddles are not an integral element of communication within our society, being required to answer such items would jeopardize our students' abilities to perform well on the test. Finally, imagine the outrage that would result if our students' educational placements and eventual ability to sustain a livelihood were determined on the basis of their performance on this test.

While such a scenario may seem absurd, it accurately represents the experiences of many Native Canadians and cultural minority groups (e.g., O'Coffey et al., 1995). Wes Darou, a senior counsellor and consultant at the Canadian International Development Agency, describes his experiences working with Native counsellors. The counsellors repeatedly reported working with students who, on the basis of their performance scores on the Wechsler Intelligence Scale for Children (WISC-R), were streamed into special-education programs. These allocations were made despite well-documented concerns about the lack of adequate norms for Native populations, language barriers, detrimental effects on self-esteem following testing, lack of predictive validity between test results and Native students' academic success, and the overall incompatibility of the tests with the goals of Native educational systems (Darou, 1992; Senior, 1993).

While advocates such as Darou (1992) and Senior (1993) acknowledge that the results of standardized tests can be used to help create optimal learning environments for students, they are adamant that if test results continue to be used in inappropriate and harmful ways there is no place for these measures within school systems.

designed to be culture-fair, students with more education score higher on them than do their less-educated counterparts.

These attempts to produce culture-fair tests remind us that conventional intelligence tests probably are culturally biased, yet the effort to create a truly culture-fair test has not yet succeeded. It is important to consider also that what is viewed as intelligent in one culture might not be thought of as intelligent in another culture (Greenfield, 1997; Suzuki & Valencia, 1997). In most Western cultures, students are considered intelligent if they are both smart (have considerable knowledge and can solve verbal problems) and fast (can process information quickly). In contrast, in the Buganda culture in Uganda, students who are wise, slow in thought, and say the socially correct thing are considered intelligent. And in the widely dispersed Caroline Islands, one of the most important dimensions of intelligence is the ability to navigate by the stars.

Ability Grouping and Tracking Another controversial issue is whether it is beneficial to use students' scores on an intelligence test to place them in ability groups. Two types of ability grouping have been used in education: between-class and within-class.

Between-Class Ability Grouping (Tracking) **Between-class ability grouping (tracking)** *consists of grouping students based on their ability or achievement.* Tracking has long been used in schools as a way to organize students, especially at the secondary level (Slavin, 1990, 1995). The positive view of tracking is that it narrows the range of skill in a group of students, making it easier to teach them. Tracking is said to prevent less able students from "holding back" more talented students.

A typical between-class grouping in schools involves dividing students into a post-secondary preparatory track and a general track. Within the two tracks, further ability groupings might be made, such as two levels of math instruction for post-secondary-bound students. Another form of tracking takes place when a student's abilities in different subject areas are taken into account. For example, the same student might be in a high-track math class and a middle-track English class.

Critics of tracking argue that it stigmatizes students who are consigned to low-track classes (Smith-Maddox & Wheelock, 1995). For example, students can become labelled as "low-track" or "the dummy group." Critics also say that low-track classrooms often have less-experienced teachers, fewer resources, and lower expectations (Wheelock, 1992). Further, critics stress that tracking is used to segregate students according to ethnicity and socioeconomic status, because higher tracks have fewer students from ethnic minority and impoverished backgrounds. In this way, tracking can actually replay segregation within schools. The detractors also argue that average and above-average students do not get substantial benefits from being grouped together.

Does research support the critics' contention that tracking is harmful to students? Researchers have found that tracking harms the achievement of low-track students (Brewer, Rees, & Argys, 1995; Slavin, 1990). However, tracking seems to benefit high-track students (such as those in a gifted program).

Within-Class Ability Grouping **Within-class ability grouping** *involves placing students in two to three groups within a class to take into account differences in students' abilities.* A typical within-class ability grouping occurs when elementary-school teachers place students in several reading groups based on their reading skills. A Grade 2 teacher might have one group using a Grade 3 first-term reading program; another using a Grade 2 first-term program; and a third group using a Grade 1 second-term program. Such within-class grouping is far more common in elementary than in secondary schools. The subject area most often involved is reading, followed by math. Although many elementary-school teachers use some form of within-class ability grouping, there is no clear research support for this strategy.

When any form of tracking is used, teachers need to be especially vigilant not to allow students' placement in an ability group to affect instructional approach or performance expectations. Teachers need to resist labelling groups (e.g., "low," "middle," "high") or making comparisons among them. No more than two or three groups should be formed, so that all students can be provided with adequate attention and instructional time. Tracking does not negate teachers' responsibilities to implement effective instructional strategies, resources, and support services. Furthermore, teachers need to resist any attempt to track students solely on the basis of IQ-test results, especially group-administered ones. Instead, other measures of students' knowledge and potential should be used to place students in an ability group. Finally, teachers need to consider students' placement in any group as subject to review and change. This is as true for low-track students as it is for high-track students.

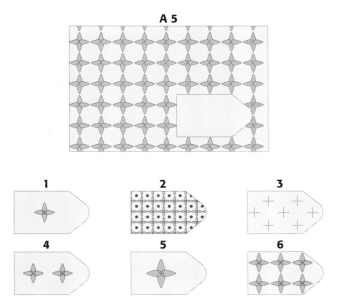

FIGURE 4.4 **Sample Item from the Raven Progressive Matrices Test** Individuals are presented with a matrix arrangement of symbols, such as the one at the top of this figure, and must then complete the matrix by selecting the appropriate missing symbol from a group of symbols.

Teaching Strategies
Related to Teacher Expectations and Intelligence Tests

✔ Remember that IQ tests are tools
  • use IQ test scores to better understand students' strengths and weaknesses
  • use IQ test scores to create optimal learning environments for students
✔ Do not use IQ test scores to create unwarranted stereotypes and negative expectations
  • do not make generalizations or formulate expectations for students on the basis of IQ test scores
  • remember that IQ test scores are a measure of current performance, not fixed potential
  • remember that maturational changes and enriched environmental experiences can advance students' intelligence
  • hold high expectations for all students
✔ Be especially cautious when interpreting the meaningfulness of IQ scores
  • avoid using IQ test results as the primary or sole indicator of competence
  • remember that intelligence consists of multiple domains
  • consider all of a student's skills, including creative and practical talents
  • find at least one domain of strength for every student
  • develop plans to help students perform better in weaker domains and capitalize on areas of competence
✔ Communicate expectations clearly
  • avoid forming expectations based on students' IQ scores and your opinions
  • "catch" students performing well—explicitly praise appropriate behaviour, and treat all students with respect and dignity
  • monitor messages to students (what, when, and how)
✔ Provide multiple opportunities for students to demonstrate their abilities
  • provide positive reinforcement to all students for good work
  • avoid criticizing students when they make mistakes
  • provide opportunities for all students to speak during class, to offer their opinions, and to share their ideas
  • provide assistance or encouragement to all students when problem solving

Self-Fulfilling Prophecies   The relationship between an individual's beliefs about his or her ability to achieve a specific goal in a specific situation and his or her subsequent behaviour is often viewed in terms of "self-fulfilling prophecy." Self-fulfilling prophecies in education have largely been associated with teacher expectations and behaviours, and students' academic achievement and intelligence levels (Jussim, 1986). Self-fulfilling prophecies may be viewed as a form of labelling students. The implications of the chosen label can be positive or negative. According to Rosenthal (1995; 1994), the more teachers believe in students' abilities to succeed the more likely they and their students will be to shape events to make this belief a reality. The inverse is also true. The more teachers believe their students lack the ability to succeed, the more likely it is that they and their students will act in unsuccessful ways.

Some researchers have argued that self-fulfilling prophecies (also known as the Pygmalian effect) have little real impact on student performance (Alpert, 2001; Cronbach, 1975). However, Schaler (1996) cautions that many parents and teachers fail to realize how much children tend to learn from the way adults think and behave. Good and Brophy (2000) and Novak and Purkey (2001) suggest that teachers and parents send a variety of positive and negative messages to children in nonverbal ways. These messages

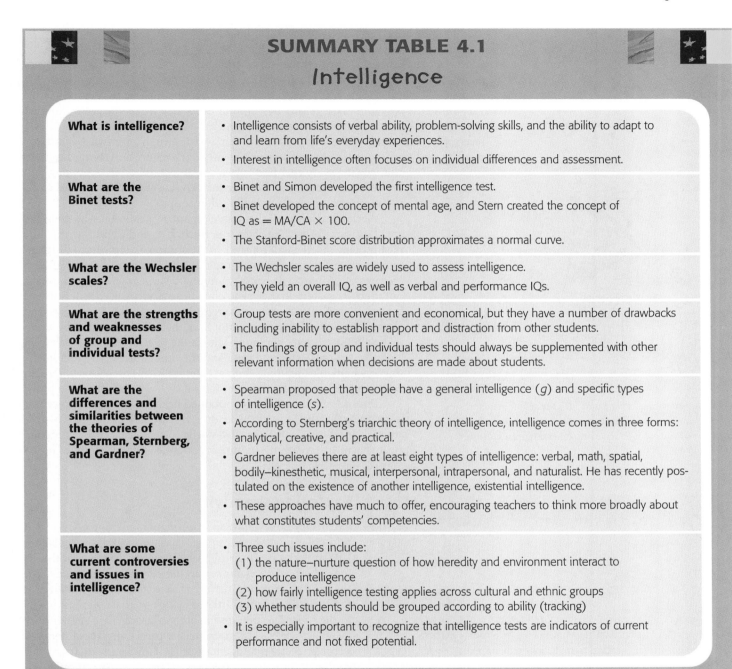

SUMMARY TABLE 4.1
Intelligence

What is intelligence?	• Intelligence consists of verbal ability, problem-solving skills, and the ability to adapt to and learn from life's everyday experiences. • Interest in intelligence often focuses on individual differences and assessment.
What are the Binet tests?	• Binet and Simon developed the first intelligence test. • Binet developed the concept of mental age, and Stern created the concept of IQ as $= MA/CA \times 100$. • The Stanford-Binet score distribution approximates a normal curve.
What are the Wechsler scales?	• The Wechsler scales are widely used to assess intelligence. • They yield an overall IQ, as well as verbal and performance IQs.
What are the strengths and weaknesses of group and individual tests?	• Group tests are more convenient and economical, but they have a number of drawbacks including inability to establish rapport and distraction from other students. • The findings of group and individual tests should always be supplemented with other relevant information when decisions are made about students.
What are the differences and similarities between the theories of Spearman, Sternberg, and Gardner?	• Spearman proposed that people have a general intelligence (*g*) and specific types of intelligence (*s*). • According to Sternberg's triarchic theory of intelligence, intelligence comes in three forms: analytical, creative, and practical. • Gardner believes there are at least eight types of intelligence: verbal, math, spatial, bodily–kinesthetic, musical, interpersonal, intrapersonal, and naturalist. He has recently postulated on the existence of another intelligence, existential intelligence. • These approaches have much to offer, encouraging teachers to think more broadly about what constitutes students' competencies.

What are some current controversies and issues in intelligence?	• Three such issues include:
	  (1) the nature–nurture question of how heredity and environment interact to produce intelligence
	  (2) how fairly intelligence testing applies across cultural and ethnic groups
	  (3) whether students should be grouped according to ability (tracking)
	• It is especially important to recognize that intelligence tests are indicators of current performance and not fixed potential.

are often unintentional and are reflected in things such as tone of voice, facial expression, and the amount of time devoted to talking or listening to students. For example, dismissing the ideas of a troublesome student may be interpreted as a message that the student is not worth bothering with. Conversely, if a teacher consistently and sincerely conveys to students a belief that they are valuable and capable, it is likely that these students will adjust their behaviour accordingly. Teachers need to be aware of what they say and how they behave toward their students. Some strategies for communicating positive expectations to create appropriate self-fulfilling prophecies are presented in the Teaching Strategies Related to Teacher Expectations and Intelligence Tests feature on page 114.

At this point we have studied a number of ideas about intelligence. A review of these ideas is presented in Summary Table 4.1.

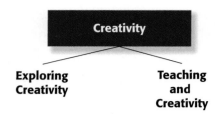

CREATIVITY

Teresa Amabile remembers that when she was in kindergarten she rushed into class every day, excited about getting to the easel and playing with all of those bright colours and big paintbrushes. She and her classmates also had free access to a table with all kinds of art materials on it. Teresa remembers telling her mother every day when she got home that she wanted to play with crayons and draw and paint.

Teresa's kindergarten experience unfortunately was the high point of her artistic interest. The next year she entered a conventional elementary school and things began to change. She no longer had free access to art materials every day, and art became just another subject for Teresa, something she had to do for an hour and a half on Friday afternoon.

Week after week, all through elementary school, it was the same art class. For Teresa, the class was restrictive and demoralizing. She recalls being given small reprints of painting masterpieces, a different one each week; one week in Grade 2, students were presented with pictures of Leonardo da Vinci's *Adoration of the Magi* and told to take out their art materials and try to copy the masterpiece. For Teresa and the other students, it was an exercise in frustration. Teresa says that elementary-school students do not have the skill development even to make all those horses and angels fit on the page, let alone make them look like the masterpiece. Teresa and the other students were not getting any help in developing their artistic skills. Needless to say, Teresa's desire to go home and paint after school each day diminished rapidly.

What do you mean, "What is it?" It's the spontaneous, unfettered expression of a young mind not yet bound by the restraints of narrative or pictorial representation.
by Sidney Harris

Teresa Amabile eventually obtained her Ph.D. in psychology and went on to become one of the leading researchers in the field of creativity. Her hope is that teachers will foster, not crush, students' enthusiasm for creativity (Conti & Amabile, 1999; Goleman, Kaufman, & Ray, 1993).

Through the Eyes of Students

The 8-Year-Old Filmmaker and Oozy Red Goop

Steven was eight years old and wanted to get a scout badge in filmmaking. His father bought him a Super 8 movie camera. Steven got the inspiration to make a horror movie.

He started imagining what he needed to do to make a movie. Needing some red, bloody-looking goop to ooze from the kitchen cabinets, he got his mother to buy 30 cans of cherries. Steven dumped the cherries into the pressure cooker and produced an oozy red goop.

His mother gave him free rein in the house, letting him virtually convert it into a child's movie studio. Steven told his mother he needed to make some costumes, which she obligingly did.

The son's name? Steven Spielberg, whose mother supported his imagination and passion for filmmaking. Of course, Spielberg went on to become one of Hollywood's greatest producers, with such films as *E.T.* and *Jurassic Park*. (Goleman, Kaufman, & Ray, 1993)

Exploring Creativity

Creativity *is the ability to think about something in novel and unusual ways and come up with unique solutions to problems.* J. P. Guilford (1967) distinguished between **convergent thinking**, *which produces one correct answer and is characteristic of the kind of thinking required on conventional intelligence tests,* and **divergent thinking**, *which produces many answers to the same question and is more characteristic of creativity* (Michael, 1999). For example, a typical convergent item on a conventional intelligence test is, "How many quarters will you get in return for 60 dimes?" The question has only one right answer. In contrast, divergent questions have many possible answers. For example, what image comes to mind when you hear the phrase "sitting alone in a dark room," or the question "What are some unique uses for a paper clip?"

Current definitions of creativity extend beyond divergent thinking (Kirton, 1999). It is believed that all individuals have creative abilities that are different in style and approach. Kirton (1999) argues that there are two types of creativity: adaptive creativity and innovative creativity. **Adaptive creativity** *is demonstrated by an individual who approaches a problem in a conventional fashion and produces a conventional solution.* **Innovative creativity** *is demonstrated by an individual who examines and manipulates a problem to produce several revolutionary solutions.*

Creative Experiences with Computers

Computer technology today offers students the hardware and software tools to express their creativity and to interact with the world around them in ways that were unimaginable even a decade ago. For example, the software programs Inspiration (Inspiration Software Inc.) and SMART Ideas® (SMART Technologies Inc.) allow students to graphically brainstorm, plan, organize, and present their ideas on a computer or on paper.

Kid-Pix (Broderbund Ltd.) enables students to organize and represent their ideas in innovative formats. These programs are based on visual learning, a preferred mode of instruction for many students and for many gifted individuals including Albert Einstein, Winston Churchill, Thomas Edison, and Leonardo Da Vinci (West, 1997). Inspiration allows students to create and use concept or mind maps to represent knowledge, visualize relationships, and construct meaning.

Kid Pix provides learners with a virtual canvas and art tools. Tools include familiar drawing objects such as paintbrushes, chalk, and crayons, but there are also unusual multimedia tools such as buckets of paint, candy, and shaving cream. The software also enables students to further express themselves creatively by adding sounds, animation, and text to their creations.

Special software packages are not the only way to encourage creativity and problem solving. Everyday software programs such as word processors and spreadsheets can also be used to foster creative thinking. If your school uses programs such as Microsoft Excel or Word you can use the drawing tools built into these applications to create simple concept maps, and the outlining function can be used as a tool for brainstorming or for finding underlying patterns or meaning. Watching students work and play with technology, it is easy to imagine why technology will have an increasingly important role to play in fostering students' creativity.

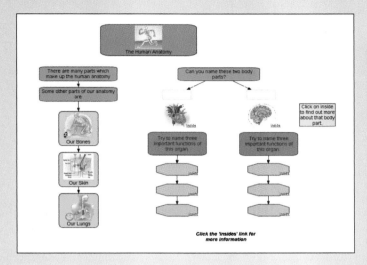

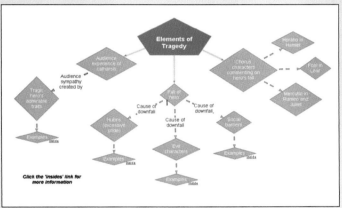

Teaching and Creativity

Ontario researcher Marci Segal (2002) defines creativity as "an attitude, behaviour and approach to using one's personal energy for improvement or experiment." Segal believes that creativity is an expression resulting from a restlessness for change. This motivation for change may be either extrinsic or intrinsic in nature. Individuals express and interpret creative acts in unique ways. This poses a challenge to teachers who seek to appraise or assess creativity in their students.

Segal believes that teachers should focus on helping students become more creative. Teachers can foster their students' creativity by having them brainstorm and participate in problem-solving activities. Teachers should provide students with learning opportunities that encourage playful thinking, intrinsic motivation, and flexibility. Above all, they should avoid any tendencies to be controlling and critical. Refer to the Teaching Strategies for Encouraging Students' Creativity feature for further suggestions about how to foster creativity.

To evaluate yourself as a role model for fostering creativity, complete Self-Assessment 4.2. Also, to read about the use of technology to stimulate creativity, see the Technology and Education box.

Through the Eyes of Teachers

Imagination as a Form of Transportation

Grade 2 teacher Beth Belcher transforms a lesson about transportation into the game of "Scattergories." After her students settle on a description of *transportation* as "a way of getting from one place to another," she divides them into teams and asks them to list as many types of transportation as they can think of. Belcher says she wants students to engage in deep thinking. If more than one team comes up with the same answer, like "car," "train," or "plane," they don't get any points. "Elevator" is a winner. And then a six-year-old girl says that "imagination" is a form of transportation, a way of getting from one place to another. Belcher says that moments like that are incredibly rewarding. (Briggs, 1998)

How Good Am I at Fostering Creativity?

For each item, respond yes or no.

	Yes	No
1. I come up with new and unique ideas.		
2. I brainstorm with others to creatively find solutions to problems.		
3. I am internally motivated.		
4. I'm flexible about things and like to play with my thinking.		
5. I read about creative projects and creative people.		
6. I'm surprised by something and surprise others every day.		
7. I wake up in the morning with a mission.		
8. I search for alternative solutions to problems rather than giving a pat answer.		
9. I spend time around creative people.		
10. I spend time in settings and activities that stimulate me to be creative.		

Examine your overall pattern of responses. What are your strengths and weaknesses in creativity? How will you practise your strengths and work to improve your weaknesses to provide students with a creative role model?

At this point, we have studied a number of ideas about creativity. A review of these ideas is presented in Summary Table 4.2. Just as there are individual differences in children's intelligence and creativity, as we see next students also vary in their learning and thinking styles.

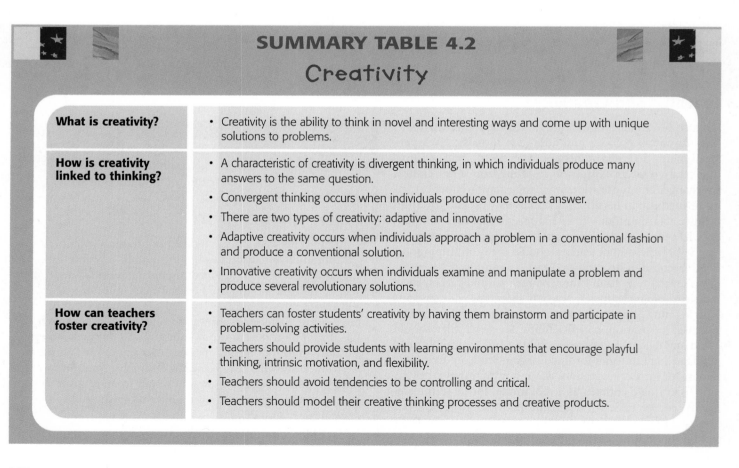

SUMMARY TABLE 4.2
Creativity

What is creativity?	• Creativity is the ability to think in novel and interesting ways and come up with unique solutions to problems.
How is creativity linked to thinking?	• A characteristic of creativity is divergent thinking, in which individuals produce many answers to the same question. • Convergent thinking occurs when individuals produce one correct answer. • There are two types of creativity: adaptive and innovative • Adaptive creativity occurs when individuals approach a problem in a conventional fashion and produce a conventional solution. • Innovative creativity occurs when individuals examine and manipulate a problem and produce several revolutionary solutions.
How can teachers foster creativity?	• Teachers can foster students' creativity by having them brainstorm and participate in problem-solving activities. • Teachers should provide students with learning environments that encourage playful thinking, intrinsic motivation, and flexibility. • Teachers should avoid tendencies to be controlling and critical. • Teachers should model their creative thinking processes and creative products.

Teaching Strategies
For Encouraging Students' Creativity

✔ Have students brainstorm
  • have students work in groups to generate creative ideas
  • require students to generate multiple ideas, accept all ideas, and expand/elaborate on others' thoughts and ideas
  • inform students that the more ideas generated, the greater the likelihood of creating a unique and/or worthy concept
  • inform students that creative people are risk takers—they are not afraid of "failing" or "being wrong"
✔ Provide students with environments that stimulate creativity
  • nurture and rely on students' curiosity
  • provide exercises and activities that encourage students to find insightful solutions to problems (e.g., Mensa puzzles and activities)
  • avoid asking questions that require rote answers
  • take students to places where creativity is valued (e.g., children's museums, art galleries, science centres)
  • invite creative people into your classroom (e.g., writer, poet, craftsperson, musician, scientist)
✔ Avoid tendencies to be controlling and critical
  • avoid telling students exactly how to complete tasks and activities
  • allow students to select areas of interest and support their choices
  • avoid hovering over students as they work
  • avoid being critical of students' creative efforts (e.g., Why is the flower bigger than you?)
✔ Encourage intrinsic motivation
  • recognize that intrinsic motivation refers to the self-driven desire to complete a task or activity (e.g., reading a novel for pleasure)
  • avoid providing external reinforcements (e.g., stickers, prizes, privileges) for tasks and activities that students are willing to perform on their own
✔ Encourage flexible and playful thinking
  • inform students that creative thinkers are flexible and "play" with problems
  • inform students that creative thinking requires effort
  • understand that humour can help students generate unusual solutions to problems and helps make extensive effort tolerable
  • model and encourage appropriate humour

LEARNING AND THINKING STYLES

Teachers will tell you that children approach learning and thinking in an amazing variety of ways. Teachers themselves also vary in their styles of learning and thinking.

Exploring Learning and Thinking Styles

The two main topics we have discussed so far—intelligence and creativity—are abilities. A style is a preferred way of using one's abilities (Sternberg, 1994, 1997b). **Learning and thinking styles** *are not abilities; rather, they are preferences in how people use their abilities.* None of us has just a single learning and thinking style; each of us has a profile of many styles. Individuals vary so much that literally hundreds of learning and thinking styles

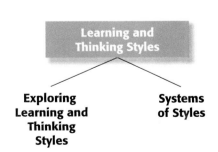

Learning and Thinking Styles

Exploring Learning and Thinking Styles   Systems of Styles

www.mcgrawhill.ca/college/santrock

have been proposed by educators and psychologists. The following coverage of learning and thinking styles is not meant to be exhaustive, but introduces widely discussed styles and links them to profiles and assessment inventories.

We will examine three of these systems: a recently proposed one (Sternberg's system of styles); one that has been used for many years (the Myers-Briggs Type Indicator); and a Canadian computer-based system (the P.E.T., or Personal Empowerment through Type inventory).

Systems of Styles

The Sternberg System of Styles   A broad system of learning and thinking styles has recently been proposed by Robert J. Sternberg (O'Hara & Sternberg, 1999; 1997b). *The main theme of the* **Sternberg System of Styles** *is that students organize and govern themselves in different ways and that these variations correspond to the different forms of government that exist around the world.* As shown in Figure 4.5, Sternberg's system consists of 13 learning and thinking styles under five categories: functions, forms, levels, scope, and leaning.

FIGURE 4.5   Sternberg's System of Learning and Thinking Styles

Style	Characteristics	Example
Functions		
Legislative	Creates, invents, designs, with little structure	Likes science projects, writing stories, music, and original artworks
Executive	Follows directions with structure	Solves problems, writes assigned papers, learns assigned information
Judicial	Judges and evaluates people and things	Critiques work of others, writes critical essays, gives feedback
Forms		
Monarchic	Devotes all energy and resources to one thing at a time	Immerses self in a single project
Hierarchic	Sets priorities for what tasks to do and time	Budgets time for doing homework
Oligarchic	Performs many tasks at once, but has difficulties setting priorities	Devotes time to reading comprehension items at expense of decoding
Anarchic	Dislikes systems, guidelines, and practically all constraints	Essays written in stream-of-consciousness form
Levels		
Global	Focuses on whole, generalities, abstractions	Writes an essay on the global message and meaning of art
Local	Focuses on details, specifics, concrete examples	Writes an essay describing the details of art and how they interact
Scope		
Internal	Works alone, focuses inward, and self-sufficient	Completes projects independently
External	Works with others, focuses outward, interdependent	Completes projects as part of a group
Leaning		
Liberal	Completes tasks in new ways, defies conventions	Prefers an open-classroom setting, enjoys "tinkering" with equipment
Conservative	Completes tasks in tried-and-true ways, follows conventions	Prefers traditional classroom setting, operates equipment in traditional manner

www.mcgrawhill.ca/college/santrock

Method of Instruction	Most Compatible Styles
Lecture	Executive/hierarchical
Thought-based questioning	Judicial/legislative
Cooperative learning	External
Problem solving of given problems	Executive
Projects	Legislative
Small-group recitation	External/executive
Small-group discussion	External/judicial
Reading	Internal/hierarchical
For details	Local/executive
For main ideas	Global/executive
For analysis	Judicial
Memorization	Executive/local/conservative

FIGURE 4.6   **Linking Sternberg's Styles with Teaching Methods**

Sternberg believes that each student tends to adopt one style in each of the five categories, although the student's style might vary with the task or situation. For example, a student who likes to work independently in a biology class (internal scope) might prefer to do social studies projects with others (external scope).

Sternberg stresses that teachers should vary their teaching styles to match up with individual students' styles. This works best when teachers have a full range of styles that they can call on when interacting with students. Figure 4.6 shows which teaching methods link up best with students' styles. Notice that the oligarchic and anarchic learning styles have been omitted from Figure 4.6 because they are incompatible with just about any method of instruction. However, teachers who have students with an oligarchic style need to help them set priorities, because these students try to do too many things at once. And teachers with students who have an anarchic style need to help the students learn to engage in self-regulation, because they tend to approach problems in a random way and don't like guidelines.

In Sternberg's research, teachers tend to overestimate how compatible their own styles are with those of their students. Also, teachers' styles differ not only across schools, but also across grades and subjects. This suggests that the learning context often places demands on teachers that require them to adapt their style to the environment. Sternberg says that teachers of younger students need to be more legislative and less executive than teachers of older students. Groups of students also differ. Students from low-income backgrounds tend to be more judicial, oligarchic, local, and conservative than middle-socioeconomic-status students.

The Myers-Briggs Type Indicator   The **Myers-Briggs Type Indicator** *(1998) is based on Carl Jung's theory of psychological types.* Briefly, Jung's theory states that individuals differ with respect to how they perceive the world and in how they reach conclusions. Consequently, they differ in their interests, reactions, values, motivations, and skills. The Myers-Briggs Type Indicator provides scores across four dichotomies (Myers, 1962):

- *Extraversion/introversion (EI).* This involves whether students focus on the outer world of people or the inner life of ideas. Extraverts enjoy spending time interacting with others while introverts prefer more solitary activities like studying alone in a library. We will have more to say about extraversion/introversion later in the chapter when we discuss personality traits.
- *Sensing/intuiting (SN).* Sensing students like to gather extensive information through their senses before they take action. By contrast, intuiting students rely on their intuition in making up their mind about something.

- *Thinking/feeling (TF).* Thinkers use systematic reasoning and logically analyze problems. They avoid letting their emotions become involved in making decisions. By contrast, feelers trust their emotions.
- *Judging/perceiving (JP).* Judgers evaluate and criticize. They enjoy debating and arguing about an issue. By contrast, perceivers use their perceptual skills to develop aesthetic appreciation. Perceivers especially enjoy art and craft activities.

When students complete the Myers-Briggs inventory, they are given scores on these pairs of characteristics and are provided feedback about which ones they prefer (Cohen & Swerdlik, 1999). A four-letter code designation (e.g., *ISFP,* standing for introverted, sensing, feeling, and perceiving) corresponds to an academic style with its own strengths and weaknesses. Some teachers believe that knowing students' Myers-Briggs profiles can help them improve their instructional strategies.

The Personal Empowerment through Type (P.E.T.) Inventory The **Personal Empowerment through Type (P.E.T.) inventory** *is a Canadian, computer-based personality and learning-style assessment tool fashioned with the Myers-Briggs in mind.* Developed by Patricia Cranton and Robert Knoop, the P.E.T. Inventory is based on the theories of Carl Jung and identifies the dimensions by which people perceive the world around them and make decisions or judgments. The Web-based inventory correlates personality preferences with learning styles, teaching styles, conflict resolution, leadership, management, problem solving, stress, and teamwork. The instrument was field tested with teachers and students in Ontario and New Brunswick. The P.E.T. includes a Personality Profile that enables teachers to profile their personality preferences relative to the demands of teaching. A Student Self-Check feature enables students to map their preferred learning styles and learn about successful strategies. A sample of the P.E.T. inventory is available online at **www.vitalknowledge.com**.

Teaching Strategies
For Students with Diverse Learning and Thinking Styles

✔ Honour students' diverse learning and thinking styles appropriately
  - recognize differences between ability and intelligence
  - recognize that style involves how students use their abilities and intelligence
  - recognize that every student possesses a combination of learning and thinking styles
✔ Monitor students' learning and thinking styles
  - evaluate whether students are using optimal learning and thinking styles (e.g., question-answering to process information deeply versus reading without reflection)
  - recognize that some learning and thinking styles (i.e., Sternberg's global and local styles) are equally effective
  - recognize that students learn best when their learning and thinking styles parallel their teacher's style
  - evaluate your dominant learning and thinking styles
  - expand the range of learning and thinking styles that you present to students
✔ Recognize that learning and thinking styles can vary across contexts
  - recognize that students' learning and thinking styles can vary across schools, grades, and subjects (e.g., impulsive when creating art but reflective when completing a jigsaw puzzle)
  - help students develop appropriate learning and thinking styles across diverse contexts

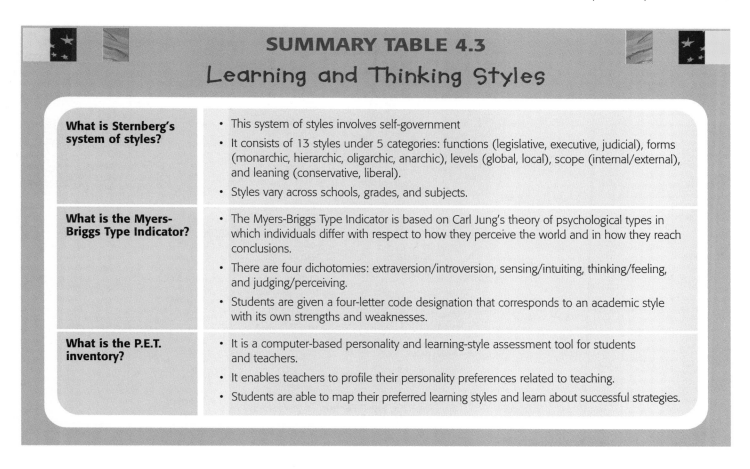

SUMMARY TABLE 4.3
Learning and Thinking Styles

What is Sternberg's system of styles?	• This system of styles involves self-government • It consists of 13 styles under 5 categories: functions (legislative, executive, judicial), forms (monarchic, hierarchic, oligarchic, anarchic), levels (global, local), scope (internal/external), and leaning (conservative, liberal). • Styles vary across schools, grades, and subjects.
What is the Myers-Briggs Type Indicator?	• The Myers-Briggs Type Indicator is based on Carl Jung's theory of psychological types in which individuals differ with respect to how they perceive the world and in how they reach conclusions. • There are four dichotomies: extraversion/introversion, sensing/intuiting, thinking/feeling, and judging/perceiving. • Students are given a four-letter code designation that corresponds to an academic style with its own strengths and weaknesses.
What is the P.E.T. inventory?	• It is a computer-based personality and learning-style assessment tool for students and teachers. • It enables teachers to profile their personality preferences related to teaching. • Students are able to map their preferred learning styles and learn about successful strategies.

At this point we have studied a number of ideas about learning and thinking styles. A review of these ideas is presented in Summary Table 4.3. Next, we will turn our attention to personality and temperament, which also need to be considered when individual differences and children's education are evaluated.

PERSONALITY AND TEMPERAMENT

Not only is it important to be aware of individual variations in children's cognition, it also is important to understand individual variations in their personality and temperament.

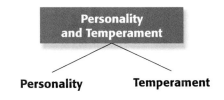

Personality

Personality *refers to distinctive thoughts, emotions, and behaviours that characterize the way an individual adapts to the world.* Think about yourself for a moment. What is your personality like? Are you outgoing or shy? considerate or caring? friendly or hostile? These are some of the characteristics involved in personality. As we see next, one view stresses that there are five main factors that make up personality.

The "Big Five" Personality Factors As with intelligence, psychologists are interested in identifying the main dimensions of personality (Ryckman, 2000). Some personality researchers believe they have identified the **"big five" personality factors:** *emotional stability, extroversion, openness to experience, agreeableness, and conscientiousness* (see Figure 4.7). A number of research studies point toward these factors as important dimensions of personality (Costa, 2000; Costa & McRae, 1995, 1998; Hogan, 1987; McNulty, 2000).

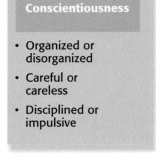

Emotional Stability	Extroversion	Openness
• Calm or anxious	• Sociable or retiring	• Imaginative or practical
• Secure or insecure	• Fun-loving or sombre	• Interested in variety or routine
• Self-satisfied or self-pitying	• Affectionate or reserved	• Independent or conforming

Agreeableness	Conscientiousness
• Softhearted or ruthless	• Organized or disorganized
• Trusting or suspicious	• Careful or careless
• Helpful or uncooperative	• Disciplined or impulsive

FIGURE 4.7   **The "Big Five" Factors of Personality**

Thinking about personality in terms of the "big five" factors can give you a framework for thinking about the personalities of your students. Your students will differ in their emotional stability, how extroverted or introverted they are, how open to experience they are, how agreeable they are, and how conscientious they are. However, some experts believe that the "big five" do not capture all of personality. They say that the range of personality also should include such factors as how positive (joyous, happy) or negative (angry, sad) students are, as well as how assertive they are.

Person–Situation Interaction   In discussing learning and thinking styles, we indicated that students' styles can vary across subjects. The same is true for personality characteristics. According to the concept of **person–situation interaction**, *the best way to characterize an individual's personality is not in terms of personal traits or characteristics alone, but also in terms of the situation involved.* Researchers have found that students choose to be in some situations and avoid others (Ickes, Snyder, & Garcia, 1997).

Suppose you have an extrovert and an introvert in your class. According to the theory of person–situation interaction, you can't predict which one will show the best adaptation unless you consider the situation they are in. The theory of person–situation interaction predicts that the extrovert will adapt best when he is asked to collaborate with others, and that the introvert will adapt best when he is asked to carry out tasks independently. Similarly, the extrovert likely will be happier when socializing with lots of people, the introvert when in a more private setting alone or with a friend.

In sum, personality traits are subject to change across all situations. The context or situation matters (Burger, 2000; Derlega, Winstead, & Jones, 1999). Monitor situations in which students with varying personality characteristics seem to feel most comfortable and provide them with opportunities to learn in those situations. If a particular personality trait is detrimental to the student's school performance (perhaps one student is so introverted that he fears working in a group), think of ways you can support the student's efforts to change.

Temperament

Temperament is closely related to personality and to learning and thinking styles. **Temperament** *is a person's behavioural style and characteristic ways of responding.* Some students are active, others are calm. Some respond warmly to people, others fuss and fret. Such descriptions involve variations in students' temperaments.

Scientists who study temperament seek to find the best ways to classify temperaments. The most well known classification was proposed by Alexander Chess and Stella Thomas (Chess & Thomas, 1977; Thomas & Chess, 1991). They believe that there are three basic styles, or clusters, of temperament:

- An **easy child** *is generally in a positive mood, quickly establishes regular routines, and easily adapts to new experiences.*
- A **difficult child** *tends to react negatively, has aggressive tendencies, lacks self-control, and is slow to accept new experiences.*
- A **slow-to-warm-up child** *has a low activity level, is somewhat negative, shows low adaptability, and displays a low intensity of mood.*

A difficult temperament or a temperament that reflects a lack of control can place a student at risk. In one study, adolescents with a difficult temperament had unusually high incidences of drug abuse and stressful events (Tubman & Windle, 1995). In another study, being identified as "out of control" (irritable and distractible) at three to five years of age was related to acting out and behavioural problems at 13 to 15 years of age (Caspi et al., 1995). Across the same age span, a temperament factor labelled "approach" (friendliness, eagerness to explore new situations) was associated with a low incidence of anxiety and depression.

New classifications of temperament continue to be forged (Kagan, 2000). In a recent review of temperament, Mary Rothbart and John Bates (1998) concluded that the best framework for classifying temperament involves a revision of Chess and Thomas' categories (easy, difficult, and slow-to-warm-up). The classification of temperament now focuses more on (1) positive affect and approach, (2) negative affect, and (3) effortful control (self-regulation).

Specific teaching practices can help teachers better understand and relate to students' temperaments (Sanson & Rothbart, 1995). Teachers should demonstrate respect for individuality. The goal of good teaching might be accomplished in one way with one student and in another way with another student, depending on the students' temperaments. Another consideration is the structure of the students' environment. For example, crowded, noisy classrooms are not conducive to learning for a "difficult" child.

Teachers should be aware of problems associated with labelling students. While acknowledging that some students are harder to teach than others is often helpful, labelling students as "difficult" may become a self-fulfilling prophecy.

At this point, we have discussed a number of ideas about personality and temperament. A review of these ideas is presented in Summary Table 4.4.

Through the Eyes of Teachers

Learning to Play Together

Grades 7 through 9 are critical times for students in terms of developing a set of morals and a sense of social justice. I encourage my students to respect themselves and others, and I pay close attention to how I interact with them. Consistency and fairness are vital. I try to avoid bantering or joking with students, as they tend to interpret everything at a personal level. They never forget how you treat them. As a music teacher, I emphasize the need for harmony in both music and in life.

I remember one year when two would-be percussionists broke into a fistfight during class. They made it very clear that they did not want to work together or even be in the same room. I kept them after school to talk about music, something we all cared about. I challenged them to show me they could be skilled musicians by performing a difficult percussion duet. Over the course of several weeks, they met with me before and after school to practise their respective parts. During this time, they also learned how to relate to each other in a professional manner and were able to perform the duet as part of a spring concert. By then, they had developed a true friendship—one that exists to this day.

Kirk D. White
Intermediate-Level Music Teacher
Prince Edward Island

Everyone must form himself as a particular human being.

Johann Wolfgang von Goethe
German Poet, 19th Century

SUMMARY TABLE 4.4
Personality and Temperament

What is personality?	• Personality refers to distinctive thoughts, emotions, and behaviours that characterize the way an individual adapts to the world.
What are the "big five" personality factors?	• The "big five" provide teachers with a framework for thinking about students' personality characteristics. • These "big five" factors are emotional stability, extroversion, openness to experience, agreeableness, and conscientiousness.
What is temperament?	• Temperament refers to a person's behavioural style and characteristic way of responding.
What are the three basic temperament styles?	• The three basic temperament styles are "easy," "difficult," and "slow-to-warm-up." "Easy" students readily adapt to new experiences. "Difficult" students lack self-control and resist new experiences. "Slow-to-warm-up" students do not adapt readily and demonstrate low activity levels.

Mr. Kumar and his colleague Ms. Kaufman had just attended a workshop on adapting instruction to children's learning styles. Ms. Jacobson and her colleague Mr. Lee had just attended a workshop on adapting instruction to cover Gardner's nine intelligences, or frames of mind. The four met in the teachers' workroom and began to discuss what they had learned.

"Well," said Mr. Kumar, "this certainly explains why some students seem to want to sit and listen to me talk, while others like to be more actively involved. Maria obviously is an executive type; she likes lectures. Alexander, on the other hand, must be legislative. He just loves to work on projects and can't stand it when I tell him how to do things."

"No, I don't think so," Ms. Jacobson replied. "I think Maria's high in verbal intelligence. That's why she can make sense out of your lectures. She writes well, too. Alexander likes to do things with his hands. He's higher in spatial and bodily–kinesthetic intelligence."

"No, no, no," Mr. Kumar responded. "Learning styles explain their differences much better. Here, look at this."

At that point, Mr. Kumar showed Ms. Jacobson the handouts from the workshop he and Ms. Kaufman had attended. Mr. Lee took out the handouts from the workshop that he and Ms. Jacobson had attended. They began comparing notes. All four of them recognized students consistent with information described in the handouts.

Ms. Kaufman became visibly upset. "You mean they're telling us that we have to adapt our classrooms to the students' personalities now, too?!" she exclaimed. "Just when I thought I had it all figured out. Used to be we just had to consider IQ. Now this. We have 25 kids in our classes. How can we possibly adapt to all these differences? What are we supposed to do—have 25 different lesson plans?"

- What are the issues in this case?
- To what extent should teachers adapt their instruction to the strengths, learning styles, and personalities of their students? Why?
- What will you do in your classroom to accommodate individual differences such as students' intellectual strengths, learning styles, and personalities?
- What other individual differences might you be called upon to accommodate? How will you do this?

CHAPTER REVIEW

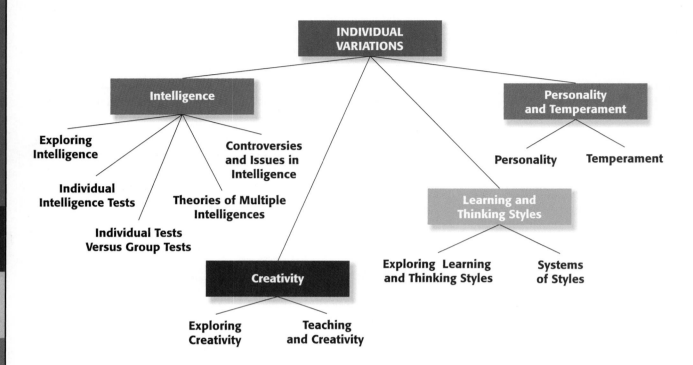

To obtain a detailed review of this chapter, study these four summary tables:

KEY TERMS

intelligence 102
individual differences 102
mental age (MA) 102
intelligence quotient (IQ) 102
normal distribution 103
triarchic theory of
     intelligence 105
culture-fair tests 111

between-class ability grouping
     (tracking) 113
within-class ability grouping 113
creativity 116
convergent thinking 116
divergent thinking 116
adaptive creativity 116
innovative creativity 116

learning and thinking styles 119
Sternberg System of Styles 120
Myers-Briggs Type Indicator
     121
Personal Empowerment through
     Type (P.E.T.) Inventory 122
personality 123
"big five" personality factors 123

person–situation interaction 124
temperament 125
easy child 125
difficult child 125
slow-to-warm-up child 125

PROFESSIONAL DEVELOPMENT/PORTFOLIO ACTIVITIES

1. When Students Say No

What do you do when students misbehave or just say no to you? Some teachers find that thinking through some strategies is a good way to prevent small classroom problems from becoming bigger problems. Consider the following scenario: While you are reading a story to the class, a student is intentionally defying your repeated requests to be quiet. How do you control your emotions in this situation? What will you do? Write down some different strategies that might work for you in these types of situations.

2. Community Creativity Resources

Conduct a brainstorming session with your colleagues to come up with a list of community resources that are most likely to stimulate students' creativity. Consider students at the kindergarten, elementary-school, intermediate-grade, and high-school levels. Discuss strategies for using each of these resources in the classroom.

3. A Response Scenario

You are generally a lighthearted and jovial teacher who uses humour to help spark and maintain student interest. In a lunchroom conversation with another teacher, it is suggested that your personality would not fit with the serious nature of teaching science and math. How would you respond? Write a short essay on the role of teaching style on student learning; include this essay in your portfolio.

INTERNET ACTIVITIES

1. Learning Styles and Multiple Intelligences

Visit the Online Learning Centre to link to personality profiles and learning-style instruments. Many sites allow you to take such intelligence profiles online and then provide you with interesting information similar to the multiple intelligences ideas of Howard Gardner. Try one of the online quizzes and see whether the results agree with your assessment of yourself. How would you classify your temperament? What are the implications of your personality traits in the classroom? What are the strengths and challenges that a teacher with these traits would have? What strategies do you see yourself using to accommodate students who may have frames of mind or preferences for learning that are different from your own?

2. Howard Gardner's Theory

How could you conduct a lesson about Howard Gardner's theory of multiple intelligences in your classroom? Why do you think it is important for students to be aware of this theory and its implications for education and society? How could you involve students in planning lessons and projects that utilize many learning styles?

Visit the *Educational Psychology* Online Learning Centre at
www.mcgrawhill.ca/college/santrock
to access Websites related to the above Internet Activities as well as chapter quizzes,
a searchable glossary, and other learning and study tools.

5 Sociocultural Diversity

Preview

Ours is a diverse, multicultural world that teems with a multitude of ethnic groups, customs, and values. Our sociocultural world also involves gender. How best to educate children from such diverse cultural backgrounds, as well as girls and boys, are topics of considerable interest today. These are some of the questions we will explore in this chapter:

- What is the best way to help impoverished children learn and cope?

- How can you help students respect and appreciate cultural and ethnic diversity?

- What controversies are involved in multicultural education?

- How extensive are ethnic and gender biases in schools? What can be done about these biases?

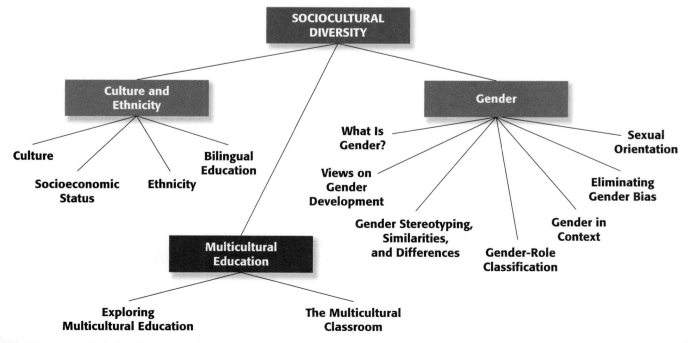

SOCIOCULTURAL DIVERSITY

Culture and Ethnicity
- Culture
- Socioeconomic Status
- Ethnicity
- Bilingual Education

Multicultural Education
- Exploring Multicultural Education
- The Multicultural Classroom

Gender
- What Is Gender?
- Views on Gender Development
- Gender Stereotyping, Similarities, and Differences
- Gender-Role Classification
- Gender in Context
- Eliminating Gender Bias
- Sexual Orientation

Teaching Stories: Mel Hurtig

Mel Hurtig is a Canadian political activist and author. In his 1999 text *Pay the Rent or Feed the Kids: The Tragedy and Disgrace of Poverty in Canada*, he explores the devastating effects of poverty on students, their families, and their teachers. In one poignant example, he describes the efforts of an elementary-grade student to help feed her younger siblings.

"...I could just barely see a little girl hiding under the stairs. Just then the noon bell went off. The little girl leapt to her feet, ran along the side of the building, disappeared into a door, quickly reappeared and motioned across the schoolyard. Immediately, two small children, a boy and a girl, maybe five and four years of age, came running across the yard. All three vanished into the school.

"The principal told me that the older girl, who was seven, was sneaking her younger brother and sister into the school's hot lunch program. She did this several times near the end of each month.

One of the new teachers noticed what was happening, and in a non-confrontational way, questioned the girl, who began to cry with shaking shoulders, deep sobs and tears rolling down her face. There was no father in the family. Their mother had been sick in bed for months. They always ran out of food before the end of the month. The utility bill had to be paid; if it wasn't child welfare would take the kids away from their mother. There was nothing in the house to eat."

Sadly, this story is not an uncommon one. The school's hot lunch program had become a lifeline for this family, much as similar programs have provided similar lifelines to countless other families. Hurtig argues that children from poor families suffer academically, socially, and emotionally. He calls upon all Canadians to become active in the fight against poverty.

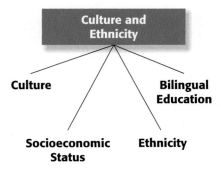

Culture and Ethnicity

Culture

Socioeconomic Status

Bilingual Education

Ethnicity

CULTURE AND ETHNICITY

Canadian researcher Daniel Yon states that race and identity are negotiated on a daily basis among culturally and ethnically diverse students (Yon, 2000). Historically, many ethnic people have found themselves at the bottom of Canada's economic and social order. They have been disproportionately represented among the poor and the inadequately educated (Ross, Scott, & Kelly, 1999). It is estimated that by 2016, visible minorities will comprise about 20 percent of the adult population and about 25 percent of the child population in Canada (Esses & Gardner, 1996); the percentage of individuals from minority backgrounds is expected to be even higher in urban centres such as Toronto, Vancouver, and Montreal. These demographic changes will challenge our understanding of the term "minority" and reconfirm the need to help students develop respect and tolerance for people from different cultural and ethnic backgrounds.

Culture

Culture *refers to the behaviour patterns, beliefs, and all other products of a particular group of people that are passed on from generation to generation.* These products result from the inter-actions among groups of people and their environments over many years (Thomas, 2000). A cultural group can be as large as Canada or as small as an isolated Inuit community. What-ever its size, the group's culture influences the behaviour of its members (Berry, 2000).

Psychologist Donald Campbell and his colleagues (Brewer & Campbell, 1976; Campbell & LeVine, 1968) found that people in all cultures tend to

- believe that what happens in their culture is "natural" and "correct" and what happens in other cultures is "unnatural" and "incorrect,"
- perceive their cultural customs as universally valid,
- behave in ways that favour their cultural group,
- feel proud of their cultural group, and
- feel hostile toward other cultural groups.

Psychologists and educators who study culture are often interested in comparing what happens in one culture with what happens in one or more other cultures. **Cross-cultural studies** *involve such comparisons, providing information about the degree to which people are similar and the degree to which certain behaviours are specific to certain cultures.*

Comparisons of North American students with Chinese, Japanese, and Taiwanese students revealed that North American students tended to go about their work more independently, whereas Asian students were more likely to work in groups (Stevenson, 1995). These differences in cultures have been described with two terms: individualism and collectivism (Triandis, 1997, 2000). **Individualism** *refers to a set of values that give priority to personal goals rather than to group goals.* Individualist values include feeling good, personal distinction, and independence. **Collectivism** *consists of a set of values that support the group. Personal goals are subordinated to preserve group integrity, interdependence of the group's members, and harmonious relationships.* Many Western cultures such as Canada, the United States, Great Britain, and the Netherlands are described as individualistic. Many Eastern cultures such as China, Japan, India, and Thailand are labelled collectivistic. Mexican culture also has stronger collectivistic characteristics than United States culture. However, Canada has many collectivistic subcultures, such as Native Canadian, Asian-Canadian and Caribbean-Canadian.

Many of psychology's basic concepts have developed in individualistic cultures such as those found in Canada and the United States. Consider the flurry of *self-* terms in psychology that have an individualistic focus: *self-actualization, self-esteem, self-concept, self-efficacy, self-reinforcement, self-criticism, self-serving bias, self-doubt,* and so on. These *self-* terms all were created by North American psychologists, leading some critics to argue that this type of psychology is strongly tilted toward individualistic rather than collectivist values (Lonner, 1990). Regardless of their cultural background, people need a positive sense of self and connectedness to others to develop fully as human beings.

Socioeconomic Status

Most countries have many subcultures. One of the most common ways of categorizing subcultures involves socio-economic status.

What Is Socioeconomic Status? Andrea and Brian come from families of differing socioeconomic status. What does this mean? **Socioeconomic status (SES)** *refers to the categorization of people according to their economic, educational, and occupational characteristics.* The most emphasis is given to distinctions between individuals of low and middle socio-economic status. Socioeconomic status carries certain inequities. Low-SES individuals often have less education, less power to influence a community's institutions (such as schools), and fewer economic resources.

Poverty Definitions of poverty differ around the globe. Gro Harlem Brundtland, a former prime minister of Norway, defined poverty as "…lack of opportunity, lack of freedom. It is hunger, malnutrition, disease and lack of basic social services. It is a policy failure that degrades people—those who suffer it and those who tolerate it" (Hurtig, 1999, p. 8).

Canada does not have an official baseline measure for poverty. Therefore, Canadian social agencies and organizations use a variety of standards when defining poverty and the poor in Canada (*Canadian Fact Book on Poverty*, 2000). The most widely accepted poverty standard is the "lower-income level" measure developed by Statistics Canada. However, Novic (2000) reported that this figure is often much higher than the annual income levels of poor families in Canada. In 1996, this measure set the poverty line at $25,668 for a family of three living in a large metropolitan city; Novic argued that a more realistic average annual family income to establish poverty is $16,700. Regardless of the figure used to establish poverty, this number cannot describe the conditions that Canada's poor endure on a daily basis.

Through the Eyes of Teachers

Providing Choices to Students from Low-Income Families

My school offers an innovative breakfast program. Specifically, the program is based on flexible hours where students are free to come and go before school begins and during the mid-morning recess. Hosting a flexible program encourages families to provide what they can, when they can, but also presents them with additional support in times of need. Food for the breakfast program is acquired through school fundraising projects and donations from local grocery stores and community organizations. Parent volunteers and teachers run the program cooperatively.

Every day, I remind my students that a nutritious breakfast makes for a good day. You can think better and learn better when you have food energy. When I notice that students are lethargic, I approach them privately, "Are you feeling okay? Did you have breakfast?" If students reply negatively, I suggest that they get a snack during recess. In my experience, I have found that when students have access to breakfast programs, they do better in school. At the end of each day, I take a moment to reflect on what I have done to help my students reach their full potential. I realize that without this breakfast program, that job would be more difficult.

Juliana Crysler
23-Year Elementary-School Teacher
Ontario

Who Are Individuals Living in Poverty in Canada? While specific measures of poverty vary across the country collectively, the data consistently indicate that there are millions of Canadians living in poverty. According to the 1996 Census Report, more than 5.2 million Canadian families, or 20.9 percent of the population, had an annual income below the lower-income level of $25,668 established by Statistics Canada for that year. The report notes that the Canadian groups most affected by poverty include Aboriginals (30 percent), visible minorities (27 percent), and people with disabilities (24 percent). Homeless people, seniors, and single unemployed men and women are also over-represented in poverty statistics. Overall, approximately 16 percent of Canadians live below the poverty line.

Women tend to be overrepresented in poverty statistics. Statistics Canada has consistently reported single-parent families as one of the poorest groups in Canada, with single mothers comprising about 55 percent of these single-parent families. Census information highlights that women, young or old, are 1.3 times more likely than men to be impoverished. According to Statistics Canada (1997), the poverty rate for single-parent mothers with children under the age of seven is about 65 percent. In other words, six out of ten Canadian families led by single mothers under the age of 25 live in poverty. Wilson and Steinman (2000) reported that women currently account for 51 to 58 percent of Canadians receiving emergency groceries from a food bank. Figure 5.1 illustrates the rising poverty rates for single mothers from 1971 to 1997.

FIGURE 5.1 **Poverty Rates for Single Women with Children, 1971–1997**

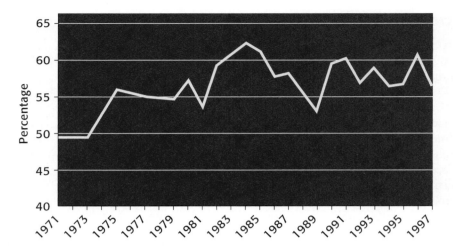

Source: Statistics Canada, "Poverty Rates for Single Women with Children 1971-1997," adapted from the Statistics Canada publication *The Daily*, Catalogue 11-001, 1997.

These data are especially poignant for Aboriginal children from large urban areas, where approximately 46 percent live in single-parent families (Statistics Canada, 1998). This statistic is only one disturbing aspect associated with child poverty. Children represent the most vulnerable group in Canadian society, and it is heart-rending to realize that approximately 16.5 percent of all Canadian children endure the harsh realities of being poor (Canadian Council on Social Development, 2001). These children face hunger and poor housing conditions, as well as limited academic, recreational, and social opportunities. Figure 5.2 provides national and provincial comparisons of child poverty.

What does it mean for children to be poor in Canada? Consider the following comments from students and their parents about what it means to be poor (Report Card 2000: Child Poverty in British Columbia; see **www.firstcallbc.org/publications/reportcard2000.pdf**).

- "Pretending that you forgot your lunch"
- "Being afraid to tell your mom that you need new gym shoes"

	Incidence (%)	Number (to the 1,000)
Canada	19.6	1,384
Newfoundland	23.3	30
Prince Edward Island	14.5	5
Nova Scotia	21.2	46
New Brunswick	20.2	34
Quebec	20.9	343
Ontario	19.8	537
Manitoba	21.5	58
Saskatchewan	18.6	48
Alberta	15.8	116
British Columbia	18.7	166

FIGURE 5.2 **Child Poverty in Canada**
Children under the age of 18 living in families whose total before-taxes income falls below the Statistics Canada lower-income cutoff.

Sources: Canadian Council on Social Development (1997); National Council of Welfare, 1999.

- "Being teased for the way you dress"
- "Not getting to go to birthday parties"
- "Not getting to go on school trips"
- "Feeling guilty that I cannot buy books at the school book club."
- "Swallowing your pride and asking for things for your children such as school clothes and other 'hand-me-downs' in order to get by."
- "Having to say NO to treats for the kids, to a regular haircut, and to buying new shoes or winter clothes."

The Consequences of Poverty   Increasingly, teachers in Canadian schools are being called upon to address the consequences of child poverty, including poor health, learning disabilities, and negative attitude. Low-income children are more likely to encounter hurdles to healthy development than children from middle-income families. According to the Canadian Council on Social Development (2001), low-income children are more likely to experience low birth weight; poor vision, speech, mobility, dexterity, and cognition; and emotional and physical pain. Moreover, children living in poverty are also less likely to live in safe neighbourhoods and are at a disproportionately higher risk for exposure to environmental contaminants. Figure 5.3 illustrates the relationship between household income and children's functional health.

Aboriginal families living on reservations endure some of the worst living conditions throughout the country. In 1992, it was estimated that only half of all on-reserve housing units were suitable for habitation, with 31 percent having neither potable water nor appropriate sanitation disposal systems (Ecumenical Coalition for Economic Justice, 1996). According to 1995 census records, three out of five Aboriginal children (60 percent) under six years of age live in poor families. The poverty rate for children in the general population during the same period was much lower, at one in four (25 percent).

While Aboriginals have made gains in education over time, they have experienced little advancement relative to other Canadians. In 1996, approximately 54 percent of Aboriginal people over the age of 15 had not completed high school, compared to 35 percent of the general population (Statistics Canada, 1998). The post-secondary education gap between Aboriginals and other Canadians is significant. In 1996, only 3.3 percent of Aboriginals held university degrees, compared to 13.5 percent of other Canadians (Statistics Canada, 1998). On a positive note, Aboriginals are more likely than other Canadians to return to school as adults. According to the 1996 census data, more than 12 percent of Aboriginals between 25 and 35 years of age were full-time students, compared to 6 percent of all other Canadians (Statistics Canada, 1998).

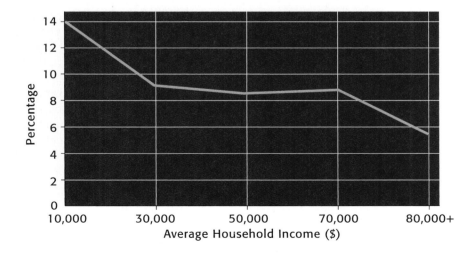

Source: Prepared by the Canadian Council on Social Development Using the National Longitudinal Survey of Children and Youth, 1994–95.

FIGURE 5.3   Household Income and Functional Health
Percentage of children (4–11 years) who experience lower functional health as related to average household income.

In summary, while Canada's economy has prospered conditions for Canada's poor have remained relatively dismal. While poor families may be making modest income gains, these are often insufficient with respect to the rising costs of education. For example, between 1992 and 1999 average family school expenditures for items like textbooks and tuition almost doubled (Canadian Council on Social Development, 2002). Wilson and Steinman (2000) suggests that for many working poor across Canada the choice is often between paying the rent or putting food on the table—educating their children is a secondary consideration after basic survival.

If your plan is for a year,
* plant rice.*
If your plan is for a decade,
* plant trees.*
If your plan is for a lifetime,
* educate children.*

                                    Confucius
        Chinese Philosopher, 6th Century B.C.

Educating Students from Low-SES Backgrounds   The schools that children from impoverished backgrounds attend often have fewer resources than the schools that students from higher-income neighbourhoods attend. These schools are more likely to have students with lower achievement test scores, graduation rates, and post-secondary attendance (Mustard et al., 1997; Ross, Scott, & Kelly, 1999; Ross & Roberts, 2000).

Student life in low-income areas also differs dramatically from that for students from more affluent areas. There are fewer co-curricular activities, clubs, or enrichment opportunities. These students often arrive at school hungry and inadequately dressed; few have adequate clothing for the Canadian winter. Many of these students suffer from severe emotional stress. They do not go on field trips, to hockey games, or to the movies. They do not have computers in their homes or places to go in the summer. Many rely on school lunch programs for daily meals (Hurtig, 1999), and live in areas where crime and violence are a way of life.

In a study reported by Statistics Canada 2002a, young people from disadvantaged homes in Ontario lagged behind their peers in basic literacy. According to Hurtig (1999), disadvantaged students score so poorly on standardized tests that they drag down the provincial rating to well below the national average. As a result, some affluent parents send their children to private schools and hire tutors, while less advantaged students are left to cope with bigger class sizes and fewer programs. Hurtig laments that this was not always the case with the Canadian educational system: "Children from low-income families were treated like other kids, they were encouraged to stay in school, they could afford to go to college or university without incurring massive debts" (Hurtig, 1999).

Unfortunately, family ability to pay for higher education is a key factor in how many teens continue with their education. Figure 5.4 illustrates how average household income correlates with teen employment and education. As family income increases, the percentage of teenagers (16–19 years of age) who are unemployed or not in school drops by 50 percent. These data suggest that disadvantaged families continue to be disadvantaged unless they are provided with educational and employment opportunities.

A number of community and school projects have been developed across Canada to address poverty and related issues. For example, Canadian Feed the Children's *Applecheck* program is a community initiative developed in partnership with the Apple Growers of Ontario. The program supplies fresh apples to school-based nutrition programs throughout the Greater Toronto Area. In 2000, more than 158,000 apples were distributed to 150 breakfast and snack programs across Toronto.

In Quebec, the Mathématique en famille/Math at Home program is an example of a school–family collaboration designed to promote children's mathematical skills in low-income school areas. The program trains parents to provide support for their children in learning mathematics through the use of games. Parents are provided with classroom materials as well as ideas and activities for linking learning to real-life situations. The Mathématique en famille/Math at Home program provides a venue for parents to help their children learn math skills and enjoy mathematics.

Children from low socioeconomic backgrounds often do not have access to technology relative to their peers from more affluent environments. The Programme for International Student Assessment (PISA) indicates that while 8 of every 10 Canadian students ages 15 to 17 use a computer/Internet at home nearly every day, students from low socioeconomic families are less likely to have access to computers/Internet at home. This is especially true for females. Gender disparities were negligible for students in high-socioeconomic-status

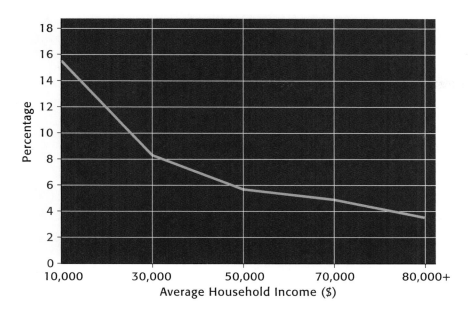

FIGURE 5.4   **Sixteen- to Nineteen-Year-Olds Not Employed and Not in School**
Percentage of teens (16–19 years of age) who are not employed or in school, as compared to average household income.

Note: Two-parent families with teens aged 16–19.
Source: Prepared by the Canadian Council on Social Development Using the Survey of Consumer Finances, 1996.

families. Corbett and Willms (2002) argue that universal access to the Internet is essential if computers are to become an effective learning tool. Two programs aimed at helping schools and students with computer and Internet access are the Computers for Schools Project and the Community Access Program. The first program recycles computers donated by government and business organizations for schools and families in low-income areas, and the second program provides low-cost public access to the Internet on evenings and weekends.

At this point we have studied a number of ideas about culture and socioeconomic status. A review of these ideas is presented in Summary Table 5.1. Next, we will explore ethnicity.

Ethnicity

Ethnicity *includes many characteristics of a person's background, including race, origin or ancestry, identity, language, and religion* (Statistics Canada, 2002b). Traditionally, the three primary determinants of ethnicity are ancestry, race, and identity. For the purposes of collecting information about the Canadian population, *race* refers to skin colour, *origin* or *ancestry* refers to the roots or ethnic background of a person, and *identity* refers to an individual's self-perception of his or her ethnic background.

It is important to remember that within any ethnic group there is a great deal of variability. What may initially appear to be similarities may actually represent substantial differences upon closer inspection. For instance, the term "Asian" is used to describe people from diverse nations including Japan, China, the Philippines, Korea, and Vietnam. Similarly, the term "Native Canadian" is often used to describe all Native people across Canada, including such diverse groups as the Dene, Inuit, Huron, Ottawa, and Métis. See the Diversity and Education box on page 140 to read about one program designed to promote students' tolerance and respect for those from culturally and ethnically diverse backgrounds.

Ethnicity and Schools   With the exception of Aboriginal children, recent statistics (Guppy & Davies, 1998) suggest that students from diverse ethnic backgrounds participate in school to the same extent as their "non-ethnic" peers. There are still concerns, however,

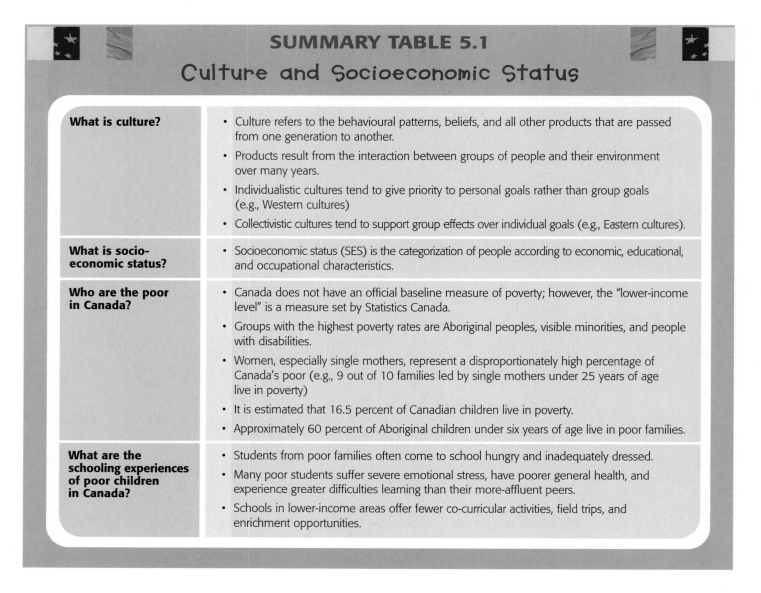

SUMMARY TABLE 5.1
Culture and Socioeconomic Status

What is culture?	• Culture refers to the behavioural patterns, beliefs, and all other products that are passed from one generation to another. • Products result from the interaction between groups of people and their environment over many years. • Individualistic cultures tend to give priority to personal goals rather than group goals (e.g., Western cultures) • Collectivistic cultures tend to support group effects over individual goals (e.g., Eastern cultures).
What is socio-economic status?	• Socioeconomic status (SES) is the categorization of people according to economic, educational, and occupational characteristics.
Who are the poor in Canada?	• Canada does not have an official baseline measure of poverty; however, the "lower-income level" is a measure set by Statistics Canada. • Groups with the highest poverty rates are Aboriginal peoples, visible minorities, and people with disabilities. • Women, especially single mothers, represent a disproportionately high percentage of Canada's poor (e.g., 9 out of 10 families led by single mothers under 25 years of age live in poverty) • It is estimated that 16.5 percent of Canadian children live in poverty. • Approximately 60 percent of Aboriginal children under six years of age live in poor families.
What are the schooling experiences of poor children in Canada?	• Students from poor families often come to school hungry and inadequately dressed. • Many poor students suffer severe emotional stress, have poorer general health, and experience greater difficulties learning than their more-affluent peers. • Schools in lower-income areas offer fewer co-curricular activities, field trips, and enrichment opportunities.

that for a variety of reasons participation in school might not be equal across all ethnic groups. For example, a Canadian study examined the type of challenges faced by educators teaching Aboriginal students in a large, urban school. Researchers concluded that most of the challenges were "task-related" rather than "person-related." Two issues were especially relevant: students' preparedness for school, and their ability to adjust to school structure. Students from different cultural backgrounds may learn in diverse ways, and educators need to understand and integrate these styles into their teaching methodologies. In addition, for some cultural or ethnic groups parental distrust of mainstream education may be a significant challenge. In general, the authors concluded that educators and administrators were not prepared to adequately meet the educational needs of students from diverse backgrounds (Danyluk & da Costa, 1999).

There is also a concern that the percentage of teachers who represent minority groups is not proportional to the student population (Danyluk, Ross, & da Costa, 1999). That is, there is a shortage of teacher role models for students from diverse cultural and ethnic backgrounds. Data culled from the 1996 Statistics Canada census report indicate that of the more than 240,000 government-certified teachers and counsellors in Canada, only

Teaching Strategies
For Working with Children in Poverty

✔ Work cooperatively with parents
  - avoid stereotyping
  - recognize that parents from poor communities can be talented, caring, and responsible individuals
  - provide support and training to parents who wish to be involved in their children's school experiences
  - honour volunteerism
✔ Provide a dynamic curriculum
  - make special efforts to motivate students and reinforce their learning attempts
  - emphasize effective thinking and problem-solving
  - recognize that parents hold different achievement standards for their children
  - recognize that parents differ in their ability to provide their children with academic supervision or assistance
✔ Avoid creating tension between students
  - promote school-based efforts to meet students' physical and safety needs and overall well-being
  - avoid favouring the products or performances of students who have greater opportunities and resources (e.g., dance lessons, sports, money for projects)
  - subsidize school trips and activities so that all students can participate
  - minimize fundraising activities
✔ Provide students with mentors
  - recognize that all students benefit from having mentors, especially those from low-income backgrounds
  - recruit appropriate mentors from within the community whenever possible
  - identify individuals in communities whose wisdom and experiences defy stereotypes—invite these individuals to participate in your classroom

21,835 were representative of diverse cultural groups. This number represents 5.57 percent of the total teaching and counselling population in Canada. At the same time, students from diverse cultures accounted for 17.1 percent of the total population of school-aged children (Moll, 2000).

Issues associated with ethnicity and education are complex. Ethnicity and culture play a part in how students view their own abilities and how they seek help with learning. For example, many immigrant or first-generation students do not ask for appropriate help because they do not know what they need, what to ask for, or how to go about asking for this help. Assisting these students to understand and feel part of the Canadian school system is an important first step in helping them learn.

A project by Ottawa's Broken English Theatre Company represents a community-based effort to help immigrant secondary-school students acclimatize to the Canadian school system. Project "FIT-IN?!" provides immigrant students with means for identifying and giving voice to issues that affect them in our multicultural society. Under the direction of professional drama educators, students create and perform dramatizations at schools throughout the community. Local presentations culminate in a "Multi-Colourful Festival"

Diversity and Education
The "Profiles of Canada" Project

An important goal of multicultural and equity education is to reduce prejudice. Teachers can use multimedia technologies and distance-learning technologies to combat prejudice by establishing learning exchanges among students from diverse cultural backgrounds (Anderson, 1998). Information and communication technology can also be used to promote positive self-concept and foster positive relationships among students. Video conferencing, audio-graphic conferencing, and electronic mail have all been used as tools for promoting intercultural exchanges and understanding. These technologies enable students from various countries and cultures to work together, exchange ideas, and build understanding and intergroup tolerance (Cifuentes & Murphy, 2000).

One popular forum for sharing information about multicultural communities is the Statistics Canada and SchoolNet Canada GrassRoots Program "Profiles of Canada." The Profiles of Canada project supports schools and students in using StatsCan data to develop portraits of different cultures and communities that contribute to the Canadian mosaic. An example of such a profile is the result of a collaboration between students from Templeton School and Vancouver Technical School in Vancouver, British Columbia. The project, "The Impact of Immigration on Vancouver," documents how the city developed at the turn of the century with a focus on the contributions of immigrants to neighbourhoods like Chinatown and Little Italy. The student-created Website, at **http://vantech.vsb.bc.ca/project**, includes photos of the neighbourhoods that they researched.

Throughout the project, students from both schools were provided with opportunities to celebrate their diversity. Consider the following reflection from one student at Vancouver Technical School:

> Our school is extremely multicultural, consisting of many ethnic groups. Everyone dresses pretty much alike, with the exception of a few who prefer to dress in their traditional clothing. Furthermore, most students interact with each other no matter what their ethnicity. Most people have learned to look beyond people's skin colour and get to know others before judging them. This is very wise, because we can actually learn a lot from each other without having to go to another country.

The Profiles of Canada project provides a rich resource for teachers looking to share cultural information and cultural experiences with their classes. Information about the Profiles of Canada project can be found at **www.statscan.ca/english/kits/grassroots/96.htm**.

held at the National Archives of Canada on the International Day for the Elimination of Racial Discrimination. Additional information about Project "FIT-IN?!" is available at **http://brokenenglishtheatre.com/Project.htm#fitin**.

Prejudice, Discrimination, and Bias   **Prejudice** *is defined as an unjustified negative attitude toward an individual based on her or his membership in a group.* The group toward which the prejudice is directed might be determined by ethnicity, sex, age, or virtually any other "difference" (Aboud, 1988; Monteith, 2000).

People who oppose prejudice and discrimination often have contrasting views about educational gains made to date. Some individuals value and praise the strides that have been made in reducing discrimination. Others criticize our schools and other institutions because they believe that many forms of discrimination and prejudice still exist (Murrell, 2000).

Some people view prejudice as a learned attitude. Children are not born with prejudicial notions. When and how do children acquire negative attitudes about others? It is often assumed that children acquire their negative attitudes by observing their parents and by interacting with peers who already possess such attitudes. Research carried out by Frances Aboud and her colleagues (Aboud, 1988; Aboud & Doyle, 1996) suggests that children as young as five can be prejudiced.

In an attempt to reduce prejudice among elementary-school students, Aboud and Doyle (1996) paired Montreal students in Grades 3 and 4 with a friend who possessed a higher level of racial tolerance. The students were then asked to discuss race. The attitudes of students who began the study with the highest levels of prejudice changed as a function of these discussions. Teachers played a large role in directing the discussion, encouraging students to find out more about a person in order to understand what he or she was really like. According to Aboud and Doyle, one of the cognitive abilities that is essential in reducing prejudice is the ability to reconcile different opinions or perspectives. Teachers can play a critical role in encouraging children to develop an accepting attitude and an ability to appreciate multiple perspectives by encouraging them to critique opposing perspectives on points of value, character, and reasoning rather than making judgments based on stereotypes, bias, or prejudice. Overall, the findings suggest that open, honest, and purposeful discussions about racial issues are necessary to foster changes in negative attitudes (Aboud, 1988).

Yet, teachers may not be cognizant of subtle forms of prejudice and bias that exist in their classrooms. Consequently, educators must strive to create a classroom atmosphere that is "inviting" (Novak, 2002). Teachers can easily misinterpret students' cultural mannerisms or behaviours. For example, one educator described gently forcing a Native student's head up while reprimanding him for inappropriate behaviour in the hallway. She misinterpreted the student's downward gaze as a sign of disrespect and disinterest, unaware that in the child's culture it was a sign of respect (Elliott et al., 2001). There are also cases where well-meaning teachers, acting out of a misguided sense of caring and tolerance, fail to challenge students from culturally diverse backgrounds to perform at their optimal capacity. Such teachers prematurely accept a low level of performance from these students, substituting warmth and affection for high academic standards (Spencer & Dornbusch, 1990).

Diversity and Differences   Historical, economic, and social experiences produce both prejudicial and legitimate differences between various ethnic groups. Individuals who live in a particular ethnic or cultural group adapt to the values, attitudes, and stresses of that culture. Their behaviour might be different from one's own, yet be functional for them. Recognizing and respecting these differences is an important aspect of getting along in a diverse, multicultural world (Spencer, 2000).

Unfortunately, the emphasis often placed on differences between visible minority groups and the cultural majority has been damaging to ethnic-minority individuals. For too long, virtually all differences were thought of as *deficits*, or inferior characteristics on the part of the ethnic minority group.

Another important dimension of every ethnic group is its diversity. Not only is Canadian culture diverse—so is every ethnic group within the Canadian culture. As we will see next, language is another factor in Canada's cultural diversity.

Bilingual Education

Canada has two official languages, English and French; English is the primary language for approximately three-quarters of the population. Most French speakers (francophones) live in Quebec, where they form the provincial majority. However, there are French minority groups in all parts of Canada, with the largest concentrations in New Brunswick, Ontario, and Manitoba. New Brunswick is Canada's only official bilingual province and has a very active and successful bilingual education program. This bilingual model has been implemented around the world in countries as such as China, Finland, and the United States. Parents, students, governments, and educators continue to recognize the value of knowing two or more languages.

An elementary-school English–Cantonese teacher instructing students in Chinese.

Bilingual education *is broadly defined as the use of two languages as a medium of instruction.* In Canada, bilingual education focuses primarily on English and French. Historically, this focus has been the result of an attempt to recognize Canadian society as an "ethnic mosaic." In the 1980s, the federal government adopted official policies for bilingualism (Official Languages Act, 1988) and multiculturalism (Canadian Multiculturalism Act, 1985).

The Canadian Charter of Rights and Freedoms (1982) legislates that public education will be available in both official languages where population numbers warrant. The primary objective of most bilingual education programs is to provide students with an opportunity to acquire a level of proficiency in the two official languages. In English-speaking Canada, schools implement these policies in one of two ways. The first is by making French mandatory until Grade 9; however, unless students are particularly capable and motivated it is difficult to become bilingual following such an approach. The second approach is through French immersion programs.

Immersion Programs While the intent of all immersion programs is to produce bilingual students, they differ in terms of entry and time spent in the program. There are three stages at which students can begin their immersion experience. *Early immersion,* which is the most popular route, usually begins at kindergarten. *Middle immersion* begins when students are in the intermediate grades, and *late immersion* begins at the secondary-school level. *Total immersion* programs start with 100-percent immersion in the second language with a gradual reduction after a few years. *Partial immersion* provides about 50-percent immersion in the second language, especially during the initial years.

In the 1980s, bilingual education became a provincial priority in New Brunswick and a wide variety of immersion programs were introduced. Today, the enrolment in these programs remains relatively high, with about 23 percent of the province's youth participating in immersion programs (versus about 5 percent of the student population across Canada) (Rehorick, 2001). As a result, there has been a marked increase in the number of New Brunswick's youth (15- to 19-year-olds) who can speak both official languages. While only 29.2 percent of youth spoke both languages in 1981, the percentage rose to 49.3 percent in 1996. Nationally, the percentage has risen from 17.7 percent to 24.2 percent (Rehorick, 2001).

Heritage Language Programs While only English and French have official-language status in the Canadian Constitution (BNA Act, 1867), Canada is home to many other ethnic groups representing a variety of languages. Including other languages as part of the school curriculum depends on the activism of individual ethnic groups, the resources available to them, and the motivation of the members of the community. The *heritage language program* is an example of one successful initiative. Participating in a heritage language program allows students to develop language skills (e.g., Italian, German, Ukranian, Urdu) and a sensitivity for the culture being studied. The goal is to encourage students to take pride in their own culture and promote respect for members of other cultures.

In general, students who study a second language perform as well academically as students who participate in single-language programs (Cummins, 1991; Cummins & Danesi, 1990). What is more difficult to assess, however, is the extent to which these students benefit from their encounters with different cultures and languages. In general, most Canadians value bilingualism and acknowledge the importance of bilingual education (Rossell & Baker, 1996).

At this point we have discussed many ideas about ethnicity and bilingual education. A review of these ideas is presented in Summary Table 5.2. Next, we continue our exploration of cultural and ethnic aspects of children's education by examining multicultural education.

SUMMARY TABLE 5.2
Ethnicity and Bilingual Education

What is ethnicity?	• Ethnicity includes characteristics of an individual's race, origin or ancestry, identity, language, and religion. • The most common means of determining ethnicity are race, ancestry, and identity. • Within any ethnic group there is a great deal of diversity.
What is the relationship between ethnicity and schools?	• School participation rates across ethnic groups have grown dramatically. • With the exception of Aboriginal children, recent statistics suggest that students from diverse ethnic backgrounds participate in school to the same extent as their "non-ethnic" peers. • Students from ethnically and culturally diverse cultures may learn in unique ways that educators need to understand and integrate into their curriculum. • Ethnically and culturally diverse students benefit from same-culture teacher role models. • There is a shortage of teachers representing diverse cultural and ethnic backgrounds.
How can teachers manage prejudice?	• Prejudice is an unjustified negative attitude toward an individual because of membership in a racial or cultural group. • Students can acquire negative attitudes toward other people by observing their parents and peers.
What is prejudice?	• Class discussions about race are necessary to foster changes in negative attitudes. • Teachers can help reduce prejudice by encouraging students to consider different perspectives, assisting them to reconcile different opinions, and leading class discussions about these issues.
What is ethnic diversity?	• Canadian culture includes a variety or diversity of cultural and ethnic groups. • The values and attitudes of different cultural and ethnic groups are the result of historical, economic, and social experiences. These can produce both legitimate and prejudicial differences between and among ethnic groups. • Differences between ethnic and cultural groups and the cultural norm are often viewed inaccurately as deficits.
What is bilingual education?	• Bilingual education is the use of two languages as a medium of instruction. • Canada has two official languages, English and French, which are the focus of bilingual education. • The Canadian Charter of Rights and Freedoms legislates that public education will be available in both official languages whenever feasible.
What are immersion programs?	• Immersion programs have the goal of producing bilingual students; programs differ in terms of entry and time spent in the program. • Early immersion begins at kindergarten. • Middle immersion begins in the intermediate grades. • Late immersion begins at the secondary-school level. • Total immersion starts with 100-percent immersion in the second language with a gradual reduction after a few years. • Partial immersion provides about 50-percent immersion in the second language, especially during the initial years.

> ### Teaching Strategies
> For Working with Linguistically and Culturally Diverse Children
>
> ✔ Demonstrate respect for students' first languages and cultures
>   - recognize that students are cognitively, linguistically, and emotionally connected to the languages and cultures in their homes
>   - learn at least a few words in students' first languages
>   - demonstrate some knowledge of students' first cultures
>   - collaborate with other teachers, parents, students, and community groups to learn more about linguistically and culturally diverse children
> ✔ Modify instruction and evaluation forms
>   - ensure that all students feel appreciated and valued
>   - recognize that second-language learning can be a difficult and lengthy process
>   - model appropriate use of English
>   - provide students with opportunities to use newly acquired vocabulary and language
>   - recognize that students who do not acquire second-language proficiency after two to three years may also experience difficulties in their first language
>   - recognize that reading and writing proficiency needed for understanding academic content may take up to four years to acquire
>   - acknowledge that students demonstrate their knowledge and skills in different ways
>   - provide linguistically independent opportunities for students to demonstrate their knowledge and skills
> ✔ Involve parents in the learning process
>   - encourage and assist parents in recognizing the value of knowing more than one language
>   - provide parents with strategies to support and maintain home-language learning
>   - recognize that students can acquire English even when a different language is used at home

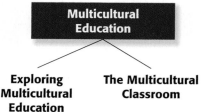

MULTICULTURAL EDUCATION

Canada's *Multiculturalism Act* (1985) proclaimed that it is the policy of the Government of Canada to facilitate the acquisition, retention, and use of all languages that contribute to the multicultural heritage of the nation. However, the goal of the Multiculturalism Act is more than language facilitation. Multicultural education is education that values diversity and includes the perspectives of a variety of cultural groups on a regular basis. Multicultural education in Canada has three primary objectives: to build personal and collective confidence among members of all ethnic groups, to promote tolerance and positive intergroup attitudes, and to support the absence of prejudice toward ethnic minorities (Berry, 1984; Berry & Laponce, 1994; Weinfeld, 1994). This mandate requires a multidisciplinary approach to curriculum development and program delivery where "multicultural literacy" becomes an essential goal in the educational process.

Exploring Multicultural Education

Empowering Students The term **empowerment** *refers to providing people with the intellectual and coping skills to succeed and make this a more just world.* In the 1960s to

1980s, multicultural education was concerned with empowering students and better representing minority and cultural groups in curricula and textbooks. Empowerment continues to be an important theme of multicultural education today. In this view, schools should give students the opportunity to learn about the experiences, struggles, and visions of many different ethnic and cultural groups. The hope is that this will raise minority students' self-esteem, reduce prejudice, and provide more-equal educational opportunities. The hope also is that it will help all students become more tolerant of those who differ from themselves.

Nieto (1992) and Kanu (2002) provide the following recommendations:

- *The school curriculum should be openly antiracist and antidiscriminatory.* Students should feel free to discuss issues of ethnicity and discrimination.
- *Multicultural education should be a part of every student's education.* This includes having all students study different cultural perspectives. Multicultural education should be reflected everywhere in the school, including bulletin boards, lunch rooms, and assemblies.
- *Students should be trained to be more conscious of culture.* This involves assisting students to be more skilful at analyzing culture and more aware of the historical, political, and social factors that shape their views of culture and ethnicity. The hope is that such critical examination will motivate students to work for political and economic justice.

The Multicultural Classroom

A number of strategies and programs are available to improve relations among children from different ethnic groups. To begin, we will discuss one of the most powerful strategies.

The Jigsaw Classroom Aronson (1986) developed the concept of the **jigsaw classroom**, *which involves having students from different cultural backgrounds cooperate by doing different parts of a project to reach a common goal.* Aronson used the term *jigsaw* because he saw the technique as much like a group of students cooperating to put different pieces together to complete a jigsaw puzzle.

How might this work? Consider a class of students from a variety of ethnic backgrounds. The lesson concerns the discovery of insulin by Banting and Best. The class might be broken up into groups of six students each, with the groups being as equally mixed as possible in terms of ethnic composition and achievement level. The lesson about the discovery is divided into six parts, and one part is assigned to each member of each six-person group. All students in each group are given an allotted time to study their parts. Then the groups meet, and each member works to teach her or his part to the group. Learning depends on the students' interdependence and cooperation in reaching the same goal. We will further discuss cooperative learning in Chapter 9.

Sometimes the jigsaw classroom strategy is described as creating a superordinate goal or common task for students. Team sports, drama productions, and music performances are additional examples of contexts in which students cooperatively and often very enthusiastically participate to reach a superordinate goal.

Positive Personal Contact with Others from Different Cultural Backgrounds
Contact by itself does not do the job of improving relationships. For example, in the United States, busing ethnic minority students to predominantly white schools or vice versa has not reduced prejudice or improved interethnic relations (Aboud, 1988). What matters is what happens after students arrive at a school.

Relations improve when students talk with each other about their personal worries, successes, failures, coping strategies, interests, and so on. When students reveal personal information about themselves, they are more likely to be perceived as individuals than simply as members of a group. Sharing personal information frequently produces this discovery: People from different backgrounds share many of the same hopes, worries, and feelings. Sharing personal information can help break down in-group/out-group and we/they barriers (Aboud & Doyle, 1996).

Positive personal contact that involves sharing doubts, hopes, ambitions, and much more is one way to improve interethnic relations.

Technology Connections with Students around the World

Traditionally, classroom instruction consisted of students interacting with their teachers and peers in the classroom. With advances in information and communication technologies, students now can learn with others from around the world. Two programs that use communications technology to connect students from diverse cultures and languages are the European Schools Project's *Teletrip*, and iEARN-Canada's *I Have a Dream*.

Teletrip

The European Schools Project's "Teletrip" program supports students' learning by combining local educational interests with international peer collaboration. The project provides teachers and students with opportunities to participate in Internet-based, cooperative learning activities aimed at improving teaching, learning, and cultural understanding and cooperation. Teletrip started at the University of Amsterdam, where various European and international groups partnered to devise cultural and curriculum learning activities. Teletrips are collaborative distance learning projects designed by teachers from participating countries to address topics of mutual interest such as pollution, tourism, energy, and the environment. Teletrips encourage students to engage in research at the local level and to communicate their findings to pupils in partner schools around the world using a foreign language and electronic communication system. Information about Teletrip can be found at **www.esp.uva.nl**.

I Have a Dream

The iEARN-Canada "I Have a Dream" project is an online showcase of students' essays, poems, drawings, and multimedia presentations about peace in the new millennium. The project, which started in 2000, hopes to establish a "Web of Peace" using Martin Luther King Jr.'s words as a starting point for reflection. The project designers aspire to encourage tolerance, understanding, and respect for others regardless of their race, gender, colour, or religion. iEARN-Canada is an affiliate of the International Education and Resource Network (iEARN), a nonprofit, global telecommunications community of more than 5,000 primary schools, secondary schools, and youth organizations in more than 95 countries. The online community supports students and teachers across the world in their attempt to contribute to peaceful cooperation among people. Information about the I Have a Dream project and other iEARN educational initiatives can be found at **www.iearn-canada.org**.

Perspective-Taking Exercises and activities that help students consider other people's perspectives can improve interethnic relations. For example, students can be encouraged to write stories or act out plays that involve prejudice or discrimination. In this way, students "step into the shoes" of students who are culturally different from themselves and feel what it is like to not be treated as an equal (Cushner, McClelland, & Safford, 1996).

In language arts, students can study familiar stories and be asked to take the perspective of different characters. A retelling of the familiar story "Little Red Riding Hood" from the perspective of the wolf is *The Maligned Wolf* (Fearn, 1972). As students read the story, they become aware of biases against various groups, such as wolves, and the perspectives of different characters within the same story. Students also can be asked to rewrite the story from the perspectives of other characters, such as the grandmother. They also can be asked to retell other stories from different points of view, such as the story of "Cinderella" from the stepmother's view (Prutzman & Johnson, 1997).

Studying people from different parts of the world also encourages students to understand different perspectives (Mazurek, Winzer, & Majorek, 2000). In social studies, students can be asked why people in certain cultures have customs different from their own. Teachers can also encourage students to read books on many different cultures.

An increasing number of Internet Websites allow students to communicate with students in other parts of Canada and around the world. Among these projects are the European Schools Project's "Teletrip" and the iEARN-Canada "I Have a Dream" Project. (For additional information about these programs, see the Technology and Education box.)

Critical Thinking and Emotional Intelligence Students who learn to think deeply and critically about interethnic relations are likely to decrease their prejudice and stereotyping of others (Aboud & Doyle, 1996). Students who think in narrow ways are often prejudiced. However, when students learn to ask questions, think first about issues rather than respond automatically, and delay judgment until more complete information is available, they become less prejudiced.

Emotional intelligence benefits interethnic relations. Recall from Chapter 3 that being emotionally intelligent means having emotional self-awareness, managing your emotions, reading emotions, and handling relationships. Consider how the following emotionally intelligent skills can help students to improve their relations with diverse others: understanding the causes of one's feelings, being good at managing one's own anger, being good at listening to what other people are saying, and being motivated to share and cooperate.

Promoting Awareness and Tolerance   One goal of multicultural education is to encourage the development of "multicultural citizenship." The multicultural citizen is inclusive, celebrates diversity, and promotes ethnic tolerance and mutual respect. The following are some general teaching strategies that teachers can use in their classrooms:

- Create a multicultural classroom environment by displaying images of children from various ethnic and cultural groups. The books you select for students also should reflect this diversity.
- Select play materials, art materials, and classroom activities that encourage ethnic and cultural understanding. Use dramatic play to illustrate nonstereotypical roles and families from diverse backgrounds.
- Use "persona" dolls. The 16 dolls represent diverse ethnic and cultural backgrounds. Each doll is given a life story designed to reduce bias.

Teaching Strategies
For Multicultural Education

✔ Learn about distinct cultural and ethnic groups
  - acquire information about the cultural and ethnic backgrounds of your students
  - seek out resources from relevant cultural and ethnic community centres
✔ Provide a culturally and ethnically diverse curriculum
  - support students' attempts to study concepts such as similarities, differences, prejudice, and discrimination
  - provide curriculum that is sensitive to students' developmental needs (e.g., racism and oppression may be developmentally inappropriate concepts for students in the primary grades)
  - use trade books, films, videotapes, and recordings that present cultural and ethnic perspectives
  - recognize racist content
✔ Be sensitive to students' cultural and ethnic backgrounds
  - view students positively regardless of their ethnicity
  - remember that students learn best when teachers hold high achievement expectations
  - reinforce students' learning attempts
  - respond to students' ethnic attitudes sensitively
  - do not accept the belief that children "do not see colour"
✔ Be sensitive to parents' cultural and ethnic backgrounds
  - recognize that most parents, regardless of their ethnicity or cultural background, are interested in their children's education and want them to succeed
  - recognize that parents from diverse cultural and ethnic backgrounds may have mixed emotions and beliefs about education based on their personal experiences
  - view all parents as equal partners and assist them in becoming involved in their children's education
  - encourage parents from diverse cultural and ethnic backgrounds to participate in the classroom and/or school

www.mcgrawhill.ca/college/santrock

- Help students resist stereotyping and discriminating against others. Make it a firm rule that no aspect of a child's or an adult's identity is an acceptable target of teasing or exclusion.
- Participate in consciousness-raising activities to better understand your cultural views and address any stereotypes or biases you might have.
- Establish genuine parent–teacher dialogue that opens up discussion of each other's views; exchange information on how children develop prejudices; and share information on how to increase tolerance.

Building Caring School Environments   Canadian teachers are increasingly concerned about the rise of violent confrontations and intolerance among students from different cultural backgrounds. One approach that may be helpful in addressing this issue is to create safer, more caring school environments and teach tolerance and cooperation as part of the school curriculum.

According to Marquardt (2001), reducing violence toward students from culturally diverse groups can be addressed through teaching conflict-resolution skills. Marquardt points to a variety of programs across the provinces that help schools create caring and safer environments. For example, in Nova Scotia the League of Peaceful Schools has developed a peer-mediation program for nonviolent conflict resolution. In Alberta, the provincial government has implemented the Safe and Caring Schools (SACS) initiative to promote safe and caring learning and teaching environments. The Ontario Human Rights Commission developed "Teaching Human Rights in Ontario" (THRIO, 2001) as an educational package for teachers to use when helping students learn about the provisions of the Ontario Human Rights Code and the work of the Commission.

In Chapter 12, a number of conflict-resolution programs are described. For instance, the Pacific Path is a comprehensive conflict-resolution and peer-mediation program developed in Montreal and is available for elementary- and secondary-school students in both French and English (Vadeboncoeur, Rondeau, & Begin, 2001).

At this point, we have studied many ideas about multicultural education. Following are some teaching strategies for facilitating multicultural education in the classroom. A review of the ideas covered in this section is presented in Summary Table 5.3. We will now turn our attention to an examination of gender issues associated with teaching and learning.

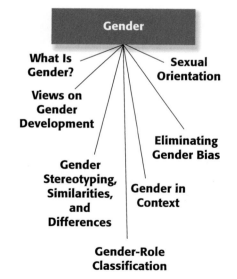

GENDER

A well-known nineteenth-century nursery rhyme by J. O. Halliwell goes like this:

What are little boys made of?
  Frogs and snails and puppy dogs' tails.
What are little girls made of?
  Sugar and spice and all that's nice.

What differences does the rhyme imply exist between boys and girls? Are any of them valid? Issues of real and perceived gender differences can be vital to effective teaching.

What Is Gender?

Gender *refers to the sociocultural dimensions of being female or male.* Gender is distinguished from **sex**, *which involves the biological dimensions of being female or male.* **Gender roles** *are the social expectations that prescribe how males and females should think, act, and feel.*

Views on Gender Development

There are various ways to view gender development. Some stress biological factors in the behaviour of males and females, others emphasize social influences, others emphasize cognitive factors.

SUMMARY TABLE 5.3
Multicultural Education

What is the goal of the Canadian Multiculturalism Act (1985)?	• The Canadian Multiculturalism Act (1985) aims to foster mutual respect and equitable participation in society for Canadians of all races, creeds, and colours. • It also promotes the acquisition, retention, and use of all languages that contribute to the multicultural heritage of Canada.
What is multicultural education?	• Multicultural education is a multidisciplinary approach to curriculum development and program delivery that focuses on "multicultural literacy" as an essential learning goal. • Multicultural education values diversity and includes the perspectives of various cultural groups.
What is empowerment?	• Empowerment is defined as providing people with the intellectual and societal skills needed to succeed. • In multicultural education, empowerment develops as students learn about the experiences, struggles, and visions of various ethnic and cultural groups.
What is a jigsaw classroom?	• The jigsaw classroom involves having students from different cultural backgrounds cooperate in doing different parts of a project to reach a common or superordinate goal.
How can multiculturalism be promoted in the classroom?	• Encourage the development of "multicultural citizenship," which celebrates diversity, promotes ethnic tolerance, and encourages mutual respect. • Encourage the sharing of personal worries, successes, failures, and coping strategies. • Provide students with opportunities to participate in perspective-taking exercises. • Promote critical thinking and emotional intelligence (e.g., understanding the causes of feelings, managing anger, listening to others, and being willing to communicate).

Biological Views In humans the 23rd pair of chromosomes (the sex chromosomes) determine whether a fetus is a female (XX) or a male (XY). No one denies the presence of genetic, biochemical, and anatomical differences between the sexes. Even gender experts with a strong environmental orientation acknowledge that girls and boys are treated differently because of their physical differences and their different roles in reproduction. What is at issue is the directness or indirectness of biological and environmental influences. For example, androgen is the predominant sex hormone in males. If a high androgen level directly influences brain functioning, which in turn increases some behaviour like aggression or activity level, then the biological effect is direct. If a child's high androgen level produces strong muscle development, which in turn causes others to expect the child to be a good athlete and, in turn, leads the child to participate in sports, then the biological effect on behaviour is more indirect.

Some biological approaches address differences in the brains of females and males (Eisenberg, Martin, & Fabes, 1996). One approach focuses on differences between females and males in the corpus callosum, the massive band of fibres that connects the brain's two hemispheres. Other approaches emphasize variations in the left and right hemispheres of the brains of males and females. At present, these are controversial views. What we do know is that the brains of females and males are far more similar than they are different. We also know that the brain has considerable plasticity and that experiences can modify its growth.

In sum, biology is not destiny when gender attitudes and behaviour are at issue. Children's socialization experiences matter a great deal.

Socialization Views The **social-learning theory of gender** *emphasizes that children's gender development occurs through observation and imitation of gender behaviour, as well as through reinforcement and punishment of gender behaviour* (Bassey & Bandura, 1999). Parents often use rewards and punishments to teach their daughters to be feminine ("Karen, you are being a good girl when you play gently with your doll") and masculine ("Keith, a big boy like you is not supposed to cry").

Many parents encourage boys and girls to engage in different types of play and activities. Girls are more likely to be given dolls and, when old enough, are more likely to be assigned babysitting duties. Girls are encouraged to be more nurturing than boys. Fathers are more likely to engage in aggressive play with their sons than with their daughters. Parents allow their adolescent sons to have more freedom than their adolescent daughters.

Peers also extensively reward and punish gender-related behaviour. Gender roles begin to be defined in toddlerhood and become associated with specific tasks early in the preschool years (Durkin & Nugent, 1998). In elementary school, boys usually hang out with boys and girls with girls. It is easier for "tomboy" girls to join boys' groups than for "feminine" boys to join girls' groups, because of our society's greater sex-typing pressure on boys. Developmental psychologist Eleanor Maccoby (1997), who has studied gender for a number of decades, believes that peers play an especially important gender-socializing role, teaching each other what is acceptable and unacceptable gender behaviour.

Imms (2000) offers a pluralistic interpretation of how boys construct and interpret their understanding of what it means to be male. Imms contends that the concept of multiple masculinities is the most realistic gauge for describing or analyzing the behaviour of boys in school. The concept of multiple masculinities runs counter to the generalized sex-role theory, which states that there is a common or all-encompassing definition of what it means to be male. The concept of multiple masculinities adopts this flexible view of masculinity and suggests that there are no absolute "manly" qualities that all males must possess. Hence, boys do not adopt predetermined gender roles as they mature, nor do they construct in isolation their versions of what it means to be male. According to the multiple masculinities approach, boys construct their gender identities and ideas based on a variety of culturally derived beliefs and ongoing interactions with others.

Television and increasingly the Internet play a gender-socializing role, portraying females and males in particular gender roles. Even with the onset of more diverse programming in recent years, researchers still find that television, radio, print, and other media such as the Internet present males and females in stereotypical or exaggerated gendered roles (Thompson & Zerbinos, 1997; Sobieraj, 1996). In one analysis of rap videos on TV, teenage girls were primarily shown as concerned with dating, shopping, and their appearance (Signonelli, 1997). They were rarely depicted as interested in school or career plans. Attractive girls were mainly pictured as "airheads," and unattractive girls as intelligent.

Weinman and Haag (1999) observed that in some cases computer-based materials for classroom use not only reinforced gender stereotypes but also exacerbated gender-based imbalances. After analyzing a representative sample of mathematics software games and simulations used in elementary schools, they found that 40 percent of the software had characters that were identifiable as male or female, but that only 12 percent of these characters were female. Moreover, the female characters were consistently depicted in the passive stereotypical roles of mother or princess.

Through the Eyes of Teachers

Gender Socialization

The classroom is a micro-society where interactions between and among students and teachers are gendered in terms of cultural norms and attitudes about how girls and boys should behave and how they should be taught. Teacher language and behaviour can play a large part in creating and reinforcing gender stereotypes, and teachers need to reflect on their practices regularly. For instance, I have stopped using the phrase "boys and girls" in favour of more neutral phrases like "grade-fours" or "class" when addressing my students. When I ask my students to line up, it is either by saying "grade-fours line up please" or by picking students randomly. In these simple ways, I am hoping to minimize gender stereotypes. I believe that teachers should encourage students to behave in manners that are school-appropriate, not gender-specific.

Liz McAnanama
Elementary-School Teacher
New Brunswick

Schools and teachers also have gender-socializing influences on boys and girls. We will discuss these influences later in the chapter.

Cognitive Views Two cognitive views on gender are (1) cognitive developmental theory and (2) gender schema theory (Martin, Ruble, & Szkrybalo, 2002). According to the **cognitive developmental theory of gender**, *children's gender typing occurs after they have developed a concept of gender.* Once they consistently conceive of themselves as female or male, children organize their world on the basis of gender. Initially developed by Lawrence Kohlberg (1966), this theory argues that gender development proceeds this way: "I am a girl. I want to do girl things. Therefore, the opportunity to do girl things is rewarding." Kohlberg believes that it is not until children reach Piaget's concrete operational stage of thinking at about six or seven years of age that they understand gender constancy—that a male is still a male regardless of whether he wears pants or a skirt or whether his hair is long or short (Kohlberg, 1966).

Gender schema theory *states that an individual's attention and behaviour are guided by an internal motivation to conform to gender-based sociocultural standards and stereotypes.* A gender schema is a cognitive structure, or network of associations, that organizes and guides an individual's perceptions along gender lines. Gender schema theory suggests that "gender-typing" occurs when children are ready to encode and organize information along the lines of what is considered appropriate or typical for females and males in a society (Rodgers, 2000).

At this point we have discussed a number of ideas about what gender is and views on gender development. A review of these ideas is presented in Summary Table 5.4. Next, we will continue our exploration of gender, starting with gender stereotyping, similarities, and differences.

Gender Stereotyping, Similarities, and Differences

How pervasive is gender stereotyping? What are the real differences between boys and girls?

Gender Stereotyping **Gender stereotypes** *are broad categories that reflect impressions and beliefs about what behaviour is appropriate for females and males.* All stereotypes, whether they relate to gender, ethnicity, or other categories, refer to an image of what the typical member of a category is like. Many stereotypes are so general they are ambiguous. Consider the categories of "masculine" and "feminine." Diverse behaviours can be assigned to each category, such as scoring a touchdown or growing facial hair for "masculine," playing with dolls or wearing lipstick for "feminine." And the behaviours that make up a category can be modified in the face of cultural change. At one point in history, muscular development might be thought of as masculine, at another time a more lithe, slender physique might be the quintessential masculine body. Earlier in the twentieth century, being dependent was thought to be an important dimension of femininity, whereas today a much greater emphasis is placed on females' sensitivity to others in relationships. Which behaviours are popularly held also can fluctuate according to socioeconomic circumstances. For example, more low-income than middle-class individuals have a rough-and-tough image of masculinity.

Gender stereotyping changes developmentally. Stereotypical gender beliefs begin to take root during the early childhood years, increase in the early elementary-school years, and then decline somewhat in the middle and late elementary-school years (Conger & Galambos, 1997; Galambos & Leadbeater, 2000). In early adolescence, gender stereotyping might increase again. As their bodies change dramatically during puberty, boys and girls are often confused and concerned about what is happening to them. The safest strategy for boys is to become the very best male possible (i.e., "masculine"), and the safest strategy for girls is to become the very best female possible (i.e., "feminine"). Thus, gender intensification created by pubertal change can produce greater stereotyping in young adolescents (Galambos et al., 1985).

Stereotypes are often negative and can be wrapped in prejudice and discrimination. **Sexism** *is prejudice and discrimination against an individual because of the person's sex.* A

We know of no culture that has said, articulately, that there is no difference between men and women except in the way they contribute to the creation of the next generation.

Margaret Mead
American Anthropologist and Author, 20th Century

www.mcgrawhill.ca/college/santrock

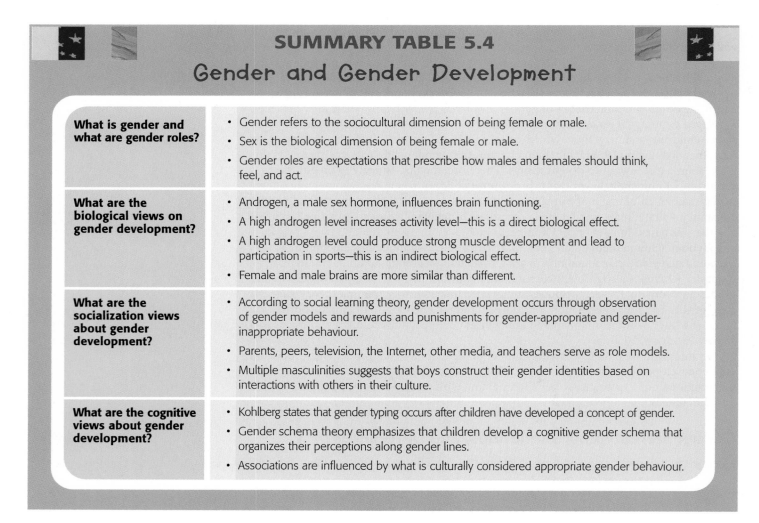

SUMMARY TABLE 5.4

Gender and Gender Development

What is gender and what are gender roles?	• Gender refers to the sociocultural dimension of being female or male. • Sex is the biological dimension of being female or male. • Gender roles are expectations that prescribe how males and females should think, feel, and act.
What are the biological views on gender development?	• Androgen, a male sex hormone, influences brain functioning. • A high androgen level increases activity level—this is a direct biological effect. • A high androgen level could produce strong muscle development and lead to participation in sports—this is an indirect biological effect. • Female and male brains are more similar than different.
What are the socialization views about gender development?	• According to social learning theory, gender development occurs through observation of gender models and rewards and punishments for gender-appropriate and gender-inappropriate behaviour. • Parents, peers, television, the Internet, other media, and teachers serve as role models. • Multiple masculinities suggests that boys construct their gender identities based on interactions with others in their culture.
What are the cognitive views about gender development?	• Kohlberg states that gender typing occurs after children have developed a concept of gender. • Gender schema theory emphasizes that children develop a cognitive gender schema that organizes their perceptions along gender lines. • Associations are influenced by what is culturally considered appropriate gender behaviour.

High quality sport and recreation programs...could significantly reduce the incidence of behaviour and emotional disorders in children and youth.

Dan Offord
Canadian Psychiatrist and Researcher,
Contemporary

person who says that a woman cannot be a competent engineer is expressing sexism. So is a person who says that a man cannot be a competent early-childhood teacher. Later in this chapter, when we discuss gender in the schools, we will describe some strategies for creating a nonsexist classroom.

Exploring Gender Similarities and Differences in Academically Relevant Domains
Many aspects of students' lives can be examined to determine similarities and differences between boys and girls (Crawford & Unger, 2000). In the following sections, we will look at physical performance, academic performance, and social skills.

Physical Activity Because physical education is an integral part of our educational system, it is important to address gender similarities and differences in physical performance (Eisenberg, Martin, & Fabes, 1996). In general, boys outperform girls in athletic skills such as running, throwing, and jumping. According to the Canadian Fitness and Lifestyle Research Institute (CFLRI Report, 1996), girls and boys in the elementary grades spend equal amounts of time per week on physical activities. However, participation rates in physical activities differ dramatically for girls and boys during adolescence (13 to 17 years of age). Teenage boys spend 40 percent more time (up to five hours more per week) in physical activity than teenage girls. Moreover, the types of activities that boys engage in during these years tend to be of higher physical intensity than those that girls select. For example, the CFLRI report indicates that adolescent boys tend to select basketball, running, and baseball as favourite activities, while girls opt for biking, swimming, walking, and

social dancing. The stereotyping of certain activities along gender lines plays a role in shaping participation rates and attitudes toward what activities are appropriate for boys and girls (CFLRI, 1996).

Most schools in Canada have teams and activities available for both boys and girls. Despite evidence that girls are interested and participate in sports activities, schools need to continue to encourage girls to participate in sports. The Canadian Fitness and Lifestyle Institute's Physical Activity Monitor (2000) reports that there is still a need for daily physical education programs for all students in Canadian schools, but especially for young girls between the ages of 12 and 19. According to Statistics Canada's National Population Health Survey (1999), only 36 percent of female youths between 12 and 19 years of age are physically active. In an attempt to improve the participation rates of girls in athletic activities, the Canadian Association for the Advancement of Women and Sport and Physical Activity suggests that schools encourage girls to participate in sports by providing a wide range of activity choices. These options should emphasize participation over skill, provide female-only gym time, and ensure that there is equity in school sports posters, photographs, award systems, and assemblies.

As reflected in this tug-of-war battle between boys and girls, the playground in elementary school is like going to "gender school." Elementary-school children show a clear preference for being with and liking same-sex peers. Eleanor Maccoby has studied children's gender development for many years. She believes peers play especially strong roles in socializing each other about gender roles.

Math and Science   Even though the literature on gender differences in academic achievement is extensive, researchers disagree on a few key issues. For example, it was traditionally thought that girls did not perform as well as boys in a variety of academic areas, especially in math and science (Eisenberg, Martin, & Fabes, 1996). These traditional notions have recently been challenged. For example, Ross (2000) states that gender differences in mathematical performance consistently favour females when course-taking opportunities are kept constant. However, while Ross notes that this is a switch from achievement patterns that existed only a decade ago, he points out that boys tend to outperform girls in some mathematical areas that rely on risk-taking. Ross suggests that boys may be more likely to invent mathematical procedures rather than accept algorithms provided for them by teachers, and this tendency provides them with some advantages in certain mathematical areas.

Other research suggests that gender differences in mathematics and science abilities are minimal (Brussiere et al., 2001; Ma, 1999) and decline over time (Nowell & Hedges, 1998). These minimal differences between boys and girls in mathematics and science may be attributable to a variety of other factors including teacher gender-based interactions (Battista, 1990), parental expectations (Ramos & Sanchez, 1995), and school programs and educational policies (Durost, 1996). Ross (2000) suggests that some of the differences between boys and girls in these subject areas might be explained by classroom behaviours, such as boys' tendencies to dominate whole-class discussions.

"So according to the stereotype, you can put two and two together, but I can read the handwriting on the wall."

Teachers need to be aware of their integral role in encouraging academic achievement in all of their students. Ross (2000) argues that if teachers want to overcome learning issues associated with culture, socioeconomic status, and gender in math and science they will need to teach students how to work together. He suggests that students should be placed in mixed ability, culture, and gender groups that increase their chances of working together and sharing ideas. Group members should be required to generate multiple solutions to solving problems, explicitly describe their strategies, and defend their solutions. These cooperative groups should also be carefully balanced to reduce socially isolating conditions. (See Chapter 9 for additional information about using cooperative learning groups in the classroom.)

Reading and Writing   Gender differences found in other academic areas, such as reading, may also be the result of a variety of compounding factors. The Program for International Student Assessment (Brussiere et al., 2001) is an international survey designed to assess the knowledge and skills of 15-year-olds in reading, mathematics, and science. The most recent survey reported that in all countries, including Canada, girls performed significantly better than boys in reading and writing. The report suggests that girls tend to possess attitudes that contribute to success in reading and writing, including an enjoyment of reading, seeing value in schooling, and more focused career and education expectations. These characteristics, which are correlated with reading and writing success, do not seem to be as valued or as readily discernable in boys.

Some gender researchers believe that gender differences in math, science, reading, and writing are due to the nature of experiences that boys and girls have, as well as societal attitudes toward these subject areas. For example, there are far more male than female math and science models (Stage & Maple, 1996). Boys take more math and science courses than girls do. Teachers and parents tend to hold higher expectations for boys than for girls in math and science (Brussiere et al., 2001). Teachers play a meaningful role in shaping the attitudes and attributions of their students toward math, science, reading, and writing. For math and science, this means recognizing the need to promote these subjects as viable career choices for boys and girls. For reading and writing, this means needing to help *all* students enjoy these experiences.

Social Skills   Traditionally, the literature around gender differences suggests that girls have better social skills than boys do. These skills include relationship and self-regulation skills.

Relationship Skills   Sociolinguist Deborah Tannen (2001) distinguishes between rapport talk and report talk. **Rapport talk** *is the language of conversation and a way of establishing connections and negotiating relationships.* **Report talk** *is talk that gives information.* Making a speech is an example of report talk. Males hold centre stage through such verbal performances as storytelling, joking, and lecturing with information. Females enjoy private talk more and conversation that is relationship-oriented (Werthner, 2001).

Tannen says that boys and girls grow up in different worlds of talk. Parents, siblings, peers, teachers, and others talk to girls and boys differently. The play of boys and girls is different. Boys tend to play in large groups that are hierarchically structured, and their groups usually have a leader who tells the others what to do and how to do it. Boys' games have winners and losers, and boys often argue about who won. Boys often boast of their skill and argue about who is best at what. In contrast, girls are more likely to play in small groups or pairs, and the centre of a girl's world is often a best friend. In girls' friendships and peer groups, intimacy is pervasive. Turn-taking is more characteristic of girls' games than boys' games. Much of the time, girls simply like to sit and talk with each other, with their primary concern focused on being liked by others.

In sum, Tannen and other gender experts, such as Carol Gilligan (1982, 1998), believe that girls are more relationship-oriented than boys are. They also believe that this relationship orientation should be prized as being more important than our culture currently takes it to be. The clear implication is for teachers to value and support children's relationship skills in the classroom.

Aggression and Self-Regulation   Social and developmental research suggests that small but real gender differences exist in children's physical aggression from early childhood through adolescence (Eagly & Steffen, 1986; Knight, Fabes, & Wilson, 1996). The difference is especially pronounced for children who are reactively aggressive. **Reactively aggressive** *children are those whose aggressive behaviour is triggered by events or the behaviour of others.* These children differ from **proactively aggressive** *children, whose aggressive behaviour is intentional or proactive.* Brendgen, Vitaro, Tremblay, and Lavoie (2001) suggest that reactively aggressive children are often reacting to perceived hostile intent. They do not handle teasing or failure well, and they tend to misinterpret social cues. These children are less skilled at sharing, negotiating, and compromising with their peers, which combined with a lack of self-regulation leads to behavioural difficulties. Self-regulation is the important ability to monitor and control one's emotions and behaviour. Boys usually show less self-regulation than girls do, and this low self-control has been associated with problematic behaviour (Eisenberg, Martin, & Fabes, 1996). Brendgen et al. maintain that proactively aggressive children have better self-regulation skills than reactively aggressive children. See Chapter 7 for more information about the development of self-regulation and the characteristics of self-regulatory learning.

Gender-Role Classification

The concept of gender-role classification involves categorization of persons in terms of personality traits. In the past, a well-adjusted boy was supposed to be independent, aggressive, and powerful. A well-adjusted female was supposed to be dependent, nurturant, and uninterested in power. Masculine characteristics were considered by society to be healthy and good; feminine characteristics were considered undesirable.

In the 1970s, as more females and males began to express open dissatisfaction with the burdens imposed by rigid gender expectations, alternatives to femininity and masculinity were proposed. Instead of restricting masculinity to male competency and femininity to female competency, it was proposed that individuals could have both "masculine" and "feminine" traits. This thinking led to the development of the concept of **androgyny**, *which refers to the presence of desirable masculine and feminine characteristics in the same person* (Bem, 1977; Spence & Helmreich, 1978). The androgynous boy might be assertive ("masculine") and nurturant ("feminine"). The androgynous girl might be powerful ("masculine") and sensitive to others' feelings ("feminine"). Measures have been developed to assess androgyny. One of the most widely used measures is the Bem Sex-Role Inventory. To see whether your gender-role classification is masculine, feminine, or androgynous, complete Self-Assessment 5.1.

Gender researchers such as Sandra Bem argue that androgynous individuals are more flexible, competent, and mentally healthy than their masculine or feminine counterparts. To some degree, though, which gender-role classification is "best" depends on the context. For example, feminine orientations might be more desirable in close relationships because of the expressive nature of these relationships, and masculine orientations might be more desirable in traditional academic and work settings because of the achievement demands in these contexts.

Of special concern are adolescent boys who adopt a strong masculine role. Researchers have found that high-masculinity adolescent boys often engage in problem behaviours, such as delinquency, drug abuse, and unprotected sexual intercourse (Martino, 2000). They present themselves as virile, macho, and aggressive, and often do poorly in school (Bouchard & St. Amand, 2000).

Gender-role critics believe that gender-role classifications lead to too much stereotyping. They suggest instead that parents should rear their children to be competent individuals, not masculine, feminine, or androgynous.

To be meek, patient, tactful, modest, honorable, brave, is not to be either manly or womanly, it is to be humane.

Jane Harrison
English Writer, 20th Century

www.mcgrawhill.ca/college/santrock

What Gender-Role Orientation Will I Present to My Students?

The items to the right are from the Bem Sex-Role Inventory. To find out whether your gender-role classification is masculine, feminine, or androgynous, rate yourself on each item from 1 (never or almost never true) to 7 (always or almost always true).

	1	2	3	4	5	6	7
1. self-reliant							
2. yielding							
3. helpful							
4. defends own beliefs							
5. cheerful							
6. moody							
7. independent							
8. shy							
9. conscientious							
10. athletic							
11. affectionate							
12. theatrical							
13. assertive							
14. flatterable							
15. happy							
16. strong personality							
17. loyal							
18. unpredictable							
19. forceful							
20. feminine							
21. reliable							
22. analytical							
23. sympathetic							
24. jealous							
25. has leadership abilities							
26. sensitive to the needs of others							
27. truthful							
28. willing to take risks							
29. understanding							
30. secretive							

	1	2	3	4	5	6	7
31. makes decisions easily							
32. compassionate							
33. sincere							
34. self-sufficient							
35. eager to soothe hurt feelings							
36. conceited							
37. dominant							
38. soft spoken							
39. likable							
40. masculine							
41. warm							
42. solemn							
43. willing to take a stand							
44. tender							
45. friendly							
46. aggressive							
47. gullible							
48. inefficient							
49. acts as a leader							
50. childlike							
51. adaptable							
52. individualistic							
53. does not use harsh language							
54. unsystematic							
55. competitive							
56. loves children							
57. tactful							
58. ambitious							
59. gentle							
60. conventional							

Scoring

Masculinity Score

Add ratings for items 1, 4, 7, 10, 13, 16, 19, 22, 25, 28, 31, 34, 37, 40, 43, 46, 49, 55, and 58
Divide the total by 20

Femininity Score

Add ratings for items 2, 5, 8, 11, 20, 23, 26, 29, 32, 35, 38, 41, 44, 47, 50, 53, 56, and 59
Divide the total by 20

Interpretation

If your masculinity score is greater than 4.9 (the approximate median for the masculinity scale) and your femininity score is greater than 4.9 (the approximate femininity median), then you would be classified as androgynous on Bem's scale.

Gender In Context

Earlier we said that the concept of gender-role classification involves categorizing people in terms of personality traits. However, recall from our discussion of personality in Chapter 4, Individual Variations, that it is beneficial to think of personality in terms of person–situation interaction rather than personality traits alone.

Helping Behaviour and Emotion   To see the importance of also considering gender in context, let's examine helping behaviour and emotion. The stereotype is that females are better than males at helping. But it depends on the situation. Females are more likely than males to volunteer their time to help children with personal problems and engage in caregiving behaviour. However, in situations where males feel a sense of competence or that involve danger, males are more likely to help (Eagly & Crowley, 1986). For example, a male is more likely than a female to stop and help a person stranded by the roadside with a flat tire.

She is emotional, he is not. That's the master emotional stereotype. However, like helping behaviour, emotional differences in males and females depend on the particular emotion involved and the context in which it is displayed (Shields, 1991; Strayer & William, 1997; Strayer, 2002). Males are more likely to show anger toward strangers, especially male strangers, when they feel they have been challenged. Males also are more likely to turn their anger into aggressive action. Emotional differences between females and males often show up in contexts that highlight social roles and relationships. For example, females are more likely to discuss emotions in terms of relationships, and they are more likely to express fear and sadness.

Culture   The importance of considering gender in context is most apparent when examining what is culturally prescribed behaviour for females and males in different countries around the world (Greene, 2000). In Canada there is now more acceptance of androgyny and similarities in male and female behaviour. However, many Canadian students still struggle to define their gender roles and identities. Pon (2000) describes how Asian-Canadian students are often stereotyped as excelling in academics and being disciplined students. Pon argues that many Asian-Canadian students find this "model minority" label oppressive and restrictive. These students are caught between two cultures and realities: the reality of Asian-Canadian experiences, and the false expectations of Canadian cultural stereotypical beliefs about Asians. This research also suggests that the struggle with conflicting cultural identities can negatively affect students' academic achievement and attitudes toward school.

In many other countries roles have remained gender-specific. For example, in Egypt the division of labour between Egyptian males and females is dramatic. Egyptian males are socialized and schooled to work in the public sphere; females are socialized to remain in the private world of home and child-rearing. The Islamic religion that predominates in Egypt dictates that the man's duty is to provide for his family and the woman's is to care for her family and household. Any deviation from this traditional masculine and feminine behaviour is severely disapproved of. Likewise, in China, although women have made some strides, the male role is still dominant.

Eliminating Gender Bias

How gendered are social interactions between teachers and students? What can teachers do to reduce or eliminate gender bias in their classrooms?

Through the Eyes of Students

The Importance of Family

Families are important because they are always there to help you and care for you. Some kids live with their moms and dads. Some kids live with their moms and visit their dads. Some kids live with their moms some of the time and with their dads at other times. Some kids live with their grandparents or with their stepmom and stepdad. Some live with foster parents. It doesn't matter who you live with, they are still your family.

Moms and dads can help you learn new things and help you with your schoolwork. If you struggle with a question, they give you hints and ideas. If you are a studying for a test, they ask you questions. If you are doing a project, they can help you get information or give you materials. Brothers and sisters can help too, but they can also be mean. Even when you fight with your brother or sister, you still have to live with them. They are still part of your family.

Heather and Sarah
Grade 4 Students
Soccer, Drama, Bowling, and Swimming Fans
Ontario

www.mcgrawhill.ca/college/santrock

What are some of the ways that teachers interact with students on the basis of gender?

Teacher–Student Interaction   Following are some of the ways that teachers and students interact with each other on the basis of gender (Beal, 1994; Sadker & Sadker, 2000; Sadker, Sadker, & Long, 1997):

- In a typical classroom, girls are more compliant, boys more rambunctious. Boys demand more attention, girls are more likely to quietly wait their turn. Teachers are more likely to scold and reprimand boys, as well as send them to school authorities for disciplinary action. Educators worry that girls' tendency to be compliant and quiet comes at a cost: diminished assertiveness.
- In many classrooms, teachers spend more time watching and interacting with boys while girls work and play quietly on their own. Most teachers don't intentionally favour boys by spending more time with them, yet somehow the classroom frequently ends up with this type of gendered profile.
- Boys get more instruction than girls and more help when they have trouble with a question. Teachers often give boys more time to answer a question, more hints at the correct answer, and further tries if they provide the wrong answer.
- Boys are more likely than girls to get lower grades and to be grade repeaters, yet girls are less likely to believe that they will be successful.
- Girls and boys enter Grade 1 with roughly equal levels of self-esteem. Yet by the intermediate-grade years, girls' self-esteem is significantly lower than boys' (American Association of University Women, 2001).
- When elementary-school children are asked to list what they want to do when they grow up, boys describe more career options than girls do.

Sexual Harassment   **Sexual harassment** *is a form of power and dominance of one person over another.* In a school setting, sexual harassment may be as innocuous as disrespectful comments or as severe as bullying (Connolly et al., 2000). Sexual harassment can result in harmful consequences for the victim, especially when the perpetrators are teachers and other adults who have considerable power and authority over students (Lee et al., 1995; Firpo-Triplett, 1997).

Sexual harassment does occur in schools (Bracey, 1997). In one study of students in Grades 8 to 11, 83 percent of the girls and 79 percent of the boys said that they had been sexually harassed. Over the last decade, there has been an increased number of reports of sexual harassment by both girls and boys. In one study, 16 percent of students reported that they had been sexually harassed by a teacher (American Association of University Women, 2001). Girls now report being more severely harassed than boys. Examples of harassment by students and teachers include:

- sexual comments, jokes, gestures, or looks
- sexual messages about a student on bathroom walls and other places, or sexual rumours spread about the student
- spying on a student who was dressing or showering at school
- flashing or mooning
- comments that a student was a gay or lesbian
- touching, grabbing, or pinching in a sexual manner
- intentionally brushing up against a student in a sexual way
- pulling a student's clothing off or down

Through the Eyes of Teachers

Recognizing the Many Types of Love

Throughout most schools in Canada, including my own, the first part of February is allocated to celebrating Valentine's Day. Following the student council meeting, our Grade 7 representative explained how tickets could be purchased for the Valentine's Day in-school dance. One ticket would cost $2.00, while two tickets could be bought for $3.00. To qualify for this discount, however, a boy and a girl had to buy the tickets. This, we were told, was to discourage two friends from buying the tickets in order to get the discount.

I was flabbergasted and astonished that none of the other teachers or students seemed concerned about this policy. To me, this policy presented a very limited view of what I wanted students to learn about the meaning of friendship and love. I asked to speak at the next meeting of the student council. At the meeting, I explained that love and friendship are important for everyone, and that love isn't something that only happens between boys and girls—students love their parents, friends love their friends, and sometimes boys love other boys and girls love other girls. These are different kinds of love and friendship and we should respect them all. I concluded that I believed that the Valentine policy should be changed in order to recognize all these types of love and friendship. When I left the meeting, the student council met in camera and voted to change the ticket policy. I was proud of the students—they were willing to take action to make their school a better place for everyone.

John J. Guiney
Elementary-School Teacher
Ontario

Teaching Strategies
For Eliminating Gender Bias

✔ Provide a gender-fair curriculum
  - help students learn about non-stereotypical male and female roles (e.g., female engineer; male childcare provider)
  - help students identify females and males performing similar tasks at home and at work
  - help students learn new skills and complete the same tasks in a non-sexist manner
  - invite individuals who have non-stereotypical jobs (e.g., female construction worker, male flight attendant) to participate in your classroom
✔ Discuss gender bias with students
  - help students critically assess print and media materials for gender bias
  - supplement gender-biased materials with gender-fair ones
  - do not accept gender-biased language in the classroom
✔ Be an effective role model
  - analyze seating plans for segregation based on gender or ethnicity
  - monitor group membership for segregation based on gender or ethnicity
  - have a colleague monitor your questioning and reinforcement patterns to ensure that you are providing equal attention and support to boys and girls
  - use nonbiased language (e.g., avoid using the pronoun *he* when referring to inanimate objects or unspecified persons)
  - replace terms such as *fireman, policeman,* and *cleaning woman* with terms like *firefighter, police officer,* and *cleaning person*
  - ask students to provide and use gender-fair terminology
  - be aware of issues associated with gender equity in education, including personal rights
  - do not tolerate gender inequity, discrimination, or harassment

  - blocking or cornering a student in a sexual way
  - being forced to kiss someone, or do some other sexual activity (American Association of University Women, 1993)

Sexual Orientation

Tremblay and Ramsay (2000) define **sexual orientation** *as an enduring emotional, romantic, sexual or affective attraction to another person.* Sexual orientation exists along a continuum that extends from exclusive homosexuality to exclusive heterosexuality. Sexual orientation is different from sexual behaviour because it refers to feelings and self-concept.

Canada prides itself on being a multicultural society that promotes human rights. Sexual orientation is one of the protected categories in the Canadian Charter of Rights and Freedoms, along with race, gender, disability, place of origin, and religion. However, while sexual orientation is protected by law in Canada, a climate of tolerance in our schools still needs to be promoted.

While exact data on the numbers of students who are gay or lesbian is difficult to ascertain, researchers suggest that between 10 and 30 percent of students are homosexual or have an immediate family member who is homosexual. Homophobia is the fear of

SUMMARY TABLE 5.5
Exploring Gender

What is gender stereotyping?	• Stereotypes involve an image of what the typical member of a category is like. • Gender is viewed in terms of person–situation interaction, not as a personality trait. • Gender stereotypes are broad categories that reflect impressions and beliefs about what behaviours are appropriate for females and males.
What is sexism?	• Sexism is prejudice and discrimination against a person because of his or her sex. • Sexism is a negative stereotype.
Are there differences between the genders?	• There are substantial differences between boys and girls in physical performance, aggression, and relationship skills. • There are small differences in academic skills, such as math, science, and verbal skills.
What is gender-role classification and androgyny?	• The concept of androgyny evolved in the 1970s. • Androgyny is the notion that individuals have both masculine and feminine positive characteristics. • Gender-role classification assesses how masculine, feminine, or androgynous an individual is.
How are teacher–student interactions gender biased?	• Girls receive less instruction than boys; by the intermediate grades girls have lower self-esteem. • Boys receive more attention than girls, yet receive lower grades. • Boys list more career options than girls.
What is sexual orientation?	• Sexual orientation is an enduring emotional, romantic, sexual, or affective attraction to another person and exists along a continuum based on exclusive homosexuality to exclusive heterosexuality. • Sexual orientation differs from sexual behaviour because it refers to feelings and self-concept. • In Canada, sexual orientation is protected under the Canadian Charter of Rights and Freedoms.

people who are perceived to be different. It feeds on stereotyping and prejudice, and can lead to discrimination and severe harassment (Tremblay & Ramsay, 2000). According to the McCreary Centre Society's (1999) survey of gay youth in British Columbia, 28 percent of students reported that their teachers made homophobic remarks, while 82 percent said other students made homophobic remarks. Sixty-three percent of the respondents reported being verbally abused, 34 percent being threatened with violence, and 17 percent being physically assaulted. Without proper support, these gay and lesbian students are vulnerable to loss of self-esteem, severe emotional disorders, and suicide. Studies indicate that suicide may be the leading cause of death among gay youth. Tremblay (1995) reported that 62.5 percent of the suicide attempts made by male youth in Alberta were by homosexual youth. School can be a hostile environment for these students. Teachers need to work to eliminate homophobic actions by creating inclusive environments where students discuss and practise conflict resolution and perspective-taking. For example, novel discussions and role-plays can provide opportunities for building awareness of the harmful nature of intolerance.

At this point we have discussed many further ideas about gender. A review of these ideas is presented in Summary Table 5.5. In the next chapter, we will continue our exploration of individual variations by studying learners who are exceptional.

Larry is a 17-year-old boy in the Grade 12 physics class in which you are student teaching. You have heard him and a number of other students complaining about gender bias on the part of their teacher, Mr. Clinton. One day you overhear Larry being reprimanded by Mr. Clinton for an altercation he had with Annie, a female classmate.

"It isn't fair, Mr. Clinton," Larry says. "Annie took my MP3 player and broke it. Why should I get in trouble for wanting her to pay for it?"

"Now, Larry," admonishes Mr. Clinton. "You know Annie would never break your MP3 player on purpose. You go apologize to her for yelling at her and I will see you after school."

Larry walks away with a very angry look on his face, muttering. "Girls in this class can get away with anything. They never get in trouble."

You have heard this from other student teachers working with Mr. Clinton, but have never really believed it. Over the course of the next three weeks you pay closer attention to Mr. Clinton's behaviour, especially with respect to the way he treats male and female students. You notice that girls receive more positive attention than boys do, and girls seem to get easier questions to answer. Boys are sent to the office frequently and girls are not. If a boy asks Mr. Clinton for an extension he often expresses disappointment, while girls are rarely refused. In class, the girls are called up to volunteer more frequently than boys. Their work receives more praise as well. The boys receive the brunt of disciplinary attention, with Mr. Clinton commenting "I don't know what to do with the boys in this class! They just don't seem to want to work or behave."

- Based on the ideas and information presented in your text to this point, as well as your own experiences, what do you believe is happening in this classroom?
- What are the possible influences on Mr. Clinton's behaviour?
- What influence do you believe Mr. Clinton's behaviour will have on his students? Why?
- If you were a student teacher in this classroom, what, if anything, would you do? Why?
- How can you minimize gender bias in your own classroom?

CHAPTER REVIEW

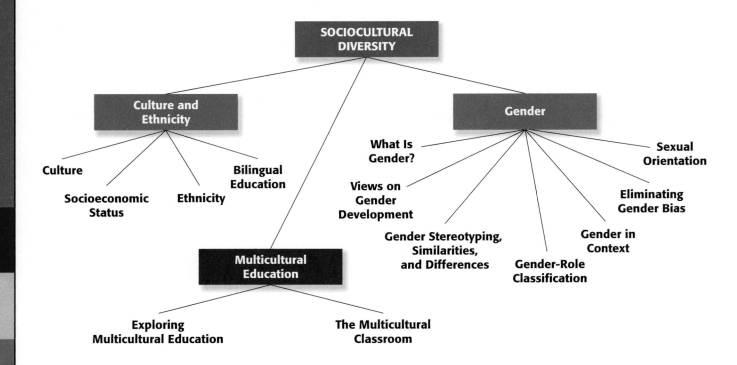

To obtain a detailed review of this chapter, study these five summary tables:

KEY TERMS

culture 132
cross-cultural studies 132
individualism 132
collectivism 132
socioeconomic status
    (SES) 133
ethnicity 137

prejudice 140
bilingual education 142
empowerment 144
jigsaw classroom 145
gender 148
sex 148
gender roles 148

social-learning theory of
    gender 150
cognitive developmental
    theory of gender 151
gender schema theory 151
gender stereotypes 151
sexism 151

rapport talk 154
report talk 154
reactively aggressive 155
proactively aggressive 155
androgyny 155
sexual harassment 158
sexual orientation 159

PROFESSIONAL DEVELOPMENT/PORTFOLIO ACTIVITIES

1. Ethnic and Gender Diversity

The different lived experiences of your students produce attitudes and opinions that may vary greatly from your own. Consider individuals from different cultural and ethnic backgrounds. How will you react to distinct ideas and opinions in your classroom? In your portfolio, outline your classroom goals for students' social behaviour and attitudes toward people who are different from them.

2. Diversity Ideas

With three or four other students in your class, come up with a list of specific diversity goals for your future classroom. Next, brainstorm and share some innovative activities that facilitate positive diversity experiences as discussed in this chapter.

3. Multiculturalism and You

Canada is regarded as a nation where people from a variety of ethnic and cultural backgrounds live and work together. Education can play a large role in fostering an understanding of other cultures; yet, the usefulness of multicultural education is vigorously debated. What is your position on the debate about multicultural education? Discuss how multicultural perspectives should be integrated into academic subjects.

4. Harassment Is as Harassment Does

Consider the following scenario. You are a single, first-year teacher who is popular and friendly with everyone at your school. A colleague continually places cartoons depicting culturally offensive stereotypes in your staff mailbox. You ask the colleague to refrain, but the cartoons continue to appear in your mailbox. Is this harassment? If only you are aware of this situation, is it worth reporting? What should you do and why? Write a brief statement on your position with respect to harassment in the teaching profession to include in your portfolio.

INTERNET ACTIVITIES

1. How Do We Measure Up?

Search the Statistics Canada Website or other online resources to find provincial or territorial data on children living in poverty. How does your region of Canada measure up in terms of children's socioeconomic status and school success? What are some of the implications of living in poverty for students and teachers? How can teachers help students from poor socioeconomic environments overcome some of the hurdles they face in achieving academic success?

2. Diversity Learning

Analyze and evaluate a lesson plan or learning activity at the Diversity Learning Website (www.diversitylearning.ca) How could it best be implemented in your future classroom? What improvements or enhancements would make the plan or activity more effective?

Connect to the Online Learning Centre at www.mcgrawhill.ca/ college/santrock **to explore possible answers.**

Visit the *Educational Psychology* Online Learning Centre at
www.mcgrawhill.ca/college/santrock
to access Websites related to the above Internet Activities as well as chapter quizzes,
a searchable glossary, and other learning and study tools.

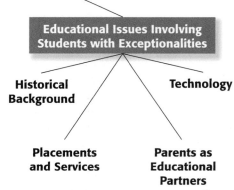

6 Learners Who Are Exceptional

Preview

For many years, public schools did little to educate students with exceptionalities. However, in the last several decades, legislation has mandated that students with exceptionalities receive a free, appropriate education. And increasingly, students with exceptionalities are being educated in the regular classroom. These are some of the questions we will explore in this chapter:

- What are the challenges of educating students with various exceptionalities and the best strategies for teaching them?

- Should students who are gifted be provided with special educational opportunities?

- What are the legal aspects of working with students who have exceptionalities?

- Should students with exceptionalities be taught mainly in the regular classroom or in a specialized setting?

- What challenges are involved in educating students with exceptionalities in the regular classroom?

- What technologies are available for educating students with exceptionalities?

LEARNERS WHO ARE EXCEPTIONAL

Learners Who Are Exceptional and Strategies for Teaching Them

- **Who Are Students with Exceptionalities?**
- **Learning Disabilities**
- **Attention Deficit Hyperactivity Disorder**
- **Emotional and Behavioural Disorders**
- **Speech and Language Disorders**
- **Developmental Disabilities/ Intellectual Disabilities**
- **Sensory Impairments and Physical Exceptionalities**
- **Students Who Are Gifted**

Educational Issues Involving Students with Exceptionalities

- **Historical Background**
- **Placements and Services**
- **Parents as Educational Partners**
- **Technology**

Teaching Stories: Kimberly Maich

Kimberly Maich is a special-education teacher in New-foundland. Over the years, she has assumed many additional roles beyond special educator including language arts teacher, computer teacher, and vice principal. Here she describes her work with Samuel, a student she met while co-teaching Grade 3.

"Samuel looked like every other boy in the class. In reality, he was profoundly deaf in one ear (unilateral hearing impairment). While a teacher for the hearing impaired monitored his academic progress, Samuel was fully integrated into the classroom setting. We structured his academic program around the accommodations and modifications outlined in his Individual Support Service Plan (ISSP), which for the most part were relatively straightforward and easy to implement. For instance, we ensured that he was seated against the wall with his 'good ear' toward the class, we touched his shoulder when we wanted his attention, and we double-checked that he understood verbal directions. Samuel also wore an FM system, or what is commonly referred to as a phonic ear. The system requires the speaker to wear a small clip microphone that feeds into a receiver headset. The system helped ensure that Samuel was not distracted by other sounds when we were speaking. Samuel removed his headset during whole-class discussions.

"Using the system also provided a unique opportunity to include other students in Samuel's ISSP. The Walkman-like device quickly became a prized possession. When students made presentations (e.g., sharing narratives, performing a play) we allowed them to pass around the microphone so that Samuel would not miss the presentation. His peers enjoyed trying the microphone and were quite amazed that they could hear each other from afar without any wires or buttons to push. Everyone giggled at my jokes about needing to shut the microphone off when entering the bathroom or staff room. Allowing them to wear the microphone demystified the equipment and helped them gain an understanding of how Samuel 'heard' the world around him—it helped them accept Samuel as a valued member of the class."

Learners Who Are Exceptional and Strategies for Teaching Them

- Who Are Students with Exceptionalities?
- Learning Disabilities
- Attention Deficit Hyperactivity Disorder
- Emotional and Behavioural Disorders

LEARNERS WHO ARE EXCEPTIONAL AND STRATEGIES FOR TEACHING THEM

Students with exceptionalities include students with disabilities and students who are gifted. Most often, the term "exceptionality" is associated with special education and some form of disability. However, students who are gifted are also identified as exceptional and may qualify for special-education resources. While we will discuss both types of exceptionalities in this chapter, our focus will be on students with disabilities.

Who Are Students with Exceptionalities?

Statistics Canada (1999) has estimated that 1 in every 10 elementary-school children receives some form of special education; approximately two-thirds of these students are male. Students receive special education for a variety of reasons, including sensory and physical handicaps, intellectual limitations, communication and behavioural disorders, and other problems that affect learning. These conditions may be mild or severe, chronic or acute, and contained or pervasive (Bohatyretz & Lipps, 1999). The majority of children who receive special education (approximately 59 percent) spend the greatest part of the school day in the regular classroom, from which they are periodically withdrawn to a special-education classroom or resource room for additional instruction or support. Some 16 percent of special-education students are never withdrawn from the classroom. A small number of students with exceptionalities (approximately 8 percent) are withdrawn full-time or attend residential schools. According to the parents of children who receive special-education services, the majority of children look forward to attending school and have as many friends as other children (Bohatyretz & Lipps, 1999).

Students with learning disabilities account for almost half of all students who receive special education (Figure 6.1). According to the Learning Disabilities Association of Canada (2002), learning disabilities include various disorders that may affect the acquisition, organization, retention, understanding, or use of verbal or nonverbal information. These disorders affect learning in individuals who otherwise demonstrate at least average abilities essential for thinking and/or reasoning. As such, learning disabilities differ from intellectual

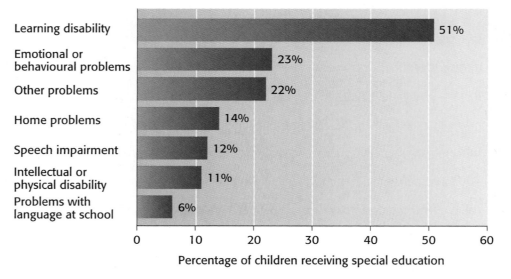

Learning disability — 51%
Emotional or behavioural problems — 23%
Other problems — 22%
Home problems — 14%
Speech impairment — 12%
Intellectual or physical disability — 11%
Problems with language at school — 6%

Percentage of children receiving special education

Notes:
Respondents may belong to more than one category.
Co-efficients of variation for these percentages are between 17% and 33% and should be interpreted with caution due to the higher levels of error associated with these estimates.
Source: "Reasons why children receive special education," adapted from the Statistics Canada, Longitudinal Survey of Children and Youth, School Component, 1994-1995.

FIGURE 6.1 **The Diversity of Students Who Have an Exceptionality**

limitations. Approximately one-quarter (23 percent) of students receive special-education services because they experience emotional or behavioural problems, while the rest receive support for a number of conditions including speech or language impairments and intellectual or physical disabilities.

The concepts of impairments, disabilities, and handicaps are distinct and can often be confusing. A *disability* involves a limitation of a person's functioning that restricts the individual's abilities (e.g., performing the activities needed to read or process information in a meaningful way); it is important to remember that the term "disability" does not mean or imply inability. *Impairment* refers to a loss or abnormality of body structure, physiological structure, or psychological function (e.g., loss of vision, restriction in hearing, or inability to relate to others). Finally, a *handicap* is defined as a condition or restriction imposed on a person who has a disability or impairment by society, the physical environment, or the person's own attitudes (e.g., access to facilities, transportation, employment).

Driven by the belief that all children can achieve their full potential if they are provided with appropriate opportunities, instructional methods, resources, and a supportive environment, educators and other professionals today choose to speak of "children with disabilities" or "children with exceptionalities" rather than "disabled children." This change in language is an important one, as it emphasizes the person and not the disability or handicap. Regardless of language, children with disabilities, impairments, and handicaps continue to be a major concern for classroom teachers. Henteleff (1997) notes that students with mild or moderate learning disabilities are increasingly not identified as such, and thus they may be lost in the general classroom setting and become marginalized. Even with the ideal of children's rights guaranteed or acknowledged in documents such as the UN Convention on the Rights of the Child (1990), the Canadian Charter of Rights and Freedoms (1982), and provincial education acts, approaches to and the application of special education across Canada vary from jurisdiction to jurisdiction.

In the following sections we look at some of the characteristics of specific exceptionalities and present appropriate teaching approaches for working with students who have them.

Learning Disabilities

Paula doesn't like kindergarten and can't seem to remember the names of her classmates or teacher. Bobby's Grade 3 teacher complains that his spelling is awful. Eleven-year-old Tim says that reading is really hard for him and that a lot of times the words don't make much sense. Each of these students may have a learning disability.

Characteristics   According to the definition developed by the Learning Disabilities Association of Ontario (2001) and adopted by the Learning Disabilities Association of Canada (2002), children with learning disabilities demonstrate (1) impairments in one or more psychological processes related to learning despite having average to above-average intelligence, (2) unexpectedly low academic achievement, or at times average to above-average achievement attained only at the expense of unrealistically high levels of effort and/or educational support, and (3) no other diagnosed problem or disability, such as an intellectual disability (developmental delay).

Learning disabilities range in severity and interfere with the acquisition and use of oral language (e.g., listening, speaking, understanding), reading (e.g., decoding, comprehension), written language (e.g., spelling, written expression), and/or mathematics (e.g., computation, problem solving). Learning disabilities may also cause difficulties with organizational skills, social perception, and social interaction (Learning Disabilities Association of Ontario, 2002; Kamphaus, 2000; Keogh & MacMillan, 1996; Wong, 1998).

About half of all students identified as exceptional in Canada have a learning disability, making learning disabilities the highest incidence of exceptionality. According to school principals who participated in the Canadian National Longitudinal Survey of Children and Youth (1997), an average of 12 percent of school children have a learning disability. The incidence of learning disabilities may increase by another 3 to 5 percent with the inclusion of students with attention deficit hyperactivity disorder (ADHD). In many provinces there is no separate category for children with ADHD, and they are often included in the general categories of learning disabilities or behavioural disorders. Because of the significant interest in ADHD today, we will discuss it specifically later in the chapter.

In both Canada and the United States, the number of children identified with a learning disability has increased dramatically (as high as 198 percent) over the past 15 years (Gresham, 1997; Winzer, 2002). Some experts say that the dramatic increase in children classified as having a learning disability reflects poor diagnostic practices and overidentification. They believe that teachers are sometimes too quick to label children with the slightest learning problem as having a learning disability instead of recognizing that the problem might rest in ineffective teaching (Nikiforuk, 1998). Other experts believe that the increase in children being classified as having a learning disability is justified (Hallahan, Kaufmann, & Lloyd, 1999).

Diagnosing a learning disability is a difficult task. A learning disability often encompasses co-ocurring conditions that can include problems in listening, concentrating, speaking, reading, writing, reasoning, math, or social interaction. Thus, individual children with a learning disability can have very different profiles (Henley, Ramsey, & Algozzine, 1999; Hutchinson, 2002). Learning disabilities can also appear in association with such medical conditions as lead poisoning and fetal alcohol syndrome (Learning Disabilities Association of Ontario, 2001), or other disabilities such as communication disorders and emotional behavioural disorders (Learning Disabilities Association of Ontario, 2001; Glassberg, Hooper, & Mattison, 1999).

About four times as many boys as girls are classified as having a learning disability (Winzer, 2002). This gender difference has been given various explanations, such as greater biological vulnerability for boys, greater instance of language and reading difficulties for boys, and referral bias (i.e., boys are more likely to be referred by teachers because of their disruptive, hyperactive behaviour).

The most common problem for children with a learning disability involves reading, especially the phonological skills needed to understand how sounds and letters combine to make words. **Dyslexia** *is a severe impairment in the ability to read.* As well, children with a learning disability often have difficulties in handwriting, spelling, or composition (dysgraphia). They may write extremely slowly, their writing products may be virtually illegible, and they may make numerous spelling errors because of their inability to match up sounds and letters.

In previous decades, difficulties in math were given little attention. Increasingly, though, math is being recognized as an academic area in which learning disabilities occur. Students with **dyscalculia** *(a learning disability in math)* may make an abundance of computational errors or use inefficient strategies in solving math problems.

Current classification of learning disabilities involves an "either/or" determination: A student either has a learning disability or does not have a learning disbility. Yet, in reality, learning disabilities vary in their intensity (Reschly, 1996; Terman et al., 1996). Severe learning disabilities, such as dyslexia, have been recognized for more than a century and are relatively easy to diagnose. However, most children with a learning disability have a milder form, which often makes them hard to distinguish from children without a learning disability. In the absence of nationally accepted criteria for classification, there continues to be considerable variability in the identification of students with a learning disability from one province to the next, and even one teacher to the next.

Although learning disabilities may change in their expression (or observable difficulties) and severity as individuals mature and as environments change, they are lifelong (Learning Disabilities Association of Ontario, 2001). Conflicting ideas exist with respect to the future of students with learning disabilities. While some researchers report positive educational, occupational, and social/ interpersonal outcomes, others indicate higher high-school dropout rates, unemployment, underemployment, and social/ emotional difficulties (Adelman & Vogel, 1998; Hocutt, 1996; Pueschel et al., 1995; Wagner & Blackorby, 1996). Presumably, the quality of supports and services provided to these students will greatly influence their future success.

Improving outcomes for students with learning disabilities is a critical and challenging task for educators. At this time, there is no one intervention or program that is effective for all students with learning disabilities (Terman et al., 1996; Winzer, 2002).

Identification   Diagnosing a child with a learning disability, especially in a mild form, is very difficult. A student with a learning disability typically does not look disabled, can communicate verbally, and does not stand out in a crowd (Larsen, 1997). Some teachers may mistakenly leap to the conclusion that a student has a learning disability when a particular teaching strategy or approach proves ineffective.

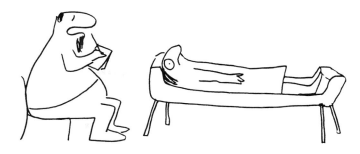

"Your feelings of insecurity seem to have started when Mary Lou Gurnblatt said, 'Maybe I don't have a learning disability—maybe you have a teaching disability.'"
©1975 Tony Saltzman. Phi Delta Kappan.

The classroom teacher usually makes the initial suggestion that a student may have a possible learning disability, ideally in consultation with other professionals in the school such as a learning-resource teacher or a special-education teacher. Medical examinations and hearing and vision tests are used to eliminate the possibility of a physical disorder. The student then completes a number of psychological evaluations (to verify normal intelligence) and educational assessments (e.g., oral reading, reading comprehension, math, general knowledge) to confirm a learning disability (Overton, 2000; Winzer, 2002). Tests of visual motor skills, language, and memory may also be used for diagnosis.

In the early-childhood years, disabilities are often identified in receptive and expressive language. Input from parents and teachers is considered before making a final diagnosis. For many school systems, the trigger for assessing students with learning disabilities is a two-grade-level lag in reading (Purcell-Gates, 1997). This approach can be a major impediment to identifying disabilities at the age when help can be the most effective—during the first two years of elementary school. If the two-grade lag is rigidly interpreted, many children do not receive assistance even if they are showing clear signs of a learning disability. To promote the early identification of students with possible learning disabilities, the Learning Disabilities Association of Ontario has launched a Web-based teaching tool that includes a screening tool (Dynamic Screening & Intervention Model; Simner, 2001) and resource data bank (see Figure 6.2). Teachers can use the tool to complete systematic observations, develop profiles for at-risk students, and plan intervention activities.

Intervention Strategies   Many interventions have focused on improving students' reading ability (Fitzgerald & Shanahan, 2000; Gunning, 2002; Lyon & Moats, 1997). In the primary grades, emphasis is placed on developing phonemic awareness; most students with reading disabilities demonstrate insufficiently developed phonemic awareness, with phonemic awareness being the predictor of reading ability in the middle grades (Cunningham & Stanovich, 1997). Most students with learning disabilities respond favourably to these interventions (e.g., Martinussen, Kirby, & Das, 1998; Schneider et al., 1999).

Children with severe phonological deficits that lead to poor decoding and word-recognition skills respond to intervention more slowly than children with mild to moderate reading problems (Torgesen, 1995). Also, the success of even the best-designed reading intervention depends on the training and skills of the teacher (Moats & Lyon, 1996).

Unfortunately, not all children who have a learning disability that involves reading will receive early intervention. Students whose learning disabilities go unrecognized do not benefit from standard interventions and require more time and effort in any subsequent remediation (Lyon, 1996; Torgesen et al., 1997). In older students, insufficiently developed phonological awareness is often followed by difficulties in reading comprehension and writing (Abbott & Berninger, 1999; Graham & Wong, 1993; Lovett & Steinbach, 1997). Effective remedial programs must be comprehensive, explicit, continuous, address all the major components of reading (phonic decoding, fluency, vocabulary, spelling, composition),

Learning Disabilities Association of Ontario
The Web Based Teaching Tool
An Early Intervention Screening Tool for SK-1 Educators

Learning Disabilities Association of Ontario — Search Pages for Early Intervention Screen.

Start Search

Or search for Teaching Materials below

Teaching Materials:

Teaching materials are educational programs and other products used to assist a teacher in the implementation of curriculum.

(Please Note: If no search options are made then no results will be returned. However, the more checkboxes you select, the slower the search results will appear.)

1. Choose Resource language Preference(s):
☐ English   ☐ French

2. Choose Curriculum Area(s):
☐ Social Skills   ☐ Oral language
☐ Motor Development   ☐ Mathematical Abilities
☐ Organizational Skills   ☐ Phonological Awareness
☐ Reading and Writing Skills

3. Choose Learning Environment(s):
☐ Partners   ☐ Independent
☐ Take Home   ☐ One to One
☐ Small Group   ☐ Whole Class
☐ Large Group

4. Choose Teaching Material Type(s) and/or cost(s):

Teaching Material Types: Teaching Material Cost Range:
☐ Workshop   ☐ $100+
☐ Kit   ☐ $50-100
☐ Video   ☐ $0-50
☐ Audio Cassette   ☐ Ministry Licensed
☐ Chalkboard
☐ Web Site
☐ CD
☐ Software
☐ Game
☐ Book
☐ Program

5. Choose Psychological Process(es):
☐ Processing Speed   ☐ Executive Functioning

http://www.earlyintervention.ca/servlet/resources

Teacher's School Readiness Inventory

Instructions: Using the five point rating scale below, rate the child on each of the following items. Add all of your ratings to obtain the child's total score.

1. In-class distractibility, attention span and memory span: Is the child distracted by other children; does the child have difficulty remembering and following instructions and remembering the details of content of materials presented in class?

1 = highly distractible	2	3	4	5 = very good attention span
○	○	○	○	○

2. Verbal fluency: Does the child tend to use precise words and convey abstract ideas reasonably well when asked to describe events?

1 = poor verbal fluency	2	3	4	5	5 = very good verbal fluency
○	○	○	○	○	○

3. Interest and participation: Does the child show interest, enthusiasm, and eagerness to participate in various classroom activities and does the child readily convey this overall sense of enthusiasm to other children or to adults?

1 = very unenthusiastic	2	3	4	5	5 = very enthusiastic
○	○	○	○	○	○

4. Letter Identification skills: Approximately how many upper case letters can the child name correctly?

Learning Disabilities Association of Ontario
Early Intervention Screening Tool Kit for K-1 Educators —
Promoting Early Intervention for Learning Disabilities

Teacher: Ms. Tamara J. Bahr   Student: Harry H. Potter

Screenings

1) TSRI Screening
 • Teacher's School Readiness Inventory

2) Step Two
 • Yopp Singer or Rosner

3) Observational Checklists
 • Phonological Awareness
 • Mathematical Abilities
 • Oral Language
 • Reading and Writing Skills
 • Organizational skills
 • Motor Skills
 • Social Skills

All Current Results

Student Profile

Name: Harry H. Potter
Date of Birth: January 1, 1992
School: Idao Test School

Edit this Student Record

FIGURE 6.2   The Learning Disabilities Association of Ontario's Web-based Teaching Tool to Promote the Early Identification of Students with Possible Learning Disabilities

and incorporate metacognitive and/or motivational techniques to encourage independent reading (Foorman et al., 1997; Gaskins et al., 1996; Torgesen et al., 1997).

Deficits in basic reading skills are the most common target of intervention studies because they are the most frequent form of learning disability, are identifiable, and represent an area about which we have considerable knowledge (Lyon, 1996). Interventions for other types of learning disabilities have been developed, but they have not been as extensively researched.

Analysis of intervention studies with children with learning disabilities suggests that a combination of direct-strategy instruction and the provision of metacognitive information produces the greatest gains (Bulter, 1995, 1998; Swanson & Hoskyn, 1998). This type of instruction is especially effective for enhancing students' reading comprehension, vocabulary, and creativity. Other effective instructional components include small interactive groups, technology, and augmentation of teacher instruction (such as homework). Nikiforuk (1998) believes that good learning is the foundation for any education, and good learning requires good teaching. Moreover, good teaching is based on the assumption that all children can be taught. Unfortunately, according to critics such as Nikiforuk, poor children and students with exceptionalities are often the recipients of poor-quality instruction. He argues that schools and teachers can teach most children how to read and write, but it requires providing teachers with adequate professional development and making schools accountable.

Attention Deficit Hyperactivity Disorder

Matthew has attention deficit hyperactivity disorder, and the outward signs are fairly typical. He has trouble attending to the teacher's instructions and is easily distracted. He can't sit still for more than a few minutes at a time, and his handwriting is messy. His mother describes him as very fidgety.

Characteristics   **Attention deficit hyperactivity disorder (ADHD)** *is a disability in which children consistently show one or more of the following characteristics over a period of time: (1) inattention, (2) hyperactivity, and (3) impulsivity.* ADHD is typically associated with activity and attentional difficulties that start before the age of seven (Barkley, 1998). Children who are *inattentive* have difficulty focusing on any one thing and might become bored with a task after only a few minutes. They often ignore details, make careless errors, and lose or forget things. These students have difficulty following instructions, completing activities, and staying organized. Children who are *hyperactive* show high levels of physical activity and almost always seem to be in motion. They often fidget and squirm and move about the classroom at inappropriate times. They experience difficulties working or playing quietly and are often described as talking constantly and excessively. Impulsivity is another symptom of hyperactivity. Children who are *impulsive* have difficulty curbing their reactions and often do not think before they speak or act (e.g., blurting out answers in the classroom, not waiting their turn, or interrupting others).

Children with ADHD may also have a variety of subtype symptoms that can confound and complicate treatment. For example, Barkley (1998) suggests that learning disabilities, particularly reading impairments, may be a subtype category for ADHD students. The hyperactivity component may also be categorized as *pervasive* (occurring at home and school) or *situational* (only in one setting). Some researchers have argued that motivation, not attention, is the problem in ADHD. Benninger (1989) argued that ADHD arises out of an inability to self-regulate, an impairment of the ability to recognize and respond to consequences, or an insensitivity to reinforcement or punishment. Usually the ADHD diagnosis includes individualized testing for cognitive abilities and achievement, medical screening, and behavioural checklists (Hutchinson, 2002). While a physician is required to make the diagnosis of ADHD, parents and teachers are increasingly asked to provide input. Children must present six or more symptoms within either the inattention or hyperactivity-impulsivity categories as described in the DSM-IV (Diagnostic and Statistical Manual of Mental Disorders; American Psychiatric Association, 1994). These symptoms must be present for at least six months and to a degree that is developmentally deviant by the age of seven.

There is controversy about the increased diagnosis of ADHD (Terman et al., 1996). Some experts attribute the increase mainly to heightened awareness of the disorder. Others are concerned that many children are being misdiagnosed without undergoing extensive professional evaluation based on input from multiple sources.

Through the Eyes of Teachers

Understanding Students with Learning Disabilities

I hated going to school. I cried every night and literally made myself sick. I thought school was my parents' way of punishing me. I felt inadequate, feared failure, and rarely took risks. One evening, I begged my mother to help me be "normal." I was identified with a learning disability when I was 11 years old.

As a teacher with a learning disability, I reflect on these memories frequently. I promised myself that I would never let a child hate learning or believe that he or she was incapable of success. I understand and empathize with students who are struggling, feel isolated, stupid, misunderstood, or frightened. I am always trying to present information to them in a meaningful way.

Catherine Kitchura
Teacher Candidate with a Learning Disability
York University

Many children with ADHD show impulsive behaviour, such as this child who is jumping out of his seat and throwing a paper airplane at other children. How would you handle this situation if this were to happen in your classroom?

Signs of ADHD can be present in the preschool years. Parents and preschool or kindergarten teachers might notice that the child has an extremely high activity level and limited attention span. They might say the child is "always on the go," "can't sit still even for a second," or "never seems to listen." Many children with ADHD are difficult to discipline, have little tolerance for frustration, and have problems in peer relations. Other common characteristics of children with ADHD include general immaturity and clumsiness.

Although signs of ADHD are often present in the preschool years, their classification often doesn't take place until the elementary-school years (Guyer, 2000; Pueschel et al., 1995). The increased academic and social demands of formal schooling, as well as stricter standards for behavioural control, often illuminate the problems of the child with ADHD (Whalen, 2000). Teachers typically report that these students have difficulty working independently, completing schoolwork, and organizing work, and that they require greater amounts of supervision than their peers. Restlessness and distractibility also are often noted. These problems are more likely to be observed in repetitive or taxing tasks, or tasks that students perceive to be boring (such as completing worksheets or doing homework). These students are often described as being more talkative and intrusive than others. They often interrupt others and present themselves as bossy and socially immature. Such children may have few friends and tend toward rough play when interacting with classmates.

It was previously believed that ADHD decreased in adolescence, but now it is believed that this often is not the case. Estimates suggest that ADHD decreases in only about one-third of adolescents. Increasingly, it is recognized that these problems also can continue into adulthood.

Definitive causes of ADHD have not been found. For example, scientists have not been able to identify causal sites in the brain. However, a number of causes have been proposed, such as low levels of certain neurotransmitters (chemical messengers in the brain), prenatal and postnatal abnormalities, and environmental toxins such as lead. Heredity might play a role, as 30 to 50 percent of children with ADHD have a sibling or

Teaching Strategies
For Students Who Have Learning Disabilities and ADHD

✔ Use explicit or direct teaching methodologies
  - state lesson objectives verbally
  - present objectives visually (e.g., board, overhead projector)
  - repeat and "break down" instructions for classroom assignments and homework activities
  - use concrete examples to illustrate abstract concepts
  - provide students with immediate and specific feedback about the use of appropriate learning processes and skills (see Chapter 8)

✔ Activate and use students' relevant prior knowledge
  - use students' experiences as a starting point for instruction
  - connect learning to real-life experiences
  - use literature that relates to students' interests and hobbies
  - provide students with choices and allow them to engage in self-determination whenever possible

✔ Provide accommodations as required
  - remember that accommodations do not alter the amount of learning that students need to demonstrate, but rather provide them with opportunities to demonstrate that knowledge
  - seek the advice and resources of the special-education resource teacher whenever possible
  - design assessment tasks that allow students to demonstrate their knowledge in a variety of ways
  - alter teaching and assessment practices to better facilitate students' learning (e.g., underline key concepts, answer two out of three questions, use untimed tests, give extra time)

✔ Provide modifications as required
  - make adjustments with respect to the nature of the academic work in an effort to increase students' confidence and feelings of success (e.g., oral report versus written report)
  - seek the advice and resources of the special-education resource teacher whenever possible
  - clarify that accommodation and modification practices provide all students with equal chances to learn versus providing some students with unfair learning advantages

✔ Facilitate students' organizational and study skills
  - encourage students to adopt effective organizational and study skills by modelling these skills
  - incorporate organizational and study skills into classroom routines (e.g., use long-term and short-term calendars, break projects into steps)

✔ Facilitate students' reading and writing skills
  - refer students to an appropriate professional for diagnosis of reading and/or writing difficulties
  - provide advance notice for reading and writing assignments
  - provide class time for reading and writing assignments
  - allow students to use relevant compensatory technology (e.g., hand-held electronic dictionaries, talking word processors, taped books)
  - use peer and adult tutors (see Chapter 9)

✔ Use behaviour-management techniques when necessary
  - develop behaviour-management plans for individual students as required (see also Chapter 7)
  - follow the principles of positive reinforcement
  - provide meaningful and specific feedback frequently

parent who has the disorder. It is important to note that there is no convincing evidence that social factors, diet, or poor parental management/parenting style cause ADHD (Bassarath, 2001; Woodrich, 1994).

Medication and ADHD   The problem behaviours of some children with ADHD can be temporarily controlled with prescriptive stimulants (Swanson et al., 1993). Two classes of medications are commonly used to treat children with ADHD: psycho-stimulants and antidepressants, with the former being the more widely used (Hutchinson, 2002). The most commonly prescribed stimulants include Ritalin, Dexedrine, and Cylert. In Canada, Ritalin consumption increased significantly from 1990 to 1997 (Maté, 2000), leading some critics to believe that physicians are too quick to prescribe the stimulant to children (Clay, 1997). A child should be given medication only after a complete assessment that includes a physical examination. Typically, a small dose is administered as a trial to examine its effects. If the child adequately tolerates the small dose, the dosage might be increased. Teachers may be called upon to administer medication when a dosage is required during the school day. The teacher plays an important role in observing whether the medication level is too high, making the child dazed and lethargic.

Current best practice in the management of ADHD combines psychological intervention (e.g., cognitive–behavioural management, family counselling), specific teaching pedagogy, and medical interventions. It is important for teachers and parents not to convey to children with ADHD the message that medication is the answer to all of their academic difficulties (Hallahan & Kaufmann, 2000). Children with ADHD should be encouraged to take responsibility for their behaviour in addition to any help that medication may provide them.

Emotional and Behavioural Disorders

Most children have emotional problems at some time during their school years. A small percentage have problems that are so serious and persistent that they are classified as having an emotional or behavioural disorder. **Emotional and behavioural disorders** *consist of serious, persistent, and pervasive problems that involve relationships, aggression, depression, and fears associated with personal or school matters, as well as other inappropriate socioemotional characteristics.* In Canada, 6 to 10 percent of school-aged children are identified with emotional or behavioural disorders (Dwort & Rathgeber, 1998; Smith et al., 2001). These students represent just under one-quarter of all those receiving special-education services. In general, the instances of emotional and behavioural disorders are lowest in the early elementary grades and highest in the late elementary and early secondary grades, with a subsequent decrease in the later secondary-school years (Hallahan & Kauffman, 1997).

There is no single definition of emotional and behavioural disorders, and students demonstrate varied characteristics (Council for Exceptional Children, 1998). Accordingly, a variety of terms have been used to describe emotional and behavioural disorders, including *conduct disorder* (e.g., disruptive, aggressive to others), *socialized aggression* (e.g., delinquency, truancy, gang membership), *attention problems/immaturity* (e.g., easily distractible, poor concentration, impulsive), *anxious/withdrawn* (e.g., self-conscious, reticent, insecure), *psychotic behaviour* (e.g., hallucinations, verbal gibberish), and *motor excess* (e.g., hyperactive, hypertalkative). Students with emotional and behavioural disorders often demonstrate symptoms consistent with several of these categories (Smith et al., 2001).

Autism and Asperger Syndrome   **Autism** and **Asperger syndrome (AS)** *are lifelong developmental disorders that affect children's social interactions, language, and behaviours.* In general, autism is the more severe of the two disorders. Some children with autism never learn to speak; others show communication and social irregularities (Mesibov, 2000). The majority of children with autism demonstrate some level of developmental disability. In a very small number of cases children with autism present *splinter skills*, such as incredible calendar skills or artistic abilities (Hutchinson, 2002). Some display autistic behaviours many times a day, others more sporadically. Social deficits include failing to make eye contact and rarely seeking others for interaction or affection. Communication deficiencies include poor synchrony and lack of reciprocity in conversation, as well as stereotyped, repetitive use of language. Stereotyped patterns can include compulsive rituals and self-stimulatory actions such as rocking, spinning, and finger flicking. Autistic individuals also can become distressed over small changes in their environment. Rearrangement of events or even the furniture can cause children who are autistic to get extremely upset, reflecting their inflexibility in adapting to new routines. Individuals with Asperger syndrome present severe impairments in social interactions and demonstrate repetitive patterns of behaviours and activities. However, they will usually demonstrate age-appropriate language, as well as cognitive and self-help behaviours and skills (Hutchinson, 2002).

There is no separate disability category for autism or Asperger syndrome in most parts of Canada. Instead, these students are often identified with developmental disabilities, communication disorders, or learning disabilities (Smith et al., 2001). Autism and Asperger syndrome are also included under the terms "spectrum of autistic disorders" and "pervasive developmental disabilities" (Hutchinson, 2002). Autism is a relatively rare disorder, occurring in 4 to 5 persons out of 10,000 births. Males are three times more likely than females to be affected (Hashimoto, 1989). Children with this condition are usually identified before three years of age. The prevalence of Asperger syndrome is more difficult to estimate, with many of these children being included under the diagnosis of autism. Autism and Asperger syndrome are organic disorders; children born with rubella and fragile X syndrome are more likely to develop autism than others (Smith et al., 2001). There is no evidence that family socialization causes autism or Asperger syndrome (Rutter & Schopler, 1987).

Students with autism and Asperger syndrome benefit from well-structured classrooms, individualized instruction, or small-group instruction (Pueschel et al., 1995). Since students with autism and Asperger syndrome are *hypersensitive* to sensory stimuli and are easily distracted and anxious, they function best in classrooms where auditory and visual distractions are minimized. As with children who have developmental disabilities, applied behavioural analysis procedures sometimes have been effective in helping autistic children learn more effectively (Alberto & Troutman, 1995). These students also benefit from explicit teaching and modelling of social skills, social interaction, and social cognition (Steiner-Bell, 1998). Keyboards, sign boards, and other visual aids may also be used to help students with autism to communicate.

Aggressive, Out-of-Control Behaviours   A small proportion of children who are classified as having emotional and behavioural disorders and who engage in disruptive, aggressive, defiant, or dangerous behaviours are removed from the classroom; approximately 80 percent of students with emotional and behavioural disorders are educated in their regular schools (Smith et al., 2001). These children are much more likely to be boys than girls, and are more likely to come from communities characterized by poverty (Hutchinson, 2002). Students with a serious emotional and behavioural disturbance are more likely than any other students with a disability to initially be classified as having a disability-related problem during the secondary-school years. However, the majority of these students began to show signs of their emotional problem in the elementary-school years (Wagner, 1995).

When students present severe emotional and behavioural disorders, teachers often enlist the services and supports of community mental health organizations and other institutions. Classroom teachers and special educators spend a great deal of time and energy helping these children adapt to the classroom environment and develop effective learning and social skills (Hocutt, 1996; Wagner, 1995).

In Chapter 3, we discussed juvenile antisocial behaviour, school violence, rejected students, and improving students' social skills. Many of the comments and recommendations we made there apply to children with a serious emotional disturbance. In Chapter 7, Behavioural Approaches, Social Cognitive Approaches, and Teaching, and Chapter 12, Managing the Classroom, we will say more about strategies and plans for effectively working with students who show emotional and behavioural problems.

www.mcgrawhill.ca/college/santrock

Depression, Anxiety, and Fears Some children turn their emotional problems inward. Their depression, anxiety, or fears become so intense and persistent that their ability to learn is significantly compromised. All children feel depressed from time to time, but most get over their despondent, down mood in a few hours or a few days. However, for some children the negative mood is more serious and longer-lasting. **Depression** *is a type of mood disorder in which the individual feels worthless, believes that things are not likely to get better, and behaves lethargically for a prolonged period of time.* When children show these signs for two weeks or longer, they likely are experiencing depression. Poor appetite and not being able to sleep well also can be associated with depression.

Depression is much more likely to appear in adolescence than in childhood and has a much higher incidence in girls than in boys (Culbertson, 1997). Experts on depression say that this gender difference is likely due to a number of factors. Females tend to ruminate on their depressed mood and amplify it, whereas males tend to distract themselves from the negative mood; girls' self-images are often more negative than those of boys during adolescence (Nolen-Hosekema, 1990; Davis & Nolen-Hoeksema, 2001).

Be vigilant in recognizing the signs of depression in students. Because it is turned inward, depression is far more likely to go unnoticed than aggressive, acting-out behaviours. If you think that a student has become depressed, talk with the student's parents and discuss the possibility of obtaining professional counselling. Cognitive therapy has been especially effective in helping individuals become less depressed, as have some drug therapies (Beckham, 2000; Coyne, 2000; Mahoney, 1991).

Anxiety involves a vague, highly unpleasant feeling of fear and apprehension (Kowalski, 2000). It is normal for children to be concerned or worried when they face life's challenges, but some students have such intense and prolonged anxiety that it substantially impairs their school performance. Some students also have personal or school-related fears that interfere with their learning. If a student shows marked or substantial fears that persist, discuss the matter with the parents and recommend professional counselling or clinical help. Some behavioural therapies have been especially effective in reducing excessive or inaccurate anxiety and fear (Baldwin & Baldwin, 1998). More information about anxiety appears in Chapter 11, Motivating Students to Learn.

In this section, we explored a number of ideas about learning disabilities, attention deficit hyperactivity disorder, and emotional and behavioural disorders. A review of these ideas is presented in Summary Table 6.1. Next we will study students who have less common exceptionalities.

Speech and Language Disorders

Learners Who Are Exceptional and Strategies for Teaching Them

- Speech and Language Disorders
- Sensory Impairments and Physical Exceptionalities
- Developmental Disabilities/Intellectual Disabilities

There are many types of speech and language disorders. **Speech and language disorders** *include a number of speech problems (such as articulation disorders, voice disorders, and fluency disorders) and language problems (difficulties in receiving information and expressing language).* Approximately 12 percent of students who receive special-education services have a speech or language impairment.

Exploring Specific Speech and Language Disorders **Articulation disorders** *are problems in pronouncing sounds correctly.* A child's articulation at six or seven years is still not always error-free, but it should be by age eight. A child with an articulation problem might find communication with peers and the teacher difficult or embarrassing. As a result, the child might avoid asking questions, participating in discussions, or communicating with peers. Articulation problems can usually be improved or resolved with speech therapy, though it might take months or years.

Voice disorders *are reflected in speech that is hoarse, harsh, too loud, too high-pitched, or too low-pitched.* Children with cleft palate often have a voice disorder that makes their speech difficult to understand. If a child speaks in a way that is consistently difficult to understand, refer the child to a speech therapist.

Fluency disorders *often involve what is commonly called "stuttering."* Stuttering occurs when a child's speech has a spasmodic hesitation, prolongation, or repetition. The anxiety

SUMMARY TABLE 6.1

Learning Disabilities, Attention Deficit Hyperactivity Disorder, and Emotional and Behavioural Disorders

What are the characteristics of students with learning disabilities?	• Normal or above normal intelligence • Difficulties in at least one academic area • Difficulties are not attributed to a diagnosed problem or disorder (i.e., cerebral palsy) • Difficulty with reading is the most common learning disability • Often experience difficulties with handwriting, spelling, composition, and math • Dyslexia is a severe impairment of the ability to read and spell; dyscalculia is an impairment of the ability to pick appropriate strategies for mathematics.
How are learning disabilities identified and treated?	• Classroom teacher usually suggests possibility of a learning disability • Specialists provide formal evaluation and diagnosis • Many learning disability interventions target reading skills • Success of learning disability interventions depends on the skills and training of the teacher
What is attention deficit hyperactivity disorder (ADHD)?	• A disability in which students consistently demonstrate inattentive, hyperactive, and/or impulsive behaviours • Although signs of ADHD may be present in early childhood, diagnosis of ADHD usually does not occur until the elementary-school years. • Many experts recommend a combination of academic, behavioural, and medical interventions
What are emotional and behavioural disorders?	• Severe, persistent difficulties with relationships, aggression, depression, phobias, or other socioemotional behaviours • Depression, anxiety, and fears can become so intense and persistent that students' ability to learn is significantly compromised
What is autism/ Asperger syndrome?	• Autism and Asperger syndrome involve deficiencies in social relationships, abnormalities in communication, and restricted, repetitive, and stereotyped patterns of behaviour. • Autism is an organic brain dysfunction; there is no evidence that it is caused by family socialization. • Students with autism and Asperger syndrome benefit from a well-structured classroom and individualized instruction.

many children feel because they stutter often just makes their stuttering worse. Speech therapy is recommended.

Language disorders *involve significant impairments in children's receptive (e.g., listening) and expressive (e.g., speaking) language* (Boyles & Contadino, 1997). Language disorders therefore involve difficulties in understanding and expressing thoughts in correct sentences (OAFCCD, 1996). These impairments can negatively affect a child's ability to be educated. Treatment by a language therapist generally produces improvement in the child with a language disorder, but the problem usually is not eradicated (Goldstein & Hockenberger, 1991). Language disorders include difficulties in these areas:

Teaching Strategies
For Students Who Have Receptive and Expressive Language Disorders

Receptive Language Disorders

✔ Use a multisensory approach
  - supplement verbal information with written and/or visual materials and directions
✔ Monitor the speed at which information is presented
  - slow down and repeat information and directions
  - have students reiterate directions before starting a task
✔ Provide students with extra response time
  - allow students with receptive language disorders 10–15 seconds longer to respond than their peers

Expressive Language Disorders

✔ Focus on content of message versus delivery of message
✔ Provide alternative formats for students to demonstrate knowledge
  - allow students with expressive language disorders to present information in a written format versus a verbal one
✔ Provide students with choices or provide the initial sound in word-finding problems
  - phrase questions as a choice among alternatives (e.g., "Is this a *wat*, or is this a *rat*?") versus as an open-ended response (e.g., "This is a *rat*, not a *wat*; say *rat*")
✔ Prepare students for verbal question-answering
  - tell students when you will be calling on them
  - allow students preparatory time to formulate a response
  - provide students with extra time when responding

- Expressing ideas clearly
- Phrasing questions properly to get the desired information
- Understanding and following oral directions
- Following conversation, especially when it is rapid and complex

These difficulties involve both receptive and expressive language.

Receptive language *consists of linguistic information that is received by the brain.* Children with a receptive-language disorder have a glitch in the way they receive information. Information comes in, but the child's brain has difficulty responding to it quickly, which can cause the child to appear disinterested or aloof.

Once a message is received and interpreted, the brain needs to form a response. **Expressive language** *involves the ability to express one's thoughts.* Some children can easily understand what is said to them, but they have difficulties when they try to form a response and express themselves.

There are several observable characteristics of children who have an oral expressive-language disorder (Boyles & Contadino, 1997):

- They might appear shy and withdrawn, and have problems interacting socially.
- They might give delayed responses to questions.
- They might have a problem finding the correct words.
- Their thoughts might be disorganized and disjointed, frustrating the listener.
- They might omit integral parts of the sentence or information needed for understanding.

Many children with language disorders also experience learning difficulties. For instance, children who experience difficulty with the production of speech sounds may have under-

No one means all he says, and yet very few say all they mean, for words are slippery and thought is viscous.

Henry Brooks Adams
American Historian and Author, 19th Century

developed phonemic awareness, which in turn may impede their early reading and spelling attempts. Difficulties with receptive language may result in impaired comprehension across subject areas. Students who experience speech and language disorders typically receive therapy from a speech and language pathologist, with parents, teachers, and other school volunteers providing follow-up exercises (Reid, 1996). Teachers can play important roles in promoting the social and academic well-being of children with speech and language disorders in the classroom. Teachers can create an accepting environment by not allowing other students to tease or mock these children; by modelling effective speech patterns when talking to students with language disorders (e.g., speaking clearly, pausing appropriately, using straightforward language and simple grammatical sentences); and by focusing on the content of students' speech rather than on how it is produced (Nelson & Sturm, 1997).

TYPE OF DEVELOPMENTAL DISABILITY	IQ RANGE
Mild	55–70
Moderate	40–54
Severe	25–39
Profound	Below 25

FIGURE 6.3 **Classification of Developmental Disabilities Based on IQ**

Developmental Disabilities/Intellectual Disabilities

Characteristics   The most distinctive characteristics of **developmental disabilities**, or what are sometimes called **intellectual disabilities**, are *limited intellectual functioning and adaptive skills*. Long before formal tests were developed to assess intelligence, individuals with developmental disabilities were identified by a lack of age-appropriate skills in learning and in caring for themselves. Adaptive skills include skills needed for self-care such as dressing, toileting, feeding, self-control, and peer interaction. The low intelligence and low adaptiveness should be evident in childhood, and should not follow a long period of normal functioning that is interrupted by an accident or other type of brain injury.

Classification and Types of Developmental Disabilities   In the past, people with developmental disabilities were identified as either *mild, moderate, severe,* or *profound* based on their IQ range (mild = 55–70; moderate = 40–54; severe = 25–39; profound = below 25) (see Figure 6.3). However, because categorizations based on IQ ranges are not perfect predictors of functioning, the American Association of Mental Retardation (1993) developed a new classification system based on the degree of support required for individuals to function at their highest level (Hallahan & Kaufman, 2000). As shown in Figure 6.4, the new categories include *intermittent, limited, extensive,* and *pervasive*. These

Intermittent	Supports are provided "as needed." The individual may need episodic or short-term support during life-span transitions (such as job loss or acute medical crisis). Intermittent supports may be low- or high-intensity when provided.
Limited	Supports are intense and relatively consistent over time. They are time-limited but not intermittent. Require fewer staff members and cost less than more intense supports. These supports likely will be needed for adaptation to the changes involved in the school–to–adult period.
Extensive	Supports are characterized by regular involvement (e.g., daily) in at least some setting (such as home or work) and are not time-limited (for example, extended home-living support).
Pervasive	Supports are constant, very intense, and are provided across settings. They may be of a life-sustaining nature. These supports typically involve more staff members and intrusiveness than the other support categories.

FIGURE 6.4 **Classification of Developmental Disabilities Based on Levels of Support**

FIGURE 6.5 A Child with Down Syndrome
What causes a child to develop Down syndrome?

new definitions have not yet been adopted by Ministries of Education across Canada, where general practice is to identify students with developmental disabilities as either *mild* or *severe.*

Mild Developmental Disabilities   About 2 percent of Canadians have mild developmental disabilities (about eight students for every 400 school-aged children). The most commonly identified form of mild developmental disability is Down syndrome, which is genetically transmitted (see Figure 6.5). The majority of these children receive all their instruction in the regular classroom. While students with mild developmental disabilities experience difficulty attaining the academic skills associated with their grade level, they are usually able to live independently and develop into self-sufficient adults. In general, students with mild developmental delays pass through the same cognitive, language, and social developmental stages as other students, but at a much slower rate. These students usually demonstrate delays in short-term memory and attention. They can experience delays in fine motor coordination and present less developed expressive and receptive vocabularies. They may demonstrate poor social adjustment, appearing immature or shy, refusing to cooperate, or being less prepared to initiate and pay attention during conversation (Hutchinson, 2002).

Severe Developmental Disabilities   Considerably fewer individuals are diagnosed with severe developmental disabilities compared to mild developmental disabilities. About one in every 1,000 Canadians are diagnosed with this disability. The category of severe developmental disabilities now includes what was previously identified as moderate, severe, and profound. Accordingly, the amount of care that these individuals will require varies dramatically, with some individuals requiring life-long care and support. Like children with mild developmental disabilities, students with severe developmental disabilities may experience difficulties focusing their attention and retaining information; they may be easily frustrated and act impulsively; they may demonstrate poor physical dexterity and coordination; and they may act inappropriately in social situations. Furthermore, they experience these difficulties to a greater extent than children with mild developmental disabilities (Hutchinson, 2002). Children with severe developmental disabilities are also more likely to show signs of other neurological complications such as cerebral palsy, epilepsy, hearing impairment, visual impairment, and other metabolic birth deficits that affect the central nervous system (Terman et al., 1996). At school, these students often receive a modified curriculum that is functional (focused on the acquisition of life skills) and community-based (Farran & Shonkoff, 1994).

Teachers can do a great deal to facilitate the learning and socialization of children with mild and severe developmental disabilities, starting by promoting a classroom environment that is inclusive and inviting. Teachers can help other students understand that *equity does not mean sameness.* Other teaching strategies are listed in Teaching Strategies For Use with Students Who Have Developmental Disabilities.

Brain Damage   Brain damage can result from many different infections and environmental hazards (Das, 2000; Hallahan & Kaufmann, 2000). Infections in pregnancy, such as rubella (German measles), syphilis, herpes, and AIDS, can cause developmental disabilities in the child. Meningitis and encephalitis are infections that can develop in childhood. They cause inflammation in the brain and can produce developmental disabilities.

Environmental hazards that can result in developmental disabilities include head injuries, malnutrition, birth injury, and chemical substance abuse on the part of the pregnant woman. **Fetal alcohol syndrome (FAS)** *involves a cluster of abnormalities, including developmental disabilities and facial abnormalities, that appear in the offspring of mothers who drink alcohol heavily during pregnancy.*

Sensory Impairments and Physical Exceptionalities

You might have students in your class who have sensory or physical disabilities.

The currently accepted description is "children with exceptionalities" rather than "disabled children" or "handicapped children." Why the changes in terminology?

Visual Impairments   Some students might have mild vision problems that have not been corrected. If you notice students squinting a lot, holding books close to their face to read them, rubbing their eyes frequently, and complaining that things appear blurred or that words move about on the page, refer them to the appropriate school professionals to have their vision checked (Boyles & Contadino, 1997). Many will only need corrective lenses. However, a small portion of students (about 1 in every 1,000 students) have more serious visual problems and are classified as visually impaired. This includes students who have low vision and students who are blind.

Children with **low vision** *have a visual acuity of between 20/70 and 20/200 (on the familiar Snellen scale in which 20/20 vision is normal) with corrective lenses.* Children with low vision can read large-print books or with the aid of a magnifying glass. Children who are **blind** *cannot use their vision in learning and must use their hearing and touch to learn.* Approximately 1 in every 1,000 students in Canada is visually impaired. Of these students, approximately 80 percent are print users, with the remaining children being potential Braille users (Gillon & Young, 2002). Many children who are visually impaired have normal intelligence and function very well academically with appropriate supports and learning aids. However, multiple disabilities are not uncommon in visually impaired and blind students. Students who have multiple disabilities often require a range of support services to meet their educational needs.

An important task in working with a student who has visual impairments is to determine the modality (such as touch or hearing) through which the student learns best (Bowe, 2000).

When developing and implementing a curriculum suitable for students with visual impairments and blindness, teachers will need to work closely with the vision teacher and other professionals and paraprofessionals. Generally, teachers will need to provide modifications and accommodations with respect to the presentation of information (e.g., increased use of verbal directions, enlarged print), classroom environment (seating arrangements, open spaces, consistent placement of furniture), resources (e.g., large-print books, Braille texts, note takers, adaptive technologies including speech-activated word processors), and assessment practices (e.g., additional time for tests and homework, verbal rather than written tests) (Bayha, 1998; Gillon & Young, 2002).

I pass, like night, from land to land;

I have strange power of speech;

That moment that his face I see,

I know the man that must hear me:

To him my tale I teach.

Samuel Taylor Coleridge
British Poet and Author, 19th Century

Teaching Strategies
For Use with Students Who Have Developmental Disabilities

✔ Teach to students' levels of intellectual functioning
  • remember that students with developmental disabilities will function intellectually at a lower level than other students in the class
  • individualize instruction to meet the needs of each student
  • move to a lower level if students do not respond appropriately to the provided level of instruction
  • consider the vocational skills that students will need for employment and modify the curriculum accordingly
✔ Provide concrete examples
  • provide clear and simple directions
  • reiterate instructions frequently
✔ Provide opportunities for frequent practice
  • break larger tasks into a series of smaller ones
  • repeat each step several times
  • allow students to overlearn a concept to facilitate retention
✔ Be sensitive to students' self-esteem
  • avoid comparisons with other students
  • encourage other students to be accepting and tolerant of those with developmental disabilities
✔ Set positive expectations for students' learning
  • remember that students with development disabilities can achieve academically
  • set goals that maximize learning
  • include parents of students with developmental disabilities when making programming decisions
✔ Use the principles of applied behaviour analysis
  • use positive reinforcement to improve students' maintenance, social, and academic skills
  • use principles of behaviour management and techniques (Chapter 7)
✔ Use the services of educational assistants and volunteers
  • use the services of school-based personnel and volunteers from the community to increase the amount of one-on-one instruction that students with developmental disabilities receive

Hearing Impairments   A hearing impairment can make learning very difficult for children. Children who are born deaf or experience a significant hearing loss in the first several years of life usually do not develop normal speech and language. You also might have some children in your class who have hearing impairments that have not yet been detected. If you have students who turn one ear toward a speaker, frequently ask to have something repeated, don't follow directions, or frequently complain of earaches, colds, and allergies, consider having the student's hearing evaluated by a specialist, such as an audiologist (Hutchinson, 2002; Patterson & Wright, 1990).

Many children with hearing impairments receive supplementary instruction. Educational approaches to help students with hearing impairments learn fall into two categories: oral and manual. **Oral approaches** *include using lip reading, speech reading (a reliance on visual cues to teach reading), and whatever hearing the student has.* **Manual approaches** *involve sign language and finger spelling.* Sign language is a system of hand movements

Through the Eyes of Students and Parents

Learning the True Meaning of Inclusion

Gloria Christianson has learned a lot about inclusion over the past 19 years. Her son, Scott, was born deaf and blind with a variety of cognitive and physical exceptionalities that left him in a wheelchair and challenged his everyday functioning.

When Scott entered the school system, Gloria realized that there were many parents, teachers, and students who were afraid of him. But she also realized that there were students who were not afraid of him and that Scott was capable of developing and sustaining true friendships. She wanted Scott to be included fully in his friends' worlds, and for them to be included in his.

Scott's friends were an essential part of his inclusion in school and life. They understood Scott at a personal level that many adults, including some of his teachers, couldn't. They became Scott's advocates. They were included in his IPRC meetings and helped develop his individual education program. They willingly learned deaf–blind signing and they were the ones who introduced him to his new teachers and classmates and taught them how to communicate with him.

They demanded that Scott's experiences not be unreasonably different or separated from their own. For example, Scott's high school had an elevator that could be used only by educational assistants and their charges. Scott's friends lobbied the principal arguing that it was unfair and unnatural to interrupt their discussions with Scott so that he could be left with his educational assistant to use the elevator while they ran to meet him on another floor. Fortunately, the principal recognized the importance of adapting school policies to meet Scott's interests, rather than having Scott adapt to them. From then on, Scott's friends were allowed to ride the elevator with him.

Scott graduated from high school with his friends in September 2002, and his friends were with Scott when he passed away in October 2002. Scott's friends never treated him as someone "special"—he was just one of the gang.

Gloria and Scott Christianson
Ontario

that symbolize words. Finger spelling consists of "spelling out" each word by signing each letter of each word. A total-communication approach that includes both oral and manual approaches is increasingly being used with students who are hearing impaired (Hallahan & Kaufmann, 2000; Heward, 1996).

A number of medical and technological advances also have improved the learning of children with hearing impairments (Boyles & Contadino, 1997). These advances and technologies include cochlear implants (a surgical procedure), placing tubes in the ears (a surgical procedure for middle-ear dysfunction), hearing aids and FM amplification systems, and telecommunication devices, such as the teletypewriter-telephone and RadioMail (using the Internet).

Teachers will also need to adapt their teaching and communication strategies when working with students who have hearing impairments. Specifically, teachers should always demonstrate patience, speaking slowly and providing students with ample time to process information. Teachers should focus on speaking distinctly versus shouting and be conscious of reducing distractions and background noises whenever possible. They should also be aware of their body position when speaking with students with hearing impairments, making sure that they are facing students and that their mouths, lips, and facial features are not obscured (Himber, 1989).

Physical Disabilities and Chronic Medical Conditions Physical disabilities in children can include orthopaedic impairments, such as cerebral palsy and epilepsy. Many children with physical disabilities require special education as well as related services, such as transportation, physical therapy, school health services, and psychological services.

Orthopaedic Impairments **Orthopaedic impairments** *involve restrictions in movement because of muscle, bone, or joint problems.* Depending on the severity of the restriction, some children might have only limited restriction, others might not be able to move at all. Some children cannot control the movement of their muscles. Orthopaedic impairments can be caused by prenatal or perinatal problems, or they can be due to disease or accident during the childhood years. With the help of adaptive devices and medical technology, many children with orthopaedic impairments function well in the classroom (Boyles & Contadino, 1997).

Cerebral palsy *is a disorder that involves a lack of muscular coordination, shaking, or unclear speech.* The most common cause of cerebral palsy is lack of oxygen at birth. In the most common type of cerebral palsy, which is called spastic, children's muscles are stiff and difficult to move. The rigid muscles often pull the limbs into contorted positions. In a less common type, *ataxia,* the child's muscles are rigid one moment and floppy the next moment, making movements clumsy and jerky.

Computers especially can help children with cerebral palsy learn. If they have the coordination to use the keyboard, they can do their written work on the computer. A pen with a light can be added to a computer and used by the student as a pointer. Many children with cerebral palsy have unclear speech. For these children, speech and voice synthesizers, communication boards, talking notes, and page turners can improve their communication.

Epilepsy **Epilepsy** *is a nervous disorder characterized by recurring sensorimotor attacks or movement convulsions.* Epilepsy comes in different forms (Barr, 2000). In one common form, called *simple absent seizures* (petit mal), seizures are brief in duration (often less than 30 seconds) and they might occur anywhere from several to a hundred times a day. Often they occur as brief staring spells, although motor movements such as twitching of the eyelids might appear. In another common form of epilepsy labelled *tonic-clonic* (grand mal), the child loses consciousness and becomes rigid, shakes, and displays jerking motions. The most severe portion of tonic-clonic seizure lasts for about three to four minutes. Children who experience seizures are usually treated with one or more anti-convulsant medications, which often are effective in reducing the seizures but do not always eliminate them. When they are not having a seizure, students with epilepsy show normal behaviour. If you have a student in your class who has a seizure disorder, become well acquainted with the procedures for monitoring and helping the child during a seizure. Also, if a student seems to "space out" a lot in your class, especially under stress, it might be worthwhile to explore whether the problem is boredom, drugs, or potentially a neurological condition. One individual was diagnosed with mild epilepsy late in high school after he had several accidents while learning to drive. The only prior indication was that he did poorly on some of his tests in school and said that he seemed to just space out on them. His teachers thought he was malingering, but the spacing out likely represented the beginning signs of mild epilepsy.

In this section we explore a number of ideas about speech and language disorders, developmental/intellectual disabilities, sensory impairments, cerebral palsy, and epilepsy. A review of these ideas is presented in Summary Table 6.2. In the next section, we will discuss students who are gifted.

SUMMARY TABLE 6.2

Students with Speech and Language Disorders, Developmental/Intellectual Disabilities, Sensory Impairments, and Physical Exceptionalities

What are speech and language disorders?	• Articulation disorders involve difficulty pronouncing words correctly. • Voice disorders involve speech that is too hoarse, loud, or high- or low-pitched. Children with a cleft palate often have voice disorders. • Fluency disorders generally involve stuttering. • Language disorders involve significant impairments in children's receptive (ability to interpret information) and expressive (ability to express thoughts) language.
What are developmental/ intellectual disabilities and how are they classified?	• Developmental or intellectual disabilities involve limited intellectual functioning and adaptive skills. • Mild, moderate, severe, and profound were former classifications used when describing developmental disabilities. Intermittent, limited, extensive, and pervasive are new classifications based on the level of support required to function. • Currently students with developmental disabilities are classified as either mild or severe, with the latter category including the former designations of moderate, severe, and profound. • Children with mild developmental disabilities experience difficulty attaining the academic skills associated with their grade level. • Children with severe developmental disabilities are likely to have other neurological complications such as cerebral palsy, epilepsy, and visual or hearing impairments.
What are visual impairments?	• One in every 1,000 students in Canada is visually impaired. • 80 percent of these students read large-print books or read with the aid of a magnifying glass; 20 percent of the students are potential Braille users.
What are hearing impairments?	• Classroom indicators of possible hearing impairment include turning one ear toward a speaker, asking for things to be repeated, following spoken directions, and complaining of earaches, colds, or allergies. • Oral approaches to helping students with hearing impairments include lip reading and speech reading. • Manual approaches include sign language and finger spelling. • Medical and technological advances for helping students with hearing impairments include cochlear implants, surgery, hearing aids, and telecommunication devices such as the Teletype telephone and Internet Radio Mail.
What is cerebral palsy?	• Cerebral palsy is an orthopaedic disorder that involves a lack of muscular coordination, shaking, or unclear speech. It is most often caused by a lack of oxygen at birth. • The most common type of cerebral palsy is called spastic, in which muscles are stiff and difficult to move and often pull limbs into contorted positions. • Ataxia is a less common form, in which muscles are rigid one moment and floppy the next. • Computers with special keyboards or light pointers are helpful for children with cerebral palsy for written work and communication.
What is epilepsy?	• Epilepsy is a nervous disorder characterized by recurring sensorimotor attacks or movement convulsions. Treatment usually involves one or more anticonvulsant medications. • There are two forms of epileptic seizures: simple absent seizures and tonic-clonic. • Simple absent (petit mal) seizures are brief in duration (30 seconds) and may occur from several to several hundred times a day, with symptoms such as brief staring or twitching of eyelids. • Tonic-clonic (grand mal) seizures involve losing consciousness and rigid shaking or jerking motions that can last up to three or four minutes.

Learners Who Are Exceptional and Strategies for Teaching Them

Students Who Are Gifted

Students Who Are Gifted

The final form of exceptionality we will review is quite different from the disabilities and disorders we have discussed so far. While it is estimated that children who are gifted or otherwise "developmentally advanced" (Keating, 1990) comprise between 3 and 5 percent of students in Canadian schools (Hutchison, 2002), there is no universally accepted definition or measure of giftedness for all provinces or territories. The definition of giftedness most frequently cited in North America is the Marland definition, adopted by The United States Office of Education in 1972 (Alberta Learning, 2000). This definition relies on the professional diagnosis of children who, by virtue of outstanding abilities, are capable of high performance or potential in any one or more of the following areas: general intellectual ability, specific academic aptitude, creative or productive thinking, leadership, or visual and performing arts.

Traditionally, giftedness has been identified using standardized tests and intelligence measures including IQ categories such as mildly gifted (IQ of 115–129), moderately gifted (IQ of 130–144), highly gifted (IQ of 145–159), and extraordinarily gifted (IQ of 160+). Increasingly, however, the single-criterion identification of giftedness such as using IQ scores has given way to the use of multiple-criteria identification using a variety of sources including teacher nominations, behavioural checklists, parent nominations, peer nominations, and self-nominations (Alberta Learning, 2000). These changes, in part, reflect changes in the definitions of giftedness that incorporate newer and broader conceptions of intelligence, such as Gardner's theory of multiple intelligences (Davidson, 2000; Gardner & Hatch, 1989; Gardner, 1983), Renzulli's enrichment triad model (MacRae & Lupart, 1991; Renzulli & Reis, 1985) and Gagné's differentiated model of gifted and talented (Gagné, 1997; 1993).

Gardner's theory of intelligences is presented in Chapter 4; we will now look briefly at Renzulli and Gagné's contributions to the definition of giftedness. According to Renzulli's enrichment model, gifted students demonstrate higher than average ability in three important areas: cognitive abilities (high verbal fluency, the ability to generalize and abstract information, excellent retention), task commitment (goal setting, perseverance, and sometimes perfectionism, which can be detrimental), and creativity (curiosity, questioning, combining and transforming ideas). Renzulli's model suggests that students who are gifted learn in different ways than other children. Gifted children tend to learn at a faster rate, process information better, have better recall, and possess better awareness of strategies and when to use them than other children.

Gagné's model (1993) of differentiated giftedness and talent provides another valuable perspective on giftedness by making a clear distinction between giftedness and talent. Gagné (1993) defines *giftedness* as the possession and use of untrained and spontaneously expressed natural abilities (aptitudes or gifts), in at least one ability domain, to a level that places a child among the top 15 percent of his or her age peers. *Talent* is the systematic development of these natural gifts to a level of mastery in at least one field of human activity that places a child's achievement within the upper 15 percent of age peers who are active in that field. The Gagné model describes five aptitude domains: intellectual, creative, socio-affective, sensorimotor, and "others" (e.g., extrasensory perception).

Gagné (1993, 1997) argues that natural abilities are the basic elements or talents, and teachers can provide a systematic approach to learning and training that is needed to develop raw ability into high-performance talent. Students' natural abilities can be readily observed in the tasks they are asked to perform in school. For example, intellectual abilities are needed to learn to read, creative abilities are needed to produce original work in art or music, and physical abilities are needed in sports or metal-working classes. Gagné also argues that children cannot be talented without first being gifted. However, it is possible to have above-average natural abilities that are never developed into talents, as evidenced by the academic underachievement of some intellectually gifted children. The Gagné model also notes that intrapersonal factors (e.g. motivation, temperament, and personality) and environmental factors (e.g. surroundings, life events, parents, teachers, siblings, peers, and chance) may exert positive or negative influences on the process of talent development.

Wesley Chu is a student who is gifted in the domain of music. He is precocious, marches to the tune of a different drummer, and has a passion to master his domain.

The Gardner, Renzulli, and Gagné models of intelligence, giftedness, and talent have all contributed to the growing recognition and acceptance of the notion of different kinds of giftedness. This includes a greater acceptance of the idea of "dual exceptionalities," where individuals may be both gifted and have a learning disability.

Canadian Wesley Chu is no stranger to the child prodigy scene. Shortly after his third birthday, Wesley started playing the piano. One year later, Wesley became the youngest person to achieve all nine grades at the Royal Conservatory of Music. By the age of five, he became the youngest person to pass his Grade 10 music exam and composed his first composition, "Sonatina in C Major." He performed his second composition, "The Playground," before the Queen of England as part of Canada Day festivities in Ottawa. At seven, he released a five-song CD. When Wesley turned nine, he signed a worldwide recording contract with Warner Classics International, and at age ten released his first major-label CD, *Wesley's World*.

This native Albertan has appeared on many television shows, including the *VII Annual Vatican Christmas Concert*, where he met his Holiness Pope John Paul II and performed his original composition "Christmas in Bethlehem" with the prestigious Orchestra Sinfonica Italiana and Piccoli Musici di Bergamo choir. In 2002, Wesley was invited to perform at the United Nations "Voices and Visions" concert honouring Nelson Mandela. When asked about his plans for the future, Wesley responded "I want to be an astronaut, a scientist, a cartoonist, an inventor and … a pianist." (For more on Wesley, see **www.wesleychu.com/biography.html**.)

The Classic Terman Studies   Lewis Terman (1925) followed into the adult years the lives of approximately 1,500 children whose Stanford-Binet IQs averaged 150. Their developmental outcomes were impressive. For the 800 men, 78 obtained doctorates (they include two past presidents of the American Psychological Association), 48 earned M.D.s, and 85 earned law degrees. These figures are 10 to 30 times greater than the educational achievements of the 800 men of the same age chosen randomly as a comparison control group.

Of the 672 women studied, two-thirds graduated from college in the 1930s, and one-fourth attended graduate school (Terman & Oden, 1959). The gifted women in Terman's study represented a cohort whose childhood, and most of their adulthood, was lived prior to the women's movement and the prevalence of the dual-career couple and the single-parent family (Tomlinson-Keasey, 1993). Studies of gifted girls and women today suggest that they have a stronger confidence in their cognitive abilities than did their gifted counterparts in Terman's study (Tomlinson-Keasey, 1997).

As a group, Terman's gifted were intellectually precocious but they were not emotionally disordered or maladjusted. This finding also has appeared in a number of studies of children who are gifted—namely, that they are as well adjusted as, or are better adjusted than, children who are not gifted (Hutchinson, 2002; Smith et al., 2001; Winner, 1996). However, children who are extremely precocious (such as those having an IQ of 180 or higher) often show more adjustment problems than children who are not gifted (Keogh & MacMillan, 1996).

Steven Ceci (1990) has argued that an analysis of the Terman group's development brings up an important point. It was not just their high IQs that gained them success. Many of Terman's gifted came from upper-income families, and their parents had high achievement expectations for them and played a guiding role in their success. However, a few of the most successful gifted individuals in Terman's study did come from low-income families. Thus, success in life for individuals who are gifted doesn't require being born into material wealth.

Educating Students Who Are Gifted   Underchallenged gifted children can become disruptive, skip classes, and lose interest in achieving. Sometimes these children just disappear into the woodwork, becoming passive and apathetic toward school (Rosselli, 1996).

Three program options for gifted children include (Hertzog, 1998):

• *Special grouping*. Historically, this has been the common way to educate children who are gifted. The special classes during the regular school day are called "pullout" programs (Schiever & Maker, 1997). Some special classes also are held after school, on Saturdays, or in the summer.

- *Acceleration and enrichment in the regular classroom setting.* The majority of students who are gifted spend most of the day in general-education classrooms where they may participate in either acceleration and/or enrichment programs. Acceleration allows students to move through the regular curriculum at a rapid pace. Enrichment programs provide students with topics, materials, experiences, and skills that are beyond the depth of coverage associated with the regular curriculum. Most enrichment activities include some form of acceleration (Gellens, 2002).
- *Mentor, apprenticeship, work/study, and/or community service programs.* Some experts believe these are important, underutilized ways to motivate, challenge, and effectively educate children who are gifted (Gellens, 2002; Pleiss & Feldhusen, 1995).

The wave of educational reform has brought into the regular classroom many strategies that once were the domain of separate gifted programs. These include an emphasis on problem-based learning, having children do projects, creating portfolios, and critical thinking. Combined with the increasing emphasis on educating all children in the regular classroom, many schools now try to challenge and motivate students who are gifted in the regular classroom (Hertzog, 1998). Some schools also include after-school or Saturday programs or develop mentor apprenticeship, work/study, or community service programs. Thus, an array of in-school and out-of-school opportunities is provided.

An ongoing debate focuses on whether students who are gifted should be placed in acceleration or enrichment programs (Feldhusen, 1997). An **acceleration program** *moves students through the curriculum as quickly as they are able to progress.* Acceleration programs include early entrance (to kindergarten, Grade 1, intermediate grades, secondary school, or university), skipping grades, taking extra courses or honours courses, and taking advanced-placement classes. **Curriculum compacting** *is a variation of acceleration in which teachers skip over aspects of the curriculum that they believe students who are gifted do not need.*

An **enrichment program** *provides students with opportunities for learning that are usually not present in the curriculum.* Enrichment opportunities can be made available in the regular classroom; through "pullout" to a special class; through a gifted education resource teacher who consults with the regular classroom teacher; through independent study in after-school, Saturday, or summer sessions and in apprenticeship and mentoring programs; and through work/study arrangements. One type of enrichment program, the *schoolwide enrichment model*, includes developing students' critical and creative thinking skills, and giving them opportunities to select areas of study (Renzulli & Reis, 1997). Students are identified for this type of program by multiple criteria that include creativity and commitment.

Research evaluation of acceleration and enrichment programs has not revealed which approach is best (Winner, 1997). Some researchers have found support for acceleration programs (Kulik, 1992), although critics say a potential problem of grade skipping is that it places students with others who are physically more advanced and socio-emotionally different (Gross, 1993). Other researchers have found support for enrichment programs (Delcourt et al., 1994; Renzulli & Reis, 1997).

Ellen Winner (1997) argues that too often students who are gifted are socially isolated and underchallenged in the classroom. It is not unusual for them to be ostracized and labelled "nerds" or "geeks" (Silverman, 1993). A gifted student who is the only such child in the room does not have the opportunity to learn with students of like ability. Many eminent adults report that school was a negative experience for them, that they were bored and sometimes knew more than their teachers (Bloom, 1985). Winner recommends that these students be allowed to attend advanced classes in their domain of exceptional ability. For example, some especially precocious intermediate-grade students are allowed to take university classes in their area of expertise.

At this point we have studied a number of ideas about children who are gifted. A review of these ideas is presented in Summary Table 6.3 and elaborated in the Diversity and Education box. Next, we will continue our exploration of learners who have exceptualities by examining the many changes that are taking place in their education.

Diversity and Education
Economically Disadvantaged Gifted Students

Some critics argue that too many children in gifted programs are not really gifted, but are instead bright, cooperative, and, usually, white and middle-class. They believe that the mantle of brilliance is cast on many children who are simply "smart normal." Others are concerned that some students who are potentially gifted, especially those who come from ethnic minority backgrounds or from economically disadvantaged backgrounds, are at high risk for not being identified as such. Young boys and adolescent girls also are at risk for being unrecognized. Teachers play a critical role in the initial identification of students who will be assessed for giftedness. As the reliance on informal as well as formal assessment measures grows, teachers are increasingly being called upon to add their insights and observations about students' everyday performances (Smith et al., 2001).

Economically disadvantaged gifted students have more in common with other gifted students than they have with other children from low-income families (Begoray & Slovinsky, 1997). For example, many possess creativity and leadership skills and are accomplished at solving real-life problems (Begoray & Slovinsky, 1997). However, classroom teachers sometimes find it difficult to recognize economically disadvantaged gifted students because they are not trained to look for them.

The Shad Valley Program is an example of gifted-education programming in Canada. This summer program for gifted high school students is offered annually at eight Canadian universities. The program, in operation since 1981, is designed to link high-school students with universities and introduce them to the communities of science, technology, and business (Shad, 2002). The program places students in challenging work terms that complement university workshops and seminars. Research data from the program, focusing on the participation of high-achieving females who have potential in the sciences (Lupart & Wilgosh, 1997), suggest that these female students view their participation as a unique and valuable opportunity to collaborate and network with their peers. This program model is heralded as an exemplary method for the promotion of a gender-balanced science culture in Canada (Lupart & Wilgosh, 1998).

EDUCATIONAL ISSUES INVOLVING STUDENTS WITH EXCEPTIONALITIES

The legal requirement that schools serve all children with an exceptionality is fairly recent. We will explore the legal aspects of working with children who have an exceptionality, profile the placements and services available for children with exceptualities, discuss factors that affect the outcomes for children receiving special-education services, as well as examine the roles of parents and technology in educating these children.

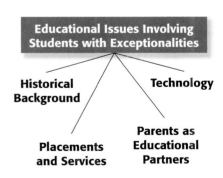

Historical Background

The educational services provided to students with exceptionalities have changed dramatically over the past half-century. Prior to the 1950s, there was no obligation for Canadian schools to educate students with exceptionalities. Instead, the onus was on parents and caregivers to provide appropriate education for their children. As parents and support organizations became more vocal in demanding public schooling for children with exceptionalities, school boards began to develop segregated programs for these students. However the prevailing attitude with respect to special education in the 1950s remained one of

SUMMARY TABLE 6.3
Students Who Are Gifted

What are the characteristics of gifted students?	• Children who are considered gifted are those who have above-average intelligence and/or superior talent in some domain, such as art, music, or mathematics. • Broader definitions acknowledge both demonstrated skills and potential abilities. • Some students demonstrate outstanding abilities in more than one area; others demonstrate skills in specific areas or may have accompanying disabilities. • Some critics argue that too many students in "gifted programs" aren't really gifted but are instead bright, cooperative, and, usually, white. • Others are concerned that students who are potentially gifted, especially young boys, adolescent girls, and students from ethnic minority groups or from socially and/or economically disadvantaged backgrounds, are at risk for being unidentified.
What were the findings from the Terman studies?	• These studies revealed the successful lives of many children who are gifted. Many of the Terman gifted not only had superior IQs but also came from high-income families in which their parents guided and monitored their achievement.
What programs exist for students who are gifted	• Educational programs available for children who are gifted include special grouping ("pullout" programs); acceleration, enrichment, mentor, and apprenticeship programs; and work/study or community service programs.

"looking after the less fortunate: one of social responsibility or liberal educational services as part of residential programs or as part of self-contained, isolated classrooms within a school." These students rarely interacted with other students or teachers in the school (Smith et al., 1991). Curriculum designed for students with special needs during this period tended to focus on vocational training aimed at helping students find employment. Many students with exceptionalities who were less outwardly apparent or more behavioural in nature (the term learning disability was first used in 1963) were viewed as poor candidates for education, and public education for students who were gifted was a virtual nonentity until the 1970s (Weber & Bennet, 1999).

In the 1970s a series of landmark reports, for example *One Million Children: A National Study of Canadian Children with Emotional and Learning Disorders* (Roberts & Lazure, 1970) and *Standards for Education of Exceptional Children in Canada* (Hardy et al., 1971), were published questioning the value of special-education programs that paralleled regular education programs. Increasing public support for the integration of children with exceptionalities into the regular classroom slowly led to school boards mainstreaming or integrating students with exceptionalities into general education programs when it was deemed appropriate.

The 1970s were also marked by a series of court cases questioning the decisions of school boards to place students with exceptionalities in segregated classes. Legal advocacy has led to the increasing involvement of parents or their representatives in the day-to-day decision making associated with education for children with exceptionalities (Weber & Bennett, 1999). The mid-1970s in the United States saw the development of the Education for All Handicapped Children Act of 1975, which mandated that students with disabilities be provided an appropriate education designed to meet their unique needs in the least restrictive environment possible. The Act also required that students with disabilities be educated to the maximum extent appropriate with peers without disabilities (i.e., mainstreamed), and codified important practices such as consultation with parents and written individual education plans (IEPs) for students (Kayale, 2000). For Canadian educators the Act highlighted the benefits and potential difficulties associated with implementing the least-restrictive environment; defining what the term "least-restrictive environment" means has led to many legal challenges.

By the 1980s, the national trend was moving from integration toward inclusion, which emphasized that students with exceptionalities should be fully included in school programs and activities (Smith et al., 1991). Inclusion differed from integration in several ways. One important differentiation was the underlying assumption that children with exceptionalities belong in the general classroom and that their schooling experiences should prepare them for the highest degree of independence possible (Liu & Pearson, 1999). In the 1980s, Canada also developed the Canadian Charter of Rights and Freedoms (1982), which constitutionally guaranteed the education rights of minorities and those with exceptionalities. In the early 1990s, Canada also ratified the United Nations' Convention on the Rights of the Child (1989), which defined and outlined a number of children's rights including the rights for children with exceptionalities to safety and education. While the Canadian Charter of Rights and Freedoms and Canada's endorsement of the U.N. Convention on the Rights of the Child provide greater security and entitlement to children with exceptionalities, the struggle for equality and appropriate education is not over. Pellat (1997) notes that some provinces and territories have objected (and, thus, not complied) to the ratification of the U.N. Convention on the grounds that the promotion of children's rights undermines parental authority. While Canada has moved forward in its understanding and approach to educating students with exceptionalities, there is still a long way to go.

Placements and Services

Obtaining Services for Students with Exceptionalities   In Canada, prior to the 1970s, a medical model approach that relied heavily on formal assessments by outside professionals was central to obtaining services for learners with exceptionalities. Since then, teachers have played a more hands-on role in the obtaining of services for and assessment of their students (Weber & Bennett, 1999). Typically, when a teacher suspects that a child may have an exceptionality and may benefit from a modified program, the teacher will contact that student's parents and discuss general behavioural or instructional processes that might resolve the difficulty. The teacher may also bring forward that student's name, along with observations and other relevant documentation (e.g., samples of schoolwork, school records), to a team assembled to complete an assessment for the student and help with instructional planning and placement decisions. Usually, the team consists of the regular teacher, the special-education teacher (or resource teacher, special-education consultant, or school psychologist), the principal, and pertinent community members (e.g., a social worker, occupational therapist, and/or speech and language pathologist). The student's parents—and, when appropriate, the student—are also invited to participate on this team. If a paraprofessional support person (educational assistant or resource teacher) has been assigned to work with the student, he or she will also serve on the team.

The primary purpose of this assessment is to identify a student's strengths and learning needs. The assessment protocol may consist of both formal (e.g., standardized tests) and informal measures (e.g., curriculum-based assessment, observation, criterion-referenced testing) as deemed appropriate by the team or required by the school board (Smith et al., 2001). Specifically, the classroom teacher and other school-based members of the team usually carry out the informal assessments, while professionals in the community complete the formalized measures. In some communities where there are long waiting lists for assessment services, parents may elect to pay for the services of a professional. Based on the assessment findings, the appropriateness of the current instructional program is reviewed with the goal of implementing specific accommodations and/or modifications that will allow the student to experience optimal success in the general classroom. The assessment process continues with an evaluation of the effectiveness of these program accommodations and modifications, which in turn incite further decisions about curriculum modifications and the provision of special-education services. The results of this process are translated into an individualized education plan (IEP).

We, the peoples of the United Nations ...reaffirm faith in fundamental human rights, in the dignity and worth of the human person....

Preamble to the Charter of
the United Nations
June, 1945

Increasingly, children with exceptionalities are being taught in the regular classroom, as is this child with a developmental delay.

The Individualized Education Plan (IEP) The individualized education plan—also known as the individualized program plan (IPP), the personal program plan (PPP), or the individualized student support plan (ISSP)—is the formal document that outlines the educational program for students with exceptionalities. Ideally, the school team prepares and regularly reviews the IEP in consultation with the student's parents. In most provinces and territories, an IEP is required whenever significant changes are made with respect to a student's learning expectations, curriculum, or teaching approaches (Hutchinson, 2002). Although the name and the specific format of the IEP may vary across provinces and territories, the plan is required to include the following components:

• *Present level of functioning*: Provides an overview of the student's current performance level, including information gathered from formal and informal testing procedures
• *Long-term goals*: Specific, realistic, measurable goals that meet the direct needs of the individual learner. Goals may include items related to learning in the curriculum, independence in the community, and career planning.
• *Short-term goals*: The specific steps and processes required to achieve long-term objectives. Short-term goals may be written only after long-term objectives are identified and tasks analyzed for prerequisite knowledge and skills.
• *Instructional strategies, supports, and services*: These outline any changes to the instructional format and modifications to the curriculum. May include the use of assistive or adaptive technologies and other equipment as required. May also outline professional support services including occupational therapy or speech and language remediation.
• *Timelines*: Ideally, the IEP is implemented immediately after it is written. A date for formal review is usually set for the end of the school year in which the IEP was established or reviewed. Parents and other member of the school team will be invited to attend the review session.
• *Participants' roles and responsibilities*: Provides an overview of the roles and responsibilities of all individuals involved in the educational program including the classroom teacher, special-education teacher, parent, and student.
• *Evaluation procedures*: Outlines the assessment procedures that will be used to evaluate the effectiveness of the educational program. Assessment should be ongoing and occur in the learning environment.

I have learned silence from the talkative, toleration from the intolerant, and kindness from the unkind; yet strange, I am ungrateful to those teachers.

Kahlil Gibran
*Lebanese Poet, Philosopher, and Artist,
20th Century*

The Regular Classroom Teacher With the increase in inclusion, the regular classroom teacher is responsible for providing more of the education of children with disabilities than in the past. The techniques outlined in Teaching Strategies for Maintaining an Effective Inclusive Classroom on page 193 can help you provide a more effective education for these children.

The Resource Teacher The resource teacher (sometimes called the learning assistance teacher, the learning program teacher, or the curriculum resource teacher) can provide valuable services for many children who have exceptionalities. Most children with exceptionalities spend the majority of their school day in a regular classroom and a small portion of their day in a resource room where a resource teacher works with them. In a typical arrangement, a student might spend a brief amount of time in the resource room and the remainder of time in the regular classroom. In many situations, resource teachers work with these students to improve their reading, writing, or mathematical skills.

It is important for the regular classroom teacher and the resource teacher to collaborate and coordinate their efforts. In some cases, the resource teacher will work with the student in the regular classroom setting rather than seeing the student in a resource room.

www.mcgrawhill.ca/college/santrock

Teaching Strategies
For Maintaining an Effective Inclusive Classroom

✔ Increase your knowledge base
- become more knowledgeable about the types of students with exceptionalities in your classroom
- keep up to date on the technology that is available for educating students with exceptionalities
- read professional journals that specialize in the education of students with exceptionalities (e.g., *Exceptional Children, Teaching Exceptional Children, Journal of Learning Disabilities*)
- join professional organizations that specialize in the education of students with exceptionalities (e.g., Council for Exceptional Children)
- enrol in post-secondary and continuing-education courses that focus on students with exceptionalities and effective educational programming for them
- encourage your school to provide increased support and training about how to teach children with exceptionalities

✔ Use relevant support services
- carry out all components of students' individual education plans
- become acquainted with and use available support services in your school and board
- seek out potential support services in the community, including the use of volunteers

✔ Avoid using diagnoses as explanations
- be cautious about using labels as causal explanations (e.g., "Larry has trouble reading because he has a learning disability," versus "Larry needs special help with reading")
- evaluate students' progress and not their labels—labels have a way of staying with children even after students' performances have improved
- use labels to consider the best conditions for improving students' learning and overall school experience

✔ Help all students understand and accept those with exceptionalities
- provide all students with information about individuals with exceptionalities
- provide opportunities for students without exceptionalities to interact positively with students with exceptionalities (e.g., peer tutoring and cooperative learning activities)
- provide opportunities for students to help those with special needs

✔ Remember that all students benefit from effective strategies
- be caring, accepting, and patient
- hold positive expectations for all students' learning
- help students with their social and communication skills as well as their academic skills
- be enthusiastic about students' learning
- monitor students' learning and provide prompt, effective, and explicit feedback

The Special-Education Teacher   In Canada, some teachers have extensive training in special education. These teachers (sometimes called methods and resource teachers) will work with many students, including those who experience difficulties in school but who have not been identified as exceptional. Some children with exceptionalities will spend time with the special-education teacher for part of the school day and be mainstreamed

www.mcgrawhill.ca/college/santrock

Working Effectively with Paraprofessionals

Working with a teaching assistant, or educational assistant, sometimes can be a challenging and intimidating experience, especially for beginning teachers. Many paraprofessionals have worked in the school system for numerous years. As a teacher, you need to acknowledge the expertise and experience that paraprofessionals bring to your classroom.

When you first begin working with teaching assistant, spend some time getting acquainted. Ask about his or her background, special interests, and area(s) of expertise. Clearly express your commitment to your students' social, emotional, and intellectual well being, as well as your willingness to assume responsibility for all the children in your classroom, including those with exceptionalities.

It is critical to view your relationship with paraprofessionals as that of a team where all members work collaboratively to provide *all* students with optimal learning experiences. Working as part of a collaborative team means clearly identifying members' roles and responsibilities, participating in program planning, reviewing students' progress, and celebrating the successes of your students.

Dr. Vianne Timmons
Former Teacher and Dean, Faculty of Education
Vice President Academic Development
University of Prince Edward Island
Editor of *Exceptionality Education Canada*

Only from the alliance of one person working with another are great things born.

Antoine de St. Exupéry
French Essayist and Novelist, 20th Century

the rest of the day. In an inclusive model, special-education teachers play a critical support role for regular classroom teachers, helping them develop and deliver programs for students with exceptionalities.

Professional and Paraprofessional Support Services In addition to regular classroom teachers, resource teachers, and special-education teachers, a number of other special-education personnel provide services for children with exceptionalities. These include teacher aides, psychologists, counsellors, school social workers, nurses, physicians, occupational therapists, physical therapists, and speech and hearing specialists. Transportation services may also be provided if needed.

Teacher aides (also known as educational assistants, or educational aides) can help the regular classroom teacher provide individualized instruction for students with exceptionalities. Some teacher aides are certified to work with students who have exceptionalities. Psychologists might be involved in assessing whether a student has an exceptionality and might be part of the team that creates the IEP. They and counsellors might also work with some students who have an exceptionality. School psychologists might make recommendations to teachers about ways that students with an exceptionality can learn more effectively. School social workers often help to coordinate family and community services for students with an exceptionality. Nurses and physicians might conduct medical assessments and/or prescribe medication for students with exceptionalities. Physical therapists and occupational therapists might be involved in helping students recover from remediable physical or cognitive impairments. Speech and hearing specialists may be included when their skills will help improve students' communication and listening skills.

Parents as Educational Partners

Educators and researchers increasingly recognize how important it is for teachers and parents to jointly guide the learning of children with exceptionalities (Williams & Cartledge, 1997). Refer to Teaching Strategies for Communicating with Parents, on page 195, for an outline of effective strategies.

Collaborative Consultation and Interactive Teaming In the last two decades, experts on educating children with exceptionalities have increasingly advocated more collaborative consultation (Idol, 1997; O'Shea & O'Shea, 1997). In **collaborative consultation**, *people with diverse expertise interact to provide services for children.* Researchers have found that collaborative consultation often results in gains for students, as well as improved skills and attitudes for teachers (Idol, Nevin, & Paolucci-Whitcomb, 1994).

Ideally, collaborative consultation encourages shared responsibility in planning and decision making. It also enables educators with diverse expertise to construct effective alternatives to traditional educational approaches (Pugach & Johnson, 1995). When collaborative consultation is used, many students remain in the regular classroom and the regular classroom teacher is actively involved in planning the students' education (Bryant & Bryant, 1998).

Increasingly, the term *interactive teaming* is being used (Thomas, Correa, & Morsink, 1995). Interactive team members are professionals and parents who collaborate to provide direct or indirect services to children (Coben et al., 1997). They share knowledge

Teaching Strategies
For Communicating with Parents of Students with Exceptionalities

✔ Appreciate each student as an individual
- discuss the student's strengths as well as areas of difficulty
- focus on the student's positive-growth areas at the beginning and end of each conversation

✔ Place yourself in the parents' shoes
- realize that parents often experience frustration, anger, and disappointment trying to help their children
- relay compassion and an appropriate degree of hope for their children

✔ Provide parents with relevant information
- engage parents in ongoing conversation about the nature of their child's exceptionality and implications for the child's schooling experience
- work cooperatively with parents to establish realistic learning goals
- discuss relevant resources that can be used to facilitate the student's schooling experience
- discuss how popular magazines, newspapers, movies, television, and radio can sometimes provide inaccurate information about children with exceptionalities
- encourage parents to discuss anything they read or hear pertaining to their child's exceptionality with you or other school personnel
- share behaviour-management techniques with parents

✔ Avoid presenting yourself as the "expert"
- recognize that each meeting with a parent is an opportunity to learn more about an individual student
- recognize parents as equal partners
- encourage parents to ask questions and express their emotions
- acknowledge when you are unable to answer parents' questions and attempt to find the information for them

✔ Avoid stereotyping students
- do research about the student, the exceptionality, and the available options
- avoid making conscious or unconscious stereotypical judgments about students and their parents based on their socioeconomic status, ethnicity, family structure, religion, or gender
- remember that conscious or unconscious biases undermine effective communication

✔ Reach out to parents to establish and maintain effective communication
- inform parents that they play an important role in helping you and other school professionals understand and educate their children
- recognize that parents know their children better than you do
- support the attendance of parents at individualized education plan (IEP) sessions and other school meetings

and skills, teaching other members their expertise when appropriate. Actual team sizes vary, and teams change in composition depending on the complexity of the child's needs. Persons involved can include educational, medical, administrative, vocational, and allied health specialists, social services personnel, and parents.

Through the Eyes of Parents

Parents as Partners

Teachers need to keep parents informed and involved in their children's learning and development at school. Conversely, parents need to be willing to work with school staff and participate in events offered by the school. All of our boys' schools have offered training workshops, support groups, and information nights. We've learned a lot about how to help our sons become self-directed learners by taking part in these activities. Teachers are experts about learning, but parents are experts about their own children. Working together creates the best environment for student learning. We became involved in our sons' schools because we wanted to help them succeed in school and shape the environment that they grew up in.

Les and Susan Wagner
Parents of Three Boys, Computer Entrepreneur & Nurse
British Columbia

Technology

Two types of technology that can be used to improve the education of students with exceptionalities are instructive technology and assistive technology (Blackhurst, 1997). **Instructive technology** *includes various types of hardware and software, combined with innovative teaching methods, to accommodate students' learning needs in the classroom.* This technology can include videotapes, computer-assisted instruction, or complex hypermedia programs in which computers are used to control the display of audio and visual images stored on videodisc. The use of telecommunication systems, especially the Internet and its World Wide Web, hold considerable promise for improving the education of all students.

 Assistive technology *consists of various services and devices to help students with disabilities function within their environment.* Examples include communication aids, alternative computer keyboards, and adaptive switches (see Figure 6.6). To locate such services, educators can use computer databases such as the Device Locator System (Academic Software, 1996).

 Teams of educators and other professionals often combine these technologies to improve the learning of students with disabilities (Elkind, 2000). For example, students who are unable to use their hands to operate a computer keyboard might use a voice-operated computer (assistive technology) that provides instruction from a software program that was designed to provide spelling instruction (instructional technology). To read about traditional and constructivist technologies, see the Technology and Education box on the next page.

 At this point we have studied many ideas about educational issues involving children with exceptionalities. An overview of these ideas is presented in Summary Table 6.4. In the next chapter we will turn our attention to behavioural approaches, social cognitive approaches, and teaching.

Traditional and Constructivist Technologies for Students with Exceptionalities

Traditional applications of technology for working with students with exceptionalities involve the use of computer-based tutorials, drill and practice, and games. These applications are used to improve the decoding and vocabulary skills of children with learning disabilities, especially those who have reading problems. Game-type software is often used to motivate children with a learning exceptionality.

Increasingly, tutorial or drill and practice applications of technology are being replaced by constructivist computer-based learning environments. Such environments focus on developing students' understanding and thinking skills through the use of real-world problem-based simulations. For example, Science Court, an Ontario Ministry of Education licensed software program, has a module that is aimed at the Grade 6 curriculum and reviews scientific phenomena (e.g., electric current) in an entertaining and thought-provoking way. The software has many scenarios presented as cartoons, which lead students through a science problem that

eventually is resolved as a court case. The case can be solved by having students view the video, meet in small groups, talk about and plan a solution, and wait for the final verdict. The software is accompanied by time for student group work, completion of the worksheets, and doing an experiment (**www.yrbe.edu.on.ca/~cecw/docs/software/profiles/ScienceCourt.PDF**). The use of problem-based simulations and programs has been shown to be both motivational and fun for students (Kosakowski, 2000).

Other constructivist technology applications that can be used effectively with children with exceptionalities are cognitive organizers, for example Idea Fisher and Inspiration. Word prediction software, voice recognition software, and text reader programs can also be used to help individuals with exceptionalities write or work on a computer, use e-mail, and access the Internet (DiPetta & Woloshyn, 2000).

(a)

(b)

FIGURE 6.6 Special Input Devices
These special input devices can help students with physical exceptionalities use computers more effectively.
(a) A student uses a special input device attached to the student's head to send signals to the computer.
(b) Many students with physical disabilities such as cerebral palsy cannot use a conventional keyboard and mouse. Many can use alternative keyboards effectively.

SUMMARY TABLE 6.4
Educational Issues Involving Students with Exceptionalities

What is the historical background around educating students with exceptionalities?	• Between 1950 and 1970 students with exceptionalities were either in residential education programs or isolated in special classrooms. • Landmark reports in the 1970s questioned the value of segregated education programs and proposed services based on individual needs rather than categories of exceptionalities. • The Canadian Charter of Rights and Freedoms (1982) and legal challenges around segregated classes led to mainstreaming and integration, as well as to more parental involvement in children's educational planning • Mainstreaming involves the integration of students with exceptionalities into general education programs. • Inclusion assumes that children with exceptionalities belong in general classrooms and that schooling should prepare students for the highest level of independence possible.
How are services for students with exceptionalities obtained?	• Classroom teachers play key roles in obtaining services for students with exceptionalities. • Teachers contact professionals or paraprofessionals to carry out assessments. • Parents and other members of the school team develop individualized education plans (IEPs).
What is an individualized education plan (IEP)?	• IEPs are personal program plans that outline learning expectations, curriculum, and teaching approaches for a student with an exceptionality. • IEPs include short- and long-term goals, supports and services, timelines, participants' roles, and evaluation procedures.
What is an inclusive classroom?	• Inclusion supports the assumption that students with exceptionalities belong in the classroom and that their schooling experiences should prepare them for the highest degree of independence possible. • The regular classroom teacher is supported by special-education support personnel. • Students are provided with an increased understanding of and acceptance for others.
What are the roles of resource teachers, special-education teachers, professionals, and paraprofessionals?	• Resource teachers provide individual services for students with exceptionalities. • Special-education teachers have extensive training in special education and also work with students who experience difficulties in school but who have not been identified as exceptional. • Special-education teachers support regular classroom teachers and help them develop and deliver programs for students with exceptionalities. • Professionals and paraprofessionals support and work collaboratively with the classroom teacher.
What are instructive and assistive technologies, constructivist applications, and the World Wide Web?	• Instructive technologies (or instructional technologies) are applications of technology for teaching and learning (e.g. computers and audio/visual equipment) • Assistive technologies are defined as devices that are used to help compensate for or overcome learning difficulties (e.g. speech synthesizers, text-readers, and books on tape). • Constructivist applications are interactive uses of technology that promote understanding and thinking skills, often through the use of real-world simulations. • The World Wide Web and other information and communication technologies assist isolated or homebound students to develop a sense of community and belonging.

Before the school year starts, Mr. Drago always holds a "get-acquainted" meeting with the parents of his incoming kindergartners. He does this so that he can explain what the children will be doing in kindergarten, his educational philosophy, his expectations, and the procedure for dropping students off at school. Especially important, this meeting provides parents with an opportunity to ask questions and voice any concerns they may have. This is what he typically hears from parents:

"Joaquim still naps in the afternoon. Is there any way we can have him changed to the morning class?"

"Ashley has severe asthma. She'll need to have her nebulizer close by in case she has an asthma attack. Do you know how to use one?"

"I just know that Stephen won't be able to sit still for very long. Do you allow the children to move a lot?"

"I sure hope you give the kids a lot of time to be active. Maura won't be able to sit still for long, either."

"Alex is very advanced for his age. What can you do to challenge him?"

"Amanda is advanced, too." "So is my Tony."

"Well, John seems to be behind. I just don't know what to do with him. He doesn't speak very well."

Mr. Drago listens respectfully to each concern or question and provides the following response: "I'll do everything I can to ensure your children have a good year in my class. All children are different and learn at different rates, so I'm not too worried about a child who is a little behind or ahead. I think we'll all do fine together."

The school year begins uneventfully. The children enjoy playing with each other and appear to have adjusted to school nicely. Mr. Drago uses the children's free-play time to observe them. While there are obvious differences between the children, he has specific concerns only for Maura, Stephen, and Alex. Their lack of attention and inability to sit still during story time is beginning to be a bit disruptive. Mr. Drago makes a note to himself to talk to their parents about this behaviour. Each day at the beginning of class, the students have calendar time. Mr. Drago marks off the day of the month on the calendar with a large X and discusses the weather. He then writes a statement on the blackboard describing the day's weather. On the tenth day of school, he writes on the board "Today is sunny and hot." He then reads the statement to the students so that they might begin to make word associations: "Today is sunny and warm."

Alex quickly shouts out, "That's not what you wrote! You wrote today is sunny and hot." Mr. Drago is astounded.

Later, during free-play time, he asks Alex to sit with him. Alex looks longingly at the trucks, but grudgingly complies. "Alex, will you read this book to me?"

"Sure," replies Alex, and does so flawlessly.

"Do you have this book at home?" asks Mr. Drago.

"Yep. Lots of others, too."

"How about this one? Do you have it?"

"Nope."

"Well then, suppose you try to read this one to me."

"Okay, but then can I go play with the trucks?"

"Certainly."

Alex reads the book to Mr. Drago, missing only a few words, and then rushes off to play with the trucks.

The next day during calendar time, Mr. Drago asks the class, "If today is the fifteenth day of the month and there are thirty days in the month, how could we find out how many days are left?"

The children call out, "We could count the days that don't have X's on them."

"Very good," replies Mr. Drago.

Alex looks puzzled. "What's wrong, Alex?" asks Mr. Drago.

"Why don't we just subtract?" he asks.

What are the issues in this case?

- How should Mr. Drago approach the parents of the students he believes might be gifted?
- Is it appropriate for him to recommend testing of any of the children? Why or why not?
- If Alex can already read and subtract, are there other skills he has likely mastered? If so, what might they be? How might this impact his experiences in kindergarten?
- How might Mr. Drago best program for a child like Alex?

CHAPTER REVIEW

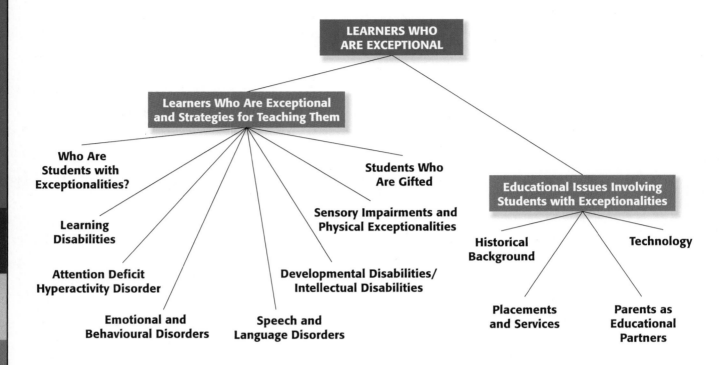

LEARNERS WHO ARE EXCEPTIONAL

- **Learners Who Are Exceptional and Strategies for Teaching Them**
  - Who Are Students with Exceptionalities?
  - Learning Disabilities
  - Attention Deficit Hyperactivity Disorder
  - Emotional and Behavioural Disorders
  - Speech and Language Disorders
  - Developmental Disabilities/Intellectual Disabilities
  - Sensory Impairments and Physical Exceptionalities
  - Students Who Are Gifted
- **Educational Issues Involving Students with Exceptionalities**
  - Historical Background
  - Technology
  - Placements and Services
  - Parents as Educational Partners

To obtain a detailed review of this chapter, study these four summary tables:

KEY TERMS

dyslexia 168
dyscalculia 168
attention deficit hyperactivity
   disorder (ADHD) 171
emotional and behavioural
   disorders 174
autism 174
Asperger syndrome 174

depression 176
speech and language disorders 176
articulation disorders 176
voice disorders 176
fluency disorders 176
language disorders 177
receptive language 178
expressive language 178

developmental disabilities/
   intellectual disabilities 179
fetal alcohol syndrome (FAS) 180
low vision 181
blind 181
oral approaches 182
manual approaches 182
orthopaedic impairments 184

cerebral palsy 184
epilepsy 184
acceleration program 188
curriculum compacting 188
enrichment program 188
collaborative consultation 194
instructive technology 196
assistive technology 196

 PROFESSIONAL DEVELOPMENT/PORTFOLIO ACTIVITIES

1. **Role Reversal**

    Place yourself in the role of a parent who has just been noti-
    fied by the school that your child has a learning disability. In
    your portfolio, write down your thoughts on the following
    questions: What feelings are you likely to be having as a parent?
    As a parent, what questions do you want to ask your child's
    teacher? Now, write down how you, as the teacher, will
    respond to these questions.

2. **Individual Education Planning**

    Teachers who work with children with exceptionalities typi-
    cally develop an individualized education plan (IEP) for each
    child. What is an IEP? Find sample IEPs from local schools

    and discuss in class how all students could benefit from receiving
    the type of feedback presented in an IEP. How could you use
    an IEP as a model for tailoring your instruction to meet the
    needs of all students?

3. **An ADHD Strategy**

    Imagine that you have two students in your classroom who
    have been diagnosed with ADHD. Research and write a report
    on some of the strategies for helping these children succeed
    in the classroom. Why is family support so important? As
    the classroom teacher, what actions will you take to maintain
    ongoing communication with the family? Place your finished
    report in your portfolio.

 INTERNET ACTIVITIES

1. **Internet Resources for Special Needs**

    A number of Canadian and international organizations have
    created special-needs Websites for teachers. Find three such
    Websites and report to the class on what they offer teachers
    in terms of resources and tools for working with students in
    your classroom.

2. **Technologies for Living**

    The Internet provides a variety of resources and tools for
    helping students with exceptionalities participate fully in the

    online world. What specific tools or software might students
    with learning difficulties benefit from? Search for these tools
    on the Web and make a list of the resources and sites that you
    find. Share this list with your class or include it in your portfolio.

    Connect to the Online Learning Centre at www.mcgrawhill.ca/
    college/santrock **to explore possible answers.**

Online
*Learning*Centre

Visit the *Educational Psychology* Online Learning Centre at
www.mcgrawhill.ca/college/santrock
to access Websites related to the above Internet Activities as well as chapter quizzes,
a searchable glossary, and other learning and study tools.

7 Behavioural Approaches, Social Cognitive Approaches, and Teaching

Preview

Virtually everyone agrees that helping students learn is an important function of schools. However, not everyone agrees on the best way to learn. In this chapter we will explore the behavioural and social cognitive approaches to learning. These are some of the questions we will examine:

- What are some different ways that students learn?

- What are some alternatives to punishing students when you want them to behave?

- How can you use observational learning to improve students' behaviour?

- What strategies can be used to improve students' self-regulatory skills?

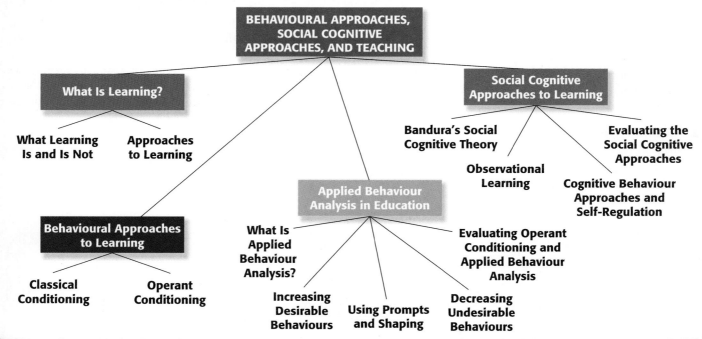

BEHAVIOURAL APPROACHES, SOCIAL COGNITIVE APPROACHES, AND TEACHING

What Is Learning?
- What Learning Is and Is Not
- Approaches to Learning

Behavioural Approaches to Learning
- Classical Conditioning
- Operant Conditioning

Applied Behaviour Analysis in Education
- What Is Applied Behaviour Analysis?
- Increasing Desirable Behaviours
- Using Prompts and Shaping
- Decreasing Undesirable Behaviours
- Evaluating Operant Conditioning and Applied Behaviour Analysis

Social Cognitive Approaches to Learning
- Bandura's Social Cognitive Theory
- Observational Learning
- Evaluating the Social Cognitive Approaches
- Cognitive Behaviour Approaches and Self-Regulation

Teaching Stories: Larry Ash

Larry Ash is the head of mathematics, science, and Canadian and world studies at an inner-city secondary school in Ontario. The school provides alternative education services for students who, for a variety of reasons (academic difficulties, behavioural conduct, truancy), have been removed from mainstream schools. Below, Larry talks about his philosophy of classroom management.

"Students feel secure when the teacher has control of the classroom. Students need to know that they can speak freely in class and take academic risks. They need to know that the teacher will not tolerate derogatory comments or disrespectful behaviour. I believe teachers earn students' respect by consistently enforcing rules and their consequences in a non-confrontational manner.

"During the first few days of class, I give my students a handout entitled 'Larry's Expectations.' The list outlines the rules and regulations for my classroom and the school. There are not many items on the list, but they are important ones. I watch my students carefully and call on them when they break a rule. In a calm and non-confrontational manner, I explain to them how they have strayed from the expected behaviour and what they need to do to rectify the situation. Indeed, these first few days of class set the tone for the remainder of the year.

"For instance, one school policy is that students cannot enter a classroom late after the first five minutes of class without an admittance slip. At the beginning of the year, I take a great deal of time to explain this rule and why it is important. The first time a student arrives late, I allow the student to enter the class and I reiterate the school policy. The next time that student arrives late, I apologize that I cannot allow him or her into the class. Then I provide the student with the day's work and state that I look forward to seeing him tomorrow when he arrives on time. It is very important that I do not allow the student to stay in class despite any excuse that he or she may have or regardless of how much I may want that student in my class. I act consistently every time a student arrives late. If I bend the rules once, only once, trust and respect are lost for the rest of the year."

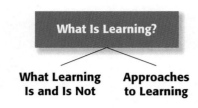

What Learning Is and Is Not   Approaches to Learning

Experience is a great teacher.

Aristotle
Greek Philosopher, 4th Century B.C.

WHAT IS LEARNING?

Learning is a central focus of educational psychology. When people are asked what schools are for, a common reply is: "To help children learn."

What Learning Is and Is Not

When children learn how to use a computer, they might make some mistakes along the way, but at a certain point they will get the knack of the behaviours required to use the computer effectively. The children will change from being individuals who cannot operate a computer into being individuals who can. Once they have learned how to use a computer, they don't lose those skills. It's like learning to drive a car. Once you have learned how, you don't have to learn all over again. Thus, learning involves a *relatively permanent* influence on behaviour, which comes about through *experience*. Putting these pieces together, we arrive at a definition: **Learning** is a *relatively permanent change in behaviour that occurs through experience.*

Not everything we know is learned. Recall our discussion of heredity and experience, or nature and nurture, in Chapter 2. We inherit some capacities—they are inborn or innate, not learned. For example, we don't have to be taught to swallow, to flinch at loud noises, or to blink when an object comes too close to our eyes. However, most human behaviours do not involve heredity alone. When children use a computer in a new way, work harder at solving problems, ask better questions, explain an answer in a more logical way, or listen more attentively, the experience of learning is at work.

The scope of learning is broad (Domjan, 2000). It involves academic behaviours and nonacademic behaviours. It occurs in schools and everywhere else that children experience their world.

Approaches to Learning

A number of approaches to learning have been proposed, including behavioural and cognitive approaches.

Behavioural The learning approaches that we discuss in the first part of this chapter are called *behavioural*. **Behaviourism** *is the view that behaviour should be explained by observable experiences, not by mental processes.* For the behaviourist, behaviour is everything that we do that can be directly observed: a child creating a poster, a teacher smiling at a child, one student assisting another student, and so on. **Mental processes** *are defined by psychologists as the thoughts, feelings, and motives that each of us experiences but that cannot be observed by others.* Although we cannot directly see thoughts, feelings, and motives, they are no less real. They include children thinking about ways to create the best poster, a teacher feeling good about students' efforts, and students' inner motivation to control their behaviour.

For the behaviourist, these thoughts, feelings, and motives are not appropriate subject matter for a science of behaviour because they cannot be directly observed. Classical conditioning and operant conditioning, two behavioural views that we will discuss shortly, adopt this stance. Both of these views emphasize **associative learning**, *which consists of learning that two events are connected (associated).* For example, associative learning occurs when a student associates a pleasant event with learning something in school, such as the teacher smiling when the student asks a good question. The discussion of applied behaviour analysis later in the chapter also reflects the behavioural view of focusing on observable behaviour and associative learning.

Cognitive Psychology became more *cognitive* in the last part of the twentieth century. This cognitive emphasis has become the basis for numerous approaches to learning (Case, 1999; Driscoll, 2000; Roeddiger, 2000). We discuss four main cognitive approaches to learning in this book: social cognitive; cognitive information processing; cognitive constructivist; and social constructivist. The *social cognitive* approaches, which emphasize how behaviour, environment, and person (cognitive) factors interact to influence learning, will be covered later in this chapter. The second set of approaches, *cognitive information processing,* focuses on how children process information through attention, memory, thinking, and other cognitive

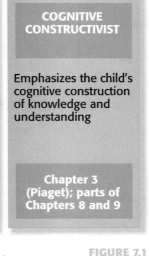

BEHAVIOURAL	SOCIAL COGNITIVE	COGNITIVE INFORMATION PROCESSING	COGNITIVE CONSTRUCTIVIST	SOCIAL CONSTRUCTIVIST
Emphasizes experiences, especially reinforcement and punishment, as determinants of learning and behaviour	Emphasizes interaction of behaviour, environment, and person (cognitive) factors as determinants of learning	Emphasizes how children process information through attention, memory, thinking, and other cognitive processes	Emphasizes the child's cognitive construction of knowledge and understanding	Emphasizes collaboration with others to produce knowledge and understanding
First part of this chapter (7)	**Last part of this chapter (7)**	**Chapter 8**	**Chapter 3 (Piaget); parts of Chapters 8 and 9**	**Chapter 3 (Vygotsky); Chapter 9**

FIGURE 7.1   **Approaches to Learning**

processes. They will be explored in Chapter 8. The third set of approaches, *cognitive constructivist*, emphasizes the child's cognitive construction of knowledge and understanding. They initially were presented in the form of Piaget's and Case's theory in Chapter 2 and will be further examined in Chapters 8 and 9. The fourth set of cognitive approaches, *social constructivist*, focuses on collaboration with others to produce knowledge and understanding. The social constructivist approaches initially were introduced in the form of Vygotsky's theory in Chapter 2 and they will be further evaluated in Chapter 9.

Adding these four cognitive approaches to the behavioural approaches, we arrive at five main approaches to learning that we discuss in this book: behavioural, social cognitive, cognitive information processing, cognitive constructivist, and social constructivist. All contribute to our understanding of how children learn. A summary of the five approaches is presented in Figure 7.1.

At this point, we have discussed a number of ideas about what learning is and various approaches to learning. A review of these ideas is presented in Summary Table 7.1. Let's now explore the behavioural approaches in greater detail.

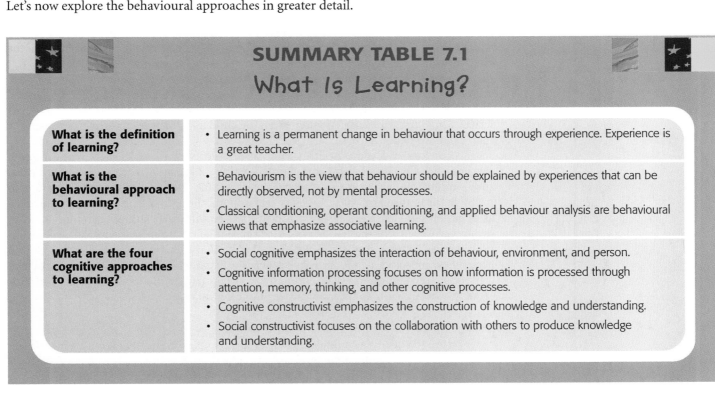

SUMMARY TABLE 7.1
What Is Learning?

What is the definition of learning?	• Learning is a permanent change in behaviour that occurs through experience. Experience is a great teacher.
What is the behavioural approach to learning?	• Behaviourism is the view that behaviour should be explained by experiences that can be directly observed, not by mental processes. • Classical conditioning, operant conditioning, and applied behaviour analysis are behavioural views that emphasize associative learning.
What are the four cognitive approaches to learning?	• Social cognitive emphasizes the interaction of behaviour, environment, and person. • Cognitive information processing focuses on how information is processed through attention, memory, thinking, and other cognitive processes. • Cognitive constructivist emphasizes the construction of knowledge and understanding. • Social constructivist focuses on the collaboration with others to produce knowledge and understanding.

Behavioural Approaches to Learning

Classical Conditioning   Operant Conditioning

BEHAVIOURAL APPROACHES TO LEARNING

The behavioural approaches emphasize the importance of children making connections between experiences and behaviour (Greeno, Collins, & Resnick, 1996). The first behaviourist approach we will examine is classical conditioning.

Classical Conditioning

In the early 1900s, Russian physiologist Ivan Pavlov was curious to know how the body digests food. In his experiments, he routinely placed meat powder in a dog's mouth, which caused the dog to salivate. Pavlov began to observe that the meat powder was not the only stimulus that caused the dog to salivate. The dog salivated in response to a number of stimuli associated with the food: the sight of the food dish, the sight of the person who brought the food into the room, and the sound of the door closing when the food arrived.

Ivan Pavlov (1849–1936), the Russian who developed the concept of classical conditioning.

Exploring Classical Conditioning **Classical conditioning** *is a type of learning in which an organism learns to connect or associate stimuli. In classical conditioning, a neutral stimulus (such as the sight of a person) becomes associated with a meaningful stimulus (such as food) and acquires the capacity to elicit a similar response.* To fully understand Pavlov's (1927) theory of classical conditioning, one must understand two types of stimuli and two types of responses: unconditioned stimulus (US), unconditioned response (UR), conditioned stimulus (CS), and conditioned response (CR).

Figure 7.2 summarizes the way classical conditioning works. An **unconditioned stimulus (US)** *is a stimulus that automatically produces a response without any prior learning.* Food was the US in Pavlov's experiments. An **unconditioned response (UR)** *is an unlearned response that is automatically elicited by the US.* In Pavlov's experiments, the dog's salivation in response to food was the UR. A **conditioned stimulus (CS)** *is a previously neutral stimulus that eventually elicits a conditioned response after being associated with the US.* Among the conditioned stimuli in Pavlov's experiments were various sights and sounds that occurred prior to the dog's actually eating the food, such as the sound of the door closing before the food was placed in the dog's dish. A **conditioned response (CR)** *is a learned response to the conditioned stimulus that occurs after US–CS pairing.*

Classical conditioning can be involved in both positive and negative experiences of students in the classroom. For example, a song could be neutral for the student until the child joins in with other classmates to sing it with accompanying positive feelings.

Similarly, students can develop fear of the classroom if they associate the classroom with criticism, so the criticism becomes a CS for fear, as Figure 7.2 suggests. Classical conditioning also can be involved in test anxiety. For example, a student fails and is criticized, which produces anxiety; thereafter, the child associates tests with anxiety, so they then can become a CS for anxiety (see Figure 7.3).

School fear and some health problems also might involve classical conditioning mechanisms. Certain physical complaints—asthma, headaches, ulcers, high blood pressure—might be partly due to classical conditioning. We usually say that such health problems are caused by stress. Often what happens, though, is that certain stimuli, such as a parent's or teacher's heavy criticism, are conditioned stimuli for physiological responses. Over time, the frequency of the physiological responses can produce a health problem. A teacher's persistent criticism of a student can cause the student to develop headaches, muscle tension, and so on. Anything associated with the teacher, such as classroom learning exercises and homework, might trigger the student's stress and subsequently be linked with ulcers or other physiological responses.

Mechanisms of Classical Conditioning: Generalization, Discrimination, and Extinction In studying a dog's responses to various stimuli, Pavlov rang a bell before giving meat powder to the dog. By being paired with the US (meat), the bell became a CS and elicited the dog's salivation. After a time, Pavlov found that the dog also responded

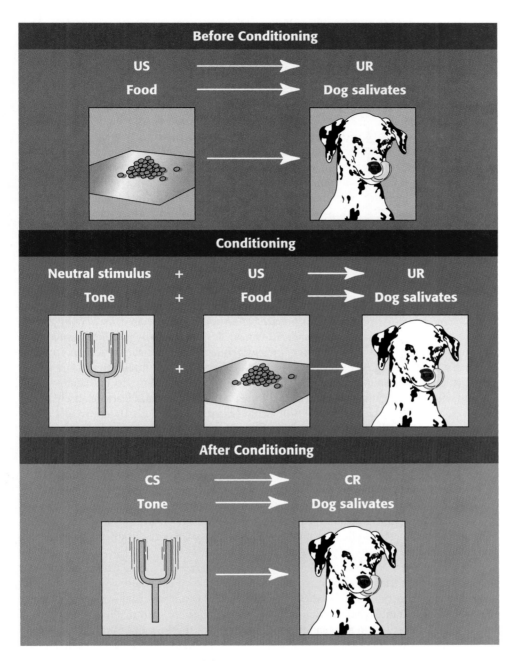

FIGURE 7.2   Pavlov's Classical Conditioning

In one experiment, Pavlov presented a neutral stimulus (tone) just before an unconditioned stimulus (food). The neutral stimulus became a conditioned stimulus by being paired with the unconditioned stimulus. Subsequently, the conditioned stimulus (tone) by itself was able to elicit the dog's salivation.

to other sounds, such as a whistle. The more bell-like the noise, the stronger the dog's response. **Generalization** *in classical conditioning involves the tendency of a new stimulus similar to the original conditioned stimulus to produce a similar response.* Let's assume that the test the student was criticized on was a biology test. When the student begins to prepare for a chemistry test, she also becomes very nervous because these two subjects are closely related in the sciences. Thus, the student's anxiety generalizes from taking a test in one subject to taking a test in another.

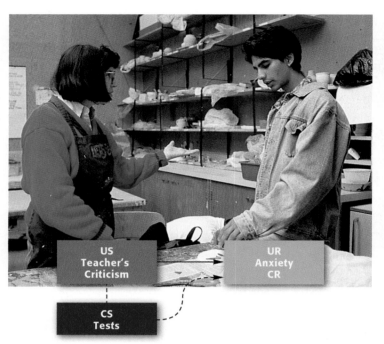

US
Teacher's
Criticism

UR
Anxiety
CR

CS
Tests

FIGURE 7.3 **Classical Conditioning Involved in Teachers' Criticism of Students and Tests**

Discrimination *in classical conditioning occurs when the organism responds to certain stimuli but not others.* To produce discrimination, Pavlov gave food to the dog only after ringing the bell and not after any other sounds. Subsequently, the dog responded only to the bell. In the case of the student taking tests in different classes, she doesn't become nearly as nervous about taking an English test or a history test, because they are very different subject areas.

Extinction *in classical conditioning involves the weakening of the conditioned response (CR) in the absence of the unconditioned stimulus (US).* In one session, Pavlov rang the bell repeatedly but did not give the dog any food. Eventually the dog quit salivating. Similarly, if the student who gets nervous while taking tests begins to do much better on tests, her anxiety will fade.

Systematic Desensitization   Sometimes the anxiety and stress associated with negative events can be eliminated by classical conditioning. **Systematic desensitization** *is a method based on classical conditioning that reduces anxiety by getting the individual to associate deep relaxation with successive visualizations of increasingly anxiety-producing situations.* Imagine that you have a student in your class who is extremely nervous about talking in front of the class. The goal of systematic desensitization is to get the student to associate public speaking with relaxation rather than anxiety. Using successive visualizations, the student might practise systematic desensitization two weeks before the talk, then a week before, four days before, two days before, the day before, the morning of the talk, on entering the room where the talk is to be given, on the way to the podium, and during the talk.

Desensitization involves a type of counterconditioning (McNeil, 2000; Schunk, 1996). The relaxing feelings that the student imagines (US) produce relaxation (UR). The student then associates anxiety-producing cues (CS) with the relaxing feelings. Such relaxation is incompatible with anxiety. By initially pairing a weak anxiety-producing cue with relaxation and gradually working up the hierarchy (from two weeks before the talk to walking up to the podium to give the talk), all of the anxiety-producing cues should generate relaxation (CR).

Chances are you will have students who fear speaking in front of the class, or have other anxieties, and there may be circumstances in your own life where you might benefit from replacing anxiety with relaxation. For example, it is not unusual for some teachers to feel very comfortable when talking in front of their students but to get very nervous if asked to give a presentation at a teaching conference. Counsellors and mental health professionals have been very successful at assisting individuals to overcome their fear of public speaking using systematic desensitization.

Evaluating Classical Conditioning   Classical conditioning helps us understand some aspects of learning better than others. It excels in explaining how neutral stimuli become associated with unlearned, involuntary responses (LoLordo, 2000). Classical conditioning can also help us understand a variety of physiological and behavioural relations, including addiction and withdrawal (Kim & Siegel, 2001) and fear and anxiety (Allan & Siegel, 1997). However, it is not as effective in explaining voluntary behaviours, such as why a student studies hard for a test or likes history better than geography. For these areas, operant conditioning is more relevant.

Operant Conditioning

Our examination of operant conditioning begins with a general definition, then turns to the views of Thorndike and Skinner.

What Is Operant Conditioning? **Operant conditioning** *(also called instrumental conditioning) is a form of learning in which the consequences of behaviour produce changes in the probability that the behaviour will occur.* Operant conditioning's main architect was B. F. Skinner, whose views built on the connectionist views of E. L. Thorndike.

Thorndike's Law of Effect At about the same time that Ivan Pavlov was conducting classical conditioning experiments with dogs, E. L. Thorndike (1906) was studying cats in puzzle boxes. Thorndike placed a hungry cat inside a box and put a piece of fish outside. To escape from the box, the cat had to learn how to open the latch inside the box. At first the cat made a number of ineffective responses. It clawed or bit at the bars and thrust its paw through the openings. Eventually the cat accidentally stepped on the treadle that released the door bolt. When the cat was returned to the box, it went through the same random activity until it stepped on the treadle once more. On subsequent trials, the cat made fewer and fewer random movements, until it immediately clawed the treadle to open the door. Thorndike's **law of effect** *states that behaviours followed by positive outcomes are strengthened and that behaviours followed by negative outcomes are weakened.*

The key question for Thorndike was how the correct stimulus-response (S-R) bond strengthens and eventually dominates incorrect stimulus-response bonds. According to Thorndike, the correct S-R association strengthens, and the incorrect association weakens, because of the *consequences* of the organism's actions. Thorndike's view is called *S-R theory* because the organism's behaviour is due to a connection between a stimulus and a response. As we see next, Skinner's approach significantly expanded on Thorndike's basic ideas.

Skinner's Operant Conditioning Operant conditioning, in which the consequences of behaviour lead to changes in the probability that the behaviour will occur, is at the heart of B. F. Skinner's (1938) behaviourism. Consequences—rewards or punishments—are contingent on the organism's behaviour.

Mechanisms of Operant Conditioning: Reinforcement and Punishment **Reinforcement (reward)** *is a consequence that increases the probability that a behaviour will occur.* In contrast, **punishment** *is a consequence that decreases the probability a behaviour will occur.* For example, you might tell one of your students, "Congratulations. I'm really proud of how good the story that you wrote is." If the student works harder and writes an even better story the next time, your positive comments are said to reinforce or reward the student's writing behaviour. If you frown at a student for talking in class and the student's talking decreases, your frown is said to punish the student's talking.

Reinforcement can be complex. "Reinforcement" means to strengthen. In **positive reinforcement**, *the frequency of a response increases because it is followed by a stimulus*, as in the example in which the teacher's positive comments increased the student's writing behaviour. Similarly, complimenting parents on being at a parent–teacher conference might encourage them to come back again. Positive reinforcement is usually welcomed and valued by the students (as when a teacher praises a student's work), but it also can be unpleasant (as when students do work they don't want to in order to get a good grade).

Conversely, in **negative reinforcement**, *the frequency of a response increases because the response either removes a stimulus or involves avoiding a stimulus.* For example, a father nags at his son to do his homework. He keeps nagging. Finally, the son gets tired of hearing the nagging and does his homework. The son's response (doing his

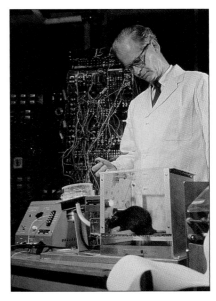

B. F. Skinner (1904–1990) was the main architect of the concept of operant conditioning.

Reward and punishment . . . these are the spur and reins whereby people are set on work and guided.

John Locke
English Philosopher, 17th Century

"Once it became clear to me that, by responding correctly to certain stimuli, I could get all the bananas I wanted, getting this job was a pushover."

homework) removed the unpleasant stimulus (nagging). Punishment is used to reduce the probability that a negative behaviour will reoccur. Punishment involves the administration of an aversive stimulus or the loss of a privilege. **Positive punishment** *involves the administration of an unwelcome consequence* (e.g., detention, additional homework, extra chores). **Negative punishment** *involves the removal of a valued item* (e.g., fieldtrip, class computer, free time). It is important to recognize that while negative reinforcement is a proactive strategy, punishment is not. That is, once students misbehave punishment does not provide them with the opportunity to rectify the situation.

One way to remember the distinction between positive and negative reinforcement is that in positive reinforcement something is added or obtained. In negative reinforcement, something is subtracted, avoided, or escaped. It is also easy to confuse negative reinforcement and punishment. To keep these terms straight, remember that negative reinforcement increases the probability a response will occur, while punishment decreases the likelihood it will occur. Figure 7.4 summarizes the concepts of positive reinforcement, negative reinforcement, positive punishment, and negative punishment and presents examples of each.

Generalization, Discrimination, and Extinction In our coverage of classical conditioning, we discussed generalization, discrimination, and extinction. These processes also are important dimensions of operant conditioning. Remember that in classical conditioning, generalization is the tendency of a stimulus similar to the conditioned stimulus to produce a response similar to the conditioned response. **Generalization** *in operant conditioning means giving the same response to similar stimuli.* Especially of interest is the extent to which behaviour generalizes from one situation to another. For example, if a teacher's praise gets a student to work harder in class, will this generalize to the student working harder out of class on homework assignments? Or if the teacher praises the student for asking good questions related to English, will this generalize to history, math, and other subjects?

Remember that in classical conditioning, discrimination means responding to certain stimuli but not others. **Discrimination** *in operant conditioning involves differentiating among stimuli or environmental events.* For example, a student knows that the tray on the teacher's desk labelled "Math" is where she is supposed to place today's math work, while another tray labelled "English" is where today's English assignments are to be put. This might sound overly simple, but it is important because students' worlds are filled with such discriminative stimuli. Around school these discriminative stimuli might include signs that say, "Stay out," "Form a line here," and so on. We will have more to say about discriminative stimuli later in the section on applied behaviour analysis.

	Positive (something is applied)	Negative (something is removed)
Reinforcement Goal: Increase desired behaviour	**Positive Reinforcement** A teacher praises a student for helping a classmate.	**Negative Reinforcement** A teacher stops "glaring" at an inattentive student once the student refocuses on the task at hand.
Punishment Goal: Decrease undesired behaviour	**Positive Punishment** A student receives a detention for speaking aloud during a lecture.	**Negative Punishment** A student loses computer time after pushing another child.

Both reinforcement and punishment come in positive and negative forms. Reinforcement increases a desired behaviour. Punishment decreases an undesired behaviour.

FIGURE 7.4 **Reinforcement and Punishment**

Behavioural Approaches to Learning **211**

In operant conditioning, **extinction** *occurs when a previously reinforced response is no longer reinforced and the response decreases.* In the classroom, the most common use of extinction is for the teacher to withdraw attention from a behaviour that the attention is maintaining. For example, in some cases a teacher's attention inadvertently reinforces a student's disruptive behaviour, as when a student speaks without raising his hand and the teacher immediately talks to him. If this happens on a regular basis, the student might learn that speaking out of turn is a good way to get the teacher's attention. If the teacher withdraws her attention, speaking out might cease. We will have more to say about extinction in our discussion of applied behaviour analysis.

At this point we have discussed a number of ideas about the behavioural approaches of classical and operant conditioning. A review of these ideas is presented in Summary Table 7.2.

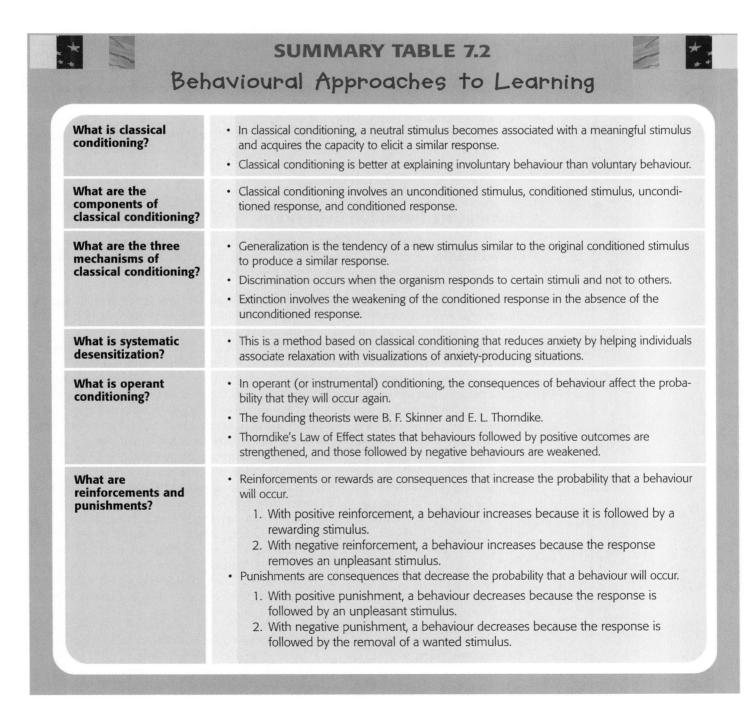

SUMMARY TABLE 7.2
Behavioural Approaches to Learning

What is classical conditioning?	• In classical conditioning, a neutral stimulus becomes associated with a meaningful stimulus and acquires the capacity to elicit a similar response. • Classical conditioning is better at explaining involuntary behaviour than voluntary behaviour.
What are the components of classical conditioning?	• Classical conditioning involves an unconditioned stimulus, conditioned stimulus, unconditioned response, and conditioned response.
What are the three mechanisms of classical conditioning?	• Generalization is the tendency of a new stimulus similar to the original conditioned stimulus to produce a similar response. • Discrimination occurs when the organism responds to certain stimuli and not to others. • Extinction involves the weakening of the conditioned response in the absence of the unconditioned response.
What is systematic desensitization?	• This is a method based on classical conditioning that reduces anxiety by helping individuals associate relaxation with visualizations of anxiety-producing situations.
What is operant conditioning?	• In operant (or instrumental) conditioning, the consequences of behaviour affect the probability that they will occur again. • The founding theorists were B. F. Skinner and E. L. Thorndike. • Thorndike's Law of Effect states that behaviours followed by positive outcomes are strengthened, and those followed by negative behaviours are weakened.

What are reinforcements and punishments?	• Reinforcements or rewards are consequences that increase the probability that a behaviour will occur.
	  1. With positive reinforcement, a behaviour increases because it is followed by a rewarding stimulus.
	  2. With negative reinforcement, a behaviour increases because the response removes an unpleasant stimulus.
	• Punishments are consequences that decrease the probability that a behaviour will occur.
	  1. With positive punishment, a behaviour decreases because the response is followed by an unpleasant stimulus.
	  2. With negative punishment, a behaviour decreases because the response is followed by the removal of a wanted stimulus.

www.mcgrawhill.ca/college/santrock

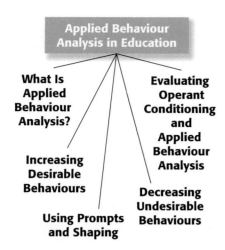

APPLIED BEHAVIOUR ANALYSIS IN EDUCATION

Many applications of operant conditioning have been made outside of research laboratories in the wider worlds of classrooms, homes, business settings, hospitals, and other real-world settings.

What Is Applied Behaviour Analysis?

Applied behaviour analysis *is the specific and comprehensive use of principles of operant conditioning to the development of abilities and self-direction skills of learners.* Originally conceived for children with exceptionalities, it is often confused with behaviour modification. Behaviour modification has often been associated with an emphasis on technique over the ethics of practice; applied behaviour analysis stresses a positive approach rather than a punitive or aversive one. Applied behaviour analysis involves a team approach (Bailey et al., 1986; Shook, Hartsfield, & Hemingway, 1995; Thyer, 1996).

Three uses of applied behaviour analysis are especially important in education: increasing desirable behaviour, using prompts and shaping, and decreasing undesirable behaviour (Alberto & Troutman, 1995). Applications of applied behaviour analysis often use a series of steps (Hayes, 2000). These often begin with some general observations and then turn to determining the specific target behaviour that needs to be changed, as well as observing its antecedent conditions. Behavioural goals are then set, particular reinforcers or punishers are selected, a behaviour management program is carried out, and the success or failure of the program is evaluated.

Increasing Desirable Behaviours

Five operant conditioning strategies can be used to increase a child's desirable behaviours: choose effective reinforcers; make reinforcers contingent and timely; select the best schedule of reinforcement; consider contracting; and use negative reinforcement effectively.

Choose Effective Reinforcers   Not all reinforcers are the same for every child. Applied behaviour analysts recommend that teachers find out what reinforcers work best with which students—that is, individualize the use of particular reinforcers. For one student it might be praise, for another it might be getting to spend more time participating in a favourite activity, for another it might involve being a hall monitor for a week, and for yet another it could be getting to surf the Internet. To find out the most effective reinforcers for a student, you can examine what has motivated the child in the past (reinforcement history), what the student wants but can't easily or frequently get, and the child's perception of the reinforcer's value. Some applied behaviour analysts recommend asking students which reinforcers they like best (Raschke, 1981). Another recommendation is to consider novel reinforcers to reduce boredom. Natural reinforcers like praise and privileges are generally recommended over material rewards like candy, stars, and money (Hall & Hall, 1998).

Activities are some of the most common reinforcers used by teachers. Named after psychologist David Premack, the **Premack principle** *states that a high-probability activity can serve as a reinforcer for a low-probability activity.* The Premack principle is at work when an elementary-school teacher tells a student, "When you complete your writing assignment, you can play a game on the computer" or an early-education teacher says, "If you pick up the blocks, then you may help Mrs. Manson prepare the snacks." The use of the Premack principle is not restricted to a single student. It also can be used with the entire class. A teacher might tell the class, "If all of the class gets their homework done by Friday, we will take a field trip next week."

Make the Reinforcer Contingent and Timely   For a reinforcer to be effective, the teacher must give it only after the child performs the particular behaviour. Applied-behaviour analysts often recommend that teachers make "If . . . then" statements to students. For example, "Tony, *if* you finish ten math problems, *then* you can go out to play." This makes it clear to Tony what he has to do to get the reinforcer. Applied behaviour analysts say that it is important to make the reinforcer *contingent* on the child's behaviour. That is, the student has to perform the behaviour to get the reward. If Tony did not complete ten math problems and the teacher still lets him go out to play, the contingency has not been established.

Reinforcers are more effective when they are given in a timely way, as soon as possible after the child performs the target behaviour. This helps children see the contingency connection between the reward and their behaviour. If the student completes the target behaviour (such as doing the ten math problems by midmorning) and the teacher doesn't give the child playtime until late afternoon, the student might have trouble making the contingency connection.

Use the Best Schedule of Reinforcement   Most of the examples given so far assume *continuous reinforcement*; that is, the child is reinforced every time she or he makes a response. In continuous reinforcement, children learn very rapidly, but when the reinforcement stops (the teacher stops praising), extinction also occurs rapidly. In the classroom, continuous reinforcement is rare. A teacher with a classroom of 25 or 30 students can't praise a child every time the student makes an appropriate response.

Partial reinforcement involves reinforcing a response only part of the time. Skinner (1953) developed the concept of **schedules of reinforcement**, *which are partial reinforcement timetables that determine when a response will be reinforced.* The four main schedules of reinforcement are fixed-ratio, variable-ratio, fixed-interval, and variable-interval.

On a **fixed-ratio schedule**, *a behaviour is reinforced after a set number of responses.* For example, a teacher might praise the student only after every fourth correct response, not after every response. On a **variable-ratio schedule**, *a behaviour is reinforced after an average number of times, but on an unpredictable basis.* For example, a teacher's praise might average out to being given every fifth response but be given after the second correct response, after eight more correct responses, after the next seven correct responses, and after the next three correct responses.

Interval schedules are determined by time elapsed since the last behaviour was reinforced. On a **fixed-interval schedule**, *the first appropriate response after a fixed amount of time is reinforced.* For example, a teacher might praise a student for the first good question the child asks after two minutes have elapsed, or give a quiz every week. On a **variable-interval schedule**, *a response is reinforced after a variable amount of time has elapsed.* On this schedule, the teacher might praise the student's question-asking after 3 minutes have gone by, then after 15 minutes have gone by, after 7 minutes have gone by, and so on. Giving a pop quiz at uneven intervals also reflects a variable-interval schedule.

What is the effect of using these schedules of reinforcement with children?

- Initial learning is usually faster, with continuous rather than partial reinforcement, which means that when a behaviour is first being learned, continuous reinforcement works better. However, partial reinforcement produces greater persistence and greater resistance to extinction than continuous reinforcement does (Hackenberg, 2000). Thus, once a response is mastered, partial reinforcement works better than continuous reinforcement.
- Children on fixed schedules show less persistence and faster response extinction than children on variable schedules. The most persistence is shown by children on a variable-interval schedule. This schedule produces slow, steady responding because children don't know when the wait is going to be over. As we mentioned earlier, a pop quiz is a good example of the variable-interval schedule. If the teacher

Through the Eyes of Teachers

Learn Their Names

I am horrible at learning new names, but I have come to realize that knowing your students' names is the teacher's best classroom-management tool. It is very difficult to yell, "Hey you, be quiet." However, "Chantal, could you finish your conversation after class?" has a tremendous effect. I also move around the classroom a lot. Students find it uncomfortable to chat to their friends when you are standing beside them. Another strategy is to stand in front of the class and say nothing. Don't look nervous, just wait and be patient. When the students quiet down, thank them and proceed with the lesson. If they start to talk again, just stop and wait again.

Greg Voigt
Senior High School General Sciences and Biology Teacher
Alberta

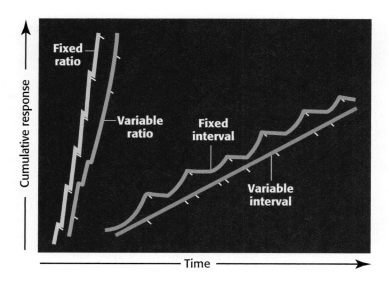

FIGURE 7.5 **Schedules of Reinforcement and Different Patterns of Responding**
In this figure, each hash mark indicates the delivery of reinforcement. Notice on the fixed-interval schedule the drop-off in responding after each response, on the variable-interval schedule the high, steady rate of responding, on the fixed-interval schedule the immediate drop-off in responding after reinforcement and the increase in responding just before reinforcement (which results in a scallop-shaped curve), and on the variable-interval schedule the slow, steady rate of responding.

starts making the pop quiz more predictable (giving it once a week, on Fridays), students will begin to show the stop-start work pattern that characterizes the fixed-interval schedule. That is, they won't work hard for most of the week, then toward the end of the week they will start cramming for the quiz. Thus, if your goal as a teacher is to increase students' persistence after the behaviour has been established, variable schedules work best, especially the variable-interval schedule (Lee & Belfiore, 1997). Figure 7.5 shows the different response patterns associated with the different schedules of reinforcement.

Consider Contracting **Contracting** *involves putting reinforcement contingencies in writing.* If problems arise and children don't uphold their end of the bargain, the teacher can refer the students to the contract they agreed to. Applied behaviour analysts suggest that a classroom contract should be the result of input from both the teacher and the student. Classroom contracts have "If . . . then" statements and are signed by the teacher and child, then dated. A teacher and student might agree on a contract that states that the child agrees to be a good citizen by doing _____, _____ and _____. As part of the contract, the teacher agrees to provide a specific response or reward if the student behaves in this manner. In some instances, the teacher asks another student to sign the contract as a witness to the agreement.

Use Negative Reinforcement Effectively Remember that in negative reinforcement, the frequency of response increases because the response removes an aversive (unpleasant) stimulus (Alberto & Troutman, 1995). A teacher who says, "Thomas, you have to stay in your seat and finish writing your story before you join the other students in making a poster," is using negative reinforcement. The negative condition of being left in his seat while the other children are doing something enjoyable will be removed if Thomas finishes the story he should have completed earlier. In another example of negative reinforcement, Maria stops her disruptive behaviour in order to avoid being ridiculed by her peers.

Using negative reinforcement has some drawbacks. Sometimes when teachers try to use this behavioural strategy, children throw a tantrum, run out of the room, or destroy materials. These negative outcomes happen most often when students don't have the skills or capabilities to do what the teacher asks of them. We will discuss such self-regulatory skills later in this chapter.

Using Prompts and Shaping

Earlier in our discussion of operant conditioning, we indicated that discrimination involves differentiating among stimuli or environmental events. Students can learn to discriminate among stimuli or events through differential reinforcement. Two differential reinforcement strategies available to teachers are prompts and shaping (Alberto & Troutman, 1995).

Prompts A **prompt** *is an added stimulus or cue that is given just before a response and increases the likelihood that the response will occur.* A reading teacher who holds up a card with the letters *w-e-r-e* and says, "Not was, but . . ." is using a verbal prompt. An art teacher who places the label *watercolours* on one group of paints and *oils* on another also is using prompts. Prompts help get behaviour going. Once the students consistently show the correct responses, the prompts are no longer needed.

Instructions can be used as prompts. For example, as the art period is drawing to a close, the teacher says, "Let's get ready for reading." If the students keep doing art, the teacher adds the prompt, "Okay, put away your art materials and come with me over to the reading area." Some prompts come in the form of hints, as when the teacher tells students to line up "quietly." Bulletin boards are common locations for prompts, frequently displaying reminders of class rules, due dates for projects, the location of a meeting, and so on. Some prompts are presented visually, as when the teacher cups a hand around her ear when a student is not speaking loudly enough.

Shaping   When teachers use prompts, they assume that students can perform the desired behaviours. But sometimes students do not have the ability to perform them. In this case, shaping is required. **Shaping** *involves teaching new behaviours by reinforcing successive approximations to a specified target behaviour.* Initially, you reinforce any response that in some way resembles the target behaviour. Subsequently, you reinforce a response that more closely resembles the target, and so on until the student performs the target behaviour, and then you reinforce it.

Suppose you have a student who has never completed 50 percent or more of her math assignments. You set the target behaviour at 100 percent, but you reinforce her for successive approximations to the target. You initially might provide a reinforcer (some type of privilege, for example) when she completes 60 percent, then the next time only when she completes 70 percent, then 80, then 90, and finally 100 percent.

Consider also a boy's shy behaviour. The target behaviour is to get him to approach a group of peers and talk with them. Initially you might need to reinforce him for simply smiling at a classmate. Next, you might reinforce him only if he says something to a classmate. Next, you might reinforce him only if he engages in a prolonged conversation with a classmate. And finally, you should reward him only if he engages in the target behaviour, joining in with a group of peers and talking with them.

Shaping can be an important tool for the classroom teacher, because most students need reinforcement along the way to reaching a learning goal. Shaping can be especially helpful for learning tasks that require time and persistence to complete. However, when using shaping, remember to implement it only if the other types of positive reinforcement and prompts are not working. Also remember to be patient. Shaping can require the reinforcement of a number of small steps en route to a target behaviour, and these might take place only over an extended period of time.

Decreasing Undesirable Behaviours

When teachers want to decrease students' undesirable behaviours (such as teasing, dominating a class discussion, or being disrespectful to the teacher), what are their options? Applied behaviour analysts Paul Alberto and Anne Troutman (1995) recommend that when teachers want to decrease a student's undesirable behaviour, they should consider using these steps in this order:

1. Use differential reinforcement.
2. Terminate reinforcement (extinction).
3. Remove desirable stimuli.
4. Present aversive stimuli (punishment).

Thus, the teacher's first option should be differential reinforcement. Punishment should be used only as a last resort and always in conjunction with providing the student information about appropriate behaviour.

Use Differential Reinforcement   In differential reinforcement, the teacher reinforces behaviour that is more appropriate or that is incompatible with what the child is doing. For example, the teacher might reinforce a student for doing learning activities on a computer rather than playing games with it, for being courteous rather than interrupting, for being seated rather than running around the classroom, or for doing homework on time rather than late.

Terminate Reinforcement (Extinction)   The strategy of terminating reinforcement involves withdrawing positive reinforcement from a child's inappropriate behaviour.

Teaching Strategies
For Using Time-Out

✔ Keep students in the classroom whenever possible
  • have students use a time-out location in the classroom (e.g., corner, pulled-out desk, laying heads on desks) for minor misbehaviours
  • allow students to view others completing the current activity and receiving positive reinforcements for their efforts
  • add to the time-out if students start yelling or acting inappropriately
✔ Use time-out when the present activity is reinforcing
  • do not place students in a time-out location that is reinforcing
  • have students return to regular activities as soon as the time-out is over
  • welcome students back to the group, but do not positively reinforce their time-out behaviours
✔ Identify the behaviour that has resulted in the time-out
  • specify the behaviour that has resulted in the time-out (e.g., You tore up Corey's paper and need to use the time-out to reflect on how you can tell Corey you are sorry)
  • do not engage in conversations or arguments about why the misbehaviour occurred
  • do not accept lame excuses about why the misbehaviour occurred
  • identify reoccurring behaviours and have students return to the time-out location
✔ Use time-out to encourage reflection and proactive behaviours
  • allow students to select time-out as a preventive strategy
  • encourage students to reflect on appropriate behaviour while in time-out
  • have students articulate their behavioural plan when returning from time-out
✔ Record time-out sessions
  • record students' names, duration spent in time-out, and associated behaviours
  • record location of time-out, especially if outside the classroom (e.g., hallway, library, principal's office)
  • monitor the effectiveness and ethical use of time-out sessions

Many inappropriate behaviours are maintained by positive reinforcement, especially the teacher's attention. Applied behaviour analysts point out that this can occur even when the teacher gives attention to an inappropriate behaviour by criticizing, threatening, or yelling at the student. Many teachers find it difficult to determine whether they are giving too much attention to inappropriate behaviour. A good strategy is to get someone to observe your classroom on several occasions and chart the patterns of reinforcement you use with your students. If you become aware that you are giving too much attention to a student's inappropriate behaviour, ignore that behaviour and give attention to the student's appropriate behaviour. Always combine taking attention away from inappropriate behaviour with giving attention to appropriate behaviour. For instance, when a student stops monopolizing the conversation in a group discussion, compliment the student on her improved behaviour.

Remove Desirable Stimuli   Suppose you have tried the first two options, and they haven't worked. A third option is to remove desirable stimuli from the student. Two strategies for accomplishing this are "time-out" and "response cost."

Time-Out   The most widely used strategy that teachers use to remove desirable stimuli is **time-out**. *In other words, take the student away from positive reinforcement.* In general, time-out is used as a reactive strategy. However, teachers should also consider using time-out

Study this picture carefully and discuss the appropriateness of this time-out strategy. What are some guidelines for using "time-out"?

in a proactive manner by encouraging students to recognize the warning signs of potential problem situations or conflicts and take steps toward preventing them. In these situations, students could be encouraged to take a "personal time-out." In this manner, time-out can be used to provide students with an opportunity to calm down, reflect on the problematic behaviour, and focus on a more positive approach.

Response Cost (Negative Punishment) A second strategy for removing desirable stimuli involves **response cost**, *which refers to taking a positive reinforcer away from a student, as when the student loses certain privileges*. For example, after a student misbehaves, the teacher might take away 10 minutes of recess time or the privilege of being a class monitor. Response cost typically involves some type of penalty or fine. As with the time-out, response cost should always be used in conjunction with strategies for increasing the student's positive behaviours.

Present Aversive Stimuli (Positive Punishment) Most people associate the presentation of aversive (unpleasant) stimuli with punishment, as when a teacher yells at a student. However, in accordance with the definition of punishment given earlier in the chapter, the consequence has to decrease the undesirable behaviour (Branch, 2000). All too often, though, aversive stimuli are not effective punishments, in that they do not decrease the unwanted behaviour. Applied behaviour analysts say that some teachers turn too quickly to aversive stimuli when trying to get a student's behaviour in line. This might occur because the teacher was harshly disciplined at home when growing up, has developed a style of handling stress by yelling or screaming, feels that he or she can effectively exercise such power over smaller charges, or is unaware of how positive reinforcement can be used to reduce unwanted student behaviours.

The most common types of aversive stimuli that teachers use are verbal reprimands. These are more effectively used when the teacher is near the student rather than across the room and when used together with a nonverbal reprimand such as a frown or eye contact (Van Houten et al., 1982). Reprimands are more effective when they are given immediately after unwanted behaviour rather than later, and when they are quick and to the point. Such reprimands do not have to involve yelling and shouting, which often just raise the noise level of the classroom and present the teacher as an uncontrolled model for students. Instead, a firmly stated "stop doing that" with eye contact is often sufficient to stop unwanted behaviour. Another strategy is to take the student aside and reprimand the student in private rather than in front of the entire class.

www.mcgrawhill.ca/college/santrock

Through the Eyes of Teachers

Creating a Community Agreement

At the beginning of the school year, I have students describe the optimum classroom environment—what it looks like, sounds like, and feels like. Based on this description, we devise a "community agreement." We also describe and post the characteristics of successful students and effective teachers. Throughout the year, we refer back to these documents as a way of reminding ourselves about our responsibilities. Students need to understand that there are boundaries for acceptable behaviour and that there are logical consequences associated with crossing them. I need to remember that if I am considerate, consistent, and fair with my expectations for students, there will be relatively few classroom-management issues.

Alan Wasserman
Guidance Counsellor and Career Education Teacher
Ontario

One discredited aversive stimulus for classroom use is physical punishment. Physical punishment of students detrimentally affects the relationship between teachers and students (Durrant, 1999; Durrant, Broberg, & Rose-Krasnor, 1999). As an aversive strategy, physical punishment rarely achieves long-term compliance. It also magnifies ethical concerns associated with punishment.

In sum, numerous problems are associated with using aversive stimuli as punishment:

- Intense punishment like yelling or screaming presents students with an out-of-control model for handling stressful situations.
- The use of punishment can appear to validate verbal and physical aggression.
- Punishment can instill fear, rage, or avoidance in students. Skinner's biggest concern was that punishment teaches avoidance. For example, a student who experiences a punitive teacher might show a dislike for the teacher and not want to come to school.
- When students are punished, they might become so aroused and anxious that they can't concentrate clearly on their work for a long time after the punishment has been given.
- Punishment tells students what not to do rather than what to do. If you make a punishing statement such as "No, that's not right," always accompany it with positive feedback, such as "but why don't you try this."
- What is intended as punishment can turn out to be reinforcing. A student might learn that misbehaving will not only get the teacher's attention but also put the student in the limelight with classmates.

A final lesson in all of this is to spend a lot more class time monitoring what students do right rather than what they do wrong. Too often it is disruptive behaviour, not competent behaviour, that catches a teacher's attention. Every day make it a point to scan your classroom for positive student behaviours that you ordinarily would not notice, and give students attention for them.

Evaluating Operant Conditioning and Applied Behaviour Analysis

Operant conditioning and applied behaviour analysis have made contributions to teaching practice (Axelrod, 1996). Reinforcing and punishing consequences are part of teachers' and students' lives. Teachers give grades, praise and reprimand, smile and frown. Learning about how such consequences affect students' behaviour improves your capabilities as a teacher. Used effectively, behavioural techniques can help you manage your classroom. Reinforcing certain behaviours can improve some students' conduct and, used in conjunction with the time-out, can increase desired behaviours in some incorrigible students.

Critics of operant conditioning and applied behaviour analysis argue that the whole approach places too much emphasis on external control of students' behaviour. They say that a better strategy is to help students learn to control their own behaviour and become internally motivated. Critics also point to potential ethical problems when operant conditioning is used inappropriately, as when a teacher immediately resorts to punishing students instead of first considering reinforcement strategies, or punishes a student without also giving the student information about appropriate behaviour. Others, like Ontario educational consultant Ron Morrish, argue that good behaviour should not be negotiable. That is, teachers should set high expectations for student behaviours versus providing them with "if … then" contingencies (Morrish, 2000). Cunningham and his colleagues also argue that parents could play a more significant role in the management of students with behavioural difficulties if they are given opportunities to participate in school-based parent training programs (Cunningham et al., 2000). Finally, when teachers spend a lot of time using applied behaviour analysis, they might focus too much on student conduct and not enough on academic learning. We will have much more to say about student conduct in Chapter 12, Managing the Classroom.

At this point we have discussed many ideas about applied behaviour analysis in education. A review of these ideas is presented in Summary Table 7.3. Critics of operant conditioning believe that denying the importance of cognitive factors ignores the richest aspects of the student's existence—their thoughts. Next, we will explore some of these cognitive factors.

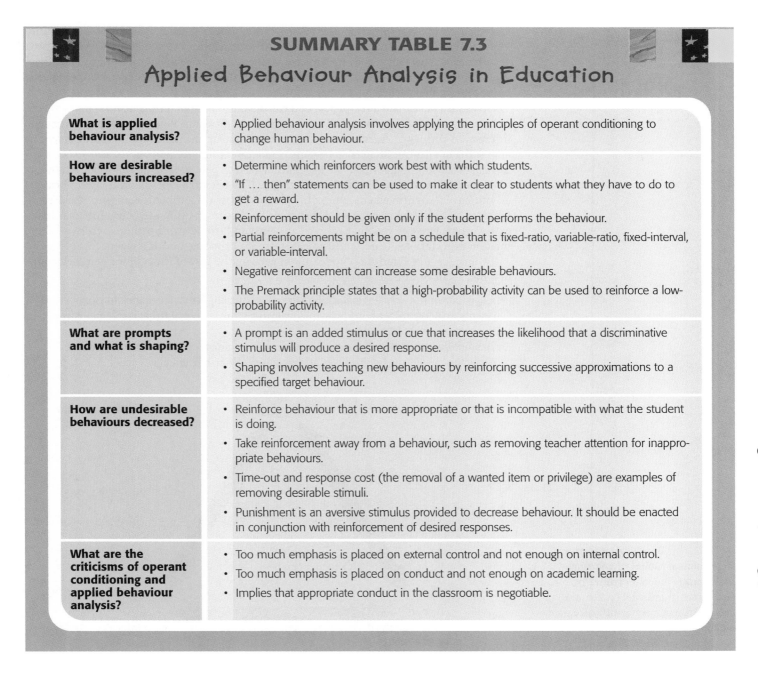

SUMMARY TABLE 7.3
Applied Behaviour Analysis in Education

What is applied behaviour analysis?	• Applied behaviour analysis involves applying the principles of operant conditioning to change human behaviour.
How are desirable behaviours increased?	• Determine which reinforcers work best with which students. • "If … then" statements can be used to make it clear to students what they have to do to get a reward. • Reinforcement should be given only if the student performs the behaviour. • Partial reinforcements might be on a schedule that is fixed-ratio, variable-ratio, fixed-interval, or variable-interval. • Negative reinforcement can increase some desirable behaviours. • The Premack principle states that a high-probability activity can be used to reinforce a low-probability activity.
What are prompts and what is shaping?	• A prompt is an added stimulus or cue that increases the likelihood that a discriminative stimulus will produce a desired response. • Shaping involves teaching new behaviours by reinforcing successive approximations to a specified target behaviour.
How are undesirable behaviours decreased?	• Reinforce behaviour that is more appropriate or that is incompatible with what the student is doing. • Take reinforcement away from a behaviour, such as removing teacher attention for inappropriate behaviours. • Time-out and response cost (the removal of a wanted item or privilege) are examples of removing desirable stimuli. • Punishment is an aversive stimulus provided to decrease behaviour. It should be enacted in conjunction with reinforcement of desired responses.
What are the criticisms of operant conditioning and applied behaviour analysis?	• Too much emphasis is placed on external control and not enough on internal control. • Too much emphasis is placed on conduct and not enough on academic learning. • Implies that appropriate conduct in the classroom is negotiable.

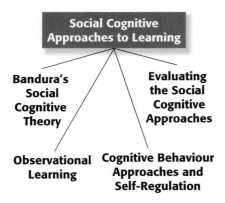

SOCIAL COGNITIVE APPROACHES TO LEARNING

Students' thoughts affect their behaviour and learning. In this section, we will explore several variations on this theme, beginning with social cognitive theory.

Bandura's Social Cognitive Theory

Social cognitive theory *states that social and cognitive factors, as well as behaviour, play important roles in learning.* Cognitive factors might involve the student's expectations for success; social factors might include students' observing their parents' achievement behaviour.

Albert Bandura (1986, 1997, 1998, 2000) is one of the main architects of social cognitive theory. Bandura was born in Mundare, Alberta and went to a small country school. He attended the University of British Columbia and was introduced to the study of behaviour by chance when he enrolled in a psychology course so that he could share a ride to the university. He became so interested in the subject that three years later he graduated with the Bolcan Award in psychology. Bandura went on to a distinguished career at Stanford University, making numerous and significant contributions to the field.

Bandura says that when students learn, they can cognitively represent or transform their experiences. Recall that in operant conditioning, connections occur only between environmental experiences and behaviour.

Bandura developed a **reciprocal determinism model** *that consists of three main factors: behaviour, person (cognitive), and environment.* As shown in Figure 7.6, these factors can interact to influence learning: Environmental factors influence behaviour, behaviour affects the environment, person (cognitive) factors influence behaviour, and so on. Bandura uses the term person, but we have modified it to person (cognitive) because so many of the person factors he describes are cognitive. The person factors Bandura describes that do not have a cognitive bent are mainly personality traits and temperament. Recall from Chapter 4, Individual Variations, that such factors might include being introverted or extroverted, active or inactive, calm or anxious, and friendly or hostile. Cognitive factors include expectations, beliefs, attitudes, strategies, thinking, and intelligence.

Consider how Bandura's model might work in the case of the achievement behaviour of a high-school student we will call Sondra:

- *Cognition influences behaviour.* Sondra develops cognitive strategies to think more deeply and logically about how to solve problems. The cognitive strategies improve her achievement behaviour.
- *Behaviour influences cognition.* Sondra's good grades lead her to have positive expectancies about her abilities and give her self-confidence.

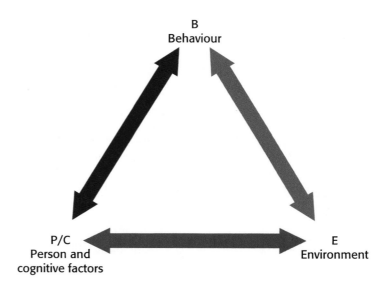

FIGURE 7.6   Bandura's Reciprocal Determinism Model of Learning
In Bandura's model, cognitive/person factors, environmental factors, and behaviour reciprocally influence each other. What are some examples of person (cognitive) factors in learning?

- *Environment influences behaviour.* The school Sondra attends recently developed a pilot study-skills program to help students learn how to take notes, manage their time, and take tests more effectively. The study-skills program improves Sondra's achievement behaviour.
- *Behaviour influences environment.* The study-skills program is successful in improving the achievement behaviour of many students in Sondra's class. The students' improved achievement behaviour stimulates the school to expand the program so that all students in the high school participate in it.
- *Cognition influences environment.* The expectations and planning of the school's principal and teachers made the study-skills program possible in the first place.
- *Environment influences cognition.* The school establishes a resource centre where students and parents can check out books and materials on improving study skills. The resource centre also makes study-skills tutoring services available to students. Sondra and her parents take advantage of the centre's resources and tutoring. These resources and services improve Sondra's thinking skills.

In Bandura's learning model, person (cognitive) factors play important roles. The person (cognitive) factor that Bandura (1997, 1998, 2000) has emphasized the most in recent years is **self-efficacy**, *the belief that one can master a situation and produce positive outcomes.* Bandura says that self-efficacy has a powerful influence over behaviour. For example, a student who has low self-efficacy might not even try to study for a test because he doesn't believe it will do him any good. We will have much more to say about self-efficacy in Chapter 11, Motivating Students to Learn.

Canadian researcher Albert Bandura has been one of the leading architects of social cognitive theory.

Observational Learning

Our exploration of observational learning focuses on the nature of observational learning, Bandura's classic Bobo doll study, and Bandura's contemporary model.

What is Observational Learning? **Observational learning**, *also called imitation or modelling, is learning that occurs when a person observes and imitates someone else's behaviour.* The capacity to learn behaviour patterns by observation eliminates tedious trial-and-error learning. In many instances, observational learning takes less time than operant conditioning.

The Classic Bobo Doll Study The following experiment by Bandura (1965) illustrates how observational learning can occur even by watching a model who is not reinforced or punished. The experiment also illustrates a distinction between learning and performance.

Equal numbers of kindergarten children watched one or another of three films in which a model beat up an adult-size plastic toy called a Bobo doll (see Figure 7.7). In the first film, the aggressor was rewarded with candy, soft drinks, and praise for aggressive behaviour. In the second film, the aggressor was criticized and spanked for the aggressive behaviour. And in the third film, there were no consequences for the aggressor's behaviour.

Subsequently, each child was left alone in a room filled with toys, including a Bobo doll. The child's behaviour was observed through a one-way mirror. Children who watched the films in which the aggressor's behaviour either was reinforced or went unpunished imitated the aggressor's behaviour more than did the children who saw the aggressor be punished. Boys were more aggressive than girls. An important point in this study is that observational learning occurred just as extensively when modelled aggressive behaviour was not reinforced as when it was reinforced.

A second important point in this study focuses on the distinction between *learning* and *performance.* Just because students don't perform a response doesn't mean they didn't learn it. In Bandura's study, when children were rewarded (with stickers or fruit juice) for imitating the model, differences in the children's imitative behaviour in the three conditions were eliminated. Bandura believes that when a child observes behaviour but makes no observable response, the child may still have acquired the modelled response in cognitive form.

We are in truth more than half what we are by imitation.

Lord Chesterfield
English Statesman, 18th Century

FIGURE 7.7 **Bandura's Classic Bobo Doll Study: The Effects of Observational Learning on Children's Aggression**
In the left frame, an adult model aggressively attacks the Bobo doll. In the right frame, a kindergarten-age girl who has observed the model's aggressive actions follows suit. In Bandura's experiment, under what conditions did the children reproduce the model's aggressive actions?

Media Violence Perhaps one of the most interesting questions arising from Bandura's initial research is the influence of media violence on children. For many years now, there has been a lively debate regarding the link between media violence and aggression. A number of studies and meta-analyses have demonstrated a link between exposure to media violence and aggression (Bushman & Anderson, 2001; Wood, Wong, & Chachere, 1991). Others, however, have questioned the validity of these studies, especially with respect to the manner in which these researchers collected their data (e.g., Bloom, 2002; Ferguson, 2002). While most researchers agree that exposure to media violence will not necessarily result in aggressive and violent behaviours, it is difficult to predict how other factors such as a predisposition toward violence or living in an environment where violence is tolerated impacts the development of these behaviours. A preventive strategy that is gaining some momentum involves making students aware of violence associated with media as part of the school curriculum (Gutwill & Hollander, 2002).

Bandura's Contemporary Model of Observational Learning Since his early experiments, Bandura (1986) has focused on the specific processes that are involved in observational learning. These include attention, retention, motor reproduction, and reinforcement or incentive conditions (see Figure 7.8):

- *Attention.* Before students can imitate a model's actions, they must attend to what the model is doing or saying. A student who is distracted by two other students who are talking might not hear what a teacher is saying. Attention to the model is influenced by a host of characteristics. For example, warm, powerful, atypical people command more attention than do cold, weak, typical people. Students are more likely to be attentive to high-status models than to low-status models. In most cases, teachers are high-status models for students.

- *Retention.* To reproduce a model's actions, students must code the information and keep it in memory so that it can be retrieved. A simple verbal description or a vivid image of what the model did assists students' retention. For example, the teacher might say, "I'm showing the correct way to do this. You have to do this step first, this step second, and this step third" as she models how to solve a math problem. A video with a colourful character demonstrating the importance of considering other students' feelings might be remembered better than if the teacher just tells the students to do this. Such colourful characters are at the heart of the popularity of *Sesame Park* with children. Students' retention will be improved when teachers give logical and clear demonstrations. In the next chapter, we will further examine the role of memory in children's learning.

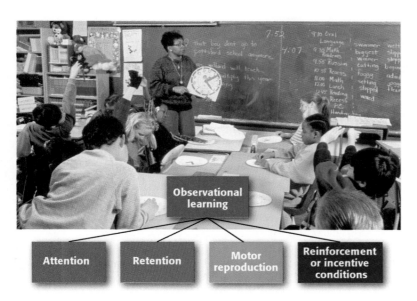

FIGURE 7.8 **Bandura's Model of Observational Learning**
In Bandura's model of observational learning, four processes need to be considered: attention, retention, motor reproduction, and reinforcement or incentive conditions. How might these processes be involved in this classroom situation in which a teacher is demonstrating how to tell time?

- *Motor reproduction.* Children might attend to a model and code in memory what they have seen but, because of limitations in their motor ability, not be able to reproduce the model's behaviour. A 13-year-old might watch basketball player Steven Nash and golfer Lorrie Kane execute their athletic skills to perfection, or observe a famous pianist or artist perform their skills, but not be able to reproduce their motor actions. Teaching, coaching, and practice can help children improve their motor performances.
- *Reinforcement or incentive conditions.* Often children attend to what a model says or does, retain the information in memory, and possess the motor skills to perform the action, but are not motivated to perform the modelled behaviour. This was demonstrated in Bandura's classic Bobo doll study when children who saw the model being punished did not reproduce the punished model's aggressive actions. However, when they subsequently were given a reinforcement or incentive (stickers or fruit juice), they did imitate the model's behaviour.

Bandura believes that reinforcement is not always necessary for observational learning to take place. But if the child does not reproduce the desired behaviours, three types of reinforcement can help do the trick: (1) Reward the model, (2) reward the child, or (3) instruct the child to make self-reinforcing statements such as "Good, I did it!" or "Okay, I've done a good job of getting most of this right, now if I keep trying I will get the rest." We will have much more to say about such self-management strategies shortly.

You will be an important model in students' lives and you have many options for providing students with an array of competent models. To evaluate the roles that models and mentors have played in your own life and can play in your students' lives, complete Self-Assessment 7.1 on page 227. In the next section, we continue our exploration of approaches that have ties to behaviourism but believe that cognitive factors are important aspects of students' learning.

Children need models more than critics.

Joseph Joubert
French Essayist, 19th Century

Cognitive Behaviour Approaches and Self-Regulation

Operant conditioning spawned applications to education and other real-world settings, and the interest in cognitive behavioural approaches has also produced such applications.

Cognitive Behaviour Approaches   In the **cognitive behaviour approaches**, *the emphasis is on getting students to monitor, manage, and regulate their own behaviour rather than let it be controlled by external factors.* In some circles, this has been called *cognitive behaviour modification.* Cognitive behaviour approaches stem from both cognitive psychology,

Teaching Strategies
Involving Observational Learning

✔ Remember that you are a model for students
  • acknowledge that teachers and students spend considerable time together
  • recognize that students will deduce your good and bad habits, expectations for student learning, level of enthusiasm, stress management and coping strategies, learning styles, and many other behaviours
✔ Demonstrate and teach new behaviours
  • frequently model new behaviours and skills (e.g., problem solving, reading, writing, anger management, conflict resolution)
  • focus students' attention on the relevant details of the learning task/situation
  • make demonstrations clear and follow a logical sequence of steps
✔ Use peers as models when appropriate
  • recognize that students will deduce their peers' good and bad habits, expectations for learning, enthusiasm, stress management and coping strategies, learning styles, and other behaviours
  • consider that students are often motivated to imitate high-status models
  • encourage older students to be models, as they usually hold higher status than same-age peers
  • encourage struggling students who use effective process skills and who place considerable effort in the learning process to be models (Chapter 9)
✔ Use mentors as models
  • recognize that mentors are individuals whom students look up to and respect, who serve as competent models, and who are willing to work with students to help them achieve their goals
  • invite guests who may serve as potential mentors into your classroom
  • take students on fieldtrips to see skilled community individuals/mentors "at work" or "performing" whenever possible
  • find a mentor for yourself, preferably a veteran teacher whose past experiences parallel your own
✔ Be aware of media models
  • monitor the models that students observe on television, video, the Internet, and other media
  • be prepared to identify positive role models that students can relate to
  • be prepared to discuss the role of media in youth culture
  • help students make critical and insightful conclusions about role models presented in popular media

with its emphasis on the effects of thoughts on behaviour, and behaviourism, with its emphasis on techniques for changing behaviour. Cognitive behaviour approaches try to change students' misconceptions, strengthen their coping skills, increase their self-control, and encourage constructive self-reflection (Kendall, 2000; Meichenbaum, 1993).

Self-instructional methods *are cognitive behaviour techniques aimed at teaching individuals to modify their own behaviour.* Donald Meichenbaum, Distinguished Professor Emeritus at the University of Waterloo, Ontario, is generally regarded as the founder of cognitive behavioural modification. In a survey reported in *American Psychologist,* he was voted one of the ten most influential psychotherapists of the century. His book *Cognitive Behaviour Modification: An Integrative Approach* is considered a classic in its field. Meichenbaum explains that self-instructional methods help people alter what they say to themselves.

Diversity and Education
Aboriginal Role Models, Mentors, and Programs in Children's Education

There are far more white than minority role models in Canadian classrooms. Teachers who are able to act as cultural and educational role models for their students can play an important role in encouraging Native students to stay in school and provide positive examples of "possible selves." According to the 1991 *Aboriginal Peoples Survey—Schooling, Work, and Related Activities, Income, Expenses, and Mobility*, 17 percent of Native people between the ages of 15 and 49 reported either completing no formal schooling or possessing less than a Grade 9 level of education. In the past, many Aboriginal children who attended formal schools were placed in residential schools, where they were separated from their families and communities. The focus in these schools was on the assimilation of Aboriginal students into mainstream society. Boys of Native descent were often placed in higher grades because of their physical size and strength and their ability to carry out caretaking chores around the schools. Over the past decade, these residential programs have been associated with disturbing allegations of verbal, physical, and sexual abuse. Aboriginal students who have suffered this abuse report they are unable to complete their academic studies in a successful fashion or adjust to community living after residential schooling. For a more detailed history of the effects of residential schools on Native students, see *Impact of Residential Schools and Other Root Causes of Poor Mental Health: Nechi Training Research and Health Promotions Institute Report* (Hodgson, 1990).

In an attempt to provide Aboriginal students with cultural role models and links to Aborginal philosophy and traditions, a number of innovative education programs have been established across Canada. Two such programs are the Aboriginal Elder/Outreach Program and the Dene Kede Curriculum Program.

Saskatchewan's Aboriginal Elder/Outreach Program
In response to an identified need to increase the involvement of Aboriginal peoples in the education of their children, and to improve Aboriginal students' self-esteem and academic achievement, Education Saskatchewan developed the Aboriginal Elder/Outreach Program in 1999. The program acknowledges the role of Aboriginal Elders, outreach workers, cultural advisers, and other Aboriginal resource people as role models and mentors in creating culturally affirming school environments. The project involves more than 70 schools in some 20 school districts in Saskatchewan, and is expanding because of the involvement and support of the Aboriginal community in shaping the program and its direction. For further information on the program see *On Course: Bringing Aboriginal Resource People into Schools* (Saskatchewan Education, 1999).

Dene Kede Program: Northwest Territories
The Dene Kede program was developed to assist Dene students adopt a Dene perspective and become responsible and capable members of the Dene community. Culture-based education implies that the culture of the community is the culture of the school. That is, the culture of the school should reflect the culture of the community with respect to physical appearance, communication style, leadership style, and teaching strategies. The Dene Kede curriculum was developed in conjunction with Dene elders and is taught by Dene teachers. The curriculum focuses on helping students develop responsible, skilful, and respectful relationships with the spiritual world, the land, other people, and themselves. The program's success is evidence of how well the Dene have integrated their world view into community schools and curriculum. For further information about the Dene Kede program, visit the Website at **www.newteachersnwt.ca/culture_based_education2.html.**

www.mcgrawhill.ca/college/santrock

Educational Lessons from Franklin the Turtle

Franklin the Turtle has touched the hearts and minds of many young Canadians. The animated turtle is a featured character in storybooks, audiobooks, CD-ROMS, and a television program. Franklin the Turtle is the product of Canadian author Paulette Bourgeois and illustrator Brenda Clark. Bourgeois' storylines come from her own childhood and parenting experiences, tales from other parents, and letters from children. As a result, children identify with Franklin the Turtle because he encounters issues that are related to their own.

These issues include emotions such as being afraid, getting lost, or having a bad day. In other episodes, Franklin learns to cope in new situations such as going to school, visiting a hospital, riding a bike, and making new friends. Franklin also encounters family issues like wanting a pet, getting a new baby sister, telling fibs, and being messy. Franklin's thoughts and feelings are explicitly stated, as are his strategies for overcoming these problems and dilemmas.

Teachers can introduce educational lessons with relevant Franklin anecdotes. While sharing stories, teachers can encourage their students to predict outcomes associated with critical events,

"If you were Franklin, what would you do?" Throughout these stories, Franklin struggles over choosing what is right and what is wrong. Teachers can use these stories to model effective decision making and to encourage observational learning. Franklin's stories come with a moral or some value that contributes not only to his growth, but also to the personal growth of his audience.

Imagine a situation in which a high-school student is extremely nervous about taking a standardized test. The student can be encouraged to talk to himself in more positive ways. Following are some self-talk strategies that students and teachers can use to cope more effectively with such stressful situations (Meichenbaum, Turk, & Burstein, 1975):

- *Prepare for anxiety or stress*
  "What do I have to do?"
  "I'm going to develop a plan to deal with it."
  "I'll just think about what I have to do."
  "I won't worry. Worry doesn't help anything."
  "I have a lot of different strategies I can use."

- *Confront and handle the anxiety or stress*
  "I can meet the challenge."
  "I'll keep on taking just one step at a time."
  "I can handle it. I'll just relax, breathe deeply, and use one of the strategies."
  "I won't think about my stress. I'll just think about what I have to do."

- *Cope with feelings at critical moments*
  "What is it I have to do?"
  "I knew my anxiety might increase. I just have to keep myself in control."
  "When the anxiety comes, I'll just pause and keep focusing on what I have to do."

- *Use reinforcing self-statements*
  "Good, I did it."
  "I handled it well."
  "I knew I could do it."
  "Wait until I tell other people how I did it!"

In many instances, the strategy is to replace negative self-statements with positive ones. For example, a student might say to herself, "I'll never get this work done by tomorrow." This can be replaced with positive self-statements like these: "This is going to be tough but I think I can do it." "I'm going to look at this as a challenge rather than a stressor." "If I work really hard, I might be able to get it done." Or in having to participate in a class

Models and Mentors in My Life and My Students' Lives

My Models and Mentors
List the most important role models and mentors in your life. Then describe what their positive modelling and mentoring have meant to your development.

Role Models and Mentors   **Their Contributions**

1. _____   _____

2. _____   _____

3. _____   _____

The Type of Role Model I Want to Be for My Students
Describe which characteristics and behaviours you believe are the most important for you to model for your students.

1. _____

2. _____

3. _____

How I Will Incorporate Models and Mentors in My Classroom
Describe a systematic plan for bringing models and mentors into your students' lives.

_____

_____

_____

_____

Who Will Be My Education Mentor? What Would My Ideal Education Mentor Be Like?
Describe your ideal mentor.

_____

_____

_____

_____

_____

_____

_____

_____

_____

_____

www.mcgrawhill.ca/college/santrock

discussion, a student might replace the negative thought "Everyone else knows more than I do so what's the use of saying anything" with positive self-statements like these: "I have as much to say as anyone else." "My ideas may be different, but they are still good." "It's okay to be a little nervous; I'll relax and start talking." Figure 7.9 shows posters that students in one Grade 5 class developed to help them remember how to talk to themselves while listening, planning, working, and checking.

Talking positively to oneself can help teachers and students reach their full potential. Uncountered negative thinking has a way of becoming a self-fulfilling prophecy. You think

POSTER 1
While Listening

1. Does this make sense?
2. Am I getting this?
3. I need to ask a question before I forget.
4. Pay attention.
5. Can I do what the teacher is asking?

POSTER 2
While Planning

1. Do I have everything together?
2. Do I have my friends tuned out so I can get this done?
3. I need to get organized first.
4. What order can I do this in?
5. I know this stuff.

POSTER 3
While Working

1. Am I working fast enough?
2. Stop staring out the window and get back to work.
3. How much time is left?
4. Do I need to stop and start all over?
5. This is hard for me but I can manage it.

POSTER 4
While Checking

1. Did I finish everything?
2. What do I need to recheck?
3. Am I proud of this work?
4. Did I write all of the words?
5. I think I'm finished. I organized myself.

FIGURE 7.9 **Some Posters Developed by a Grade 5 Class to Help Them Remember How to Effectively Talk to Themselves**

you can't do it, and so you don't. If negative self-talk is a problem for you, at random times during the day ask yourself, "What am I saying to myself right now?" Moments that you expect will be potentially stressful are excellent times to examine your self-talk. Also monitor your students' self-talk. If you hear students saying, "I can't do this" or "I'm so slow I'll never get this done," spend some time getting them to replace their negative self-talk with positive self-talk.

Cognitive behaviourists recommend that students improve their performance by monitoring their own behaviour. Teachers can encourage students to monitor their own progress by having them keep records of how many assignments they have finished, how many books they have read, how many homework papers they have turned in on time, how many days in a row they have not interrupted the teacher, and so on. In some cases, teachers place these self-monitoring charts on the walls of the classroom. Alternatively, if the teacher thinks that negative social comparison with other students will be highly stressful for some students, then keeping private records (in a notebook, for example) that are periodically checked by the teacher is probably the better strategy.

Self-Regulatory Learning **Self-regulatory learning** *consists of the self-generation and self-monitoring of thoughts, feelings, and behaviours in order to reach a goal.* These goals might be academic (improving comprehension while reading, becoming a more organized writer, learning how to do multiplication, asking relevant questions) or they might be socioemotional (controlling one's anger, getting along better with peers). What are some of the characteristics of self-regulated learners? Self-regulatory learners (Winne, 1995, 1997)

- set goals for extending their knowledge and sustaining their motivation
- are aware of their emotional makeup and have strategies for managing their emotions
- periodically monitor their progress toward a goal
- fine-tune or revise their strategies based on the progress they are making
- evaluate obstacles that may arise and make the necessary adaptations

Researchers have found that high-achieving students are often self-regulatory learners (Butler 1998a, 1998b, 2002a; Pintrich, 2000; Zimmerman, 1998, 2000). For example, compared with low-achieving students, high-achieving students set more specific learning goals, use more strategies to learn, self-monitor their learning more, and more systematically evaluate their progress toward a goal.

A Model of Self-Regulatory Learning Teachers, tutors, mentors, counsellors, and parents can help students become self-regulated learners (Randi & Corno, 2000; Weinstein, Husman, & Dierking, 2000; Zimmerman, Bonner, & Kovach, 1996). University of British Columbia researcher Deborah Butler (1998a, 1998b, 2002a, 2002b) developed the "strategic content learning" model of self-regulation. The model consists of five components: (1) analyzing task demands, (2) selecting, adapting, or creating personalized strategies, (3) implementing and monitoring strategies, (4) self-evaluating performance, and (5) revising goals or strategies (see Figure 7.10). The model can be applied across one-on-one, small-group, and whole-class instruction (Butler, 2002), and is especially beneficial when working with secondary and post-secondary students who have learning disabilities (Butler, 2002a).

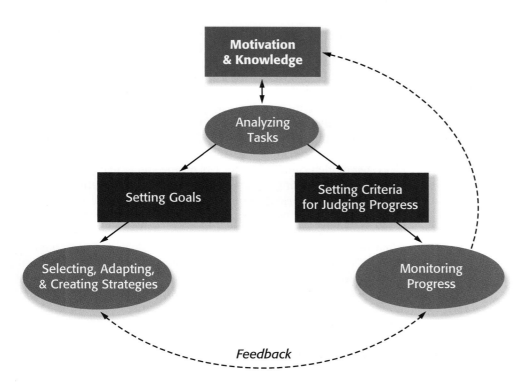

FIGURE 7.10   **Butler's Strategic Content Learning Model**

To better understand the role that teachers can play in helping their students develop self-regulatory behaviours, Butler presents the following example of a secondary-school student who is struggling to complete his academic tasks in an efficient and timely manner:

> Nick, a grade-10 student, consults his academic planner. He is dismayed to find that his history project is due Friday, since he hasn't even started researching. He groans out loud when he realizes that his science lab should be finished by the next block. He'll have to say that he forgot it at home and try to finish it tonight. His math homework is also due tomorrow, he thinks, so he'll have to do that too. But he considers whether he should even bother, given how hopeless he is at math. As he slams closed his agenda, his dismay turns to panic. He recalls that, on top of everything else, he has to write a paragraph for English. He wonders for a moment what a "narrative" paragraph even is, before deciding not to think any more about that one. (p. 84)

When helping students like Nick become self-regulated learners, teachers need to consider a multitude of factors including their prior knowledge, self-perceptions, attributes for success, and motivational beliefs. Teachers also need to guide students through each component of the strategic content learning model. Butler (2002a) provides the following suggestions for supporting Nick with his math homework.

- Begin by having Nick "talk aloud" while completing one to two math problems. Focus on identifying Nick's strengths and challenges.
- Guide Nick through the processes of task analysis, strategy use (e.g., drawing a picture, checking work, reviewing worked examples), and self-monitoring. Through the iterative process of evaluating and modifying strategies, Nick eventually will learn how to construct personally effective strategies across varying task demands.
- Recognize successful efforts and help Nick identify the strategies that he used to produce that outcome. Have Nick record these strategies as part of a "running record" that he can review, test, and refine over time.
- Encourage Nick to verbalize new insights and to try out new ideas. This type of dialogue is believed to be critical for helping students acquire knowledge and skills that can be transferred across learning tasks.

Butler (2002a) stresses that the primary emphasis of this model is *not* on teaching pre-defined strategies per se, as this type of didactic instruction excludes students from experiencing learning as a problem-solving exercise. Rather, the emphasis is on working collaboratively with students to discover a personalized strategic approach to learning that meets the unique needs of the individual and the task.

Social Origins of Self-Regulation   The development of self-regulation is influenced by many factors, among them modelling and self-efficacy (Schunk & Zimmerman, 1997).

Models are important sources for conveying self-regulatory skills. Among the self-regulatory skills that models can engage in are planning and managing time effectively, attending to and concentrating, organizing and coding information strategically, establishing a productive work environment, and using social resources. For example, students might observe a teacher engage in an effective time-management strategy and verbalize appropriate principles. By observing such models, students can come to believe that they also can plan and manage time effectively, which creates a sense of self-efficacy for academic self-regulation and motivates students to engage in those activities.

Self-efficacy can influence students' choices of tasks, effort expended, persistence, and achievement (Bandura, 1997, 2000; Schunk & Zimmerman, 1997). Compared with students who doubt their learning capabilities, those with high self-efficacy for acquiring a skill or performing a task participate more readily, work harder, persist longer in the face of difficulty, and achieve at a higher level. Self-efficacy can have a strong effect on achievement, but it is not the only influence. High self-efficacy will not result in competent performance when requisite knowledge and skills are lacking. We will further explore self-efficacy, setting goals, planning, and self-regulation in Chapter 11, Motivating Students to Learn.

Teachers who encourage students to be self-regulatory learners convey the message that they are responsible for their own behaviour, for becoming educated, and for becoming contributing citizens to society. Another message conveyed by self-regulatory learning is that learning is a personal experience that requires active and dedicated participation by the student (Zimmerman, Bonner, & Kovach, 1996).

 Through the Eyes of Students

How to Keep Students on Task

Students are well behaved if they're challenged and if teachers do fun and interesting things instead of making students write a whole bunch of notes. We do experiments in science where we really have to think. We learn important information without even realizing it because we're having lots of fun.

In math, we work in groups or we're allowed to work with a friend. My friend and I are really good at math so we work together to figure out answers. If we end up with different answers, we check the answer book. Our math teacher always leaves the answer book open on his desk. Nobody copies from the book, because we want to figure out the answer. I like this better than doing corrections, because it's easier to figure out what I did wrong when I know the correct answer. It makes everything more fun and I look forward to math now.

Nicole
Grade 7 Student
Skating, Reading, Swimming, and Shopping Enthusiast
Saskatchewan

Through the Eyes of Teachers

Helping Students Become Self-Regulated Learners

Self-evaluation is a strategy that I like to use in my classroom. I use self-evaluation to monitor and improve my own teaching. I also use it to empower my students to monitor their behaviours and learning.

At the end of each day, I select a few students and ask them to explain whether they had a "good" or "bad" day. I try not to say much during these sessions, allowing students to use their own words to tell me about their day. If the student had a good day, I reinforce the positive behaviours that contributed to this success. If the student claims to have had a poor day, I try to find something positive to comment on and discuss strategies that the student can use to make tomorrow a better one. In this way, my students can begin to self-assess their actions and regulate their behaviours.

I also use self-evaluation when teaching students to monitor their academic work. Prior to beginning any classroom work, we discuss task expectations. After, I walk around the classroom asking students to evaluate their efforts—first by re-stating what is expected of them, and then by describing what they are doing to meet these expectations. As they describe their efforts, they can start to make connections between how they approach academic work and whether they meet task expectations.

Anita Wong
Kindergarten Teacher
Ontario

Evaluating the Social Cognitive Approaches

The social cognitive approaches have made important contributions to educating children. While keeping the behaviourists' scientific flavour and emphasis on careful observation, they significantly expanded the emphasis of learning to include social and cognitive factors. Considerable learning occurs through watching and listening to competent models and then imitating what they do. The emphasis in the cognitive behaviour approach on self-instruction, self-talk, and self-regulatory learning provides an important shift from learning controlled by others to taking responsibility for one's own learning (Higgins, 2000). These self-enacted strategies can significantly improve students' learning.

Critics of the social cognitive approaches come from several camps. Some cognitive theorists believe the approaches still focus too much on overt behaviour and external factors and not enough on the details of how cognitive processes such as thinking, memory, problem solving, and the like actually take place. Some developmentalists criticize them for being nondevelopmental, in the sense that they don't specify age-related, sequential changes in learning. Others worry that students with severe developmental or intellectual disabilities (e.g., fetal alcohol syndrome, acquired brain injury) may be unable to link consequences with behaviour or regulate their behaviour. And humanistic theorists fault them for not placing enough attention on self-esteem and caring, supportive relationships. All of these criticisms also can be, and have been, levelled at the behavioural approaches, such as Skinner's operant conditioning, discussed earlier in the chapter.

At this point, we have discussed many aspects of the social cognitive approaches. A review of these ideas is presented in Summary Table 7.4. This chapter focused on the cognitive approaches to learning that still retain some behavioural leanings. In the next chapter, we will examine approaches with a purely cognitive bent.

SUMMARY TABLE 7.4
Social Cognitive Approaches to Learning

What is social cognitive theory?	• Social cognitive theory states that a person can master a situation and produce positive outcomes. • This is accomplished through interactions between the person (cognitive), behaviour, and environment. • Albert Bandura is the main theorist.
What is observational learning?	• It is learning that occurs when a person observes and imitates another's behaviour. This is also called imitation or modelling.
What is the classic Bobo doll study?	• In this experiment, Bandura illustrated how observational learning can occur even by watching a model who is not reinforced or punished. The experiment also demonstrates a distinction between learning and performance.
What are cognitive behaviour approaches?	• These approaches emphasize having students monitor, manage, and regulate their own behaviour rather than allowing it to be externally controlled. This is also called cognitive behaviour modification. • Cognitive behaviour approaches try to change students' misconceptions, strengthen their coping skills, increase their self-control, and encourage constructive self-reflection. • Cognitive behaviourists believe that students can improve their performance by monitoring their behaviour.
What is self-regulatory learning?	• Self-regulatory learning consists of self-generation and self-monitoring of thoughts, feelings, and behaviours to reach a goal. It gives students responsibility for their learning. • The strategic content learning model involves analyzing task demands, selecting, adapting, or creating personalized strategies, implementing and monitoring strategies, self-evaluating performance, and revising goals or strategies.
What are the criticisms of cognitive social approaches?	• Too much emphasis is placed on behaviour and external factors and not enough on the details of cognitive processes. • These approaches are non-developmental and do not give enough attention to self-esteem and caring, supportive relationships.

Adam, a student in Mr. Potter's Grade 10 French class, is disruptive from time to time. He is also very bright.

One day Adam began talking very loudly to the other students, laughing and telling jokes. Mr. Potter chose to ignore Adam's behaviour in the hope that he would stop on his own. Adam didn't stop. Instead, his behaviour became more raucous. Still Mr. Potter ignored it. Soon Adam was making enough noise that Mr. Potter was afraid that students in the neighbouring classrooms would be disturbed. He verbally reprimanded Adam.

Adam was a bit quieter for the next few minutes. After that, however, he once again became loud and disruptive. Again Mr. Potter verbally reprimanded him. This time he also told Adam that if he continued with his disruptive behaviour he would have to go to the office. Adam's behaviour became even more disruptive. Mr. Potter sent him to the office.

When Adam arrived at the office it was full of people—teachers getting their mail and making copies, volunteers signing in, students who were ill, students sent on errands, and other students who had been sent for disciplinary reasons. The school secretary told Adam to have a seat, which he did. He conversed with every person who entered the office, as well as those who were there when he arrived. Half an hour after his arrival, he was sent back to class. He behaved quite well for the rest of the day, to Mr. Potter's relief.

The next day, when students were given seatwork in Mr. Potter's class, Adam once again became disruptive. He loudly told jokes to his classmates, laughed until tears were streaming down his face, and threw a paper airplane across the room. Mr. Potter reprimanded him and asked him to stop. When Adam didn't comply, Mr. Potter sent him to the office again. Once more the office was bustling with activity.

Over the course of the next two weeks, Adam was sent to the office for disrupting class each day, always during seatwork assignments. Mr. Potter was perplexed. Even more perplexing was that within three school days other students were becoming disruptive as well, requiring that they too be sent to the office. Consider the principles of behavioural learning theories while answering these questions:

- What are the issues in this case?
- Why did Adam continue to disrupt class despite the consequences?
- What has Adam learned? What has Mr. Potter learned?
- Why did the other students join Adam in his disruptive behaviour?
- What could Mr. Potter have done differently? What could he do next?

CHAPTER REVIEW

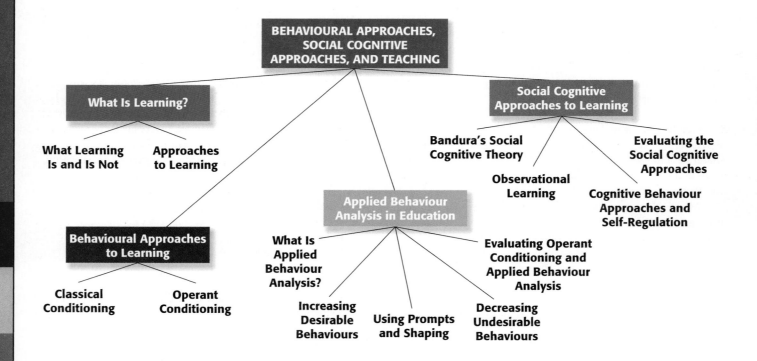

BEHAVIOURAL APPROACHES, SOCIAL COGNITIVE APPROACHES, AND TEACHING

What Is Learning?
- What Learning Is and Is Not
- Approaches to Learning

Behavioural Approaches to Learning
- Classical Conditioning
- Operant Conditioning

Applied Behaviour Analysis in Education
- What Is Applied Behaviour Analysis?
- Increasing Desirable Behaviours
- Using Prompts and Shaping
- Decreasing Undesirable Behaviours
- Evaluating Operant Conditioning and Applied Behaviour Analysis

Social Cognitive Approaches to Learning
- Bandura's Social Cognitive Theory
- Observational Learning
- Evaluating the Social Cognitive Approaches
- Cognitive Behaviour Approaches and Self-Regulation

To obtain a detailed review of this chapter, study these four summary tables:

 KEY TERMS

learning 204
behaviourism 204
mental processes 204
associative learning 204
classical conditioning 206
unconditioned stimulus (US) 206
unconditioned response (UR) 206
conditioned stimulus (CS) 206
conditioned response (CR) 206
generalization (classical conditioning) 207

discrimination (classical conditioning) 208
extinction (classical conditioning) 208
systematic desensitization 208
operant conditioning 209
law of effect 209
reinforcement (reward) 209
punishment 209
positive reinforcement 209
negative reinforcement 209
positive punishment 210
negative punishment 210

generalization (operant conditioning) 210
discrimination (operant conditioning) 210
extinction (operant conditioning) 211
applied behaviour analysis 212
Premack principle 212
schedules of reinforcement 213
fixed-ratio schedule 213
variable-ratio schedule 213
fixed-interval schedule 213
variable-interval schedule 213

contracting 214
prompt 214
shaping 215
time-out 216
response cost 217
social cognitive theory 220
reciprocal determinism model 220
self-efficacy 221
observational learning 221
cognitive behaviour approaches 223
self-instructional methods 224
self-regulatory learning 228

PROFESSIONAL DEVELOPMENT/PORTFOLIO ACTIVITIES

1. What to Do, What to Do

Prompt and effective handling of potential behaviour problems can minimize classroom disruptions. In a group with two or three of your colleagues, discuss appropriate strategies for handling each of the following students:

- Christina, a girl who likes to intermittently utter profanities
- Bruce, a boy who tells you to quit bugging him when you ask him questions
- Larissa, a student who frequently talks with other students around her while you are teaching a lesson

In your portfolio, write about the nature of these disruptions and how you might possibly handle them.

2. The Power of Imitation

An important principle of Bandura's social cognitive theory is that exposure to positive role models can alter students' attitudes. Bandura emphasizes the importance of modelling as a way of teaching. Does a teacher's behaviour and attitude in the classroom influence students' behaviours and attitudes? Do television, movies, magazines, music videos, and other media affect how students behave in the classroom? How might you overcome the effects modelling that these media present to your students?

3. A Self-Regulation Scenario

Consider the following scenario. Jane is a high school student who doesn't have adequate self-regulatory skills, and consequently this is causing her serious academic problems. She does not plan or organize, she has poor study strategies, and she does not manage her time well. Using Butler's model, design an effective self-regulation program for Jane and include the plan in your portfolio.

INTERNET ACTIVITIES

1. Behaviour Tips from the Web

You have a student who constantly forgets to bring books and materials to class. Searching the Web for tips on how to change student behaviour you will find numerous Websites that are dedicated to how to change negative behaviour. How will you know if these Websites are providing you with good information? Assess the information you find on recommended behavioural approaches in light of the information presented in this chapter.

2. Websites for Students Who Are Gifted

Together with three or four other students in your class, come up with a list and description of software programs or Websites that you think would benefit children who are gifted. One good source of information on such software is the Journal of Electronic Learning. Share the results of your search with your colleagues.

Connect to the Online Learning Centre at www.mcgrawhill.ca/ college/santrock **to explore possible answers.**

Visit the *Educational Psychology* Online Learning Centre at
www.mcgrawhill.ca/college/santrock
to access Websites related to the above Internet Activities as well as chapter quizzes,
a searchable glossary, and other learning and study tools.

8 The Cognitive Information-Processing Approach and Teaching

Preview

Students thirst to know and understand. In their efforts to know and understand, they process information. These statements reflect a cognitive information-processing approach, the focus of this chapter. These are some of the questions we will explore:

- What are the key features of the information-processing approach?
- How do students construct their memory?
- How do students think, and what are the best ways to guide their thinking?
- How can you effectively teach so that students will transfer their learning from the classroom to other contexts?
- What is metacognition? How can you help students use better strategies in remembering and solving problems?

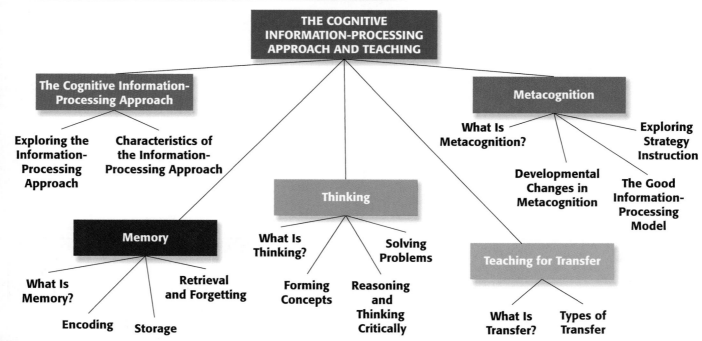

THE COGNITIVE INFORMATION-PROCESSING APPROACH AND TEACHING

The Cognitive Information-Processing Approach
- Exploring the Information-Processing Approach
- Characteristics of the Information-Processing Approach

Memory
- What Is Memory?
- Encoding
- Storage
- Retrieval and Forgetting

Thinking
- What Is Thinking?
- Forming Concepts
- Reasoning and Thinking Critically
- Solving Problems

Metacognition
- What Is Metacognition?
- Developmental Changes in Metacognition
- Exploring Strategy Instruction
- The Good Information-Processing Model

Teaching for Transfer
- What Is Transfer?
- Types of Transfer

When Nature her great masterpiece
design'd,
And fram'd her last, best work,
the human mind.

Robert Burns
Scottish Poet, 18th Century

Teaching Stories: Michael Riordon

For more than 16 years, Michael Riordan (a classroom teacher, special educator, and principal) has been using explicit strategy instruction to help elementary-school students learn to problem-solve in school and in life. Michael uses a teaching technique that he calls the "Freeze Frame" to help students transfer problem-solving strategies to academic tasks.

"The Freeze Frame method is a technique that I use to periodically 'freeze' instruction in order to identify the connection between a strategy or concept and a context where the strategy or concept might be useful. In the early stages of learning a new problem-solving strategy, I freeze the class and state the connections for the students explicitly. I model a form of self-talk or thinking aloud to highlight the connections that I want the students to make. With practice, the students begin to make the connections themselves.

"Recently, I used the Freeze Frame approach to teach students how to organize and communicate chart information. First, I introduced a variety of charts to students with examples from several subject areas. During instruction, I called out 'Freeze Frame!' when I wanted the students to reflect on the process that we were using versus the content we were studying. I asked them questions like, 'Where else might I use charts? How do these charts make the information easier to understand?

What is included in the different charts? Where have I seen charts like these used before?'

"When discussing dinosaurs as part of another class, I presented the students with a collection of data and used Freeze Frame to ask, 'How many dinosaurs have I been asked to compare? How many attributes are involved in the comparisons? What kind of chart can I use to make sense of this? If each item represents a cell in my chart, how many cells are required? I don't think I'll be doing much with dinosaurs in my life, but what if I had to make a decision about buying my new bike. How could I use a chart to make that decision?'

"I also make sure to model my thinking with respect to these questions. I might say, 'In order to make a good comparison between dinosaurs, I will need to look at cells that have the same information. Can I write a sentence that compares the three dinosaurs and what they eat? Can I write a sentence comparing each of the bikes and the features that they have? What kinds of charts might I use to answer these questions?'

"I use the Freeze Frame technique to create teachable moments for my students—moments that move beyond the specific subject area or curriculum concept that we are studying and extend to how we can problem-solve effectively in the 'real world.'"

The Cognitive Information-Processing Approach

Exploring the Information-Processing Approach

Characteristics of the Information-Processing Approach

THE COGNITIVE INFORMATION-PROCESSING APPROACH

How capable are children? Proponents of the information-processing approach believe they are highly capable. Children attend to information being presented and tinker with it. They develop strategies for remembering. They form concepts. They reason and solve problems.

Exploring the Information-Processing Approach

The **information-processing approach** *emphasizes that children manipulate information, monitor it, and strategize about it. Central to this approach are the processes of memory and thinking.* According to the information-processing approach, children develop a gradually increasing capacity for processing information, which allows them to acquire increasingly complex knowledge and skills (Stevenson, Hofer, & Randel, 1999).

Some information-processing approaches have stronger constructivist leanings than others. Those that do have a constructivist bent see teachers as cognitive guides for academic tasks and children as learners who are trying to make sense of these tasks (Mayer, 1996, 1999). Piaget's and Case's cognitive developmental theories, described in Chapter 2, exemplify the cognitive constructivist approach. So do some information-processing approaches in this chapter (Ceci, 2000). Information-processing approaches that emphasize a more passive child who simply memorizes information provided by the environment are not constructivist.

Behaviourism and its associative model of learning was a dominant force in psychology until the 1950s and 1960s, when many psychologists began to acknowledge that they could not explain children's learning without referring to mental processes such as memory and thinking (Sternberg, 1999). The term *cognitive psychology* became a label for approaches that sought to explain behaviour by examining mental processes. Although a number of factors stimulated the growth of cognitive psychology, none was more important than the development of computers. The first modern computer, developed by John von Neumann in the late 1940s, showed that inanimate machines could perform logical operations. This suggested that some mental operations might be carried out by computers, possibly telling us something about the way human cognition works. Cognitive psychologists often draw analogies to computers to help explain the relation between cognition and the brain. The physical brain is described as the computer's hardware, cognition as its software. And although computers and software aren't perfect analogies for brains and cognitive activities, the comparison contributed to our thinking about the child's mind as an active information-processing system nonetheless.

> Our life is what
> our thoughts make it.
>
> Marcus Aurelius
> *Roman Emperor and Philosopher,*
> *2nd Century* A.D.

Characteristics of the Information-Processing Approach

Robert Siegler (1998) described three main characteristics of the information-processing approach:

- *Thinking.* In Siegler's view, thinking is information processing. In this regard, Siegler provides a broad perspective on thinking. He says that when children perceive, encode, represent, and store information from the world, they are engaging in thinking. Siegler believes that thinking is highly flexible, which allows individuals to adapt and adjust to many changes in circumstances, task requirements, and goals. However, there are some limits on the human's remarkable thinking abilities. Individuals can attend to only a limited amount of information at any point in time, and there are limits on how fast we can process information. Later in the chapter we will explore children's attention in more depth.
- *Change mechanisms.* Siegler argues that in information processing the main focus should be on the role of mechanisms of change in development. He believes that four main mechanisms work together to create changes in children's cognitive skills: encoding, automaticity, strategy construction, and generalization. **Encoding** *is the process by*

which information gets into memory. Siegler states that a key aspect of solving problems is to encode the relevant information and ignore the irrelevant parts. Because it often takes time and effort to construct new strategies, children must practise them in order to eventually execute them automatically and maximize their effectiveness. The term **automaticity** *refers to the ability to process information with little or no effort.* With age and experience, information processing becomes increasingly automatic on many tasks, allowing children to detect connections among ideas and events that they otherwise would miss. The third and fourth change mechanisms are strategy construction and generalization. **Strategy construction** *involves the discovery of a new procedure for processing information.* Siegler says that children need to encode key information about a problem and coordinate the information with relevant prior knowledge to solve the problem. To fully benefit from a newly constructed strategy, children need to generalize, or apply, it to other problems. Later in the chapter, we will discuss generalization under the topic of transfer of learning. **Transfer** *occurs when the child applies previous experiences and knowledge to learning or problem solving in a new situation.*

• *Self-modification.* The contemporary information-processing approach argues that children play an active role in their development. They use knowledge and strategies that they have learned in previous circumstances to adapt their responses to a new learning situation. In this manner, children build newer and more sophisticated responses from prior knowledge and strategies. The importance of self-modification in processing information is exemplified in **metacognition**, *which means cognition about cognition, or "knowing about knowing"* (Flavell, 1999; Flavell & Miller, 1998). We will study metacognition in the final section of this chapter and especially will emphasize how students' self-awareness can enable them to adapt and manage their strategies during problem solving and thinking.

Now that we have studied some general properties of the information-processing approach, let's examine some of its main cognitive processes in greater detail. We will begin with memory. Some of the aspects of memory that we will explore are encoding, automatization, and strategies, which are critical change mechanisms according to Siegler's view of information processing.

MEMORY

Twentieth-century playwright Tennessee Williams once commented that life is all memory except for that one present moment that goes by so quickly that you can hardly catch it going. But just what is memory?

What Is Memory?

Memory *is the retention of information over time.* Educational psychologists study how information is initially placed or encoded into memory, how it is retained or stored after being encoded, and how it is found or retrieved for a certain purpose later. Memory anchors the self in continuity. Without memory you would not be able to connect what happened to you yesterday with what is going on in your life today. Today, educational psychologists emphasize that it is important not to view memory in terms of how children add something to it but rather to underscore how children actively construct their memory (Schneider & Bjorklund, 1998).

The main body of our discussion of memory will focus on encoding, storage, and retrieval. Thinking about memory in terms of these processes should help you to understand it better (see Figure 8.1). For memory to work, children have to take information in, store it or represent it, and then retrieve it for some purpose later.

As you learned earlier, encoding is the process by which information gets into memory. **Storage** *is the retention of information over time.* **Retrieval** *means taking information out of storage.* Let's now explore each of these three important memory activities in greater detail.

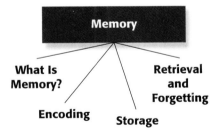

...There exists in the mind of man a block of wax, ... Let us say that this tablet is a gift of Memory.

Plato
Greek Philosopher,
4th Century B.C.

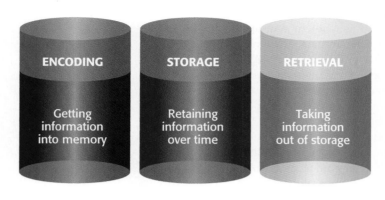

FIGURE 8.1   Processing Information in Memory
As you read about the many aspects of memory in this chapter, it should help you to think about the organization of memory in terms of these three main activities.

Encoding

In everyday language, encoding has much in common with attention and learning. When a student is listening to a teacher, watching a movie, listening to music, or talking with a friend, she or he is encoding information into memory. Although children can perform some activities automatically, to perform many others they must pay **attention**, *which refers to concentrating and focusing mental resources.* One critical skill in paying attention is doing it *selectively* (Pashler, 1998). As the teacher gives instructions for completing a task, students need to attend to what she is saying and not be distracted by other students who are talking. As students study for a test, they need to focus selectively on the book they are reading and tune out or eliminate other stimuli such as the sound of a television. In one research study, 8-year-old children tended to use exhaustive attentional searches to find information, whereas 11-year-olds used more selective attentional strategies in searching for information (Davidson, 1996).

Being able to *shift* from one activity to another when appropriate is another challenge related to attention. For example, learning to write good stories requires shifting among the competing tasks of forming letters, composing grammar, structuring paragraphs, and conveying the story as a whole. Older children and adolescents are better than younger children at making appropriate shifts of attention.

Another problem for many young children is that they focus too much on the attention-grabbing aspects of a task or situation rather than on what is important. They focus on *salient* aspects of a situation rather than on its *relevant* aspects. For example, when preschoolers watch a video on which a clown is giving directions for solving a problem, they often focus more on the clown's attention-grabbing appearance than on the instructions he is giving. By the middle of elementary school, children are better at focusing their attention on the relevant dimensions of a task (Ridderinkhof & van der Molen, 1995; Ridderinkhof, van der Molen, & Band, 1997). This change often signals greater reflection and less impulsiveness. Of course, there are individual differences in attention, and some elementary-school children need help in attending to the relevant dimensions of a task rather than the salient dimensions.

One reason older children are better at deploying attention than younger children is that they are more likely to construct a plan of action to guide their attentional efforts when they are trying to solve a problem. However, younger children often can effectively use attention-focusing strategies when these are provided to them. Possibly school experiences help children become more aware of their own attentional capabilities, or perhaps as they develop they come to understand that their mind works best when it is active and constructive (Lovett & Pillow, 1996). Attending to something relevant is an active, effortful process that draws on mental resources, rather than a passive process of receiving the available information.

Rehearsal   **Rehearsal** *is the conscious repetition of information over time to increase the length of time information stays in memory.* Rehearsal does not hold more information in memory, it just keeps the same information in memory longer. Rehearsal works best when individuals need to remember a list of items for a brief period of time. When they must retain information over long periods of time, as when they are studying for a test they won't take until next week, other strategies usually work better than rehearsal. A main reason that rehearsal does not work well for retaining information over the long term is that rehearsal often involves just rotely repeating information without imparting any meaning to it. When students construct their memory in meaningful ways, they remember better. As we will see next, they also remember better when they process material deeply and elaborate it.

Teaching Strategies
For Helping Students Pay Attention

✓ Encourage students to pay attention
  - tell students the importance of paying attention for memory and learning
  - have students practise giving undivided attention to a task
  - reward attention with verbal praise
✓ Help students develop and monitor their attention
  - use instructional comments, cues, or gestures to signal important information
  - have students use cues/phrases like "alert," "focus," or "zero" when they need to focus
  - have students keep a record of the number of times their minds wander
✓ Make learning interesting
  - relate to-be-learned concepts to students' interests
  - integrate novel, unusual, or surprising exercises into lessons
  - use dramatic and interesting questions
✓ Actively engage students in the learning process
  - use a variety of instructional formats, provide hands-on activities, and use relevant community resources including guest speakers
  - integrate relevant media and technology into your classroom
  - reflect on features that catch students' attention and incorporate them into your instruction (e.g., use of colourful images)
✓ Avoid providing students with too much information too quickly
  - have students activate relevant prior knowledge or provide students with this information prior to learning new concepts
  - provide students with only a few concepts at a time
  - repeat critical information
✓ Program for individual differences in students' attentional skills
  - be aware that some students with exceptionalities have severe difficulties paying attention
  - eliminate distractions in the classroom
✓ Maintain students' attention once you have obtained it
  - avoid focusing and/or calling on specific students
  - spread your attention and requests so that each student has an equal chance of being called on

Deep Processing Following the discovery that rehearsal is not an efficient way to remember information over the long term, Fergus Craik and Robert Lockhart (1972) proposed that we can process information at a variety of levels. Their **levels of processing theory** *states that the processing of memory occurs on a continuum from shallow to deep, with deeper processing producing better memory.* The sensory or physical features of stimuli are analyzed first at a shallow level. This might involve detecting the lines, angles, and contours of a printed word's letters or a spoken word's frequency, duration, and loudness. At an *intermediate* level of processing, the stimulus is recognized and given a label. For example, a four-legged, barking object is identified as a dog. Then, at the *deepest* level, information is processed semantically, in terms of its meaning. For example, if a child sees the word *boat*, at the shallow level she might notice the shapes of the letters, at the intermediate level she might think of the characteristics of the word (for instance, that it rhymes with *coat*), and at the deepest level she might think about the last time she went fishing with her dad on a boat and the kind of boat it was. Researchers have found that individuals remember information better when they process it at a deeper level (Craik, 2000; Hunt & Ellis, 1999).

Elaboration   Cognitive psychologists soon recognized, however, that there is more to good memory than just depth of processing. They discovered that when individuals use elaboration in their encoding of information, their memory benefits. **Elaboration** *is the extensiveness of information processing involved in memory.* Thus, when you present the concept of democracy to students, they likely will remember it better if they come up with good examples of it. Thinking of examples is a good way to elaborate information. For instance, self-reference is an effective way to elaborate information. If you are trying to get students to remember the concept of fairness, the more they can generate personal examples of inequities and equities they have personally experienced, the more likely it is that they will remember the concept. Likewise, students are more likely to remember the concept of aerodynamics if they associate it with the last time they flew a kite, rather than just rehearsing the words that define aerodynamics. Thinking about personal associations with information makes the information more meaningful and helps students remember it.

One reason elaboration works so well in producing good memory is that it adds to the *distinctiveness* of memory code (Schneider & Pressley, 1997; Willoughby et al., 2000). To remember a piece of information, such as a name, an experience, or a fact about geography, students need to search for the code that contains this information among the mass of codes in their long-term memory. The search process is easier if the memory code is unique (Hunt & Kelly, 1996). The situation is not unlike searching for a friend at a crowded airport—if your friend is 6 feet 3 inches tall and has flaming red hair, it will be easier to find him in the crowd than if he has more common features. Also, as a person elaborates information, more information is stored. And as more information is stored, it becomes easier to differentiate the memory from others. For example, students can improve their learning about the Canadian provinces and territories (e.g., Apples were first cultivated in Nova Scotia; British Columbia is the province with the greatest number of lizards) by using their existing knowledge of Canada to support new information (e.g., Nova Scotia was one of the first provinces settled; British Columbia is densely forested) versus reading the information repeatedly (Woloshyn & Stockley, 1995; Woloshyn, Wood, & Willoughby, 1994).

Constructing Images   When we construct an image of something, we are elaborating the information. For example, how many windows are there in the apartment or house where your family has lived for a substantial part of your life? Few of us ever memorize this information, but you probably can come up with a good answer, especially if you reconstruct a mental image of each room. Take a "mental walk" through the house, counting the windows as you go.

Canadian researcher Allan Paivio (1971, 1986; Sadoski & Paivio, 2001) believes that memories are stored in one of two ways: as a verbal code or as an image code. For example, you can remember a picture by a label (the *Mona Lisa*, a verbal code) or by a mental image. Paivio states that the more detailed and distinctive the image code, the better your memory of the information will be. We will have more to say about imagery later in the chapter when we discuss memory strategies.

Organization   When students organize information when they are encoding it, their memory benefits. To understand the importance of organization in encoding, complete the following exercise: Recall the 12 months of the year as quickly as you can. How long did it take you? What was the order of your recall? Your answers are probably "a few seconds" and "in natural order" (January, February, March, and so on). Now try to remember the months in alpha-

Through the Eyes of Students

How Do You Remember?

Information goes in through your eyes and ears and you process it and then you do it. To remember information you think about it often and you write it down. The teacher will make you write it down or she'll remind you of it often. She sounds serious and she'll wait until everybody is there and settled down.

Leah
Grade 4 Student,
Painting and Movie Enthusiast
Newfoundland

betical order. Did you make any errors? How long did it take you? There is a clear distinction between recalling the months in natural order and alphabetically. This exercise is a good one to use with your students to help them understand the importance of organizing their memories in *meaningful* ways.

The more you present information in an organized way, the easier your students will remember it. This is especially true if you organize information hierarchically or outline it. Also, if you simply encourage students to organize information, they often will remember it better than if you give them no instructions about organizing (Mandler, 1980).

Chunking *is a beneficial organizational memory strategy that involves grouping or "packing" information into "higher-order" units that can be remembered as single units.* Chunking works by making large amounts of information more manageable and more meaningful. For example, consider this simple list of words: *hot, city, book, forget, tomorrow, smile.* Try to hold these in memory for a moment, then write them down. If you recalled all six words, you succeeded in holding 30 letters in your memory.

Storage

After children encode information, they need to retain or store the information. Among the most prominent aspects of memory storage are the three main stores, which vary according to time: sensory memory, working (or short-term) memory, and long-term memory. (See Figure 8.2 for Baddeley's memory model.)

Memory's Time Frames   Individuals remember some information for less than a second, some for about half a minute, and other information for minutes, hours, years, even a lifetime. The three types of memory that vary according to their time frames are *sensory memory* (which lasts a fraction of a second to several seconds); *short-term memory* (also called *working memory*; lasts about 30 seconds), and *long-term memory* (which lasts up to a lifetime).

Sensory Memory   **Sensory memory** *holds information from the world in its original sensory form for only an instant,* not much longer than the brief time a student is exposed to the visual, auditory, and other sensations. Its information is quickly lost unless students engage in mental processes like rehearsal to transfer it into short-term or long-term memory.

Students have a sensory memory for sounds for up to several seconds, sort of like a brief echo. However, their sensory memory for visual images lasts only for about one-fourth of a second. Because sensory information lasts for only a fleeting moment, an important task for the student is attending to the sensory information that is important for learning.

Short-Term (Working) Memory   **Short-term memory** (often called **working memory**) *is a limited-capacity memory system in which information is retained for as long as 30 seconds, unless the information is rehearsed or otherwise processed further, in which case it can be retained longer.* Compared to sensory memory, short-term memory is limited in capacity

Frank and Ernest

FRANK & ERNEST reprinted by permission of Newspaper Enterprise Association, Inc.

Through the Eyes of Teachers

Knowing All the Answers

I will never forget the first time that a student asked a question to which I did not know the answer. Being a diligent teacher, I responded that I would, "check the text." Looking somewhat confused, the student continued, "Don't you know what the answer is? Aren't you supposed to know what you're teaching? Why do we need to know it if you don't?"

I panicked briefly but then realized that this was a teachable moment. I could turn this potentially dismal situation into an educationally rich one. I started by confirming that these were important questions that we should address as a class. I asked the students what was more important—knowing where and how to find unknown information or being able to memorize it. I explained that I had no interest in having them memorize content in order to regurgitate it on a test or some other form of assessment. I also confessed that although I was a teacher, I did not always have all the answers. There was no fountain of knowledge that I could turn on or off at will. Finally, I explained that my responsibility as their teacher was to help them learn how to find information, critically reflect on it, and make sense of it. I expected them to be able to conduct research to find answers for their own questions and for the queries of others.

Paul Allen
Associate Professor, Faculty of Education
University of New Brunswick
Former Secondary-School Teacher
New Brunswick

"Can we hurry up and get to the test? My short-term memory is better than my long-term memory."
© 1985: reprinted courtesy of Bill Hoest and Parade Magazine.

but relatively longer in duration. Its limited capacity intrigued George Miller (1956), who described this in a paper with a catchy title: "The Magical Number Seven, Plus or Minus Two." Miller pointed out that on many tasks, students are limited in how much information they can keep track of without external aids. Usually the limit is in the range of 7 ± 2 items.

The most widely cited example of the 7 ± 2 phenomenon involves **memory span**, *the number of digits an individual can repeat back without error in a single presentation*. How many digits individuals can repeat back depends on how old they are. In one study, memory span increased from 2 digits in 2- to 3-year-olds, to 5 digits in 7-year-olds, to 6 or 7 digits in 13-year-olds (Dempster, 1981). Many college students can handle lists of 8 or 9 digits. Keep in mind that these are averages and individuals differ. For example, many 7-year-olds have a memory span of fewer than 6 or 7 digits, others have a memory span of 8 or more digits.

Related to short-term memory, British psychologist Alan Baddeley (1993, 1998, 2000, 2001) proposed that **working memory** is a three-part system that temporarily holds information as people perform tasks. Working memory is a kind of mental "workbench" where information is manipulated and assembled to help us make decisions, solve problems, and comprehend written and spoken language. Notice that working memory is not like a passive storehouse, with shelves to store information until it moves to long-term memory. Rather, it is a very active memory system (Engle, 2002).

Figure 8.2 shows Baddeley's view of working memory and its three components: phonological loop, visual-spatial memory, and central executive. Think of them as an executive (central executive) with two assistants (phonological loop and visual-spatial working memory) to help do your work.

- The *phonological loop* is specialized to briefly store speech-based information about the sounds of language. The phonological loop contains two separate components: an acoustic code, which decays in a few seconds, and rehearsal, which allows individuals to repeat the words in the phonological store.
- *Visual-spatial working memory* stores visual and spatial information, including visual imagery. Like the phonological loop, visual-spatial working memory has a limited capacity. The phonological loop and visual-spatial working memory function independently. You could rehearse numbers in the phonological loop while making spatial arrangements of letters in visual-spatial working memory.
- The *central executive* integrates information not only from the phonological loop and visual-spatial working memory, but also from long-term memory. In Baddeley's view, the central executive plays important roles in attention, planning, and organizing behaviour. The central executive acts much like a supervisor who monitors which information and issues deserve attention and which should be ignored. It also selects which strategies to use to process information and solve problems. As with the other two components of working memory—the phonological loop and visual-spatial working memory—the central executive has a limited capacity.

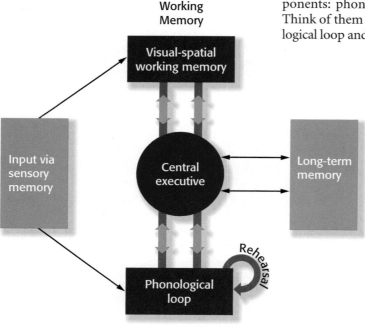

FIGURE 8.2   Working Memory
In Baddeley's working-memory model, working memory is like a "mental workbench" where a great deal of information processing is carried out. Working memory consists of three main components. The phonological loop and visual-spatial working memory serve as assistants in helping the central executive do its work. Input from sensory memory goes to the phonological loop, where information about speech is stored and rehearsal takes place, and visual-spatial working memory, where visual and spatial information, including imagery, are stored. Working memory is a limited-capacity system and information is stored there only for a brief time. Working memory interacts with long-term memory, using information from long-term memory in its work and transmitting information to long-term memory for longer storage.

Let's examine an aspect of life in which working memory is involved. In one recent study, verbal working memory was impaired by negative emotion (Gray, 2001). In other words, when people are feeling bad about something, their working memory may become less efficient. In another recent study, college students who wrote about a negative emotional event showed sizeable improvement in working memory, compared to students who wrote about a positive emotional event and those in a control group who wrote about their daily schedule (Klein & Boals, 2001). The writing effect on working memory was associated with higher grades. An important implication of this study is its demonstration that working memory is malleable and can be affected by an experience such as writing about one's emotional experiences (Miyake, 2001). For example, students with math anxiety often experience deficiencies in working memory when doing math problems because of intrusive thoughts and worries about math (Ashcraft & Kirk, 2001). Such students might benefit from writing about their math anxiety.

Long-Term Memory **Long-term memory** *is a type of memory that holds enormous amounts of information for a long period of time in a relatively permanent fashion.* A typical human's long-term memory capacity is staggering. The distinguished computer scientist John von Neumann put the size at 2.8 × 10 (280 quintillion) bits, which in practical terms means that long-term memory storage is virtually unlimited. Even more impressive is the efficiency with which individuals can retrieve information. It often takes only a moment to search through this vast storehouse to find the information we want. Think about your own long-term memory. Who was the first prime minister? Who was your Grade 1 teacher? When were you born? Where do you live? You can answer thousands of such questions instantly. Of course, not all information is retrieved so easily from long-term memory. Later in this chapter we will examine ways that students can retrieve hard-to-recall information.

A Model of the Three Memory Stores Richard Atkinson and Richard Shiffrin (1968) proposed the original three-stage model of memory from which Baddeley's more complex model evolved. According to the **Atkinson-Shiffrin model**, *memory involves a sequence of these three stages: sensory memory, short-term (working) memory, and long-term memory.* As we have seen, much information makes it no farther than the sensory memories of sounds and sights. This information is retained only for a brief instant. However, some information, especially that to which we pay attention, is transferred to short-term memory, where it can be retained for about 30 seconds (or longer with the aid of rehearsal). Atkinson and Shiffrin claimed that the longer information is retained in short-term memory through the use of rehearsal, the greater its chance is of getting into long-term memory.

Contemporary experts on memory such as Baddeley (1998) and Bartlett (1998) argue that memory doesn't always work in a neatly packaged three-stage sequence, as Atkinson and Shiffrin proposed. These contemporary experts stress that working memory uses long-term memory's contents in more flexible ways than simply retrieving information from it.

Some contemporary psychologists equate the terms *short-term memory* and *working memory*; others believe that these terms should not be used interchangeably. In most instances they prefer the concept of working memory because of its active, constructive emphasis. They believe that the Atkinson-Shiffrin model places too much emphasis on rehearsal and that the concept of working memory provides a more accurate picture of research results on memory.

Now that we have studied memory's time frames and several models of memory that focus on these, let's examine the contents of long-term memory in more depth.

Long-Term Memory's Contents Just as different types of memory can be distinguished by how long they last, memory can be differentiated on the basis of its contents. For long-term memory, many contemporary psychologists accept the hierarchy of contents described in Figure 8.3. In this hierarchy, long-term memory is divided into the subtypes of declarative and procedural memory. Declarative memory is subdivided into episodic memory and semantic memory.

I come into the fields and spacious palaces of my memory, which house treasures of countless images of things of every manner.

St. Augustine
*Christian Church Father,
5th Century A.D.*

www.mcgrawhill.ca/college/santrock

FIGURE 8.3   Classification of Long-Term Memory's Contents

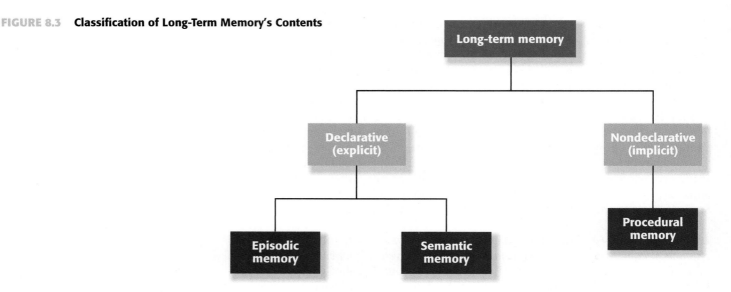

Declarative and Procedural Memory   **Declarative memory** *is the conscious recollection of information, such as specific facts or events that can be verbally communicated.* Declarative memory has been called "knowing that," and more recently has been labelled "explicit memory." Demonstrations of students' declarative memory could include recounting an event they have witnessed or describing a basic principle of math. However, students do not need to be talking to be using declarative memory. If students simply sit and reflect on an experience, their declarative memory is involved.

Procedural memory *is knowledge in the form of skills and cognitive operations. Procedural memory cannot be consciously recollected, at least not in the form of specific events or facts.* This makes procedural memory difficult, if not impossible, to communicate verbally. Procedural memory is sometimes called "knowing how," and recently it also has been described as "implicit memory" (Schacter, 2000). When students apply their abilities to perform a dance, ride a bicycle, or type on a computer keyboard, their procedural memory is at work. It also is at work when they speak grammatically correct sentences without having to think about how to do it.

Episodic and Semantic Memory   Cognitive psychologist Endel Tulving (1972, 2000) distinguishes between two subtypes of declarative memory: episodic and semantic. **Episodic memory** *is the retention of information about the where and when of life's happenings.* Students' memories of the first day of school, who they had lunch with, or the guest who came to talk with their class last week are all episodic.

Semantic memory *is a student's general knowledge about the world.* It includes:

• Knowledge of the sort learned in school (such as knowledge of geometry)
• Knowledge in different fields of expertise (such as knowledge of chess, for a skilled 15-year-old chess player)
• "Everyday" knowledge about meanings of words, famous people, important places, and common things (such as what being "street smart" means, or who Nelson Mandela or Celine Dion is)

Semantic memory is independent of the person's identity with the past. For example, students might access a fact—such as "Ottawa is the capital of Canada"—and not have the foggiest idea when and where they learned it.

Content Knowledge and How It Is Represented in Long-Term Memory   Does what students already know about a subject affect their ability to remember new information about that subject? How do students represent information in their memory?

Knowledge in different fields of experience, such as knowledge of chess, involves semantic memory.

Content Knowledge   Our ability to remember new information about a subject does depend considerably on what we already know about it (Keil, 1999). For example, a student's ability to recount what she saw when she was at the library is largely governed by what she already knows about libraries, such as where books on certain topics are located, how to check books out, and so on. If she knew little about libraries, the student would have a much harder time recounting what was there.

The contribution of content knowledge to memory is especially evident when we compare the memory of experts and novices in a particular knowledge domain. An expert is the opposite of a novice (someone who is just beginning to learn a content area). Experts demonstrate especially impressive memory in their areas of expertise. One reason why children remember less than adults is that they are far less expert in most areas.

In areas where children are experts, their memory is often extremely good. In fact, it often exceeds that of adults who are novices in that content area. This was documented in a study of 10-year-old chess experts (Chi, 1978). These children were excellent chess players, but not especially brilliant in other ways. Similar to most 10-year-olds, their memory spans for digits were shorter than an adult's. However, when they were presented chess boards, they remembered the configurations far better than did the adults who were novices at chess.

How do students acquire such a rich knowledge base? Their expertise is developed over a long period of time in which they show considerable motivation to learn more about a topic. Expert knowledge in areas like chess, music, tennis, and many other domains often requires considerable amounts of practice over many years (Frensch & Buchner, 1999; Schneider & Bjorklund, 1998).

Network Theories   **Network theories** *describe how information in memory is organized and connected.* They emphasize nodes in the memory network. The nodes stand for labels or concepts. Consider the concept "bird." One of the earliest network theories described memory representation as

Knowledge is power.

Francis Bacon
English Philosopher, 17th Century

Through the Eyes of Teachers

Focus on Teaching Learning Strategies

Students need to learn how to learn. Content changes rapidly. As teachers, we need to focus on teaching students effective learning strategies and skills. This is the most important information that we teach our students. I believe that course content is a vehicle for teaching learning skills, self-awareness, independent work habits, initiative, and organization.

David Tallach Miller
Secondary-School Science, Mathematics, and Computer Science Teacher,
Board Consultant, and Adult Educator
Ontario

hierarchically arranged with more concrete concepts ("canary," for example) nestled under more abstract concepts (like "bird"). However, it soon was realized that such hierarchical networks are too neat to accurately portray how memory representation really works. For example, students take longer to answer the question "Is an ostrich a bird?" than to answer the question "Is a canary a bird?" Thus, today memory researchers envision the memory network as more irregular and distorted. A *typical* bird, such as a canary, is closer to the node or centre of the category "bird" than is the atypical *ostrich*.

Experts in a particular area usually have far more elaborate networks of information about that area than novices do (see Figure 8.4). The information they represent in memory has more nodes, more interconnections, and better hierarchical organization. It's not that experts have a better memory than novices in general; their memory is superior in a particular domain.

Schema Theories   Long-term memory has been compared to a library of books. The idea is that our memory stores information, just as a library stores books. In this analogy, the way students retrieve information is said to be similar to the process they use to locate and check out a book. However, the process of retrieving information from long-term memory is not as precise as the library analogy suggests. When we search through our long-term memory storehouse, we don't always find the *exact* "book" we want, or we might find the "book" we want but discover that only "several pages" are intact—we have to *reconstruct* the rest.

Schema theories *state that when we reconstruct information, we fit it into information that already exists in our mind.* A **schema** *is information—concepts, knowledge, information about events—that already exists in a person's mind.* Schemas from prior experiences influence the way we encode, make inferences about, and retrieve information. Unlike network theories, which assume that retrieval involves specific facts, schema theory claims that long-term memory searches are not very exact. We often don't find precisely what we want, and we have to reconstruct the rest. Often when asked to retrieve information, we fill in the gaps between our fragmented memories with a variety of accuracies and inaccuracies.

We have schemas for all sorts of information. If you tell a story to your class and then ask the students to write down what the story was about, you likely will get many different versions. That is, your students won't remember every detail of the story you told and will reconstruct the story with their own particular stamp on it. Suppose you tell your class a story about a young family growing up during the pioneer era in Western

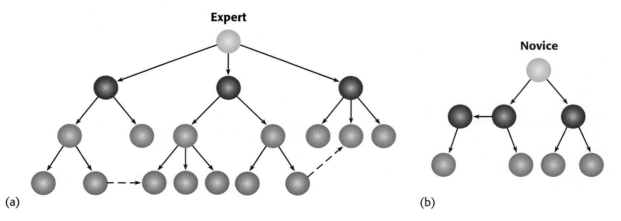

FIGURE 8.4   An Example of How Information Is Organized in the Mind of an Expert and a Novice
(a) An expert's knowledge is based on years of experience in which small bits of information have been linked with many other small pieces, which together are placed in a more general category. This category is in turn placed in an even more general category of knowledge. The dotted lines are used as pointers, associations between specific elements of knowledge that connect the lower branches and provide mental shortcuts in the expert's mind. *(b)* The novice's knowledge shows far fewer connections, shortcuts, and levels than an expert's knowledge.

Canada. One student might reconstruct the story by saying that there was a family of cowboys, another might describe two boys and two girls, and someone else might say that the family lived in Alberta. The reconstruction and distortion of memory is nowhere more apparent than in the memories given by people involved in a trial. In criminal court trials the variations in people's memories of what happened underscores how we reconstruct the past rather than take an exact photograph of it.

A **script** *is a schema for an event.* Scripts often have information about physical features, people, and typical occurrences. This kind of information is helpful when teachers and students need to figure out what is happening around them. In a script for an art activity, students likely will remember that you will instruct them on what to draw, that they are supposed to put on smocks over their clothes, that they must get the art paper and paints from the cupboard, that they are to clean the brushes when they are finished, and so on. For example, a student who comes in late to the art activity likely knows much of what to do because he has an art activity script.

Retrieval and Forgetting

After students have encoded information and then represented it in memory, they might be able to retrieve some of it but might also forget some of it.

Retrieval   When we retrieve something from our mental "data bank," we search our store of memory to find the relevant information. Just as with encoding, this search can be automatic or it can require effort. For example, if you ask your students what month it is, the answer might immediately spring to their lips. That is, the retrieval may be automatic. But if you ask your students to name the guest speaker who came to the class two months earlier, the retrieval process likely will require more effort.

An item's position on a list also affects how easy or difficult it will be to remember it. The **serial position effect** *is that recall is better for items at the beginning and end of a list than for items in the middle.* Suppose that, when you give a student directions about where to go to get tutoring help, you say: "Left on Queen, right on Central, left on Balboa, left on Elm, and right on King." The student likely will remember "Left on Queen" and "Right on King" better than "Left on Balboa." The **primacy effect** *is that items at the beginning of a list tend to be remembered.* The **recency effect** *is that items at the end of a list also tend to be remembered.* Figure 8.5 shows a typical serial position effect with a slightly stronger recency effect than primacy effect. The serial position effect applies not only to lists, but also to events. If you spread out a lesson on history over a week and then ask students about it the following Monday, they likely will have the best memory for what you told them on Friday of last week and the worst memory for what you told them on Wednesday of last week.

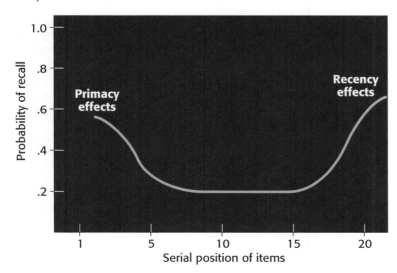

FIGURE 8.5   Serial Position Effect
When a person is asked to memorize a list of words, the words memorized last usually are recalled best, those at the beginning next best, and those in the middle least efficiently.

Teaching Strategies
For Helping Students Remember and Study Effectively

✓ Encourage students to activate their relevant prior knowledge when studying new concepts
  • have students reflect on personal experiences and background knowledge
  • have students paraphrase information and provide their own meanings
✓ Help students organize information when encoding
  • use advanced/graphic organizers
  • have students practise arranging and reworking information
✓ Provide students with memory mnemonics
  • *Method of loci*: Students develop images of to-be-remembered items (e.g., Greek gods and goddesses: Zeus, Neptune, Athena) and mentally store them in a familiar location (e.g., house). Students remember items by mentally walking through the familiar location and retrieving items (Zeus on the roof, Neptune in the bathtub, Athena in the library)
  • *Rhymes*: Examples of mnemonic rhymes include the spelling rule "*i* before *e* except after *c*"; the month rule "Thirty days hath September, April, June, and November"; the bolt-turning rule "Right is tight, left is loose"; and the alphabet song
  • *Acronyms*: Students create a word from the first letters of the to-be-remembered items; for example, the acronym HOMES for remembering the Great Lakes (Huron, Ontario, Michigan, Erie, and Superior)
  • *Keyword mnemonic*: Students form an interactive mental image that incorporates the meaning of the to-be-remembered word, and a familiar word or image that shares an acoustic element. For example, the word "carlin" (meaning "old woman"), which could be remembered by creating a mental image of a car being driven by an old woman (Sadoski & Paivio, 2001).
✓ Encourage students to extend and consolidate their learning
  • encourage and guide regular review
  • encourage students to ask themselves questions while reading/studying (e.g., Why is this important? How does this relate to what I already know?)
  • discourage cramming as a study method
✓ Help students learn how to take good notes
  • encourage students to use paraphrasing strategies
  • *Summarizing*: Have students listen for several minutes and then record the main idea. Repeat this process.
  • *Outlining*: Provide students with outlines and advance organizers that differentiate between main ideas and supporting ones or subtopics
  • *Concept maps*: Visually portray information in a "spider-like" or "bubble" fashion that represents hierarchical relations among concepts
✓ Encourage students to preview, question, reflect, and review when reading (PQ4R)
  • *Preview*: Encourage students to survey headings and illustrations to gain an overall sense of the organization of the material.
  • *Question*: Encourage students to ask themselves questions while reading
  • *Read*: Encourage students to be active readers, monitoring whether they understand information while reading versus being empty readers whose eyes just track words
  • *Reflect*: Encourage students to periodically stop reading and reflect on the material, thereby increasing its meaningfulness—encourage students to think out applications and interpretations of information and to connect it to information that they already know
  • *Recite*: Encourage students to self-test
  • *Review*: Encourage students to re-read and to re-study information that they don't remember or understand well

Another factor that affects retrieval is the nature of the cues people use to prompt their memory. Students can learn to create effective cues. For example, if a student has a "block" about remembering the name of the guest who came to class two months ago, she might go through the alphabet, generating names with each letter. If she manages to stumble across the right name, she likely will recognize it.

Another consideration in understanding retrieval is the **encoding specificity principle**: *that associations formed at the time of encoding or learning tend to be effective retrieval cues.* For example, imagine that a 13-year-old child has encoded this information about Mother Teresa: She was born in Albania, lived most of her life in India, became a Roman Catholic nun, was saddened by seeing people sick and dying in Calcutta's streets, and won a Nobel Prize for her humanitarian efforts to help the poor and suffering. Words such as *Nobel Prize*, *Calcutta*, and *humanitarian* then can be used as retrieval cues when the child tries to remember her name, what country she lived in, and her religion. The concept of encoding specificity is compatible with our earlier discussion of elaboration: the more elaboration children use in encoding information, the better their memory of the information will be. Encoding specificity and elaboration reveal how interdependent encoding and retrieval are.

Yet another aspect of retrieval is the nature of the retrieval task itself. **Recall** *is a memory task in which individuals must retrieve previously learned information, as students must do for fill-in-the-blank or essay questions.* **Recognition** *is a memory task in which individuals only have to identify ("recognize") learned information, as is often the case on multiple-choice tests.* Many students prefer multiple-choice items because they provide good retrieval cues, which fill-in-the-blank and essay items don't do.

Forgetting   One form of forgetting involves the cues we just discussed. **Cue-dependent forgetting** *is retrieval failure caused by a lack of effective retrieval cues* (Nairne, 2000). The notion of cue-dependent forgetting can explain why a student might fail to retrieve a needed fact for an exam even when he is sure he "knows" the information. For example, if you are studying for a test in this course and are asked a question about a distinction between recall and recognition in retrieval, you likely will remember the distinction better if you possess the cues "fill-in-the-blank" and "multiple-choice," respectively.

The principle of cue-dependent forgetting is consistent with **interference theory**, *which states that we forget not because we actually lose memories from storage, but rather because other information gets in the way of what we are trying to remember.* For a student who studies for a biology test, then studies for a history test, and then takes the biology test, the information about history will interfere with remembering the information about biology. Thus, interference theory implies that a good study strategy is to study last what you are going to be tested on next if you have multiple courses to study for. That is, the student taking the biology test would have benefited from studying history first and studying biology afterward. This strategy also fits with the recency effect we described earlier. Take a moment and think about how your knowledge of interference theory can help you when you review for students what you plan to test next.

Another source of forgetting is memory decay. According to **decay theory**, *new learning involves the creation of a neurochemical "memory trace," which will eventually disintegrate. Thus, decay theory suggests that the passage of time is responsible for forgetting.* Memories decay at different speeds. Some memories are vivid and last for long periods of time, especially when they have emotional ties. We can often remember these "flashbulb" memories with considerable accuracy and vivid imagery. For example, consider the night of your high school graduation, when you were first accepted into college or university, an early romantic experience, and where you were when you heard about Princess Diana's death. Chances are, you can retrieve this information even though the events happened a long time ago. To evaluate your own memory and study strategies, complete Self-Assessment 8.1.

At this point we have studied many ideas about cognitive information-processing approaches and memory. A review of these ideas is presented in Summary Table 8.1.

SUMMARY TABLE 8.1
The Cognitive Information–Processing Approach and Memory

What is the information-processing approach?	• This approach emphasizes that children manipulate information, monitor it, and strategize about it. Central to this approach are the processes of memory and thinking. • Elements of the model include thinking, change mechanisms (encoding, automaticity, strategy construction, generalization), and self-modification (metacognition).
What is memory?	• Memory is the retention of information over time and involves encoding, storage, and retrieval. • Attention, rehearsal, deep processing, elaboration, constructing images, and organization are processes involved in encoding. • Storage is the retention of information in the sensory, working (or short-term), and long-term memory • Retrieval is the process of reactivating and reconstructing data stored in the long-term memory. It is influenced by the serial position effect (memory is better for items at the beginning and end of lists than in the middle), how effective retrieval cues are, encoding specificity, and the memory task (such as recall versus recognition).
What is the Baddeley model of working memory?	• Baddeley's model describes working memory as a limited capacity system and a kind of mental "workbench." • Working memory consists of an "executive" and two subsystems (phonological loop and visual-spatial sketchpad). • Working memory interacts with long-term memory using information from long-term memory for its work and sending information to long-term memory for longer storage.
What is the Atkinson-Shiffrin stage model of memory?	• The Atkinson-Shiffrin model states that memory involves a sequence of three stages: sensory, short-term, and long-term memory.
What are the subtypes of memory?	• Memory can be differentiated on the basis of content and divided into declarative and procedural memory subtypes. • Procedural or implicit memory is the knowledge of skills and cognitive operations about how to do something. • Declarative or explicit memory is the conscious recollection of information. Declarative memory is further subdivided into episodic and semantic memory. Episodic memory is the retention of information about the where and when of life's happenings; semantic memory is general knowledge about the world.
How is information represented in long-term memory?	• There are two theories about how information is represented: network theories (focus on how information is organized and connected, with emphasis on nodes), and schema theories (students often reconstruct information and fit it into an existing schema).
What is forgetting?	• Forgetting may be due to cue-dependent forgetting (failure to use effective retrieval cues), interference theory (other information gets in the way of what we are trying to remember), and decay (losing information over time).

How Effective Are My Memory and Study Strategies?

For each item, respond 1 = Never, 2 = Sometimes, 3 = Moderate, 4 = Almost always, 5 = Always

	1	2	3	4	5
1. I study for understanding rather than memorize material in a rote fashion.					
2. I organize information hierarchically as part of my memory strategies.					
3. I use mnemonic strategies.					
4. I spread out my studying to consolidate my learning.					
5. I ask myself questions about what I have read or about class activities.					
6. I have a good note-taking system.					
7. I use the PQ4R method or a similar study method.					
TOTAL					

Scoring and Interpretation
31–35 = Your memory and study strategies are solid
26–30 = Your memory and study strategies are reasonably good
7–25 = Your memory and study strategies could be improved

THINKING

What does it mean to think? How can teachers help students to become better thinkers?

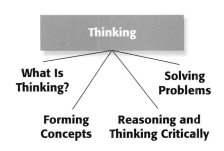

What Is Thinking?

Thinking *involves manipulating and transforming information in memory. This often is done to form concepts, reason, think critically, and solve problems.* Students can think about the concrete, such as a vacation at the beach or how to win at a video game, or if they are in high school they can think in more abstract ways, such as pondering the meaning of freedom or identity. They can think about the past (what happened to them last month) and the future (what their lives will be like in the year 2020). They can think about reality (such as how to do better on the next test) and fantasy (what it would be like to meet Wayne Gretzky or land a spacecraft on Mars).

The next sections explore forming concepts, reasoning, thinking critically, and solving problems.

Forming Concepts

Forming concepts is an important aspect of constructing information.

What Are Concepts? **Concepts** *are categories used to group objects, events, and characteristics on the basis of common properties.* Concepts are elements of cognition that help to simplify and summarize information (Medin, 2000). Imagine a world in which we had no concepts: we would see each object as unique and would not be able to make any generalizations. If we had no concepts, we would find the most trivial problems to be time-consuming and even impossible to solve. Consider the concept of a book. If a student were not aware that a book is sheets of paper of uniform sizes, all bound together along one edge, and full of printed words and pictures in some meaningful order, each time the student encountered a new book she would have to figure out what it was. In a way, then, concepts keep us from "reinventing the wheel" each time we come across a new piece of information.

I think, therefore I am.

Rene Descartes
*French Philosopher and Mathematician,
17th Century*

Concepts also aid the process of remembering, making it more efficient. When students group objects to form a concept, they can remember the concept, then retrieve the concept's characteristics. Thus, when you assign math homework, you probably won't have to go through the details of what math is or what homework is. Students will have embedded in their memory a number of associations with math and homework. In ways such as this, concepts not only help to jog memory, but they also make communication more efficient. If you say, "It's time for art," students know what this means because they have the relevant concepts. You don't have to go into a lengthy explanation of what art is. Thus, concepts help students to simplify and summarize information, as well as to improve the efficiency of their memory, communication, and time use.

Students form concepts through direct experiences with objects and events in their world. For example, in forming a concept of cartoons, children might initially experience TV cartoon shows, then read comic strips, and eventually look at some political caricatures. Students also form concepts through experience with symbols (things that stand for or represent something else). For example, words are symbols. So are math formulas, graphs, and pictures.

Some concepts are relatively simple, clear, and concrete, whereas others are more complex, fuzzy, and abstract (Barsalou, 2000). The former are easier to agree on. For example, most people can agree on the meaning of "baby." But we have a harder time agreeing on what is meant by "young" or "old." We agree on whether something is an apple more readily than on whether something is a fruit. Some concepts are especially complex, fuzzy, and abstract, like the concepts involved in theories of economic collapse or string theory in physics.

Exploring Concept Formation Further understanding of concept formation involves the features of concepts, definitions and examples of concepts, concept maps and hierarchical organization, hypothesis testing, and prototype matching.

Features An important aspect of concept formation is learning the key features, attributes, or characteristics of the concept. These are the defining elements of a concept, the dimensions that make it different from another concept. For example, in our earlier example of the concept of book, the key features include sheets of paper, being bound together along one edge, and being full of printed words and pictures in some meaningful order. Other characteristics such as size, colour, and length are not key features that define the concept of book. Consider also these critical features of the concept of dinosaur: extinct, gigantic, and reptile. Thus, in the case of the concept of dinosaur, the feature "size" is important.

Definitions and Examples of Concepts An important aspect of teaching concepts is to clearly define them and give carefully chosen examples of them. The *rule–example* strategy is an effective strategy for teaching that involves defining a concept and giving examples of it (Tennyson & Cocchiarella, 1986). This strategy consists of four steps:

1. *Define the concept.* As part of defining it, link it to a superordinate concept and identify its key features or characteristics. A superordinate concept is a larger class into which it fits. Thus, in specifying the key features of the concept of dinosaur, you might want to mention the larger class into which it fits: reptiles.
2. *Clarify terms in the definition.* Make sure that the key features or characteristics are well understood. Thus, in describing the key features of the concept of dinosaur, it is important for students to know what a reptile is: a cold-blooded, usually egg-laying vertebrate with an external covering of scales or horny plates that breathes by means of lungs.
3. *Give examples to illustrate the key features or characteristics.* With regard to dinosaurs, one might give examples and descriptions of different types of dinosaurs, such as triceratops, brontosaur, and stegosaur. The concept can be further clarified by giving examples of other reptiles that are not dinosaurs, such as snakes, lizards, crocodiles,

To call forth a concept a word is needed; to portray a phenomenon, a concept is needed. All three mirror one and the same reality.

Antoine Laurent Lavoisier
French Scientist and Father of Modern Chemistry, 18th Century

and turtles. Indeed, giving non-examples of a concept as well as examples is often a good strategy for teaching concept formation. More examples are required when you teach complex concepts and when you work with less sophisticated learners (Moore, 1998).

4. *Provide additional examples. Ask students to categorize these, explain their categorization, or have them generate their own examples of the concept.* Other dinosaur types might be given, such as pterodactyl, ornitholestes, and dimetrodon, or students could be asked to generate these examples. They also might be asked to think up other non-examples of dinosaurs, such as dogs, cats, and whales.

Concept Maps A **concept map** *is a visual representation of a concept's connections and hierarchical organization.* Getting students to create a map of a concept's features or characteristics can help them to learn the concept. The concept map also might embed the concept in a superordinate category and include examples and non-examples of the concept. The visual aspects of the concept map relate to our earlier discussion of the use of imagery in memory. You might create a concept map with the assistance of students, or let them try to develop it individually or in small groups. Figure 8.6 shows an example of a concept map (or what we sometimes call "cognitive maps") for the concept of dinosaur.

Hypothesis Testing **Hypotheses** *are specific assumptions and predictions that can be tested to determine their accuracy.* Students benefit from the practice of developing hypotheses about what a concept is and is not (Ross, 2000). One way this is done is to come up with a rule about why some objects fall within a concept and others do not. Here is an example of how you can give your students practice in developing such hypotheses: Present your students with the picture of geometric forms shown in Figure 8.7. Then silently select the concept of one of those geometric forms (such as "circle" or "green circle")

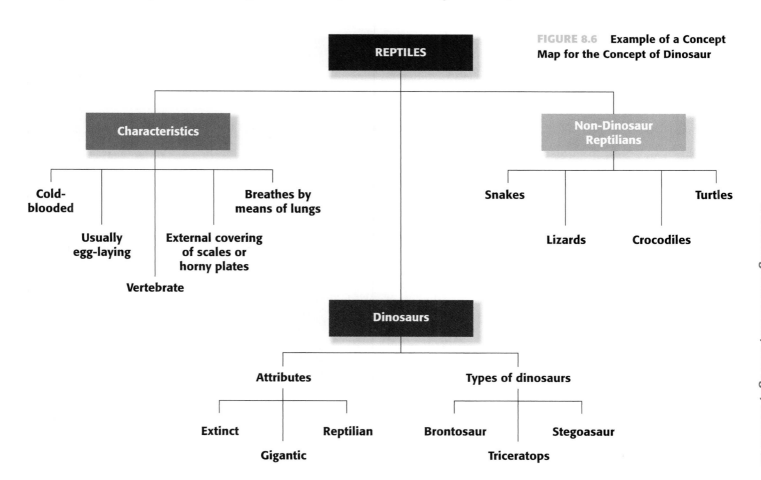

FIGURE 8.6 **Example of a Concept Map for the Concept of Dinosaur**

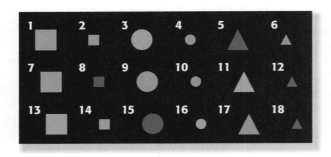

FIGURE 8.7 **Getting Students to Generate Hypotheses About a Concept**

You can use arrangements like the one shown here to help students generate hypotheses about what concept you have in mind. This encourages students to develop the most efficient strategies for understanding what a concept is. For example, you might select the concept "squares and green triangles" or "green triangles and blue squares" and ask students to figure out what concept you're thinking of. You also can let students take turns selecting the concept.

and ask your students to develop hypotheses about what concept you have selected. They zero in on your concept by asking you questions related to the geometric forms and eliminating non-examples. You might also let the students take turns "being the teacher"—they select a concept and answer questions from the other students as they generate hypotheses about what the concept is. Work with your students on developing the most efficient strategies for identifying the correct concept.

Prototype Matching In **prototype matching**, *individuals decide whether an item is a member of a category by comparing it with the most typical item(s) of the category* (Rosch, 1973). The more similar the item is to the prototype, the more likely it is that the individual will say the item belongs to the category; the less similar, the more likely the person will judge that it doesn't belong in the category. For example, a student's concept of a football player might include being big and muscular like an offensive lineman. But some football players, such as many field goal kickers, are not so big and muscular. An offensive lineman is a more prototypical example of a football player than a field goal kicker. When students consider whether someone belongs in the category "football player," they are more likely to think of someone who looks like an offensive lineman than to think of someone who looks like a field goal kicker. That is, members of a category can vary greatly and still have qualities that make them a member of that category.

Teaching Strategies
For Helping Students Form Concepts

✓ Use the rule–example strategy
  • define the concept
  • clarify the terms in the definition
  • give illustrative examples
  • provide additional practice categorizing examples.
✓ Help students learn what a concept IS NOT
  • list the characteristics of the concept
  • list examples of things that are not the concept
✓ Make concepts clear and complete
  • present a new concept through an illustration and then ask students for more examples
  • relate new concepts to existing concepts
  • ask students for prototypical and non-prototypical examples of a concept
✓ Encourage students to create concept maps
  • have students visually map out the hierarchical organization of concepts
  • have students arrange concepts from the general to the specific
✓ Ask students to generate hypotheses about a concept
  • encourage students to think of and develop hypothesis-solving strategies
  • check for students' understanding of a concept and its application to other contexts
  • have students read further about the concept and consider how the concept can be applied in different contexts

Reasoning and Thinking Critically

Let's explore some different types of reasoning, beginning with the distinction between inductive and deductive reasoning.

Inductive Versus Deductive Reasoning **Inductive reasoning** *involves reasoning from the specific to the general.* That is, it consists of drawing conclusions about all members of a category based on observing only some members. When a student in a literature class reads only a few of Stephen Leacock's humorous essays and is asked to draw conclusions from them about the general nature of Leacock's humour, inductive reasoning is being tapped. When a student is asked whether a concept learned in math class applies to other domains, such as business or science, inductive reasoning also is being called for.

Deductive reasoning *is reasoning from the general to the specific. It consists of working with general statements and deriving a specific conclusion* (Johnson-Laird, 2000). Many puzzles and riddles call on students to engage in deductive reasoning. In some educational domains, such as math and science, students typically learn about a general rule and then are asked to decide whether the rule applies or does not apply to various specific situations. This also involves deductive reasoning.

Reasoning About Analogies An **analogy** *is a type of formal reasoning that involves four parts, with the relation between the last two parts being the same as the relation between the first two.* Educators can use analogies to stimulate critical and creative thinking. Analogies can be used to teach connections and reinforce relationships. In math, a lesson may begin with this analogy: subtraction : addition :: _____ : multiplication. (The answer is "division.")

Critical Thinking Currently, there is considerable interest in critical thinking among psychologists and educators, although it is not an entirely new idea (Gardner, 1999; Runco, 1999; Moldoveanu & Langer, 1999; Sternberg, 2000). The famous educator John Dewey (1933) proposed a similar idea when he talked about the importance of getting students to think reflectively. The well-known psychologist Max Wertheimer (1945) talked about the importance of thinking productively rather than just guessing at a correct answer. **Critical thinking** *involves thinking reflectively and productively, and evaluating the evidence.* Here are some ways teachers can consciously build critical thinking into their lesson plans:

- Ask not only what happened but also "how" and "why."
- Examine supposed "facts" to determine whether there is evidence to support them.
- Argue in a reasoned way rather than through emotions.
- Recognize that there is sometimes more than one good answer or explanation.
- Compare various answers to a question and judge which is really the best answer.
- Evaluate and possibly question what other people say rather than immediately accepting it as the truth.
- Ask questions and speculate beyond what we already know to create new ideas and new information.

Jacqueline and Martin Brooks (1993) lament that few schools really teach students to think critically. In their view, schools spend too much time on getting students to give a single correct answer in an imitative way rather than encouraging students to expand their thinking by coming up with new ideas and rethinking earlier conclusions. They believe that too often teachers ask students to recite, define, describe, state, and list rather than to analyze, infer, connect, synthesize, criticize, create, evaluate, think, and rethink.

Brooks and Brooks point out that many successful students complete their assignments, do well on tests, and get good grades, yet don't ever learn to think critically and deeply. They believe our schools turn out students who think too superficially, staying on the surface of problems rather than stretching their minds and becoming deeply engaged in meaningful thinking.

What are some good strategies for nurturing children's critical thinking?

www.mcgrawhill.ca/college/santrock

Daniel Perkins and Sarah Tishman (1997) work with teachers to incorporate critical thinking into classrooms. The following are some of the critical thinking skills they encourage teachers to help their students develop:

- *Open-mindedness.* Get your students to avoid narrow thinking and to explore options. For example, when teaching Canadian literature, teachers might ask students to generate multiple critiques of W.O. Mitchell's *Who Has Seen the Wind?*
- *Intellectual curiosity.* Encourage your students to wonder, probe, question, and inquire. Getting students to recognize problems and inconsistencies also is an aspect of intellectual curiosity. In history class, this might mean looking beyond culturally biased views of history by reading accounts by First Nations authors.
- *Planning and strategy.* Work with your students to help them develop plans, set goals, find direction, and seek outcomes. In physical education, this might involve determining the best strategy to win a basketball or baseball game.
- *Intellectual carefulness.* Encourage your students to check for inaccuracies and errors, to be precise, and to be organized. For example, when students write a paper, they learn to structure the content and check the facts that they include.

Solving Problems

Let's examine what problem solving means and some steps involved in problem solving.

Exploring Problem Solving **Problem solving** *involves finding an appropriate way to attain a goal.* Consider these tasks that require students to engage in problem solving: creating a project for a science fair, writing a paper for an English class, getting a community to be more environmentally responsible, or giving a talk on the factors that cause people to be prejudiced.

Efforts have been made to specify the steps that individuals go through in effectively solving problems (Bransford & Stein, 1993). Following are four such steps.

1. *Find and Frame Problems* Before a problem can be solved, it has to be recognized. In the past, most problem-solving exercises given to students involved well-defined problems with well-defined solutions and operations for attaining the solutions. Schools need to place more emphasis on encouraging students to identify problems instead of just trying to solve well-defined textbook problems. Many real-life problems are ill-defined: They are vague and don't have clear ways of being solved.

Consider the student faced with creating a science fair project. The student has identified a general problem but needs to zero in on a specific area for the project, such as biology, physics, computer science, psychology, and so on. Exploring such alternatives and then making a decision on which problem area to pursue is an important aspect of problem solving. Then the student must narrow the problem even more. If the student decides to do a project on psychology, she will need to specify the area, such as perception, memory, thinking, or personality. Then the student will have to find a problem within that domain. For example, the student might choose the area of memory and focus on this problem: How reliable are people's memories of traumatic events they have experienced? After considerable exploring and refining, the student has narrowed the topic to a point at which strategies for solving it can be generated.

In sum, an important educational agenda is to give students opportunities to find problems and generate the problems they think need to be solved. Serve as a guide and consultant in helping them frame a meaningful problem and define it clearly.

2. *Develop Good Problem-Solving Strategies* Once students find a problem and clearly define it, they need to develop strategies for solving it. Among the effective strategies are setting subgoals, using algorithms, and calling on heuristics.

Subgoalling *involves setting intermediate goals that put students in a better position to reach the final goal or solution.* Students might do poorly in solving problems because they don't generate subproblems or subgoals. Let's return to the science fair project on the reliability of people's memory for traumatic events they have experienced. What might be some subgoalling strategies? One might be locating the right books and research journals on thinking; another might be interviewing teachers about the strategies they use to encourage deep thinking. At the same time as the student is working on this subgoalling strategy, the student likely will benefit from establishing further subgoals in terms of what she needs to accomplish along the way to her final goal of a finished science project. If the science project is due in three months, she might set the following subgoals: finishing the first draft of the project two weeks before the project is due; having the research completed a month before the project is due; being halfway through the research two months before the project is due; having three teacher interviews done two weeks from today; and starting library research tomorrow.

Notice that in establishing the subgoals, we worked backward in time. This is often a good strategy (Reed, 2000). Students first create a subgoal that is closest to the final goal and then work backward to the subgoal that is closest to the beginning of the problem-solving effort.

Algorithms *are strategies that guarantee a solution to a problem.* When students solve a multiplication problem by a set procedure, they are using an algorithm. When they follow the directions for diagramming a sentence, they are using an algorithm. Life would be easy if all its problems could be solved by algorithms. But many real-world problems are not so straightforward. They require the use of heuristics.

Heuristics *are strategies or guidelines that can suggest a solution to a problem but don't guarantee a solution.* Consider a student who has just gotten his driver's licence. He is going to drive over to a friend's house he has never been to before. He drives through an unfamiliar part of town and soon realizes that he is lost. If he knows that the correct direction to turn is north, he might use the heuristic of turning onto the next road that goes in that direction. This strategy might work, but it also might fail. The road might end or it might veer east.

A **means–end analysis** *is a heuristic in which one identifies the goal (end) of a problem, assesses the current situation, and evaluates what needs to be done (means) to decrease the difference between the two conditions.* Another name for means–end analysis is *difference reduction.* Means–end analysis also can involve the use of subgoalling, which we described earlier (Anderson, 1993). Means–end analysis is commonly used in solving problems. Consider a 14-year-old girl who has to write her first essay in high school. She assesses her current situation, in which she is just starting to think about the essay. Then she maps out a plan to organize her writing with the goal of answering the essay question. Her "means" include reading the suggested materials, going to the library to research the topic, and exploring the Internet for additional information.

3. Evaluate Solutions   Once we think we have solved a problem, we might not know whether our solution is effective unless we evaluate it. It helps to have in mind a clear criterion for the effectiveness of the solution. For example, what will be the student's criterion for effectively solving the problem of doing a science fair project? Will it be simply getting it completed? receiving positive feedback about the project? winning an award? winning first place? the self-satisfaction of having set a goal, planned for it, and reached it?

4. Rethink and Redefine Problems and Solutions over Time   An important final step in problem solving is to continually rethink and redefine problems and solutions over time (Bereiter & Scardamalia, 1993). People who are good at problem solving are motivated to improve on their past performances and to make original contributions. Thus, the student who completed the science fair project can look back at the project and think about ways the project can be improved. The student might use feedback from judges or information from others who talked with the student about the project to tinker with and fine-tune it.

Obstacles to Solving Problems   Some common obstacles to solving problems are these: fixation, confirmation bias, lack of motivation, and lack of persistence.

Fixation   It is easy to fall into the trap of becoming fixated on a particular strategy for solving a problem. **Fixation** *involves using a prior strategy and failing to look at a problem from a fresh, new perspective.* **Functional fixedness** *is a type of fixation in which an individual fails to solve a problem because she or he views the elements involved solely in terms of their usual functions.* A student who uses a shoe to hammer a nail has overcome functional fixedness to solve a problem.

A **mental set** *is a type of fixation in which an individual tries to solve a problem in a particular way that has worked in the past.* For example, some individuals have a mental set about using a pen and paper rather than a computer to write. They feel comfortable with a pen and paper because they can see the entire document. It takes time to break out of this mental set. Once this is accomplished, the goal of writing the document will become much easier. You might have a similar mental set against using the new computer and video technology available for classroom use. A good strategy is keep an open mind about such changes and monitor whether your mental set is keeping you from trying out new technologies that can make the classroom a more exciting learning atmosphere for students.

Confirmation Bias   **Confirmation bias** *is the tendency to search for and use information that supports our ideas rather than refutes them.* Thus, in solving a problem, a student might have an initial hypothesis that a certain approach is going to work. He tests out the hypothesis and finds out that it is right some of the time. He concludes that his hypothesis was right rather than further exploring the fact that it didn't work some of the time.

We tend to seek out and listen to people whose views confirm our own rather than listen to dissenting views. Thus, you might have a particular teaching style, such as lecturing, that you like to use. If so, you probably will have a tendency to listen more to other teachers who use that style than to teachers who prefer other styles, such as collaborative problem solving by students. Be aware of how easy it is for you and your students to fall into the trap of using confirmation bias to support your ideas and problem-solving efforts.

Lack of Motivation and Persistence   Even if your students already have great problem-solving abilities, that hardly matters if they are not motivated to use them (Pintrich, 2000; Sternberg & Spear-Swerling, 1996). It is especially important for students to be internally motivated to tackle a problem and persist at finding a solution to it. Some students avoid problems or give up too easily.

An important task for teachers is to devise or steer students toward problems that are meaningful to them and to encourage and support them in finding solutions. Students are far more motivated to solve problems that they can relate to their personal lives than textbook problems that have no personal meaning for them. Problem-based learning takes this real-world personal focus. For an in-depth look at how to motivate students to learn, refer to Chapter 11.

Problem-based Learning   **Problem-based learning** *emphasizes solving authentic problems like those that occur in daily life* (Jones, Rasmussen, & Moffit, 1997; Feuerstein, Jackson, & Lewis, 1998). One example of problem-based learning is the Canadian National Marsville Program. Based out of the Challenger Learning Centre at the Ontario Science Centre, the program strives to enhance the scientific and technical problem-solving skills of students in Grades 5 through 12 (**http://mars2001.enoreo.on.ca**).

Marsville is a fictional cosmic village and is the final destination of the first human mission to Mars. Prior to the mission, students must prepare for challenges associated with daily life in a futuristic space society and strive to cooperatively solve these problems.

To facilitate their students' learning experience, teachers attend a full-day workshop and they are provided with the necessary curriculum, activities, and resources. There is a focus on Canada's role in the development of space and communication technologies.

Teaching Strategies
To Help Students Become Better Thinkers

✓ Assist students to identify real-world problems
  - use authentic, real-world problems in contrast to textbook problems, which too often do not have much meaning for students
  - develop problems that are relevant to students' lives
  - ask questions that stimulate thinking and develop a deeper understanding of a topic (e.g., "Compare the French Revolution and the War of 1812. How were they similar? How were they different?")
✓ Monitor students' effective and ineffective thinking through the four problem-solving steps
  - find and frame problems
  - develop good problem-solving strategies
  - evaluate solutions
  - rethink and redefine problems and solutions over time
✓ Assist students to construct their own thinking
  - value students' questions
  - view students as thinkers with emerging theories about the world
  - seek students' points of view
  - seek elaboration of students' initial responses
  - nurture students' intellectual curiosity
  - engage students in the construction of their own knowledge structures
  - promote knowledge acquisition from multiple sources other than just textbooks
✓ Use technology effectively
  - incorporate into your classroom programs that use technology in creative and meaningful ways (e.g., the Canadian National Marsville Program)
  - use relevant television presentations to foster students' problem-solving and thinking skills (e.g., *Sesame Park*)
✓ Provide role models for thinking
  - invite community members and business professionals into your class or plan a field trip to their job site
  - model good thinking practices
✓ Involve and support parents
  - offer parents relevant references and Websites (e.g., Word Problems for Kids)
✓ Keep up to date on the latest developments in thinking and problem solving

Throughout the program, expert mentors from universities and the private sector volunteer their time and offer suggestions for the development of the Mars colonies.

Teachers begin by dividing their classes into small groups or mission teams. Mission teams are partnered with other teams from nearby schools to cooperatively design systems that will support them on the Martian settlement. The mission teams propose technological solutions for support systems including air, energy, communication, health and recreation, waste management, temperature control, transportation, and food/water supplies. The mission teams communicate through writing or e-mail. A Web-based conferencing system is set up and the mission teams create Web pages to display their work. These activities continue for several weeks.

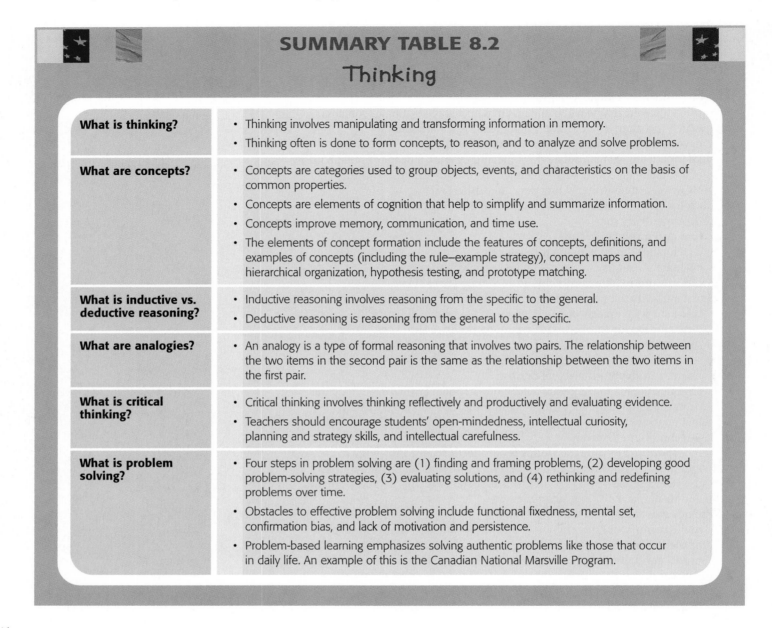

SUMMARY TABLE 8.2
Thinking

What is thinking?	• Thinking involves manipulating and transforming information in memory. • Thinking often is done to form concepts, to reason, and to analyze and solve problems.
What are concepts?	• Concepts are categories used to group objects, events, and characteristics on the basis of common properties. • Concepts are elements of cognition that help to simplify and summarize information. • Concepts improve memory, communication, and time use. • The elements of concept formation include the features of concepts, definitions, and examples of concepts (including the rule–example strategy), concept maps and hierarchical organization, hypothesis testing, and prototype matching.
What is inductive vs. deductive reasoning?	• Inductive reasoning involves reasoning from the specific to the general. • Deductive reasoning is reasoning from the general to the specific.
What are analogies?	• An analogy is a type of formal reasoning that involves two pairs. The relationship between the two items in the second pair is the same as the relationship between the two items in the first pair.
What is critical thinking?	• Critical thinking involves thinking reflectively and productively and evaluating evidence. • Teachers should encourage students' open-mindedness, intellectual curiosity, planning and strategy skills, and intellectual carefulness.
What is problem solving?	• Four steps in problem solving are (1) finding and framing problems, (2) developing good problem-solving strategies, (3) evaluating solutions, and (4) rethinking and redefining problems over time. • Obstacles to effective problem solving include functional fixedness, mental set, confirmation bias, and lack of motivation and persistence. • Problem-based learning emphasizes solving authentic problems like those that occur in daily life. An example of this is the Canadian National Marsville Program.

Michael Carter, a satellite systems engineer from Ottawa and mentor for the program, states that intermediate-level students need to more greatly appreciate the role of science in today's society. Carter provides problem-solving opportunities by highlighting basic physical properties and then challenging students to test their assumptions. "If they can dream it," according to Carter, "then they can find a way to build it."

Every year in the spring, the mission teams meet at several different sites across Canada to construct the Marsville Cosmic Village. Each of the mission teams brings forward its technological solutions. The mission teams share their problem-solving strategies with other participants across the country and then debrief about their experiences.

Scientific Problem-Solving on the Web and Television

Sci Squad, a television series aired on the Discovery Channel, is featured on the Website **http://kids.discovery.com**. Sci Squad was created by Pierre Valette and Bill Jersey and is a joint production of Discovery Kids, KCTS/Seattle Public Television, Quest Productions, and Cinar.

Sci Squad is a virtual scientific problem-solving agency that is able to handle any sort of science emergency, query, or challenge. Television episodes focus on helping students self-discover the answers to several authentic science-based problems. For example, students can demonstrate that a rollercoaster is aerodynamically safe in "Loop-De-Loop"; in "Look Up Noses," they can learn about the human sense of smell.

Online, students become "agents" by completing the Sci Squad missions. They are encouraged to test out theories and they receive feedback and encouragement for their solution attempts. As missions are successfully completed, the agents receive credits or points that are accumulated to comprise their Sci Squad ranking. In this way, agents move through the ranks and tackle assignments that are increasingly more complex and challenging.

Here is an example of one of the first missions.

Hi Sci Squad,

My older brother is totally into skydiving, and it completely amazes me how he manages to land in the right place each time. He jumps out of the plane way before the plane is directly over the target!

Now my Mom is trying to get him to stop because she says it's just luck. Can you please help me figure out what's going on? Someday I want to be able to try it!

Grounded,
Carmen Chapman
Chilliwack, British Columbia

What follows are a series of interactive examples that explore the movement of a launched ball. The agent is directed to pay attention to how the speed of the falling ball correlates with where the ball lands. Agents are then provided opportunities to test their hypothesis with a simulated model of a skydiver and a target. Finally, a complete explanation with proof is offered for the solution.

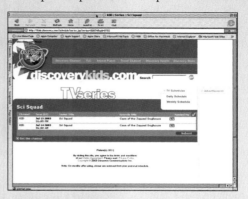

Diversity and Education
HISTOR!CA

HISTOR!CA is a non-partisan registered charity committed to providing the best possible Canadian history education to all students. The organization sponsors programs and resources that encourage Canadian youth to explore their history at the community as well as the national level (**www.histori.ca**). To this end, HISTOR!CA supports several educational initiatives such as history-teacher training workshops, the *Canadian Encyclopedia* (a reference source), heritage fairs, the *Heritage Minutes* (Canadian history mini-movies), and YouthLinks.

YouthLinks is supported by both private- and public-sector funding and has partnered with such institutions as Université de Sherbrooke, Université de Moncton, Simon Fraser University, Queen's University (Kingston, Ontario), and York University (Toronto, Ontario). The goal of the YouthLinks program is to help develop students' critical thinking and research skills and to provide educators with relevant resources and teaching strategies. YouthLinks connects secondary-school students with their peers worldwide to work collaboratively on Canadian history projects. This Web-based venue allows students to post their ideas and resources. Project themes are of global importance and include topics such as immigration or human security. Youth participate in online discussions and then collaboratively write and edit their projects. Their work can ultimately be published in the *YouthLinks* magazine.

www.mcgrawhill.ca/college/santrock

How Effective Are My Thinking Strategies?

For each item, respond 1 =Very much unlike me, 2 = Somewhat unlike me,
3 = Somewhat like me, 4 = Very much like me

	1	2	3	4
1. I am aware of effective and ineffective thinking strategies.				
2. I periodically monitor the thinking strategies I use.				
3. I am good at reasoning.				
4. I use good strategies for forming concepts.				
5. I am good at thinking critically and deeply about problems and issues.				
6. I construct my own thinking rather than just passively accept what others think.				
7. I like to use technology as part of my effort to think effectively.				
8. I have good role models for thinking.				
9. I keep up-to-date on the latest educational developments in thinking.				
10. I use a system for solving problems like the four-step system described in the text.				
11. I'm good at finding and framing problems.				
12. When solving problems, I use strategies like subgoalling and working backward.				
13. I don't fall into problem-solving traps like fixating, having a confirmation bias, not being motivated, and lacking persistence.				
14. When solving problems, I set criteria for my success and evaluate how well I have met my problem-solving goals.				
15. I make a practice of rethinking and redefining problems over an extended period of time.				
16. I love to work on problem-solving projects.				
TOTAL				

Scoring and Interpretation

60–68 points = Your thinking strategies are very good
50–59 points = Your thinking strategies are moderately good
Below 50 points = Your thinking strategies can be improved

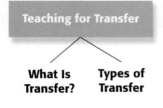

Teaching for Transfer

What Is Transfer?   **Types of Transfer**

TEACHING FOR TRANSFER

An important educational goal is for students to be able to take what they learn in one situation and apply it to new situations. An important goal of schooling is that students will learn something in school and be able to apply it outside of the classroom. Schools are not functioning effectively if students do well on tests in language arts but can't write a competent letter as part of a job application. Schools also are not effectively educating students if the students do well on math tests in the classroom but can't solve math problems on a job, such as effectively performing accounting procedures. Teaching for transfer helps students make the connection between what they learned in school and applying it outside of the classroom in new contexts.

What Is Transfer?

As you learned at the beginning of this chapter, *transfer* occurs when a person applies previous experiences and knowledge to learning or problem solving in a new situation (Gentile, 2000; Mayer & Wittrock, 1996). Thus, if a student learns a concept in math and then uses this concept to solve a problem in science, transfer has occurred. It also has occurred if a student reads and studies about the concept of fairness in school and subsequently treats others more fairly outside the classroom.

Types of Transfer

Transfer can be characterized as either near or far and also as either low-road or high-road (Schunk, 2000).

Near or Far Transfer   **Near transfer** *occurs when situations are very similar. If the classroom learning situation is similar to the transfer situation, near transfer is at work.* For example, if a geometry teacher instructs students in how to logically prove a concept, and then tests the students on this logic in the same room in which they learned the concept, near transfer is involved.

Far transfer *means the transfer of learning to a situation that is very different from the one in which the initial learning took place.* For instance, if a student gets a part-time job in an architect's office and applies what was learned in geometry class to helping the architect analyze a spatial problem that is quite different than any problem the student encountered in geometry class, far transfer has occurred.

Low-Road or High-Road Transfer   Gavriel Salomon and David Perkins (1989) distinguished between low-road and high-road transfer. **Low-road transfer** *occurs when previous learning automatically, often unconsciously, transfers to another situation.* This occurs most often with highly practised skills in which there is little need for reflective thinking. For example, when competent readers encounter new sentences in their native language, they read them automatically.

By contrast, **high-road transfer** *is conscious and effortful.* Students consciously establish connections between what they learned in a previous situation and the new situation they now face. High-road transfer is *mindful*—that is, students have to be aware of what they are doing and think about the connection between contexts. High-road transfer implies abstracting a general rule or principle from previous experience and then applying it to the new problem in the new context. For example, students might learn about the concept of subgoalling (setting intermediate goals) in math class. Several months later, one of the students thinks about how subgoalling might benefit him in completing a lengthy homework assignment in history. This is high-road transfer.

An example of transfer training is the PASS Reading Enhancement Program (PREP), which was developed by Das (2001) at the University of Alberta. This reading program is founded on the premise that transfer of principles can be facilitated through inductive inference (Carlson & Das, 1996; as cited in Das, 2001). Students develop their ability to use reading strategies such as rehearsal, categorization, monitoring, prediction, and sounding through experience with graduated tasks. Low-road transfer is encouraged by providing tasks that require the application of successive strategies; this practice fosters automaticity. High-road transfer is facilitated through training in controlled processing strategies that are linked to reading authentic materials. Das (2001) refers to this transfer as the bridging component in which the students manage abstract thinking processes.

METACOGNITION

We just discussed the importance of teaching in ways that help students transfer knowledge and strategies to new situations. Some cognitive psychologists believe that what is called a metacognitive strategy improves transfer.

What Is Metacognition?

As you read at the beginning of this chapter, metacognition is cognition about cognition, or "knowing about knowing" (Ferrari & Sternberg, 1998; Flavell, 1999; Flavell & Miller,

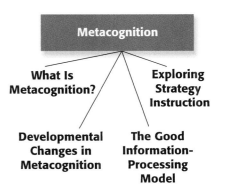

Teaching Strategies
For Helping Students Transfer Information

✓ Provide students with many opportunities for real-world learning
  - provide students with real-world problem-solving and thinking challenges
  - consider what your students need to know for success in life
    (e.g., communication skills, interpersonal skills, and teamwork skills)
✓ Root concepts in applications
  - present a concept, define it (or get students to help you define it),
    and then ask students to generate examples and non-examples
  - challenge students to apply the concept to their personal lives or to
    other contexts
✓ Teach for depth of understanding and meaning
  - encourage students to actively construct meaning and make meaning
    out of material
  - avoid teaching for the retention of facts
✓ Teach strategies that will promote generalization
  - provide students with information about the importance of the strategy
    and how to use the strategy
  - provide students with opportunities to rehearse and practise
    using the strategy
  - assess students' abilities to recall how to use the strategy
  - provide students with new problems that require them
    to use familiar strategies, but that appear to be different

1998). A distinction can be made between metacognitive knowledge and metacognitive activity (Ferrari & Sternberg, 1998). **Metacognitive knowledge** *involves monitoring and reflecting on one's current or recent thoughts* (Flavell, Miller, & Miller, 1993). This includes both *factual knowledge*, such as knowledge about the task, one's goals, or one's self, and *strategic knowledge*, such as how and when to use specific procedures to solve problems. **Metacognitive activity** *occurs when students consciously adapt and manage their thinking strategies during problem solving and purposeful thinking* (Ferrari & Sternberg, 1998; Kuhn et al., 1995). Thus, students' awareness and use of the self-regulatory learning strategies involves metacognition.

Metacognitive skills have been taught to students of all ages and abilities in order to promote learning across the content areas (e.g., language arts: Glaubman, Glaubman, & Ofir, 1997; Lambert, 2000; math: Kramarski, Mevarech, & Lieberman, 2001; and science: Georghiades, 2000), to enhance critical thinking and problem solving skills (e.g., Halpern, 1998, Mevarech, 1999), and even to increase positive social interactions (e.g., Rosenthal, 1997). Metacognitive training is especially effective when it is accompanied by strategy instruction. Mevarech (1999) observed that Grade 7 students who were provided with metacognitive training as part of strategic instruction in mathematical problem solving outperformed their peers who were provided with strategy instruction; these students in turn outperformed their peers who received neither kind of training.

Many experts on children's thinking (Ciardiello, 1998; Kuhn, 1999a, 1999b; Schneider & Bjorkland, 1998; Schneider & Pressley, 1999) believe that metacognition should be a stronger focus of efforts to help children become better critical thinkers, especially in the intermediate grades and high-school levels. They distinguish between first-order cognitive skills, which enable children to know about the world (and have been the main focus of critical thinking programs), and second-order cognitive skills—*meta-knowing skills*—which involve knowing about one's own (and others') knowing.

Developmental Changes in Metacognition

The majority of developmental studies classified as "metacognitive" have focused on metamemory, or knowledge about memory. This includes general knowledge about memory, such as knowing that recognition tests are easier than recall tests. It also encompasses knowledge about one's own memory, such as a student's ability to monitor whether she has studied enough for a test that is coming up next week.

By five or six years of age, children usually know that familiar items are easier to learn than unfamiliar ones, that short lists are easier than long ones, that recognition is easier than recall, and that forgetting is more likely to occur over time (Lyon & Flavell, 1993). However, in other ways young children's metamemory is limited. They don't understand that related items are easier to remember than unrelated ones and that remembering the gist of a story is easier than remembering information verbatim (Kreutzer, Leonard, & Flavell, 1975; O'Sullivan, 1996). By Grade 5, students understand that gist recall is easier than verbatim recall. Young children also have an inflated opinion of their memory abilities. For example, in one study a majority of young children predicted that they would be able to recall all ten items on a list of ten items. When tested, none of the young children managed this feat (Flavell, Friedrichs, & Hoyt, 1970). As they move through the elementary-school years, children give more realistic evaluations of their memory skills (Joyner & Kurtz-Costes, 1997; Schneider & Pressley, 1997).

Young children also have little appreciation for the importance of "cognitive cueing" for memory. Cognitive cueing involves being reminded of something by an external cue or phrase, such as "Don't you remember, it helps you to learn a concept when you can think of an example of it." By seven or eight years of age, children better appreciate the importance of such cognitive cueing for memory.

The Good Information-Processing Model

Pressley and his colleagues (Pressley, Borkowski, & Schneider, 1989; Schneider & Pressley, 1997) have developed a metacognitive model called the *good information-processing model*. It emphasizes that competent cognition results from a number of interacting factors. These include strategies, content knowledge, motivation, and metacognition. They believe that three factors add to children's cognitive success:

1. Children are taught by parents or teachers to use a particular strategy. With practice, they learn about its characteristics and advantages for learning *specific knowledge*. The more intellectually stimulating children's homes and schools are, the more specific strategies they will encounter and learn to use.
2. Teachers may demonstrate similarities and differences in multiple strategies in a particular domain, such as math, which motivates students to see shared features of different strategies. This leads to better *relational knowledge*.
3. Students recognize the general benefits of using strategies, which produces *general-strategy knowledge*. They learn to attribute successful learning outcomes to the efforts they make in evaluating, selecting, and monitoring strategy use (*metacognitive knowledge and activity*).

Exploring Strategy Instruction

Many educators believe that the key to education is helping students learn a rich repertoire of strategies that result in solutions of problems (McCormick & Pressley, 1997). Good thinkers routinely use strategies and effective planning to solve problems. Good thinkers also know when and where to use strategies (metacognitive knowledge about strategies). Understanding when and where to use strategies often results from the learner's monitoring of the learning situation. Pressley argues that when students are given instruction about effective strategies, they often can apply strategies that they previously have not used on their own.

Through the Eyes of Teachers

Learning to Read and Reading to Learn

I have noticed that some of my Grade 7 students are overwhelmed by their science textbooks. They are big and thick and for some students this is the first time they have really been called upon to work with a text. Up until now, the focus has been on "learning to read." Now, I am expecting them to "read to learn." I have to teach them strategies and skills like finding the main idea of a passage, using a glossary, and understanding information contained in figures or graphs. Without my help, some students, usually those with adult assistance, will figure out these skills over time. Others, however, will struggle, become discouraged, and eventually give up. That is why it is essential to provide all students with these strategies and skills.

Catherine Little
Grade 7, 8, & 9 Science and Mathematics Teacher
York University Faculty of Education Alumni Association
Excellence in Teaching Award Recipient
Science Olympiad Outstanding Coach
Ontario

How can teachers help children improve their metacognitive regulation of strategies?

Students learn best when they are taught learning strategies (Allen, 1998; Gallagher & Woloshyn, 1999; Gaskin, 1998; Pressley et al., 1998; Pressley, Yokoi, & Rankin, 1996; Woloshyn & Elliott, 1998). **Strategy instruction** *requires that teachers model appropriate learning strategies frequently.* As part of this modelling teachers need to verbalize the steps in the strategy, as well as the parameters associated with its use; teachers often share relevant personal learning experiences. They then need to provide students with opportunities to practise using the strategy, guiding their attempts to do so until they can carry out the strategy independently. Throughout this process, teachers help students "discover" that the strategic approach to learning is superior to a non-strategic one, in part by encouraging them to compare the quality of their work before and after using the strategy. Finally, teachers need to continually prompt students to transfer and generalize strategy use across the curriculum (Woloshyn, Elliott, & Kaucho, 2001).

Learning how to use strategies effectively takes time and motivation. Initially, many students require substantial time and extensive guidance and support to learn how to execute the strategies. Once students have demonstrated proficiency in the use of one strategy, they can be introduced to another so that they can develop a repertoire of effective strategies. With practice, students will learn to execute strategies faster and more competently.

Teachers, too, typically need extensive in-service and ongoing mentoring to become proficient strategy instructors (Duffy, 1993; Woloshyn, Elliott, & Riordon, 1998). As part of an initiative designed to promote students' use of effective learning strategies, Woloshyn and her colleagues (Woloshyn et al., 1998) hosted a professional development forum where local teachers met over the course of 18 months to develop their skills as strategy instructors and share their use of effective strategies in the classroom. At the end of the program the teachers commented on the importance of labelling strategic processes, introducing strategies apart from curriculum before integrating them into course content, and being conscious of why and how information and/or skills are presented to students. So great was their belief that students benefited from strategy instruction that at the end of the program they elected to become mentors for other teachers.

Proficient learners use multiple strategies in memory and problem solving (Schneider & Bjorklund, 1998; Siegler, 1998). Most children benefit from generating a variety of alternative strategies and experimenting with different approaches to a problem, discovering what works well, when, and where (Schneider & Bjorklund, 1998). This is especially true for children from the middle elementary-school grades on, although some cognitive psychologists believe that even young children should be encouraged to practise varying strategies (Siegler, 1998).

At this point, we have examined a number of ideas about teaching for transfer and metacognition. A review of these ideas is presented in Summary Table 8.3. In the next chapter, we will continue our exploration of children's learning, especially focusing on collaborative learning and learning in groups, as well as a number of strategies for teaching children in specific areas such as reading, writing, math, and science.

Teaching Strategies
For Using Strategy Instruction in the Classroom

✓ State content and process objectives
- tell students what information they will learn
- inform students what strategy they will use to help them learn this information

✓ Share a personal learning story related to strategy use
- tell students about a learning task where you did not use an appropriate strategy and as a consequence did not perform well
- tell students about a similar learning task where you did use the appropriate strategy and ultimately performed well

✓ State why strategy is useful
- remind students that using a relevant learning strategy will help them learn effectively
- emphasize that using a learning strategy requires considerable cognitive effort and attention but that the resulting learning gains warrant these efforts

✓ State when and where strategy can be used
- tell students about any prerequisites/requirements necessary to use the strategy effectively (e.g., some prior knowledge to use self-questioning strategies)
- provide students with examples of other learning tasks where it would be appropriate to use the strategy

✓ Model the strategy
- verbalize/think aloud the steps involved in carrying out the strategy
- verbalize/think aloud your success using the strategy, as well as any modifications you are required to make to the strategy
- call upon individual students to verbalize/think aloud during strategy use once they have gained some proficiency using the strategy

✓ Provide students with guided strategy instruction
- review strategy steps and the rationale for using the strategy prior to beginning a task
- ask students about next steps when they are completing a task
- re-model the strategy to individual students or groups as needed

✓ Encourage students to use strategy across related learning tasks
- question students about appropriate strategies prior to beginning new learning tasks
- provide students with information about appropriate strategies when necessary

✓ Convince students that strategy really works
- have students compare their work before and after using the strategy
- have students seek the opinions of others (teachers, parents, peers) about the quality of their work.

Source: Adapted from Woloshyn, Elliott, and Kaucho (2001).

SUMMARY TABLE 8.3
Teaching for Transfer and Metacognition

What is transfer?	• Transfer occurs when students apply previous experiences and knowledge to learning or problem solving in a new situation. • Near transfer occurs when situations are similar. • Far transfer occurs when situations are very different. • Low-road transfer occurs when previous learning automatically transfers to another situation. • High-road transfer is conscious.
What is metacognition?	• Metacognition is knowing about knowing, and it involves both metacognitive knowledge and metacognitive activity. • The majority of metacognitive studies focus on metamemory, or what students know about how memory works. • Students' metamemory improves through the elementary-school years.
What is the good information-processing model?	• The good information-processing model consists of three components: – developing specific knowledge about a particular strategy. – developing relational knowledge by examining similarities and differences across multiple strategies. – learning to attribute successful learning outcomes to strategy use.
How do students benefit from strategies and strategy instruction?	• Effective learners possess a rich repertoire of strategies. • Students benefit when they are provided strategy instruction. • Strategy instruction requires teachers to model effective strategies, provides students with opportunities to practise using them, and encourages them to monitor their learning as a function of strategy use. • It takes time to learn a new strategy and use it independently. • Most students benefit from using multiple strategies, and knowing which ones work best across various tasks and activities.

George has a test next week in his Grade 9 history class. He is having considerable difficulty remembering terms, names, and facts. On his last test, he identified General Brock as a Second World War hero, and Saigon as the capital of Japan. Historical dates are so confusing to him that he does not even try to remember them. In addition, George has difficulty spelling.

The test will consist of 50 multiple-choice items and two essay items. In general, George does better on essay items. He purposely leaves out any names about which he is uncertain and always omits dates. Sometimes he mixes up his facts and often loses points for misspelled words. He has greater difficulty on objective items. Sometimes, more than one answer will appear to be correct. Other times, he is sure he is correct, only to discover later that he was mistaken.

Before the last test, George tried to design some mnemonic devices to help him understand. He used acronyms, such as HOMES (for Huron, Ontario, Michigan, Erie, and Superior) to remember the names of the Great Lakes. While he remembered his acronyms quite well, he could not recall what each letter stood for. The result was a test paper filled with acronyms. Another time a classmate suggested that George try using concept maps. This classmate lent George the concept maps she had designed for her own use. George looked at them and found them to be very busy and confusing—he couldn't figure out what they even meant. They were not at all useful to him.

George has decided he needs some help if he is to pass this class, and has sought you out.

- What are the issues in this case?
- With what type of learning is George having difficulty?
- What type of learning is easier for George?
- Design a study-skills program for George using principles from the cognitive information-processing approach.

CHAPTER REVIEW

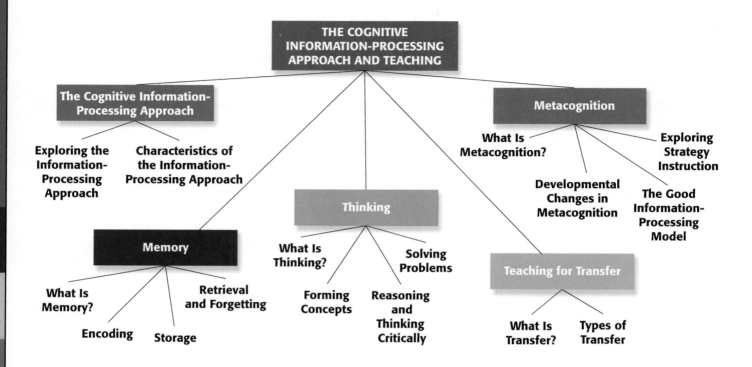

To obtain a detailed review of this chapter, study these three summary tables:

KEY TERMS

information-processing
   approach 238
encoding 238
automaticity 239
strategy construction 239
transfer 239
metacognition 239
memory 239
storage 239
retrieval 239
attention 240
rehearsal 240
levels of processing theory 241

elaboration 242
chunking 243
sensory memory 243
short-term (working)
   memory 243
memory span 244
working memory 244
long-term memory 245
Atkinson-Shiffrin model 245
declarative memory 246
procedural memory 246
episodic memory 246
semantic memory 246

network theories 247
schema theories 248
schema 248
script 249
serial position effect 249
primacy effect 249
recency effect 249
encoding specificity principle
   251
recall 251
recognition 251
cue-dependent forgetting 251
interference theory 251

decay theory 251
thinking 253
concepts 253
concept map 255
hypotheses 255
prototype matching 256
inductive reasoning 257
deductive reasoning 257
analogy 257
critical thinking 257
problem solving 258
subgoalling 258
algorithms 259

PROFESSIONAL DEVELOPMENT/PORTFOLIO ACTIVITIES

1. Memory and Study Strategies

Knowing how to study is as important as what you study. Working in a group with two or three of your colleagues, brainstorm ways to help students develop better memory and study strategies. Consider how you might use computers to help students learn effective note-taking strategies. Share classroom activities or ideas that you have seen for helping students improve their use of memory in school.

2. How Do You Study?

How you study reveals a great deal about your views of teaching and learning. In a group with two or three of your colleagues, share stories of how you studied for a major exam or test. Describe and compare your typical study routines. What do these routines suggest about your strategies for learning? In relation to the memory research presented in this chapter, discuss how you could improve your study techniques.

3. Linking Past and Present Knowledge

Information-processing theorists view prior knowledge and the environment as intimately connected to learning. Together with your colleagues, share stories of how you each have struggled to understand new ideas or information. Now consider how you might determine your students' prior knowledge about a specific lesson or topic. Discuss how you intend to present new information to your class. Develop a lesson plan that reveals how you would assess your students' prior knowledge in a particular area. Include this lesson plan in your portfolio.

4. A Response to a Question on Memory

Memory, like many other human abilities, changes with age and development. How would you respond to a Grade 2 student who asks you, "Why can't I ever remember things?" How would you respond to that same question from a Grade 10 student? Place your responses in your portfolio.

INTERNET ACTIVITIES

1. Computers as Memory Models

The information-processing model of memory is often compared to how a computer works. What can we learn from comparing how people think to how computers think? Using a search engine, find an online article or Website that discusses artificial intelligence (AI) or compares how people and computers think. Based on what you have read in this chapter and what you have found on the Internet, what have we learned about how human memory works from studying how computers function?

2. Webquest Workout

Increasingly, there is an emphasis on using the Internet as a tool in the classroom. Webquests are Internet-based projects planned around a specific topic or theme. Search the Internet and find three Webquests on topics that are of interest to you. Critique the three Webquests based on what the information-processing model suggests about teaching and learning. Report the results of your critique to your colleagues.

Connect to the Online Learning Centre at www.mcgrawhill.ca/college/santrock **to explore possible answers.**

Visit the *Educational Psychology* Online Learning Centre at
www.mcgrawhill.ca/college/santrock
to access Websites related to the above Internet Activities as well as chapter quizzes, a searchable glossary, and other learning and study tools.

www.mcgrawhill.ca/college/santrock

Social Constructivist Approaches, Domain-Specific Approaches, and Teaching

Preview

Children do some of their thinking by themselves, but as social beings their cognition is often collaborative. Much of this chapter focuses on the collaborative thinking advocated by social constructivist approaches. In the last part of the chapter, we will examine some domain-specific constructivist approaches. The questions we will explore in this chapter include these:

- What does it mean to take a social constructivist approach in teaching?

- What are some good strategies for including peers in students' learning?

- What is the best way to structure small-group work?

- What are some educational approaches that emphasize collaborative learning?

- What are some specific cognitive and social constructivist approaches to teaching reading, writing, math, and science?

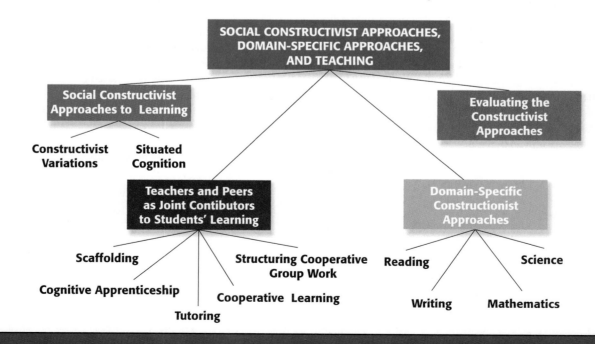

SOCIAL CONSTRUCTIVIST APPROACHES, DOMAIN-SPECIFIC APPROACHES, AND TEACHING

Social Constructivist Approaches to Learning

Constructivist Variations   Situated Cognition

Teachers and Peers as Joint Contibutors to Students' Learning

Scaffolding   Structuring Cooperative Group Work

Cognitive Apprenticeship   Cooperative Learning

Tutoring

Evaluating the Constructivist Approaches

Domain-Specific Constructionist Approaches

Reading   Science

Writing   Mathematics

Teaching Stories: Carol McCullough

Carol McCullough is a special-education teacher. For several years, she worked at a First Nations reserve in Alberta and taught English as a second language to adult learners. Carol currently works with the Bow Valley College Adult Literacy program. She describes the philosophy underpinning the program as meeting the learning needs of adults who have encountered barriers to their literacy development by offering flexible programming and individualized instruction. She describes the program in greater detail below.

"One of my guiding principles as program coordinator and literacy tutor trainer is to help tutors realize the importance of linking literacy learning to 'real-world success.' Real-world success means ensuring that learners take the literacy skills they learn here and apply them in a meaningful way outside the classroom. When adults can see a practical return with respect to their time in the literacy classroom, their motivation for learning increases.

"Our programs are staffed by a combination of instructors, educational assistants, and specially trained volunteers. Everyone is required to take a training program that includes a review of adult learning theories and educational strategies. The program staff work with clients either on an individual basis or as part of a small group. The instructional focus is to enhance our clients' skill levels so that there is an immediate benefit to their daily living. The tutor and client establish learning objectives and activities collaboratively. For example, one of my clients wanted to enrol in a nursing attendant care program. As part of her curriculum here, we studied drug names (spelling and vocabulary) and practised creating reports about fictitious patients (writing). She practised reading from the nursing attendant course manual.

"The primary goal of the Bow Valley College Adult Literacy program is to promote life-long learning by helping individuals realize that they can use their newly developed literacy skills to create a better quality of life for themselves and their families."

An isolated individual does
not exist.

Antoine de Saint-Exupéry
French Essayist and Novelist, 20th Century

SOCIAL CONSTRUCTIVIST APPROACHES TO LEARNING

The social constructivist approaches involve a number of innovations in classroom learning. Before we study these innovations, let us first consolidate our knowledge about constructivist variations and where the social constructivist approaches fit in the overall constructivist framework.

Constructivist Variations

Constructivism *emphasizes that individuals learn best when they actively construct knowledge and understanding in light of their own experiences* (Palincsar, 1998). In other words, the learner is inventing and building representations of reality, rather than simply discovering what is already out there. In the last chapter, our main focus was on the cognitive information–processing approaches to learning, which included some ideas about how students use information-processing skills to think in constructivist ways. Earlier in this book we described Piaget's and Vygotsky's theories of development, both of which are constructivist. According to all of these constructivist approaches, students author their own knowledge. In this chapter, the focus is on social constructivist approaches.

In general, **social constructivist approaches** *emphasize the social contexts of learning and that strategies and knowledge of the world are mutually constructed* (Palincsar, 1998). In other words, individuals learn and construct representations with reference to their social milieu. Vygotsky's social constructivist theory is especially relevant for the current chapter. Vygotsky's model is a social child embedded in a sociohistorical backdrop. Moving from Piaget to Vygotsky, the conceptual shift is from the individual to collaboration, social interaction, and sociocultural activity (Rogoff, 1998). Piaget believed that students construct knowledge by transforming, organizing, and reorganizing previous knowledge and information. Vygotsky believed that students construct knowledge through social interactions with others. The content of this knowledge is influenced by the culture in which the student lives, which includes language, beliefs, and skills.

The implication of Piaget's model is that teachers should provide support for students to explore their world and develop understanding. The implication of Vygotsky's model is that teachers should create many opportunities for students to learn with the teacher and with peers in co-constructing knowledge (Kozulni, 2000). In both Piaget's and Vygotsky's models, teachers serve as facilitators and guides rather than directors and moulders of children's learning.

Sometimes the distinctions among constructivist approaches are not clear-cut (Marshall, 1996). For example, when teachers serve as guides for students in discovering knowledge, there are social dimensions to the construction. And the same is true for processing information. If a teacher creates a brainstorming session for students to come up with good memory strategies, social interaction is clearly involved.

Some sociocultural approaches, like Vygotsky's, emphasize the importance of culture in learning. For example, culture can determine what skills are important (e.g., computer skills, communication skills, teamwork skills). Others focus more exclusively on the immediate social circumstances of the classroom, as when students collaborate to solve a problem.

In one recent analysis of the social constructivist approach, it was suggested that teachers need to "look at learning through the eyes of children" (Oldfather et al., 1999). These are some of the characteristics of social constructivist classrooms that were noted in this analysis (Oldfather et al., 1999):

- An important goal orientation is the construction of collaborative meaning.
- Teachers closely monitor students' perspectives, thoughts, and feelings.
- Teachers and students are learning and teaching.
- Social interaction permeates the classroom.
- The curriculum and the physical contents of the classroom reflect students' interests and are infused with their cultures.

Situated Cognition

Situated cognition *is an important assumption in the social constructivist approaches. It refers to the idea that thinking is located (situated) in social and physical contexts, not within an individual's mind.* Situated cognition conveys the idea that knowledge is embedded in and connected to the context in which the knowledge developed (King, 2000). If this is so, it makes sense to create learning situations that are as close to real-world circumstances as possible. Our discussion of problem-based learning in Chapters 8 and 10 provides similar emphasis.

Later in this chapter we will explore constructivist approaches in a number of specific domains or situations, such as reading, writing, math, and science. However, the extent to which instructional practices can be generalized across different domains, such as reading and science, is an important issue in educational psychology; teachers are required to create a balance between general and situation-specific learning contexts.

What is the nature of the social constructivist approach to education?

TEACHERS AND PEERS AS JOINT CONTRIBUTORS TO STUDENTS' LEARNING

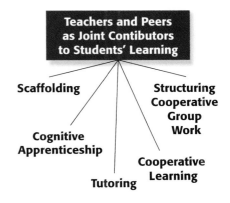

The idea that teachers and peers can be joint contributors to students' learning involves the concepts of scaffolding, cognitive apprenticeship, tutoring, and cooperative learning (Rogoff, 1998).

Scaffolding

Scaffolding *is a technique of changing the level of support over the course of a teaching session; a more-skilled person (a teacher or a more-advanced peer) adjusts the amount of guidance to fit the student's current performance level.* When a learning task is new, the teacher might use direct instruction. As the student's competence increases, less guidance is provided. Think of scaffolding in learning like the scaffolding used to build a bridge. The scaffolding provides support when needed, but it is adjusted or removed as a project unfolds (Soderman, Gregory, & O'Neill, 1999).

Cognitive Apprenticeship

Developmental psychologist Barbara Rogoff (1990) believes that an important aspect of education is **cognitive apprenticeship**, *in which an expert stretches and supports a novice's understanding of, and use of, the culture's skills.* The term *apprenticeship* underscores the importance of activity in learning and highlights the situated nature of learning. In a cognitive apprenticeship, teachers often model strategies for students. Then, teachers or skilled peers support students' efforts at doing the task. Finally, they encourage students to continue their work independently.

Parental engagement in cognitive apprenticeships with their children is correlated with their educational experiences and family income (Sloat & Willms, 2000). Canadian parents with more economic resources involve their children in cognitive apprenticeships more often than parents with fewer resources. These parents—in particular mothers—read to their children frequently, buy them educational toys, and recognize teachable moments associated with everyday experiences (e.g., setting up a lemonade stand or playing grocery shopping as a way of teaching math concepts). Children from these homes tend to be more linguistically and numerically proficient than their counterparts from "poorer" homes (Beals, De Temple, & Dickinson, 1994; Lancy, 1994; Willms, 1996). The trend continues throughout the school years, with high-socioeconomic-status parents tending to be more involved in their children's educational and schooling experiences than low-socioeconomic-status parents (Sloat & Willms, 2000).

Tutoring

Tutoring also involves a cognitive apprenticeship between an expert and a novice. Tutoring can take place between an adult and a child, or between a more-skilled child and a less-skilled child.

Individual Tutoring Over the past two decades, numerous one-on-one tutoring programs have been developed. One of the most influential and best-known programs is Reading Recovery.

Reading Recovery Reading Recovery involves highly skilled teachers tutoring Grade 1 students who are at risk for reading problems (Clay, 1993; Roehrig, Pressley, & Sloup, 2001; Wasik & Slavin, 1993). Sessions usually begin with the student reading a familiar book. Reading familiar text helps the student develop fluency and increases his or her confidence as a reader. The student is then asked to read a less familiar book, usually a book that has been introduced in the previous tutoring session. The teacher will keep a running record of the student's successes and errors during this reading. These observations will also help the teacher determine the nature of the instruction for the present tutorial session. The formal tutoring session then proceeds with some form of word study. As part of this lesson, the concept of reading by analogy (i.e., using known patterns to help decode or write unfamiliar words) will also be reinforced. The teacher will then assist the student to write a brief response to the story. The session concludes with the reading of a new text that carries over to the next tutorial session. Homework activities include continued practice reading and working with the cut-up sentences. Students are usually seen daily for about 30 minutes over 12 to 20 weeks.

Evaluations of the Reading Recovery program have been mixed (Elbaum et al., 2000; Smith-Burke, 2001). Overall, students who successfully complete the program in Grade 1 read better than their non-participating peers immediately after the program, and in some cases up to Grade 3 (Moore & Wade, 1998; Smith-Burke, 2001). However, the advantages of Reading Recovery can fade if students are not provided with proper instructional support, especially as they progress into the intermediate grades (Pinnell, 1997; Shanahan & Barr, 1995). James Kepron from Brandon University in Manitoba describes other concerns associated with the intervention program, including high costs for training teachers and delivering programs in isolated areas (Kepron, 1998).

More positively, there is increasing agreement that teachers can use Reading Recovery methods when providing either small-group or whole-class reading and writing instruction. For instance, B.C. researcher Deborah Begoray concluded that low-achieving Grade 2 students attained average grade-cohort reading levels after participating in a small-group, pull-out program based on Reading Recovery strategies. Roehrig, Pressley, and Sloup (2001) observed that teachers trained in Reading Recovery often transfer these associated reading strategies to their work in the regular classroom, thereby providing all students with high-quality reading and writing instruction. The Diversity and Education box on page 279 describes how Reading Recovery methods have been used with ESL students.

Teacher Aides, Volunteers, and Mentors Some students will need additional individual help beyond the time their classroom teacher can provide. Teacher aides, volunteers, and mentors can play an important role here. Carefully evaluate students who you believe could benefit from one-on-one tutoring and then scour the community for individuals who might be able to volunteer their time (e.g., parents, university students, retirees). In the following section, we describe one program that has capitalized on such community volunteer resources.

Howard Street Tutoring Program Chicago's Howard Street Tutoring Program is one of the longest-running volunteer tutoring programs in North America (Morris, Shaw, & Perney, 1990; Morris, 1992; Morris, 2001; Wasik, 1998). Program staff are adult volunteers—

university students, parents, and retirees—many who return to the program year after year. Prior to working directly with the students, volunteers receive training from a program supervisor (e.g., a graduate student in reading, or a reading specialist) and are provided with materials necessary to carry out the 45-minute tutoring sessions. Each session follows a predictable pattern where tutors and students participate in some form of guided reading (e.g., echo reading, partner reading, alternative reading, independent student reading). Readers are directed to *The Howard Street Tutoring Manual: Teaching At-Risk Readers in the Primary Grades* by Morris (1999) for more detailed information about the structure of the volunteer program, as well as the specific activities included during the tutoring sessions.

Peer Tutors   Fellow students also can be effective tutors. In peer tutoring, one student teaches another. In *cross-age peer tutoring*, the peer is older. In *same-age peer tutoring*, the peer is from the same class. Cross-age peer tutoring usually works better than same-age peer tutoring. An older peer is likely to be more skilled than a same-age peer, and being tutored by a same-age classmate is more likely to embarrass a student and create a negative social comparison.

Researchers have found that peer tutoring often benefits students' achievement (Fuchs et al., 1997; Harper et al., 1999; Mathers et al., 1998; Putman, 1997; Taylor, Hansen, & Justice-Swanson, 1997). And in some instances, the tutoring benefits the tutor as well as the tutee, especially when the older tutor is a low-achieving student. Teaching something to someone else is one of the best ways to learn.

Effective peer-tutoring programs require careful preparation and supervision. Taylor and her colleagues (Taylor et al., 1997) describe a peer-tutoring program where struggling Grade 4 readers were paired with poor Grade 2 readers. As a part of this program, the older students met with their teachers and the reading coordinator every Monday and Tuesday to plan their tutoring sessions for the remainder of the week. During these 45-minute planning sessions, teachers modelled effective teaching and reading strategies (e.g., question-answering, reading-by-analogy, prediction) and provided opportunities for the older students to practise these skills. Tutors also used this time to practise reading books that they would read aloud to the younger students. On Friday, the tutors wrote a letter to an adult mentor describing their tutoring experiences over the week, documenting any

Diversity and Education
The Reading Recovery Program

The Reading Recovery approach has been used to help Canadian ESL students acquire beginning literacy skills (Hodgson & Price, 1997). Hodgson and Price describe a Reading Recovery project at a middle school in Etobicoke, Ontario, where an ESL teacher trained in the Reading Recovery method designed individualized reading programs for students who had arrived from a variety of countries (including Algeria, Poland, and Spain) with minimal or no English-language skills. In the morning, the teacher worked one-on-one with each student. During the remainder of the day, these students worked with other ESL students. The combination of individual instruction and group experiences proved highly successful.

Hodgson and Price believe that "sharing" is a key Reading Recovery technique. They recommend using techniques to model and promote writing skills and using pictures as anchors for literary discussions.

Further information about the Reading Recovery Program can be found online at the Canadian Institute of Reading Recovery: **www.yrbe.edu.on.ca/~read/rr/cirr.htm**. Information about the Hodgson and Price study using Reading Recovery with ESL learners may be found at **www.ritslab.ubc.ca/teslcan/read.htm#refer**.

questions or concerns. The training cycle was repeated, with the mentor providing written feedback for the Monday session. Over the 14-week program, both tutors and younger students demonstrated substantial gains in their reading skills.

Similar gains have been reported by others using peer-tutoring programs in elementary and secondary classrooms (Allsopp, 1997; DuPaul & Henningson, 1993; Fuchs et al., 2001). In one well-recognized research study, Fuchs and others (1997) evaluated the effectiveness of a classwide peer-tutoring program for three types of learners: low-achieving students with exceptionalities, low-achieving students without exceptionalities, and average-achieving students. Twelve schools were randomly assigned to experimental (peer tutoring carried out) and control (no peer tutoring) groups. The peer-tutoring program was conducted during regularly scheduled reading instruction 3 days a week for 35 minutes each day and lasted for 15 weeks. The training of peer tutors emphasized helping students practise reading aloud from narrative text, reviewing and sequencing information, summarizing large chunks of connected texts, stating main ideas, predicting and checking story outcomes, and other reading strategies. Pre- and post-treatment reading achievement data were collected. Irrespective of the type of learner, students in the peer-tutoring classrooms showed greater reading progress over the 15 weeks than their counterparts who did not receive peer tutoring. The beneficial effects of peer tutoring are not limited to reading instruction. Class-wide peer-tutoring programs have also improved students' mathematical and problem-solving skills (Allsopp, 1997; Bogan, 1997; Fuchs & Fuchs, 2001; Gardner et al., 2001).

Cooperative Learning

Cooperative learning *occurs when students work in small groups to help each other learn.* Cooperative learning groups vary in size, although a typical group will have about four students. In some cases, cooperative learning is done in dyads (two students). When students are assigned to work in a cooperative group, the group usually stays together for weeks or months. However, working in cooperative groups should occupy only a portion of the school day.

Components of Cooperative Learning   Three decades of research document that instructing students to use cooperative learning techniques improves their academic and social performances (Antil et al., 1998; Blumfield et al., 1996; Kahl & Woloshyn, 1994; Shachar & Sharan, 1994; Sharon, 1994; Slavin, 1990, 1995). Cooperative learning involves more than simply placing students into groups (Kagan, 2001; Natasi & Clements, 1991; Thousand, Villa, & Nevin, 1994). Johnson and Johnson (1991, 1994, 2000) believe that certain environmental conditions must pre-exist and that students must possess critical skills before they can collaborate effectively. These components include positive interdependence (where an individual student's success is dependent on the success of his or her group); positive face-to-face interactions (where students develop a sense of sharing, understanding, and accumulated group knowledge); interpersonal and small-group skills (e.g., effective communication, conflict resolution, and decision-making); individual accountability (where each student is required to demonstrate his or her own learning); and critical reflection.

Positive Interdependence   As part of many cooperative-learning activities, students are often asked to acquire distinct bodies of knowledge and present that information to others. When students are responsible for teaching concepts to others, they tend to learn the material more effectively. Students' learning can further be enhanced by providing them with specific training with respect to how to engage in effective cognitive processing (Berg, 1993; Meloth & Deering, 1992, 1994). For instance, Canadian researchers Kahl and Woloshyn (1994) demonstrated that students who received instruction in both question-answering and cooperative learning prior to completing an academic activity demonstrated superior learning than did students who received training in only question-answering or cooperative learning. Students' learning can also be improved if some type of recognition

Teaching Strategies
For Volunteer and Peer Tutoring

Volunteer Tutoring

✔ Have a specialist serve as a supervisor or coordinator
- possess a sound knowledge and understanding of the reading and writing processes
- assess students and provide an accurate description of their reading and writing abilities
- develop initial curriculum, lessons, and materials for tutoring sessions
- supervise daily program operations
- carry out ongoing assessment of students' skills and adjust program accordingly
- communicate and coordinate services with students' classroom teachers

✔ Provide tutors with training and ongoing support
- able to work constructively with other adults
- provide intensive training including a review of program materials and resources
- capitalize on tutors' strengths
- provide constructive feedback and suggestions regularly
- provide ongoing training addressing areas of difficulty

✔ Provide structured and concentrated tutoring sessions
- use activities that are consistent with empirically validated programs (e.g., Reading Recovery)
- train tutors to use explicit instruction, modelling, and scaffolding procedures
- provide intensive programming over the school year (e.g., one to two hours per week)
- keep tutor–student pairings consistent
- provide tutors and students access to high-quality literature

✔ Reward and honour volunteers

Sources: Morrow and Woo (2001), Wasik (1998), and Goodlad and Hirst (1989)

Peer Tutoring

✔ Use cross-age tutoring
- avoid using same-age tutoring
- set aside a regular time in the day for peer tutoring

✔ Provide tutors with appropriate training
- provide tutors with clear objectives and guidelines for the learning activity
- model appropriate peer-tutoring strategies
- model appropriate questioning strategies
- provide tutors with opportunities to practise tutoring
- invite tutors to ask questions about their assignments
- provide tutors with opportunities to reflect on their tutoring experiences

✔ Have students participate as tutor and learner
- help students appreciate that they can benefit from being in the position of tutor as well as learner
- avoid pairing friends
- avoid overusing high-achieving students as peer tutors

✔ Communicate with parents about tutoring sessions
- provide parents with information about the effectiveness of peer tutoring
- provide parents with opportunities to observe peer-tutoring sessions
- explain to parents that their children will be provided opportunities to be the tutor as well as the learner

or reward is provided to the group so that members sense it is in their own best interest to help each other learn (Slavin, 1995). In this way, cooperative learning promotes increased interdependence and connection with others (Johnson & Johnson, 1999).

Positive Face-to-Face Interactions   Effective cooperative learning requires that time be spent on team-building skills. For teachers, this involves thinking about how to start team building at the beginning of the school year, helping students become better listeners, providing students with opportunities to practise contributing to a team product, having students discuss the value of a team leader, and working with students to help them overcome difficult situations. Positive peer interactions and student decision making can enhance students' motivation to learn (Sapon-Shevin, 1999). In one study, Grade 5 and 6 Israeli students were given a choice of continuing to do school work or going out to play. Only the students in cooperative learning groups elected to forgo recess (Sharan & Shaulov, 1990).

www.mcgrawhill.ca/college/santrock

Interpersonal and Small-Group Interactions   One way to facilitate small-group work is to assign specific roles to students. The following are some roles that students can assume in a group (Kagan, 1992):

- Encourager—brings out reluctant students and is a motivator
- Praiser—shows appreciation of other students' work
- Gatekeeper—equalizes participation of students in the group
- Coach—helps with academic content
- Question commander—ensures that students ask questions and that the group answers them
- Checker—makes sure the group understands the material
- Taskmaster—keeps the group on task
- Recorder—writes down ideas on task
- Reflector—thinks about and evaluates the group's progress
- Quiet captain—monitors the group's noise level
- Materials monitor—obtains and returns supplies

Another approach is to designate some students as "summarizers" and others as "listeners." Researchers have consistently found that summarizing benefits learning more than listening, so if these roles are used, all members should be provided with opportunities to be summarizers (Dansereau, 1988).

Roles help groups function smoothly and provide all members with a sense of importance. Although we have described several different roles that can be used in groups, most experts recommend that groups not exceed five or six members. Accordingly, some members can fill multiple roles, and all roles do not always have to be filled.

Individual Accountability   Without some method of assessing individuals' contributions and efforts to the learning process, some students may either allow others to complete the work (i.e., "social loafing") or be left out because of the belief that they have little to contribute. Therefore, it is critical for educators to assess the knowledge of individual students as well as the group product, for instance by requiring all students to complete a fact-based quiz as well as handing in a group project when determining their achievement scores (Michaelson, Fink, & Knight, 1997).

Through the Eyes of Teachers

Putting Students First

For me, putting students first means expressing respect and concern for my students—both as learners and as individuals. The role of teacher has changed quite dramatically over the past decade. We can no longer stand in front of our classes and simply tell students what to do and how to do it. Instead, we need to assume the roles of facilitators, mentors, and guides. We need to help students work through a variety of activities based on their abilities and interests. We need to help students develop cooperative skills, yet still hold them accountable for their own learning. We have the complex task of preparing students for life beyond the school walls.

Lynn Facey
Elementary-School Teacher
New Brunswick

Critical Reflection   Advocates of cooperative learning maintain that students need to engage in thoughtful and reflective dialogue in order to experience maximal learning and social gains, and to generalize skills across new learning situations (Johnson & Johnson, 2000). Specifically, students need to discuss whether they achieved the social and academic goals established at the beginning of the task. Teachers need to provide students with instructional time and support to have these discussions. When working with a group of educators from Ontario schools, Elliott and Woloshyn (1996) observed that there was a tendency for some teachers to trivialize this component of instruction. While many teachers required students to critically assess the effectiveness of their group interactions, others either ignored the stage or asked the students for a simple response.

Preparing Students to Work Cooperatively   The decision to use cooperative learning in the classroom requires careful preparation and planning on the part of teachers. Specifically, teachers must consider how they will introduce cooperative skills and how they will structure student groups.

Gradual and Explicit Instruction   Teachers report that cooperative learning often works best when students have previously worked together on team-building activities. Teachers are encouraged to have students work on personal and interpersonal communication skills and other cooperative skills for a short period each day across several weeks before beginning a cooperative learning project. Ideally, students should work with just one or two others while mastering these skills using familiar materials and "easy" tasks. As students gain skills and begin to appreciate the value of working cooperatively versus competitively, teachers should gradually increase the size of the group. (For suggestions about group-building, communication, and problem-solving activities, see Abrami et al., 1995.)

Teachers should also model effective communication and interpersonal processes and provide students with associated "what," "when," and "why" information—for example, *What* does good listening look like (sound like, feel like, etc.); *When* is it appropriate to listen; *Why* is good listening important (Mitchell et al., 2003).

> Man is a knot, a web, a mesh into which relationships are tied.
>
> Antoine de Saint-Exupéry
> *French Novelist and Essayist, 20th Century*

Structuring Cooperative Group Work

Composing the Group   Teachers often ask how they should assign students to small groups in their class. The cooperative learning approaches featured in this chapter generally recommend heterogeneous groups with diversity in ability, ethnic background, socioeconomic status, and gender (Johnson & Johnson, 2000). The reasoning behind heterogeneous grouping is that it maximizes opportunities for peer tutoring and support, improves cross-gender and cross-ethnic relations, and ensures that each group has at least one student who can do the work (Kagan, 1992).

Heterogeneous Ability   One of the main reasons for using heterogeneous-ability groups is that they benefit low-ability students, who can learn from higher-ability students. However, some critics argue that such heterogeneous groupings hold back high-ability students. In most studies, though, high-achieving students perform equally well on achievement tests after working in heterogeneous groups or homogeneous groups (Hooper et al., 1989). In heterogeneous groups, high-ability students often assume the role of "teacher" and explain concepts to other students. In homogeneous groups, high-ability students are less likely to assume this teaching role. One potential problem with heterogeneous groups is that when high-ability, low-ability, and medium-ability students are in a group, the medium-ability students may be excluded to some extent (high-ability and low-ability students might form teacher–student relationships). Therefore, medium-ability students might perform better in groups where most or all of the students have medium abilities.

Ethnic, Socioeconomic, and Gender Heterogeneity   One of the initial reasons cooperative learning groups were formed was to improve interpersonal relations among students from different ethnic and socioeconomic backgrounds. The hope was that interaction under conditions of equal status in cooperative groups would reduce prejudice.

Some experts recommend that, when forming ethnically and socioeconomically heterogeneous groups, careful attention be given to a group's composition (Miller & Harrington, 1990). One recommendation is to not make the composition too obvious. Thus, you might vary different social characteristics (ethnicity, socioeconomic status, and gender) simultaneously, such as grouping together a middle-income black female, a white male from a low-income family, and so on. Another recommendation is to not form groups that have only one minority student, if at all possible; this avoids calling attention to the student's "solo status."

In mixed-gender groups, males tend to be more active and dominant (Tannen, 1990). Thus, when mixing females and males, an important task for teachers is to encourage girls to speak up and boys to allow girls to express their opinions and contribute to the group's functioning. A general strategy is to have an equal number of girls and boys. In groups of five or six children in which only one member is a girl, the boys tend to ignore the girl (Webb, 1984).

Cooperative Learning Approaches   A number of cooperative learning approaches have been developed, including student-teams-achievement divisions (STAD) and the jigsaw classroom.

STAD (Student-Teams-Achievement Divisions)   STAD involves team recognition and group responsibility for learning in mixed-ability groups (Slavin, 1994). Rewards are given to teams whose members improve the most over their past performances. Students are assigned to teams of four or five members. The teacher presents a lesson, usually over one or two class sessions. Next, students study worksheets based on the material presented by the teacher. Students monitor their team members' performance to ensure that all members have mastered their material. Teams practise working on problems together and study together, but the members take quizzes individually. The resulting individual scores contribute to the team's overall score. An individual's contribution to the team score is based on that individual's improvement (rather than an absolute score), which motivates students to work hard because each contribution counts. In some STAD classrooms, a weekly class newsletter is published that recognizes both team and individual performances.

The STAD approach has been used in a variety of subjects (math, reading, social studies) and with students at different grade levels. It is most effective for learning situations that involve well-defined objectives or problems with specific answers or solutions. These include math computation, language use, geography skills, and science facts.

The Jigsaw Classroom   Developed by Aronson and his colleagues (1978), *Jigsaw I* is a cooperative learning approach in which six-member teams work on material that has been broken down into parts. Each team member is responsible for a part. Members of different teams who have studied the same part convene, discuss their part, and then return to their teams, where they take turns teaching their part to other team members.

 Through the Eyes of Teachers

An Eye-Level Meeting of the Minds

Grade 9 history teacher Jimmy Furlow believes that students learn best when they have to teach others. He has groups of students summarize textbook sections and put them on transparencies to help the entire class prepare for a test. Furlow lost both legs in Vietnam but he rarely stays in one place, moving his wheelchair around the room, communicating with students at eye level. When the class completes their discussion of all the points on the overhead, Furlow edits their work to demonstrate concise, clear writing and help students zero in on an important point (Marklein, 1998).

Grade 9 history teacher Jimmy Furlow converses with a student in his class.

Robert Slavin (1994) created *Jigsaw II*, a modified version of Jigsaw I. Whereas Jigsaw I consists of teams of six, Jigsaw II usually has teams of four or five. All team members study the entire lesson rather than one part, and individual scores are combined to form an overall team score, as in STAD. After they have studied the entire lesson students become expert in one aspect of the lesson; students with the same topic then meet in expert groups to discuss it. Subsequently, they return to their teams and help other members of the team learn the material.

At this point we have studied a number of ideas about social constructivist approaches and teachers and peers as joint contributors to students' learning. A review of these ideas is presented in Summary Table 9.1. Next, we will describe some programs that reflect a social constructivist approach to learning.

Teaching Strategies
For Developing Students' Team-Building Skills

✔ Teach interpersonal and communication skills
  - model critical interpersonal and communication skills
  - discuss the importance of effective interpersonal and communication skills
  - provide students with opportunities to practise interpersonal and communication skills apart from academic tasks
  - provide students with opportunities to discover that being cooperative is more effective than being competitive
✔ Provide instruction gradually
  - provide students with opportunities (short intervals over several weeks) to work cooperatively on familiar tasks prior to completing difficult ones
  - have students work in pairs before completing tasks in small groups
  - provide opportunities for all members to experience being a valued team member
✔ Help students become better listeners
  - model for students how to take turns listening
  - ask students to develop behavioural descriptions for good listening (e.g., looking at the speaker, paraphrasing information, summarizing key ideas)
  - have students practise good listening
  - contrast poor listening experiences with good listening experiences
✔ Provide students with opportunities to contribute to a common product
  - have students contribute individual components to create a single product (e.g., single sentence to create a story; single picture to create a collage)
  - discuss each person's contribution to the product
  - discuss how working together is beneficial
✔ Explore the potential value of a team leader
  - discuss specific behaviours and manners of effective team leaders (e.g., helps the group get organized, keeps the group on task, shows enthusiasm, helps resolve disagreements)
  - model leadership skills
  - provide students with opportunities to practise leadership skills (e.g., role-play)
  - select a group leader or help students nominate someone for this position
  - ensure that every student has an opportunity to assume the role of leader
  - provide assistance to leaders as required

Source: Aronson and Patnoe (1996).

www.mcgrawhill.ca/college/santrock

SUMMARY TABLE 9.1

Social Constructivist Approaches to Learning, and Teachers and Peers as Joint Contributors to Students' Learning

What is constructivism?	• Constructivism emphasizes that individuals learn best when they actively construct knowledge and understanding in light of their own experiences. • The learner is inventing and building representations of reality, rather than simply discovering what is already out there. • Piaget's theory is a constructivist theory.
What are social constructivist approaches to learning?	• Social constructivist approaches emphasize the social contexts of learning and that strategies and knowledge of the world are mutually constructed. • Individuals learn and construct representations with reference to their social milieu. • Vygotsky's theory is a social constructivist theory.
What are situated cognition, scaffolding, and cognitive apprenticeships?	• Situated cognition refers to the idea that thinking is located (situated) in social and physical contexts, not within an individual's mind. • Scaffolding involves changing levels of support over the course of a teaching session, with more-skilled individuals providing guidance to fit the student's current performance. • Cognitive apprenticeship involves a novice and an expert, who stretches and supports the novice's understanding and use of the culture's skills.
What is tutoring?	• Tutoring involves a cognitive apprenticeship between an expert and a novice. • Tutoring can take place between an adult and a child, or a more-skilled child and a less-skilled child. • Classroom aides, volunteers, and mentors can serve as tutors to support teachers and classroom learning. • In many cases, students benefit more from cross-age tutoring than from same-age tutoring. • Tutoring can benefit not only the learner but also the tutor.
What is cooperative learning?	• Cooperative learning includes five components: positive interdependence, positive face-to-face interactions, interpersonal and small-group skills, individual accountability, and critical reflection. • Cooperative learning can improve students' achievement, especially when group goals and individual accountability are instituted. • Cooperative learning approaches include STAD (Student-Teams-Achievement Divisions), the jigsaw classroom (I and II), group investigation, and cooperative scripting.
How are cooperative groups best structured?	• Heterogeneous groups with diversity in ability, ethnicity, socioeconomic status, and gender are usually recommended. • Structuring small-group work involves attention to team-building skills. • Spend several weeks at the beginning of the school year on building team skills. • Assign students different roles to help the group function smoothly.

DOMAIN-SPECIFIC CONSTRUCTIVIST APPROACHES

In this section of the chapter, we examine constructivist approaches that have been developed for reading, writing, mathematics, and science.

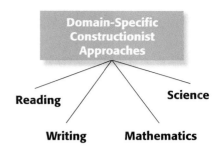

Reading

We will describe several approaches to teaching reading, including the *basic-skills-and-phonetics approach*, the *whole-language approach*, and the *balanced-instruction approach*. (We have also described several effective reading intervention programs at the beginning of this chapter.) In general, the basic-skills-and-phonetics approach emphasizes decoding skills and therefore is more reflective of the cognitive constructivist view (Tierney & Readence, 2000). The whole-language approach focuses on becoming immersed in the world of print and therefore fits more within a social constructivist framework. There is every reason to believe that students learn to read best when they are exposed to both decoding skills and whole-language experiences. Balanced instruction, which emphasizes the importance of modelling strategic processes in the context of authentic learning experiences and materials, contains elements of both cognitive and social constructivist frameworks.

Approaches to Reading   *Reading* is the ability to understand written discourse. Students cannot be said to read if all they can do is respond to flash cards, as in some early child-training programs. Early reading requires mastering the basic language rules of phonology, morphology, syntax, and semantics. A student who has poor grammatical skills for speech and listening and does not understand what is meant by "The car was pushed by a truck" when it is spoken will not understand its meaning in print either. Likewise, a student who cannot determine what pronouns refer to (as in John went to the store with his dog. It was closed.) will not do well in reading comprehension.

What are some approaches to teaching students how to read? Education and language experts continue to debate how students should be taught reading (Rayner, 2000). The debate is between those who advocate a basic-skills-and-phonetics approach, those who emphasize a whole-language approach, and those who support a balanced-instruction approach:

- **Basic-skills-and-phonetics approach.** *This approach involves teaching both phonemic awareness (breaking apart and manipulating sounds in words) and phonics (learning that sounds are represented by letters of the alphabet, which can then be blended together to form words).* Early reading resources should involve simple materials (Meyer, 2002). Only after students have learned phonological rules should they be given books and poems.
- **Whole-language approach.** *This approach assumes that reading instruction should parallel students' natural language learning.* From the outset, reading materials should be whole and meaningful. That is, in early reading instruction, students should be presented materials in their complete form, such as stories and poems. In this way, they learn to understand language's communicative function. The whole-language approach implies that all words are essentially "sight" words, which the student recognizes as a whole without detecting how the individual letters contribute to sounds. In the whole-language approach, reading should be connected with writing and listening skills. Also in this approach, reading is often integrated with other skills and subjects such as science and social studies. Most whole-language approaches have students read real-world, relevant materials, such as newspapers and books, and ask them to write about them and discuss them.
- **Balanced-instruction approach.** *This approach is a combination of reading approaches; namely, the basic-skills-and-phonetics approach, and the whole-language approach* (Asselin, 1999; Freppon & Dahl, 1998; Pressley, 1998; Tompkins, 1997; Weaver, 1998). Specifically, students receive instruction in phonemic awareness (sounds in

words), phonics, and other decoding skills, while simultaneously being exposed to print in authentic literature. Most language experts believe that a combination of the two approaches should be followed (Freppon & Dahl, 1998; Spear-Swerling & Sternberg, 1994).

Which approach is best? Researchers have found that students can benefit from all three approaches. They have found strong evidence that the basic-skills-and-phonetics approach should be used in teaching reading but that students also benefit from the whole-language approach of being immersed in a natural world of print (Fox & Hull, 2002; Graham & Harris, 1994; Wilson et al., 2001). The Canadian Psychological Association also supports a balanced approach to teaching reading (Simner, 1998). The Association contends that the whole-language philosophy, which minimizes the role of phonics instruction, is not appropriate for all students (Simner, 1998). Instead, Simner states that the Association believes phonological awareness training programs are effective in helping children to become successful readers.

In a recent study, Michael Pressley and his colleagues (2001) examined literacy instruction in five classrooms. Classroom effectiveness was evaluated based on students' academic and literacy performance. In the most effective classrooms, teachers exhibited excellent classroom-management based on positive reinforcement and cooperation; balanced teaching of skills, literature, and writing; scaffolding and matching task demands to students' skill levels; encouragement of student self-regulation; and strong connections across subject areas. In general, the extensive observations did not support any particular reading approach (such as whole-language or basic-skills-and-phonetics); rather, excellent instruction involved multiple, well-integrated components. An important point in this study is that effective reading instruction involves more than a specific reading approach—it also includes effective classroom management, encouragement of self-regulation, and other components.

Cognitive Constructivist Approaches   Cognitive constructivist approaches to reading emphasize decoding and comprehending words, constructing meaning, and developing expert reader strategies.

Decoding and Comprehending Words   The cognitive constructivist approach emphasizes the cognitive processes involved in decoding and comprehending words. Important in this regard are certain metacognitive skills and a general automaticity of information processing.

Metacognition is involved in reading in the sense that good readers develop control of their own reading skills and have an understanding of how reading works. For example, good readers know that it is important to comprehend the gist of what an author is saying.

Teachers can help students develop good metacognitive strategies for reading by getting them to monitor their own reading, especially when they run into difficulties. Here are some metacognitive strategies that teachers can help students use to improve their reading (Miholic, 1994; Pressley & Afflerbach, 1995; Singhal, 2001):

- Overview text before reading.
- Look for important information while reading and pay more attention to it than other information; ask yourself questions about the important ideas or relate them to something you already know.
- Attempt to determine the meaning of words not recognized (use the words around a word to figure out its meaning, use a dictionary, or temporarily ignore it and wait for further clarification).
- Monitor text comprehension.
- Understand relationships between parts of text.
- Recognize when you might need to go back and reread a passage (you didn't understand it, to clarify an important idea, it seemed important to remember, or to underline or summarize it for study).
- Adjust pace of reading depending on the difficulty of the material.

Constructing Meaning In the cognitive approach, text has meaning that a reader must construct, not simply decode. Readers actively construct this meaning by using their background knowledge and knowledge of words and how they are linked (Heilman, Blair, & Rupley, 2002). According to some prominent educational theorists, prior knowledge is the most important single factor that affects learning (e.g., Ausubel, 1968). When students possess prior knowledge that is consistent with information presented in a text, their learning for new information is considerably greater than when they do not possess this knowledge (Lipson, 1984; Pearson, Hansen, & Gordon, 1979). Learning is especially enhanced when students are directed to activate their relevant prior knowledge before reading (e.g., Stockley, Woloshyn, & Bond, 1998; Woloshyn & Stockley, 1995). In one study, students who were knowledgeable about baseball retained more new information from a passage about the game, even if they were poor readers, than did readers who knew little about the game, even if they were skilled readers (Recht & Leslie, 1988). However, when students possess prior knowledge that is inconsistent with text information, also known as *alternative frameworks or misconceptions*, their learning can be inhibited (Taber, 1998, 2000, 2001; Taber & Watts, 1997). In this sense, prior knowledge is a double-edged sword.

Developing Expert Reading Strategies In the cognitive approach, researchers have tried to focus not so much on whether one teaching approach, such as whole language, is better than another, such as phonics. Rather, they have searched for the underlying cognitive processes that explain reading. This search has led to an interest in strategies, especially the strategies of expert readers compared with those of novice readers. Researchers advise teachers to guide students in developing good reading strategies.

Michael Pressley and his colleagues (1992) developed the *transactional strategy instruction approach (TSI)*, a cognitive constructivist method for reading instruction that emphasizes the use of specific strategies training to help students develop their reading capabilities. Janzen (1996) described the components of transactional strategy instruction including the careful selection of reading content based on students' interests, the provision of direct explanation and instruction about how and when to use specific strategies, and the provision of explicit feedback. Janzen notes that TSI strategies can also be used in other subject areas and tasks; therefore, teachers are encouraged to teach reading strategies as part of other subject areas.

Social Constructivist Approaches

The social constructivist approaches bring the social dimensions of reading to the forefront (Hiebert & Raphael, 1996). Two social constructivist assumptions about reading are that (1) the social context plays an important role in reading, and (2) knowledgeable readers in the culture assist less-knowledgeable readers in learning to read.

The contribution of the social context to reading includes such factors as how much emphasis the culture places on reading, the extent to which children have interacted with books before they enter formal schooling, the teacher's communication skills, the extent to which teachers provide students with opportunities to discuss what they have read with the teacher and their peers, and the mandated reading curriculum. Whereas cognitive constructivists emphasize students' construction of meaning, social constructivists stress that meaning is socially negotiated. What they mean by "socially negotiated" is that meaning involves not only the reader's contribution but also the context in which the text is read, along with the purpose for reading. Social constructivist approaches emphasize the importance of providing students with opportunities to engage in meaningful dialogue about the books they have just read. One way of doing this is through reciprocal teaching.

Reciprocal Teaching **Reciprocal teaching** *involves students taking turns leading a small-group discussion.* Reciprocal teaching requires students to discuss complex passages, collaborate, and share their expertise and perspective about a particular topic. It requires carefully planned interactions between students, with some teachers electing to use a modified version of the jigsaw classroom. As students begin to read about a topic area,

www.mcgrawhill.ca/college/santrock

they participate in "crosstalk" sessions. These are whole-class activities in which groups periodically summarize where they are in their learning activity and get input from the other groups. "Mini jigsaws" (small groups) also are used. At both the whole-class and mini-jigsaw level, if group members can't understand what a student is saying or if that student is unable to answer questions from his/her peers, he or she must continue to explore the topic area and present it again later. Students are then grouped into reciprocal teaching seminars in which each student is an expert on one subtopic, teaches that part to the others, and also participates in constructing questions based on the unit.

Reciprocal teaching also can involve interactions between a teacher and a student. In reciprocal teaching, teachers initially explain the strategies and model how to use them in making sense of the text. Then they ask students to demonstrate the strategies, giving them support as they learn them. As in scaffolding, the teacher gradually assumes a less active role, letting the student assume more initiative. For example, Annamarie Palincsar and Ann Brown (1984) used reciprocal teaching to improve students' abilities to enact certain strategies to improve their reading comprehension. In this teacher-scaffolded instruction, teachers worked with students to help them generate questions about the text they had read, clarify what they did not understand, summarize the text, and make predictions. Figure 9.1 portrays a teacher–student dialogue that reflects reciprocal teaching. Research on reciprocal teaching suggests that it is a very effective strategy for improving reading comprehension (Brown & Palincsar, 1989; Webb & Palincsar, 1996).

To ask questions of a wise person is the beginning of wisdom.

German Proverb

Book Clubs   **Book clubs** *involve peer learning and consist of student-led discussions of literature* (McMahon, 1994; McMahon, Raphael, & Goatley, 1995; Raphael & McMahon, 1994; Raphael et al., 2001). Teachers serve as guides but give students considerable responsibility for how text discussions evolve. Conducted in this manner, book clubs often involve a range of discussions, as students make connections to their own lives, clarify points of confusion in the texts, draw inferences to fill in gaps left by the texts, and critique the quality of the texts.

Frank, Dixon, and Brandts (2001) suggest that students benefit the most from book clubs when they are provided with opportunities to talk about books they have self-selected. Reporting on a community literacy initiative involving book clubs in Leeds, England, Tanner (2000) observed that when students were allowed to select their own reading as part of a book club they enjoyed and valued being part of the club and believed they gained from it. In Canada, many teachers form book clubs as after-school or summer activities that extend and support classroom reading programs. The Internet has also affected how teachers and schools create and operate book clubs. For example, the Calgary Public Library provides a virtual book club, where students can check out student and librarian recommendations for good books, teachers can find information about how to start up a school book club or a virtual book club, and classes can talk to other classes around the country in online book discussion groups. The Calgary book club site can be found at **www.chapteraday.com/library/calgary**.

Book clubs in school or online reflect the social constructivist principle that meaning is socially negotiated. Book clubs also help fill a void that exists in many classrooms: a focus on talking about text.

School/Family/Community Connections   From the social constructivist perspective, schools are not the only sociocultural context that is important in reading. Families and communities are also important (McGhee & Richaels, 2000).

Through the Eyes of Teachers

Working with English as Second Language (ESL) Students

When I work with students whose first language is not English, I tell them that I did not always speak English. I share with them some of my own experiences from when I first came to Canada. I confide to them how worried I was about my ability to learn English and adapt to Canadian culture. Sometimes my classes watch the videotape *You Can Make It Too!*, which documents my experiences as a new immigrant. I was a participant in this video, produced by the Toronto District School Board, and I use it to help students talk about their own experiences of coming to a new land. I explain to them that there are many children who have had similar experiences of their own and that there are many people who are committed to helping them thrive in their new home. I hope that by sharing my story, I can help students feel more at ease in my classroom and with each other.

Anita Ghazariansteja
Secondary School Science/Chemistry Teacher
Toronto District School Board
Recipient of the 2002 Ontario Secondary School Teachers' Federation
Status of Women Award for Outstanding Female Educator
Ontario

READING:
Cats also "talk" by making other sounds. Some scientists think cats may have as many as 100 different calls. Cats have calls for greeting people, for showing hunger, for making a threat to another cat, and even for scolding their kittens. When a cat is frightened or angry, it may growl, spit, hiss, or scream.

39. T: C_____, as a teacher, can you ask someone a question about this information? [pause] Sometimes it helps if you're having a hard time to summarize what I just told you. [pause] What was I telling you about, what kind of information?
40. S2: About different ways they talk.
41. T: You mean there are [sic] more than one way for them to communicate?
42. S2: A hundred ways.
43. T: I did talk about that. They communicate with a hundred different sounds. Why do they need all those different sounds?
44. S2: To tell people stuff.
45. S6: To see if their babies are okay.
46. T: Possibly. Now, with that information, C_____, knowing that they have all those different ways to talk and to communicate, can you think of a question to ask? You can start your question with the word what . . . or when . . . or why.
47. S2: Why do they purr?
48. T: Who is they?
49. S2: The cats.
50. T: Okay, let's have that information in your sentence. Why . . .
51. S2: Why do the cats purr?
52. S5: To tell them what they want.
53. T: Can you tell us a little bit more?
54. S5: [not audible]
55. T: Would it sound the same way for all those things?
56. S5: No.
57. T: So that's why it needs a hundred sounds. So, I might say, if I were going to ask a question, why do cats have so many different sounds or calls?
58. S3: Because they have so many different colours in their fur.
59. T: I said calls, not colours. Why do they have so many different calls, or sounds? [pause] Think of what R_____ told us. Do they always want the same thing?
60. S3: No.
61. T: Then why do they have so many different ones? Is it so they can communicate what they really want?

FIGURE 9.1 **Reciprocal Teaching and Reading**

Of special concern are the language experiences of students from low-income families. Researchers have found that, on the average, children from low-income homes receive only half as much language experience in their early years as children from middle and higher-income families (Hart & Risley, 1999; Sloat & Willms, 2000). At-risk students who do not engage in reading out of school fall farther behind as they go through the elementary-school years (Sloat & Willms, 2000). Most students who are avid readers report that they have at least one other person to talk with about their reading and about what to read next (Sloat & Willms, 2000). Many parents of at-risk students have their own reading difficulties as well as problems in obtaining books (Gunning, 2000; Jalongo, 2000; Robinson, McKenna, & Wedman, 2000).

A number of adult programs and home-school partnerships have been established in recognition of the critical role that families play in children's literacy development, including the National Centre for Family Literacy in Alberta (**www.famlit.ca**). In general, family literacy programs offer four levels of participation: (1) direct parent/direct child (direct instruction for parents and children); (2) direct parent/indirect child (focus on parent literacy development with the assumption that children will benefit indirectly); (3) indirect adult/direct child (focus on child literacy development, providing parents

Writers in Electronic Residence (WIER)

Trevor Owen founded the Writers in Electronic Residence (WIER) program in 1988. The goal of WIER is to connect Canadian writers with students and their teachers through online conferences. Professional writers offer revision advice to students of all grade levels who post their writings. The students' writing may include poems, narratives, and short stories. The writers' responses are often rich with suggestions about how students can augment their work. Other students across the nation are also welcome to offer their comments, akin to a virtual peer-editing process.

Three panels of professional writers exist for students in each of the elementary, intermediate, or high-school levels. These distinguished Canadian writers head up six classes to form what is called an "electronic literary salon." A few salons are grouped into a conference, so that over the course of the program the students experience the input not only of several writers, but also of other students from across Canada. Examples of the students' writing are selected each year and posted by division level in the link titled "The WIER Taps."

Teachers may register through an online application at **www.wier.ca**. Three program terms are offered in the fall, winter, and spring; each term is 12 weeks long. Teachers select the program term that complements their curriculum.

As a result of participating in WIER, students generally demonstrate a greater appreciation of writing and view themselves more confidently as developing writers. Furthermore, they show significant improvement in their writing, which can be traced to the professional writers' suggestions and online communications. There is also a marked improvement in their attitudes toward Canadian writers and literature.

with adjunct instruction); and (4) indirect parent/indirect child (providing little or no explicit literacy instruction). In general, programs that focus their efforts directly on parent and child literacy are more effective than those that are not as specific in their focus.

One example of such a home-school program is the Family Learning Program developed by Adele Thomas and her colleagues at Brock University in Southern Ontario. Expanding on the Kenan model (Seaman, Popp, Darling, 1991; Philliber, Spillman, & King, 1996) developed at the National Centre for Family Literacy, Thomas worked with a local school board to offer young parents—many who had low literacy skills and all who had not completed secondary school—an opportunity to earn a high-school diploma while completing courses designed to promote positive parent–child interactions. During the program, which was staffed by a secondary-school teacher and early childhood educator, the parents participated in a variety of courses relating to nutrition, parenting, and family literacy. Lessons were grounded in everyday experiences, with assignments consisting of family literacy activities (e.g., shared reading, reading response, question asking). Each half-day session began with "circle time," where parents and their children participated in a shared reading. For the remainder of the session, children participated in a parallel program where they were provided with opportunities to interact with their peers and develop their own literacy and social skills. Overall, participation in the Family Learning Program resulted in improved parenting skills as well as literacy gains for both parents and their children (Thomas, 1998; Thomas & Stiefelmeyer, 1999a, 1999b).

Writing

How do students learn to write? Here, as with reading, we will explore cognitive and social constructivist approaches to writing. There are many ways that the writing skills of young authors can be enhanced. The Technology and Education box above features the Writers in Electronic Residence (WIER) program, which connects Canadian writers with students through online conferences. As well, teachers should consider how to incorporate both reading and writing into their classroom activities. Self-Assessment 9.1 offers a checklist of such literacy-enhancing opportunities.

How Do I Plan to Incorporate Reading and Writing into My Classroom?

By incorporating many of these reading and writing activities in your classroom, you will significantly improve your students' literacy and enhance their opportunities for success in a world that places a high value on reading and writing skills.

	Yes	No
Computer technology, such as the WIER Program		
Whole-language opportunities such as using newspapers, magazines, and fiction and nonfiction books, as well as trying to integrate subject areas		
Phonological awareness and word–sound decoding-skill activities		
Reciprocal teaching		
Reading strategies, such as monitoring and summarizing		
Book clubs		
Involving parents in students' reading and writing activities		
Working with students on writing as a problem-solving activity		
Emphasizing the social context in writing		
Having students write "real texts" about meaningful experiences		
Having regular student–teacher writing conferences		
Setting up writing projects on which students collaborate with each other		
Bringing in expert writers, such as authors and newspaper editors or writers, to talk with students		
Giving students "writing to learn" opportunities		
Giving students free-writing assignments		
Giving students creative-writing assignments		
Giving students formal writing opportunities		

Cognitive Constructivist Approaches   Cognitive approaches to writing emphasize many of the same themes that we discussed with regard to reading, such as constructing meaning and developing strategies (Kellogg, 2000; Olson, 2001). Planning, problem-solving, revising, and metacognitive strategies are thought to be especially important in improving students' writing.

Planning   Planning, which includes outlining and organizing content information, is an important aspect of writing (Levy & Randsell, 1996). Students need to be shown how to outline and organize a paper, and they need to be given feedback about the competence of their efforts.

Problem Solving   Much of the instruction in writing in schools involves teaching students how to write sentences and paragraphs properly. However, there is more to writing than avoiding run-on sentences or making sure that paragraphs support topic sentences (Mayer, 1999). More fundamentally, writing is a broader sort of problem solving. One psychologist called the problem-solving process in writing "the making of meaning" (Kellogg, 1994).

As problem solvers, writers need to establish goals and work to attain them. It also is helpful to think of writers as constrained by their need for integrated understanding of the subject, knowledge of how the language system works, and the writing problem itself.

You just jot down ideas as they occur to you. The jotting is simplicity itself—it is the occurring which is difficult.

Stephen Leacock
Canadian Author and Humorist,
20th Century

www.mcgrawhill.ca/college/santrock

Through the Eyes of Students

The Devl and the Babe Goste

Anna Mudd is the six-year-old author of "The Devl and the Babe Goste." Anna has been writing stories for at least two years. Her story includes poetic images, sophisticated syntax, and vocabulary that reflect advances in language development.

The writing problem includes the purpose of the paper, the audience, and the role of the writer in the paper to be produced (Flower & Hayes, 1981).

Revising Revising is a major component of successful writing (Mayer, 1999). Revising involves writing multiple drafts, getting feedback from individuals who are knowledgeable about writing, and learning how to use the critical feedback to improve the writing. It also includes detecting and correcting errors. Researchers have found that older and more skilled writers are more likely to revise their writing than younger and less skilled writers (Bartlett, 1982; Hayes & Flower, 1986).

Metacognition When we emphasize knowledge of writing strategies, we move into the area of metacognition. In one study, students 10 to 14 years of age were asked to write a paper that would be of interest to students in their own age range (Scardamalia, 1981). In carrying out this project, the students were hampered by a lack of planning, not recording ideas in notes for later use, and not monitoring their writing progress by rereading and rewriting. The results are indicative of the fact that many intermediate-level students do not have good knowledge of the planning and organizational strategies required by good writing and need to be taught these skills (Harris & Graham, 1996; Indrisano & Squire 2000; Marchisan, 2001; Perry & Drummond, 2002).

Monitoring one's writing progress is especially important in becoming a good writer (Graham & Harris, 2001). This includes being receptive to feedback and applying what one learns in writing one paper to making the next paper better.

Social Constructivist Approaches As in reading, social constructivist approaches emphasize that writing is best understood as culturally embedded and socially constructed rather than internally generated. In the social constructivist approach to reading, the teacher's role shifts from transmitting knowledge to helping students restructure their knowledge. In this regard, both teachers and peers can serve as the more-knowledgeable reader. This social constructivist strategy also can be applied to writing (Dauite, 2001; Schultz & Fecho, 2001).

The Social Context of Writing The social constructivist perspective focuses on the social context in which writing is produced. It is important that students participate in a writing community to understand author–reader relationships and that they learn to recognize how their perspective might differ from that of other people (Hiebert & Raphael, 1996).

To see the importance of social context in writing, consider two students. One, Darjit, is a nine-year-old East Indian student who has lived in the Toronto area of Ontario his entire life (McCarthey, 1994). He reads and writes extensively, keeps scientific journals, and participated in classrooms with a strong emphasis on writing in his earlier school years. He is enthusiastic about his writing topic, a tribute to his grandmother who recently died. Darjit's teacher encourages him to write about her death, discussing various writing possibilities on this topic with him during their student–teacher writing conference. She and Darjit talk about the best ways to structure and organize the paper. His final writing product is a moving account of his grandmother's life and death. Darjit's teacher believes that writing plays an important role in education, and she communicates this enthusiastically to her students.

Contrast Darjit's writing experience with that of another East Indian student, Nabja, whose parents recently immigrated to the city. Although his English is good, Nabja has had few classroom experiences in which he has practised writing about his personal experiences, and he has never done any writing on his own outside the classroom. He feels very uncomfortable when the teacher asks him to write about personal experiences. In the student–teacher writing conference, Nabja is reluctant to discuss his feelings. Nabja's teacher has been mandated by the school board to include writing experiences in different subjects. She is not enthusiastic about this and spends little time working with Nabja to improve his writing.

As evidenced by Darjit's and Nabja's situations, the social context plays an important role in writing. Some students bring a rich background of writing to the classroom, others have little writing experience. In some classrooms the teacher places a high value on writing, in others the teacher treats writing as being less important.

Writing "Real Texts" about Meaningful Experiences, and Student–Teacher Writing Conferences In the social constructivist approach, students' writing should include opportunities to create "real" texts, in the sense of writing about personally meaningful situations. For example, Darjit, whose teacher frequently asks students to write about personal experiences, wrote about his grandmother's life and death and his teacher gave him considerable support for writing about this emotional experience. Student–teacher writing conferences play an important support role in helping students become better writers.

Peer Collaboration in Writing While working in groups, writers experience the processes of inquiry, clarification, and elaboration that are important in good writing (Webb & Palincsar, 1996). Students often bring diverse experiences to bear as they collaborate in writing text. Such rich, shared collaboration can produce new insights about what to write about and how (Daiute & Dalton, 1993).

Without explicit and guided instruction, however, collaborative writing experiences may differ among students. For instance, female and male students may differ in their approach to peer editing, especially when working with students of the same gender. According to Mary Styslinger, a high-school English teacher, female students tend to be highly involved in the editorial process. They readily question one another, focusing on the content of the written work versus its mechanics. Female students respond favourably to working together, balancing the ability to provide constructive feedback while supporting each other's writing efforts. Male students, on the other hand, are more reluctant to participate in such conversations. Their discussions tend to be more disconnected and task-orientated, with greater emphasis on writing mechanics (Styslinger, 1999).

School/Family/Community Connections For more than eight years, Deborah Berrill, a researcher and pre-service instructor at Queen's University, has recruited teacher candidates to serve as pen pals for local primary-grade students (Berrill & Gall, 1999). As part of this year-round program, emergent Grade 1 and 2 writers are matched with teacher candidates. In order to instill a sense of commitment, rapport, and community among the writers, the program is officially kicked off with a field trip where students visit the local university to meet their pen pals. These relationships are further developed and maintained through biweekly letter writing.

These letter-writing sessions provide students with a forum to support and enhance each other's writing efforts, as well as an opportunity for their teachers to provide explicit instruction with respect to writing. Berrill describes the efforts of one classroom teacher to create such a constructivist environment:

> On the days when the letters arrive, the students congregate on the carpet where they are individually called to the teacher's chair to receive them. Each student's letter is opened and read aloud (by either the teacher or the student) to the entire class. During the reading, time is taken to discuss relevant letter-writing protocol (e.g., mailing and return addresses, figures of speech, vocabulary, punctuation, question-asking and answering). After the reading,

Teaching Strategies
For Incorporating Writing into the Curriculum

✔ Use writing as a learning tool
- include writing across all subject areas (e.g., sciences, math, social sciences)
- have students write summaries about the main ideas of new content
- have students write novel examples illustrating new content
- have students record outstanding questions or concerns that were not answered as part of their studies

✔ Use free-writing assignments
- allow students to write openly about a topic (i.e., do not provide a question or direction for this writing beyond the general topic area)
- include a time limit for this writing (5–15 minutes is usually sufficient)
- encourage students to ask questions, record new ideas, and establish connections while writing

✔ Use creative-writing assignments
- encourage students to write using a number of genres (e.g., poetry, short stories, personal essays, narrative stories, expository essays)
- provide students with opportunities to write creatively about various topics
- encourage students to use writing as a vehicle for self-exploration and personal reflection

✔ Use formal writing assignments
- provide students with opportunities to write formally, as a forum for making formal arguments and as a vehicle for self-expression
- relate writing assignments to real-world events (e.g., "Global warming: Real fears or hype?" or "Are people really prejudiced?")
- model how to generate a writing topic, structure a paper and carry out editing and proofreading functions
- model effective planning and time-management skills
- require students to include an objective point of view, precise writing style, and evidence in support of their conclusions
- model how to use and cite references and provide students with opportunities to practise these skills

Source: Halonen (1999).

Reprinted by permission of United Features Syndicate, Inc.

all students are encouraged to ask questions or make comments about the letter, often providing the writer with potential responses for subsequent letters. Following the reading of the last letter, students return to their seats to begin the process of writing their reply letters.

Berrill notes that the letter-reading experience differs from most classroom reading/writing activities in that each student belongs to a community of readers/writers. Every student is called upon to be a "reading meaning-maker" regardless of his or her reading ability or background. Every student's letter is valued and every student is expected to be a letter-writer.

Mathematics

Controversy in Math Education   Mathematics education is currently swirled in controversy over whether a cognitive approach or a practice approach should be followed (Batcheldar, 2000; Stevenson, 2000; Stevenson, Hofer, & Randel, 1999). Some proponents of the cognitive approach argue against memorization and practice in teaching mathematics. They emphasize a constructivist approach to mathematical problem solving. Others assume that speed and automaticity are fundamental to effective mathematics achievement and emphasize that such skills can be acquired only through practice. In recent years, the constructivist approach has become increasingly popular. In this approach, effective instruction focuses on involving students in solving a problem or developing a concept and in exploring the efficiency of alternative solutions.

The field of mathematics education is undergoing dramatic change (Riedsel & Schwartz, 1999). In the low-tech past, shopkeeper paper-and-pencil math might have worked, but that no longer is the case in the high-tech age of computers and other electronic challenges that require new ways of understanding math. To meet these new challenges, the guide *Principles and Standards for School Mathematics*, **www.standards.nctm.org** (National Council of Teachers of Mathematics [NCTM], 2000), was developed. The National Council of Teachers of Mathematics is the world's largest mathematics education organization, with more than 100,000 members in Canada and the United States. Its primary mandate is to provide the necessary standards and leadership so that all students receive the highest-quality mathematics education possible. To this end, the council has also created the online guide *Illuminations*, to assist teachers when implementing the *Principles and Standards for School Mathematics*. The guide contains multimedia math lessons, Web resources, research reports, and articles, and can be found at **www.illuminations.nctm.org**. These standards emphasize that teaching math should involve giving students opportunities to

- solve meaningful math problems,
- develop critical reasoning skills,
- make connections to prior knowledge, and
- discuss math concepts with each other.

In general, these standards emphasize that teachers should guide students in making sense of math problems rather than directing them to complete computational drills.

Mathematical Thinking   Children already have a substantial understanding of numbers before they enter Grade 1. For example, in Ontario, students should understand the concepts of set and whole numbers, count verbally to 30, and use cardinal and ordinal numbers by the end of kindergarten. They are expected to create and extend simple patterns and be able to collect, display, and interpret data as part of their daily activities. They are expected to measure and compare length, weight, mass, capacity, and temperature of objects, and demonstrate awareness of the passage of time. In addition, students are expected to describe basic spatial relationships (e.g., above/below, near/far, in/out), and identify three-dimensional objects (e.g., cans, blocks, balls, cones) and two-dimensional shapes (e.g., circle, square, rectangle, triangle) (Ontario Ministry of Education, 1998).

As they continue in school, students learn many more-advanced kinds of numerical skills (Ginsburg, Klein, & Starkey, 1997). People often think that students just either learn or fail to learn what they are taught. In fact, what they learn often reflects their own thinking as much as anything they are taught. This is true even in the case of basic addition and subtraction, which might be thought to involve only the simplest of learning procedures, memorization.

Arithmetic   In most instruction aimed at helping students learn basic arithmetic facts (e.g., How much is 3 plus 9?), the goal is to teach children how to retrieve the answer from memory. For a period of several years after they enter school, however, children use a mix of strategies, including ones that no one ever taught them. Thus, on a problem such as 3 + 9, students in Grades 1, 2, and 3 will retrieve the answer from memory, some will count from 1, some will count from 9, and some will reason that 9 is 1 less than 10, that $3 + 10$ is 13, and therefore $3 + 9$ must be 12. These last two strategies are rarely taught by teachers or parents, yet children frequently use them anyway.

From his research laboratory at the University of Saskatchewan, Jamie Campbell and his colleagues (e.g., Campbell & Xue, 2001) have identified solution strategies that young students use when solving simple arithmetic problems. According to Campbell, students most often use procedural strategies such as counting, decomposition, and transformation when they are unable to retrieve solutions directly from memory. Over time, students become both much faster and more accurate when solving problems, in part because they increasingly use the faster and more accurate strategies, such as retrieval, and in part because they execute each of the strategies more quickly and accurately. Eventually, they solve all of these problems consistently, correctly, and very quickly.

As they progress through the elementary-school grades, students learn to solve multidigit arithmetic problems and problems involving fractions. Much of what's involved in learning these more advanced arithmetic skills is overcoming misconceptions. For example, in learning multidigit subtraction, students need to overcome "buggy" rules (named for the "bugs" that appear in faulty computer programs). Suppose a Grade 3 student is given the following four problems and generates the answers shown here:

$$
\begin{array}{cccc}
306 & 453 & 204 & 370 \\
-43 & -274 & -177 & -89 \\
\hline
343 & 179 & 177 & 281 \\
\end{array}
$$

Can you figure out what the student was doing wrong?

Analysis of the problems indicates that the student was following a "buggy" rule. The difficulty with these subtraction problems arose only when the problem involved borrowing across a zero; the student answered correctly on the problem that did not involve a zero and on the problem in which the zero was in the rightmost column. When it was necessary to borrow across a zero, the student proceeded in a consistent, but wrong, way that involved subtracting the zero from the number beneath it, rather than the reverse, and then not decrementing the number next to the zero (presumably because nothing had been borrowed from it). Such buggy algorithms are quite common in subtraction for students in Grades 3, 4, and 5 (VanLehn, 1986).

In an attempt to combat the "bugs" that interfere with students' learning, teachers should help students understand that mathematics is something you "do," not something you "remember." Canadian researchers Friesen and Stone (1996) suggest that teachers use arithmetic exploration or activity-based learning with their students. Students should be encouraged to participate in a cycle of exploration, discovery, reflection, and articulation when acquiring mathematical skills. They believe that such instruction will motivate students and help them view math as "fun." Group work should be promoted and teachers should ensure that all students are able to paraphrase concepts using their own words. Activities should be designed that allow for innovative solutions and interpretations.

Algebra   Students develop far more powerful mathematical reasoning when they learn algebra. A single equation can represent an infinite variety of situations. Even many students who get A's and B's in algebra classes, however, do so without understanding what they are learning—they simply memorize the equations.

One method to enhance students' beginning algebra skills is to use peer tutors. In one study (Allsopp, 1997), 14- and 15-year-old peer tutors were able to model higher-order thinking skills to students who were beginning high-school algebra. The tutors were trained by their teachers to deliver direct instruction including the use of effective learning strategies. Mnemonics were used to help students organize and remember problem-solving steps and concrete manipulatives were used to illustrate abstract concepts. This instruction was especially beneficial for students who were at risk for math failure (Allsopp, 1997).

Some Constructivist Principles   According to the constructivist perspective, students need to be provided with opportunities to explore and discover mathematical processes.

It is especially important that students are provided with opportunities to discuss problem-solving strategies (Ernest, 1997; Noddings, 1990). The following principles should be followed when teaching mathematics (Ernest, 1997; Noddings, 1990; Middleton & Goepfert, 1996).

Make Math Realistic and Interesting   Build your teaching of math around realistic and interesting problems. These problems might involve some kind of conflict, suspense, or crisis that motivates students' interest. The math problem-solving activities might centre on the student, community issues, scientific discoveries, or historical events. Math game-playing provides a motivating context for learning math. Questions that teachers use during game playing, such as "What do you need to roll on the dice to move your piece to number 10 on the board?" are more meaningful than decontextualized problems. Connecting math with other subject areas, such as science, geography, reading, and writing, also is recommended.

Thinking versus Rote Memorization   Math activities should be based on well-defined cognitive objectives. Activities should provide for knowledge extension and exploration. That is, students should be encouraged to construct their own understanding of a mathematical concept, test it, and revise their understanding accordingly (Ernest, 1997; Noddings, 1990).

Consider the Prior Knowledge of the Student   Students bring some knowledge of math prior to their arrival to the classroom, the starting point from which to continue their knowledge and understanding of mathematics (Ernest, 1997; Noddings, 1990). Evaluate what knowledge the students bring to the unit and the context in which instruction will take place. Provide sufficient information so that students are able to come up with a method for solving math problems, but withhold enough information so that they need to stretch their minds to solve the problems.

Make the Math Curricula Socially Interactive   Develop math projects that require students to work together to come up with a solution. Build into the math curriculum opportunities for students to use and improve their communication skills. Generate math projects that engender discussion, argument, and compromise. Constructivist teachers need to be skilled in structuring the social climate of the classroom so that students can discuss, reflect on, and make meaning of mathematical tasks (Ernest, 1997; Noddings, 1990).

Innovative Math Projects   The interest in making math instruction more constructivist has spawned a number of innovative programs (Middleton & Goepfert, 1996). These include programs for primary, junior/intermediate, and high school. We will describe a program at each level.

Primary   The Galileo Educational Network Association (GENA) works with educational organizations in Canada and the United States to provide a research-based approach to professional development for practitioners. Through an ongoing relationship with the University of Calgary, GENA sponsors teacher workshops designed to encourage the teaching of mathematics through exploration and investigation. GENA also encourages teachers to organize math fairs that provide students with the opportunity to develop their own math problems and entice their schoolmates, parents, and guests to work through their problems. At C. Ian McLaren Elementary School in Black Diamond, Alberta, a group of Grade 1 and 2 students hosted such a math fair. The teachers believed that their students' math performance was enhanced through the provision of engaging inquiry-based learning opportunities (MacNeil, 2002).

Junior and Intermediate   Students in the junior and intermediate grades can also participate in fun and challenging mathematics competitions. Recently, the Canadian Mathematics Competition hosted an annual competition for Grade 7 and 8 students called the "Gauss." The Ontario Mathematics Olympiad (O.M.O.) is another annual event. As part of this event, students are required to solve questions based on the curriculum. Some questions are answered individually, while others are answered as a team (O.A.M.E., 2002).

Through the Eyes of Teachers

The Joy of Problem Solving

I became a mathematics teacher because I enjoy solving problems and I wanted to share this joy with others. Solving a math problem is like solving a mystery or finishing a puzzle—I want my students to experience this sense of satisfaction in the context of mathematics.

Mathematics instruction should follow a blend of rehearsal/rote memorization and constructivism. I use both approaches to varying degrees depending on the skill set I want students to acquire. For example, I believe that it is more important for students to know how and when to use a formula than to simply recite it.

Teaching problem solving has changed since I went to school. Now, there is an emphasis on cooperative learning methods and the use of technology. These tools enable me to push students beyond the textbook questions, to engage them in constructing knowledge and to evaluate their ability to apply thinking and inquiry skills in the context of real-world problems.

Alice Kong
Secondary School Mathematics Teacher
Ontario

High School The Centre for Education in Mathematics and Computing at the University of Waterloo in Ontario organizes an annual Canadian Mathematics Competition open to students at all levels of high school. Competitions that emphasize written communication and thinking skills include "Fryer" (Grade 9), "Galois" (Grade 10), and "Hypatia" (Grade 11). The Euclid is a contest for students in their fifth year of high school, which emphasizes Euclidean geometry. The Centre for Education in Mathematics and Computing recognizes that problem solving is one of the most important components of teaching mathematics and hopes that its competitions help promote this awareness among members of society (Centre for Education in Mathematics, 2002). For further information about the competition, visit **www.cemc.uwaterloo.ca**.

Technology and Math Instruction The NCTM's *Principles and Standards for School Mathematics* (2000) recommend that calculators be used at all levels of mathematics instruction. Some access to computers is also necessary, if students are to be adequately educated for future careers. In many school systems, adequate funds for computers is a major issue. One recommendation by math curriculum experts James Middleton and Polly Goepfert (1996) is that instead of purchasing a lab full of low-end computers, schools should purchase one really good, top-of-the-line computer for each math classroom, along with a projection device or large-screen monitor. This allows students to participate in using significant technology every day. Teachers are also encouraged to familiarize themselves with mathematical software and Websites. For instance, various provincial mathematics associations such as the British Columbia Association of Mathematics Teachers (**www.bctf.ca/bcamt**) and the Ontario Association for Mathematics Education (**www.oame.on.ca**) provide access to math resources, software reviews, and Weblinks.

Connecting with Parents Teachers should encourage parents' active participation in their children's education. Parents can demonstrate that using math is a valuable tool by opening a bank account for their children, or by reading and following recipes together. Positive parental modelling emphasizes that math is a subject necessary for everyday life (Fotoples, 2000). Parental involvement is also essential if students experience math anxiety. Parents might consider having family math nights. Schools can offer resources, such as math manipulations or games like Mathblaster, that parents can use at home (Fotoples, 2000). As a teacher, you are also a mathematics coach—building self-confidence while refining the math skills of your students.

Continue to Be an Active Learner Yourself Friesen and Stone (1996) believe that few students will enjoy learning mathematics unless their teachers enjoy teaching it. If you teach math, one good active step is to join the National Council of Teachers of Mathematics (NCTM) and use its resources. NCTM has annual conferences, publishes an annual yearbook with stimulating chapters on recent developments in math education, and publishes journals such as *Mathematics Teacher*. For more information about NCTM, visit **www.nctm.org**.

Science

With an emphasis on discovery and hands-on laboratory investigation, many science teachers now help their students construct their knowledge of science (Abruscato, 2000; Tolman & Hardy, 1999). Constructivist teaching emphasizes that children have to build their own scientific knowledge and understanding. At each step in science learning, they need to interpret new knowledge in the context of what they already understand. Rather than putting fully formed knowledge into students' minds, in the constructivist approach teachers help them construct scientifically valid interpretations of the world and guide them in altering their scientific misconceptions (Chin, Mumby, & Krugly-Smolska, 1997; Martin, Sexton, & Gerlovich, 1999; Resnick & Chi, 1988).

Scientific Thinking   Students' problem solving is often compared to that of scientists. Both children and scientists ask fundamental questions about the nature of reality. Both also seek answers to problems that seem utterly trivial or unanswerable to other people (e.g., Why is the sky blue?). Both are granted by society the time and freedom to pursue answers to the problems they find interesting. This "child as scientist" metaphor has led researchers to ask whether students generate hypotheses, perform experiments, and reach conclusions concerning the meaning of their data in ways resembling those of scientists (Clinchy, Mansfield, & Schott, 1995).

Scientific reasoning often is aimed at identifying causal relations. In some ways, students' causal inferences are similar to those of scientists. For example, like scientists, they place a great deal of emphasis on causal mechanisms (Frye et al., 1996). Their understanding of how events are caused weighs more heavily in their causal inferences than do even such strong influences as whether the cause happened immediately before the effect (Shultz et al., 1986).

There also are important differences between the reasoning of students and the reasoning of scientists, however. This is true even of preadolescents who have had some instruction in school regarding the scientific method. One difference comes in the preadolescents' much greater difficulty in separating their prior theories from the evidence that they have obtained. Often, when they try to learn about new phenomena, they maintain their old theories regardless of the evidence (Chin, Mumby, & Krugly-Smolska, 1997; Kuhn, Schauble, & Garcia-Mila, 1992).

Another difference is that they are more influenced by happenstance events than by the overall pattern of occurrences (Kuhn, Amsel, & O'Laughlin, 1988). They also have difficulty designing new experiments that can distinguish conclusively among alternative causes. Instead, they tend to bias the experiments in favour of whichever hypothesis they began with, and sometimes they will see the results as supporting their original hypothesis even when the results directly contradict it (Schauble, 1990). Thus, although there are important similarities between students and scientists, in their basic curiosity and in the kinds of questions they ask, there are also important differences in their ability to design conclusive experiments and in the degree to which they can separate theory and evidence (Schauble, 1996).

Constructivist Teaching Strategies   Some contemporary constructivist approaches to teaching science include exploring everyday science problems that help students think about how science works and the social contexts of science (Linn, Songer, & Eylon, 1996).

Science in Elementary Schools

Exploring Everyday Science Problems   Most students are far more interested in science that addresses problems relevant to their lives than they are in discussing abstract theories. *Logical Reasoning in Science and Technology* (Aikenhead, 1991) is one curriculum that reflects such an emphasis. As part of this curriculum, which is used in Saskatchewan, Nova Scotia, and Newfoundland and Labrador, students are provided with an opportunity to connect science to real-world issues and practices. Students work collaboratively to gain an understanding about problems associated with societal issues such as the consumption of alcohol. For example, students at Brother Rice High School in St. John's, Newfoundland explore the role of alcohol in the death of Princess Diana while learning about the mechanics of Breathalyzer tests and their role as courtroom evidence. Consistent with constructivist approaches, the program encourages students to be active learners and emphasizes the connections between science, technology, and society.

Some critics of this and other constructivist approaches argue that too much attention is given to inquiry skills and not enough is given to discipline-specific information (American Association for the Advancement of Science, 1993; National Research Council, 1999). These

www.mcgrawhill.ca/college/santrock

researchers remind teachers that no one form of instruction can adequately meet the learning needs of all students. Instead, teachers are encouraged to develop a repertoire of teaching and instructional practices, creating balance between teacher-led and student-led approaches.

The Social Contexts of Science When considering the social contents of science, teacher–student and student–student collaborative interactions are stressed. Students investigate environmental science problems, create group or individual reports, and support each other as part of a community of science learners.

The Kids as Global Scientists project (Songer, 1993, 1996) is one program that captures the theme of the social contexts of science. For more than a decade, intermediate-grade students from around the world have been invited to enhance their knowledge and understandings of atmospheric sciences. As part of this program, students are first provided with the mandate to collect local weather data (using real time and archival satellite and weather imagery). Students then share this information with their peers around the world in an effort to gain a better understanding of severe weather and global environmental issues.

An Innovative National Science Program Let's Talk Science is a national organization committed to improving scientific literacy for all Canadians. In existence since 1991, the program has grown from a small outreach program housed at London's University of Western Ontario to a national organization encompassing 15 universities across seven provinces. Committed to the idea that science is an important and relevant subject area for all Canadians, the Let's Talk Science team of teachers, scientists, and graduate-student volunteers is continuously adding to its constructivist-based science workshops, programs, and conferences.

The organization offers three major programs: science activities for students from kindergarten to Grade 12, professional-development activities for classroom teachers, and community outreach. The In Your Community umbrella of programs provide after-school and summer programming for elementary-school students. Through the use of fun, hands-on activities, participants are encouraged to develop their understanding of scientific principles, literacy skills, and peripheral skills such as communication and problem solving. To promote science as a family interest, many of the activities include a take-home component. The organization also offers in-class workshops where Let's Talk Science staff and volunteers work with classroom teachers to provide science workshops for students. The Partnership Program matches graduate science students with classroom teachers for about eight months of the school year. As part of the program, science students visit the classroom, host visits to the university, and serve as a science resource for the school.

Enhancing the professional development of those directly involved in science instruction is another primary objective of the program. To this end, the organization offers several workshops and summer institutes. Let's Talk Science also offers more extensive and ongoing professional development and mentoring opportunities with university science faculty and graduate-student volunteers.

Finally, as part of the community outreach program, Let's Talk Science staff advocate for the advancement of science and science education throughout the country. To promote public awareness and advocacy, the organization hosts science presentations and demonstrations for community organizations (e.g., Guides, Scouts) and at community events (e.g., exhibitions, shows).

More than 500,000 Canadian youth and educators have participated in one or more of the Let's Talk Science programs from 1996 to 2003. The workshops have positively influenced students' and teachers' attitudes toward science and have helped teachers develop confidence in themselves as science instructors (Allison & Allison, 2001). For more about Let's Talk Science programs, contact the national office at 1-866-352-3060, or visit **www.letstalkscience.uwo.ca**.

Science in Secondary Schools In most high schools, science is taught in this sequence: biology, chemistry, physics. Many students take only the biology course or the biology–chemistry sequence and never enrol in physics. An increasing number of scientists argue that science courses should be taught in the opposite sequence and that the science

Peer tutors have been shown to help students enhance their mathematics and science skills.

subjects also should be taught in a more integrated fashion (Chin, Mumby, & Krugly-Smolska, 1997; Council of Ministers of Education Canada, 1995; Siegfried, 1998). They believe that to understand biology, students need to know a lot of chemistry. Life is made of molecules and survives by such processes as photosynthesis and respiration. Teaching biology first and chemistry second, in their view, is like watching *The Empire Strikes Back* before *Star Wars*. Likewise, understanding chemistry without knowing something about physics is difficult. Chemistry is based on energy changes and the forces between atoms, which are the subject matter of physics. The science curriculum also should include real-world problems that tie physics, chemistry, and biology together. And it should explore these aspects of scientific thinking: theory, prediction, skepticism, and methods for assessing evidence. In short, students need to be provided with opportunities to experience how science works versus being "told" about the process.

Another Innovative Science Program The Ontario Science Centre provides secondary-school students with a unique opportunity to participate in a hands-on science curriculum while earning university preparation science credits (Ontario Science Centre, 2002). In existence for more than 20 years, the Science School is the only program in the country where local secondary-school students can enrol in residential courses in biology, chemistry, physics, and calculus. Students participate in workshops and cooperative learning activities led by distinguished scientists in the fields of biotechnology, engineering, and space science. Because the Science School places a strong emphasis on the importance of science in the community and the importance of communicating science to all citizens, students are required to earn work-experience hours as part of their Science in Society course. Collectively, the science curriculum is intended to enhance students' scientific understanding, as well as help them acquire the essential communication and collaborative skills required for a successful career in the sciences. For more information about the Ontario Science Centre and the Science School, visit **www.ontariosciencecentre.ca**.

EVALUATING THE CONSTRUCTIVIST APPROACHES

Many contemporary educational psychologists are enthusiastic about constructivist approaches that portray the child as an active constructor of meaning (Anderson et al., 1996; Marshall, 1997). At many points in this book we have chronicled constructivist approaches to students' learning. This has included William James and John Dewey's initial infusion of constructivism into educational psychology early in the twentieth century (Chapter 1), Piaget's cognitive constructivism and Vygotsky's social constructivism (Chapter 2), constructivist emphases in moral education (values education, cognitive moral education) (Chapter 3), constructivist teaching strategies for improving children's creative thinking (Chapter 4), constructivist aspects of critical thinking and solving problems (Chapter 8), as well as the social constructivist dimensions of collaborative learning and cognitive and social constructivist strategies in domain-specific areas such as reading, writing, math, and science (this chapter). We will continue to present constructivist teaching strategies in the remaining chapters of this text.

Though constructivism has taken on an increasingly popular role in educational reform, not all educational psychologists and teachers embrace it. As we saw earlier in our discussion of science, some critics argue that too much attention is given to inquiry skills and not enough to the content of the discipline. This criticism also has been levelled at whole-language approaches to teaching reading, which are constructivist. Critics also say that many constructivist approaches are too relativistic and vague. And critics argue that constructivism is a general approach and theory that has not yet been proven to be the best approach to teaching children. We believe that students are best served when teachers adopt a repertoire of teaching and learning strategies rather then relying exclusively on either direct or constructivist approaches.

At this point we have examined a number of ideas about domain-specific constructivist approaches and evaluating the constructivist approaches. A review of these ideas is presented in Summary Table 9.2. In the next chapter, we will explore the roles of planning, instruction, and technology in teaching and learning.

Evaluating the Constructivist Approaches

That's what makes a man great; his flashes of insight, when he pierces through the nonsense of his time, and gets at something that really matters.

Robertson Davies
Canadian Author, 20th Century

www.mcgrawhill.ca/college/santrock

SUMMARY TABLE 9.2
Domain–Specific Constructivist Approaches, and Evaluating the Constructivist Approaches

What are constructivist approaches in reading?	• The basic-skills-and-phonics approach emphasizes decoding skills and is reflective of the cognitive constructivist view. • The whole-language approach focuses on becoming immersed in the world of print and fits within a social constructivist framework. • The balanced-instruction approach emphasizes the importance of modelling and strategic processes in the context of authentic learning experiences and contains elements of both cognitive and social constructivist frameworks. • Metacognitive strategies, as well as automatic and effortful processes, are involved in decoding and comprehending words. • Reciprocal teaching is a valuable technique in helping students improve their reading. Book clubs and some family literacy programs also reflect the social constructivist perspective.
What are constructivist approaches in writing?	• Cognitive constructivist approaches to writing emphasize constructing meaning and developing strategies. Planning, problem-solving, revising, and metacognitive strategies are thought to be especially important in improving students' writing. • Social constructivist approaches to writing focus on the social context in which writing is produced. This social context includes the importance of students participating in a writing community to understand author/reader relationships and perspective taking. • Social constructivist approaches to writing include writing "real texts" about meaningful experiences, teacher–student writing conferences, and peer collaboration.
What are constructivist approaches in mathematics?	• Children have a substantial understanding of numerical concepts before they enter Grade 1. As they proceed through school, students learn many more advanced kinds of numerical skills. • Currently, there is controversy in math education about whether curricula should be more cognitively or more practically oriented. • Reforms focus on making math education more meaningful, making connections to prior knowledge, and discussing math concepts.
What are constructivist approaches in science?	• Students' thinking skills share certain characteristics of those of scientists (e.g., questioning of reality, emphasis on causal mechanisms), but also differ in important ways (e.g., more influenced by happenstance, more inclined to retain old beliefs, difficulty separating theory and evidence). • Constructivist approaches to science emphasize hands-on laboratory investigations and discovery learning. Let's Talk Science and the Ontario Science Centre's Science School are excellent examples of science programs that have a constructivist orientation. • The sequence of science courses at the secondary-school level is controversial, with critics calling for a reversed order of instruction and greater integration across the sciences.
What controversy is associated with constructivist approaches?	• Many contemporary educational psychologists are enthusiastic about the constructivist approaches that portray the student as an active constructor of meaning. • Some critics say the constructivist approaches do not adequately teach content, are relativistic, and are vague. • Students may be best served when teachers adopt a repertoire of teaching and learning strategies rather then relying on either direct or constructivist approaches exclusively.

Denna has a test in her Grade 11 math class this Friday. In preparation, she has spent the last several evenings studying the statistical formulas for measures of central tendency and variability. To do this, she has quizzed herself repeatedly. In the beginning she got them confused, but after repeated practice she can now recite the formula for each without fail. She is certain that she will have no difficulties on the test.

When she receives her test on Friday, the first thing she does is write down all of the formulas before she can forget them, certain that they will be all she needs to do well on the test. After writing down the formulas, she begins reading the test. Here is the first question:

Mr. Peters' math class received these scores on last week's test:

45, 54, 65, 68, 70, 72, 72, 73, 75, 78, 80, 80, 80, 80, 82, 83, 84, 84, 84, 84, 84, 85, 86, 87, 87, 88, 90, 91, 92, 92, 92, 93, 94, 95, 95, 95, 96, 96, 97, 97, 98, 98, 99, 99, 99, 99

Find the mean, median, mode, variance, and standard deviation.

Denna anxiously looks at her list of formulas. She knows which formula goes with each measure. For instance, she knows that the formula for the mean is $\Sigma x / n$. The problem is that she doesn't know what Σx represents. She is reasonably sure that "/n" means she is to divide by n, but what is n? When looking at the rest of the formulas, she realizes that she does not understand the other symbols as well. She stares at the test in dismay. After all that studying and careful memorization, she can't complete a single problem on the test.

- What are the issues in this case?
- What went wrong for Denna?
- What should she do differently if she wants to do better on her next test?
- If you were Denna's teacher, how would you help your students to prepare for this type of test?
- Explain how the assessment protocol could be better linked to the instruction.

CHAPTER REVIEW

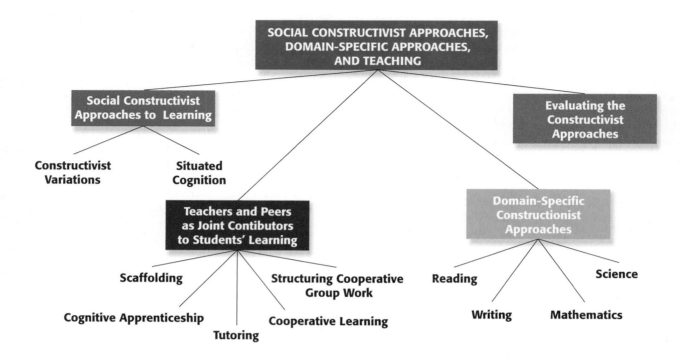

To obtain a detailed review of this chapter, study these two summary tables:

KEY TERMS

constructivism 276
social constructivist
    approaches 276

situated cognition 277
scaffolding 277
cognitive apprenticeship 277
cooperative learning 280

basic skills-and-phonetics
    approach 287
whole language approach 287

balanced-instruction
    approach 287
reciprocal teaching 289
book clubs 290

 PROFESSIONAL DEVELOPMENT/PORTFOLIO ACTIVITIES

1. What Is Transfer?

In a short paper, define and describe the concept of "transfer." Consider the issues of retaining subject matter and students' application of skills. Explain how you might make the transfer skills more successful. Place this essay in your portfolio.

2. Are You a Problem Solver?

Describe the characteristics of a person who is an effective problem solver. How does open-ended problem solving lead to knowledge and skills that are transferable? Why is the transfer of knowledge so critical in learning new subjects or skills? Why are these skills so important in today's society?

3. Scaffolding, Cognitive Apprenticeship, and Tutoring

Social constructivist approaches to teaching and learning involve a variety of specific strategies such as scaffolding, cognitive apprenticeship, tutoring, and cooperative learning. How are these strategies similar and how are they different? Which strategies would you use to teach word-recognition skills in Grade 2, writing skills in Grade 5, and social skills in Grade 8? Why?

 INTERNET ACTIVITIES

1. Creative Lessons on the Web

The Internet is a valuable resource for lesson plans and classroom activities. Find an online lesson plan Website, select two or three lesson plans, and evaluate them for their educational value. Do the lessons foster students' creative and divergent thinking? What roles do the teacher and the classroom environment play in fostering such creativity? Explain how you would modify the online lessons to approximate your particular teaching approach and classroom environment. How would these lessons help students develop creative and divergent thinking skills?

2. A Website Evaluation Activity

Find and evaluate a Website that could be used in a social studies classroom. Does this resource portray events from several different perspectives? What kinds of historical artifacts are provided for student review and analysis? Will students be challenged to think critically about past events or current social issues? How would you design a lesson or project using this Website?

Connect to the Online Learning Centre at www.mcgrawhill.ca/college/santrock **to explore possible answers.**

Visit the *Educational Psychology* Online Learning Centre at
www.mcgrawhill.ca/college/santrock
to access Websites related to the above Internet Activities as well as chapter quizzes, a searchable glossary, and other learning and study tools.

www.mcgrawhill.ca/college/santrock

10 Planning, Instruction, and Technology

Preview

In this chapter, we will examine teaching and learning primarily at the level of the overall lesson or unit, often making use of the learning principles discussed in Chapters 7 to 9. We will focus on teacher-centred and learner-centred lesson planning, and will study many dimensions of incorporating technology into lesson planning and instruction. Some central questions include:

- What are the most effective ways to plan?
- What objectives should you keep in mind when planning lessons?
- How should homework be handled at different grade levels?
- What strategies should be followed in learner-centred planning and instruction?
- How can the curriculum be integrated?
- What are some guidelines for choosing and using technology?

PLANNING, INSTRUCTION, AND TECHNOLOGY

Planning
- Instructional Planning
- Time Frames and Planning

Teacher-Centred Lesson Planning and Instruction
- Teacher-Centred Lesson Planning
- Evaluating Teacher-Centred Instruction
- Direct Instruction and Teacher-Centred Instructional Strategies

Learner-Centred Lesson Planning and Instruction
- Learner-Centred Principles
- Three Learner-Centred Instructional Strategies
- Integrating the Curriculum
- Evaluating Learner-Centred Instruction

Technology and Education
- The Technology Factor
- The Technology Landscape
- Technology and Sociocultural Diversity
- The Realities of Information and Communication Technology and Education

Teaching Stories: Reg Hawes

For more than 15 years, Reg Hawes has been a social science and history teacher. Reg began his career as a secondary-school teacher and has assumed a variety of roles, including head of the history and contemporary studies department. He has also worked for the Ontario Ministry of Education. He is currently cross-appointed at the University of Toronto Schools and the Ontario Institute for Studies in Education. Below, Reg recalls his first experiences with simulations as an instructional tool and elaborates on how he uses them in his classrooms.

"My interest in simulations started in high school in Lanigan, Saskatchewan. Shakespeare's Julius Caesar *was required reading for Grade 10 English. Our teacher, Mr. Harrison, didn't have us complete 'conventional' activities, like memorizing soliloquies or plot lines. Instead, he had us simulate what a trial for the conspirators who assassinated Julius Caesar might have looked like. The only requirement was that any evidence used in the trial be drawn from the text. We delved into the book with an enthusiasm that I had never witnessed before in an English class. The trial lasted four days. The defence and the prosecution presented copious details from the text and used all of their creativity to simulate the trial conditions. To this day, I suspect*

that I, and many of my classmates, remember more details about Julius Caesar than any other literary work we were required to study.

"Today, I use simulations frequently as part of my social science and history classes and my students respond favourably to them. For instance, as part of a Grade 9 social studies unit entitled Coming to Canada, I ask students to research immigration policies and assume the identity of an immigrant. The culminating activity involves a town-hall meeting where the Minister of Finance announces cutbacks to community support programs for immigrants, such as ESL and daycare. In the simulated meeting, students are required to make informed arguments to defend the rights of immigrants and maintain community programs. I have also used simulations to recreate the trial of Louis Riel and debate the legitimacy of the Vietnam War (from the perspective of the president, soldiers, war protestors, Vietnamese citizens, etc.).

"Simulations offer an authentic learning experience for students. By researching and exploring the topic at hand, students develop a profound understanding of and empathy for the people and events that they are studying."

Planning

Instructional Planning | Time Frames and Planning

If you plan the day's transactions and follow that plan, you carry the thread that will guide you through the maze of the busiest life. But if you make no plan, chaos will reign.

Victor Hugo
French Novelist and Playwright, 19th Century

PLANNING

It has been said that when people fail to plan, they plan to fail. Many successful people attribute their accomplishments to effective planning. For example, Lee Iacocca (1984), former chairman of Chrysler Corporation, credits his success to his weekly planner. Our introduction to planning describes what instructional planning is and the time frames of planning.

Instructional Planning

Planning is a critical aspect of being a competent teacher (Parkay & Mass, 2000). While spontaneous (or "aha!") teaching moments are wonderful events, good planning is necessary to ensure that students and teachers are ready and able to make the most of these teachable opportunities when they come along. **Instructional planning** *involves developing a systematic, organized strategy for planning lessons.*

Instructional planning finds its beginnings in the systematic-design model of instruction and behavioural psychology. The instructional-design model divides learning into small, clearly observable and sequential steps that can be monitored and reinforced. While some have criticized the model for being too technical or mechanistic in its approach to addressing cognitive processes and environmental interactions, we believe that the model is useful for teachers with respect to setting objectives, sequencing instruction, and assessing and evaluating student learning. Teachers need to decide what they are going to teach, the sequence in which the material is going to be taught, the best methods for instruction, and techniques for reinforcing the learning (Cranton, 2000).

It might seem tedious to spend so much time planning and writing out lesson, unit, and yearly plans. However, such planning provides a standard with which to compare how well curriculum and lessons are meeting educational goals. Furthermore, students appreciate lessons that make the best use of instructional time. This is not to suggest that planning prescribes a rigid format or an inflexible teaching script that must be adhered to in all cases. Rather, lesson plans will vary with the type of lesson, the educational objectives, and the needs and interests of students.

Ministries of Education, school boards, and individual schools often mandate instructional planning for their teachers. Many principals require teachers to keep written plans, and in some cases teachers may be asked to submit lesson plans several weeks in advance. In some jurisdictions, lesson plans are required to be posted on school Websites so that parents can be informed about what and how their children are learning. Written lesson plans provide a starting point for critically examining performance and improving practice. Principals or supervisors may refer to these plans when observing classroom teachers. Finally, lesson plans allow substitute teachers to keep classes on track and focused.

Time Frames and Planning

Developing systematic time plans involves knowing what needs to be done and when to do it, or focusing on "task" and "time." Here is one helpful six-part task and time plan (Douglass & Douglass, 1993):

What Needs to Be Done

1. *Set instructional goals* (What do I expect to accomplish?)
2. *Plan activities* (What do I have to do to reach the goals?)
3. *Set priorities* (Which tasks are more important than others?)

The Time to Do It

4. *Make time estimates* (How much time will each activity take?)
5. *Create schedules* (When will we do each activity?)
6. *Be flexible* (How will I handle unexpected occurrences?)

Robert Yinger (1980) identified five time frames of teacher planning: yearly planning, term planning, unit planning, weekly planning, and daily planning. Figure 10.1 illustrates

these time frames and shows planning for them. Yinger also recommends that teachers attend to four areas when planning: goals, sources of information, form, and criteria for evaluating the effectiveness of the planning. Figure 10.1 shows what is involved in these areas across the five different time frames.

Although planning is a key dimension of successful teaching, don't overplan to the point of becoming an automaton. Develop organized plans and try to carry them out, but be flexible; as a year, month, week, or day unfolds, adapt to changing circumstances. A controversial current event or necessary topic might emerge that you did not originally include. Monitor and rework your plans as the school year goes by to suit these changing circumstances.

If you plan effectively, you won't have to keep all of the details of a lesson in mind all of the time (Middleton & Goepfert, 1996). Your plan lets you focus on the immediate dialogue you are having with students and guides the interactive aspect of your instruction.

> You've got to be careful if you don't know where you are going because you might not get there.
>
> Yogi Berra
> *American Baseball Star, 20th Century*

Time Span	Teacher's Planning Activities
Yearly planning	• Planning that is general in nature; used to establish broad content areas, sequencing, and materials • Involves data provided from the school, the school board, and the provincial education ministry
Term planning	• Focuses on detailing the content to be covered in the upcoming term and establishes a weekly schedule of units, lessons, and activities • Considers time and available resources • Considers information gathered from students
Unit planning	• Develops a sequence of meaningful, comprehensive, integrated, and organized learning experiences • Based on an awareness of students' abilities, learning styles, and interests • Considers available materials, time, learning goals, and facilities
Weekly planning	• Consists of weekly activities that maintain continuity and regularity of activities • Connected to a unit plan and adjusted to address special needs and foreseeable interruptions (e.g., assemblies, holidays, special events) • Uses and displays data collected from students' performances in preceding weeks
Daily planning	• Involves setting up and arranging the class for the next day • Involves activities and adjusting the daily schedule in accordance with last-minute changes or school events. • Daily planning can be written on the blackboard or discussed with students

FIGURE 10.1   Five Time Spans of Teacher Planning and Their Occurrence over the School Year

Many teachers rely heavily on published teachers' guides or textbook structures to direct their instructional planning. This can have positive benefits because, with activities or lessons developed for the entire time, you can focus more on the day-to-day aspects of teaching. However, you might want to go into greater depth about some topics and develop larger projects for the entire term than are included in the teachers' guides.

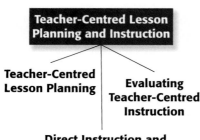

TEACHER-CENTRED LESSON PLANNING AND INSTRUCTION

Traditionally, the focus in North American schools has been on teacher-centred lesson planning and instruction. In this approach, the teacher is the central figure in planning and goal setting for the classroom. Teacher-centred instruction is highly structured and places responsibility for classroom activities, management, and socioemotional climate squarely in the hands of the teacher.

Teacher-Centred Lesson Planning

Lesson planning in a teacher-centred approach includes creating behavioural objectives, analyzing tasks, and developing instructional taxonomies.

Creating Behavioural Objectives   **Behavioural objectives** *are statements that communicate proposed changes in students' behaviour to reach desired levels of performance.* Behavioural objectives should be specific, clear, and explicitly stated (Cranton, 2000; Mager, 1962). Learning to write behavioural objectives is something that requires practice and, often, feedback from other teachers (Cranton, 2000). Robert Mager (1962) maintains that behavioural objectives should consist of three parts:

- *Students' behaviours.* Teachers need to focus on what the students will learn and describe these activities as observable behaviours.
- *Conditions under which the behaviour will occur.* These are statements about how the behaviours will be evaluated or tested.
- *Performance criteria.* These statements focus on what level of performance is considered acceptable in the activities or behaviours.

Recently, Cranton (2000) proposed the addition of another component to this list— flexibility. For example, these behavioural objectives can be applied to a secondary-school history class where students are required to describe five causes of the Riel Rebellion (students' behaviour). Suppose that the statement of objectives outlines that students would be required to list and discuss these five causes in an essay (conditions under which the behaviour will occur), and that presenting and discussing four of the five causes would be considered acceptable performance (performance criteria). These performance criteria are not clear and could be improved by adding that presenting and discussing four out of five of the causes presented in class would be considered acceptable performance (flexibility).

Analyzing Tasks   Another key aspect of teacher-centred planning is task analysis. Task analysis is based on the assumption that learning is hierarchical and that specific elements must precede others in order for learning to occur (Gagne, 1975). Therefore, **task analysis** *breaks down complex tasks into their component parts* (Alberto & Troutman, 1996). A basic framework for analyzing tasks involves the following steps (Cranton, 2000):

- Selecting the objectives that will form the basis for the analysis
- Considering one objective at a time and making a list of the prerequisites that students must possess
- Itemizing what students must know in order to learn the particular skill or objective
- Ordering or arranging the items into a hierarchical "tree structure"

• Testing the analysis with colleagues and then in class
• Evaluating how well it worked in terms of meeting stated objectives
• Modifying the order as needed

Flexibility—the willingness to discuss objectives with students and to modify objectives if they are not clear or comprehensive—is vital in writing effective behavioural objectives.

Developing Instructional Taxonomies   Teacher-centred approaches to lesson planning and instruction have involved the development and use of instructional taxonomies. A **taxonomy** *is a classification system.* One of the most common taxonomies used in education is Bloom's taxonomy, which consists of three categories or domains: cognitive, affective, and psychomotor.

The Cognitive Domain   Bloom's cognitive domain focuses on knowledge and the development of cognitive skills such as recognition, recall, procedural patterning, judgment, and decision making. The cognitive domain is divided into six major categories ranked in a hierarchical fashion (Bloom et al., 1956, 1964b, 1994):

Knowledge. The focus of this category is on the recall or recognition of information. For example, an objective from this domain of learning might be to *recite* "O Canada" from memory, or to *list* the safety rules for operating machinery as part of a shop class.

Comprehension. At this level students should understand information and be able to explain it in their own words. An objective aimed at this level might ask students to *explain* in their own words what is meant by "in loco parentis" or to *discuss* how a specific safety rule can be used to prevent accidents.

Application. This level is categorized by the use of knowledge to solve real-life problems. For example, an objective at this level might be to *demonstrate* what has been learned about using a word processor to create a brochure, or to *solve* word problems in mathematics using specific formulas or equations.

Analysis. The focus in this category involves breaking down complex information into smaller parts and examining interrelationships with other information. For example, students could be asked to compare Canadian approaches to representative democracy with those of the United States. In a transportation shop class, students might be asked to *classify* assorted engine parts by their primary functions.

Synthesis. This category is aimed at the combination of elements and the creation of new information. For example, an objective might ask students to *predict* what communications technology might look like in ten years based on existing technologies, or to *design* a machine to perform a specific task.

Evaluation. This is the highest level of the cognitive domain and involves judgment and decision making. For example, an objective written at this level might require students to *critique* the implications of the Kyoto Accord for different sectors of Canadian society, or to *assess* the contributions made by Canadian scientists to the North American space program.

Although Bloom's taxonomy is presented as a hierarchy, where higher-order objectives are built on lower-order ones, many educators tend to strip the objectives of their level. Instead, they use objectives as a comprehensive way of considering different cognitive goals.

Bloom's cognitive objectives are useful for planning assessment. For example, teachers often use true/false, matching, short-answer, or multiple-choice test items to assess knowledge and comprehension of materials presented in class. Essay questions, class discussions, projects, and portfolios are used for assessing students' application, analysis, synthesis, and evaluation skills.

The Affective Domain   The affective taxonomy consists of five objectives related to emotional responses, such as feelings, values, motivations, and attitudes toward tasks (Krathwohl, Bloom, & Masia, 1964; Bloom, 1986). Each of the five objectives requires students to demonstrate some degree of commitment or emotional intensity:

Receiving. This first level of the affective domain focuses on becoming aware of, or attending to, something in the environment. For example, an objective based on this category might ask students to listen carefully to an Aboriginal speaker describing her life in the Far North, or to remember the names of new students as they are introduced to the class.

Responding. This category involves motivation to learn and demonstrate new behaviours as a result of experience. An objective at this level might involve students' motivation to read more books following a presentation by a guest speaker about the importance of reading.

Valuing. This level is categorized by becoming involved or committed to some experience. For example, an objective at this level might be to have students appreciate or value reading as a life-long skill and interest.

Organizing. This affective level is characterized by the integration of new values into an already-existing set of values. For example, an organizing objective might be to have students start an after-school club or activity group.

Value characterizing. The highest level of the affective domain represents acting in accordance with a specific value and being firmly committed to it. For example, an objective at this level might involve students exercising every day of the school year as a way of demonstrating the value of physical activity.

The Psychomotor Domain   Most people link the idea of motor activity with physical education, dance, or athletics, but many other activities such as keyboarding and working with calipers and other instruments are relevant as well. Bloom's objectives in the psychomotor domain include:

Reflex movements. Reactions are characterized as involuntary responses to a stimulus, without conscious thought. For example, students might be expected to extend their hands to catch a ball that is tossed at them.

Basic fundamentals. Basic voluntary and purposeful movements or manipulations of objects characterize this level. For example, an objective at this level might be to have students turn a knob on a microscope to bring an object into focus.

Perceptual abilities. The aim of this category is to use human senses to guide movements and manipulations. A perceptual objective might be to have students distinguish the difference in how an engine sounds when it is running "rich" or "lean," and what that implies for making appropriate adjustments to fuel intake.

Physical abilities. This domain level is characterized by general skills in endurance, strength, agility, and flexibility. An objective at this stage might be to have students develop their stamina in running long distances, or to practise hitting a ball with a bat.

Skilled movements. At this level, complex physical skills are executed with some degree of proficiency. For example, a skilled-movement objective for culinary-arts students might be to break an egg into a bowl with one hand. For dance students, an objective might be to accomplish a *très jeté*.

Non-discussive movements. This level of the psychomotor domain categorizes the ability to communicate feelings or emotions through bodily movements or actions. For example, a learning objective at this level might be to have visual-arts students express their reactions to a piece of music.

Bloom's taxonomies for the cognitive, affective, and psychomotor domains are used by many teachers to help plan instruction. In the past, instructional planning tended to focus on cognitive or behavioural objectives. Bloom's taxonomy provides for a more expansive consideration of skills by including the affective and psychomotor domains. Figure 10.2 presents useful action verbs associated with each of Bloom's categories that can be used when developing instructional objectives.

Direct Instruction and Teacher-Centred Instructional Strategies

Direct instruction is a structured, teacher-centred approach that is characterized by teacher direction and control, high teacher expectations for students' progress, maximum time spent on academic tasks, and minimal negative affect (Joyce & Weil, 1996; Woloshyn, Elliott, & Kaucho, 2001; see Chapter 8 for a more detailed discussion about direct instruction). Teacher direction and control take place when the teacher chooses students' learning tasks, directs students' learning of the tasks, and minimizes the amount

FIGURE 10.2 **Action Verbs for Writing Objectives in the Cognitive, Affective, and Psychomotor Domains**

COGNITIVE DOMAIN

Category	Associated Verbs
Knowledge	List, read, identify, define, indicate, describe, name, quote, underline
Comprehension	Translate, transform, summarize, paraphrase, illustrate, interpret, estimate, interpolate, extrapolate, classify, categorize, re-organize, explain, predict
Application	Apply, generalize, relate, use, employ, transfer, graph, exemplify, illustrate, tabulate, calculate, compute, derive, calibrate
Analysis	Analyze, contrast, compare, distinguish, detect, edit, discriminate
Synthesis	Produce, constitute, modify, originate, propose, plan, design, combine, organize, synthesize, develop, formulate
Evaluation	Judge, argue, validate, predict, assess, decide, appraise, conclude, evaluate, explain, criticize

AFFECTIVE DOMAIN

Category	Associated Verbs
Receiving	Accept, differentiate, listen, separate, select, share, agree
Responding	Approve, applaud, comply, follow, discuss, volunteer, practise, spend time with, paraphrase
Valuing	Argue, debate, deny, help, support, protest, participate, subsidize, praise
Organizing	Discuss, compare, balance, define, abstract, formulate, theorize, organize
Value characterizing	Change, avoid, complete, manage, resolve, revise, resist, require

PSYCHOMOTOR DOMAIN

Category	Associated Verbs
Reflex movements	Blink, stretch, relax, jerk, straighten up
Basic fundamentals	Walk, run, jump, push, pull, manipulate, catch, grasp, stand
Perceptual abilities	Follow, dodge, maintain, identify, read, write, list, balance, trace, brush, print, pronounce
Physical abilities	Hop, skip, jump, run, touch, lift, push, pull, tap, float, hit, throw, toss, strum
Skilled movements	Draw, dance, ski, skate, paint, build, volley, race, whistle, march, somersault, hammer, sculpt, sketch
Non-discussive movements	Pantomime, mimic, direct, perform, communicate, gesture, use body movement

of non-academic talk. Teacher-centred instructional strategies that reflect direct instruction include orienting; lecturing, explaining, and demonstrating; questioning and discussing; mastery learning; seatwork; and homework.

Orienting   Establish a framework for new learning by orienting or preparing students to receive new information before presenting and explaining it (Joyce & Weil, 1996). To orient students for new learning, teachers can (1) review the previous day's activities, (2) discuss the lesson's objectives, (3) provide clear, explicit instructions about the work to be done, and (4) give an overview of the day's lesson. Orienting and structuring lessons in this way has been linked to improved student achievement (Fisher et al., 1980; Cavalier & Klein, 1998).

Diversity and Education
The Internet and Cultural Diversity in the Classroom: WebQuests

One of the most effective ways to use the Internet in your classroom to promote multicultural exploration and diversity is through project-centred small-group activities that encourage active learning and the social construction of knowledge. WebQuests are project-based activities that students find engaging and teachers find effective in making good use of student Internet time. Moreover, Webquests are a means for exploring the cultural interests of diverse student groups and tailoring resources and materials to suit student needs and interests in a cooperative learning format. Ritchie (1999) described collaborative WebQuest projects as opportunities for students to exchange information with people from other countries, cultures, languages, ethnicities, or religions. WebQuest activities that focus on cultural issues or investigation help students feel part of the global community outside the classroom.

WebQuest activities base most or all of the information used by learners on resources found on the World Wide Web. WebQuests are designed to focus on *using* information (rather than looking for it) and to support learners' thinking in analysis, synthesis, and evaluation. The WebQuest model was developed in 1995 by Bernie Dodge at the University of San Diego. Dodge outlines two types of WebQuests: short-term and longer-term. The instructional goal of a short-term WebQuest is knowledge acquisition and integration. At the end of a short-term WebQuest, usually one to three class sessions, students will have examined and explored new information and constructed their own understanding of it. Longer-term WebQuests are designed to provide students with opportunities for extending and refining knowledge. A longer-term WebQuest typically takes from one week to one month to complete and involves analyzing a body of knowledge, transforming it, and demonstrating understanding by creating a product that others can respond to either in class or on the computer.

"Dispelling the Myth: A Study of Cultures" is an example of a WebQuest developed to explore cultural diversity for students in Grades 4 to 6. The WebQuest scenario describes a fight between two students. The fight started when one of the students made fun of the other student's lunch; the lunch was a traditional Mexican meal. When the students returned to the classroom, a class meeting was held to discuss the incident. During the class discussion, the point was made that students need to respect each other's culture and heritage, and one student shouts out that he can't respect a culture he doesn't understand. Thus begins a WebQuest on Mexican and American cultures.

Whitehorse Elementary School in the Yukon uses cultural WebQuests extensively to provide students with cultural experiences and learning that they would not otherwise be able to obtain. The Whitehorse Elementary Web page lists a variety of cultural WebQuests from around the globe, including "Dispelling the Myth." The Whitehorse Web page is located at **www.yesnet.yk.ca/schools/wes/webquests/countries**. Further information and examples of WebQuests can be found at the Bernie Dodge Website: **http://webquest.sdsu.edu/**.

Advance organizers *are teaching activities and techniques that establish a framework and orient students to material before it is presented* (Ausubel, 1960). You can use advance organizers when you begin a lesson to help students see the "big picture" of what is to come and how information is meaningfully connected.

Advance organizers come in two forms: expository and comparative (Mayer, 1984). **Expository advance organizers** *provide students with new knowledge that will orient them to the upcoming lesson*. The chapter-opening and within-chapter cognitive maps in this book are expository advance organizers. They provide you with new information about what you will study in the chapter and its main sections, and they are analogous to providing an overall outline of what a lesson will be about. Another way to provide an expository advance organizer is to describe the lesson's theme and why it is important to study this topic. For example, in orienting secondary-school students to exploring the influence of France and French culture on Canada, the teacher might say that they are going to study the *couriers du bois*—who they were, what their lives were like, and their artifacts. To heighten student interest, the teacher might suggest that the class is going to study "worlds in collision," as European settlers were unfamiliar with the native North American culture that they encountered. The teacher emphasizes how exploring these themes will help everyone in the class see the world around them through new eyes.

Comparative advance organizers *introduce new material by connecting it with what students already know.* For example, in the history class mentioned above the teacher could suggest that the French influence in Canada is a mirror of contemporary North American influence on Europe, because the transatlantic flow of ideas and resources changed life on both continents. The teacher then asks students to further consider how the French influence on Canada connects with the Spanish invasion of Mexico, which they examined last week.

Lecturing, Explaining, and Demonstrating Lecturing, explaining, and demonstrating are common teacher activities in the direct-instruction approach. Researchers have found that effective teachers spend more time explaining and demonstrating new material than do their less-effective counterparts (McKeachie, 1998; Rosenshine, 1985).

Questioning and Discussing Questions play a key role in the teaching and learning process, enabling teachers and students to define what is known, to examine new ideas and concepts, and to apply and extend familiar knowledge (Morgan & Saxton, 1994; Weinstein, 1997). Questioning is also a necessary part of developing metacognition and effective thinking. Questions are most often categorized as factual, conceptual, or contextual. Morgan and Saxton (1991) proposed an alternative approach to questioning that focuses on the question's purpose or the teacher's intent. Questions viewed from this perspective are intended to elicit information, shape understanding, or encourage reflection.

Questions that elicit information are often used as lead-ins for higher-level questions that focus on understanding or reflection. For example, a teacher might ask what year the Battle of Hastings occurred, and then ask for the political or social causes of the battle.

Questions that shape understanding encourage students to elaborate on and express their thoughts and feelings about the material being studied. For example, when assessing why soldiers fought in the Battle of Hastings a teacher might ask students to consider the viewpoints of the clergy, the leaders of the battle, common soldiers, and modern society.

Finally, questions that encourage reflection require students to explore their ideas and feelings. For example, a teacher might ask a class to defend the view that Eminem is a great musician. For further ideas about how to use questions to elicit information, shape students' understanding, and encourage reflection, see the Teaching Strategies on page 319.

Neil Postman (1979) has suggested that questioning and discussing are as much a part of language arts as reading and writing, but are often neglected in students' schooling. When using questions and discussions it is important to respond to each student's learning needs while maintaining the group's interest and attention. It is important to distribute participation widely while also retaining the enthusiasm of eager volunteers. An additional challenge is allowing all students to contribute while still maintaining the focus of the lesson.

Through the Eyes of Teachers

The Value of Higher-Level-Thinking Questions

Using higher-level-thinking questions challenges our students to think beyond the obvious and encourages them to forge a link between their thoughts and experiences. As they listen to discussions that follow from asking higher-level questions, students learn from their peers. They enjoy the challenge associated with these questions and, with repeated practice, become more proficient at developing their thoughts and presenting advanced answers. It is vital that our students develop higher-level-thinking skills if they are to be our future leaders.

Janice King
Grade 5 Teacher and 24-Year Teaching Veteran
Former Math Enrichment Instructor, Remedial Math Instructor, Vice-Principal, and Principal
Newfoundland

Teaching Strategies
For Lecturing

✔ Be prepared
  • know the content area
  • spend time organizing lecture information and activities
  • be familiar with alternative points of view
  • anticipate areas of difficulty and be prepared to provide clarification
✔ Capture students' interest
  • relate lecture content to students' previous experiences, background knowledge, and interests
  • supplement lectures with multimedia resources (e.g., video clips, demonstrations, hands-on activities, handouts)
  • provide students with opportunities to present their perspectives and viewpoints
  • provide alternative viewpoints, especially when addressing controversial issues
  • vary the pace of the lecture (e.g., provide background information; place students in small discussion groups and have them complete an activity)
  • synthesize information after a discussion or inquiry
✔ Follow a regular format
  • begin with advance organizers or previews
  • highlight key concepts or new ideas verbally and visually (e.g., using blackboard, overhead projector, liquid crystal display)
  • relate new information to familiar content
  • elicit student responses regularly to ensure understanding
  • review information as necessary
  • provide students with instructions before having them complete tasks
  • provide a summary or overview of main ideas
  • provide a preview for future lectures and activities

Sources: deWinstanley and Bjork (2002); Henson (1988).

The fool wonders, the wise man asks.

Benjamin Disraeli
British Politician and Author, 20th Century

A special concern in questioning technique is that male students are more likely than female students to dominate classroom discussions or to impulsively respond to questions. Studies have shown that boys call out in class eight times more than girls do and that teachers tend to direct questions, praise, and criticism to boys three times more often than they do to girls (Canadian Teachers' Federation, 1992). Other studies from the U.S. and the U.K. confirm that males are much more likely to call out answers in response to teacher questions than are females (Anderson, 2000). Teachers need to be sensitive to gender patterns in their classrooms, reflecting on the nature and purpose of the questions they pose to boys and girls and explicitly teaching students how to participate in classroom discussions in an equitable fashion.

Mastery Learning **Mastery learning** *involves learning one concept or topic to a predefined exemplary degree or level before moving on to a more difficult one.* Mastery learning as developed by Benjamin Bloom provides a general model for learning that is not based on internal psychological processing theory. Instead, mastery learning relies on an input–output approach that focuses on outcomes by providing a framework to help teachers design activities that ensure high levels of student achievement (Bloom, 1976). A mastery-learning approach involves the following procedures (Bloom, 1971; Carroll, 1963):

• Explicitly establishing the learning task and the level of achievement to be mastered (typically, this standard is the level where an A student performs).

Teaching Strategies
For the Effective Use of Questions

✔ Use good questioning techniques
- develop clear, purposeful, and logically sequenced questions
- monitor your responses to students' questions; avoid "yes/no" responses
- extend students' queries into higher-level, probing questions
- avoid asking rhetorical questions
- distinguish questions addressed to individuals, small groups, and the whole class
- do not allow individuals or small groups of students to dominate responses or discussion
- be especially aware of gender-biased and minority-biased question–answer patterns
- ensure that all students have the opportunity to ask and respond to questions (e.g., use a checklist, draw names randomly)
- provide sufficient time for students to formulate responses and queries
- model effective questioning format
- encourage and reinforce students' questioning and answering efforts

✔ Use questions to elicit information
- use questions to establish and maintain classroom rules and procedures (e.g., "What do we need to do to ensure that this experiment runs smoothly and without interruption?")
- use questions to establish and maintain good instructional practices (e.g., "Can the people at the back hear me clearly?")
- use questions to establish and maintain a positive climate in the classroom ("How can we demonstrate respect for others in this classroom?")
- use questions to elicit information as "lead-ins" for higher-level questions that focus on understanding and reflection (e.g., "What year did the Battle of Hastings occur?" followed by, "What were some of the political or social causes for the battle?")

✔ Use questions to shape students' understandings
- use questions that focus on connections (e.g., How does the vision of urban life in the novel *A Tale of Two Cities* compare with life in today's urban centres?")
- use questions to rethink, restate, or clarify content, intent, attitudes, opinions, and biases (e.g., "What does the author really mean in that paragraph?", "How does the author want us to behave during our daily lives?")
- encourage students to make inferences and provide interpretations (e.g., "How would a soldier describe the Battle of Hastings?", "How would the clergy describe this battle?")

✔ Use questions to encourage reflection
- use questions to develop creativity through supposition or hypothesizing (e.g., "Why couldn't all the King's horses put Humpty Dumpty back together again?")
- encourage students to develop personal meanings (e.g., What does this novel tell you about living your life well?")
- encourage students to make projections and develop future actions (e.g., How can we address high levels of uncertainty in our lives?")

Sources: Morgan and Saxton (1991), Sternberg and Spear-Swirling (1996), and Weinstein and Migano (1997).

- Breaking the learning task into units aligned with instructional objectives.
- Planning instructional procedures that include corrective feedback measures (e.g., tutoring, small-group instruction, remedial instruction) for students who do not attain mastery.
- Providing evaluation before the end of a unit or course that determines whether students have mastered materials at an acceptable level.

Mastery learning has been shown to be more effective in some subject areas than others. Schrunk (1996) reports on the positive effects of using the mastery approach in remedial reading. A mastery approach in remedial reading allows students to progress at their own speed based on their skills, motivations, and the time available. In general, the success of mastery learning depends on the skills of the teacher with respect to planning and implementing the approach in the classroom.

Seatwork *Seatwork* refers to the practice of having students work independently at their desks. Seatwork is often used to enable teachers to monitor how individuals in a class are doing or to address varying levels of student ability. When assigning seatwork, teachers need to ensure that the work is clear and meaningful and matched to students' ability levels. The most common teacher complaint about seatwork is the time and effort involved in collecting, correcting, recording, returning, and discussing assignments with students. Students also struggle with seatwork when they are uncertain about how to ask for help from teachers or peers. Some of the challenges associated with seatwork for teachers and students are presented in Figure 10.3.

An alternative to pencil-and-paper seatwork is the use of learning centres that encourage collaborative learning and peer interaction. For example, teachers might establish science learning centres, with simple experiments. In math, learning centres might focus on math challenges or puzzles, or they might consist of manipulative activities that help students grasp abstract ideas or relationships. In art classes, learning centres might be based on holiday or thematic projects or curriculum skills (e.g., quilting or origami). In writing classes, centres might involve class story-writing activities such as add-on stories or scripts; in social studies classes, centres might be established to gather data and create charts about population trends.

Computer stations are often used as learning centres. In Ontario, a valuable resource for computer-based learning centres is the Ontario Software Acquisition Program. The program was developed by English and French representatives from across the province who advise the Ministry of Education on the acquisition of provincial software licences for schools. The resource lists software licensed to public-funded schools and provides information about how to link software content to curricular goals. Programs that can be used as part of computer-based learning centres include Digital Field Trip to the Wetlands (which uses simulations and models to help students discover and understand the origin and his-

FOR THE TEACHER	FOR THE STUDENT
1. Keeping track of what the rest of the class is doing	1. Completing assigned work on their own
2. Keeping students on task	2. Understanding how and when to obtain the teacher's help
3. Addressing the varying paces at which students work ("ragged" endings)	3. Understanding the norms for assisting peers
4. Selecting or creating seatwork that is clear and meaningful	4. Learning how to be effective in obtaining help from peers
5. Matching seatwork to students' varying levels of achievement	
6. Collecting, correcting, recording, and returning seatwork assignments	

FIGURE 10.3 **Challenges of Seatwork for Teachers and Students**

Teaching Strategies
For Using Seatwork

✔ Provide meaningful seatwork
- check seatwork for clarity, meaningfulness, and appropriateness
- develop seatwork activities that challenge students to think reflectively, deeply, and creatively
- avoid overusing worksheets—use ones that are well-organized, attractive, and functional
- avoid seatwork that consists of trivial tasks
- selected alternatives to seatwork include reading, writing, ongoing projects, learning centres, computer work, cross-age tutoring

✔ Prepare students for seatwork
- describe seatwork assignments clearly
- provide students with introductory explanations and explain the importance of seatwork
- model how seatwork should be completed
- teach students what to do if they are unable to complete seatwork (e.g., seek teacher assistance, seek peer assistance, skip troublesome questions until assistance is available, use relevant resources in the classroom)
- ask questions that assess students' understanding of seatwork
- inform students what to do when they are finished (e.g., computer work, free reading, journal writing, bellwork, ongoing project).

✔ Monitor students during seatwork
- circulate around the room during the first 5 to 10 minutes to answer questions
- convene with small groups when appropriate
- circulate around the room prior to reconvening with small groups
- ask questions to determine students' understanding of seatwork and appropriate process
- be prepared to stop seatwork if small groups or the whole class appear not to understand, or not to be able to complete seatwork

Source: Weinstein and Mignano (1997).

tory of natural features of the landscape, for example lakes and river flats) and Eyewitness Virtual Reality Earth Quest (which provides an interactive, multimedia environment for the study of earth sciences). Figure 10.4 provides some suggestions for learning centres.

Homework   *Homework* represents another important instructional decision for teachers. While there is some evidence that the amount of time spent on homework is positively related to student achievement, it is also recognized that this positive relationship is influenced by such factors as grade level, the quality of the homework assigned, and the effort and care students take in completing it (National Center for Education Statistics Report, 1996).

The findings from a meta-analysis exploring the effects of homework (Cooper et al., 1998) suggest that for students up to Grade 6 homework does not significantly affect achievement. After Grade 6, however, the relationship between homework and achievement changes for the positive. When students carefully complete task-appropriate homework, their academic achievement increases.

A key aspect of the debate about whether elementary-school children should be assigned homework is the type of homework assigned (Begley, 1998). What is good homework? Especially for younger children, the emphasis should be on homework that

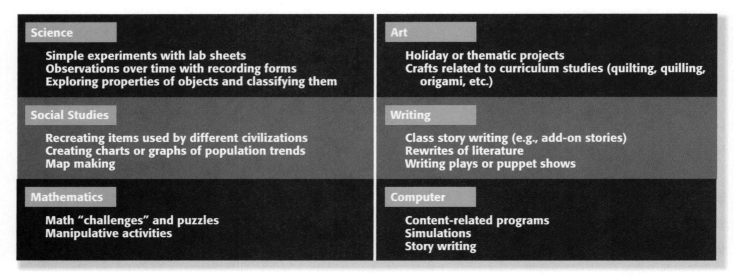

Science	Art
Simple experiments with lab sheets Observations over time with recording forms Exploring properties of objects and classifying them	Holiday or thematic projects Crafts related to curriculum studies (quilting, quilling, origami, etc.)
Social Studies	**Writing**
Recreating items used by different civilizations Creating charts or graphs of population trends Map making	Class story writing (e.g., add-on stories) Rewrites of literature Writing plays or puppet shows
Mathematics	**Computer**
Math "challenges" and puzzles Manipulative activities	Content-related programs Simulations Story writing

FIGURE 10.4 **Suggestions for Learning Centres**

"I don't have my homework because my little brother put a Pop-Tart® in my disk drive!"

 Through the Eyes of Students

Thoughts about Homework

Homework is work that you don't finish at school and have to take home. It takes me about 10 minutes to do my homework, which is just a little bit of time. The teacher usually gives special math or special stories for homework because they are important. If you don't get your homework done at home at night, then you have to do it during recess. If you practise your homework over and over again, it will make you smarter.

Olivia
Grade 1 Student
Enjoys Ballet, Soccer, and Swimming
Ontario

I do my homework as soon as I get home. If I get stuck doing my homework I ask my Mom to help me. Once I get it, she asks me to do the question again on my own. The good part about doing homework is that I enjoy spending time with my Mom. The bad part about doing homework is that there is too much of it—teachers give you too much homework. I spend at least an hour and a half doing homework each night. I know that in Grade 6, I am going to get a lot more. It won't be easy.

Sanjay
Grade 5 Student and Hockey Fanatic
Ontario

I believe that homework is an integral part of the learning process. Homework should provide students with opportunities to extend their learning. Sometimes, however, homework just involves completing menial tasks. I believe that students should be able to express their true understanding of the subject material by completing homework activities. I spend two or three hours doing my homework every day. That's a lot of time, but it's time well spent if it helps me prepare for university or a career.

Kevin
Grade 11 Student
Passionate about Piano, Electric Guitar, Trombone, History, and Literature
Ontario

fosters a love of learning and hones study skills. Short assignments that can be quickly completed should be the goal. With young children, long assignments that go uncompleted or completed assignments that bring a great deal of stress, tears, and tantrums should be avoided. Too often teachers assign homework that duplicates without reinforcing material that is covered in class.

Some educational psychologists believe that the main reason homework has not been effective in elementary school is that it has focused too much on subject matter and not enough on developing attitudes toward school, persistence, and responsible completion of assignments (Corno, 1998). They believe that it is not homework perse that benefits students, but rather homework that provides opportunities for the student to take responsibility. They believe that teachers need to inform parents about guiding their children in these aspects of doing their homework: setting goals, managing their time, controlling their emotions, and checking their work. Teachers and parents can use homework in the early grades to help children wrestle with goal setting and follow-through.

Cooper (1989, 2001) suggests the following about homework:

Why is parental involvement an important part of effective homework strategies? How can teachers best prepare parents to assist their children to complete homework?

- Homework has more positive effects when it is distributed over a period of time rather than done all at once. For example, doing 10 math problems each night for five nights is recommended, rather than doing 50 over the weekend.
- Homework effects are greater for math, reading, and English than for science and social studies.
- For intermediate-grade students, one or two hours of homework a night is optimal. High-school students benefit from even more hours of homework, but it is unclear what a maximum number of hours ought to be.

Homework can be a valuable tool for increasing learning, especially in intermediate and secondary school. However, it is important to make homework meaningful, monitor it, provide students with feedback on it, and involve parents in the process. In many elementary schools throughout Canada, teachers keep parents informed about the objectives of homework assignments through weekly letters, school newsletters, and Websites. For example, Beaconsfield Junior High in St. John's, Newfoundland provides parents with online access to a homework Website that lists assignments by course and teacher. The site also provides direct e-mail access to each teacher, as well as an online newsletter with detailed information about school activities. The Beaconsfield Junior High homework Website can be found at **www.bjh.k12.nf.ca**.

Evaluating Teacher-Centred Instruction

Advocates of the teacher-centred approach believe that it is the best method for teaching basic skills needed in reading, math, science, and languages. Teacher-centred instruction is behaviourally oriented and, therefore, highly structured, dividing learning into carefully sequenced sub-lessons aimed at meeting a larger curricular goal. Hirsch (1996) suggests that teacher-centred approaches are superior to student-centred ones because they focus on specific skills and measurable outcomes. Research on teacher-centred instruction has provided valuable suggestions for classroom practice, including holding high expectations for students' progress, providing adequate academic learning time, using high-level thinking questions, and developing meaningful seatwork and homework assignments.

Teacher-centred instruction is not without criticism, however. Windschitl (1999) argues that teacher-centred approaches do not encourage student participation, offer inadequate opportunities for hands-on learning, tend to lead to passive rote learning, and do not take into account students' interests, inclinations, or socioemotional development. Moreover, critics argue that teacher-centred approaches to learning promote external rather than internal motivation, rely too heavily on paper-and-pencil tests, and provide few opportunities for real-world applications and collaborative learning. Such criticisms are often levelled by advocates of learner-centred instruction, which we will examine next.

At this point we have discussed a number of ideas about planning and teacher-centred lesson planning and instruction. A review of these ideas is presented in Summary Table 10.1.

SUMMARY TABLE 10.1

Planning, and Teacher–Centred Lesson Planning and Instruction

What is instructional planning?	• Instructional planning provides a systematic, organized blueprint for teaching that promotes student learning.
What is the relationship between time frames and planning?	• Effective planning addresses tasks (e.g., goals, activities, and priorities) and time (e.g., estimates and schedules) issues. • Effective planning incorporates various time frames ranging from yearly planning to daily planning.
What is teacher-centred lesson planning and instruction?	• Teacher-centred lesson planning relies on the teacher to choose behavioural objectives (statements of observable change in performance linked to learning goals), analyze tasks (breaking down complex tasks into component parts), and select instructional taxonomies (Bloom's cognitive, affective, and psychomotor domains).
What are the three domains of Bloom's taxonomy?	• The cognitive domain focuses on knowledge and the development of cognitive skills. It is divided into six major categories (knowledge, comprehension, application, analysis, synthesis, and evaluation). • The affective domain consists of five objectives related to emotional responses (receiving, responding, valuing, organizing, and value characterizing). • The psychomotor domain links instruction with motor activity in six domains (reflex movements, basic fundamentals, perceptual abilities, physical abilities, skilled movements, and non-discussive movements).
What are teacher-centred instructional strategies?	• Teacher-centred strategies include orienting students (establishing a context or framework for students); lecturing (presenting and explaining new material); demonstrating (showing how to do something); and discussing and questioning (question and answer sessions). • Other teacher-centred strategies include mastery learning (learning one concept or topic at a high level before moving on to a new one), seatwork (a teacher-structured opportunity to informally assess and assist individual students using paper-and-pencil activities), and homework. • Researchers have found that the effects of homework on primary students' achievement are minimal. Homework has more positive effects for intermediate and secondary-school students. When homework is given, it is important to make it meaningful, and provide feedback about it to students.
What criticism exists about teacher-centred instructional strategies?	• Critics of teacher-centred instruction argue that it leads to passive, rote learning and rigid and structured classrooms, and that it focuses on basic skills, extrinsic motivation, and paper-and-pencil tests, paying insufficient attention to students' socioemotional development.

LEARNER-CENTRED LESSON PLANNING AND INSTRUCTION

Just as the behavioural approaches described in Chapter 7 provide the conceptual underpinnings for teacher-centred lesson planning and instruction, the cognitive information-processing and constructivist approaches discussed in Chapters 2, 8, and 9 form the theoretical backdrop for learner-centred lesson planning and instruction.

Learner-Centred Principles

Learner-centred approaches *to teaching and learning move the focus of instructional planning and delivery away from the teacher and toward the student.* In the 1990s, interest in this redirection of instructional focus led to the creation of a number of reform and research groups in the United States, including the Presidential Task Force on Psychology in Education, 1992; the Workgroup of the American Psychological Association, 1995; and the Learner-Centered Principles Workgroup, 1997. Collectively these groups developed 14 guiding principles for learner-centred education and school reform. These principles are outlined in "Learner-Centered Psychological Principles: A Framework for School Reform and Redesign," available online on the American Psychological Association Website at **www.apa.org/ed/lcp.html**.

The psychological principles offered in support of learner-centred education are divided into four categories:

1. *Cognition and metacognition.* Examines the nature and goals of the learning process, as well as the construction of knowledge, strategic thinking, thinking about thinking, and the context of learning.
2. *Motivation and affect.* Examines the motivational and emotional influences on learning, intrinsic motivation, and the effects of motivation on effort.
3. *Development and social.* Examines developmental and social influences on learning.
4. *Individual differences.* Examines the nature and implications of individual differences on learning, including the implications of diversity on educational standards and assessment.

In Canada, the increasing use and implementation of information and communication technologies in schools has helped promote more learner-centred approaches to teaching and learning. The TeleLearning Network of Centres of Excellence, a national consortium of more than 200 private and public organizations researching and promoting technologies for learning, argues that as information and communication technology is integrated into the Canadian education system a paradigm change from teacher-centred to learner-centred instruction is required; such a shift should stress knowledge building and active collaborative learning (Harasim, 1999).

Three Learner-Centred Instructional Strategies

We have already discussed a number of strategies that teachers can consider in developing learner-centred lesson plans. These especially include the teaching strategies based on the theories of Piaget and Vygotsky (Chapter 2), constructivist aspects of thinking (Chapter 8), and cognitive and social cognitive approaches (Chapter 9).

Three learner-centred strategies that can help you with your lesson planning are problem-based learning and project-based learning, essential questions, and discovery learning.

Problem-Based Learning and Project-Based Learning   *Problem-based learning* and *project-based learning* describe a range of instructional strategies that engage students in authentic, reality-based tasks for learning. Students are given "real-world" problems or projects to solve that allow for more than one solution path or answer. Both problem-based learning and project-based learning are learner-centred approaches to instruction where the role of the teacher is that of guide or facilitator. Students engaged in problem-based or project-based learning activities work in cooperative groups to search for resources and materials, and problem-solve as they go along.

Problem- and project-based approaches have been shown to promote independent learning, raise students' metacognitive awareness, and motivate students by providing real-world situations and rationales for learning activities (Albanese & Mitchell, 1993). Moreover, because the strategies focus on substantive rather than superficial exploration of material, these approaches help students retain and understand information (Pross, 2002).

Problem-based learning and project-based learning are not identical. Problem-based learning has been widely adopted for medical-school instruction since its introduction at McMaster University Medical School in Hamilton, Ontario in the late 1960s (Pross, 2002). Problem-based learning is also extensively used in professional preparation practices (Ryan et al., 1994). Project-based learning is more widely used in K–12 classrooms. Project-based learning tends to focus on the production of an end product, or "artifact," that requires specific content knowledge or skills to produce. Students begin a project by researching a topic, designing a product, and developing a plan. Problems are addressed as part of the production process. Projects vary in scope and time frame, and end products vary in terms of technology and the quality or complexity of the finished artifact. One example of project-based learning was developed by Nancy Mitchell for her Grade 2–4 students at Whitehorse Elementary School in the Yukon. The project requires students to use Plasticine, aluminum foil, and paper to create boats that would float and hold 100 cubic centimetres of cargo. A complete description of several school projects is available at **www.yesnet.yk.ca/schools/wes/themes.html**.

The focus in problem-based learning, however, is not on the production of an artifact but rather on problem-solving processes. Students are presented with a problem situation or scenario that they must solve. Problems are designed to be "fuzzy" in order to simulate the complexity of real-world situations. The problem-based approach uses a general-inquiry model for student learning (Allen, 1998). The following is an example of a problem-based learning scenario presented to students during a Grade 10 history class.

> You have been hired as consultants for a major motion picture filming in Vancouver. Although the story, set in the early 1800s, is fictional, the director wants every historical detail in the film to be as accurate as possible. Many of the film's scenes are planned to take place around a native encampment with a large and imposing totem pole. Your task is to determine what this totem should look like—including its images, size, and colours. You will also need to determine the vicinity of the pole, and the activities that occur around it. Finally, you will recommend a location where the filming of the totem scenes could take place. Include notes about what aspects of the setting would need to be altered, either physically or through special effects, in order to be historically accurate.

Essential Questions **Essential questions** *are questions that require one to make a decision or plan a course of action.* Jacobs (1997) states that essential questions are questions that reflect the heart of the curriculum. Essential questions pique students' curiosity and cause them to think. Essential questions are creative choices that explore a variety of perspectives, make interrelationships explicit, and encourage elaboration. For example, a lower-knowledge-level question in a history class might be, "What was the political effect of the War of 1812 on Upper Canada?" This question can be transformed into a higher-order essential question by making it thought-provoking—redefining it as a question that requires a variety of perspectives and the interrelationship and elaboration of ideas, such as "Is the War of 1812 still being battled today in Ontario?"

Proponents of the essential-questions strategy argue that too often lesson planning and instruction become rigid, stiff, and dull. For example, consider the essential question for a high-school history curriculum: "What is personal responsibility to a community?" Compare the possible reactions to that essential question with the following: "What events, things, people, and places in my community affect my life, and how?"

Writing creative and motivational essential questions takes patience and practice. Avoid asking simple "what is" questions, such as "What is the Canadian Charter of Rights and Freedoms?" While "what is" questions are important, they do not require students to make decisions or contemplate actions and responses. An essential question on the Charter might ask, "How does the Canadian Charter of Rights and Freedoms affect your life as a citizen of Canada?" A question phrased in this way requires students to choose among various options and defend that decision.

Discovery Learning **Discovery learning** *is learning in which students build an understanding of a subject, topic, or concept based on their experiences with the material.* Students examine and question data provided by the teacher to discover the underlying principle or meaning in a lesson. Discovery learning is an inquiry-based approach to

www.mcgrawhill.ca/college/santrock

We are what we repeatedly do. Excellence, then, is not an act, but a habit.

Aristotle
Greek Philosopher and Teacher,
4th Century B.C.

teaching and learning that stands in contrast to the direct-instruction approach, where the teacher directly demonstrates, explains, or presents information to learners. John Dewey (1933) wrote that, "There is an intimate and necessary relation between the processes of actual experience and education"; Jerome Bruner (1966) stated that, "Emphasis on discovery in learning has precisely the effect on the learner of leading him to be a constructionist, to organize what he is encountering in a manner not only designed to discover regularity and relatedness, but also to avoid the kind of information drift that fails to keep account of the uses to which information might have to be put."

Advocates of discovery learning argue that the approach feeds students' natural curiosity, encourages students to think for themselves, and aids in retention of learning because it makes use of students' personal associations with learning rather than relying on associations made by the teacher. Teachers can facilitate discovery learning by providing students with activities that stimulate their natural curiosity and by helping students recognize and identify connections among concepts. Concept maps, diagrams, outlines, and summaries are methods that teachers can use to help students recognize the interrelationships among ideas. Teachers also encourage discovery learning when they pose creative questions that ask students to come up with plausible and defensible answers. For example, a math teacher could ask students to define a relationship between the area of one ceiling tile and the area of the whole ceiling, or a science teacher could ask how technology might improve human beings.

Most discovery approaches used in North American schools today do not involve "pure" discovery methods, in which students are encouraged to learn on their own and instruction is minimal. Rather, teachers rely on *guided* discovery learning, in which they encourage, question, and direct students to facilitate their understanding.

Critics of discovery learning argue that the process often requires special materials and extensive preparation on the part of the teacher. Moreover, in order for discovery learning to be effective, students must have basic knowledge about the problem being investigated and must know how to apply problem-solving strategies.

Integrating the Curriculum

Integrated curriculum is a central theme in learner-based approaches to planning and instruction. By linking and sharing information across different subject areas, students construct an understanding of the interconnectedness of ideas and information (Drake, 1998; Mallery, 2000).

Drake (1998) describes a number of ways that curricula in Canadian schools can be integrated, and examines multidisciplinary and interdisciplinary approaches. Multidisciplinary programs are defined as programs that incorporate two or more subject areas connected to a specific theme; the separate procedures from the individual disciplines of study that influence how the subject is taught and assessed shape the overall program. Content within multidisciplinary programs is labelled as belonging to one subject area (e.g., history in history, and English in English). The North York Board of Education's project *Learning through the Arts: Fusing Artists into the Curriculum* is an example of a multidisciplinary curriculum. Through the services of the Royal Conservatory of Music and various arts organizations, foundations, and corporate sponsors, students from seven schools are taught by a minimum of three artists. Teachers follow through with each artist's specific skills by integrating these techniques into classroom instruction; for example, an artist's workshop on painting with water colours could be followed up in class as part of a painting unit or lesson.

Through the Eyes of Teachers

Integrating the Curriculum for Student Motivation

If students are going to learn in your classroom, then you will need to connect the curriculum to their interests. Think about your favourite learning experiences during elementary school. You probably will recall completing an assortment of special projects or thematic units.

As a teacher, you will need to deliver lessons and units that not only fulfill specific learning expectations, but also inform students and their parents that they have unlimited potential. For example, creating a weather station, carrying out a community history project, or using the Internet to link students with their peers throughout the country or the world are all ways of helping them become excited about learning. These are the learning experiences that they will remember over their lifetimes.

Dan Forbes
18-Year Elementary/Middle School Teacher
TOBA Award for Physical Education Program, 2001
Roy C. Hill Award for Important Educational Innovation, 1999
Prime Minister's Certificate of Achievement for Teaching Excellence, 1997
Manitoba

FRAGMENTED
Periscope—one direction; one sighting; narrow focus on single discipline

Description
The traditional model of separate and distinct disciplines, which fragments the subject areas.

Example
Teacher applies this view in math, science, social studies, language arts OR sciences, humanities, fine and practical arts.

CONNECTED
Opera glass—details of one discipline; focus on subtleties and interconnections

Description
Within each subject area, course content is connected topic to topic, concept to concept, one year's work to the next, and relates idea(s) explicitly.

Example
Teacher relates the concept of fractions to decimals, which in turn relates to money, grades, etc.

NESTED
3-D glasses—multiple dimensions to one scene, topic, or unit

Description
Within each subject area, the teacher targets multiple skills: a social skill, a thinking skill, and a content-specific skill.

Example
Teacher designs the unit on photosynthesis to simultaneously target consensus seeking (social skill), sequencing (thinking skill), and plant life cycle (science content).

SEQUENCED
Eyeglasses—varied internal content framed by broad, related concepts

Description
Topics or units of study are rearranged and sequenced to coincide with one another. Similar ideas are taught in concert while remaining separate subjects.

Example
English teacher presents a historical novel depicting a particular period while the history teacher teaches that same historical period.

SHARED
Binoculars—two disciplines that share overlapping concepts and skills

Description
Shared planning and teaching take place in two disciplines in which overlapping concepts or ideas emerge as organizing elements.

Example
Science and math teachers use data collection, charting, and graphing as shared concepts that can be team-taught.

WEBBED
Telescope—broad view of an entire constellation as one theme, webbed to the various elements

Description
A fertile theme is webbed to curriculum contents and disciplines; subjects use the theme to sift out appropriate concepts, topics, and ideas.

Example
Teacher presents a simple topical theme, such as the circus, and webs it to the subject areas. A conceptual theme, such as conflict, can be webbed for more depth in the theme approach.

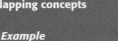
THREADED
Magnifying glass—big ideas that magnify all content through a metacurricular approach

Description
The metacurricular approach threads thinking skills, social skills, multiple intelligences, technology, and study skills through the various disciplines.

Example
Teaching staff targets prediction in reading, math, and science lab experiments while social studies teacher targets forecasting current events, and thus threads the skill (prediction) across disciplines.

INTEGRATED
Kaleidoscope—new patterns and designs that use the basic elements of each discipline

Description
This interdisciplinary approach matches subjects for overlaps in topics and concepts with some team teaching in an authentic integrated model.

Example
In math, science, social studies, fine arts, language arts, and practical arts, teachers look for patterning models and approach content through these patterns.

FIGURE 10.5 **Integrating the Curriculum**

Fogarty's multidisciplinary and interdisciplinary strategies for integrating the curriculum.

Most approaches to integration tend to be interdisciplinary. Interdisciplinary approaches are defined by disciplines that remain readily identifiable even though content is interconnected. The disciplines are connected by one or more common elements, essential learnings, and skills or standards that are made explicit to the students. In this approach, all elements of curriculum are interconnected and assessment and reporting reflect selected standards and instructional strategies. Fogarty (1991; Fogarty & Stoher, 1995) provides several curricular strategies including within-discipline approaches, cross-discipline approaches, and intrinsic approaches that educators can use for integrated curriculum. Figure 10.5 shows three ways the curriculum can be integrated within a discipline and five ways it can be integrated across disciplines. Traditionally, the fragmented model has been used to plan curriculum. This model involves little or no integration, and learners are essentially left to their own devices to make connections or integrate concepts. More recently, many schools have adopted the interdisciplinary strategy of webbed integration, in which teachers select a theme around which to construct curriculum. A theme can be a topic, concept, event, novel, project, movie, or song (Fogarty & Stoher, 1995).

Evaluating Learner-Centred Instruction

Proponents of the learner-centred approach refer to the four factors in support of the Learner-Centered Principles Workgroup (1997) instructional approach: cognitive and metacognitive factors, motivational and affective factors, developmental and social factors, and individual differences. Teachers use elements from these four factors when they develop activities that help students actively construct understanding; set learning goals; plan; think deeply and creatively; monitor their learning; solve real-world problems; focus on internal motivation; learn in developmentally appropriate ways; become aware of learning preferences and styles; and collaborate effectively with others.

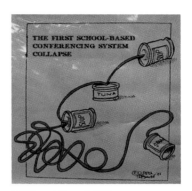

© DiPetta & Banwell, 1998

Critics of learner-centred instruction argue that it pays too much attention to the *process* of learning (e.g., learning creatively and collaboratively), and not enough to academic content (such as the facts of history; Hirsch, 1996). They also note that learner-centred instruction tends to work better in subjects with "fuzzy" or ill-defined problems (such as the social sciences and humanities; Feng, 1996) than in subjects that demand more structured domain knowledge (such as mathematics and science). In these latter subject areas, critics maintain that teacher-centred approaches are more effective in providing students with basic skills and content knowledge. Critics also suggest that the approach is ineffective with beginning-level students, who may not have the knowledge or skills necessary to make decisions about what or how to learn.

Teacher-centred and learner-centred approaches to planning and instruction have been presented as separate and discrete concepts, but teachers tend not to use them in an either/or manner. Rather, most teachers include elements of both approaches in their planning and instruction to make the classroom a positive learning environment for all students.

At this point we have discussed many ideas about learner-centred lesson planning and instruction. A review of these ideas is presented in Summary Table 10.2.

TECHNOLOGY AND EDUCATION

Technology is such an important aspect of modern education that it is woven throughout this book. Here, we explore the technology factor, the technology landscape, technology and sociocultural diversity, and the realities of information and communication technology and education.

The Technology Factor

Students today are growing up in a world that is far different technologically from the world in which their parents and grandparents went to school. For example, consider the changes that have occurred in information and communication technologies since the 1990s that would have been considered science fiction in your parents' day: video cell phones, wristwatch digital cameras, digital paper. The innovation of digital paper—a synthetic that can be used for notepads, catalogues, and textbooks—allows students to write or capture text directly into a computer. Students can point to a reference in a textbook made with digital paper and get the most current information available about the topic from an Internet or intranet site.

We live in an information-based society that increasingly relies on technology and technologically aware workers and citizens in business, industry, and everyday life. The need for education to prepare students to live and work in this information society is highlighted in government, industry, and media reports. According to an Industry Canada analysis, information and communication technology has increased the skill requirements for workers, and this demand for workers with technology skills is expected to increase (Betts, 1998). Betts also notes that there is a significant widening of the wage gap between university-educated workers and those with a lower level of educational attainment. While the information society relies on basic skills and competencies such as communication skills, problem-solving, and critical and creative thinking, how people acquire and develop these competencies in today's technologically oriented world is being challenged

SUMMARY TABLE 10.2
Learner–Centred Lesson Planning and Instruction

What is learner-centred instruction?	• Learner-centred instruction moves the focus of instructional planning and delivery away from the teacher and toward students. • The principles of learner-centred instruction include cognitive and metacognitive factors, motivational and affective factors, developmental and social factors, and individual differences.
What are some learner-centred instructional strategies?	• Learner-centred instructional strategies include project-based and problem-based learning, essential questions, and discovery learning. • Project-based approaches (e.g., create a foil and paper ship that floats and holds 100 one-centimetre cubes) focus on product. • Problem-based approaches focus on process (e.g., preventing an egg from breaking if you drop it from a height of 10 metres). • Essential questions reflect the heart of the curriculum and require students to make a decision or plan a course of action (Jacobs, 1997). • Discovery learning requires students to build an understanding of a subject, topic, or concept through interaction with relevant materials.
What is curriculum integration?	• Integrated curriculum is a central theme in learner-based instruction and involves linking and sharing information across different subject areas (Drake, 1998; Mallery, 2000). • Multidisciplinary programs are defined by separate procedures within the discipline that influence how the subject is taught and assessed. • Interdisciplinary approaches have disciplines that remain readily identifiable even though content is interconnected by one or more common elements, themes, essential learnings, and skills or standards that are made explicit to the students. Most approaches to integration are interdisciplinary.
What are the criticisms of learner-centred instruction?	• Critics argue that learner-centred instruction pays too much attention to the process of learning (learning creatively and collaboratively), and not enough to academic content (such as facts of history) (Hirsch, 1996). • Appears to work better in subjects areas with "fuzzy" problems, such as the social sciences and humanities (Feng, 1996). • Viewed as ineffective with beginning-level students.

and extended in ways and at a pace that few people had to cope with in previous eras (Harasim, 1994; Owston, 2000; Owen & Owston, 1998; Tapscott, 1998).

Technology has been part of school curricula for many decades, but until recently the technologies used were relatively simple and changed slowly. To underscore how dramatically technology in schools has changed, consider that the *total* number of computers in schools in Canada and the United States in 1983 was less than 60,000, but by 2000 there were close to half a million connected computers in schools in Canada alone (Drouin, 2000). A 1999 survey of U.S. and Canadian schools, shown in Figure 10.6, illustrates that Canada compares favourably with the United States in terms of the ratio of students per Internet-connected computer. At the secondary level the ratio was 7:1 (i.e., seven students for every Internet-connected computer), at the intermediate level the ratio was 8:1, and at the elementary level the ratio was 9:1 (Drouin, 2000). The survey also reports that nine out of every ten Canadian students attended a school that had Internet access for educational purposes.

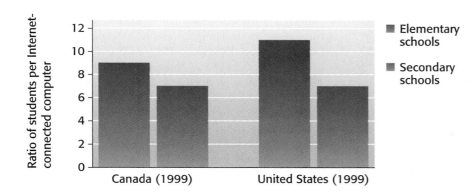

FIGURE 10.6 **School Internet Connectivity in Canada and the United States**

Source: Drouin, 2000

One important implication of the rapid spread of information and communication technology throughout Canada's schools is the need for a prudent approach toward implementing and integrating computers into the curriculum and the culture of education (DiPetta, Novak, & Marini, 2002). Another implication is the need for greater attention to, and focus on, school-to-work transitions and preparing students for learning within a rapidly changing technology landscape (Courchene, 2002).

The Technology Landscape

The landscape for information and communication technology in schools is expanding dramatically. It includes computer-assisted instruction; word processing; computer programming; games, simulations, and microworlds; CD-ROMs and videodiscs; hypertext and hypermedia; and computer-mediated communications.

Computer-Assisted Instruction **Computer-assisted instruction (CAI)** *is an instructional approach that uses computers to individualize and deliver content based on learners' characteristics and needs.* CAI is closely associated with the concept of mastery learning and direct instruction. The CAI approach uses the capabilities of the computer to control the rate of progress and the amount and type of instructional and test material that each student uses. The computer can also create reports of student progress and analyze student data for course effectiveness reports. There are many forms of computer-assisted instruction, including drill and practice, tutorial, testing, and dialogue. Simulations and games are often associated with CAI programs because of their impact on student motivation (Bankay & Woloshyn, 1999).

Drill-and-practice programs *provide students with structured, computer-based activities that promote the acquisition of knowledge or skill through repetitive practice.* Drill-and-practice programs are most commonly associated with basic skills instruction in science, math, and reading, and they may use games or simulations to increase motivation. Proponents of drill-and-practice computer applications argue that these programs offer structured reinforcement of previously learned concepts using question and answer interactions and feedback.

Critics of drill-and-practice computer programs argue that the programs encourage rote learning, make little significant difference in student learning, and do not develop higher-order thinking skills (Johnson, 1996; Robertson, 1998). Moreover, critics suggest that drill-and-practice software is ill-matched with curriculum guidelines, and is often designed to cover a narrow sector of a subject domain (Means & Olson, 1994).

Tutorial programs *are designed to replicate what human tutors do to guide and facilitate students' learning.* Tutorial programs adapt their pace according to how students respond. In a typical tutorial, the student will be asked a number of questions and then the computer program will branch off in directions that are most likely to benefit the student's learning. The computer technology can also eliminate or reduce some types of student errors. For example, an action-research project investigating the use of math tutorial software with Grade 7 geometry students at Dickenson High School in Alberta found that students benefited because the computer program removed the tedium of drawing and numbering grids, erasing errors, and correcting errors resulting from poorly constructed grids (Happon & Griffiths, 1997).

www.mcgrawhill.ca/college/santrock

Through the Eyes of Teachers

Using Computers in the Classroom

I work with young adults who are returning to school to complete their high-school diplomas so that they can continue their studies at the college or university level. Our program is a mastery-oriented one, where students set their own learning pace. Since computers hold such a critical role in our society, we provide students with plenty of opportunities to acquire computer skills throughout the program. Students are also required to take an introductory computer course that reviews word processing, data entry, spreadsheet application, multimedia presentation, and Internet use. We then integrate computer and information technology throughout all of the remaining course modules, with the expectation that students apply these introductory skills. For instance, as part of our science course we require students to conduct research about the nature of technology as it relates to science, culture, and society. In this manner, we hope that students will learn more than how a piece of technology works—we hope that they will learn to consider its potential impact on human behaviour and values.

Jennifer Auld-Cameron
Secondary-School Science Teacher for More Than 10 Years
Community College Instructor
Nova Scotia

Critics of computer-assisted instruction argue that the programs place too much emphasis on external rather than internal motivation. They note that CAI provides considerable corrective feedback as students attempt to master a topic, feedback that is largely based on the behavioural concept of operant conditioning and which encourages rote learning. Merrill et al. (1996) counter that recent versions of CAI embody more cognitive principles of learning, focusing on capturing and holding student attention, prior learning, and the positive transfer of information.

Word Processing   In the early days of the twentieth century, schools promoted learning to type on a typewriter as an essential skill for university and career preparation. Today, using computer software for word processing is viewed as a basic skill in both education and the world of work. In 1990, the Department of Education for Newfoundland and Labrador developed a word-processing course based on the rationale that more than half of the workforce in North America is involved in processing or exchanging information through computers. In addition to this, more than 70 percent of all new jobs are computer-related or involve computer use.

Educationally, the use of word processors has been associated with improvements in writing and spelling skills and attitudes toward writing for regular, special education, and English as a second language students (Maddox, Johnston, & Willis, 1997; McNaughton, Hughes, & Ofiesh, 1997; Owston & Wideman, 1996; MacArthur, 1996; Zordell, 1990). The capability of quickly and easily highlighting information, changing font size and colour, checking spelling and grammar, and moving blocks of text within a document are features that students and teachers have found helpful and motivational for student writing.

Word-processing technology also plays a significant role in special education as an assistive technology. Optical character recognition (OCR) and voice recognition software, text-reader programs, voice synthesizer software, and adaptive keyboards are all tools that have enabled students with exceptionalities to use computers and word-processing programs to support and enhance their learning (see Chapter 6). These integrated word-processing technologies are increasingly used to help students organize their work, conduct research, take notes, and communicate with peers. As well, support personnel make use of word-processing features such as flowcharting, mind mapping, outlining, and Internet communications such as voice e-mail and Web features.

Computer Programming as a Learning Tool   Seymour Papert (1980), the creator of the Logo programming language, argued that by learning a programming language children learn to think logically and independently. There are many different programming languages, ranging from the simple, such as Basic or Logo, to the more complex, such as C++. Regardless of their complexity, all programming languages share common building blocks and tools. Therefore, learning any computer language helps in learning others. Logo was designed for students to use with a graphic or mechanical "turtle" that moved around a computer screen or table top in response to their programming efforts. Recent versions of Logo programs incorporate the Logo language, Java scripting, multimedia graphics, word-processing capabilities, animation, and problem-solving tools in an Internet-based environment called a "microworld." According to Papert, these microworlds encourage students to explore and ask questions about their own learning in a way that makes their thinking explicit and thereby helps them discover both how to think and how to learn.

Recent studies of Logo suggest that when the program is used in a constructivist environment that involves guidance and scaffolding, the planning skills, math skills, problem-solving, and logical thinking skills required in learning and working with Logo transfer positively to other learning contexts (Lehrer, Lee, & Jeong, 1994; Cognition and Technology Group at Vanderbilt, 1996).

Games, Simulations, and Microworlds **Instructional (or educational) games** *are computer-based learning activities that are rule-based and involve some form of competition* (Dempsey, Rasmussen, & Lucassen, 1996). Computer-based educational games capitalize on the motivation and interest sparked by the multimedia and animation capabilities of modern technology.

"I see what's wrong with your calculator—it's the remote control to your TV."

Categories or types of games include adventure games, simulations, competitions, cooperation games, programming games, puzzle games, and business and management games (Leemkuil, de Jong, & Ootes, 2000). Over the past two decades many children have grown up on a steady stream of video games, and manufacturers have been quick to develop computer-learning activities based on the video-game format. Two of the most popular and successful examples of the educational game format are *Where in the World Is Carmen Sandiego?*, which places students in the role of a detective tracking down criminals in a number of countries, and *Mathblaster*, which has a variety of math-related, arcade-style games. Both of these games are fun to play and provide practice in domain-specific subject areas.

Computer simulations *are applications that place learners in computer-learning environments that model real-world situations.* Simulations resemble games in that they contain a model of some kind of system; learners can change variable values, make specific actions, and observe the consequences of their actions. However, while the object of a game is to win, the object of a simulation is to experience the consequences of choices or decisions based on roles that have responsibilities and privileges. Moreover, while the events in a game are typically rule-based and linear in nature, simulations rely on a dynamic set of relationships among several variables. Simulations offer vivid portrayals of environments or worlds that students could not directly participate in otherwise. For example, most medical schools in Canada and the United States and virtually all secondary schools no longer use live-animal laboratories in physiology courses and science curricula. Instead, using a problem-based format and simulation software such as SymBioSys.21, students repeat manoeuvres until they are mastered—without the risk and anxiety that accompanies working on a living organism (Cohen, 2000).

Microworlds *are computer-generated educational environments intended to support students in the active exploration of a subject-matter domain.* These computer-based interactive models or representations of real or imagined worlds are structured to behave according to the laws and conditions defined by a particular subject. Exploring these created worlds enables students to experience the nature of the particular subject through their own explorations or through teacher-guided activities. Papert (1993), who created one of the first microworlds using the Logo programming language, stated that these scaled-down simulations of real environments enable learners to construct knowledge by exploring and designing new worlds. An interesting microworld is the *Temple of Alife* (**http://alife.fusebox.com/index.html**). The site is the creation of artists and scientists interested in exploring artificial life, a field of study that models living biological systems using complex mathematical algorithms. The site offers a number of microworlds, including Planet Wator, which is set up so visitors can carry out a study of aquatic life on the planet's surface, gathering data about climatic conditions and animal life. As visitors change, ecosystem-conditions consequences are reflected in the new data about the planet. Other examples of microworld simulations include SimCity and SimAnt, which explore the development of a city and an ant colony, respectively.

Educational microworlds, simulations, and games are social constructivist approaches to learning that involve peer collaboration and experimentation. These social constructivist concepts have also contributed to the development of computer-supported intentional learning environments (CSILE), a computer-based environment developed by Marlene

Scardamalia and Carl Bereiter (1996, 1999) at the Ontario Institute for Studies in Education of the University of Toronto. Scardamalia and Bereiter analyzed how discourse in knowledge-building communities contrasts with the learning discourse that most often happens in schools; they concluded that schools need to be restructured as communities in which the construction of knowledge is supported as a collective goal. The role of educational technology should be to replace classroom discourse patterns with those having more immediate and natural extensions to knowledge-building communities outside of school walls. CSILE was designed to reframe classroom discourse to support knowledge building. The Technology and Education box on p. 335 presents more information about CSILE and the role that educational technology can play in social learning.

CD-ROMs and Videodiscs **CD-ROMs** *are compact discs with read-only memory.* These discs resemble those used in digital CD players, and allow for the storage and presentation of large amounts of multimedia educational materials and activities. One CD-ROM can store the total amount of information available in a full set of encyclopedias. Advancements in CD-ROM technology, including the ability to write CD-ROMs with home or school computers, are changing the way that many schools and teachers present information or lessons. CD-ROMs can be used to present information, expand on previously learned material, allow students to self-explore a topic, and as a resource for report writing and research. The use of educational CD-ROMs has been shown to help develop students' critical thinking and creativity skills and encourage collaborative work among students (Marlow, 2001).

Videodiscs *are laser-readable discs that are used to store and present multimedia materials and resources.* Advantages associated with the use of this technology in the classroom include the quality of the graphic representations, the amount of data that can be stored, and the fact that they do not require a computer. However, advancements in CD-ROM technology may soon make videodiscs less attractive to teachers and schools (Maddox, Johnston, & Willis, 1997).

Hypertext and Hypermedia **Hypertext** *can be defined as a non-linear system for writing and presenting text on a computer so that readers can access the content material at several levels and connect it to related documents and resources.* When individual words, phrases, or graphics are formatted as "hypertext hot links" using hypertext markup language (html), learners using browser software (e.g., Netscape or Internet Explorer) can click on a link and view that material wherever it is stored on the World Wide Web. Hypertext is used in many CD-ROMs to enable non-linear exploration of content.

Hypermedia *refers to multimedia information (text, visual, audio and/or animated information) presented in a hypertext non-linear format.* Links in hypermedia enable students to browse through introductory materials or examine topics of interest in greater detail. Hypertext and hypermedia have become virtually synonymous terms; hypertext may include pictures or graphics, just as text in books may include photos or images. Increasingly people use the term *hypertext* to refer to media presented in a non-linear, linked format. The multimedia and self-selection aspects of hypermedia or hypertext are appealing to many students and have been shown to positively affect students' attitudes toward learning (MacGregor, 1999; Szabo, 2000). Jonassen (1996) argues that students probably learn more by developing and working on their own hypermedia presentations than by trying to absorb material from ready-made ones. A software tool used in many Canadian schools for designing hypermedia is HyperStudio. This multimedia authoring software has drawing tools and audio, video, animation, and text components that students can use to create active rather than passive presentations. Figure 10.7 shows the opening screen of a hypermedia program about Beethoven's Fifth Symphony; Figure 10.8 is an example of a Grade 7 geography hyperstudio project on understanding how one's identity is connected to a "birth" land.

Computer-Mediated Communication **Computer-mediated communication (CMC)** *refers to communication, most often text-based, that is conducted or facilitated through the*

Computer Supported Intentional Learning Environments (CSILE)

A CSILE site might include more than one classroom. A typical classroom has eight networked computers (Bereiter, 1999, 2002; Bereiter & Scardamalia, 1999; Scardamalia & Bereiter, 1996). CSILE classrooms are connected to form a communal base for the entire school. Students are encouraged to enter their views and questions, compare perspectives, and reflect on joint understanding of ideas. Students work both individually and collaboratively. Students can add a comment or attach a graphic note, such as a picture or diagram, to another student's entry. However, only the original author of the note can edit or delete the notes. Authors are informed when a comment has been attached to one of their notes.

Following is an example of work done within one combined Grade 5/6 CSILE classroom (Bruer, 1989). The focus was on ecology, with one group working on the topic of fossil fuels. The group began with a kitchen scene that one student had previously created as a CSILE note. The students took this as a learning challenge to identify the uses of fossil fuels in an ordinary kitchen. Different students examined different parts of the kitchen, exploring such topics as the generation of electricity and the origin of natural gas. This information led to the posting of notes explaining how the fossil fuels were used. The notes were attached to pictures of the various kitchen objects. The computer system allowed notes to be posted hierarchically. For example, a student could begin with a kitchen scene and click on the refrigerator. This would open a picture of the refrigerator's interior. Clicking on various items in the refrigerator then would bring up pictures and text about the fossil fuels. This learning exercise unfolded in a museum-like way, with every detail of daily life made interesting.

CSILE helps students understand how knowledge and understanding are socially constructed and gives students opportunities to reflect on, revise, and transform their thinking. Students learn that thinking is not a brief, cursory exercise. Rather it takes place over an extended time and often needs to be modified based on feedback from a community of learners. Research evaluations indicate that students in CSILE classrooms perform better on standardized achievement tests of language and math, give deeper explanations of concepts, are better at solving problems, and have a more positive attitude toward learning than students in conventional classrooms (Scardamalia & Bereiter, 1996, 1999).

For more information about CSILE visit the Computer Supported International Learning Website at the University of Toronto: **http://csile.oise.utoronto.ca/**.

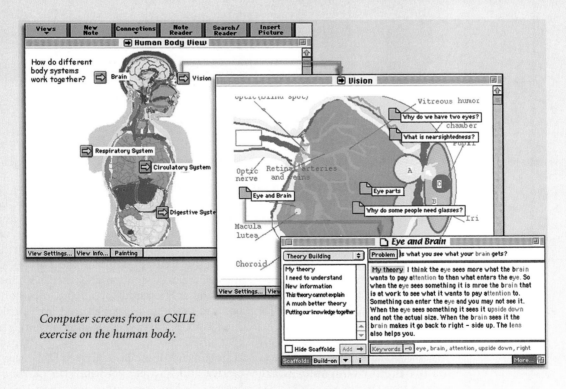

Computer screens from a CSILE exercise on the human body.

use of computers and computer networks. CMC includes e-mail and computer conferencing. Computer-mediated communication in education is sometimes referred to as *educational telecommunications.* The *Internet,* the *Net,* or the *information highway* are all terms used to describe the growing global computer network that forms the core of computer-mediated communication.

FIGURE 10.7 An Example of Hypermedia: Beethoven's 5th
This screen is the opening menu of the hypermedia, *Beethoven's 5th*. It includes text, graphics, and CD-quality sound.

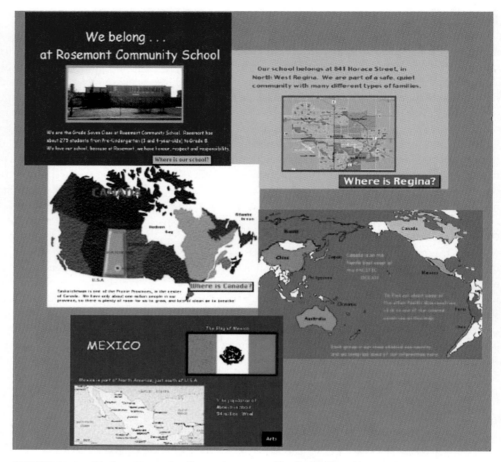

FIGURE 10.8 Student HyperStudio Projects on Identity and Native Land

Source: http://wblrd.sk.ca/~bestpractice/multimedia/example3.html

The Internet The **Internet** *is a global network of interconnected computers and resources that provides students and teachers with an incredible array of information.* The Internet provides quick access to current, up-to-date material. Canada is one of the most connected countries in the world; on March 30, 1999, Canada became the first country to connect all its public schools (including First Nations schools) and public libraries to the information highway (SchoolNet, 2000). In the 2001 Speech from the Throne, the federal government committed to providing Canadian students and teachers with increased access to high-speed Internet service in schools. The rapid spread and adoption of the Internet as an educational environment and tool reinforces the need for teachers and administrators to think carefully about how the Internet is used to promote student growth and learning (DiPetta, Novak, & Marini, 2002).

According to the United Nations Human Development Report (Fukuda Parr, 2002), industrialized countries in North America and Europe, with only 15 percent of the world's population, account for 88 percent of all Internet users. Less than 1 percent of people in South Asia are online, even though it is home to one-fifth of the world's population. Africa, with more than 700 million people, has less than 1 million Internet users. England, on the other hand, has more than 10.5 million Internet users. Interestingly, only 2 percent of the world's population has access to the phone lines needed for Internet connectivity, and even if telecommunications systems were in place, most of the world's poor would still be excluded from the Internet because of illiteracy. Moreover, since 80 percent of the Websites on the Internet are currently in English, a language understood by only 10 percent of the global population, much of the Internet remains a foreign place for the majority of the world.

The **World Wide Web (WWW, the Web)** *is a hypermedia interface for searching and retrieving materials on the Internet.* While the original Internet was largely text-based and required knowledge of computer-based commands and systems, the World Wide Web interface uses "move and click" mouse commands and multimedia Web pages. Libraries, museums, universities, schools, companies, and individuals display information on the Web, all of which can be accessed by students with a mouse click. Web indexes or subject guides (e.g., Yahoo) and search engines (e.g., Google) can help students find information on the Web by sorting through and finding relevant material from among the millions of Websites available. Finding relevant or appropriate material on the Web is becoming increasingly time-consuming.

E-mail *stands for "electronic mail" and is another valuable educational tool, as messages can be exchanged simultaneously not only between individuals but also among large groups.* E-mail is a means for staying in touch with parents and peers, and a vehicle for student activities such as e-mail pen pals.

Internet Cautions The Internet and the Web can be valuable tools for helping students learn (Roblyer & Edwards, 2000), but they are not without risk or cost (Owston, 1999). There are many technical, infrastructure, and support considerations associated with the effective use of Internet technology in schools. Finding information on the Web is often very frustrating for students, especially when they receive thousands of irrelevant, useless, or non-working URLs. Moreover, there are many inappropriate and offensive sites that students may stumble across as they search for material.

The rapid adoption and spread of Internet access in Canadian schools has also meant that many schools and administrations have had little time to develop appropriate and effective policies and guidelines for secure and safe student Internet use (DiPetta, Novak, & Marini, 2002). Most jurisdictions across the country are moving quickly to develop policies and guidelines to help teachers, parents, and students avoid the many potholes associated with the information superhighway. Moreover, teachers need to be knowledgeable and feel comfortable using the Internet in their lessons. When used effectively, the Internet can provide access to a world of knowledge, experiences, and resources that students would otherwise not be able to reach (Garner & Gillingham, 1998).

Technology and Sociocultural Diversity

Technology brings with it certain social issues and concerns. For example, will the impact of the increased use of computers and computer-based technologies in North American schools widen the learning gap between rich and poor students, or between male and female students (Oberg & Gibson, 1999; Owen & Owston, 2001; Weinman & Haag, 1999)? The problem of computer access and use is compounded by the far greater presence of computers in the homes of middle-income and higher-income families than in lower-income ones. The diffusion of computer technology in Canadian society has not been equitable. Despite its status in the world as an Internet-connected country, tremendous differences exist in the ratio of students to Internet-connected computers, with averages ranging from 15:1 for elementary schools in Nova Scotia to 5:1 for secondary schools in Manitoba (CESC 2000).

Moreover, how computers are used in schools varies as a function of school focus, teacher training, and cultural interests and attitudes. Schools with teachers who have little or no training in how to use computers tend to use them for drill-and-practice activities. In contrast, schools where teachers are trained and supported in using technology are more likely to use computers for active, constructivist activities or applications (Laferriere, Breuleux, & Bracewell, 1999; Wideman & Owston, 2001). Creating equitable access to, and use of, computers in our schools will require innovative approaches for providing minority students with computers and increasing training opportunities for teachers.

Teaching Strategies
For Using Technology in the Classroom

✔ Become aware of how to work with technology in the classroom
  - incorporate word-processing in classroom activities (e.g., bulletins, newsletters, and note taking)
  - use computer simulations as a means of developing deep understanding of a topic
  - experiment with CD-ROMs as multimedia information sources for student work
  - explore how laser discs, microworlds, hypertext, and hypermedia can be used in lessons

✔ Look for ways to use technology as part of research and learning
  - assist students in using search engines and search tools to find information on the Internet
  - use e-mail to connect students and classroom activities with students and teachers in other schools
  - participate in collaborative learning exercises that involve technology (e.g., online teacher discussion forums and conferences)

✔ Choose technology that presents positive models for students
  - discuss with your students the benefits and dangers associated with computer technology
  - present technology use as a means for increasing cooperation and communication among students
  - develop lessons that demonstrate how important technological literacy is for students' futures (e.g., jobs and careers)

The Realities of Information and Communication Technology and Education

Maddux, Johnson, and Willis (1997) identified two different types of computer use in education: Type I applications, "which make it easier, quicker, or more efficient to teach the same things in the same ways we have always taught them," and Type II applications, "which make available new and better ways of teaching" (cited in Harlow & Johnson, 1998).

The number of computers connected to the Internet in Canadian schools has increased tremendously in the past decade. Yet, despite the potential for creating new and innovative approaches for student learning, many schools and teachers still struggle with how best to implement and use information and communication technology.

Attempts to promote the use of information and communication technologies in the classroom over the past two decades have not been as successful as anticipated. Computers are still used too often for drill-and-practice activities rather than for active constructive learning (Laferriere et al., 1999). Reasons for this reality are varied and include computer illiteracy on the part of teachers and administrators (Haugland & Wright, 1997), commercially developed courseware that does not dovetail with educational theory or classroom practice (Reinking, 1989), and the lack of hardware, software, and professional-development resources (CESC, 2000).

More positively, teacher candidates in faculties of education throughout the country are learning to work with information and communication technologies and are expected to use these tools in their teaching practice. We believe that these teachers will be the agents of change who will develop the tools and practices that will map and redefine the landscape of how technology is used in education. To evaluate your own readiness with respect to technological skills and attitudes, see Self-Assessment 10.1.

Evaluating My Skills and Attitudes toward Technology

Use this form to rate your school's readiness for teaching with technology. Rate each statement from 1 to 5, with 1 = Do not agree and 5 = Absolutely agree.

	1	2	3	4	5

People

Teachers, administrators, parents, students, and staff are informed about and involved in discussions on how ICT* is used at this school

Administrators encourage professional development in ICT

Teachers support and encourage all students in using ICT

Teachers provide all students with opportunities to work with ICT

Parents feel their ICT opinions and concerns are considered by teachers and administrators

Places

Technology adds to and fits in well with the clean, well-maintained, and attractive appearance of the schools

Network computers are available in labs, the library, classrooms, and student work areas

Virtual work and communication spaces on school-based conferencing systems or bulletin boards are kept updated and provide relevant information for teachers, students, and parents

Work areas are well-lit, uncluttered, accessible to all, and conveniently located

The school's Web pages present ICT policies and information in clear, accurate, and jargon-free language

Policies

Teachers, administrators, parents, students, and staff are informed about and involved in ICT policy development

User policies and general rules for ICT are clear, well-posted, and fairly administered

It is a policy that teachers are updated, supported, and recognized for working with technology in their classes

School policy encourages teachers and non-teaching staff to use technology for professional development

Policy links ICT with the attainment of specific and explicit academic goals

Programs

Technology programs involve out-of-school experiences that link to the community and the world

Programs encourage teachers and students to explore technology, its uses, and its meaning for society

Programs allow students some choice in determining their technology activities

Programs are planned with interests, life and career goals, and technology skills in mind

Programs are flexible and support student access to learning in a variety of ways including, but not limited to, online education

Processes

Parents receive a response to an e-mail or phone request within a reasonable period of time

Administrators and teachers routinely use ICT to communicate with parents, students, and the community

Teachers maintain clear and reasonable technology goals and assignments, keeping in mind student learning styles and interests

Teachers are available for students online but also in person before and after school

All students have the right and feel welcome to use the labs and equipment when necessary

Scoring and Interpretation

This self-assessment scale is based on the theory and practice of invitational education (DiPetta, Novak, & Marini, 2002). The results can provide school-based groups with a starting point for discussing the use of computer technology from a technologically prudent and people-centred perspective.

*ICT = Information and communication technology

Reprinted with permission from Inviting Online Education; DiPetta, Novak, and Marini (2002) Phi Delta Kappa Fastback #498.

At this point we have studied many ideas about information and communication technology in education. A review of these ideas is presented in Summary Table 10.3.

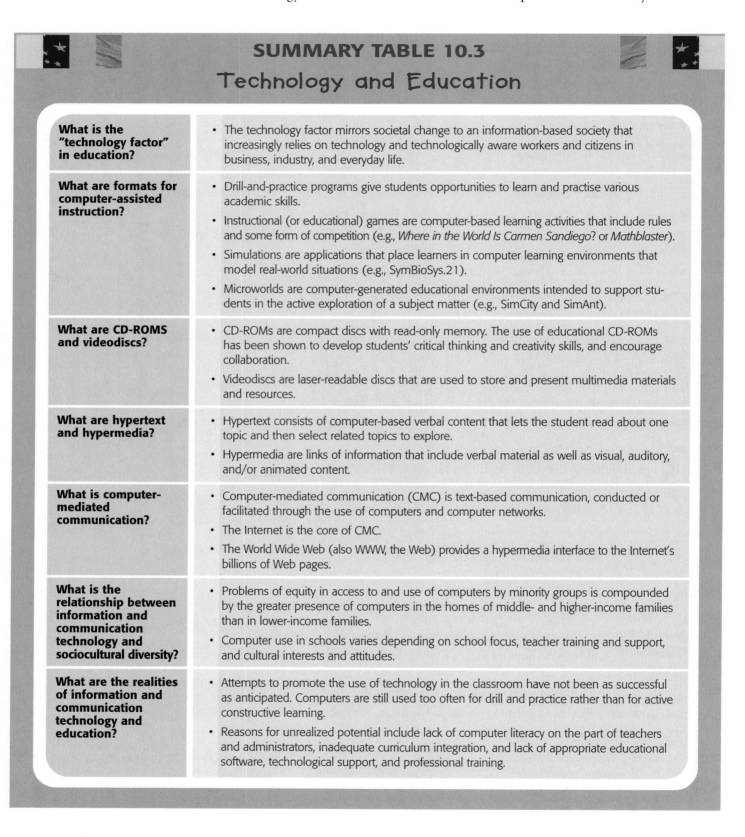

SUMMARY TABLE 10.3
Technology and Education

What is the "technology factor" in education?	• The technology factor mirrors societal change to an information-based society that increasingly relies on technology and technologically aware workers and citizens in business, industry, and everyday life.
What are formats for computer-assisted instruction?	• Drill-and-practice programs give students opportunities to learn and practise various academic skills. • Instructional (or educational) games are computer-based learning activities that include rules and some form of competition (e.g., *Where in the World Is Carmen Sandiego?* or *Mathblaster*). • Simulations are applications that place learners in computer learning environments that model real-world situations (e.g., SymBioSys.21). • Microworlds are computer-generated educational environments intended to support students in the active exploration of a subject matter (e.g., SimCity and SimAnt).
What are CD-ROMS and videodiscs?	• CD-ROMs are compact discs with read-only memory. The use of educational CD-ROMs has been shown to develop students' critical thinking and creativity skills, and encourage collaboration. • Videodiscs are laser-readable discs that are used to store and present multimedia materials and resources.
What are hypertext and hypermedia?	• Hypertext consists of computer-based verbal content that lets the student read about one topic and then select related topics to explore. • Hypermedia are links of information that include verbal material as well as visual, auditory, and/or animated content.
What is computer-mediated communication?	• Computer-mediated communication (CMC) is text-based communication, conducted or facilitated through the use of computers and computer networks. • The Internet is the core of CMC. • The World Wide Web (also WWW, the Web) provides a hypermedia interface to the Internet's billions of Web pages.
What is the relationship between information and communication technology and sociocultural diversity?	• Problems of equity in access to and use of computers by minority groups is compounded by the greater presence of computers in the homes of middle- and higher-income families than in lower-income families. • Computer use in schools varies depending on school focus, teacher training and support, and cultural interests and attitudes.
What are the realities of information and communication technology and education?	• Attempts to promote the use of technology in the classroom have not been as successful as anticipated. Computers are still used too often for drill and practice rather than for active constructive learning. • Reasons for unrealized potential include lack of computer literacy on the part of teachers and administrators, inadequate curriculum integration, and lack of appropriate educational software, technological support, and professional training.

Mrs. Rumer was new to teaching Grade 3 at Hillside Elementary School. Before the school year began, she met with other new teachers and their mentors for planning sessions. The administration appeared to be aware of just how much planning is necessary for successful teaching. Mrs. Rumer openly shared her ideas with her mentor, Mr. Spowart, and the rest of the group.

"I really want to have a learner-centred classroom," Mrs. Rumer said. "I'd like to use aspects of problem-based learning, and guided discovery. I also intend to integrate the curriculum as much as possible and use computers. I think the students will learn so much more that way than if I use teacher-centred instruction."

Mr. Spowart smiled and said, "Well, they'll probably have more fun, but I doubt that their test scores will reflect much learning. We really need to prepare our students to meet provincial standards, Mrs. Rumer. To do that, you'd better throw in some good old-fashioned direct instruction."

Several other teachers readily agreed. "You'll make yourself crazy trying to integrate the curriculum, too. Besides, the intermediate-grade teachers will just tear it all apart again." Another teacher said, "I use my classroom computer all the time, and the kids really like it."

The other teachers' comments surprised Mrs. Rumer. She had learned about learner-centred instruction as part of her teacher training. She wanted her students to be active in the construction of their knowledge, not merely vessels into which she poured information. She also thought that by integrating the curriculum, the students would see the connections between various disciplines. The principal assured her that if she wanted to give an integrated, learner-centred approach a try, she would have that freedom.

With this assurance, Mrs. Rumer began making lists of everything she would have to plan for in order to have an effective learner-centred classroom. She began by going through the curriculum guide for Grade 3 and made a list of all the expectations. After doing this, she realized her job was going to be a daunting one.

- What are the issues in this case?
- Where should Mrs. Rumer go from here?
- How can she take a curriculum that has been taught in a teacher-centred manner and convert it to a learner-centred curriculum? Should she? Why or why not?
- How can she incorporate technology into the curriculum so that the computers become more than "electronic flash cards"?

CHAPTER REVIEW

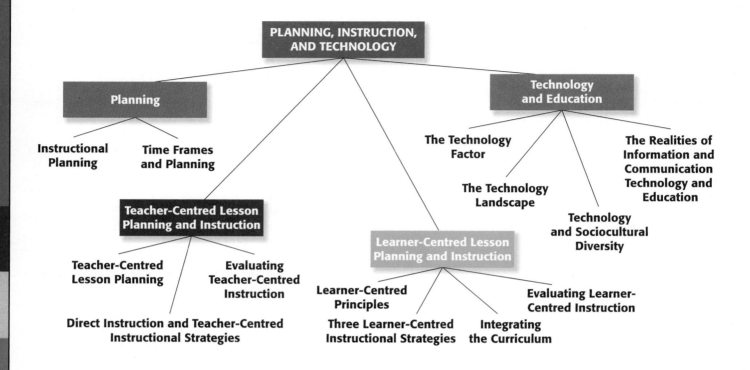

PLANNING, INSTRUCTION, AND TECHNOLOGY

- Planning
  - Instructional Planning
  - Time Frames and Planning
  - Teacher-Centred Lesson Planning and Instruction
    - Teacher-Centred Lesson Planning
    - Evaluating Teacher-Centred Instruction
    - Direct Instruction and Teacher-Centred Instructional Strategies
- Learner-Centred Lesson Planning and Instruction
  - Learner-Centred Principles
  - Three Learner-Centred Instructional Strategies
  - Integrating the Curriculum
  - Evaluating Learner-Centred Instruction
- Technology and Education
  - The Technology Factor
  - The Technology Landscape
  - Technology and Sociocultural Diversity
  - The Realities of Information and Communication Technology and Education

To obtain a detailed review of this chapter, study these three summary tables:

KEY TERMS

instructional planning 310
behavourial objectives 312
task analysis 312
taxonomy 313
advance organizers 316
expository advance
   organizers 316
comparative advance
   organizers 317

mastery learning 318
learner-centred approaches
   325
essential questions 326
discovery learning 326
computer-assisted instruction
   (CAI) 331
drill-and-practice programs 331
tutorial programs 331

instructional (or educational)
   games 333
computer simulations 333
microworlds 333
CD-ROM 334
videodisc 334
hypertext 334
hypermedia 334

computer-mediated
   communication (CMC) 334
Internet 336
World Wide Web (WWW, the
   Web) 337
e-mail 337

PROFESSIONAL DEVELOPMENT/PORTFOLIO ACTIVITIES

1. Working with Technology

More and more schools are incorporating technology into the curriculum. How will you work with computer and information technology to help your students learn? How will you encourage your students to independently work with technology? Write a brief essay on how you will teach with technology as well as teach about technology in your classroom. Include this essay in your portfolio.

2. Computers and You

The way we use computers in our classrooms is influenced by the type of experiences we have had dealing with computers in our own lives. Working with one of your colleagues, share your best and worst experiences working with computers. Based on what you discuss and what you know about computer technology, how might you create positive computer experiences for your students? How would you work with only one computer in your class? How would you use a computer lab? What role are computers likely to play in your classroom?

3. Clouds and Computers

You have been asked to teach a Grade 5 lesson on cloud formation. What teaching methods or strategies might you use? Suppose your school has recently established an Internet computer lab and you believe that your students could benefit from using it for this unit. How could you use the lab to help your students learn about clouds? What problems do you see in planning to use the lab for a unit on clouds? How might you overcome these problems?

 INTERNET ACTIVITIES

1. Virtual Museum Trips

Museums, art galleries, and historical sites throughout the world are increasingly using the Internet to provide virtual tours of their exhibits. A number of Websites, such as those for the Ontario Science Centre (www.ontariosciencecentre.ca), the Provincial Museum of Alberta (www.pma.edmonton.ab.ca), and the Saskatchewan Science Centre (www.sciencecentre.sk.ca), offer a variety of hands-on science projects that emphasize discovery and exploration. Visit one of these online science museums and discuss how its resources can help you teach science in your classroom.

2. Student Learning and the Net

The Internet has become a major source of information for students, who need to be able to critically evaluate the information they find on the Web before they use it. As well, students need to learn what plagiarism means with regard to information they take from the Web. Design a lesson that helps students learn what plagiarism is and how to correctly use information they find on the Internet.

Connect to the Online Learning Centre at www.mcgrawhill.ca/ college/santrock **to explore possible answers.**

 Visit the *Educational Psychology* Online Learning Centre at
www.mcgrawhill.ca/college/santrock
to access Websites related to the above Internet Activities as well as chapter quizzes,
a searchable glossary, and other learning and study tools.

Preview

In Chapter 10, you learned that motivation is a key component of learner-centred psychological principles. Indeed, motivation is a critical aspect of teaching and learning. Unmotivated students won't expend the necessary energy and effort to learn. Highly motivated students are eager to come to school and learn. These are some of the questions we will explore in this chapter:

- How can teachers get students to become more internally motivated?
- How can teachers get students to develop a better sense of mastering their environment?
- What are some good strategies to help students set goals and plan?
- How does anxiety interfere with students' achievement, and what can teachers do about it?
- How important is social motivation in students' lives?
- Once students are motivated, how can teachers keep them motivated?
- What are the best strategies for motivating hard-to-reach, low-achieving students?

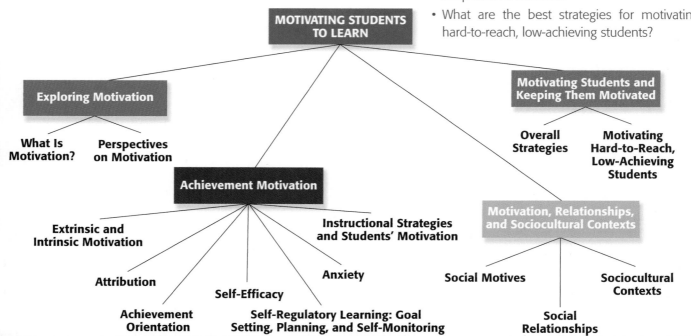

MOTIVATING STUDENTS TO LEARN

Exploring Motivation
- What Is Motivation?
- Perspectives on Motivation

Achievement Motivation
- Extrinsic and Intrinsic Motivation
- Attribution
- Achievement Orientation
- Self-Efficacy
- Self-Regulatory Learning: Goal Setting, Planning, and Self-Monitoring
- Instructional Strategies and Students' Motivation
- Anxiety

Motivation, Relationships, and Sociocultural Contexts
- Social Motives
- Social Relationships
- Sociocultural Contexts

Motivating Students and Keeping Them Motivated
- Overall Strategies
- Motivating Hard-to-Reach, Low-Achieving Students

The art of teaching is the art of awakening the curiosity of young minds.

Anatole France
French Novelist and Poet, 20th Century

Teaching Stories: Erica Bawn

Over her 20-year career in Nova Scotia schools, Erica Bawn has been the recipient of several teaching awards including the CAPHERD Young Professional Award. The former physical education teacher and past chair of the Nova Scotia School Athletic Federation is now a middle-school principal. Erica believes that creating a supportive learning community is essential for students in the middle grades. Below, she describes her school's Positive Participation Program, interdisciplinary instruction approach, and schoolwide initiatives, which she believes help to foster a sense of school purpose and community for students and teachers.

"Friendship, social acceptance, and peer pressure are especially powerful influences on students' lives during the middle-school years. One of our primary goals at Evangeline Middle School is to ensure that our school culture is a caring and positive one that helps instill a sense of self-worth and responsibility in our students. To do this, we created the Positive Participation Program to encourage students to take initiative with respect to doing positive things around the school. A positive initiative can include anything from picking up litter to tutoring students or being a good friend. For each positive initiative that students make, they can receive a ballot from a teacher that enters them in a school draw for prizes. Prizes are drawn at a Positive Participation Program assembly, held every second Wednesday. The assemblies also provide an opportunity to further develop a sense of school community by having students participate in spirit-building activities (e.g., music, skits, games).

"As well, we view interdisciplinary instruction as a form of authentic learning. We see our students as 'knowledge workers' using information to solve problems in the real world. In order to prepare to solve a real-world task, it is sometimes necessary to receive formal instruction. That is, students often need to possess special knowledge and skills to solve a problem. However, providing students with this type of instruction without a clear link to the 'real world' is a virtual guarantee for their disinterest and failure. Thus, we emphasize connections between school learning and 'real life' to develop and foster a positive learning environment.

"We also employ a schoolwide initiatives program to help develop appropriate behaviour and to provide students with a sense of belonging. A schoolwide initiative includes students and teachers working together toward a common goal. Examples of schoolwide goals have included a three-day trip to Prince Edward Island, citizenship projects, and cultural events. The attraction of a schoolwide initiative does not rest in the exotic nature of the initiative, but in the opportunity it provides for students and teachers to work together. Schoolwide initiatives enhance school climate, heighten teacher efficacy, and reduce student misconduct."

Exploring Motivation

What Is
Motivation?

Perspectives
on Motivation

EXPLORING MOTIVATION

Terry Fox was born in Winnipeg, Manitoba and raised in Port Coquitlam, B.C. He undertook one of the greatest long-distance runs in history (McNally, 1990)—averaging a marathon (42 km) a day for 5 months, he ran 5,373 km across Canada. What makes his feat truly remarkable is that before the run he lost a leg to cancer. Terry Fox called his journey the Marathon of Hope, and although he didn't reach his ultimate goal of crossing the entire country his efforts have resulted in the contribution of millions of dollars to cancer research. Terry Fox was undoubtedly a motivated person. What does it mean to be motivated?

What Is Motivation?

Motivation *is the drive to satisfy a need and the reason why people behave the way they do. Motivated behaviour is energized, directed, and sustained.* Why did Terry Fox complete his run? When Terry was hospitalized with cancer, he told himself that if he survived he would do something to help fund cancer research. Thus, the motivation for his run was to give purpose to his life by helping other people with cancer.

Terry Fox's behaviour was energized, directed, and sustained. Running across Canada, he encountered unforeseen hurdles: severe headwinds, heavy rain, snow, and icy roads. Because of these conditions, he was averaging only 13 km a day after the first month, far below what he had planned. But he kept going and picked up the pace in the second month until he was back on track to reach his goal. His example stands as a testimonial to how motivation can help each of us prevail.

Terry Fox's story is portrayed in the classroom film *The Power of Purpose*; the film includes actual footage from the Marathon of Hope, and helps students see themselves in a positive manner. One Grade 6 teacher showed the film to her class and then asked her students to write down what they learned from it. One student wrote, "I learned that even if something bad happens to you, you have to keep going, keep trying. Even if your body gets hurt, it can't take away your spirit."

As with Terry Fox's marathon run, a student's motivation in the classroom involves why the student is behaving in a particular way and the extent to which the student's behaviour is energized, directed, and sustained. If a student doesn't complete an assignment because he is bored, lack of motivation is involved. If a student encounters challenges in researching and writing a paper, but persists and overcomes the hurdles, motivation is involved.

Perspectives on Motivation

Different psychological perspectives explain motivation in different ways. We explore three of these perspectives: behavioural, humanistic, and cognitive.

The Behavioural Perspective   The behavioural perspective emphasizes external rewards and punishments as keys in determining students' motivation. **Incentives** *are positive or negative stimuli or events that can motivate students' behaviour.* Advocates of the use of incentives emphasize that they add interest or excitement to the class, and direct attention toward appropriate behaviour and away from inappropriate behaviour (Emmer, Everton, & Worsham, 2000; Stipek, 2002).

Incentives that classroom teachers use include numerical scores and letter grades, which provide feedback about the quality of work, and checkmarks or stars for competently completing work. Other incentives include giving students recognition—for example, by displaying their work, giving them a certificate of achievement, placing them on the honour roll, or verbally mentioning their accomplishments. Another type of incentive focuses on allowing students to do something special, such as a desirable activity, as a reward for good work. This might include extra time at recess, playing computer games, a field trip, or even a party. (See Chapter 7 for an in-depth discussion about using reward and punishment.) In our discussion of intrinsic and extrinsic motivation, we will look more closely at the issue of whether incentives are a good idea.

Terry Fox, during his run across Canada to raise funds for cancer research.

© Lynn Johnston Productions, Inc. Reproduced by permission.

The Humanistic Perspective   The **humanistic perspective** *stresses students' capacity for personal growth, freedom to choose their destiny, and positive qualities.* This perspective is closely associated with Abraham Maslow's (1954, 1971) view that motivation can be associated with a "hierarchy of needs." As outlined in Figure 11.1, Maslow's **hierarchy of needs** *offers a seven-step model for explaining human motivation and behaviour* (Maslow, 1968, 1987). According to Maslow, individuals progress to growth needs only when lower-level needs have been met. The first four levels of Maslow's model (physiological needs, safety needs, belonging and love needs, and esteem needs) are also known as deficiency needs. Maslow maintained that, from an educational perspective, failure to address or meet *deficiency* needs interferes or limits students' abilities to focus on complex tasks and learn—a student who is being bullied at school may have little interest in studying French, or a child who comes to school hungry may not be able to focus on reading a story. The idea that deficiency needs affect learning has had many implications for education and educators.

Over the last decade, schools across the country have assumed greater responsibility in helping students fulfill basic needs. For example, in 2001 about 137,000 Canadian children participated in the School Breakfast Program (Breakfast for Learning, 2002), designed to provide students with a nutritious meal at the start of the day so that they are better prepared to learn. Consistent with Maslow's hierarchy of needs, students who arrive at school hungry do not perform well academically and are more likely to exhibit behavioural problems. Fortunately, innovations like the School Breakfast Program can do much to turn this situation around, promoting positive attitudes toward school and enhancing students' academic performance.

The upper three levels of Maslow's hierarchy (the need to understand and know, aesthetic needs, and the need for self-actualization) are referred to as *growth* (or *being*) needs. These needs tend to be self-reinforcing, highlighting individuals' strengths. For example, a student who is motivated to understand how birds fly and who decides she enjoys learning about flight and space is likely to want to work toward her goal of becoming a pilot or an astronaut.

Self-actualization, *the highest and most elusive of Maslow's needs, has been given special attention. It is the motivation to develop one's full potential as a human being.* The realization of personal potential is self-fulfillment (Maslow, 1971). In Maslow's view, self-actualization is possible only after the lower needs have been met. Maslow cautions that most people stop maturing after they have developed a high level of esteem and therefore never become self-actualized.

FIGURE 11.1 Maslow's Hierarchy of Needs Abraham Maslow developed the hierarchy of human needs to show how we have to satisfy certain basic needs before we can satisfy higher-level growth needs.

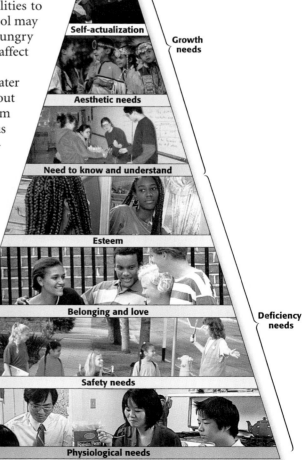

The idea that human needs are hierarchically arranged is appealing but controversial. Critics of Maslow's hierarchy point out that some people may be motivated to meet a variety of needs at the same time. Such evidence suggests that people may move up and down the hierarchy or place different emphasis on meeting different needs. For example, some students may place the need to be popular above the need for personal safety. Others may place aesthetic needs such as the desire to write or create music before the need for belonging and love.

Critics also challenge that the proposed hierarchy does not hold across different cultures, (Hoffman, 1989). For example, a student from a country where individualism is not the cultural norm might put love and belonging needs ahead of safety needs. An individual who is suddenly confronted with the loss of a job or an illness might revert to lower-level concerns for meeting physiological or safety needs.

'Tis a lesson you should heed,
Try, try again
If at first you don't succeed,
Try, try again.

Thomas H. Palmer
*American Author of Teachers' Manuals,
19th Century*

The Cognitive Perspective   According to the cognitive perspective, students' thoughts guide their motivation. Researchers in this area explore students' internal motivation to achieve, their attributions about success or failure, and their beliefs about whether they can effectively control their environment, including their thoughts about goal setting, planning, and monitoring goal progress (Pintrich & Schunk, 2002). The cognitive perspective holds that both cognitive and motivational variables need to be considered in

Through the Eyes of Teachers

Motivation and Learning

Catherine Little, a junior-high-school teacher and instructional leader for more than a decade, reflects on the long-term impact that teachers have on their students after asking former students what they remembered about her classes. Here, she talks about what teachers can do to ensure that students are motivated to recall and use what they have learned in class.

One of the most professionally informative things I have done as a teacher is ask former students what they learned from me as their teacher. Most of their responses validated not the content that I taught in my classes but rather the skills and values that students learned while we were together. For example, many former students recalled two of my classroom-management techniques. Some mentioned that I overused the first technique, the use of the light switch as a class signal, but most mentioned that they appreciated another technique, the use of reading aloud in science class. They said that my reading aloud at the start of science classes helped them settle into the class and calm themselves and this helped them do better in all their classes. They found calmness to be something they valued and many used reading as a way to calm themselves even when they weren't in my class. Another student said that the most important thing she learned from me was to be nice to people even if you felt like screaming at them and she learned this not from what I taught but from how I taught.

  I guess what I learned from my former students is that one never knows when something, anything, no matter how seemingly small or insignificant, can make a huge impact on a student's life.

Catherine Little
Science and Math Teacher, Grades 7, 8, and 9
Former Head of Science Department
York University Faculty of Education Alumni Excellence in Teaching Award Recipient
Science Olympiad Outstanding Coach
Ontario

Source: Little, C. (2001). What matters to students. *Educational Leadership. A publication of the Association for Supervision and Curriculum Development. 61–64.*

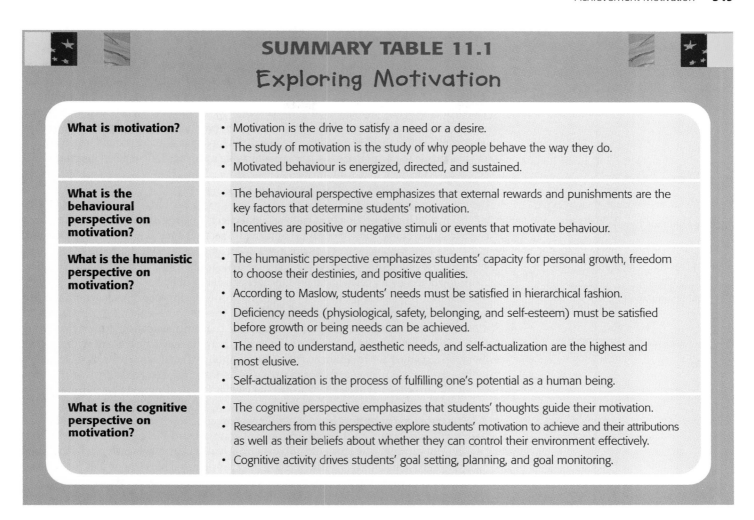

SUMMARY TABLE 11.1
Exploring Motivation

What is motivation?	• Motivation is the drive to satisfy a need or a desire. • The study of motivation is the study of why people behave the way they do. • Motivated behaviour is energized, directed, and sustained.
What is the behavioural perspective on motivation?	• The behavioural perspective emphasizes that external rewards and punishments are the key factors that determine students' motivation. • Incentives are positive or negative stimuli or events that motivate behaviour.
What is the humanistic perspective on motivation?	• The humanistic perspective emphasizes students' capacity for personal growth, freedom to choose their destinies, and positive qualities. • According to Maslow, students' needs must be satisfied in hierarchical fashion. • Deficiency needs (physiological, safety, belonging, and self-esteem) must be satisfied before growth or being needs can be achieved. • The need to understand, aesthetic needs, and self-actualization are the highest and most elusive. • Self-actualization is the process of fulfilling one's potential as a human being.
What is the cognitive perspective on motivation?	• The cognitive perspective emphasizes that students' thoughts guide their motivation. • Researchers from this perspective explore students' motivation to achieve and their attributions as well as their beliefs about whether they can control their environment effectively. • Cognitive activity drives students' goal setting, planning, and goal monitoring.

accounting for student learning (Puhan & Huigin, 2002). Cognitive activity drives students' goals, expectancies, and beliefs, which in turn have an important role in determining what students choose to do, their level of persistence, and their ultimate success.

Thus, whereas the behaviourist perspective views students' motivation as a consequence of external incentives, the cognitive perspective argues that external pressures should be de-emphasized. The cognitive perspective recommends that students should be given more opportunities and responsibility for controlling their own achievement outcomes.

The cognitive perspective on motivation fits with the ideas of R. W. White (1959), who proposed the concept of **competence motivation**, *the idea that people are motivated to deal effectively with their environment, to master their world, and to process information efficiently.* White believed that people behaved this way because they have an internal motivation to effectively interact with the environment.

A review of our discussion of perspectives on motivation is presented in Summary Table 11.1.

ACHIEVEMENT MOTIVATION

Achievement motivation involves a desire to reach goals through one's own efforts. The current interest in achievement motivation has been fuelled by the cognitive perspective. The emphasis in this form of motivation is on planning and establishing realistic goals, mastering the tasks needed to achieve these goals, problem-solving, and monitoring progress. However, before discussing these specific issues, we will examine the most controversial topic in achievement motivation: intrinsic versus extrinsic motivation.

Achievement Motivation
- Extrinsic and Intrinsic Motivation
- Attribution
- Achievement Orientation
- Self-Efficacy
- Self-Regulatory Learning: Goal Setting, Planning, and Self-Monitoring
- Anxiety
- Instructional Strategies and Students' Motivation

www.mcgrawhill.ca/college/santrock

Extrinsic and Intrinsic Motivation

Extrinsic motivation *involves the use of external incentives such as rewards and punishments.* The behavioural perspective emphasizes the importance of extrinsic motivation in achievement. The humanistic and cognitive approaches stress the importance of intrinsic motivation in achievement. **Intrinsic motivation** *involves internal factors such as self-determination, curiosity, challenge, and effort.* Some students study hard because they want to make good grades or avoid parental disapproval (i.e., extrinsic motivation). Other students study hard because they are internally motivated to achieve high standards in their work (i.e., intrinsic motivation).

Self-Determination and Personal Choice Enzle, Wright, and Redondo (1996) provided a model for predicting how motivational effects might generalize or transfer across various activities. The authors' definition of intrinsic motivation is consistent with Deci and Ryan's (1994) view that human beings are innately driven to be autonomous or self-directing rather than controlled by external forces. Thus, intrinsically motivated behaviour is action that is undertaken by an individual with no other goal than the activity itself.

Events that foster a sense of self-determination or competence in learners tend to enhance or at least maintain intrinsic motivation. Events that weaken learners' sense of self-determination or competence tend to decrease their intrinsic motivation. Providing students with choices about how to complete an activity and providing them with positive feedback about their performance will enhance their intrinsic motivation. Contrarily, providing students with rewards based on doing a task (an external motivator), providing them with negative feedback, or being overly controlling tend to reduce intrinsic motivation.

The idea that extrinsic motivation has a negative effect on intrinsic motivation is not unchallenged. University of Alberta professors Cameron and Pierce (2002) contend that rewards do not always stifle students' intrinsic motivation for a subject or activity. They argue that rewards can often lead students to better academic achievement and fuel intrinsic motivation for an activity.

The following list provides suggestions for promoting students' self-determination and choice in your classroom:

- Explain to students the importance of learning activities.
- Be attentive to students' feelings, especially when they are being asked to complete activities they do not enjoy.
- Allow students to make personal choices—whenever possible, let students select topics for book reports, writing assignments, and research projects. Provide options for presenting completed work; for example, students may elect to present with a partner or small group, or to incorporate drama or art as part of their presentation.
- Allow students to divide themselves into self-selected interest groups. Have students work on relevant research topics with other students who share similar interests.

> People who are unable to motivate themselves must be content with mediocrity, no matter how impressive their other talents.
>
> Andrew Carnegie
> *American Industrialist and Philanthropist,*
> *19th Century*

These students were given an opportunity to write and perform their own play. These kinds of self-determining opportunities can enhance students' motivation to achieve.

- Create learning centres where students can work individually or collaboratively with others on various projects. Integrate learning centres throughout the curriculum (e.g., language arts, social studies, computers). Provide students with optional activities within each centre.

Optimal Experiences and Flow Mihaly Csikszentmihalyi (1990, 1993, 2000) has developed ideas that are relevant to understanding motivation. He has studied the optimal experiences of people for more than two decades and reports that these optimal experiences involve feelings of deep enjoyment and happiness. Csikszentmihalyi uses the term *flow* to describe optimal experiences in life. **Flow** *can be defined as the feeling we get when engaged in activities that provide us with both a sense of meaning and a degree of happiness.* Flow occurs most often when people develop a sense of mastery and are absorbed in a state of concentration while they engage in an activity, and when individuals are engaged in challenges they find neither too difficult nor too easy (Csikszentmihalyi, 1993).

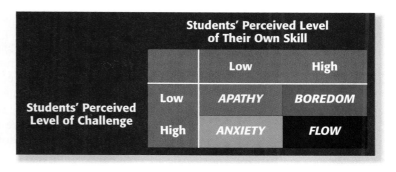

FIGURE 11.2 **Outcomes of Perceived Levels of Challenge and Skill**

Perceived levels of challenge and skill can result in different outcomes (see Figure 11.2; Brophy, 1998). Flow is most likely to occur in areas in which students are challenged and perceive themselves as having a high degree of skill. When students' skills are high but the activity provides little challenge, the result is boredom. When both the challenge and skill levels are low, students feel apathy. And when students face a challenging task that they don't believe they have adequate skills to master, they experience anxiety.

Flow emphasizes the need to increase students' intrinsic motivation. Teachers can use several techniques to encourage students to achieve maximum levels of flow. Start by being knowledgeable about the subject matter and showing enthusiasm when you teach. Present yourself as a model who is intrinsically motivated. Work hard to maintain an optimal match between your instructional challenges and students' skills; that is, encourage students to achieve challenging but reasonable goals. Finally, provide students with both instructional and emotional support that encourages them to tackle learning with confidence and a minimum of anxiety (Csikszentmihalyi, Rathunde, & Whalen, 1993).

Next, we examine the role that extrinsic rewards play in either undermining or promoting intrinsic motivation.

Effects of Rewards The usefulness of classroom rewards is a topic of lively debate. On one hand, critics maintain that rewards can undermine learning. For instance, in one study, students who had a strong interest in art and did not expect a reward spent more time drawing than did students who also had a strong interest in art but knew they would be rewarded for drawing (Lepper, Greene, & Nisbett, 1973). Others argue that rewards can motivate students (Eisenberger & Cameron, 1998), particularly if used to convey information about students' competencies (Bandura, 1982; Deci, 1975). When rewards convey information about mastery, they are more likely to promote students' feelings of competence. However, rewards used as incentives can lead to perceptions that students' behaviours were caused by external rewards and not by their own motivation to be competent.

For more than 30 years, researchers have attempted to determine whether extrinsic rewards undermine intrinsic motivation. Some researchers believe that verbal rewards can be used to enhance students' intrinsic motivation (Cameron & Pierce, 1994, 1996, 2002; Cameron, Banko, & Pierce, 2001). They also believe that intrinsic motivation is maintained when tangible rewards such as gold stars and money are offered contingent on task performance or given unexpectedly (Eisenberger & Cameron, 1996). Others argue that these researchers have not considered some of the negative effects of rewards on motivation (Kohn, 1996; Lepper, Keavney, & Drake, 1996; Ryan & Deci, 1996). For instance, Deci and his colleagues concluded that expected, tangible rewards undermine students' intrinsic motivation, and recommend that teachers be cautious when using reward-based incentive systems.

"Your son has made a career choice, Mildred. He's going to win the lottery and travel a lot."
© 1986; Reprinted courtesy of Bunny Hoest and Parade Magazine.

To better understand the difference between using rewards to control students' behaviour and using them to provide information about mastery, consider this example (Schunk, 1996, 2001): A teacher puts a reward system in place in which the more work students accomplish, the more points they will earn. Students will be motivated to work to earn points because the points can be exchanged for privileges. The points also provide information about their capabilities. As students complete more work, they accumulate more points, and are more likely to feel confident in their abilities. In contrast, if points are provided simply for spending time on a task, the task might be perceived as a means to an end. Because the points don't convey anything about capabilities, students are likely to perceive the rewards as controlling their behaviour.

Thus, rewards that convey information about students' mastery can increase intrinsic motivation by increasing their sense of competence. However, negative feedback, such as criticism that carries the implication that students are incompetent, can undermine intrinsic motivation, especially if students already have doubts about their abilities (Stipek, 1996; 2001).

Developmental Changes   Many psychologists and educators believe that an important goal of teaching is to help students develop a greater sense of independence, internalization, and intrinsic motivation. However, researchers have found that as students move from the early elementary-school years to the high-school years their intrinsic motivation decreases, with the biggest drop occurring between Grades 6 and 7 (Harter, 1981, 1996). This decline in intrinsic motivation seems to be accompanied by an increase in extrinsic motivation and persisting reports from students that school is boring and irrelevant (Harter, 1996). A recent study confirmed these findings and extended them to consider the role of subject area. While students' intrinsic motivation showed the largest decline in mathematics, there was no significant change in other subject areas, such as social studies (Gottfried, Fleming, & Gottfried, 2001).

Why the shift toward extrinsic motivation as students progress through the grades? There are many explanations, ranging from changes in grading practices to changes in school environment. For instance, it may well be the case that the increase in specificity that accompanies the change from letter grades (e.g., S=Satisfactory, N=Needs improvement) to numerical evaluation (e.g., 78%, 85%) makes tracking students' performance easier and also facilitates comparison between students. It is also the case that the change to numerical evaluation is followed by acknowledgment of the high achievers on such measures as class honour rolls and principals' lists.

According to Jacquelynne Eccles and her colleagues, too many schools do not reflect an adequate person–environment fit. What does this mean?

Transition to High School According to Eccles and her colleagues, changes in the school climate may help explain the decline in students' intrinsic motivation in the later-elementary and secondary-school grades (Eccles, 2000; Wigfield, Eccles, & Pintrich, 1996). On the whole, high schools tend to be larger, more bureaucratic, and more impersonal than elementary schools. In such an environment, the sense of community is undermined and there is little opportunity for students and teachers to get to know each other (Lee, Bryk, & Smith, 1993; Bryk, 1994; Lee & Smith, 1994). Research suggests that as students progress through elementary schools and into high schools they encounter an environment that is increasingly less personal, more formal, more evaluative, and more competitive. Students are also more likely to compare themselves with other students, because they are graded increasingly in terms of their relative performance on assignments and standardized tests (Bryk, 1994; Lee & Smith, 1994). Such a climate can be especially harmful for the intrinsic motivation of students who are not doing well academically. This decline in intrinsic motivation also seems to permeate other aspects of students' lives. For instance, declining intrinsic motivation has been correlated with declining willingness to engage in sports and other co-curricular activities (Vallerand, 1999; Vallerand & Rousseau, 2001).

Person–environment fit *refers to the lack of fit between the elementary- and secondary-school environments and the needs of young adolescents, resulting in increasingly negative self-evaluations and attitudes toward school.* Consider that just when adolescents are seeking more autonomy, teachers become more controlling. Similarly, just when students are seeking independence from their parents and need greater support from other adults, teacher–student relationships become more impersonal. Finally, just when adolescents are becoming more self-conscious, there comes an increased emphasis on grades and other competitive comparisons (Eccles, 2000).

The work of Barry J. Fraser and his colleagues provides additional evidence about the importance of person–environment fit (Ferguson & Fraser, 1998; Fraser, 1994, 1998). In an Australian study, high-school students reported more negative perceptions about their classroom environments than did elementary-school students. The results also revealed that students expressed the greatest satisfaction in classrooms with more affiliation, autonomy, and teacher support (Ferguson & Fraser, 1998).

Evaluating Intrinsic and Extrinsic Motivation There is ample evidence in support of the importance of establishing a classroom climate in which students are intrinsically motivated to learn (Eccles, 2000; Hennessey & Amabile, 1998; Lepper, 1998). Teachers can enhance students' learning experiences by creating classrooms that are personal, uncompetitive, and intrinsically challenging. Students are more motivated to learn when they are provided with choices, faced with challenges that match their skills, and receive rewards that have informational value. Thus, praise can enhance students' intrinsic motivation if it contains information about specific competencies and is not perceived as a control agent.

Attribution

Attributions *are perceived causes of outcomes.* **Attribution theory** *states that in their effort to make sense of their own behaviour or performance, individuals are motivated to discover its underlying causes.* Students are like intuitive scientists—they seek to explain the cause behind what happens (Weary & Jacobson, 1997; Weiner, 2000). For example, a secondary-school student asks, "Why am I not doing well in this class?" or "Did I get a poor grade because I did not study well, because the teacher made up a difficult test, or both?" The search for a cause or explanation is most likely to be initiated when students' expectations are violated, such as when unexpected and important events end in failure (Graham & Weiner, 1996). For example, when a good student receives a lower grade than expected, he or she will be more likely to initiate a search for explanations. Some of the most frequently inferred causes of success and failure are ability, effort, task difficulty, and luck.

Dimensions of Causal Attributions   Three dimensions have been identified as particularly important to causal attributions: (1) *locus*, whether the cause is internal or external to the individual; (2) *stability*, the extent to which the cause remains the same or changes; and (3) *controllability*, the extent to which the individual can control the cause (Weiner, 1986, 1992). For example, a student might perceive his aptitude as internal, stable, and uncontrollable. The student also might perceive chance or luck as external, variable, and uncontrollable. Figure 11.3 lists common causal attributes used by students as a function of locus, stability, and controllability.

Students' perceptions of success or failure as due to internal or external factors influence their self-esteem. Students who perceive their success as due to an internal reason, such as effort, are more likely to have higher self-esteem following success than students who believe that their success is due to an external reason, such as luck. In the aftermath of failure, internal attributions lead to decreased self-esteem.

Students' perceptions of stability also influence their expectations of success. If students ascribe a positive outcome to a stable cause, such as aptitude, they will expect future success. If they attribute a negative outcome to the same stable cause, they will expect future failure. When students attribute failure to unstable causes such as bad luck or lack of effort, they might believe that they will succeed in the future because the cause of their failure is changeable.

Students' perceptions of the stability of a cause influence their expectation of success (Graham & Weiner, 1996). When students perceive that they are prevented from succeeding because of external factors that other people could have controlled (such as noise or bias), they often become angry. When students perceive that they have not done well because of internally controllable causes (such as not making enough effort or being negligent), they often feel guilty. When students perceive that others do not achieve their goals because of uncontrollable causes (such as lack of ability or a physical handicap), they feel pity or sympathy. And when students fail because of internally uncontrollable factors (such as low ability), they feel shame, humiliation, and embarrassment.

To see how attributions affect subsequent achievement strivings, consider these two students (Graham & Weiner, 1996):

1. Vartan fails his math test. He subsequently seeks tutoring and increases his study time.
2. Saira also fails her math test, but decides to drop out of school.

Vartan's negative outcome (failing the test) motivated him to search for the reasons behind his low grade. He attributes the failure to himself, not blaming his teacher or bad luck. He also attributes the failure to an unstable factor—lack of preparation and study time. Thus, he perceives that his failure is due to internal, unstable, and also controllable

FIGURE 11.3 Combinations of Causal Attributions and Explanations for Failure

When students fail or do poorly on a test or assignment, they often generate causal attributions in an attempt to explain their poor performance. The explanations reflect eight combinations of Weiner's three main categories of attributions: locus (internal-external), stability (stable-unstable), and controllability (controllable-uncontrollable).

Combination of Causal Attributions	Reason Students Give for Failure
Internal-Stable-Uncontrollable	Low aptitude
Internal-Stable-Controllable	Never study
Internal-Unstable-Uncontrollable	Sick the day of the test
Internal-Unstable-Controllable	Did not study for this particular test
External-Stable-Uncontrollable	School has tough requirements
External-Stable-Controllable	The instructor is biased
External-Unstable-Uncontrollable	Bad luck
External-Unstable-Controllable	Friends failed to help

factors. Because the factors are unstable, Vartan has a reasonable expectation that he can still succeed in the future. And because the factors are controllable, he also feels guilty. His expectations for success enable him to overcome his deflated sense of self-esteem. His hope for the future results in renewed goal-setting and increased motivation to do well on the next test.

Saira's negative outcome (also failing the test) led her to drop out of school rather than resolving to study harder. Her failure also stimulated her to make causal attributions. Saira ascribed failure to herself and attributed her poor performance to lack of ability, which is internal, unstable, and uncontrollable. Because the perceived cause is internal, her self-esteem suffered. Because it is stable, she anticipated failure in the future and adaopted a helpless feeling that she could not do anything about it. And because it is uncontrollable, she feels ashamed and humiliated. In addition, her parents and teacher tell her they feel sorry for her but don't provide any recommendations or strategies for success, furthering her belief that she is incompetent. With low expectations for success, low self-esteem, and a depressed mood, Saira decides to drop out of school.

Teachers can use the information provided in Figure 11.3 to help students develop controllable attributions. For example, a teacher could ask a couple of questions, such as "To what extent do you think your score on the test was influenced by personal factors (things about you) rather than external factors (the test, the room, the teacher)?" and "To what extent do you think your score on the test was caused by elements that you can't control versus elements that you can control?" Where appropriate, teachers should redirect students' attributes regarding failure to reflect a lack of effort rather than a lack of ability, task difficulty, or luck.

Some students may not differentiate between quantity and quality; teachers need to help students appreciate the difference between the quantity of effort and the quality of their work. Hence, the teacher must make it quite clear that the target of praise is the effort as well as the quality of the work produced. The repeated focus on the quality of the effort will lead students to realize that what is important is not only the amount of effort, but also the quality. For example, it is not the number of hours spent working on a paper that is important; rather, it is the quality of the finished product.

Brophy (1998) recommends that teachers present students with realistic scenarios where models struggle to overcome difficulties before experiencing success. Brophy believes that such scenarios will help students be better able to address frustration, persist in the face of difficulties, and constructively cope with failure. This is opposed to the usual strategy of providing students with models who handle tasks with ease and succeed with little effort or perseverance.

Achievement Orientation

Researchers have identified mastery as one of three types of achievement orientation: mastery, helpless, and performance. According to Dweck and her colleagues (Henderson & Dweck, 1990; Dweck & Leggett, 1988), students show two distinct responses to challenging or difficult circumstances: a mastery orientation or a helpless orientation. Children with a **mastery orientation** *focus on the task rather than on their ability, have positive affect (suggesting they enjoy the challenge), and generate solution-oriented strategies that improve their performance.*

Mastery-oriented students often rely on self-directed instructions to remind themselves to pay attention, to think carefully, and to remember strategies that have worked in the past (Anderman, Maehr, & Midgley, 1996). The mastery orientation is analogous to the attributional combination of internal–unstable–controllable. Mastery-oriented students believe that their ability can be changed and improved, and are more likely to endorse such statements as, "Being smart is a goal you can achieve."

Mastery orientation also has much in common with Csikszentmihalyi's concept of "flow," or being absorbed in a state of concentration during an activity. Mastery-oriented students immerse themselves in a task and focus their concentration on developing their skills rather than worrying about whether they are going to outperform others. In a state of flow, students become so attuned to what they are doing they are oblivious to distractions.

May you live all the days of your life.

Jonathan Swift
English Writer, 18th Century

In contrast, students with a **helpless orientation** *focus on their personal inadequacies, often attribute their difficulty to a lack of ability, and display negative affect (including boredom and anxiety).* The helpless orientation is akin to the attributional combination of internal–stable–uncontrollable. Thus, helpless-oriented students believe that ability is basically fixed and cannot be changed, and are more likely to endorse such statements as, "How smart you are stays the same."

The third type of achievement orientation is **performance orientation**, *which involves being concerned with outcome rather than with process.* For performance-oriented students, winning is most important and happiness is thought to be a result of winning. In contrasting mastery orientation with performance orientation it becomes clear that for mastery-oriented students, effectively interacting with their environment is of primary importance. These students like to win, but winning is not as important as it is to performance-oriented students; rather, developing their skills is of greater importance.

Performance-oriented students who are not confident of their success face a special problem (Stipek, 1996). If they try and fail, they often take their failure as evidence of low ability. By not trying at all, they can maintain an alternative, more personally acceptable explanation for their failure. This dilemma leads some students to engage in behaviour that protects them from an image of incompetence in the short run but interferes with their learning and achievement in the long run (Covington, 1992). To avoid the attribution of low ability, some of these students simply don't try, or they cheat. Others might resort to more subtle image-protecting strategies such as procrastinating, making excuses, working halfheartedly, or setting unrealistic goals.

What can teachers do to increase mastery orientation and lessen the occurrence of helpless and performance orientation? According to a study by Mueller and Dweck (1998), teachers need to be careful when praising students. Students who receive praise for their intelligence and achievements often blame poor performance on a lack of intelligence. Students who are praised for the quality of their efforts usually demonstrate a determination to learn strategies that will help them improve their performance. Complimenting students for their intelligence and general performance may lead them to believe that high grades are more important than mastering new concepts. More importantly, it appears that one of the unintended consequences of praising students' abilities is that it might backfire by making them more performance-oriented—and thus vulnerable to the effects of inevitable setbacks. In short, judicious use of praise that is focused on highlighting students' efforts is more likely to promote mastery orientation.

Self-Efficacy

Self-efficacy *is the belief that one can master a situation and produce positive outcomes.* According to Bandura (2000), self-efficacy affects how people feel, think, and act. Low self-efficacy is associated with depression, anxiety, and helplessness. A strong sense of competency facilitates general cognitive processes and builds confidence in the ability to think clearly, make good plans, and execute them. Students with high self-efficacy set higher goals and persevere to attain them. Once an action has been started, students with high self-efficacy invest more effort into its successful completion and persist with the task longer than students with low self-efficacy. More importantly, when setbacks occur, students with high self-efficacy recover quickly. Bandura (1994, 1997, 1998, 2000) believes that self-efficacy is a critical factor in whether students achieve in school. Self-efficacy has much in common with intrinsic motivation and achievement orientation. Self-efficacy is the belief that "I can"; helplessness is the belief that "I cannot" (Stipek, 1996). Students with high self-efficacy have a positive, "can-do" attitude and endorse such statements as "I know that I will be able to learn the material in this class," and "I expect to be able to do well at this activity."

According to Schunk (1989, 1991, 1999), self-efficacy influences students' choices of activities. Students with low self-efficacy tend to avoid many learning tasks, especially those that are challenging. Students with high self-efficacy are more likely to expend greater effort and persist longer at a learning task.

That's what makes a man great; his flashes of insight, when he pierces through the nonsense of his time, and gets at something that really matters.

Robertson Davies
Canadian Author, 20th Century

Teaching Strategies
For Improving Students' Self-Efficacy

✔ Teach goal setting
- help students establish realistic long-term goals
- help students break long-term goals into a series of short-term ones
- help students monitor short-term-goal performance
- help students monitor progress toward long-term goals
- provide students with performance-contingent rewards (i.e., those that reward mastery versus task engagement)

✔ Teach relevant strategies
- explicitly teach strategies needed to achieve goals (e.g., problem solving, critical thinking)
- explicitly teach strategies that will assist students to focus on the task at hand (e.g., outlining, summarizing)
- inform students about how using effective strategies facilitates goal acquisition
- help students understand the connection between strategy use and performance

✔ Monitor students' affect
- make sure students are not overly aroused or anxious
- discourage students from worrying or agonizing about their performance
- provide students with supportive statements (e.g., "You can do this," "You have the right skills to do this task," "You know what strategies you need to use here")
- encourage students, other teachers, and parents to use similar statements of support

✔ Provide appropriate mentors and models
- be a positive role model—cope effectively and master challenges
- help students recognize successful peers (especially ones who are similar to themselves) and the strategies they use
- have students explain how they mastered specific tasks
- help students recognize successful adults and the strategies they use
- use cooperative and collaborative learning processes

Source: Stipek (1996)

As a teacher, your self-efficacy also influences the quality of learning that your students will experience in your classroom. According to Melby (1995), teachers with low self-efficacy often have little confidence in their ability to manage their classroom, become easily stressed and angered at students' misbehaviours, are pessimistic about students' abilities to improve, adopt a custodial view of their profession, and rely on restrictive and punitive modes of discipline. When their students fail to learn, teachers with low self-efficacy are inclined to attribute low student ability as the causal reason.

Teachers with high self-efficacy tend to view difficult students as reachable and teachable. They regard learning problems as surmountable and are more likely to develop ingenious strategies when helping struggling students. Students learn much more from teachers with a high sense of efficacy than from those who are beset by self-doubt (Ashton & Webb, 1986). While observing students during computer classes, Ross and his colleagues noted that students led by teachers with high computer confidence demonstrated greater knowledge and skills as well as increased computer self-efficacy when compared to students led by teachers with low computer confidence (Ross, Hogaboam-Gray, & Hannay, 2001).

While the ability to transmit subject matter is one aspect of instructional self-efficacy, it also includes the belief that one can maintain an orderly classroom, create an exciting place

for students to learn, enlist community resources, and involve parents in their children's learning (Bandura, 1997).

Bandura (1997) also described the characteristics of efficacious schools, where high expectations and standards for achievement are pervasive and teachers and principals work together to improve instruction. Masterful leadership promotes teachers' sense of instructional efficacy, which in turn encourages them to regard their students as capable individuals, set challenging academic standards, and provide students with appropriate supports for achieving their goals.

In low-achieving schools, principals function more as administrators and disciplinarians (Coladarci, 1992). Teachers spend less time actively teaching and monitoring students' academic progress, and tend to "write off" a high percentage of students as unteachable (Brookover et al., 1979). Not surprisingly, students in these environments are likely to exhibit low self-efficacy and a sense of academic futility.

At this point we have studied a number of ideas about extrinsic and intrinsic motivation, attribution, achievement orientation, and self-efficacy. A review of these ideas is presented in Summary Table 11.2. Next, we will continue our coverage of achievement motivation by studying goal setting, planning, and self-monitoring.

Self-Regulatory Learning: Goal Setting, Planning, and Self-Monitoring

Self-regulatory learning *consists of the self-generation of thoughts, feelings, and behaviours to reach a goal.* In this section, we will focus on three important components of self-regulatory learning: goal setting, planning, and self-monitoring.

Goals Researchers have found that self-efficacy and achievement improve when students set goals that are specific, proximal, and challenging (Bandura, 1997; Schunk, 1996; Schunk & Ertmer, 2000). Consider the nonspecific, fuzzy goal "I want to be successful" versus the more concrete, specific goal "I want to make the honour roll by the end of the semester."

Goals can have two characteristics: time and difficulty. Students should be encouraged to set both long-term (distal) and short-term (proximal) goals. However, when students set long-term goals, such as "I want to graduate from high school," or "I want to go to university," they need to make sure that they also set short-term goals as steps along the way, such as "Getting an A on the next math test," or "Doing all of my homework by 4 p.m. Sunday." Students do better if they focus their attention predominantly on short-term goals, as they will be able to judge their progress more accurately than if they focus on long-term goals. Students should also be encouraged to work in small increments and be reminded that a house is built one brick at a time and that an artist paints one stroke at a time.

Teachers need to help their students develop accurate self-judgment so that they can improve on their ability to set specific educational goals. Have students practise setting goals by recording them, clarifying and assessing them, and developing strategies for meeting them. For instance, students can be more productive if they set specific goals to work toward each time they study, such as completing 20 math problems, reading two chapters of a book, and writing a one-page summary for a project.

Another general strategy is to encourage students to set challenging but attainable goals. Strong interest and involvement in activities is sparked by challenges and goals that are optimally matched to students' skill levels. Goals that are easy to reach generate little interest or effort, and goals that are unrealistically high can result in repeated failures that lower students' self-efficacy.

Nicholls (1979; Nicholls et al., 1990) distinguishes between three types of goals: ego-involved, task-involved, and work-avoidant. Students who set **ego-involved goals** *strive to maximize favourable evaluations and minimize unfavourable ones.* Ego-involved students might focus on how smart they will appear and how many other students they can outperform. On the other hand, students who have **task-involved goals** *focus on mastering tasks.* They concentrate on how well they can complete the task and what they will learn during the process. These students become absorbed in their schoolwork and are

www.mcgrawhill.ca/college/santrock

The highest wisdom I know is that success is conquered by those who conquer it each day anew.

Johann Wolfgang von Goethe
German Poet and Playwright, 19th Century

SUMMARY TABLE 11.2
Extrinsic and Intrinsic Motivation, Attribution, Achievement Orientation, and Self–Efficacy

What are the two types of motivation?	• Extrinsic motivation is based on external incentives such as rewards and punishment. • In some situations, rewards can undermine performance. • When rewards are used, they should convey information about task mastery rather than external control. • Intrinsic motivation is based on internal factors such as self-determination, curiosity, challenge, and effort. • Intrinsic motivation promotes self-determination and personal characteristics. • Providing students with choice and providing opportunities for them to take responsibility increases intrinsic motivation. • Researchers have found that as students move from the early elementary-school years to high school their intrinsic motivation decreases.
What is flow?	• Csikszentimihalyi uses the term flow to describe life's optimal experiences that involve a sense of mastery and absorbed concentration in an activity. • Flow is most likely to occur when students are challenged and perceive themselves as having a high degree of skill.
What is person–environment fit?	• Person–environment fit is the relationship between individuals' need for autonomy and organizations' need for control. • As students progress through school, there is often a lack of fit between adolescents' needs for autonomy and schools' needs for increasing control. • The mismatch can result in students' acquiring negative self-evaluations and attitudes toward school.
What are attributions and attribution theory?	• Attributions are perceived causes of outcomes. • Attribution theory states that in an attempt to make sense of their own behaviour or performance, individuals are motivated to discover its underlying causes. • Weiner identified three dimensions of causal attributions: locus (internal/external), stability (stable/unstable), and controllability (controllable/uncontrollable). Combinations of these dimensions produce different explanations for failure and success. • Students who perceive success as due to internal reasons, such as effort, have higher self-esteem than those students who believe that their success is due to external reasons, such as luck. • Students who ascribe a positive outcome to a stable cause will expect success; those who attribute a negative outcome to a stable cause will expect failure.
What are achievement orientations?	• A mastery orientation focuses on the task rather than ability, involves positive affect, and includes solution-oriented strategies. • A helpless orientation focuses on personal inadequacies, attributes difficulty to lack of ability, and involves negative affect (such as boredom or anxiety). • A performance orientation focuses on concern for achievement versus the achievement process.
What is self-efficacy?	• Self-efficacy is the belief that one can master a situation and produce positive outcomes. • Bandura believes that self-efficacy is a critical factor in whether students do well academically. • Low-efficacy students avoid many learning tasks, especially those that are challenging. • Low-efficacy teachers become mired in classroom problems. • High-efficacy students work eagerly at challenging learning tasks and are more likely to persist until they master a concept or a skill. • High-efficacy teachers believe all students can learn, and that learning difficulties are surmountable with extra effort and good strategies.

Through the Eyes of Teachers

Helping Students Achieve Their Goals

Goal-setting programs in elementary grades can be powerful tools for helping students take charge of their own learning. However, I have seen a number of goal-setting programs that have not been successful over the long term. Sometimes, there was a lack of follow-through by the teacher or by the students. Sometimes, goals were too curriculum-oriented and were not relevant to students' lives. Other times, students set genuine and realistic learning goals but lacked the necessary skills or knowledge to achieve them. If teachers are to help students become successful goal setters, they must teach them how to set realistic targets, help them develop necessary skills and attitudes, and provide classroom environments where goal attainment is part of the daily routine. While this is not a simple task, it is one well worth pursuing.

Hillary Elliott
Elementary-School Teacher
Alberta

not concerned about comparing their performance to that of other students. Students with **work-avoidant goals** *try to exert as little effort as possible on a task*. For example, students with work-avoidant behaviours might simply answer "yes" or "no" to a question that requires an elaboration.

Creating an environment that fosters the development of task-involved goals rather than ego-involved or work-avoidant goals requires conscious effort on the part of teachers. This is especially true when students make the transition from elementary to high school, as they are likely to increase their motivation to focus on performance goals rather than mastery goals (Eccles, Wigfield, & Schiefele, 1998). In one research study, both teachers and students reported that task-involved goals were more common in intermediate grades than in elementary school (Midgley, Anderson, & Hicks, 1995). In addition, the elementary-school teachers reported using task-focused goals more than intermediate-grade teachers did. At both levels, the extent to which the teachers were task-focused was linked with the students' and the teachers' sense of personal efficacy. Not unexpectedly, personal efficacy was lower for the intermediate- than the elementary-school participants. Thus, it is especially important that intermediate-grade teachers include task-focused goals in their instruction.

To encourage students to set task-focused goals, the Learning Skills Program at the University of Victoria recommends that teachers use the acronym SMART. This acronym stands for goals that are **S**pecific, **M**anageable, **A**ttainable, **R**ealistic, and **T**imely. Goals that are SMART help students avoid procrastinating and encourage them to be accountable. In general, the Learning Skills Program seeks to assist students in the development of efficient study techniques and learning methods. The institute offers workshops to students regularly on such topics as time management and increasing motivation. For more information about the Learning Skills Program, visit **www.coun.uvic.ca/learn/timemgt.html**.

Planning   Being a good planner means managing time effectively, setting priorities, and being organized. While helping students set goals is a valuable activity, it is just as important to encourage them to plan how they will reach their goals (Elliot, McGregor, & Gable, 1999; Randi & Como, 2000).

You might start by providing students with a calendar on which they can record the dates of exams, papers, homework assignments, and other tasks and activities. Ask them to think about how many days or weeks they will need to study for exams or write papers. Have them include the days or weeks during which these tasks will be their main priority. Tell them that their term calendar is not etched in stone; encourage them to monitor it regularly and evaluate whether they need to modify it (for example, you might add another assignment or change a test date, or students might find that they need more study time than they originally predicted for a particular course).

An important educational objective, especially for the older students, is to develop a realistic sense of the time required to finish various tasks. This type of information is valuable for developing planning ability. To assist students in this endeavour, photocopy a blank weekly plan. The form should have the days of the week across the top, and the headings "Planned" and "Actual" under each day. The 24 hours of the day should be listed vertically on the left side in a column. Have students fill in their class hours, leisure activities (e.g., sports, music practice, watching TV), and other routine activities like sleeping and eating. A good strategy is to have students create this plan at the end of the week. Then have them monitor it the next week to see how effectively they carried out their plan.

After students have created term and weekly plans, give them practice in setting priorities for the next day. A critical skill for good time managers is setting priorities. An effective way to help students set priorities is to have them create manageable to-do lists. Their goal should be to make up the list in the evening and then complete all of the items the next day. Have them identify the top-priority tasks and make sure that they complete those.

The University of Guelph in Ontario has posted a resource about how to make effective academic to-do lists. The first step is to record all school-related assignments, projects, and tests, along with their due dates. Next, estimate the time that it will take to complete these tasks. These estimates may span across several days or weeks. Students should consider the due dates and then prioritize which tasks should be completed first. All of the tasks should be ranked in order of importance as a means of prioritizing time. Encourage students to complete all tasks within their due dates. For more information, visit **www.learningcommons.uoguelph.ca**.

Students will be surprised at the types of discoveries they can make when they analyze their time-use plans. Some students will be totally unaware of how much time they waste, underestimate how much time they need to study, and be far less effective at using time than they imagined. Other students will learn that proper time management requires planning, organization, and self-discipline, but that the results are worth it.

Schools have not given students adequate opportunities to practise time-management skills. Recently, many schools in Canada have required students to use school planners or agendas, sometimes as early as Grade 1. As part of this program, teachers model how to record homework assignments and upcoming events. The agenda can also be used as a communication log between home and school.

If you are going to be an elementary- or secondary-level teacher, commit to working with students to improve their time-management skills. The following are some general strategies that you can use to teach students how to manage time effectively and increase achievement:

- Be proactive—avoid the tendency to be reactive. Students rarely plan or manage their available time for studying. Most students tend to complete their assignments on a reactive basis at the last minute. Encourage them to be more proactive and develop term plans, weekly plans, and daily to-do lists.
- Provide students with regular work and study times.
- Provide students with regular work and study areas—ensure that these areas have appropriate lighting and are free from noise and other distractions.
- Help students learn to say no to distractions—encourage them to say no when friends or siblings call upon them when they are working or studying. Encourage students to negotiate alternative plans with their friends and siblings when they have finished the task at hand.
- Provide students with rewards for their successes—encourage students to delay desirable activities (e.g., playing with friends, watching TV, playing electronic games) and use them as rewards for completing their work.

Self-monitoring   Older students not only should plan their next week's activities, but also should monitor how well they are progressing with their plan. Once students engage in a task, they need to monitor their progress, judge how well they are doing, and evaluate the outcomes to regulate what they do in the future (Eccles, Wigfield, & Schiefele, 1998). Using these strategies will improve their achievements, and will help them develop critical skills that they can apply to life beyond school (Butler 1998a, 1998b, 2002a; Zimmerman, Bonner, & Kovach, 1996). Researchers have found that high-achieving students often are self-regulatory learners (Butler 1998a, 1998b, 2002a; Pressley, 1995; Schunk & Zimmerman, 1994; Zimmerman & Risemberg, 1997). For instance, high-achieving students self-monitor their learning and evaluate their progress toward goals more than low-achieving students do. Encouraging students to self-monitor their learning conveys the message that students are responsible for their own behaviour and that learning requires active, dedicated participation.

Teachers can foster self-monitoring by providing checklists that break down tasks and by guiding students in self-monitoring activities. A checklist can be created for any task or activity to track progress and identify elements of the task that need greater attention. Teachers may need to offer structure or guidance to help students learn to successfully monitor their work. With prudence, students can move from relying on a teacher's guidance to setting and monitoring guides independently. According to Butler's self-regulation model of strategic content learning (see Chapter 7), there needs to be an ongoing emphasis on collaboration between student and teacher to ensure that the approach to learning meets the needs of the student and the task (Butler 1998a, 1998b, 2002a).

Anxiety

Anxiety *is a vague, highly unpleasant feeling of fear and apprehension.* It is normal for students to be concerned or worried when they face school challenges, such as doing well on a test. Indeed, researchers have found that many successful students have moderate levels of anxiety (Bandura, 1997). However, some students have high levels of anxiety and worry constantly, which can significantly impair their ability to achieve.

Some students' high anxiety levels are the result of parents' unrealistic achievement expectations and pressure. Many students experience increasing anxiety as they reach higher grade levels, where they face more frequent evaluation, social comparison, and, for some, experiences of failure (Eccles, Wigfield, & Schiefele, 1998). Elevated anxiety can result in a range of internalizing and externalizing outcomes such as depression, poor academic performance, and behaviour problems. Cognitive and behavioural coping skills can provide students with strategies to manage elevated anxiety.

A number of programs have been created to reduce an individual child's high anxiety level (Wigfield & Eccles, 1989). Some intervention programs emphasize relaxation techniques. These programs often are effective at reducing anxiety, but they do not always lead to improved achievement. Other types of intervention programs aim at reducing anxiety by focusing on the worry aspect, attempting to change the negative, self-damaging thoughts of anxious students and replacing them with positive, task-focused thoughts (Meichenbaum & Deffenbacher, 1988; Roeser, Eccles, & Sameroft, 2000; Roeser, Eccles, & Stroebel, 1998). For example, most high-school students write final exams in the gymnasium. The lack of familiarity with the examination environment could cause additional anxiety in students. In preparing for a final exam, a student may wish to develop a "self-talk script" that would involve visualizing the gym on the morning of the exam, as well as imagining writing the exam in the gym. Part of the script would involve instructions for taking slow and deliberate deep breaths while engaging in positive self-talk with self-affirming statements, such as "I know the material—I can do this question." According to Hains and colleagues, these cognitive-based programs appear to be effective in reducing anxiety and improving students' achievement (Hains & Szyjakowski, 1990; Hains & Ellman, 1994).

Instructional Strategies and Students' Motivation

Ames (1992) examined how the various tasks used in instruction, teacher–student relations, and the nature of evaluation and recognition can influence students' motivational patterns in such areas as intrinsic motivation, attributions involving effort-based strategies, and active engagement. Figure 11.4 provides a summary of the research in the area. It is worth noting that the motivational concepts in Figure 11.4 reflect many of the ideas on achievement motivation we have discussed so far in this chapter.

The direction of causality in Figure 11.4 goes from teacher to student, implying that the teacher influences students' motivation rather than students influencing the teacher (Eccles, Wigfield, & Schiefele, 1998). However, students' own beliefs about effective instructional and motivational strategies need to be considered. For instance, one study found that students and teachers often had different perspectives on motivational practices.

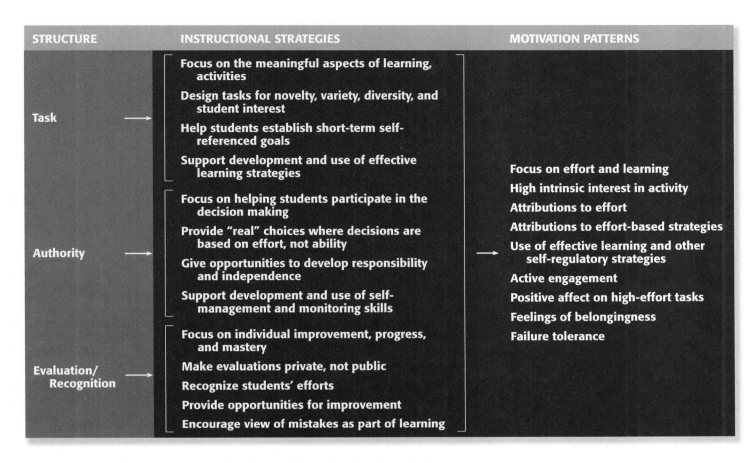

STRUCTURE	INSTRUCTIONAL STRATEGIES	MOTIVATION PATTERNS
Task →	Focus on the meaningful aspects of learning, activities Design tasks for novelty, variety, diversity, and student interest Help students establish short-term self-referenced goals Support development and use of effective learning strategies	Focus on effort and learning High intrinsic interest in activity Attributions to effort Attributions to effort-based strategies
Authority →	Focus on helping students participate in the decision making Provide "real" choices where decisions are based on effort, not ability Give opportunities to develop responsibility and independence Support development and use of self-management and monitoring skills	→ Use of effective learning and other self-regulatory strategies Active engagement Positive affect on high-effort tasks Feelings of belongingness Failure tolerance
Evaluation/ Recognition →	Focus on individual improvement, progress, and mastery Make evaluations private, not public Recognize students' efforts Provide opportunities for improvement Encourage view of mistakes as part of learning	

FIGURE 11.4 **Links Between Instructional Strategies and Students' Motivation**

Students thought that extrinsic rewards like gold stars and money were more effective in motivating them than praise, which teachers believed was more effective (Nolen & Nicholls, 1994).

An important aspect of instructional strategies not included in Ames's model is teacher expectancies. Students' motivation and performance are influenced by teachers' expectations, with most students trying to match the expectations placed on them. Therefore, if teachers have high expectations of students, it is quite likely that their students will try hard to do well. Unfortunately, it is also the case that when teachers have low expectations, students are unlikely to exert the effort needed to perform well. A number of studies have examined the role of teachers' expectations. Teachers often have more positive expectations for high-ability students than for low-ability students, with these expectations influencing their behaviour toward them. When compared to interaction with low-ability students, teachers require high-ability students to work harder, wait longer for them to respond to questions, respond to them more elaborately, criticize them less often, praise them more often, are friendlier to them, call on them more often, seat them closer to the teachers' desks, and are more likely to give them the benefit of the doubt (Brophy, 1985, 1998). Thus, it is critical that teachers monitor their expectations for all students. Fortunately, researchers have found that with support teachers can adapt and raise their expectations for students with low abilities (Weinstein, Madison, & Kuklinski, 1995).

At this point we have studied a number of ideas about goal setting, planning, and self-monitoring; anxiety; and instructional strategies and students' motivation. A review of these ideas is presented in Summary Table 11.3. Next, we will explore the nature of social motives, relationships, and sociocultural contexts, as we continue to examine various aspects of achievement.

www.mcgrawhill.ca/college/santrock

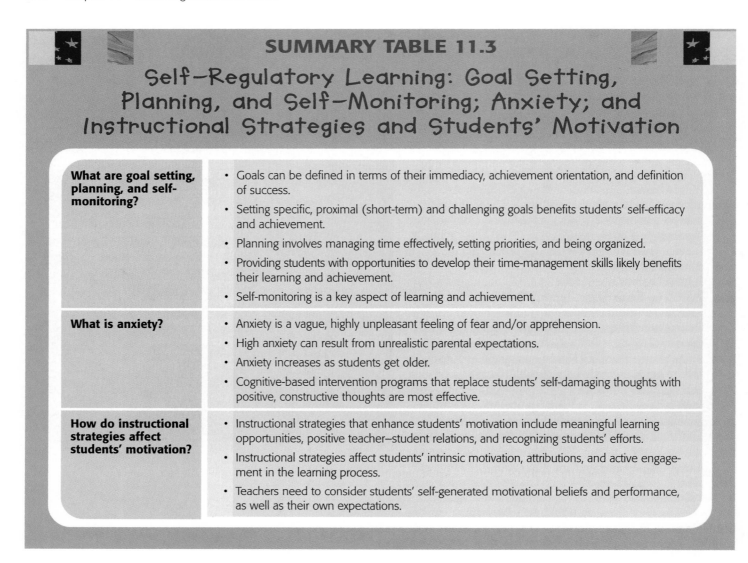

SUMMARY TABLE 11.3

Self–Regulatory Learning: Goal Setting, Planning, and Self–Monitoring; Anxiety; and Instructional Strategies and Students' Motivation

What are goal setting, planning, and self-monitoring?	• Goals can be defined in terms of their immediacy, achievement orientation, and definition of success. • Setting specific, proximal (short-term) and challenging goals benefits students' self-efficacy and achievement. • Planning involves managing time effectively, setting priorities, and being organized. • Providing students with opportunities to develop their time-management skills likely benefits their learning and achievement. • Self-monitoring is a key aspect of learning and achievement.
What is anxiety?	• Anxiety is a vague, highly unpleasant feeling of fear and/or apprehension. • High anxiety can result from unrealistic parental expectations. • Anxiety increases as students get older. • Cognitive-based intervention programs that replace students' self-damaging thoughts with positive, constructive thoughts are most effective.
How do instructional strategies affect students' motivation?	• Instructional strategies that enhance students' motivation include meaningful learning opportunities, positive teacher–student relations, and recognizing students' efforts. • Instructional strategies affect students' intrinsic motivation, attributions, and active engagement in the learning process. • Teachers need to consider students' self-generated motivational beliefs and performance, as well as their own expectations.

Motivation, Relationships, and Sociocultural Contexts

Social Motives — Sociocultural Contexts — Social Relationships

MOTIVATION, RELATIONSHIPS, AND SOCIOCULTURAL CONTEXTS

Motivation has a social component. Students have not only achievement motives, but also social motives. Our coverage of the social dimensions of motivation focuses on students' social motives, social relationships, and sociocultural contexts.

Social Motives

How are students' social lives at school related to their motivation to achieve academically? Every day students work at establishing and maintaining social relationships, with these social worlds influencing their lives at school. Researchers have found that students who display socially competent behaviour are more likely to excel academically than those who do not (Juvonen & Wentzel, 1996; Wentzel, 1997). Beyond this relationship, researchers still know relatively little about how students' social worlds are related to their motivation to learn in the classroom (Covington, 2000).

Social motives *are needs and desires that are learned through experiences with the social world.* According to Henry Murray's (1938) early work on social needs (or motives), humans have a **need for affiliation**, *which is the motive to be with other people to establish, maintain, and restore warm, close, personal relationships.* Students' social needs change as they progress through the grade levels, perhaps ranging from the need to have one or more close friends in the early years, to a desire to be popular with peers in the later elementary years, and to feeling a powerful attraction to someone they love in the high-school years. Though each student has a need for affiliation, some students have a stronger need than others (O'Conner & Rosenblood, 1996). Some students like to be surrounded by lots of friends. For example, some high-school students believe that something is drastically missing from their lives if they don't have a girlfriend or boyfriend. Other students don't have such strong needs for affiliation. They do not feel a need to have several close friends around at all times and do not experience anxiety if they are without a romantic partner.

Parents, peers, and teachers comprise the major sources of approval and social motivation for most students. However, the strength or importance of any one of these sources will fluctuate, depending on the age of the student and the environmental context. For instance, in the elementary-school years most students are more motivated to please their parents than their peers (Berndt, 1979; Juvonen & Wentzel, 1996). By the end of elementary school, parent approval and peer approval are about equal (Steinberg, 2000). According to Wentzel (1991), the quality of peer relationships has a strong impact on social adjustment and subsequent performance at school. High-school students usually experience an increase in peer influence and then a significant shift away from it. For example, at the beginning of high school peer conformity outstrips compliance to parents, with the importance of peer influence peaking around 14 years of age (Gándara, 2000). By the end of high school, conformity to peers drops off somewhat as students become more autonomous and independent in their decision making (Juvonen & Wentzel, 1996).

Adolescence is an especially critical time in the development of students' achievement and social motivation. In general, adolescence marks an increase in students' negative attitudes toward learning and a gradual decline in academic motivation (Henderson & Dweck, 1990; Hymel et al., 1996). Furthermore, new academic and social pressures

Through the Eyes of Students

When Mom and Dad Ask about My Day

I like it when I come home from school, because my Mom asks me what I did there. I tell her all about the work we did and if we watched a movie, I tell her about that too. I like telling her about playing with my friends at school. When I talk to my Mom and Dad about the good part of my day at school, I tell them about my friends and the fun stuff. If I don't feel good, then I usually have had a bad day at school, and I tell them about that too. When my Mom asks me what I learned, I tell her that I learned about words and that I learned about this language, but I forget the name of it. I really like talking to my Mom and Dad about school.

Aldo
Grade 1 Student
Dinosaur Expert Who Loves Soccer, Baseball, and Reading
Nova Scotia

Adolescence is a critical juncture in the achievement orientation of many students. Why is it such a critical juncture?

require adolescents to assume greater responsibilities. Adolescents' social interests compete with time required for academic studies. Ambitions in one area can undermine the attainment of goals in another, as when academic achievement leads to social disapproval. In early adolescence, many students must choose whether they will spend more time pursuing social goals or academic ones. The results of these decisions may have long-term consequences in terms of their educational and occupational attainment.

Social Relationships

Schools and families represent complex social systems. Teachers use a variety of teaching methods to try to make learning stimulating for students; these efforts can be enhanced, or in some cases hindered, by certain family characteristics. Hence, students' relationships with parents, peers, friends, teachers, mentors, and others can have profound effects on their achievement and social motivation.

Parents   Research has been carried out studying the relationship between parenting and students' motivation. Specifically, researchers have examined demographic characteristics, child-rearing practices, and home experiences (Eccles, Wigfield, & Schiefele, 1998; Wigfield & Eccles, 2002).

Demographic Characteristics   Parents can have a great deal of influence on the school experience of their children. For example, the degree of parental involvement is directly related to students' academic achievement even in high school (see Figure 11.5). The higher the grades attained, the greater the likelihood that the parents were involved in the child's education.

The socioeconomic status of the family can also be an important factor. For instance, parents with more education are more likely to be involved in their children's educational experiences than parents with less education. They are also more likely to have intellectually stimulating materials at home such as books, educational toys, computers, and musical instruments (Hurtig, 1999). When parents' time and energy are largely consumed by other

Survey Items	Self-reported Grades			
	Mostly A's	Mostly B's	Mostly C's	Mostly D's
Mother keeps close track of how well child does in school.	92%	89%	84%	80%
Father keeps close track of how well child does in school.	85%	79%	69%	64%
Parents almost always know child's whereabouts.	88%	81%	72%	61%
Child talks with mother or father almost every day.	75%	67%	59%	45%
Parents attend PTA meetings at least once in a while.	25%	22%	20%	15%
Child lives in household with both parents.	80%	71%	64%	60%

FIGURE 11.5   Parents' Involvement and High-School Students' Grades

functions beyond their children, students' motivation can suffer. Living in a single-parent family, having parents who are consumed by their work, and living in a large family can sometimes harm students' achievement (Lipman, Offord, & Dooley, 1996).

Family–school connections can also be affected by other factors linked to socioeconomic status, such as parents' mental health. While studying 4,300 Canadian boys and girls aged 6 to 11, Ryan and Adams (2000) observed a relationship between parental mental health and socioeconomic status. Families with higher socioeconomic status have greater levels of social support and thus are better able to manage the effects of depression than are families with lower socioeconomic status. Parents without such social support are more likely to become dysfunctional and are less likely to take the steps necessary to address their depression, which can interfere with their children's school success.

Child-Rearing Practices   According to Eccles and colleagues, even though demographic factors can affect students' motivation, parents' child-rearing practices have even greater effects (Eccles, 1993; Eccles, Wigfield, & Schiefele, 1998; Wigfield & Eccles, 2002).

The following are some positive parenting practices that result in improved student motivation and achievement:

- Knowing enough about the child to provide the right amount of challenge and the right amount of support
- Providing a positive emotional climate, which motivates children to internalize their parents' values and goals
- Providing open, ongoing two-way communication
- Modelling motivated achievement behaviour (i.e., working hard and persisting with challenging tasks)

Teachers need to be aware, however, that while parenting practices have an impact on students' motivation and achievement, challenges that students encounter cannot be attributable solely to their parents' child-rearing practices.

Home Experiences   In addition to general child-rearing practices, parents can influence students' achievement motivation by providing specific experiences at home. Reading to one's preschool children and providing reading materials in the home are positively related to students' later reading achievement and motivation (Wigfield & Asher, 1984). Indeed, researchers have documented that children's skills and work habits when they enter kindergarten are among the best predictors of academic motivation and performance throughout the elementary and secondary-school years (Entwisle & Alexander, 1993).

Peers   Peers can affect students' motivation through social comparison, social competence and motivation, co-learning, and group influences (Eccles, Wigfield, & Schiefele, 1998). Students can compare themselves with their peers on where they stand academically and socially (Ruble, 1983). Adolescents are more likely than younger children to engage in social comparison, although adolescents are prone to deny that they ever compare themselves with others (Harter, 1990). Positive social comparisons usually result in higher self-esteem, negative comparisons in lower self-esteem. Students are most likely to compare themselves with the students who are most similar to them in age, ability, and interests.

Students who are more accepted by their peers and who have good social skills often do better in school and have positive academic achievement motivation (Asher & Coie, 1990; Wentzel, 1997). In contrast, rejected students, especially those who are highly aggressive,

Through the Eyes of Teachers

Parental Involvement and Support

As a guidance counsellor and parent, I know that adolescence is a time when parent–child relationships can be challenged by students attempting to assert their independence. Students often attempt to exclude their parents from their school activities. However, it is especially important that parents remain involved in their children's education during the adolescent years. They need to establish realistic expectations for their children. This is not the time for the parents or teachers to assume the role of "friend." Instead, parents, teachers, and students should endeavour to develop mutual respect through open communications.

I encourage families to develop a homework schedule. Opening lines of communication between home and school is an important part of this process. I suggest that families schedule homework for the early evening and build in some type of recreational activity closer to bedtime. This "fun" time can help motivate children to complete homework. Denial of privileges if homework isn't done should be for that evening, not for the long term. I believe in using natural consequences and positive reinforcement. Extended unrelated punishment can only lead to animosity.

David Adams
Retired, 30-Year Junior-High-School Teacher and Guidance Counsellor
Newfoundland

are at risk for a number of achievement problems, including low grades and school dropout (Olweus, 2001; William-Savin & Berndt, 1990).

In Chapter 9, Social Constructivist Approaches, Domain-Specific Approaches, and Teaching, we highlighted the role of peers in collaborative and cooperative learning, as well as peer tutoring. Peers can help each other learn material through discussion in small groups, and peer tutoring often brings achievement gains to the tutor as well as the student being tutored.

Early work on the role of the peer group in students' achievement focused on its negative role in distracting adolescents from a commitment to academic learning (Goodlad, 1984). More recently, the peer group has been viewed as a positive or negative influence depending on its motivational orientation. If the peer group has high achievement standards, it will support students' academic achievement. But, if a low-achieving student joins a low-achieving peer group or clique, the student's academic work can deteriorate even further (Kinderman, McCollam, & Gibson, 1996).

Negative Peer-Modelling   In recent years, many surveys have measured both the prevalence and the correlates of risk-taking behaviours such as smoking, drug and alcohol consumption, and unprotected sexual activity. One of the most persistent findings is that students are much more likely to participate in a risk-taking activity if their friends participate in it. For example, Greenlund, Johnson, Webber, and Berenson (1997) found that students in Grades 3 through 6 were almost five times as likely to smoke if their best friend smoked. Similarly, Brook, Whiteman, Czeisler, Shapiro, and Cohen (1997) found that one of the best predictors of young adults' smoking was whether they had smoking friends when they were adolescents.

Positive Peer-Modelling   While a substantial amount of research suggests that peer influence peaks around 14 years of age, there is also emerging evidence that peer pressure may continue throughout later adolescence (Gándara, 2000). One form of peer pressure that is of great interest to teachers is that of the "broader reference group." These are individuals with whom a student may never interact, but who represent the kind of person they aspire to be. For example, a female astronaut who speaks at a school may inspire a female student to pursue a career in science; a former paper carrier who earned an academic scholarship in order to afford university may inspire a student to take on a part-time job. Thus, the creation of a culture of high expectations in schools continues to be an important goal for teachers.

Teachers   Early studies of the teacher's role in student motivation focused on the importance of the teacher's warmth and supportiveness. More recently, researchers have expanded their interests to also include instructional strategies, managerial style, and academic expectations (Eccles, Wigfield, & Schiefele, 1998; Ryan & Pintrich, 1997).

Students' motivation is optimized when teachers provide challenging tasks in a mastery-oriented environment that includes good emotional and cognitive support, meaningful and interesting materials, and encouragement and support for autonomy and initiative (Eccles, Wigfield, & Schiefele, 1998).

According to Ryan and Pintrich (1997), teachers need to realize that the substantial social pressures faced by teenagers might force them to adopt counterproductive strategies. They found that students who needed the most help in math were also the ones who were most concerned about what their peers would think if they asked for help. Avoiding looking stupid was their number-one concern; these students were reluctant to ask for help for fear of appearing less smart than other students, even if it resulted in falling behind or performing badly on tests. Teachers and parents need to promote an atmosphere where asking for help is not perceived as a sign of weakness, and must encourage students to avoid making comparisons with others and to concentrate on their own progress.

Consistent with Bandura's ideas about self-efficacy, the motivation and achievement climate of the entire school affects student motivation. Schools with high expectations and academic standards and academic and emotional support for students often have students who are motivated to achieve. The importance of setting high expectations, using collaborative approaches, and linking with the community is highlighted in a study undertaken by Human Resources Development Canada and the Canadian Education Association (1996). Exemplary schools are dedicated to enhancing the working conditions of teachers, are committed to equity and inclusion, and have policies that reflect sensitivity and diversity in decision making (Gaskell, 1995).

Teachers and Parents   When teachers and parents combine their efforts to shape students' development, the impact can be quite significant (Epstein, 1994, 1995, 1996; Hickman, 1996). Thus, it is important to explore strategies that teachers can use to involve parents in their children's education. In the past, schools have given little attention to how teachers can enlist parents as partners in improving students' achievement. There is considerable current interest in how to build this partnership. When teachers systematically and frequently inform parents about their children's progress and help them get involved in their children's learning activities, students often achieve more (Epstein, 1994, 1996).

A model of parent–teacher partnership can be found at Labrador City Collegiate. The school, which is situated in the southwest part of Labrador close to the Quebec border, houses 500 students in Grades 7 to 12. Here parents play many roles, including chauffeur, caterer, office clerk, guest speaker, and coach. In some cases, parents help out in the classroom by supervising and administering tests and assisting in setting up science demonstrations and experiments. Sometimes parents listen to students read, monitor homework assignments, and even help students organize their lockers and schedules. As part of this partnership, parents see their efforts as rewarding and appreciate the personal contact with school staff. In turn, staff members make the parents feel welcomed and appreciated.

According to Connolly, Hachette, and McMaster (1998), when parents become involved in classroom activities such as organizing a reading club, supervising pizza day, or assisting in the school, they convey a clear message to their children that school is important. Children's perception of parental support is related to their school achievement (Connolly, Hachette, & McMaster, 1998). High parental educational aspirations contributed to students' positive attitude toward school and, ultimately, their school success. In this sense, it is especially important for teachers to create an inviting atmosphere for parents so that they will be more likely to become and stay involved in school activities.

Sociocultural Contexts

In this section we will focus on how socioeconomic status, ethnicity, and gender can influence motivation and achievement.

Socioeconomic Status and Ethnicity   Why is it that students from certain cultural and ethnic backgrounds appear to do well in school? The answer to this question is complex. However, it is important to recognize that diversity exists within every cultural group in terms of their definition of achievement. It also is important to distinguish between difference and deficiency. Too often, the achievements of students from many ethnic backgrounds have been interpreted in terms of *deficits* when they are simply *culturally different* (Jones, 1994). In many cases, differences in achievements can be directly linked to other factors such as socioeconomic status, achievement aspirations, and beliefs about the importance of effort (Gibbs, 1989; Schultz, 1993).

Many investigations have overlooked the socioeconomic status of ethnic students. However, when ethnicity and socioeconomic status are simultaneously investigated, socioeconomic status is a better predictor of achievement than is ethnicity. Students from middle- and upper-income families fare better than their counterparts from lower-income backgrounds across a host of achievement situations, including expectations for success, achievement aspirations, and recognition of the importance of effort (Gibbs, 1989; Schultz, 1993). It seems that poverty impacts students' school achievements negatively, regardless of cultural background (Linver, Brooks-Gunn, & Kohen, 2002; Yeung, Linver, & Brooks-Gunn, 2002).

Membership in a cultural or ethnic group is not the most significant factor in determining school achievement. Rather, it is the sharing of certain beliefs and values related

Diversity and Education
Marie Battiste

In an effort to support the achievement motivation of students from diverse ethnic backgrounds, teachers look to exemplary individuals who, through their accomplishments and actions, can provide inspiration and become effective role models. Dr. Marie Battiste is one of these unique individuals.

Dr. Marie Battiste is an outstanding role model for all Canadians. While she calls Saskatchewan her home, she has travelled across Canada and around the world, teaching, guiding, and inspiring audiences ranging from school children to diplomats. Dr. Battiste is a Mi'kmaq born in the Potlo'tek First Nation in Nova Scotia. As an adult, she worked for many years on the impoverished Eskasoni Reserve in a variety of roles including teacher, administrator, and curriculum developer. Throughout her doctoral studies at Harvard and Stanford University, she focused her attention on Mi'kmaw literacy. Her writings on Aboriginal education have resulted in such influential books as *First Nations Education in Canada: The Circle Unfolds, Reclaiming Indigenous Voice and Vision,* and *Protecting Indigenous Knowledge.* Her tireless quest to ensure that indigenous voices are heard has made her a well-known authority at both the national and international level.

Dr. Battiste's extensive contributions have earned her numerous awards including the White Eagle Feather, the Queen's Award for Service to the Community, and the Nova Scotia Social Studies Curriculum Development Award. Other awards include two honorary doctorate degrees—one from Saint Mary's University in Halifax and the other from the University of Maine at Farmington. Students and teachers alike can draw inspiration from Dr. Battiste's dedication to the learning and teaching processes, as well as her passion for the preservation of Aboriginal culture.

Source: www.usask.ca/education/people/battistem.htm, January 10, 2003.

to school success that is important. Students who believe that effort is the main reason for school success are more likely to do well academically than those who believe that achievement is largely determined by luck (Chen & Uttal, 1998; Graham, 1994; Graham, Taylor, & Hudley, 1998; Stevenson et al., 1990). While exploring the experiences of Chinese youth adjusting to the North American educational environment, Chen, Lee, and Stevenson (1996) concluded that these students held high achievement aspirations. In addition, the students reported a strong belief that if they worked hard they would do well in school.

Cultural belief systems can affect school achievement in other ways. For example, people in North America are likely to believe that certain abilities such as intelligence are innate and, therefore, uncontrollable. They also are more likely to perceive a direct link between intelligence and school achievement (Ogbu, 1983; Hess, 1986; Stevenson et al., 1990). While we do not wish to overgeneralize, it is important to highlight the fact that this type of belief system reduces the likelihood that "effort" or "persevering" will be properly appreciated. In contrast, people from cultures that believe that effort (a controllable factor) is the main cause of achievement are more likely to emphasize the importance of "working harder" (Ogbu, 1983).

Another challenge faced by many students from ethnically diverse backgrounds, especially those living in poverty, is the lack of high-achieving adults in their cultural group who can serve as positive role models (McLoyd, 1998; Spencer & Markstrom-Adams,

1990). According to Bandura's research (1997), role models and mentors can influence the aspirations of young people and motivate them to succeed in school and in life. Greater efforts need to be made to increase the number of mentors in the lives of students from all ethnic backgrounds.

Gender   While, there are some differences in motivation and attributions, female and male students' competence-related beliefs vary by achievement context. For example, boys tend to have higher competency beliefs than girls for math and sports, and girls tend to have higher competency beliefs for English, reading, and social activities (Dick & Rallis, 1991; Eccles et al., 1993; Eccles, 1994; Eccles et al., 1999).

Lorenz and Lupart (2001) investigated factors that contributed to elementary- and high-school students' participation in math and science. Working with approximately 1,400 Grade 7 and Grade 10 students from Calgary, the researchers found differences in students' expectations for success in math, language arts/English, and science as a function of gender. Female students held high expectations for success in language courses, and careers that required writing and speaking ability. Male students held high expectations for success in math courses, and careers that required math and science ability.

According to Lorenz and Lupart, teachers need to do more to orient students to a range of career options. Teachers should aim to create learning environments where science is relevant to females, and to create language courses that are relevant to males. Direct links between these activities and careers will help students appreciate the links between the courses they are currently taking and their future careers.

The Women in Engineering and Science (WES) program, developed by the National Research Council of Canada (NRC), is designed to encourage academically talented female students to pursue professional careers in science and engineering. The program, aimed at students entering university, provides significant financial support and offers access to some of the most well-known researchers in the field of engineering and science in Canada. The students are hired for two to three years to work on research projects during the summer or during co-op work terms. Students who participate in the program are partnered with scientists who act as guides and mentors. Participants have the opportunity to experience first-hand the various aspects of their chosen career and build important relationships with future colleagues and mentors.

At this point we have discussed many ideas about social motives, relationships, and sociocultural contexts. A review of these ideas is presented in Summary Table 11.4.

MOTIVATING STUDENTS AND KEEPING THEM MOTIVATED

Throughout this chapter we have discussed many strategies for helping students become motivated to learn. In this section we revisit those strategies, provide further examples, and add some final thoughts on motivating students. We also will discuss some specific strategies for motivating hard-to-reach, low-achieving students.

Overall Strategies

As outlined in the Teaching Strategies for Motivating Students box on page 373, some general approaches for improving your students' motivation include being a competent model, holding high expectations, encouraging students' intrinsic motivation, and guiding students in setting goals, planning, and self-monitoring. To evaluate your own motivational makeup, complete Self-Assessment 11.1.

Parents are an especially important potential resource for enhancing student motivation. Whenever possible, involve them as partners with you in motivating students to learn. Make sure to tell them how much you value their role in providing a motivating atmosphere. In cases where students are not achieving, meet with the parents and invite them to help you develop appropriate strategies. When parents are uncooperative or do

Motivating Students and Keeping Them Motivated

Overall Strategies → **Motivating Hard-to-Reach, Low-Achieving Students**

Life is a gift . . . Accept it.
Life is an adventure . . . Dare it.
Life is a mystery . . . Unfold it.
Life is a struggle . . . Face it.
Life is a puzzle . . . Solve it.
Life is an opportunity . . . Take it.
Life is a mission . . . Fulfill it.
Life is a goal . . . Achieve it.

—Author Unknown

SUMMARY TABLE 11.4
Motivation, Relationships, and Sociocultural Contexts

What are social motives?	• Social motives are needs and desires that are learned through experience with the social world.
	• The need for affiliation involves the motive to be with other people, which consists of establishing, maintaining, and restoring warm, close personal relationships.
	• Teacher and peer approval are important factors in students' sense of social approval.
	• Peer conformity peaks in early adolescence, a time of important decisions about whether to pursue academic or social motives.
How can parents, peers, and teachers affect students' motivation?	• Parents' educational level and time spent at work can affect students' motivation.
	• The provision of specific experiences and materials (such as reading materials) also affects students' motivation.
	• Social comparison, social competence, co-learning, and peer groups influence students' motivation.
	• Teachers' instructional and managerial style affects students' motivation.
	• Enlisting parents as partners in the educational process facilitates students' motivation.
How do socioeconomic status, ethnicity, and gender affect students' motivation?	• The quality of schools for many socioeconomically impoverished students is lower than for their middle-income and upper-income peers.
	• Special concerns focus on valuing cultural diversity, as well as teasing apart the influences of socioeconomic status and ethnicity.
	• Students from some ethnically diverse backgrounds are more likely to emphasize "effort" than "luck."
	• Gender differences in achievement involve attributions, beliefs, and values.
	• Males tend to hold high expectations for their math and science abilities, and girls tend to have high expectations for success in their writing and speaking abilities.
	• Teachers need to do more to orient students to a range of career options and create learning environments where science is relevant to females and language is relevant to males.

Curiosity has its own reason for existing.

Albert Einstein
American Scientist,
20th Century

not possess the necessary skills or abilities to work with you, try to find mentors who are willing to help students succeed.

Students often find the opportunity to interact with positive role models or mentors to be quite motivating. This is especially important for students who do not have access to adult models in their immediate family or community. Ellis, Small-McGinley, and Hart (1998) reported on a volunteer-based mentor program designed to support literacy development in young students. The program was implemented in the primary division of two large schools in Alberta that were considered "high-need" schools. Mentors were all adults who could commit to coming to the school at least one hour every week to share a snack, read, and do other language-based activities with the students. They included university professors, education students, parents, retired teachers and principals, friends and relatives of school staff, and employees of a nearby bank. When matching mentors with students, teachers considered the needs of children and the characteristics of the mentors. For example, students who already had social support outside of school but struggled academically were matched with university students who were more likely to try new instructional ideas.

Teaching Strategies
For Motivating Students

✔ Create an atmosphere that promotes learning
  - establish high achievement expectations and standards
  - do not accept low-quality work or minimal efforts
  - challenge students to do their best
  - inform students that it is their responsibility to put forth their best effort
  - place inspiring quotes and other literature in visible locations
  - use achievement as a unit theme
✔ Help students achieve expectations
  - explicitly communicate your expectations to students
  - monitor students' progress
  - communicate your confidence in students' abilities to meet academic challenges
  - provide students with supportive statements (e.g., "I know you can do this," "Keep working and you will be able to solve this problem")
  - recognize when students need to learn specific skills and provide appropriate instruction
  - recognize when students' emotions are hindering their progress and provide appropriate intervention
  - encourage students to take pride in their accomplishments
✔ Encourage students' intrinsic motivation
  - encourage students to make commitments to activities
  - encourage students to express confidence that they will succeed
  - encourage students to acquire the skills and strategies necessary for success
  - provide students with choices
  - provide learning activities that stimulate students' interest and curiosity
  - use rewards to provide feedback about mastery
  - do not use rewards as a method of control
✔ Help students establish goals
  - provide classroom time for goal setting and plan development
  - provide classroom time for students to monitor their progress toward goals
  - help students establish short-term goals
  - provide students with opportunities to establish priorities
  - have students complete time-management exercises
✔ Use technology effectively
  - provide students with opportunities to use educational software
  - provide students with opportunities to use technology to enhance their academic products
  - provide students with opportunities to use technology to interact with other students
✔ Be a model
  - convey positive attitudes about learning, effort, and achievement
  - express curiosity and enthusiasm
  - emphasize that learning is an important goal in itself
  - share stories about setting goals and the strategies you used to achieve them
  - share stories about being persistent and using effort to achieve goals
  - reflect on your own motivation to be a teacher
  - reflect on how you can sustain your motivation to teach

Evaluating My Motivation

For each item, respond 1 = Not like me, 3 = Somewhat like me, or 5 = Very much like me

	1	2	3	4	5
1. I am aware of the hierarchy of motives and which ones are the most important for me.					
2. I am intrinsically motivated.					
3. I have high expectations and standards for success.					
4. My life has many moments of flow.					
5. I am aware of the people in my life who have motivated me and what it is they did that motivated me.					
6. I make achievement-related attributions that emphasize effort.					
7. I have a mastery motivation orientation rather than a helpless or performance orientation.					
8. I am motivated to learn and succeed because of my aspirations, not because I want to protect my self-worth or avoid failure.					
9. I have high self-efficacy.					
10. I have high instructional self-efficacy in terms of my ability to manage my classroom effectively.					
11. I regularly set goals, plan how to reach those goals, and systematically monitor my progress toward the goals.					
12. I set specific, proximal, and challenging goals.					
13. I am a good time manager, regularly doing weekly plans, monitoring my use of time, and doing "to do" lists.					
14. I am good at learning from my mistakes.					
15. I don't let anxiety or other emotions get in the way of my motivation.					
16. I have a good support system and have positive close relationships with people who can help me sustain my motivation.					

Scoring and Interpretation

Items rated 4 or 5 = Your motivation is working to your advantage. You are likely to be a positive motivational role model for students.

Items rated 3 or less = You should spend some time thinking about how you can improve these aspects of your motivational life. You are not likely at this point to be a positive motivational model for students.

Over the course of the program, students' academic and social performances improved. Teachers reported that the students were highly appreciative of having someone who was there just for them. Students became highly motivated to read and would eagerly anticipate the arrival of their mentors.

Motivating Hard-to-Reach, Low-Achieving Students

According to Brophy (1998), there are two main types of hard-to-reach and low-achieving students: discouraged students who lack the confidence and motivation to learn, and uninterested or alienated students. We will begin our discussion of intervention strategies by focusing on discouraged students.

Rebuilding Discouraged Students' Confidence and Motivation to Learn
Discouraged students include (1) low achievers with low ability who have difficulty keeping up and have developed low achievement expectations, (2) students with failure syndrome, and (3) students obsessed with protecting their self-worth by avoiding failure.

Learning and Animation: Artists and Educators Working Together

For more than 14 years, Tony Tarantini has been using his art and design skills to communicate educational messages to children through multimedia animation. An art and film instructor at Sheridan College in Oakville, Ontario, Tarantini also works as an animation artist with Nelvana Studios, an all-Canadian entertainment company that produces animated children's programs such as *Franklin, Care Bears, George Shrinks,* and Scholastic's *The Magic School Bus.*

Tarantini notes that in Canada, the Canadian Radio-television and Telecommunications Commission (CRTC) mandates that a teaching objective must be specified for every animated children's episode and that this message must be explicitly stated in the script. Animated programs, therefore, are a study in both design and creativity. Each animation starts with an idea and an educational goal that the production team (consisting of writers, directors, producers, and artists) must make come alive for viewers. The challenge for Tony Tarantini and the rest of the creative production team is figuring out how to hook students by communicating the script's vision in a way that motivates them. Motivating students to learn from animated stories is partly a function of the animation team's ability to hook students into the story, and partly a function of educators

and parents discussing and reinforcing the positive ideas and themes raised in the story. "Teacher kits" provide questions and activities that link the animated storyline to curriculum and educational goals.

Tarantini believes that advances in digital editing and multimedia production technology over the past decade have afforded animators with new opportunities and means to expand their creative visions, explore new horizons, and set new limits with respect to what they can achieve with animation. However, while multimedia animation can capture children's attention and introduce new ideas in exciting and entertaining ways, it is teachers and parents making sense of the animated stories by working with students that makes this medium a powerful educational tool.

Tarantini comments that children and adults today have access to some of the most sophisticated animation ever. It is worth remembering, however, that multimedia animation for education is only as good as the artists and educators who work together to make these animated stories a starting point for teaching and not an end in themselves. For further information about animation in education, visit the Animation World Network at **www.awn.com**.

Low-Ability, Low-Achieving Students with Low Expectations for Success These students need to be consistently reassured that they can meet the goals and challenges you have set for them and that you will give them the help and support they need to succeed. However, they need to be reminded that you will accept their progress only as long as they make a real effort. They might require individualized instruction materials or activities. Help them set learning goals and provide them with support for reaching these goals. Recognize gains in their progress, even though they may not yet have the ability to perform at the same level as the rest of the class (Brophy, 1998).

Students with Failure Syndrome **Failure syndrome** *refers to having low expectations for success and giving up at the first sign of difficulty.* Failure-syndrome students are different from low-achieving students, who fail despite putting forth their best effort. Failure-syndrome students don't put forth enough effort, often beginning tasks in a halfhearted manner and giving up quickly at the first hint of a challenge. It is important to keep in mind that students come to school with a range of abilities, and some students unfortunately will have reduced capabilities for a number of reasons. For example, some students, especially in the early grades, show failure-syndrome tendencies due to emotional immaturity. However, most symptoms of failure syndrome are developed through social learning (Brophy, 1998). These students often have low self-efficacy or attribution problems, ascribing their failures to internal, stable, and uncontrollable causes such as low ability.

A number of strategies can be used to increase the motivation of students who display failure syndrome. Especially beneficial are cognitive retraining methods, such as efficacy retraining, attribution retraining, and strategy training (see Figure 11.6).

According to Brophy (1998), teachers may be most effective when they insist on better effort from these students. Teachers should convey an "incremental" view of ability, expressing confidence that improvements will be sustained over time.

Students Motivated to Protect Their Self-Worth by Avoiding Failure Some students are so interested in protecting their self-worth and avoiding failure that they become distracted from pursuing learning goals and engage in ineffective learning strategies. These students protect their self-worth by handicapping themselves. Self-handicappers choose

TRAINING METHOD	PRIMARY EMPHASIS	MAIN GOALS
Efficacy training	Improve students' self-efficacy perceptions	Teach students to establish and obtain specific, proximal, and challenging goals. Monitor students' progress and frequently support students by saying things like "I know you can do it." "You have the necessary skills for this task." "Keep using your strategies." Use adult and peer modelling effectively. Individualize instruction and tailor it to students' knowledge and skills. Keep social comparison to a minimum. Be an efficacious teacher and have confidence in your abilities. View students with a failure syndrome as challenges rather than as losers.
Attribution and achievement orientation retraining	Change students' attributions and achievement orientation	Teach students to attribute failures to factors that can be changed, such as insufficient knowledge or effort and ineffective strategies. Work with students to develop a mastery orientation rather than a performance orientation by helping them focus on the achievement process (learning the task) rather than the achievement product (winning or losing).
Strategy training	Improve students' domain- and task-specific skills and strategies	Help students to acquire and self-regulate their use of effective learning and problem-solving strategies. Teach students what to do, how to do it, and when and why to do it (i.e., explicit instruction).

FIGURE 11.6 Cognitive Retraining Methods for Increasing the Motivation of Students Who Display Failure Syndrome

obstacles to successful performance that enable them to deflect the cause of failure away from their competence and onto an obstacle (Covington, 1997; Tice & Baumeister, 1990). For example, a self-handicapper might work at their part-time job the night before a final exam. Consequently, their poor exam performance is justified by the fact that studying was not possible due to the evening of work.

Following are some of their strategies for protecting self-esteem and avoiding failure (Covington & Teel, 1996):

- *Nonperformance.* The most obvious strategy for avoiding failure is to not try. Students' nonperformance tactics include appearing eager to answer a teacher's question but hoping the teacher will call on another student, sliding down in the seat to avoid being seen by the teacher, and avoiding eye contact. These might seem like minor deceptions, but they can portend other more chronic forms of noninvolvement such as dropping out and excessive absences.
- *Sham effort.* To avoid being criticized for not trying, some students appear to participate but do so more to avoid punishment than to succeed. Some student behaviours that reflect a sham effort are asking a question even though they already know the answer, adopting a pensive, quizzical expression, and feigning focused attention during a class discussion.
- *Procrastination.* Students who postpone studying for a test until the last minute can blame their failure on poor time management, thus deflecting attention away from the possibility that they are incompetent. A variation on this theme involves students who take on so many activities and responsibilities that they have an excuse for not doing any one of them in a highly competent manner.
- *Setting unreachable goals.* By setting goals so high that success is virtually impossible for any student to achieve, students can avoid the implication that they are incompetent.
- *The academic wooden leg.* In this strategy, students admit to a minor personal weakness to avoid acknowledging the greater feared weakness of being incompetent. For example, the student might blame a failing test score on anxiety. Having test anxiety is not as devastating to a personal sense of self-worth as is lack of ability.

According to Covington and his colleagues (Covington, 1992, 1997, 1998; Covington & Teel, 1996; Covington, Teel, & Parecki, 1994), there are a number of strategies that teachers can use to help students reduce their preoccupation with protecting their self-worth and avoiding failure. These instructional strategies and teaching techniques include:

• Providing students with assignments that are inherently interesting and curiosity provoking. The assignments should challenge but not overwhelm their skills. Allow students some choice of activities. As their expertise increases, increase the level of challenge accordingly.
• Requiring that students who tend to procrastinate hand in an outline or first draft a week or two before the final paper is due. According to McKeachie (1999) these students are then forced to plan ahead.
• Establishing a reward system so that all students, not just the brightest, highest-achieving ones, can attain rewards if they put forth effort. Make sure that rewards reinforce students for setting meaningful goals. Reinforce the act of learning as a desirable goal.
• Helping students set challenging but realistic goals, and provide them with the academic and emotional support to reach those goals.
• Emphasizing the association between effort and self-worth. Encourage students to take pride in their efforts and minimize social comparison.
• Encouraging students to develop positive beliefs about their abilities.
• Improving your relationship with students by emphasizing your role as a resource person who will guide and support their learning efforts rather than an authority figure who controls their behaviour.

Motivating Uninterested or Alienated Students According to Brophy (1998), the most difficult motivational problem involves students who are apathetic, uninterested in learning, or for whom achieving in school is not an important value. Reaching apathetic students requires sustained efforts to resocialize their attitudes toward school achievement (Murdock, 1999). Such efforts include working on developing a positive relationship; if uninterested or alienated students do not like you, it is hard to motivate these students to complete any achievement goals. Show patience, but be determined to help students maintain steady progress in spite of setbacks or resistance. Incorporate students' interests whenever possible when developing assignments, and teach them strategies for making academic work more enjoyable. Help them understand that they are creating their own difficulties, and find ways to guide them to take pride in their work. Finally, consider enlisting the aid of community mentors or older students whom you believe uninterested or alienated students will respect.

"Connections" is an example of an intervention program developed to help alienated secondary-school students. Developed in North Bay, Ontario, the program has captured the attention and support of some well-known individuals including Lynn Johnston, the award-winning cartoonist of the popular comic strip *For Better or For Worse*.

The program offers a holistic blend of services for students who are experiencing difficulties fitting in with mainstream high-school culture. Some of the students in the program have learning difficulties, some have problems at home, some are bullied, and others are victimized and isolated. The program offers participants an environment where they feel accepted and valued. Through mentoring and volunteering, participants are provided with opportunities to acquire valuable knowledge and skills.

The four guiding principles of Connections include volunteering, recreational activities, a breakfast program, and mentoring. To provide students with a sense of belonging, they become involved in non-profit organizations by helping out at community events. Once a week students go to the YMCA, where they participate in activities such as golf, curling, horseback riding, and canoe trips. One morning per week students are provided with a nutritious breakfast, while they discuss relevant issues or events or receive instruction about anger management, study strategies, or other relevant skills. Finally, students are matched with adults in the community who can serve as role models and provide career guidance. Sometimes university students serve as mentors, and they often invite the youth to visit campus. The goal is to help the participants become less intimidated by these settings and come to see them as places that they could attend one day. For more information about Connections, see **www.youth-connections.ca**.

At this point we have explored a number of ideas about motivating students and keeping them motivated. A review of these ideas is presented in Summary Table 11.5. Motivating students to learn is an important dimension of classroom life. So is managing the classroom effectively, the topic of the next chapter.

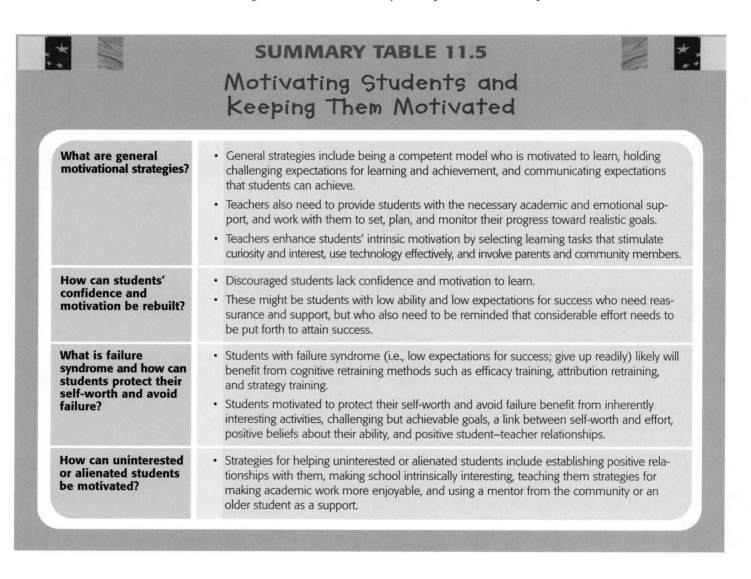

SUMMARY TABLE 11.5

Motivating Students and Keeping Them Motivated

What are general motivational strategies?	• General strategies include being a competent model who is motivated to learn, holding challenging expectations for learning and achievement, and communicating expectations that students can achieve. • Teachers also need to provide students with the necessary academic and emotional support, and work with them to set, plan, and monitor their progress toward realistic goals. • Teachers enhance students' intrinsic motivation by selecting learning tasks that stimulate curiosity and interest, use technology effectively, and involve parents and community members.
How can students' confidence and motivation be rebuilt?	• Discouraged students lack confidence and motivation to learn. • These might be students with low ability and low expectations for success who need reassurance and support, but who also need to be reminded that considerable effort needs to be put forth to attain success.
What is failure syndrome and how can students protect their self-worth and avoid failure?	• Students with failure syndrome (i.e., low expectations for success; give up readily) likely will benefit from cognitive retraining methods such as efficacy training, attribution retraining, and strategy training. • Students motivated to protect their self-worth and avoid failure benefit from inherently interesting activities, challenging but achievable goals, a link between self-worth and effort, positive beliefs about their ability, and positive student–teacher relationships.
How can uninterested or alienated students be motivated?	• Strategies for helping uninterested or alienated students include establishing positive relationships with them, making school intrinsically interesting, teaching them strategies for making academic work more enjoyable, and using a mentor from the community or an older student as a support.

Marjana teaches Grade 2 in an economically disadvantaged elementary school. Many of her students read below grade level. Some of her students have had little exposure to reading outside of school, and most do not choose to read during their free time at school. Knowing that reading skills are important to future success in school, Marjana is justifiably concerned.

In an effort to entice her students to read more, Marjana develops a reading incentive program. She places a large chart on the classroom wall to track student progress. Each time a student completes a book, he or she tells Marjana, who then places a star next to the student's name. Each student who reads five books per month receives a small prize from the class prize box. The student who reads the most books in any given month receives a larger prize. When Marjana tells her students about the new incentive program, they are very enthusiastic.

"This is great!" says Markus. "I'm gonna get the most stars!"

"No, you won't," says Peter. "Sami will. She's always got her nose stuck in a book. She's the best reader in the class."

Sami is a very good reader. She is reading well above grade level and generally favours novels from the young adult section of the library. These books are rather lengthy and take her quite some time to finish. However, she really enjoys them. Marjana has brought her several from her own collection as well, since none of the classroom books seem to interest Sami.

The first week of the program is quite exciting. Every day the students tell Marjana about the books they have read. The chart begins to fill with stars. By the end of the week all the students have at least one star next to their name except Sami. During the last week of the month many students choose reading as a free-time activity. The students are anxious to ensure that they will earn at least one prize, and many are devouring books in anticipation of being the month's top reader. At the end of the month, 23 of Marjana's 25 students have five stars on the chart. The only exceptions are Sami, who has only one star, and Michael, who had chicken pox during the month. True to his word, Markus receives the most stars—15. The students excitedly choose their prizes.

The following month the reading frenzy continues. This time Sami joins her classmates in their accumulation of stars and receives 30, making her the top reader. Markus is right behind her with 25. Every student in the class earns at least five stars, entitling all to a prize. Because they are all reading so much, Marjana gives them a Friday afternoon party at which they watch an animated movie and eat popcorn.

A similar pattern is repeated over the next several months. The star chart fills quickly. Marjana is thrilled with their progress. She decides that after the test, she will drop the incentive program and just quietly keep track of how much her students read. After doing this she notices that once again very few students are reading during their free time. Even Sami is no longer reading when she is finished with her other work.

- What are the issues in this case?
- Analyze the case from the perspectives of extrinsic and intrinsic motivation.
- Analyze the case from a goal-orientation perspective.
- Why do you think Sami went from receiving one star the first month to receiving 30 stars the next? Why does she no longer read in her free time at school?
- What are the problems with this type of incentive program? How might an incentive program be developed that does not undermine students' motivation to read?

CHAPTER REVIEW

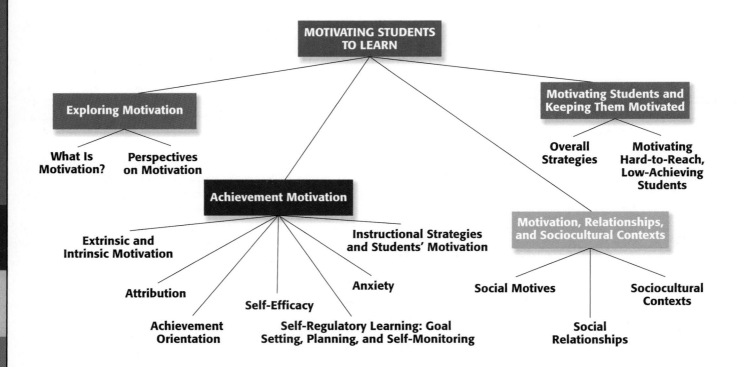

To obtain a detailed review of this chapter, study these five summary tables:

 KEY TERMS

motivation 346	extrinsic motivation 350	mastery orientation 355	task-involved goals 358
incentives 346	intrinsic motivation 350	helpless orientation 356	work-avoidant goals 360
humanistic perspective 347	flow 351	performance orientation 356	anxiety 362
hierarchy of needs 347	person–environment fit 353	self-efficacy 356	social motives 364
self-actualization 347	attributions 353	self-regulatory learning 358	need for affiliation 364
competence motivation 349	attribution theory 353	ego-involved goals 358	failure syndrome 375

PROFESSIONAL DEVELOPMENT/PORTFOLIO ACTIVITIES

1. The Relationship between Self-Efficacy and Attribution

Two new concepts have been covered in this chapter: self-efficacy and attribution. Self-efficacy is an individual's belief in his or her ability to achieve. Attribution is the reason a person gives to explain his or her success or failure. Differentiate between these two concepts by writing a two-page essay. Consider the following question: What is the relationship between a student's self-efficacy and the student's potential attributions?

2. Attribution Style

As a teacher, your attribution style will have an impact on the way you interact with your students. Visit the Weblinks section of the Online Learning Centre to find instruments designed to assess attribution style. Try a few of these assessment tools. Do you find them accurate? Compare the results and synthesize this information in one page. Now, apply your knowledge to the following situation. Suppose a student tells you that she lacks the ability to succeed in your class. How would you respond? How would you describe your student's locus of control and attribution style? How could your style affect the way you teach and interact with this particular student?

3. Maintaining Student Motivation

As a teacher, maintaining student motivation will be an ongoing process. Using the information you learned in this chapter, write a personal mission statement that reflects how you intend to sustain a motivationally rich classroom. What would such a classroom include? What types of activities would you carry out? Include possible interventions to improve the motivation of the following types of students:

- a 7-year-old who has low expectations for success and gives up easily
- a 10-year-old who works overtime because he has a strong fear of failure
- a 13-year-old who is quiet in the classroom and underestimates her skills

INTERNET ACTIVITIES

1. In Search of Motivation

At-risk students are typically characterized as unmotivated underachievers who are often placed in classes that emphasize remediation. What are some successful alternatives to remediation that focus on student motivation? Find an exemplary model for teaching at-risk students on the Web, and summarize its program components. Illustrate why students in the program become motivated to achieve.

2. Setting Goals

Reflect on your teaching goals and what you hope to accomplish in the classroom. Take yourself through the process of setting a goal. Design a goal-setting activity that you could integrate into your classroom. Why are goals an important element of students' learning experiences?

Connect to the Online Learning Centre at www.mcgrawhill.ca/college/santrock **to explore possible answers.**

12 Managing the Classroom

Preview

In educational circles, it is commonly said that no one pays any attention to good classroom management until it is missing. When classrooms are effectively managed, they run smoothly and students are actively engaged in learning. When they are poorly managed, they can become chaotic settings in which learning is a foreign activity. These are some of the questions we will explore in this chapter:

- What are the essential challenges of managing a classroom?
- What are some good strategies for establishing and maintaining classroom rules?
- What are some good teaching strategies for improving communication skills?
- How can the classroom be physically designed to make it more manageable?
- How can teachers effectively deal with fighting and student hostility?

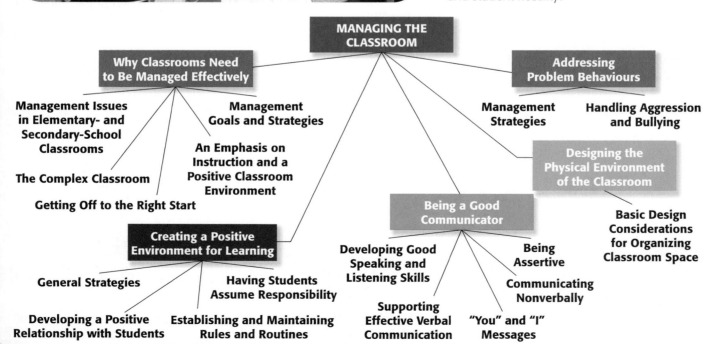

MANAGING THE CLASSROOM

Why Classrooms Need to Be Managed Effectively

- Management Issues in Elementary- and Secondary-School Classrooms
- The Complex Classroom
- Getting Off to the Right Start
- Management Goals and Strategies
- An Emphasis on Instruction and a Positive Classroom Environment

Creating a Positive Environment for Learning

- General Strategies
- Developing a Positive Relationship with Students
- Having Students Assume Responsibility
- Establishing and Maintaining Rules and Routines

Being a Good Communicator

- Developing Good Speaking and Listening Skills
- Supporting Effective Verbal Communication
- Being Assertive
- "You" and "I" Messages
- Communicating Nonverbally

Addressing Problem Behaviours

- Management Strategies
- Handling Aggression and Bullying

Designing the Physical Environment of the Classroom

- Basic Design Considerations for Organizing Classroom Space

Teaching Stories: Karel Sury

With more than 30 years of teaching and administrative experience, Karel Sury knows first-hand how violence can negatively affect a school and community. While principal of a vocational school in Ontario, Karel came face-to-face with a gunman who wounded two students and a teacher. The incident led to the development of a crisis-management plan for the school board, and prompted the creation of the Ontario Secondary School Principals' Task Force on Safe Schools and the Ministry of Education's Safe School Plan for Ontario. Karel describes the incident below.

"Principals and teachers should not view violence as something that might happen in their schools. Rather, they need to proactively plan for when it will occur. I was unprepared for the young man who appeared in the hallway of my school brandishing a gun in one hand and a large hunting knife in the other.

"I was forced to make an on-the-spot decision about how to best address this situation. When I first saw him in the hallway I didn't know who the young man was or what he was capable of doing. I thought I could talk to him and calm him down. I remember him shouting, 'You don't believe I'm serious, do you?' as he started firing shots into the walls and ceiling of the school. A bullet ricocheted off the wall and into the arm of a teacher who was coming down the hall to help me. At the same time, two girls rounded the corner. The gunman shot one of them in the abdomen and chased the other down

the hall. With the help of some other teachers, I moved the wounded girl into my office. Someone called the police while I used the intercom to warn students and teachers to leave the hallways and go into their classrooms and lock the doors.

"Eventually the teenage gunman found the second girl. She had broken off a relationship with the boy prior to transferring to my school. He shot her in the thigh and would have killed her if not for two events. As the girl lay wounded and crying on the ground a teacher rushed out to place himself between the gunman and the girl. At the same moment, another teenage boy appeared in the hallway. The gunman recognized the new arrival as the girl's new boyfriend and chased after him. I could now hear police sirens in the distance and the gunman must have heard them too because he fled the school by a rear door. He was captured a few hours later.

"While the gunman did not mortally wound anyone, his actions affected our school for a very long time. The nine teachers who had contact with the gunman had to join a support group to learn how to cope with their reactions. Similarly, hundreds of students at the school spent time with counsellors and social workers. The incident challenged everyone's basic assumption that the school was a safe environment."

Why Classrooms Need to Be Managed Effectively

Management Issues in Elementary- and Secondary-School Classrooms

Management Goals and Strategies

An Emphasis on Instruction and a Positive Classroom Environment

The Complex Classroom

Getting Off to the Right Start

WHY CLASSROOMS NEED TO BE MANAGED EFFECTIVELY

Effective classroom management maximizes students' learning opportunities (Levin & Nolan, 2000). Experts in classroom management report that there has been a change in thinking about the best way to manage classrooms. The older view emphasized creating and applying rules to control students' behaviours. The newer view focuses more on students' needs for nurturing relationships and opportunities for self-regulation (Weinstein, 1999). There is greater emphasis on guiding students to become more proficient at self-discipline and less on externally controlling them (Freiberg, 1999; Skiba & Peterson, 1999). In other words, the role of the teacher is changing from director to facilitator. As part of their new management role, teachers place greater emphasis on caring, self-regulation, and prevention.

As you develop and refine your classroom-management strategies, it is important to recognize that your classroom is part of a larger school community and that your approach to discipline and classroom management needs to be consistent with the policies and practices of your school and colleagues (Emmer, Evertson, & Worsham, 2003). We will begin our tour of effective classroom management by exploring how management issues sometimes differ in elementary and secondary classrooms.

Management Issues in Elementary- and Secondary-School Classrooms

Elementary- and secondary-school classrooms share many of the same management issues, including the design of the physical environment, the creation of a positive learning atmosphere, the establishment of rules and routines, the handling of problematic behaviours, and the use of good communication strategies.

However, some differences in elementary and secondary schools have implications for the way these classrooms need to be managed. In elementary schools, teachers interact with the same children most, if not all, of the day. In turn, elementary students spend much more time with the same peer group than do their high-school counterparts. Having to interact with the same people in close proximity for such a long time can breed feelings of confinement, boredom, and even dislike for fellow classmates (Emmer, Evertson, & Worsham, 2003; Evertson et al., 1994).

Secondary-school teachers face different challenges. They often encounter five to six groups of adolescents for brief periods on a daily basis, resulting in greater need to focus on time management and instructional content. Because secondary-school teachers spend considerably less time with individual students, it also makes it difficult to establish personal relationships with them. Secondary-school students' problems can be more long-standing and more deeply ingrained, and therefore more difficult to modify, than those of elementary-school students. Also, in secondary schools discipline problems are frequently more severe, the students potentially more unruly and even dangerous. They may challenge rules and routines more readily and demand more elaborate and logical explanations of them than do elementary-school students. Hallway socializing can carry into the classroom, and every class requires a "settling down" process. Effective classroom management requires you to become familiar with the challenges faced in both environments. Regardless of level, however, all classrooms can be complex.

Class Size One of the conditions that is often suggested as having a strong effect on classroom climate and effectiveness is class size (Ziegler, 1997). **Class size** is defined as *the number of students in a given classroom*, but class size is often associated and confused with the term *pupil–teacher ratio*. The **pupil–teacher ratio** (**PTR**) is generally defined as *the number of students in a school divided by all of the certified teachers in that school—*including librarians, learning resource teachers, and administrators, who may have little or no contact with students in the classroom. According to the Education Improvement

Commission Report for Ontario (1997), pupil–teacher ratios are used as the primary measure of class size. Because of workplace collective agreements, the ratios are often calculated by dividing the total number of students within a board by the total number of certified teachers under contract in that board (including part-time and occasional teachers). The pupil–teacher ratio is calculated differently across school boards and jurisdictions throughout Canada; thus, no consistent format for gathering data on either PTR or class size currently exists. According to one national survey of school boards conducted by the Alberta government (Alberta Learning, 2001), elementary class sizes average around 19 students per class for kindergarten and 24 students per class for Grades 1 to 6. Secondary-school figures range between 20 and 27 students per class.

Determining the effects of class size on teaching and learning outcomes is complex and often involves factors such as teachers' abilities and training. According to a meta-analysis of current educational research, students benefit when class sizes are kept low (fewer than 20 students per class) (British Columbia Teachers' Federation, 2001; Tremblay, Ross, & Berthelot, 2002; Manitoba Association of School Trustees, 2001). Smaller class size is especially beneficial for students from lower socioeconomic backgrounds and for those students from home environments that preclude parental or adult involvement in their educational experiences (Alberta Teachers Association, 2001). The benefits of smaller class size for these students include more contact time with teachers, greater opportunities to ask questions, more individualized help, and more classroom time spent on teaching (Lytton & Pyryt, 1998).

The research on the effects of class size on student achievement has largely focused on the primary grades; information about the effects of class size on later grades is either extrapolated from the early-grades research or unavailable (Manitoba Association of School Trustees, 2001). In the United States, the California Class Size Reduction initiative (CSR) limited primary class sizes to 20 or fewer students and tracked nearly 1.8 million primary-grade students. Teachers in the CSR program reported more in-depth coverage of content, more time for enrichment activities, and less time disciplining students or dealing with classroom-management problems than teachers in larger classes (CSR Report, 1999).

Research on the effects of class size over time is also scarce. One of the few available longitudinal studies compared the effects of class sizes on student achievement by tracking some 11,000 students from elementary through secondary school (British Columbia Teachers' Federation, 2001). The findings suggest that students who were in small classes for the first four years of their schooling performed better on national standardized tests starting in Grade 3 and continuing through Grade 12.

The Complex Classroom

Even beyond the dynamics of class size and pupil–teacher ratio, classrooms are complex, fast-moving, and dynamic environments that if left unmanaged can develop into problem centres for teachers. According to Doyle (1986), teachers need to be aware of the characteristics of classrooms and be prepared to manage them. We describe six of the most important characteristics below.

- *Classrooms are multidimensional.* Classrooms are the setting for many activities, including the academic and the social. Teachers have to monitor all of these activities in order to keep students on track. As we see next, work has to be assigned, monitored, collected, and evaluated at the same time that students' individual needs are considered and addressed. Similarly, social interactions should be monitored to ensure that the students' ability to share and get along with each other is maintained.
- *Activities occur simultaneously.* Many academic and social activities occur simultaneously. For instance, one cluster of students might be writing at their desks, another might be discussing a story with the teacher, one student might be picking on another, others might be talking about what they are going to do after school, and so on.

- *Events happen quickly.* Negative events often occur rapidly in classrooms and frequently require immediate responses from teachers. Such events may involve two students arguing about the ownership of a notebook, a student complaining that another is copying her answers, a student speaking out of turn, or two students bullying a classmate.
- *Events are often unpredictable.* Even though you might carefully plan the day's activities, unanticipated events do occur: a fire alarm goes off; a student gets sick; a computer won't work; the heat goes off in the middle of the winter; and so on.
- *There is little privacy.* Classrooms are public places where students observe how the teacher addresses discipline problems, unexpected events, and frustrating circumstances. Some teachers report that they feel like they are in a "fishbowl" or constantly on stage. Much of what happens to one student is observed by the entire class, with students making attributions about what is occurring. In one case, they might perceive that the teacher is being unfair, while in another they might appreciate her sensitivity to a student's feelings.
- *Classrooms have histories.* Students have memories about what happened earlier in their classroom. They remember how the teacher handled a discipline problem, which students have received more privileges than others, and whether the teacher abides by his promises. Because the past affects the future, it is important for teachers to be consistent and sensitive to students' perceptions and to manage the classroom today in a way that will support rather than undermine learning tomorrow. This means that the first several weeks of the school year are critical for establishing effective management principles.

Getting Off to the Right Start

The beginning of the school year is critical for the establishment of work habits and healthy student–student and student–teacher interactions. During the first few days and weeks of school, your students will learn procedures and routines that they will need for the remainder of the school year. Getting off to a good start requires careful planning and execution. You will want to outline your rules and procedures concretely and attain your students' cooperation in following them. In some cases, this may include having students participate in the generation of classroom rules and their associated consequences. In addition, you will want to engage your students in activities that ensure their academic success so that they will feel optimistic about their ability to do well in your classroom. This will also help students develop a positive attitude toward school and provide them with confidence to tackle more difficult tasks later. Take special care to show your students that you are someone who can be approached when they need information. Move around the room, monitor students' progress, and provide assistance as needed. Finally, remember to maintain your authority in the classroom. Even if you have stated your rules and expectations explicitly, some students will forget and others will test your willingness to enforce them. During the first weeks of school, it is especially important that you clearly and consistently establish the boundaries between acceptable and unacceptable classroom behaviours (Emmer, Evertson, & Worsham, 2003). Taking the time during these weeks to establish expectations, rules, and routines will help your class run smoothly and set the tone for a positive classroom environment.

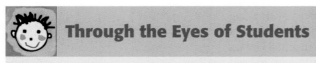

Through the Eyes of Students

Rules Are Everywhere

Rules, rules, rules! Rules are everywhere at school and at home. Some of them I agree with and some of them I don't. I think the rule about not speaking when the teacher is talking is a good one. If everyone talks at the same time, we won't hear the teacher and no one will know what to do. Also, you need to raise your hand if you have a question. If you don't, everyone will be talking at the same time and the teacher will have to give out detentions.

The rule about not eating in class is a bad one because we get hungry. Even though I don't like the rule, I understand that the teacher wants us to concentrate on our work and not on our food. Finally, it is very important that you always ask to leave the classroom if you have an appointment or need to go to the washroom. If you don't tell the teacher that you are leaving, she might think that you are missing or have been hurt.

Marcus
Grade 3 Student
Excellent Basketball Player
Ontario

An Emphasis on Instruction and a Positive Classroom Environment

Historically, the effectively managed classroom has been described as a "well-oiled machine," but a more appropriate metaphor for today's effectively managed classroom is "beehive of activity" (see Figure 12.1) (Randolph & Evertson, 1995). In the past, teachers emphasized maintaining discipline in their classrooms. Today, teachers are more likely to focus their efforts on developing a positive classroom climate in order to promote and support their students' learning (Emmer, Evertson, & Worsham, 2003). This shift represents a greater emphasis toward proactive strategies rather than becoming immersed in reactive disciplinary tactics (Paintal, 1999). Researchers in educational psychology consistently find that teachers who competently guide and structure classroom activities are more effective than teachers who emphasize their disciplinary role (Brophy, 1996).

Management Goals and Strategies

Effective classroom management has two main goals: to help students spend more time on learning and less time on non–goal-directed activity, and to prevent students from developing academic and emotional problems. Kounin and his colleagues (Kounin, 1970, 1983; Kounin & Gump, 1974) carried out a number of studies to identify characteristics of effective classroom managers. They concluded that these teachers were more skilled at managing transitions, preventing misbehaviours, and maintaining group focus than were their colleagues.

Help Students Spend More Time on Learning and Less Time on Non–Goal-Directed Behaviour   According to educational researchers such as Weinstein (1997) and Leonard (2001), actual instructional time in a typical classroom falls short of the learning time mandated by schools. When factoring in activities such as lunch and recess breaks, instructional time can constitute as little as 40 percent of a typical school day (Garvie, 1994; Gilman & Knoll, 1984). In other words, a great deal of time is taken up by interruptions, transitions, and misbehaviours.

Through the Eyes of Teachers

Helping Students Develop Time-Management Skills

"Clancy's Corner" is what my classes know as a corner of the blackboard that I use for recording upcoming events, assignments, and tests. I have marked off a square for each of my classes. I begin and end each class by insisting that the students record their work for the next few days into their agendas or personal calendars. It could be homework questions, lab preparation, readings, or even a "day off." Students fall easily into this routine and come to rely on this communication format. Some teachers believe that this type of organizational activity takes too much time away from the curriculum. I disagree. It provides students with an opportunity to organize and prepare for learning. It demonstrates to students that you, the teacher, are not frenzied or hurried and it provides you with an opportunity to observe your students. Finally, it provides everyone with a structured opportunity to exchange information and ask questions.

Christina Clancy
13-Year Secondary-School Science Teacher
Ontario

FIGURE 12.1   The Effectively Managed Classroom
"Well-Oiled Machine" or "Beehive of Activity"?

> ## Teaching Strategies
> ### For Increasing Academic Learning Time
>
> ✔ Maintain flow between activities
> - complete one activity before starting another—avoid switching from one activity to another and then returning to the first
> - do not interrupt the flow of a class to address behaviours that are irrelevant (e.g., posture) or distracting (e.g., gum chewing)
> - use negative reinforcement techniques such as proximity and the "teacher glare" to address problematic behaviours whenever possible
>
> ✔ Minimize transition time
> - recognize that misbehaviours (e.g., hitting, yelling, and using obscenities) are twice as likely to occur during transitions than during activities
> - prepare students for upcoming transitions
> - establish routines for transitions
> - define lesson boundaries
>
> ✔ Hold students accountable
> - recognize that students are more likely to make good use of class time when they know you will assess their work
> - clearly communicate assignments and all associated requirements
> - explain what needs to be done and why it is important to do it
> - explain where and how students should obtain help if needed
> - provide activities in advance for students who complete assigned work before their peers
> - help students establish goals and plan and monitor their progress
> - maintain good records of students' performance
>
> **Source:** Weinstein (1997)

Leonard (2001) observed the nature and extent of instructional interruptions across three rural school districts in Western Canada. He concluded that there is a large amount of time taken up by non-instructional activities such as school assemblies, public announcements, telephone calls, visits, fundraising activities, and clerical tasks. Almost half of the teachers (46.4 percent) lamented that such interruptions result in serious distractions and disruptions to classroom time, well beyond a temporary loss of focus. Effective classroom management will help you maximize your instructional time and your students' learning time.

Prevent Students from Developing Problems A well-managed classroom not only fosters meaningful learning but also helps prevent academic and emotional problems from developing. Well-managed classrooms keep students busy with active, appropriately challenging tasks. Well-managed classrooms have activities in which students become absorbed and motivated to learn and clear rules and regulations students must abide by. In such classrooms, students are less likely to develop academic and emotional problems. By contrast, in poorly managed classrooms, students' academic and emotional problems are more likely to fester. The academically unmotivated student becomes even less motivated. The shy student becomes more reclusive. The bully becomes meaner.

The importance of classroom management and the factors that can challenge teachers are reviewed in Summary Table 12.1. In the next section, we will explore specific techniques and strategies that teachers can use to make the classroom a positive environment for learning. These approaches include developing a positive relationship with students, establishing and maintaining rules and routines, and having students assume responsibility for their actions.

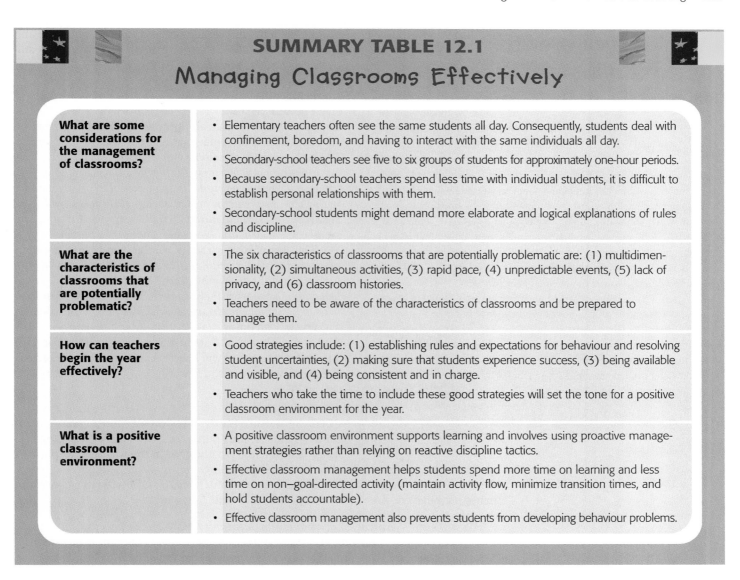

SUMMARY TABLE 12.1
Managing Classrooms Effectively

What are some considerations for the management of classrooms?	• Elementary teachers often see the same students all day. Consequently, students deal with confinement, boredom, and having to interact with the same individuals all day. • Secondary-school teachers see five to six groups of students for approximately one-hour periods. • Because secondary-school teachers spend less time with individual students, it is difficult to establish personal relationships with them. • Secondary-school students might demand more elaborate and logical explanations of rules and discipline.
What are the characteristics of classrooms that are potentially problematic?	• The six characteristics of classrooms that are potentially problematic are: (1) multidimensionality, (2) simultaneous activities, (3) rapid pace, (4) unpredictable events, (5) lack of privacy, and (6) classroom histories. • Teachers need to be aware of the characteristics of classrooms and be prepared to manage them.
How can teachers begin the year effectively?	• Good strategies include: (1) establishing rules and expectations for behaviour and resolving student uncertainties, (2) making sure that students experience success, (3) being available and visible, and (4) being consistent and in charge. • Teachers who take the time to include these good strategies will set the tone for a positive classroom environment for the year.
What is a positive classroom environment?	• A positive classroom environment supports learning and involves using proactive management strategies rather than relying on reactive discipline tactics. • Effective classroom management helps students spend more time on learning and less time on non–goal-directed activity (maintain activity flow, minimize transition times, and hold students accountable). • Effective classroom management also prevents students from developing behaviour problems.

CREATING A POSITIVE ENVIRONMENT FOR LEARNING

Students need a positive environment for learning. We will discuss some general classroom-management strategies for providing this environment, including how to effectively establish and maintain rules and how to encourage students to cooperate.

General Strategies

General strategies including using an authoritative strategy and effectively managing the group's activities will be covered in the next section.

Using an Authoritative Strategy   The authoritative classroom-management strategy is derived from Diana Baumrind's (1971, 1996) parenting styles, which were discussed in Chapter 3. Like authoritative parents, authoritative teachers have students who tend to be self-reliant, delay gratification, get along well with their peers, and show high self-esteem. An **authoritative strategy of classroom management** *encourages students to be independent thinkers and doers but still involves effective monitoring.* Authoritative teachers

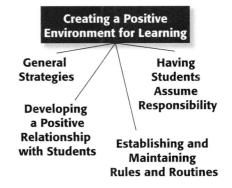

Creating a Positive Environment for Learning

General Strategies

Developing a Positive Relationship with Students

Having Students Assume Responsibility

Establishing and Maintaining Rules and Routines

Through the Eyes of Teachers

Seating Plans and Student Success

In my experience, the design and the physical arrangement of the classroom have an enormous influence on students' behaviours and participation in class. I like to arrange my classroom so that I can walk around it easily. This allows me to monitor and interact with my students, staying on top of any potentially problematic behaviour.

I seat students in groups as a way of fostering positive peer relations and providing them with opportunities to develop and practise cooperative skills. Unfortunately, these skills don't happen simply by placing students' desks together. You need to show students how to work effectively in a group, how to ask for help, and how to address disagreements and other conflicts.

When my students are working on assignments, I like to keep group structure flexible. Sometimes they work independently, sometimes they select a partner, and sometimes I assign them to a group. I change seating arrangements about once a month so that the students have the opportunity to develop new friendships and work with everyone in the class.

Karen Forgrave
Elementary-School Teacher
Ontario

engage students in considerable verbal give-and-take and show a caring attitude toward them. However, they still declare limits when necessary. Authoritative teachers clarify rules and regulations, establishing these standards with input from students.

The authoritative strategy contrasts with two ineffective strategies: authoritarian and permissive. The **authoritarian strategy of classroom management** *is restrictive and punitive. The focus is mainly on keeping order in the classroom rather than on instruction and learning. Authoritarian teachers place firm limits and controls on students and have little verbal exchange with them. Students in authoritarian classrooms tend to be passive learners, fail to initiate activities, express anxiety about social comparison, and have poor communication skills.*

The **permissive strategy of classroom management** *offers students considerable autonomy but provides them with little support for developing learning skills or managing their behaviour. Not surprisingly, students in permissive classrooms tend to have inadequate academic skills and low self-control.*

Overall, an authoritative strategy will benefit your students more than authoritarian or permissive strategies. An authoritative strategy will help your students become active, self-regulated learners.

Managing Group Activities   We described some aspects of Jacob Kounin's (1970) work on classroom management earlier in the chapter. Kounin concluded that effective teachers differ from ineffective ones not in the way they respond to students' misbehaviours but instead in how competently they manage the group's activities. Here we focus on some of the differences between effective and ineffective classroom managers. Effective classroom managers focus on the following:

- *"Withitness."* **Withitness** *is a management strategy in which teachers show students that they are aware of what is happening. These teachers closely monitor students on a regular basis. This allows them to detect inappropriate behaviour early before it gets out of hand.* Teachers who are not "with it" are likely to not notice such misbehaviours until they gain momentum and spread.
- *Simultaneous management.* Some teachers seem to have one-track minds, addressing only one issue at a time. This ineffective strategy often leads to frequent interruptions in the flow of the class. For example, one teacher was working with a reading group when she observed two boys talking to each other. She immediately got up, went over to the other side of the room, addressed their misbehaviour, and then returned to the reading group. However, by the time she returned to the reading group, the students in the group had become bored and were starting to misbehave. In contrast, effective managers are able to deal with overlapping situations in less disruptive ways. For example, in the reading group situation, a teacher might quickly respond to the students by providing a visual prompt that they should stop talking and refocus on their work, in a way that does not significantly alter the flow of the reading group's activity.
- *Continuity.* Effective managers keep the flow of a lesson moving smoothly, maintaining students' interest and not giving them opportunities to be easily distracted. Earlier in the chapter when we discussed strategies for increasing academic learning time, we mentioned some ineffective activities of teachers that can disrupt the flow of a lesson. These included flip-flopping, unnecessarily pulling away from an ongoing event, and dwelling too long on something that students already understand. Another teacher action that disrupts the lesson's flow is called "fragmentation," in which the teacher breaks an activity into components even though the activity could be performed

as an entire unit. For example, a teacher might individually ask six students to do something, such as get out their art supplies, when all six could be asked to do this as a group. In another fragmented teaching situation, a teacher who was making the transition from spelling to math told students to close their spelling books, then put away their red pencils, then close their spelling books (again), next to put their spelling books on their desks but keep them out of the way. Then the teacher told the students to take out their math books and put them on their desks but keep everything off their desks but the math books. Next, the students were told to get out their black pencils. Clearly, this segmented teaching disrupted the flow of the transition from spelling to math.

• *Challenging activities.* Kounin also found that effective classroom managers engage students in a variety of challenging but not overly hard activities. The students frequently worked independently rather than being directly supervised by a teacher who hovered over them.

Developing a Positive Relationship with Students

When most of us think about a favourite teacher, we think of someone who sincerely cared for us. Showing that you genuinely care about students as individuals apart from their academic work helps to gain their cooperation. It is easy to get caught up in the pressing demands of academic achievement and classroom business and to ignore students' socio-emotional needs.

A review of the contemporary literature exploring the characteristics of effective schools reveals that creating an environment where students feel safe and secure can be as important to their academic and their general life success as establishing effective rules and routines (Collinson, Killeavy, & Stephenson, 1999; Creemers, 1996; Henchey & Raham). Developing such rapport and trust with students, or what is otherwise referred to as an "ethic of care" (Flinders & Noddings, 2001; Katz, Noddings, & Strike, 1999; Noddings, 1996, 2003), requires teachers and schools to be genuinely concerned about their students' overall well being. Teachers need to recognize the very real effects of students' socioeconomic realities and genuinely support their learning efforts, emphasizing effort over achievement. They need to be sensitive to their students' needs, as well as their fears and anxieties. Students need to believe that they are being treated fairly. The classroom atmosphere should be one that is relaxed and pleasant, with educational activities presented as inviting experiences. Figure 12.2 presents some teacher guidelines for developing positive relationships with students.

1. Give students a friendly "hello" at the door.
2. Have brief one-on-one conversations about things that are happening in your students' lives.
3. Write brief notes of encouragement.
4. Use students' names in class.
5. Show enthusiasm about being with students (even late in the day, week, or year).
6. Share relevant personal stories that help students see you as a real person. Always take into account level of understanding and emotional vulnerability in disclosing information about yourself to them.
7. Be an active listener who carefully attends to what the students are saying.
8. Let students know that you are there to support and help them.
9. Keep in mind that developing positive, trusting relationships takes time. This especially is the case for students from high-risk environments, who might not initially trust your motives.

FIGURE 12.2   Guidelines for Establishing Positive Relationships with Students

As part of a two-year study of 12 secondary schools in low-income urban environments throughout British Columbia, Alberta, and Quebec, Henchy and his colleagues (2001) described the characteristics of schools that practised the **ethic of care**. Specifically, *in these schools teachers expressed positive attitudes and held high expectations for their students*. The focus was on students' needs, with teachers coordinating their instruction and integrating content materials. Teachers and students were able to articulate a commitment to core values and there was a general sense of engagement and belonging among teachers and students alike. Special efforts were made to motivate students and make learning relevant, with students participating in many hands-on and cooperative learning activities. There were also efforts to develop and enhance community–school connections among students, teachers, parents, extended family members, and community organizations. Establishing positive community relationships is critical when creating a climate of care, especially when working in ethnically diverse settings. Joanne Tompkins (1998) provides an especially moving account of the importance of community when describing her experiences as principal in a local Inuit school on Baffin Island.

Establishing and Maintaining Rules and Routines

There is some debate about whether students should be allowed to participate in establishing classroom rules. Some experts on classroom management believe that sharing responsibility with students for making classroom decisions increases the students' commitment to these decisions (Evertson et al., 1997; MacDonald & Healy, 1999; Risley & Walther, 1995). Regardless of whether teachers invite students to participate in the development of rules and routines, they need to consider carefully which ones they will adopt well before their students arrive at school. Carol Weinstein (1997) describes four principles that teachers can use when establishing classroom rules and routines:

- *Rules should be reasonable and necessary.* Ask yourself whether your rules are appropriate for your grade level and whether there are good reasons underlining them. For instance, a secondary-school teacher may have the rule that students must come to class on time. Students are clearly told that if they are late they will receive a detention, even on the first violation. The rule is explained at the beginning of the semester, along with the reason behind it—if they are late they may miss important information.
- *Rules should be clear and comprehensible.* Make sure to explicitly state what each rule means and encompasses, especially when using general rules such as "Be prepared"; that is, explain what these rules look like, sound like, and feel like (e.g., having your homework, notebook, and pen with you every day, waiting silently for instructions, and clearing your mind of distracting thoughts). If you invite students to help you develop classroom rules, also have them generate examples of such general rules. Remember that you can veto student-generated rules you believe are inappropriate.
- *Rules should be consistent with instructional goals.* Ensure that your rules do not interfere with or inhibit students' learning. For example, some teachers become so concerned with having orderly, quiet classrooms that they restrict students from interacting with each other and from engaging in collaborative activities.
- *Classroom rules should be consistent with school rules.* Be familiar with your school's rules and routines (e.g., hallway and cafeteria procedures). Many schools have handbooks in which school rules and student codes of conduct are specified. Make sure to review the school rules along with your classroom rules at the beginning of the school year.

Rewarding Appropriate Behaviour   Once you have established your classroom rules and routines, you will want to reinforce students' commitment to them throughout the school year. It will be especially important that you consider how rewards can be used in effectively managing the classroom. Following are some guidelines for using rewards. For a more extensive discussion of rewards and enhancing student motivation, review Chapters 7 and 11.

- *Choose effective reinforcers.* Find out which reinforcers work best with which students, and individualize reinforcement. For one student, the most effective reward might be praise; for another, it might be getting to do a favourite activity. Remember that pleasurable activities often are especially valuable in gaining students' cooperation. You might tell a student, "When you complete your math problems, you can go to the media area and play a computer game."
- *Use prompts and shaping effectively.* Remember that if you wait for students to perform perfectly, it might never happen. A good strategy is to use prompts and shape students' behaviour by rewarding improvement. Some prompts come in the form of hints or reminders, such as "Remember the rule about lining up." Shaping involves rewarding a student for successive approximations to a specified target behaviour. Thus, you might initially reward a student for getting 60 percent of her math problems right, then for 70 percent the next time, and so on.
- *Use rewards to promote mastery.* Rewards that impart information about students' mastery can increase their intrinsic motivation and sense of responsibility. However, rewards that are used to control students' behaviour are less likely to promote self-regulation and responsibility. For example, a student might benefit from being selected "student of the week" because he or she engaged in a number of highly productive, competent activities. However, the student likely will not benefit from being given the reward for sitting still at a desk: the latter is an effort by the teacher to control the student, and students in heavily controlled learning environments tend to act like pawns.

Having Students Assume Responsibility

Earlier in this chapter, we discussed the importance of developing an authoritative atmosphere in the classroom and allowing students to assume some responsibility for the development of classroom rules and routines. Many educational experts also believe that students' commitment to school increases when teachers encourage them to assume greater responsibility for their overall learning. The following are some guidelines for encouraging students to share and assume responsibility in the classroom:

- *Solicit students' input.* Involve students in the planning and implementation of school and classroom initiatives. This type of participation can increase students' sense of self-confidence and belonging.
- *Have students consider motives.* Encourage students to judge their own behaviours. Rather than pass judgment, ask questions that motivate them to evaluate their own actions (e.g., Does your behaviour reflect class rules? What's the rule?). When presented with such questions, some students may try to blame others or change the subject. In these situations, you will need to stay focused and guide them toward accepting responsibility.
- *Do not accept excuses.* When teachers allow students to make excuses, they allow them to pass on or avoid responsibility. Try not to entertain any discussion about excuses. Rather, ask students what they can do the next time a similar situation develops. It is important, however, that teachers be able to differentiate between excuse making and legitimate circumstances. Your knowledge of students as individuals will help you determine this difference.
- *Provide adequate time.* It takes time and considerable practice for students to learn to assume responsibility for their behaviours. Many students' misbehaviours are ingrained habits that will take a long time to change. There may be many times that your patience will be challenged by students who avoid assuming responsibility.
- *Allow students to generate solutions.* An increasingly popular approach in classroom management is to provide students with class time to meet as a group to discuss problematic behaviours and other issues of concern (e.g., "town hall" or "focus group" sessions). As part of these discussions, students need to be challenged to generate feasible solutions to problem situations. Teachers must ensure that ground rules are established prior to these discussions and that there is an atmosphere of trust and good rapport in the classroom.

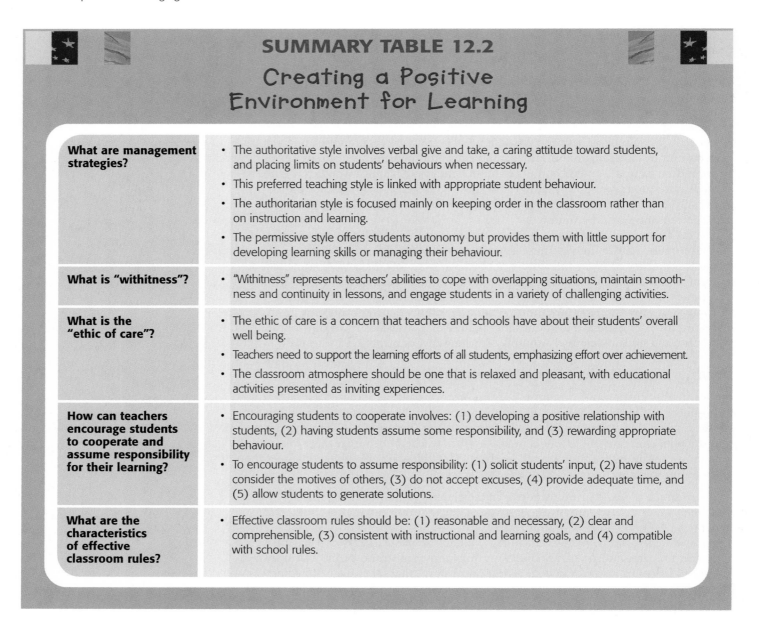

SUMMARY TABLE 12.2
Creating a Positive Environment for Learning

What are management strategies?	• The authoritative style involves verbal give and take, a caring attitude toward students, and placing limits on students' behaviours when necessary. • This preferred teaching style is linked with appropriate student behaviour. • The authoritarian style is focused mainly on keeping order in the classroom rather than on instruction and learning. • The permissive style offers students autonomy but provides them with little support for developing learning skills or managing their behaviour.
What is "withitness"?	• "Withitness" represents teachers' abilities to cope with overlapping situations, maintain smoothness and continuity in lessons, and engage students in a variety of challenging activities.
What is the "ethic of care"?	• The ethic of care is a concern that teachers and schools have about their students' overall well being. • Teachers need to support the learning efforts of all students, emphasizing effort over achievement. • The classroom atmosphere should be one that is relaxed and pleasant, with educational activities presented as inviting experiences.
How can teachers encourage students to cooperate and assume responsibility for their learning?	• Encouraging students to cooperate involves: (1) developing a positive relationship with students, (2) having students assume some responsibility, and (3) rewarding appropriate behaviour. • To encourage students to assume responsibility: (1) solicit students' input, (2) have students consider the motives of others, (3) do not accept excuses, (4) provide adequate time, and (5) allow students to generate solutions.
What are the characteristics of effective classroom rules?	• Effective classroom rules should be: (1) reasonable and necessary, (2) clear and comprehensible, (3) consistent with instructional and learning goals, and (4) compatible with school rules.

Summary Table 12.2 outlines teaching styles associated with positive learning environments, as well as specific strategies that teachers can adopt to create such environments in their classrooms. Because so much of creating a positive learning environment is contingent on possessing effective communication skills, in the next section we describe how teachers can enhance verbal and nonverbal communications for both themselves and their students.

BEING A GOOD COMMUNICATOR

Teachers need to possess good communication skills to manage their classrooms and constructively resolve conflicts. To accomplish this, you will need to be able to communicate verbally and nonverbally and to be assertive.

Developing Good Speaking and Listening Skills

Becoming an Effective Speaker   You and your students will benefit considerably if you have effective speaking skills and you work with your students on developing their speaking skills. You will be speaking in your class every day in both formal and informal ways, and you should work to provide your students with similar speaking opportunities. These activities give students opportunities to improve their speaking, organizational, and thinking skills.

The Saskatchewan Department of Education offers some helpful suggestions to guide both teachers and students through the speaking process. These suggestions are divided into activities that should occur prior to, during, and after the actual speaking event. Prior to speaking, individuals should select a topic, decide on a presentation format, determine the purpose for speaking, and consider the intended audience. During the speech, the orator should actively engage the audience using such techniques as questioning, conversation, and discussion. After the event, the speaker should take time to reflect on his or her performance and set personal goals for improving his or her speaking ability. For additional information, refer to the Saskatchewan Department of Education Website (**www.sasked.gov.sk.ca**).

People often list public speaking as their single greatest fear. If we gave students more opportunities to practise public speaking, this fear likely would diminish. To help your students overcome this fear, give them plenty of opportunities to talk in front of a group and provide them with supportive advice (Santrock & Halonen, 1999). When they prepare for their talk, have them rehearse the talk a number of times until they are confident they know the material. Let them know that most people fear talking in front of groups, but that once they do it their fear subsides. Most teachers and students acknowledge that public speaking is a valuable activity (SchoolNet News Network, 2001). The opportunity to speak publicly also provides students with the opportunity to voice their opinions. Teachers add that public speaking improves confidence and forces students to think on their feet.

Working with students on their speaking skills also provides an excellent opportunity to invite someone from the community to talk to your class. If a local college or university has a communications department, contact the department and ask one of their faculty to talk with your students about speaking skills or other aspects of communication. You also might have heard someone give a speech that you thought was outstanding; invite the speaker to come to your class and give students tips on how to give a great talk.

Developing Good Listening Skills   Effectively managing your classroom will be easier if you and your students have good listening skills. Listening is a critical skill for making and keeping relationships. If you are a good listener, students, parents, and other teachers and administrators will be drawn to you. If your students are good listeners, they will benefit more from your instruction and will have better social relationships. Good listeners actively listen and don't just passively absorb information. **Active listening** *means giving full attention to the speaker, focusing on both the intellectual and the emotional content of the message.*

The Teaching Resources Office (TRACE) at the University of Waterloo offers some basic strategies for active listening (retrieved from **www.uwaterloo.ca**). One could adapt these strategies when working with students in the primary grades:

- *Stop.* Focus on the other person. Consider the speaker's thoughts and feelings. Consciously focus on quieting your own internal commentary, and step away from your own concerns to think about those of the speaker. Give your full attention to the speaker.
- *Look.* Pay attention to nonverbal communication, without letting yourself be distracted. Notice body language and nonverbal cues to allow for a richer understanding of the speaker's message.
- *Listen.* Listen for the essence of the speaker's thoughts. Seek an overall understanding of what the speaker is trying to communicate, rather than reacting to the individual words or terms that he or she uses.
- *Be empathetic.* Imagine how you would feel in the speaker's position. Be empathetic to the feelings of the speaker, while maintaining a calm centre within yourself. You need not be drawn into all of his or her problems or issues, as long as you acknowledge what he or she is experiencing.
- *Ask questions.* Use questions to clarify your understanding, as well as to demonstrate interest in what is being said.

Listening strategies that can be used when working with students in the upper elementary and secondary levels include (Santrock & Halonen, 1999):

- *Pay careful attention.* This shows the person that you are interested in what she or he is saying. Maintain good eye contact and lean forward slightly when another person is speaking to you.
- *Paraphrase.* State in your own words what the other person has just said. You can start your paraphrase with words like "Let me see, what I hear you saying is …" or "Do you mean … ?" Use paraphrasing when someone says something that is important.
- *Synthesize themes and patterns.* The conversation landscape can become strewn with bits and pieces of information that are not tied together in meaningful ways. A good active listener puts together a summary of the main themes and feelings the speaker has expressed over a reasonably long conversation. The following sentence stems can help you and your students get started in synthesizing the themes of a conversation:

"One theme you keep coming back to is …"
"Let's go over what we have been covering so far …"

> The reason we have two ears and only one mouth is so we can listen more and talk less.
>
> Zeno of Citum
> *Greek Philosopher, 3rd Century* B.C.

Through the Eyes of Teachers

Developing Verbal Communication Skills

Sometime early in the school year, usually during the first week of school, my students and I talk about the characteristics of effective communication, or "good talk." I tell them that over the course of the school year we will have many opportunities to communicate with each other, to share ideas, tell stories, and talk about things that interest and excite us. However, I also point out that there will be rules for how we talk and communicate in class. I call these rules "good manners," and I ask the students if they know any good manners for speaking and listening. Together, we develop a set of rules that will guide our conversations throughout the year. The rules usually include listening politely and attentively, waiting for the speaker to finish before responding, and using appropriate and positive language.

I place the rules on chart paper and post them at the front of class. Before student presentations or small-group work, I refer to the chart and ask the class to consider how to apply these rules to the task at hand. Helping students develop their verbal communication skills also provides them with tools for resolving problems and understanding that real communication is more than just talking.

Arlene Bartolacci
Elementary-School Teacher
Nova Scotia

- *Provide feedback in a competent manner.* Verbal or non-verbal feedback gives the speaker an idea of how much progress the speaker is making in getting a point across. Good listeners give feedback quickly, honestly, clearly, and informatively. To evaluate your listening skills, complete Self-Assessment 12.1.

Supporting Effective Verbal Communication

Students' speaking skills develop best in interactive classrooms where time is provided for them to share and listen to each other's ideas. A safe atmosphere is critical for the development of productive talk in the classroom, especially for those students who may come from backgrounds that differ from the classroom norm. Classrooms should be places where students can ask and answer meaningful questions and where teachers and students collaborate with each other to communicate ideas and information (see **www.sasked.gov.sk.ca/docs/mla/speak005.html**).

Classrooms can also contain barriers to effective communication (see **www.adm.uwaterloo.ca/infotrac/barriersandstrategies.html**). Teachers should be especially sensitive to the following:

- *Lacking clarity.* Be as precise and clear as possible about information. Do not use colloquialisms or jargon.
- *Using stereotypes and generalizations.* Be careful not to buy into stereotypes, or to make generalizations about people, places, or things. Using biased language and general labels tends to create barriers when attempting to communicate and connect with other people.

Reflecting on My Active Listening Skills

For each item, respond 1 = Rarely, 2 = Usually, 3 = Always

I listen and pay attention to what the speaker is saying.

I use body language that is open and receptive (e.g., face the speaker, nod encouragement, lean toward the speaker).

I refrain from interrupting the speaker.

I paraphrase what the speaker has said.

I ask for clarification when uncertain about the speaker's intent.

I provide honest and sincere feedback.

I provide clear and informative feedback.

I refrain from criticizing the speaker.

I avoid labelling or judging the speaker.

I refrain from offering answers or advice when not asked to do so.

Look over your self-ratings. Work on improving any items on which you did not rate yourself a 2 or higher.

1	2	3

- *Jumping to conclusions.* Do not assume you know the reasons or implications associated with certain events. Make sure you have all the necessary information, and then speak clearly about the facts versus their meanings or interpretations.
- *Using disconfirming responses.* Be careful about failing to provide a response, interrupting, or making irrelevant comments. This may discourage students from participating in the conversation.
- *Lacking confidence.* Lacking confidence about your speaking abilities can create a barrier to effective communication and can hinder your ability to make your needs and opinions known.

"You" and "I" Messages

How often have you been involved in a conversation in which someone says something like this:

"Why are you being so negative?"
"You did not do what you said you were going to do."
"You are not very considerate."

These are examples of what communication experts call "**you**" messages, *an undesirable style in which speakers appear to judge people and place them in a defensive position.* "You" communication does not always literally include the word *you.* "You" is implied when someone says:

"That was a really stupid thing to say" (which means, "What you said was really stupid.")
"Stay out of my life" (which means, "You are intruding in my life.")

It is easy for you and your students to fall into the trap of using too many "you" messages and not enough "**I**" **messages**, *which are less provocative. "I" messages reflect the speaker's true feelings better than judgmental "you" statements.*

Communication experts recommend replacing "you" messages with "I" messages:

"I'm angry that this has gotten so negative."
"I don't like it when promises get broken."
"I'm hurt when my feelings aren't taken into account."

Many communication experts believe that most interpersonal communication is nonverbal.

"You" messages consume conversation with judgments about the other person. "I" messages help to move the conversation in a more constructive direction by expressing your feelings without judging the other person. Monitor your own conversation from time to time to make sure you are using "I" messages rather than "you" messages. Also monitor your students' conversations and guide them toward using more "I" messages.

Communicating Nonverbally

In addition to what you say, you also communicate by how you fold your arms, cast your eyes, move your mouth, cross your legs, or touch another person. Nonverbal communication accounts for more than half of the "messages" that individuals convey (Canadian Association of Student Activity Advisors; see **http://casaa-resources.net**). Here are some examples of some common behaviours by which individuals communicate nonverbally:

- Lift an eyebrow in disbelief
- Clasp their arms to isolate or protect themselves
- Shrug their shoulders when they are indifferent
- Wink one eye to show warmth and approval
- Tap their fingers when they are impatient
- Slap their forehead when they forget something

Many communication experts believe that most interpersonal communication is nonverbal. Of particular relevance here, 82 percent of teachers' messages are nonverbal, making this a more influential mode of communication than verbal communication (Kirova, 2001). Even a person sitting in a corner silently reading is nonverbally communicating something, perhaps that he or she wants to be left alone. When you notice your students blankly staring out the window, they are likely communicating that they are bored. Because it is hard to mask nonverbal communication, it is important to recognize how it can communicate your true feelings.

Facial Expressions and Eye Communication People's faces disclose emotions and reveal what really matters to them. A smile, a frown, or a puzzled look all communicate. Most North Americans seek eye contact with people they like and avoid eye contact with people they dislike. However, ethnic variations in eye contact exist, with Japanese Canadians and Native Canadians avoiding eye contact more than European Canadians. In general, smiling and maintaining eye contact with your students indicates that you like them.

When studying the lives of children who had recently immigrated to Canada, Kirova (2003) found that the interactions between teachers and these linguistically diverse students were predominantly nonverbal. Teachers need to be aware of the roles and functions of nonverbal behaviour in communication. Teachers use nonverbal communication to indicate their level of support, interest, trust, and concern. Direct and frequent eye contact can not only improve students' attention and increase the amount of information that students retain, but also contribute to their participation and positive self-esteem (Kirova, 2003; Woolfolk & Brooks, 1985).

Touch Touch can be a powerful form of communication. Touch especially can be used when consoling someone who has undergone a stressful or unfortunate experience. For example, if a student's parent has become seriously ill or died, a student's parents recently became divorced, or a student has lost a pet, gently touching the student's hand while consoling him or her can add warmth to the communication. Because of concerns about sexual harassment and potential lawsuits, many teachers have refrained from touching students at all. Tiffany Field (1995), director of the Touch Research Institute at the University of Miami (Florida) and a leading expert in developmental psychology, believes that teachers should use touch appropriately and courteously in their interaction with students.

Talking and eloquence are not the same: to speak, and to speak well, are two things.

Ben Jonson
English Dramatist, 17th Century

Space   Each of us has a personal space that at times we don't want others to invade. Not surprisingly, given the crowdedness of the classroom, students report that having their own space where they can put their materials and belongings is important to them. Make sure that students all have their own desks or spaces. Tell students that they are entitled to have this individual space and that they should respect other students' spaces.

Silence   In our fast-paced, modern culture we often act as if there is something wrong with anyone who remains silent for more than a second or two after something is said to them. In Chapter 10 we indicated that after asking a question of students, many teachers rarely remain silent long enough for students to think reflectively before giving an answer. By being silent, a good listener can:

- Observe the speaker's eyes, facial expressions, posture, and gestures for communication
- Think about what the other person is communicating
- Wonder what the other person is feeling
- Consider the most appropriate response

Of course, silence can be overdone and is sometimes inappropriate. It is rarely wise to listen for an excessive length of time without making some verbal response. Interpersonal communication should be a dialogue, not a monologue.

Being Assertive

There are four main styles in which people address conflict in their lives: aggressive, manipulative, passive, or assertive. People who use an **aggressive style** *run roughshod over others. They are demanding, abrasive, and act in hostile ways.* Aggressive individuals are often insensitive to others' rights and feelings. People who use a **manipulative style** *try to get what they want by making people feel guilty or sorry for them.* Rather than take responsibility for meeting their own needs, they play the role of the victim or the martyr. People who use a **passive style** *are nonassertive and submissive.* They let others run roughshod over them. Passive individuals don't express their feelings and don't let others know what they want.

In contrast, people with an **assertive style** *express their feelings, ask for what they want, and say no to things they don't want.* When people act assertively, they act in their own best interests. They stand up for their legitimate rights and express their views openly. Assertive individuals insist that misbehaviour be corrected, and they resist being coerced or manipulated (Evertson et al., 1997). In the view of assertiveness experts Robert Alberti and Michael Emmons (1995), assertiveness builds positive, constructive relationships.

Of the four styles of addressing conflict, acting assertively is by far the best choice. Following are some strategies for becoming a more assertive individual (Bourne, 1995):

- *Evaluate your rights.* Determine your rights in the situation at hand. For example, you have the right to make mistakes and to change your mind.
- *State the problem to the person involved in terms of its consequences for you.* Clearly outline your point of view, even if it seems obvious to you. This allows the other person to get a better sense of your position. Describe the problem as objectively as you can without blaming or judging. For example, you might tell a student:

"I'm having a problem with your humming in class. It is bothering me, so please don't do it anymore."
"When you come in late, it disrupts the class and you miss important information."
"Saying that to another student hurts his feelings."

- *Express your feelings about the particular situation.* When you express your feelings, even others who completely disagree with you can tell how strongly you feel about the situation. Remember to use "I" messages rather than "you" messages.
- *Make your request.* This is an important aspect of being assertive. Simply ask for what you want (or don't want) in a straightforward manner.

As a practising teacher, if you feel that you are too aggressive, manipulative, or passive, work on being more assertive. The key to being an assertive educator is to make assertive requests. The University of Saskatchewan suggests five components to communicating assertively:

- *Use assertive nonverbal behaviour.* Establish eye contact, square your shoulders, remain calm, and be self-confident.
- *Keep your request simple.* One or two easy-to-understand sentences is adequate. For example, you might tell a student, "We need to go to the principal to get this straightened out."
- *Avoid asking for more than one thing at a time.* For example, don't ask the principal for a new computer and a new projector.
- *Don't apologize for your request.* Make direct requests such as, "I want you to …"; don't say "I know this is an imposition on you, but …" What if the other person responds with criticism, tries to make you feel guilty, or makes sarcastic remarks? Simply repeat your assertive request directly, strongly, and confidently.
- *Describe the benefits of the request.* Describing the benefits of cooperating with the request can be an honest offer of mutual give-and-take rather than manipulation.

Following this sequence conveys the message to students that positive results will occur if specific actions are taken. Consequently, this leaves students feeling in control of changing their behaviour.

So far in this chapter, we have discussed the importance of creating a positive learning environment. We have also discussed a number of ideas about being a good communicator. A review of these ideas is presented in Summary Table 12.3. Teachers will also want to consider the physical management of their classrooms. In the next section, we describe several classroom-arrangement styles and considerations for organizing classroom space.

If your aim is control, it must be self-control first.

If your aim is management, it must be self-management first.

Anonymous

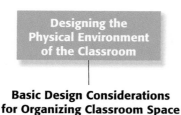

Designing the Physical Environment of the Classroom

Basic Design Considerations for Organizing Classroom Space

DESIGNING THE PHYSICAL ENVIRONMENT OF THE CLASSROOM

When thinking about how to effectively manage their classrooms, some teachers overlook the importance of the physical layout. Planning the physical environment of a classroom involves much more than creating bulletin boards or moving student desks together. Teachers can use space and physical resources in their classrooms to promote a positive and safe learning environment. The design and use of classroom space for such things as learning centres, talk circles, or cooperative groups depends, in part, on matching the instructional style of the teacher with the learning styles of the students, as well as analyzing the purpose or goals of the instructional activities. In this section, we will examine some of the pedagogical planning and design issues associated with the physical environment of classrooms, including multi-level classrooms and open-concept arrangements.

Basic Design Considerations for Organizing Classroom Space

John Dewey wrote that a democratic society "must have a type of education which gives individuals a personal interest in social relationships and control, and the habits of mind which secure social change without introducing disorder" (p. 115). Since teachers and students spend the majority of the school day in classrooms, it seems prudent that students be involved in the setup and operation of classroom space. Classroom space is a valuable asset, and classroom layout can either help or hinder student learning and teacher effectiveness. Certain classroom layouts may be unsuitable for specific lessons or instructional approaches. For example, a cluttered and disorganized wood shop may be unsafe for a large class or activity-based lessons. A classroom seating arrangement that places students in rows may not be the best arrangement for encouraging cooperative interaction or discussion, and a circle seat configuration may not be the best arrangement for a lecture or student presentation. Below are some basic considerations that you can use when arranging your classroom.

- *Consider the instructional activities your classroom space will be used for and what resources you will need to support these activities.* For example, if you are planning on using technology or machinery such as lathes or milling machines, then sufficient space and access to power and ventilation systems must be considered. Work areas for

SUMMARY TABLE 12.3
Being a Good Communicator

How can teachers help students develop effective speaking skills?	• Prior to speaking, students should choose a speaking topic, decide on a presentation format, determine the purpose for speaking, and consider the intended audience. • During the speech, students should actively engage with the audience through communication and interaction. • After the event, students should take time to reflect on their performance and set personal goals for improving their speaking ability.
What is active listening?	• Active listening occurs when a person gives full attention to the speaker and focuses on the intellectual and the emotional content of the message. • Active listening strategies for primary students include stopping, looking, listening, being empathetic, and asking questions. • Active listening strategies for intermediate and secondary students include paying careful attention to the person who is talking, maintaining eye contact, paraphrasing, synthesizing, and giving meaningful feedback.
What are barriers to effective verbal communication?	• Barriers to effective verbal communication include lack of clarity, using stereotypes and generalizations, jumping to conclusions, using disconfirming responses, and lacking confidence.
What are "you" and "I" messages?	• "You" messages imply judgments of people and place them in defensive positions. • "I" messages are less provocative and better reflect speakers' true feelings.
How do we communicate nonverbally?	• The majority of communication is nonverbal and usually reflects how people really feel. • Nonverbal communication involves facial expressions, eye communication, touch, space, and silence.
How do people address conflict?	• The four styles that people use to address conflict are aggressive, manipulative, passive, and assertive. • Individuals with an aggressive style are demanding, abrasive, and act in hostile ways. • Individuals with a manipulative style try to get what they want by making people feel guilty or sorry for them, rather than taking control of their own needs. • Individuals with a passive style are nonassertive and submissive and do not let others know what they want. • Individuals with an assertive style act in their own best interests, insist that misbehaviours be corrected, and resist being coerced or manipulated. • The assertive style is the best strategy for dealing with conflict as it builds positive, constructive relationships.

activities such as art, drama, or science need special consideration with respect to traffic patterns, safety, and security. Finally, consider the need to display student work (Machnaik, 2002).

• *Focus on student safety and security as key elements when planning classroom layout and arrangement.* It is important to be able to monitor all students at all times. Plan layouts so that you have a clear view of students, resources, and activities. Prepare and rehearse contingency plans for emergencies. Finally, ensure that all students can see you by walking about the classroom and checking for blind spots (Brownlie & King, 2000).

www.mcgrawhill.ca/college/santrock

• *Organize and monitor access to required materials and supplies in order to promote efficient use of resources and instructional time.* Plan where students will be working or interacting. Consider how materials will be located or retrieved by students. Develop transitional plans and routines that are time-efficient and promote student learning (Everston, Emmer, & Worsham, 2000).

For an innovative idea about how technology can be used to optimize classroom space, see the Technology and Education box on page 403.

Classroom-Arrangement Styles A number of classroom-arrangement styles provide options for both large and small classes. Each style has benefits and constraints that teachers must consider when making plans and decisions. For example, in the traditional *auditorium style* seating arrangement, all students face the teacher and are seated in rows designed to inhibit face-to-face student interactions and provide centralized teacher control. Alternatively, in *face-to-face style* seating arrangements, students face each other to enable discussion and interaction. This style, however, also increases the risk of distraction from other students. In *small-group style* and *offset style* seating arrangements, small groups of students are seated around a common work area designed to balance the need for student interaction and teacher-directed activities. Figure 12.3 illustrates some of these seating arrangements. Two other arrangement styles that have been shown to affect classroom management, instructional format, and student learning are *open-concept schools* and *multi-level classrooms*.

Open-concept schools *have teachers and students moving freely among rooms, sharing materials and resources.* Open-concept schools and classrooms gained initial popularity in the 1960s. In Canada, the Hall-Dennis Report on Education (Ontario, 1986) advocated for open-concept schools. The report suggested that self-contained classrooms tend to emphasize achievement of basic skills and a standardized approach to learning, while open-concept schools emphasize attitudes, feelings, and a variety of learning approaches. Following the release of the report a number of open-concept schools were built throughout Ontario; many still exist today. Open-concept classrooms require considerable teacher planning, collaboration, and management to avoid becoming too noisy or too busy.

FIGURE 12.3 Variations of Classroom Seating Arrangements

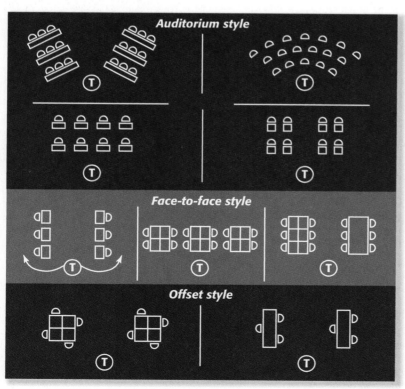

Multi-level classrooms *resemble open-concept schools in that a number of different grade levels are present in the same class space.* Horsman (1997) describes some of the strategies adopted by Saskatchewan schools when working in a multi-level classroom, including curriculum mapping, thematic teaching, independent study, peer tutoring, and experiential learning. According to Horsman, successful instruction in these skills depends on teachers embracing the philosophy that the classroom truly represents a "community of learners."

The T-Zone or Action Zone Research suggests that in classrooms where the students' seats are arranged in rows and the teacher's desk is placed at the front, teachers tend to interact most often with those students seated in the "T" formation at the front and centre of the class (Flanders, 1970). Figure 12.4 illustrates this T formation (which has also been called the "action zone," because students seated here are likely to receive the greatest amount of teacher attention and are most likely to initiate discussion). Focusing on the action zone tends to marginalize students seated at the fringes of the class. In an attempt to counteract the centralizing tendency of the

Optimizing Classroom Space Using Whiteboard Conversion Kits

Many of the elementary and secondary schools that have been built in recent years have been wired to support technology for group and collaborative learning activities. However, purchasing new information and communication technologies—or even modifying an older school or classroom—is often prohibitively expensive for many school boards. For example, interactive or electronic whiteboards are tools that many teachers would like to have in their classrooms. Electronic whiteboards can integrate a variety of materials including pictures from the Internet, graphs from spreadsheets, text, sound, and student and teacher annotations. The boards can facilitate collaborative work and free students from the demands of note taking. They can also be used to provide instructional support to students with visual or physical impairments. But electronic whiteboards are typically large pieces of equipment that take up a great deal of classroom space. Furthermore, related equipment can cost thousands of dollars, placing them out of reach of many K–12 school boards.

Recent innovations that convert standard classroom whiteboards into electronic whiteboards may help older schools seeking to incorporate technology into the classroom. Mimio and eBeam are two companies offering clip-on conversion kits to convert a standard whiteboard into an electronic copy-board; the kits cost about the same as a regular computer. The Mimio and eBeam conversion systems enable a standard whiteboard to detect the movement of a dry-erase marker pen (inside a special case), which functions as a computer mouse on the surface of the board. The conversion kits include all the hardware and software needed to enable teachers and students to work on a standard whiteboard while still capturing and saving the materials, as well as to broadcast notes, charts, or graphics over the Web in real time. Additional information about Mimio and eBeam technology can be found at **www.mimio.com** and **www.e-beam.com**, respectively.

action zone, teachers are encouraged to move about the classroom, establish eye contact with all students, monitor how often and with whom they interact, and have students change seats on a regular basis (about every six to eight weeks).

Personalizing Classroom Space   It is also important to personalize classroom spaces in order to engage students and create a positive learning environment. The need to personalize learning spaces is often most noticeable in secondary schools, where six or seven different classes might use the same space throughout the course of a day (Weinstein & Mignano, 1997). Teachers can personalize classrooms by posting students' artistic efforts, written works, or other products.

At this point, we have considered some ideas with respect to the physical layout of the classroom. A review of these ideas is presented in Summary Table 12.4. Despite teachers' best efforts to create inviting classrooms and be proactive with respect to classroom management, there will be times when they are called upon to address students' misbehaviours. In the next section, we explore strategies that teachers can use when addressing problem behaviours.

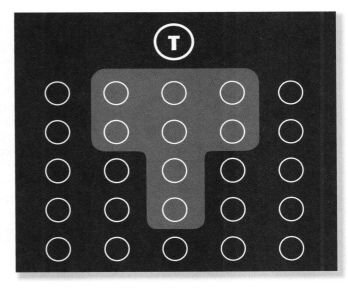

FIGURE 12.4   **The Action Zone**
"Action zone" refers to the seats in the front and centre of row arrangement. Students in these seats are more likely to interact with the teacher, ask questions, and initiate discussion than students seated in more peripheral locations.

ADDRESSING PROBLEM BEHAVIOURS

In any classroom, a certain amount of problematic behaviour is to be expected. However, with proper preparation and timely interventions, many of these instances can be prevented or managed in such a way that the level of disruption is minimal. It is important that you develop a comprehensive plan to address problem behaviours that includes preventive strategies and reactive interventions.

Addressing Problem Behaviours

Management Strategies   Handling Aggression and Bullying

SUMMARY TABLE 12.4
Designing the Physical Classroom Environment

What are the basic design principles for the classroom?	• The basic principles include reducing congestion in high-traffic areas, making sure that you can easily see all students, making frequently used materials and supplies easily accessible, and making sure that all students can see whole-class presentations.
What are considerations for organizing the physical classroom space?	• The basic organizational considerations are (1) classroom arrangement style (auditorium, face-to-face, small-group style, offset), (2) personalizing the classroom, (3) considering what activities students will be engaged in, (4) drawing up a floor plan, and (5) involving students in the classroom design and being flexible in redesigning it.
What are open-concept schools and multi-level classrooms?	• Open-concept schools have teachers and students moving freely between rooms, sharing materials and resources. • Multi-level classrooms have a number of different grade levels in the same class space.

Striking a Balance between Preventive Strategies and Reactive Interventions

The development of a comprehensive classroom-management strategy must take into account a larger view of discipline, one that aims to strike a healthy balance between proactive and reactive strategies. Unfortunately, most intervention programs are focused on management of problematic behaviours after they occur, leaving prevention approaches largely neglected (Nansel et al., 2001; Spivak & Prothrow-Stith, 2001).

However, many experienced teachers know that prevention is the best intervention. For example, setting up the classroom to be an inviting environment not only encourages academic performance, but also serves to prevent many discipline problems. While there is no denying the importance of reactive strategies, we are suggesting that teachers place greater emphasis on the development of proactive ones so that a healthy balance can be obtained between these two modes of intervention.

Prevention Planning

GENERAL PREVENTION GUIDELINES   Prevention plans are based on the premise that solid work and planning ahead of time will reduce the number and severity of problem behaviours. For teachers, prevention planning involves self-reflection and an analysis of personal teaching style and classroom environment. Teachers should reflect on their assumptions about problematic behaviours, asking themselves why students misbehave and what are the goals of interventions that "punish" bad behaviours. It is also important to view misbehaviour along a continuum of behaviours, ranging from relatively minor offences (e.g., hiding someone's book) to more serious ones (e.g., causing harm to others). Planning for prevention generally means being prepared and willing to learn about your students. Every student is unique and comes to school with a complex set of circumstances. Learn about your students by asking questions and becoming knowledgeable about their interests and concerns.

PREVENTION STRATEGIES   Prevention strategies are aimed at preparing students with the knowledge, skills, and practice needed to cope with problem situations before they escalate. Teachers, with the help of their students, can develop a classroom code of conduct that details the types of prosocial behaviours that are expected from everyone, as well as

Teaching Strategies
For Designing a Classroom Arrangement

✔ Consider the curriculum
  - consider activities that students will need to complete
  - allow space for whole-class instruction, reading aloud, small-group instruction, drama and art, hands-on laboratory activities, and presentations
  - consider resources and special equipment needed for subject areas (e.g., sink for science, electric outlets for computers)
✔ Create a floor plan
  - draw several floor plans to scale
  - create moveable desks and other "furniture"
  - select the most appropriate floor plan
  - include options with respect to student seating
  - have students participate in the design of the floor plan whenever possible
  - include space for students to keep their personal items
✔ Monitor classroom arrangement
  - evaluate the effectiveness of your classroom arrangement regularly
  - be aware of problematic behaviours that result from classroom arrangement (e.g., increased misbehaviour during story time because of crowding around the teacher)
  - be willing to change student seating and floor plan (e.g., use semicircle for story time)

Sources: Weinstein (1997), and Weinstein and Mignano (1997)

the consequences associated with misbehaviour. Copies of codes should be prominently displayed and sent home to keep parents informed.

Another prevention strategy is inviting community members with specialized skills or knowledge into your classroom. For example, police officers and public health nurses are often willing to talk to students about risks and consequences of inappropriate behaviour.

Finally, recognize that some cases of misbehaviour can be an indicator of other difficulties. Factors such as mental health disorders, drug use, or emotional and psychological problems can manifest and have serious adverse effects on students' behaviour. Learn about the resources available in your school, board, and community so that you can be better prepared to address such serious difficulties.

Management Strategies

Managing problematic behaviours is the one area that most teachers would prefer to avoid. However, every teacher must be prepared for the challenges presented in this part of the job. It is helpful if intervention strategies are conceptualized along a continuum, ranging from minor, to moderate, to serious (Evertson, Emmer, & Worsham, 2003). When assessing the seriousness of a behaviour, you may also want to consider its severity, chronicity, and frequency. **Severity** *refers to the overall potential impact of the misbehaviour and can range from simple misdemeanours* (e.g., throwing spitballs) *to more serious offences* (e.g., bringing a gun to school). **Chronicity** *refers to the pervasiveness of the behaviour* (e.g., across science, language arts, and recess), and **frequency** *refers to how often it occurs* (e.g., every week, once a year). The combination of these three dimensions will determine the type of intervention required.

"How come when you say we have a problem, I'm always the one who has the problem?"

Minor Interventions Some problems require only minor interventions. These problems involve behaviours that, if infrequent, usually don't disrupt class activities and learning. For example, students might call out to the teacher out of turn, leave their seats without permission, engage in social talk when it is not allowed, eat candy in class, and so on. When only minor interventions are needed for problem behaviours, the following strategies can be effective (Evertson, Emmer, & Worsham, 2000, 2003).

- *Use nonverbal cues.* Establish eye contact with students. Signal by placing your finger on your lips, shaking your head, or using a hand signal to stop the behaviour.
- *Keep the activity moving.* Sometimes transitions between activities take too long or a break in activity occurs when students have nothing to do. In these situations, students might leave their seats, socialize, crack jokes, and begin to get out of control. A good strategy is not to correct students' minor misbehaviours in these situations, but rather start the next activity in a more timely fashion. By effectively planning the day, you should be able to eliminate these long transitions and gaps in activity.
- *Move closer to students.* When students start misbehaving, simply moving nearer to them will often cause the misbehaviour to stop.
- *Redirect the behaviour.* If students get off-task, remind them of what they are supposed to be doing. You might say, "Okay, remember, everybody is supposed to be working on their math problems."
- *Give needed instruction.* Sometimes students engage in minor misbehaviours when they haven't comprehended how to do the task they have been assigned. Unable to effectively do the activity, they fill the time by engaging in misbehaviour. Solving this problem involves careful monitoring of students' work and providing guidance when needed.
- *Directly and assertively telling students to stop.* Establish direct eye contact with students; be assertive, and tell students to stop the behaviour. Make your statement brief, and monitor the situation until the students comply. This strategy can be combined with redirecting their behaviour.
- *Provide students with choices.* Place responsibility in the students' hands by saying that they have a choice of either behaving appropriately or receiving a negative consequence. Be sure to tell students what the appropriate behaviour is and what the consequences are for not performing it. For example, an elementary-school teacher might say, "Remember, appropriate behaviour means not eating candy in class. If you choose to do that, you won't be allowed to play games on the computer."

Remember, effective teachers are always vigilant for opportunities to reinforce desired behaviours. The next two sections will describe moderate and serious interventions.

Moderate Interventions Some misbehaviours require a stronger intervention than those described above—for example, when students abuse privileges, disrupt activities, goof off, or interfere with your instruction or other students' work. Following are some moderate interventions for dealing with these types of problems (Evertson, Emmer, & Worsham, 2000, 2003).

- *Withhold a privilege or desired activity.* Inevitably, you will have students who abuse privileges they have been given, such as freedom to move around the classroom or to work on a project with friends. In these cases, you can revoke the privilege.
- *Create a behavioural contract. Contracting* involves putting reinforcement contingencies into writing. If problems arise and students don't uphold their end of the bargain, the teacher can refer to the contract the students agreed to. The contract should reflect input from both the teacher and the students.
- *Isolate or remove students. Time-out* involves removing students from positive reinforcement. If you use a time-out, be sure to review the procedures outlined in Chapter 7, including identifying students' behaviours that resulted in the time-out (e.g., "You are being placed in time-out for 10 minutes because you destroyed Derrek's artwork"). If the misbehaviour occurs again, re-identify it and place students in another time-out. After the time-out, don't comment about how well the students behaved during the time-out, just return them to the activity that was interrupted.

- *Impose a penalty.* A small amount of repetitious work can be used as a penalty for misbehaviour. For instance, students may have to write an extra page, or run an extra lap. However, the problem with penalties is that they can harm students' attitudes toward the subject matter.
- *Impose a detention.* Students can also serve a detention for their misbehaviours, at lunch, recess, before school, or after school. The length of the detention should initially be short—no more than 10 to 15 minutes. As with the time-out, you will need to keep a record of the detention.

Serious Interventions   Some misbehaviours represent serious concerns. Examples include bullying, sexual harassment, use of illegal substances, and violent behaviours. While it is unlikely that you will see many of these extreme behaviours, you must be prepared to meet these challenges by acting in a consultative, consistent, and timely fashion. The following are some intervention strategies that can be used when addressing serious behavioural problems.

- *Consult with others.* Seek the advice of colleagues, administrators, and professionals so that you are better prepared to address the incident. It is quite likely that students who commit serious offences repeatedly have needs that cannot be met by the school alone. In these cases, it is important to have a protocol that can be implemented quickly.
- *Know the law.* Become knowledgeable about the provincial and territorial laws governing educational institutions and become familiar with the policies and protocols used by your school board. Identify situations in which you have some discretion over the handling of the incident (e.g., broken lab equipment) and those in which you do not (e.g., reports of abuse, possession of weapons).
- *Suspension and expulsion.* Each school board has its own set of policies and procedures regarding the expulsion and suspension of students. Expulsion and suspension are distinct and serious responses to students' infractions. Expulsion involves the school board–approved removal of a student for an extended period of time. The behaviours of expelled students are often considered injurious to themselves or to others. In contrast, suspension is the temporary loss of privileges or removal of a student from the classroom, bus, or school property. Consequently, suspensions may be in-school or out of school and may be for as little as half a day.
- *Prepare for the students' re-entry.* Following a serious incident, it is important that students' re-entry into the school environment be managed properly. Parents and students will need to meet with school staff and administrators to discuss what has been learned from the incident and what plans are in place to prevent its recurrence. In some cases, students may be required to apologize formally, redress wrongs, attend counselling, or perform community service.

Working with Parents   Regardless of the level of intervention you use when addressing students' problematic behaviours, you will want to include parents whenever possible. It is important that parents understand that you are trying to form a partnership with them in order to help their children. In many cases, just informing parents can sometimes cause students to become more aware of the consequences of their actions and motivate them to improve their behaviour. When conferencing with parents, have docu-

Through the Eyes of Teachers

Tips on Classroom Management and Discipline

- Make sure students know your expectations—academic and behavioural—from the first day of school.
- Exude confidence, even if you don't feel it. Have high but realistic expectations for your students and yourself.
- Teach "bell-to-bell."
- Observe and talk with teachers who seem to have a teaching style and values regarding teaching that are similar to your own; they are often helpful in suggesting strategies that will fit your style.
- Avoid power struggles. Yelling and condescending remarks usually make things worse.
- Students love knowing what to expect next. List on your board the agenda for the day. Set priorities for what needs to be done before free time.
- Set guidelines and see that they are followed. Change them if necessary.
- Having students help create classroom rules and procedures often ensures more buy-in.
- Be clear with your students about what you expect. Let them see it in writing as well as hear it.
- Be consistent.
- A master teacher can provide you with encouragement and alternative approaches to curriculum frustrations or student struggles.
- Listen to your students. Immediate care is necessary if a student expresses fear for his or her safety at school or at home.

mented evidence available. Be careful not to create the impression that you are blaming them for their children's misbehaviours. To increase the likelihood of forming a cooperative partnership, keep the focus on the behaviour and not the students. Briefly describe the problem and state that you would appreciate any support that they can provide.

Working with Peer Mediators Students sometimes can be very effective in persuading other students to behave appropriately (Cunningham et al., 1998). In cases where students become involved in conflicts on the playground or in the classroom, peers can play a significant role in finding a resolution. If appropriately trained and supervised, peer mediators can be quite effective in resolving conflicts between students. There are a number of peer-mediation programs available, including "Peacemakers," "Friends in the Neighbourhood," and the Canadian "Pacific Path."

Working with Community Mentors In Chapter 11, we emphasized the importance of having at least one person in a student's life who cares about them and supports their development. We also described programs (e.g., "Connections") that are designed to help students who are experiencing difficulties at school. Look around the community for potential mentors, especially for students from high-risk backgrounds.

Handling Aggression and Bullying

According to Statistics Canada (1999), while the overall rate of youth-related crime has decreased, aggressive and violent incidents among youth have increased by approximately 40 percent over the past 10 years. In many schools, it is now common for students to fight, bully each other, or threaten each other and their teachers. A survey of British Columbia youth revealed that only 39 percent of Grade 8 students and 58 percent of Grade 12 students reported feeling safe at school (The McCreary Centre Society Report, 1996). In another survey involving more than 700 British Columbia teachers, about half of the participants reported experiencing some form of violence (either direct or indirect) over the previous school year, with a total of 81 percent reporting being the victim of violence at some point in their careers.

> Good nature is more agreeable in conversation than wit and gives a certain air to the countenance which is more amiable than beauty.
>
> Joseph Addison
> *English Essayist, 18th Century*

Fighting Most provinces have implemented some version of *zero tolerance*, which usually involves adopting a "get-tough" attitude accompanied by a very strict and highly structured set of punitive consequences designed to eliminate antisocial behaviour. While a zero-tolerance policy might be a deterrent, teachers should be prepared to act in the event of a fight. According to Evertson, Emmer, and Worsham (2003), teacher intervention is likely to be influenced by the grade level of the students involved. At the elementary-school level, fighting can usually be terminated by firmly and decisively telling students to stop. Afterward, keep the students separated, request that all others leave the area, and appoint someone to inform other members of the staff.

In cases involving secondary-school students, you may not be able to intervene alone without risking injury to yourself; you will probably need the help of two or more adults. Work out a strategy to request quick support when needed. The period following a fight is critical. It is important that the participants have time to cool off, followed by an opportunity to present their version of the story. Ideally, your role should remain that of an instructor. In other words, avoid acting as both judge and jury.

Defiance or Hostility toward Teachers The most important element of handling a defiant or hostile student is to avoid setting up conditions for a power struggle. According to Evertson, Emmer, and Worsham (2003), if acts of defiance or hostility are permitted to continue, there is the real possibility that they will escalate and spread. Your reaction should be guided by the severity of the event. If it is a minor incident, try to defuse the situation by addressing the student privately. In cases where the event is more serious, you may need to ask the student to leave the classroom. Allow yourself and the student some time to calm down, and consider your next steps.

If the student persists to the point of becoming completely uncooperative, you will need the help of other teachers or the main office. In these stressful circumstances, it is important to remain calm and avoid power struggles with students (Evertson, Emmer, & Worsham, 2003).

Bullying In Chapter 3, we defined bullying as the repeated and intentional abuse of physical and psychological power. Recent studies have reported that bullying is one of the most pervasive and underrated socioeducational problems facing elementary- and secondary-school students (Boivin, Hymel, & Hodges, 2001; Craig, Pepler, Connolly, & Henderson, 2001; Marini, Fairbairn, & Zuber, 2001).

Research findings suggest that bullying behaviours have an earlier onset than previously thought, that the number of students affected is relatively high (15 to 25 percent), that the range of behaviours involved is quite severe, and that the consequences associated with bullying are long-lasting (Craig, Pepler, & Atlas, 2000; Kochenderfer & Ladd, 1996; Loeber & Hay, 1997; Olweus, 2001; Pepler & Craig, 1995; Smith, Cowie, Olafsson, & Liefooghe, 2002). Students who participate in bullying (i.e., bullies, victims, and bystanders) are quite diverse in nature, defying any simplified attempt at characterizing them. For instance, bullies may range from students who lack social skills to those who purposefully exploit victims' weaknesses (Marini, McWhinnie, & Lacharite, 2003).

A number of intervention programs aimed at reducing bullying behaviours have been developed and implemented (e.g., Elsea & Smith, 1998; Olweus, 1993; Pepler, Craig, Ziegler, & Charach, 1994). While the rate of success varies from program to program, the more successful interventions use a systematic approach whereby bullying is addressed at a number of levels, including school board policies, instructional materials, and remedial support. Pepler and her colleagues have implemented and evaluated one such program, and reported a reduction in bullying incidences as a function of its use. The program consists of a comprehensive intervention involving the entire school system. School administrators and teachers present students with books, videotapes, and activities that are designed to increase their awareness of bullying behaviours and how they can be prevented. Parents are also involved by attending workshops and in some cases assisting in playground supervision (Pepler et al., 1994). Using a similar multi-level intervention, Elsea and Smith (1998) reported a 17-percent reduction in victims and a 7-percent decrease in the number of identified bullies, while Olweus (1993) reported a 50-percent decrease in bullying incidents.

School boards that want to implement an anti-bullying program can select from a variety of available options, depending on the level of prevention they wish to emphasize. A comprehensive prevention program based on the Public Health Model outlines three levels of prevention: primary, secondary, and tertiary (Marini, Bombay, Hobin, Winn, & Dumyn, 2000). The following are examples of intervention programs at each level.

"… and suddenly there were teachers all over the place!"

Primary Prevention These programs are aimed at developing positive attitudes and social skills across the entire school population; they attempt to increase students' empathy and level of caring, and are especially useful in the early grades. An example is the Roots of Empathy program developed by Mary Gordon (2000) and aimed at junior and senior kindergartens. The program nurtures students' empathy by arranging for a mom-and-baby visit to the classroom once a month over a ten-month period. The teacher works with the students before, during, and after each visit to facilitate learning about one's emotions, as well as how others feel. Rock, Hammond, and Rasmussen (2002) evaluated an intervention program that focused predominantly on developing empathy, and reported a 73-percent reduction in incidents of bullying. It is believed that this is accomplished through building the students' prosocial behaviour tendencies along with their capacity to be empathetic. Consequently, there is a decrease in antisocial behaviour.

Secondary Prevention These programs are aimed at increasing awareness about the warning signs of peer aggression and victimization as well as reducing risks. Instructional materials such as plays and books are effective secondary prevention tools. Peer-mediation programs have also proven to be appropriate secondary prevention measures.

Teaching should be such that what is offered is perceived as a valuable gift and not as a hardship.

Albert Einstein
American Scientist, 20th Century

www.mcgrawhill.ca/college/santrock

Peer mediation can be effective provided they are properly supervised.

Teaching Strategies
For Reducing Bullying

✔ Develop an identification system
  • recognize physical, social, cognitive, and emotional signs of bullying (Chapter 3)
  • identify who holds power (i.e., bully)
  • identify who lacks power (i.e., victim)
  • identify the audience for the bullying behaviour (i.e., bystanders)
✔ Implement an anti-bullying program
  • develop codes of conduct for the school and classroom
  • hold regular discussions about bullying (i.e., talk circles, debates, role-playing)
  • provide all students with negotiation and conflict-resolution training
  • use older students as mediation models
  • assign students roles of importance on a rotational basis
  • develop a school-wide reinforcement plan to catch students "being good"
  • collaborate with relevant community organizations
✔ Provide alternative activities
  • offer a diverse selection of extracurricular activities
  • offer extracurricular activities during lunch and recess sessions
  • offer extracurricular activities before and after school
  • allow students access to supervised areas during lunch and recess (e.g., classroom, library, study hall)

Cunningham and his colleagues (Cunningham, Cunningham, & Martorelli, 1997) assessed the effectiveness of using a peer-mediation program for elementary-school students from junior kindergarten to Grade 5. Mediation teams made up of Grade 5 students received 15 hours of conflict-resolution training where they participated in role-playing, case-analysis, and problem-solving activities. Following training, the mediators were successful in resolving about 90 percent of the conflicts in which they intervened. Furthermore, the occurrence of physical aggression on the playground decreased from 65 percent to 51 percent. More importantly, these effects were maintained up to one year following the training. According to Cunningham, teacher support is an important factor in determining the success of any secondary intervention program.

Other examples include the Edmonton-based TAB program (Teasing and Bullying: Unacceptable Behaviour Program; Langevin, 1998) and the Pacific Path program. TAB aims at encouraging students to take responsible action against teasing and bullying. Students are encouraged to mobilize bystanders and use conflict-resolution strategies. The Pacific Path program was developed in Montreal and promotes conflict resolution and peer mediation as a schoolwide intervention for elementary- and secondary-school students (Vadeboncoeur, Rondeau, & Begin, 2001). The program has students complete a variety of activities including personal reflection, group discussion, and role-playing. Instructional emphasis is directed toward the themes of violence, self-image, and peer influence. Results culled from participants in the Pacific Path program indicated a 20-percent increase prosocial behaviour (Vadeboncoeur, Rondeau, & Begin, 2001).

Tertiary Prevention These programs are aimed at helping those students identified as bullies and victims to change their respective roles. Through counselling, bullies are directed to replace their negative behaviours with more positive and socially acceptable interactions. For victims, the focus is on empowerment through role playing, assertiveness training, and inclusion activities. While there are relatively few programs that focus specifically on the protagonists of bullying, one of them is worth noting: the Shared Concern method, originally developed by Pikas (2002), is based on the belief that bullies

Diversity and Education
Farheen Hasan and the Afgan Women's Organization of Canada

A special concern for Canadian educators is to promote tolerance and respect for diverse religious and cultural practices that are increasingly becoming part of urban school life. Approximately 650,000 Muslims currently call Canada home; while they come from all parts of the world, most follow the common Islamic practices of not drinking alcohol, dressing modestly, and praying five times a day. This growing Muslim Canadian population is often misunderstood and stereotyped as being violent and disrespectful toward women (Jafri, 1998).

Misunderstanding and fear of Muslims, especially in the wake of recent world events, has led to discrimination, bullying, and sometimes violence against Muslim students in Canadian schools. Many of these students acknowledge feeling insecure about their dual identities as Muslims and Canadians (Jafri, 1998).

Increasing awareness and understanding of Muslim Canadians is crucial to reducing tensions in schools, increasing

tolerance, and optimizing Muslim students' learning experiences. Farheen Hasan is a Muslim Canadian and a member of the Afgan Women's Organization. The group is dedicated to explaining the principles of Islam to other Canadians. As a Pakastani Muslim and a journalist, Hasan is involved in a project called "Muslim Women: Improving Portrayals in Canadian Media"; the project is aimed at studying how Afghans, Arabs, and Muslims, especially women, were portrayed in the media in the six-month period after the events of September 11, 2001. Its ultimate goal is to improve relations between Afghan, Arab, and Muslim communities in Canada, as well as with the media and the Canadian public.

Every community has individuals like Farheen Hasan who are committed to providing positive cultural role models for teachers and students. If the need for such a role model arises in your school, make a commitment to scour the community for such talented, informed, and concerned cultural representatives.

Teaching Strategies
For Conflict Resolution

✔ Create a supportive environment
- do not focus on changing individuals' behaviours—focus on transforming the school environment
- create situations that foster cooperation versus competition
- explicitly teach students communication and social skills
- model how to resolve conflicts constructively
- do not attempt to eliminate all conflict—moderate conflict can increase students' achievement, motivation to learn, and problem-solving skills

✔ Reduce in-school risk factors
- monitor students' academic performances and provide remedial instruction as necessary
- monitor students' social interactions and provide social skills training as necessary
- promote a sense of belonging for all students
- provide an assortment of extracurricular and learning activities

✔ Teach students how to resolve conflicts
- teach students negotiation strategies (e.g., define what you want, describe your feelings, explain underlying reasons, consider the other person's perspective, generate three possible resolutions, agree on the best course of action)
- teach students mediation strategies (e.g., stop the hostilities, ensure that individuals are committed to resolution, facilitate the negotiation process, formalize the agreement)
- borrow from established programs (e.g., Peacemakers, Friends in the Neighbourhood)
- provide instruction to as many students as possible

Source: Johnson & Johnson (1995)

www.mcgrawhill.ca/college/santrock

SUMMARY TABLE 12.5
Addressing Problematic Behaviours

What do teachers need to consider prior to implementing a prevention program?	• Teachers should develop a personal philosophy of student behaviour, classroom management, and remediation • Teachers need to understand that problematic behaviour occurs across a continuum ranging from minor to serious, and realize that some level of problematic behaviour is to be expected. • Teachers also need to understand that students' individual circumstances can affect their behaviours.
What are examples of minor, moderate, and serious management interventions?	• Minor interventions involve using nonverbal cues and proximity-redirecting behaviours, and providing students with choice. • Moderate interventions include withholding a privilege or a desired activity, creating a behavioural contract, isolating or removing students, and imposing a penalty or detention. • Serious interventions include consulting with others, suspension and expulsion, and preparing for students' re-entry into the school.
What are the types of strategies for handling aggression?	• Fighting is deterred by a zero-tolerance policy, which is a set of punitive consequences designed to eliminate antisocial behaviour. • Defiance or hostility toward teachers is best handled by avoiding power struggles. • Bullying should be addressed at a number of levels including school board policies, instructional material, and remedial support.
What is the distinction between primary, secondary, and tertiary prevention programs?	• Primary programs are aimed at developing positive attitudes and social skills across the entire school population. • Secondary programs are aimed at increasing awareness about the warning signs of aggression and victimization, and reducing risks. • Tertiary programs present conflict resolution and peer mediation as school-wide initiatives.
What are successful conflict-resolution programs based on?	• Successful conflict-resolution programs are based on three principles: (1) creating a supportive context, (2) decreasing in-school risk factors, and (3) teaching all students how to resolve conflicts constructively.

and victims can eventually come to resolve their differences. In this mediation-centred treatment process, a therapist works with bullies to help them accept responsibility for their actions. The victims are counselled to help them feel like they are not scapegoats. Depending on the severity of the incidences, meetings are held separately; in other words, the therapist may have to use shuttle diplomacy between the bully and the victim. At the end of the process an agreement is made and sealed with a "communication contract." Although there are no systematic evaluations of this approach, both Duncan (1996) and Pikas (2002) have reported positive results.

See the Diversity and Education box for a description of one program dedicated to enhancing students' acceptance and increasing their prosocial behaviours to ethnically and culturally diverse groups.

At this point, we have discussed many ideas about how to manage students' misbehaviours. A review of these ideas is presented in Summary Table 12.5.

Mr. Stolz was a new Grade 7 language arts teacher. Prior to beginning his new position, he developed a classroom-management plan that mirrored the code of conduct for the school. He expected the students to behave respectfully toward him and their classmates. He also expected them to respect school property and the learning environment. Minor behavioural infractions were to result in a verbal warning. Further infractions would net more severe consequences in steps: a detention, a referral to the office, and a call to the student's parents. Mr. Stolz was pleased with his management plan. He distributed it to students on the first day of class. He also distributed it to parents at the annual "Back to School" night during the first week of school.

Darius, a very social boy, was one of Mr. Stolz's students who spent much of his class time talking to other students rather than working. Mr. Stolz tried moving him to different parts of the room. He tried seating him next to students to whom he had never seen him talk. This had no impact on his behaviour. He simply made new friends and continued chatting, sometimes disrupting the class in the process. He tried seating Darius next to girls. This seemed to make things even worse.

Darius was very bright in addition to being very social. Although he was only in Grade 7, he was taking algebra with a group of mathematically advanced Grade 8 students. The algebra teacher, Mrs. Apple, and Darius had a very good relationship. He never disrupted her class or misbehaved in any way. Mrs. Apple was amazed to hear that Darius did not always behave appropriately in his other classes.

One day Darius was particularly talkative in class. Mr. Stolz asked him to stop talking. He did, but resumed his chatter within five minutes. When he began talking again, Mr. Stolz took him aside and told him loudly, "That's it, Darius. I'm going to have you removed from algebra class. You know taking that class is a privilege, not a right."

Darius was stunned. He sat quietly for the rest of the period, but did not participate. He made no eye contact with Mr. Stolz or any other students. The rest of the day was something of a blur to him. He had no idea how he would explain this to his parents.

When Darius told his mother he was going to be removed from algebra for his behaviour in language arts, she immediately went to see Mr. Stolz. She tried to tell Mr. Stolz that to remove Darius from algebra would be to deny him the free and appropriate public education to which he (and all other students) was entitled. Mr. Stolz held his ground and insisted that he could and would have his placement altered.

- What are the issues in this case?
- Is removal from algebra class an appropriate consequence for Darius? Why or why not?
- What do you think Darius' mother will do now?
- How do you think Mrs. Apple will react when she hears about the situation?
- What should Mr. Stolz do?

CHAPTER REVIEW

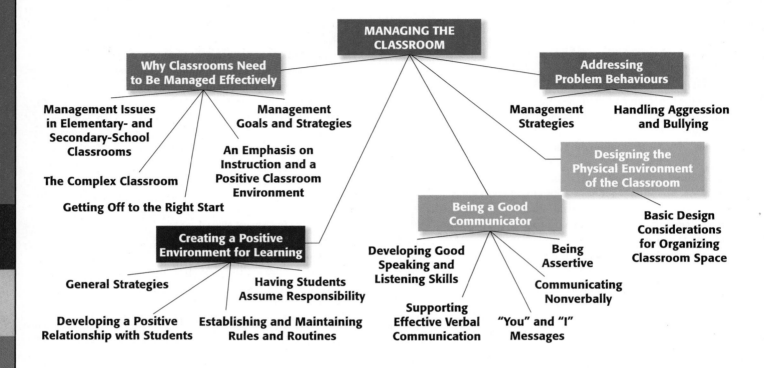

MANAGING THE CLASSROOM

Why Classrooms Need to Be Managed Effectively

- Management Issues in Elementary- and Secondary-School Classrooms
- The Complex Classroom
- Management Goals and Strategies
- An Emphasis on Instruction and a Positive Classroom Environment
- Getting Off to the Right Start

Creating a Positive Environment for Learning

- General Strategies
- Developing a Positive Relationship with Students
- Having Students Assume Responsibility
- Establishing and Maintaining Rules and Routines

Being a Good Communicator

- Developing Good Speaking and Listening Skills
- Supporting Effective Verbal Communication
- Being Assertive
- Communicating Nonverbally
- "You" and "I" Messages

Addressing Problem Behaviours

- Management Strategies
- Handling Aggression and Bullying

Designing the Physical Environment of the Classroom

- Basic Design Considerations for Organizing Classroom Space

To obtain a detailed review of this chapter, study these five summary tables:

 KEY TERMS

class size 384
pupil–teacher ratio 384
authoritative strategy of classroom management 389
authoritarian strategy of classroom management 390

permissive strategy of classroom management 390
"withitness" 390
ethic of care 392
active listening 395
"you" messages 397

"I" messages 397
aggressive style 399
manipulative style 399
passive style 399
assertive style 399
open-concept schools 402

multi-level classroom 402
severity 405
chronicity 405
frequency 405

PROFESSIONAL DEVELOPMENT/PORTFOLIO ACTIVITIES

1. Interventions for Aggression

Aggressive incidents can disrupt the learning process and create a negative classroom atmosphere. It is important for teachers to possess a range of intervention strategies that allow them to act promptly and consistently when students misbehave.

Imagine that these incidents take place in your classroom. In writing, describe how you would handle each one. Include these scenarios and their interventions in your portfolio.

- a Grade 2 girl yells out at you when you are working with another student
- a small, Grade 5 boy tells you that two much larger boys are bullying him
- two Grade 9 boys begin fighting on the other side of the classroom
- a Grade 11 girl openly defies you in front of the class and refuses to cooperate

2. Are Rules Meant to Be Broken?

In your portfolio, write down what you think are the ten most important classroom-conduct rules. For each rule, include two possible consequences that you may consider if students break the rules. Get together with three or four of your colleagues and share your rules and consequences. Reflect on the comments that your colleagues have made and evaluate the appropriateness of your rules and their consequences. Include your final copy of your classroom-conduct rules in your portfolio.

3. Disclosing the Self

In the context of teaching, self-disclosure is the process of letting students know who you are as a person. Self-disclosure is often an important component of relationship building. However, teachers need to consider how open they should be with their students. Write a personal reflection on how you will develop positive relationships with your students. What guidelines will you follow to establish proper boundaries?

4. Discipline Put to the Theory Test

Interview school counsellors at an elementary, intermediate, or secondary school. Ask them to describe the discipline policies at their schools and how well they work. Also ask them to describe the most difficult student problem they have ever dealt with and how it was handled. Write up that problem as a case study. Consult relevant educational psychology theory from this text to evaluate the case.

 # INTERNET ACTIVITIES

1. Classroom Design

Classroom design and organization can influence the learning environment. Using the Internet as a resource, list several descriptors that depict your ideal classroom environment. Anticipate challenges, and discuss how you could compensate for a classroom lacking storage space, natural light, or special areas for computer or group work. If you have access to a computer assisted design program (such as AutoSketch), use it to draw a floor layout of your classroom. Experiment with different design layouts for your learning environment.

2. The Rules Go to the Net

Setting clear expectations is a preventive measure for potential classroom behavioural difficulties. These expectations can be framed to focus on positive social interactions rather than the negative difficulties of antisocial behaviours. It is important to develop a list of rules for your classroom that are positively framed. After you have developed these rules, review the list and think about these questions: Are the rules worded in a positive manner? Are they appropriate and understandable for your target grade level? Did you consider involving your students in creating the rules? Post these rules on your school's Website, or create a site for your class.

Connect to the Online Learning Centre at www.mcgrawhill.ca/college/santrock **to explore possible answers.**

 Visit the *Educational Psychology* Online Learning Centre at
www.mcgrawhill.ca/college/santrock
to access Websites related to the above Internet Activities as well as chapter quizzes,
a searchable glossary, and other learning and study tools.

13
Standardized Tests and Teaching

Preview

Standardized tests are widely used to evaluate students' learning and achievement. Although they are increasingly used to compare students' performance in different schools, districts, provinces, territories, and countries, they are not without controversy. These are some of the questions we will explore in this chapter:

- What is the teacher's role in preparing students for and administering standardized tests?
- What criteria are used to evaluate standardized tests?
- What is involved in provincial/territorial–mandated tests?
- What are some good strategies for interpreting test results?
- What are some guidelines for communicating test results to parents?
- What are some issues and controversies involving standardized tests?

STANDARDIZED TESTS AND TEACHING

The Nature of Standardized Tests
- What Is a Standardized Test?
- The Purposes of Standardized Tests
- Criteria for Evaluating Standardized Tests

Standardized Aptitude, Achievement, and Psychoeducational Tests
- Comparing Aptitude, Achievement, and Psychoeducational Tests
- Psychoeducational Assessment
- Student Testing across the Provinces and Territories
- Types of Standardized Achievement Tests

The Teacher's Role
- Preparing Students to Take Standardized Tests
- Administering Standardized Tests in the Classroom
- Understanding and Interpreting Test Results
- Communicating Test Results to Parents

Issues in Standardized Testing
- Standardized Tests and Alternative Assessments
- In Search of a Balanced Approach
- Diversity and Standardized Testing

Teaching Stories: Sharon Sulley-Kean

Sharon Sulley-Kean is an experienced educator who has taught in several provinces including Alberta and Newfoundland and Labrador. She is the recipient of the Deputy Minister's Award for Excellence in Education. Throughout her 12-year teaching career, Sharon has assumed many roles beyond teaching in a contained classroom, including special educator, coordinator of short-term behavioural programs, and itinerant teacher for speech programming. Across all her roles, she has helped teachers and students prepare for standardized tests. Here, she offers a number of test-preparation tips for teachers and students.

"I'm often surprised when teachers ask me to help them prepare their classes to take a standardized test. While many standardized tests are designed to assess students' knowledge of specific content areas, teachers should not try to teach this content in a last-moment effort to increase students' performance scores. Such instruction usually places too much emphasis on the rote learning of material. Instead, teachers should focus on reducing students' anxiety and developing their test-taking skills. Teachers can help reduce student stress by using a variety of test formats throughout the year. Analyzing test results with a class can further prepare students for the next test. Talking about effective study strategies is especially beneficial in helping students develop their test-taking skills.

"Teachers should teach students how to logically select responses when completing multiple-choice questions. I tell students to guess when they are uncertain about the correct answer, but only when there is no penalty for guessing. I also encourage students to eliminate erroneous options before making an educated guess. I tell them to stay with their initial response when they are uncertain, as they are more likely to make an error if they change their response. Students also need to be reminded to show their work and provide lots of detail so that the grader can understand their thought processes.

"When preparing students for essay or case study questions, I teach them to create a brief outline by jotting down a few words about each of the ideas they want to discuss. Numbering these items is an easy way to determine their order of presentation. I encourage students to be direct by stating the main point and an overview of their essay as part of the introductory statement. These are the points that should be discussed in greater detail throughout the remainder of the essay. Supporting these points with examples or quotations is also part of an effective essay-writing strategy.

"When teachers know how to help prepare their students for standardized tests they reduce student test-taking anxiety and help them demonstrate their true understanding of the content area."

THE NATURE OF STANDARDIZED TESTS

Chances are, you have taken a number of standardized tests. In kindergarten, you may have taken a school readiness test, in elementary school you may have taken some basic skills or achievement tests, and in high school you may have taken a test required for graduation. Let's explore the concept of standardized testing.

What Is a Standardized Test?

A **standardized test** *is a commercially prepared test that assesses students' performance under uniform conditions. A standardized test often allows a student's performance to be compared with the performance of other students at the same age or grade level, in many cases on a national basis.* How are such standardized tests different from the tests you will construct as a teacher to assess your students' achievement? Teacher-made tests tend to focus on instructional objectives for a particular classroom. Standardized tests attempt to include material that is common across most classrooms (Gay & Airasian, 2000; Airasian, 1997). Some other ways standardized tests differ from teacher-made tests are that standardized tests have norms, have more extensive assessments of the test's validity, and have more extensive evaluations of the test's reliability. We will explore these aspects of standardized tests shortly, but first let's examine the purposes of standardized tests.

The Purposes of Standardized Tests

Standardized tests vary in their method of delivery and purpose. Individualized tests are administered to a student by an examiner in a one-on-one setting. Group tests are delivered to a whole class or cohort of students at the same time. In general, standardized tests provide educators with additional information about students' performance. Educators who may recommend the use of standardized tests include school administrators and teachers, the local school board, or the provincial ministry/department of education. Standardized tests may also be used to:

- *Provide information about students' progress.* Standardized tests are a source of information about how well students are performing. Students in one class might get A's but perform at a mediocre level on a provincial/territorial standardized test, and students in another class might get C's and do extremely well on the same standardized test. Without an external, objective marker like a standardized test, individual classroom teachers have difficulty knowing how well their students are performing compared to students elsewhere in the province, territory, or country.
- *Diagnose students' strengths and weaknesses.* Standardized tests also can provide information about students' learning strengths or weaknesses (Cascio, 2000; Popham, 2000). For example, a student who is not doing well in reading might be given one or more standardized tests to pinpoint where the learning weaknesses are. When standardized tests are given for diagnostic purposes, they usually are given individually rather than to a group of students.
- *Provide evidence for placement of students in specific programs.* Standardized tests can be used to make decisions about whether a student should be allowed to enter a specific program. In elementary school, a standardized test might be used to provide information for determining which students will receive resource assistance. In high school, a standardized test might be used to determine students' course selections. Students also might take standardized tests to determine their suitability for particular careers.
- *Help administrators evaluate programs.* If a school changes to a new educational program, the school administration will want to know how effective the new program is. One way to determine this is to give students relevant standardized tests to see how they are performing under the new program. For example, a school might change from a direct-instruction approach to a social-constructivist approach. Students' scores on a relevant standardized test can be used along with other evidence to determine the effectiveness of the change.

• *Contribute to accountability.* Schools and teachers are increasingly being held accountable for students' learning. Standardized tests are being used to determine how effectively schools are using tax dollars, although this is controversial (Aiken, 2000). Interest in accountability has led to the creation of **minimum competency tests**, *which assess skills that students are expected to have mastered before they can be promoted to the next grade or permitted to graduate.* For example, in British Columbia Grade 12 students must write provincial examinations for every subject that they complete. These examinations are worth 40 percent of their final course marks, and students must pass them to earn course credit (Government of British Columbia, 2002). Similarly, in Alberta Grade 12 diploma examinations in core academic courses account for 50 percent of students' final grades (Government of Alberta, 2002); in Manitoba, seniors are required to write final exams in English and mathematics that account for 30 percent of their final grade (Manitoba Education, Training and Youth, 2002). Other provinces have comparable minimum competency tests.

High-stakes testing *is using tests in a way that will have important consequences for the student, affecting decisions such as whether the student will be promoted a grade, graduate, or get a scholarship.* Later in the chapter we will discuss provincial/territorial–mandated tests, which are increasingly being used to make such "high-stakes" decisions.

For now, though, note that an important theme throughout this chapter is that a standardized test should not be the only method for evaluating students' learning. Nor should standardized tests by themselves be considered sufficient information in holding schools accountable for students' learning (Popham, 2000).

Criteria for Evaluating Standardized Tests

Among the most important criteria for evaluating standardized tests are *norms, reliability,* and *validity*.

Norms   To understand an individual student's performance on a test, it needs to be compared with the performance of a **norm group**, *a group of similar individuals who previously had been given the test by the test maker.* The test is said to be based on **national norms** *when the norm group consists of a nationally representative group of students.* For example, a standardized test for Grade 4 reading vocabulary and comprehension might be given to a national sample of Grade 4 students. The scores of the representative sample of thousands of Grade 4 students become the basis for comparison. This norm group should include students from urban, suburban, and rural areas; different geographical regions; private and public schools; boys and girls; and different ethnic groups. Based on the student's score on the standardized reading vocabulary and comprehension test, the teacher can determine whether a student is performing above, on level with, or below a national norm (Aiken, 2000). The teacher also can see how the class as a whole is performing in relation to the general population of students.

In addition to national norms, standardized tests also can have special group norms and local norms. **Special group norms** *consist of test scores for subgroups from the national sample.* For example, special group norms might be available for students from low, middle, and high socioeconomic groups; for inner-city, suburban, and rural schools; for public and private schools; for female and male students; and for students from different ethnic groups. **Local norms** *are sometimes available for standardized tests.* These allow comparison of a student's performance to that of students in the same class, school, or board. Thus, evaluations of a student's test performance might differ depending on what norm group is used.

Reliability   **Reliability** *means the extent to which a test produces a consistent, reproducible measure of performance.* Reliable measures are stable, dependable, and relatively free from errors of measurement (Fekken, 2000; Popham, 2000). It is important to note, however, that measures of reliability do not include an assessment of the appropriateness of the test tool. Rather, the role of reliability is to determine the consistency of an assessment tool. Reliability can be measured in several ways, including test–retest reliability, alternate forms reliability, and split-half reliability.

Test–retest reliability *is the extent to which a test yields the same performance when students are given the same test on two different occasions.* Thus, if the standardized Grade 4 reading test is given to a group of students today and then given to them again a month later, the test would be considered reliable if the students' scores were consistent across the two testings. There are two negative features of test–retest reliability: students sometimes do better the second time they take the test because of their familiarity with it, and some students may have learned information in the time between the first test and the second test that changes their performance.

Alternate forms reliability *involves giving different forms of the same test on two different occasions to the same group of students to determine how consistent the scores are.* The test items on the two forms are similar but not identical. This strategy eliminates the likelihood that students will perform better on the second test administration due to their familiarity with the items, but it does not eliminate a student's increase in knowledge and familiarity with the procedures and strategies in testing.

Split-half reliability *involves dividing the test items into two halves, such as the odd-numbered and even-numbered items. The scores on the two sets of items are compared to determine how consistently the students performed across each set.* When split-half reliability is high, we say that the test is internally consistent. For example, on the standardized Grade 4 reading test, the students' scores on the odd-numbered and even-numbered items could be compared. If they scored similarly on the two sets of items, we could conclude that the science test had high split-half reliability.

Reliability is influenced by a number of errors in measurement. A student can have adequate knowledge and skill yet still not perform consistently across several tests because of a number of internal and external factors. *Internal factors* include health, motivation, and anxiety. *External factors* include inadequate directions given by the examiner, ambiguously created items, poor sampling of information, and inefficient scoring. When students perform inconsistently across the same or similar tests of their knowledge and skill, careful analysis should be made of internal and external factors that may have contributed to the inconsistency.

Validity **Validity** *is the extent to which a test measures what it is intended to measure.* Four important types of validity are content validity, criterion validity, construct validity, and instructional validity.

A valid standardized test should have good **content validity**, *which refers to the test's ability to sample the content that is to be measured.* This concept is similar to "content-related evidence." For example, if a standardized Grade 7 math test purports to assess both computational and problem-solving skills, then the test should include both items that measure content information about math and items that measure problem-solving skills.

Another form of validity is **criterion validity**, *which is the test's ability to predict a student's performance as measured by other assessments or criteria.* How might criterion validity be assessed for the standardized math test? One method is to get a representative sample of Grade 7 teachers to evaluate the competence of the students in their math classes and then compare those competence ratings with the students' scores on the standardized tests. Another method is to compare the scores of students on the standardized test with the scores of the same students on a different test that was designed to test the same material.

Criterion validity can be either concurrent or predictive (Gregory, 2000; Krueger, 2000). **Concurrent validity** *refers to the relation between the test's scores and other criteria that are currently (concurrently) available.* For example, does the standardized Grade 7 math test correspond to students' grades in math this term? If it does, we say that test has high concurrent validity.

Predictive validity *refers to the relation between test scores and the student's future performance.* For example, scores on the Grade 7 math test might be used to predict how many math classes different students will take in high school, whether intermediate-level girls say they are interested in pursuing a career that includes mathematics, or whether students will win an award in mathematics at some point in the future.

A third type of validity is **construct validity**. A construct *is an unobservable trait or characteristic of a person, such as intelligence, creativity, learning style, personality, or anxiety.* Construct validity consists of the extent to which there is evidence that a test measures a particular construct. Construct validity is the broadest of the three types of validity we have discussed and can include evidence from concurrent and predictive validity (Gronlund, 1998). Construct validity also might include a description of the development of the test, the pattern of the relations between the test and other significant factors (such as high correlations with similar tests and low correlations with tests measuring different constructs), and any other type of evidence that contributes to understanding the meaning of test scores. Because a construct typically involves abstract qualities, obtaining these various forms of evidence can help us determine whether the construct is valid.

Instructional validity *is the extent to which the assessment is a reasonable sample of the classroom practice* (Payne, 1997). Consider a math class where the teacher tests students on their ability to solve multiplication problems. For instructional validity, it is important that the teacher instructs students in how to solve the problems and gives them adequate opportunities to practise this skill prior to assessment.

Validity and reliability are related. A test that is valid is reliable, but a test that is reliable is not necessarily valid. People can respond consistently on a test but the test might not be measuring what it purports to measure. To understand this, imagine that you have three darts to throw. If all three fall close together, you have reliability. However, you have validity only if all three hit the bull's-eye (see Figure 13.1).

At this point we have studied a number of ideas about the nature of standardized tests. A review of these ideas is presented in Summary Table 13.1.

Valid and reliable   Reliable but not valid

FIGURE 13.1 Links between Reliability and Validity
A test that is valid is reliable, but a test that is reliable is not necessarily valid. This is illustrated by the dart-throwing analogy. All three darts may land far away from the bull's-eye but land in about the same place. To be valid, though, all three darts have to hit the bull's-eye or be very close to it, which also means they have to be reliable.

STANDARDIZED APTITUDE, ACHIEVEMENT, AND PSYCHOEDUCATIONAL TESTS

There are two main types of standardized tests: aptitude tests and achievement tests. Psychoeducational tests are comprised of one of each of these two types. We will first define these types of tests and compare them, then consider some different types of achievement tests, and finally describe provincial and territorial tests.

Comparing Aptitude, Achievement, and Psychoeducational Tests

An **aptitude test** *is used to predict a student's ability to learn a skill or accomplish something with further education and training.* Aptitude tests are norm-referenced (i.e., a student's performance is compared to a norming group). Aptitude tests include general mental ability tests like the intelligence tests (Wechsler Intelligence Scale for Children–Third Edition, and Stanford-Binet) that we described in Chapter 4, Individual Variations, and specific aptitude tests used to predict success in an academic subject or occupational area. For example, one aptitude test might be given to students to predict their future success in math, another might be given to predict whether an individual is likely to do well in sales or medicine.

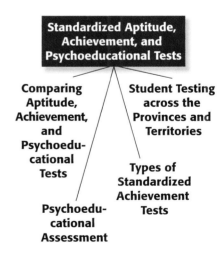

Standardized Aptitude, Achievement, and Psychoeducational Tests

Comparing Aptitude, Achievement, and Psychoeducational Tests

Psychoeducational Assessment

Student Testing across the Provinces and Territories

Types of Standardized Achievement Tests

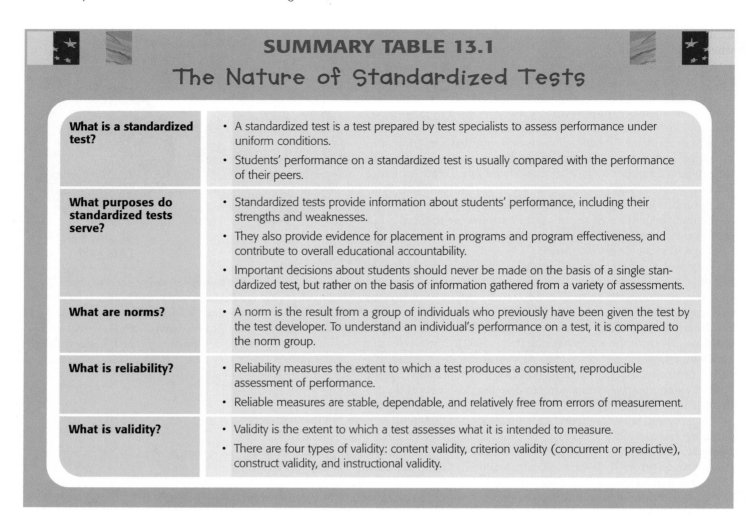

SUMMARY TABLE 13.1

The Nature of Standardized Tests

What is a standardized test?	• A standardized test is a test prepared by test specialists to assess performance under uniform conditions. • Students' performance on a standardized test is usually compared with the performance of their peers.
What purposes do standardized tests serve?	• Standardized tests provide information about students' performance, including their strengths and weaknesses. • They also provide evidence for placement in programs and program effectiveness, and contribute to overall educational accountability. • Important decisions about students should never be made on the basis of a single standardized test, but rather on the basis of information gathered from a variety of assessments.
What are norms?	• A norm is the result from a group of individuals who previously have been given the test by the test developer. To understand an individual's performance on a test, it is compared to the norm group.
What is reliability?	• Reliability measures the extent to which a test produces a consistent, reproducible assessment of performance. • Reliable measures are stable, dependable, and relatively free from errors of measurement.
What is validity?	• Validity is the extent to which a test assesses what it is intended to measure. • There are four types of validity: content validity, criterion validity (concurrent or predictive), construct validity, and instructional validity.

> Nothing in education is so astonishing as the amount of ignorance it accumulates in the form of inert facts.
>
> Henry Brooks Adams
> *Historian and Author, 19th Century*

An **achievement test** *measures what the student has learned or what skills the student has mastered.* Examples of achievement tests include the Canadian Cognitive Abilities Test (CCAT; Nelson), the Canadian Test of Basic Skills (CTBS; Nelson) and the Canadian Achievement Test (CAT-3; Canadian Test Centre). Achievement tests may be *norm-referenced, criterion-referenced*, or both. A norm-referenced test is one in which an individual's score is compared to a distribution of scores obtained from a standardized group. In contrast, an individual's score is compared to a predetermined standard or level of performance on a criterion-referenced test. An achievement test that is both norm-referenced and criterion-referenced is one that compares the performance of an individual to his/her peers and evaluates how much material the individual has learned according to a set standard (Aiken, 2000). However, the distinction between the two types of standardized tests is sometimes blurred. Both types of tests assess a student's current status, both include similar types of questions, and the results of the two kinds of tests usually are highly correlated.

A **psychoeducational assessment** *comprises two general test batteries: aptitude (intelligence) and achievement.* In Canada, many examiners use the Weschler Intelligence Scale for Children (Third Edition) (WISC-III; Harcourt Canada). This assessment includes Canadian norming data. The WISC-III is a time-sensitive series of assessments that is divided into verbally mediated subtests and visually oriented subtests. The WISC-III cannot be completed more than once every two years. An alternative aptitude measure is the Stanford-Binet (Fourth Edition) (Nelson). While this measure is not time-sensitive,

Canadian norms do not exist. There are a variety of achievement test measures that are used frequently, including the Wechsler Individual Achievement Test (WIAT; The Psychological Corporation) and the Wide Range Achievement Test (Third Edition) (WRAT-3; Jastak Assessment Systems).

Psychoeducational Assessment

When parents and educators suspect that a student is not realizing his or her academic potential, two steps are taken to obtain information and recommend appropriate action.

The first step in the process is a diagnosis of the student's cognitive strengths and weaknesses; the second step is a designation or labelling of the student's needs. Generally, a psychoeducational assessment is completed to provide a diagnosis of the student's difficulties, as well as an understanding about how these difficulties impact the student's educational performance. This assessment is completed or supervised by a registered psychologist who is either appointed by the school board or in private professional practice (Canadian Psychological Association, 1996). In Canada, a registered psychologist is obligated to provide a diagnosis based on criteria cited in the *Diagnostic and Statistical Manual of Mental Disorders—Fourth Edition* (DSM-IV). This manual is considered the standard for diagnosis of mental disorders. In Chapter 6, we described some common diagnoses, including developmental delays (receptive and expressive), learning disabilities, and motor systems disabilities.

A psychoeducational report is a confidential legal document that is retained in the student's official school records. The diagnosis is presented by a registered psychologist to the student's school. There are four designations of exceptionality: intellectual, communication, behaviour, and medical. The psychoeducational report also makes recommendations with respect to how educators can take advantage of students' natural strengths and talents while compensating for their weaknesses. Instructional placement and resources are addressed as part of the individualized education plan, described in Chapter 6.

Figure 13.2 is an outline of a typical psychoeducational report. Most comprehensive documents follow this prescribed format, which includes information about the student, assessment measures, findings, conclusions, and recommendations.

Types of Standardized Achievement Tests

There are numerous types of standardized achievement tests. One common way to classify them is as survey batteries, specific subject tests, or diagnostic tests (Payne, 1997).

Survey Batteries A **survey battery** *is a group of individual subject-matter tests designed for a particular level of student.* Survey batteries are widely used in school testing programs. For example, the Canadian Achievement Tests (CAT-3; Canadian Test Centre) include reading/language and mathematics tests ranging across Grades 1 through 12. The subject-matter tests for reading/language include comprehension, vocabulary, and mechanics and expression. The mathematics test includes problem-solving tasks that require students to apply mathematics skills and concepts. There are supplemental tests of word analysis, spelling, language/writing conventions, computations, and numerical estimation. In their early years, survey batteries consisted of multiple-choice items to assess students' content knowledge. However, recent editions have increasingly included more open-ended items that evaluate students' thinking and reasoning skills.

Through the Eyes of Professionals

The Value of Psychoeducational Assessment

Students who are experiencing difficulties in school are often referred to my clinic for a psychoeducational assessment. The purpose of this assessment is to determine how a student's academic performance compares to the student's cognitive abilities. The results of the psychoeducational assessment are used to determine students' learning needs and the characteristics of their ideal learning environment. Once the assessment is complete, a report is prepared containing a summary of the test results as well as recommendations for educational programming. A detailed feedback session with a communication of the diagnosis takes place with the student and parents. The report's learning strategies and resource information is then used in the school to help create an individualized education plan. Some people believe that such a diagnosis provides students with an excuse not to work. I believe that it provides an explanation about how they work best.

Jill M. Pickett, Ph.D., C.Psych.
Clinical Psychologist
Ontario

FIGURE 13.2 An Outline of a Psychoeducational Report

Name

Date of Birth

Parents/Guardians

Dates of Assessment *(assessments are completed over the course of several days)*

Age at Assessment *(in years and months)*

School Placement

Reason for Referral *(identifies the parties who have requested the assessment)*

Tests Administered *(specific names of assessments)*

Test Behaviour *(observations and anecdotal comments)*

Relevant History *(pertinent information provided by the parents/guardians regarding family, developmental, behavioural and health history of the student)*

Academic History *(brief highlights of school records and teachers' comments)*

Results of Assessment Findings *(scores for intellectual/aptitude, memory, and academic/achievement testing)*

Comments and Conclusions *(diagnostic statement based on behavioural observations, background history, and assessment findings)*

Recommendations *(regarding school placement, medication, or academic instruction)*

Psychologist's Signature *(person responsible for the diagnosis)*

Tests for Specific Subjects Some standardized achievement tests assess skills in a particular area such as reading or mathematics. Because they focus on a specific area, they usually assess the skill in a more detailed, extensive way than a survey battery. Two examples of specific-area tests that involve reading are the Woodcock Reading Mastery Tests and the Gates-MacGinitie Reading Diagnostic Test. Some standardized subject-area tests cover topics such as chemistry, psychology, or computer science that are not included in survey batteries.

Diagnostic Tests As stated earlier, diagnosis is an important function of standardized testing. **Diagnostic tests** *are achievement tests that measure select skills in a specific subject area with the purpose of diagnosing an individual's relative strengths and weaknesses. Diagnostic tests are available in reading, arithmetic, and spelling* (Aiken, 2000). In many cases, diagnostic testing is done after considerable instruction already has taken place. An achievement test is sometimes used for diagnostic purposes (such as one of the reading tests mentioned above). In many circumstances, however, a combination of observations and achievement tests will be used. A typical diagnostic sequence might involve (1) informal observations by the teacher, (2) a survey battery, (3) a group diagnostic test, and (4) an individual diagnostic test (Payne, 1997). Note that in this sequence, diagnostic tests can often be given in a group format or an individual format. Reading and mathematics are the two areas in which standardized tests are most often used for diagnosis.

Student Testing across the Provinces and Territories

As schools are increasingly being held accountable, public and government tests have taken on more powerful roles (Foot, 2001). Mandatory provincial and territorial tests are examples of high-stakes testing. The results of these evaluations are being used to make decisions about educational practices that contribute to students' progress and achievement. The results of these tests provide some form of public accountability in attempting to identify whether learning objectives have been met (Clarke, Madaus, Horn, & Ramos, 2000). Standardized tests are being used as part of graduation requirements for students in provinces including British Columbia and Manitoba.

Some form of standardized testing is mandated in ten of the Canadian provinces and territories including Alberta, British Columbia, Manitoba, New Brunswick, Newfoundland, Nova Scotia, Ontario, Quebec, Saskatchewan, and the Yukon. Following is a brief summary of each testing program (see also Figure 13.3).

Alberta—Provincial Achievement Tests   In Alberta, all students in Grades 3, 6, 9, and 12 write provincial achievement tests in the month of June. Grade 3 students write language arts and mathematics tests; Grade 6 and 9 students complete tests in language arts, mathematics, science, and social studies. Students in Grade 12 write diploma examinations. The provincial achievement tests are largely comprised of multiple-choice questions that account for 50 percent of students' final grades. Test results are reported for individual students and publicly announced for each school, school jurisdiction, and the province (Government of Alberta, 2002).

British Columbia—Provincial Examinations   The British Columbia Provincial Exam Program was created in 1984 to ensure that Grade 12 students meet provincial standards of achievement in academic subjects. A secondary goal of the program is to provide a benchmark measure for access to post-secondary programs. For graduating students, the provincial exam score is worth 40 percent of their final course grades. The exams are each two hours in length and comprise multiple-choice and written-response questions. Students have one year from the time they complete a course to write the corresponding provincial exam (Government of British Columbia, 2002).

Manitoba—Provincial Assessment Program   Manitoba has both optional and mandatory student testing. In the Fall, a mandatory test of reading and numeracy is given to Grade 3 students. Teachers are provided with the results of this testing immediately in order to plan appropriately for the current school year. Mandatory standard tests are also administered each term for secondary-school English and mathematics. These test scores count for 30 percent of the students' final grades. There also are optional tests for Grade 6 English and Senior 1 mathematics; the decision to administer these optional tests is made by school boards (Manitoba Education, Training and Youth, 2002).

New Brunswick—Provincial Assessments   The Evaluation Branch of the Department of Education of New Brunswick is responsible for monitoring student achievement. At the elementary level, provincial assessments are administered at Grades 3 and 5 for language arts, mathematics, and science. At the intermediate level, Grade 8 students complete a mathematics assessment and an English-language proficiency assessment. Successful completion of the latter exam is a requirement for graduation. In Grade 11, students are tested in mathematics and English, with these examinations counting for 30 percent of their final grades (Department of Education, New Brunswick, 2002).

Newfoundland and Labrador—Public Examinations   Newfoundland periodically requires that students in Grades 3 and 6 write public examinations in language arts. Students in Grade 9 are tested in core French, math, and science. The results from these criterion-referenced tests are used to assess achievement of learning outcomes. Students in Grade 12 write mandatory public examinations in each of their courses; these exams are worth 50 percent of their final course grades (Department of Education, Newfoundland, 2002).

FIGURE 13.3 **Student Testing across the Canadian Provinces and Territories.**

Province/Territory	Testing Program	Grade Level/Description
Alberta	Provincial Achievement Tests	Grade 3 (language arts and math) Grades 6 and 9 (language arts, math, science, and social studies) Grade 12 (diploma examinations in core academic courses)
British Columbia	Provincial Examinations	Grade 12 (provincial examinations—every subject)
Manitoba	Provincial Assessment Program	Grade 3 (reading and numeracy) Senior (English and mathematics) Optional Grade 6 and Senior 1 (mathematics)
New Brunswick	Provincial Assessments	Grades 3 and 5 (language arts, mathematics, science) Grade 8 (mathematics and English) Grade 11 (mathematics and English)
Newfoundland and Labrador	Public Examinations	Periodic testing in Grades 3 and 6 Grade 9 (French, mathematics, and science) Grade 12 (public examinations—every subject)
Nova Scotia	Program of Learning Assessment (PLANS)	Grades 5 and 8 (mathematics) Grades 6 and 9 (language arts) Grade 12 (chemistry, English, mathematics, physics)
Ontario	Education Quality and Accountability Office (EQAO)	Grades 3 and 6 (reading, writing, mathematics) Grade 9 (mathematics) Grade 10 (literacy)
Quebec	Uniform Ministry Examinations	Secondary IV and V (selected uniform examinations)
Saskatchewan	Provincial Learning Assessment Program	Grades 5, 8, and 11 (mathematics, language arts, technological literacy, critical/creative thinking)
Yukon	Student Assessment Program	Grades 3, 6, and 9 (mathematics and language arts) Grades 11 and 12 (language proficiency index) Grade 12 (British Columbia provincial examinations—every subject)

Nova Scotia—Program of Learning Assessment (PLANS)

Provincial assessments are completed in elementary, intermediate, and senior high schools across Nova Scotia. Mathematics is assessed for students in Grades 5 and 8; language arts is examined for students in Grades 6 and 9. The provincial assessments are designed to review curriculum topics from the two previous grades, as well as the current grade. In Grade 12, students complete the Nova Scotia Examinations (NSE) for chemistry, English, mathematics, and physics. These examinations are administered in January and June and account for 30 percent of students' final course grades (Nova Scotia Department of Education, 2002).

Ontario—Education Quality and Accountability Office (EQAO)

In Ontario, an arm's-length testing agency (EQAO) conducts province-wide standardized tests for students in Grades 3 and 6 in reading, writing, and mathematics. At the Grade 9 level, testing is administered in mathematics, and at the Grade 10 level a literacy test is mandated to measure student achievement in reading and writing. Successful completion of the province-wide Grade 10 literacy test is a requirement to obtain a secondary-school diploma. Testing will commence for Grade 4 and 7 language arts, science, and technology, and for Grade 5 and 8 mathematics and social studies. Thereafter, changes are expected at the secondary level. In 2004–05, Grade 9 science will be tested; in 2005–06 Grade 10 history will be tested; and in 2006–07 Grade 11 English and mathematics will be tested. Secondary-school students will also be required to complete tests at the end of each course, with these examinations accounting for 20 percent of their final mark (EQAO, 2001).

Quebec—Uniform Ministry Examinations

Every year, the Ministère de l'Éducation selects a certain number of subjects for which it will prepare uniform examinations, and publishes the June results. Examples of these subjects include English, language arts, physical science, provincial history, and French reading. These uniform examinations are administered to Secondary IV and Secondary V students. Students' final course grades consist of their performance on the provincial examinations as well as their school marks. The provincial examinations are compulsory prerequisites for certain college programs (Gouvernement du Québec, 1998).

Saskatchewan—Provincial Learning Assessment Program

In Saskatchewan, the Assessment and Evaluation Unit monitors and assesses students' learning from kindergarten to Grade 12. Student achievement in Grades 5, 8, and 11 is measured in mathematics, language arts, technological literacy, and critical and creative thinking. In addition, students and teachers complete questionnaires in an attempt to provide contextual data around student learning. These data are used to inform educational decision-making. A document is released annually that reports on the performance of Saskatchewan's students (Saskatchewan Department of Education, 2002).

Yukon—Student Assessment Program

Since 1999, the Yukon has implemented a comprehensive testing strategy to measure the numeracy and literacy skills of students in the primary, junior, intermediate, and secondary grades. The Yukon Department of Education mandates assessments at Grades 3, 6, and 9 for mathematics and language arts. For Grades 11 and 12, a language proficiency index is administered, with these results forwarded

Through the Eyes of Students

Standardized Testing

I took the provincial Grade 10 literacy test seriously. Schoolwork has always been unappealing to me and I wanted to be well prepared. During the weeks before the test, I spent most of my free time doing practice exercises from a booklet given to us by the school. I also attended an after-school preparatory program.

I wrote the exam in my regular classroom with 12 other students. Writing in my own classroom with familiar faces around me was better than having to write in an unfamiliar room with strangers. The test consisted of reading passages and a timed writing assignment. I found the writing to be the most difficult part because it was difficult to develop a plan and edit my work in the time provided. I liked the multiple-choice and fill-in-the-blank questions better because all I needed to do was select the correct response. I did well on the test because I've developed good study skills—I studied for the test by using the practice information and by working with my tutor and parents.

Ryan
Grade 10 Student
Avid Card and Stamp Collector
Ontario

Through the Eyes of Professionals

Standardized Assessment

The Yukon Territories has participated in the School Achievement Indicators Program (SAIP) since 1994. These tests are given on a cyclical basis to 13- and 16-year-olds in reading/writing, science, and math. In 2007, SAIP will be replaced by the Pan-Canadian Assessment Program (PCAP), which is an updated testing program. While still enabling comparison to previous years of SAIP data, the new program will potentially allow the Yukon to compare results internationally to ensure that curricula and programs are appropriate.

The Yukon also tests every year in math and language arts in Grades 3, 6, and 9 as part of the Yukon Achievement Tests, while students in Grade 12 write B.C. provincial examinations for graduation. The Yukon Achievement Tests are a tool for parents and teachers to determine if individual students are learning what they are expected to learn. The department and the schools also use these results to monitor and improve student learning. The SAIP and PCAP tests are more of a broad-based assessment. They are used to evaluate our education system as a whole in a national and, after 2007, potentially an international context.

Lee Kubica
Education Director of Programs and Services
Yukon Department of Education
(Source: Excerpt from Press Release, April 8, 2003.)

to post-secondary institutions. Students in Grade 12 are also required to write the British Columbia provincial examinations in each subject area (Government of Yukon, Department of Education, 2002).

Evaluating Provincial/Territorial–Mandated Achievement Tests The use of provincial/territorial achievement tests is very controversial (Linn, 2000). Supporters of the tests argue that they are the best way to hold schools accountable for students' learning (Cibulka, 1999). Without the tests, say their supporters, schools and teachers are more likely to slack off and not put as much effort into educating students. Supporters also believe that the tests provide valuable feedback about which areas of learning need greater attention.

Critics of the provincial and territorial tests argue that they encourage teachers to teach for the test (Gallagher, 2000; O'Neil & Tell, 1999). That is, because teachers know that their students will be tested and they want their class to do well, they narrow their instruction to match the content of the tests. Many teachers say that the provincial and territorial standardized tests infringe on their ability to teach what they believe is best for their students, and divert valuable class time from instruction and learning.

The Canadian Psychological Association and the Canadian Association of School Psychologists have published a joint position statement with respect to provincial testing (Simner, 2000). They express a collective concern that the media tend to encourage the public to compare schools based on the outcomes of mandated tests. The media rarely acknowledge other factors that influence students' test performance, including motivation and absenteeism (Simner, 2000). The Canadian Psychological Association and the Canadian Association of School Psychologists warn that making schools solely responsible for students' test performances places unnecessary pressures on teachers, administrators, and students (Simner, 2000).

National Assessment: School Achievement Indicators Program (SAIP) Since 1993, the Council of Ministers of Education has assessed student achievement in mathematics, problem solving, reading, writing, science, and inquiry. The goal of the School Achievement Indicators Program (SAIP) is to determine whether students reach similar levels of performance at about the same age. The assessments are designed to complement existing ones in each province and territory. The performance of 13- and 16-year-olds is measured, with results provided to each provincial/territorial Minister of Education so that they can re-evaluate their respective curricula and school systems (School Achievement Indicators Program, 2002).

Content areas evaluated as part of SAIP change annually. The first cycle of assessment began in 1993 with an evaluation of mathematics. The reading and writing assessment followed in 1994, and the science assessment was administered in 1996. The second cycle of assessments was administered from 1997 to 1999, and the third cycle began in 2001. Test questions are taken from previous assessments as well as recent instruments that reflect new pedagogical and curricular innovations. Questions are reviewed by a national panel of teachers and ministry officials in an attempt to reduce cultural and gender bias (School Achievement Indicators Program, 2002).

Achievement on the SAIP assessments is quantified over five levels. Level 1 is representative of knowledge and skills typically acquired during early elementary education. Level 3 skills meet the expectations of the panel and represent performance at intermediate-grade levels. Level 5 is exemplified in students who have skills typical of those at or near the end of secondary school.

In the most recent assessment of mathematics (2001), two-thirds of the 13-year-old students reached Level 2 and more than 25 percent reached Level 3 in both content and problem solving. Half of the 16-year-olds reached Level 3, and more than 10 percent attained Levels 4 or 5 (School Achievement Indicators Program, 2002).

For the last Science II assessment (1999), 13-year-old and 16-year-old Canadian students scored higher in science knowledge and skills than they did on the initial test in 1996. Moreover, there were no significant differences in achievement scores between males and females. For both the written assessment and practical task assessment, half of the 13-year-olds obtained Level 3. Similarly, more than three-quarters of the 16-year-olds obtained Level 3.

World-Class Standards: The Programme for International Student Assessment (PISA) The Programme for International Student Assessment (PISA) examines the skills and knowledge of 15-year-olds across 32 countries. The first international assessments were carried out in 2000 and sought to address questions such as: How well are young adults prepared to meet the challenges of the future? Are they able to analyze, reason, and communicate their ideas effectively? Are some kinds of school policies and practices more effective than others? (Council of Ministers of Education Canada, 2001). The goal of PISA is to provide countries with benchmarks for their students' performance. Results from PISA are invaluable to educators, social policy analysts, and advocacy groups. For instance, researchers and analysts can access PISA results when addressing barriers that face young adults when pursuing higher education or gaining employment.

PISA attempts to assess students' capacity to use their knowledge and skills in order to meet employment requirements in a modern society. Presumably, students must understand and master key concepts from their school curriculum in order to apply knowledge and test performance in real-life situations. Specifically, PISA assesses literacy in reading, mathematics, and science. Reading literacy is defined as the ability to understand, interpret, reflect on, and evaluate written texts. Mathematical literacy is the capacity to identify, understand, and engage in mathematics and to make well-founded judgments about the role of mathematics in society. Science literacy refers to the ability to think scientifically in a world in which science and technology shape our lives. The assessment includes a two-hour written test and a 30-minute background questionnaire (PISA, 2002). As part of these questionnaires students are surveyed about their attitudes and approaches to learning, as well as their beliefs in their own abilities, motivation to learn, and willingness to self-regulate their learning.

In 2000, about 1,200 schools across Canada were randomly selected to participate in PISA. In general, Canadian students scored above international averages across all subject areas (Council of Ministers of Education, 2001). For instance, Canadian students placed third behind Finland and Korea in reading. In mathematics, Canadian students were sixth behind Japan, Korea, New Zealand, Finland, and Australia. Similarly, Canadian students ranked fifth behind Korea, Japan, Finland, and the United Kingdom in science (see Figure 13.4 and **www.pisa.oecd.org/knowledge/summary/b.htm**).

At this point we have discussed many ideas about standardized aptitude and achievement tests. A review of these ideas is presented in Summary Table 13.2.

The Programme for International Student Assessment (PISA) assesses literacy in reading, mathematics and science in 32 countries.

THE TEACHER'S ROLE

The teacher's role in standardized testing involves preparing students for the test, administering the tests in the classroom, understanding and interpreting test results, and communicating test results to parents.

Preparing Students to Take Standardized Tests

James McMillan (1997) described the teacher's role in preparing students to take standardized tests. It is important for all students to have an opportunity to do their best. One way to do this is to make sure that students have good test-taking skills.

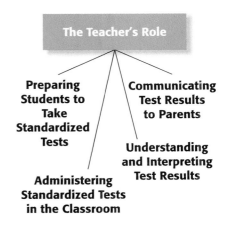

SUMMARY TABLE 13.2
Standardized Aptitude, Achievement, and Psychoeducational Tests

What are aptitude, achievement, and psychoeducational assessments?	• Aptitude tests predict students' abilities to learn (e.g., intelligence tests). • Achievement tests measure what students have learned, or the skills they have mastered (e.g., comprehension, mathematics computations). • A psychoeducational assessment is comprised of two general test batteries: aptitude and achievement. • A psychoeducational assessment is usually administered by a registered psychologist for the purposes of diagnosing students' cognitive strengths and weaknesses.
What are the types of standardized achievement tests?	• Survey batteries are subject-matter tests that are designed for particular levels of students. • Diagnostic tests pinpoint students' strengths and weaknesses following instruction. • Achievement tests may be norm-referenced, criterion-referenced, or both.
What is the purpose of testing by the provinces and territories?	• Results of provincial/territorial testing are used to make decisions about educational practices and indicate areas for improvement. • Currently, ten provinces and territories mandate student testing. • Some provinces include mandatory testing as a graduation requirement.
What is the School Achievement Indicators Program (SAIP)?	• The Council of Ministers of Education carries out assessment of student achievement in mathematics, problem solving, reading, writing, science knowledge, and inquiry. • The performance of 13- and 16-year-olds is measured. • Results are used by provincial/territorial ministries of education to evaluate school curriculum and systems.
What is the Programme for International Student Assessment (PISA)?	• The Programme for International Student Assessment (PISA) is an assessment of the skills and knowledge of 15-year-olds across 32 countries. • The PISA assesses students' reading, mathematics, and science literacies. • It is assumed that students must understand and master key concepts from their school curriculum in order to apply this knowledge in real-life situations.

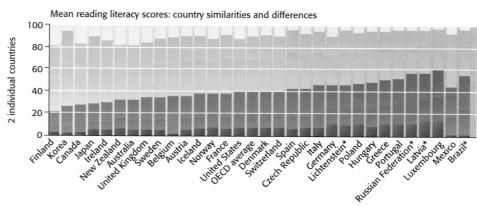

a. Mean reading literacy scores: country similarities and differences

FIGURE 13.4 **Programme for International Student Assessment (PISA, 2000) International Reading and Mathematics Scores**

b.   Mean mathematical literacy scores: country similarities and differences

FIGURE 13.4   (continued)

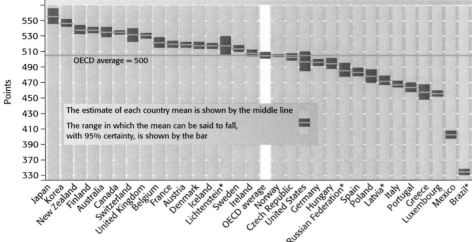

*Non-OECD country

It also is important for you to communicate a positive attitude about the test to students. Explain the nature and purpose of the test. Describe the test as an opportunity and a challenge rather than an ordeal. Avoid saying anything that can cause students to be nervous about the test. If you observe that some students are so anxious that their performance on the test will be hindered, consider having a counsellor talk with them about ways to reduce their test anxiety.

In this era of high-stakes testing in which scores on standardized tests can have serious consequences for students, teachers, and schools, many schools are establishing programs designed to improve students' test-taking skills (Payne, 1997). There are some important test-taking strategies that teachers will want to discuss with their students (Linn & Gronlund, 2000). First, inform students to read the test instructions and test items carefully. Students should follow directions carefully when wording responses and check that the appropriate response is marked on the answer sheet. While working through the test items, students should work quickly enough to complete the test, skipping difficult items and returning to them later. If students need to guess, they should eliminate as many false alternatives as possible. Finally, if time permits, students should go back and check their responses. Researchers have found that coaching or training students to take a test slightly boosts their scores (Linn & Gronlund, 2000).

When tests have high stakes attached to them, and when teachers are held responsible for their students' scores, testing protocols are susceptible to manipulation (Earl, 1999). Teachers may feel the pressure to engage in instructional practices that are more test-like, often at the expense of good instructional pedagogy. Non-assessed areas of the curriculum may be ignored and instruction may become focused on memorization as opposed to thinking (Earl, 1999). Teachers must recognize that the ultimate test-taking strategy is good teaching.

Administering Standardized Tests in the Classroom

Most standardized test developers spell out in considerable detail how the test should be administered (Airasian, 1997; Gay & Airasian, 2000). This includes how to set up the testing room, what to do while students take the test, how to distribute the test and answer sheets, and how to time the tests.

The physical testing environment should be well lighted and well ventilated. Students should have adequate work space. Seat students in a manner that will avoid distractions or cheating. Hang a sign on the door to the room that says something like "Testing in Progress—Do Not Disturb" (McMillan, 1997).

If the teacher is administering the test, he or she should follow word for word the script that is included in the test manual, to ensure that the test is being given under standardized conditions (Gay & Airasian, 2000). If this script is not followed exactly, comparisons of the students' performance with the population of students on which the norms for the test were established could be invalid (Airasian, 1997). Be sure to write the start and finish times for the test on the board. At start time, tell students clearly to begin. Make sure students stop when the time has expired.

After students have completed the test, teachers are often required to count the booklets and answer sheets. Also record any incidents that you observed that might invalidate students' scores.

Understanding and Interpreting Test Results

Knowledge of some basic descriptive statistics will help you interpret standardized tests. We will discuss these basic statistics as well as some ways that test results are commonly reported.

Understanding Descriptive Statistics   Although we are discussing statistics here to help you understand standardized tests, the information about statistics also can help you with many other aspects of classroom assessment, such as interpreting students' scores on tests you have created and administered. Our primary focus here is on **descriptive statistics**, *which are mathematical procedures that are used to describe and summarize data (information) in a meaningful way* (Hockenbury, 1997). We will study frequency distributions, measures of central tendency, measures of variability, and the normal distribution.

Frequency Distributions   The first step in organizing data involves creating a **frequency distribution**, *a listing of scores, usually from highest to lowest, along with the number of times each score appears.* Imagine that a test was given and 21 students received the following scores on the test: 96, 95, 94, 92, 88, 88, 86, 86, 86, 86, 84, 83, 82, 82, 82, 78, 75, 75, 72, 68, and 62. Figure 13.5a shows a frequency distribution for these scores. Frequency distributions often are presented graphically. For example, a **histogram** *is a frequency distribution in the form of a graph. Vertical bars represent the frequency of scores per category.* Figure 13.5b shows a histogram for the 21 scores. A histogram is often called a bar graph. Notice in the histogram that the horizontal axis (x-axis) indicates the obtained scores and the vertical axis (the y-axis) presents how often each score occurs.

Although representing a group of scores *graphically* can provide insight about students' performance, so can statistical techniques that represent scores *numerically*. These techniques involve the concepts of central tendency and variability, each of which we will discuss.

FIGURE 13.5   A Frequency Distribution and Histogram

Score	Frequency
96	1
95	1
94	1
92	1
88	2
86	4
84	1
83	1
82	3
78	1
75	2
72	1
68	1
62	1

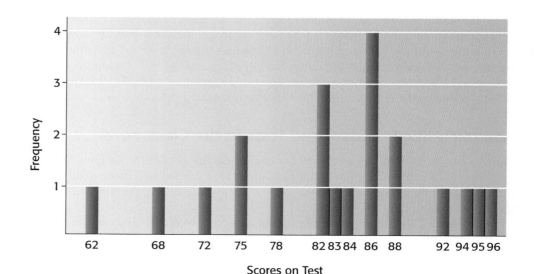

Measures of Central Tendency   A **measure of central tendency** *is a number that provides information about the average or typical score in a set of data. There are three measures of central tendency: mean, median, and mode.* The **mean** *is the numerical average of a group of scores, commonly labelled as M (Mn) of X (mean of X) by statisticians.* The mean is computed by adding all the scores and then dividing by the number of scores. Thus, the mean for the 21 students' test scores provided in our example is 1740/21 = 82.86. The mean is often a good indicator of the central tendency of a group of scores.

The **median** *is the score that falls exactly in the middle of a distribution of scores after they have been arranged* (or ranked) *from highest to lowest.* In our example of 21 test scores, the 11th ranked score of 84 is the median.

The **mode** *is the score that occurs most often.* The mode can be determined by looking at the frequency distribution or histogram. In our example of 21 scores, the mode is 86 (the score occurring most often—4 times). The mode is most revealing when its value is much more frequent than the other values or scores. For example, in the 21 scores in our example, if 15 of the 21 scores had been the same, then the mode probably would be the best measure of central tendency for the data. In this case, the mean and median would be less meaningful.

There can be two or more modes. For example, in our example of 21 students taking a test, if four students had scored 86 and four students had scored 75 (instead of the 2), then the set of scores would have had two modes (86 and 75). A set of scores with two modes is called a *bimodal distribution.* It is possible for a set of scores to have more than two modes, in which case it is called a *multimodal distribution.*

Measures of Variability   In addition to obtaining information about the central tendency of a set of scores, it is also important to know about their variability. **Measures of variability** *tell us how much the scores vary from one another.* Two measures of variability are range and standard deviation.

The **range** *is the distance between the highest and lowest scores.* The range of the 21 students' test scores in our example is 34 points (96 − 62 = 34). The range is a rather simple measure of variability and it is not used often. The most commonly used measure of variability is standard deviation.

Standard deviation *is a measure of how much a set of scores varies on the average around the mean of the scores. Stated another way, it reveals how closely scores cluster around the mean. The smaller the standard deviation, the less the scores tend to vary from the mean. The greater the standard deviation, the more the scores tend to spread out from the mean.* Calculating a standard deviation is not very difficult, especially if you have a calculator that is capable of computing square roots. To calculate a standard deviation, follow these four steps:

1. Compute the mean of the scores.
2. From each score, subtract the mean and then square the difference between the score and the mean. (Squaring the scores will eliminate any minus signs that result from subtracting the mean.)
3. Add the squares and then divide that sum by the number of scores minus one.
4. Compute the square root of the value obtained in step 3. This is the standard deviation.

The formula for these four steps is

$$\sqrt{\frac{\Sigma(\chi-\overline{\chi})^2}{N-1}}$$

where χ = the individual score minus the mean, represented by $\overline{\chi}$, N = the number of scores, and Σ means "the sum of."

"Tonight, we're going to let the statistics speak for themselves."
Drawing by Koren: © 1974 The New Yorker Magazine, Inc.

Applying this formula to the test scores of the 21 students:

1. We already computed the mean of the scores and found that it was 82.86.
2. Subtract 82.86 from the first score: $96 - 82.86 = 13.14$. Square 13.14 to get 172.66. Save the value and go on to do the same for the second score, the third score, and so on.
3. Add the 21 squares to get 1543.28. Divide the sum by (21–1): $1543.28/20 = 77.16$.
4. Find the square root of 77.16. The result is 8.78, the standard deviation.

$$\sqrt{\frac{1543.28}{21}} = \sqrt{77.16} = 8.78$$

Many calculators have statistics modes and are capable of directly calculating means and standard deviations. To evaluate your knowledge of and skills in computing the various measures of central tendency and variability we have described, complete Self-Assessment 13.1. Mastering these kinds of descriptive statistics is useful not only for classroom work but also for understanding research results.

The standard deviation is a better measure of variability than the range because the range represents information about only two bits of data (the highest and lowest scores), whereas the standard deviation represents combined information about all the data. It is usually more helpful to know how much test scores are spread out or clustered together than to know the highest and lowest scores. If a teacher gives a test and the standard deviation turns out to be very low, it means the scores tend to cluster around the same value. That could mean that everyone in the class learned the material equally well, or that the test was too easy and is not discriminating very effectively between students who mastered the material and those who did not. Conversely, if the standard deviation is a large value, it means that there is a large variation among scores. Some students found the test easy, while others found it difficult.

The standard deviation is also useful in assessing the true meaning of multiple measures of central tendency. For instance, what does it mean when two classes complete the same test and produce roughly equal means but radically different standard deviation scores? This likely signifies that the students in the class with the relatively smaller standard deviation measure have performed somewhat homogeneously, whereas the class with the larger standard deviation has varied scores. Possible reasons why students in one class have such discrepant scores should be explored.

The Normal Distribution In a **normal distribution**, *most of the scores cluster around the mean. The farther above or below the mean we travel, the less frequently each score occurs. A normal distribution is also called a "bell-shaped curve" or "bell curve."* Many characteristics, such as human intelligence measured by intelligence tests, athletic ability, weight, and height, follow or approximate a normal distribution. We presented the normal distribution for intelligence in Chapter 4, Individual Variations. We show it again here to illustrate what a normal distribution, or "bell-shaped curve," looks like and focus more on its statistical properties (see Figure 13.6).

Evaluating My Knowledge of and Skill in Computing Measures of Central Tendency and Variability

Examine each of the following statements and place a checkmark next to the statement if you feel confident of your knowledge of the concept and your skill in computing the measure or using the instrument.

I know what a frequency distribution is.

I can describe what a histogram is and know how to create one.

I understand what a mean is and know how to compute it.

I understand what a median is and know how to calculate it.

I know what a mode is and know how to compute it.

I know what a range is and know how to arrive at it.

I can discuss what a standard deviation is and know how to compute it.

I have a good calculator and know how to use it to compute basic descriptive statistics.

✓

For any items that you did not check off, go back and study the concept again. If you are still not confident about computing the various measures, keep practising. For example, sometimes students need to compute a number of standard deviations before they get a sense of the concept and what it means.

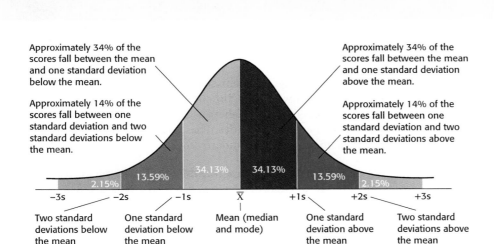

FIGURE 13.6 **The Normal Distribution**

Figure 13.6 illustrates several important characteristics of a normal distribution. First, it is symmetrical. Because of this symmetry, the mean, median, and mode are identical in a normal distribution. Second, its bell shape shows that the most common scores are near the middle. The scores become less frequent the farther away from the middle they appear (that is, as they become more extreme). Third, the normal distribution incorporates information about both the mean and the standard deviation, as indicated in Figure 13.6. The area on the normal curve that is one standard deviation above the mean and one standard deviation below it represents 68.26 percent of the scores. At two standard deviations above and below the mean, 95.42 percent of the scores are represented. Finally, at three standard deviations above and below the mean, 99.74 percent of the scores are included. If we apply this information to Figure 13.6, which shows the normal distribution of IQ scores in the population, we can see that 68 percent of the population has an IQ between 85 and 115, 95 percent between 76 and 126, and 99 percent between 55 and 145.

Interpreting Test Results Understanding descriptive statistics provides the foundation for effectively interpreting test results. A **raw score** *is the number of items the student*

Calculators: Implications for Assessment and Evaluation

The Mathematics Council of the Alberta Teachers' Association (MCATA) recently published a position paper stating that calculators have a valuable role in encouraging students to be creative and independent problem solvers. Specifically, calculators can be an invaluable tool when developing concepts, exploring and demonstrating mathematical relationships and patterns, organizing and displaying data, decreasing time spent on tedious computations, developing understandings of computational algorithms, and creating geometric displays that simulate real-world situations (Alberta Program of Studies for K–12 Mathematics, 1997). The calculators used in classrooms today have evolved greatly from their original counterparts, with some having more memory and computational capacity than the first generation of home computers. Advancements in calculator capability and power have significant implications for equitable assessment and evaluation of student learning.

In 1997, MCATA provided a number of recommendations for calculator use in Alberta schools. These recommendations are especially timely given that many of the newer calculators used by students on the Grade 9 and 12 provincial tests and diploma examinations have alphanumeric capabilities. That is, these calculators are mini-display computers that can store notes or formulas, calculate quadratic equations, and generate graphs or charts. These technologies, which students are currently allowed to use when taking exams, raise equity issues about access and training.

MCATA recommends that all students have access to equivalent technologies as part of their schooling experience. The group also recommends that provincial examinations be completed in two parts: one where students would write without the use of technology and another where students would be required to use technologies such as a scientific calculator (after receiving training in their use as part of their regular classroom instruction).

answered correctly on the test. Raw scores, by themselves, are not very useful because they don't provide information about how easy or difficult the test was or how the student fared compared with other students. Test publishers usually provide teachers with many different kinds of scores that go beyond raw scores. These include percentile rank scores, stanine scores, grade-equivalent scores, and standard scores.

Percentile Rank Scores A **percentile rank score** *reveals the percentage of the distribution that lies at or below the score. It also provides information about the score's position in relation to the rest of the scores. Percentile ranks range from 1 to 99.* If a student has a percentile rank of 81 on a test, it means that the student performed as well as or higher on the test than 81 percent of the sample who made up the norm group. Note that percentiles do not refer to percentages of items answered correctly on the test.

Stanine Scores A **stanine score** *describes a student's test performance on a nine-point scale ranging from 1 to 9.* Scores of 1, 2, and 3 are usually considered to be below average; 4, 5, and 6 average; and 7, 8, and 9 above average. As in the case of a student's percentile rank score, a stanine score in one subject area (such as science) can be compared with the student's stanine score in other areas (such as math, reading, and social studies).

A stanine refers to a specific percentage of the normal curve's area. The correspondence between a stanine score and a percentile rank is shown in Figure 13.7. A stanine score provides a more general index of a student's performance, while a percentile rank score yields a more precise estimation.

Grade-Equivalent Scores A **grade-equivalent score** *is expressed in terms of the grade level of students who are actually in a given grade.* This often is represented in year and month, such as 4.5, which stands for Grade 4, fifth month in school. A grade equivalent of 6.0 stands for the beginning of Grade 6. In some test reports a decimal is omitted, so that 45 is the same as 4.5 or 60 is the same as 6.0.

Stanine Score	Percentile Rank Score
9	96 or Higher
8	89–95
7	77–88
6	60–76
5	40–59
4	23–39
3	11–22
2	4–10
1	Below 4

FIGURE 13.7 **The Relation between Stanine Score and Percentile Rank Score**

Grade-equivalent scores should be used only to interpret a student's progress, not for grade placement. Many educators believe that because grade-equivalent scores are often misleading and misinterpreted, other types of scores, such as standard scores, are more appropriate to use.

Standard Scores   A **standard score** *is expressed as a deviation from the mean, which involves the concept of standard deviation that we discussed earlier.* The term standard as used in "standard score" does not refer to a specific level of performance or expectation but rather to the standard normal curve (McMillan, 1997). Actually, the stanine scores and grade-equivalent scores we already have profiled are standard scores. Two additional standard scores we will evaluate here are *z*-scores and *T*-scores.

A ***z*-score** *provides information about how many standard deviations a raw score is above or below the mean.* Calculation of a *z*-score is done using this formula:

$$z\text{-score} = \frac{X - \overline{X}}{SD}$$

where X = any raw score, $\overline{X}$ = mean of the raw scores, and SD equals the standard deviation of the raw score distribution.

Consider again our example of 21 students taking a test. What would a student's *z*-score be if the student's raw score were 86? Using the formula above it would be

$$\frac{86 - 82.86}{8.57} = .37$$

Thus, the raw score of 86 is .37 of a standard deviation above the mean. The *z*-score mean is 0 and the standard deviation is 1.

A ***T*-score** *is a standard score in which the mean is set at 50 and the standard deviation is set at 10.* The following formula can be used to compute a *T*-score:

$$T\text{-score} = 50 + 10(z)$$

For example, a *T*-score of 70 is the same as a *z*-score of 2, and a *T*-score of 40 is the same as a *z*-score of -1. For the raw score of 86, the corresponding *T*-score is, therefore, 54.

Figure 13.8 presents an overall comparison of many of the types of standardized scores you will see on test reports. Most raw standardized test scores are forced into a normal curve representation.

Don't Overinterpret Test Results   Use caution in interpreting small differences in test scores, especially percentile-rank and grade-equivalent test scores (Airasian, 1997). All tests have some degree of error.

A good strategy is to think of a score not as a single number but as a location in a band or general range. Small differences in test scores are usually not meaningful. Some test reports include **percentile bands**, *a range of scores (rather than a single score) around a mean value expressed in percentiles, such as 75th to 85th percentile.* A percentile rank of 6 to 8 points or a 2- to 5-month grade-equivalence difference between two students rarely indicates any meaningful difference in achievement.

When considering information from a standardized test, don't evaluate it in isolation. Evaluate it in conjunction with other information you know about the student and your classroom instruction (Airasian, 1997). Most manuals that accompany standardized tests warn against overinterpretation.

Communicating Test Results to Parents

Teachers often present and interpret students' scores on standardized tests during a parent–teacher conference. Teachers should be aware of the fact that parents often misinterpret these statistics. For example, as previously noted, percentile rank scores are not

www.mcgrawhill.ca/college/santrock

FIGURE 13.8 **Some Commonly Reported Test Scores Based on the Normal Curve**

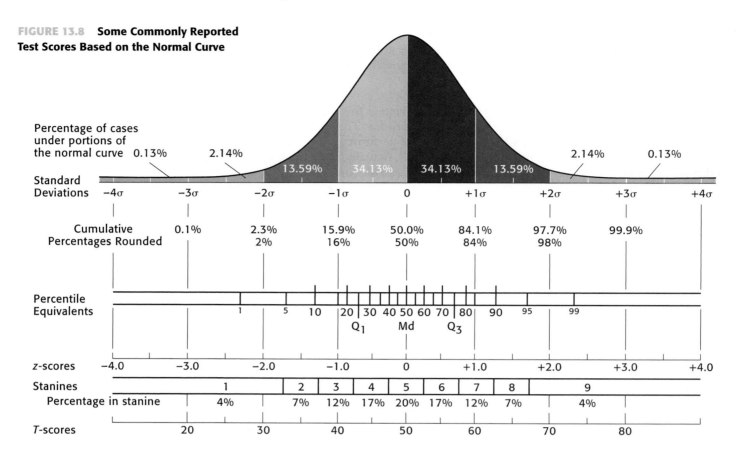

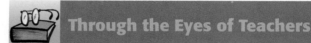

Through the Eyes of Teachers

Communicating Test Results to Parents

Standardized testing can provide valuable information that teachers and parents can use to overcome barriers to student learning. Standardized test results can offer an early indication that students are experiencing some form of learning difficulty. The advantage of an early diagnosis is that it prompts early intervention. Students who may otherwise be overlooked in the classroom because there is no clear or obvious symptom of a learning difficulty can be provided with appropriate programming. Communicating test results to parents and interpreting the results for them in a meaningful manner can help circumvent future academic difficulties.

On the other hand, communicating poor test results to parents can sometimes create a negative self-fulfilling prophecy. Once students are identified—or labelled—as having some form of learning difficulty, parents and teachers may unconsciously limit the opportunities available to them. Students may also sense that they have not performed well. They may feel that they have disappointed their parents, which in turn can negatively affect their self-esteem. It is important to communicate test results in a positive manner, focusing on what can be done rather than dwelling on what has not occurred.

Jennifer Auld-Cameron
10-Year Secondary-School Computer Teacher
Community College Instructor
Nova Scotia

the same as the percentage of items answered correctly on a test. Often, parents do not understand this distinction and they become confused by the fact that a percentile rank score between 26 and 84 is within an "average" range of scores. A brief explanation of the differentiation of these statistics may alleviate some of the confusion. A suggestion offered by McEwan (1998) is that teachers might hold a meeting to discuss and explain test scores to all parents. A representative from the school board or district could also be available to talk to parents who want a more detailed explanation of statistics. Refer to the Teaching Strategies box on page 440 for more strategies for communicating test results to parents.

At this point, we have discussed a number of ideas about the teacher's role in standardized testing. A review of these ideas is presented in Summary Table 13.3.

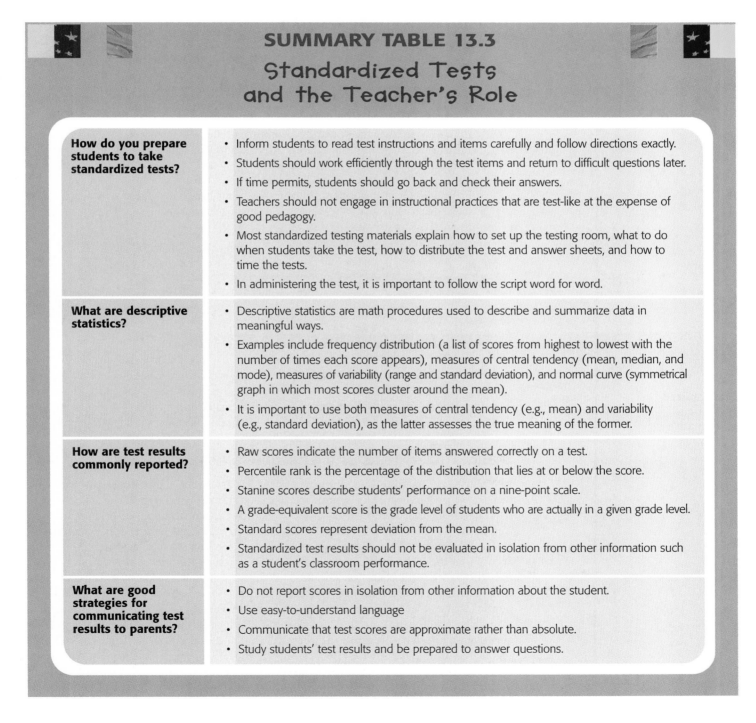

SUMMARY TABLE 13.3
Standardized Tests and the Teacher's Role

How do you prepare students to take standardized tests?	• Inform students to read test instructions and items carefully and follow directions exactly. • Students should work efficiently through the test items and return to difficult questions later. • If time permits, students should go back and check their answers. • Teachers should not engage in instructional practices that are test-like at the expense of good pedagogy. • Most standardized testing materials explain how to set up the testing room, what to do when students take the test, how to distribute the test and answer sheets, and how to time the tests. • In administering the test, it is important to follow the script word for word.
What are descriptive statistics?	• Descriptive statistics are math procedures used to describe and summarize data in meaningful ways. • Examples include frequency distribution (a list of scores from highest to lowest with the number of times each score appears), measures of central tendency (mean, median, and mode), measures of variability (range and standard deviation), and normal curve (symmetrical graph in which most scores cluster around the mean). • It is important to use both measures of central tendency (e.g., mean) and variability (e.g., standard deviation), as the latter assesses the true meaning of the former.
How are test results commonly reported?	• Raw scores indicate the number of items answered correctly on a test. • Percentile rank is the percentage of the distribution that lies at or below the score. • Stanine scores describe students' performance on a nine-point scale. • A grade-equivalent score is the grade level of students who are actually in a given grade level. • Standard scores represent deviation from the mean. • Standardized test results should not be evaluated in isolation from other information such as a student's classroom performance.
What are good strategies for communicating test results to parents?	• Do not report scores in isolation from other information about the student. • Use easy-to-understand language • Communicate that test scores are approximate rather than absolute. • Study students' test results and be prepared to answer questions.

Teaching Strategies
For Communicating Test Results to Parents

✔ Report test scores in context
  • provide parents with information about students' performances across a number of classroom assessments
  • avoid emphasizing the findings from any one assessment, especially a standardized test
  • provide parents with exemplars of students' work that emphasize strengths as well as areas for improvement
✔ Use clear language
  • use terms that are readily understood
  • avoid using jargon or obscure test language
  • provide parents with information about percentile scores or bands whenever possible
  • provide parents with visual aids such as graphs and charts when describing students' performances
✔ Be informed and reassuring
  • inform parents that test results are approximate
  • inform parents about the various internal and external factors that can affect students' performances
  • familiarize yourself with students' test scores
  • be prepared to interpret and summarize test scores
  • use a discussion format when talking with parents and invite them to ask questions

Source: McMillan (1997)

Issues in Standardized Testing

Standardized Tests and Alternative Assessments

In Search of a Balanced Approach

Diversity and Standardized Testing

ISSUES IN STANDARDIZED TESTING

As we have already mentioned, standardized testing is controversial. One debate concerns how standardized tests compare with alternative methods of assessment. Another is about whether standardized tests discriminate against ethnic minority students and students from low-income backgrounds (for an extended discussion, refer to Chapter 4).

Standardized Tests and Alternative Assessments

Alternative assessments include various performance assessments, such as oral presentations, real-world problems, projects, and portfolios (systematic and organized collections of students' work that demonstrate their skills and accomplishments). Which is the best way to assess student performance—standardized tests that mainly rely on multiple-choice questions, or alternative assessments? Wilson (1999), an educator at Queen's University, argues that the large-scale standardized testing practices that have grown in popularity over the past decade serve to evaluate curriculum implementation over authentic student learning. This evaluation of the curriculum is provoked by both political and economic factions that require reports on student achievement (Wilson, 1999). This agenda is in direct juxtaposition to the current trend in education in which classroom teachers are engaging in dynamic methods of instruction and evaluation (Wilson, 1999). Some argue that this dynamic view of learning is more valid, and accordingly should be reflected in all facets of assessment (Wilson, 1999). Alternative assessments that are meaningful, involve higher-level thinking skills, and emphasize constructivist and social-constructivist approaches to learning are representative of this type of assessment (Wiggins, 1992). When alternative assessments are used, it is important that they meet acceptable standards for validity, reliability, administration, and scoring.

Ronald Hambleton (1996) concluded that multiple-choice standardized testing is not likely to be completely abandoned in the foreseeable future, but he predicts that we will see more of a balance in assessment with inclusion of writing tasks, performance tests, computer simulation exercises, hands-on projects, and portfolios of work. We will say more about alternative assessments in the next chapter.

Diversity and Standardized Testing

A special concern that we discussed in earlier chapters is cultural bias in tests and the importance of creating culturally responsive tests for diagnostic and instructional purposes (Bigelow, 1999; Gay, 1997; Sandoval et al., 1999). Because of the potential for cultural bias in standardized tests, it is important to assess students using a variety of methods. As we indicated earlier, many assessment experts believe that performance and portfolio assessments reduce some of the inequity that characterizes standardized tests for ethnic minority students and students from low-income backgrounds. In Chapter 14, alternatives including authentic, portfolio, and performance-based assessments will be discussed. For more about fair and equitable assessment for all students, see the Diversity and Education box.

The test of first-rate intelligence is the ability to hold two opposed ideas in the mind at the same time, and still retain the ability to function.

F. Scott Fitzgerald
American Author, 20th Century

In Search of a Balanced Approach

Educators in the 21st century are attempting to balance effective assessment practices along with the call to be accountable publicly (Earl, 1999). Provincial and territorial governments are calling for accountability through formal student testing and more centralized curricula (Earl, 1999). However, when too much emphasis is placed on formal

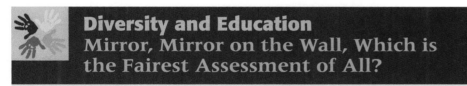

Diversity and Education
Mirror, Mirror on the Wall, Which is the Fairest Assessment of All?

In order to promote fair and unbiased assessment practices, the *Principles for Fair Student Assessment Practices for Education in Canada* was developed by members of a joint advisory committee. The committee included representation from the Canadian Education Association, Canadian School Boards Association, Canadian Association for School Administrators, Canadian Teachers' Federation, Canadian Guidance and Counselling Association, Canadian Association of School Psychologists, Canadian Council for Exceptional Children, Canadian Psychological Association, Canadian Society for the Study of Education, and the provincial and territorial ministries/departments of education. These guidelines identify issues that need to be considered when ensuring the fair and equitable assessment of all Canadian students.

There are three subsections in the document, addressing assessment development, information collection, and scoring procedures; guidelines focus on ethical, fair, and unbiased practices. For example, the panel recommends that when developing assessment methods, students' backgrounds and prior experiences need to be considered. As well, consideration should be given to content and language that could be viewed as sensitive, sexist, or offensive. When collecting assessment information, alternate procedures should be in place for students with exceptionalities and for students with limited language proficiency. The document is available from the Centre for Research in Applied Measurement and Evaluation at the University of Alberta (mailing address: 3–104 Education Building North, University of Alberta, Edmonton, Alberta, T6G 2G5).

assessment results, the educational focus shifts away from enhancing learning toward increasing test scores (Earl, 1999).

Accordingly, a balanced approach to assessment is a high priority for educators across the country (Wilson, Squire, & Craig, 2000). The Canadian Teachers' Federation adopts the position that there is little evidence to support the use of standardized tests from a pedagogical standpoint (Froese-Germain, 1999). The results of standardized tests are often misused and the significance of the data is overemphasized. According to the official Standards of Practice developed by the Ontario College of Teachers, educators are required to use multiple methods when assessing and evaluating students. Furthermore, they must be able to communicate this information clearly to parents (Wilson et al., 2000). Teachers are encouraged to use a combination of teacher-developed assessment measures as well as standardized ones when assessing student learning and classroom practice (Earl, 1999).

At this point we have explored many ideas about issues in standardized testing. A review of these ideas is presented in Summary Table 13.4. In the next chapter, we will examine a broader range of strategies for assessing students' learning.

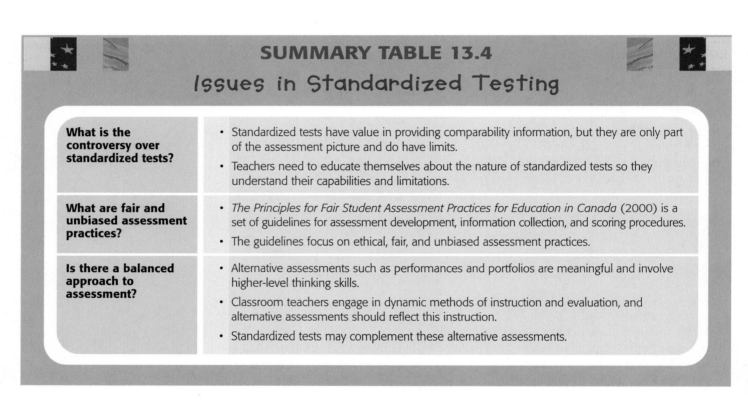

SUMMARY TABLE 13.4
Issues in Standardized Testing

What is the controversy over standardized tests?	• Standardized tests have value in providing comparability information, but they are only part of the assessment picture and do have limits. • Teachers need to educate themselves about the nature of standardized tests so they understand their capabilities and limitations.
What are fair and unbiased assessment practices?	• *The Principles for Fair Student Assessment Practices for Education in Canada* (2000) is a set of guidelines for assessment development, information collection, and scoring procedures. • The guidelines focus on ethical, fair, and unbiased assessment practices.
Is there a balanced approach to assessment?	• Alternative assessments such as performances and portfolios are meaningful and involve higher-level thinking skills. • Classroom teachers engage in dynamic methods of instruction and evaluation, and alternative assessments should reflect this instruction. • Standardized tests may complement these alternative assessments.

Ms. Carter is a Grade 3 teacher responsible for preparing her students for a standardized test given each spring to measure student achievement and ability in math, science, reading, writing, and social studies. This test is required by the Ministry of Education to assess the degree to which students have met or exceeded territorial standards. This test yields individual, school, and board scores, and compares these to territorial averages. In addition, the local school board uses a nationally normed test to assess both achievement and cognitive ability. This achievement test yields individual scores as they relate to national norms. These scores are reported as percentile-rank scores and grade-equivalent scores. The cognitive ability test yields percentile-rank scores and IQ-type scores.

Ms. Carter is not thrilled about giving her students so many standardized tests. She says, "Sometimes it seems all we do is prepare for these tests and take them." She makes sure she has taught her students appropriate test-taking strategies. She also tries to give her students experience that mirrors the standardized tests, such as filling in bubbles on answer sheets and taking tests with time limits. She also sends notes home to parents asking them to ensure that their children get adequate sleep and eat breakfast during testing weeks.

During testing, she always hangs a sign on the door communicating that she does not wish to be disturbed. She reads the instructions verbatim and asks her students if they have any questions prior to beginning the test. She tries to keep the testing situation as low-key as possible for her students.

Test results are routinely distributed to parents with student report cards. Parent–teacher conferences are conducted the week following distribution. Parents inevitably have many questions about standardized test scores:

"Ms. Carter, what does this grade equivalent mean? It says here that Emily has a grade equivalent of 4.3. Does that mean we should ask to have her placed in Grade 4?"

"Ms. Carter, John scored at the 90th percentile on language, but he's getting C's in your class. I just don't understand."

"Ms. Carter, how can it be that my daughter scored in the 60th percentile on the ability test and the 70th on the achievement test, and doesn't meet territorial standards in math?"

"Ms. Carter, how can my son score in the 40th percentile on the ability test and the 80th percentile on the achievement test? That just doesn't make any sense!"

- What are the issues involved in this situation?
- Examine Ms. Carter's testing procedures. What does she do incorrectly? How might this reduce the validity of the students' scores?
- How would you answer each of the parents' questions?

CHAPTER REVIEW

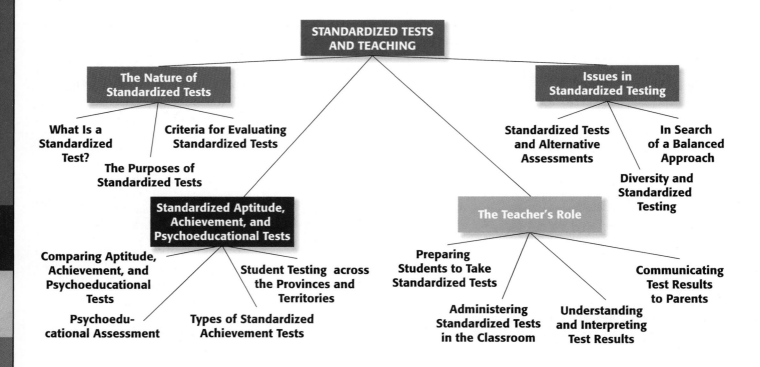

To obtain a detailed review of this chapter, study these four summary tables:

 KEY TERMS

standardized test 418
minimum competency tests 419
high-stakes testing 419
norm group 419
national norms 419
special group norms 419
local norms 419
reliability 419
test–retest reliability 420
alternate forms reliability 420
split-half reliability 420

validity 420
content validity 420
criterion validity 420
concurrent validity 420
predictive validity 420
construct validity 421
instructional validity 421
aptitude test 421
achievement test 422
psychoeducational assessment 422

survey battery 423
diagnostic tests 424
descriptive statistics 432
frequency distribution 432
histogram 432
measure of central tendency 433
mean 433
median 433
mode 433
measures of variability 433
range 433

standard deviation 433
normal distribution 434
raw score 435
percentile rank score 436
stanine score 436
grade-equivalent score 436
standard score 437
z-score 437
T-score 437
percentile bands 437

PROFESSIONAL DEVELOPMENT/PORTFOLIO ACTIVITIES

1. Standardized Testing—Good or Bad?

The use of standardized tests by provinces as a means for assessing student learning and teaching effectiveness has received mixed reactions from teachers and education researchers. Some believe that standardized tests provide the accountability needed to improve education. On the other hand, some individuals maintain that standardized tests do not accurately reflect students' understanding or ability. Below you will find a series of statements about standardized testing. Evaluate each statement and explain why you agree or disagree with what has been stated. Include the responses in your portfolio.

a) Province-wide standardized testing based on multiple-choice questions will lead to a "dumbing-down" of instruction.

b) Standardized provincal tests do not tell teachers anything they do not already know about their students.

c) Standardized tests that are designed to measure student achievement can also speak to the quality of students' education.

2. Talking to Parents about Test Results

An important part of student assessment is talking to parents about what test results and evaluations mean. It often helps to be able to graphically display how students are doing in your class. Below you will find a set of history class test scores that can be plotted as a histogram and frequency distribution. Create a frequency distribution and histogram for the scores. Calculate the mean, median, and mode of the scores as well as the standard deviation. Draw a normal curve with the information provided and plot a student grade of 75 percent. Use the information you have to plan what you would say to a parent whose child has received a grade of 75 percent on the test.

Student history scores: 98, 96, 94, 94, 92, 90, 90, 88, 86, 86, 86, 82, 80, 80, 80, 80, 80, 78, 75, 72, 70, 68, 64.

3. Assessment and Accommodation

You have a student with a reading disability who is preparing to take a standardized test. Consider what type of accommodations might help this student. Make two columns on a piece of paper. In the first column, list the ways that students with disabilities might receive unfair treatment due to standardized testing. In the other column, list modifications or accommodations that teachers can make to overcome these problems. Place the list in your portfolio.

 INTERNET ACTIVITIES

1. Performance Testing versus Standardized Testing

Performance assessment and standardized tests differ in both style and substance. Search the Internet to find definitions of both performance assessment and standardized tests. Describe the situations in which you would be tested with a standardized test and the situations in which you would be tested with a performance assessment.

2. Multiple-Choice Tests

One of the most common forms of teacher-constructed tests is the multiple-choice test. Pick a partner from your class, select a subject area, and write three multiple-choice questions each for that subject area. Trade questions with your partner and critique them. Identify strengths and weaknesses and discuss strategies for developing effective multiple-choice questions.

Connect to the Online Learning Centre at www.mcgrawhill.ca/college/santrock **to explore possible answers.**

Visit the *Educational Psychology* Online Learning Centre at
www.mcgrawhill.ca/college/santrock
to access Websites related to the above Internet Activities as well as chapter quizzes,
a searchable glossary, and other learning and study tools.

14 Assessing Students' Learning

Preview

Assessment of students' learning has recently generated considerable interest in educational circles. This interest has focused on such issues as the extent to which teachers should incorporate provincial and territorial "standards" in their teaching and assessment, as well as the degree to which teachers should use traditional tests or alternative assessments such as performance assessments. These are some of the questions we will explore in this chapter:

- How can assessment be made an integral part of teaching?
- What does it take to construct high-quality assessments?
- What are traditional tests?
- What are authentic, performance, and portfolio assessments?
- What are some good strategies for grading and reporting students' performance?
- How can computers be used in assessment and grading?

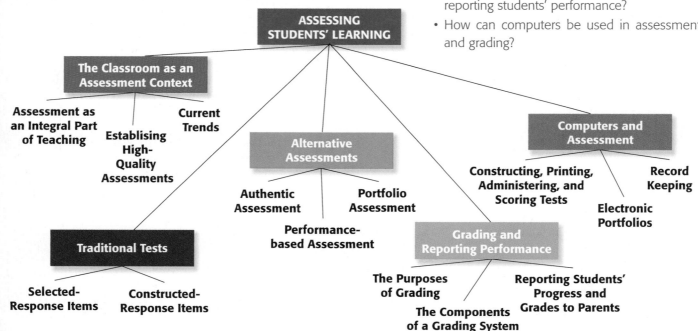

ASSESSING STUDENTS' LEARNING

The Classroom as an Assessment Context
- Assessment as an Integral Part of Teaching
- Establishing High-Quality Assessments
- Current Trends

Traditional Tests
- Selected-Response Items
- Constructed-Response Items

Alternative Assessments
- Authentic Assessment
- Performance-based Assessment
- Portfolio Assessment

Grading and Reporting Performance
- The Purposes of Grading
- The Components of a Grading System
- Reporting Students' Progress and Grades to Parents

Computers and Assessment
- Constructing, Printing, Administering, and Scoring Tests
- Electronic Portfolios
- Record Keeping

*A*ny fact of intellect, character or skill means a tendency to respond in a certain way to a certain situation.

Edward Lee Thorndike
A Founder of Educational Psychology, 20th Century

Teaching Stories: Randolph Rodgers

Randolph Rodgers is an elementary-school teacher working in Newfoundland. With more than 30 years of classroom experience, Randolph understands that assessment is a vital component of classroom teaching. Below, he describes how he ensures that all students are assessed in appropriate and relevant ways.

"Teachers should keep in mind that test results are not always accurate. Sometimes there are mitigating reasons for students' poor performances (e.g., having a bad day, or misunderstanding the test directions). Teachers should never make decisions about students' abilities on the basis of single test results.

"Teachers need to use a variety of assessment instruments and approaches in order to meet the needs of individual students. I once had a student who was performing below grade average and presenting symptoms consistent with a language-processing deficiency. He clearly struggled with any reading- or writing-based assessment. One day I decided to use a verbal-based assessment, and was surprised at how much the student was able to articulate. By changing the format of assessment, I was able to develop a more accurate assessment of his true abilities.

"Teachers also need to remember the strong link between assessment and instruction. I recall a student who was exceptionally strong in art, but demonstrated difficulties with her short-term memory. I changed my instructional approach to appeal to her visual orientation with the thought of using her strength in art to enhance her memory. I encouraged her to add drawings beside her notes; I used colours to highlight important terms, phrases, and ideas; I recorded information in chart format; and I taught the class an assortment of visual mnemonics. Similarly, I modified my assessment methods to reflect a more visually oriented style. While I was attempting to be responsible to the learning needs of this individual student, I was also helping the other students in the class develop effective study skills and understand the importance of learning styles."

The Classroom as an
Assessment Context

Assessment as
an Integral Part
of Teaching

Current
Trends

Establising High-
Quality Assessments

THE CLASSROOM AS AN ASSESSMENT CONTEXT

When you think of assessment, what are some other words that come to mind? You might think of *evaluation*. While the two terms are often used interchangeably, in an educational psychology context each term represents a distinct process. According to the *Statements of Principle on Assessment and Evaluation* (Canadian Teachers' Federation, 1999), assessment involves the gathering of reliable information pertaining to students' knowledge and understanding of critical concepts. This information may include social, economic, and educational factors and resources that influence student and system performance. Evaluation is the process of making judgments, based in part on assessment data. Assessment and evaluation are continuous processes that inform decision making at classroom and system levels (Canadian Teachers' Federation, 1999). In this chapter, you will discover that contemporary views of assessment are quite complex and involve more than just tests.

Assessment as an Integral Part of Teaching

Teachers spend more time on assessment than you might imagine. In one analysis, they spent 20 to 30 percent of their professional time dealing with assessment matters (Stiggins, 1987, 2000). With so much time spent on assessment, it is important that it be done well. Assessment expert James McMillan (1997, 2000) believes that competent teachers frequently evaluate their students in relation to learning goals and adapt their instruction accordingly. Assessment not only documents what students know and can do, but also affects their learning and motivation. These ideas represent a change in the way assessment is viewed, away from the concept that assessment is an isolated outcome done only after instruction is finished and toward the concept of integrating assessment with instruction.

According to the *Statements of Principle on Assessment and Evaluation* (Canadian Teachers' Federation, 1999), classroom teachers have the primary responsibility for assessing and evaluating student achievement with the intent of supporting student learning. Accordingly, decisions regarding evaluation and assessment should focus on what is valuable, and not simply on what is measurable (Canadian Teachers' Federation, 1999). The design, interpretation, and application of information derived from assessment and evaluation are complex tasks. Teachers should consider integrating instruction and assessment in terms of three time frames: before instruction, during instruction, and after instruction. Figure 14.1 provides a review of assessment questions that teachers can ask themselves at these three stages (Beauchamp, McConaghy, Parsons, & Sanford, 1996).

Before-Instruction Assessment   Imagine that you want to know how well your students can solve a certain level of math problem before you begin formal instruction on a more advanced level. You might look at your students' prior grades and their scores on standardized math tests, and also observe your students for several days to see how well they perform. These assessments are designed to answer this question: "What math skills are my students able to demonstrate?" If the results of your assessment indicate that students lack prerequisite knowledge and skills, you will decide to begin with materials that are less difficult for them. If they do extremely well on your before-instruction assessment, you will move your level of instruction to a higher plane. Without this pre-instructional assessment, you run the risk of having a class that is overwhelmed (your instruction level will be too advanced) or bored (your instruction level will be too low).

Much of before-instruction assessment is informal observation. In the first several weeks of school, you will have numerous opportunities to observe students' characteristics and behaviours. Be sensitive to whether a student is shy or outgoing, has a good or weak vocabulary, speaks and listens effectively, is considerate of others or is egocentric, engages in appropriate or inappropriate behaviour, and so on. Also focus on the student's nonverbal behaviour for cues that might reveal nervousness, boredom, frustration, or a lack of understanding. For example, a student might say that things are fine but come into class every day with a downturned head and sad look.

www.mcgrawhill.ca/college/santrock

FIGURE 14.1   **Before-, During-, and After-Instruction Assessment Questions**

Before-Instruction Assessment Questions

• Why am I using this type of assessment?

• Why am I assessing students at this time?

• What is my goal?

• What am I assessing?

• What do I want to learn about the students through this assessment?

• What do I want the students to learn from this assessment?

• Is my assessment based on my instructional objectives?

• Are my students well prepared for the assessment?

• Are students' different ability levels considered?

• What is my follow-up activity?

• Is there anything about the assessment that would be difficult or confusing for my students?

During-Instruction Assessment Questions

• Are the students aware of the evaluation criteria process?

• Does the assessment document changes in students' learning? (i.e., direction and amount of change or skill development)

• Does the assessment evaluate the process of learning?

After-Instruction Assessment Questions

• Did the students understand what was asked of them?

• Were the students prepared? Is this evident in the results?

• What changes would, could, or should I make in the future?

• Is there an assessment tool that would be more appropriate?

After you have made informal observations, you will need to interpret them. That is, what does the student's behaviour mean? Are a downturned head and sad look clues to a lack of self-esteem regarding academic skills, or possibly stressful circumstances at home? Are the student's poor listening skills due to a lack of motivation?

Guard against developing expectations that will distort your perception of a student. It is virtually impossible not to have expectations about students. Because teacher expectations are potentially powerful influences on students' learning, some teachers don't even want to look at students' prior grades or standardized test scores. Whether you do or do not examine such assessment information, work on making your expectations realistic. If you err, err in the direction of having overly positive expectations for students.

A good strategy is to treat your initial impressions of students as hypotheses to be confirmed or modified by subsequent observation and information. Some of your initial observations will be accurate, others will need to be revised. As you try to get a sense of what your students are like, refrain from believing hearsay information, from making enduring judgments based on only one or two observations, and from labelling the student (Airasian, 1997).

Some teachers also administer textbook review or diagnostic pretests in subject areas to examine students' levels of knowledge and skills. And many schools are increasingly collecting samples of students' work in portfolios, which can accompany them from grade to grade. The portfolios provide teachers with far more concrete, less biased information to evaluate than other teachers' hearsay comments. We will describe portfolios in greater depth later in the chapter.

During-Instruction Assessment   **Formative assessment** *is assessment during the course of instruction rather than after it is completed.* Your ongoing observation and mon-

Through the Eyes of Teachers

Marking in Math Class

Over the long run, marking students' daily work or assignments can become a tedious process. However, teachers must always remember that if marking isn't carried out in a sensitive manner, it can hurt students emotionally and negatively affect their attitudes toward the subject area and learning in general. Receiving grades for tests or daily exercises can be a positive experience for students when it affirms their learning efforts. On the other hand, it can also be a painful experience for students who have worked hard but perform poorly. Struggling students see many more X's than check marks on their work and this can be discouraging. I recall an English teacher who stopped marking grammatical and spelling errors whenever it became obvious that a student was experiencing difficulties. She believed that too many corrections on a student's work only served to mortify the student. I feel the same way about marking mathematics assignments and tests.

When a student is struggling with a mathematical concept or methodology, I stop marking and write a note asking the student to see me. I generally begin our dialogue by verifying that learning mathematics can be difficult and that I made many mistakes when I was a student. I quickly qualify that after receiving some additional help, I was able to succeed in mathematics and that I believe they can be successful too. Together we develop a plan for improving the student's performance, focusing on what can be done before the next test or assignment. A little bit of success goes a long way. Once students experience some success, they usually want more of it and will be very willing to make the extra effort to achieve it.

Tess Miller
Secondary-School Math Teacher
Teaching Assistant, Queen's University
Ontario

itoring of students' learning while you teach provides you with information about what to do next. Assessment during instruction helps you set your teaching at a level that challenges students and stretches their thinking. It also helps you to detect which students need your individual attention. Good assessment is parallel to good instruction. Experienced teachers believe that good teaching and effective assessment are complementary skills that are often difficult to distinguish (Columba, 2001).

Assessment during instruction takes place at the same time as you make many other decisions about what to do, say, or ask next to keep the classroom running smoothly and to help students actively learn (Airasian, 1997). It requires listening to students' answers, observing other students for indications of understanding or confusion, framing the next question, and scanning the class for possible misbehaviour (Doyle, 1986; Manitoba Education and Training, 1997). At the same time, the teacher must be aware of the pace of the activity, the sequence of choosing students to answer, the relevance and quality of the answers, and the logical development of the content. When the class is divided into small groups, the teacher might need to monitor and regulate several different activities simultaneously. (An extended discussion about the inherent dangers of perceived teacher expectations and within-class grouping is provided in Chapter 4.)

Verbal questions are an especially important aspect of assessment during instruction. Some teachers ask as many as 300 to 400 questions a day, not only to stimulate students' thinking and inquiry but also to assess their knowledge and skill level (Columbia, 2001; Christensen, 1991; Morgan & Saxton, 1991). We recommend that teachers follow the general IRE (initiate, respond, and evaluate) pattern when using questions in the classroom. In this sequence the teacher asks a question, the student responds, and the teacher evaluates the response for concordance to the answer he or she is seeking (Earl & Katz, 2000). A detailed discussion about how to provide thinking-based questions as part of classroom instruction is provided in Chapter 10.

After-Instruction Assessment **Summative assessment** *is assessment after instruction is finished.* Assessment after instruction provides information about how well your students have mastered the material, whether students are ready for the next unit, what grades students should be given, what comments you should make to parents, and how you should adapt your instruction (McMillan, 1997, 2000). Summative assessment is most meaningful for students when they are aware of the process required to complete the task and the evaluation criteria ahead of time (Principles for Fair Student Assessment Practices for Education in Canada, 2002). As a final caution, the Canadian Teachers' Federation (1999) notes that there are many forms, methods, and approaches to assessment—none of which in isolation is an adequate measure of student, program, or system performance.

Establishing High-Quality Assessments

It is difficult to obtain information about everything students know. Rather, your assessment will probably be a sample of students' learning (Gredler, 1999; Weber, 1999). Assessment is considered to be of a high level of quality when it yields reliable, valid, and unbiased information about students' performance (Stiggins, 1997, 2000; McMillan, 1997).

Reliability   **Reliability** *is defined as the extent to which an assessment produces a consistent, reproducible measure of performance. Reliable measures are stable, dependable, and relatively free from errors of measurement* (see Chapter 13). If a history teacher gives students three tests over a period of several months and the students perform in a consistent manner on the tests, the assessments can be considered reliable. Reliability also involves the consistency of the inferences teachers make about students based on assessment information (Payne, 1997).

Validity   **Validity** *refers to the extent to which an assessment measures what it is intended to measure* (see Chapter 13). An important strategy for validity in classroom assessment is to systematically link learning targets, content, instruction, and assessment (McMillan, 1997). The most important source of information for validity in your classroom will be **content-related evidence,** *the extent to which the assessment reflects what you have been teaching* (McMillan, 1997).

If a test you give does a balanced job of sampling the full range of content that has been taught, and students get 80 percent of the answers correct, it is reasonable to conclude that the students probably learned about 80 percent of the content. On the other hand, if the test you give samples only part of the material and students get 80 percent correct, the test results give no clear indication about how much of the overall content the students actually learned.

Adequately sampling content is clearly an important goal of valid assessment (Mehrens, 1997; Trice, 2000). Use your best professional judgment when sampling content. An increasing trend is to use multiple methods of assessment, which can provide a more comprehensive sampling of content. Thus, the teacher might assess students' knowledge of a geography chapter using multiple-choice questions, several essay questions, and a project to complete. Always ask yourself whether your assessments of students are adequate samples of their performance. For example, is the completed geography project all that you will use to grade the student, or will you include information about the students' effort and class participation in your grading?

Linking instruction and assessment leads to consideration of an important type of validity in the classroom called **instructional validity,** *the extent to which the assessment is a reasonable sample of what actually went on in the classroom* (Payne, 1997). For example, a classroom assessment should measure what the teacher taught and whether students had an adequate opportunity to learn the material. Consider a math class in which the teacher gives students a test on their ability to solve multiplication problems. For instructional validity, it is important that the teacher competently instructed students in how to solve the problems and gave students adequate opportunities to practise this skill.

An important strategy for validity in classroom assessment is to systematically link learning targets, content, instruction, and assessment (McMillan, 1997). Imagine that you are a science teacher and that one of your learning targets is to get students to think more critically and creatively in designing science projects. Ask yourself what content is important to achieve this learning target. For instance, will it help students to read biographies of famous scientists that include information about how they came up with their ideas? Also ask yourself what learning targets you will emphasize in instruction. For your target regarding students' science projects, it will be important for you to carry through in your instruction on the theme of helping students to think critically and creatively about science.

Fairness   High-quality classroom assessment is not only valid and reliable, but also fair (McMillan, 1997). Assessment is fair when all students have an equal opportunity to learn and demonstrate their knowledge and skill. Assessment is fair when teachers have developed appropriate learning targets, provided competent content and instruction to match those targets, and chosen assessments that reflect the targets, content, and instruction. The document *Principles for Fair Student Assessment Practices for Education in Canada* (1993) provides teachers with a set of guidelines to help ensure that assessment is authentic, accurate, and fair. The report was written by the Joint Advisory Committee from the Centre for Research in Applied Measurement and Evaluation, and is endorsed by the Canadian School Boards Association, the Canadian Teachers' Federation, the

Teaching Strategies
For Fair Assessment Practices

✔ Develop and select methods of assessment
- align assessment methods with the purpose and context of the assessment
- ensure that methods support conclusions about a student's knowledge, skills, attitudes, and behaviours
- relate methods to the goals of instruction and the instructional approaches used
- use more than one assessment method to allow for the background and prior knowledge of students
- avoid content and language that is sensitive, sexist, or that might offend a student

✔ Collect assessment information
- provide students with a variety of opportunities to demonstrate the knowledge, skills, attitudes, or behaviours being assessed
- inform students about why assessment data is collected and how it will be used
- ensure that directions are clear, complete, and suited to the age, ability, and grade level of the students
- interact consistently with students (e.g., if one student needs a question clarified on a test, clarify it for the whole class)
- use alternate procedures for students with special needs

✔ Judge and score student performance
- consistently apply procedures for judging student performance
- prepare scoring procedures before an assessment is used
- inform students of how their performance will be scored or judged
- do not include factors not relevant to the assessment in the scoring procedure

✔ Summarize and interpret results
- provide accurate information about student performance by linking it to the goals and objectives of instruction
- clearly explain how comments and grades are formulated to students and parents
- base comments and grades on more than one assessment result
- separately grade achievement, effort, participation, and other behaviours

✔ Report assessment findings
- ensure that assessment reports are clear, accurate, and of practical value to the audiences for whom they are intended
- describe the goals and objectives of instruction in both written and oral reports
- address both weaknesses and strengths in the report
- provide conference opportunities between teachers and parents/guardians

Source: Adapted from *Principles for Fair Student Assessment Practices for Education in Canada*, 1993.

Canadian Association for School Administrators, and the Canadian Society for the Study of Education. Refer to the Teaching Strategies box above for a summary of the report.

Fair assessments are unbiased and do not discriminate against certain students because of their ethnic background, gender, or disability. David Payne (1997) believes it is important to create a philosophy of **pluralistic assessment**, *which includes being responsive to cultural diversity in the classroom and at school.* Assessment and evaluation of students, whether carried out at the classroom level or beyond, must take into account gender differences as well as cultural, linguistic, socioeconomic, and other forms of diversity (Canadian Teachers' Federation, 1999). This usually includes performance assessments during instruction and after instruction. Performance assessments that can be used as part of plu-

Diversity and Education
Rekindling Traditions: A Culturally Responsive Approach to Native Education

The "Rekindling Traditions: Cross-Cultural Science and Technology Units" project (CCSTU) is designed to help make Western science and engineering accessible to Aboriginal students in ways that do not conflict with their cultural identities; that is, in ways that do not force students to set aside their culture's view of the physical world when they study science at school.

Aikenhead (1997) and Battiste (2000) suggest that one of the principal reasons why more Aboriginal students do not participate in science and engineering courses or programs concerns the cultural gap that exists between many Aboriginal worldviews and the Western rationalist worldview typically expressed in science classes. The CCSTU project is a joint initiative among several Saskatchewan school divisions, Saskatchewan Education, and the University of Saskatchewan. Program developers have created cross-cultural science and technology units that include not only culturally sensitive strategies for teaching and assessing students, but also a *prototype process* for adapting curriculum materials to better suit local culture.

Cajete (1999) argues that successful cross-cultural instructional approaches put students in touch with their cultural roots and selves, facilitate their discovery for the complexity of nature, and help them recognize how various Aboriginal people live on the land using practical skills that mediate between students' cultural views and the Western science view. Cajete suggests that teachers can help students develop a cross-cultural worldview that bridges Western and Aboriginal beliefs about science and the environment through activities that engage students in using all of their senses to observe, appreciate, and explore their local environment.

The CCSTU project developers contend that if instruction is not meaningfully set in the context of the local community, students will find the science curriculum culturally foreign and inaccessible. Culturally sensitive approaches to teaching science focus on instruction as a *cross-cultural* event. Culturally sensitive instruction varies among local contexts and communities. For example, a biology student in Nunavut might focus on fish and marine biology, while a biology student in Alberta might study flora and fauna instead. Further information about the CCSTU project and case studies developed by the team can be found at **http://capes.usask.ca/ccstu/stories.html**.

ralistic assessment include portfolios, projects, demonstrations, interviews, and oral presentations. This does not mean abandoning objective measurement in the form of multiple-choice exams and essay questions, but rather making sure that a variety of methods are used including at least some performance assessments. To read further about culturally responsive strategies in assessing students, see the Diversity and Education box.

Current Trends

Following are some current trends in classroom assessment (Hambleton, 1996; McMillan, Myran, & Workman, 2002):

- *Using at least some performance-based assessment.* Historically, classroom assessment has emphasized the use of **objective tests**, *such as multiple-choice, which have relatively clear, unambiguous scoring criteria.* In contrast, **performance assessments** *require students to conduct an experiment, carry out a project, solve a real-world problem, create a portfolio, or perform some other task.* Performance assessments require students to create answers or products that demonstrate their knowledge or skill.
- *Examining higher-order cognitive skills.* Rather than assess only content knowledge, as many objective tests do, a current trend is to evaluate students' higher-order

Man, unlike any other thing organic or inorganic in the universe, grows beyond his work, walks up the stairs of his concepts, emerges ahead of his accomplishments.

John Steinbeck
American Author, 20th Century

cognitive skills, such as problem solving, critical thinking, decision making, drawing inferences, and strategic thinking.

- *Using multiple assessment methods.* In the past, assessment meant using a test—often a multiple-choice test—as the sole means of assessing students' learning. A current trend is to use multiple methods to assess students. Thus, a teacher might use any number of these methods: a multiple-choice test, an essay, an interview, a project, a portfolio, or even having students evaluate themselves. Multiple assessments provide a broader view of the students' learning and achievement than a single measure.
- *Having high performance standards.* Another trend is the demand for high performance standards, even "world-class" performance standards, for interpreting educational results. Some experts say that world-class performance standards are driving contemporary classroom assessment by setting goals or targets (Taylor, 1994).
- *Using computers as part of assessment.* Traditionally, computers have been used to score tests, analyze test results, and report scores. Today, computers increasingly are being used to construct and administer tests, as well as to present different assessment formats to students in a multimedia environment. With continued advances in technology, assessment practices in the twenty-first century are very different from traditional paper-and-pencil tests (van der Linden, 1995).

Trends in assessment also include emphasizing integrated rather than isolated skills, providing more feedback, and making standards and criteria public rather than private and secretive. We will revisit many of these current trends later in this chapter.

At this point we have studied many ideas about the classroom as an assessment context. A review of these ideas is presented in Summary Table 14.1.

TRADITIONAL TESTS

Traditional Tests

Selected-Response Items   Constructed-Response Items

Traditional tests are typically paper-and-pencil tests in which students select from choices, calculate numbers, construct short responses, or write essays. Our coverage of traditional tests focuses on two main types of item formats in assessment: (1) selected-response items and (2) constructed-response items.

Selected-Response Items

Selected-response items *have an objective item format in which students' responses can be scored on quick inspection. A scoring key for correct responses is created and can be applied by an examiner or by a computer.* True/false, multiple-choice, and matching items are the most widely used types of items in selected-response tests. We also will describe several other recently developed objective-item formats.

True/False Items   In true/false items, students mark whether a statement is *true* or *false*. For example:

Ottawa is the capital of Canada.   True   False

True/false items are useful for outcomes where there are only two possible alternatives. These items place less demand on reading ability than do multiple-choice items, and a relatively large number of items can be answered during a typical testing period. Teachers regard true/false tests as easy to score, objective, and reliable.

There are a few cautions and limitations associated with this test format. When devising questions, teachers should not take statements directly from a text; this encourages rote memorization with little understanding of the material. It is difficult for teachers to write statements that reflect a high level of thinking and are free from ambiguity. When a statement is identified correctly as false, there is no evidence that students know the correct response. Further, no diagnostic information can be gleaned from students' incorrect answers. Teachers should take note that students' scores on true/false tests are more influenced by guessing than with any other item type.

SUMMARY TABLE 14.1

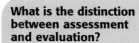

The Classroom as an Assessment Context

What is the distinction between assessment and evaluation?	• Assessment is the gathering of reliable information pertaining to students' knowledge and understanding, including social, economic, and educational factors and resources that influence student and system performance. • Evaluation is the process of making judgments, based in part on assessment data.
What are before-instruction, during-instruction, and after-instruction assessment?	• Before-instruction assessment involves informal observations, pre-tests in subject areas, and examination of students' learning portfolios from previous grades. • During-instruction assessment involves formative measures. • Questioning is an efficient method for monitoring students' progress and for detecting learning and instructional difficulties. • Summative assessment is assessment after instruction. It usually involves tests.
What is a high-quality assessment?	• High-quality assessments are reliable, valid, and fair. • Reliability is the extent to which an assessment produces a consistent, reproducible measure of performance. • Validity is the extent to which an assessment measures what it is intended to measure • Validity is also a measure of how accurate and useful teachers' inferences are. • Content-related validity measures the extent to which the assessment reflects what has been taught. • Instructional validity is the extent to which an assessment is a reasonable sample of what went on in the classroom. • Fairness requires that all students have an equal opportunity to learn and demonstrate their knowledge and skills. • Gender, cultural, linguistic, and socioeconomic diversity are considered as part of fair assessment.
What are current trends in assessment?	• Current trends in assessment include performance-based assessment, examining higher-order thinking skills, using multiple assessment methods, having high performance standards, and using computers.

Multiple-Choice Items A **multiple-choice item** *consists of two parts: the stem, plus a set of possible responses.* The stem is a question or statement, and it is followed by a set of possible answers from which to choose. Incorrect alternatives are called *distractors*. Students need to select the correct choice from among the distractors. For example:

What is the capital of Canada?   (Stem)
     a. Victoria   (Distractor)
     b. Ottawa   (Answer)
     c. St. John's   (Distractor)
     d. Toronto   (Distractor)

Multiple-choice items provide a broad indicator of achievement. Multiple-choice tests are highly structured and provide teachers with an opportunity to measure lower and higher-level learning outcomes. Students' incorrect responses can provide diagnostic information,

www.mcgrawhill.ca/college/santrock

Teaching Strategies
For Writing True/False Questions

✔ Include only one central idea
  • avoid including more than one idea in any one statement
  • avoid using complicated sentences that tax students' reading abilities
    – Example (the first item is better than the second item):

    Toronto is the capital of Ontario.
    Toronto is the capital of Ontario, has one of the largest immigrant populations in Canada, and is the province with the greatest number of bankruptcies.

✔ Keep statements short
  • use simple vocabulary
  • use simple sentence structure
  • avoid including extraneous information
    – Example (the first item is better than the second item):

    Toronto is the capital of Ontario.
    The capital of Ontario is a large, ethnically diverse metropolis known as Toronto.

✔ Use precise wording
  • use statements that can be evaluated for accuracy readily
  • ensure that true statements are "true" under all circumstances
  • avoid using absolutes (e.g., always, never, all, none, only)
  • avoid using qualifiers (e.g., might, possible)
  • avoid using vague terms (e.g., seldom, frequently, often)
    – Example (the first item is better than the second item):

    According to 1998 polls, the majority of Canadians supported sending troops to Kuwait.
    A lot of people believe that the Gulf War might have been justified.

✔ Use negatives sparingly
  • avoid using double negatives
  • highlight negatives
    – Example (the first item is better than the second item):

    In the presence of high heat, oxygen bonds readily to hydrogen.
    In the presence of high heat, oxygen is *not* unlikely to bond with hydrogen.

✔ Provide source information for opinion statements
  • Use opinion statements sparingly
  • Only cite critical opinions
    – Example (the first item is better than the second item):

    According to Ghandi, the first Prime Minister of India, violence is never acceptable.
    Some important world leaders believe that violence is never acceptable.

Source: Adapted from Gronlund (1998)

and test scores are less influenced by guessing than with true/false items. Scoring multiple-choice items is easy, objective, and reliable.

There are a few limitations associated with multiple-choice items. The multiple-choice format is ineffective for measuring some types of problem solving and the organization and expressing of ideas. As well, students' scores can be influenced by reading ability and comprehension. Constructing good multiple-choice items can be time consuming, and it is often difficult to find plausible distractors. Refer to Figure 14.2 for suggestions on how to write effective multiple-choice questions.

Who was Sir John A. Macdonald?
a) A Tory
b) The first Prime Minister of Canada
c) A catalyst in uniting Canada and a practitioner of porkbarrel politics
d) Lanny Macdonald's great-grandfather

Better question format:
Which of the following is Paul Henderson most famous for?
a) He once played for the Toronto Maple Leafs and the Calgary Flames
b) He scored the winning goal in the final game of the 1972 Canada–Soviet series
c) He was the only Toronto Maple Leaf to win the Lady Byng trophy

- **Avoid** using an incomplete statement in the stem. The stem should contain enough information to stand on its own.

- **Do** provide responses that are similar in grammatical structure and length.

- **Do** provide one response that is absolutely the correct answer.

- **Do** provide distractors that have an element of plausibility in them. Distractors are intended to distract—not trick—students who are unprepared.

Which of the following is not a vegetable?
a) Carrot
b) Banana
c) Potato
d) Tomato
e) C and D
f) A and B

Better question format:
The defining characteristic of fruit is that it does not grow underground. Which of the following is NOT a fruit?
a) A tomato
b) An apple
c) A blueberry
d) A beet

- **Avoid** using negative terms and complicated "within-choices" questions. Such questions usually cause confusion, increase reading difficulty, and require an unjustifiable amount of time to solve. If a negative has to be used in the stem, emphasize it (e.g., capital letters, underlining, italics).

- **Avoid** using "none of the above" or "all of above." About four choices are usually appropriate.

Which of the following does not belong?
a) Giotto
b) Raphael
c) Dante
d) Rembrandt

Better question format:
Which artist best represents the Dutch painting style?
a) Giotto
b) Raphael
c) Dante
d) Rembrandt

- **Be prepared** for unforeseen but valid responses from students. For example, the teacher may have expected the students to choose (c) since Dante was a writer, not a painter. However, some students may have chosen (d) because Rembrandt was Dutch while the other three were Italian.

FIGURE 14.2   How to Write Effective Multiple-Choice Questions

Source: Adapted from Gronlund (1998); Haladyna (1997); Linden (1996); and Sax (1997).

Scoring Multiple-Choice Items   Students below Grade 4 probably should answer questions on the test page rather than on a separate answer sheet. Young elementary-school students tend to respond slowly and lose their place easily when they have to use a separate answer sheet (Sax, 1997). Using a separate answer sheet with older students often reduces scoring time because the answers usually can fit on only one page. If you hand-score multiple-choice tests, consider preparing a scoring stencil by cutting or punching holes in the answer sheet in the locations of the correct answers.

For most classroom requirements, simply count the number of answers marked correctly. Some teachers penalize students for guessing by deducting for wrong answers, but assessment experts say that this probably is not worth the extra bother and frequently leads to mistakes in scoring (Sax, 1997).

Matching Items   Used by many teachers with younger students, matching requires students to connect one group of stimuli correctly with a second group of stimuli (Hambleton, 1996). Matching is especially well suited for assessing associations or links between two sets of information. In a typical matching format, a teacher places a list of terms on the left side of the page and a description or definition of the terms on the right side of the page. The students' task is to draw lines between the columns that correctly link terms with their definitions or descriptions. In another format, a space is left blank next to each term and students write in the correct number or letter of the description/definition. When using matching, limit the number of items to be matched to no more than eight or ten. Many experts recommend using no more than five or six items per set (Linden, 1996).

Criticisms of matching-items assessments are that they tend to ask students to connect trivial information, and that most matching tasks require students to connect information they have memorized, although items can be constructed that measure more complex cognitive skills (Sax, 1997).

Other Objective Assessment Formats   Other objective or selected-response formats include audiovisuals and problem sets (Hambleton, 1996).

Using Audiovisuals to Set the Context   The audiovisual format takes advantage of the ease with which we now can create and show slides and videotapes. Students are presented with a problem in an audiovisual format and asked to make decisions about what is going on or how to solve the problem. Students select answers from sets of options, just like in a paper-and-pencil multiple-choice test. The main advantages of this audiovisual format are that it can depict the real world and can be used to evaluate higher-level cognitive skills. The main drawbacks are the costs in time and money.

Problem Sets   **Problem sets** *involve writing two or more multiple-choice or objective short-answer items that are related to the same material, such as an illustration, graph, or passage.* To arrive at correct answers, students have to apply their knowledge and skills. For example, in math class a graph might be displayed together with a series of multiple-choice items. In history or social studies, a map might be used for this purpose. Some students report that the problem-set format seems more realistic than a set of discrete, independent items.

How Good Are Your Test Items?   One way to evaluate the quality of your test items is to conduct an item analysis. Two methods for doing this involve computing the difficulty level of the items and determining how well they discriminate between students who scored high and those who scored low on the entire test (Gronlund, 1998; Linn & Gronlund, 1999; Linden, 1996).

The **item-difficulty index** *is the percentage of students who obtain the correct answer on an item.* To compute the difficulty index for each item, go through the following steps:

1. Rank-order the scores on the test from highest to lowest.
2. Identify the high-scoring group and the low-scoring group. With 30 students you might choose the 10 students who scored the highest on the test and the 10 students who scored the lowest. A good strategy is to select the top-scoring one-third of students and the bottom-scoring one-third of students.
3. Determine the percentage of high scorers and low scorers passing an item. In one example, 8 of 10 students in the high-scoring group correctly answered the item, which equals 80 percent; 4 of 10 students in the low-scoring group answered it correctly, which equals 40 percent.
4. To obtain the item-difficulty index, add the percentage correct in the high and low groups and then divide by 2. Add a percent sign to the answer. Thus, in our example,

$$\frac{80 + 40}{2} = 60\%$$

When the item difficulty index is 75 percent or higher, the item is usually interpreted as easy in terms of difficulty level; when the index is 25 percent or less, the item is usually interpreted as hard, or low, in difficulty level. All other percentages—including the 60 percent in our example—are usually interpreted as average in difficulty level. Assessment experts recommend that most of the items be in the 40- to 60-percent range with only a few hard items (0 to 25 percent) or easy (75 to 100 percent) items.

The **item-discrimination index** *reflects the item's ability to discriminate between individuals who scored high and those who scored low on the entire test.* Obtain the item-discrimination index by subtracting the percentage correct in the low-scoring group from the percentage correct in the high-scoring group. Then, add a decimal point to the answer. Thus, in our example:

$$80 - 40 = .40$$

This item-discrimination index has a decimal point, and its value ranges from 0 to 1.00. If the index is 0 to .19, there was little or no difference between the high- and low-scoring groups on the item; if the index is .20 to .39, the item discriminated moderately well between the high- and low-scoring groups; if the index is .40 or greater, the item strongly discriminated between the high- and low-scoring groups (which was the case for the item in our example: .40). If the item-discrimination index is below .20, you likely will want to improve the item or eliminate it; if it is .20 to .39, you might want to keep the item but improve it; and if the index is .40 or above, you likely will want to keep the item as it is.

The first time you compute item difficulty and item-discrimination indices, they might seem more complicated than they really are. After you have done several of these, the computations should become easier for you to complete.

Constructed-Response Items

Constructed-response items *require students to write out information rather than select a response. Short-answer and essay items are the most commonly used forms of constructed-response items.* In scoring, many constructed-response items require judgment on the part of the examiner.

Short-Answer Items   A **short-answer item** *is a constructed-response format in which students are required to write a word, short phrase, or several sentences in response to a task.* For example, a student might be asked:

Who discovered insulin?

The short-answer format allows recall and could provide a problem-solving assessment of a wide range of material. The disadvantages of short-answer questions are that they can require judgment to be scored and typically measure rote learning.

Sentence completion is a variation of the short-answer item, in which students express their knowledge and skill by completing a sentence. For example, a student might be asked to complete this sentence stem: *The name of the person who discovered insulin is* _____.

York University professors Nield and Wintre (1986) surveyed students about their preferences and attitudes regarding test item format. Students preferred short-answer formats and multiple-choice questions (with the option to explain their answers) over other formats such as true/false, fill-in-the-blank, or essay questions.

Essays   **Essay items** *allow students more response freedom, but require more writing than other formats. Essay items are especially good for assessing students' understanding of material, higher-level thinking skills, ability to organize information, and writing skills.* Here are some examples of high-school essay questions:

- What are the strengths and weaknesses of a democratic approach to government?
- Describe the main themes of the novel you just read.
- Argue that Canada is a gender-biased nation.

Essay items can require students to write anything from a few sentences to much more extended responses. In some cases, teachers ask all students to answer the same essay question(s). In others, teachers let students select from a group of items the item(s) they want to write about, a strategy that makes it more difficult to compare students' responses across essays.

Suggestions for writing good essay items include these (Sax, 1997):

- *Specify limitations.* Be sure to inform students about the length of the desired answer and the weight that will be given to each item in determining scores or judgments.
- *Structure and clarify the task.* Clearly state what students are supposed to write about. A poorly worded item is "Who was Sir John A. Macdonald?" This could be answered in five words: "First Prime Minister of Canada." In cases like this, ask yourself what you want students to tell. The following more-structured essay items would require more thinking on the part of the student:

> Contrast the two periods of administration of Sir John A. Macdonald.
> Describe two major accomplishments of Pierre Trudeau's political life.
> What was important about each accomplishment?

- *Ask questions in a direct way.*

Essay questions can be used to assess the highest levels of cognitive learning (analysis, synthesis, evaluation). Yet it can be difficult to relate essay responses to intended learning outcomes because of students' freedom to select, organize, and express ideas. Teachers generally find that it takes less time to prepare an essay item than to prepare a selection of multiple-choice items. However, the process of scoring essays is time consuming, subjective, and may be unreliable; students' scores may be raised by their strong writing skills and their ability to bluff. Conversely, students' scores may be lowered by poor handwriting, misspelling, and grammatical errors.

One tool for assisting students in answering essay-item questions and facilitating teacher scoring and evaluation of essay items is the rubric. Rubrics are assessment scales that consist of a set of teacher or teacher–student defined criteria that describe levels of expectations. Rubrics provided prior to a task inform students about areas upon which they should focus their attention and study efforts. Rubrics provided after a test provide

www.mcgrawhill.ca/college/santrock

 Through the Eyes of Teachers

Rubrics Are a Teacher's Best Friend

Rubrics are a teacher's best friend! Keep them simple and, whenever possible, have students participate in developing the scoring criteria. Discuss the rubric with students so that they know how they will be evaluated before they start an assignment. Put yourself in their shoes. How many times did one of your teachers start a class by holding up the best assignment and saying, "This is what I expected"? How can students hit the target if they don't know where it is? I confess that when I first started teaching, I graded students' work in the same manner. I would find the brightest students' work and grade those assignments first. Their work became the baseline against which I compared the remaining students' work. Needless to say, many students were unhappy with their results using this format, and some questioned the basis for their grades. Since I started providing my students with rubrics, they have a much better sense of my expectations and how they will be evaluated.

Greg Voigt
Senior-High-School General Sciences and Biology Teacher
Member of the Assessment for Learning Committee
Alberta

Teaching Strategies
For Scoring Essays

✔ Avoid scoring bias
 • randomly assign numbers or aliases to student papers
 • match numbers or aliases with student names when recording scores
✔ Evaluate all answers to the same question together
 • read and score students' responses to one item before moving to another item
 • reread papers before handing them back to students
✔ Scoring can be holistic or analytical
 • holistic scoring focuses on the whole paper and assigns an overall letter or number grade
 • analytical scoring focuses on scoring various criteria separately and then adding up all the points to attain an overall grade or score
✔ Prepare a policy for dealing with errors, problems, or complaints
 • decide if grammar, spelling, and writing style will influence scoring and how
 • discuss the policy for errors, problems, or complaints with students prior to testing
✔ Provide feedback on the paper
 • write overall comments about the paper at the start or the end, along with brief comments throughout (e.g., "Unclear," "What does this mean and how does it apply to the question?" "An example here would support your statement")
 • written comments throughout provide opportunities to focus on how to improve essay-writing skills
✔ Outline and discuss what constitutes good or acceptable answers with students
 • prepare a rubric or scoring guide and discuss this with students prior to testing
 • follow the guide and discuss results with students afterward as a way to improve student skills in essay writing

students with clear and specific indicators about how they have performed and how they can improve. Rubrics are a template for focused analytical and objective measurement of students' learning.

At this point we have discussed a number of ideas about traditional tests. A review of these ideas is presented in Summary Table 14.2.

ALTERNATIVE ASSESSMENTS

There are alternatives to the traditional assessments that we just discussed. One current trend is to include performance assessments that require students to perform a task such as carry out a project, solve a real-world problem, or create a learning portfolio (Gronlund, Linn, & Davis, 2000; Popham, 2000). Alternative assessments are needed to make instruction compatible with contemporary views of learning and motivation.

Consider several alternative assessments that an intermediate-level arts teacher devised (Combs, 1997). She gave students a menu of options to choose from that included such formats as book reports, artwork, videos, and creating models. For example, in a unit on mystery, students might choose to write a report on an author of mystery stories, write an original mystery, make a children's mystery book, or conduct an interview with a private investigator. Each of these options comes with a detailed set of instructions and a scoring guide for quality control. Figure 14.3 provides another example, including directions and a scoring guide, of an alternative assessment for a unit on family history.

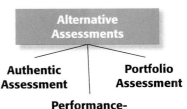

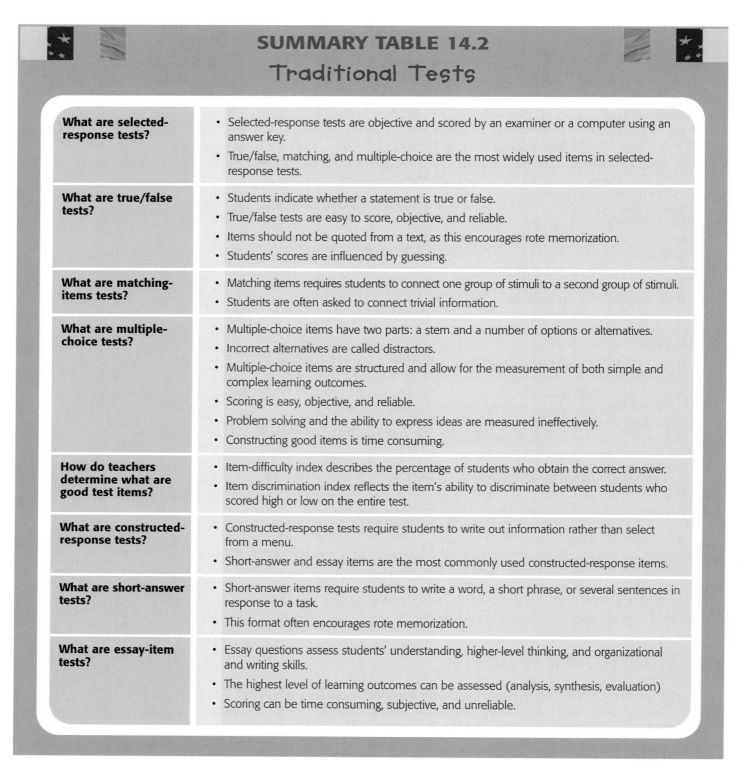

SUMMARY TABLE 14.2
Traditional Tests

What are selected-response tests?	• Selected-response tests are objective and scored by an examiner or a computer using an answer key. • True/false, matching, and multiple-choice are the most widely used items in selected-response tests.
What are true/false tests?	• Students indicate whether a statement is true or false. • True/false tests are easy to score, objective, and reliable. • Items should not be quoted from a text, as this encourages rote memorization. • Students' scores are influenced by guessing.
What are matching-items tests?	• Matching items requires students to connect one group of stimuli to a second group of stimuli. • Students are often asked to connect trivial information.
What are multiple-choice tests?	• Multiple-choice items have two parts: a stem and a number of options or alternatives. • Incorrect alternatives are called distractors. • Multiple-choice items are structured and allow for the measurement of both simple and complex learning outcomes. • Scoring is easy, objective, and reliable. • Problem solving and the ability to express ideas are measured ineffectively. • Constructing good items is time consuming.
How do teachers determine what are good test items?	• Item-difficulty index describes the percentage of students who obtain the correct answer. • Item discrimination index reflects the item's ability to discriminate between students who scored high or low on the entire test.
What are constructed-response tests?	• Constructed-response tests require students to write out information rather than select from a menu. • Short-answer and essay items are the most commonly used constructed-response items.
What are short-answer tests?	• Short-answer items require students to write a word, a short phrase, or several sentences in response to a task. • This format often encourages rote memorization.
What are essay-item tests?	• Essay questions assess students' understanding, higher-level thinking, and organizational and writing skills. • The highest level of learning outcomes can be assessed (analysis, synthesis, evaluation) • Scoring can be time consuming, subjective, and unreliable.

Authentic Assessment

Traditional assessment has involved the use of paper-and-pencil tests that are far removed from real-world contexts. An increasing trend is to assess students with items that more closely reflect reality (Palomba & Bantai, 1999). **Authentic assessment** *means evaluating students' knowledge or skills in a context that approximates the real world or real life as closely as possible.* The emphasis is on the process as well as the product. Learning

Family Unit Option
Family Tree Poster

Directions:
Make a poster of your family tree, you must go back at least 3 generations. Provide as much information about family member as possible, including but not limited to birthdate, death date (if not living), occupation, place of birth, accomplishments, etc. In addition, provide at least two anecdotes about your family's history (how they came to live in our town, special notoriety, honours, awards, medals, etc.). You must write out your family tree! (You may not make a copy of a commercially prepared family tree and paste it on the poster.) Make your poster attractive and neat!

Scoring Guide

25	Family tree includes at least three generations prior to you
25	In addition to names, most entries include information such as birth, death, and place of birth
25	Poster includes at least two anecdotes about interesting or well-known family members
15	Poster is neatly and attractively typed or written by you
10	Mechanics, spelling, usage

FIGURE 14.3 **Example of an Alternative Assessment**

is an ongoing process leading toward the achievement of an established outcome, with students' progress being recorded along the way. With authentic assessment, both teachers and students are involved in formative assessments. Instructional modifications follow as a natural outcome of authentic assessment, as these tools provide teachers with critical information about how to guide students' learning efforts (Montgomery, 2000).

Critics of authentic assessment argue that such assessments are not necessarily superior to more conventional assessments, such as multiple-choice and essay tests (Terwilliger, 1997). They say that the proponents of authentic assessment rarely present data in support of the validity of authentic assessments. Because authenticity is learner-specific, it is difficult to make reliable judgments about performances across students. Little is known about judgment reliability in authentic assessments (Tanner, 2001). Others argue that authentic assessments do not examine knowledge and basic skills adequately. Finally, it may be difficult to measure students' learning immediately following authentic instruction, as considerable time and practice is needed before they can demonstrate skills proficiently (Campbell, 2000).

Performance-based Assessment

Moving from traditional assessment with objective tests to performance-based assessment has been described as going from "knowing" to "showing" (Burz & Marshall, 1996). *Performance-based assessment* requires students to complete tasks that demonstrate their ability to apply knowledge and skills, or to put their understanding into action, in simulated or real-life situations (Muraki, Hombo, & Lee, 2000). Many performance-based assessments include an emphasis on open-ended tasks that assess higher-order thinking (Hambleton, 1996). Most assessment activities have no correct, objective answer. Assessment may take place over an extended interval and may be based on a group or individual performance. Figure 14.4 outlines a performance-based assessment tool in science (Solano-Flores & Shavelson, 1997). In this example, students must model a problem and monitor their observations. Solutions are proposed and students' performances are scored for accuracy and scientific reasoning.

Performance-based assessments use direct methods of evaluation, such as writing samples to assess writing skills and verbal presentations to assess speaking skills. Observing students give oral presentations is a

Performance-based assessment requires students to complete tasks that demonstrate understanding in action.

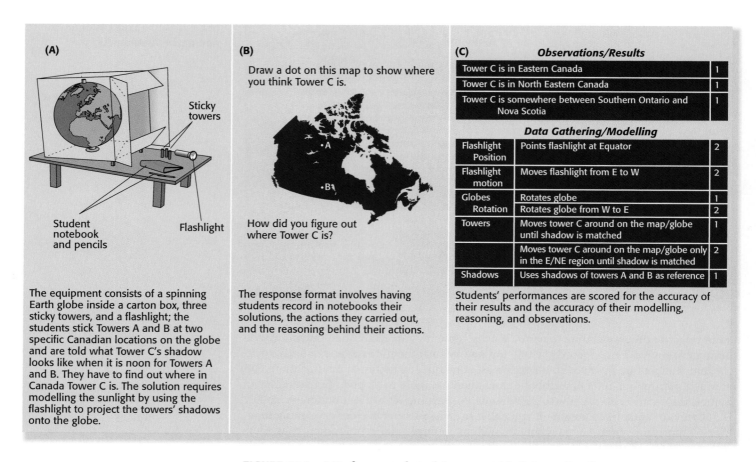

(A)

Sticky towers

Student notebook and pencils

Flashlight

The equipment consists of a spinning Earth globe inside a carton box, three sticky towers, and a flashlight; the students stick Towers A and B at two specific Canadian locations on the globe and are told what Tower C's shadow looks like when it is noon for Towers A and B. They have to find out where in Canada Tower C is. The solution requires modelling the sunlight by using the flashlight to project the towers' shadows onto the globe.

(B)

Draw a dot on this map to show where you think Tower C is.

•A

•B

How did you figure out where Tower C is?

The response format involves having students record in notebooks their solutions, the actions they carried out, and the reasoning behind their actions.

(C)

Observations/Results	
Tower C is in Eastern Canada	1
Tower C is in North Eastern Canada	1
Tower C is somewhere between Southern Ontario and Nova Scotia	1

Data Gathering/Modelling		
Flashlight Position	Points flashlight at Equator	2
Flashlight motion	Moves flashlight from E to W	2
Globes Rotation	Rotates globe	1
	Rotates globe from W to E	2
Towers	Moves tower C around on the map/globe until shadow is matched	1
	Moves tower C around on the map/globe only in the E/NE region until shadow is matched	2
Shadows	Uses shadows of towers A and B as reference	1

Students' performances are scored for the accuracy of their results and the accuracy of their modelling, reasoning, and observations.

FIGURE 14.4   A Performance-based Assessment in Science: Daytime Astronomy

more direct assessment than asking them a series of questions about speaking skills on a paper-and-pencil test. Similarly, allowing students to use calculators or computers in solving math problems on tests reflects closer ties to the real world than requiring students to do them with only paper and pencil. When students have to solve math problems in the real world, they likely will use calculators and computers.

In many performance-based activities, there is no correct, objective answer. For example, there is no correct answer when students give talks in class, create paintings, perform gymnastic routines, or design science projects.

Some performance-based assessments evaluate how effectively a group of students perform, not just how the students perform individually. A group of students might be assigned to create a science project rather than having each student do a project individually. Evaluation can include both each individual's contribution and the group's product. Group projects are often complex and allow for the assessment of cooperative skills, communication skills, and leadership skills. In traditional assessment, assessment occurs in a single time frame. For example, a teacher gives a multiple-choice test and students are allowed an hour to take it. However, it is not unusual for performance assessments to involve sustained work over days, weeks, and even months (Bracken, 2000). For example, a student might be evaluated once each month on the progress the student is making on a science project, and then receive a final evaluation when the project is completed. Some performance assessments involve having students evaluate their own performances. This emphasis shifts responsibility away from teachers and places it more squarely on students' shoulders. For example, students might be asked to judge the quality of their own dance performance, oral presentation, or dramatic acting.

Many performance-based assessments give students considerable freedom to construct their own responses rather than narrowing their range of answers. Although this

Criteria That Are General and Not Well Organized

Speaks clearly and slowly
Makes eye contact
Shows good effort
Understands the topic
Organizes effectively

Pronounces correctly
Exhibits good posture when presenting
Presents with feeling
Has an enthusiastic attitude

Criteria That Are Specific and Well Organized

I. PHYSICAL EXPRESSION
Stands straight and faces audience
Changes facial expression with changes in the tone of the report
Maintains eye contact with audience

II. VOCAL EXPRESSION
Speaks in a steady, clear voice
Varies tone to emphasize points
Speaks loudly enough to be heard by audience
Paces words in an even flow
Enunciates each word

III. VERBAL EXPRESSION
Chooses precise words to convey meaning
Avoids unnecessary repetition
States sentences with complete thoughts or ideas
Organizes information logically
Summarizes main points at conclusion

FIGURE 14.5 **Examples of Performance Criteria for Oral Presentations**

makes scoring difficult, it provides a context for evaluating students' higher-order thinking skills, such as the ability to think deeply about an issue or a topic (Wiggins, 1993; Muraki, Hombo, & Lee, 2000).

Guidelines for Using Performance-based Assessment Guidelines for using performance-based assessments cover four general issues (Airasian, 1997): establishing a clear purpose; identifying performance criteria; providing an appropriate setting; and scoring or rating the performance.

Make sure that any performance-based assessment has a clear purpose and that a clear decision can be made from the assessment (McKinley, Boulet, & Hambleton, 2000). The purposes can be diverse: to assign a grade, to evaluate students' progress, to recognize the important steps in a performance, to generate products to be included in a learning portfolio, to provide concrete examples of students' work for admission to university, and so forth.

Performance criteria *are specific behaviours that students need to perform effectively as part of the assessment.* Establishing performance criteria helps you to go beyond general descriptions (e.g., "Do an oral presentation," or "Complete a science project") of what students need to do. Performance criteria help you make your observations more systematic and focused. As guidelines, they direct your observations. Without such criteria, your observations can be unsystematic and haphazard. Communicating these performance criteria to students at the beginning of instruction lets students know how to focus their learning. Figure 14.5 contrasts examples of weak and effective criteria for oral presentations.

Once you have clearly defined the performance criteria, it is important to specify the setting in which you will observe the performance or product. You may want to observe behaviours directly in the regular flow of classroom activity, in a special context you create in the classroom, or in a context outside the classroom. As a rule, it is a good idea to observe students on more than one occasion, because a single performance might not fairly represent the students' knowledge or skills.

Finally, you will need to score or rate the performance, either holistically or analytically. The performance criteria you established earlier provide the key dimensions for scoring. Some teachers use scales to rate students' performance. For example, a teacher could rate each of the criteria listed in Figure 14.5 on a four-point scale: 1 = never, 2 = seldom, 3 = usually, and 4 = always.

Evaluating Performance-based Assessments   Many educational psychologists endorse the increased use of performance-based assessment (Eisner, 1999; Neil, 1997; Stiggins, 1997). They believe performance-based assessments involve students more in their learning, often encourage higher-order thinking skills, can measure what is really important in the curriculum, and can tie assessment more to real-world, real-life experiences.

Evaluating performance-based assessments can pose a challenge to teachers who are seeking to measure students' work objectively and consistently. This is especially the case when the performance-based assessment includes a written component. Technology may offer some support to teachers attempting to objectively score essays. For example, The Electronic Essay Rater (e-rater) analyzes essay features based on characteristics specified by a six-point rating scale that measures syntactic variety, structure analysis, and content analysis; agreement between the e-rater and human raters is relatively high (Muraki, Hombo, & Lee, 2000).

Although support for performance-based assessment is high in many areas of Canada and the United States, effective implementation faces several hurdles (Hambleton, 1996). Performance assessment often takes considerably more time to construct, administer, and score than objective tests. Also, many performance-based assessments do not meet the standards of validity and reliability outlined by such groups as the American Educational Research Association and the Canadian Psychological Association (Guidelines for Education and Psychological Testing, 1996). To have validity, the content contained in performance-based assessments should be relevant, replicable, and related to other measures and constructs (Miller & Linn, 2000).

Although planning, constructing, and scoring performance tests is challenging, teachers should make every effort to include performance assessments as one aspect of their assessment repertoire (Mabry, 1999).

Portfolio Assessment

Interest in portfolio assessment has mushroomed in recent years. Portfolios represent a significant departure from traditional tests of learning. Figure 14.6 summarizes the contrast between portfolios and traditional testing.

What Is a Portfolio?   A **portfolio** *consists of a systematic and organized collection of a student's work that demonstrates the student's skills and accomplishments* (Lankes, 1995). A portfolio is a purposeful collection of work that tells the story of the student's progress and achievements (Arter, 1995). It is much more than a compilation of student papers stuffed into a manila folder or a collection of memorabilia pasted into a scrapbook (Barton & Collins, 1997; Hatch, 2000). To qualify for inclusion in a portfolio, each piece of work should be created and organized in a way that demonstrates progress and purpose. Portfolios can include many different types of work, such as writing samples, journal entries, videotapes, art, teacher comments, posters, interviews, poetry, test results, problem solutions, recordings of foreign language communication, self-assessments, and any other expression of the student that the teacher believes demonstrates the student's skills and accomplishments. Portfolios can be collected on paper, in photographs, and on audiotape, videotape, computer disk, or CD-ROM. Assessment expert Joan Herman (1996) states that portfolio assessment has become increasingly popular because it is a natural way to integrate instruction and assessment.

Four classes of evidence that can be placed in students' portfolios are artifacts, reproductions, attestations, and productions (Barton & Collins, 1997). **Artifacts** *are documents or products, such as papers and homework, that are produced during normal academic work in the classroom.* **Reproductions** *consist of documentation of a student's work outside the classroom, such as special projects and interviews.* For example, a student's

Traditional Tests	Portfolios
• Separate learning, testing, and teaching	• Link assessment and teaching to learning
• Fail to assess the impact of prior knowledge on learning by using short passages that are often isolated and unfamiliar	• Address the importance of students' prior knowledge as a critical determinant to learning by using authentic assessment activities
• Rely on materials requesting only literal information	• Provide opportunities to demonstrate inferential and critical thinking that are essential for constructing meaning
• Prohibit collaboration during the assessment process	• Represent a collaborative approach to assessment involving both students and teachers
• Often treat skills in isolated contexts to determine achievement for reporting purposes	• Use multi-faceted activities while recognizing that learning requires integration and coordination of communication skills
• Assess students across a limited range of assignments that may not match what students do in classrooms	• Represent the full range of instructional activities that students are doing in their classrooms
• Assess students in a predetermined situation where the content is fixed	• Can measure students' abilities to perform appropriately in unanticipated situations
• Assess all students on the same dimensions	• Measure students' achievements while allowing individual differences
• Address only achievement	• Address improvement, effort, and achievement
• Seldom provide vehicles for assessing students' abilities to monitor their own learning	• Implements self-assessment by having students monitor their learning
• Are mechanically scored or scored by teachers who have little input into the assessment	• Engage students in assessing their progress and/or accomplishments and establishing ongoing learning goals
• Rarely include items that assess emotional responses to learning	• Provide opportunities to reflect upon feelings about learning

FIGURE 14.6   **Contrasting Traditional Tests and Portfolios**

description of an interview with a local scientist about the scientist's work is a reproduction. **Attestations** *represent the teacher's or other responsible person's documentation of the student's progress.* For example, a teacher might write evaluative notes about a student's oral presentation and place them in the student's portfolio. **Productions** *are documents the student prepares especially for the portfolio.* Productions consist of three types of materials: goal statements, reflections, and captions. Students generate goal statements about what they want to accomplish with their portfolio, write down their reflections about their work and describe their progress, and create captions that describe each piece of work in the portfolio and its importance.

Using Portfolios Effectively   Effective use of portfolios for assessment requires establishing the portfolio's purpose, involving the student in decisions about it, and evaluating the portfolio.

Establishing Purpose   Portfolios can be used for different purposes (Lyons, 1999). Two broad purposes are to document growth and to show best work. A **growth portfolio** *consists of the student's work over an extended time frame (throughout the school year or even longer) to reveal the student's progress in meeting learning targets.* Growth portfolios also are sometimes referred to as "developmental portfolios." Growth portfolios are especially helpful in providing concrete evidence of how much a student has changed or learned over time. As students examine their portfolios, they can see for themselves how much they have improved. One example of this type of portfolio is the French-language portfolio used

www.mcgrawhill.ca/college/santrock

in L.A. Matheson Secondary School in Surrey, British Columbia. As part of French instruction, students are required to produce a personal scrapbook that reflects what they have learned about themselves and the French language throughout the year. The scrapbook portfolio includes samples of students' work, cultural items collected outside the classroom, and reflective writings. The scrapbook is assessed at several designated times during the year by the students and the teacher using student/teacher–generated criteria, and is presented publicly at the end of the school year.

A **best-work portfolio** *showcases the student's most outstanding work.* Sometimes it is even called a "showcase portfolio." Best-work portfolios are more selective than developmental portfolios and often include the student's latest product. Best-work portfolios are especially useful for parent–teacher conferences, future teachers, and admission to higher education programs. Best-work or showcase portfolios are becoming more common in Canadian programs. Evans (1999), a faculty member of the Ontario Institute for Studies in Education at the University of Toronto, describes the UNITE project, which requires Grade 9 students to complete a cross-curricular portfolio. Students include samples of work that represent personal accomplishments in writing, social science, math, art, drama, and music throughout the school year. Students are also required to make reflective entries for each item, providing a rationale for their selections. Portfolios are shared with parents and other teachers. Evans (1999) states that portfolio assessment fits best with subjects like history and social studies where there is a clear congruency among learning outcomes, pedagogical strategies, and performance standards, and where constructivist models of teaching have emphasized process-oriented and authentic learning outcomes.

Involving Students in Selecting Portfolio Materials   Many teachers let students make at least some of the decisions about the portfolio's contents (Shaklee et al., 1997). Student-led parent conferences allow students to demonstrate to parents what they have learned (Little & Allan, 1988). When students are allowed to choose the contents for their own portfolios, a good strategy is to encourage self-reflection by having them write a brief description about why they selected each piece of work (Airasian, 1997). In this way, portfolios can enhance students' critical thinking, self-reflection, and articulation skills (Earl & Katz, 2000). It is important to explain to students at the beginning of the year what portfolios are and how they will be used. You also should have a number of student–teacher conferences throughout the year to review students' progress and help them to plan future work for the portfolio (McMillan, 1997; Weldin & Tumarkin, 1999).

Evaluating Portfolios   Clear and systematic performance criteria are essential for effectively using portfolios (Linn & Gronlund, 2000; Ruiz-Primo, Li, Ayala, & Shavelson, 2000). Clear learning targets for students makes developing performance criteria much easier. Ask yourself what knowledge and skills you want your students to possess. This should be the focus of your teaching and your performance criteria. Scoring and judging portfolios is time consuming (Airasian, 1997). Teachers must evaluate not only each individual item but also the portfolio as a whole. When the portfolio's purpose is to provide descriptive information about the student for the teacher at the next grade level, no scoring or summarizing of the portfolio might be necessary. However, when its purpose is to diagnose, reflect improvement, provide evidence for effective instruction, motivate students to reflect on their work, or determine students' grades, summary scoring and judgments need to be made. Checklists and rating scales are commonly used for this purpose. As with other aspects of portfolio assessment, some teachers provide students the opportunity to evaluate and critique their own work.

Evaluating the Role of Portfolios in Assessment   Learning portfolios have several strengths: their comprehensive nature captures the complexity and completeness of students' works and accomplishments. They provide opportunities for encouraging student decision-making and self-reflection. They moti-

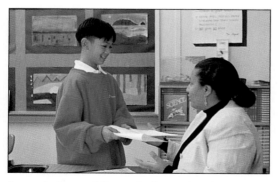

Increasingly, portfolios and other authentic assessment methods are finding a place beside traditional paper-and-pencil assessments.

Planning My Assessment Philosophy

Rate each of the assessments on this scale: 1 = Use often, 2 = May use, 3 = Will not use.

	1	2	3
1. Informal observations as a part of before-instruction assessment			
2. Structured exercises as a part of before-instruction assessment			
3. Observation during instruction			
4. Questions during instruction			
5. Assessments of students' affect			
6. True/false items			
7. Multiple-choice items			
8. Matching items			
9. Audiovisual context setting			
10. Problem sets			
11. Short-answer items			
12. Essays			
13. Authentic assessment			
14. Experiments			
15. Projects			
16. Oral presentations			
17. Interviews			
18. Performances			
19. Exhibitions			
20. Growth portfolios			
21. Best-work portfolios			

vate students to think critically and deeply. And they provide an excellent mechanism for evaluating student progress and improvement.

Learning portfolios also have several weaknesses: They take considerable time to coordinate and evaluate. Their complexity and uniqueness mean that they are difficult to evaluate, and their reliability is often much lower than for traditional tests. Teachers are sometimes required to make difficult decisions about the amount and kind of assistance that they should give to students during portfolio assembly. Finally, teachers may find themselves evaluating their own performances as portfolio readers (Callahan, 2001).

Even with these weaknesses in mind, most educational psychology experts and educational organizations, such as the National Council for the Social Studies and the Canadian Teachers' Federation, support the use of portfolios and similar alternatives to traditional tests (NCSS, 2002; Canadian Teachers' Federation, 1999).

We have discussed many types of assessment, and this is a good time to consider what your classroom assessment philosophy will be. Self-Assessment 14.1 above may help you form this philosophy.

At this point we have studied a number of ideas about alternative assessments. A review of these ideas is presented in Summary Table 14.3.

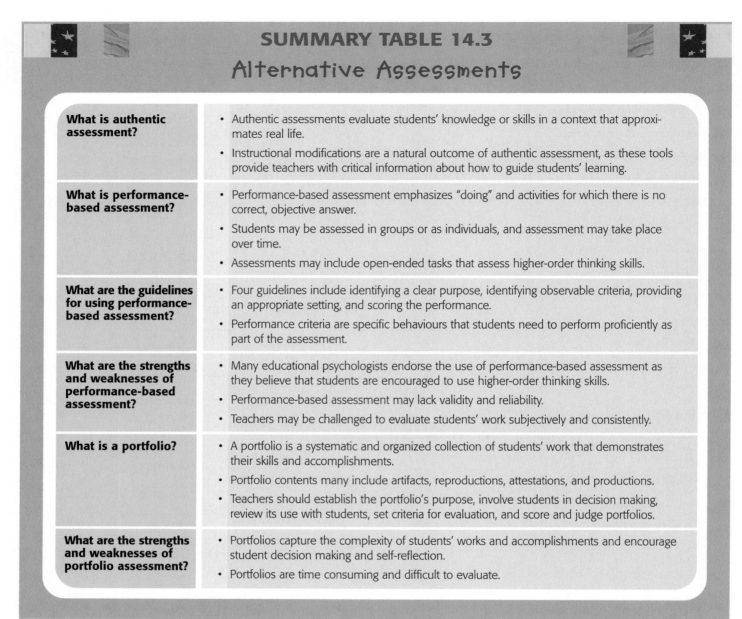

SUMMARY TABLE 14.3
Alternative Assessments

What is authentic assessment?	• Authentic assessments evaluate students' knowledge or skills in a context that approximates real life. • Instructional modifications are a natural outcome of authentic assessment, as these tools provide teachers with critical information about how to guide students' learning.
What is performance-based assessment?	• Performance-based assessment emphasizes "doing" and activities for which there is no correct, objective answer. • Students may be assessed in groups or as individuals, and assessment may take place over time. • Assessments may include open-ended tasks that assess higher-order thinking skills.
What are the guidelines for using performance-based assessment?	• Four guidelines include identifying a clear purpose, identifying observable criteria, providing an appropriate setting, and scoring the performance. • Performance criteria are specific behaviours that students need to perform proficiently as part of the assessment.
What are the strengths and weaknesses of performance-based assessment?	• Many educational psychologists endorse the use of performance-based assessment as they believe that students are encouraged to use higher-order thinking skills. • Performance-based assessment may lack validity and reliability. • Teachers may be challenged to evaluate students' work subjectively and consistently.
What is a portfolio?	• A portfolio is a systematic and organized collection of students' work that demonstrates their skills and accomplishments. • Portfolio contents many include artifacts, reproductions, attestations, and productions. • Teachers should establish the portfolio's purpose, involve students in decision making, review its use with students, set criteria for evaluation, and score and judge portfolios.
What are the strengths and weaknesses of portfolio assessment?	• Portfolios capture the complexity of students' works and accomplishments and encourage student decision making and self-reflection. • Portfolios are time consuming and difficult to evaluate.

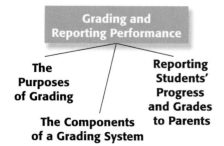

Grading and Reporting Performance

The Purposes of Grading

The Components of a Grading System

Reporting Students' Progress and Grades to Parents

GRADING AND REPORTING PERFORMANCE

Grading *means translating descriptive assessment information into letters, numbers, or other marks that indicate the quality of students' learning or performances.*

The Purposes of Grading

Grading is carried out to communicate meaningful information about students' learning and achievements. In this process, grades serve four basic purposes (Airasian, 1997):

- *Administrative.* Grades help determine students' class rank, credits for graduation, and whether they should be promoted to the next grade.
- *Informational.* Grades can be used to inform students, parents, and others (such as admissions officers) about their work. Grades represent the teacher's summary judgment about how well students have met instructional objectives and learning targets.

- *Motivational.* As we saw in Chapter 11, Motivating Students to Learn, teachers should promote students' intrinsic motivation. Nonetheless, in an educational world in which grades are given, many students work harder because they are motivated to achieve high grades and they fear low grades (extrinsic motivation). Some teachers do not like to give low grades because they believe they diminish students' motivation to learn. However, some critics believe that grade inflation—especially in the form of giving high grades for mediocre performance—provides students with a false belief that they are learning and achieving more than they actually are. The result is that many students discover they can perform well below their ability and still achieve high grades.
- *Guidance.* Grades help students, parents, and counsellors to select appropriate courses and levels of work for students. They provide information about which students might need special services and what types of future educational programs students will likely be able to complete.

While studying how beginning teachers grade students, Shulha (1999), a Queen's University professor, concluded that grading is a complex process influenced by the teacher, the learner, the learning environment, and the quality of the assessment strategies selected to generate information.

The Components of a Grading System

Grades reflect teachers' judgments. Three main types of teacher judgments underlie the grading system (Airasian, 1997): (1) What standard of comparison will be used for grading? (2) What aspects of students' performance will be used to establish grades? and (3) How will different kinds of evidence be weighted when giving grades?

Teachers must consider not only the context of the classroom but also the needs, interests, and abilities of their students when grading (Shulha, 1999). Canadian researchers Wilson and Martinussen (1999) found that beginning teachers allowed their expectations about how a student might perform to affect their judgments about that student's performance. In general, teachers placed greater weight on academic performance, effort, and improvement and less emphasis on homework (McMillan, Myran, & Workman, 2002).

Standards of Comparison   A student's performance can be graded by comparing it to the performance of other students (norm-referenced grading) or to predefined standards of performance (criterion-referenced grading).

Norm-referenced grading *is a grading system based on comparison of a student's performance with that of other students in the class or of other classes and other students.* Students who get high grades perform better than most of their classmates, students who get low grades perform more poorly than most of their classmates. Norm-referenced grading is commonly referred to as *grading on the curve.* In norm-referenced grading, the grading scale determines what percentages get particular grades. In most instances, the scale is created so that the largest percentage of students receive C's. This is a typical breakdown of grades: 15 percent A's, 25 percent B's, 40 percent C's, 15 percent D's, and 5 percent F's. In assigning grades, instructors often look for gaps in the range of scores. If six students score between 92 and 100 and 10 students score between 81 and 88, and there are no scores between 88 and 92, the teacher would assign a grade of A to the 92–100 scores and a B to the 81–88 scores. Norm-referenced grading has been criticized for reducing students' motivation, increasing their anxiety, increasing negative interactions among students, and hindering learning.

Through the Eyes of Students

Tests and Report-Card Grades

I do very well on French and social science tests. I do not do so well on science tests. I like the type of tests where you have to circle the right answer because they are easy to answer and do not take a long time to finish. When I get nervous, I do not do as well as I could.

I am trying to improve my grade in math. My goal is to practise a little every day, and I ask my parents to quiz me on my math facts. I also like it when my teacher comments on what I could do better. I hope to receive a better grade in math on my next report card.

Katie
Grade 5 Student
Loves Reading, Swimming, Playing Clarinet, and Collecting Stamps and Coins
Nova Scotia

"Your grading curve and my learning curve don't intersect."

Criterion-referenced grading *is a grading system based on comparison with predetermined standards.* All students who reach a particular level get the same grade. Sometimes criterion-referenced grading is called *absolute grading.* Typically, criterion-referenced grading is based on the proportion of points attained on a test or the level of mastery reached in a performance skill, such as giving an oral presentation and meeting all the predetermined criteria. Criterion-referenced grading is recommended over norm-referenced grading.

In theory, the standard established is supposed to be absolute, but in practice it doesn't always work out that way (McMillan, 1997). For example, a school board often develops a percentage grading system that goes something like this: A = 94–100, B = 87–93, C = 77–86, D = 70–76, F = Below 70. Although this system is absolute in the sense that every student must get 94 points to earn an A and every student who does not get at least 70 points gets an F, teachers and classrooms vary enormously in what constitutes mastery of material to get a 94, an 87, a 77, or a 70. One teacher might give very hard tests, another very easy tests.

Many teachers use different cutoff scores than the ones just mentioned. Some teachers argue that low grades discourage student motivation and refuse to give D's or F's; others won't fail students unless their scores fall below 50.

Aspects of Students' Performance   Over the course of a grading period, students will likely have created many products that can be evaluated and used to formulate their grades. These can include test and quiz results, as well as various alternative assessments such as oral reports, projects, interviews, and homework. Increasingly, portfolios are being used to grade students' work. Grades should be based mainly on academic performance, but teacher ratings of motivation and effort can be factored in as well.

Many teachers use tests as the main, or even sole, basis for assigning grades. A good strategy is to base an overall grade on a series of tests and other types of assessments. Thus, a semester grade in geography might be based on two major tests, a final examination, eight quizzes, homework, two oral reports, and a project. Basing a grade on a series of tests and different types of assessment helps to balance out students' strengths and weaknesses, as well as compensate for a poor performance or two because of internal and external sources of measurement errors.

Some educators advocate factoring affective characteristics such as motivation and effort into grades, especially by giving borderline students a plus or minus. Thus, a teacher might convert a B to a B+ if the student was highly motivated, put forth considerable effort, and actively participated in the class—or to a B– if the student was poorly motivated, made little effort, and did not actively participate. However, other educators believe that grades should be based on academic performance only. One of the problems with including factors such as effort in grades is the difficulty in determining the reliability and validity of effort.

Weighting Different Kinds of Evidence   You will need to determine how much weight to give the different components of students' work. Thus, in the earlier example of a geography class, the teacher will have to decide how much weight to give the major tests, final examination, quizzes, homework, oral report, and project. The teacher might arrive at a weighting system that looks something like this:

Major tests (2)	20%
Final examination	25%
Quizzes	20%
Homework	5%
Oral report	10%
Project	20%

Many teachers do not use homework as a component for a grade. However, there have been increasing calls for more rigorous use of homework as a means of improving public education. Canadian schools have considered raising grading and homework standards as a means to ensure quality education and as a criterion for funding to

I'd suggest instead of writing that little Billy lies about doing his homework, you write that he has difficulty distinguishing between factual and imaginary material.

© DiPetta, Benwell, 2003

schools (Betts & Ferrall, 1997). There are many implications to a more homework-focused system in schools. For example, if a student fails to turn in a certain number of homework assignments, some teachers lower the student's grade. Also, when a student's grade depends heavily on homework or other work outside class, parents might be tempted to do their child's work to ensure a good grade. Including homework as a component of grading also favours students who have better home environments. As with other aspects of classroom assessment, your judgment is involved in how you synthesize information to arrive at a student's grade.

Reporting Students' Progress and Grades to Parents

Grades are the most common method of informing students about their progress and performance in the classroom (Airasian, 1997). However, grades by themselves provide limited information, are usually given infrequently, do not specify how the student is learning, and rarely include information about the student's motivation, cooperation, and classroom behaviour. Because of these limitations, both grades and comments are needed to give parents a full portrait of the student. In a Canadian study of beginning teachers, only 13 percent provided comments specific enough to improve students' current work or extend their learning on future performances (Shulha, 1999). Teachers need to make conscious efforts to include comments that can extend and enhance students' learning and describe how this learning is transferable to future curriculum. A word of caution: although it is important to include positive, encouraging comments about students, parents appreciate being explicitly informed when their children are having difficulties.

Through the Eyes of Teachers

The Importance of Observation

As a teacher, you need concrete examples of student behaviour to support your assessment and evaluation activities. Observation is an important assessment tool for gathering examples of student behaviour, especially in the primary grades. I use large index cards to make observation records for each student in my kindergarten class. Every day, I select a few students for observation and monitor what they say and do during class activities. For example, during circle time, I will watch a student retell a story, recording any comprehension or pronunciation errors. I date each observation session so that I can monitor students' growth—academic and social—throughout the year.

I use information from the index cards when completing report cards and during interviews with parents. I draw examples from the information recorded on the index cards, as well as information obtained from other types of assessment tools including student portfolios and workbooks. Observational records are excellent tools for gathering and organizing information about student behaviour.

Anita Wong
Kindergarten Teacher
Ontario

The Report Card The report card is a standard method of reporting students' progress and grades to parents. The form of judgments on report cards varies from one school board to another, and, in many cases, from one grade level to another. Some report cards convey letter grades (typically A, B, C, D, and F, sometimes also allowing pluses and minuses). Some report cards convey numerical scores (such as 91 in math, 85 in English, and so on). Other report cards have a pass/fail category in one or more subjects. Yet other report cards have checklists indicating skills or objectives that the student has attained. Some report cards have categories for affective characteristics, such as effort, cooperation, and other appropriate and inappropriate behaviours. Many report cards also have space for a teacher's written, summative comments.

In the higher elementary-school grade levels and secondary schools, letter grades are mainly used, although these might be accompanied by other information such as written comments. Checklists of skills and objectives are mainly used at the primary-grade level. In many school boards, there is spirited debate about what form of grading should be used and what should be included on report cards.

Written Progress Reports Another reporting strategy is to provide parents with a weekly, biweekly, or monthly report of students' progress and achievement (McMillan, 1997). These written reports can include the student's performance on tests and quizzes, projects, oral reports, and so on. They also can include information about the student's motivation, cooperation, and behaviour, as well as suggestions for how parents can help students improve their performance.

> Teaching Strategies
> For Parent-Teacher Conferences
>
> ✔ For academic, social, or behavioural problems that affect classroom teaching, teachers should:
>   • focus on problem solving and helping students
>   • be professional, punctual, and courteous by welcoming parents and sitting eye-to-eye
>   • promise only what they can deliver
>   • apologize when they are wrong
> ✔ For parents' concerns with the curriculum, materials, assessment methods, or classroom management, teachers should:
>   • listen to parents' concerns and comments
>   • be open, empathize, and remember that parents are advocating for their child
>   • consider the cultural differences and backgrounds of parents
>   • be open to constructive criticism
>   • show parents examples of students' work
> ✔ For problems identified by students such as bullying, disagreements with peers/teachers, or curriculum that is too challenging, teachers should:
>   • gather all the facts and define the problem
>   • work with parents, other professionals, and the students to identify several possible solution strategies
>   • discuss the solution choices with the parents and the student and focus on helping the student
>   • implement the chosen plan; monitor and adjust as needed
>
> **Source:** Adapted from McKewan (1998)

"I don't know why you're so surprised by his poor grades. Every day you asked him what he did at school, and every day he answered, 'Nothing.'"

Parent–Teacher Conferences   Parent–teacher conferences are another way to communicate information about grades and assessment. Such conferences are both a responsibility and an opportunity (Payne, 1997). Parents have a right to know how their child is doing in school and how their child might improve. Conferences provide an opportunity for giving parents helpful information about how they can be partners with you in helping their child learn more effectively. Refer to the Teaching Strategies box above for more suggestions.

Computers and Assessment

Constructing, Printing, Administering, and Scoring Tests

Record Keeping

Electronic Portfolios

COMPUTERS AND ASSESSMENT

Computers can be used to construct, print, administer, and score tests, provide a medium for portfolios, and maintain student records (Gronlund, 1998). Concerns about the validity and reliability of assessment using a computer are no different than for paper-and-pencil measures.

Constructing, Printing, Administering, and Scoring Tests

One way computers can aid test construction is through item-banking. This consists of maintaining test item files that can be retrieved for preparing a test. Items typically are coded by subject area, instructional level, instructional objective measured, and item difficulty.

Computers can be used to print tests from the item bank. The coded information about each item makes it possible to create different forms of tests, such as a test arranged by instructional objective or increasing difficulty.

E-Portfolios in Teaching and Learning

Manitoba's departments of Education and Youth and Advanced Education and Training define electronic portfolios (e-portfolios) as a "selective and purposeful" collection of student work samples that are created in digital form, scanned from original hand work or photographs, or captured using a digital or video camera (see **www.edu.gov.mb.ca/ks4/tech/imym/faqs/portfolios.html#1**).

E-portfolios are also a means for connecting students to learning communities that span the classroom, school, or globe. Scardamalia and Bereiter (2000) suggest that schools, universities, cultural institutions, service organizations, and businesses can network electronically to create computer-supported intentional learning environments. (CSILE, a software program to create intentional learning environments online, is discussed in this text in Chapter 10.) Scardamalia and Bereiter observed that students who used the CSILE network system for learning were better able to comprehend difficult information, demonstrated higher-quality

reflections, provided greater depth of explanation, and demonstrated more mature beliefs about learning than did students who were not provided the opportunity to participate in CSILE. These findings suggest that the social construction of knowledge takes place in electronic learning environments and helps students make meaning of learned concepts.

According to Barrett (1998), e-portfolio assignments should include a statement of learning goals, guidelines for selecting materials (to keep the collection from growing haphazardly), work samples chosen by the student and the teacher, teacher feedback, student self-reflections, evaluation rubrics, and examples of exemplary work. Barrett states that the ways in which e-portfolios are used best will depend on the nature and purpose of the assessment, the available technology, and any constraints associated with storage and presentation of the portfolio.

Computers also can be used directly in the administration of tests. The student is presented with test items on a computer screen and answers the items accordingly. After the test is administered, the computer can be used to score the test and arrange the scores in different ways. Computer scoring especially can be helpful in relieving teachers from the time-consuming task of scoring test-item responses. Although the assessment data can be analyzed by a computer, computers are not capable of including common sense, intuition, and judgment of effort in their analysis. Much of what is involved in making decisions about performance scores relies on the teacher's interpretation and judgment, just as with paper-and-pencil measures (Jones, 1999).

Electronic Portfolios

As we saw earlier in the chapter, portfolio assessment is increasingly common. The terms *electronic portfolio* and *computer-based portfolio* are used to describe portfolio work that is saved in an electronic format (Lankes, 1995; 1998). The record can include text, graphics, sound, and video (Barrett, 1994; Lankes, 1998). Thus, students can save writing samples, math solutions, samples of art work, depictions of science projects, and multimedia presentations in an electronic portfolio. A single computer with a large storage capacity can store portfolios for all the students in a class. If a number of students store multimedia material, a floppy or hard disk might not have sufficient storage. An alternative is to store students' portfolios on a "rewritable" compact disc (CD-RW, a compact disc that stores text, sound, graphics, and video). A computer-based portfolio allows for easy transfer of information from teacher to teacher or school to school. The vision is that student transcripts will eventually be replaced with electronic portfolios that include a full history of the student's classroom performances, work samples, and activities. To read further about electronic portfolios, see the Technology and Education box above.

Record Keeping

Record keeping is a burden for many teachers. Assessment information represents a considerable chunk of this record keeping. Computer technology can help to reduce the burden of record keeping (Maddux, Johnson, & Willis, 1997). For example, electronic grade

www.mcgrawhill.ca/college/santrock

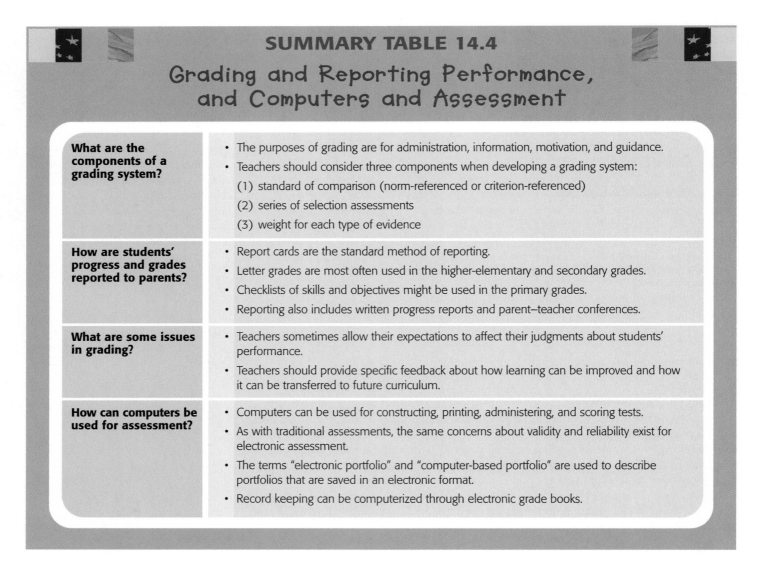

SUMMARY TABLE 14.4

Grading and Reporting Performance, and Computers and Assessment

What are the components of a grading system?	• The purposes of grading are for administration, information, motivation, and guidance. • Teachers should consider three components when developing a grading system: (1) standard of comparison (norm-referenced or criterion-referenced) (2) series of selection assessments (3) weight for each type of evidence
How are students' progress and grades reported to parents?	• Report cards are the standard method of reporting. • Letter grades are most often used in the higher-elementary and secondary grades. • Checklists of skills and objectives might be used in the primary grades. • Reporting also includes written progress reports and parent–teacher conferences.
What are some issues in grading?	• Teachers sometimes allow their expectations to affect their judgments about students' performance. • Teachers should provide specific feedback about how learning can be improved and how it can be transferred to future curriculum.
How can computers be used for assessment?	• Computers can be used for constructing, printing, administering, and scoring tests. • As with traditional assessments, the same concerns about validity and reliability exist for electronic assessment. • The terms "electronic portfolio" and "computer-based portfolio" are used to describe portfolios that are saved in an electronic format. • Record keeping can be computerized through electronic grade books.

books can keep track of students' grades in a course. Electronic grade books are available in many shapes and sizes—teachers can create their own using spreadsheet software (e.g., Microsoft Excel, or Lotus 1-2-3), or use one of the ready-made programs available as freeware (e.g., ClassRoom Windows, MarkBook 2002 for PCs, Grade Machine for Macs). MarkBook is currently one of the most commonly used grading programs in North America. The program can help teachers in managing data, planning student assessment, and reporting and communicating student achievement.

Electronic grade books can save teachers hours of work by automatically calculating and updating midterm and final grades, analyzing class results, printing anonymous lists, or exporting student results to other electronic systems. Some electronic grade book programs have parent access options.

Teachers can also acquire Web-based tools for managing attendance rosters and grade books through organizations like TeleEducation New Brunswick, an organization committed to the use of technology in education (**http://teleeducation.nb.ca**).

At this point we have studied a number of ideas about grading and performance, as well as computers and assessment. A review of these ideas is presented in Summary Table 14.4.

Mr. Huber was using traditional, multiple-choice tests in his Grade 12 history class. The students seemed bored with studying for these tests and with his lectures. Therefore, for the unit on ancient Mesopotamia, he decided to allow the students to complete a project instead of taking a test. Along with his student teacher, Ms. Benjamin, he gave these choices:

Construct a test covering the chapter on Mesopotamia.
Create a game about Mesopotamia.
Create a diorama about Mesopotamia.
Write a play about life in Mesopotamia.
Create artifacts from Mesopotamia that an archaeologist might find.

Ms. Benjamin told the students that they could not use a computer to complete their project.

Andrea, a student in the class, decided to write a test for her project. She carefully read the chapter and constructed questions as she went along. She used short-answer questions because she was worried about constructing good multiple-choice questions. It had been her experience that the distractors used in these questions were often confusing. She felt the same way about true/false questions. She wanted to make her questions as clear as possible because she didn't want her classmates to be mad at her when they took her test.

Andrea carefully printed each question and then created an answer key, which she intended to use to grade her classmates' tests. The final product consisted of 25 short-answer questions. She was very proud of her work the day she turned it in.

Mr. Huber looked at her test and told her, "This isn't acceptable. Why didn't you type it?"

"Ms. Benjamin told us we couldn't use computers."

"That isn't what she meant. She meant you couldn't use the Internet," responded Mr. Huber. "Take it home and type it. Turn it in tomorrow."

Andrea left the room, very upset. She took her test home, and carefully typed both the test and the key. She turned them in the next day. Three days later, Andrea received these marks:

Content: **B+** Should have included a variety of question types, such as multiple-choice, matching, and true/false.
Mechanics: **A** Nicely typed. Correct spelling used.
Accuracy: **B**
Effort: **C−**
Grade: **C**

Andrea was upset with her grade. "C-minus for effort?! I worked really hard on this! I even had to do it twice, 'cause of stupid Ms. Benjamin!" She took her grade sheet and test home and showed it to her mother. Andrea's mother was equally upset, particularly about the low grade for effort. She called Mr. Huber, asking to see the guidelines for the project and the grading rubric. Mr. Huber was unable to provide either. She asked him the difference between content and accuracy. He could not tell her. She also asked him how he had measured effort, to which he responded, "I consider what I expect from a student and then what they give me."

- What are the issues involved in this situation?
- What did Mr. Huber do wrong?
- How should he have gone about developing his alternative assessments?
- How should he have developed his grading guide?
- What do you think of the practice of including an effort grade on students' projects? Why?

CHAPTER REVIEW

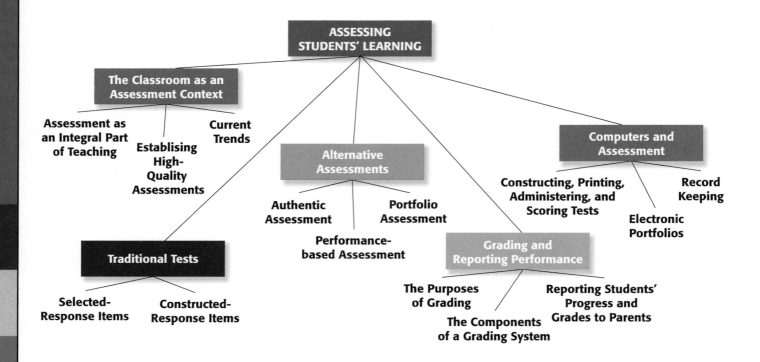

To obtain a detailed review of this chapter, study these four summary tables:

 KEY TERMS

formative assessment 449
summative assessment 450
reliability 451
validity 451
content-related evidence 451
instructional validity 451
pluralistic assessment 452
objective tests 453

performance assessments 453
selected-response items 454
multiple-choice item 455
problem sets 458
item-difficulty index 458
item-discrimination index 459
constructed-response item 459
short-answer item 459

essay items 459
authentic assessment 462
performance criteria 465
portfolio 466
artifacts 466
reproductions 466
attestations 467
productions 467

growth portfolio 467
best-work portfolio 468
grading 470
norm-referenced grading 471
criterion-referenced grading 472

PROFESSIONAL DEVELOPMENT/PORTFOLIO ACTIVITIES

1. What's the Difference?

There is significant disagreement about the value of standardized tests versus alternative assessment methods such as performance and portfolio assessment. Write a brief statement of your views on student assessment. Do standardized tests provide an accurate picture of student ability, or do they provide only a portion of the assessment picture? What are the limits of standardized tests? What is your assessment plan for students in your classroom? When you have finished writing your assessment statement, put it in your portfolio.

2. Your Tests Are Biased!

Talking to parents about their children's grades or evaluation is sometimes a difficult task. With a colleague, consider and respond to the following scenario. At a parent–teacher meeting a father and mother suggest that their son, who earns A's in other classes, is getting B's in your class because your tests are inherently biased against boys. Throughout the year you have used a variety of assessment methods and you have maintained portfolios of students' work. How do you respond to these parents? How can teachers guard against writing or using biased assessment instruments?

3. Assessment Now and Then

With a colleague, discuss the aims of assessment before, during, and after instruction. Reflect on the best teacher you had in high school and what methods of assessment he or she used. Share your reflections with your colleagues.

INTERNET ACTIVITIES

1. E-Portfolios

Paired with someone from your class, browse the Web to find examples of K–12 electronic student portfolios. What are the typical components or artifacts that go into an electronic portfolio? What are some of the benefits for teachers and students of using electronic portfolios to showcase and archive student work? What are some of the tools or skills that you will need to help your students create e-portfolios? Where might you find resources or help to create e-portfolios?

2. Assessment Rubrics

Your Grade 7 students are engaged in a one-week collaborative project researching and writing essays on models of symbiotic relationships in the animal and human world. You want to ensure that they not only learn the subject matter but also practise writing research essays. Using the Internet as a resource, plan a scoring rubric for this project that outlines what you expect from a good essay on the topic at this age and grade level. Will students be graded as a group, independently, or both? Will they conduct self- or peer-assessments? What are their goals and responsibilities? Include the rubric in your portfolio.

Connect to the Online Learning Centre at www.mcgrawhill.ca/college/santrock to explore possible answers.

Glossary

A

acceleration program   A program for children who are gifted in which they are moved through the curriculum as quickly as they are able to progress.   188

accommodation   In Piaget's theory, the process in which children adjust a schema to new information.   43

achievement test   A type of test that measures what the student has learned or what skills the student has mastered.   422

action research   Research aimed at solving a specific classroom or school problem, improving teaching and other educational strategies, or making a decision regarding a specific location.   23

active listening   The practice of giving full attention to a speaker, focusing on both the intellectual and the emotional content of the message.   395

adaptive creativity   The type of creativity demonstrated by an individual who approaches a problem in a conventional fashion and produces a conventional solution.   116

adolescence   The period of transition from childhood to adulthood, entered at about age 10 to 12 and exited around age 18 to 22.   35

adolescent egocentrism   The heightened self-consciousness that is reflected in adolescents' beliefs that others are as interested in them as they themselves are. Also includes a sense of personal uniqueness.   48

advance organizers   Teaching activities and techniques that establish a framework and orient students to material before it is presented.   316

aggressive style   A way of dealing with conflict in which people run roughshod over others, being demanding, abrasive, and acting in hostile ways.   399

algorithms   Strategies that guarantee a solution to a problem.   259

alternate forms reliability   The extent to which students' scores are consistent on two different forms of the same test (the test items on the two sets are similar but not identical).   420

analogy   A type of formal reasoning that involves four parts, with the relation of the last two parts being the same as the relation of the first two parts.   257

androgyny   The presence of desirable masculine and feminine characteristics in the same person.   155

animism   In preoperational thought, the belief that inanimate objects have "lifelike" qualities and are capable of action.   45

anxiety   A vague, highly unpleasant feeling of fear and apprehension.   362

applied behaviour analysis   Application of principles of operant conditioning in order to change human behaviour.   212

aptitude test   A type of test used to predict a student's ability to learn a skill or accomplish something with further education and training.   421

articulation disorders   Problems in pronouncing sounds correctly.   176

artifacts   Portfolio documents or products, such as student papers and homework, that are produced during normal academic work in the classroom.   466

assertive style   A way of dealing with conflict in which individuals express their feelings, ask for what they want, and say no to things they don't want; the most desirable strategy for handling conflict.   399

assimilation   In Piaget's theory, the process in which children incorporate new knowledge into existing knowledge.   43

assistive technology   Various services and devices to help children with disabilities function in their environment.   196

associative learning   Learning that two events are connected (associated).   204

Atkinson-Shiffrin model   A model of memory that involves a sequence of three stages: sensory memory, short-term (working) memory, and long-term memory.   245

attention deficit hyperactivity disorder   A disability in which children consistently show one or more of the following characteristics over a period of time: (1) inattention, (2) hyperactivity, and (3) impulsivity.   171

attention   Concentration and focusing of mental resources.   240

attestations   Portfolio items that represent the teacher's or other responsible person's documentation of the student's progress.   467

attribution theory   The theory that individuals are motivated to discover the underlying causes of their own behaviour or performance in their effort to make sense of it.   353

attributions   Perceived causes of outcomes.   353

authentic assessment   Evaluating a student's knowledge or skill in a context that approximates the real world as closely as possible.   462

authoritarian parenting   A restrictive and punitive parenting style in which there is little verbal exchange between parents and children. Associated with children's socially incompetent behaviour.   71

authoritarian strategy of classroom management   A management style that is restrictive, punitive, and firmly controlled; the focus being mainly on keeping order rather than instruction and learning. Teachers allow little verbal exchange with students, and students often become passive learners when taught in this style.   390

authoritative parenting   A positive parenting style that encourages children to be independent but still places limits and controls on their actions. Extensive verbal give-and-take is allowed, and parents are nurturant and supportive. Associated with children's socially competent behaviour.   71

authoritative strategy of classroom management   A management style that encourages students to be independent thinkers and doers but still involves effective monitoring. Authoritative teachers engage students in considerable verbal give-and-take and show a caring attitude toward them, but still declare limits when necessary.   439

autism and Asperger syndrome   Often-severe developmental disorders with an onset in infancy that includes deficiencies in social relationships, abnormalities in communication, and restricted, repetitive, and stereotyped patterns of behaviour.   174

automaticity   The ability to process information with little or no effort.   239

autonomy versus shame and doubt   Erikson's second psychosocial stage (late infancy and toddler years).   70

B

balanced-instruction approach   An approach to reading instruction that is a combination of the basic-skills-and-phonetics approach and the whole-language approach.   287

basic-skills-and-phonetics approach   An approach to reading instruction that stresses phonetics and basic rules for translating symbols into sounds. Early reading instruction should involve simplified materials.   287

behavioural objectives   Statements that communicate proposed changes in students' behaviour to reach desired levels of performance.   312

behaviourism   The view that behaviour should be explained by observable experiences, not by mental processes.   204

best-work portfolio   A portfolio that showcases the student's most outstanding work.   468

between-class ability grouping (tracking)   Grouping students according to their ability or achievement.   113

"big five" personality factors Emotional stability, extroversion, openness, agreeableness, and conscientiousness. Researchers have found that these five factors point to important dimensions in personality. 123

bilingual education An educational approach whose aim is to teach academic subjects to immigrant children in their native languages (most often Spanish) while gradually adding English instruction. 142

biological processes Changes that stem from the child's physical nature, including genetic inheritance. 34

blind An inability to use one's vision in learning; implies a need use hearing and touch to learn. 181

book club A small group that meets to discuss books that all members of the group have read; a useful tool for peer learning and for giving students experience in leading small-group discussions. 335

C

care perspective A moral perspective that views people in terms of their connectedness, emphasizing relationships and concerns for others. Gilligan believes this approach should be incorporated more in understanding moral development. 87

case study An in-depth look at an individual. 19

CD-ROM Compact disc read-only memory. Small storage disks similar to laser digital compact discs for music. 334

centration In preoperational thought, focusing (or centring) attention on one characteristic to the exclusion of all others. 45

cerebral palsy A disorder that involves a lack of muscular coordination, shaking, or unclear speech. 184

character education A direct approach to moral education that involves teaching students basic moral literacy to prevent them from engaging in immoral behaviour and doing harm to themselves and others. 88

chronicity The pervasiveness of misbehaviour. 405

chronosystem In Bronfenbrenner's ecological theory, the sociohistorical contexts of development. 69

chunking A beneficial organizational memory strategy that involves grouping or "packing" information into "higher-order" units that can be remembered as single units. 243

class size The number of students in a given classroom. 384

classical conditioning A type of learning in which an organism learns to connect or associate stimuli. A neutral stimulus becomes associated with a meaningful stimulus and acquires the capacity to elicit a similar response. 206

classifying Dividing things into different sets or subsets and considering their interrelationships. 46

cognitive apprenticeship A learning relationship between a novice and an expert who stretches and supports the novice's understanding of and use of the culture's skills. 277

cognitive behaviour approaches Approaches to learning that emphasize getting students to monitor, manage, and regulate their own behaviour rather than let it be controlled by external factors. 223

cognitive developmental theory of gender Kohlberg's theory that children's gender typing occurs after they have developed a concept of gender. 151

cognitive moral education An approach to moral education based on the belief that students should learn to value things like democracy and justice as their moral reasoning develops. Kohlberg's theory has been the basis for a number of cognitive moral education programs. 88

cognitive processes Changes in thinking, intelligence, and language. 35

collaborative consultation An educational strategy in which people with diverse expertise interact to establish competent services for children; increasingly used in the education of children with disabilities. 194

collectivism A set of values that give priority to the group rather than the individual. 132

comparative advance organizers Advance organizers that introduce new material by connecting it with what students already know. 317

competence motivation R. W. White's concept that people are motivated to deal effectively with their environment, to master their world, and to process information efficiently. 349

computer simulations Computer learning environments that model real-world situations. 333

computer-assisted instruction (CAI) Instruction that is provided by a computer; closely linked with mastery learning. 331

computer-mediated communication (CMC) Communication through electronic exchanges; sometimes referred to as telecommunications or educational telecommunications; includes the Internet and e-mail. 334

computer simulations Computer learning environments that model real-world situations. 380

concept map A visual presentation of a concept's connections and hierarchical organization. 255

concepts Categories used to group objects, events, and characteristics on the basis of common properties. 253

concrete operational stage Piaget's third stage, lasting from about 7 to 11 years of age. Involves using operations, logical reasoning instead of intuitive reasoning (but only in concrete situations), and classification. 46

concurrent validity A form of criterion validity that refers to the relation between a test score and other criteria that are currently (concurrently) available. 420

conditioned response (CR) A learned response to a conditioned stimulus that occurs after a US–CS pairing. 206

conditioned stimulus (CS) A previously neutral stimulus that eventually elicits a conditioned response after being associated with the US. 206

confirmation bias The tendency to search for and use information that supports our ideas rather than refutes them. 260

conservation The idea that some characteristic of an object stays the same even though the object might change in appearance. 45

construct validity A broad form of validity that can include concurrent and predictive validity, as well as other evidence regarding the extent to which a test measures a particular construct (an unobservable trait or characteristic of a person, such as intelligence). 421

constructed-response item Assessment items that require students to write out answers rather than select a response from a menu; they usually do not allow objective scoring but require judgment on the part of the examiner. Short-answer and essay items are the most common examples. 459

constructivism An approach to learning that emphasizes that individuals actively construct knowledge and understanding. Children are encouraged to explore their world, discover knowledge, reflect, and think critically. 9, 276

content validity A test's ability to sample the content that is to be measured. 420

content-related evidence The extent to which assessment reflects the material that has been taught. 501

continuity in development Gradual, cumulative developmental change. 36

contracting Putting reinforcement contingencies into a written agreement. 214

control group A comparison group in an experiment that is treated in every way like the experimental group except for the manipulated factor. 20

controversial children Children frequently nominated both as someone's best friend and as being disliked by peers. 77

conventional reasoning In Kohlberg's theory, the second level of moral development. At this level, internalization is intermediate. Individuals abide internally by certain standards, but these essentially are the standards imposed by other people. 86

convergent thinking A pattern of thinking in which individuals produce one correct answer, characteristic of the kind of thinking required on conventional intelligence tests; a term coined by Guilford. 116

cooperative learning Learning that occurs when students work in small groups to help each other learn. 280

correlational research Research whose goal is to describe the strength of the relation between two or more events or characteristics. 19

creativity The ability to think about something in novel and unusual ways and come up with unique solutions to problems. 116

criterion validity A test's ability to predict a student's performance as measured by other assessments or criteria. 420

criterion-referenced grading A grading system based on comparison with predetermined standards. 472

critical thinking Thinking reflectively and productively, and evaluating the evidence. 257

cross-cultural studies Studies that compare what happens in one culture with what happens in other cultures, providing information about the degree to which people are similar and to what degree certain behaviours are specific to certain cultures. 132

cross-sectional research Research that studies groups of people all at one time. 21

cue-dependent forgetting Memory retrieval failure caused by a lack of effective retrieval cues. 251

culture The behaviour patterns, beliefs, and all other products of a particular group of people that are passed down from generation to generation. 132

culture-fair tests Tests of intelligence that are intended to be free of cultural bias. 111

curriculum compacting A variation of acceleration in which teachers skip over aspects of the curriculum that they believe are not needed by children who are gifted. 188

D

decay theory The theory that new learning involves the creation of a neurochemical "memory trace," which will eventually disintegrate. Thus, decay theory suggests that the passage of time is responsible for forgetting. 251

declarative memory The conscious recollection of information, such as specific facts or events that can be verbally communicated. 246

deductive reasoning Reasoning from the general to the specific. 257

dependent variable The factor that is measured as the result of an experiment. 20

depression A type of mood disorder in which the individual feels worthless, believes that things are not likely to get better, and behaves in a lethargic manner for a prolonged period of time. 176

descriptive statistics Mathematical procedures that are used to describe and summarize data (information) in a meaningful way. 432

development The pattern of biological, cognitive, and socioemotional changes that begins at conception and continues through the life span. 34

developmental/intellectual disabilities Limited intellectual functioning and adaptive skills. 179

developmentally appropriate education Education based on knowledge of the typical development of children within an age span (age appropriateness) as well as the uniqueness of the child (individual appropriateness). 80

diagnostic testing A relatively in-depth evaluation of a specific area of learning; its purpose is to determine the specific learning needs of a student so those needs can be met through regular or remedial instruction. 424

difficult child A child who tends to react negatively, has aggressive tendencies, lacks self-control, and is slow to accept new experiences. 125

discontinuity in development Distinctive, stagelike developmental change. 36

discovery learning Learning in which students construct an understanding on their own. 326

discrimination (in classical conditioning) The response of organism to certain stimuli and not others. 208

discrimination (in operant conditioning) Differentiating among stimuli or environmental events. 210

divergent thinking A pattern of thinking in which individuals produce many answers to the same question; more characteristic of creativity than convergent thinking; a term coined by Guilford. 116

drill-and-practice programs Computer programs that give students opportunities to learn and practise academic skills, such as mathematics, science, and reading. 331

dyscalculia A learning disability in math. 168

dyslexia A category of learning disabilities involving a severe impairment in the ability to read and spell. 168

E

early adulthood The period beginning in the late teens or early twenties and stretching into the thirties. 35

early childhood Sometimes called the "preschool years," the period from infancy to about 5 or 6 years. 35

Early Years Program that represents a partnership among government, communities, and parents to positively affect young children's lives and prepare them for school. 81

early–later experience issue The degree to which early experiences (especially in infancy and/or early childhood) or later experiences are viewed as the key determinants of development. 36

easy child A child who is generally in a good mood, quickly establishes regular routines, and easily adapts to new routines. 125

ecological theory Bronfenbrenner's theory that analyzes the environment's influence on children's development in terms of five systems: microsystem, mesosystem, exosystem, macrosystem, and chronosystem. 68

educational psychology The branch of psychology that specializes in understanding teaching and learning in educational settings. 4

egocentrism In preoperational thought, the inability to distinguish one's own perspective from someone else's perspective. 44

ego-involved goals When students set goals that strive to maximize favourable evaluations and minimize unfavourable ones. 358

elaboration The extensiveness of information processing involved in memory. 242

e-mail Electronic mail; messages can be sent to and received from individuals as well as large numbers of people at once. 337

emotional and behavioural disorders Serious, persistent problems that involve relationships, aggression, depression, fears associated with personal or school matters, as well as other inappropriate socioemotional characteristics. 174

emotional intelligence Emotional self-awareness and the ability to manage emotions, read emotions, and handle relationships. 91

empowerment Providing people with the intellectual and coping skills to succeed and make this a more just world. 144

encoding The process by which information gets into memory. 238

encoding specificity principle Associations formed at the time of encoding or learning tend to be effective retrieval cues. 251

enrichment program A program for children who are gifted that provides opportunities for learning that usually are not present in the curriculum. 188

epilepsy A nervous disorder characterized by recurring sensorimotor attacks or movement convulsions. 184

episodic memory Declarative memory that involves the retention of information about the where and when of life's happenings. 246

essay items Assessment items that require extensive writing. They allow more freedom of response than other item formats and can be especially good for assessing understanding, higher-level thinking skills, ability to organize information, and writing skills. 459

essential questions Questions that reflect the heart of the curriculum, the most important things a teacher thinks students should explore and learn. 326

ethic of care Occurs in schools where teachers express positive attitudes and hold high expectations for their students. 392

ethnic gloss The use of an ethnic label such as Asian, Italo-Canadian, Latino, or Native Canadian in a superficial way that makes an ethnic group seem more homogeneous than it really is. 26

ethnicity A shared pattern of characteristics such as cultural heritage, nationality, race, religion, and language. 137

exosystem In Bronfenbrenner's ecological theory, other settings (in which the student does not play an active role) that influence what teachers and students experience in their immediate context. 68

experiment A carefully regulated procedure in which one or more of the factors believed to influence the behaviour being studied is manipulated and all other factors are held constant. 19

experimental group   A group whose experience is manipulated in an experiment.   20

experimental research   Research involving experiments that permit the determination of cause.   19

expository advance organizers   Advance organizers that provide students with new knowledge that will orient them to an upcoming lesson.   316

expressive language   The ability to express one's thoughts.   178

extinction (in classical conditioning)   The weakening of a conditioned response in the absence of the unconditioned stimulus.   208

extinction (in operant conditioning)   A decrease in the frequency of a response when it is no longer reinforced.   211

extrinsic motivation   Response to external incentives such as rewards and punishments.   350

F

failure syndrome   A pattern of having low expectations for success and a tendency to give up at the first sign of difficulty.   375

far transfer   Transfer of learning to a situation that is very different from the one in which the initial learning took place.   265

fetal alcohol syndrome (FAS)   A cluster of abnormalities (including mental retardation and facial abnormalities) that appear in the offspring of mothers who drink alcohol heavily during pregnancy; appears in about one-third of the offspring of pregnant alcoholic women.   180

fine motor skills   Skills involving finely tuned movements, such as the finger dexterity required for writing and drawing.   38

fixation   Using a prior strategy and failing to look at a problem from a fresh, new perspective.   260

fixed-interval schedule   A reinforcement schedule in which the first appropriate response after a fixed amount of time is reinforced.   213

fixed-ratio schedule   A reinforcement schedule in which a set number of responses elapses and then the first appropriate response is reinforced.   213

flow   Csikszentmihalyi's concept that optimal life experiences occur most often when people develop a sense of mastery and are absorbed in a state of concentration when they are engaged in an activity.   351

fluency disorders   Various disorders that involve what is commonly called "stuttering."   176

formal operational stage   Piaget's fourth and final cognitive stage, which emerges at about 11 to 15 years of age. Individuals move beyond reasoning only about concrete experiences and think in more abstract, idealistic, and logical ways.   46

formative assessment   Assessment during the course of instruction rather than after it is completed.   449

frequency   How often misbehaviour occurs.   405

frequency distribution   A listing of scores, usually from highest to lowest, along with the number of times each score appears.   432

functional fixedness   A type of fixation in which the individual fails to solve a problem because she or he views the elements involved solely in terms of their usual functions.   260

G

gender   The sociocultural dimensions of being female or male.   148

gender roles   Expectations that prescribe how males and females should think, feel, and act.   148

gender schema theory   The theory that the individual's attention and behaviour are guided by an inner motivation to conform to gender-based sociocultural standards and stereotypes.   151

gender stereotypes   Broad categories that reflect impressions and beliefs about what behaviour is appropriate for females and males.   151

generalization (in classical conditioning)   The tendency of a new stimulus similar to an original conditioned stimulus to produce a similar response.   207

generalization (in operant conditioning)   Giving the same response to similar stimuli.   210

generativity versus stagnation   Erikson's seventh psychosocial stage (forties, fifties).   70

grade-equivalent score   A score expressed in terms of the grade level of students who are actually in the given grade level. Because it often is misinterpreted, other types of scores, such as standard scores, are more appropriate to use.   436

grading   Translating descriptive assessment information into numbers, letters, or other marks that indicate the quality of the student's learning or performance.   470

gross motor skills   Skills involving large-muscle activities, such as running and playing sports.   38

growth portfolio   A portfolio of the student's work over an extended time frame, which reveals how much the student has changed or learned over time.   467

H

helpless orientation   An outlook in which children focus on their personal inadequacies, often attribute their difficulty to a lack of ability, and display negative affect (including boredom and anxiety). This orientation undermines their performance.   356

heuristics   Strategies or guidelines that can suggest a solution to a problem but do not guarantee a solution.   259

hidden curriculum   According to Dewey, the pervasive moral atmosphere every school has even if it doesn't have a program of moral education.   88

hierarchy of needs   Maslow's view that certain basic needs must be satisfied before higher needs can be satisfied. In this view, needs must be satisfied in this sequence: physiological, safety, love and belongingness, esteem, cognitive, aesthetic, and self-actualization.   347

high-road transfer   Conscious and effortful transfer of learning to a new situation.   265

high-stakes testing   Using test results in a way that has important consequences for the student, affecting decisions such as whether the student will be promoted to the next grade, graduate, or get a scholarship.   419

histogram   A frequency distribution presented in the form of a graph, in which vertical bars represent the frequency of scores per category.   432

humanistic perspective   A perspective that stresses our capacity for personal growth, our freedom to choose our destiny, and our positive qualities.   347

hypermedia   Computer-based content that includes linked verbal, visual, auditory, and/or animated content.   334

hypertext   Computer-based verbal content with embedded links that lets students read about one topic and then select related topics to explore.   334

hypotheses   Specific assumptions and predictions that can be tested to determine their accuracy.   16, 255

hypothetical-deductive reasoning   Developing hypotheses about ways to solve problems and systematically reaching conclusions; a form of reasoning Piaget believed adolescents become capable of as they become formal operational thinkers.   48

I

"I" messages   A desirable style of communication in which speakers reflect their own true feelings better than when they use "you" messages.   397

identity achievement   The identity status in which individuals have adequately explored alternative courses of action and made a commitment.   85

identity diffusion   The identity status in which individuals have neither explored meaningful alternatives nor made a commitment.   85

identity foreclosure   The identity status in which individuals have made a commitment but have not explored meaningful alternative courses of action.   85

identity moratorium   The identity status in which individuals are in the midst of exploring alternative courses of action but have not yet made a commitment.   85

identity versus identity confusion   Erikson's fifth psychosocial stage (adolescence).   70

idiographic needs   The needs of the individual, not of the group.   27

incentives   In the behavioural perspective, positive or negative stimuli that can motivate behaviour.   346

independent variable   The manipulated, influential, experimental factor in an experiment.   20

individual differences   The stable, consistent ways in which people are different from one another.   102

individualism A set of values that give priority to personal goals rather than to group goals. 132

inductive reasoning Reasoning from the specific to the general. 257

indulgent parenting A parenting style in which parents are highly involved with their children but place few limits or restrictions on their behaviours; associated with children's socially incompetent behaviour, especially low self-control. 72

industry versus inferiority Erikson's fourth psychosocial stage (elementary-school years). 70

infancy The period from birth to 18–24 months. 35

infinite generativity The ability to produce an endless number of meaningful sentences using a finite set of words and rules. 55

information-processing approach An approach to learning that emphasizes that individuals manipulate information, monitor it, and strategize about it. Central to this approach are the processes of memory and thinking. 238

initiative versus guilt Erikson's third psychosocial stage (early childhood years). 70

innovative creativity The type of creativity demonstrated by an individual who examines and manipulates a problem to produce several revolutionary solutions. 116

instructional games Computer-based activities that capitalize on the increased motivation and interest that comes from encasing learning in an animated, visually displayed game. 333

instructional planning A systematic, organized strategy for planning lessons. 310

instructional validity The extent to which the assessment is a reasonable sample of what actually went on in the classroom. 421, 451

instructive technology Various types of hardware and software, combined with innovative teaching methods, to accommodate students' learning needs in the classroom. 196

integrity versus despair Erikson's eighth psychosocial stage (sixties to death). 70

intelligence Verbal and problem-solving skills, and the ability to adapt to and learn from life's everyday experiences. Not everyone agrees on what constitutes intelligence. 102

intelligence quotient (IQ) A person's tested mental age divided by chronological age, multiplied by 100. 102

interference theory The theory that we forget, not because we lose memories from storage, but because other information gets in the way of what we are trying to remember. 251

internalization The developmental change from behaviour that is externally controlled to behaviour that is internally controlled. 86

Internet A worldwide system that connects thousands of computer networks, providing an incredible array of information that students can access; the core of computer-mediated communication. 336

intimacy versus isolation Erikson's sixth psychosocial stage (early adulthood). 70

intrinsic motivation Internal motivational factors such as self-determination, curiosity, challenge, and effort. 350

intuitive thought substage The second substage in preoperational thought, lasting from about four to seven years of age. Children begin to use primitive reasoning, ask countless questions, and seem sure of their knowledge but are unaware of how they know what they know. 45

item-difficulty index The percentage of students who obtain the correct answer on an item. 458

item-discrimination index A numeric value, from 0 to 1.00, that reflects the item's ability to discriminate among individuals who scored high and those who scored low on the entire test. 459

J

jigsaw classroom Having students from different cultural backgrounds cooperate by doing different parts of a project to reach a common goal. 145

justice perspective A moral perspective that focuses on the rights of individuals; Kohlberg's theory is a justice perspective. 87

L

laboratory A controlled setting from which many of the complex factors of the real world have been removed. 18

language A form of communication, whether spoken, written, or signed, that is based on a system of symbols. 55

language disorders Disorders involving significant impairments in receptive and expressive language. 177

law of effect Thorndike's concept that behaviours followed by positive outcomes are strengthened, and that behaviours followed by negative outcomes are weakened. 209

learner-centred approaches Approaches to teaching and learning that move the focus of instructional planning and delivery away from the teacher and toward the student. 325

learning A relatively permanent change in behaviour that occurs through experience. 204

learning and thinking styles People's individual preferences regarding how they use their abilities. 119

levels of processing theory Craik and Lockhart's theory that the processing of memory occurs on a continuum from shallow to deep, with deeper processing producing better memory. 241

local norms In standardized testing, the scores of a group that is more locally based than a national group; examples include scores of students in the same class, school, or board. 419

longitudinal research Research that studies the same individuals over a period of time, usually several years or more. 21

long-term memory The memory system that holds enormous amounts of information for a long period of time in a relatively permanent fashion. 245

low vision Visual acuity between 20/70 and 20/200 with corrective lenses. 181

low-road transfer The automatic, often unconscious, transfer of learning to another situation. 265

M

macrosystem In Bronfenbrenner's ecological theory, the broader culture in which students and teachers live. 69

manipulative style A way of dealing with conflict in which individuals try to get others to feel sorry for them or to feel guilty. 399

manual approaches Educational approaches to help children with hearing impairments; they involve sign language and finger spelling. 182

mastery learning Learning one concept or topic thoroughly before moving on to a more difficult one. 318

mastery orientation An outlook in which children focus on the task rather than their ability, have positive affect, and generate solution-oriented strategies that improve their performance. 355

maturation The orderly sequence of changes dictated by the child's genetic blueprint. 35

mean A measure of central tendency that is the numerical average of a group of scores; commonly labelled M or Mn of X (mean of X) by statisticians. 433

means–end analysis A heuristic in which one identifies the goal (end) of a problem, assesses the current situation, and evaluates what needs to be done (means) to decrease the difference between the two conditions. 259

measure of central tendency A number that provides information about the average or typical score in a set of data; the three measures of central tendency are the mean, median, and mode. 433

measures of variability Measures that show how much scores vary; two measures of variability are range and standard deviation. 433

median The score that falls exactly in the middle of a distribution of scores after they have been ranked from highest to lowest; a measure of central tendency. 433

memory span The number of digits an individual can report back without error in a single presentation. 244

memory The retention of information over time, involving these main activities: encoding, storage, and retrieval. 239

mental age (MA) An individual's level of mental development relative to others, a concept developed by Binet. 102

mental processes The thoughts, feelings, and motives that each of us experiences but that cannot be observed by others. 204

mental set   A type of fixation in which an individual tries to solve a problem in a particular way that has worked in the past.   260

mesosystem   In Bronfenbrenner's ecology theory, the system composed of linkages between microsystems.   68

metacognition   Cognition about cognition; "knowing about knowing."   239

metacognitive activity   The conscious adaptation and management of thinking strategies during purposeful thinking and problem solving.   266

metacognitive knowledge   Monitoring and reflecting on one's current or recent thoughts.   266

microsystem   In Bronfenbrenner's ecological theory, a setting in which individuals spend considerable time. Examples of such contexts are the student's family, peers, schools, and neighbourhoods. The student has direct interactions with others in these settings.   68

microworlds   Scaled-down, computer-based simulations of real environments in which learners construct knowledge as they explore and design new worlds.   333

middle and late childhood   Sometimes called the "elementary-school years," the period from about 6 to 11 years of age.   35

minimum competency tests   Tests that assess skills students are expected to have mastered before they can be promoted to the next grade or permitted to graduate.   419

mode   The score that occurs most often in a set of scores; a measure of central tendency.   433

moral development   Development with respect to the rules and conventions about just interactions between people.   86

morphology   The language system for combining morphemes, which are meaningful strings of sounds that contain no smaller meaningful parts.   56

motivation   Why people behave the way they do. Motivated behaviour is energized, directed, and sustained.   346

multi-level classrooms   Resemble open-concept schools in that a number of different grade levels are present in the same class space.   402

multiple-choice item   A selected-response item that consists of two parts: a stem and number of options or alternatives.   455

myelination   A biological process in which many cells of the brain and nervous system are covered with an insulating layer of fat cells. This increases the speed at which information travels through the nervous system.   37

Myers-Briggs Type Indicator   A classification system that is based on Carl Jung's theory of psychological types.   121

N

national norms   The scores on a standardized test of a nationally representative group of individuals; a student's score is evaluated in relation to this group's scores.   419

naturalistic observation   Observations that take place out in the real world instead of in a laboratory.   18

nature–nurture controversy   The debate about whether development is primarily influenced by maturation (biological inheritance, "nature") or primarily by experience (environment, "nurture").   36

near transfer   Transfer of learning when situations are very similar. For example, if the classroom learning situation is similar to the transfer situation, near transfer is involved.   265

need for affiliation   The motive to be with other people; involves establishing, maintaining, and restoring warm, close, personal relationships.   364

negative affectivity (NA)   The range of negative emotions, including anxiety, anger, guilt, and sadness.   91

negative punishment   The removal of a valued item.   210

negative reinforcement   The removal of an aversive (unpleasant) stimulus after the occurrence of a response, causing the response to increase in frequency.   209

neglected children   Children infrequently nominated as a best friend but not disliked by their peers.   76

neglectful parenting   A form of permissive parenting in which parents are uninvolved in their children's lives; associated with children's lack of social competence, especially low self-control.   72

neo-Piagetians   Developmental psychologists who believe that Piaget got some things right but that his theory needs revision. They give more emphasis to information processing.   49

network theories   Theories that describe how information in memory is organized and connected, with an emphasis on nodes in the memory network.   247

nomothetic research   Research conducted at the level of the group.   26

norm group   In standardized testing, the group of students previously given the test by the test maker for purposes of calibration; a student's score on a standardized test is evaluated in relation to this group's scores.   419

norm-referenced grading   A grading system based on comparison of a student's performance with that of other students in the class or of other classes and other students.   471

normal distribution   A distribution in which most of the scores cluster symmetrically around the mean. The farther above or below the mean a score is, the less frequently it occurs. A normal distribution also is called a "bell-shaped curve" or "bell curve."   103, 434

O

object permanence   An important infant accomplishment in Piaget's theory that involves understanding that objects and events continue to exist even when they cannot be seen, heard, or touched.   44

objective tests   Tests with clear, unambiguous scoring criteria; multiple-choice tests are objective tests.   453

observational learning   Learning that occurs when a person observes and imitates someone else's behaviour; also called imitation or modelling.   221

open-concept schools   Schools where teachers and students move freely among rooms, sharing materials and resources.   402

operant conditioning   A form of learning in which the consequences of behaviour produce changes in the probability that the behaviour will occur; also called instrumental conditioning.   209

operations   In Piaget's theory, mental representations that are reversible.   45

oral approaches   Educational approaches to help children with hearing impairments; they include lip reading, speech reading, and whatever hearing the child has.   182

orthopaedic impairments   Restrictions in movement abilities due to muscle, bone, or joint problems.   184

P

participant observation   Research in which the observer-researcher is actively involved as a participant in the activity or setting.   24

passive style   A way of dealing with conflict in which individuals are nonassertive and submissive.   399

peers   Children of about the same age or maturity level.   75

percentile bands   A range of scores (rather than a single score) around a mean value expressed in percentiles, such as 75th to 85th percentile.   437

percentile rank score   A score that expresses the percentage of a distribution of scores that lie at or below a given raw score; percentile ranks range from 1 to 99.   436

performance assessments   Assessments that require students to perform a task, such as write an essay, conduct an experiment, carry out a project, solve a real-world problem, or create a portfolio.   453

performance criteria   Specific behaviours that students are expected to effectively perform as part of an assessment.   465

performance orientation   An outlook in which children are concerned with performance outcome rather than performance process. For performance-oriented students, winning is what matters.   356

permissive strategy of classroom management   A management style that offers students considerable autonomy but provides them with little support for developing skills or managing their behaviour. Taught in this manner, students often do not develop adequate academic skills and do not learn self-control.   414

Personal Empowerment through Type (P.E.T.) inventory   A Canadian, computer-based personality and learning-style assessment tool fashioned with the Myers-Briggs in mind.   122

personality The distinctive thoughts, emotions, and behaviours that characterize the way an individual adapts to the world.   123

person–environment fit The fit between the needs of students (person) and the type of schooling (environment) they experience. Eccles and her colleagues argue that a lack of fit between the intermediate-level environment and the needs of young adolescents produces increasingly negative self-evaluations and attitudes toward school.   353

person–situation interaction The view that the best way to conceptualize personality is not in terms of personal traits alone but also in terms of the situation involved.   124

phonology The sound system of a language.   56

pluralistic assessment Assessment that is responsive to cultural diversity in the classroom and at school.   452

popular children Children frequently nominated as a best friend and rarely disliked by their peers.   76

portfolio A systematic and organized collection of a student's work that demonstrates the student's skills and accomplishments.   466

positive affectivity (PA) The range of positive emotions, whether high energy or low energy; joy and happiness are examples of PA.   91

positive punishment The administration of an unwelcome consequence.   210

positive reinforcement A stimulus that follows a response and increases the frequency of the response.   209

postconventional reasoning In Kohlberg's theory, the third and highest level of moral development. At this level, morality is completely internalized and not based on external standards.   86

pragmatics The system of rules for the use of appropriate conversation.   56

preconventional reasoning In Kohlberg's theory, the lowest level of moral development. At this level the child shows no internalization of moral values. Moral reasoning is controlled by external punishments and rewards.   86

predictive validity A form of criterion validity that refers to the relation between a test score and the student's future performance.

prejudice An unjustified negative attitude toward an individual because of the individual's membership in a group.   140

Premack principle The principle that a high-probability activity can be used as a reinforcer for a low-probability activity.   212

preoperational stage Piaget's second stage, lasting approximately from two to seven years of age. It is more symbolic than sensorimotor thought, does not involve operational thought, is egocentric, and is intuitive rather than logical.   44

primacy effect Items at the beginning of a list tend to be remembered.   249

proactively aggressive Children whose aggressive behaviour is intentional or proactive.   155

problem-based learning An approach to learning that emphasizes solving authentic problems like those that occur in daily life.   260

problem sets Two or more assessment items that are related to the same stimulus, such as an illustration, graph, or passage.

problem solving Finding an appropriate way to attain a goal.   258

procedural memory Knowledge in the form of skills and cognitive operations about how to do something. This knowledge cannot be consciously recollected, at least not in the form of specific facts.   246

productions Documents that a student prepares especially for a portfolio.

program-evaluation research Research that is designed to make decisions about the effectiveness of a particular program.   22

prompt An added stimulus or cue that is given just prior to a response and increases the likelihood that the response will occur.   214

prosocial behaviour Behaviour that focuses on the positive side of moral development. Includes being altruistic, fair, sharing, and generally empathetic.   88

prototype matching Deciding whether an item is a member of a category by comparing it with the most typical item(s) of the category.   256

psychoeducational assessment Comprises two general test batteries: aptitude (intelligence) and achievement.   422

puberty A maturational phase that occurs mainly in early adolescence, involving changes in height, weight, and sexual functions.   40

punishment A consequence that decreases the probability a behaviour will occur.   209

pupil–teacher ratio (PTR) The number of students in a school divided by all of the certified teachers in that school (including librarians, learning resource teachers, and administrators).   384

Q

qualitative research methods Methods that are primarily nonexperimental and concerned with identifying and describing themes underlying human experience or the experience of a particular phenomenon.   16

quantitative research methods Methods that are primarily experimental in nature and concerned with the causal relationships between dependent and independent variables.   16

R

random assignment In experimental research, the assignment of participants to experimental and control groups by chance.   20

range The distance between the highest and lowest scores in a set of scores; a measure of variability.

rapport talk The language of conversation and a way of establishing connections and negotiating relationships; usually preferred by females more than by males.   154

raw score The number of items a student gets correct on a test.

reactively aggressive Children whose aggressive behaviour is triggered by events or the behaviour of others.   155

recall A memory task in which individuals must retrieve previously learned information, as for fill-in-the-blank or essay questions.   251

recency effect Items at the end of a list tend to be remembered.   249

receptive language Linguistic information that is received by the brain.   179

reciprocal determinism model Bandura's social cognitive model in which three main factors—behaviour, environment, and person (cognition)—interact to influence learning.   220

reciprocal teaching Students taking turns to lead small-group discussion.   289

recognition A memory task in which individuals only have to identify ("recognize") learned information, as for multiple-choice items.   251

rehearsal Conscious repetition of information over time to increase the length of time information stays in memory.   240

reinforcement (reward) A consequence (either positive or negative) that increases the probability that a behaviour will occur.   209

rejected children Children infrequently nominated as a best friend and disliked by their peers.   78

reliability The extent to which an assessment produces a consistent, reproducible measure of performance; reliable measures are stable, dependable, and relatively free from errors of measurement.

report talk Talk that gives information; usually preferred by males more than by females.   154

reproductions Portfolio documentation of a student's work outside the classroom, such as special projects and interviews.

response cost Taking a positive reinforcer away from the student, as when the student loses certain privileges.   217

retrieval Taking information out of storage.   239

S

scaffolding The technique of changing the level of support over the course of a teaching session; the more-skilled person adjusts the amount of guidance to fit the student's current performance level.   52, 277

schedules of reinforcement Partial reinforcement timetables that determine when a response will be reinforced.   213

schema A concept or framework that exists in an individual's mind to organize and interpret information.   43, 248

schema theories Theories that when people reconstruct information, they fit it into information that already exists in their minds. 248

scientific method A method for discovering accurate information that includes these steps: conceptualize the problem, collect data, draw conclusions, and revise research conclusions and theory. 16

scientific research Objective, systematic, and testable research that aims at reducing the likelihood that conclusions will be based on personal beliefs, opinions, and feelings. 16

script A schema for an event. 249

selected-response items Assessment items with an objective format in which students select an answer from several given choices rather than construct the answer themselves. A scoring key is created and can be applied by an examiner or by a computer to score students' responses.

self-actualization The highest and most elusive of Maslow's needs, involving the motivation to develop one's full potential as a human being. 347

self-efficacy The belief that one can master a situation and produce positive outcomes. 221, 356

self-esteem The global, evaluative dimension of the self, also referred to as self-worth or self-image, that reflects an individual's overall confidence and satisfaction. 83

self-instructional methods Cognitive behaviour techniques aimed at teaching individuals to modify their own behaviour. 224

self-regulatory learning The self-generation of thoughts, feelings, and behaviours to reach a goal. 228, 358

semantic memory Declarative memory of general knowledge about the world. 246

semantics The language system that involves the meaning of words and sentences. 56

sensorimotor stage Piaget's first stage, which lasts from birth to about two years of age. Infants construct an understanding of the world by coordinating their sensory experiences with their motor actions. 44

sensory memory The memory system that holds information from the world in its original sensory form for only an instant. 243

serial position effect Recall is better for items at the beginning and end of a list than for items in the middle. 249

seriation The concrete operation that involves ordering stimuli along some quantitative dimension (such as length). 46

service learning A form of education that promotes social responsibility and service to the community. 88

severity The overall potential impact of misbehaviour. 405

sex The biological dimensions of being female or male. 148

sexism Prejudice and discrimination against an individual because of the person's sex. 151

sexual harassment A form of power and dominance of one person over another. 158

sexual orientation An enduring emotional, romantic, sexual or affective attraction to another person. 159

shaping Teaching new behaviours by reinforcing successive approximations to a specified target behaviour. 215

short-answer item A constructed-response assessment item in which students are required to write a word, a short phrase, or several sentences in response to a task. 459

short-term (working) memory The limited-capacity memory system in which information is retained for as long as 30 seconds, unless the information is rehearsed, in which case it can be retained longer. 243

situated cognition An important assumption in social constructivist approaches that thinking is located (situated) in social and physical contexts, not within an individual's mind. 277

slow-to-warm-up child A child who has a low activity level, is somewhat negative, shows low adaptability, and displays a low intensity of mood. 125

social cognitive theory Bandura's view that social and cognitive factors, as well as behaviour, play important roles in learning. 220

social constructivist approach An emphasis on the social contexts of learning and knowledge as mutually built and constructed, characteristic of Vygotsky's theory. 276

social motives Needs and desires that are learned through experiences with the social world. 364

social-learning theory of gender The theory that gender development occurs through observation and imitation of gender behaviour, as well as reinforcement and punishment of gender behaviour. 150

socioeconomic status (SES) The categorization of people according to their economic, educational, and occupational characteristics. 133

socioemotional processes Changes in the child's relationships with other people, emotion, and personality. 35

special group norms In standardized testing, scores of subgroups from a national sample. 419

speech and language disorders A number of speech problems (such as articulation disorders, voice disorders, and fluency disorders) and language problems (which involve difficulties in receiving and expressing language). 176

split-half reliability A method of checking the reliability of a test by dividing the test items into two halves, such as the odd-numbered and even-numbered items; the scores on the two sets are compared to determine how consistently students performed across the sets. 420

standard deviation A measure of variability that reveals how much a set of scores varies on the average around the mean of the scores; that is, this measure shows how closely scores cluster around the mean. The smaller the standard deviation, the less variability from the mean, and vice versa. 433

standard score A score expressed as a deviation from the mean. 437

standardized test A test that is prepared by test specialists to assess performance under uniform conditions; allows a student's performance to be compared with other students' performance, often on a national basis. 18, 418

stanine score A score that describes a student's test performance on a scale ranging from 1 to 9. 436

Sternberg System of Styles A system of learning styles with the theme that students organize and govern themselves in different ways and that these variations correspond to the different forms of government that exist around the world. 120

storage The retention of information in memory over time. 239

strategy construction The discovery of a new procedure for processing information. 239

strategy instruction Requires that teachers model appropriate learning strategies frequently. 268

subgoalling Setting intermediate goals that put one in a better position to reach a final goal or solution. 258

summative assessment Assessment after instruction is finished. 450

survey battery A group of individual subject-matter tests that is designed for a particular level of students. 423

symbolic function substage In Piaget's theory, a substage of preoperational thought occurring roughly between two and four years of age. The young child gains the ability to represent mentally an object that is not present. 44

syntax The language system that involves the way words are combined to form acceptable phrases and sentences. 56

systematic desensitization A method based on classical conditioning that reduces anxiety by getting the individual to associate deep relaxation with successive visualizations of increasingly anxiety-producing situations. 208

T

task analysis Breaking down a complex task into its component parts. 312

task-involved goals When students focus on mastering tasks. 358

taxonomy A classification system. 313

teacher-as-researcher Also called "teacher-researcher"; the idea that classroom teachers can conduct their own systematic studies to improve their educational practices. 23

temperament A person's behavioural style and characteristic ways of responding. 125

test–retest reliability The extent to which a test yields the same performance when a student is given the same test on two different occasions. 420

theory An interrelated, coherent set of ideas that helps to explain and make predictions. 16

thinking Manipulating and transforming information in memory; often done to form concepts, reason, think critically, and solve problems. 253

time-out The extinction strategy most widely used by teachers to remove desirable stimuli. The student is taken away from positive reinforcement. 216

top-dog phenomenon Moving from the top position to the lowest position in a transition from one level of schooling to another (such as an elementary school to an intermediate school). 82

transfer The process by which a person applies previous experiences and knowledge to learning or problem solving in a new situation. 239

transitivity In concrete operational thought, a mental concept about the relations between classes that underlies the ability to logically combine relations to understand certain conclusions. 46

triarchic theory of intelligence Sternberg's view that intelligence comes in three main forms: analytical, creative, and practical. 105

trust versus mistrust Erikson's first psychosocial stage (first year of life). 70

T-score A standard score in which the mean is set at 50 and the standard deviation is set at 10. 437

tutorial programs Computer-based activities designed to replicate what human tutors do to guide and facilitate students' learning. 331

U

unconditioned response (UR) An unlearned response that is automatically elicited by the US. 206

unconditioned stimulus (US) A stimulus that automatically produces a response without any prior learning. 206

V

validity The extent to which a test measures what it is intended to measure. 420, 451

variable-interval schedule A reinforcement schedule in which a response is reinforced after a variable amount of time has elapsed. 213

variable-ratio schedule A reinforcement schedule in which a behaviour is reinforced after an average number of times, but on an unpredictable basis. 213

videodiscs Large laser discs used to store visual images. 334

voice disorders Disorders reflected in speech that is hoarse, harsh, too loud, too high-pitched, or too low-pitched. 176

W

whole-language approach An approach to reading instruction based on the idea that instruction should parallel children's natural language learning. Reading materials should be whole and meaningful. 287

within-class ability grouping The placement of students in different groups within a class to take into account differences in students' abilities. 113

"withitness" A management style described by Kounin in which teachers show students that they are aware of what is happening, closely monitoring students on a regular basis. This especially helps teachers detect inappropriate behaviour before it gets out of hand. 390

work-avoidant goals When students try to exert as little effort as possible on a task. 358

working-memory model Alan Baddeley's model in which working memory is a kind of mental "workbench" that lets individuals manipulate, assemble, and construct information when they make decisions, solve problems, and comprehend written and spoken language. The model consists of a general "executive" and two subsystems (articulatory loop and visuospatial scratchpad). 244

World Wide Web (the Web) A hypermedia information retrieval system that links a variety of Internet materials; can include text, graphics, sound, and animation. 337

Y

"you" messages An undesirable form of communication that suggests the speaker is judging people and placing them in a defensive position. 397

Z

zone of proximal development (ZPD) In Vygotsky's theory, the term for the range of tasks that are too difficult for children to master alone but that can be learned with guidance and assistance from adults or more-skilled children. 51

z-score A standard score that provides information about how many standard deviations a raw score lies above or below the mean. 437

References

A

Abbott, S. P., & Berninger, V. W. (1999). It's never too late to remediate: Teaching word recognition to students with reading disabilities in Grades 4–7. *Annals of Dyslexia, 49,* 223–250.

Aboud, F. E. (1988). *Children and prejudice.* New York, NY: B. Blackwell.

Aboud, F. E., & Doyle, A. B. (1996). *Does talk of race foster prejudice or tolerance in children?* Retrieved 7 December 2002, from http://www.cpa.ca/cjb-snew/1996/ful_aboud.html.

Abrami, P. C., Chambers, B., Poulsen, C., De Simone, C., d'Apollonia, S., & Howden, J. (1995). *Classroom connections: Understanding and using cooperative learning.* Toronto, ON: Harcourt Brace.

Abruscato, J. (2000). *Teaching children science: A discovery approach* (5th ed.). Boston: Allyn & Bacon.

Academic Software. (1996). *Adaptive Device Locator System* [computer program]. Lexington, KY: Author.

Adelman, P. B., & Vogel, S. A. (1998). Adults with learning disabilities. In B. Wong (Ed.), *Learning about learning disabilities (2nd ed.).* San Diego, CA: Academic Press.

Aiken, L. R. (2000). *Psychological testing and assessment* (10th ed). Boston: Allyn & Bacon.

Aikenhead, G. (1997). Toward a First Nations cross-cultural science and technology curriculum. *Science Education, 81(2),* 217–239.

Aikenhead, G. S. (1991). *Logical reasoning in science & technology.* Toronto, ON: John Wiley of Canada.

Airasian, P. W. (1997). *Classroom assessment* (3rd ed.). New York: McGraw-Hill.

Albanese, M. A., & Mitchell, S. (1993). Problem-based learning: A review of literature on its outcomes and implementation issues. *Academic Medicine, 68(1),* 52–81.

Alberta Learning. (2001). Optimizing Human Potential: Alberta Learning 2001–2002 Annual Report. Retrieved 2 December 2002, from http://www.learning.gov.ab.ca/annualreport/2002/introduction.pdf.

Alberta Program of Studies for K–12 Mathematics. (1997). *The common curriculum framework for K–12 mathematics: Western Canadian protocol for collaboration in basic education.* Retrieved 5 December 2002, from: http://www.learning.gov.ab.ca/studentprograms/math/k9Math/math.pdf.

Alberta Teachers Association. (2001). Class size is important: Latest research. Retrieved December 7, 2002, from http://www.teachers.ab.ca/peac/factsheets.cfm?p_ID=140&p_att1s=PEAC1.

Alberti, R. E., & Emmons, M. L. (1995). *Your perfect right* (8th ed.). San Luis Obispo, CA: Impact.

Alberto, P. A., & Troutman, A. C. (1995). *Applied behavior analysis for teachers* (4th ed.). Englewood Cliffs, NJ: Merrill.

Alberto, P. A., & Troutman, A. C. (1999). *Applied behavior analysis for teachers* (5th ed.). Englewood Cliffs, NJ: Merrill.

Allan, L. G., & Siegel, S. (1997). Assessing a new analysis of contingent color aftereffects. *Cognition, 64,* 207–222.

Allen, D. (1998). Bringing problem-based learning to the introductory biology classroom. In A. McNeal & C. D'Avanzo (Eds.), *Student active science* (Ch. 15). Retrieved 6 November 2002, from: http://www.saunderscollege.com/lifesci/studact/chapters/ch15.html.

Allen, L. (1998). An integrated strategies approach: Making word identification instruction work for beginning readers. *The Reading Teacher, 52(3),* 254–268.

Allison, D., & Allison, P. (2001). *Building life skills through science education.* Final report for the project Let's Talk Science. London, ON.

Allsopp, D. H. (1997). Using classwide peer tutoring to teach beginning algebra problem-solving skills in heterogeneous classrooms. *Remedial & Special Education, 18(6),* 367–380.

American Association for the Advancement of Science. (1993). Benchmarks for science literacy: Project 2061. New York: Oxford University Press.

American Association of University Women (2001). Hostile hallways: Bullying, teasing, and sexual harassment in school. Washington, DC: Author.

American Association of University Women Educational Foundation. (1998). *Gender gaps: Where schools still fail our children.* Washington, DC: Author.

American Association of University Women. (1993). *Hostile hallways.* Washington, DC: Author.

Ames, C. (1992). Classroom goals, structures, and student motivation. *Journal of Educational Psychology, 84,* 261–271.

Anderman, E. M., Maehr, M. L., & Midgley, C. (1996). Declining motivation after the transition to middle school: Schools can make a difference. Unpublished manuscript, University of Kentucky, Lexington.

Anderson, J. A. (2000, September). *Teacher questioning and pupil anxiety in the primary classroom.* Paper presented at the British Educational Research Association Conference, Research Student Symposium, Cardiff University, England.

Anderson, J. R. (1993). Problem solving and learning. *American Psychologist, 48,* 35–44.

Anderson, L., Blumenfeld, P., Pintrich, P. R., Clark, C. M., Marx, R. W., & Peterson, P. (1996). Educational psychology for teachers: Reforming our courses, rethinking our roles. *Educational Psychologist, 30,* 143–157.

Anderson, S. E. (1998). Integrating multimedia multicultural methods into an educational psychology course. *Journal of Technology and Teacher Education, 6(2–3),* 169–182.

Anselmi, D. L. (1998). *Questions of gender.* New York: McGraw-Hill.

Antil, L. R., Jenkins, J. R., Wayne, S. K., & Vadasy, P. F. (1998). Cooperative learning: Prevalence, conceptualizations, and the relation between research and practice. *American Educational Research Association, 35(3),* 419–454.

Arends, R. I., Winitzky, N. E., & Tannenbaum, M. D. (1998). *Introduction to education: Exploring teaching.* New York: McGraw-Hill.

Aronson, E. E. (1986, August). *Teaching students things they think they already know about: The case of prejudice and desegregation.* Paper presented at the meeting of the American Psychological Association, Washington, DC.

Aronson, E. E., Blaney, N., Sephan, C., Sikes, J., & Snapp, M. (1978). *The jigsaw classroom.* Beverly Hills, CA: Sage.

Aronson, E., & Patnoe, S. (1996). *The jigsaw classroom* (2nd ed.). Boston: Addison-Wesley.

Arter, J. (1995). *Portfolios for assessment and instruction.* ERIC Document Reproduction Service No. ED388890.

Ashcraft, M. H., & Kirk, E. P. (2001). The relationships among working memory, math anxiety, and performance. *Journal of Experimental Psychology: General, 130,* 224–237.

Asher, S. R., & Cole, J. D. (Eds.). (1990). *Peer rejection in childhood.* New York: Cambridge University Press.

Ashton, P. T., & Webb, R. B. (1986). *Making a difference: Teachers' sense of efficacy and student achievement.* White Plains, NY: Longman.

Asselin, M. (1999). Balanced literacy. *Teacher Librarian, 27(1),* 69–70.

Atkinson, R. C., & Shiffrin, R. M. (1968). Human memory: A proposed system and its control processes. In K. W. Spence & J. T. Spence (Eds.), *The psychology of learning and motivation* (Vol. 2). San Diego: Academic Press.

Ausubel, D. P. (1960). The use of advance organizers in the learning and retention of meaningful verbal material. *Journal of Educational Psychology, 51,* 267–272.

Axelrod, S. (1996). What's wrong with behavioral analysis? *Journal of Behavioral Education, 6,* 247–256.

B

Baddeley, A. (1993). Working memory and conscious awareness. In A. F. Collins, S. E. Gatherhole, M. A. Conway, & P. E. Morris (Eds.), *Theories of memory*. Mahwah, NJ: Erlbaum.

Baddeley, A. (1998). *Human memory* (rev. ed.). Boston: Allyn & Bacon.

Baddeley, A. (2000). Short-term and working memory. In E. Tulving & F. I. M. Craik (Eds.), *The Oxford handbook of memory*. New York: Oxford University Press.

Baddeley, A. (2001). *Is working memory still working?* Paper presented at the meeting of the American Psychological Association, San Francisco.

Bailey, J. S., Shook, G. L., Iwata, B. A., Reid, D. H., & Repp, A. C. (Eds.). (1996). *Behavior analysis in developmental disabilities 1968–1985 from the Journal of Applied Behavior Analysis*. Kalamazoo. MI: Association for Behavior Analysis.

Baldwin, J. D., & Baldwin, J. L. (1998). *Behavior principles in everyday life*. Upper Saddle River, NJ: Prentice Hall.

Bandura, A. (1965). Influence of models' reinforcement contingencies on the acquisition of imitative responses. *Journal of Personality and Social Psychology, 1*, 589–596.

Bandura, A. (1982). Self-efficacy mechanism in human agency. *American Psychologist, 37*, 122–147.

Bandura, A. (1986). *Social foundations of thought and action*. Englewood Cliffs, NJ: Prentice Hall.

Bandura, A. (1994). *Self-efficacy: The exercise of control*. New York: W. H. Freeman.

Bandura, A. (1997). *Self-efficacy: The exercise of control*. New York: W. H. Freeman.

Bandura, A. (1998). Self-efficacy. In H. S. Friedman (Ed.), *Encyclopedia of mental health* (Vol. 3). San Diego: Academic Press.

Bandura, A. (2000). Self-efficacy. In A. Kazdin (Ed.), *Encyclopedia of psychology*. Washington, DC, & New York: American Psychological Association and Oxford University Press.

Bandura, A. (2000). Social cognitive theory. In A. Kazdin (Ed.), *Encyclopedia of psychology*. Washington, DC, and New York: American Psychological Association and Oxford University Press.

Bankay, D., & Woloshyn, V. E. (1998). The future of computer-based literacy instruction for adult learners: Putting new technologies to good use. *Brock Education, 8*, 29–43.

Banks, J. A., & Banks, C. A. (Eds.). (1997). *Multicultural education* (3rd ed.). Boston: Allyn & Bacon.

Barkley, R. A. (1998). *Attention-deficit hyperactivity disorder: A handbook for diagnosis and treatment*. New York: Guilford.

Barr, W. B. (2000). Epilepsy. In A. Kazdin (Ed.), *Encyclopedia of psychology*. Washington, DC, and New York: American Psychological Association and Oxford University Press.

Barrett, H. C. (1994). Technology-supported assessment portfolios. *Computing Teacher, 21* (6), 9–12.

Barrett, H. C. (1998, March). Electronic teaching portfolios. Paper based on a presentation at the Society for Technology and Teacher Education (SITE), Washington, DC. Retrieved 5 January 2003, from: http://transition.alaska.edu/www/portfolios/SITEArt.html.

Barsalou, L. W. (2000). Concepts: Structure. In A. Kazdin (Ed.), *Encyclopedia of psychology*. Washington, DC, and New York: American Psychological Association and Oxford University Press.

Bartlett, E. J. (1982). Learning to revise: Some component processes. In M. Nystrand (Ed.), *What writers know*. New York: Academic Press.

Bartlett, J. C. (1998, July). Personal communication. Program in Psychology, University of Texas at Dallas.

Barton, J., & Collins, A. (1997). Starting Out: Designing your portfolio. In J. Barton & A. Collins (Eds.), *Portfolio assessment: A handbook for educators*. Boston: Addison-Wesley.

Bassarath, L. (2001). ADHD: The latest research findings. *Antisocial Behaviour in Youth, 19(1)*. Retrieved June 2002, from http://www.iay.org.

Bassey, K., & Bandura, A. (1999). Social cognitive theory of gender development and differentiation. *Psychological Review, 106(4)*, 676–713.

Batchelder, W. (2000). Mathematical psychology. In A. Kazdin (Ed.), *Encyclopedia of psychology*. Washington, DC, and New York: American Psychological Association and Oxford University Press.

Battista, M. T. (1990). Spatial visualization and gender differences in high school geometry. *Journal for Research in Mathematics Education, 21(1)*, 47–60.

Battiste, M. (Ed.), (2000). Reclaiming indigenous voice and vision. Vancouver, BC: University of British Columbia Press.

Baumrind, D. (1971). Current patterns of parental authority. *Developmental Psychology Monographs, 4* (1, Part 2).

Baumrind, D. (1996, April). Unpublished review of J. W. Santrock's *Children,* 5th ed. (New York: McGraw-Hill).

Bayha, B. (1998). *The Internet: An inclusive magnet for teaching all students*. Oakland, CA: Internet Handbook, World Institute on Disability.

BCTF News (2001). *Teachers rally to promote primary class-size limits*. Retrieved December 2, 2002, from: http://www.bctf.ca/publications/newsreleases/archive/2001/2001-01-26b.html.

Beal, C. (1994). *Boys and girls: The development of gender roles*. New York: McGraw-Hill.

Beals, D. E., De Temple, J. M., & Dickinson, D. K. (1994). Talking and listening that support early literacy development of children from low-income families. In D. K. Dickinson (ed.) *Bridges to literacy: Children, families, and schools*. Cambridge, MA: Blackwell Publishers.

Beatty, B. (1998). From laws of learning to a science of values: Efficiency and morality in Thorndike's educational psychology. *American Psychologist, 53*, 1145–1152.

Beauchamp. L., Parsons, J., McConaghy, G., & Sanford, K. (1996). Teaching from the outside in. Edmonton, Alberta: Les Editions Duval, Inc.

Beckham, E. E. (2000). Depression. In A. Kazdin (Ed.), *Encyclopedia of psychology*. Washington, DC, and New York: American Psychological Association and Oxford University Press.

Begley, S. (1998, March 30). Homework doesn't help. *Newsweek,* pp. 30–31.

Begoray, D. (2001). The literacy groups project: Investigating the use of Reading Recovery techniques with small groups of grade two students. *Alberta Journal of Educational Research, 67(2)*, 141–155.

Begoray, D., & Slovinsky, K. (1997). Pearls in shells: Preparing teachers to accommodate gifted low income populations. *Roeper Review, 20(1)*, 45–50.

Bem, S. L. (1977). On the utility of alternative procedures for assessing psychological androgyny. *Journal of Consulting and Clinical Psychology, 45*, 196–205.

Bennett, W. (1993). *The book of virtues*. New York: Simon & Schuster.

Benninger, W. (1989). A teacher's guide to recognizing psychological and behavioral problems of students. Teaching material available from MHS, at http://www.mhs.com/.

Bereiter, C. (1999). In search of high impact. In L. Harasim (Ed.), *Wisdom & wizardry: Celebrating the pioneers of online education* (pp. 8–9). Vancouver, BC: Telelearning, Inc.

Bereiter, C. (2002). *Education and mind in the knowledge age*. Mahwah, NJ: Lawrence Erlbaum Associates.

Bereiter, C., & Scardamalia, M. (1989). Intentional learning as a goal of instruction. In L. B. Resnick (Ed.), *Knowing, learning, and instruction. Essays in honor of Robert Glaser*. Hillsdale, NJ: Erlbaum.

Bereiter, C., & Scardamalia, M. (1993). *Surpassing ourselves: An inquiry into the nature and implications of expertise*. Chicago: Open Court.

Berg, K. F. (1993). *Structured Cooperative Learning and Achievement in a High School Mathematics Class*. (ERIC Document Reproduction Service No. ED412696).

Berger, E. H., & Pollman, M, J. (1996). Multiple intelligences: Enabling diverse learning. *Early Childhood Education Journal, 23* (No. 4), 249–253.

Berko Gleason, J. (2000). Language. In M. H. Bornstein & M. E. Lamb (Eds.), *Developmental psychology* (4th ed.). Mahwah, NJ: Erlbaum.

Berko, J. (1958). The child's learning of English morphology. *Word, 14*, 150–177.

Berliner, D. C. (1988, February). *The development of expertise in pedagogy*. Paper presented at the meeting of the American Association of Colleges for Teacher Education, New Orleans.

Berndt, T. J. (1979). Developmental changes in conformity to peers and parents. *Developmental Psychology, 15*, 608–616.

Berndt, T. J. (1996). Transitions in friendship and friends' influence. In J. A. Graeber, J. Brooks-Gunn, & A. C. Petersen (Eds.), *Transitions through adolescence*. Mahwah, NJ: Erlbaum.

Berndt, T. J., & Keefe, K. (1996). Friends' influence on school adjustment: A motivational analysis. In J. Juvonen & K. R. Wentzel (Eds.), *Social motivation*. New York: Cambridge University Press.

Berrill, D. P. & Gall, M. (1999). On the carpet: Emergent writer/readers' letter sharing in a penpal program. *Language Arts, 76(6)*, 470–478.

Berry, J. W. (1984). Multicultural policy in Canada: A social psychological analysis. *Canadian Journal of Behavioural Science, 16*, 353–370.

Berry, J. W. (2000). Cultural foundations of behavior. In A. Kazdin (Ed.), *Encyclopedia of psychology*. Washington, DC, and New York: American Psychological Association and Oxford University Press.

Berry, J. W., & Laponce, J. A. (1994). Evaluating research on Canada's multiethnic and multicultural society: An introduction. In J. W. Berry & J. A. Laponce (Eds.), *Ethnicity and culture in Canada: The research landscape (pp. 3–16)*. Toronto, ON: University of Toronto Press.

Bersoff, D. N. (Ed.). (1999). *Ethical conflicts in psychology* (2nd ed.). Washington, DC: American Psychological Association.

Betts, J. R. (1998). The implications of technological change for human resource policy. Industry Canada, Strategies Micro-economic policy report #7. Retrieved December 16, 2002, from: http://strategis.ic.gc.ca/SSG/ra01718e.html.

Betts, J. R., & Ferrall, C. (1997). Policies for improving public schools. *Policy Options, 18(6)*, 35–39.

Bigelow, B. (1999, April). Why standardized tests threaten multiculturalism. *Educational Leadership, 56*, 37–40.

Billips, L. H., & Rauth, M. (1987). Teachers and research. In V. Richardson-Koeler (Ed.), *Educator's handbook*. White Plains, NY: Longman.

Bjorklund, D. F. (2000). Middle childhood: Cognitive development. In A. Kazdin (Ed.), *Encyclopedia of psychology*. Washington, DC, and New York: American Psychological Association and Oxford University Press.

Blackhurst, A. E. (1997, May/June). Perspectives on technology in special education. *Teaching Exceptional Children*, pp. 41–47.

Bloom, B. (1976). *Human characteristics and school learning*. New York, McGraw-Hill.

Bloom, B. (1986). What we're learning about teaching and learning: A summary of recent research. *Principal, 66(2)*, 6–10.

Bloom, B. S. (1971). Mastering learning. In J. H. Block (Ed.), *Mastery learning*. New York: Holt, Rinehart & Winston.

Bloom, B. S. (Ed.). (1985). *Developing talent in young people*. New York: Ballantine.

Bloom, B. S., & Krathwohl, D. (Eds.). (1956). *Taxonomy of education objectives: Handbook 1. Cognitive domain*. New York: Longman, Green.

Bloom, B. S., Engelhart, M. D., Frost, E. J., Hill, W. H., & Krathwohl, D. R. (1956). *Taxonomy of educational objectives*. New York: David McKay.

Bloom, B. S., Mesia, B. B., & Krathwohl, D. R. (1964). *Taxonomy of Educational Objectives* (two vols: The Affective Domain & The Cognitive Domain). New York. David McKay Co.

Bloom, L. (1998). Language acquisition in its developmental context. In W. Damon (Ed.), *Handbook of child psychology* (4th ed., Vol. 2). New York: Wiley.

Bloom, R. W. (2002). On media violence: Whose facts? Whose misinformation? *American Psychologist, 57*, 447–448.

Boekaerts, M., Pintrich, P., & Zeidner, M. (Eds.). (2000). *Handbook of self-regulation*. San Diego: Academic Press.

Bogan, E. (1997). Three equations for an equitable math program. *Educational Leadership, (April)*, 46–47.

Bohatyretz, S., & Lipps, G. (1999). Diversity in the classroom: Characteristics of elementary students receiving special education. *Education Quarterly Review, 6*, 7–19.

Boivin, M., Hymel, S., & Hodges, E. V. E. (2001). Toward a process view of peer rejection and harassment. In J. Juvonen, & S. Graham (Eds.), *Peer harassment in school: The plight of the vulnerable and victimized* (pp. 265–289). New York: The Guilford Press.

Borko, H., & Putnam, R. T. (1996). Learning to teach. In D. C. Berliner & R. C. Calfee (Eds.), *Handbook of educational psychology*. New York: Macmillan.

Bornstein, M. H. (1995). (Ed.). *Handbook of parenting* (Vols. 1–3). Mahwah, NJ: Erlbaum.

Bouchard, P., & St-Amand, J.C. (2000). Gender identities and school success. *The Alberta Journal of Educational Research, 46(3)*, 280–284.

Bourne, E. J. (1995). *The anxiety and phobia workbook*. Oakland, CA: New Harbinger.

Boyles, N. S., & Contadino, D. (1997). *The learning differences sourcebook*. Los Angeles: Lowell House.

Bowe, F. G. (2000). *Physical, sensory, and health disabilities*. Upper Saddle River, NJ: Merrill.

Bowlby, J. (1989). *Secure attachment*. New York: Basic Books.

Boyles, N. S., & Contadino, D. (1997). *The learning differences sourcebook*. Los Angeles: Lowell House.

Bracey, G. W. (1997, May). The culture of sexual harassment. *Phi Delta Kappan*, pp. 725–726.

Bracken, B. A. (Ed.). (2000). *Psychoeducational assessment of preschool children*. Boston: Allyn & Bacon.

Branch, M. N. (2000). Punishment. In A. Kazdin (Ed.), *Encyclopedia of psychology*. Washington, DC, and New York: American Psychological Association and Oxford University Press.

Bransford, J. D., & Stein, B. S. (1993). *The IDEAL problem solver*. New York: W. H. Freeman.

Bransford, J. D., Brown, A. L., & Cocking, R. R. (Eds.). (1999). *How people learn*. Washington, DC: National Academy Press.

Breakfast for Learning (2002). Who we are: Our mission. Retrieved 12 December 2002, from: http://www.breakfastforlearning.ca/english/who_we_are_a1/index.html.

Bredekamp, S., & Copple, C. (1997). (Eds.) *Developmentally appropriate practice in early childhood programs* (rev. ed.). Washington, DC: National Association for the Education of Young Children.

Brendgen, M., Vitaro, F., Tremblay, R. E., & Lavoie, F. (2001). Reactive and proactive aggression: Predictions to physical violence in different contexts and moderating effects of parental monitoring and caregiving behavior. *Journal of Abnormal Child Psychology, 29*, 293–304.

Brewer, D. J., Rees, D. I., & Argys, L. M. (1995). Detracking America's schools. *Phi Delta Kappan, 77*, 210–215.

Brewer, M. B., & Campbell, D. I. (1976). *Ethnocentrism and intergroup attitudes*. New York: Wiley.

Briggs, T. W. (1998, November 24). In the classroom with our All-USA teachers. *USA Today*, p. 9D.

Bronfenbrenner, U. (1986). Ecology of the family as a context for human development: Research perspectives. *Developmental Psychology, 22*, 723–742.

Bronfenbrenner, U., & Morris, F. (1998). The ecology of developmental processes. In W. Damon (Ed.), *Handbook of child psychology* (5th ed., Vol. 1). New York: Wiley.

Brook, J. S., Whiteman, M., Czeisler, L. J., Shapiro, J., & Cohen, P. (1997). Cigarette smoking in young adults: Childhood and adolescent personality, familial, and peer antecedents. *The Journal of Genetic Psychology, 158*, 172–188.

Brookover, W. B., Beady, C., Flood, P., Schweitzer, U., & Wisenbaker, J. (1979). *School social systems and student achievement: Schools make a difference*. New York: Praeger.

Brooks, J. G. & Brooks, M. G. (1993). *The case for constructivist classrooms*. Alexandria, VA: Association for Supervision and Curriculum Development.

Brooks-Gunn, J. (1996, March). *The uniqueness of the early adolescence transition*. Paper presented at the meeting of the Society for Research on Adolescence, Boston.

Brooks-Gunn, J., & Paikoff, R. (1997). Sexuality and development transitions during adolescence. In J. Schulenberg, J. Maggas, & K. Hurrelmann (Eds.), *Health risks and developmental transitions during adolescence*. New York: Cambridge University Press.

Brophy, J. (1996). *Teaching problem students*. New York: Guilford.

Brophy, J. (1998). *Motivating students to learn*. New York: McGraw-Hill.

Brown, A. L. (1997). Transforming schools into communities of thinking and learning about serious matters. *American Psychologist, 52*, 399–413.

Brown, A. L., & Campione, J. C. (1996). Psychological learning theory and the design of innovative environments. In L. Schuable & R. Glaser (Eds.), *Contributions of instructional innovation to understanding learning*. Mahwah, NJ: Erlbaum.

Brown, A. L., & Palincsar, A. S. (1989). Guided, cooperative learning and individual knowledge acquisition. In L. B. Resnick (Ed.), *Knowing, learning, and instruction*. Mahwah, NJ: Erlbaum.

Brown, R. (1973). *A first language: The early stages.* Cambridge, MA: Harvard University Press.

Brownlie, F., & King, J. (2000). *Learning in safe schools: Creating classrooms where all students belong.* Markham, ON: Pembroke Publishers Ltd.

Bruer, J. (1989). *1989 Report.* St. Louis: James S. McDonnell Foundation.

Bryant, D. P., & Bryant, B. R. (1998). Using assistive technology adaptations to include students with learning disabilities in cooperative learning activities. *Journal of Learning Disabilities, 31,* 41–54.

Bryk, A. S. (1994). More good news that school organization matters. Issues in restructuring schools (Issue Report No. 7). Madison, WI: University of Wisconsin, Center on Organization and Restructuring of Schools.

Buhrmester, D., & Furman, W. (1987). The development of companionship and intimacy. *Child Development, 61,* 1387–1398.

Burger, J. M. (2000). *Personality* (5th ed.). Belmont, CA: Wadsworth.

Burz, H. L., & Marshall, K. (1996). Performance-based curriculum for mathematics: From knowing to showing. ERIC Document Reproduction Service No. ED400194.

Bushman, B. J., & Anderson, C. A. (2001). Media violence and the American public: Scientific facts versus media misinformation. *American Psychologist, 56,* 477–489.

Bussière, P., Cartwright, F., Crocker R., Ma, X., Oderkirk, J., & Zhang, Y. (2001) *Measuring Up: The Performance of Canada's Youth in Reading, Mathematics and Science.* Human Resources Development Canada, Statistics Canada, Council of Ministers of Education, Canada. Retrieved January 2003, from http://www.cmec.ca/pisa/2000/indexe.stm.

Butler, D. L. (1998a). The Strategic Content Learning approach to promoting self-regulated learning. In B. J. Zimmerman & D. Schunk (Eds.), *Developing self-regulated learning: From teaching to self-reflective practice* (pp. 160–183). New York: Guildford Publications, Inc.

Butler, D. L. (1998b). The Strategic Content Learning approach to promoting self-regulated learning: A summary of three studies. *Journal of Educational Psychology, 90,* 682–697.

Butler, D. L. (2002a). Individualizing instruction in self-regulated learning. *Theory into Practice, 41,* 81–92.

Butler, D. L. (2002b). Qualitative approaches to investigating self-regulated learning: Contributions and challenges. *Educational Psychologist, 37,* 59–63.

C

Cajete, G. A. (1999). Igniting the sparkle: An indigenous science education model. Skyand, NC: Kivaki Press.

Calabrese, R. L., & Schumer, H. (1986). The effects of service activities on adolescent alienation. *Adolescence, 21,* 675–687.

Calderhead, J. (1996). Teachers: Beliefs and knowledge. In D. C. Berliner, & R. C. Calfee (Eds.), *Handbook of educational psychology.* New York: Macmillan.

Calfee, R. C. (1999). Educational Psychology. In A. Kazdin (Ed.), *Encyclopedia of psychology.* Washington, DC, and New York: American Psychological Association and Oxford U. Press.

Calhoun, E. F. (1993). Action research: Three approaches. *Educational Leadership, 51(2),* 62–65.

Calhoun, E. M. (1994). *How to use research in the self-renewing school.* Alexandria, VA: Association for Supervision and Curriculum Development.

Callahan, S. (2001). When portfolios become a site of ethical conflict: Using student portfolios for teacher accountability. *Educational Assessment, 7(3),* 177–200.

Cameron, J. R., & Pierce, W. D. (1996). The debate about rewards and intrinsic motivation. *Review of Educational Research, 66,* 39–62.

Cameron, J., & Pierce, W. D. (2002). *Rewards and intrinsic motivation: Resolving the controversy.* Bergin & Garvey Press.

Cameron, J., Banko, K. M., & Pierce, W. E. (2001). Pervasive negative effects of rewards on intrinsic motivation: The myth continues. *The Behavior Analyst, 24(1),* 1–44.

Campbell, D. (2000). Authentic assessment and authentic standards. *Phi Delta Kappan, 81(5),* 405–407.

Campbell, D. T., & LeVine, D. T. (1968). Ethnocentrism and intergroup relations. In R. Abelson & others (Eds.), *Theories of cognitive consistency.* Chicago: Rand McNally.

Campbell, F. A., & Ramey, C. T. (1994). Effects of early intervention on intellectual and academic achievement: A follow-up study of children from low-income families. *Child Development, 65,* 684–698.

Campbell, F. A., Pungello, E. P., Miller-Johnson, S., Burchinal, M., & Ramey, C. T. (2001). The development of cognitive and academic abilities: Growth curves from an early childhood educational experiment. *Developmental Psychology, 37,* 231–243.

Campbell, J. I. D., & Xue, Q. (2001). Cognitive arithmetic across cultures. *Journal of Experimental Psychology: General, 130 (2),* 299–315.

Campbell, L., Campbell, B., & Dickinson, D. (1999). *Teaching and learning through multiple intelligences* (2nd ed.). Boston: Allyn & Bacon.

Canadian & World Encyclopedia. (1998). Toronto, ON: McClelland & Stewart.

Canadian Charter of Rights and Freedoms. (1982).

Canadian Council on Social Development. (2001). The Progress of Canada's Children. Ottawa, ON: The Canadian Council on Social Development.

Canadian Council on Social Development. (2002). Child poverty: It's more than just a number game. Ottawa, ON: The Canadian Council on Social Development.

Canadian Fact Book on Poverty. (2000). (Ross, D. P., Scott, K. J., & Smith, P. J.): Ottawa, ON: Canadian Council on Social Development.

Canadian Fitness and Lifestyle Research Institute (CFLRI). (1996). How Canadians spend their time. *Progress in Prevention, Bulletin No. 7.* Ottawa, ON: Authors.

Canadian Psychological Association. (1996). *CPA accredited programmes.* Retrieved 7 December 2002, from: http://www.cpa.ca/accredlist.htm.

Canadian Teachers' Federation. (1992). *The better idea book: A resource book on gender, culture, science and schools.* Ottawa, ON: Author.

Canadian Teachers' Federation. (1999). Assessment and Evaluation: Policy. Retrieved 6 December 2002, from: http://www.ctf-fce.ca/e/what/other/assessment/testing-policy.html.

Carlson, J. S., & Das, J. P. (1996). A process approach to remediating word decoding deficiencies in Chapter 1 Children. *Learning Disability Quarterly, 20(2),* 93–102.

Carroll, J. B. (1963). A model of school learning. *Teachers College Record, 64,* 723–733.

Cascio, W. (2000). Test utility. In A. Kazdin (Ed.), *Encyclopedia of psychology.* Washington, DC, & New York: American Psychological Association and Oxford U. Press.

Case, R. (1985). *Intellectual development: Birth to adulthood.* NY: Academic Press.

Case, R. (1987). Neo-Piagetian theory: Retrospect and prospect. *International Journal of Psychology, 22,* 773–791.

Case, R. (1992a). *The mind's staircase: Exploring the conceptual underpinnings of children's thought and knowledge.* Hillsdale, NJ: Lawrence Erlbaum Associates.

Case, R. (1992b). The role of the frontal lobes in the regulation of cognitive development. *Brain and Cognition, 20,* 51–73.

Case, R. (1997). The development of conceptual structures. In D. Kuhn & R. S. Siegler (Eds.), *Carmichael's handbook of child development: Vol. 2. Perception, cognition and language* (5th ed., pp. 745–800). NY: McGraw Hill.

Case, R. (1997, April). *A dynamic model of general numerical understanding and its development in specific contexts.* Paper presented at the meeting of the Society for Research in Child Development, Washington, DC.

Case, R. (1998). The development of conceptual structures. In W. Damon (Ed.), *Handbook of child psychology* (5th ed., Vol. 2). New York: Wiley.

Case, R. (1998). Conceptual development in the child and in the field: A personal view of the Piagetian legacy. In E. Scholnick & S. Gelman (Eds). *Conceptual representation: The Piagetian legacy* (pp. 23–51). Hillsdale, NJ: Erlbaum.

Case, R. (1999). Cognitive development. In M. Bennett (Ed.) *Developmental psychology: Achievements and prospects* (pp. 36–54). Philadelphia: Taylor & Francis.

Case, R. (2000). Conceptual structures. In M. Bennett (Ed.), *Developmental psychology.* Philadelphia: Psychology Press.

Case, R., & McKeough, A. (1990). Schooling and the development of central conceptual structures: An example from the domain of children's narrative. *International Journal of Educational Psychology, 8,* 835–855.

Case, R., Griffin, S. & Kelly, W. (1999). Social class gradients in mathematical ability and their responsiveness to compensatory education. In D. Keating & C. Hertzman (Eds.), *Tomorrow's society, today's children: The health and developmental wealth of nations* (pp. 125–150). New York: Guilford.

Case, R., Okamoto, Y., Griffin, S., McKeough, A., Bleiker, C., Henderson, B., et al. (1996). The role of central conceptual structures in the development of children's thought. *Monographs of the Society for Research in Child Development, 61* (1–2), 1–266 .

Caspi, A., Henry, B., McGee, R. O., Moffitt, T. E., & Silva, P. A. (1995). Temperamental origins of child and adolescent behavior problems: From age three to age fifteen. *Child Development, 66,* 55–68.

Cavalier, J., & Klein, J. (1998). Effects of cooperative versus individual learning and orienting activities during computer-based instruction. *Educational Technology, Research and Development, 46(1),* 5–17.

Ceci, S. J. (1990). *On intelligence . . . more or less: A bioecological treatise.* Upper Saddle River, NJ: Prentice Hall.

Ceci, S. J. (2000). Memory: Constructive processes. In A. Kazdin (Ed.), *Encyclopedia of psychology.* Washington, DC, and New York: American Psychological Association and Oxford U. Press.

Ceci, S. J., Rosenblum, T., deBruyn, E., & Lee, D. Y. (1997). A bio-ecological model of intellectual development. In R. J. Sternberg & E. Grigorenko (Eds.), *Intelligence, heredity, and environment.* New York: Cambridge University Press.

CESC (Canadian Education Statistics Council). (2000). *Education Indicators in Canada: Report of the Pan-Canadian Education Indicators Program 1999.* Retrieved 14 December 2002, from: http://www.cesc.ca/pceip/pceipen.pdf.

Chalmers, A. (1995). Insights into gender, identity and equity. In Lisa Pedrini (Ed.), *Tools for gender equity.* A B.C. Teachers' Federation Research Project. Retrieved 20 January 2003, from: http://www.bctf.bc.ca/ResearchReports/94sw01/Articles/Article1.html.

Charles, C. M. (1997). *Introduction to educational psychology* (3rd ed.). New York: Longman.

Chen, C., & Uttal, D. H. (1988). Cultural values, parents' beliefs, and children's achievement in the United States and China. *Human Development, 31,* 351–358.

Chen, C., Lee, S. Y., & Stevenson, H. W. (1996). Long-term prediction of academic achievement of American, Chinese, and Japanese adolescents. *Journal of Educational Psychology, 88,* 750–759.

Chess, S., & Thomas, A. (1977). Temperamental individuality from childhood to adolescence. *Journal of Child Psychiatry, 16,* 218–226.

Chi, M. T. H. (1978). Knowledge structures and memory development. In R. S. Siegler (Ed.), *Children's thinking.* Mahwah, NJ: Erlbaum.

Chin, P., Mumby, H., & Krugly-Smolka, E. (1997). Science: Secondary school curriculum. Background Research Commissioned by the Ontario Ministry of Education and Training. Toronto, ON: Queen's Printer Ontario. Retrieved May 2002, from http://www.stao.org/backgrnd.htm.

Chira, S. (1993, June 23). What do teachers want most? Help from parents. *New York Times,* sec. 1, p. 7.

Chomsky, N. (1957). *Syntactic structures.* The Hague: Mouton.

Christensen, C. R. (1991). The discussion teacher in action: Questioning, listening, and response. In C. R. Christensen, D. A. Garvin, & A. Sweet (Eds.), *Education for judgment.* Boston: Harvard University Business School.

Ciardiello, A. V. (1998). Did you ask a good question today? Alternative cognitive and metacognitive strategies. *Journal of Adolescent an Adult Literacy, 42(3),* 210–219.

Cifuentes, L. & Murphy, K. L. (2000). Promoting multicultural understanding and positive self-concept through a distance learning community: Cultural Connections. *Educational Technology Research and Development, 48 (1),* 69–83.

Clarke, M. M., Madaus, G. F., Horn, C. L., & Ramos, M. A. (2000). Retrospective on educational testing and assessment in the 20th century. *Journal of Curriculum Studies, 32*(2), 159–181.

Clay, M. M. (1993). *Reading Recovery: A guidebook for teachers in training.* Portsmouth, NH: Heinemann.

Clay, M. M., & Cazden, C. B. (1990). A Vygotskian Interpretation of Reading Recovery. In L. Moll (Ed.), *Vygotsky and education.* New York: Oxford University Press.

Clay, R. A. (1997, December). Are children being overmedicated? *APA Monitor,* pp. 1, 27.

Clinchy, B. M., Mansfield, A. F., & Schott, J. L. (1995, March). *Development of narrative and scientific modes of thought in middle childhood.* Paper presented at the meeting of the Society for Research in Child Development, Indianapolis.

Coben, S. S., Thomas, C. C., Sattler, R. O., & Morsink, C. V. (1997). Meeting the challenge of consultation and collaboration: Developing interactive teams. *Journal of Learning Disabilities, 30,* 427–432.

Cognition and Technology Group at Vanderbilt. (1997). *Designing environments to reveal, support, and expand our children's potentials.* Paper presented at the meeting of the Society for Research in Child Development, Washington, DC.

Cohen, M. J. (2000). *Live animal laboratories in physiology teaching.* Medical Research Modernization Committee paper. Retrieved 15 December 2002, from: http://www.mrmcmed.org/lal.html.

Cohen, R. J., & Swerdlik, M. E. (1999). *Psychological testing and assessment* (4th ed.). Mountain View, CA: Mayfield.

Coladarci, T. (1992). Teachers' sense of efficacy and commitment to teaching. *Journal of Experimental Education, 60,* 323–337.

Colby, A., Kohlberg, L., Gibbs, J., & Lieberman, M. (1983). A longitudinal study of moral judgment. *Monographs of the Society for Research in Child Development, 48* (21, Serial No. 201).

Cole, M. (1999). Culture in development. In M. H. Bornstein & M. E. Lamb (Eds.), *Developmental psychology* (4th ed.). Mahwah, NJ: Erlbaum.

Cole, M. (2001). Culture-free versus culture-based measures of cognition. In R. J. Sternberg (Ed.), *The nature of cognition (pp. 645–664).* Massachusetts: The MIT Press.

Cole, N., & Willmingham, W. W. (1997). *Gender and fair assessment.* Mahwah, NJ: Lawrence Erlbaum and Associates.

Collins, M. (1996, Winter). The job outlook for '96 grads. *Journal of Career Planning,* pp. 51–54.

Collinson, V., Killeavy, M., & Stephenson, H. J. (1999). Exemplary teachers: Practicing in ethics of care in England, Ireland, and the United States. *Journal for Just and Caring Education, 5(4),* 349–366.

Columba, L. (2001). Daily classroom assessment. *Education, 122*(2), 372–375.

Combs, D. (1997, September). Using alternative assessment to provide options for student success. *Middle School Journal,* pp. 3–8.

Cone, J. (1999). Observational assessment. In P. C. Kendall, J. N. Butcher, & G. Holmbeck (Eds.), *Handbook of research methods in clinical psychology.* New York: Wiley.

Conger, J. J., & Galambos, N. L. (1997). *Adolescence and youth: Psychological development in a changing world (5th ed.).* New York: Addison Wesley Longman.

Connell, D. (1998, April 6). Commentary, *Newsweek,* p. 24.

Connolly, J., Hachette, V., & McMaster, L. (1998). Academic achievement in early adolescence: Do school attitudes make a difference? Investing in Children: A National Research Conference (Workshop Paper #w-98-14Es). Retrieved 15 December 2002, from: http://www.hrdc-drhc.gc.ca/sp-ps/arb-dgra/conferences/nlscyconf/w-98-14es-e.pdf.

Connolly, J., Pepler, D. J., Craig, W. M., & Tardash, A. (2000). Bullies and their conceptions of romantic relationships. *Journal of Child Maltreatment, 5.*

Conti, R., & Amabile, T. (1999). Motivation/drive. In M. A. Runco & S. Pritzker (Eds.), *Encyclopedia of creativity.* San Diego: Academic Press.

Cooper, H. (1989). Synthesis of research on homework. *Educational Leadership, 47* (3), 85–91.

Cooper, H., Lindsay, J. J., Nye, B., & Greathouse, S. (1998). Relationships among attitudes about homework, amount of homework assigned and completed, and student achievement. *Journal of Educational Psychology, 90,* 70–83.

Corbett B. A., & Willms, J. D. (2002, April). Canadian students' access to and use of information and communication technology. Paper presented at 2002 Pan-Canadian Education Research Agenda Symposium "Information Technology and Learning." Montreal, Quebec.

Corno, L. (1998, March 30). Commentary. *Newsweek,* p. 51.

Costa, P. (2000). NEO Personality Inventory. In A. Kazdin (Ed.), *Encyclopedia of psychology*. Washington, DC, and New York: American Psychological Association and Oxford University Press.

Costa, P. T., & McRae, R. R. (1998). Personality assessment. In H. S. Friedman (Ed.), *Encyclopedia of mental health* (Vol. 3). San Diego: Academic Press.

Council for Exceptional Children. (1998). *CEC's comments on the proposed IDEA regulations*. Washington, DC: Author.

Council of Ministers of Education Canada. (1995). *A Report on Education in Canada*. Toronto, ON. Retrieved 15 September 2002, from: http://www.cmec.ca/reports/rprt95e.htm.

Council of Ministers of Education, Canada. (2001). *Measuring Up: The performance of Canada's youth in reading, mathematics and science—OECD PISA Study: First Results for Canadians aged 15*. Retrieved 5 December 2002, from: http://www.cmec.ca/pisa/2000/CanadaReport.en.pdf.

Courchene, T. J. (2002). *Knowledge and human capital: The winning combo for the information era*. Paper presented at the TD Forum on Canada's Standard of Living. Retrieved from http://www.td.com/economics/standard/full/Courchene.pdf.

Couture J. (1997). Teachers' work: Living in the culture of insufficiency. In M. Moll (Ed.), *Tech high: Globalization and the future of Canadian education* (pp. 139–166). Halifax, NS: Canadian Centre for Policy Alternatives and Fernwood Publishing.

Covington, M. V. (1992). *Making the grade: A self-worth perspective on motivation and school reform*. New York: Cambridge University Press.

Covington, M. V. (1997). A motivational analysis of academic life in college. In R. P. Perry & J. C. Smart (Eds.). *Effective teaching in higher education: Research and practice*. New York: Agathon Press.

Covington, M. V. (1998, April). *Caring about learning: The nature and nurturing of subject-matter appreciation*. Paper presented at the meeting of the American Educational Research Association, San Diego.

Covington, M. V., & Teel, K. T. (1996). *Overcoming student failure*. Washington, DC: American Psychological Association.

Covington, M. V., Teel, K. M., & Parecki, A. D. (1994, April). *Motivation benefits of improved academic performance among middle-school African American students through an effort-based grading system*. Paper presented at the meeting of the American Educational Research Association, New Orleans.

Covington, M.V. (2000). A motivational analysis of academic life in college. In R.P. Perry & J.C. Smart (Eds.). *Effective teaching in higher education: Research and practice*. New York: Agathon Press.

Cowley, G. (1998, April 6). Why children turn violent. *Newsweek*, pp. 24–25.

Coyne, J. C. (2000). Mood disorders. In A. Kazdin (Ed.), *Encyclopedia of psychology*. Washington, DC, and New York: American Psychological Association and Oxford U. Press.

Craig, W. M., Pepler, D. J., Atlas, R. (2000). Observations of bullying on the playground and in the classroom. *International Journal of School Psychology, 21*, 22–36.

Craig, W. M., Pepler, D., Connolly, J., & Henderson, K. (2001). Developmental context of peer harassment in early adolescence: The role of puberty and the peer group. In J. Juvonen & S. Graham (Eds.), *Peer Harassment in School: The Plight of the Vulnerable and Victimized* (pp. 242–261). New York: Guilford.

Craik, F. I. M. (2000). Memory: Coding processes. In A. Kazdin (Ed.), *Encyclopedia of psychology*. Washington, DC, and New York: American Psychological Association and Oxford U. Press.

Craik, F. I. M., & Lockhart, R. S. (1972). Levels of processing: A framework for memory research. *Journal of Verbal Learning and Verbal Behavior, 11*, 671–684.

Cranton, P. (2000). *Planning instruction for adult learners* (2nd ed.). Toronto, ON: Wall & Emerson.

Crawford, C., & Krebs, D. L. (Eds.) (1998). *Handbook of Evolutionary Psychology: Ideas, Issues and Applications*. Hillsdale, NJ: Erlbaum Associates.

Crawford, M., & Unger, R. (2000). *Women and gender* (3rd ed.) New York: McGraw-Hill.

Creemers, B. (1996). The school effectiveness knowledge base. In D. Reynolds *et al.* (Eds.), *Making good schools. Linking school effectiveness and school improvement* (pp. 36–58). London: Routledge.

Cronbach, L. J. (1975). Beyond the two disciplines of scientific psychology. *American Psychologist, 30*, 116–127.

Csikszentmihalyi, M. (1990). *Flow*. New York: Harper & Row.

Csikszentmihalyi, M. (1993). *The evolving self*. New York: HarperCollins.

Csikszentmihalyi, M. (2000). Creativity: An overview. In A. Kazdin (Ed.), *Encyclopedia of psychology*. Washington, DC, and New York: American Psychological Association and Oxford University Press.

Csikszentmihalyi, M., Rathunde, K., & Whalen, S. (1993). *Talented teenagers: The roots of success and failure*. Cambridge, UK: Cambridge University Press.

CSR Research Consortium. (1999). Executive Summary: Class Size Reduction in California: The 1998–99 Evaluation Findings. CSR Research Consortium Web site: www.classize.org.

Culbertson, F. M. (1997). Depression and gender. *American Psychologist, 52*, 25–31.

Cummins, J. (1991). Empowering minority students: A framework for intervention. In M. Minami and B. P. Kennedy (Eds.), *Language issues in literacy and bilingual/multicultural education*. Harvard Educational Review Reprint Series. Cambridge, MA: Educational Board Harvard University.

Cummins, J., & Danesi, M. (1990). *Heritage Languages: The Development and Denial of Canada's Linguistic Resources*. Toronto: Garamond Press.

Cunningham, A. E., & Stanovich, K. E. (1997). Early reading acquisition and its relation to reading experience and ability 10 years later. *Developmental Psychology, 33*, 934–945.

Cunningham, C. E., Boyle, M. H., Offord, D. R., Racine, Y. A., Hundert, J., Secord, M., & McDonald, J. (2000). Tri-Ministry Study: Correlates of school-based parenting course utilization. *Journal of Consulting and Clinical Psychology, 68(5)*, 928–933.

Cunningham, C. E., Cunningham, L. J., & Martorelli, V. (1997). *Coping with conflict at school: the collaborative student mediation project manual*. Hamilton, ON: COPE Works, 1997.

Cunningham, C. E., Cunningham, L. J., Martorelli, V., Tran, A., Young, J., & Zacharias, Y. R. (1998). The effects of primary division, student-mediated conflict resolution programs on playground aggression. *Journal of Child Psychology and Psychiatry and Allied Disciplines, 39(5)*, 653–662.

Cushner, K., McClelland, A., & Safford, P. (1996). *Human diversity and education* (2nd ed.). New York: McGraw-Hill.

D

Daiute, C., & Dalton, B. (1993). Collaboration between children learning to write: Can novices be masters? *Cognition and Instruction, 10*, 281–333.

Damon, W. (2000). Moral development. In A. Kazdin (Ed.), *Encyclopedia of psychology*. Washington, DC, and New York: American Psychological Association and Oxford University Press.

Dansereau, D. F. (1988). Cooperative learning strategies. In C. E. Weinstein, E. T. Goetz, & P. A. Alexander (Eds.), *Learning and study strategies*. Orlando, FL: Academic Press.

Danyluk, R. C., & da Costa, J. L. (1999, April). Identifying and addressing challenges encountered by educators of aboriginal children in an urban setting. Paper presented at the American Educational Research Association Annual Meeting, Montreal, QC. (ED 429 958; p. 23).

Darou. W. G. (1992). Native Canadians and intelligence testing. *Canadian Journal of counseling, 26(2)*, 96–99.

Das, J. P. (2000). Mental retardation. In A. Kazdin (Ed.), *Encyclopedia of psychology*. Washington, DC, and New York: American Psychological Association and Oxford University Press.

Das, J. P. (2001). *PASS reading enhancement program: PREP*. Retrieved April 16, 2002, from http://www.quasar.ualberta.ca/ddc/development/prep.html.

Dauite, C. (2001). Social relational knowing in writing development. In J. Byrnes & E. Amsel (Eds.), *Language, literacy, and cognitive development*. Mahwah, NJ: Erlbaum.

Davidson, J. (2000). Giftedness. In A. Kazdin (Ed.), *Encyclopedia of psychology*. Washington, DC, and New York: American Psychological Association and Oxford University Press.

Davidson, R. J. (1996). The effects of decision characteristics on children's selective search of predecisional information. *Acta Psychologica, 92*, 263–281.

Davis, C. G. & Nolen-Hoesekema, S. (2001). Loss and meaning: How do people make sense of loss? *American Behavioral Scientist, 44*, 726–741.

Deaux, K. (1996). Social identification. In E. T. Higgins & A. Kruglanski (Eds.), *Social psychology: Handbook of basic mechanisms and processes* (pp. 777–798). New York: Guilford Press.

Deci, E. L. (1975). *Intrinsic motivation.* New York: Plenum.

Deci, E., & Ryan, R. (1994). Promoting self-determined education. *Scandinavian Journal of Educational Research, 38,* 3–14.

Dempsey, J. V., Rasmussen, K., & Lucassen, B. (1996*). The instructional gaming literature: Implications and 99 sources* (COE Technical report 96-1). Mobile, AL: University of South Alabama, College of Education. Retrieved December 15, 2002, from: http://www.coe.usouthal.edu/TechReports/TR96_1.PDF.

Dempster, F. N. (1981). Memory span: Sources of individual and developmental differences. *Psychological Bulletin, 89,* 63–100.

Department of Education, New Brunswick. (2002). *Anglophone Sector: Educational Programs and Services.* Retrieved December 2002, from http://gnb.ca/0000/anglophone-e.asp.

Department of Education, Newfoundland. (2002). *Public Examinations Handbook 2001.* Retrieved December 2002, from http://www.gov.nf.ca/edu/pub/public/public.htm.

Derlega, V., Winstead, B., & Jones, W. (1999). *Personality: Contemporary theory and research* (2nd ed.). Belmont, CA: Wadsworth.

de Villers, J. (1996). Towards a rational empiricism: Why interactionism isn't behaviorism any more than biology is genetics. In M. E. Rice (Ed.), *Towards a genetics of language.* Mahwah, NJ: Erlbaum.

de Villiers, J. G., & de Villiers, P. A. (1999). Language development. In M. H. Bornstein & M. E. Lamb (Eds.), *Developmental psychology: An advanced textbook* (4th ed.). Mahwah, NJ: Erlbaum.

Dewey, J. (1933). *How we think.* Lexington, MA: D. C. Heath.

Dick, T. P., & Rallis, S. F. (1991). Factors and influences on high school students' career choices. *Journal for Research in Mathematical Education, 22(4),* 28192.

DiPetta, T., & Woloshyn, V. E. (2001). Voice recognition for online literacy: Continuous voice recognition technology in adult literacy training. *Education and Information Technologies, 6(4),* 225–241.

DiPetta, T., Novak, J. M., & Marini, Z. A. (2002). *Inviting online education.* Phi Delta Kappa Education Foundation. Fastback, 498. Bloomington, Indiana: Phi Delta Kappa Educational Foundation.

Dishion, T. J., & Spracklen, K. M. (1996, March). *Childhood peer rejection in the development of adolescent substance abuse.* Paper presented at the meeting of the Society for Research on Adolescence. Boston.

Domino, G. (2000). *Psychological testing.* Upper Saddle River, NJ: Prentice Hall.

Domjan, M. (2000). Learning: An overview. In A. Kazdin (Ed.), *Encyclopedia of psychology.* Washington, DC, and New York: American Psychological Association and Oxford University Press.

Doolittle, P. (1997). Vygotsky's zone of proximal development as a theoretical foundation for cooperative learning. *Journal on Excellence in College Teaching, 8,* 81–101.

Douglass, M. E., & Douglass, D. N. (1993). *Manage your work yourself* (updated ed.). New York: American Management Association.

Doyle, J. A., & Paludi, M. A. (1998). *Sex and gender* (4th ed.). New York: McGraw-Hill.

Doyle, W. (1986). Classroom organization and management. In M. C. Wittrock (Ed.), *Handbook of research on teaching* (3rd ed.). New York: Macmillan.

Drake, S. M. (1998). *Creating integrated curriculum: Proven ways to increase student learning.* Thousand Oaks, CA: Corwin Press, Inc.

Driscoll, M. (2000). *Psychology of learning for instruction* (2nd ed.). Boston: Allyn & Bacon.

Drouin, J. (2000a). *SchoolNet online connectivity survey report.* Retrieved December 12, 2002, from: http://www.schoolnet.ca/home/e/connectivityresearch.asp.

Drouin, J. (2000b). *Internet connectivity comparison between Canadian and United States schools.* Retrieved 12 December 2002, from: http://www.schoolnet.ca/home/e/connectivityresearch.asp.

Drummond, R. J. (2000). *Appraisal procedures for counselors and helping professionals* (4th ed.). Upper Saddle River, NJ: Merrill.

Dryfoos, J. (1998). *Safe passage: Making it through adolescence in a risky society.* New York: Oxford University Press.

Duffy, G. G. (1993). Rethinking strategy instruction: Four teachers' development and their low achievers' understandings. *Elementary School Journal, 93(3),* 231–247.

Duncan, A. (1996). The Shared Concern Method for resolving group bullying in schools. *Educational Psychology in Practice, 12(2),* 94–98.

Dunphy, D. C. (1963). The social structure of urban adolescent peer groups. *Society, 26,* 230–246.

DuPaul, G. J., & Henningson, P. N. (1993). Peer tutoring effects on the classroom performance of children with Attention Deficit Hyperactivity Disorder. *School Psychology Review, 22(1),* 134–143.

Durkin, K., & Nugent, B. (1998). Kindergarten children's gender-role expectations for television actors. *Sex Roles, 38(5/6),* 387–402.

Durost, R. (1996). Single sex math classes: What and for whom? One school's experiences. *Bulletin, 80,* 27–31.

Durrant, J. E. (1999). Evaluating the success of Sweden's corporal punishment ban. *Child Abuse and Neglect, 23,* 435–448.

Durrant, J. E., Broberg, A., & Rose-Krasnor, L. (1999). Predicting use of physical punishment during mother–child conflicts in Sweden and Canada. In P. Hastings & C. Piotrowski (Eds.), *Maternal beliefs about child rearing. New directions for child & adolescent development, 86,* 25–42.

Dweck, C. S., & Leggett, E. (1988). A social cognitive approach to motivation and personality. *Psychological Review, 95,* 256–273.

Dwort, D., & Rathgeber, A. (1998). Confusion reigns: Definitions of behaviour exceptionalities in Canada. *Exceptionality Education Canada, 8(1),* 3–19.

E

Eagly, A. H., & Crowley, M. (1986). Gender and helping behavior: A meta-analytic review of the social psychological literature. *Psychological Bulletin, 100,* 283–308.

Eagly, A. H., & Steffen, V. J. (1986). Gender and aggressive behavior: A meta-analytic review of the social psychological literature. *Psychological Bulletin, 111,* 3–22.

Earl, L. M. (1999). Assessment and accountability in education: Improvement or surveillance? *Education Canada, 39(3),* 4–6.

Earl, L., & Katz, S. (2000). The paradox of classroom assessment. *Orbit, 30(4),* 8–10.

Eccles, J. (1994). Understanding women's educational and occupational choices. *Psychology of Women Quarterly, 18,* 585–609.

Eccles, J. (2000). Social patterns, achievements, and problems. In A. Kazdin (Ed.), *Encyclopedia of psychology.* Washington, DC, & New York: American Psychological Association and Oxford U. Press.

Eccles, J. S. (1993). School and family effects on the ontogeny of children's interests, self-perceptions, and activity choice. In J. Jacobs (Ed.), *Nebraska symposium on motivation.* Lincoln: University of Nebraska Press.

Eccles, J. S. (2000). Adolescence: Social patterns, achievements, and problems. In A. Kazdin (Ed.), *Encyclopedia of psychology.* Washington, DC, & New York: American Psychological Association and Oxford University Press.

Eccles, J. S., & Harold, R. D. (1996). Family involvement in children's and adolescents' schooling. In A. Booth & J. E. Dunn (Eds.), *Family-school links.* Mahwah, NJ: Erlbaum.

Eccles, J. S., Lord, S., & Buchanan, C. M. (1996). School transitions in early adolescence: What are we doing to our young people? In J. A. Graeber, J. Brooks-Gunn, & A. C. Petersen (Eds.), *Transitions in adolescence.* Mahwah, NJ: Erlbaum.

Eccles, J. S., Wigfield, A., & Schiefele, U. (1998). Motivation to succeed. In W. Damon (Ed.), *Handbook of child psychology* (5th ed., Vol. 3). New York: Wiley.

Eccles, J. S., Wigfield, A., Harold, R., & Blumenfeld, P. B. (1993). Age and gender differences in children's self- and task-perceptions during elementary school. *Child Development, 64,* 830–847.

Eccles, J., Barber, B., Jozefowicz, D., Malenchuk, O., & Vida, M. (1999). Self-evaluations of competence, task values, and self-esteem. In N. Johnson, M. Roberts, & J. Worell (Eds.). *Beyond appearance: A new look at adolescent girls.* Washington, DC: American Psychological Association.

Echols, L. D., West, R. F., Stanovich, K. E., & Zehr, K. S. (1996). Using children's literacy activities to predict growth in verbal cognitive skills: A longitudinal investigation. *Journal of Educational Psychology, 88(2),* 296–304.

Education Improvement Commission. (1999). Progress report to the Education Improvement Commission: Overview. Retrieved October 6, 2002, from: http://www.ocdsb.edu.on.ca/General_Info/EIC/EIC_Director/Default.htm.

Eisenberg, N., & Fabes, R. A. (1998). Prosocial development. In W. Damon (Ed.), *Handbook of child psychology* (5th ed., Vol. 3). New York: Wiley.

Eisenberg, N., Martin, C. L., & Fabes, R. A. (1996). Gender development and gender effects. In D. C. Berliner & R. C. Calfee (Eds.), *Handbook of educational psychology.* New York: Macmillan.

Eisenberger, R., & Cameron, J. (1998). Reward, intrinsic interest, and creativity: New findings. *American Psychologist, 53,* 676–679.

Eisner, E. W. (1999, May). The uses and limits of performance assessment. *Phi Delta Kappan, 80,* 658–661.

Elbaum, B., Vaughn, S., Tejero Hughes, M., & Watson Moody, S. (2000). How effective are one-to-one tutoring programs in reading for elementary students at risk for reading failure? A meta-analysis of the intervention research. *Journal of Educational Psychology, 92(4),* 605–619.

Elkind, D. (1978). Understanding the young adolescent. *Adolescence, 13,* 127–134.

Elkind, J. I. (2000). Technology and disabilities. In A. Kazdin (Ed.), *Encyclopedia of psychology.* Washington, DC, and New York: American Psychological Association and Oxford University Press.

Elliot, A. J., McGregor, H. A., & Gable, S. (1999). Achievement goals, study strategies, and exam performance: A mediational analysis. *Journal of Educational Psychology, 91,* 549–563.

Elliott, A., & Woloshyn, V. (1996). Adopting collaborative learning strategies in the classroom. *The Canadian School Executive, 15(9),* 3–9.

Elliott, A., Woloshyn, V., Richards, M. & Mitchell, C. (Eds.) (2001). *Collaboration uncovered: The forgotten, the assumed and the unexamined.* Westport, CT: Greenwood Publishing Group.

Ellis, J., Small-McGinley, J., & Hart, S. (1998). Mentor-supported literacy programs in elementary schools. *Alberta Journal of Educational Research, 44(2),* 149–162.

Elsea, M., & Smith, P. K. (1998). The long-term effectiveness of anti-bullying work in primary schools. *Educational Researcher, 40,* 203–218.

Emery, R. E. (1999). *Marriage, divorce, and children's adjustment* (2nd ed.). Thousand Oaks, CA: Sage.

Emig, V. B. (1997). A multiple intelligences inventory. *Educational Leadership, 55(1),* 47–50.

Emmer, E. T., Evertson, C. M., & Worsham, M. E. (2000). *Classroom management for secondary teachers* (5th ed.). Boston: Allyn & Bacon.

Emmer, E. T., Evertson, C. M., & Worsham, M. E. (2003). *Classroom management for secondary teachers* (6th ed.). Boston: Allyn & Bacon.

Engle, R. W. (2002). Working memory capacity as executive attention. *Current Directions in Psychological Science, 11,* 19–23.

Entwisle, D. R., & Alexander, K. L. (1993). Entry into the school: The beginning school transition and educational stratification in the United States. *Annual Review of Sociology, 19,* 401–423.

Enzle, M. E., Wright, E. F., & Redondo, I. M. (1996). Cross-Task Generalization of Intrinsic Motivation Effects. *Canadian Journal of Behavioural Science, 28.* Retrieved 16 December 2002, from: http://www.cpa.ca/cjbsnew/1996/ful_enzle.html.

Epstein, J. L. (1996). Perspectives and previews on research and policy for school, family, and community partnerships. In A. Booth & J. F. Dunn (Eds.), *Family-school links.* Mahwah, NJ: Erlbaum.

Epstein, J. L. (1997, June 6). Commentary, *Wall Street Journal,* sec. 1, p. 1.

EQAO. (2001). *Education Quality and Accountability Office: Ontario Provincial Report on Achievement 2000–2001—English language elementary schools.* Retrieved 5 December 2002, from: http://www.eqao.com/eqao/home_page/pdf_e/01/01P081e.pdf.

Erikson, E. H. (1968). *Identity: Youth and crisis.* New York: W. W. Norton.

Ernest, P. (1997). *Social constructivism as a philosophy of mathematics.* Albany, NY: State University of New York Press.

Esses, V. M., & Gardner, R. C. (1996). Multiculturalism in Canada: Context and current status. *Canadian Journal of Behavioural Science, 8(3),* 145–152. Retrieved 12 December 2002, from: http://www.cpa.ca/cjbsnew/1996/ful_edito.html.

Evans, M. (1999). Civics. Secondary Policy Document for Ontario Ministry of Education and Training Secondary Curriculum, Grades 9 and 10: Canadian and World Studies (new compulsory secondary school Civics course for Canadian and World Studies—primary author).

Evans, M. A. (1996). Reticent primary grade children and their more talkative peers: Verbal, nonverbal, and self-concept characteristics. *Journal of Educational Psychology, 88 (4),* 739–749.

Evertson, C. M., Emmer, E. T., & Worsham, M. E. (2003). *Classroom management for elementary teachers* (6th ed.). Boston: Allyn & Bacon.

Evertson, C. M., Emmer, E. T., Clements, B. S., & Worsham, M. E. (1994). *Classroom Management for Elementary Teachers.* Boston, MA: Allyn & Bacon.

F

Farkas, G. (2001). *Poverty and children's vocabulary development.* Unpublished manuscript, Pennsylvania State University.

Farran, D. C. & Shonkoff, J. P. (1994). Developmental disabilities and the concept of school readiness. *Early Education and Development, 5 (2),* 141–151.

Farrington, D. P. (2000). Explaining and preventing crime: The globalization of knowledge—The American Society of Criminology 1999 presidential address. *Criminology 38(1),* 1–24.

Fearn, L. (1972). *The maligned wolf.* San Diego: Kabyn Press.

Fekken, G. C. (2000). Reliability. In A. Kazdin (Ed.), *Encyclopedia of psychology.* Washington, DC, & New York: American Psychological Association and Oxford University Press.

Feldhusen, J. F. (1997). Secondary services, opportunities, and activities for talented youth. In N. Colangelo & G. A. Davis (Eds.), *Handbook of gifted education.* Boston: Allyn & Bacon.

Feng, Y. (1996). Some thoughts about applying constructivist theories to guide instruction. *Computers in the Schools, 12,* 71–84.

Ferguson, C. J. (2002). Media violence: Miscast causality. *American Psychologist, 57,* 446–448.

Ferguson, P., & Fraser, B. (1998). Student gender, school size and changing perceptions of science learning environments during the transition from primary to secondary school. *Research in Science Education, 28(4),* 387–397.

Fernandez, P., & Thompson, S. (2000). Frontier College: A century of lifelong learning outside the boxes. *Education Canada, 40(2),* 12–14.

Ferrari, M., & Sternberg, R. J. (1998). The development of mental abilities and styles. In W. Damon (Ed.), *Handbook of child psychology* (Vol. 2). New York: Wiley.

Feuerstein, R., Jackson, Y., & Lewis, J. (1998). Feuerstein's IE and structural cognitive modifiability. In R. Samuda (Ed.), *Advances in Cross-Cultural Assessment.* Thousand Oaks, CA: Sage.

Field, T. (Ed.). (1995). *Touch in early development.* Mahwah, NJ: Erlbaum.

Firpo-Triplett, R. (1997, July). *Is it flirting or sexual harassment?* Paper presented at the Working with America's Youth conference, Pittsburgh.

Fisher, C. W., Berliner, D. C., Filby, N. N., Marliave, R., Ghen, L. S., & Dishaw, M. M. (1980). Teaching behaviors, academic learning time, and student achievement: An overview. In C. Denham & A. Lieberman (Eds.), *Time to learn.* Washington, DC: National Institute of Education.

Fitzgerald, J., & Shanahan, T. (2000). Reading and writing relations and their development. *Educational Psychologist, 35 (1),* 39–50.

Flake, C., Kuhs, T., Donnelly, A., & Ebert, C. (1995). Teacher as researcher: Reinventing the role of teacher. *Phi Delta Kappan, 76,* 405–407.

Flanders, N. A. (1970). *Analyzing teaching behavior.* Reading, MA: Addison-Wesley.

Flavell, J. H. (1999). Cognitive development. *Annual Review of Psychology* (Vol. 50). Palo Alto, CA: Annual Reviews.

Flavell, J. H., & Miller, P. H. (1998). Social cognition. In W. Damon (Ed.), *Handbook of child psychology* (Vol. 2). New York: Wiley.

Flavell, J. H., Friedrichs, A., & Hoyt, J. (1970). Developmental changes in memorization processes. *Cognitive Psychology, 1,* 324–340.

Flavell, J. H., Miller, P. H., & Miller, S. A. (1993). *Cognitive development* (3rd ed.). Englewood Cliffs, NJ: Prentice Hall.

Flavell, J. H., Miller, P. H., & Miller, S. A. (2002). *Cognitive development* (4th ed.). Upper Saddle River, NJ: Prentice Hall.

Flinders, D. J., & Noddings, N. (2001). *Multiyear teaching: The case for continuity.* Bloomington, IN: Phi Delta Kappa International.

Flower, L. S., & Hayes, J. R. (1981). Problem-solving and the cognitive processes in writing. In C. Frederiksen & J. F. Dominic (Eds.), *Writing: The nature, development, and teaching of written communication.* Mahwah, NJ: Erlbaum.

Flynn, J. R. (1984). *The mean IQ of Americans: Massive gains.* New York: Harper & Row.

Fogarty, R. (1991). *The mindful school.* Arlington Heights, IL: IRI/Skylight.

Fogarty, R., & Stoehr, J. (1995). *Integrating curricula with multiple intelligences: Teams, themes and threads.* Palatine, IL: Skylight.

Foorman, B. R., Francis, D. J., Beeler, T., Winikates, D., & Fletcher, J. M. (1997). Early interventions for children with reading problems: Study designs and preliminary findings. *Learning Disabilities: A Multidisciplinary Perspective, 8,* 63–71.

Foot, D. (2001). Canadian education: Demographic change and future challenges. *Education Canada, 41*(1), 24–27.

Fotoples, R. M. (2000). Overcoming math anxiety. *Kappa Delta Pi Record (Summer),* 149–151.

Fox, B., & Hull, M. (2002). *Phonics for the teacher of reading* (8th ed.). Upper Saddle River, NJ: Merrill.

Fraenkel, J. R., & Wallen, N. (2000). *How to design and evaluate research in education.* New York: McGraw-Hill.

Frank, C., Dixon, C., & Brandts, L. (2001). Bears, trolls, and pagemasters: Learning about learners in book clubs. *The Reading Teacher, 54*(5), 448–462.

Frederick, J. A., & Boyd, M. (1998). The impact of family structure on high school completion. *Canadian Social Trends,* Spring, 12–14 (Catalogue No. 11-008). Ottawa, Ontario: Statistics Canada.

Freiberg, H. J. (1999). Sustaining the paradigm. In H. J. Frieberg (Ed.), *Beyond behaviorism: Changing the classroom management paradigm.* Boston: Allyn & Bacon.

Frensch, P. A., & Buchner, A. (1999). Domain-generality versus domain-specificity in cognition. In R. J. Sternberg (Ed.), *The nature of cognition* (pp. 137–172). Cambridge, MA: The MIT Press.

Freppon, P. A., & Dahl, K. L. (1998). Balanced instruction: Insights and considerations (Theory and research into practice). *Reading Research Quarterly, 33*(2), 240–51.

Friesen, S., & Stone, M. (1996). Great explorations. *Applying Research to the Classroom, 14*(2), 6–11.

Froese-Germain, B. (1999). *Standardized testing: Undermining equity in education.* Ottawa, ON: Canadian Teachers' Federation.

Frye, D., Zelazo, P. D., Brooks, P. J., & Samuels, M. C. (1996). Inference and action in early causal reasoning. *Developmental Psychology, 32,* 120–131.

Fuchs, L. S., & Fuchs, D. (2001). Principles for the prevention and intervention of mathematics difficulties. *Learning Disabilities: Research & Practice, 16*(2), 85–95.

Fuchs, L. S., Fuchs, D., Hamlett, C. L., Phillips, N. B., Karns, K., & Dutka, S. (1997). Enhancing students' helping behavior during peer-mediated instruction with conceptual mathematical explanations. *Elementary School Journal, 97,* 223–250.

Fuchs, L. S., Fuchs, D., Karns, K. (2001). Enhancing kindergartners' mathematical development: Effects of peer-assisted learning strategies. *Elementary School Journal, 101*(5), 495–510.

Fukuda-Parr, S. (2002). *Human Development Report 2002: Deepening Democracy in a Fragmented World.* Retrieved 12 December 2002, from: http://www.worldbank.org/wbi/B-SPAN/subhdreport.htm.

Furman, W., & Buhrmester, D. (1992). Age and sex differences in perceptions of networks of personal relationships. *Child Development, 63,* 103–115.

Furth, H. G., & Wachs, H. (1975). *Thinking goes to school.* New York: Oxford University Press.

 G

Gage, N. L. (1978). *The scientific basis of the art of teaching.* New York: Teachers College Press.

Gagné, F. (1993). Constructs and models pertaining to exceptional human abilities. In K. A. Heller, F. J. Monks, & A. H. Passow (Eds.), *International Handbook of Research and Development of Giftedness and Talent* (pp. 63–85). Oxford: Pergamon Press.

Gagne, F. (1997). A differentiated model of giftedness and talent. *Gifted,* July, 15–16.

Gagne, R. M. (1975). *Essentials of Learning for Instruction.* New York: Holt, Rinehart, & Winston.

Galambos, N. L., & Leadbeater, B. J. (2000). Trends in adolescent research for the new millennium. *International Journal of Behavioral Development, 24,* 289–294.

Galambos, N. L., & Tilton-Weaver, L. C. (1998). Multiple risk behaviour in adolescents and young adults. *Health Reports, 10*(2), 9–20 (Catalogue No. 82-003-XPB). Ottawa, ON: Statistics Canada.

Galambos, N. L., Petersen, A. C., Richards, M., & Gitleson, I. B. (1985). The Attitudes toward Women Scale for Adolescents (AWSA). *Sex Roles, 13,* 343–356.

Gallagher, C. (2000). A seat at the table: Teachers reclaiming assessment through rethinking accountability. *Phi Delta Kappan, 81,* 502–507.

Gallagher, T., & Woloshyn, V. E. (1999). Comparing explicit multiple-spelling strategy instruction with traditional language arts instruction in eighth-grade students. *Brock Education, 8*(2), 36–46.

Gándara , P. (2000). *Interventions for Excellence: What we know about nurturing high achievement in underrepresented students.* Washington DC: National Academy of Sciences.

Garbarino, J. (2000). The effects of community violence. In L. Balter & C. S. Tamis-LeMonda (Eds.), *Child psychology: A handbook of contemporary issues.* Philadelphia: Psychology Press.

Gardner, H. (1983). *Frames of mind.* New York: Basic Books.

Gardner, H. (1993). *Multiple intelligences.* New York: Basic Books.

Gardner, H. (1999). *The disciplined mind.* New York: Simon & Schuster.

Gardner, H. (1999). *Intelligence reframed.* New York: Basic Books.

Gardner, H., & Hatch, T. (1989). Multiple intelligences go to school: Educational implications of the theory of multiple intelligences. *Educational Researcher, 18*(8), 4–9.

Gardner, H., Feldman, D. H., & Krechevsky, M. (Eds.). (1998). *Project Spectrum.* New York: Teachers College Press.

Gardner, R., Cartledge, G., Seidl, B., Woolsey, M. L., Schley, G. S., & Utley, C. A. (2001). Mt. Olivet after-school program: Peer-mediated interventions for at-risk students. *Remedial and Special Education, 22*(1), 22–33.

Garner, R., & Gillingham, M. G. (1998). The Internet in the classroom: Is it the end of transmission-oriented pedagogy? In D. Reinking, M. McKenna, L. Labbo, & R. Kieffer (Eds.), *Literacy for the 21st century: Handbook of literacy and technology* (pp. 221–231). Mahwah, NJ: Erlbaum.

Garvie, E. (1991). An integrative approach with young learners. In C. Brumfit, J. Moon, & R. Tongue (Eds.). *Teaching English to children: From practice to principle* (pp. 115–126). Longman.

Gaskell, J. (1995). Secondary schools in Canada: *The national report of the Exemplary Schools Project.* Toronto: The Canadian Education Association.

Gaskin, I. (1998). There is more to teaching at-risk readers and delayed readers than good reading instruction. *The Reading Teacher, 5*(7), 534–547.

Gaskins, I. W., Ehri, L. C., Cress, C., O'Hara, C., & Donnelly, K. (1996). Procedures for word learning: Issues and recommendations. In L. J. Meltzer (Ed.), *Strategy assessment and instruction for students with learning disabilities* (pp. 271–292). Austin, TX: PRO-ED.

Gay, G. (1997). Educational equality for students of color. In J. A. Banks & C. M. Banks (Eds.), *Multicultural Education* (3rd ed.). Boston: Allyn & Bacon.

Gay, L. R., & Airasian, P. (2000). *Educational research* (6th ed.). Upper Saddle River, NJ: Merrill.

Gellens, S. (2000). *Activities that build the young child's brain.* Sarasota, FL: Early Childhood Association of Florida.

Gelman, R., & Brennerman, K. (1994). Domain specificity and cultural specificity are not inconsistent. In L. A. Hirschfeld & S. Gelman (Eds.), *Mapping out domain specificity in cognition and culture.* New York: Cambridge University Press.

Gentile, J. R. (2000). Learning, transfer of. In A. Kazdin (Ed.), *Encyclopedia of psychology.* Washington, DC, and New York: American Psychological Association and Oxford University Press.

Georghiades, P. (2000). Beyond conceptual change learning in science education: Focusing on transfer, durability and metacognition. *Educational Research, 42(2),* 119–139.

Gibbs, J. T. (1989). Black American adolescents. In J. T. Gibbs & L. N. Huang (Eds.), *Children of color.* San Francisco: Jossey-Bass.

Gibson, S., & McKay, R. (2001). What constructivist theory and brain research may offer social studies. *Canadian Social Studies, 35(4).* Retrieved May 21, 2002 from: http://www.quasar.ualberta.ca.css.

Gilligan, C. (1982). *In a different voice.* Cambridge, MA: Harvard University Press.

Gilligan, C. (1996). The centrality of relationships in psychological development: A puzzle, some evidence, and a theory. In G. G. Noam & K. W. Fischer (Eds.), *Development and vulnerability.* Mahwah, NJ: Erlbaum.

Gilligan, C. (1998). *Minding women: Reshaping the education realm.* Cambridge, MA: Harvard University Press.

Gillon, G. T. & Young, A. A. (2002). The phonological-awareness skills of children who are blind. *Journal of Visual Impairment & Blindness, 96(1),* 38–49.

Gilman, D. A., & Knoll, S. (1994). Increasing instruction time: What are the priorities and how do they affect the alternatives? *NAASP Bulletin, (March),* 41–44.

Gingras, J. (2001). Toxic playground: Understanding the environmental influences that increase the risk of childhood weight disturbance and recommendations for prevention. A discussion paper for the South Frasier Health Region. Retrieved May 20, 2002, from: http://www.jacquigingras.com.

Ginsburg, H. P., Klein, A., & Starkey, P. (1998). The development of children's mathematical thinking. In I. E. Sigel & K. A. Renninger (Eds.), *Handbook of child psychology* (5th ed., Vol. 4). New York: Wiley.

Glassberg, L. A., Hooper, S. R., & Mattison, R. E. (1999). Prevalence of learning disabilities at enrollment in special education students with behavioral disorders. *Behavioral Disorders, 25(1),* 9–21.

Glaubman, R., Glaubman, H., & Ofir, L. (1997). Effects of self-directed learning, story comprehension, and self-questioning in kindergarten. *Journal of Educational Research, 90(6),* 361–374.

Gleason, J. B., & Ratner, N. (1998). *Psycholinguistics* (3rd ed.). Fort Worth, TX: Harcourt Brace.

Godin G., & Michaud, F. (1998). STD and AIDS prevention among young people. In *Canada health action: Building on the legacy: Vol. 1. Children and youth* (pp. 357–400). Ottawa: National Forum on Health, Health Canada,

Goldin-Meadow, S. (2000). Language development, syntax, and communication. In A. Kazdin (Ed.), *Encyclopedia of psychology.* Washington, DC, and New York: American Psychological Association and Oxford University Press.

Goldstein, H., & Hockenberger, E. (1991). Significant progress in child language intervention: An 11-year retrospective. *Research in Developmental Disabilities, 12,* 401–424.

Goleman, D. (1995). *Emotional intelligence.* New York: Bantam.

Goleman, D., Kaufman, P., & Ray, M. (1993). *The creative spirit.* New York: Plume.

Good, T. L., & Brophy, J. E. (2000). *Looking in Classrooms (8th ed.).* NY, NY: Longman.

Goodlad, J. I. (1984). *A place called school.* New York: McGraw-Hill.

Goodnough, K. (2001). Multiple intelligence theory: A framework for personalizing science curricula. *School Science & Mathematics, 101(4),* 180–194.

Gordon, M. (2000). The roots of empathy program. *Newsletter of the Infant Mental Health Promotion Project (IMP), 27(Spring),* 2–5.

Gottfried, A. E., Fleming, J. S., & Gottfried, A. W. (2001). Continuity of academic intrinsic motivation from childhood to early adolescence: A longitudinal study. *Journal of Educational Psychology.*

Gouvernement du Quebec. (1998). *Ministere de l'Education—Uniform ministry examination.* Government Document (ISBN 2-550-32656-3).

Government of Alberta. (2002). *Alberta Learning–Policy 2. 1. 3: Use and reporting of results on provincial assessments.* Retrieved 5 December 2002, from: http://www.learning.gov.ab.ca/educationguide/pol-plan/polregs/213.asp.

Government of British Columbia. (2002). *Ministry of Education—Provincial examinations.* Retrieved 6 December 2002, from: http://www.bced.gov.bc.ca/exams/handbook/chapter1/whatareexams.htm.

Government of Canada. (1996). Census Families in Private Households by Selected Household and Dwelling Characteristics, Showing Family Structure, for Canada, 1996 Census, Ottawa, Ontario: Statistics Canada.

Government of Yukon, Department of Education. (2002). *Student Assessment Programs.* Retrieved December 2002, from: http://www.gov.yk.ca/depts/education/ess/assessment/index.html.

Graham, L., & Wong, B. (1993). Two models of teaching a question–answering strategy for enhancing reading comprehension. *Journal of Learning Disabilities, 26,* 270–279.

Graham, S. (1992). Most of the subjects were white and middle class. *American Psychologist, 47,* 629–637.

Graham, S. (1994). Motivation in African Americans. *Review of Educational Research, 64,* 55–117.

Graham, S. (1996). What's "emotional" about social motivation? A comment. In J. Juvonen & K. R. Wentzel (Eds.), *Social motivation.* New York: Cambridge University Press.

Graham, S., & Harris, K. R. (1994). The effects of whole language on children's writing: A review of the literature. *Educational Psychologist, 29,* 187–192.

Graham, S., & Harris, K. R. (2001). The role of self-regulation and transcription skills in writing and writing development. *Educational Psychologist, 35,* 3–12.

Graham, S., & Weiner, B. (1996). Theories and principles of motivation. In D. C. Berliner & R. C. Calfee (Eds.), *Handbook of educational psychology.* New York: Macmillan.

Graham, S., Taylor, A. Z., & Hudley, C. (1998). Exploring achievement values among ethnic minority early adolescents. *Journal of Educational Psychology, 90,* 606–620.

Gray, J. R. (2001). Emotional modulation of cognitive control: Approach-withdrawal states of double-dissociate spatial from verbal two-back task performance. *Journal of Experimental Psychology: General, 130,* 436–452.

Graziano, A. M., & Raulin, M. L. (2000). *Research methods* (4th ed.). Boston: Allyn & Bacon.

Gredler, M. (1999). *Classroom assessment and learning.* Boston: Addison Wesley.

Greene, B. (2000). Gender and culture. In A. Kazdin (Ed.), *Encyclopedia of psychology.* Washington, DC, and New York: American Psychological Association and Oxford U. Press.

Greenfield, P. M. (1997). You can't take it with you: Why ability assessments don't cross cultures. *American Psychologist, 52(10),* 1115–1124.

Greenfield, P. M. (2000). Culture and development. In A. Kazdin (Ed.), *Encyclopedia of psychology.* Washington, DC, and New York: American Psychological Association and Oxford University Press.

Greenlund, K. J., Johnson, C. C., Webber, L. S., & Berenson, G. S. (1997). Cigarette smoking attitudes and first use among third-through sixth-grade students: The Bogalusa Heart Study. *American Journal of Public Health, 87(8),* 1345–1348.

Greeno, J. G. (1993). For research to reform education and cognitive science. In L. A. Penner, G. M. Batche, H. M. Knoff, & D. L. Nelson (Eds.), *The challenge in mathematics and science education: Psychology's response.* Washington, DC: American Psychological Association.

Greeno, J. G., Collins, A. M., & Resnick, L. (1996). Cognition and learning. In D. C. Berliner & R. C. Calfee (Eds.), *Handbook of educational psychology.* New York: Macmillan.

Greenough, W. (1997, April 21). Commentary: *U.S. News & World Report,* p. 79.

Greenough, W. (2000). Brain development. In A. Kazdin (Ed.), *Encyclopedia of psychology.* Washington, DC, and New York: American Psychological Association and Oxford University Press.

Gregory, R. J. (2000). *Psychological testing* (3rd ed.). Boston: Allyn & Bacon.

Gresham, F. (1997, November/December). We need a better way to identify students with learning disabilities. *CEC Today,* 14.

Griffin, S., & Case, R. (1997). Rethinking the primary school math curriculum: an approach based on cognitive science. *Issues in Education, 3,* 1–65.

Gronlund, N. E. (1998). *Assessment of student achievement.* Boston: Allyn & Bacon.

Gronlund, N. E., Linn, R. L., & Davis, K. M. (2000). *Measurement and assessment in teaching.* Upper Saddle River, NJ: Prentice Hall.

Grotevant, H. D. (1998). Adolescent development in family contexts. In W. Damon (Ed.), *Handbook of child psychology* (5th ed., Vol. 3). New York: Wiley.

Guild, P. B. (1998). Multiple intelligence, learning styles, brain-based education: Where do the messages overlap? *Schools-in-the-Middle, 7(4),* 38–40.

Guilford, J. P. (1967). *The structure of intellect.* New York: McGraw-Hill.

Gunning, T. G. (2000). *Creating literacy instruction for all children* (3rd ed.). Boston: Allyn & Bacon.

Gunning, T. G. (2002). *Assessing and correcting reading and writing difficulties.* Boston, MA: Allyn and Bacon.

Guppy, N., & Davies, S. (1998). Education in Canada: Recent Trends and Future Challenges. Ottawa, ON: Statistics Canada, Minister of Industry.

Gutwill, S., & Hollander, N. C. (2002). Zero tolerance or media literacy: A critical psychoanalytic perspective on combating violence among children. *Journal for the Psychoanalysis of Culture & Society, 7,* 263–273.

Guyer, B. (2000). *ADHD.* Boston: Allyn & Bacon.

H

Hackenberg, T. D. (2000). Schedules of reinforcement. In A. Kazdin (Ed.), *Encyclopedia of psychology.* Washington, DC, and New York: American Psychological Association and Oxford University Press.

Hains, A. A. & Szyjakowski. (1990). A cognitive stress-reduction intervention program for adolescents. *Journal of Counseling Psychology, 37,* 79–84.

Hains, A. A., & Ellman, S. W. (1994). Stress inoculation training as a preventative intervention for high school youths. *Journal of Cognitive Psychotherapy, 8,* 219–232.

Haladyna, T. M. (1997). *Writing test items to evaluate higher-order thinking.* Boston: Allyn & Bacon.

Hall, W. (1998, February 24). I.Q. scores are up, and psychologists wonder why. *Wall Street Journal,* pp. B11–12.

Hall, R. V., & Hall, M. L. (1998). *How to select reinforcers* (2nd ed.). Austin: Pro-Ed.

Hallahan, D. P. & Kauffman, J. M. (2000). *Exceptional learners* (8th ed.). Boston: Allyn & Bacon.

Hallahan, D. P., & Kauffman, J. M. (1997). *Exceptional learners: Introduction to special education* (5th ed.). Boston: Allyn & Bacon.

Hallahan, D., Kauffman, J., & Lloyd, J. (1999). *Introduction to learning disabilities* (2nd ed.). Boston: Allyn & Bacon.

Hall-Dennis Report on Education—Ontario. (1968). *Living and Learning: The Hall-Dennis report.* Toronto: Government of Ontario, Department of Education.

Halonen, J. A. (1999). Writing and speaking. In J. W. Santrock & J. A. Halonen, *Mastering the college experience.* Belmont, CA: Wadsworth.

Halpern, D. F. (1998). Teaching critical thinking for transfer across domains: Dispositions, skills, structure training, and metacognitive monitoring. *American Psychologist, 53(4),* 449–455.

Hambleton, R. K. (1996). Advances in assessment models, methods, and practices. In D. C. Berliner & R. C. Calfee (Eds.), *Handbook of educational psychology.* New York: Macmillan.

Hamburg, D. A. (1997). Meeting the essential requirements for healthy adolescent development in a transforming world. In R. Takanishi & D. Hamburg (Eds.), *Preparing adolescents for the 21st century.* New York: Cambridge University Press.

Happon, P., & Griffiths, D. (1997). What benefit might be derived from the use of tutorial programs and how might one use a common drawing program to improve grade seven students understanding of geometry? Edmonton, AB: Project Pegasus, Edmonton Public Schools. Retrieved November 12, 2002, from: http://www.epsb.ca/pd/pegasus/dickinsfield.htm.

Harasim, L. (1994, September). Trouble in paradise. *Update Newsletter, 6(3).* Published by the Centre for Systems Science, Simon Fraser University, Burnaby, BC. Retrieved 12 November 2002, from: http://www.css.sfu.ca/update/vol6/6.3-trouble-in-paradise.html.

Harasim, L. (1999). Telelearning network centres of excellence. Plenary address at Telelearning '99 Conference: Wizardry & Wisdom Connecting the History and the Future of Online Education. Montreal, Quebec. Retrieved 12 November 2002, from: http://www.telelearn.ca/conference99/index.html#keynotes.

Hardy, M. I., McLeod, J., Minto, H., Perkins, S. A., & Quance, W. R. (1971). *Standards for education of exceptional children in Canada: The SEECC Report.* Toronto: Leonard Crainford.

Harlow, S. D., & LaMont Johnson, D. (1998). An epistemology of technology. *Educational Technology Review, 9(2–3),* 15–18.

Harper, G. F., Maheady, L., Mallette, B., & Karnes, M. (1999). Peer tutoring and the minority child with disabilities. *Preventing School Failure, 43,* 45–51.

Harris, J. L., Kamhi, A. G., & Pollock, K. E. (2001). *Literacy in African American communities.* Mahwah, NJ: Erlbaum.

Harris, K. R., & Graham, S. (1996). *Making the writing process work: Strategies for composition and self-regulation (Cognitive Strategy Training).* Cambridge, MA: Brookline Books.

Hart, B., & Risley, T. (1999). *Advantage and disadvantage.* Baltimore: Paul H. Brookes.

Harter, S. (1981). A new self-report scale of intrinsic versus extrinsic orientation in the classroom: motivational and informational components. *Developmental Psychology, 17,* 300–312.

Harter, S. (1981). A new self-report scale of intrinsic versus extrinsic orientation in the classroom: Motivational and informational components. *Developmental Psychology, 17,* 300–312.

Harter, S. (1990). Self and identity development. In S. S. Feldman & G. R. Elliott (Eds.), *At the threshold: The developing adolescent.* Cambridge, MA: Harvard University Press.

Harter, S. (1996). Teacher and classmate influences on scholastic motivation, self-esteem, and level of voice in adolescents. In J. Juvonen & K. R. Wentzel (Eds.), *Social motivation.* New York: Cambridge University Press.

Harter, S., & Marold, D. B. (1992). Psychosocial risk factors contributing to suicide ideation. In G. Noam & S. Borst (Eds.), *Child and adolescent suicide.* San Francisco: Jossey-Bass.

Hartup, W. W. (1983). Peer relations. In P. H. Mussen (Ed.), *Handbook of child psychology* (4th ed., Vol. 4). New York: Wiley.

Hartup, W. W. (2000). Middle childhood: Socialization and social context. In A. Kazdin (Ed.), *Encyclopedia of psychology.* Washington, DC, & New York American Psychological Association and Oxford University Press.

Hartup, W. W., & Stevens, N. (1997). Friendships and adaptation in the life course. *Psychological Bulletin, 121,* 355–370.

Hashimoto, T. et al. (1989). *Magnetic resonance imaging in autism: Preliminary report. Neuropediatrics, 20(3),* 142–146.

Hatch, T. (2000, April). *Portfolios and the scholarship of teaching.* Paper presented at the meeting of the American Educational Research Association, New Orleans.

Haugland, S. W., & Wright, J. L. (1997). *Young children and technology: A world of discovery.* New York: Allyn & Bacon.

Hayes, J. R., & Flower, L. S. (1986). Writing research and the writer. *American Psychologist, 41,* 1106–1113.

Hayes, S. C. (2000). Applied behavior analysis. In A. Kazdin (Ed.), *Encyclopedia of psychology.* Washington, DC, and New York: American Psychological Association and Oxford University Press.

Health Canada. (1995). *Turning points: Canadians from coast to coast set a new course for healthy child and youth development* (Catalogue No. H21-125/1995E). Ottawa: Health Canada.

Health Canada. (1998a). *National population health survey (NPHS), 1996–97.* Unpublished data.

Health Canada. (1998b). *Personal health practices: A closer look at the determinants. Health Canada Web site: Retrieved June 2002* http://www.hc-sc.gc.ca/hppb/lcdc/publicat/ccdr/98vol24/24sl/stde_e.html.

Health Canada. (1999). *Healthy development of children and youth: The role of determinants of health.* Retrieved June, 2002, from http://www.hc-sc.gc.ca/hppb/childhood-youth/spsc.html.

Heilman, A. W., Blair, T. R., & Rupley, W. H. (2002). *Principles and practices of teaching Reading* (10th ed.). Upper Saddle River, NJ: Merrill.

Henchey, N., & Raham, H. (2003, January). *Schools that make a difference: Twelve Canadian secondary schools in low-income settings.* Paper presented to the International Congress for School Effectiveness and improvement, Sydney, Australia. Retrieved January 20, 2003, from: http://www.saee.ca/lCSEIpaper_Jan03.pdf.

Henchey, N., Dunnigan, M., Gardner, A., Lessard, C., Muhtadi, N., Raham, H., & Violato, C. (2001). *Schools that make a difference: Final report.* Kelowna, BC: Society for the Advancement of Excellence in Education.

Henderson, V. L., & Dweck, C. S. (1990). Motivation and achievement. In S. S. Feldman & G. R. Elliott (Eds.), *At the threshold: The developing adolescent.* Cambridge, MA: Harvard University Press.

Henley, M., Ramsey, R., & Algozzine, R. (1999). *Characteristics and strategies for teaching students with mild disabilities* (3rd ed.). Boston: Allyn & Bacon.

Hennessey, B. A., & Amabile, T. M. (1998). Reward, intrinsic motivation, and creativity. *American Psychologist, 53*, 674–675.

Henteleff, Y. (1997). *Special needs children and the youth justice system: Sliding off the scales of justice.* Ottawa, ON: Learning Disabilities Association of Canada.

Herman, J. (1996). Commentary in "The latest on student portfolios." *NEA Today, 15* (4), 17.

Herrnstein, R. J., & Murray, C. (1994). *The bell curve: Intelligence and class structure in modern life.* New York: Free Press.

Hertzog, N. B. (1998, January/February). Gifted education specialist. *Teaching Exceptional Children,* pp. 39–43.

Hess, J. D. (1994). *The Whole World Guide to Culture Learning.* Yarmouth, Maine: Intercultural Press.

Hetherington, E. M. (1995, March). *The changing American family and the well-being of others.* Paper presented at the meeting of the Society for Research in Child Development, Indianapolis.

Hetherington, E. M. (1999). *Should we stay together for the sake of the children?* Unpublished manuscript, Department of Psychology, University of Virginia, Charlottesville.

Hetherington, E. M., Bridges, M., & Isabella, G. M. (1998). What matters? Five perspectives on the association between marital transitions and children's adjustment. *American Psychologist, 53*, 167–184.

Hewitt, J. S., & Whittier, K. S. (1997). *Today's schools.* Boston: Allyn & Bacon.

Hickman, C. W. (1996). *The future of high school success: The importance of parent involvement programs.* Retrieved 13 December 2002, from: http://horizon.unc.edu/projects/hsj/hickman.asp.

Hiebert, E. H., & Raphael, T. E. (1996). Psychological perspectives on literacy and extensions to educational practice. In D. C. Berliner & R. C. Calfee (Eds.), *Handbook of educational psychology.* New York: Macmillan.

Higgins, A., Power, C., & Kohlberg, L. (1983, April). *Moral atmosphere and moral judgement.* Paper presented at the biennial meeting of the Society for Research in Child Development, Detroit.

Higgins, E. T. (2000). Self-regulation. In A. Kazdin (Ed.), *Encyclopedia of psychology.* Washington, DC, and New York: American Psychological Association and Oxford University Press.

Hightower, E. (1990). Adolescent interpersonal and familial precursors of positive mental health at midlife. *Journal of Youth and Adolescence, 19*, 257–275.

Himber, C. (1989). *How to survive hearing loss.* Washington, DC: Gallaudet University Press.

Hirsch, E. D. (1996). *The schools we need: And why we don't have them.* New York: Doubleday.

Hockenbury, D. (1997). Statistical appendix. In J. W. Santrock, *Psychology* (5th ed.). New York: McGraw-Hill.

Hocutt, A. M. (1996). Effectiveness of special education: Is placement the critical factor? *Future of Children, 6* (1), 77–102.

Hodgson, M. (1990). *Impact of residential schools and other root causes of poor mental health.* Edmonton, AB: Nechi Institute.

Hodgson, S., & Price, B. (1997, April). Reading Recovery and the ESL Learner: More Than a Marriage of Convenience. TESL Canada Session. Retrieved 12 December 2002, from: http://www.ritslab.ubc.ca/teslcan/read.htm.

Hoff, E. (2001). *Language development* (2nd ed.). Belmont, CA: Wadsworth.

Hoff-Ginsburg, E., & Tardif, T. (1995). Socioeconomic status and parenting. In M. H. Bornstein (Ed.). *Children and parenting* (Vol. 2). Hillsdale, NJ: Erlbaum.

Hoffman, E. (1989). *The right to be human. A biography of Abraham Maslow.* Wellingborough, UK: Crucible.

Hogan, D. M., & Tudge, J. (1999). Implications of Vygotsky's theory for peer learning. In A. M. O'Donnell & A. King (Eds.), *Cognitive perspectives on peer learning.* Mahwah, NJ: Erlbaum.

Hogan, K., & Pressley, M. (Eds.). (1997). *Scaffolding student learning: Instructional approaches and issues (Advances in learning & teaching).* Boston: Brookline Books.

Hogan, R. T. (1987, August). *Conceptions of personality and the prediction of job performance.* Paper presented at the meeting of the American Psychological Association, New York City.

Hooper, S., Ward, T. J., Hannafin, M. J., & Clark, H. T. (1989). The effects of aptitude composition on achievement during small group learning. *Journal of Computer-Based Instruction, 16*, 102–109.

Horsman, H. (1997). *Learning together in multi-level classrooms.* Saskatoon, SK: Saskatchewan Professional Development Unit.

Howes, C., & Tonyan, H. (2000). Peer relations. In L. Balter & C. S. Tamis-LeMonda (Eds.), *Child psychology: A handbook of contemporary issues.* Philadelphia: Psychology Press.

Hunt, R. R., & Ellis, H. C. (1999). *Fundamentals of cognitive psychology* (6th ed.). New York: McGraw-Hill.

Hunt, R. R., & Kelly, R. E. S. (1996). Accessing the particular from the general: The power of distinctiveness in the context of organization. *Memory and Cognition, 24*, 217–225.

Hurtig, M. (1999). *Pay the rent or feed the kids: The tragedy and disgrace of poverty in Canada.* Toronto: McClelland & Stewart.

Hutchinson, N. L. (2002). *Inclusion of exceptional learners in Canadian schools: A practical handbook for teachers.* Toronto, ON: Pearson Education Canada.

Hymel, S., Comfort, C., Schonert-Reichl, K., & McDougall, P. (1996). Academic failure and school dropout: The influence of peers. In J. Juvonen & K. R. Wentzel (Eds.). (1996). *Social motivation: Understanding children's school adjustment* (pp. 313–345). New York, NY: Cambridge University Press.

I

Iacocca, L. (1984). *Iacocca: An autobiography.* New York: Bantam.

Ickes, W., Snyder, M., & Garcia, S. (1997). Personality influences or the choice of situations. In R. Hogan, J. Johnson, & S. Briggs (Eds.), *Handbook of personality psychology.* San Diego: Academic Press.

Idol, L. (1997). Key questions related to building collaborative and inclusive schools. *Journal of Learning Disabilities, 30*, 384–394.

Idol, L., Nevin, A., & Paolucci-Whitcomb, P. (1994). *Collaborative consultation.* Austin, TX: PRO-ED.

Imms, W. (2000). Multiple masculinities and the schooling of boys. *Canadian Journal of Education, 25(2)*, 152–165.

Indrisano, R., & Squire, J.R. (Eds.) (2000). *Perspectives on writing: Research, theory, practice.* Newark, DE: International Reading Association.

Insight Canada Research. (1992). *The adolescent female and birth control.* Toronto: Insight Canada Research.

J

Jackson, P. W. (1968). *Life in classrooms.* New York: Holt, Rinehart & Winston.

Jacobs, H. H. (1997). *Mapping the big picture: Integrating curriculum and assessment K–12.* Alexandria, VA: Association for Supervision and Curriculum Development.

Jafri, G. J. (1998). *The portrayal of Muslim women in Canadian mainstream media: A community-based analysis.* Afghan Women's Organization. Retrieved December 15, 2002, from http://www-mirror.media-awareness.ca/eng/issues/minrep/resource/reports/jafri.pdf.

Jalongo, M. R. (2000). *Early childhood language arts: Meeting diverse literacy needs through collaboration with families and professionals* (2nd ed.). Boston: Allyn & Bacon.

James, W. (1899/1993). *Talks to teachers.* New York: W. W. Norton.

Jayachandran, J. (2000). Contributions of socioeconomic, sociopsychological, and biological factors to fertility differentials in Canada. *Canadian Studies in Population, 27(2)*, 329–354.

Jensen, A. R. (1969). How much can we boost IQ and academic achievement? *Harvard Educational Review, 39*, 1–123.

Jensen, A. R. (1980). *Bias in Mental Testing.* New York: The Free Press.

Johnson, B., & Christensen, L. (2000). *Educational research.* Boston: Allyn & Bacon.

Johnson, D. (1996). Evaluating the impact of technology: The less simple answer. *From Now On The Educational Technology Journal, 5*, 5. Retrieved 12 November 2002, from: http://www.fromnowon.org/eschool/secrets.html.

Johnson, D. W., & Johnson, F. P. (2000). *Joining Together: Group Theory and Group Skills* (7th ed.). Boston, MA: Allyn and Bacon.

Johnson, D. W., & Johnson, R. T. (1991). *Teaching students to be peacemakers.* Edina, MN: Interaction.

Johnson, D. W., & Johnson, R. T. (1994). *Learning together and alone* (2nd ed.). Englewood Cliffs, NJ: Prentice Hall.

Johnson, D. W., & Johnson, R. T. (1995, February). Why violence prevention programs don't work— And what does. *Educational Leadership*, pp. 63–68.

Johnson, M. K., Beebe, T., Mortimer, J. T., & Snyder, M. (1998). Volunteerism in adolescence: A process perspective, *Journal of Research on Adolescence, 8,* 309–332.

Johnson-Laird, P. (2000). Reasoning. In A. Kazdin (Ed.), *Encyclopedia of psychology.* Washington, DC, and New York: American Psychological Association and Oxford University Press.

John-Steiner, V., & Mahn, H. (1996). Sociocultural approaches to learning and development: A Vygotskian framework. *Educational Psychologist, 31,* 191–206.

Jonassen, D. H. (1996). *Computers in the classroom: Mindtools for critical thinking.* Columbus, OH: Merrill/Prentice-Hall.

Jones, B. D. (1999). Computer-rated essays in the English composition classroom. *Journal of Educational Computing Research, 20,* 169–188.

Jones, B. F., Rasmussen C. M., & Moffitt, M. C. (1997). *Real-life problem solving.* Washington, DC: American Psychological Association.

Jones, J. M. (1994). The African American: A duality dilemma? In W. J. Lonner & R. Malpass (Eds.), *Psychology and culture.* Boston: Allyn & Bacon.

Joyce, B., & Weil, M. (1996). *Models of teaching* (5th ed.). New York: McGraw-Hill.

Joyner, M. H., & Kurtz-Costes, B. (1997). Metamemory development. In N. Cowan (Ed.), *The development of memory in childhood.* Hove East Sussex, UK: Psychology Press.

Jussim, L. (1986). Self-fulfilling prophecies: A theoretical and integrative review. *Psychological Review, 93(4),* 429–445.

Juvonen, J., & Wentzel, K. R. (1996). *Social motivation: Understanding children's school adjustment.* New York: Cambridge University Press.

k

Kagan, J. (2000). Temperament. In A. Kazdin (Ed.), *Encyclopedia of psychology.* Washington, DC, and New York: American Psychological Association and Oxford U. Press.

Kagan, S. (1992). *Cooperative learning.* San Juan Capistrano, CA: Resources for Teachers.

Kagan, S. (2001). *Cooperative learning.* San Clemente, CA: Kagan Cooperative Learning.

Kahl, B., & Woloshyn, V. E. (1994). Using elaborative interrogation in cooperative learning settings: One good strategy deserves another. *Applied Cognitive Psychology, 8,* 465–478.

Kahn, A. (1999). *The schools our children deserve.* Boston: Houghton Mifflin.

Kail, R., & Pellegrino, J. W. (1985). *Human intelligence.* New York: W. H. Freeman.

Kalchman, M., & Case, R. (1998). Teaching mathematical functions in primary and middle school: An approach based on neo-Piagetian theory. *Scientia, Paedogogica Experimentalis, XXXV (1),* 7–53.

Kamphaus, R. W. (2000). Learning disabilities. In A. Kazdin (Ed.), *Encyclopedia of psychology.* Washington, DC, and New York: American Psychological Association and Oxford University Press.

Kanu, Y. (2002). In their own voices: First Nations students identify some cultural mediators of their learning in the formal school system. *Alberta Journal of Educational Research, XLVII(2),* 1–24.

Karau, S. J., & Williams, K. D. (2001). Understanding individual motivation in groups: The collective effort model. In M.E. Turner (Ed.), *Group at work: Theory and research* (pp. 113–141). Mahwah, NJ: Lawrence Erlbaum.

Katz, L., & Chard, S. (1989). *Engaging the minds of young children: The project approach.* Norwood, NJ: Ablex.

Katz, M., Noddings, N., & Strike, K. (Eds.). (1999). *Justice and caring: The search for common ground in education.* NY: Teachers College Press.

Kaufman, A. S., & Lictenberger, E. O. (2002). *Assessing adolescent and adult intelligence* (2nd ed.). Boston: Allyn & Bacon.

Kayale, K. A. (2000). History, rhetoric, and reality. *Remedial & Special Education, 21(5),* 21–25.

Keating, D. P. (1990). *Adolescent thinking.* In S. S. Feldman & G. R. Elliott (Eds.), *At the threshold: The developing adolescent* (pp. 54–89). Cambridge, MA: Harvard University Press.

Keil, F. (1999). Cognition. In M. Bennett (Ed.), *Developmental psychology.* Philadelphia: Psychology Press.

Kellogg, R. T. (1994). *The psychology of writing.* New York: Oxford University Press.

Kellogg, R. T. (2000). Writing. In A. Kazdin (Ed.), *Encyclopedia of psychology.* Washington, DC, and New York: American Psychological Association and Oxford University Press.

Kendall, P. (2000). Cognitive behavior therapy. In A. Kazdin (Ed.), *Encyclopedia of psychology.* Washington, DC, and New York: American Psychological Association and Oxford U. Press.

Kennedy, M. (1999). Infusing educational research with decision making. In G. J. Cizek (Ed.), *Handbook of educational policy.* San Diego: Academic Press.

Keogh, B. K., & Macmillan, D. L. (1996). Exceptionality. In D. Berliner & R. Calfee (Eds.), *Handbook of educational psychology.* New York: Macmillan.

Kepron, J. P. (1998). Reading recovery: Response from the field. *McGill Journal of Education, 33(1),* 85–99.

Kim, J. A., & Siegel, S. (2001). The role of cholecystokinin in conditional compensatory responding and morphine tolerance. *Behavioral Neuroscience, 115,* 704–709.

Kinderman, T. A., McCollam, T. L., & Gibson, E. (1996). Peer networks and students' classroom engagement during childhood and adolescence. In J. Juvonen & K. R. Wentzel (Eds.), *Social motivation.* New York: Cambridge University Press.

King, A. (2000). Situated cognition. In A. Kazdin (Ed.), *Encyclopedia of psychology.* Washington, DC, and New York: American Psychological Association and Oxford University Press.

Kirova, A. (2003). Accessing children's experiences of loneliness through conversations. *Field Methods, 15(1),* 1–12.

Kirton, M. J. (1999). *Manual: Kirton adaptation-innovation inventory (3rd ed.)* Hatfield, UK: Occupational Research Centre.

Klein, K., & Boals, A. (2001). Expressive writing can increase working memory capacity. *Journal of Experimental Psychology: General, 130,* 520–533.

Knight, G. P., Fabes, R. A., & Higgins, D. A. (1996). Concerns about drawing causal inferences from meta-analyses: An example in the study of gender differences in aggression. *Psychological Bulletin, 119,* 410–421.

Kochenderfer, B. J., & Ladd, G. W. (1996). Peer victimization: Cause or consequences of school maladjustment? *Child Development, 67,* 1293–1305.

Kohlberg, L. (1966). A cognitive-developmental analysis of children's sex-role concepts and attitudes. In E. E. Maccoby (Ed.), *The development of sex differences.* Palo Alto, CA: Stanford University Press.

Kohlberg, L. (1976). Moral stages and moralization: The cognitive-developmental approach. In T. Lickona (Ed.), *Moral development and behavior.* New York: Holt, Rinehart & Winston.

Kohlberg, L. (1986). A current statement of some theoretical issues. In S. Modgil & C. Modgil (Eds.), *Lawrence Kohlberg.* Philadelphia: Falmer.

Kohn, A. (1996). By all available means: Cameron and Pierce's defense of extrinsic motivators. *Review of Educational Research, 66,* 5–32.

Kosakowski, J. (2000). The benefits of information technology. *Education and Technology Yearbook, 25,* 53–56.

Kounin, J. S. (1970). *Discipline and management in classrooms.* New York: Holt, Rinehart & Winston.

Kounin, J. S. (1983). *Discipline and group management in classrooms.* Malabar, FL: Robert E Krieger Publishing Co.

Kounin, J. S., & Gump, P. V. (1974). Signal systems of lesson settings and the task-related behavior of preschool children. *Journal of Educational Psychology, 66(4),* 554–562.

Kowalski, R. M. (2000). Anxiety. In A. Kazdin (Ed.), *Encyclopedia of psychology.* Washington, DC, and New York: American Psychological Association and Oxford University Press.

Kozulin, A. (2000). Vygotsky, Lev. In A. Kazdin (Ed.), *Encyclopedia of psychology.* Washington, DC, and New York: American Psychological Association and Oxford University Press.

Kramarski, B., Mevarech, Z. R., & Lieberman, A. (2001). Effects on multilevel versus unilevel metacognitive training on mathematical reasoning. *Journal of Educational Research, 94(5),* 292–300.

Krathwohl, D. R., Bloom, B. S., & Masia, B. B. (1964). *Taxonomy of educational objectives. Handbook II: Affective domain.* New York: David McKay.

Kreutzer, L. C., & Flavell, J. H. (1975). An interview study of children's knowledge about memory. *Monographs of the Society for Research in Child Development, 40* (1, Serial No. 159).

Krueger, R. (2000). Validity. In A. Kazdin (Ed.), *Encyclopedia of psychology.* Washington, DC, & New York: American Psychological Association and Oxford University Press.

Kuhn, D. (1999a). A developmental model of critical thinking. *Educational Researcher, 28,* 16–25.

Kuhn, D. (1999b). Metacognitive development. In L. Balter & S. Tamis-Lemonda (Eds.), *Child psychology: A handbook of contemporary issues.* Philadelphia: Psychology Press.

Kuhn, D., Amsel, E., & O'Laughlin, M. (1988). *The development of scientific thinking skills.* Orlando, FL: Academic Press.

Kuhn, D., Garcia-Mila, M., Zohar, Z., & Anderson, C. (1995). Strategies for knowledge acquisition. *Monographs of the Society for Research in Child Development, 60* (4, Serial No. 245), 1–127.

Kuhn, D., Schauble, L., & Garcia-Mila, M. (1992). Cross-domain development of scientific reasoning. *Cognition and Instruction, 9,* 285–327.

Kulik, J. A. (1992). An analysis of the research on ability grouping. *Monograph of the National Research Center on the Gifted and Talented* (No. 9204). Storrs: University of Connecticut.

Kupersmidt, J. B., & Coie, J. D. (1990). Preadolescent peer status, aggression, and school adjustment as predictors of externalizing problems in adolescence. *Child Development, 61,* 1350–1363.

L

Labinowicz, E. (1980). *The Piaget primer: Thinking, learning, teaching.* Reading, MA: Addison-Wesley.

Laferrière, T., Breuleux, A., & Bracewell, R. (1999). *Benefits of using information and communication technologies (ICT) for teaching and learning in K–12/13 classrooms.* Ottawa, ON: Industry Canada.

Lam, T. C. M. (1995). Individualization of objectives: A model of educational program evaluation. *Evaluation Practice, 16(1),* 13–28.

Lambert, M. A. (2000). Tips for teaching: Using cognitive and metacognitive learning strategies in the classroom. *Preventing School Failure, 44(2),* 81–82.

Lancy, D. F. (Ed.). (1994). *Children's emergent literacy: From research to practice.* Westport, CT: Praeger Publishers.

Langevin, M. (1998). *Teasing and bullying: Unacceptable behaviour (TAB).* Field testing report (Revised edition). Edmonton, Alberta: Institute for Stuttering Treatment and Research.

Lankes, A. M. (1998). Portfolios: A new wave in assessment. *The Journal, 25(9),* 18–20.

Lankes, A. M. D. (1995). *Electronic portfolios: A new idea in assessment.* ERIC Document Reproduction Service No. ED390377.

Larsen, L. (1997, June 18). Commentary in "Diagnosing learning problems can be difficult for parents and teachers." *USA Today,* p. D8.

Learner-Centered Principles Work Group. (1997). *Learner-centered psychological principles: A framework for school reform and redesign.* Washington, DC: American Psychological Association.

Learning Disabilities Association of Ontario. (2001). About LD, promoting early intervention: Draft definition. Retrieved June 2002, from http://www.ldao.on.ca/defdraft.html.

Lee, D. L., & Belfiore, P. J. (1997). Enhancing classroom performance: A review of reinforcement schedules. *Journal of Behavioral Education, 7,* 205–217.

Lee, L. C. (1992, August). *In search of universals: What ever happened to race?* Paper presented at the meeting of the American Psychological Association, Washington, DC.

Lee, V. E., & Smith, J. B. (1994). High school restructuring and student achievement. Issues in Restructuring Schools (Report No. 7). Madison, WI: University of Wisconsin-Madison, Center on Organization and Restructuring of Schools.

Lee, V. E., Bryk, A. S., & Smith, J. B. (1993). The organization of effective secondary schools. *Review of Research in Education, 19,* 171–267.

Lee, V. E., Croninger, R. G., Linn, E., & Chen, X. (1995, March). *The culture of sexual harassment in secondary schools.* Paper presented at the meeting of the Society for Research in Child Development, Indianapolis.

Leemkuil, H., de Jong, T., & Ootes, S. (2000). *Review of educational use of games and simulations.* Knowledge Management Interactive Training System Report—Project number IST-1999-13078. Retrieved from http://kits.edte.utwente.nl/documents/D1.pdf.

Lehrer, R., Lee, M., & Jeong, A. (1994). *Reflective teaching of LOGO.* Unpublished manuscript. Department of Educational Psychology, University of Wisconsin, Madison.

Leinhardt, G., & Greeno, J. G. (1986). The cognitive skill of teaching. *Journal of Educational Psychology, 78,* 75–95.

Leonard, L. J. (2001). Erosion of instructional time: Teacher concerns. Paper Presented at the Thirtieth Annual Meeting of the Mid-South Educational Research Association. Little Rock, Arkansas.

Leonard, P. (1999). Understanding the dimensions of school culture: Value orientations and value conflicts. *Journal of Educational Administration and Foundations, 13(2),* 27–53.

Lepper, M. R. (1998). A whole much less than the sum of its parts. *American Psychologist, 53,* 675–676.

Lepper, M. R., Keavney, M., & Drake, M. (1996). Intrinsic motivation and extrinsic rewards: A commentary on Cameron and Pierce's Meta-analysis. *Review of Educational Research, 66,* 5–32.

Lepper, M., Greene, D., & Nisbett, R. (1973). Undermining children's intrinsic interest with intrinsic rewards: A test of the overjustification hypothesis. *Journal of Personality and Social Psychology, 28,* 129–137.

Levesque, J., & Prosser, T. (1996). Service learning connections. *Journal of Teacher Education, 47,* 325–334.

Levin, J., & Nolan, J. F. (2000). *Principles of classroom management: A professional decision-making model* (3rd Ed.). Boston: Allyn & Bacon.

Levy, C. M., & Randsell, S. (Eds.). (1996). *The science of writing.* Mahwah, NJ: Erlbaum.

Linden, K. W. (1996). *Cooperative learning and problem solving.* Prospect Heights, IL: Waveland Press.

Linn, M. C., Songer, N. B., & Eylon, B. (1996). Shifts and convergences in science learning and instruction. In D. C. Berliner & R. C. Calfee (Eds.), *Handbook of educational psychology.* New York: Macmillan.

Linn, R. L. (2000). Assessments and accountability. *Educational Research, 29,* 4–15.

Linn, R. L., & Gronlund, N. E. (2000). *Measurement and assessment in teaching* (8th ed.). Upper Saddle River, NJ: Prentice Hall.

Linver, M. R., Brooks-Gunn, J., & Kohen, D. E. (2002). Family processes as pathways from income to young children's development. *Developmental Psychology, 38,* 719–734.

Lipman, E. L., Offord, D. R., & Dooley, M. D. (1996). What do we know about children from single-mother families? Questions and answers from the National longitudinal survey of children and youth. In *Growing up in Canada: National longitudinal survey of children and youth* (Catalogue No. 89-550-MPE). Ottawa, ON: Human Resources Development Canada.

Lipsitz, J. (1984). *Successful schools for young adolescents.* New Brunswick, NJ: Transaction Books.

Lipson, M. Y. (1982, December). The Relationship between Oral Reading Miscues and Category of Replacement Errors of Cloze Passages. Paper presented at the Annual Meeting of the National Reading Conference, Clearwater Beach, FL.

Little, N., & Allan, J. (1988). *Student-led parent conference.* Los Angeles: UCLA Graduate School of Education, RAND Institute on Education Training.

Liu, J. & Pearson, D. (1999). *Teachers' attitude toward inclusion and perceived professional needs for an inclusive classroom.* (ED 438274) Princeton: Eric Clearing House.

Loeber, R., & Hay, D. (1997). Key issues in the development of aggression and violence from childhood to early adulthood. *Annual Review of Psychology, 48,* 371–410.

LoLordo, V. M. (2000). Classical conditioning. In A. Kazdin (Ed.), *Encyclopedia of psychology.* Washington, DC, and New York: American Psychological Association and Oxford University Press.

Lonner, W. J. (1990). An overview of cross-cultural testing and assessment. In R. W. Brislin (Ed.), *Applied cross-cultural psychology.* Newbury Park, CA: Sage.

Lovett, S. B., & Pillow, B. H. (1996). Development of the ability to distinguish between comprehension and memory: Evidence from goal-state evaluation tasks. *Journal of Educational Psychology, 88,* 546–562.

Lovett, M. W., & Steinbach, K. A. (1997). The effectiveness of remedial programs for reading disabled children of different ages: Does the benefit decrease for older children? *Learning Disability Quarterly, 20,* 189–210.

Lubinski, D. (2000). Measures of intelligence: Intelligence tests. In A. Kazdin (Ed.), *Encyclopedia of psychology.* Washington, DC, and New York: American Psychological Association and Oxford University Press.

Lyon, G. R. (1996). Learning disabilities. *Future of Children, 6* (1), 54–76.

Lupart, J., & Wilgosh, L. (1997). Undoing underachievement and promoting societal advancement of women and girls. *Gifted Education International, 12,* 159–169.

Luria, A., & Herzog, E. (1985, April). *Gender segregation across and within settings.* Paper presented at the biennial meeting of the Society for Research in Child Development, Toronto.

Lyon, G. R. (1996). Learning disabilities. *Future of Children, 6* (1), 54–76.

Lyon, G. R., & Moats, L. C. (1997). Critical conceptual and methodological considerations in reading intervention research. *Journal of Learning Disabilities, 30,* 578–588.

Lyon, T. D., & Flavell, J. H. (1993). Young children's understanding of forgetting over time. *Child Development, 64,* 789–800.

Lyons, N. (1999, May). How portfolios can shape emerging practice. *Educational Leadership, 56,* 63–67.

Lytle, S. L., & Cochran-Smith, M. (1990). Learning from teacher research: A working typology. *Teachers College Record, 92*(1), 83–102.

Lytton, H., & Pyryt, M. C. (1998). Predictors of achievement in basic skills: A Canadian effective schools study. *Canadian Journal of Education, 23,(3),* 281–301.

M

Ma, X. (1999). Dropping out of advanced mathematics: the effects of parental involvement. *Teachers College Record, 101*(1), 60–81.

Mabry, L. (1999, May). Writing to the rubric: Lingering effects of traditional standardized testing on direct writing assessment. *Phi Delta Kappan, 80,* 673–679.

MacArthur, C. A. (1996). Using technology to enhance the writing processes of students with learning disabilities. *Journal of Learning Disabilities, 29,* 344–354.

Maccoby, E. E. (1995). The two sexes and their social systems. In P. Moen, G. H. Elder, & K. Luscher (Eds.), *Examining lives in context.* Washington, DC: American Psychological Association.

Maccoby, E. E. (1997, April). Discussant, *Missing pieces in the puzzle: Biological contributions to gender development.* Symposium at the meeting of the Soceity for Research in Child Development, Washington, DC.

MacDonald, R. E., & Healy, S. (1999). *A Handbook for Beginning Teachers (2nd ed).* Boston, MA: Allyn & Bacon.

MacGregor, S. K. (1999). Hypermedia navigation profiles: Cognitive characteristics and information processing strategies. *Journal of Educational Computing Research, 20,* 189–206.

Machnaik, J. (2002). Best practices: Effective instructional methods and techniques. Retrieved 7 January 2003, from: http://wblrd.sk.ca/~bestpractice/.

MacNeil, J. (2002). Problem solving key to success at students' math fair. Okotoks *Western Wheel, 27(39).* Retrieved May 2002, from Galileo Educational Network Association at http://www.galileo.org/about.html.

MacRae, L., & Lupart, L. L. (1991). Issues in identifying gifted students: How Renzulli's model stacks up. *Roeper Review, 14(2),* 53–58.

Maddux, C. D., Johnson, D. L., & Willis, J. W. (1997). *Educational computing* (2nd ed.). Boston: Allyn & Bacon.

Mager, R. (1962). *Preparing instructional objectives* (2nd ed.). Palo Alto, CA: Fearon.

Magnusson, D. (1988). *Individual development from an interactional perspective.* Mahwah, NJ: Erlbaum.

Mahoney, M. (1991). *Human change processes.* New York: Basic Books.

Mallery, A. L. (2000). *Creating a catalyst for thinking: The integrated curriculum.* Boston: Allyn & Bacon.

Mandler, G. (1980). Recognizing: The judgment of previous occurrence. *Psychological Review, 87,* 252–271.

Manitoba Association of School Trustees. (2001). Submission to the commission on class size and composition (November, 2001). Retrieved 7 January 2003, from: http://www.mast.mb.ca/Communications/Publications/Class_Size. PDF.

Manitoba Education, Training and Youth. (2002). *Assessment and Evaluation: Overview of the provincial assessment program.* Retrieved December 2002, from http://www.edu.gov.mb.ca/ks4/assess/index.html.

Marchisan, M. L., & Alber, S. R. (2001). The write way: Tips for teaching the writing process to resistant writers. *Intervention in School and Clinic, 36,* 154-162.

Marcia, J. E. (1980). Identity in adolescence. In J. Adelson (Ed.), *Handbook of adolescent psychology.* New York: Wiley.

Marcia, J. E. (1998). Optimal development from an Eriksonian perspective. In H. S. Friedman (Ed.), *Encyclopedia of mental health* (Vol. 2). San Diego: Academic Press.

Marini, Z. A. (1992). Synchrony and asynchrony in the development of children's scientific reasoning. In R. Case (Ed.), *The mind's staircase: Exploring the conceptual underpinnings of children's thought and knowledge* (pp. 53–73). Hillsdale, NJ: Lawrence Earlbaum Associates.

Marini, Z. A. (2000, October). *A tribute to Robbie Case: Builder of developmental staircases and bridges.* Symposium conducted at the meeting A Design for Development: The legacy of Robbie Case, Toronto, Ontario, Canada.

Marini, Z. A., & Case, R. (1989). Parallels in the development of preschoolers' knowledge about their physical and social worlds. *Merrill-Palmer Quarterly, 35,* 63–88.

Marini, Z. A., & Case, R. (1994). The development of abstract reasoning about the physical and social world. *Child Development, 65,* 147–159.

Marini, Z. A., Bombay, K., Hobin, C., Winn, D., & Dumyn, P. (2000). From peer victimization to peer mediation: A public health approach to the prevention and management of school bullying. *Brock Education, 10,* 1–29.

Marini, Z. A., Fairbairn, L., & Zuber, R. (2001). Peer harassment in individuals with developmental disabilities: Towards the development of a multidimensional bullying identification model. *Developmental Disabilities Bulletin, 29,* 170–195.

Marini, Z. A., McWhinnie, M., & Lacharite, M. (2003). Preventing school bullying: Identification and intervention strategies involving bystanders. *Teaching & Learning, 2*(2), 1–6.

Marini, Z. A., Spear, S., & Bombay, K. (1999). Peer victimization in middle childhood: Characteristics, causes and consequences of school bullying. *Brock Education, 9,* 32–47.

Marlow, E. (2001). *Assessing the quality of CD-ROMs in the curriculum.* Experiments in Education. (ERIC Document Reproduction Service No. ED453287).

Marquardt, R. (2001). Education for Peace, Human Rights, Democracy, International Understanding and Tolerance. Council of Ministers of Education Canada document. Retrieved 5 December 2002, from http://www.cmec.ca/international/unesco/pax.en.pdf.

Marshall, H. H. (1996). Implications of differentiating and understanding constructivist approaches. *Educational Psychologist, 31,* 243–240.

Marshall, H. H. (1997). Clarifying and implementing contemporary psychological perspectives. *Educational Psychologist, 31* (1), 29–34.

Martin, C. L., Ruble, D. N., & Szkrybalo, J. (2002). Cognitive theories of early gender development. *Psychological Bulletin, 128,* 903–933.

Martin, R., Sexton, C., & Gerlovich, J. (1999). *Science for all children: Lessons for constructing understanding.* Boston: Allyn & Bacon.

Martino, W. (2000). Mucking around in class, giving crap, and acting cool: Adolescent boys enacting masculinities at school. *Canadian Journal of Education, 25(2),* 102–112.

Martinussen, R., Kirby, J. R., & Das, J. P. (1998). Instruction in successive and phonological processing to improve reading acquisition skills of at-risk kindergarten children. *Developmental Disabilities Bulletin, 26(2),* 19–39.

Maslow, A. H. (1954). *Motivation and personality.* New York: Harper & Row.

Maslow, A. H. (1971). *The farther reaches of human nature.* New York: Viking Press.

Mata, F. (1997). Intergenerational transmission of education and socio-economic status: A look at immigrants, visible minority and Aboriginals. In *Survey of labour and income dynamics* (Working Paper Series Catalogue No. 97-07). Ottawa: Statistics Canada.

Maté, G. (2000). *Scattered minds: A new look at the origins and healing of attention deficit disorder.* Toronto: Alfred A. Knopf Canada.

Mathes, P. G., Howard, J. K., Allen, S. H., & Fuchs, D. (1998). Peer-assisted learning strategies for first-grade readers: Responding to the needs of diverse learners. *Reading Research Quarterly, 33,* 62–94.

Mayer, R. E. (1984). Twenty-five years of research on advance organizers. *Instructional Science, 8,* 133–169.

Mayer, R. E. (1999). *The promise of educational psychology.* Upper Saddle River, NJ: Prentice Hall.

Mayer, R. E., & Wittrock, M. C. (1996). Problem-solving transfer. In D. C. Berliner & R. C. Calfee (Eds.), *Handbook of educational psychology.* New York: Macmillan.

Mazurek, K., Winzer, M. A., & Majorek, C. (2000). *Education in a global society.* Boston: Allyn & Bacon.

McCain, M. N., & Mustard, F. (1999), *Reversing the brain drain: Early study: Final report,* Ontario Children's Secretariat, Toronto, Ontario.

McCarthey, S. (1994). Opportunities and risks of writing from personal experience. *Language Arts, 71,* 182–191.

McCormick, C. B., & Pressley, M. (1997). *Educational psychology.* New York: Longman.

McCreary Centre Society. (1996). Adolescent health survey (summary). Retrieved 6 October 2002, from http://www.mcs.bc.ca.

McEwan, E. K. (1998). *How to deal with parents who are angry, troubled, afraid or just plain crazy.* Thousand Oaks, CA: Corwin Press, Inc.

McKeachie, W. J. (1998). *Teaching tips. (10th ed).* Lexington, MA: D.C. Heath.

McKeachie, W. J. (1999). *Teaching tips (10th ed).* New York: Houghton Mifflin.

McKeough, A. (2000, October). *Central social structures in childhood and adolescence: Mapping the development of narrative thought.* Symposium conducted at the meeting A Design for Development: The legacy of Robbie Case, Toronto, ON.

McKinley, D. W., Boulet, J. R., & Hambleton, R. K. (2000, August). *Standard-setting for performance-based assessment.* Paper presented at the meeting of the American Educational Research Association, New Orleans.

McLoyd, V. C. (1998). Children in poverty: Development, public policy, and practice. In W. Damon (Ed.), *Handbook of child psychology* (5th ed., Vol. 4). New York: Wiley.

McLuhan, M. (1964). *Understanding media: The extensions of man.* New York: McGraw-Hill.

McMahon, S. I. (1994). Student-led book clubs: Traversing a river of interpretation. *New Advocate, 7,* 109–125.

McMahon, S. I., Raphael, T. E., & Goatley, V. J. (1995). Changing the context for classroom reading instruction: The Book Club project. In J. Brophy (Ed.), *Advances in research on teaching.* Greenwich, CT: JAI Press.

McMillan, J. H. (1997). *Classroom assessment.* Boston: Allyn & Bacon.

McMillan, J. H. (2000). *Educational research* (3rd ed.). Upper Saddle River, NJ: Merrill.

McMillan, J. H., Myran, S., & Workman, D. (2002). Elementary teachers' classroom assessment and grading practices. *Journal of Educational Research, 95*(4).

McNally, D. (1990). *Even eagles need a push.* New York: Dell.

McNaughton, D., Hughes, C., & Ofiesh, N. (1997). Proofreading for students with learning disabilities: Integrating computer and strategy use. *Learning Disabilities Research and Practice, 12,* 16–28.

McNeil, D. (2000). Systematic desensitization. In A. Kazdin (Ed.), *Encyclopedia of psychology.* Washington, DC, and New York: American Psychological Association and Oxford University Press.

McNulty, J. (2000). Five-factor model of personality. In A. Kazdin (Ed.), *Encyclopedia of psychology.* Washington, DC, and New York: American Psychological Association and Oxford U. Press.

McShane, D. A., & Plas, J. M. (1984). The cognitive functioning of American Indian children: Moving from the WISC to the WISC-R. *The School Psychology Review, 13,* 61–73.

Means, B., & Olson, K. (1994). The link between technology and authentic learning. *Educational Leadership, 51(7),* 15–18.

Medin, D. L. (2000). Concepts: An overview. In A. Kazdin (Ed.), *Encyclopedia of psychology.* Washington, DC, and New York: American Psychological Association and Oxford University Press.

Mehrens, W. A. (1997, Summer). The consequences of consequential validity. *Educational Measurement, 16,* 16–18.

Meichenbaum D. H., & Deffenbacher J. L. (1988). Stress inoculation training. *The Counseling Psychologist, 16,* 60–90.

Meichenbaum, D. (1993). Cognitive behavior modification. In F. H. Kanfer & A. P. Goldstein (Eds.), *Helping people change: A handbook of methods.* New York: Pergamon.

Meichenbaum, D., Turk, D., & Burstein, S. (1975). The nature of coping with stress. In I. Sarason & C. Spielberger (Eds.), *Stress and anxiety.* Washington, DC: Hemisphere.

Melby, L. C. (1995). *Teacher efficacy and classroom management: A study of teacher cognition, emotion, and strategy usage associated with externalizing student behavior.* Ph.D. dissertation, University of California at Los Angeles.

Meloth, M. S., & Deering, P. D. (1992). Effects of two cooperative conditions on peer-group discussions, reading comprehension and metacognition. *Contemporary Educational Psychology, 17(Apr),* 175–93.

Meloth, M. S., & Deering, P. D. (1994). Task talk and task awareness under different cooperative learning conditions. *American Educational Research Journal, 31(1),* 138–165.

Merrill, P. F., Hammons, K., Vincent, B. R., & Reynolds, M. N. (1996). *Computers in education* (3rd ed.). Boston: Allyn & Bacon.

Mesibov, G. (2000). Autistic disorder. In A. Kazdin (Ed.), *Encyclopedia of psychology.* Washington, DC, and New York: American Psychological Association and Oxford U. Press.

Mevarech, Z. R. (1999). Effects of metacognitive training embedded in cooperative settings on mathematical problem solving. *Journal of Educational Research, 92(4),* 195–205.

Meyer, R. J. (2002). *Phonics exposed.* Mahwah, NJ: Erlbaum.

Michael, W. (1999). Guilford's view. In M. A. Runco & S. Pritzker (Eds.), *Encyclopedia of creativity.* San Diego: Academic Press.

Michaelsen, L. K., Fink, L. D., & Knight, A. (1997). Designing effective group activities: Lessons for classroom teaching and faculty development. In D. Denure (Ed.), *To improve the academy* (Vol. 16, pp. 373–398). Fort Collins, CO: Professional and Organizational Development Network in Higher Education.

Middleton, J., & Goepfert, P. (1996). *Inventive strategies for teaching mathematics.* Washington, DC: American Psychological Association.

Midgley, C., Anderman, E., & Hicks, L. (1995). Differences between elementary school and middle school teachers and students: A goal theory approach. *Journal of Early Adolescence, 15,* 90–113.

Miholic, V. (1994). An inventory to pique students' metacognitive awareness of reading strategies. *Journal of Reading, 38,* 84–86.

Miller, G. A. (1956). The magical number seven, plus or minus two: Some limits on our capacity for information processing. *Psychological Review, 48,* 337–442.

Miller, M. D., & Linn, R. L. (2000). Validation of performance-based assessments. *Applied Psychological Measurement, 24(4),* 367–378.

Miller, N., & Harrington, H. J. (1990). A situational identity perspective on cultural diversity and teamwork in the classroom. In S. Sharan (Ed.), *Cooperative learning: Theory and research.* New York: Praeger.

Miller-Jones, D. (1989). Culture and testing. *American Psychologist, 44,* 360–366.

Mills, G. E. (2000). *Action research: A guide for the teacher-researcher.* Columbus, OH: Merrill.

Minuchin, P. P., & Shapiro, E. K. (1983). The school as a context for social development. In P. H. Mussen (Ed.), *Handbook of child psychology* (4th ed., Vol. 4). New York: Wiley.

Miyake, A. (2001, September). Commentary in S. Carpenter. A new reason for keeping a diary. *Monitor on Psychology, 32,* 68–70.

Moats, L. C., & Lyon, G. R. (1996). Wanted: Teachers with knowledge of language. *Topics in Language Disorders, 16,* 73–86.

Moldoveanu, M. C., & Langer, E. (1999). Mindfulness. In M. A. Runco & S. Pritzker (Eds.), *Encyclopedia of creativity.* San Diego: Academic Press.

Monteith, M. (2000). Prejudice. In A. Kazdin (Ed.), *Encyclopedia of psychology.* Washington, DC, and New York. American Psychological Association and Oxford University Press.

Montgomery, K. (2000). Authentic tasks and rubrics: Going beyond traditional assessments in college teaching. *College Teaching, 50(1),* 34–38.

Moore, K. D. (1998). Classroom teaching skills (4th ed.). New York: McGraw-Hill.

Moore, M., & Wade, B. (1998). Reading and comprehension: A longitudinal study of ex-Reading Recovery students. *Educational Studies, 24(2)*, 195–203.

Morgan, N., & Saxton, J. (1991). *Teaching, questioning, and learning.* New York: Routledge.

Morgan, N., & Saxton, J. (1994). *Asking better questions.* Markham, ON: Pembroke Publishers.

Morra, S. (2002). Il contributto di Robbie Case allo studio dell'apprendimento. *Eta Evolutiva, 72,* 98–109.

Morris, D. (1992). *Case Studies in Teaching Beginning Readers: The Howard Street Tutoring Manual.* Fieldstream Publications

Morris, D. (1999). *The Howard Street tutoring manual: Teaching at-risk reading in the primary grades.* NY, NT: Guilford Press.

Morris, D. (2001). The Howard Street Tutoring Model: Using volunteer tutors to prevent reading failure in the primary grades. *Tutoring Programs for Struggling Readers.* Chapter 9, pp. 177–192.

Morris, D., Shaw, B., & Perney, J. (1990). Helping low readers in grade 2 and 3: An after-school volunteer tutoring program. *Elementary School Journal, 91,* 132–150.

Morrish, R. (2000). *With all due respect: Keys for building effective school discipline.* Fonthill, ON: Woodstream Publisher, Inc.

Morrison, G. S. (2000). *Teaching in America* (2nd ed.). Boston: Allyn & Bacon.

Mueller, C. M., & Dweck, C. S. (1998). Praise for intelligence can undermine children's motivation and performance. *Journal of Personality and Social Psychology, 75,* 33–52.

Muraki, E., Hombo, C. M., & Lee, Y. (2000). Equating and linking of performance assessments. *Applied Psychological Measurement, 24(4),* 325–337.

Murdock, T. B. (1999). The social context of risk: Status and motivational predictors of alienation in middle school. *Journal of Educational Psychology, 91,* 62–75.

Murray, H. A. (1938). *Explorations in personality.* Cambridge, MA: Harvard University Press.

Murrell, A. J. (2000). Discrimination. In A. Kazdin (Ed.), *Encyclopedia of psychology.* Washington, DC, and New York: American Psychological Association and Oxford University Press.

Mustard, F., Offord, D., Goldenberg, K., & Young, S. (1997). In K. Guy (ed.) *Our Promise to Children.* Ottawa, ON: Health Canada.

Myers, I. B. (1962). *The Myers-Briggs Type Indicator.* Palo Alto, CA: Consulting Psychologists Press.

N

Nairne, J. S. (2000). Forgetting. In A. Kazdin (Ed.), *Encyclopedia of psychology.* Washington, DC, and New York: American Psychological Association and Oxford University Press.

Nakamura, K. (2001). The acquisition of polite language by Japanese children. In K. E. Nelson, A. Aksu-Koc, & C. E. Johnson (Eds.), *Children's language* (Vol. 10). Mahwah, NJ: Erlbaum.

Nansel, T. R., Overpeck, M., Pilla, R. S., Ruan, W. J., Simons-Morton, B., & Scheidt, P. (2001). Bullying behaviors among U.S. youth: Prevalence and association with psychosocial adjustment. *Journal of the American Medical Association, 285,* 2094–2100.

Nash, J. M. (1997, February 3). Fertile minds. *Time,* pp. 50–54.

NASSP. (1997, May/June). Students say: What makes a good teacher? *Schools in the Middle,* 15–17.

Natasi, B. K., & Clements, D. H. (1991). Research on cooperative learning: Implications for practice. *The Social Psychology Review, 120(1),* 110–131.

National Association for the Education of Young Children. (1996). *How to choose a good early childhood program.* Washington, DC: Author.

National Center for Education Statistics Report. (1996, November). *Education indicators: An international perspective* (Catalogue No. NCES 96-003). Ottawa, ON: Author.

National Center for Education Statistics. (1997). *School-family linkages.* Unpublished manuscript. Washington, DC: U.S. Department of Education.

National Council of Teachers of English. (1997). Parent involvement: Linking home and School. *School Talk, 2(4),* 1–6.

National Council of Teachers of Mathematics. (1998). *Mathematics in the middle.* Reston, VA: National Middle School Association, Columbus, OH.

National Council of Teachers of Mathematics. (2000). *Principles and standards for school mathematics.* Reston, VA: Author.

National Research Council. (1999). *How people learn.* Washington, DC: National Academic Press.

NCSS (National Council for the Social Studies). (2002). National Standards for Social Studies Teachers. Retrieved January 5, 2003, from: http://www.socialstudies.org/standards/teachers/.

Neil, D. M. (1997, September). Transforming student assessment. *Phi Delta Kappan,* pp. 34–40, 58.

Neissor, U. (1997). Rising scores on Intelligence tests. *American Scientist, 85(5),* 440–447.

Nelson, N. W., & Sturm, J. M. (1997). Formal classroom lessons: New perspectives on a familiar discourse event. *Language, Speech, and Hearing Services in Schools, 28(3),* 255–273.

Neugarten, B. L. (1988, August). *Policy issues for an aging society.* Paper presented at the meeting of the American Psychological Association, Atlanta.

Newman, J. M. (2000, January). Action research: A brief overview. *Forum Qualitative Sozialforschung / Forum: Qualitative Social Research, 1(1).* Retrieved May 7, 2002, from: http://qualitative-research.net/fqs.

Nicholls, J. G. (1979). Development of perception of own attainment and causal attribution for success and failure in reading. *Journal of Educational Psychology, 71,* 94–99.

Nicholls, J. G., Cobb, P., Wood, T., Yackel, E., & Pataschnick, M. (1990). Assessing students' theories of success in mathematics: Individual and classroom differences. *Journal for Research in Mathematics Education, 21,* 109–122.

Nield, A. F., & Wintre, M. G. (1986). Multiple-choice questions with an option to comment: Student attitudes and use. *Teaching of Psychology, 13(4),* 196–199.

Nieto, S. (1992). *Affirming diversity: The sociopolitical context of multicultural education.* White Plains, NY: Longman.

Nikiforuk, A. (1998). Foreword to *Teach your children well: A solution to some of North America's educational problems,* by Michael Maloney. Cambridge, MA: Cambridge Center for Behavioral Studies.

Noddings, N. (1990). Constructivism in mathematics education. In R. B. Davis, C. A. Maher, & N. Noddings (Eds.), *Constructivist views of teaching and learning mathematics,* JRME Monograph No. 4, Reston, VA.

Noddings, N. (1996). Rethinking the benefits of the college-bound curriculum. *Phi Delta Kappan,* 285–289.

Noddings, N. (2003). *Caring: A feminine approach to ethics and moral education (2nd ed.).* Berkeley, CA: The University of California Press.

Nolen, S. B., & Nicholls, J. G. (1994). A place to begin (again) in research on student motivation: teachers' beliefs. *Teaching and Teacher Education, 10,* 57–69.

Nolen-Hoesekema, S. (1990). *Sex differences in depression.* Stanford, CA: Stanford University Press.

Nova Scotia Department of Education. (2002). *Program of Learning Assessment for NS (PLANS).* Retrieved December 2002, from http://plans.ednet.ns.ca/about.shtml.

Novak J. M., & Purkey W. W. (2001). *Invitational education.* Bloomington, IN: Phi Delta Kappa Educational Foundation Fastback.

Novak, J. M. (2002). *Inviting Educational Leadership: Fulfilling potential & applying an ethical perspective to the educational process.* London, Great Britain: Pearson Publishing.

Novick, R. (1998). Learning to read and write: A place to start. Portland, OR: Northwest Regional Educational Laboratory. Retrieved 5 May 2002, from http://www.nwrel.org/cfc/publications/learningreadwrite.html.

Nowell, A., & Hedges, L. V. (1998). Trends in gender differences in academic achievement from 1960 to 1994: An analysis of differences in mean, variance and extreme scores. *Sex Roles, 39,* 21–43.

O

O'Coffey, T., Simoes, D., Madden, C., Murphy, T., Gifford, S., Kim, J., et al. (1995). *A review of the Canadian Journal of behavioural science.* Retrieved June 2002, from http://www.sfu.ca/wwwpsyb/issues/1995/winter/ocoffey.htm.

O'Conner, S. C., & Rosenblood, L. K. (1996). Affiliation motivation in everyday experience: A theoretical comparison. *Journal of Personality and Social Psychology, 70,* 513–522.

O'Hara, L., & Sternberg, R. J. (1999). Learning styles. In M. A. Runco & S. Pritzker (Eds.), *Encylopedia of creativity.* San Diego: Academic Press.

O'Neil, J., & Tell, C. (1999, September). Why students lose when "tougher standards" win: A conversation with Alphi Kohn. *Educational Leadership, 57,* 18–23.

O'Shea, D. J., & O'Shea, L. J. (1997). What have we learned and where are we headed? Issues in collaboration and school reform. *Journal of Learning Disabilities, 30,* 376–377.

O'Sullivan, J. T. (1996). Children's metamemory about the influence of conceptual relations on recall. *Journal of Experimental Child Psychology, 62(1),* 1–29.

OAFCCD. (1996). *Ontario Association for Families of Children with Communication Disorders: Provincial Model of Speech and Language Service for Children.* Ontario, Canada.

Oberg, D., & Gibson, S. (1999). What's happening with Internet use in Alberta schools? *The Alberta Journal of Educational Research, XLV(3),* 239–252.

Official Languages Act. (1998). Policy and Communications Branch, Office of the Commissioner of Official Languages, Ottawa, Canada.

Ogbu, J. (1983). Minority status and schooling in plural societies. *Comparative Education Review, 27,* 168–190.

Oldfather, P., West, J., White, J., & Wilmarth, J. (1999). Learning through children's eyes: Social constructivism and the desire to learn. Washington, DC: American Psychological Association.

Oller, D. K. (2000). *The emergence of speech capacity.* Mahwah, NJ: Erlbaum.

Olson, L. (2001). Overboard on testing? *Editorial Projects in Education, 20* (No. 17), 23–30.

Olweus, D. (1993). *Bullying at school: What we know and what we can do.* Cambridge, MA: Blackwell Publishers.

Olweus, D. (2001). Peer harassment: A critical analysis and some important issues. In J. Juvonen & S. Graham (Eds.), *Peer harassment in school: The plight of the vulnerable and victimized* (pp. 3–20). New York: The Guilford Press.

Ontario Association for Mathematics Education. (2002). Retrieved 6 July 2002, from: http://www.oame.on.ca.

Ontario Ministry of Education. (1998). Science and Technology: The Ontario Curriculum, Grades 1–8. Retrieved 6 July 2002, from: http://www.edu.gov.on.ca/eng/document/curricul/scientec/scientec.html.

Ontario Science Centre. (2002). *Science Centre School.* Retrieved 6 July 2002, from http://www.ontariosciencecentre.ca/school/osc_school/about.asp.

Overton, T. (2000). *Assessment in special education* (3rd ed.). Upper Saddle River, NJ: Merrill.

Owen, T., & Owston, R. (1998). *The learning highway: Smart students and the Internet* (3rd ed.). Toronto, ON: Key Porter.

Owston, R. (1999). Strategies for Evaluating Web-based Learning. Annual Meeting of the American Educational Research Association (AERA). Montreal, QC. Retrieved 12 November 2002, from: http://www.edu.yorku.ca/~rowston/aera99.html.

Owston, R. (2000, April). *A meta-evaluation of six cases studies of web-based learning.* A paper presented at the Annual Meeting of the American Educational Research Association, New Orleans, GA. Retrieved 12 November 2002, from: http://www.edu.yorku.ca/~rowston/aera2000.html.

Owston, R., & Wideman, H. (1996). *Word processors and children's writing in a high computer access setting.* Retrieved 12 November 2002, from: http://www.edu.yorku.ca/~rowston/written.html.

P

Paintal, S. (1999). Banning corporal punishment of children. *Childhood Education, 76,* 36–40.

Paivio, A. (1971). *Imagery and verbal processes.* Fort Worth, TX: Harcourt Brace.

Paivio, A. (1986). *Mental representations: A dual coding approach.* New York: Oxford University Press.

Palincsar, A. S. (1998). Social constructivist perspectives on teaching and learning. *Annual Review of Psychology, 49,* 345–375.

Palincsar, A. S., & Brown, A. L. (1984). Reciprocal teaching of comprehension-fostering and comprehension-monitoring activities. *Cognition and Instruction, 1,* 117–175.

Palomba, C., & Banta, T. W. (1999). *Assessment essentials.* San Francisco: Jossey-Bass.

Panofsky, C. (1999, April). *What the zone of proximal development conceals.* Paper presented at the meeting of the Society for Research in Child Development, Montreal.

Papert, S. (1980). *Mindstorms: Children, computers, and powerful ideas.* New York: Basic Books.

Papert, S. (1993). *The children's machine: Rethinking school in the age of the computer.* New York: Basic Books.

Parcel, G. S., Simons-Morton, G. G., O'Hara, N. M., Baranowksi, T., Kolbe, L. J., & Bee, D. E. (1987). School promotion of healthful diet and exercise behavior. *Journal of School Health, 57,* 150–156.

Parkay, F. W., & Hass, C. G. (2000). *Curriculum planning: A contemporary approach* (7th ed.). Boston: Allyn & Bacon.

Parke, R. D., & Buriel, R. (1998). Socialization in the family: Ethnic and ecological perspectives. In W. Damon (Ed.), *Handbook of child psychology* (5th ed., Vol. 3). New York: Wiley.

Pascual-Leone, J. (1970). A mathematical model for the transition rule in Piaget's developmental stages. *Acta Psychologia, 63,* 301–345.

Pascual-Leone, J. (1990). Reflections on life-span intelligence, consciousness, and ego development. In C. N. Alexander & E. J. Langer (Eds.), *Higher stages of human development* (pp. 258–285). New York: Oxford University Press.

Pascual-Leone, J., & Smith, J. (1969). The encoding and decoding of symbols by children. *Journal of Experimental Child Psychology, 8,* 328–355.

Pashler, H. (Ed.) (1998). *Attention.* Philadelphia: Psychology Press.

Patterson, K., & Wright, A. E. (1990, Winter). The speech, language, or hearing-impaired child: At-risk academically. *Childhood Education,* pp. 91–95.

Pavlov, I. P. (1927). *Conditioned reflexes.* New York: Dover.

Payne, D. A. (1997). *Applied educational assessment.* Belmont, CA: Wadsworth.

Pearson, P. D., Hansen, J., & Gordon, C. (1979). The effect of background knowledge on young children's comprehension of explicit and implicit information. *Journal of Reading Behavior, 11,* 201–210.

Pellat, A. (1997). Feasibility study: Subsidized guardianship. A report completed for Alberta Family Social Services.

Pepler, D. J., Craig, W., Ziegler, S., & Charach, A. (1994). An Evaluation of an Anti-Bullying Intervention in Toronto Schools. *Canadian Journal of Community Mental Health, 13,* 95–100.

Pepler, D., & Craig, W. (1995). A peek behind the fence: Naturalistic observations of aggressive children with remote audiovisual recording. *Developmental Psychology, 31,* 548–553.

Perkins, D. (1999). The many faces of constructivism. *Educational Leadership, 57,* No. 3, 6–11.

Perkins, D., & Tishman, S. (1997, March). Commentary in "Teaching today's pupils to think more critically." *APA Monitor,* p. 51.

Perry, C. (1999). *Creating Health Behavior Change: How to Develop Community-Wide Programs for Youth.* Thousand Oaks, CA: Saga Publications.

Perry, N., & Drummond, L. (2002). Helping young students become self-regulated researchers and writers. *Reading Teacher, 56(3),* 298–310.

Petersen, A. C. (2000). Puberty and biological maturation. In A. Kazdin (Ed.), *Encyclopedia of psychology.* Washington, DC, and New York: American Psychological Association and Oxford U. Press.

Philliber, W. W., Spillman, R. E., & King, R. E. (1996). Consequences of family literacy for adults and children: Some preliminary findings. *Journal of Adolescent & Adult Literacy, 39(7),* 558–565.

Piaget, J. (1952). *The origins of intelligence in children.* New York: International Universities Press.

Piaget, J., & Inhelder, B. (1969). *The child's conception of space.* New York: Norton.

Pikas, A. (2002). New developments of the shared concern method. *School Psychology International, 23(3),* 307–326.

Pinnell. G. G. (1997). Reading Recovery: A summary of research. In J. Flood, S. B. Heath & D. Lapp (Eds.). *Handbook of research on teaching literacy through the Communicative and visual arts.* (pp. 638–654). New York: MacMillan.

Pintrich, P. R. (2000). Learning and motivation. In A. Kazdin (Ed.), *Encyclopedia of psychology.* Washington, DC, and New York: American Psychological Association and Oxford University Press.

Pintrich, P. R. (2000). The role of goal orientation in self-regulated learning. In M. Boekaerts, P. R. Pintrich, & M. Zeidner (Eds.), *Handbook of self-regulation.* San Diego: Academic Press.

Pintrich, P. R., & Schunk, D. H. (2002). *Motivation in education* (2nd ed.). Upper Saddle River, NJ: Prentice Hall.

Pleiss, M. K., & Feldhusen, J. F. (1995). Mentors, role models, and heroes in the lives of gifted children. *Educational Psychologist 30,* 159–169.

Plomin, R. (2000). Behavior genetics. In M. Bennett (Ed.), *Developmental psychology: Achievements and prospects.* Philadelphia: Psychology Press.

Poest, C. A., Williams, J. R., Witt, D. D., & Atwood, M. E. (1990). Challenge me to move: Large muscle development in children. *Young Children, 45,* 4–10.

Pon, G. (2000). Importing the Asian model minority discourse into Canada: Implications for social work and education. *Canadian Social Work Review, 17(2).*

Popham, W. J. (2000). *Classroom assessment* (3rd ed.). Boston: Allyn & Bacon.

Popham, W. J. (2000). *Modern educational measurement* (3rd Ed.). Boston: Allyn & Bacon.

Postman, N. (1979). *Teaching as a conserving activity.* New York: Laurel Press.

Pressley, M. (1995). More about the development of self-regulation: Complex, long-term, and thoroughly social. *Educational Psychologist, 30,* 207–212.

Pressley, M. (1998). *Reading instruction that works: The case for balanced teaching.* NY, NY: The Guilford Press.

Pressley, M., & Afflerbach, P. (1995). *Verbal protocols of reading.* Mahwah, NJ: Erlbaum.

Pressley, M., Borkowski, J. G., & Schneider, W. (1989). Good information processing: What it is and what education can do to promote it. *International Journal of Educational Research, 13,* 857–867.

Pressley, M., Schuder T., SAIL Faculty and Administration, German, J., & El-Dinary, P. B. (1992). A researcher-educator collaborative interview study of transactional comprehension strategies instruction. *Journal of Educational Psychology, 84,* 231–246.

Pressley, M., Wharto-McDonald, R., Allington, R., Block, C. C., Morrow, H. L., Tracey, D., Baker, K., Brooks, G., Cronin, J., Nelson, E., & Woo, D. (2001). A study of effective first grade literacy instruction. *Scientific Studies of Reading, 15,* 35–58.

Pressley, M., Wharton-McDonald, R., Mistretta-Hampston, J., & Echevarria, M. (1998). Literacy instruction in 10 fourth- and fifth- grade classrooms in upstate New York. *Scientific Studies of Reading, 2(2),* 159–194.

Pressley, M., Yokoi, L., & Rankin, J. (1996). A survey of instructional practices of primary teachers nominated as effective in promoting literacy. *Elementary School Journal, 96(4),* 333–384.

Price, R. H. (2000). Prevention and intervention. In A. Kazdin (Ed.), *Encyclopedia of psychology.* Washington, DC, and New York: American Psychological Association and Oxford U. Press.

Principles for Fair Student Assessment Practices for Education in Canada. (1993). Edmonton, Alberta: Joint Advisory Committee.

Programme for International Student Assessment. (2002). *PISA (Program for International Student Assessment): What PISA is?* Retrieved 10 December 2002, from: http://www.pisa.oecd.org/pisa/summary.htm.

Pross, H. (2002). *Problem-based learning at Queen's University.* Kingston, ON: Queen's University. Retrieved 12 November 2002, from: http://meds.queensu.ca/medicine/pbl/.

Prutzman, P., & Johnson, J. (1997). Bias awareness and multiple perspectives: Essential aspects of conflict resolution. *Theory into Practice, 36,* 27–31.

Pueschel, S. M., Scola, P. S., Weidenman, L. E., & Bernier, J. C. (1995). *The special child.* Baltimore: Paul H. Brookes.

Pugach, M. C., & Johnson, L. J. (1995). *Collaborative practitioners, collaborative schools.* Denver: Love.

Puhan, G. & Huiqin, H. (2002, April). *Cognition versus motivation: What causes performance differences in science?* Poster presented at the annual meeting of the National Council on Measurement in Education, New Orleans, LA.

Purcell-Gates, V. (1997, June 18). Commentary in "Diagnosing learning problems can be difficult for parents and teachers." *USA Today,* p. D8.

Putnam, J. A. (1997). *Cooperative learning in diverse classrooms.* Columbus, OH: Merrill, Prentice Hall.

R

Ramey, C. T., Bryant, D. M., Campbell, F. A., Sparling, J. J., & Wasik, B. H. (1988). Early intervention for high-risk children. The Carolina Early Intervention Program. In R. H. Price, E. L. Cowen, R. P. Lorion, & J. Ramos-McKay (Eds.), *14 ounces of prevention.* Washington, DC: American Psychological Association.

Ramos, L., & Sanchez, A. R. (1995). Mexican-American high school students: Educational aspirations. *Journal of Multicultural Counseling and Development, 23,* 122–221.

Randi, J., & Corno, L. (2000). Teacher innovations in self-regulated learning. In M. Boekaerts, P. R. Pintrich, & M. Zeidner (Eds.), *Handbook of self-regulation.* San Diego: Academic Press.

Randi, J., & Corno, L. (2000). Teacher innovations in self-regulated learning, In M. Boekaerts, P. R. Pintrich, & M. Zeidner (Eds.), *Handbook of self-regulation.* Boston: American Psychological Association.

Randolph, C. H., & Evertson, C. M. (1995). Managing for learning: Rules, roles, and meanings in a writing class. *Journal of Classroom Instruction, 30,* 17–25.

Raphael, T. E., Kehus, M., & Damphouse, K. (2001). *Book Club for middle school.* Lawrence, MA: Small Planet Communications.

Raphael, T., & McMahon, S. (1994). Book Club: An alternative framework for reading instruction. *The Reading Teacher, 48(2),* 102–116.

Raschke, D. (1981). Designing reinforcement surveys: Let the student choose the reward. *Teaching Exceptional Children, 14,* 92–96.

Rayner, K. (2000). Reading. In A. Kazdin (Ed.), *Encyclopedia of psychology.* Washington, DC, and New York: American Psychological Association and Oxford University Press.

Recht, D. R., & Leslie, L. (1988). Effect of prior knowledge on good and poor readers' memory of text. *Journal of Educational Psychology, 80,* 16–20.

Reed, S. (2000). Problem solving. In A. Kazdin (Ed.), *Encyclopedia of psychology.* Washington, DC, and New York: American Psychological Association and Oxford University Press.

Rehorick, S. (2001). *La formation des enseignants et des enseignantes du français langue seconde, clé du succès des programmes pour les jeunes Canadiens et Canadiennes.* Paper presented at XIXe Biennale de la langue française, Jeunesse et langue française, Hull, Quebec. Retrieved March 2003, from http://www. unb. ca/slec/about/biennale_eng. html.

Reid, J. (1996). Pupils with special educational needs: The role of speech & language therapists. *Interchange, 43.*

Reinking, D. (1989). Misconceptions about reading that affect software development. *The Computing Teacher, 16(4),* 27–29.

Renzulli, J. S., & Reis, S. M. (1985). *The school wide enrichment model: A comprehensive plan for educational excellence.* Mansfield Center, CN: Creative Learning Press.

Renzulli, J. S., & Reis, S. M. (1997). The schoolwide enrichment model. In N. Colangelo & G. A. Davis (Eds.), *Handbook of gifted education.* Boston: Allyn & Bacon.

Reschly, D. (1996). Identification and assessment of students with disabilities. *Future of Children, 6 (1),* 40–53.

Resnick, L. B., & Chi, M. T. H. (1988). Cognitive psychology and science learning. In M. Druger (Ed.), *Science for the fun of it: A guide to informal science education.* Washington, DC: National Science Teachers Association.

Ridderinkhof, K. R., & van der Molen, M. (1995). A psychophysiological analysis of developmental differences in the ability to resist interference. *Child Development, 66(4),* 1040–1056.

Ridderinkhof, K. R., van der Molen, M., & Band, G. P. H. (1997). Sources of interference from irrelevant information: A developmental study. *Journal of Experimental Child Psychology, 65(3),* 315–341.

Riedsel, C. A., & Schwartz, J. E. (1999). *Essentials of elementary mathematics* (2nd ed.). Boston: Allyn & Bacon.

Rigby, K. (1996, August). *What to do about bullying: An Australian perspective.* Paper presented at the conference Putting the Brakes on Violence. North York, ON.

Risley, D. S., & Walther, B. (1995). *Creating responsible learners.* Washington, DC: American Psychological Association.

Ritchie D. (1999). Using the web effectively in the classroom. *QUICK, 72,* 8–12. Retrieved online from http://education.qut.edu.au/lloydm/mdb383/zerolecture.rtf.

Roberts, C. A., & Lazure, M. D. (1970*). One million children: A national study of Canadian children with emotional and learning disorders.* Toronto: Leonard Crainford.

Robertson, S. (1998). Paradise lost: Children, multimedia and the myth of interactivity. *Journal of Computer Assisted Learning, 14,* 31–39.

Robinson, R. D., McKenna, M. C., & Wedman, J. M. (2000). *Issues and trends in literacy education* (2nd ed.). Boston: Allyn & Bacon.

Roblyer, M. D., & Edwards, J. (2000). *Integrating educational technology into teaching* (2nd ed.). Upper Saddle River, NJ: Prentice Hall.

Rock, E. A., Hammond, M., & Rasmussen, S. (2002). School Based Program to Teach Children Empathy and Bully Prevention. Paper retrieved December 12, 2002, from: http://ericcass.uncg.edu/virtuallib/bullying/1071.html.

Rodgers, C. (2000). Gender schema. In A. Kazdin (Ed.), *Encyclopedia of psychology.* Washington, DC, and New York: American Psychological Association and Oxford University Press.

Roediger, H. (2000). Learning: Cognitive approach for humans. In A. Kazdin (Ed.), *Encyclopedia of psychology.* Washington, DC, and New York: American Psychological Association and Oxford University Press.

Roehrig, A. D., Pressley, M., & Sloup, M. (2001). Reading strategy instruction in regular primary-level classrooms by teachers trained in Reading Recovery. *Reading & Writing Quarterly, 17,* 323–348.

Roeser, R. W, Eccles, J. S., & Sameroft, A. J. (2000). School as a context of early adolescents' academic and social-emotional development: a summary of research findings. *The Elementary School Journal, 100(5),* 443–471.

Roeser, R. W., Eccles, J. S., & Strobel, K. R. (1998). Linking the study of schooling and mental health: Selected issues and empirical illustrations at the level of the individual. *Educational Psychologist, 33(4),* 153–176.

Rogoff, B. (1998). Cognition as a collaborative process. In D. Kuhn & R. S. Siegler (Eds.), *Handbook of child psychology* (5th ed., Vol. 2). New York: Wiley.

Rosch, E. H. (1973). On the internal structure of perceptual and semantic categories. In T. E. Moore (Ed.), *Cognition and the acquisition of language.* New York: Academic Press.

Rosenshine, B. (1985). Direct instruction. In T. Husen & T. N. Postlethwaite (Eds.), *Encyclopedia of education* (Vol. 3). New York: Pergamon.

Rosenthal, M., & Andrea, L. (1997). Stop and think! Using metacognitive strategies to teach students social skills. *Teaching Exceptional Children, 29(3),* 29–31.

Rosenthal, R. (1994). Interpersonal expectancy effects: A 30-year perspective. *Current Directions in Psychological Science, 3(6),* 176–179.

Rosenthal, R. (1995). Critiquing Pygmalion: A 25-year perspective. *Current Directions in Psychological Science, 4(6),* 171–172.

Ross, B. H. (2000). Concepts: Learning. In A. Kazdin (Ed.), *Encyclopedia of psychology.* Washington, DC, and New York: American Psychological Association and Oxford University Press.

Ross, D. P., & Roberts, P. (2000). Income and Child Well-being: A new perspective on the poverty debate. Ottawa, ON: Canadian Council on Social Development.

Ross, D. P., Scott, K., & Kelly, M. (1996). *Child poverty: What are the consequences?* Ottawa, ON: Centre for Internal Statistics, Canadian Council on Social Development.

Ross, D. P., Scott, K., & Kelly, M. (1999). *Child Poverty: What are the Consequences?* Ottawa, ON: Canadian Council on Social Development.

Ross, J. (2000) Mathematics reform: Do some students benefit more than others. *Orbit magazine, 31(3),* Toronto, ON: University of Toronto Press.

Ross, J. A., Hogaboam-Gray, A., & Hannay, L. (2001). Effects of teacher efficacy on computer skills and computer cognitions of K–3 students. *Elementary School Journal, 102(2),* 141–156.

Rossell, C., & Baker, R. (1996). The educational effectiveness of bilingual education. *Research in the Teaching of English, 30(1),* 7–74.

Rosselli, H. C. (1996, February/March). Gifted students. *National Association for Secondary School Principals,* pp. 12–17.

Rothbart, M. K., & Bates, J. E. (1998). Temperament. In W. Damon (Ed.), *Handbook of child psychology* (5th ed., Vol. 3). New York: Wiley.

Rubin, K. H. (2000). Peer relation. In A. Kazdin (Ed.), *Encyclopedia of psychology.* Washington, DC, and New York: American Psychological Association and Oxford University Press.

Rubin, K. H., Bukowski, W., & Parker, J. G. (1998). Peer interactions, relationships, and groups. In W. Damon (Ed.), *Handbook of child psychology* (5th ed., Vol. 3). New York: Wiley.

Rubin, K. H., Coplan, R. J., Nelson, L. J., Dheah, C. S. L., & Lagace-Seguin, D. G. (2000). Peer relationships in childhood. In M. H. Bornstein & M. E. Lamb (Eds.), *Developmental psychology* (4th Ed.). Mahwah, NJ: Erlbaum.

Ruble, D. (1983). The development of social comparison processes and their role in achievement-related self-socialization. In E. T. Higgins, D. N. Ruble, & W. W. Hartup (Eds.), *Social cognition and development.* New York: Cambridge University Press.

Ruiz-Primo, M., Li, M., Ayala, C., & Shavelson, R. (2000, April). *Students' science journals as an assessment tool.* Paper presented at the meeting of the American Educational Research Association, New Orleans.

Runco, M. (1999). Critical thinking. In M. A. Runco & S. Pritzker (Eds.), *Encyclopedia of creativity.* San Diego: Academic Press.

Russell, T. (2000). *Introducing pre-service teachers to teacher research.* Paper presented at the meeting of the American Education Research Association, New Orleans, LA.

Rutter, M., & Schopler, E. (1987). Autism and pervasive developmental disorders: Concepts and diagnostic issues. *Journal of Autism and Pervasive Developmental Disorders, 17,* 159–186.

Ryan, A. M., & Patrick, H. (1996, March). *Positive peer relationships and psychosocial adjustment during adolescence.* Paper presented at the meeting of the Society for Research on Adolescence, Boston.

Ryan, R. M., & Deci, E. L. (1996). When paradigms clash: Comments on Cameron and Pierce's claim that rewards do not undermine intrinsic motivation. *Review of Educational Research, 66,* 33–38.

Ryan, A. M., & Pintrich, P. R. (1997). "Should I ask for help?" the role of motivation and attitudes in adolescents' help seeking in math class. *Journal of Educational Psychology, 89 (2),* 329–341.

Ryan, B., & Adams, G. (2000). The Family–School Connection. *Transition Magazine, 30*(1). Retrieved 14 December 2002, from: http://www.vifamily.ca/tm/301/1.htm.

Ryan-Finn, K. D., Cauce, A. M., & Grove, K. (1995, March). *Children and adolescents of color: Where are you? Selection, recruitment, and retention in developmental research.* Paper presented at the meeting of the Society for Research in Child Development, Indianapolis.

Rychman, R. M. (2000). *Theories of personality* (7th ed.). Belmont, CA: Wadsworth.

S

Sadker, D. M. P., & Sadker, D. M. (2000). *Teachers, schools, and society* (5th ed.). New York: McGraw-Hill.

Sadker, M., Sadker, D., & Long, L. (1997). Gender and educational equality. In J. A. Banks & C. A. M. Banks (Eds.), *Multicultural education* (3rd ed.). Boston: Allyn & Bacon.

Sadoski, M., & Paivio, A. (2001). *Imagery and text: A dual coding theory of reading and writing.* Mahwah, NJ: Lawrence Erlbaum Associates.

Salomon, G., & Perkins, D. (1989). Rocky roads to transfer: Rethinking mechanisms of a neglected phenomenon. *Educational Psychologist, 24,* 113–142.

Sandoval, J., Scheuneman, J. D., Ramos-Grenier, J., Geisinger, K. F., & Frisby, C. (Eds.). (1999). *Test interpretation and diversity: Achieving equity in assessment.* Washington, DC: American Psychological Association.

Sanford, A. J. (2000). Semantics. In A. Kazdin (Ed.), *Encyclopedia of psychology.* Washington, DC, and New York: American Psychological Association and Oxford University Press.

Sanson, A. V., & Rothbart, M. K. (1995). Child temperament and parenting. In M. H. Bornstein (Ed.), *Handbook of parenting* (Vol. 4). Hillsdale, NJ: Erlbaum.

Santrock, J. W. (1998). *Adolescence* (7th ed.). New York: McGraw-Hill.

Santrock, J. W., & Halonen, J. S. (1999). *The guide to college success.* Belmont, CA: Wadsworth.

Sapon-Shevin, M. (1999). *Because we can change the world: A practical guide to building cooperative, inclusive classroom communities.* Boston: Allyn & Bacon.

Saskatchewan Department of Education. (2002). *Saskatchewan Learning: Assessment & Evaluation Unit.* Retrieved 5 December 2002, from: http://www.sasked.gov.sk.ca/k/pecs/ae.

Sax, G. (1997). *Principles of educational and psychological measurement and evaluation* (4th ed.). Belmont, CA: Wadsworth.

Scardamalia, M. (1981). How children cope with the cognitive demands of writing. In C. Frederiksen & J. F. Dominic (Eds.). *Writing: The nature, development, and teaching of written communication.* Mahwah, NJ: Erlbaum.

Scardamalia, M., & Bereiter, C. (1996). Computer support for knowledge-building communities. In T. Koschmann (Ed.), *CSCL: Theory and practice of an emerging paradigm* (pp. 249–268). Mahwah, NJ: Lawrence Erlbaum Associates.

Scardamalia, M., & Bereiter, C. (1999). Schools as knowledge-building organizations. In D. Keating & C. Hertzman (Eds.), *Today's children, tomorrow's society: The development health and wealth of nations* (pp. 274–289). New York: Guilford.

Scarr, S. (1996). Best of human genetics. *Contemporary Psychology, 41,* 149–150.

Schacter, D. L. (2000). Memory systems. In A. Kazdin (Ed.), *Encyclopedia of psychology.* Washington, DC, and New York: American Psychological Association and Oxford University Press.

Schaefer, A. C. (2001, Spring). *Demographic overview: Teacher workload issues and stress survey.* BCTF Research Report, Section III 2001-WLC-05. Retrieved 2003/02/22, from http://www.bctf.bc.ca/ResearchReports/2001wlc05/report.html.

Schaler, J. A. (1996). Thinking about drinking: The power of self-fulfilling prophecies. *The International Journal of Drug Policy, 7*(3), 187–192.

Schauble, L. (1990). Belief revision in children: The role of prior knowledge and strategies for generating evidence. *Journal of Experimental Child Psychology, 49,* 31–57.

Schauble, L. (1996). The development of scientific reasoning in knowledge-rich contexts. *Developmental Psychology, 32,* 102–119.

Schiever, S. W., & Maker, C. J. (1997). Enrichment and acceleration: An overview and new directions. In N. Colangelo & G. A. Davis (Eds.), *Handbook of gifted education.* Boston: Allyn & Bacon.

Schneider, W., & Bjorklund, D. F. (1998). Memory. In W. Damon (Ed.), *Handbook of child psychology* (5th ed., Vol. 2). New York: Wiley.

Schneider, W., & Pressley, M. (1997). *Memory development between 2 and 20 (2nd ed.)* Mahwah, NJ: Lawrence Erlbaum Associates.

Schneider, W., Ennemoser, M., Roth, E., & Kuspert, P. (1999). Kindergarten prevention of dyslexia: Does training in phonological awareness work for everybody? *Journal of Learning Disabilities, 32,* 429–436.

SchoolNet News Network. (2001). *Speaking publicly!* News report by Lillian. Student Magazine (Vol. 7, March). Retrieved 5 October 2002, from: http://www.snn-rdr.ca/snn/march2001/speeches.html.

SchoolNet Report. (2000, December). Evaluation of the SchoolNet initiative: Final report (Project No. 34436). Retrieved November 15, 2002, from: http://www.schoolnet.ca/home/e/documents/SN_evaluationE.pdf.

Schuell, T. J. (1996). The role of educational psychology in the preparation of teachers. *Educational Psychologist, 3* (1), 5–14.

Schultz, G. F. (1993) Socioeconomic advantage and achievement motivation: Important mediators of academic performance in minority children in urban schools. *Urban Review, 25*(3), 221–232.

Schultz, K., & Fecho, B. (2001). Society's child: Social context and writing development. *Educational Psychologist, 35,* 51–62.

Schunk, D. H. (1989). Self-efficacy and cognitive skill learning. In C. Ames & R. Ames (Eds.), *Research on motivation and education* (Vol. 3). Orlando: Academic Press.

Schunk, D. H. (1991). Self-efficacy and academic motivation. *Educational Psychologist, 25,* 71–86.

Schunk, D. H. (1996). *Learning theories* (2nd ed.). Englewood Cliffs, NJ: Merrill.

Schunk, D. H. (1996). Social cognitive theory and self-regulated learning. In B. J. Zimmerman & D. H. Schunk (Eds.), *Self-regulated learning and academic achievement.* Mahwah, NJ: Erlbaum.

Schunk, D. H. (1999, August). *Social-self interaction and achievement behavior.* Presidential address, Division 15, presented at the meeting of the American Psychological Association, Boston.

Schunk, D. H. (2000). *Learning theories: An educational perspective* (3rd ed.). Upper Saddle River, NJ: Prentice Hall.

Schunk, D. H. (2001). Social cognitive theory and self-regulated learning. In B. J. Zimmerman & D. H. Schunk (Eds.), *Self-regulated learning and achievement* (2nd ed.). Mahwah, NJ: Erlbaum.

Schunk, D. H., & Ertmer, P. A. (2000). Self-regulation and academic learning: Self-efficacy enhancing intervention. In M. Boekarts, P. Pintrich, & M. Zeidner (Eds.), *Handbook of self-regulation.* San Diego: Academic Press.

Schunk, D. H., & Zimmerman, B. J. (Eds.). (1994). *Self-regulation of learning and performance: Issues and educational applications.* Mahwah, NJ: Erlbaum.

Schunk, D. H., & Zimmerman, B. J. (1997). Social origins of self-regulatory competence. *Educational Psychologist, 32,* 195–208.

Scott, N. H. (1999). *Supporting new teachers: A report on the 1998–99 beginning teacher induction program in New Brunswick.* (ERIC Document Reproduction Services No. ED437347)

Seaman, D., Popp, B., & Darling, S. (1991). *Follow-up Study of the Impact of the Kenan Trust Model for Family Literacy.* Louisville, Kentucky: National Center for Family Literacy.

Segal, M. (2002). *Another look at creativity styles: Reporting on research and a new question.* Retrieved 21 October 2002, from http://www.tri-network.com/articles/kaimbti.html.

Seidman, E. (2000). School transitions. In A. Kazdin (Ed.), *Encyclopedia of psychology.* Washington, DC, & New York: American Psychological Association and Oxford University Press.

Senge, P. (2000). *Schools that learn: A Fifth Discipline Fieldbook for educators, parents, and everyone who cares about education.* NY, NY: Doubleday.

Senior, S. (1993). Canadian Native intelligence studies: A Brief review. *Canadian Journal of Native Education, 20(1),* 148–156.

Serow, R. C., Ciechalski, J., & Daye, C. (1990). Students as volunteers. *Urban Education, 25,* 157–168.

Serpell, R. (2000). Culture and Intelligence. In A. Kazdin (Ed.), *Encyclopedia of psychology.* Washington, DC, and New York: American Psychological Association and Oxford University Press.

Shachar, H., & Sharan, S. (1994). Cooperative learning and school organization. In S. Sharan (Ed.). *Handbook of Cooperative Learning Methods.* Westport, CT: Greenwood Press.

Shad. (2002). *Shad Valley Program: Information.* Retrieved December 6, 2002, from http://www.shad.ca/home.html.

Shaklee, B. D., Barbour, N. E., Ambrose, R., & Hansford, S. J. (1997). *Designing and using portfolios.* Boston: Allyn & Bacon.

Shanahan, T., & Barr, R. (1995). Reading Recovery: An independent evaluation of the effects of an early instructional intervention for at-risk learners. *Reading Research Quarterly, 30(4),* 958–996.

Sharan, S. (Ed.). (1994). *Handbook of Cooperative Learning Methods.* Westport, CT: Greenwood Press.

Sharan, S., & Shaulov, A. (1990). Cooperative learning, motivation to learn, and academic achievement. In S. Sharan (Ed.), *Cooperative learning.* New York: Praeger.

Shields, S. A. (1991). Gender in the psychology of emotion: A selective research review. In K. T. Strongman (Ed.), *International review of studies on emotion.* New York: Wiley.

Shook, G. L., Hartsfield, F., & Hemingway, M. (1995). Essential content for training behavior analysis practitioners. *The Behavior Analyst, 18,* 83–91.

Shulha, L. (1999). Understanding novice teachers' thinking about student assessment. *Alberta Journal of Educational Research, 45*(3), 288–303.

Shultz, T. R., Fisher, G. W., Pratt, C. C., & Rulf, S. (1986). Selection of causal rules. *Child Development, 57,* 143–152.

Siegfried, T. (1998, July 13). In teaching scientific subjects, high schools are out of order. *Dallas Morning News,* p. 9D.

Siegler, R. S. (1998). *Children's thinking* (3rd ed.). Upper Saddle River, NJ: Erlbaum.

Signorielli, N. (1997, April). Reflections of girls in the media: A two-part study on gender and media. Kaiser Family foundation and Children NOW. Retrieved December 3, 2002, from http://www.childrennow.org/media/mc97/ReflectSummary.html#top.

Silverman, L. K. (1993). A developmental model for counseling the gifted. In L. K. Silverman (Ed.), *Counseling the gifted and the talented.* Denver: Love.

Simner, M. L. (1998). *Promoting reading success: Phonological Awareness Activities for the Kindergarten Child.* Ottawa, ON: Canadian Psychological Association.

Simner, M. L. (2000). A joint position statement by the Canadian Psychological Association and the Canadian Association of School Psychologists on the Canadian Press Coverage of the Province-wide Achievement Test Results. Retrieved December 7, 2002, from: http://www.cpa.ca/documents/joint_position.html.

Simner, M. L. (2001). *Learning Disabilities Association of Ontario bulletin #3: Promoting early intervention for learning disabilities initiative.* Retrieved June 2002, from http://www.ldao.on.ca/pei/pei_bul3.pdf.

Singhal, M. (2001). Reading proficiency, reading strategies, metacognitive awareness, and L2 readers. *Reading Matrix, 1,* 1–6.

Skiba, R., & Peterson, R. (1999, January). The dark side of zero tolerance. *Phi Delta Kappan, 80,* 372–376.

Skinner, B. F. (1938). *The behavior of organisms.* New York: Appleton-Century-Crofts.

Skinner, B. F. (1953). *Science and human behavior.* New York: Macmillan.

Slavin, R. E. (1990). Achievement effects of ability grouping in secondary schools: A best-evidence synthesis. *Review of Educational Research, 60,* 471–500.

Slavin, R. E. (1994). *Using team learning (4th ed.).* Baltimore, MD: Johns Hopkins University, Center for Research on Elementary and Middle Schools.

Slavin, R. E. (1995). *Cooperative learning: Theory, research, and practice* (2nd ed.). Boston: Allyn & Bacon.

Slavin, R. E. (1995). Detracking and the detractors. *Phi Delta Kappan, 77,* 220–221.

Sloat, E., & Willms, J. D. (2000). The international adult literacy survey: Implications for Canadian social policy. *Canadian Journal of Education, 25*(3), 218–233.

Smith, P. K., & Sharp, S. (Eds.), (1994). *School bullying: Insights and perspectives.* London: Routledge.

Smith, P. K., Cowie, H., Olafsson, R., & Liefooghe, P. (2002). Definitions of bullying: A comparison of terms used, and age and gender differences in a fourteen-country international comparison. *Child Development, 73,* 1119–1133.

Smith, P. K., Shu, S., & Madsen, K. (2001). Characteristics of victims of school bullying: Developmental changes in coping strategies and skills. In J. Juvonen & S. Graham (Eds.), *Peer harassment in school: The plight of the vulnerable and victimized* (pp. 332–351). New York: The Guilford Press.

Smith, T. E., Polloway, E. A., Patton, J. R., Dowdy, C. A., & Heath, N. L. (2001). *Teaching students with special needs in inclusive settings.* Toronto, ON: Pearson Education Canada.

Smith-Burke, M. T. (2001). Reading Recovery®: A systemic approach to early intervention. In L. M. Morrow & D. G. Woo (Eds.). *Tutoring programs for struggling readers* (pp. 216–236). New York, NY: Guilford Press.

Smith-Maddox, R., & Wheelock, A. (1995). Untracking and students' futures. *Phi Delta Kappan, 77,* 222–228.

Snow, C., & Beals, D. (2001). Deciding what to tell: Selecting an elaborative narrative. Topics in family interaction and children's personal experience stories. In S. Blum-Kulka & C. Snow (Eds.), *Talking to adults.* Mahwah, NJ: Erlbaum.

Sobieraj, S. (1996). Beauty and the beast: toy commercials and the social construction of gender. American Sociological Association, *Sociological Abstracts,* 044.

Soderman, A. K., Gregory, K. M., & O'Neill, L. T. (1999). *Scaffolding emerging literacy.* Boston: Allyn & Bacon.

Solano-Flores, G. & Shavelson, R. J. (1997, Fall). Development of performance assessments in science: Conceptual, practical, and logistical issues. *Educational Measurement,* pp. 16–24.

Songer, N. B. (1993). Learning science with a child-focused resource: A case study of Kids as Global Scientists. In *Proceedings of the 15th Annual Meeting of the Cognitive Science Society.* Mahwah, NJ: Erlbaum.

Spearman, C. E. (1927). *The abilities of man.* New York: Macmillan.

Spear-Swerling, L., & Sternberg, R. J. (1994). The road not taken: An integrative theoretical model of reading disability. *Journal of Learning Disabilities, 27,* 91–103.

Spence, J. T., & Helmreich, R. (1978). *Masculinity and femininity. Their psychological dimensions.* Austin: University of Texas Press.

Spencer, M. B. (2000). Ethnocentrism. In A. Kazdin (Ed.), *Encyclopedia of psychology.* Washington, DC, and New York: American Psychological Association and Oxford University Press.

Spencer, M. B., & Dornbusch, S. M. (1990). Challenges in studying minority youth. In S. S. Feldman & G. R. Elliott (Eds.), *At the threshold: The developing adolescent.* Cambridge, MA: Harvard University Press.

Spencer, M. B., & Markstrom-Adams, C. (1990). Identity processes among racial and ethnic minority children in America. *Child Development, 61,* 290–310.

Spivak H., & Prothrow-Stith, D. (2001). The need to address bullying. An important component of violence prevention. *Journal of the American Medical Association, 285,* 2131–2132.

Spring, J. (2000). *The intersection of cultures* (2nd ed.). New York: McGraw-Hill.

Squire, F. (1998). Action research and standards of practice: Creating connections within the Ontario context. Paper presented at the Second International Conference on Self-Study of Teacher Education Practices, Herstmonceux Castle, UK.

Stage, F. K., & Maple, S. A. (1996). Incompatible goals: Narratives of graduate women in the mathematics pipeline, *American Educational Research Journal, 33,* 23–51.

Statistics Canada. (1997). Earnings of Men and Women. Ottawa: Minister of Industry.

Statistics Canada. (1999). *National longitudinal survey on children, survey instruments for 1994-1995, data collection, cycle 1* (Catalogue No. 89F0077XPE). Ottawa: Author.

Statistics Canada. (1999). *Youth justice statistics.* Retrieved December 13, 2002, from http://canada.justice.gc.ca/en/news/nr/1999/yoafact4.html.

Statistics Canada. (2002a). Measuring up: The performance of Canada's youth in reading, mathematics and science OECD PISA Study—First results for Canadians aged 15 (Catalogue No.: 81-590-XPE). Ottawa, Ontario: Council of Ministers of Education and Human Resources Development Canada (HRDC).

Statistics Canada. (2002b). Ethnicity: Concept and definition. Retrieved 7 December 2002, from http://www.statcan.ca/english/concepts/definitions/ethnicity.htm.

Steiner-Bell, K. (1998). Teaching emotion and belief as adapted curriculum for children with autism: A first step in addressing mind-blindness. Unpublished master's thesis. Queen's University, Kingston, ON.

Sternberg, R. J. (1986). *Intelligence applied.* Fort Worth, TX: Harcourt Brace.

Sternberg, R. J. (1994, November). Allowing for thinking styles. *Educational Leadership,* pp. 36–40.

Sternberg, R. J. (1997). *Thinking styles.* New York: Cambridge University Press.

Sternberg, R. J. (1999). Looking back and looking forward on intelligence: Toward a theory of successful intelligence. In M. Bennett (Ed.), *Developmental psychology: Achievement and prospects.* Philadelphia: Psychology Press.

Sternberg, R. J. (2000). Thinking: An overview. In A. Kazdin (Ed.), *Encyclopedia of psychology.* Washington, DC, and New York: American Psychological Association and Oxford U. Press.

Sternberg, R. J. (2002). Intelligence: The triarchic theory of intelligence. In J. W. Gutherie (Ed.), *Encyclopedia of education* (2nd ed.). New York: Macmillan.

Sternberg, R. J., & Spear-Swerling, P. (1996). *Teaching for thinking.* Washington, DC: American Psychological Association.

Sternberg, R. J., Torff, B., & Grigorenko, E. (1998, May). Teaching for successful intelligence raises school achievement. *Phi Delta Kappan,* 667–669.

Stevenson, H. G. (1995, March). *Missing data: On the forgotten substance of race, ethnicity, and socioeconomic classifications.* Paper presented at the meeting of the Society for Research in Child Development, Indianapolis.

Stevenson, H. W. (1995). Mathematics achievement of American students: First in the world by 2000? In C. A. Nelson (Ed.), *Basic and applied perspectives in learning, cognition, and development.* Minneapolis: University of Minnesota Press.

Stevenson, H. W. (2000). Middle childhood: Education and schooling. In A. Kazdin (Ed.), *Encyclopedia of psychology.* Washington, DC & New York: American Psychological Association and Oxford University Press.

Stevenson, H. W., Hofer, B. K., & Randel, B. (1999). *Middle childhood: Education and schooling.* Unpublished manuscript, Dept. of Psychology, University of Michigan, Ann Arbor.

Stevenson, H. W., Lee, H J. W., Chen, S. Y., Stigler, J. W., Hsu, C. C., & Kitamura, S. (1990). Contexts of achievement: A study of American, Chinese, and Japanese children. *Monographs of the Society for Research in Child Development, 221(55)*, 1–2.

Stiggins, R. J. (1997). *Student-Centered Classroom Assessment* (2nd ed.). Upper Saddle River, NJ: Prentice Hall Merrill Education.

Stiggins, R. J. (2000). Classroom assessment: A history of neglect, a future of immense potential. Paper presented at the Annual Meeting of the American Educational Research Association, New Orleans.

Stiggins, R. J. (2002). Where is our assessment future and how can we get from here to there? In R. W. Kissitz & W. D. Schafer (Eds.), *Assessment in educational reform: Both means and ends*. Boston: Allyn & Bacon.

Stipek, D. J. (1996). Motivation and instruction. In D. C. Berliner & R. C. Calfee (Eds.), *Handbook of educational psychology*. New York: Macmillan.

Stipek, D. J. (2002). *Motivation to learn* (4th ed.). Boston: Allyn & Bacon.

Stockley, D., Woloshyn, V. E., & Bond, R. (1998). Comparing factual retention in students with severe learning disabilities. *Brock Education, 7*, 56–67.

Strayer, J. (2002). The dynamics of emotions and life cycle identity. *Identity, 2(1)*, 47–79.

Strayer, J., & William, R. (1997). Facial and verbal measures of children's emotions and empathy. *International Journal of Behavioral Development, 20(4)*, 627–649

Styslinger, M. E. (1999). Mars and Venus in my classroom: Men go to their caves and women talk through peer revision. *English Journal, (January)*, 50–56.

Sullivan, H. S. (1953). *The interpersonal theory of psychiatry*. New York: Norton.

Sumara, D. (2002). Changing the subject: Inventing identities while learning to teach. *Alberta Teachers Association Magazine, 82(3)*, 34–37.

Sund, R. B. (1976). *Piaget for educators*. Columbus, OH: Merrill.

Suzuki, L. A., & Valencia, R. R. (1997). Race, ethnicity and measured intelligence: Educational implications. *American Psychologist, 52(10)*, 1103–1114.

Swanson, H. L., & Hoskyn, M. (1998). Experimental intervention research on students with learning disabilities: A meta-analysis of treatment outcomes. *Review of Educational Research, 68*, 277–321.

Swanson, J. M., McBrunett, K., Wigal, T., & others. (1993). The effect of stimulant medication on ADD children. *Exceptional Children, 60*, 154–162.

Szabo, M. (2000, June). Enhancing distance education through research on multimedia and hypermedia: A review of effectiveness, efficiency, access and attitude. Paper presented at the meeting of The Centre for Research in Distance and Adult Learning (CRIDALA), Open University of Hong Kong.

T

Taber, K. S. (1998). An alternative conceptual framework from chemistry education. *International Journal of Science Education, 20(5)*, 597–608.

Taber, K. S. (2000). Multiple frameworks? Evidence of manifold conceptions in individual cognitive structure, *International Journal of Science Education, 22 (4)*, 399–417.

Taber, K. S. (2001). Constructing chemical concepts in the classroom? Using research to inform practice, due to be published in *Chemical Education Research and Practice in Europe(CERAPIE), 2* , 43–51. [http://www.uoi.gr/conf_sem.cerapie]

Taber, K. S., & Watts, M. (1997). Constructivism and concept learning in chemistry—perspectives from a case study. *Research in Education, 58,* 10–20.

Tamis-LeMonda, C. S., Bornstein, M. H., & Baumwell, L. (2001). Maternal responsiveness and children's achievement of language milestones. *Child Development, 72,* 748–767.

Tannen, D. (1990). *You just don't understand!* New York: Ballantine.

Tannen, D. (2001). *I only say this because I love you: How the way we talk can make or break family relationships throughout our lives*. New York: Random House.

Tanner, D. E. (2001). *Assessing academic achievement*. Boston: Allyn & Bacon.

Tanner, D. E. (2001). Authentic assessment: A solution, or part of the problem? *High School Journal, 85(1)*, 24–29.

Tanner, J. M. (1978). *Fetus into man*. Cambridge, MA: Harvard University Press.

Tappan, M. B. (1998). Sociocultural psychology and caring psychology: Exploring Vygotsky's "hidden curriculum." *Educational Psychologist, 33,* 23–33.

Tapscott, D. (1998). *Growing up digital: The rise of the net generation*. New York: McGraw-Hill.

Taylor, B. M., Hanson, B. E., & Justice-Swanson, K. (1997). Helping struggling readers: Linking small-group instruction with cross-age tutoring. *Reading Teacher, 51*, 196–209.

Taylor, C. (1994). Assessment of measurement or standards: The peril and the promise of large-scale assessment reform. *American Educational Research Journal, 32*, 231–262.

Tennyson, R., & Cocchiarella, M. (1986). An empirically based instructional design theory for teaching concepts. *Review of Educational Research, 56*, 40–71.

Terman, L., & Oden, M. H. (1959). *Genetic studies of genius. Vol. 5: The gifted group at mid-life*. Stanford, CA: Stanford University Press.

Terman, D. L., Larner, M. B., Stevenson, C. S., & Behrman, R. E. (1996). Special education for students with disabilities: Analysis and recommendations. *Future of Children, 6 (1)*, 4–24.

Terman, L. (1925). *Genetic studies of genius: Vol. 1. Mental and physical traits of a thousand gifted children*. Stanford, CA: Stanford University Press.

Terwilliger, J. (1997). Semantics, psychometrics, and assessment reform: A close look at "authentic" assessments. *Educational Researcher, 26*, 24–27.

Tetreault, M. K. T. (1997). Classrooms for diversity: Rethinking curriculum and pedagogy. In J. A. Banks & C. A. Banks (Eds.), *Multicultural education* (3rd ed.). Boston: Allyn & Bacon.

Thomas, A. (Ed.). (1998). *Family literacy in Canada: Profiles in effective practice*. Brock University, ON: Soleil Press.

Thomas, A., & Chess, S. (1991). Temperament in adolescence and its functional significance. In R. M. Lerner, A. C. Petersen, & J. Brooks-Gunn (Eds.), *Encyclopedia of adolescence* (Vol. 2). New York: Garland.

Thomas, A., Fazio, L., & Stiefelmeyer, B. L. (1999a). *Families at School: A Guide for Educators*. Newark, DE: International Reading Association.

Thomas, C. C., Correa, V. I., & Morsink, C. V. (1995). *Interactive teaming: Consultation and collaboration in special programs* (2nd ed.). Upper Saddle River, NJ: Merrill/Prentice Hall.

Thomas, R. M. (2000). *Human development theories: Windows on culture*. Thousand Oaks, CA: Sage.

Thompson, T. and Zerbinos, E. (1997). Television cartoons: Do children notice it's a boy's world? *Sex Roles: A Journal of Research, 37*, 415–433.

Thousand, J. S., Villa, R., & Nevin, A. (Eds.). (1994). *Creativity and collaborative learning: A practical guide to empowering, students and teachers*. Baltimore, MD: Paul H. Brookes.

THRIO. (2001). Teaching Human Rights in Ontario: An educational package for Ontario schools. Developed by the Ontario Human Rights Commission. Retrieved December 5, 2002, from http://www.ohrc.on.ca/english/education/thrio-r2001.pdf.

Thurstone, L. L. (1938). *Primary mental abilities*. Chicago: University of Chicago Press.

Thyer, B. A. (1996). Behavior analysis and social welfare policy. In M. A. Mattaini & B. A. Thyer (Eds.), *Finding solution to social problems* (pp. 41–60). Washington, DC: American Psychological Association.

Tice, D. M., & Baumeister, R. F. (1990). Self-esteem, self-handicapping, and self-presentation: The strategy of inadequate practice. *Journal of Personality, 58*, 443–464.

Tierney, R. J., & Readence, J. E. (2000). *Reading strategies and practices: A compendium* (5th ed.). Boston: Allyn & Bacon.

Tolman, M. N., & Hardy, G. R. (1999). *Discovering elementary science* (2nd ed.). Boston: Allyn & Bacon.

Tomlinson-Keasey, C. (1993, August). *Tracing the lives of gifted women*. Paper presented at the meeting of the American Psychological Association, Toronto.

Tomlinson-Keasey, C. (1997, April). *Gifted women: Themes in their lives*. Paper presented at the meeting of the Society for Research in Child Development, Washington, DC.

Tompkins, G. E. (1997). *Literacy for the twenty-first century: A balanced approach*. Upper Saddle River, N. J. : Merrill.

Tompkins, J. (1998). *Teaching in a cold and windy place: Change in an Inuit school*. Toronto: University of Toronto Press.

Torff, B. (2000). Multiple intelligences. In A. Kazdin (Ed.), *Encyclopedia of psychology.* Washington, DC, and New York: American Psychological Association and Oxford U. Press.

Torgesen, J. D. (1995, December). *Prevention and remediation of reading disabilities.* Progress Report (NICHD Grant HD 30988). Bethesda, MD: National Institute of Child Health and Human Development.

Torgesen, J. K., Wagner, R. K., Rashotte, C. A., Alexander, A. W., & Conway, T. (1997). Preventive and remedial interventions for children with severe reading disabilities. *Learning Disabilities: An Interdisciplinary Journal, 8,* 51–61.

Townsend, D. J., & Bever, T. G. (2001). *Sentence comprehension.* Cambridge, MA: MIT Press.

Tremblay, M. S., & Willms, D. J. (2000). Secular trends in the body mass index of children. *Canadian Medical Association Journal, 163,* 1429–1433.

Tremblay, P. (1995). *The homosexuality factor in the youth suicide problem.* Paper presented to Sixth Annual Conference of the Canadian Association for Suicide Prevention, Banff, AB: Retrieved 27 November 2002, from: http://www.qrd.org/qrd/www/youth/tremblay/.

Tremblay, P., & Ramsay, R. (2000). *The social construction of male homosexuality and related suicide problems: research proposals for the twenty-first century.* Paper presented at the Sociological Symposium on Suicide, San Diego State University, March, 2000. The results of 5 Youth Risk Behavior Surveys are given at http://www.virtualcity.com/youthsuicide/b-gay-male-youth-suicide.htm#table-2.

Tremblay, S., Ross, N., & Berthelot, J. M. (2002). *Ontario Grade 3 student achievement.* Retrieved 4 December 2002, from: http://www.statcan.ca/english/kits/pdf/social/grade3.pdf.

Triandis, H. C. (2000). Cross-cultural psychology: The history of the field. In A. Kazdin (Ed.), *Encyclopedia of psychology.* Washington, DC, and New York: American Psychological Association and Oxford University Press.

Trice, A. D. (2000). *Handbook of classroom assessment.* Boston: Addison Wesley.

Tri-Council Policy Statement: Ethical Conduct for Research Involving Humans. (1998). Retrieved February 2003, from: http://www.nserc.ca/programs/ethics/english/policy.htm#contents).

Trimble, J. E. (1989, August). *The enculturation of contemporary psychology.* Paper presented at the meeting of the American Psychological Association, New Orleans.

Trimble, J. E. (2000). Guidelines urge researchers to take a less superficial look at minorities. In M. Waters (Ed.), *Monitor on psychology, 31(6)* Washington, DC: American Psychological Association. Retrieved 5 February 2003, from: http://www.apa.org/monitor/jun00/minorities.html.

Tubman, J. G., & Windle, M. (1995). Continuity of difficult temperament in adolescence: Relations with depression, life events, family support, and substance abuse across a one-year period. *Journal of Youth and Adolescence, 24,* 133–152.

Tuckman, B. W., & Hinkle, J. S. (1988). An experimental study of the physical and psychological effects of aerobic exercise on school children. In B. G. Melamed, K. A. Matthews, D. K. Routh, B. Stabler, & N. Schneiderman (Eds.), *Child health psychology.* Mahwah, NJ: Erlbaum.

Tulving, E. (1972). Episodic and semantic memory. In E. Tulving & W. Donaldson (Eds.), *Origins of memory.* San Diego: Academic Press.

Tulving, E. (2000). Concepts of memory. In E. Tulving & F. I. M. Craik (Eds.), *The Oxford handbook of memory.* New York: Oxford University Press.

Turiel, E. (1997). The development of morality. In W. Damon (Ed.), *Handbook of child psychology* (5th ed., Vol. 3). New York: Wiley.

V

Vadeboncoeur, J., Rondeau, N., & Bégin, H. (2001), *Évaluation des effets d'un programme de prévention de la violence par la promotion des conduites pacifiques implanté auprès d'enfants de maternelle; effets préliminaires.* Congrès de la Société québecoise de la recherche en psychologie, Chicoutimi, Quebec.

Vallerand, R. J. (1999). An integrative analysis of intrinsic and extrinsic motivation in sport. *Journal of Applied Sport Psychology, 11*(1), 142–169.

Vallerand, R. J., & Rousseau, F. L. (2001). Intrinsic and extrinsic motivation in sport and exercise: A review using the hierarchical model of intrinsic and extrinsic motivation. In R. N. Singer, H. A. Hausenblas & C. M. Janelle. *Handbook of sport psychology* (pp. 389–416). New York: Wiley.

van der Linden, W. J. (1995). Advances in computer applications. In T. Oakland & R. K. Hambleton (Eds.), *International perspectives on academic assessment.* Boston: Kluwer Academic.

Van Houten, R., Nau, P., Mackenzie-Keating, S., Sameoto, D., & Colavecchia, B. (1982). An analysis of some variables influencing the effectiveness of reprimands. *Journal of Applied Behavior Analysis, 15,* 65–83.

VanLehn, K. (1986). Arithmetic procedures are induced from examples. In J. Hiebert (Ed.), *Conceptual and procedural knowledge: The case of mathematics.* Hillsdale, NJ: Erlbaum.

VanderLely, H. K., & Ullman, M. T. (2001). Past tense morphology in specifically language impaired and normally developing children. *Language and Cognitive Processes, 16,* 177–217.

Vitaro, F., Larocque, D., Janosz, M., & Tremblay, R. E. (2001). Negative social experiences and dropping out of school. *Educational Psychology, 21,* 401–415.

Vygotsky, L. S. (1962). *Thought and language.* Cambridge, MA: MIT Press.

Vygotsky, L. S. (1978). *Mind in society.* Cambridge, MA: Harvard University Press.

Vygotsky, L. S. (1987). Thinking and speech. In R. W. Rieber & A. S. Carton (Eds.), *The collected works of L. S. Vygotsky.* New York: Plenum.

W

Wadhera, S., & Millar, W. J. (1997). Teenage pregnancies, 1974 to 1994. *Health Reports, 9(3),* 9–16 (Catalogue No. 82-003-XPB). Ottawa: Statistics Canada.

Wagner, M. (1995). Outcomes for youths with serious emotional disturbance in secondary school and early adulthood. *Future of Children 5* (2), 90–112.

Wagner, M. W., & Blackorby, J. (1996). Transition from high school to work or college: How special education students fare. *Future of Children, 6* (1), 103–120.

Wahlsten, D. (2000). Behavioral genetics. In A. Kazdin (Ed.), *Encyclopedia of psychology.* Washington, DC, and New York: American Psychological Association and Oxford U. Press.

Wasik, B. A. (1998). Volunteer tutoring programs in reading: A review. *Reading Research Quarterly, 33,* 266–292.

Wasik, B. A., & Slavin, R. E. (1993). Preventing early reading failure with one-to-one tutoring: A review of five programs. *Reading Research Quarterly, 28,* 178–200.

Waterman, A. S. (1997). An overview of service-learning and the role of research and evaluation in service-learning programs. In A. S. Waterman (Ed.), *Service learning.* Mahwah, NJ: Erlbaum.

Weary, G., & Jacobson, J. A. (1997). Causal uncertainty beliefs and diagnostic information seeking. *Journal of Personality and Social Psychology, 73,* 839–848.

Weaver, C. (1998). *Toward a balanced approach to reading in reconsidering a balanced approach to reading.* National Council of Teachers of English, Urbana, IL. [ED 418 388]

Webb, J. M., Diana, E. M., Luft, P., Brooks, E. W., & Brenna, E. L. (1997). Influence of pedagogical expertise and feedback on assessing student comprehension from nonverbal behavior. *Journal of Educational Research, 91(2),* 89–97.

Webb, N. M. (1984). Sex differences in interaction and achievement in cooperative small groups. *Journal of Educational Psychology, 76,* 33–34.

Webb, N. M., & Palincsar, A. S. (1996). Group processes in the classroom. In D. C. Berliner & R. C. Calfee (Eds.), *Handbook of educational psychology.* New York: Macmillan.

Weber, E. (1999). *Student assessment that works.* Boston: Allyn & Bacon.

Weber, K., & Bennet, S. (1999). *Special education in Ontario schools.* Toronto: Highland Press.

Weiner, B. (1986). *An attributional theory of motivation and emotion.* New York: Springer.

Weiner, B. (1992). *Human motivation: Metaphors, theories, and research.* Newbury Park, CA: Sage.

Weiner, B. (2000). Motivation: An overview. In A. Kazdin (Ed.), *Encyclopedia of psychology.* Washington, DC, & New York: American Psychological Association and Oxford University Press.

Weinfeld, M. (1994). Ethnic assimilation and the retention of ethnic cultures. In J. W. Berry & J. A. Laponce (Eds.), *Ethnicity and culture in Canada: The research landscape (pp. 238–266).* Toronto: University of Toronto Press.

Weinman J., & Haag, P. (1999). Gender equity in cyberspace. *Educational Leadership, 56(5),* 44–49.

Weinstein, C. E., Husman, J., & Dierking, D. R. (2000). Self-regulation interventions with a focus on learning strategies. In M. Moekaerts, P. R. Pintrich, & M. Zeidner (Eds.), *Handbook of self-regulation.* San Diego: Academic Press.

Weinstein, C. S. (1997). *Secondary classroom management.* New York: McGraw-Hill.

Weinstein, C. S. (1999). Reflections on the best practices and promising programs: Beyond assertive classroom discipline. In H. J. Friedberg (Ed.), *Beyond behaviorism: Changing the classroom management paradigm.* Boston: Allyn & Bacon.

Weinstein, C. S., & Mignano, A. J., Jr. (1997). *Elementary classroom management.* New York: McGraw-Hill.

Weinstein, R. S., Madison, S. M., & Kuklinksi, M. R. (1995). Raising expectations in schooling: Obstacles and opportunities for change. *American Educational Research Journal, 32,* 121–159.

Weldin, D. J., & Tumarkin, S. R. (1999). Parent involvement: More power in the portfolio process. *Childhood Education, 75,* 90–96.

Wentzel, K. R. (1991). Social competence at school: Relation between social responsibility and academic achievement. *Review of Educational Research, 61(1),* 1–24.

Wentzel, K. R. (1997). Student motivation in middle school: the role of perceived pedagogical caring. *Journal of Educational Psychology 89,* 411–419.

Wentzel, K. R., & Asher, S. R. (1995). The academic lives of neglected, rejected, popular, and controversial children. *Child Development, 66,* 754–763.

Wertheimer, M. (1945). *Productive thinking.* New York: Harper.

Werthner, P. (2001). Communicating with clarity: Guidelines to help women coaches succeed. Canadian Journal for Women in Coaching-Online, 1(3). Retrieved 11 December 2002, from: http://www.coach.ca/women/e/journal/jan2001/print_communication.htm.

Wertsch, J. (2000). Cognitive development. In M. Bennett (Ed.), *Developmental psychology: Achievements and prospects.* Philadelphia: Psychology Press.

West, T. G. (1997). In the mind's eye: Visual thinkers, gifted people with dyslexia and other learning difficulties, computer images and the ironies of creativity. Amherst, NY: Prometheus Books.

Whalen, C. (2000). Attention deficit hyperactivity disorder. In A. Kazdin (Ed.), *Encyclopedia of psychology.* Washington, DC, and New York: American Psychological Association and Oxford University Press.

Wheelock, A. (1992). *Crossing the tracks: how "untracking" can save America's schools.* New York: New Press.

White, R. W. (1959). Motivation reconsidered: The concept of confidence. *Psychological Review, 66,* 297–333.

Wideman, H. H., & Owston, R. D. (2001). Lessons learned: Three case studies of ICT in teaching and their implications for practice. In Barrell, B. R. (Ed.), *Technology, teaching and learning: Issues in the integration of technology* (pp. 163–182). Calgary, AB: Detselig Enterprises.

Wigfield, A., & Asher, S. R. (1984). Social and motivational influences on reading. In P. D. Pearson, R. Barr, M. L. Kamil, & P. Mosenthal (Eds.), *Handbook of reading research.* New York: Longman.

Wigfield, A., & Eccles, J. S. (1989). Test anxiety in elementary and secondary school students. *Journal of Educational Psychology, 24,* 159–183.

Wigfield, A., Eccles, J. S., & Pintrich, P. R. (1996). Development between the ages of 11 and 25. In D. C. Berliner & R. C. Calfee (Eds.), *Handbook of educational psychology.* New York: Macmillan.

Wiggins, G. (1992, May). Creating tests worth taking. *Educational Leadership,* pp. 26–33.

Wiggins, G. (1993, November). Assessment: Authenticity, context, and validity. *Phi Delta Kappan,* pp. 200–214.

Williams, V. I., & Cartledge, G. (1997, September/October). Notes to parents. *Teaching Exceptional Children,* pp. 30–34.

Williams-Savin, R., & Berndt, T. (1990). Friendship and peer relations. *At The Threshold,* 277–307.

Willms, J. D. (1996). Social policy renewal for Canadian children. In J. D. Willms (Ed.), *Vulnerable children: Findings from Canada's Longitudinal Study of Children and Youth.* Edmonton: University of Alberta Press.

Willoughby, T., Wood, E., McDermott, C., & McLaren, J. (2000). Enhancing learning through strategy instruction and group interaction: Is active generation of elaborations critical? *Applied Cognitive Psychology, 14(1),* 19–30.

Wilson, B., & Steinman, C. (2000). *HungerCount 2000: A Surplus of Hunger.* Toronto.

Wilson, D., Squire, F. A., & Craig, A. (2000). Standards of practice and classroom assessment. *Orbit, 30(4),* 23–25.

Wilson, M. (1999). Cultural diversity. In A. Kazdin (Ed.), *Encyclopedia of psychology.* Washington, DC, and New York: American Psychological Association and Oxford U. Press.

Wilson, R. J. (1999). Aspects of validity in large-scale programs of student assessment. *The Alberta Journal of Educational Research, XLV* (4), 333–343.

Wilson, R. J. & Martinussen, R. L. (1999). Factors affecting the assessment of student achievement. *The Alberta Journal of Educational Research, XLV[45](3),* 267–277.

Wilson, R. M., Hall, M. A., Leu, D. J., & Kinzer, C. K. (2001). *Phonics, phonemic awareness, and word analysis for teachers* (7th ed.). Upper Saddle River, NJ: Merrill.

Windschitl, M. (1999). The challenges of sustaining a constructivist classroom culture. *Phi Delta Kappa Journal, 80,* 751–755.

Winne, P. H. (1995). Inherent details in self-regulated learning. *Educational Psychologist, 30,* 173–187.

Winne, P. H. (1997). Experimenting to bootstrap self-regulated learning. *Journal of Educational Psychology, 89,* 397–410.

Winner, E. (1996). *Gifted children: Myths and realities.* New York: Basic Books.

Winsler, A., Diaz, R. M., & Montero, I. (1997). The role of private speech in the transition from collaborative to independent task performance in young children. *Early Childhood Research Quarterly, 12,* 59–79.

Winzer, M. (2002). *Children with exceptionalities in Canadian classrooms.* Toronto, ON: Pearson Education Canada.

Woloshyn, V. E. & Elliott, A. (1998). Providing seventh-and-eighth-grade students with reading and writing instructions: Comparing explicit-strategy and implicit-strategy programs. *The Reading Professor, 20(1),* 59–79.

Woloshyn, V. E., & Rye, B. J. (1995). Using Bloom's learning taxonomies to conceptualize effective sexuality education for adolescents. *The Canadian Journal of Human Sexuality, 4(3),* 155–167.

Woloshyn, V. E., & Stockley, D. B. (1995). Helping students acquire belief-inconsistent and belief-consistent science facts: Comparisons between individual and dyad study using elaborative-interrogation, self-selected study and repetitious reading. *Applied Cognitive Psychology, 9(1),* 75–89.

Woloshyn, V. E., Elliott, A., & Kaucho, S. (2001). So what exactly is explicit strategy instruction? A review of eight critical teaching steps. *The Reading Professor, 24,* 66–114.

Woloshyn, V. E., Elliott, A., & Riordon, M. (1998). Seven teachers' experiences using explicit strategy instruction in the classroom. *Journal of Professional Studies, 5,* 18–28.

Woloshyn, V. E., Wood, E., & Willoughby, T. (1994). Considering prior knowledge when using elaborative interrogation. *Applied Cognitive Psychology, 8(1),* 25–36.

Wong, B. (1998). *Learning about learning disabilities (2nd ed.).* San Diego, CA: Academic Press.

Wood, W., Wong, F. Y., & Chachere, J. G. (1991). Effects of media violence on viewers' aggression in unconstrained social interaction. *Psychological Bulletin, 109,* 371–383.

Woodrich, D. L. (1994). *Attention-deficit hyperactivity disorder: What every parent should know.* Baltimore: Paul H. Brookes.

Woolfolk, A. E., & Brooks, D. M. (1985). The influence of teachers' nonverbal behaviors on students' perceptions and performance. *Elementary School Journal, 85,* 513–528.

Workman, S. H., & Gage, J. A. (1997). Family-school partnerships: A family strengths approach. *Young Children, 52,* 10–14.

Y

Yates, M. (1995, March). *Community service and political-moral discussions among Black urban adolescents.* Paper presented at the meeting of the Society for Research in Child Development, Indianapolis.

Yeung, W. J., Linver, M., & J. B. Brooks-Gunn, J. B. (2002). How money matters for young children's development: Parental investment and family processes. *Child Development.*

Yinger, R. J. (1980). Study of teacher planning. *Elementary School Journal, 80,* 107–127.

Yon, D. A. (2000). *Elusive culture: Schooling, race, and identity in global times.* Albany, NY: State University of New York Press.

Youth Lifestyle Choices–CURA (Community University Research Alliance). (2002). Report on Youth Lifestyle Choices in the Niagara Region. Retrieved 12 June 2002, from http://www.ylc-cura.ca/pulications.html.

Z

Ziegler, S. (1997). Class size, academic achievement, and public policy. *Connections 1*(1), 1–8.

Zimmerman, B. J. (1998, April). *Achieving academic excellence: The role of self-efficacy and self-regulatory skill.* Paper presented at the meeting of the American Psychological Association, San Diego.

Zimmerman, B. J. (2000). Attaining self-regulation: A social cognitive perspective. In M. Boekaerts, P. Pintrich, & M. Seidner (Eds.), *Self-regulation: Theory, research, and application.* San Diego: Academic Press.

Zimmerman, B. J. & Risemberg, R. (1997). *Self-Regulatory dimensions of academic learning and motivation* (p. 105–125). In G. D. Phye (Ed.). Handbook of Academic Learning: Construction of Knowledge. San Diego, CA: Academic Press.

Zimmerman, B. J., Bonner, S., & Kovach, R. (1996). *Developing self-regulated learners.* Washington, DC: American Psychological Association.

Zordell, J. (1990). The use of word prediction and spelling correction software with mildly handicapped students. *Closing the Gap, 9(1),* 10–11.

Credits

Line Art and Text Credits

Chapter 1

Figure 1.1: From "Students say what makes a good teacher" in *Schools in the Middle*, May/June 1997. Copyright © 1997 National Association of Secondary School Principals. Used with permission of the National Associates of Secondary School Principals (NASSP). All rights reserved.

Chapter 2

Figure 2.1: From *Adolescence* by John Santrock. Copyright © 1998. Reprinted with permission by The McGraw-Hill Companies.

Figure 2.2: From J.M. Tanner, R.H. Whitehouse, and M. Takishi, "Standards from Birth to Weight Velocity: British Children, 1965" in *Archives of Diseases in Childhood*, 41. Copyright © 1966 British Medical Association, London, England. Reprinted by permission.

Figure 2.4a: Dennis Palmer Wolf/Project PACE

Figure 2.4b: Courtesy of Dr. Ellen Winner, Project Zero.

Figure 2.5: From *Child Development* by John Santrock. Copyright © 1998 by McGraw-Hill College Division. Reprinted with permission by The McGraw-Hill Companies.

Figure 2.8: From Berko, Word, 14:361. Copyright © 1958 International Linguistic Association, New York, NY. Reprinted by permission.

Chapter 3

Figure 3.1: CB Kopp/JB Krakow, *Child Development in the Social Context*, (page 648), © 1982 by Addison-Wesley Publishing Company, Inc. Reprinted by permission of Addison-Wesley Longman, Inc.

Figure 3.2: From *Adolescence* by John Santrock. Copyright © 1998 by McGraw-Hill College Division. Reprinted with permission by The McGraw-Hill Companies.

Figure 3.3: From *Life-Span Development* by John Santrock. Copyright ©1999 by McGraw-Hill College Division. Reprinted with permission by The McGraw-Hill Companies.

Page 77: Adapted from: Report on Youth Lifestyle Choices in the Niagara Region: Findings from the Youth Resilience Questionnaire. Retrieved from http://www.ylc-cura.ca/publications.html.

Page 78: Adapted from McClelland & Stewart (1998); Bearden, Jim and Linda Jean Butler. — *Shadd : the life and times of Mary Shadd Cary*. Toronto : NC Press Ltd., c1977. – p.233.

Page 79: Marini, Z. A., Fairbairn, L., & Zuber, R. (2001). Peer harassment in individuals with developmental disabilities: Towards the development of a multidimensional bullying identification model. *Developmental Disabilities Bulletin, 29*, 170–195.

Figure 3.5: Excerpted from *Developmentally Appropriate Practice* (pp. 54–56), S. Bredekamp, ed., 1987, Washington, D.C.: the National Association for the Education of Young Children. Copyright © 1987 by NAEYC.

Figure 3.6: From *Child Development* by John Santrock. Copyright © 1998 by McGraw-Hill College Division. Reprinted with permission by The McGraw-Hill Companies.

Chapter 4

Figure 4.1: From *Child Development* by John Santrock. Copyright © 1998 by McGraw-Hill College Division. Reprinted with permission by The McGraw-Hill Companies.

Figure 4.2: From *Child Development* by John Santrock. Copyright © 1998 by McGraw-Hill College Division. Reprinted with permission by The McGraw-Hill Companies.

Figure 4.3: "Increasing IQ Scores from 1932–1997" by Ulric Neisser Copyright © 1997. Reprinted with permission by the author.

Figure 4.4: Item A5 from Raven's *Standard Progressive Matrices*. Reprinted by permission of J. C. Raven Limited.

Figure 4.5: From "A Successful Program of Teachers Assisting Teachers" by Kent, K in *Educational Leadership* 43, 3:30–33. Used by permission of the Association for Supervision and Curriculum Development. Copyright © 1985 by ASCD. All rights reserved.

Figure 4.6: From "A Successful Program of Teachers Assisting Teachers" by Kent, K in *Educational Leadership* 43, 3:30–33. Used by permission of the Association for Supervision and Curriculum Development. Copyright © 1985 by ASCD. All rights reserved.

Chapter 5

Page 131: From *Pay the Rent or Feed the Kids: The Tragedy and Disgrace of Poverty in Canada* by Mel Hurtig. Used by permission, McClelland & Stewart Ltd. The Canadian Publishers.

Figure 5.1: Statistics Canada, "Poverty Rates for Single Women with Children 1971–1997," adapted from the Statistics Canada publication The Daily, Catalogue 11-001, 1997.

Figure 5.2: Child Poverty, Canada and the Provinces, 1997. www.ccsd.ca/factsheets.fs_cp97.htm. Canadian Council on Social Development.

Page 140: Statistics Canada. www.statcan.ca/english/kits/grassroots/96.htm. Profiles of Canada Project.

Chapter 6

Figure 6.1: "Reasons why children receive special education," adapted from the Statistics Canada, "Longitudinal Survey of Children and Youth, School Component, 1994–1995."

Chapter 7

Figure 7.5: From *Psychology*, 6e by John Santrock. Copyright ©2000 by McGraw-Hill College Division. Reprinted with permission by The McGraw-Hill Companies.

Figure 7.6: From *Life-Span Development*, 7e by John Santrock. Copyright © 1999 by McGraw-Hill College Division. Reprinted with permission by The McGraw-Hill Companies.

Figure 7.9: From *Self-Talk for Teachers and Students: Metacognitive Strategies for Personal and Classroom Use* by Manning, B. H. & Payne, B. D. Copyright © 1996 by Allyn & Bacon, a Pearson Education Company. Reprinted by permission.

Chapter 8

Figure 8.2: From *Psychology*, 6e by John Santrock. Copyright ©2000 by McGraw-Hill College Division. Reprinted with permission by The McGraw-Hill Companies.

Figure 8.4: From *The Universe Within*. Copyright © 1982 by Morton Hunt. Reprinted by permission of Simon & Schuster.

Figure 8.5: From Joel Levin, et al., "The Keyword Method in the Classroom" in *Elementary School Journal*, 80:4. Copyright © 1980 University of Chicago Press. Reprinted by permission.

Figure 8.7: From *Psychology*, by John Santrock. Copyright © 1997 by McGraw-Hill College Division. Reprinted with permission by The McGraw-Hill Companies.

Page 263: Used with permission of HISTOR!CA.

Chapter 9

Figure 9.1: From *Educational Psychologist* by Palinscar, A. S. Copyright © 1986 by Lawrence Erlbaum Associates, Inc., Publishers. Reprinted by permission.

Page 292: WIER (n.d.), Retrieved May 3, 2002, from http://www.wier.ca. Used with permission of Trevor Owen.

Chapter 10

Figure 10.1: From "A Study of Teacher Planning" by Yinger, R. J. in *The Elementary School Journal* Copyright © 1980. Reprinted by permission of the University of Chicago Press.

Figure 10.2: Reprinted by permission of Waveland Press, Inc. from K.W. Linden in *Cooperative Learning and Problem Solving*, Second Edition. (Prospect Heights, IL: Waveland Press, Inc., 1996). All rights reserved.

Figure 10.3: From *Elementary Classroom Management* by Weinstein, C. S. and Mignano, A. J. Copyright © 1997 by McGraw-Hill College Division. Reprinted with permission by The McGraw-Hill Companies.

Figure 10.4: From *Elementary Classroom Management* by Weinstein, C. S. and Mignano, A. J. Copyright © 1997 by McGraw-Hill College Division. Reprinted with permission by The McGraw-Hill Companies.

Figure 10.5: Extrapolated from "Design Options for an Integrated Curriculum" by Heidi Hayes Jacobs in Interdisciplinary Curriculum: Design and Implementation published in 1990 by the Association of Supervision and Curriculum Development, Alexandria, Virginia. Reprinted from *The Mindful School: How to Integrate the Curricula* by Robin Fogarty. Copyright © 1991 by IRI/SkyLight Professional Development, Arlington Heights, Illinois. http://skylightedu.com.

Figure 10.8: "I Belong, But Where?" HypterStudio Project by Grade seven students, Rosemont Community School, Regina, Saskatchewan.

Chapter 11

Figure 11.2: From *Motivating Students to Learn* by Brophy, J. Copyright © 1998 by McGraw-Hill College Division. Reprinted with permission by The McGraw-Hill Companies.

Figure 11.3: From Weiner, B. in *Human Motivation: Metaphors, Theories and Research.* Copyright © 1992 by Sage Publications, Inc. Reprinted by Permission of Sage Publications, Inc.

Figure 11.4: From "Classrooms: Goals, Structures, and Student Motivation" by Ames, C. Copyright © 1992 in *Journal of Educational Psychology.* Reprinted by permission of American Psychological Association, Washington, D.C.

Figure 11.5: "Parents' Involvement and High School Students' Grades NCES, 1985," *National Center for Education Statistics, U.S. Department of Education.*

Figure 11.6: From *Motivating Students to Learn* by Brophy, J. Copyright © 1998 by McGraw-Hill College Division. Reprinted with permission by The McGraw-Hill Companies.

Page 370: Used with permission of Dr. Marie Battiste.

Chapter 12

Figure 12.2: From *Secondary Classroom Management* by C. S. Weinstein. Copyright © 1996 by McGraw-Hill. Reprinted by permission of McGraw-Hill Companies.

Figure 12.4: From *Excellent Classroom Management*, 1st ed. By C. L. Rinne, figure 8.1, p. 110. Copyright © 1997 Wadsworth. Reprinted with permission of Wadsworth Publishing, a division of Thomson Learning.

Chapter 13

Figure 13.4: From John Santrock, *Psychology*, 5th ed., p. 624. Copyright © 1997 by McGraw-Hill. Reprinted with permission of The McGraw-Hill Companies.

Figure 13.8: Adapted from "The Psychological Corporation, Test Service Notebook, No. 148" by The Psychological Corporation. Reproduced with the permission of Elsevier Science (USA).

Chapter 14

Figure 14.1: From James McMillan, (2002), figure 1.1, p. 3 in *Essential Assessment of Student Achievement*, 6/e, Allyn & Bacon, p. 79. Copyright © 1998 by Pearson Education. Reprinted by permission of the publisher.

Figure 14.3: From D. Combs, "Using alternative assessment to provide options for student success" in *Middle School Journal*, 1997, Sept., p. 5, figure 1. Used with permission from National Middle School Association.

Figure 14.6: From N. J. Johnson & L. M. Rose in Portfolios. Copyright © 1997 by Rowman & Littlefield Publishing Company. Reprinted with permission.

Photo Credits

Chapter 1

Opener: Copyright © Canadian Museum of Civilization, photographer Steven Darby, 1997, image no. AC98-69-18; **p.4** (left): Copyright © Brown Brothers; (right): Columbia University Archives and Columbiana Library; **p.5** (top) Used with permission of Dr. Robert Marvin, University of Virginia; (bottom) Duke University Archives; **p.10** Copyright © Tony Freeman/Photo Edit; **p.19** Courtesy of Steve and Cindi Binder; **p.23** V.C.L./Taxi/ Getty Images; **p.25** (left): Copyright © Andy Sacks/Tony Stone Images; (right): Copyright © David Young-Wolff/ Tony Stone Images.

Chapter 2

Opener: Copyright © Richard Howard; **p.39** John Kelly/Image Bank/Getty Images; **p.43** From Penguin Dreams and Stranger Things by Berke D. Breathed. Copyright © 1985 by The Washington Post Company. By permission of Little, Brown and Company; **p.46** Drawing by Lorenz: © 1989 The New Yorker Magazine, Inc.; **p.54** (left): Copyright © 1999 Yves deBraine/ Black Star; (middle): Used with permission; (right): A.R. Lauria/Dr. Michael Cole, Laboratory of Human Cognition, University of California, San Diego; **p.57** © Glenn Bernhardt.

Chapter 3

Opener: Copyright © Tony Freeman/ Photo Edit; **p.68** Courtesy of Cornell University; **p.71** Copyright © Sarah Putman/Index Stock; **p.75** CALVIN AND HOBBES © 1993 Watterson Dist. By UNIVERSAL PRESS SYNDICATE: All rights reserved; **p.78** National Archives of Canada/ C-029977; **p.86** Drawing by Ziegler: © 1985 The New Yorker Magazine, Inc.; **p.88** (top): Copyright © Keith Carter; (bottom): Copyright © Anthony Verde Photography; p.91 © Gary Larson; **p.94** (top): Copyright © AP/World Wide Photos; (bottom): CP/Kevin Frayer.

Chapter 4

Opener: Copyright © Lawrence Migdale/Tony Stone Images; **p.105** Courtesy of Rober Sternberg; p.108 Paula Barber; **p.111** © 1991 by Sydney Harris – "You Want Proof?. . ." W.H. Freeman and Company; **p.116** By Sidney Harris; **p.117** © 2003 SMART Technologies Inc. Used with permission.

Chapter 5

Opener: Copyright © David Young-Wolff/Tony Stone Images; **p.142** Copyright © Elizabeth Crews; **p.145** SW Productions/ PhotoDisc Green/ Getty Images; **p.153** Copyright © Suzanne Szasz/ Photo Researchers; **p.154** © 1994 Joel Pett. All rights reserved; **p.158** Paula Barber.

Chapter 6

Opener: Copyright © Frank Siteman/ Photo Edit; **p.169** © 1975 Tony Saltzman. Phi Delta Kappan; **p.172** Copyright © David Young-Wolff/Photo Edit; **p.181** Copyright © Will & Deni McIntyre/ Photo Researchers; **p.183** Courtesy of Gloria Christianson; **p.186** Photograph by Caroline Connolly, Mud River Photography. Used with permission. **p.192** Copyright © Richard Hutchings/Photo Researchers; **p.197** (left): Bob Daemmrick/ Stock Boston; (right): Used by permission of Don Johnston Inc.

Chapter 7

Opener: Copyright © Elizabeth Crews; **p.206** Copyright © Sovfoto; **p.208** Copyright © Elizabeth Crews; **p.209** Nina Leen, Life Magazine, Copyright © Time, Inc.; **p.217** Copyright © B. Daemmrick/ The Image Works; **p.221** Courtesy of Albert Bandura; **p.222** Courtesy of Albert Bandura; **p.223** Copyright © Jeffry W. Myers/Corbis; **p.226** Selection from Franklin's Neighborhood by Paulette Bourgeois and illustrated by Brenda Clark, used by permission of Kids Can Press Ltd., Toronto. Illustration copyright © 1999 by Brenda Clark Illustrator Inc.

Chapter 8

Opener: Copyright © Zigy Kaluzny/Tony Stone Images; **p.244** © 1985: reprinted courtesy of Bill Hoest and Parade Magazine. **p.247** Copyright © Elizabeth Crews; **p.257** Copyright © Elizabeth Crews; **p.260** Courtesy of The Education Network of Ontario; **p.263** Copyright 2000 Discovery Communications, Inc. All rights reserved. www.discovery.com; **p.268** Bruce Ayres/ Stone/ Getty Images.

Chapter 9

Opener: Courtesy of Compton-Drew Investigative Learning Center Middle School, St. Louis, MO; **p.277** Copyright © Will Hart/ Photo Edit; **p.284** Copyright © Todd Hampton Lillard; **p.296** Reprinted by permission of United Features Syndicate, Inc.; **p.302** Courtesy of Let's Talk Science.

Chapter 10

Opener: Copyright © David Young-Wolff/ Tony Stone Images; **p.323** Copyright © Anna Palma; **p.335** This screen shot is from a second-generation CSILE product, Knowledge Forum ®, The authors of this work are Marlene Scardamalia and Carl Bereiter, directors of the CSILE research and development team at OISE/University of Toronto. The publisher is Learning in Motion (Marge Cappo, President); **p.336** (left): Screen shot from the World Book Millennium 2000. Copyright © 1999 World Book, Inc by permission of the publisher; (right): "I Belong, But Where?" HypterStudio Project by Grade seven students, Rosemont Community School, Regina, Saskatchewan.

Chapter 11

Opener: Copyright © Michael Newman/ Photo Edit; **p.346** Copyright © AP/World Wide Photos; **p.347** (cartoon): © Lynn Johnston Productions, Inc., Reproduced by permission; (first): Copyright © Lonnie Duka/Tony Stone Images; (second): CP/Mike Ridewood; (third): Paula Barber; (sixth): Copyright © David Young-Wolff/ Tony Stone Images; (seventh): Copyright © Lawrence Migdale; **p.352** © 1986; Reprinted courtesy of Bunny Hoest and Parade Magazine; **p.366** Leland Bobbe/ Taxi/ Getty Images; **p.370** Courtesy of Dr. Marie Battiste.

Chapter 12

Opener: Copyright © A. Ramey/Photo Edit; **p.387** (left): Copyright © Spencer Grant/ PhotoEdit; (right): Copyright © Elizabeth Crowes; **pp. 395, 396, 397:** Prepared for the TRACE Workshop "Developing and Maintaining Professional Relationships," June 4, 2002; TRACE Office, University of Waterloo, Ontario Canada. **p.398** Scott T. Baxter/ Photodisc Green/Getty Images; **p.410** Divino Mucciante.

Chapter 13

Opener: Copyright © Robert E. Daemmrick/Tony Stone Images/ Getty Images; **p.429** Copyright © Robert Isaacs/ Photo Researchers; **p.433** Drawing by Koren: © 1974 The New Yorker Magazine, Inc. **p.436** © Bonnie Kamin/Photo Edit.

Chapter 14

Opener: Copyright © David Young-Wolff/PhotoEdit; **p.463** Copyright © Paul Conklin; **p.468** Copyright © Michael Newman/ PhotoEdit.

Name Index

A

Aboud, F.E., 140, 141, 145, 146
Abrami, P.C., 283
Abruscato, J., 300
Adams, D., 367
Adams, G., 367
Afflerbach, P., 288
Aiken, L.R., 19, 103, 419, 422, 424
Aikenhead, G., 301, 453
Ainsworth, M.S., 5
Airasian, P., 24, 418, 431, 432, 437, 449, 450, 465, 468, 470, 471, 473
Albanese, M.A., 325
Alberta Learning, 186, 384–385
Alberta Teachers Association, 385
Alberti, R., 10, 399
Alberto, P.A., 212, 214, 215, 312
Alexander, K.L., 367
Allan, J., 468
Allan, L.G., 208
Allen, D., 268, 326
Allen, P., 6, 243
Allison, D., 302
Allison, P., 302
Allsopp, D.H., 280, 298
Amabile, T.M., 116, 353
American Association for the Advancement of Science, 1993, 301
American Association of University Women, 158, 159
American Psychiatric Association, 171
Ames, C., 362
Amsel, E., 301
Anderman, E.M., 355
Anderson, C.A., 222
Anderson, E., 360
Anderson, J.A., 318
Anderson, J.R., 259
Anderson, L., 303
Anderson, S.E., 140
Andrea, L., 266
Anselmi, D.L., 25
Antil, L.R., 280
Arends, R.I., 6
Argys, L.M., 113
Aronson, E.E., 145, 284, 285
Arter, J., 466
Ash, L., 203
Ashcraft, M.H., 245
Asher, S.R., 76, 367
Ashton, P.T., 356
Asselin, M., 287
Atkinson, R., 245, 252
Atlas, R., 409
Auld-Cameron, J., 332, 438
Ausubel, D.P., 289, 316
Axelrod, S., 218
Ayala, C., 468

B

Baddeley, A., 244, 245
Bailey, J.S., 212
Baker, R., 142
Baldwin, J., 5, 15
Band, G.P., 240
Bandura, A., 150, 220, 221, 222, 230, 232, 351, 356, 358, 362, 371
Banham, K.M., 5
Bankay, D., 33, 331
Banko, K.M., 351
Banks, C.A., 7, 10
Banks, J.A., 7, 10
Bantai, T.W., 462
Barr, 278
Barrett, H.C., 475
Barsalou, L.W., 254
Bartlett, E.J., 294
Bartlett, J.C., 245
Bartolacci, A., 395
Barton, J., 466
Bassey, K., 150
Batcheldar, W., 297
Bates, J., 125
Battista, M.T., 153
Battiste, M., 370, 453
Baumeister, R.F., 376
Baumrind, D., 71, 72, 389
Baumwell, L., 57
Bawn, E., 345
Beal, C., 158
Beals, D., 56
Beals, D.E., 277
Beauchamp, L., 448
Begin, H., 148, 410
Begley, S., 321
Begoray, D., 51
Belfiore, P.J., 214
Bem, S.L., 155
Bennett, W., 88
Bereiter, C., 259, 334, 335
Berenson, G.S., 368
Berg, K.E., 280
Berger, E.H., 109
Berkley, 391
Berko-Gleason, J., 57
Berliner, D.C., 13
Bernardo-Kusyj, C., 14
Berndt, T., 368
Berndt, T.J., 79, 365
Berrill, D.P., 295, 296
Berry, J.W., 132, 144
Bersoff, D.N., 25
Berthelot, J.M., 385
Betts, J.R., 329, 473
Bever, T.G., 56
Bigelow, B., 441
Billips, L.H., 6

B (continued)

Bjork, 318
Bjorklund, D.F., 48, 239, 247, 266, 268
Blair, T.R., 289
Bloom, B., 57, 313, 318
Bloom, B.S., 313, 318
Bloom, R.W., 222
Blumfield, 280
Boals, A., 245
Boekaerts, M., 9
Bogan, E., 280
Boivin, M., 409
Bombay, K., 78, 409
Bond, R., 289
Bonner, S., 228, 230, 361
Borko, H., 9, 13
Borkowski, J.G., 267
Bornstein, M.H., 56–57, 71
Bouchard, P., 155
Boulet, J.R., 465
Bourne, E.J., 399
Bowlby, J., 37
Boyd, M., 73
Bracey, G.W.
Bracken, B.A., 464
Branch, M.N., 217
Brandts, L., 290
Brannigan, 387
Bransford, J.D., 9, 258
Breakfast for Learning, 347
Bredekamp, S., 81
Brendgen, M., 155
Brenneman, K., 49
Breuleux, A., 337
Brewer, M.B., 113, 132
Bridges, M., 74
Briggs, T.W., 117
British Columbia Teachers' Federation, 385
Broberg, A., 218
Bronfenbrenner, U., 68, 69, 73, 74
Brook, J.S., 368
Brookover, W.B., 358
Brooks, D.M., 398
Brooks, J., 257
Brooks, M., 257
Brooks-Gunn, J., 41, 369
Brooks-Gunn, J.B., 369
Brophy, J., 10, 114, 351, 355, 363, 374, 375, 377, 387
Brown, A.L., 7, 9, 290
Brown, R., 56
Brownlie, 401
Bruner, J., 327
Brussiere, 154
Bryk, A.S., 353
Buchanan, C.M., 83
Buchner, A., 247
Buhrmester, D., 79
Bukowski, W., 76
Burger, J.M., 124

B (continued)

Buriel, R., 74
Burz, H.L., 463
Bushman, B.J., 222
Butler, D.L., 228, 229, 230, 361, 362
Byng, R., 57

C

Cajete, G.A., 453
Calabrese, R.L., 89
Calderhead, J., 13
Calfee, R.C., 4
Calhoun, E.F., 23
Calhoun, E.M., 23
Cameron, 351
Cameron, J.R., 350
Campbell, B., 106, 109
Campbell, D., 463
Campbell, D.I., 132
Campbell, D.T., 132
Campbell, F.A., 110
Campbell, J.I.D., 110, 298
Campbell, L., 106, 109
Campbell, S.J., 110
Campione, J.C., 7
Canadian Association for School Administrators, 452
Canadian Association for the Advancement of Women and Sport and Physical Activity, 153
Canadian Association of School Psychologists, 428
Canadian Core Learning Resource Metadata Protocol, 11
Canadian Council on Social Development, 134, 135, 136
Canadian Education Association, 369
Canadian Fact Book on Poverty, 133
Canadian Fitness and Lifestyle Institute, 153
Canadian Medical Association Journal, 39
Canadian National Longitudinal Survey of Children and Youth, 167
Canadian Psychological Association, 24, 423, 428
Canadian School Boards Association, 451
Canadian Society for the Study of Education, 452
Canadian Teachers' Federation, 318, 448, 450, 451, 452, 469
Carlson, J.S., 265
Carroll, J.B., 318
Carter, M., 262
Cascio, W., 418
Case, R., 36, 37, 43, 48, 49, 54, 55, 204, 205, 238
Caspi, A., 125

Garcia, S., 124
Garcia-Mila, M., 301
Gardner, H., 105, 106, 108, 257
Gardner, R., 280
Gardner, R.C., 132
Garner, R., 337
Garvie, E., 387
Gaskell, J., 369
Gaskin, I., 268
Gay, G., 441
Gay, L.R., 24, 418, 431, 432
Gelman, R., 49
Gentile, J.R., 264
Georghiades, P., 266
Gerlovich, J., 301
Gibbs, J.T., 369
Gibson, E., 368
Gibson, S., 9, 337
Gilligan, C., 87, 154
Gillingham, M.G., 337
Gilman, D.A., 387
Gingras, J., 38
Ginsburg, H.P., 297
Glaubman, H., 266
Glaubman, R., 266
Gleason, J.B., 57, 58, 59
Goatley, V.J., 290
Godin, G., 95
Goepfert, P., 299, 311
Goldin-Meadow, S., 59
Goleman, D., 91, 116
Goodlad, J.I., 368
Goodlad, S., 281
Goodnough, K., 108
Gordon, C., 289
Gordon, M., 409
Gottfried, A.E., 352
Gottfried, A.W., 352
Gouvernement du Québec, 427
Government of Alberta, 425
Government of British Columbia,
    419, 425
Government of Manitoba, 419
Government of Yukon, Department
    of Education, 428
Graham, S., 25, 90, 288, 294, 353,
    354, 370
Gray, J.R., 245
Graziano, 21
Gredler, M., 450
Greene, B., 157
Greene, D., 351
Greenfield, P.M., 49, 111, 112
Greenlund, K.J., 368
Greeno, J.G., 13, 51
Greenough, W., 110
Gregory, K.M., 277
Gregory, R.J., 105, 420
Griffin, S., 50
Griffiths, D., 331
Grigorenko, E., 105
Gronlund, N., 421
Gronlund, N.E., 431, 456, 457, 458,
    461, 468, 474
Grotevant, H.D., 71
Grove, K., 25
Guidelines for Education and
    Psychological Testing, 466

Guild, P.B., 108
Guilford, J.P., 116
Guiney, J.J., 158
Gump, P.V., 387
Gunning, T.G., 291
Guppy, N., 137
Gutwill, S., 222

H

Haag, P., 150, 337
Hachette, V., 369
Hackenberg, T.D., 213
Hains, A.A., 362
Haladyna, T.M., 457
Hall, R.V., 110
Hall-Dennis Report on Education, 402
Halonen, J.A., 296
Halonen, J.S., 395
Halpern, D.F., 266
Hambleton, R., 441
Hambleton, R.K., 453, 458, 463, 466
Hambleton, R.k., 465
Hamburg, D.A., 89
Hammond, M., 409
Hannay, L., 356
Hansen, B.E., 279
Hansen, J., 289
Happon, P., 331
Harasim, L., 325, 330
Hardy, G.R., 300
Harlow, S.D., 338
Harold, R.D., 75
Harper, 279
Harrington, H.J., 283
Harris, J.L., 290
Harris, K.R., 288, 294
Hart, B., 291
Hart, S., 372
Harter, S., 84, 352, 367
Hartsfield, F., 212
Hartup, W.W., 76, 79
Hasan, F., 411
Hass, C.G., 310
Hatch, T., 466
Haugland, S.W., 338
Hawes, R., 309
Hay, D., 409
Hayes, J.R., 294
Hayes, S.C., 212
Health Canada, 95
Healy, S., 392
Hedges, L.V., 153
Heilman, A.W., 289
Helmreich, R., 155
Hemingway, M., 212
Henchey, N., 5, 391
Henchy, 392
Henderson, K., 409
Henderson, P., 41, 93
Henderson, V.L., 355, 365
Hennessey, B.A., 353
Henningson, P.N., 280
Henson, 318
Herman, J., 466
Herrnstein, R.J., 110
Herzog, E., 79
Hess, J.D., 370

Hetherington, E.M., 74
Hewitt, J.S., 12
Hickman, C.W., 369
Hicks, L., 360
Hiebert, E.H., 289, 294
Higgins, A., 88
Higgins, E.T., 231
Hightower, E., 75
Hinkle, J.S., 38
Hirsch, E.D., 323, 329, 330
Hirst, B., 281
Hobin, C., 409
Hockenbury, D., 432
Hodges, E.V.E., 409
Hodgson, M., 225
Hodgson, S., 279
Hofer, B.K., 238, 297
Hoff, E., 56
Hoff-Ginsberg, E., 74
Hoffman, E., 348
Hogaboam-Gray, A., 356
Hogan, D.M., 52
Hogan, K., 7
Hogan, R.T., 123
Hollander, N.C., 222
Hombo, C.M., 463, 465, 466
Hooper, S., 283
Horn, C.L., 425
Horsman, H., 402
Howes, C., 75
Hoyt, J., 267
Hudley, C., 370
Hughes, C., 332
Hull, M., 288
Human Resources Development
    Canada, 369
Hunt, R.E.S., 242
Hunt, R.R., 242
Hurtig, M., 131, 133, 136, 366
Husman, J., 228
Hymel, 365
Hymel, S., 409

I

Iacocca, L., 310
Ickes, W., 124
Imms, W., 150
Indrisano, 294
Inhelder, B., 44
International Society for Technology
    in Education, 11
Isabella, G.M., 74

J

Jackson, P.W., 6
Jackson, Y., 260
Jacobs, H.H., 326, 330
Jacobson, 353
Jafir, 411
Jalongo, M.R., 291
James, W., 4, 5, 9, 15, 303
Janosz, M., 75
Janzen, 289
Jayachandran, J., 74
Jensen, A.R., 110, 112
Jeong, A., 333

John-Steiner, V., 52
Johnson, B., 16
Johnson, C.C., 368
Johnson, D., 331
Johnson, D.L., 332, 334, 338, 475
Johnson, D.W., 280, 281, 282, 283, 411
Johnson, D.W. dif yr, 89
Johnson, F.P., 280, 281, 282, 283
Johnson, L.J., 146
Johnson, R.T., 411
Johnson-Laird, P., 257
Jonassen, D.H., 334
Jones, B.D., 475
Jones, B.F., 260
Jones, J.M., 369
Jones, W., 124
Joyce, B., 314, 315
Joyner, M.H., 267
Jussim, L., 114
Justice-Swanson, K., 279
Juvonen, J., 364, 365

K

Kagan, S., 37, 125, 280, 282, 283
Kahl, B., 280
Kahn, A., 9
Kail, R., 102
Kalchman, M., 50
Kamhi, A.G., 290
Kanu, Y., 145
Katz, L., 82, 450
Katz, M., 391
Katz, S., 468
Kaucho, S., 268, 269, 314
Kaufman, A.S., 102
Kaufman, P., 116
Keavney, M., 351
Keil, F., 247
Kellogg, R.T., 293
Kelly, M., 73, 95, 132, 136
Kelly, R.R., 242
Kelly, W., 50
Kendall, P., 224
Kennedy, M., 16
Kepron, J.P., 278
Killeavy, M., 391
Kim, J.A., 208
Kinderman, T.A., 368
King, 401
King, A., 277
King, J., 317
King, R.E., 292
Kirk, E.P., 245
Kirova, 398
Kirton, M.J., 116
Kitchura, C., 171
Klein, A., 297
Klein, J., 315
Klein, K., 245
Knight, A., 282
Knight, G.P., 155
Knoll, S., 387
Knoop, R., 122
Kochenderfer, B.J., 409
Kohen, D.E., 369
Kohlberg, L., 86, 87, 88, 151
Kohn, A., 351

Nova Scotia Department of
Education, 427
Nova Scotia School Athletic
Federation, 345
Novak, J.M., 12, 88, 114, 141, 331,
336, 337, 339
Novick, R., 61, 133
Nowell, A., 153
Nugent, B., 150

O

OAFCCD, 177
O.A.M.E., 299
Oberg, D., 337
O'Coffey, T., 112
O'Conner, S.C., 365
Offord, D.R., 73, 367
Ofiesh, N., 332
Ofir, L., 266
Ogbu, J., 370
O'Hara, C., 120
Olafsson, R., 409
O'Laughlin, M., 301
Oldfather, P., 9, 276
Oller, D.K., 56
Olson, K., 331
Olson, L., 293
Olweus, D., 78, 368, 409
O'Neil, J., 428
O'Neill, L.T., 277
Ontario Institute for Studies in
Education, 12, 334
Ontario Mathematics Olympiad, 299
Ontario Ministry of Education, 297
Ootes, S., 333
O'Sullivan, J.T., 267
Owen, T., 292, 330, 337
Owston, R., 330, 332, 337

P

Paikoff, R., 41
Paintal, S., 387
Paivio, A., 242, 250
Palincsar, A.S., 276, 290, 295
Palomba, C., 462
Paludi, M.A., 25
Panofsky, C., 51
Papert, S., 332, 333
Parcel, G.S., 38
Parecki, A.D., 377
Parkay, F.W., 310
Parke, R.D., 74
Parker, J.G., 76
Parsons, J., 448
Pascual-Leone, J., 49
Pashler, H., 240
Patnoe, S., 285
Patrick, P.R., 75
Pavlov, I.P., 206
Payne, D., 452
Payne, D.A., 421, 423, 424, 431, 451, 474
Pearson, P.D., 289
Pelligrino, J.W., 102
Pepler, D., 78, 409
Perkins, D., 9, 258, 265
Perney, J., 278

Perry, C., 96, 294
Petersen, J., 41
Peterson, R., 384
Philliber, W.W., 292
Piaget, J., 43, 44, 45, 49, 50, 52, 53,
54, 55, 205, 238, 276, 325
Pickett, J.M., 423
Pierce, W.D., 350
Pierce, W.E., 351
Pikas, A., 410, 412
Pillow, B.H., 240
Pinnell, G.G., 278
Pintrich, P., 9, 260
Pintrich, P.R., 228, 348, 353, 368
PISA, 429
Plas, J.M., 110
Plomin, R., 37
Poest, C.A., 38
Pollack, K.E., 290
Pollman, M.J., 109
Pon, G., 157
Popham, W.J., 418, 419, 461
Popp, B., 292
Postman, N., 317
Power, C., 88
Premack, D., 212
Presidential Task Force on
Psychology in Education, 325
Pressley, M., 7, 242, 266, 267, 268,
278, 287, 288, 289, 361
Price, B., 279
Price, R.H., 96
Principles for Fair Student Association
Practices for Education in
Canada, 450, 451, 452
Principles of Psychology, 4
Pross, H., 325, 326
Prosser, T., 89
Prothrow-Stith, D., 404
Prutzman, P., 146
Psychological Corporation, 104
Puhan, G., 349
Purkey, W.W., 12, 114
Putman, 279
Putnam, R.T., 9, 13
Pyryt, M.C., 385

R

Raham, H., 391
Rallis, F.S., 371
Ramey, C.T., 110
Ramos, L., 153
Ramos, M.A., 425
Ramsay, R., 159
Randel, B., 238, 297
Randi, J., 228, 360
Randolph, C.H., 387
Randsell, S., 293
Rankin, J., 268
Raphael, T.E., 289, 290, 294
Raschke, D., 212
Rasmussen, C.M., 260
Rasmussen, K., 333
Rasmussen, S., 409
Rathunde, K., 351
Ratner, N., 57
Raulin, 21

Rauth, M., 6
Ray, M., 116
Rayner, K., 287
Recht, D.R., 289
Redondo, I.M., 350
Reed, S., 259
Rees, D.I., 113
Rehorick, S., 142
Reinking, D., 338
Report Card 2000; Child Poverty in
British Columbia, 134
Resnick, L., 51, 206
Resnick, L.B., 301
Ridderinkhof, K.R., 240
Riedsel, C.A., 297
Rigby, K., 78
Riordan, M., 237
Riordon, M., 268
Risemberg, 361
Risley, D.S., 392
Risley, T., 291
Ritchie, D., 316
Roberts, P., 136
Robertson, S., 331
Robinson, R.D., 291
Robyler, M.D., 337
Rock, E.A., 409
Rodgers, C., 151
Rodgers, R., 447
Roe-Krasnor, L., 218
Roediger, H., 204
Roehrig, A.D., 278
Roeser, R.W., 362
Rogoff, B., 51, 53, 276, 277
Rondeau, N., 148, 410
Rosch, E.H., 256
Rosenblood, L.K., 365
Rosenshine, B., 317
Rosenthal, M., 266
Rosenthal, R., 114
Ross, B.H., 153, 255
Ross, D.P., 73, 95, 132, 136
Ross, J.A., 154, 356
Ross, N., 385
Rossell, C., 142
Rothbart, M.K., 125
Rousseau, F.L., 353
Rubin, K.H., 75, 76, 77
Ruble, D., 367
Ruble, D.N., 151
Ruiz-Primo, M., 468
Runco, M., 10, 257
Rupley, W.H., 289
Russell, T., 23
Ryan, 326
Ryan, A.M., 75, 368
Ryan, B., 367
Ryan, R., 350, 351
Ryan-Finn, K.D., 25
Ryckman, R.M., 123
Rye, B.J., 95

S

Sadker, D.M., 10, 158
Sadker, D.M.P., 10, 158
Sadoski, M., 242, 250
Safford, S., 146

Salomon, G., 265
Sameroft, A.J., 362
Sanchez, A.R., 153
Sandoval, J., 441
Sanford, A.J., 59
Sanford, K., 448
Sanson, A.V., 125
Santrock, J.W., 395
Sapon-Shevin, M., 281
Saskatchewan Department of
Education, 225, 395, 427
Sax, G., 457, 458, 460
Saxton, J., 317, 450
Scardamalia, M., 259, 294, 334, 335
Scarr, S., 110
Schacter, D.L., 246
Schaefer, A.C., 12
Schaler, J.A., 114
Schauble, L., 301
Schiefele, U., 360, 361, 362, 366,
367, 368
Schneider, W., 239, 242, 247, 266,
267, 268
School Achievement Indicators
Program, 429
SchoolNet, 336
SchoolNet News Network, 395
Schott, L., 301
Schultz, G.F., 369
Schultz, K., 294
Schumer, H., 89
Schunk, D.H., 208, 230, 265, 320,
348, 352, 356, 358, 361
Schwartz, J.E., 297
Scott, K., 73, 95, 132, 136
Scott, N.H., 13
Seaman, D., 292
Segal, M., 117
Seidman, E., 82
Senge, P., 61
Senior, S., 112
Serow, R.C., 89
Serpell, R., 111
Sexton, C., 301
Shachar, H., 280
Shaklee, B.D., 468
Shanahan, 278
Shapiro, E.K., 79
Shapiro, J., 368
Sharan, S., 280, 281
Sharp, S., 78
Shaulov, A., 281
Shavelson, R., 468
Shavelson, R.J., 463
Shaw, B., 278
Shields, S.A., 157
Shiffrin, R., 245, 252
Shook, G.L., 212
Shu, S., 78
Shuell, 4
Shulha, L., 471, 473
Siegel, S., 208
Siegfried, T., 303
Siegler, R.S., 238
Siegler, T., 268
Signorielli, N., 150
Simner, M.L., 288, 428
Singhal, M., 288

Subject Index

A

ability grouping and tracking
  between-class ability grouping (tracking), 113
  self-fulfilling prophecies, 114–115
  within-class ability grouping, 113
Aboriginal children
  culturally responsive approach to Native education, 453
  educators' challenges, 138
  and poverty, 134, 135
  role models, mentors and programs, 225
Aboriginal Elder/Outreach Program, 225
academic to-do lists, 361
academic wooden leg, 376
acceleration program, 188
accommodation, 43
achievement motivation
  see also motivation
  achievement orientation, 355–356
  anxiety, 362
  attribution, 353–355
  described, 349
  instructional strategies and, 362–363
  self-efficacy, 356–358
  self-regulatory learning, 358–362
achievement orientation
  helpless orientation, 356
  mastery orientation, 355
  performance orientation, 356
achievement tests
  defined, 422
  diagnostic tests, 424
  national assessment, 428–429
  Programme for International Student Assessment (PISA), 429
  provincial/territorial-mandated, 425–428
  School Achievement Indicators Program (SAIP), 428–429
  specific subjects, 424
  survey battery, 423
action research, 23, 24
action zone, 402–403
active listening, 395, 397
adaptive creativity, 116
ADHD. *See* attention deficit hyperactivity disorder (ADHD)
adolescence
  see also secondary school
  achievement motivation, development of, 365–366
  ADHD in, 172

boys, onset of puberty, 41
bullying, 93–94
challenges of. *See* adolescent challenges
defined, 35
developmental changes in peer relations, 79
girls, onset of puberty, 41
hypothetical-deductive reasoning, 48
identity *versus* identity confusion, 70
language development, 60
menarche, 41
pubertal changes, 40–42
social motivation, development of, 365–366
socioemotional development, challenges of, 92–96
adolescent challenges
  bullying, extreme forms of, 93–94
  peer harassment, 93–94
  pregnancy, 95
  school dropout, 95
  school violence, 93–94
  sexually transmitted diseases (STDs), 95
  substance abuse, 92–93
  successful programs, 96
  truancy, 95
adolescent egocentrism, 48
advance organizers, 316–317
affect. *See* emotions
affective domain, 313–314
Afgan Women's Organization of Canada, 411
after-instruction assessment, 450
aggression
  in bullying, 79
  defiance, 408–409
  emotional and behavioural disorders, 175
  fighting, 408
  gender differences, 155
  hostility toward teachers, 408–409
  management of, 408–409
  proactively aggressive, 155
  reactively aggressive, 155
aggressive style, 399
agreeableness, 123
Ainsworth, Mary Salter, 5
Alberta — provincial achievement tests, 425
algebra, 298
algorithms, 259
alienated students, 377–378
alternate forms reliability, 420
alternative assessments
  authentic assessment, 462–463

performance-based assessment, 463–466
portfolio assessment, 466–469
vs. standardized tests, 440–441
American Psychological Association, 325
analogy, 257
androgyny, 155
animation, and learning, 375
animism, 45
anxiety, 176, 362
applied behaviour analysis
  community agreement, 218
  contingent and timely reinforcement, 212–213
  contracting, 214
  critics of, 218–219
  decreasing undesirable behaviours, 215–218
  defined, 212
  differential reinforcement, 214–215
  effective reinforcers, 212
  evaluation of, 218–219
  extinction, 215–216
  increasing desirable behaviours, 212–214
  negative punishment, 217
  negative reinforcement, effective use of, 214
  positive punishment, 217–218
  Premack principle, 212
  present aversive stimuli, 217–218
  prompts, 214–215
  removal of desirable stimuli, 216–217
  response cost, 217
  schedules of reinforcement, 213–214
  shaping, 215
  time-out, 216–217
aptitude tests, 421
arithmetic, 297–298
articulation disorders, 176
artifacts, 466
Asperger syndrome, 174–175
assertive style, 399–400
assessments
  see also tests
  alternative assessments, 440–441, 461–470
  authentic assessment, 462–463
  before-instruction assessment, 448–449
  and computers, 454, 474–476
  counter-related evidence, 451
  current trends, 453–454
  and diversity, 453
  fairness, 451–453
  formative assessment, 449–450

grading, 470–473
high performance standards, 454
high-quality, establishment of, 450–453
instructional validity, 451
as integral part of teaching, 448–450
mathematics, 450
multiple assessment methods, 454
objective tests, 453
performance assessments, 453
performance-based assessment, 463–466
pluralistic assessment, 452–453
portfolio assessment, 466–469
reliability, 451
reporting to parents, 473–474
rubrics, 460
summative assessment, 450
traditional tests, 454–461
validity, 451
assimilation, 43
assistive technology, 196
associative learning, 204
ataxia, 184
Atkinson-Shiffrin model of long-term memory, 245
attention, 222, 240, 241
attention deficit hyperactivity disorder (ADHD)
  in adolescence, 172
  causes of, 172–173
  characteristics, 171–174
  defined, 171
  elementary school years, classification in, 172
  learning disabilities, 167–168
  medication and, 174
  pervasive hyperactivity component, 171
  in preschool years, 172
  situational hyperactivity component, 171
  subtype symptoms, 171
  teaching strategies, 173
attestations, 467
attribution theory, 353
attributions
  defined, 353
  dimensions of causal attributions, 354–355
audiovisuals, 458
auditorium style, 402
authentic assessment, 462–463
authoritarian parenting, 71
authoritarian strategy of classroom management, 390
authoritative parenting, 71–72

V

validity
- of assessments, 451
- concurrent validity, 420
- construct validity, 421
- content validity, 420
- counter-related evidence, 451
- criterion validity, 420
- defined, 420
- instructional validity, 421, 451
- predictive validity, 420–421
- and reliability, 421
- standardized tests, 420–421

variable-interval schedule, 213
variable-ratio schedule, 213
verbal behaviour, 57
verbal skills, 106
video games, and children's health, 38–39
videodiscs, 334
visual impairments, 181
visual-spatial working memory, 244

voice disorders, 176
volunteer tutoring, 278–279, 281
Vygotsky, Lev, 5, 50
Vygotsky's theory
- assumptions, 51
- language, 52
- *vs.* Piaget's theory, 52
- scaffolding, 52
- thought, 52
- zone of proximal development, 51

W

WebQuests, 316
Wechsler Individual Achievement Test (WIAT), 423
Wechsler scales, 103
Weschler Intelligence Scale for Children (WISC-III), 422–423
whiteboard conversion kits, 403
whole-language approach, 287
Wide Range Achievement Test (WRAT-3), 423
within-class ability grouping, 113

"withitness," 390
Women in Engineering and Science (WES) program, 371
work-avoidant goals, 360
working memory
- central executive, 244
- phonological loop, 244
- three-part system, 243
- visual-spatial, 244

World Wide Web (WWW, the Web), 337
Writers in Electronic Residence (WIER), 292
writing
- cognitive constructivist approaches, 293–294
- and gender differences, 154
- metacognition, 294
- peer collaboration, 295
- planning, 293
- problem solving, 293–294
- "real texts" about meaningful experiences, 295
- revising, 294

school/family/community connections, 295–296
social constructivist approaches, 294–296
social context of, 294–295
student-teacher writing conferences, 295
written progress reports, 473

Y

"you" messages, 397–398
Youth Lifestyle Choices Community University Research Alliance (YLC-CURA), 76
YouthLinks, 263
Yukon-student assessment program, 427–428

Z

z-score, 437
zone of proximal development, 51